The Political Economy of North-South Relations

The Political Economy of North-South Relations

edited by

Toivo Miljan

broadview press

Canadian Cataloguing in Publication Data

Main entry under title:

The Political economy of north-south relations

ISBN 0–921149–11–5

1. International economic relations. 2. Developing
countries – Foreign economic relations. 3. International relations. 4. Developing countries –
Foreign relations. I. Miljan, Toivo.

HF1411.P65 1987 337'.09'04 C87–094759–1

broadview press   in the U.S.: broadview press
P. O. Box 1243   421 Center St.
Peterborough, Canada, K9J 7H5 Lewiston, N. Y. 14092

Printed and bound in Canada by
Gagné Ltd.
Cover design by Falcom Design & Communications

Table of Contents

Foreword

This book has several objectives: to bring before the American and Canadian student concerned with the inconsistencies in the relations between the First and Third Worlds a large number of systematically arranged current articles reflecting both First World and Third World views and written by both policy-makers and policy analysts in academic and policy-oriented journals.

The book has been organized in four sections, divided into fourteen chapters, each addressing a specific area of concern. Each chapter has an introduction by the editor outlining the area of concern without replicating the articles that it introduces.

The first part, titled *The Changed World,* focuses on three intractable problems: first, the rapidly changing technology-driven structure of the world economy, now firmly dominated by the advanced high technology industries, primarily in the United States, Europe and Japan. Any roles for the Third World will simply have to be reconciled with the demands of the core economies and their publics.

In the second chapter the structure of the Third World state is examined and found to vary greatly from the western competitive democratic models operated by the core states. In addition to creating conflicts between the First and the Third Worlds, the structural differences add to instability within the Third World, especially when juxtaposed with the dominant economic structures of the world.

In the final chapter of the first part the role of armaments, their transfer from the First to the Third World and their costs, are found not only to create instability in the Third World, and economic and political dependency on the First World, but also to retard economic and social development in the Third World.

In the second part, entitled *Dependence and Interdependence,* five chapters examine economic problems created or exacerbated by the differences between the economic and social structures of the First and Third Worlds. Chapter Four addresses the confusion of world trade policies during the last 30 years of the 20th century, focusing especially on problems of protectionism and the need to open First World markets to Third World goods, as part of a general freeing of market mechanisms in the world system as a whole.

Chapter Five examines the problems of investment flows from the First World to the Third World and concludes that much of the private investment and official aid to the latter has been misplaced, and is insufficient to meet the needs of integrated development of social, economic and political systems of the Third World.

Chapter Six is atypical in that it views the activities of the transnational corporations in a generally favorable light, seeing them as the principal providers of private direct investment as well as marketing channels for the transfer of technology. The growth of Third World-based TNCs (some joint ventures with the First World) is especially welcome by the newly industrializing countries of the Third World.

Chapter Seven examines the international monetary system, both generally and in several details and concludes that little has happened during the past decade to be sanguine about—the monetary crisis is still very much with us. Solutions abound, but the political will to implement them is missing.

Chapter Eight focuses on one of the saddest and most intractable problems of the day—the problem of nutrition and lack of food in large parts of the Third World, most notably Africa—amidst a surfeit of food in the rich developed North. Although many of the problems are self-generated in the South, the North is at fault as well in not permitting free access for southern agricultural commodities to northern markets and in misusing its technological and economic power in creating, rather than solving, some nutritional problems in the South.

The third part of this book, entitled *The Regions*, provides specific overviews of three main Third World regions. Although all are part of the Third World, their problems vary considerably, as does their status in the ladder of economic development and integration with the world economy. Chapter Nine considers the salient problems of Latin America, particularly an ever-increasing foreign debt burden that is and the problems that this creates for the fragile democracies of the region.

Chapter Ten deals with the plethora of serious weaknesses of Africa: its endemic low-man-on-the-ladder status, its domination by the North for over a century since its "discovery" by Europe, its serious and continuing famines and endemic internal wars. Articles in the chapter also review current proposals for solving its problems.

Chapter Eleven is much more upbeat and focuses on the "miracle" of the variants of the Japanese model of socio-economic growth applied by Korea and Taiwan, as well as on the opening up of China to world markets.

The final part of the book, titled *Dialogues with the South: Politics of Self-Interest* is divided into three chapters, each describing a set of approaches and concerns of relations between the wealthy northern hemisphere and the South.

Chapter Twelve looks at general northern approaches and views towards the south and concludes that much of these are expressions of self-interest rather than altruism.

Chapter Thirteen views the "dialogue" with the South with a jaundiced eye and sees little progress from the large amount of energy spent and reports produced in an effort to bring about a closing of the gap between the North and the South.

The final chapter brings the Marxist-Leninist North into the North-South relationship, looks at ways in which both the East and the West can cooperate in the South, and at the ideological explanations offered by Marxism-Leninism in an attempt to justify its non-cooperation hitherto with the West in the South.

Acknowledgements

The production of any book is the result of cooperation of many people; so it is with this one. I wish to acknowledge the cooperation of the publishers and owners of copyright of the articles, tables and figures that appear in this volume. The most important participants in the volume, of course, are the authors of the articles in the book. I thank both those whose articles are reprinted here, and those who provided original papers.

Wilfrid Laurier University provided me with both enthusiastic support and financial assistance in preparing the manuscript for publication. Helen Paret and Debbie Kohlruss provided unflagging support in cheerfully handling the large amount of typing necessary in compiling such a large manuscript. Without the infectious enthusiasm of Don LePan, my publisher and literary editor, this book would not have seen print. Last, and most important, I wish to thank Nadia Manin, a graduate student of political science, who so ably assisted me in the selection of the material, the writing up of the chapter introductions and in general research, for her consistent industry and availability, and her good humor in working under the pressure of an early deadline.

PART I
THE CHANGED WORLD

Chapter 1

The Techno-Economic Structure of the Contemporary World

Introduction

The internationalization of the world economy is one of the most significant events of the post-war period. General yardsticks such as trade/GNP ratios or the magnitude of current account balances and capital movements provide a measure of the increasing interdependence over this period, and of parallels with the evolution of the world economy during the century prior to the disintegration of the 1930s. The main difference is that technological change is much faster now than ever before in history; indeed, the past forty years have seen an ever-increasing acceleration of this change. Revolutionary changes in transportation and communication technology have made markets in different countries interdependent to an unprecedented degree during the past few years. As a result, trade and financial flows between countries have become super-sensitive to changes in relative prices. Another feature brought about by transportation and communication changes is the internationalization of entrepreneurship and of technology and the emergence of the transnational corporation. These new factors mean that positive or negative developments in the world economy are likely to take place and spread much more quickly than hitherto and to affect a much larger proportion of the world's population. The large number of independent states which emerged from the process of decolonization during this period has added a degree of complexity to world relations unknown in the past. At the same time the market-based multilateral trade and payments systems developed at Bretton Woods at the end of the Second World War have provided the framework for widespread and unprecedented increases in productivity and living standards in developed and less developed countries alike – although at disparate and differential rates.

Trade between developed and developing countries has become a dynamic feature of the world economy in the past two decades. Rapidly rising international investment has contributed to spreading modern technology and managerial capacity around the world. The international financial system has been a major instrument in channelling world savings into productive investments in many developing countries (though certainly not all). As a result of this progressive integration into the world economy, economic, social and demographic trends in developing countries are now having a major impact on world economic and financial affairs. This does not mean that the crucial importance for the developing countries of dynamic and sound economies in the United States, the European community and Japan has lessened. However, it is important to understand that this relationship is no longer as one-sided as it was once considered to be. Intensified economic interchange and improved cooperation with developing countries has become much more important to the efforts of the economic "engines" of this world to maintain stable growth by opening expanding markets for industries and agriculture, by contributing to competitive imports by improvements in productivity and by the curbing of inflation, as well as by providing outlets for raw materials and energy. Studies generally show that the long-run prospects for the industrialized countries are substantially better in scenarios in which the developing countries progress harmoniously; thus it is in the interest of the industrialized countries – quite aside from any moral obligation – to cooperate with and support such progress.

The interdependent world economy gives rise to opportunities for joint gains in economic welfare at the same time as it increases vulnerabilities. The more the world economy depends upon complex linkages among countries and among the various key international markets, the more vulnerable it becomes to dysfunctions, rigidities and natural or political shocks in component markets and individual economies. The more national economies are integrated in the world economy, the more they are vulnerable to changes which occur abroad. While benefits from participation in the world economy are widespread, the capacity of national economies to benefit from the opportunities of an open system and to absorb external shocks has differed both among industrial and developing countries, depending on such factors as resource endowments and factor mobility as well as the responsiveness of national economic policies. Insufficient diversification of export products and trading partners and a frequently low degree of national socio-economic integration limits the resilience of poor economies.

Interdependence thus gives rise to problems of common concern to both developed and developing countries. These include
– the need to pursue policies which effectively re-establish the conditions for sustained non-inflationary recovery and satisfactory levels of employment;
– the accumulating dangers to the preservation of the open multilateral trading system arising from the persistence of slow growth in both output and employment and from difficulties in domestic and international adjustment processes;
– the buildup of large international assets and indebtedness in a complex and interdependent world financial system;
– instability in oil markets and long-term energy balances;
– instability in agricultural markets, together with inadequate agricultural performance and problems of food security in many developing countries;
– instability of commodity markets and related problems concerning the adequacy and reliability of raw material supplies;
– population explosion in developing countries;
– major migration flows with potential for creating social and political instability.
Seminal changes have taken place during the past decade that are changing the fundamental economic and social relationships within the First World as well as those between it and the Third World. Peter F. Drucker argues that the structure of the world economy has changed as follows:
– the primary products economy has come "uncoupled" from the industrial economy;
– in the industrial economy itself, production has come "uncoupled" from employment;
– capital movements rather than trade (in both goods and services) have become the driving force of the world economy. The two have not quite come uncoupled but the link has become loose, and worse, unpredictable.[*]

If Drucker is right – and a good deal of evidence suggests that he is – then the world economy has become one that is driven by technology and by financial flows rather than by manufacturing and fluctuations in the prices of raw materials. Such a world economy clearly is dominated by and concentrated in the so-called High-Tech sectors of North America, Europe, and Japan. But, even in these sectors, it is the financial markets which appear to determine the level of activity in the high-tech industries. This means, of course, that the Third World, largely limited to raw materials extraction and low-tech industries, experiences growth in inverse proportion to that in the high-tech economies, essentially for two reasons. First, high technology requires ever-decreasing amounts of raw materials and second, the products of high technology tend to replace labour in the low-tech industries, with the result that high-tech industries tend to generate a decrease in industrial employment. This, of course, is true both in the First World and the Third World. However, the impact in the First World may be somewhat ameliorated by the increase in service sector employment. Even more serious, certainly in the short run, is the apparent uncoupling of capital movements from trade as the driving force of the world economy. In the Third World we have already seen the impact of the tremendous expansion of capital movements resulting from the "petro dollar" recycling of the late 1970s – a process carried on quite separately from the traditional trade links which in earlier days determined the ability to repay the original capital loan and which were the basis for granting loans. Much of the conflict in First and Third World relations during the 1980s and 1990s is the result of this "uncoupling" of financial flows from trade.

The chapters dealing with investment flows, the crisis of the monetary system, Latin America and Africa look in greater detail at the resultant problems. In the First World, the "uncoupling" of financial flows in the capital market from industrial production has come to the forefront only during the middle of the 1980s. The avalanche of articles and predictions at year end provides the most vivid evidence that neither governments nor economic analysts fully understand either the phenomenon or its implications for economy and society. However, it is evident that the stock markets (in all their manifestations) in all of the First World countries now move quite independently of the bottom line in economic prediction or performance. Part of this is the direct result of the technology involved in stock trading, which is now carried on largely by pre-programmed buy and sell orders executed by computers owned by the large players in the markets in New York and elsewhere.

The first article in this chapter, by Manuel Castells, provides an overview of both the developments in the structural transformation in the world economy that is either taking place in different parts of the world in the last quarter of the century, as well as a thorough reference list of the main authors who have dealt with these questions both conceptually and analytically. He analyzes in detail the problem of the new international division of labour created by high technology, and its implications for growth in the Third World. He then demonstrates how the Third World is largely bypassed by the current technological revolution, except for its military implications, consumer electronics products, and the connection of its directional centres to an integrated network of world telecommunications. Thus only a few segments of the productive structure and increasingly narrow markets participate in the process of new "peripheral industrialization." "Moreover," he points out, "new agricultural technologies are helping to increase labour redundancy in the modern, capitalist exploitations, thus accelerating rural-urban migration." In addition, "raw materials are being replaced by synthetic, advanced materials, condemning large areas of the world to economic obsolescence." This means that "functional and social distance is increasing not only between countries, but also between regions of the same country." He then examines in detail the employment impact of high technology on the First World and the eventual fall-out of this on the Third World.

The second article by W. W. Rostow, who is credited with developing the concept of crucial relationships in economic development patterns almost 30 years ago in a book entitled *The Economic Stages of Growth*, describes the increasing interdependence in the growth patterns of the First and Third World countries by using some of the basic concepts developed in that book. He demonstrates that "a high growth stage in the developing regions [leads to] increased dependence of the south on the north" and suggests why this should be so. As he puts it, "it is a central characteristic of diversified modern technology . . . that it systematically increases interdependence among countries which absorb that technology." Hence, "economic 'independence' is an illusory goal for all of us as far ahead as any of us can see." He spends the remainder of his article discussing the historical cycles which constitute the basis for the period of rapid expansion in the world economy which he believes will take place in the remainder of the 1980s and the 1990s and which ought then to be the basis for an "appropriate north-south agenda."

The final article in the chapter, by William Diebold Jr., surveys the role that the United States has played in the world economy during the past half century. The main objective of the paper is to demonstrate to Americans that the United States has a responsibility to play a leading role in the world economy if for no other reason than because the United States is not a country like any other. As he puts it, "our dollar and our missiles prove that." He also adds, "it is . . . wrong to suppose that American interests will be well served by old-fashioned narrow nationalism modified by contemporary neomercantilism." He urges Americans to seriously rethink the responsibilities that they have to the world and to turn away from the inward looking protectionist sentiments that characterize American congressional politics at the beginning of the 100th Congress, with the United States and the European Community each threatening to fight to the bitter end to ensure access for their own exports in the other's markets.

---

* Peter F. Drucker, "The Changed World Economy". *Foreign Affairs*, Spring, 1986, p. 768.

High Technology, World Development and Structural Transformation: The Trends and the Debate

Manuel Castells

I. Introduction

We have the privilege and the responsibility of living through one of the greatest technological revolutions in the history of humankind. Two major features characterize this technological revolution: it is aimed at generating and processing information; its outcome is process-oriented and, therefore, its effects are pervasive, cutting across the entire realm of human activity.

As in all historical breaking points of scientific advancement, there is a whole constellation of discoveries taking place simultaneously, according to an interconnected self-reinforcing pattern. Some of these discoveries concern new products such as special materials; others are the technical application of existing technologies, such as space navigation and operation. Yet, the core of the current technological revolution resides in the ability to generate and process information, and to introduce such capacity into the actions and functions through which we work, produce, consume, manage, enjoy ourselves, live and die. What microelectronics does is to process information in increasingly powerful, yet decreasingly costly, miniaturized circuits. What computers do, on the basis of microelectronics, is to process, and eventually generate, information, at an even greater speed, and accuracy, with increasing capacity of memory, and with a broadening range of accessibility from non-expert knowledge to the computing system, thus decentralizing and transforming it into a truly humane society, the technological question is perhaps one of the most important we will have to face. It is, in fact, a matter of life and death. This is because we are entering a historical period in which humankind is at once penetrating the secrets of life and the sources of intelligence, while risking the unleashing, at any moment, of the disintegration of matter, or the lethal mutation of life.

This report addresses these questions by examining the specific effects of new technologies in some fundamental dimensions of our socio-economic structure: the new international economy and the fate of Third World countries in such new conditions; the changing patterns of work and employment; the technological environment in which our everyday life will be taking place; and the implications of this scientific revolution for the fundamental issue of war and peace. To be sure, other aspects and dimensions of the social implications of the new technologies ought to be considered to be able to assess comprehensively their impact. But the analysis presented here is geared to a more specific purpose: to define

Originally published in *Alternatives*, vol VI, 1986. Reprinted with permission.

the conditions for social uses of new technologies that would be an alternative to the pre-vailing patterns of exploitation, oppression, and war. Such will be the last section of our report. Yet, in order to base our alternatives on the actual historical trends, we must inves-tigate the current intertwining between technology, economy, and society. Otherwise our intellectual endeavor could easily become the progressive version of futurology, something we want to avoid by all means. We want to explore the tendencies rooted in our societies not only to forecast them, but to change them, so that we do not submit to our destiny but contribute to increasing the capacity to make our human history. Yet, such capacity will depend not only on our vision and our ideals, but on our clear-sightedness in knowing where we are. And, it is our hypothesis that we are on the threshold of a major technologi-cal revolution, taking place in the midst of a world-wide process of economic restructuring, and on the edge of a dangerous realignment of macropolitical strategies.

II. High technology and economic restructuring in the aftermath of the crisis

Technological revolution does not take place in a social vacuum. It develops in a very specific socio-economic, historical context, whose characteristics deeply affect the form and goals of the uses of technology, and ultimately, of technology itself (Rosenberg, 1982; Blackburn, Coombs and Green, 1985). This is not to say that technological discoveries happen necessarily as responses to the needs of "the system." Science and research have their own pace of development, with moments of qualitative breakthroughs and accelera-tion of discovery produced by the interplay between scientific research, the institutional framework where it takes place, and the social demand for technological applications.

The current technological revolution gained its innovation during the 1970s at a time when the world economy was undergoing a major structural crisis whose causes and charac-teristics we have examined elsewhere (Castells, 1980). In the mid-1980s, the key centers of the world economy have restructured some fundamental mechanisms so that the processes of capital accumulation and social order, on which the system relies, are adequately per-formed (Camus, Delattre, Dutailly, Eymard-Duvernay, Vassille, 1981; O'Connor, 1984; Bowles, Gordon, and Weisskopf, 1983; Carnoy, Shearer and Rumberger, 1983).

Capitalism has reformed itself, through a process of social struggles and victorious politi-cal battles, and has recovered some of its dynamism, and much of its social control, by shrinking the number of people benefiting from the system and reaching out to almost the entire planet to inter-connect all segments of potential beneficiaries of this leaner, more aggressive, more determined, new type of capitalism. In recent years (around the 1970-80 period), a new model of economic growth has emerged that represents a similar departure from Keynesianism and welfare-state capitalism as that reform-minded capitalist model represented vis-à-vis liberal capitalism before the 1930s depression. Because it is one hypothesis that high technology has played a major role (as a tool, not as a cause) in this dramatic process of economic restructuring, it is necessary to outline, very schematically, the characteristics of the new model of economic policy, to pinpoint the specific role of new technologies in relationship to each one of the major economic axes (Carnoy and Castells, 1985). Such a model is not necessarily linked to a particular political party or administra-tion, or even to a country, even though the Reagan or Thatcher governments seem to be the closest examples of the fulfillment of these policies. But very similar policies have devel-oped in most West European countries, in those governed by Christian Democrats and Liberals, as well as in those governed by Socialists, and even in Communist-led regions (Italy) or Communist-participating governments (France, for a certain period). At the same time, in most Third World countries, austerity policies, inspired or dictated by the International Monetary Fund and world financial institutions, have also developed along the same lines, establishing not without contradictions and conflicts (Walton, 1985) a new economic logic that is not only capitalist but a very specific kind of capitalism that we will try to describe briefly (Carnoy and Castells, 1985). Obviously, the generalization of such a model of economic policy (which is not historically irreversible) does not imply that all governments are alike or that politics does not matter. The issue is that when a system reaches a historical limit, and the socio-political process is unable to transform it, the only possibility for society not to disintegrate is to consolidate, reinforce, and make more dynamic the already institutionalized structural logic. Because the economy (under capitalism) structures society, and because the economy is highly interdependent at an international level, individual governments in individual countries find themselves faced with the dilemma of adjusting to the dominant logic in the most advantageous manner, or having to undertake an uphill battle that is unlikely to succeed as an isolated enterprise. Thus, most countries are embarking along the lines of a new model of economic policy that is organized around a major series of measures, coming at the same time from governments and private business:

1. Control of inflation through fiscal austerity and monetary restriction, aimed at the partial disarmament of the welfare state (Taylor, 1983).

2. Reduction of labor costs, at the same time, on wages, working conditions, and social benefits. Consequently, the share of business' profit increases proportionally, all other conditions being equal (Bowles, Gordon, Weisskopf, 1983).

3. Increase of productivity of companies, and of profitability of business, by lay-offs, reduction of working time, technological innovation, and faster pace of work (Reich, 1983).

4. Restructuring of industrial sectors, disinvesting massively from those sectors, regions, and companies that become less profitable, and investing in new products and activities, generally in high-technology manufacturing, corporate services, miscellaneous consumer services, and real estate (Bluestone and Harrison, 1982). A major development within industrial restructuring (particularly in Europe and Latin America) is the shrinkage of the public sector, and the alignment of public companies on the logic of profitability.

5. Tremendous growth of the "informal economy," that is, of all kinds of cash economic activities unregulated and uncontrolled by the state, regardless of the legality of their status. This includes certainly the astronomic sum of cash flow in criminal activities (particularly in the production and distribution of drugs), but it mainly refers to undeclared salaried work, unpaid taxes, absence of compliance with health and safety regulations, labor legislation, etc., (Portes and Walton, 1981; Piore and Sabel, 1984). In countries like the United States, massive immigration from undocumented workers fuels the process of the increasing penetration of the center by the periphery. The informal economy today represents a key element of all economies alike, not only for the survival of the poor, but for the dynamism of small businesses, accounting for much of the growth and new employment (Sassen-Koob, 1984; Maldonado and Moore, 1985), and for the transfer of value from the informal sector to large corporations through subcontracting arrangements and networks of decentralized production.

6. Opening of the world market, and increasing internationalization of the economy, taking advantage of the most favorable locations for production, management, and control of the markets, within a system interconnected world-wide. This is a common strategy for both companies and governments, and paradoxically, it simultaneously triggers protectionist reactions, as soon as industrial sectors, regions, or countries, start losing in the cutthroat competition (Bienefeld and Godfrey, 1982; Little, 1982).

7. Relative control of world prices of raw materials and energy from the center, assuring the stability of the price system and exchange flows (OECD, 1984).

Of course, this sketchy presentation of the dominant economic model emphasizes its coherence and internal logic, without considering the contradictions it implies, and the potentially destructive deviations of its own rationality. For instance, in the case of the United States, the claim for fiscal austerity and a balanced budget is translated into a greater deficit, with a shift within the budget from social expenditures to military expenditures (what we call, following Herbert Marcuse, the transition from the Welfare State to the Warfare State). It is financed, without inflation, by the influx of capital from all over the world, thus drying up sources of investment everywhere else, and pushing upward the dollar, therefore wrecking the US balance of trade, in a series of connected ill-effects that threaten the whole model when considered in its actual dynamics.

Nevertheless, we think it is useful to keep in mind the characteristics of the post-Keynesian economic model of capitalism, because the technological revolution has matured precisely during its rise, and it is in fact playing a major role in the feasibility of the model's implementation. In turn, the lines of technological development are now being shaped by the predominant social and economic uses assigned to them.

The new technologies are at the core of the current process of economic restructuring in the following way:

1. *They contribute to a qualitative increase in productivity* across the board, in manufacturing, agriculture (down the line, through biotechnology), and in services. In fact, productivity growth is particularly crucial in this fundamental aspect of the economy. Because new technologies are primarily aimed at processing information, and this is precisely the subject of most services, the deepest economic impact of the new technologies will occur in services and office work (Noyelle, 1984; Stanback, 1979; Hirschhorn, 1984; Baran, 1985).

Yet, for the moment, the most immediate impact in industrial productivity has been in manufacturing, and particularly in the automobile industry. The UNIDO report on the topic (UNIDO, 1984) observes that "The position of the [automobile] industry in the industrial system has altered. No longer will it be a creator of jobs. It will be a pioneer in the introduction and use of technologies and materials of several kinds and in so doing it will transform its inter-industry linkages. These changes are unlikely to be limited to the OECD countries, even though their present force is concentrated in that area" (page 17). In fact, during the 1980s, the automobile industry is experiencing a major transformation in the production process and in the overall logic of industry, being the main user of industrial robots, and of CAD/CAM systems of flexible manufacturing. Adding the developments in new materials, it seems that in a few years the automobile industry will have shifted from an electromechanical industry to an electronics-plastics industry (UNIDO, 1984) dramatically increasing productivity and reducing employment in production. Similar trends can be observed in key industries such as electronics (Ernst, 1980; Cohen and Zysman, 1986; Jacobson and Sigurdsun, 1983), and telecommunications (Borrus, Bar, and Warde, 1984).

This impact cannot be equated to a negative effect of new technologies on employment, a more complex issue that we will examine in detail below. But, in any case, the general impact of new technologies on business tends to increase productivity and quality, reduce costs, and improve profitability, thus contributing a great deal to stimulate investment and overcome economic slump.

2. At the same time, the potential (or actual) impact of new technologies on job-suppression places management in an advantageous position regarding workers and unions, to obtain concessions in wages and working conditions in exchange for maintaining employment, or of slowing down the phasing out of jobs. Thus, although technology per se is not an instrument of capital, it is being used as a bargaining factor in the redefinition of the power relationships between management and labor, a key component of the overall economic restructuring (Institut Syndical Europeen, 1980; AFL-CIO, 1984; Bluestone and Harrison, 1984).

3. Technological change is also the source of new investment, the main engine of economic recovery, for two main reasons. On the one hand, such as written in the 1984 OEDC Report, "Higher than expected growth of non-residential private investment seems to be explained by the increase of marginal productivity of investment in those countries where the share of computers and other high technology equipment in the companies investments has significantly increased. Thus, it would seem that the profitability for a given investment increases [because of new technologies]. Investments that were previously under the threshold of profitability become profitable now. This phenomenon is particularly important in the U.S. and Japan" (p. 10, our translation from the French version of the Report).

On the other hand, in anticipation of the demand for new technologies, there is a rush of investment in the high technology sectors, thus stimulating the economy out of recession, while deeply reshaping its structure in terms of "sunrise" and "sunset" industries, regions, and countries (Bluestone and Harrison, 1984; Celada, Lopez-Groh and Parra, 1985; Markusen, 1984; Henderson and Castells, 1986).

4. New technologies stimulate markets, particularly for upper income households, by generating new products (such as home computers and new communication devices) or creating new lines of old products by introducing into them informational devices (from cars to kitchens).

5. Last, but not least, new technologies, and particularly telecommunications, constitute the material conditions necessary for the process of internationalization of the economy, probably the key feature of the new model of accumulation. Only through the integrated system of telecommunications and computers is it possible to both integrate and decentralize production, distribution, and management in a world-wide, flexible, interconnected system. The new telecommunication technologies are the electronic highways of the informational age, equivalent to the role played by the railways systems in the process of industrialization (Nicol, 1985).

Also, world production and distribution is only possible because of the twin processes of perfect standardization of parts (that can be assembled even if produced in very distant locations), and flexible customized production (that can adapt a basic product to specific characteristics targeted on the final market), (UNIDO, 1984; Henderson and Scott, 1986). Both processes are dependent upon automated production, and flexible electronic tools able to be re-programmed. The world-assembly line and the planetary bazaar, require both the electronic factory and on-line management.

Thus, new technologies are a key component of the process of economic restructuring that determines a new international division of labor whose characteristics are decisive for the making of our future world.

III. High technology, the new international division of labor and the future of the Third World

The new technologies are rendering obsolete the "new international division of labor" that emerged in different areas of the world during the 1970s as a response to the structural economic crisis (Frobel, Henricks and Kreye, 1980). Such international division of labor was mainly organized around the policies of multinational corporations that relocated their production "offshore" in countries where low wages, lack of environmental and health controls, pro-business and repressive government policies, and favorable fiscal exceptions substantially reduced production costs in comparison with the core countries (Palloix, 1977; Peet, 1984; Nayyar, 1978; Schmitz, 1984). Thus a new North-South division of labor started to take place between high-technology industries and advanced services in the North and assembly operations, low-skilled manufacturing, and extraction of natural resources in the South (Brandt, 1980). Multinational corporations were important agents in such a process, particularly in the most dynamic industries such as electronics (UNIDO, 1981; Ernst, 1980), and in those sectors that underwent global economic restructuring such as automobiles (Maxey, 1981; UNIDO, 1984). Yet, along with the multinationals, small and medium companies from the newly industrializing periphery, as in Hong Kong (Chen, 1979; Schiffer, 1983), Korea or Taiwan (Browett, 1985), followed a similar strategy of producing for the world market on the basis of their comparative advantage of low-production costs. It followed a realignment of the world economy, an intensification of world trade, and the surge of a group of newly industrialized countries (Browett, 1985; Bradford, 1982; Bienefeld and Godfrey, 1982). So, through a combination of decentralization of productive investment from the core, and of dynamism of indigenous capital in the periphery supported by development-oriented national governments, new economic actors have entered the international arena, increasingly differentiating the so-called Third World.

The development of high-technology industries and technological change are both furthering and modifying this new international division of labor. The transformation of the process takes place along different but inter-related lines that we will analyze sequentially for the sake of clarity.

1. On the one hand cheaper and more effective automation of the work process increasingly allows corporations to retain their factories in the core countries (sometimes relocating in rural areas) while still lowering their production costs (Rada, 1982; Cohen, Zysman and Associates, 1986). In fact, the threat of unemployment, and the policies of economic incentives by regional governments in the depressed regions of the United States and Europe, are enhancing the chances for an inter-regional rather than an international division of labor (Glasmeier, 1986; Sawers and Tabb, 1984; Massey, 1984). Such a possibility is being extended to sectors such as textiles and garments that were considered to have become the exclusive prerogative of the newly industrialized countries as newer, electronically-based technologies, such as laser-cutting, and CAD/CAM production lines are installed in the remaining old industries of Europe and the United States (UNIDO, 1984; Botkin, Dimancescu and Stata, 1984). Furthermore, not only has the migration of

core-countries' companies to the periphery slowed down, but there seems to be a process of "relocation back North" (Rada, 1982), apparently induced by a combination of political uncertainty abroad, higher labor costs in the first NIC countries (such as Singapore and Hong Kong), and the need for skilled personnel to handle and repair increasingly sophisticated electronics-based machinery (UNIDO, 1981, 1984).

Nevertheless, there is still a process of productive decentralization across the world that now reaches more countries in the outer periphery. The first ring of NICs (Korea, Taiwan, Hong Kong, Singapore, Malaysia and the industrialized areas of Brazil and Mexico) are now concentrating on more sophisticated and higher skilled production activities, that in the case of Korea and Singapore could even rival some West European countries (Government of Korea, 1985; Botkin, Dimancescu and Stata, 1984). Simultaneously, less developed countries, with a large pool of unskilled, extremely cheap labor, enter the productive line at the low end, particularly Thailand and the Philippines (Henderson, 1986; Lim, 1982; Akrasanee, 1977). Yet, the more automation enters the process of production and management the less low wages play a role in the comparative advantages of a given location. One of the greatest paradoxes of the effects of automation on employment is that the most directly hurt are the Third World countries whose incipient process of industrialization, however exploitative, is based upon the differential cost between unskilled labor in the core and the periphery. Probably the next round of differentiating labor costs will be between skilled labor, including engineers. And this is what countries like Singapore (but also Brazil) are trying to offer. Yet, it is not evident that the training of technical labor could be done rapidly enough, and on a scale large enough to foster a second stage of "off-shore" productive decentralization from the North's industrial base. Thus the fundamental tendency introduced by new technologies is to enhance the role of productivity, instead of focusing on direct labor costs in the overall process of capital accumulation; this therefore reinforces the position of technologically advanced economies in the new international competition.

2. Interestingly enough, while labor costs are becoming a less important factor for the location of companies because of increasing automation, the current trend points toward a greater internationalization of the companies' structure in order to locate closer to their different markets. It thus reverses the tendency of the 1970s, when export-platforms were aimed at the world market (Henderson and Scott, 1986; Lee, 1981; Balassa, 1982; Perlo, 1986). This is a fundamental point that requires some explanation.

The internationalization of the economy and the intensification of world trade in the last two decades led to national economic policies that are increasingly dependent upon their performance on the world scene. International economic competitiveness is a key political factor for any government's fate, domestically as well as in foreign affairs. To reinforce the competitive chances of its national companies, many governments have engaged in restrictive practices of trade, as well as in export incentive programs, so that national corporations can build a home base for their subsequent assault on the world economy (Zysman and Cohen, 1983). This strategy has become known as the Japanese Model (Johnson, 1982), but it is also increasingly true of many NIC countries—Korea (Rosenberg, 1980), and Brazil (Costa Souza, 1985) being the most prominent in this respect.

The EEC has stepped up its control on "unfair competition" of non-EEC countries in Europe, particularly for Japanese exports, and in advanced electronics (there is for instance a 17 percent surcharge on all imported semiconductors). In the United States in the period 1983-86, there has been a dramatic surge of public protest against imports, particularly from Japan, that, in spite of Reagan's free trade philosophy, has led to the imposition of a number of quotas on several products and even to the threat of a commercial war with Japan (*Business Week*, April 8, 1985). Because of the mounting danger of protectionist measures, companies from all countries are positioning themselves to be present in their key foreign markets, often with the support of their own governments, given the strategic importance of the conquest of international markets by national (or nationally-backed) companies. Thus, American and Japanese companies are establishing themselves in increasing numbers in the EEC; Japanese companies (particularly Toyota and Nissan) are locating in the United States; Korean companies settling in Canada; investment from all over the world is pouring into the United States, some of it into securities and real estate, but most of it in setting up new companies or buying old ones, particularly in the West and the Southwest (Schoenberger, 1985; Glickman, 1985).

Large potential markets such as Brazil, Mexico and China are being tapped by foreign investment, locating there to take over the expansion of new segments of consumers. In sum, the target is still the world market, but the strategy of multilocation is increasingly more important vis-à-vis the export-platform strategy. The consequence for the Third World is two-fold: on the one hand, most investment tends to concentrate inside the economies of the most developed countries, so substituting a North-to-North and a South-to-North pattern for the incipient North-to-South decentralization that was taking place during the 1970s. On the other hand, domestic markets within the NICs, and in the Third World in general, will have to be shared with international companies, at least in those commercial lines considered profitable. Thus, it follows an increasing dependency, although not necessarily more underdevelopment, of those Third World countries which are somewhat industrialized.

This trend fundamentally alters the current international division of labor because it strongly articulates a new productive location and presence in the market, even though such production facilities will continue to be financially and technologically dependent on the core economies. The development of new technologies plays a major role in this new pattern of the international economy. Let us see why.

3. It is, first of all, because new telecommunications technologies allow the integration of management, as well as internal technological transfer within the same company between its different units, regardless of their location (Nicol, 1983; Piercy, 1984). Thus, a country can use a multilocational strategy to penetrate markets around the world, while keeping its own internal coherence, on the basis of easy inter-personal communication and data transmission (UNCTC, 1984). This is particularly important because while "off-shore" production does not require day-to-day contact between the center and the periphery of the company (given that it generally concerns routine assembly operations), productive location close to a market implies a greater coordination of the company's strategy (UNIDO, 1984), something that is only possible thanks to the power, flexibility, and decreasing cost of new telecommunication technologies.

Secondly, this new strategy of internationalization on the basis of multilocation is, to a large extent, the result of the opportunity that high technology products and services provide to take over entire countries as protected markets in areas of the world in great need of devices that incorporate new information technologies but are still far behind the current leaders in the field of high technology manufacturing. In this sense, Western Europe appears as the most rapidly growing, promising market for high technology companies in the forthcoming years. This is why all multinationals, including the European ones, are striving to position themselves in that market. Yet the United States is still the fundamental market for high technology (particularly considering the current renovation process of industrial equipment in the United States). That explains why much of the US productive facilities of high technology companies will still remain close to their own market. Japanese and European companies are trying to penetrate the US market by investing heavily in it, or setting up joint ventures. Further, presence in the US technological milieu appears to be a prerequisite for competing in the race for industrial innovation. For instance, French-government owned electronics giant Thomson, recently acquired an almost bankrupt, highly inefficient American company Mostek, based in Dallas, to gain an additional entry into the US electronics field. Japan is the second largest industrial market in the world (Nazakawa, 1985), but its many ways of disguised protectionism are still keeping it at bay from deep penetration by foreign competition (Borrus, Millstein and Zysman, 1983; Johnson, 1982). Yet, the deregulation of Nippon Telephone Company in 1985, and the monetary and financial policies undertaken in the Fall of the same year by the Nakasone Government seem to signal an awareness by the Japanese establishment of the danger of a backlash in both the United States and the EEC, should their protectionism continue unabated. As a result, it is likely that at least a segment of the Japanese market will join the world economy, further penetrating it along a clearly defined North-North axis. High technology industries, the most dynamic industrial sector today, tend to locate both in terms of their technical labor (the key production factor) and in terms of their markets, in the OECD countries whose technological-economic lead is thereby self-reinforcing. At the same time, some new potential markets for high technology production appear in oil-producing countries (particularly in the Middle East), and in a few NICs (essentially Korea, Brazil, Mexico, India, and in a few years, China), but they are still very limited in terms of the market, and very distant from the core in their technological capability (with the important exceptions of Singapore and Korea). Much of the Third World (particularly Africa) appears to be left out from the current process of technological modernization, both in terms of markets and of production. The technological revolution for most of the world seems to be limited to the telecommunications networks of some directional centers, or to the enclaves of some large, internationally-oriented companies, and sadly enough, to increasingly sophisticated weaponry. High technology, in its process of uneven development, is profoundly altering the world's economic geography.

Thirdly, the need to access key technologies withheld by multinational corporations has motivated numerous governments to actively seek the location of these multinationals in their countries. Because of the vital need for technology transfer, corporations obtain financial, material, and legislative advantages that amount to a significant bonus to the multinational strategy (UNIDO, 1981; Balassa, 1982). Countries, and regions within countries, enter the competition to obtain the companies' favors. Since in most cases the employment effect of such locations is very limited, and government and local capital financing account for the majority of investments, it seems that the search for technological know-how is the main reason for national governments' efforts to lure high-technology companies. Thus, the technological gap is not only the consequence, but also a major cause of the new process of economic internationalization, by favoring the multilocation of new industries. We are shifting from a strategy based on export-platforms, to a new one relying on the export of the productive platform itself, so that it can penetrate national markets, and be subsidized by national governments, in exchange for some drops of the precious know-how generated by the current technological revolution.

4. At this point we should introduce in the analysis the specific economic policies through which different countries are trying to find their way out of the structural economic crisis. It is only by studying the interplay between current policies of economic restructuring and qualitative changes induced by the diffusion of new technologies that we will be able to understand the emerging international economy.

Three main factors favor the capacity of a given country in the current economic conjuncture to engage in a process of recovery (OECD, 1984; Lavard, Basevi, Blanchard, Buiter and Kleppe, 1984): the size of its domestic market; its technological capabilities; and its ability to generate public spending without the high risk of inflation (for instance, by being able to finance a budget deficit with foreign capital buying government bonds). The simultaneous action of the three factors reinforce each other, establishing a strong hierarchical relationship between countries in the international economy. If we consider how these three factors rank countries between themselves (an exercise that we will not undertake here to avoid further complicating this report), we find a common sense ordering of the world economy. The United States is at the top, closely followed by Japan; behind them (at an increasing distance) the EEC; further behind are the newly industrialized countries, mainly comprising the growth economies of the Pacific Basin, Portions of Mexico, Brazil, and India, and the incipient industrialized areas of OPEC countries; and finally the majority of Third World countries, increasingly deteriorating in their relationship to the center of the world economy, possibly with the exception of China. At the low-end of the structure a growing number of countries and regions, and therefore of people have an even looser connection with the overall economic structure. Yet it provides the basic, irreversible framework of their existence.

While this international hierarchy is well known, it is important to remind ourselves of two key facts. First, it is an interdependent *structure*, not just an order of importance; it is made up not just of distance, but of asymmetrical, actual relationships. There is not simply a separation between core and periphery but a highly differentiated, complex structure whose precise workings have to be unveiled in each specific conjuncture. Second, technological capacity is a fundamental factor in the organization of the whole structure. And it is a particularly dynamic one. Given the speed of the technological revolution, the technological gap is growing, and it will become irreversible (thus making irreversible the asymmetrical world structure) in the absence of counter-tendencies prevailing against the current trends.

This is not only true for the Third World, but for Western Europe as well. The Common Market is in fact rather uncommon because of its imperfect and arbitrary integration. The lack of flexibility of its economies, and the bureaucratization of the public sector have rendered Europe entirely dependent on the pace of the US economy to fuel its own recovery: in the last decade, in spite of the US recession, the American economy created 20 million new jobs (admittedly, including fast food teenage workers) while Western Europe lost, in net balance, about 5 million jobs. Furthermore, European high technology industries, with few exceptions, are in a shameful state. The gap between them and their Japanese and US competitors is broadening, at times leading them to surrender to technological supremacy and join the bandwagon of the victors (for instance, as in the case of Olivetti). A 1984 official report of the European Community (EEC, 1984, our translation into English) states: "Europe, because of competitive pressure, will have to embrace new technologies, one day or another. If it allows increases in the current technological gap with the US and Japan, the assimilation of new technologies will take place under the worst possible conditions. Its competitiveness will be reduced, unemployment will soar, technological dependency will translate into industrial, economic, and cultural dependency." The prospects are rather grim from a European perspective because, according to the same document, in 1984, "European industry is losing ground in information technologies. Eight out of ten personal computers sold in Europe come from American makers; nine out of ten VCRs sold in Europe come from Japan. European companies have only 30 percent of their national share of integrated circuits and only 13 percent of the world market. In this sector [integrated circuits] Europe as a whole represents one third of the world market, yet it only controls 40 percent of its own market and 10 percent of the world market. . . The situation continues to deteriorate. All European makers of mainframe computers have had to pass agreements with Japanese or American companies to obtain technology transfer" (page 5). Other estimates are even more pessimistic, and assign to Europe a mere 7 percent of the world market of semiconductors (the core of information technologies), against 53 percent to the United States and 39 percent to Japan (*The Economist*, November 24-30, 1984).

Nevertheless, Europe does have first class scientific institutions and a strong technological base that has been able to keep pace in the fields of avionics, missiles, communications equipment, nuclear power, and, to a lesser extent, in biotechnology (FAST, 1984). And yet, two major flaws seem to be causing a decisive handicap for Europe: the first is the inability to translate scientific discoveries into industrial and commercial applications; the second (not unrelated to the first), is the failure of European research and technological development in two key fields: microelectronics and computers. Because they are the core of information technologies, and because it is information technology that commands the current stream of technological innovation, it is doubtful that Europe could ever bridge the existing gap. Some European programs of technological cooperation, such as ESPRIT (FAST, 1984), are now trying to bring together resources and political will to avoid a technological dependency that in today's world will be translated in dependency *tout court*. The launching of EUREKA in 1985 under the initiative of the French government could be a major step in such a direction. Yet, EUREKA is too closely associated with the political battle against the SDI program, a battle many European governments are reluctant to join precisely because of their fear of losing access to a key source of new technologies. Overall, Europe is waking up to the awareness of the key role played by the technological revolution in the restructuring of our world. It remains to be seen if the political priority given to the technological *aggiornamento* can overcome cultural and bureaucratic resistances to the utmost effort of mobilization Europe would require to at least keep pace with the United States and Japan in the technological race. The issue concerns the entire world, and particularly the Third World. Because only if there is a technologically advanced Europe, will the Third World be able to bargain for its technological development with a plurality of partners, without being immediately confronted with the techno-political rivalry between the two superpowers, or having to choose between American or Japanese economic domination.

5. The impact of the technological revolution on the Third World in the international division of labor is even more dramatic and far-reaching. In fact, together with the process

of economic restructuring, the impact of the new technologies has laid to rest the very notion of "a Third World," if it ever existed. The situations of many countries are becoming not only different (they always were) but they even belong to contradictory processes, whose dynamics pull them apart from each other, into distinct historical constellations.

For the sake of clarity we will risk a highly schematic presentation of the differential impact of the current techno-economic restructuring for several groups of countries with specific positions in the international division of labor:

A. A first group includes the few truly newly industrialized countries, basically Korea, Taiwan, Hong Kong, and Singapore, with Malaysia striving to join them. They are connecting more and more closely to the core economies, and particularly to the dynamics of the US market. They have used new technologies both as a tool to modernize their industry, making it more competitive, and as a product-line for jumping into the world market, with the increasing sophistication of their electronics industries. For instance, Korea's electronics labor force amounted, in 1984, to about 350,000 workers (Government of Korea, 1985), that is, more than all Silicon Valley and Route 128 employees combined, although at a much lower level of skill. Therefore, one can think of the "four Asian tigers" as having joined the industrialized world, and are even likely to surpass some European countries in the near future, by being able to shift from an export strategy based on low-pricing to a new industrial competitiveness based upon the dynamic accumulation of new technologies and new technological products. It must be recalled that such an accomplishment is *not* the result of laissez faire capitalism, or of the beneficial effects of off-shore production by multinational corporations. All four cases are government-led processes of economic development (see Schiffer, 1983, and Castells, 1985, for Hong Kong; Hamilton, 1984, and Luedde-Neurath, for Korea; Wade, 1984, and Lee, 1981, for Singapore; and Chen, 1979, and Browett, 1985, for the overall argument). With the exception of Singapore, the multinationals play a minor role in exports (74 percent of Hong Kong exports and 75 percent of Korean exports come from local, non-subsidiary companies). And the domestic market is decisive for their industrial expansion, with the obvious exception of the city-states (Singapore and Hong Kong). The export-led strategy leaping forward to join the industrialized world by means of the technological revolution is clearly an exception in the overall historical trend, although it is an important exception from which we can learn many lessons about the development process and the potentials for a fruitful assimilation of new technologies. Incidentally, authoritarian regimes such as those governing the four countries are neither a precondition nor a consequence of the development process. If anything, they are likely to be undermined by the complex civil society emerging from a developed, highly internationalized economy.

B. A second group of countries corresponds to the model of the so-called "new international division of labor", experiencing dependent industrialization linked to decentralized production by multinationals or their subcontractors on the basis of cheap labor and low government regulations. The second ring of Southeast Asian countries (Lee, 1981) could be included here (Vasquez, 1985), particularly Thailand, the Philippines, and some of Malaysia, along with a number of Caribbean islands, some of them specializing in routine key-punching operations for data-processing services, beamed back and forth by satellite. Also, some areas of some countries, basically included in a different position in the world economy, might fit this model: the Mexican border regions (Perlo, 1986), the Chinese Special Economic Zones, and some Brazilian industries (such as shoes and leather) entirely aimed at exports on the basis of low labor costs. For this group of countries, the new techno-economic model has a contradictory, two-fold effect. On the one hand, production can be dispersed across the world and reunited by technological means in a single process. Also, small companies, using data transmission equipment can actually tap on the world market, while keeping a lean, flexible organization. On the other hand, automation makes industrial production in the North easier and relatively cheap, at a moment when political uncertainty and the cost of managerial and technical personnel seem to call into question some of the advantages of off-shoring. Although empirical evidence on the matter is scant, an educated guess would suggest that off-shore production will continue but at a much slower pace. The second round of peripheral industrialization will not take place on a large scale (for instance in the Philippines), on the sole basis of an export-oriented strategy. Domestic markets still will be fundamental for a lasting process of development.

C. A third category includes those countries whose population size and industrial potential make feasible, at least in theory, a process of technological modernization aimed simultaneously at their domestic market and at the world economy. Generally speaking, it would seem that technology transfer and capital accumulation will have their dynamic component in an export-oriented strategy, around which the rest of the economy would experience a gradual incorporation. Brazil, Mexico, maybe Argentina, more recently China, and to some extent India, could be examples of this specific situation. For these countries, the eruption of new technologies is a mixed blessing. On the one hand, they can accelerate their pace toward modernization, leaping over the traditional sequence of industrialization. On the other hand, their main comparative advantage (low production costs) is partly offset by automation. Besides, their need to access technological know-how places them in a much greater dependency vis-à-vis the core economies, since autonomous technological capacity cannot be developed in a few years, while the pace of innovation dramatically accelerates. For instance, if we take the example of the most industrialized country among them, Brazil (currently the tenth largest industrial output in the world), its first item for exports is military equipment, including tanks, armored cars, helicopters, and light planes. Its competitive advantage is low-price for cash-short Third World governments in need of military hardware, along with the absence of any political conditions attached to the sale. Yet, the increasing sophistication of weaponry forces Brazil to enhance its technological level very quickly if it wants to survive in this lucrative market. This will entail considerable efforts to obtain technological licensing and know-how, rendering Brazilian industry increasingly dependent on its sources of innovation in the core economies. At the same time, the modern, multinational sector of the industry will come under increasing pressure to automate to keep its share of the world market; for instance, this is the case for the Brazilian automobile industry that will be among the eight largest automobile producers in the world, and the largest in the Third World, by the end of this decade (UNIDO, 1984). Thus, new industrialization will be less labor-intensive, increasing the problem of absorption of the surplus work population whose migration from the countryside will be accelerated by the bio-technological revolution in agriculture.

This process is just beginning, given the incredibly low-level of penetration of new technologies in most semi-peripheral countries, even one as industrialized as Brazil. For instance, in 1984, in the entire Brazilian industry, there were only 50 industrial robots, 15 CAD systems, and 850 numerically controlled machine-tools in only 266 industrial companies, out of the 120,600 such companies in the whole country. All companies with some level of automated equipment are either foreign or subsidiaries of multinationals. Concerning services, a similar low-level of information technology appears to exist, for instance, less than 5 percent of banks' branches (the first service industry to use new technologies in all countries) use on-line communications systems (Costa Souza, 1985). On the other hand, because it is aware of the strategic importance of information technologies, Brazil is trying to create an endogenous base for such developments. For instance, it has forbidden the import of mini- and micro-computers, so that Brazilian computer makers can grow on the basis of their domestic market. Nevertheless, it seems doubtful that Brazil, or any other country in the Third World, could develop its own technological base without relying on technology transfer from the multinationals. But is it to the advantage of these companies to agree to such a transfer? That is why China is receiving so much attention from American, Japanese, and West European companies. In exchange for the technological and managerial know-how the Chinese expect to receive from foreign companies, these companies seek, primarily, to position themselves in a market of a billion people that will gradually increase (they hope) its purchasing power.

So, three processes simultaneously taking place are associated with techno-economic restructuring in the largest countries of the Third World: the positioning of the multinational companies in these large, protected markets, using their technological know-how as their primary bargaining chip; the strategy of these large countries to increase their competitive edge in the world economy, with technological modernization in the mid-term while still taking advantage of their low-prices through cheap labor; and the expansion of industrial capability on the basis of large domestic markets that will be served by an increasingly efficient, technologically advanced industry.

What of the compatibility between the three processes? For instance, if the price for technology transfer is opening up the domestic market to the multinationals, it will be difficult for the national companies to build up enough strength on their own ground to be able to compete abroad in a second stage (remember that Japan and Korea first developed their industrial might from protected domestic markets). On the other hand, if protectionism arises, it is unlikely that technology transfer will happen at any significant level. Take another major issue: employment, and therefore solvent demand. If large-scale automation is required to compete in the world economy in terms of quality standards, the technological modernization of the industrial base is unlikely to generate enough jobs to stimulate the urban economy and to broaden the domestic market. Instead, it will be increasing competition, by both national and multinational corporations, on a relatively small upper-level urban market.

The overall effect seems likely to be the increasing disarticulation of the national economy (and to some extent of society), not between multinational corporations and indigenous capital, but between a highly dynamic sector of the world economy, both as producer and market, and a series of destructured segments that will mix their roles as subcontracting sweatshops for the internationalized sector, as providers of goods and services for specific domestic sub-markets, and as daily inventors of survival strategies.

D. A fourth group of countries comprises the major oil-producers. In principle, their wealth (in spite of the leveling off of oil prices), makes them potential markets for technological modernization and industrialization. In some cases, as in Nigeria and Indonesia, their population size is also a major potential asset. In recent years, these countries have sought to use their financial resources to create an industrial base aimed mainly at import substitution, although still keeping in mind the world market, particularly in petrochemicals. Yet, a number of different elements have fundamentally flawed developmental processes: (a) Exacerbated nationalism and religious fanaticism, manipulated by the superpowers, have pitched countries against each other (notably Iraq and Iran), wrecking their economies, killing their people, and diverting technological modernization from industry to the army. (b) Weak political institutions, widespread corruption, and unstable domestic ethnic and cultural cleavages have channeled resources towards the bureaucracy for the personal advantage of its members. Such seems to be, particularly, the case of Nigeria during the 1970s (Lubeck, 1985). (c) The attempt to create a national industrial base, in the midst of the opening up of the international economy, turned major public investments into gigantic money losers. Hastily financed by international banks, such ventures transformed oil revenue surpluses into unpayable foreign debt, thus deepening financial dependency and halting the process of autonomous industrialization. Venezuela and Mexico are perhaps the most typical cases.

With the exception of Mexico (whose connection with the US economy makes it more susceptible to direct technological modernization), most of the oil producing countries will be users, rather than producers of new technologies. They are targeted as important potential markets by high technology corporations ready to sell the consumption of the technological revolution at a high price, while those countries maintain, by and large, a dependent economy and a traditional society. In some cases, oil-hungry governments such as France are exchanging technological products for oil, for instance with Nigeria, enlarging the practice of barter that is becoming a major factor in international trade.

But, in general, oil producers have been unable to use their resources to generate industrial development. This is partly because the coincidence of the rise of high technology with the oil bonanza has restructured the international economy. The technological dependence of oil producers on new industrial equipment is deepened and it is now more difficult to enter the competition in the world economy on the basis of heavy industry which the oil producing countries were trying to build. Political manipulation opened up profitable markets for high tech weapons. Financial greed lent massive capital to the "nouveaux riches" to tie them, and the rest of the world along, to the "global debt bomb" (Carnoy, 1985). This process refutes the assumption that capital supply is the source of development. Indeed neither the largest inflow of capital in recent history, nor the existence of unlimited technological possibilities, were able to engage countries with archaic, exploitative structures, and tied frequently to the superpowers' geopolitical games, to undertake development seriously.

E. Most of the Third World countries are being largely bypassed by the current technological revolution, except for its military implications, consumer electronics products, and the connection of its directional centers to an integrated network of world telecommunications. Thus, only a few segments of the productive structure and increasingly narrow markets participate in the process of new peripheral industrialization. Furthermore, new agricultural technology is helping increase labor redundancy in the modern, capitalist exploitations, thus accelerating rural-urban migration. numerous raw materials are being replaced by synthetic, advanced materials, condemning large areas of the world to economic obsolescence. Functional and social distance is not only increasing between countries, but also between regions of the same country. The downturn of the core economies is also hurting the export capability of most Third World countries, while they are unlikely to enter the competition in the new information technologies (Eward, 1984; Saunders, et al., 1983).

High interest rates in the center, and fluctuating exchange rates for national currencies, are imposing an unbearable burden of servicing the interest on foreign debts in increasingly depressed economies (Carnoy, 1985). Unemployment, misery, hunger, illness, and individual violence, are on the increase all over the Third World, and particularly in the large urban centers. New technologies by themselves have little influence on such trends. Yet, the peculiar world-wide economic structure to which they contribute relates to the increasing social and economic dislocation of most Third World countries. By interconnecting economically and technologically valuable elements of each country at the world level, and disconnecting social groups, regions, cities, individuals, and sometimes entire countries that do not belong to the new, dynamic techno-economic system, the current process of restructuring is fragmenting the social fabric of the planet, and recomposing only some of them, into a structure that fits predominantly the interests of dominant governments and corporations.

People, regions, countries, and governments, react against such trends. In most cases, there is a survival reaction, with the expanding informal economy defining its own rules of the game on the local shop floors of most Third World cities. Also, new unintended forms of connection between center and periphery take place—for instance, production of and trade in drugs on a huge, international scale. With the collapse of the world's tin markets, and the reluctance of foreign capital to invest in a class-conscious, highly politicized country, Bolivian peasants are tapped by drug traffickers to make coca production and (illegal) export of coca paste the major export of the country (Flores and Blanes, 1983). Such a large, uncontrolled cash-economy, in dollars, wrecks the country's monetary system, triggering unsustainable inflation. Colombia, with a stronger, more diversified economy, is at the core of cocaine traffic; Peru, Ecuador, some areas of Brazil and Mexico, are also now entering the race. Thus, new ties are being established between the center and the periphery that pervert the dreams of universal development by means of technological progress. There is still a connection between Silicon Valley and Bolivia, but it is the technological switch-off of Bolivia from the new international economy and its delinquent tie-in with cocaine traffic aimed at markets such as the one represented by Silicon Valley engineers for them to be able to keep pace with the frantic race for technological innovation.

Some countries do react against their internal fragmentation and global marginality, rallying around their national governments to strive for political autonomy and economic modernization aimed at their domestic markets, responsive to their people's needs. In different contexts, and with diverse ideologies. Mozambique, Nicaragua, and Peru are trying to keep afloat their societies without submitting to the logic of global imperatives. Yet, the path is so narrow, and aggression or opportunistic manipulation by both superpowers so blatant, that we still have no example of a country setting its own national development path with relative autonomy vis-à-vis the international economy. As soon as people and nations have to address the issue of their relationship to the world's economic structure, old and new patterns of dependency combine to close exits, and channel countries toward one of two positions: the international division of labor, currently structured around high technology industries and financial institutions, and political alignment within the power blocs organized around the superpowers striving for strategic supremacy. In both cases, Third World countries will have to deal inescapably with the new technological equation. Thus, new technologies have not transformed the world into a global village of communicative fellow humans. Rather, the new techno-economic restructuring is fragmenting people and isolating countries, to combine them into a reconstructed image made of the silent fulfillment of invisible structural interests.

* * *

[Section IV omitted]

V. Alternative technology or alternative society?

New technologies are not responsible for the shameful state of our world. In fact, it is the ultimate paradox to realize that, while we now have the economic and technological possibility of fulfilling much of humankind's historical utopias, our social and political institutions are the two barriers to their realization. Nevertheless, new technologies are so powerful and so pervasive that they do accelerate and emphasize the contradictory tendencies present in our societies. Thus, the economic uses of automation translate labor saving into job suppression, and work flexibility into union busting. Uneven development on the world scale transforms the impulse for technological innovation into an insurmountable technological gap for dependent, impoverished Third World countries. The new media reinforce the tendency toward social isolation and turn the electronic home into an individualistic inner space, open to the sounds and images of the entire planet, yet too often closed to face-to-face interaction. The most powerful innovative technologies are appropriated and kept secret, to be geared toward warfare, keeping our world a nuclear hostage of state terrorism in the competition between the superpowers. While new technologies are based upon free flows of information, hidden bureaucracies tend to channel them into the purpose of scrutinizing people to program their lives. On the edge of liberating its creativity by the means of an unprecedented technological revolution, humankind becomes the slave of its own collective monsters, fostered by the greediness of capital and the despotism of state. Under these circumstances, it is understandable that people, including intellectuals and scientists, all over the world have criticized the current technological revolution and denounced its militaristic, authoritarian, and exploitative ramifications. Consequently, some of the critics of new technologies argue for alternative paths of technological development that are closer to "human nature" and more respectful of ecological equilibrium in searching for the harmony of lost, simpler, rural-like communities. In most cases, without taking such extreme positions, the horror of the militarization and bureaucratization of the new technological environment has led responsible professionals and grass-roots groups to resist the inevitability of the current process of technological change, looking for alternative ways to handle work and everyday life. While such reactions are entirely understandable, they are, in our opinion, fundamentally confused. And this is for two basic reasons: first, because technologies are not the cause but the instrument of the devastating effects being produced in the current historical process; second, because in order to transform this process, it is crucial to recognize the ineluctability of technologically-induced structural transformations, so as to be able to address our social and political problems in their new historical terms. In other words, instead of withdrawing into the seclusion of alternative technology (which can only be a marginal phenomenon), we ought to struggle for an alternative society that will incorporate, master, and reshape the extraordinary technological discoveries that are taking place. After all, the primacy of information implies the coming of culture and symbols to the forefront of our experience and social organization, making society potentially freer to construct itself around its own desires. This is precisely why, barely out of our pre-historic era, when hunger, illness, torture, and massacres are still the actual problems faced by much of humankind today, the level of our technological development is much higher than that of our social development. The solution to this gap is not to downgrade our scientific creativity but to enhance our social organization. Such is the challenge to which this report humbly attempts to contribute.

Sociologists know that visions of a better world must be rooted in the historical workings of a given society, to have any chance of achieving the status of human experience. At the same time, such action-oriented visions cannot be reduced to linear extrapolations of current trends. The factor of will, the consciousness and purpose of human subjects, individual or collective, are an objective social process by themselves. Visions are not utopias because they connect with material, historical trends. But they are human matter, that is, a particular form of matter that is self-reflective, and can therefore act upon its own environment.

It is in this twilight zone between utopia and pragmatism that we would like to suggest potential ways to orient the technological revolution toward social uses more humane than those currently in the making.

The fundamental idea which we want to put forward is that, rather than alternative uses of technology, what we need are alternative forms of social organization capable of resisting the formidable stress to which our current institutions will be subjected by the ongoing technological revolution.

To be sure, some of the new information technologies could be put to a better use. For instance, communication technologies could be used to enhance interactive systems of popular consultation at the level of local government institutions. Or, instead of using computers for state control of people's private lives, citizens could be authorized to penetrate the informational avenues of *their* government, at whatever level, from their personal computers. Handicapped people should be rendered mobile on a large scale by using currently restricted technologies; and the blind could read by using machines already at work in the intelligence services. Biotechnology could be spread out from the commercial wishes of pharmaceutical multinationals to contribute to Third World agricultural production in the countryside, and to the Third World's serious pollution and sewage problems in its new sprawling cities.

Yet, a few well-intentioned twists to the general pattern of using new technologies will do little in comparison with the fundamental structural transformation to which new technologies are contributing along the lines we have described in this report. What we require, most urgently, is a social restructuring able to match, and to control, the techno-economic restructuring underway. We will briefly indicate what seem to be the main axes of social transformation required to articulate in a creative way the effects of technological transformation.

The first major domain in which an alternative society must emerge in the forthcoming years is work and employment. Instead of eliminating jobs or contributing to the polarization of the occupational structure, new technologies could be used, and should be used, to redefine the social nature of work. Paid working time should be reduced dramatically for everybody, so that everybody has the possibility of being employed. Productivity increases, allowed by widespread automation, could provide substantial pay for less working time, even allowing for a fair increase of private profit for employers in a capitalist economy.

What sounds utopian is in fact not much different from the actual historical transition from the condition of salaried work in the nineteenth century to labor legislation in Western Europe in the second half of this century: blue-collar workers have about one-third less working time, while their real take-home pay has increased substantially, let alone their general standards of living. When the German metalworkers' union went on strike for a 35-hour week without reduction in pay (obtaining, in fact, 38 1/2 in the automobile industry), they were putting forward the demand we propose to generalize as the overarching principle of a new social organization of work, made possible because of the coming of the information revolution: let us share paid working time, so that everybody has, at the same time, a sure job and more free time. Nevertheless, such a goal will be impossible to fulfill on a significant scale, unless it is generalized simultaneously at the international level. Otherwise, competition between countries and companies will wreck the economic foundations of those engaging in the path of social change. The example of France, reducing just one hour per week of working time in 1981, and paying heavily for it in terms of jobs and income, is quite indicative in this sense. But to speak of a generalized international policy of sharing working-time is, in fact, to speak of a fundamental transformation of values and of the principles of social and economic organization. Because for free-time/equal-pay to be more than a countercultural gadget, a number of economic and social issues have to be addressed.

Economically, we have to make explicit the relationship existing between free time and higher productivity in the workplace, so that the reduction of working time does not necessarily mean the reduction of actual production input in the work process. The connection is established precisely by the new, strategic role of information as a source of productivity. The more a worker of the information age is educated, healthy, relaxed, equilibrated, up-to-date on a variety of information and activities, integrated in his or her personal, family, and community life, the more her or his brain is alert and innovative. It is as simple as that: in the information economy, the improvement, maintenance, and repair of the human mind is the most important productivity investment that can be made. And because of the social characteristics of our species, the conditions of a more productive intellect, on a sustained basis, are precisely the possibility of enjoying a multidimensional, equilibrated, healthy, everyday life, in which the individual is not wasted but enhanced by his or her way of living. In fact, many high-tech companies already employ this philosophy for their top researchers and designers, trying to accommodate them with flexible time and to provide them with access to health clubs, recreational activities, educational improvement, and the like. Yet, most of the scientists and engineers are true workaholics and hardly live a healthy, harmonious life. But this is due to the current one-dimensionality of social change. Some individuals can express themselves in work-related innovation, while still being incapable of other experiences, with the exception of indulging themselves in compensatory consumption. So, once having bought a second BMW and still be trapped in the same traffic jams to rejoin the dullness of an anonymous suburb, the avenues of technological discovery appear as the only true open road for those human spirits able to travel along them. Therefore, the ability to become a multidimensional human being does not depend only on the free control of our time, but requires a broader cultural transformation that has to be part of the articulated process of social change constructed around the information revolution.

Such changes of the relationship between work and social life are not limited to the top of the productive scale—researchers, engineers, and managers. It could in fact permeate the entire occupational structure, if we consider three elements: (a) Most of the routine work, including services, could easily be automated. (b) Therefore, information-processing will play a major role in almost all jobs, since for each position a number of machines will have to be instructed and a variety of situations will have to be assessed and decided upon. As a matter of fact, research done in our universities on the transformation of work in the insurance companies points to the dramatic upgrading of skills in those few middle-management positions that survive automation. The problem, of course, is the downgrading of life for subsequently laid-off workers, as well as their re-entry in the labor market through even more routine, lower-paid jobs, as we have pointed out in this report. This is why upgrading of some key working positions, which are not only professionally rewarding but well-paid as well, has to go along with automation of much of the routine work, and with the sharing of the dramatically reduced working time among everyone (assuming, too, that everyone has the skills, or education, to keep up with such qualified jobs). (c) To connect the need for creativity, as generated outside the workplace, with information-processing productivity at work, on a general scale, we also have to abandon the old (yet too-present) distinction between intellectual and manual labor. Many non-scientific, non-high-tech jobs require tremendous cultural skills and professional qualifications, which take a long education and an even more supportive lifestyle to develop, for these jobs to be done properly.

Let us take just two examples among the occupations that most rapidly develop in the low-level service activities of post-industrial economies: cooks and security guards. Cooking, as everybody knows, is an art, and an art that takes sensitivity, culture, professional know-how, and even the ability to relate to changing patterns of social behaviour. We also know how much people fulfill themselves, given the chance and the time, in innovative cooking. Why shouldn't professional cooks be highly trained, sophisticated, information-processing workers, instead of junk-food frying-pan operators? The issue resides with our social organization, not with the relationship between the activity itself, the role of information technology, and the social conditions required to "produce" a good cook able to do a proper job.

Or, what could be more complex, sophisticated, and challenging than working as a security guard, trying to prevent violence or crime, to approach each situation in a sensible manner, to defuse tension, to comfort victims, to enforce a just legal procedure, to diminish pain, and to preserve personal property? Of course, one could also ask why, in such a "new society", we would still need security guards. But we are not projecting dreams, just generating visions of what technological progress makes possible if we dare to engage in the new historical stage of social struggles. And we do not foresee the end of violence and transgression of the law, since human nature includes a biological component of aggressiveness.

The information process of work has no limits, no elitist bias; it permeates the entire realm of our activity, provided we decide to enhance the quality of our life in a true multidimensional approach. At that level of structural transformation, work and social life become interpenetrated to reunite the whole meaning of human experience.

Thus, from an economic point of view, the loss of productivity linked to the reduction of the quantity of work can be more than offset by the productivity generated by the quality of work in the information economy. And such quality is produced, enhanced, and preserved by the whole development of human creativity, both physical and intellectual, allowed by a multidimensional pattern of life that requires freer and more flexible use of time, outside the rules of specific organizations. Under the productive conditions of the information age, free time and organized work could complement each other.

Nevertheless, such a profound transformation of work is unlikely to succeed (leaving aside for the moment the political obstacles to fulfilling this vision) in the absence of a dramatic cultural change and of social policies aimed at providing the material conditions for the expression of a new, multidimensional personality. The new welfare state would be one emphasizing the accessibility to the arts, to scientific knowledge, to manual work, to languages, to travel, to sports and physical fitness, to outdoor experiences, and to interactive, decentralized communications media for everyone. Many programs for youth in advanced industrial societies already do just that. But there is some implicit conception that this "play time" should be reserved for some short period for the very young and for the leftover time of the very old, once they have accomplished their period of duty. Why could not general-purpose, free activities, and focused, salaried activities be combined in a different pattern along the entire life cycle? According to sexist social rules, women can stay at home bringing up children for a few years, to work later, once their family duties have been fulfilled. What if we redistribute working time and social time between genders and between ages, reducing constrained activities and making free time potentially productive because of its enhancing of creative capabilities? The main obstacle for the development of a holistic welfare state is not economic but cultural and political. Cultural, because we have equated not being paid with not being worthwhile, and because social services are considered a redistributional matter instead of being understood as human capital formation. Political, because we associate the welfare state with centralized, costful bureaucracies, providing services or allocating payments to their passive clientele. And yet, the state is us; the services "they" deliver are of our utmost concern. Therefore, citizen participation in the management of state institutions, volunteerism, and free-work contribution could dramatically increase the capacity to generate services and to support activities. Of course, voluntary organizations must not substitute for the services and programs that people are entitled to require from the state. Also, such programs could easily be financed with increased revenues from a highly productive information economy, and decreased expenditures from a much smaller military budget, rendered obsolete by other measures we will discuss below. Thus, what we are suggesting is that *in addition* to a rationalized, flourishing welfare state, citizen participation and users' involvement could greatly expand the range and quality of public services infrastructure, from which would blossom widespread human creativity. Such a decentralized, participative structure requires, of course, a different kind of state; one that would use information technology to decentralize its power, and that would translate democratic principles into full involvement by citizens in the management and control of public affairs.

The cultural obstacles can be the most difficult to overcome. Thousands of years of submissive labor and oppressive politics have created in us the habit of conceding our working time in exchange for the preservation of our own preserved patch. Yet, as most social research on activities of the retired shows, harsh work and a harsh life leave little room for the self-expression of people, even if, and when, they are on their own time. Life is most often dried up from the inside. This is why the structural transformation we are advocating will have to start with the next generation. A revolution must take place in our schools while we set up the institutional framework and the economic policies necessary for the historical reconversion of the productive structure. Our children will have to be provided not only with computers (they will be, anyway, so in fact some major change is going on), but with the technical ability to use them *at all levels*, and with the social personality capable of entering the new world. The school system is a strategic ace in the making of the new world. If we just let the spontaneous trends of the technological revolution enter our schools as they are, we will see a dramatic reinforcement of social selection and discrimination by class, by gender, and by race. Our schools are totally obsolete, and not simply technologically, but intellectually and organizationally. The computer in the school, in every class of every school, must be accompanied by a total restructuring of the educational system, to overcome social obstacles to the acquisition of information technology, and to socialize the children of the next generation in the new world of multidimensional personality that the information age makes functionally necessary and socially desirable. To be sure, the education and socialization process does not take place only in the school, and will have to include a reorientation of the relationship between children and the media, community-based programs aimed at children's activities, and a vast educational effort toward the families, so that they can manage the cultural transition.

It is this combination of economic policies, social programs, political reform, and cultural revolution, that will help to plant alternative seeds for the future society that is now in the making. It follows very different lines, and is predicated on the power of a technological revolution confiscated and turned aside by our obsolete political bureaucracies.

Visions such as the ones we have outlined in this section might seem inappropriate when we keep in mind the current conditions in Third World countries, and the rather bleak prospects that, as we have shown, the acceleration of the historical tempo by the technological revolution, offers to them. And yet, the Third World too has to come to grips with the reality that, unless we plan alternative paths of development, the conditions for most people in most countries will dramatically worsen over the next two decades—and this not only on the economic plane, but also in the overall structure of society, as we tried to explain in Section III. The two basic problems confronting the Third World, in relation to the current technological revolution, are the increasing technological gap they will fall into, and the disconnection/reconnection process that will destabilize national societies while strengthening global power. To avoid the tremendous disruptive potential of such processes, we must develop immediate feasible alternatives that introduce a different dynamic in the relationship between new technologies and the Third World.

Third World countries will have to combine self-reliance while playing the technological game in the international arena. By no means can they afford to be left out of the current technological revolution, with its potential for improving their living conditions much faster and with less effort. On the other hand, such technology transfer should take place under the control and in the interest of Third World peoples, sometimes represented by their national governments. This is a nice, abstract principle, but extremely difficult to be concretely implemented.

An obvious bottom line is the reinforcement of the technological endogenous potential of the Third World by building cooperative advanced research institutions through the joint effort of national governments and international institutions in key areas of the world. Many of the top scientists and engineers of the OECD countries are from the Third World, and a substantial number of them would gladly return home if given the material and institutional opportunities to pursue their scientific endeavors. Furthermore, until such institutions exist on a large scale, it seems useless to continue sending Third World graduates to receive PhDs in the United States or Europe, at great cost, for their own benefit, and the further concentration of research capabilities in a few world-dominant centers. A program to stop the brain-drain starts with the creation of conditions for these brains to develop in their own countries in the first place. Given the scarce resources of most countries, the building of a few major regional international institutions in the key technological areas seems to be the most fruitful way. The United Nations could sponsor such an effort, but multinational corporations should be called in also to give support, both financially and technologically, in exchange for the access they obtain to markets and locations. If the Singapore government has been successful in building such institutions with the support of various corporations, there is no reason why other countries should not amplify the effort, particularly if they cooperate in it and receive the backing of international institutions. There is no greater priority for Third World development in the next quarter of a century than to create the conditions for the expansion of its human capital.

Along with this effort at the top, Third World governments must be helped to introduce computer literacy at a higher scale in their primary and secondary schools. It may seem ridiculous to propose such a program when schools simply do not exist for a substantial proportion of the population. Yet it is precisely because a new educational system has to be built that Third World countries should leap over the traditional stages of development to create new schools with the help of information tools and aimed at educating their people about the information age—which, as we maintain, goes far beyond just using computers.

On a third level, technological cooperation with the Third World could receive a decisive impetus by using new technologies, particularly in agriculture and health care, to deal with the fundamental problems of survival against hunger and illness. Joint programs between governments, community groups, multinational corporations, and international institutions could target specific areas and problems, and concentrate research efforts and technological training, in the same manner as companies seeking to discover a potentially profitable product. Throughout the process, the implementation of such programs at Third World sites would also train the technicians and scientists who will bring their knowledge, in the near future, to the fulfillment of the self-reliant politics on which the Third World will ultimately have to count.

The fourth fundamental axis of intervention in this area concerns the need to keep the internal coherence of national societies, in their regional context, vis-à-vis the techno-economic pattern of asymmetrical flows of domination and control, as described in Section III. Several lines of policy are available to Third World countries. The most important matter is to reinforce the social fabric at the grass-roots level and to closely connect it to national institutions and policy-making, while accepting the necessary tensions and contradictions involved in such a process. On the basis of widespread citizen participation and face-to-face interaction in the public domain, the historical roots and cultural specificities of societies offer enough resistance to the penetration of electronic flows so that new messages can be assimilated, and reinterpreted, without local cultures becoming diffused into the foreign-controlled networks of flows. Another fundamental element would be a national policy of telecommunications, including the media. This is not necessarily for governments to control messages, but for countries to set up their own systems of communication, enabling them to connect to the world network under their own terms and conditions. Telecommunications and media policies are key components of any process of national development today; yet they are often neglected in order to concentrate on apparently more urgent matters, thus undermining a country's future.

As a last example of how Third World governments could fight to avoid their increasing marginality in the world-wide system of decision flows, governments of different ideologies have an objective interest in reinforcing regional economic and political organizations, with the specific aim of dealing collectively with major transnational corporations. Only in this manner can governments avoid being played against each other in the economic strategies of world-wide organizations. After all, most governments in the Third World have more in common between themselves than with the multinationals. Since cooperation with major companies will still be a necessity for a long time, the only way out of the contradiction is to present a common front, at least at the regional level, and to debate internal differences within the regional institutions. The problem will be to set up such a system without duplicating wasteful, ineffective international bureaucracies. If there is truly a political will, the operational procedure could be extremely fast, with a very light infrastructure. For instance, a system of on-line telecommunication, monitoring several countries' economic activity on a daily basis, with ad hoc teleconferences among the key decision-makers, could reverse some of the direction of decision flows, decentralizing them, and making the world a more complex yet a more diversified and less centralized network.

The Third World must enter the technological revolution with a clear sense of its specific common interests (in spite of the diversity of situations we have shown), or the fragmentation of its societies will become the one-way terminals of a new, invisible colonization.

Thus, new technologies do transform our societies and our economies, our source of life and our abyss of death. Their pervasive, powerful influence will require all our lucidity, imagination, and courage to restore the internal equilibrium of a technologically developed, socially underdeveloped human species. People do make their own history, and ultimately all the visions we have projected will depend on the capacity of social movements and political institutions to undertake the process of structural transformation. Yet, unless people recognize the actual profile of our world, we will be fighting the shadows of our past, instead of planting the seeds of the next historical harvest.

References

AFL-CIO, *Deindustrialization and the Two-Tier Society* (Washington, DC: AFL-CIO Industrial Union Department, 1948).

N. Akrasanee, *et al.*, (editors), *Trade and Employment in Asia and the Pacific* (Quezon City, Philippines: Council of Asian Manpower Studies, 1977).

B. Balassa (editor), *Development Strategies in Semi-industrial Economics* (Baltimore: The Johns Hopkins University Press, 1982).

B. Baran, *Technological Innovation and Deregulation: the Transformation of the Labour Process in the Insurance Industry* (Berkeley: BRIE, University of California, 1985).

M. Bienefeld and Godfrey (editors), *The Struggle for Development: National Strategies in an International Context* (New York: John Wiley, 1982).

P. Blackburn, R. Coombs and K. Green, *Technology, Economic Growth, and the Labor Process* (New York: St Martin's Press, 1985).

B. Bluestone and B. Harrison, *The Deindustrialization of America* (New York: Basic Books, 1982).

B. Bluestone and B. Harrison, *The Economic State of the Union in 1984: Uneven Recovery, Uncertain Future* (Boston, MA, 1984), unpublished manuscript.

M. Borrus, F. Bar and I. Warde, *The Impacts of Divestiture and Deregulation: Infrastructural Changes, Manufacturing Transition, and Competition in the U.S. Telecommunications Industries* (Berkeley: University of California, BRIE, 1984).

M. Borrus, J. Millstein and J. Zysman, *Responses to the Japanese Challenge in High Technology Innovation, Maturity, and U.S.-Japanese Competition in the Microelectronics* (Berkeley: University of California, BRIE, 1983).

J. Botkin, D. Dimancescu and R. Stata, *The Innovators, Rediscovering America's Creative Energy* (New York: Harper & Row, 1984).

S. Bowles, D. Gordon and T. Weisskopf, *Beyond the Wasteland* (Garden City, NY. Anchor/Doubleday, 1983).

C. I. Bradford, "Newly industrializing countries in an interdependent world." *The World Economy*, vol 5, no 2, 1982, pp. 171-185.

W. Brandt, (Chairman of Commission) *North-South. A Program for Survival* (Cambridge, MA: MIT Press, 1980).

J. Browett, *Industrialization in the Global Periphery: The Significance of the Newly Industrializing Countries* (Adelaide: Flinders University of South Australia, School of Social Sciences, 1985).

Business Week, "Special Report: Collision Course. Can the U.S. Avert a Trade War with Japan?" April 8, 1985.

Business Week, "Pentagon spending is the economy's biggest gun," October 1985.

B. Camus, M. Delattre, J. C. Dutaille, F. Eymard-Duyemay and L. Vasille, *La Crise du Systeme Productie Français* (Paris: INSEE, 1981).

M. Carnoy, *Foreign Debt and Latin American Domestic Politics*, Paper delivered at the Institute of the Americas Brazil Conference, San Diego, CA, November 21-22, 1985.

M. Carnoy, *The Labor Market in Silicon Valley and its Implications for Education* (Stanford: Stanford University, School of Education, Research Report, 1985).

M. Carnoy and M. Castells, *Technology and Economy in the U.S.,* Paper for the UNESCO Conference on Technological Change, Athens, September, 1985.

M. Carnoy, D. Sheaver and R. Rumberger, *A New Social Contract* (New York: Harper & Row, 1983).

M. Castells, *The Economic Crisis and American Society* (Princeton, NJ: Princeton University Press, 1980).

M. Castells, *Public Housing and Economic Development in Hong Kong* (Hong Kong: University of Hong Kong, Centre of Urban Studies and Planning, 1985).

M. Castells, A. Barrera, P. Casals, C. Castano, P. Escario and J. Nadal, *Nuevas tecnologias, economia y sociedad en Espana* (Madrid: Alianza Editorial, 1986).

F. Celada, F. Lopez-Groh and T. Parra *Efectos espaciales de los proceses de reorganisacion del sistema productivo en Madrid* (Madrid: Communidad de Madrid, 1985).

E. K. Y. Chen, *High-Growth in Asian Economies: A Comparative Study of Hong Kong, Japan, Korea, Singapore and Taiwan* (London: Macmillan, 1979).

D. Cockroft, "New Office Technology and Employment," *International Law Review*, vol 119, no 6, Nov-Dec 1980.

S. Cohen and J. Zysman, *Manufacturing Matters* (Berkeley: University of California, BRIE, 1986).

P. R. Costa Souza, *Los impactos economicos y sociales de las nuevas tecnologias en Brasil* (Madrid: Fundesco Seminar on New Technologies in Industrialized Countries, 1985).

G. Dosi, *Technical Change and Industrial Transformation* (New York: St. Martin's Press, 1984).

M. P. Drennen, *Implications of Computer and Communications Technology for Less Skilled Service Employment Opportunities* (New York: Columbia University, Research Report to the US Department of Labor, 1983).

The Economist, "How Europe Has Failed," November 24-30, 1984.

R. S. Eward, *The Competition for Markets in International Communications* (Dedham, MA: Artech House, 1984).

EEC, Office of Economic European Community *The Europe of New Technologies*, Madrid Office, 1984 (Spanish text).

D. Ernst, *The Global Race in Micro-electronics* (Frankfurt: Campus Verlag, 1980).

FAST, *Eurofutures: The Challenges of Innovation* (London: Butterworth, 1984).

G. Flores and J. Blanes, *¿Donde va el Chapare?* (Cochambamba, Bolivia: Centro de Estudios de la Realidad Economica y Social, 1983).

F. Frobel, J. Henricks and O. Kreye, *The New International Division of Labor* (Cambridge: Cambridge University Press. 1980).

A. Glasmeier, *Spatial Differentiation of High Technology Industries* (Berkeley: University of California, Dept. of City and Regional Planning, Ph.D. Dissertation, 1986).

N. Glickman, *International Economic Change and the Cities*, Paper delivered at the Annual Conference of the American Collegiate Schools of Planning, Atlanta, GA, 1985.

R. Gordon and L. M. Kimball. *High Technology, Employment and the Challenges to Education* (Santa Cruz: University of California, Silicon Valley Research Group, 1985).

Government of Korea, *Current Status and Prospects of Information and Communication industry in Korea*, Paper delivered at the FUNDESCO Seminar on new Technologies in Industrialized Countries, Madrid: FUNDESCO, 1985.

C. Hamilton, "Class, State, and Industrialization in South Korea," *Institute of Development Studies Bulletin*, vol 5, no 2, 1984, pp. 38-43.

J. Henderson, "The new international division of labor and American semi-conductor production in South-East Asia," in: D. Watt, C. Dixon and D. Drakakis-Smith (editors), *Multinational Companies in the Third World* (London: Croom Helm, 1986).

J. Henderson and M. Castells (editors), *Global Restructuring and Territorial Development* (London: Sage, 1986).

J. Henderson and A. J. Scott, *Global Restructuring and Internationalization of the American Semiconductor Industry* (Hong Kong: University of Hong Kong, Centre of Urban Studies and Planning, 1986).

J. Henderson and A. J. Scott, "The growth and internationalization of the American semiconductor industry," in: M. Brehemy and R. McQuaid (editors), *The Development of High Technology Industry: An International Survey* (London: Croom Helm, 1986).

L. Hirschhorn, *Beyond Mechanization* (Cambridge, MA: MIT Press, 1984).

H. A. Hunt and T.L. Hunt, *Human Resource Implications of Robotics* (Kalamazoo, MI: W. E. Upjohn Institute for Employment Research, 1983).

Institut Syndical Europeen, *L'impact de la micro-electronique sur l'emploi en Europe Occidentale dans les annees 80* (Brussels: ISE, 1980).

S. Jacobsson and Sigurdson (editors), *Technological Trends and Challenges in Electronics* (Lund, Sweden: University of Lund, 1983).

H. Jansen, *Information and Communication Technologies in the Growth and Employment Crisis* (Berlin: International Conference Organized by the Government of the Federal Republic of Germany and the OECD on the Social Challenge of Information Technologies, November 28-30, 1984).

C. Johnson, *MITI and the Japanese Miracle* (Stanford: Stanford University Press, 1982).

R. E. Kutscher, *Factors Influencing the Changing Employment Structure of the U.S.*, Paper delivered at the Second International Conference of Progetto Milano, Mlilan, January 25, 1985.

B. Kuttner, "The declining middle," *The Atlantic Monthly*, July 1984, pp. 60-72.

Robert Z. Lawrence, (1984a) *The Employment Effects of Information Technologies: An Optimistic View*, Paper delivered at the OECD Conference on the Social Challenge of Information Technologies, Berlin, November 28-30, 1984.

Robert Z. Lawrence, (1984b) *Can America Compete?* (Washington, DC: The Brookings Institution, 1984).

R. Layard, G. Basevi, O. Blanchard, W. Buiter and P. Kleppe, *Europe: the Case for Unsustainable Growth* (Brussels: Centre for European Policy Studies, paper no 8-9, 1984).

E. Lee (editor), *Export-Led Industrialization and Development* (Geneva: I.L.O., Asian Employment Program, 1981).

W. Leontieff and F. Duchin, *The Impacts of Automation on Employment, 1963-2000* (New York: New York University, Institute for Economic Analysis, Research Report, 1984).

N. H. Lim, *Policies to Attract Export-oriented Industries: The Role of Export-processing Zones in the Philippines* (Freiburg: Institute of Development Policy, 1982).

I. M. D. Little, "The experience and causes of rapid labour-intensive development in Korea, Taiwan Province, Hong Kong, and Singapore and the possibilities of emulation," in: E. Lee (editor), *Export-Led Industrialization and Development* (Geneva: ILO, Asian Employment Program, 1982).

P. M. Lubeck, *Authoritarianism, Crisis, and the Urban Industrial Sector. Nigeria's Role in the International Division of Labor* (Hong Kong: Paper delivered at the ISA Conference on the Urban and Regional Impact of the New International Division of Labour, August 1985).

R. Luedde-Neurath, "State Intervention and Foreign Direct Investment in South Korea," *Institute of Development Studies Bulletin*, 15 (2), pp. 18-25.

N. Maeda, "A fact-finding study on the impact of microelectronics on employment," in: *Microelectronics, Productivity and Employment* (Paris: OECD, 1981), pp. 155-180.

L. Maldonado and J. Moore (editors), *Urban Ethnicity in the United States* (Beverly Hills: Sage, 1985).

A. Markusen, *High Tech. Job Markets, and Economic Development Prospects* (Berkeley: University of California, IURD, Working Paper, 1983).

A. Markusen, *Profit Cycles, Oligopoly, and Regional Development* (Cambridge, MA: MIT Press, 1984).

D. Massey, *Spatial Divisions of Labour* (London: Macmillan, 1984).

G. Maxey, *The Multinational Motor Corporation* (London: Croom Helm, 1981).

P. Nayyar,"Transnational corporations and manufactured exports from poor countries," *The Economic Journal*, vol 88, no 1, 1978, pp. 59-84

T. Nazakawa, *Impactos economicos y sociales de las nuevas technologieas en Japon* (Madrid: Fundesco Seminar on New Technologies in Industrialized Countries, 1985).

L. Nicol, *Information Technology, Information networks and On-Line Information Services* (Berkeley: University of California, IURD, 1983).

L. Nicol, "Communications technology: economic and spatial impacts," in: M. Castells (editor), *High Technology, Space, and Society* (Beverly Hills, CA: Sage, 1985).

T. Noyelle, *The Shift to Services*, Paper delivered at the UNIDO Conference on Regional Development and the International Division of Labor, Vienna, August 1984.

J. O'Connor, *Accumulation Crisis* (Oxford: Basil Blackwell, 1984).

OECD, (*Economic Perspectives of OECD*, Paris: OECD, Annual Report, December 1984.

C. Palloix, "The self-expansion of capital on a world scale," *Review of Radical Political Economics*, vol 9, no 2, 1977, pp. 1-28.

R. Peet, "Class Struggle, the relocation of employment, and economic crises, *Science and Society*, vol 48, no 2, 1984, pp. 38-51.

M. Perlo, "Exploring the spatial effects of the Internationalization of the Mexican economy," in: J. Henderson and M. Castells (editors), *Global Restructuring and Territorial Development* (London: Sage, 1986).

N. Piercy (editor), *The Management Implications of New Information Technology* (London: Croom Helm, 1984).

M. Piore and C. Sabel, *The Second Industrial Divide* (New York: Basic Books, 1984).

A. Portes and J. Walton, *Class, Labor, and the International System* (New York: Academic Press, 1981).

J. Rada, *Structure and Behavior of the Semiconductor Industry* (New York: United Nations Center for the Study of Transnational Corporations, 1982).

R. Reich, *The Next American Frontier* (New York: Times Books. 1983).

R. W. Riche. D. E. Hecker and J. D. Burgan, "High technology today and tomorrow: a small slice of the employment pie," *Monthly Labor Review* 1983, pp. 50-58.

N. Rosenberg, *Inside the Block Box. Technology and Economics* (Cambridge: Cambridge University Press, 1982).

W. Rosenberg, "South-Korea: export-led development—severed and unsevered," *Journal of Contemporary Asia*, vol 10, no 3, 1980, pp. 300-308.

R. W. Rumberger, "High technology and job loss." *Technology in Society* vol 6, 1984, pp. 263-284.

R. W. Rumberger and H. M. Levin, *Forecasting the Impact of New Technologies on the Future Job Market* (Stanford: Stanford University School of Education. Research Report, 1984).

S. Sassen-Koob, *Growth and Informalization at the Core: the Case of New York City* (Baltimore: The Johns Hopkins University Press, Jun 8-10 1984).

R. J. Saunders, *et al., Telecommunications and Economic Development* (Baltimore: The Johns Hopkins University Press and the World Bank, 1983).

L. Sawers and W. K. Tabb, *Sunbelt/Snowbelt. Urban Development and Regional Restructuring* (New York: Oxford University Press, 1984).

J. R. Schiffer, *Anatomy of a Laissez-faire Government: The Hong Kong Growth Model Reconsidered* (Hong Kong: University of Hong Kong, Centre of Urban Studies and Planning, 1983).

H. Schmitz, "Industrialization strategies in less developed countries: some lessons of historical experience," *Journal of Development Studies*, vol 21, no 1, 2984, pp. 1-24.

E. Schoenberger, *Direct Foreign Investment in the U.S.* (Berkeley: University of California, Dept. of City and Regional Planning, Ph.D. Dissertation, 1985).

A. J. Scott, *High Technology Industry and Territorial Development: the Rise of the Orange County Complex, 1955-84* (Los Angeles: UCLA, Department of Geography, Research Report, 1985).

G. T. Silvestri, J. M. Lukasiewicz and M. A. Einstein. "Occupational employment projections through 1995," *Monthly Labor Review*, November, 1983, pp. 37-49.

T. Stanback, *Understanding the Service Economy* (Baltimore: Johns Hopkins University Press, 1979).

C. L. Taylor (editor), *Why Governments Grow* (Beverley Hills, CA: Sage, 1983).

L. C. Thurow, "The disappearance of the middle class," *The New York Times*, February 5, 1984.

UNCTC, *Transborder Data Flows and Brazil: The Role of Transnational Corporations, Impacts of Transborder Data Flows, and Effects on National Policies* (New York: North Holland, 1984).

UNIDO, *Restructuring World Industry in a Period of Crisis. The Role of Innovation* (Vienna: UNIDO Division of Industrial Studies, Working Paper, 1981).

UNIDO, *International Industrial Restructuring and the International Division of Labor in the Automotive Industry* (Vienna: UNIDO Division of Industrial Studies, Working Paper, 1984).

N. D. Vasquez, *The impact of the New International Division of Labor on ASEAN Labor: the Philippine Case* (Hong Kong: Paper delivered at the ISA Conference on the Urban and Regional Impact of the New International Division of Labour, 1985).

R. Wade, "Dirigisme Taiwan-style," *Institute of Development Studies Bulletin*, 15(2), pp.65-70.

J. Walton, *The IMF Riot*, Paper delivered at the I.S.A. Conference on the Urban Impact of the New International Division of Labour, Hong Kong, 1985.

J. Zysman and S. Cohen, *The Mercantilist Challenge to the Liberal International Trade Order* (Washington: US Congress, Joint Economic Committee, 1983).

Terms of a North-South Economic Partnership

W. W. Rostow

Introduction

Speaking in Tokyo recently I hazarded the guess that, in the world being created by the new technologies, no single nation would dominate as did Great Britain in the early phase of the cotton textile revolution, or the United States in the early phase of the automobile age. The highly diversified character of the new technologies—which I shall below be calling the "Fourth Industrial Revolution"—decrees that we shall see a great deal of international trade and co-operation in the new sectors as well as competition. The notion of an OECD economy will gradually emerge, gather substance, and begin to co-opt the more advanced developing economies. Indeed, if one reads the economic press with that concept in mind one can observe the building or such an international economy going forward every day, transaction by transaction.[1]

As the ties among the advanced industrial countries become closer, it is essential that a fresh start be made in North-South economic relations; for those relations are increasingly important for all concerned, and they are not now in good shape. The problems confronted in the world economy and the overlap of certain authentic interests of the North and the South ought to yield a steady partnership effort in the 1980s and 1990s. That partnership does not now exist because of certain identifiable, inappropriate policies in both the North and the South. This essay seeks not only to identify our difficulties—but also to suggest how the impasse might be broken and the partnership built. I shall proceed to explore this clear but rather large theme in three steps: to state the underlying conditions which justify or even require a North-South partnership; to identify the sources of frustrations and then to outline how we might proceed.

I am, of course, aware of the danger inherent in any such exercise undertaken by one whose memory and experience of these matters reaches back to the 1950s. If one thing is clear it is that a great deal has changed over these thirty years. The North is different, the South is different, and the relations between them have changed. Moreover, the forces at work in the world economy have altered quite radically.

In fact, I would draw from the experience of the 1950s only one lesson: a North-South intellectual consensus would help the politicians of the 1980s a good deal. It was a major achievement of the intellectuals of the North and the South in the 1950s that they did achieve a consensus among themselves on which working politicians could build when circumstances impelled them to act together on development problems. The intellectual consensus covered the nature of the common interests as between the North and South: a rational—even theoretical—basis for an operational agenda and a mode for implementing the agenda. This consensus played a significant role in the pathbreaking institutional devel-

Originally published in *Millennium: Journal of International Studies*, Vol. 14, No.1, 1985

opments of the late 1950s and early 1960s; for example, the emergence of the World Bank consortia for India and Pakistan, the International Development Association, the Alliance for Progress. We need a substantively different but equivalent consensus now.

Heightened Interdependence and the S-Shaped Path of Growth

Both the economic common interests of the North and the South and the appropriate agenda for a partnership must be rooted in the realities of the world economy. The economic common interests flow from a heightened North-South interdependence which, in turn, is the product of the normally S-shaped path of economic growth (see Figure 1 and Tables 1A and 1B).

Table 1A: *Income Levels and Growth Rates, 1960-1970*

	Population 1967 (millions)	GNP for Capita 1967 US$	Average Annual Growth Rate 1960-70
United States	199	$3,670	3.2%
Group 1 ($1,750–$3,670)	307	3,120	3.4
Group 2 ($1,000–$1,750)	238	1,490	3.5
Group 3 ($700–$1,000)	444	930	6.5
Group 4 ($400–$700)	161	550	4.4
Group 5 ($200–$400)	299	270	2.9
Group 6 ($100–$200)	376	130	2.6
Group 7 ($50–$100)	1,580	90	1.7
World	3,391	$ 610	3.2%

Source: Thorkil Kristensen, *Development in Rich and Poor Countries* (New York: Praeger, 1974), pp. 156-159.

Table 1B: *Annual Average Growth Rates per Capita GDP, 1960-1973*

Stage		%
A.	Old developed	
	1. United States	3.1%
	2. Other	3.7
	Total	3.4
B.	Newly Developed	7.0
C.	Transitional	3.9
D.	Less Developed	1.8
	Total market economies	2.8
E.	Centrally Planned	3.6%

Source: Hollis Chenery and Moises Syrquin, *Patterns of Development, 1950-1970* (London and New York: Oxford University Press World Bank, 1975), Table 2B.

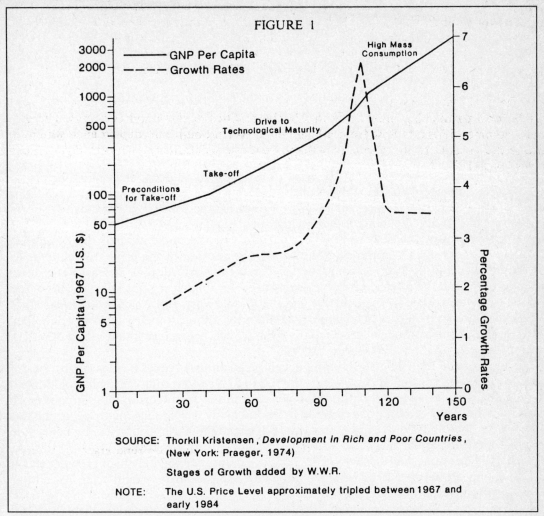

FIGURE 1

SOURCE: Thorkil Kristensen, *Development in Rich and Poor Countries*, (New York: Praeger, 1974)

Stages of Growth added by W.W.R.

NOTE: The U.S. Price Level approximately tripled between 1967 and early 1984

Figure 1 is based on cross-sectional World Bank data of recent decades. It does not, therefore, include pre-modern traditional societies. Such traditional societies, with relatively fixed technologies, tended to experience oscillations around relatively static low levels of real income per capita. The oscillations were mainly the product of harvest fluctuations, the impact of wars and of demographic cycles of various length.

What Figure 1 does capture is the following: in what I call the preconditions for take-off—say, below 1967 US $100—real income per capita tended to rise at a relatively slow rate, in recent decades damped by rates of population increase much greater than experienced at an equivalent stage in the historical past. In some cases, population increase is fully cancelling out the rise in real income.

During take-off (say, between 1967 $100 and $200) there is a marked acceleration in real income per capita reflecting the effective absorption of some modern technologies in some sectors and regions of a country. Other sectors and regions may be only modestly affected if at all.

Then comes the drive to technological maturity when modern technologies of increased sophistication are progressively diffused to an increasingly wide range of diversified industrial sectors as well as to agriculture and other primary economic activities. This is the stage when growth rates tend to be at their maximum. At its close an economy has just about absorbed the backlog of unapplied technologies the global pool has to offer, and typically GNP per capita has moved from 1967 $200 to $1000.

As a technologically mature economy turns to the supply of sophisticated durable consumer goods and services, growth rates tend to slow down for two reasons. The economy is dependent on the flow of new technologies from research and development (R&D), having exhausted the backlog previously available; and the income elasticity of demand decrees disproportionate increases in demand for services as real income rises. Historically, services have been associated with lower rates of productivity increase than manufactures, a fact that may change with the absorption of new and foreseeable technologies related to services. This S-shaped pattern has been well documented for recent decades by Thorkil Kristensen and Hollis Chenery and for the historical past, by myself.[2]

For our purposes, the central point is that most of the population of the developing regions live in societies experiencing one version or another of the drive to technological maturity and this is likely to remain true for several further decades at least. Therefore, what we might call the natural rate of growth of the developing regions is high. This is true of most of Latin America, North Africa and the Middle East, and Asia. I would place both India and China in the drive to technological maturity, although their vast low productivity rural areas and certain policy deformations slow growth below levels that might otherwise be obtained.

The high natural rates of growth in the developing countries could be clearly observed in both the 1960s and the 1970s. What the United Nations calls "Developing Market Economies" grew at an annual rate of 5.5 per cent in the first decade; 6.0 per cent in the second. In the 1970s growth was sustained in a good many developing countries, in the face of high oil prices and the deceleration of the advanced industrial countries, by heavy borrowing in private capital markets. After the second oil price increase, growth rates collapsed in the South as well as the North. I believe disproportionately high growth rates in the developing regions would be resumed if the advanced countries would bring down interest rates and move into a sustained boom.[3]

The fact that the developing countries, taken as a whole, are in the naturally high growth stage of the drive to technological maturity has heightened economic interdependence for both sides, that is, the North's dependence on the South and the South's dependence on the North have both increased.

As for the North's increased dependence on the South, it can be simply stated: the proportion of the North's exports going to the South has rapidly increased over the past decade. For example, the proportion of US exports to developing countries rose from 30 per cent in 1972 to 40 per cent in 1982. With the rise in the price of oil, import dependence on developing countries also rose: from 27 per cent of the value of imports to 42 per cent. For the North as a whole, merchandise exports to the South rose from 23 per cent to 28 per cent in the period 1973-80. Even if the North resumes higher growth rates, I would expect the trend to continue because of the naturally higher growth rates of the South at this stage of history.

The South's increased dependence on the North is reflected not only in the same figures cited for the United States, seen from the South's perspective, but from two further characteristics of their present position and prospects. First, the drive to technological maturity is, as I suggested, the stage when the backlog of existing technologies is being absorbed rapidly over a much wider front than in the past. South-South trade is increasing and will continue to do so, but most of those new technologies must, for the time being, be drawn from the North. This aspect of dependence has been heightened in recent years by the emergence from R&D of a whole new set of technologies, notably those derived from the microchip and genetics, whose implications we shall discuss later under the rubric of the Fourth Industrial Revolution. To absorb the technological flow the South needs and is capable of absorbing, the South must sell more to the North, including manufactures. The second increasingly important element in the South's dependence on the North is that, as countries move through the drive to technological maturity, their case for concessional loans weakens and, not without some withdrawal pains, they become progressively more dependent on international private capital markets for external loans. With that increasing dependence comes also the impact of interest rate fluctuations as decreed, among other things, by the domestic economic policies of advanced industrial countries, most notably the United States.

It may seem paradoxical that a high growth stage in the developing regions, reflecting great prior progress across the board in the modernisation process, should yield this phase of increased dependence of the South on the North—but an analysis of its various components suggests why it should be so. Friends in the developing world often ask: "When, if ever, will we escape from this dependence on the North?" The answer is: "Never". What will happen—and it is a process which can already be observed in some developing nations—is a transition to a much better balance in technological virtuosity and to a dignified interdependence of the kind that exists among the advanced industrial countries. It is a central characteristic of diversified modern technology, which will be heightened by the character of the Fourth Industrial Revolution, that it systematically increases interdependence among countries which absorb that technology. Economic "independence" is an illusory goal for all of us as far ahead as any of us can see.

Assuming for a moment that this argument is correct and North-South economic interdependence is destined to increase over the next generation, what should North and South do together? What about an operating agenda? Evidently, an operating agenda, if it is to serve as the basis for serious, sustained North-South co-operation must also be rooted in certain characteristics of the world economy likely to persist over the next decade and beyond.

For our purposes, I would isolate two sets of forces which I shall characterise as the Fifth Kondratieff Upswing and the Fourth Industrial Revolution. These forces constitute both the basis for the period of rapid expansion in the world economy which we should enjoy in the 1980s and 1990s and also the basis for an appropriate North-South agenda.

The Fifth Kondratieff Upswing: Maintaining the Resource Base for Continued Growth

A minor but persistent strand in the history of economic thought in the twentieth century is speculation about the possible existence of long cycles in the world economy. They are generally dated as 40-60 years in length.

Such cycles are usually associated with the name of Nicolai Kondratieff, a Russian economist working in the 1920s. He crystallised a body of price, interest rate and money wage data, beginning in the 1790s, which exhibited two and a half cycles and the beginning of a third downturn. He never developed, in his own phrase, "an appropriate theory of long waves". But he speculated in an interesting way about possible causes; for example, changes in technology, wars and revolutions, the bringing of new countries into the world economy and fluctuations in gold production. Kondratieff's successors in this line of speculation have explored each of his leads. But over the whole span since 1790, hypotheses about cycles in innovation, wars, gold discoveries, or cycles in overall growth rates break down when subjected to close analysis. The only hypothesis that does the job for the whole two century era is one centred on the prices of basic commodities relative to manufactured products. (Their relative movements over the past century, on a global basis, is captured in Figure 2).

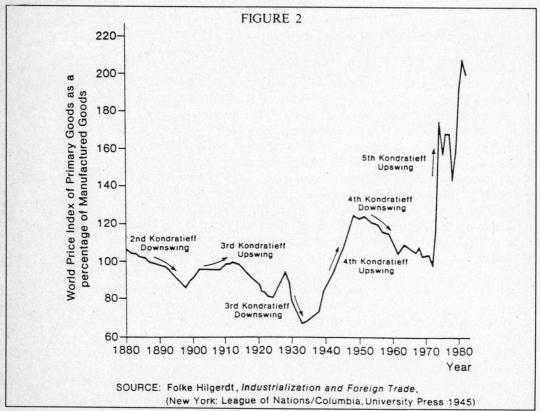

FIGURE 2

SOURCE: Folke Hilgerdt, *Industrialization and Foreign Trade*, (New York: League of Nations/Columbia, University Press 1945)

Specifically, I have taken the view that, with some foreshadowing in the second half of the 1960s, the world economy moved at the close of 1972 into the fifth protracted period of relatively high prices for basic commodities after experiencing some twenty years of absolute or relative decline in those commodities, starting in 1951. Thus, since 1951 we have lived, in my view, during the Fourth Kondratieff Downswing (when the relative prices of basic commodities fell) and a part, at least, of the Fifth Kondratieff Upswing: (Figures 3A and 3B exhibit these recent relative price movements for the United States).

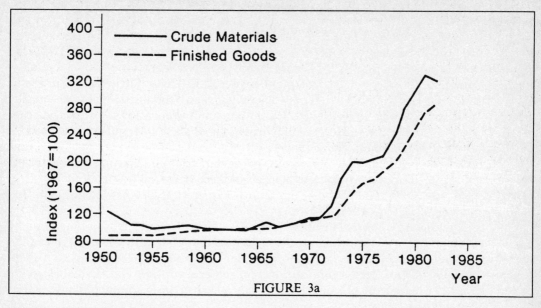

FIGURE 3a

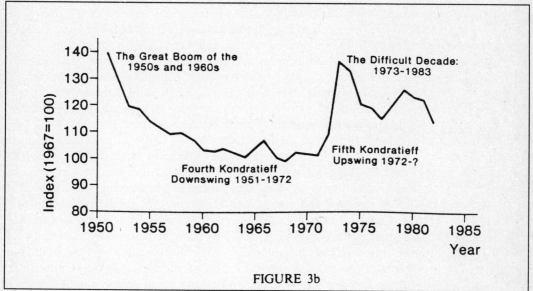

FIGURE 3b

Evidently, this theory of Kondratieff cycles is consistent with either relatively prosperous or relatively depressed Upswings or Downswings. For example, the Upswing in relative prices in the two decades before the First World War was accompanied by a relatively rapid growth phase in the world economy; the post-1972 Upswing has seen severe retardation in growth. Similarly, the inter-war Downswing in relative prices was, by and large, disastrous; the post-1951 Downswing saw the most powerful sustained boom in modern economic history. In short, relative price trends have systematically caused the price, interest rate and money wage rate phenomena Kondratieff identified but they did not determine output trends which were the outcome of the behaviour of other variables.

I would underline that the cycles Kondratieff identified were by no means smooth sine curves. There are even elements of uniformity in their irregularity. Before 1914, for example, they began with a sharp, initial rise lasting a few years, after which the relative price of basic commodities oscillated in a high range. Of the trend rise in British prices in the First Kondratieff Upswing, 66 per cent occurred between 1798 and 1801; in the second, 71 per cent between 1852 and 1854; in the third, 57 per cent between 1898 and 1900. As Figures 2 and 3 demonstrate, the world economy experienced such a convulsive rise in 1973-75, with subsequent oscillation in a high range.

The downswings also tended to assume a particular contour, starting with a sharp decelerating downward break in the relative prices of basic commodities from the peaks in 1813, 1873, 1920 and 1951. The shape of the Fourth Kondratieff Downswing in Figure 3 is therefore quite typical.

There was a third fairly consistent irregularity. The Upswings and Downswings usually exhibited an interval or cycle in which the trend movement abated or reversed, and then asserted itself again. In the British case, for example, the cycles of 1803-08, 1832-37, 1862-68, 1885-94 and 1904-08 all, to a significant degree, ran against the trend. I shall raise the question later as to whether the present relatively soft phase in basic commodity prices constitutes such an interval.

For the purposes of the North-South agenda, the central phenomenon of a Kondratieff Upswing is that a shift in the direction of investment is required towards the expansion of supplies of (or substitutes for) the high-priced commodities in relatively short supply. That shift is necessary to avoid a frustration or growth due to a relative shortage of basic commodities and progressively higher relative prices for such commodities. On the Downswing, with some interesting explicable exceptions, investment shifted towards industrial sectors, consumer goods, urban infrastructure and service sectors where the relative profitability of investment was now favourable. That happened between 1951 and 1972.

The Fifth Kondratieff Upswing began, at the close of 1972, with an explosion of grain prices, followed by a quadrupling of oil prices the next year. In both cases, exogenous events played a role; that is, the poor harvests of 1972-73 and the Middle East War of October 1973. But a deeper examination makes clear that strong endogenous forces were at work in the late 1960s which decreed, in time, a reversal of post-1951 relative price trends.

As of 1984, of course, energy, food and raw material prices are soft as compared to their levels in, say, 1980, although they are a bit higher than a year ago. But it is wholly fair to ask if the Fifth Kondratieff Downswing has begun after a much shorter upswing than in the historical past. After all, in the pre-1914 world the length of the Upswing was often determined by the time it took to open up new territories and bring them into large-scale, efficient production. Now much of the expansion will come from increases in productivity and the exploitation of already accessible resources. Moreover, the increase in energy prices was so extreme by historical standards that it might have induced more rapid compensatory adjustment than in the historical past.

On the other hand, it may well be that we have another transient break in the trend and the Fifth Kondratieff Upswing will reassert itself. Consider, for example, the following. Although energy experts, like others, differ, a majority argue that the real price of oil will resume its rise by the second half of the 1980s if the world economy generates a reasonably high and regular growth rate. In that case, a little noted aspect of the pattern of world energy consumption is likely to reassert itself, namely, the much higher rates of increase in energy consumption in the developing regions than in the advanced industrial world. For example, primary energy consumption increased in the US and Canada, between 1971 and 1981, at the rate of 0.8 per cent per annum; in Western Europe at 1.0 per cent but in Latin America, the Middle East, Africa and Asia at between 5.1 per cent and 6.6 per cent. History, in fact, is not linear, but primary energy consumption in the developing regions would exceed that in Western Europe and North America in a quarter century, if the differential expansion rates of the 1970s were to persist. The reasons for the higher energy growth rates in the developing regions include: higher real growth rates at this stage of their history than those of the advanced industrial countries; high rates of expansion of population in energy-intensive cities; the rapid absorption of energy-intensive technologies such as steel, metal-working and chemicals and high rates of expansion in motor vehicle use.

With respect to agriculture, the reason for not assuming a persistent declining price trend is different. The inescapable increase of population in the developing regions, due to age structures, despite current declines in birth rates, may add something like 2 billion human beings to the planet in the next generation; overall, the rate of increase in agricultural production in those regions is not yet matching the rate of increase in the demand for food, inducing an annual rate of growth in grain imports of more than 3 per cent. In 1982, of the 65 low-income food deficit countries in the world, either no increase or a decline in cereal production occurred in 47; in three, the gains in production were less than the rate of population growth. In addition, there is the pathology of agriculture in most of the communist states, with Hungary an important exception and China making hopeful progress.

As for raw materials, there is evidence of under-investment and distorted patterns of investment in recent years. In Latin America, for example, the tension between an understandable nationalist desire to control fully natural resources and an understandable desire of foreign investors for stable and reasonable terms for their outlays has resulted, in a number of countries, in reduced rates of raw materials development. If the world economy revives, we may encounter raw material bottlenecks. Taking precisely this view of raw material prospects, the World Bank has estimated that 1977-2000 capital requirements for additional capacity in seven key minerals would come to 1977 US $278 billion, of which $96 billion constitutes investments in the developing countries. (In 1982 dollars these figures would be about $342 billion and $118 billion, respectively).

Without dogmatism, I am inclined to believe, on balance, that the Fifth Kondratieff Upswing is not over if the world economy revives in the 1980s, and that a relative rise in basic commodity prices will assert itself during this decade. For our purposes, this means that very large additional investments must take place within the world economy in energy, agriculture and raw materials if growth is to go forward at normal rates and a still rapidly enlarging population is to be accommodated with adequate food supplies. And a high proportion of that investment must take place in the developing regions.

There is another major form of resource-related investment that should be included in this array; that is, investment in rolling back degradation or the environment and maintaining long-run supplies of clean air and water, arable land, forest, and irreplaceable areas for recreation and wildlife. These are tasks for both advanced industrial and developing countries. And systematic budgeting of investment for these purposes is clearly now an inescapable item on the national and international agenda.

We do not have the data required to estimate firmly the diversion of investment to these resource sectors required to maintain a viable world economy. Where calculations have been made, the numbers are large. For example, a World Bank estimate suggested that energy production investment requirements in the developing regions would approximate 1980 US \$683 billion, with an annual investment growth rate of 12.3 per cent, lifting the proportion or investment allocated to this purpose from 2.3 per cent of GNP in 1980 to 3.2 per cent in 1990. A good deal of this capital would have to come from abroad.

For Latin America alone, the Inter-American Development Bank estimated that in the the course of the 1980s something of the order or 1980 US \$300 billion would be required for investment in energy production, about 45 per cent or which would have to come from abroad. The proportion or GNP allocated to energy investment would, on these calculations, rise from something like 3 per cent to 4.4 per cent.

A study sponsored by the Asian Development Bank estimated that energy production investment would have to double in its developing member countries (excepting India) in the period 1980-85 relative to the level of 1975-80, if high growth rates are to be sustained.

For the United States, my colleagues and I at the University of Texas a few years ago estimated that to render the United States a marginal net energy exporter, through full exploitation of coal and synthetics, would require a rise in the proportion of energy production investment to GNP from 3.5 per cent to at least 4.2 per cent.

These resource problems are, in fact, endemic and not confined to the noncommunist world. Any analysis of the problems and prospects for the Soviet Union and the People's Republic of China over the next generation would have to include energy and agriculture high on the list of priority tasks.

I might note, parenthetically, that the concept that a North-South partnership should be built on the basis of an authentic common interest in this array of resource problems has been widely perceived without the benefit of an economic historian's conclusion that we are experiencing the Fifth Kondratieff Upswing. For example, the report of the Brandt Commission, *North-South*, devoted several chapters to this theme, although these elements in the report were overwhelmed in its public impact by an overriding plea for a massive transfer of resources from North to South on the dubious grounds that the North lacked adequate investment opportunities to achieve full employment. The report of the Herrera Commission, appointed by the Secretary-General of the Organisation of American States (OAS) to define areas for economic co-operation in the western hemisphere, isolated agriculture, energy, raw materials and certain environmental problems among its seven priority tasks. The Association of Southeast Asian Nations (ASEAN) has defined energy and agriculture as the two top priority areas for joint action. The Pacific Economic Co-operation Conference, held at Bali in November 1983, focused on agriculture, minerals and energy among its four major themes. Indeed, at Cancun in October 1981, in a little noted intervention, President Reagan showed an awareness of the need to move in this direction. Among the five principles he set out to guide North-South economic relations, he included the following as his third point: "Guiding our assistance towards the development of self-sustaining productive activities, particularly in food and energy". Unfortunately, neither Mr. Reagan's colleagues in Cancun nor his own Administration has pursued this insight seriously and systematically.

Diffusing the Fourth Industrial Revolution

A second pervasive element in the dynamics of the world economy is what I call the Fourth Industrial Revolution. I include in the Fourth Industrial Revolution innovations in microelectronics, communications, the offshoots of genetics, the laser, robots and new synthetic materials.

It may be useful to make clear both the over-simplification and the element of reality involved in the notion that inventions and innovations come in groups which justify the designation of a sequence of definable industrial revolutions.

By no means do all innovations come in such grand clusters. First, to start at the less glamorous end of the spectrum, a great deal of invention and innovation of great importance has gone on since the 1780s which consists of incremental improvements in the existing technologies. The path of this kind of refinement by small steps is subject to diminishing returns, as particular technologies age and potentialities for improvement decline. Second, innovations of varying significance, creating new industries, large and small, are initiated, in modern times, over a wide front and they are by no means all related to each other.

But economic historians and some economists have recognised that, in addition, there have been, before our time, three giant innovational clusters: factory manufactured textiles, Cort's method for making iron from coke, and Watt's steam engine, all of which came on stage in a substantial way in Britain in the 1780s; then the railroads, making considerable commercial headway in the 1830s but generating substantial booms in Britain, the American North-east, and Germany in the 1840s and leading to the revolution in steelmaking in the 1870s; and finally, electricity, a new batch of chemicals, and the internal combustion engine. These became significant around the opening of the twentieth century and, in its various elaborations, carried economic growth forward through the 1960s in the advanced industrial countries.

This grouping of innovational giants has still a good deal to commend it; although it is, of course, highly over-simplified. I should note that since the dating of the initiation of these clusters is arbitrary, one could adjust them to, say, a 60 or 70 year periodicity; but there is no rational reason to assume a uniform rhythm for such grand innovational cycles.

I turn now to three general characteristics of the new, fourth group of technologies. First, rather more than the industrial revolutions of the past, this one is closely linked to areas of basic science which themselves are rapidly evolving. When Watt produced his steam engine with a separate condenser, Cort, his method for making iron from coke, and various people made it possible, up to a point, to match the skill of Indian hands with machines in factories, all these devices could be refined and rendered progressively more efficient by skilled mechanics and engineers on the job. The users of these machines did not have to turn to basic scientists to solve their problems. And so it was with the railroad, most aspects of steel and metal-working, and even the internal combustion engine. This is clearly not the case with genetic engineering, the forthcoming rounds of computers and other dimensions of the Fourth Industrial Revolution. The fate of particular sectors and even whole national economies is likely to depend on success or failure in bringing into firm and steady partnership the domains of basic science, R&D, engineering and entrepreneurship.

A second characteristic of the Fourth Industrial Revolution is that it seems fated to be ubiquitous. It is likely to transform—indeed, it is already beginning to transform—the older basic industries. I would guess that in the advances industrial countries motor vehicles, machine tools, steel and perhaps even textiles, will be "high-tech" industries in a quite thorough-going way in a decade or so.[4] This process means that the shift of old basic industries to the developing regions to exploit low wage rates may be slower than in the past. But the new technologies will equally suffuse agriculture, forestry and animal husbandry and, as is already observable, they will have revolutionary effects on a wide range of services: communications and medical care, education and banking. Some believe the effects of the new technologies on communication will be so powerful as to constitute in effect a transport revolution; that is, the transmittal of information may substantially substitute for the movement of people.

A third characteristic of the new technologies I would underline is that, in different degree, they are and will increasingly be relevant to all the developing countries. What we call developing countries cover an enormous spectrum not only in levels of real income per capita but also, and more significantly, in their capacities to absorb efficiently the pool of existing and emerging technologies. Nevertheless, the Fourth Industrial Revolution is relevant even at the lower end of the development spectrum, for example, a good many countries in Africa south of the Sahara. There, aspects of the new technologies that bear on agriculture, forestry, animal husbandry and communications, as well, of course, on medical care, will be immediately relevant. At the other end of the spectrum, a country like South Korea has almost fully exploited the technologies of the Third Industrial Revolution. Speaking in Seoul in October 1983, I guessed that by the end of the 1980s South Korea would have for the most part completed the absorption of steel, heavy as well as light engineering, chemicals and the early forms of electronics and it would have to move rapidly to "high-tech" status to maintain its momentum.

As I noted earlier most of the population of the developing world lives in societies which I would define as in the drive to technological maturity, and they are likely to be in an intermediate position with respect to the new technologies. A country in the midst of the drive to technological maturity will be concerned simultaneously with bringing some sectors and regions forward in terms of technologies of the Third (or even earlier) Industrial Revolutions while also establishing which of the new technologies are relevant, in what sectors, and proceeding to absorb them.

But, in the course of recent travels I have become aware of the seriousness of the following question: How can a country not engaged on the frontiers of the Fourth Industrial Revolution understand where science and the R&D process are heading; in what directions practical results are likely to emerge in five or ten years' time; in what fields should talented young men and women be trained and other time-consuming preparations be made to understand and make the most of the technologies when they come "on line"?

After extended discussion I have concluded that there is considerable scope at many levels for scientists, engineers and entrepreneurs from advanced industrial countries to meet systematically with similar groups from less developed countries to discuss where the Fourth Industrial Revolution is heading in particular fields, and what forthcoming technologies are likely to be relevant to particular developing countries or to groups of such countries at similar stages of growth. I would now argue that this kind of discussion has a significant place on a sensible North-South agenda and the encouragement of such arrangements should be a regular part of the agenda of the World Bank and the three regional development banks.

Some Failures of Policy

The conclusion to be drawn from our treatment of the Fifth Kondratieff Upswing and the Fourth Industrial Revolution is simple enough: taken together they should provide both the leading sectors for a sustained period of strong expansion in the world economy and, equally, the basis for an agenda of intense North-South cooperation. The agenda for co-operation would focus mainly on joint measures, notably expanded investment, to assure the supplies of food, energy and raw materials required to permit the growth process to go forward without acute Malthusian crises or supply bottlenecks, and joint measures to assure the diffusion of the Fourth Industrial Revolution to the developing countries as the technologies it incorporates become relevant and cost effective in each country. The questions before us are, then: Why is this potential global boom not happening? Why is the potential mutually productive partnership not in place?

The boom is not happening primarily because interest rates are still too high to unleash the extremely large potential for investment in the advanced industrial countries. Without such rapid expansion in the advanced industrial countries, the developing world continues to be inhibited in five ways: its exports to the North are constrained; its export prices are weakened; beset with high unemployment, the North imposes protectionist barriers against the South; beset with serious social problems associated with the slowdown of their economies, legislators in the North accord low priority to official development lending and the high interest rates imposed to keep inflation under control render the already fragile debt position of a good many developing countries potentially dangerous to to them and to the world economy as a whole.

The fault clearly lies in those advanced industrial countries which have not supplemented conventional fiscal and monetary policy with effective income policies, as a device to control inflation. Given its role in the world economy, the worst offender has been the United States.

I am utterly convinced that, whatever the difficulties, democratic societies will have to learn to amount long-term incomes policies if they are to reconcile high sustained growth with control over inflation. The alternatives are either stop-and-go policies or chronic high unemployment. But an incomes policy is difficult to install and maintain. It is not an antiseptic technical device like, say, the maintenance of a fixed and pre-determined rate of growth in the money supply. It is a set of political, social and institutional arrangements by which a society accepts a hard fact: namely, there is no other source for a sustained increase in real wages than an increase in productivity. Societies which face up to that fact can find ways to adjust the average rate of increase of money wages to the average rate of productivity increase. A number of countries have sustained such arrangements for quite long periods of time, most notably Japan, the Federal Republic of Germany, Austria and Switzerland. They have been well rewarded.

Flying in August 1983 from Sydney to Perth, with no statistical source other than an issue of *The Economist*, I compared, through some simple arithmetic averages, the recent relative performances of three economies which have fairly effective incomes policies (Japan, the FRG and Switzerland) with the performances of three without effective incomes policies (the US, the UK and France). The results were as follows: those without incomes policies averaged twice the inflation rate, twice the unemployment rate, and had prime rates of interest one-third higher than those with effective incomes policies. In addition, those with incomes policies enjoyed average annual current account surpluses of US $7.3 billion versus deficits of US $7.2 billion for the others. I would underline that my method was oversimple, but I am confident that calculations involving many more equations and parameters, run through a sophisticated computer, would not significantly alter the general finding.

As I noted above, I have recently published a book[5] which embraces this theme, and it would be inappropriate to elaborate here the specific remedies I propose for the United States. What is clear is that the failure of some of the advanced industrial countries to reconcile sustained growth with control over inflation has been a major factor in slowing down the growth rate in the developing regions.

There have also been failures of policy in a good many developing countries which have damped real growth rates; for example, excessively slow reductions in birth rates; insufficient incentives for farmers to increase agricultural production; an excessively intrusive role of the state, where "state bourgeoisies" have developed over the past generation with interests of their own not necessarily identical with those of the nation as a whole; excessive subsidies, which consume the revenue raising capacity of the state in transfer payments; excessive protectionism and insufficient domestic competition. This catalogue, with appropriate minor modification, holds true for a good deal of Latin America, North Africa, the Middle East and Asia, including India and China.

Historically, the emergence of these problems is explicable; they are quite deeply rooted and will take time to mitigate or solve. For our purposes, I would merely note that a candid assessment would assign responsibility for the damping of growth in significant parts of the developing world to policies pursued by both Northern and Southern governments.

Similarly, I would allocate responsibility to both the South and the North for the failure to translate the palpable area of authentic overlapping interests into a working partnership. Put simply, the New International Economic Order (NIEO) initiative of the South, about which I shall have something more to say below, did not prove a helpful or viable way to go about setting up the partnership, but for a decade the North has been satisfied with fending off the NIEO without offering a serious alternative except reliance on free enterprise and canons of liberal trade violated every day in the North as well as the South.

A Proposal

How, then, would one go about organising a concrete North-South enterprise based on the analysis I have presented above? I suggest the following.

First, the enterprise should be conducted primarily on a regional basis. The ultimate task is to examine sectoral investment requirements looking a decade or more ahead, and isolating projects to be financed domestically or with foreign private or official resources. This kind of technical activity does not lend itself to global gatherings which now involve anywhere up to 150 governmental representatives.

Second, the regional groups might centre, in the western hemisphere, around the Organisation of American States and the Inter-American Development Bank; in Africa, around the African Development Bank and the Economic Commission for Africa; and in the Pacific basin, around the Asian Development Bank. The World Bank would participate in all the regional enterprises, as would relevant global organisations such as, for example, the Food and Agriculture Organisation. The US, Western Europe and Japan would also participate in the three regional ventures—although their degree of involvement might vary with their respective regional interests. India and China might well prefer, because of their size, to deal with this array of problems via the World Bank (and the kind of consortium arrangements the World Bank has managed) rather than in multilateral committees. But an association of the World Bank and the Asian Development Bank, with the work of the recently formed association for South Asian Regional Co-operation, might help move this potentially important grouping from a stage of creative diplomacy to serious business.

Third, the participants would, evidently, have to consist primarily of officials who bear serious responsibilities domestically for policy towards the sectors under examination. Where appropriate, governments may wish to engage persons from their private sectors in the process.

I have argued, then, that a solid potential basis exists for North-South partnership; that conditions for its success are Northern policies that reconcile sustained growth with control over inflation and Southern policies that begin to correct the accumulated structural distortions now damping growth in the South; that the working agenda of the partnership should focus substantially—not exclusively—on (1) expanded investment in certain resource-related fields, including the control and reversal of gross environmental degradation and (2) the accelerated diffusion of the emerging new technologies of the Fourth Industrial Revolution.

I have also argued that the work should be organised regionally and subregionally wherever possible; that it should be linked to the World Bank, the regional development banks and the relevant global functional agencies; and that it should be conducted by men and women who bear direct operational responsibility in their societies for the various sectors concerned.

This is clearly a different vision of how things should proceed from that incorporated in the NIEO, where the primary objective is to effect by one device or another a massive, undifferentiated transfer of resources from North to South, where the negotiations are conducted globally and where the negotiating officials come primarily from foreign offices. I would not expect the governments of the South to abandon the NIEO and proceed as I propose on the basis of functional, regional and sub-regional negotiations among responsible experts, working toward the formulation and financing of specific investment projects. But I would hope that the governments would not permit the existence of the NIEO to be the enemy of such functional, regional North-South efforts; and, if the latter should show promise, the NIEO might find a useful destiny, after many years of costly frustration, in focusing on a limited number of issues which can only he effectively handled on a global basis.

Standing back from this argument, what we are talking about is a set of problems, centred on the supply of resources required in every economy on the planet and on the prompt and the effective diffusion of a set of revolutionary technologies that are destined to affect the lives of every man, woman and child among us. We confront these problems of resources and technologies at a time in history which has generated passionate contentions of many kinds and in many places and a time also that shall probably be seen in retrospect as the interval of maximum pressure of man against his resources and physical environment. But if the statesmen of the planet stare hard at the problems and possibilities I have tried to evoke in this essay, it is barely possible that they will decide to act in the spirit of the poet after whom I happen to be named, Walt Whitman, who once wrote:

> One thought ever at the fore,
> That in the Divine Ship the Earth
>   Breasting Time and Space,
> All peoples together Sail,
> Sail the same voyage,
>   Are bound for the same destination.

References

This article is based on the LSE Suntory-Toyota Lecture sponsored by the International Centre for Economics and Related Disciplines (ICERD) and delivered at the London School of Economics on 13 March 1984, and was revised for publication in late March 1984. The author would like to acknowledge the unfailing support of the Institute of Economics and Statistics at Oxford in the preparation of this paper.

1. I take this lecture series, sponsored in the heart of London by two Japanese firms, to be one reflection of this process.
2. I summarise contemporary and historical evidence in W.W. Rostow, *Why the Poor Get Richer and the Rich Slow Down* (Austin, TX: University of Texas Press, 1980).
3. I discuss how this might be done in W.W. Rostow, *The Barbaric Counter-Revolution: Cause and Cure* (Austin, TX: University of Texas Press, 1983).
4. The resurgence of Jaguar may, in retrospect, mark an important turning point in British economic history.
5. See W.W. Rostow, *The Barbaric Counter-Revolution: Cause and Cure, op. cit.*

The United States in the World Economy:
A Fifty Year Perspective

William Diebold, Jr.

I

* * *

Because the immediate postwar period is now seen as a time of American hegemony, there is a tendency for people to think the United States always got its way. Careful scholars know matters are more complicated than that. But when labels become commonplace, they often mislead, and that has happened to many people in this case. There is no doubt that the United States was the greatest power in the world. That did not mean it could impose a new economic system on the postwar world. There were at least four reasons for this.

First, for a long time Americans did not realize how strong they were. Plans for the postwar economy assumed that London would continue to be a primary financial center, the pound a key currency, and Britain a leading element in a multilateral trading system. Continental Europe was expected to return to a central position in the world economy—provided Germany could be kept from becoming a menace once again. Much of Asia and Africa was still ruled from European capitals. By the time Americans came to realize their own strength, the foundations of the postwar world had been laid and Washington wisely did not change course.

The second reason the United States could not always get its way was that not all American power could be used to shape the world economy. The planes may have stretched from one horizon to the other over Tokyo Bay when the japanese surrendered on the *Missouri*, but that did nothing to rebuild factories or produce a set of rules for world trade.

Third—and most fundamental—the kind of international economic system the United States was advocating was based on cooperation among sovereign states; no country would engage in lasting cooperation unless its interests were served. Therefore, if the United States used its dominance to set up arrangements that served only American interests, they would be undone once other countries got strong enough—and if they did not get strong enough, American policy would have failed. That was clear to practical politicians as well as to postwar planners.

Finally, the Americans most concerned about the postwar world economy knew that a crucial problem was to restrain the United States. No one, in the 1940s, could feel sure that

Reprinted by permission of *Foreign Affairs*, vol. 62, no. 1, 1983. © 1983 by the Council on Foreign Relations Inc. Sections omitted are indicated by asterisks.

postwar American governments would be sufficiently different from their prewar counterparts to sustain the new lines of policy. An American commitment to international agreements known to be balanced bargains could be a potent argument for continuity and consistency.

Any careful study of the record will show that difficult and often unsatisfactory negotiation was the modality by which the postwar system was produced, not U.S. dictation. Of
course, there was a bias. The Americans did the lion's share of the drafting (and most of
the rest was British). Some things could not be done because Congress would not accept
them; others had to be done because Congress insisted. American negotiators were known
to invoke Congress as a bargaining weapon. When American performance fell short of
what would have been desirable, other countries could only rarely force a change. Foreign
governments had many irons in the fire and wanted to go along with American wishes as
much as they conveniently could. The realistic recognition that countries with difficult
balance-of-payments problems or large reconstruction needs had to be treated differently
from the United States—whose economy had expanded during the war—meant that most
foreign governments did not have to be in an uncomfortable hurry to live up to the principles they had agreed to.

This was not the only time that the United States accepted commonality in form that was
not always matched in fact. Perhaps Americans simply recognized what the situation made
reasonable, if not inevitable. To have been too stubborn or pushed too hard for full reciprocity and equality would have risked ruining the long-run prospects. Perhaps being a
hegemon helped. By the 1960s and 1970s, when Americans began to find it annoying that
other countries were not assuming more responsibility for international security and economic cooperation, Washington's power had declined.

Long before that point was reached, however, the new international economic order had
been tested in a number of ways.

II

The testing started early, with unexpected events. For all the wartime planning, the United
States was not adequately prepared for the part it was to play in European reconstruction.
Nevertheless, through a number of channels, some ten billion dollars in aid was provided
to Europe before the launching of the Marshall Plan. That famous effort was remarkable
not only as an innovation in American policy but for the efforts, cooperative and national,
it drew forth in Europe. Before the Marshall Plan was over, NATO was negotiated, rearma-
ment began, the Korean War broke out and the United States was providing military aid in
both Europe and Asia. Occupation policy in Germany was reversed and Japan was soon
given its autonomy in economic policy—two major steps that further changed the world
economy.

Not surprisingly, in these circumstances the dollar came to have a different place from
that assumed at Bretton Woods. Most countries used exchange controls and, for some
years, the International Monetary Fund could not play the central part it was supposed to
have in liberalizing and stabilizing international payments. The International Bank for
Reconstruction and Development moved slowly, was second to the United States in providing loans and could not do much in the short run to provide the underpinnings—material
and psychological—for flourishing private investment. Trade liberalization, however, was

not postponed, for two good reasons. The reduction of American tariffs while other countries continued to limit imports made an immediate contribution to righting imbalances. Had nothing been done until every country was ready to act, investment patterns would have been established that would have made later liberalization more difficult. Assistant Secretary of State Will Clayton, I was told, said it was important to act before the vested interests got their vests on.

It was not until the late 1950s that the world economy came close to matching the picture on which the new international system was based. But the contributions of improvisation and reasonably consistent adherence to the original ideas paid off. Great material progress which lasted into the 1970s seemed both to justify the new approach and to strengthen the ability of governments to cooperate.

The interplay of cause and effect is a matter for study and debate. The removal of trade barriers must have had something to do with the fact that international trade increased faster than production. But the great growth of international investment was also important and there was no general agreement covering that. Thus, the fact that the postwar depression that was widely expected did not materialize is not easily traceable to the commitments to international economic cooperation. Would cooperation have survived a serious contraction in the world economy? One way or another, the coexistence of the new order of international economic cooperation and a period of unprecedented growth and prosperity in most of the world augured well for both.

Remarkable economic changes took place in this period. Products never known before became commonplace; familiar products were produced by new processes. New firms and whole new industries appeared. All this changed the conditions of competition and helped some people while hurting others. Technological change was a big issue; there was a dispute about automation and the destruction of jobs in the 1950s and 1960s that foreshadowed today's concern about robotization and high technology. The technological revolution in agriculture—involving enormous investments made possible by public policy—began in the United States and spread to other countries. It played a constructive part in meeting the greatly increased world demand for food that resulted from the increase in population and income. But some of its other effects on international cooperation were damaging.

Naturally enough, recovery in Western Europe and Japan gave those areas greater economic weight in the world. As time passed, that was to have an effect on American policy. There were, however, other changes in the political and economic organization of the world that had a bearing on whether the international economic system set up at the end of the Second World War would work or not. That system, it should be recalled, was based on multilateral cooperation among governments that were responsible for their own national economies. With regard to international behavior, they made firm commitments on some matters and looser agreements for objectives on others. Each country was autonomous as to the character of its domestic economy (socialist, capitalist or whatever) and its performance (efficiency vs. stability, work vs. leisure, etc.), so long as it lived up to its international commitments. Reciprocity and equal treatment were basic elements in principle but imperfectly achieved in practice. Taken together, the numerous international agreements and the way governments behaved under them made up what can properly be called a new international economic system.

In principle this system was global. Most countries belonged to the United Nations, whose Economic and Social Council was expected to be more effective in guiding the world economy than it has proved to be. The major agreements on trade and finance involved only those countries willing to undertake certain obligations. In practice it was the continuing participation of several of the economically most important countries that was crucial to the system. Even among them, not everything could be reduced to rigid formulas, and occasional departures from the rules proved compatible with continuing cooperation. In practice the system has been very resilient. Nevertheless, its adaptation to some big changes in how the world is organized has left some unresolved problems.

Although the Russians were at the Bretton Woods conference, it was never clear whether they really wanted to take part in the building of a new international economic order—or how serious it would be if they did not. The cold war put that issue aside for the time being but raised new questions about the long-run economic relations of the First and Second Worlds, especially after the latter was enlarged to include Eastern Europe, China and several other countries. It proved not to be a serious disadvantage for the development of the new international economic order that the U.S.S.R. and its allies were outside and had to be dealt with by special arrangements. The biggest economic effect of the emergence of the U.S.S.R. as a superpower has come through the burdens of arms expenditures and the way strategic considerations have shaped policy on both sides, particularly for the United States. The impact of the Soviet economic system has been enormous on those who live under it but secondary for the rest of the world. East-West tensions strengthened the West's will to cooperate at certain times, but are now serious sources of divisiveness.

Far more important to the operation of the system than the omission of the Soviet bloc was the partial integration of Western Europe, something not seriously contemplated in wartime thinking about the postwar world (except by a handful of people). Though a nod was given to the possibility of customs unions and monetary groupings, the arrangements for multilateral cooperation among nation-states were not well equipped to deal with the appearance of major agglomerations. Once the path toward European integration was opened—starting with the cooperative arrangements that were part of the European end of the Marshall Plan and then, much more dramatically, with the creation of the European Coal and Steel Community in 1952—people came to expect much greater results than ever appeared. For a limited number of purposes, the European Community became a unit vis-à-vis the rest of the world; in other matters, its member-states continued to act separately; and sometimes they were in between, with preferential arrangements among themselves that were not always well regarded by the rest of the world. Without doubt, the strengthening of the European economy and the removal of historic barriers within Western Europe were major achievements of the postwar period. But the future remains unclear as to how this massive change will ultimately affect the international system, and also as to how cohesive the European Community will prove to be.

In the United States and Canada—and much less in Europe—Japan was not given much thought when plans were laid for the postwar international economic system. But by the time the peace treaty was negotiated, its economic counterpart was clear: a place would have to be found in the world economy to permit a resource-poor country with a talented, energetic people to live on economically satisfactory terms. Then came the unexpectedly rapid development of Japan into a major modern industrial power; it caught up to and often outdistanced North America and Western Europe as the premier producer of a number of key manufactures.

The liberal multilateral economic arrangements gave Japan great opportunities and the system's ability to accommodate this unexpected growth may be one of its major achievements. But neither Japan nor the other countries have done all they should. Perhaps time will permit the working out of arrangements for a fuller application of the system's rules and principles by all countries. There is, however, also a question whether Japan's economic success suggests that national and international policy principles based on the Atlantic industrial experience may be inadequate for the modern world.

No one seriously doubted that the changes in Europe and Japan, and the American reactions to them, had to be coped with if the system of international economic cooperation was to continue. But the dominant attitude toward the participation of the developing countries in the system has been that it was a secondary problem that could be temporized with. This is no longer true and was unwise from the first.

When the postwar planners thought about economic development, they looked mostly toward China but sometimes toward Latin America and Eastern Europe. They expected India to become independent but could not imagine that so many other countries would follow so quickly. Independence reversed the priorities of colonial times: growth took first place ahead of balancing the accounts. I remember an English economist who said, "I always told them there would be trouble with the balance of payments when the Indians began eating as they would like." That is not exactly what happened, but the new governments, democratic and not-so-democratic, were expected to produce results that it had taken decades—perhaps centuries—to achieve elsewhere. It was not independence alone that changed things—most Latin American countries had, after all, been governing themselves for over a century. People had new visions of what was possible; governments were judged by the standards of the mid-twentieth century welfare state, not the more rugged nineteenth century attitudes that had accompanied growth in Europe and North America. Maybe some of the most dangerous false expectations were those of economists who thought they had mastered development policy, endorsing first one formula and then another, counting too heavily on foreign aid, and using generalizations where particularization was needed.

Yet there was much success. Growth in the developing world as a whole has been high; hundreds of millions of people are better off in health, life expectancy and standards of living than their parents; most countries can earn their way in the world at much higher levels of production and consumption than ever before. The idea of new Japans entering the world scene may cause some trepidation, but surely the appearance of the NICs—the newly industrializing countries—is a mark of progress. The NICs also make another basic point. Not only are they quite different from most other developing countries but they vary greatly from one another—compare South Korea and Brazil. Differentiation is a better approach to the problems of the developing countries than treating the Third World as a whole. OPEC—the oil-producers' cartel—showed that, too.

There is, however, more evidence coming—China. How is it to be regarded? As the biggest developing country, but with a late start? As a late-starting communist country that is also less developed? As a near-NIC on the coast but with a huge hinterland? As falling into the category of countries whose absolute size makes their economy different from others, including India, the U.S.S.R., Australia, Brazil, Canada and maybe the United States? Or simply as a country different from all others, as almost any Chinese would say?

Unfortunately, the way the new international economic system dealt with these sweeping developments was all too often by giving the developing countries a special status exempt from most obligations and entitled to some kind of specially favorable treatment. For reasons that cannot be set out in detail here, this formula has not been very helpful to either set of countries. External pressure improves the performance of rich, industrialized countries; are poor countries likely to do better when fewer demands are made on them? Can the rich countries be expected to expose one domestic industry after another to competition if their access to the markets of developing countries does not improve in return?

Whenever lines are drawn on a generalized North-South basis, difficulties multiply and often lead to an impasse. To the extent that differentiation is acceptable, new possibilities arise, provided the stronger countries do not try too hard to take advantage of their positions. What is called for, I think, is not simply some improved method of bringing the developing countries into fuller participation in the international economic system that has been shaped by the older industrial countries, but a reshaping of that system itself.

Unfortunately, reshaping the international economic system to permit it to work better in a greatly changed world has not been regarded by the powers that be as a vital need—and when efforts have been made in the last decade and a half, they have not produced great success. It seems quite clear that the world is no longer as creative or farsighted in dealing with new challenges as it was in the 1940s, 1950s, and early 1960s.

This is not just nostalgia. Consider the record. By the late 1960s there was no serious doubt that the international monetary system needed reform. It proved hard to achieve. The unilateral American decision to stop exchanging dollars for gold in 1971 forced the issue and set everyone on a new course—but it hardly passes for cooperation. When a new system of floating rates was worked out, governments proved unwilling to let them swing beyond certain points and unable to agree what those points should be. The energy crisis of the 1970s ought to have seen a drawing together of the main consumer countries. But mostly their responses were divisive, and have continued that way as each country has tried to attain more security in its oil supplies. Who can be confident that the easier situation of oil supply and prices (resulting to an important degree from the depression of the early 1980s) will set these issues aside forever? In trade, the Tokyo Round took longer than the Kennedy Round and left important gaps in its achievements. At the end of a near fiasco last November, the GATT ministerial meeting called for a strengthening of the trading system, an eloquent plea from the very people who were undermining it. The record on the coordination of national economic policies is very unsatisfactory even though the effort was moved from what is usually called the working level up to the summit.

Many people see this deterioration of cooperation as primarily a product of the 1970s. Certainly that was a time of troubles. Some were new, notably the oil shocks and the souring of U.S.-Soviet relations before the most serious effort to improve them had a reasonable trial. But other developments—new heights of inflation and new lows in productivity growth, and the spread of macroeconomic failure to most major countries—were at least in part an extension of past troubles. That was also true of the difficulties with the international monetary system and with the American economy. It seems to me preferable to stress the links between the 1970s and the earlier decades than to look for what it is now fashionable to call a discontinuity.

The depression of the early 1980s is another villain in the piece. It increased all economic difficulties and pushed governments even further to let domestic pressures take priority over international considerations. Recovery will ease matters, but will not restore the status quo ante—much less create a more satisfactory state of affairs.

* * *

III

* * *

From the very beginning there have been gaps and weaknesses. The U.N. Economic and Social Council never did the coordinating and guiding that was once expected of it. Although a few U.N. agencies have dealt effectively with economic problems, the general record is not encouraging. Part of the explanation lies in the large number of countries involved in most efforts, the emphasis on national sovereignty, the frequency with which issues fall into a North-South or East-West pattern, and the unwillingness of the economically stronger countries to let themselves be outvoted on matters of substance by a majority of poorer, weaker nations. The creation in 1964 of the United Nations Conference on Trade and Development (UNCTAD) as a place where the richer and more industrialized countries have had to respond to the wishes of the developing countries has had its uses, although the material results have been fairly modest.

The industrial countries have also not been willing to push ahead with the process of cooperation and building institutions. An International Trade Organization (ITO), repeatedly said to be essential to the success of the International Monetary Fund and the World Bank, was both proposed and abandoned by the United States at a very early stage. The breaking point was an investment code unwisely asked for and then opposed by American business. (That was neither the first nor the last time that organized American business did not distinguish itself by its foresightedness.) Massive investments have done much to change the world economy, but there are still no broad multilateral agreements about them. There have also been no adequate replacements for other chapters in the ITO Charter, on commodity agreements, restrictive business practices and the relation of national economic problems to trade. We have the General Agreement on Tariffs and Trade—but significant parts of world trade escape it, and its provisions and organization are inadequate to deal with disputes stemming from the clash of national industrial policies and structural changes in the world economy. The Articles of Agreement of the IMF were drafted on the assumption that capital movements would be controlled by national action, but this does not much happen any more.

A second major source of the deterioration of cooperation lies in the problems of managing national economies. It was hardly a new thought in 1945 that governments were responsible for their economies, but the idea took on a new meaning once it was believed that governments not only should but could prevent depressions, guarantee something like full employment, and keep the unemployed, the old, the weak, and even just the feckless from the depths of poverty and its ills. This new social contract brought benefits that were not only humanitarian but economic. It is not always easy to tell them apart, as human capital is every country's major resource, and people sense that there are links between economic security and political cohesion. At the same time it is clear that welfare and security for individuals can have social costs if they reduce the flexibility of economies, put budgets out of control, blunt incentives and initiative, and foster too much consumption at the expense of investment. There are complex interrelations among intitlements, the veto power of certain groups, the political process, and both macroeconomic and structural policies.

A period of considerable success in economic management in most industrial countries has been followed by doubts about the ability of governments to govern. The backlash against government programs has underestimated their durability—perhaps because there are so many beneficiaries. Imperative as it may be to reduce the burden of some social costs, governments cannot escape responsibility for what happens to the poor, the old and the unemployed. Health as an objective of public policy is growing, not diminishing, in the importance most people attach to it. Deregulation is often highly beneficial—perhaps especially when it is opposed by those who are regulated—but there is no evidence that laissez faire is around the corner. People support most measures to improve the environment. What is increasingly being sought is clarification of objectives, costs and how to get results efficiently. Who should choose the necessary tradeoffs is a fundamental political problem.

All this makes it very hard to balance the demands of a democracy's public—which is often many publics—with a responsible overall management of the economy through traditional macroeconomic policies dealing with fiscal and monetary matters—and now with the simultaneous pursuit of a number of specific economic objectives with regard to productivity, trade, industrial structure, regional balance and other matters. Unemployment and inflation make everything more difficult and create specific pressures of their own. Naturally, these domestic pressures are the ones that every government feels the most acutely. Legislators and executives do what they think has to be done and hope that the international effects will take care of themselves or can be lived with. And if some of the burdens and costs of dealing with a domestic problem can be dumped on other countries, so much the better—if one can get away with it.

Increasingly, though, one cannot. Very few countries can cope with their so-called domestic economic problems without taking account of the international economy. They cannot safely assume that other countries will absorb whatever dislocation comes their way without reacting. Ironically, past success in cooperation has contributed to the present deterioration and that deterioration seems likely to continue. Barriers to trade and investment have come down, money moves freely around the world, the ability to insulate is limited and, regardless of a government's intentions, the effects of its actions may be felt abroad. Consequently, the gaps in the system of economic cooperation are more serious than they used to be.

At the same time, the troubles every country has with its domestic economy are harder to deal with because all economies are so exposed to one another. This is the paradox of interdependence. It is so well recognized, and so much written about these days, that there is no need to expand on the subject. It is necessary, though, to underline the basic challenge that interdependence poses. It was put clearly and forcefully by Ramsay Muir, a British Liberal, in *The Interdependent World and its Problems*, published in 1933:

We have entered a new era, the era of world-interdependence; and this interdependent world is threatened with chaos because it has not learnt how to adjust its institutions and its traditions of government to the new conditions.

The situation has been familiar for many years: national politics and international economics. There are parallels in security. We are not about to see the end of the nation-state, so the tension will continue. There could be some pulling back from interdependence: some lines can be cut, some flows dammed, in the interests of gaining a freer hand to shape the national economy and meet domestic pressures. But for most countries, the area of maneuver is very limited; reducing interdependence is likely to mean reducing resources; the cost of extensive disturbances of established patterns of production, consumption and trade is likely to seem rather high. Some of these prices may have to be paid, if only because other countries will not cooperate to reduce them. Before asking what it might be reasonable to look for in new cooperative measures, it is worth asking whether there may not be other forces at play, pushing the world economy toward greater internationalization and further limiting the ability of governments to manage domestic affairs on a purely national basis.

Business is one possibility. Its internationalization is a complex process that has been gaining ground throughout the postwar period. This is not just a matter of the spread of multinational enterprises. The late Judd Polk argued long ago that we should focus on the characteristics of international production and its financing rather than on organizational forms. In many different ways, and through various kinds of financial links, the internationalization of business changes (and may conceal) who controls what and whose assets have to cover what obligations. It alters the meaning of national policies and the reach of national measures. Private business has to negotiate with governments but also has a certain freedom of action. Is it possible that, as entrepreneurs pursue their interests in flexible and ingenious ways, they will bring about a creative adaptation of the world economy to the new interdependence? It is, but that cannot be the whole answer. There has to be some means of asserting the public interest, and neither theory nor practice says that the invisible hand of the market will do so.

Moreover, there are many public interests and they have to be blended, compromised and offset. Present (and past) practice calls for all these interests to be balanced, fused or organized in the process of arriving at something called the national interest. This is not a very sensible procedure and becomes increasingly less so as economies are internationalized and their boundaries blurred. (Does anyone doubt that what happens to American companies abroad affects American as well as foreign interests? In what sense are foreign-owned companies in the United States "American"?) Quite often, businessmen try to avoid bringing their "own" governments into disputes with other governments for fear that their own interests will be lost in the pursuit of other national aims. Surely we ought to make better use of the fact that most international economic issues involve clashes of interests within each country. Why have better ways not been invented to let private people make their cases to international bodies and foreign governments? Is it simply cultural lag? Or is it the inevitable consequence of the fact that the "consent of the governed" is asked and given entirely on a national level?

Along with business, technology has been a major force creating interdependence. The 50 years covered in this essay may have set a record in shrinking the globe. Perhaps the most dramatic economic effect has come from the almost instantaneous movement of money around the world. This technological marvel may not be all to the good. Years ago when my brother wrote one of the earliest papers on electronic banking, my wife said, "but I don't want the money taken out of my bank account as soon as I hand over my charge card." Governments may feel the same way, as they try to control their money supply.

What can you do, though, in the face of technological change? "Speed up the reaction time" is a common answer. But people are increasingly uncomfortable with the idea that they will be pushed around by machines or some disembodied force called Technology. What is the cost of resistance—to become Luddites, or laggards in a technological race all countries are forced to run? So far as one can see, most governments have opted for speeding up the race, but often get poor results. Can the race be run to the advantage of all—perhaps by increased internationalization of the effort, through private and public channels? Or do we ineluctably make it a zero-sum game if we all want the same thing—the lead?

As in the case of interdependence, we are back at a basic choice that wise men recognized long ago. In 1939, Eugene Staley wrote, in *World Economy in Transition*:

> Fundamental technological changes are pushing mankind in the direction of world-wide economic integration and interdependence, but. . . political tendencies. . . have strongly resisted that trend. . . It would be unfortunate if inability to solve the political problems connected with a world-wide economy should snatch away the productive advantages. . . offered by our technicians.

Many people, then and since, have accepted this proposition—but how much international action has been based on it?

IV

With the international economic system in a troubled state, the United States faces hard choices. In the 1930s it tried to stand aside. In the 1940s it took the lead, and by the 1950s it had, for the first time in history, played a key part in leading the world into highly developed arrangements for international cooperation. In the 1980s, it is again in a new position.

The internationalization of the American economy has outrun people's understanding of its implications. More than ever before, we cannot put our own house in order except by relating the American economy to the rest of the world. In trying to do that we have trouble because our pluralistic methods greatly complicate our dealings with other countries. It is not just a matter of government and business, Congress and the President: the courts play a key part in economic matters; it is hard to know when a ruling on the environment or something else is final; the actions of independent regulatory agencies affect foreign countries; states and cities deal with foreign investors and Canadian provinces (it makes sense for New York to buy subway cars in Canada but Michigan and Washington do not agree). In my recent work I have been repeatedly struck with how many current issues I first encountered as an undergraduate in a seminar on government and business. They were hard problems then, when we rarely looked beyond the American scene; they are harder now when the international dimensions cannot be ignored, whether we are talking about coal, steel, antitrust, banking reform, or the Securities and Exchange Commission.

Macroeconomic policies that worked fairly well in the past have broken down and have not been replaced by anything worth having. America's adaptation to changes in the world economy and in technology is very incomplete. This is reflected in selective protection, high general unemployment, extraordinarily high unemployment among some groups, the related deterioration of human capital and the educational system, the slump in productivity growth, reduced international competitiveness, low investment in times of high consumption, a variety of business practices and labor attitudes, and some aspects of inflation. The recent depression has made things worse, but recovery will not eliminate the basic problems.

On top of everything else, the United States has to cope with frustration. The world economy is not what many Americans expected it to be, or what they thought they were promised in the bargains that created the postwar institutions. The frustration that fueled the American outburst of disruptive economic nationalism in August 1971 can still be felt strongly today.

There are good grounds for some of these reactions but not for others. Americans are not free to conclude that the international economic system is tilted against them unless they also recognize that the United States has not been laggard in looking for special treatment for its own problems. It led the way in putting most agriculture outside the arrangements for trade liberalization (and now wants to push some back); it did the same for cotton textiles in 1961 and then, ten years later, for man-made fibers; since the 1950s the United States has pressed Japan to restrict exports of one product or another and then formalized such arrangements in Orderly Marketing Agreements extended to other countries. The list goes on: export subsidies that violated GATT rules; delays in conforming on other matters (American Selling Price and the injury test for countervailing duties); bilateral arrangements made without much regard to the multilateral rules (steel and autos). Foreigners have a right to ask how much weight their interests have been given in the shaping of American fiscal and monetary measures.

It is quite true that most other countries behave at least as badly as the United States in these matters and frequently worse. There is no doubt that some foreign governments and their negotiators believe they can get away with some things because the United States will not always retaliate in kind—or will not be effective if it tries, because its government is cumbersome and has its hands tied by legal limits and procedural requirements unknown in most other democracies. This only exacerbates matters and can lead to a good deal of trouble because the United States is not immune to economic nationalism. Support grows for the view that the United States should hit back, "give them a dose of their own medicine" and so on. If that approach is embodied in law, any American administration will have only limited freedom of action; if the approach gains strong political support, the forces that made for cooperation will be reversed. If that happens, they are likely to stay that way for some time to come.

Americans are in danger of misunderstanding their place in the world. Oversimplified statements about the decline of American power have confused people. How would we like it if Europe and Japan were still economic weaklings and no one in the Third World had reached the level of the NICs? The end of hegemony need not be traumatic but it requires adjustments that have not been handled very well. The United States and other countries share responsibility for this.

It is wrong to say that the United States is a country like any other. Our dollar and our missiles prove that. It is also wrong to suppose that American interests will be well served by old-fashioned narrow nationalism modified by contemporary neomercantilism. The final fallacy in this series is to believe that the loss of power means the United States has no responsibilities for the repair of the international economic system. True, the United States cannot do the job alone, but neither can anyone else. The United States has a veto but so do some others, and no one can be counted on to use it very constructively. Nothing major can be done without strong American participation and from that fact stem responsibilities.

Before they can act on these responsibilities, however, Americans have to do some serious rethinking about what they want in the world. They have to get used to defining their interests in terms of both the domestic economy and the world economy. Unless they are prepared to make some changes in both spheres, it is hard to see either why the international deterioration should come to an end, or how the American economy will overcome the obstacles to satisfactory performance at home and the ability to compete internationally.

Using the historical perspective of this paper, one could say that Americans need a sense of concern about their own economy comparable to what they had in the Great Depression—and about the world economy of the sort that they developed in the 1940s. Naturally, the measures taken in those earlier times are not right for today. It would mean little to say we need a New Deal, but let us recall that the New Deal was neither an ideology nor a fullblown program; it was highly pragmatic and comprised experimental approaches to many problems. We need some of that spirit now.

When I say we need to look at our relation to the international economy as we did in the 1940s, I do not mean that we should simply refurbish and patch up the structure of international agreements set in place then. For years my studies have shown that these arrangements are not adequate for the kind of world we live in now. It is vital to improve them, but that is only part of what needs to be done, as Miriam Camps and I have recently argued with regard to trade in *The New Multilateralism*.[1] Action will be needed in a number of fields—trade, money, energy, the debt issue and development finance, the relation of national economic policies to those of other countries, investment, industrial policy, raw materials and the movement of people. We should have long-run objectives even if they remain unattainable for some time, and also practical programs for immediate action. But we should not proclaim our adherence to such commonly heard objectives as a new Bretton Woods, or free trade, or getting the government out of the economy.

It is not "Bretton Woods" that has broken down, only the provisions for more-or-less fixed exchange rates. The replacement part—floating rates—has not performed as we hoped and itself needs repair. We also need a clearer understanding of the obligations of debtors and creditors to cope with troublesome debts. Our best chance to meet these needs is to build on the rest of the Bretton Woods system itself: the IMF, the processes that have grown up around it, and the basic principle that a common interest in money and finance requires continuous cooperation centered in an institution that both helps countries and puts pressure on them. "Free trade" has never been an American objective, is not mentioned in GATT and would not be accepted by many governments without massive and disillusioning exceptions. *Freer* trade is another matter. Getting the government out of the economy cannot be a realistic objective—for the United States or anyone else—no matter how desirable it may be to end various kinds of intervention and regulation. But there are questions about how the international impact of interventions should be handled when different governments have different practices.

It is hard to escape some use of oversimplified tags as shorthand, but to let them become the clichés of journalism, and then of speeches and policy pronouncements, is dangerous. By obscuring complexity they inhibit thought; by preaching perfection they invite accusations of hypocrisy and lay the foundations for frustration. If we want a single label, let us adopt Miriam Camps coinage, "The Management of Interdependence."[2] This is not achieved by some single act but calls for continuing, complex activities, domestic and international, which require more imagination, ingenuity and stamina than have been evident for some time.

V

It is not the United States alone that has to show these qualities—or, for that matter, do the thinking that is called for about the international system. If other countries too do not exercise their responsibilities, then any efforts the United States may make will not arrest the deterioration of the international economic system (though they may improve the position of the United States). Not every country has to cooperate and not all have to play an equal part in every activity.

Indeed, one of the most difficult questions to be faced is which countries are crucial for which activities. The formula cannot be the same as in the 1940s; and this raises a delicate, even dangerous, issue. In a world in which some degree of equal treatment and some sense of reciprocity are essential to get sovereigns to cooperate, should one wait for a broad consensus or encourage a few major countries to push ahead of the rest? And can that be done without undermining the basic character of the system?

As countries go through these processes, they should be doing more than preparing negotiating positions. They should be talking with one another about directions, objectives and constraints. They should make proposals, however tentative. If other countries do not do this, they will encourage one of the worst habits of the U.S. government, which is to work out fairly ambitious programs on its own which take realistic account of the domestic play of forces needed to get support for them—and then to present to the rest of the world programs so tailored to American needs as to incite suspicion, and so linked to political bargains in the United States as to impede negotiation.

There is no need to think in terms of major new international conferences—within or outside the U.N. framework—to discuss all these matters. The time for that is in the future and will not ever arrive if the recent deterioration of cooperation is not stemmed. There is also no need to wait for new ideas. The failures of recent years have not come from lack of imagination or of practical proposals, but from the unwillingness of governments to adopt them. Naturally, new ideas are always welcome, and sometimes they provide just the twist needed to make something acceptable and manageable. More often than not, though, new ideas can only very slowly be built into bases for practical action. (One reason the American proposals to extend the principles of trade liberalization to services led to nothing more than a two-year study in GATT was that so few people in foreign countries had done any thinking about the subject.)

Prescriptions abound, and there is no space to lay out a detailed agenda or offer the author's favorite programs in some or all fields. The agenda lies to hand. Where better to start than with the issues on which governments have failed to agree for the last decade and more?

- The unfinished business of the Tokyo Round [the Uruguay round of MTM is scheduled to consider these matters]—such as tightening the conditions under which countries can temporarily restrict disruptive imports, breathing life into the codes on subsidies and other matters already agreed upon, and moving ahead in the directions proposed at the GATT ministerial meeting of November 1982;
- Serious negotiations about fitting the NICs more fully into the world economic system, plus a realistic appraisal of the long-run trade requirements of developing countries—this last could be linked to the handling of the debt issue, the newest big question and one which governments seem more disposed to cooperate on than other matters, perhaps because their fear is greater;

– A reassessment of the energy situation before too many countries go too far on the assumption that there will never again be an oil problem;
– Finding ways to deal with clashes among national industrial policies;
– Finally coming to grips with the better management of exchange rates, which may well require going behind them and asking if it might be possible to do something about the world's money supply and the cumulative effect of national fiscal policies.

The list goes on, but this is enough to show that what is missing is not an agenda but action on it.

Many people hold very strong views on these matters. But the larger need—of repairing the damage to the international system—will not be best served if each country insists on every jot and tittle of a particular way of handling a problem. Details are immensely important in international economic relations, but imperfect arrangements often work. Logic has its limits in human affairs and the world has done quite well with arrangements that could be shown on paper to be fatally flawed. Internationally as well as nationally—and perhaps even more so—we live with a constantly changing interplay of forces which cannot always be either prevented from hurting others or channeled toward constructive results. As law is an incomplete remedy nationally, so are fixed commitments internationally—even if governments have agreed to them. James Madison laid out the fundamentals in Number 10 of *The Federalist*:

> The latent causes of faction are. . . sown in the nature of man. . . The regulation of these various and interfering interests forms the principal task of modern legislation. . .
>
> It is in vain to say that enlightened statesmen will be able to adjust these clashing interests, and render them all subservient to the public good. Enlightened statesmen will not always be at the helm. Nor, in many cases, can such an adjustment be made at all without taking into view indirect and remote considerations, which will rarely prevail over the immediate interest which one party may find in disregarding the rights of another or the good of the whole.
>
> The inference to which we are brought is, that the *causes* of faction cannot be removed, and that relief is only to be sought in the means of controlling its *effects*.

Negotiation can itself be a process of education, showing what is possible and what people will tolerate in others even if they do not accept it in principle (or for themselves). Thanks to the situation described earlier in this article—the combination of interdependence with the problems of managing national economies—there may well be a need for innovations in the way international economic negotiations are carried on. The importance of international economic organizations in the process suggests that they should be strengthened. It should not be forgotten, though, that these are intergovernmental organizations and what they do depends on what governments will have them do. The primary need is for governments to realize anew the strength of their national interests in an effective system of international economic cooperation.

Some governments might come to a different conclusion, believing themselves better off pursuing "national interests" on their own. Then everything depends on their strength, their skill in using it and what other governments do. It is hard to believe that more than one or two important countries can choose the non-cooperative course without almost all following (though they may group together in bilateral or broader combinations). It is conceivable that the interplay of many such national policies will produce more benign results than those one generally associates with a world of rivals who think of their national interests rather narrowly, that is, in terms of conventional neomercantilism.

It is conceivable—but to me it is not credible. It can be argued that in the end these policies will cause so much trouble that countries will be forced to work out compromises and to move towards a new system of economic cooperation better attuned to the end of the twentieth century than what we have now. One has to ask how long that will take and what it will cost. Nor can one really be certain that better cooperation will be the ultimate course. It is exceptional to have the kind of arrangements that have marked the last 40 years. There is no reason to suppose that it will become the normal state of affairs. At best one can take comfort from Francis Bacon's remark, "Prosperity doth best discover vice, but adversity doth best discover virtue." He was, however, also the man who said, "Hope is a good breakfast, but it is a bad supper."

As my analysis has tried to show, there are reasons for the deterioration of international cooperation. I believe we are quite far along in that undesirable process; others take a less pessimistic view. Very likely the positive arguments of these last few pages fall into the category of "giving good advice to people who don't want it." Perhaps not enough people are sufficiently alarmed; perhaps they take it too much for granted that cooperation is the natural state of things because they did not live through the process of painstaking construction of what has been good but is still inadequate.

Certainly it is easier to see why international economic cooperation should continue to deteriorate than to see where the strength for its restoration will come from. There is only fragmentary evidence of a will to deal adequately with the basic structural problems of the American economy—and that will worsen our relations with the rest of the world. So we may well be on the verge of a new era in international relations—and a very unattractive one.

The ageless baseball pitcher, Satchel Paige, used to say, "Never look back, something may be gaining on you.(cd But if you do look back, you may see that you are losing something.

References

[1] Miriam Camps and William Diebold,Jr., *The New Multilateralism*, New York: Council on Foreign Relations, 1983.

[2] Miriam Camps, *The Management of Interdependence*, New York: Council on Foreign Relations, 1974.

Chapter 2

The Third World: Political and Economic Discontinuities

Introduction

What distinguishes the Third World from the First, and even from the socialist countries of the Second, is its peripheral status economically, politically, and geographically. The seminal economic and political activities of the globe are carried on in the relatively scarcely populated wealthy and powerful states of the northern hemisphere. There are many reasons why this is so and why the Third World continues to be relegated to a peripheral position. Historically, the most important factors were colonialism and late industrialization, both of which led to penetration and domination by the metropolitan centres of the northern hemisphere. During the last two decades of the 20th century, most analysts in the First World believe that the Third World will remain peripheral well into the 21st century, mainly because of twin sets of deficiencies: the lack of differentiation among its economic, social and political systems, as well as a lack of differentiation (or division of labour) within them; and the lack of social integration both at the class level (the elite-mass gap) and nationally (the ethnic/tribal cleavages).

Although all are serious deficiencies, and are not entirely absent in all industrialized northern countries—there are problems with regional/ethnic/class discrepancies in the United States and Canada as well as parts of Europe, especially in the south—the most disruptive from our perspective are the uneven differentiations in the first set, between state structures and the political-economic system. well as the economy. The former produces a political system (irrespective of whether its label is self-described or analytically ascribed) which tends to behave on irrational power bases rather than on rationally prescribed bureaucratic categories. The contrast may best be described by juxtaposing the phrases "rule by law" and "rule by man". In Third World states, the belief that rules are binding on all members of society—even on the powerful political leaders—is generally very weakly held, especially by the ruling elites themselves. This, of course, creates a political situation in which power, more or less nakedly wielded, dominates the structures of the state. As a result, irrational power demands rather than rational economic determinants become the main—and sometimes the sole—inputs in domestic economic decisions. Perhaps this would not be all bad if both those in power and the world economic environment remained stable for long periods, since even selfish power decisions tend to produce some benefits for the subject masses if they can be consolidated. However, as the articles in chapter 1 show, change is the only stable factor in the world economy that we live in today. In the third chapter, reference is made to the rapacity with which elites in the Third World seek and use armaments both to maintain themselves in power domestically and to carry on expensive disputes with their neighbours. In this chapter the Clapham and Bratton articles analyze the authoritarian use of power purely for the purpose of maintaining oneself in power, unrestrained by "other-directed" bureaucratized rules of law.

There is also a very disruptive external impact on the domestic economic situation brought about by the power-assisted penetration of the domestic market by foreign goods, industries and finances. Quite aside from the fact that foreign industries and governments tend inevitably to put their own self-interest ahead of the interests of the Third World nation, the forms of political system prevalent in the Third World often militate against truly beneficial relationships. This is not to argue that a "rule-by-law" political system, such as the Canadian or Dutch or Finnish (all small polities and economies exposed to large capitalist neighbours) prevents foreign economic penetration (all three have high levels of foreign ownership of industry, corporate financing and market penetration); rather it is to argue that in nearly all Third World states the decisions relating to foreign economic penetration are often still based on the short-term domestic pursuit-of-power or patronage. Unfortunately, both approaches subvert rather than control the economy, prevent differentiation, support massive corruption and propagate the elite-mass gap, and lead to continuing conflict on regional, ethnic, class and economic bases, thus preventing social and national integration.

The article by Christopher Clapham describes the structure of the contemporary Third World state and shows how it is incompatible with the democratic industrialized state of the west. The reader interested in gaining a thorough understanding of the problem of managing a Third World polity and economy is well advised to read Dr. Clapham's book, *Third World Politics* (London: Croom Helm, 1985, 197 pp.).

It is both the intrusiveness of selfish power-oriented politics in the economy and the destabilizing impact of the world economy and the economic activities of the dominant industrial state that creates problems for the Third World state economically and politically, and leads to a ripple feedback effect on the world economy.

The article by David P. Rapkin and William P. Avery reviews the linkages between the world markets and domestic politics in Third World states. The article identifies two broad categories of linkage: those deriving from market volatilities of goods that the Third World imports and exports, and those deriving from capital, technology and other factors of production. The authors divide the second category into two: transnational corporations and international financial institutions. Subsequent chapters of this book develop these themes further: chapter 4 evaluates trade problems, chapter 6 transnational corporations, and chapters 5 and 7 international financial flows. Chapter 9 focusses on the impact of international debt on politics in Latin America, and chapter 10 looks at the political and economic discontinuities abetted by debt and political structures in Africa.

The Third World State

Christopher Clapham

The Nature of the Third World State

What actually happened at independence? There was a ceremony and a celebration, a lowering of the old flag and a raising of the new, a formal handover by some representative of the colonial administration of the 'instruments of government' to the designated successor. This symbolic action was also extremely exact. What the new rulers actually received was the right, usually conferred by elections before independence and confirmed by the outgoing colonial regime, to control the instruments of government – in the sense of the actual institutions – created by that regime for its own use. These institutions then constituted 'the state', and it is this state which has emerged as the key to the structure of third world politics. The state has gained a similar centrality in those few third world countries which were not subject to formal colonialism through the process of monarchical modernisation which has already been touched on, and this centrality has been maintained in regions such as Latin America in which the experience of colonialism now lies well in the past.

What distinguishes the third world state from its equivalents in other parts of the world is the combination of its power and its fragility. Of these two elements, the power is by far the more evident. What the state consists of in its most basic sense is a structure of control. Arising from the colonial setting in which the first imperative was to secure the obedience of an alien people – or in its indigenous monarchical setting to reduce the autonomy of regional potentates – it is usually strongly hierarchical. The grid of power radiates from the capital, through a set of territorial subdivisions which only rarely (in India, Nigeria, Brazil, for instance) gain the limited autonomy provided by federalism. The primary responsibility of this grid is the maintenance of order, and the servants of the state whose concern this is the regional prefect or governor, the police force and the courts and, lying in reserve, the army – are the dominant elements in the whole structure. Close beneath them and closely associated with them, however, are the agencies concerned with the economic management of the state. Appearances to the contrary, these are not primarily interested in economic 'development'. Like the colonial state from which it is descended, the third world state has to maintain itself by extracting resources from the domestic economy, and especially from the trade generated by the economy's incorporation into a global structure of exchange. Whereas the developmental functions of the state are often patchy and inadequate, sometimes almost non-existent, its extractive ones are omnipresent. Lastly come those elements of the state which are immediately concerned with providing benefits for its citizens, rather

Excerpted from Ch. 3 of *Third World Politics: An Introduction*, published by Croom Helm, 1985. Reprinted with permission.

than for the state itself: education, health and other social services. Along with the state come the people who own it. These are drawn overwhelmingly from the most educated and articulate sections of the population, and associated in most cases with those groups within society which already enjoy the greatest social status, wealth and power. The state becomes in their hands not only a source of benefits in itself, but also a means to defend themselves against domestic discontent, and in some measure also against external penetration.

Yet the state is not the all-powerful monolith which this sketch may suggest. For one thing, its power is attractive, and competition to control that power saps and subverts the state itself. In any country, control over the state is one of the central things – indeed *the* main thing – which politics is about; but where the state provides a source of power and wealth entirely disproportionate to that available from any other organised force within society, the quest for state power takes on a pathological dimension. Whereas in established Marxist-Leninist states, access to this power is rigidly channelled by the state itself and its associated party (though even then not without its characteristic traumas), few if any third world states have managed to turn themselves into self-sufficient bureaucratic apparatuses. Control over the state is a prize which can be fought for, and therefore is. In the period before independence and immediately after it, the fight takes place between formally organised political parties, with their leaders, their programmes and their support drawn from one or another section of the population in the form of votes or sometimes more direct and violent political action. Occasionally, this system survives. Much more often, it proves incapable of withstanding a situation in which the power of the state is allied with that of the most successful political party, which is then ideally placed either to attract or to repress its rivals. Even then, however, essentially the same conflict takes place, perhaps violently on the streets as the opposition groupings seek to mobilise their forces, perhaps secretly as they conspire to overthrow the government in power, or through factional manoeuvres within the government itself; one way or another, the prize of state control is too appealing to be abandoned. Exactly the same is true for the government in power, whose determination to cling on is likely to be strengthened by a growing dependence on the comforts of office, and the fear of retaliation should their opponents get in. On the state as a simple agency for extraction and control, must then be superimposed the state as a prize in political competition, and as a means by which those who win that competition can serve their ambitions and suppress their opponents. A third element is introduced when competition for control over the state is extended to include parts of the state itself among the competitors. A ruler who has very little to fear from popular opposition may easily be toppled by military coup. Where the state is by far the strongest source of organised political power, government of the state, by the state and for the state becomes extremely likely, and even rulers not directly projected into power from the ranks of the state's own servants may well fall back on it as the easiest and least risky way of running the government. This in turn, however, raises problems of political management both within the state bureaucracy, civil and military, and in the relationships between the state and the wider society – which are most conveniently examined in the chapter on military regimes.

If the state cannot be controlled, it may at least be subverted. One of the features of the third world state which prevents it from developing into a totalitarian structure of hierarchical control is the fact that it is so readily permeated by the society in which it exists. The colonial state was not so permeable. It did very largely operate as a selfcontained bureaucratic institution, responsible to its own rules and its own superiors, and open to infiltration by the society which it governed only at the lowest level, through the influence of indigenous local rulers or of locally recruited clerks, interpreters or policemen. That was possible because it was alien. Even its indigenous employees were responsible to a chain of command which led directly overseas, and had to abide by its standards on pain of losing the most privileged positions which colonialism had to offer. After independence it was different, though some sections of the bureaucracy in countries such as India or Ghana continued to cling to colonial standards – in which by this time they had acquired an interest, since these helped to protect them from the demands of their political masters. On the whole, however, civil servants became part of the indigenous political process, identifiable with the class, caste or regional group from which they came, readily suspected of serving their own particularist interests on the one hand, while subject to influence and inducement on the other. At times, indeed, civil servants turned themselves into spokesmen for political interests, especially during periods of military government when the ordinary channels of political articulation were withdrawn, and even the army could become divided between 'politicals' and 'professionals'. In the process, the boundary between state and society became blurred, as the state itself became less coherent.

What did *not* take place, however – and this again is central to the character and role of the third world state – was any merging of state and society as common expressions of a set of shared values. In part, this too was a legacy of colonial imposition. Where, as in Africa or Asia, the state was imported along with the people who ran it, the division between indigenous society and external political structure was not eradicated by the replacement of colonial by local officials. The new state was now capable of being influenced, even subverted, by political action, but it was rarely something to which loyalty was owed in itself. Something of the same effect could be found in states in the Caribbean and parts of Latin America, where the people were imported as well as the political structure, and everything was artificial, except for the national boundaries which in the island territories at least were set by the sea. In some states, such as Jamaica and Barbados, this artificial society does appear to have been welded into a national community with its own set of political institutions (copied though these are from a metropolitan model). None the less, the state in its origins was the preserve of the dominant immigrant group (characteristically the white slave owners) and used as an agency of control. Where racial divisions persist, either between dominant immigrants and subordinate indigenous groups, as in Bolivia and Peru, or between rival groups of immigrants, as in Guyana or to some degree in Trinidad, the state is still readily associated with those who control it. The most extreme example of this process is South Africa. Even in those states such as Thailand or Ethiopia which escaped colonialism, the state is often associated with a core national community, which imposes its role on peripheral areas inhabited by other peoples.

The lack of organic unity or shared values between state and society, compounded though it is by the myriad effects of social change and incorporation into the global economy and political structure, is the single most basic reason for the fragility of the third world state. Political fragility is something very different from a simple lack of state capacity. Third world states differ sharply in the amount that they can actually do. Some, such as Singapore and South Korea, are as efficiently controlled as any in the world, whereas others, such as Burma or Ethiopia, cannot even control much of their own territory. Other indicators of state capacity, such as government share of gross national product or the proportion of the population employed in internal security duties, likewise rank third world states among both the highest and lowest in the world. Fragility in the sense in which I am concerned with here, rather, is most immediately expressed in the weakness of 'legitimacy', seen as a sustained and widespread public commitment to particular forms of governmental institution which will select and sustain political leaders. The absence of such legitimacy in turn fuels governmental insecurity amounting sometimes to paranoia. Personal and political corruption likewise reflects the lack of accepted and enforceable public values. Both of these aspects of the lack of shared values accept the state as the basic framework for public action: autocrats and coup leaders seek to control the state, just as corrupt officials seek to profit by it. Neither would get anywhere once it ceased to exercise its coercive and extractive functions. The lack of value consensus none the less ultimately carries a threat to the state's own survival – the ultimate débâcle for a third world (or for that matter any) political system. Sometimes, as in Uganda, a state which (despite internal divisions) is apparently quite viable may be brought to its knees by the combined brutality and incompetence of a single leader. Some states, such as Chad, were from the start highly artificial amalgamations of disparate political factions whose divisions could easily destroy the prize for which they were contending. In Lebanon, a fragile though up to a point quite successful domestic political balance was shattered by the incursion of rival Palestinian, Israeli and Syrian armies whose conflicts were ultimately not about Lebanon at all. Other states have been forcibly split in two, like Pakistan and Bangladesh, or amalgamated, like North and South Vietnam. On the whole, the great majority of third world states have survived, due to an alliance of domestic and external interests which favours their preservation, and which will be examined further in Chapter 6; but that survival is certainly not something to be taken for granted.

This combination of power and fragility, with its accompanying disjunction between the state and any shared set of social values, in turn accounts for almost every distinctive aspect of third world politics, and the rest of this book is in a sense simply the exploration of its implications. The first question that arises is that if the state does not work according to the classic (and clearly western) model of the nation-state, in which the constitutional structure is ultimately upheld by a sense of national self-identify, then how *does* it work? It does not usually operate simply by force, yet nor is it usually ineffective; and in so far as any single general theme can be used to illuminate the diverse politics of widely scattered states, this is the theme of 'neo-patrimonialism', which is examined in the next section. A second question is, how *might* it work? This is a matter, not of the theories used by social scientists to make sense of third world politics, but of the theories devised by the leaders of third world states in order to guide or justify their own activities. Such theories, or 'ideologies' if that seems a better word for them, naturally enough reflect the structural situation and personal self-interest of those who devise them; that indeed is part of their importance. But as with theories or ideologies of colonial administration, the way in which politicians seek to make sense of the position they are in and the options which they face is always instructive, and provides at least one guide to what they actually do. What they actually do – the problem of political management – then forms the core of the subsequent chapters: the consolidation of leadership, the management or mismanagement of domestic political relationships, the economy and contacts with the outside world.

Neo-Patrimonialism and its Consequences

Forms of Authority

Both the organisation and the legitimacy of the modern state rest, in principle at least, on what Weber described as rational-legal authority. The basis of that authority is that individuals in public positions, possessing power over their fellow citizens, exercise that power in accordance with a legally defined structure directed towards a publicly acknowledged goal. What provides the element of 'authority' or morally accepted or justified power, is that goals themselves are widely accepted, and that the structures are likewise accepted as the most efficient means of achieving these goals. What is then necessary to make the structures work is a strict division between an individual's public and private roles, encapsulated in the notion of an 'office'. In office, the official acts simply as an official, exercising the powers which his office gives him and accepting the restraints which it likewise places on him, while treating other individuals impersonally according to the criteria which the office lays down, whether they be his superiors, his subordinates or the 'public' with which he deals. If he is shifted to another office, he will instantly start to behave in the way which the new office requires, while the individual who replaces him in his old office will behave as he did before. Outside the office, he reverts to the status of a private individual, having private ambitions and obligations, but unable to use his public position to achieve them.

This ideal type, obviously enough, is nowhere fully achieved. The most basic reason for the failure to achieve it is that it goes against our natural instincts as human beings, calling on us to divide into rigidly demarcated public and private compartments aspects of our lives which we would otherwise put together. It is the modern state which is artificial, together with the modern economy which underlies it, and it calls for a corresponding artificiality in the behaviour of the people who run it. In this sense it is public rather than private behaviour which is the 'problem', and it is for this reason that no state has ever fully succeeded in maintaining itself as an entirely public entity, divorced from the personal interests of its constituent individuals. Even in so far as a rational bureaucratic organisation is maintained, moreover, it may be directed to the bureaucracy or its masters rather than to public goals shared by the mass of the population. The rational-legal idea none the less retains a central importance, since it is only through this ideal that the enormous powers of the modern state can be exercised in a way which is both efficient and legitimate. From this viewpoint, perhaps the basic problem of the third world state – and hence more generally of third world politics – is its failure in most cases even to approximate to a rational-legal mode of operation.

One level at which this is evident is the formal constitution of the state itself, which should in principle provide the ultimate legal framework through which rational-legal behaviour is defined. The failure to maintain a constitution is thus the simplest measure of the failure to maintain an agreed set of state objectives and of institutions through which to achieve them. In the former colonial states, the constitutions inherited at independence have rarely lasted for long, though there are exceptions, notably in the Caribbean, where constitutional longevity has reflected some sense of political order. More often, and especially in Africa, they have been brusquely changed to suit the needs of incumbent governments, and equally easily replaced or simply abolished by their successors. In some respects, independence constitutions reflected a balance of power which became anachronistic with the act of independence itself, since the major role in formulating them was played by the departing colonial power which (especially in the case of British colonies) often showed a sensitivity to opposition and minority demands which the new regime quickly reversed. Newly drawn up indigenous constitutions, which might be expected to reflect the realities of the domestic power structure none the less rarely fared much better while constitutional upheavals have continued at a rapid rate even in states which have never experienced direct colonialism, or have now put it far behind them. In only three of the twenty Latin American states has a single constitution remained continuously in effect since 1960, while established non-colonial states such as Thailand or Turkey have changed or suspended their constitutions at intervals of ten years or less over most of the last forty years. Where a single constitution has remained in force over a substantial period, as in South Africa or in Liberia before 1980, this has as often as not been because it served as a vehicle for regulating the internal competition of a small elite group to which power has been effectively confined.

Another test of rational-legal authority lies in the behaviour of public officials, and especially the courts and the bureaucracy. This test is less stringent than that of constitutional continuity, since it concerns the internal organisation of the government rather than the overall structure of the political system. 'Going by the book' is also in some ways in the interests of bureaucrats themselves, protecting them against external pressure. However, cases can certainly be cited of both individual bureaucrats and bureaucratic structures as a whole which operate honestly and efficiently according to their rules, while judges especially sometimes show astonishing courage in resisting political pressures. The overall conclusion reached by the great majority of studies of third world bureaucracy is none the less that formal rational-legal criteria are a very inadequate guide to their behaviour.[1] And having made every qualification for the tendency of scholars investigating this behaviour to set it against a rigid ideal type which is realised nowhere in the world (and certainly not in the United States, for instance), it is still not all that surprising to find that western industrial forms of administrative institution cannot be parachuted into third world states and expected to work in the same way as they do in societies with very different values, economies and patterns of historical development.

Some of the earliest attempts to analyse authority structures in third world states, from the 1950s onwards, drew on Weber's alternative ideal type of charismatic authority. Charisma, most familiar from the example of messianic religious leaders, was a form of authority inherent in an individual, who through his own virtue and example crystallised a new concept of authority, even though this would have consistent elements drawn from previous experience, and would ultimately, if successful, be routinised in a new institutional form. It was a concept tailor-made for the nationalist leaders, then at the height of their reputations, and perhaps over-enthusiastically applied to them by scholars anxious to identify with postcolonial aspirations. Certainly, new leaders did embody the heady feelings of 'the time when politics came', and some of them did settle down to impart to their states after independence lasting aspects of their own ideologies and attitudes. None the less, charisma was always much too feeble a base on which to build any general analysis of political authority, even in those states where an appropriate leader could be identified – and some staggeringly inappropriate leaders, such as Marcos in the Philippines, were also accorded the accolade. The idea effectively died with the overthrow of Kwame Nkrumah in Ghana, one of the classic 'charismatic' leaders, in February 1966, and was buried by photographs of joyful

Ghanaians destroying the outsize statue of the man once hailed as their redeemer.

In retrospect, the idea of charisma may best be regarded as an attempt to grapple with the distinctive forms of politics which occur when new social groups are rapidly being incorporated into the political process. It was the peculiar situation in which they were working, rather than any personal quality inherent in themselves, that distinguished the nationalist leaders from 'routinised' politicians engaged in managing an existing system – even though the mobilisation of new groups often required a level of personal leadership which was reflected in the prestige accruing to the leader himself. Precisely this same process of mobilisation is evident in other situations which give rise to 'charismatic' leadership, one of the clearest examples being Juan Perón in Argentina between 1943 and 1955 – a rare case of a military leader forming his own mass urban following. Gamel Abdel Nasser in Egypt after 1952 is another example, while the relationship between 'charisma' and mobilisation is most striking of all in revolutionary leaders such as Castro in Cuba or Mao Tse-Tung in China. As a general approach to the structure of authority in third world states, however, charismatic leadership is too evidently inadequate to be worth reviving.

We can however get further through the third of Weber's authority types, that of patrimonialism. The distinctive features of patrimonialism are that, in contrast to rational-legal relationships, authority is ascribed to a person rather than an office-holder, while in contrast to charisma, that person is firmly anchored in a social and political order. As the word implies, the concept of authority which underlies it is that of a father over his children – a concept which constantly recurred in the rhetoric of such a traditionalist patrimonial ruler as Haile Selassie of Ethiopia – and the classic setting in which it is found may broadly be described as feudal. In a system held together by a patrimonial logic, those lower down the political hierarchy are not subordinates, in the sense of officials with defined powers and functions of their own, but rather vassals or retainers whose position depends on the leader to whom they owe allegiance. Neither leader nor followers have defined powers, since what matters about power is not the amount of it that you have, but rather on whose behalf you exercise it. The system as a whole is held together by the oath of loyalty, or by kinship ties (often symbolic and fictitious) rather than by a hierarchy of administrative grades and functions. When, for example, the leader of an Ethiopian army died in battle, like the Emperor Yohannes fighting the Mahdists at Metemma in 1889, the command did not automatically devolve on his immediate subordinate; instead the whole army disintegrated, there and then, into its component sections. The logic which held it together had gone, and a new army could only be formed by another individual establishing his own separate authority.

Third world states, of course, are not feudal systems, even in so far as that description can be applied to the old Ethiopian Empire, though here and there touches of pure patrimonialism survive, for example in the way that each new Saudi king builds his own palace, leaving that of his predecessor as an abandoned shell. What characterises them, rather, is *neo-patrimonialism*, a form of organisation in which relationships of a broadly patrimonial type pervade a political and administrative system which is formally constructed on rational-legal lines.[2] Officials hold positions in bureaucratic organisations with powers which are formally defined, but exercise those powers, so far as they can, as a form not of public service but of private property. Relationships with others likewise fall into the patrimonial pattern of vassal and lord, rather than the rational-legal one of subordinate and superior, and behaviour is correspondingly devised to display a personal status, rather than to perform an official function. The postal clerk who shuts down his counter half an hour early, for apparently no better reason than to spite the patient queue of people waiting to buy stamps, and the head of state who insists that all his ministers and leading officials turn up at the airport to bid him farewell on a visit abroad, are both doing essentially the same thing: demonstrating that the relationship between themselves and their clients or underlings is one of personal subordination. The implications of the same approach plague the ordinary business of government administration. It is not just that officials, treating their posts as personal fiefdoms, use them to extract bribes or to appoint relatives, though that will shortly be considered under the heading of corruption. There are characteristic problems, too, about delegation. A superior will consider that he has the right to intervene personally in any matter which comes within his jurisdiction, and will do so regardless of the chaos it may cause, before going on to intervene elsewhere. A subordinate who takes decisions without referring them upwards may be regarded as slighting the authority of his boss – since to act independently of him is implicitly to challenge him. When the boss is away, especially in the case of the head of state, the decision-making process waits on his return. If he is reluctant to make decisions, the entire system sinks into a torpor from which it may only be rescued by his overthrow and replacement by a new boss who rapidly gets things under way. Within the context of a patrimonial system, all of these features serve the valuable function of maintaining a single legitimate source of authority. Imposed upon the structure of a bureaucratic state, they can rapidly gum up the works.

Neo-patrimonialism, like charisma or rational-legality, is an ideal type, realised to a varying degree both in third world states and elsewhere. There are, however, a number of reasons why it is most often the salient type in third world societies. First, the natural human disinclination to distinguish between one's private and official self equally corresponds to the normal forms of social organisation in precolonial societies. Neo-patrimonialism is far more than just a feudal hangover. It also characterises tribal societies in which loyalty to one's kin group is the primary social value, and plural societies like the immigrant states of the new world in which status and identity were determined by ethnic group affiliation or position on a caste-like social hierarchy; that is one of the reasons why it survives in the ethnic politics of the United States. Beneath the façade of the modern state, the same principles continue to operate. They are particularly obvious in the behaviour of the non-elite mass of the population, both in the speed with which a following of claimants gathers round a successful bureaucrat or politician, and in the readiness with which the abuse of office by public officials (as it would be reckoned, at any rate, by western industrial standards) is accepted as normal behaviour, condemned only in so far as it benefits someone else rather than oneself. Further, both the artificiality of national communities, and the incorporation of the society into the global economy, help to corrode a sense of common values, and hence indirectly to encourage neo-patrimonialism, which can be readily adapted to an instrumental form, in which straightforward considerations of personal benefit and the exchange of favours come to replace the reciprocal obligations which characterise patrimonialism in its original or traditional form. Two closely linked areas in which this is particularly evident are those of corruption and patron-client relations.

Corruption

Corruption is the use of public powers in order to achieve private goals. The very concept of corruption itself thus turns on the distinction between the public and the private which underlies Weber's ideal type of rational-legal authority. In a truly patrimonial system, the idea of corruption in itself makes no sense because that distinction does not arise: there is no embezzlement because the ruler's personal income is the same as the government revenue, no nepotism because there is no criterion for appointment to office apart from the ruler's favour. In a neo-patrimonial system, on the other hand, corruption does arise because the system itself is formally constructed on the principle of rational-legality. Nor is this just a form: corruption cannot, as it were, be abolished by declaring the state to be a patrimonial one after all, and thereby appropriating the revenues for one's own personal use, as was done in effect by President Bokassa of the Central African Republic when in 1976 he declared himself to be an Emperor and sucked the national economy dry to pay for his coronation. The modern state depends on forms of organisation, and insists on exercising powers, which must ultimately rest – if they are to be rendered legitimate at all – on rational-legality. In all states, those powers are in some degree corruptly exercised, because of the inherent artificiality of the public/private distinction already noted, and the difficulty of controlling officials in even the most highly accountable system. But the dangers of corruption are at their greatest when the distinction itself is scarcely recognised, and when public office consequently becomes accepted as a route to personal wealth and power. As always in dealing with ideal types, one must beware of treating a formal model as empirical fact applicable in this case to all third world states. They both differ from one another and change over time, while in the case of a state such as Great Britain the public/private distinction was established over a period of some three hundred years, from the early seventeenth to the late nineteenth centuries, through a succession of measures which progressively established the limits of acceptable public behaviour. There is no doubt, however, that corruption is a very considerable problem almost throughout the third world, amounting in extreme cases to a system of government for purposes of personal enrichment, which has been described as 'kleptocracy' or rule by theft. This cannot plausibly be ascribed just to the moral failings of individual officials even though moral criteria may quite properly distinguish between people who, within a given system, behave with particular honesty or graft. A general phenomenon calls for a general explanation, which the idea of neo-patrimonialism most conveniently encapsulates.

Among the reasons most often given for the salience of third world corruption is the carry-over into present-day political behaviour of cultural values inherited from a patrimonial past. In some ways, this is convincing enough. The practice of gift-giving, for example, is almost universal in patrimonial societies. When a chief or some other person of authority visited the village, or when a dispute was taken before a judge, it was normal and accepted to make a gift, usually of food, to the person concerned. This gift expressed, within a tributary system, a recognition of the authority of the person who received it; *not* to make it would be taken as expressing insubordination or contempt. Even in patrimonial societies, this may readily be viewed in Marxist terms as a means by which the dominant class extracted a surplus from producers; in the context of the modern state, it is easily converted into bribery on one side, or extortion on the other. The same goes for the deeply entrenched principle of mutual support among fellow members of the extended family, village, clan, or other communal group. A highly functional response to the economic and political insecurity of subsistence agriculture, it readily converts into nepotism, or into a form of extortion from below in which a member of the community who has made good in the modern world is placed under the most intense social pressure to use his position for the benefit of those who feel that they have a valid moral claim on his services.

Yet these traditionalist explanations for corruption readily degenerate into self justifying excuses if they do not recognise the key role played by the structure of the third world state. It is unreasonable to expect a set of rational-legal values to develop among public officials without any effective mechanism for their enforcement, and the basic problem here is the weakness of accountability by the governors to the governed. Some of the constitutional aspects of this, notably the inability in most countries to establish liberal democratic forms of government which (for all their faults) provide the best means for ensuring accountability, will be discussed in the next chapter; but these rest on more general points related to the state itself, and its relations with the international system. First, there is the sheer social distance established as members of what has become an elite acquire western education and move into well-paid modern sector jobs, accompanied very often by physical distance as they move into towns where they can enjoy an appropriate life style and, even within the towns, enclose themselves in separate residential areas. While the immigrant societies of the new world lack the distinction between a 'traditional' and a 'modern' sector, they more than make up for it by the fact that income inequalities are greater in Latin America than anywhere else on earth.³ Accountability must, therefore, largely be achieved by members of the elite among themselves. Secondly, the state provides an enormous and institutionalised inequality of power. Not only is it in itself highly hierarchical, but it is unchecked by countervailing powers such as those produced by capitalism and private property in the development of the western liberal states. Similar problems are of course found in the party-state *apparats* of the Soviet bloc. In so far as officials are unchecked by their own superiors, even petty employees of government – the traffic policeman, for instance – can use their little bits of state power as a means to increase their income. Low-level government officials are often not paid much anyway, and their salaries may come irregularly owing to inefficiency or extortion higher up, or just because there is no money in the treasury; they make up the difference by collecting it from their subjects. At a higher level, senior politicians often feel that their status and role demand an ostentatious life style which falls well beyond their salary, requiring either bribery, or else perhaps opportunities for legitimate private profit made possible by their official position. India is rare in having an indigenous ascetic ethic which enables powerful men to gain status through poverty; more often, and especially in Africa, wealth is flaunted rather than concealed.

Effective control over corruption is difficult to maintain. Occasionally a head of state such as Dr Banda in Malawi, an autocrat with the rigid morality of an elder of the Kirk of Scotland, is able to enforce his own standards on his subordinates. More often, although the head of state's speeches are peppered with exhortations, these are part of the official rhetoric which no one takes very seriously. The common stereotype in which the leader is regarded as honest while his ministers are regarded as corrupt, provides the leader not just with extra moral authority, but with a threat which he can use to keep the rest in line; when he wishes to dispense with someone anyway, corruption provides a pretext for doing so. The chance of being brought to book in the wake of a military coup provides no more than an uncertain threat to a few prominent individuals; insecurity may indeed be an incentive to salt away money while the going is good. Military regimes characteristically come into power with a strong rhetorical appeal to honesty and efficiency, but even if they believe this at the time – as they may well do – it can rarely survive for long in government. Militaries, after all, form part of the same state apparatus as civilian bureaucrats and politicians; they govern through it, and benefit from the structural inequalities implicit in it. One of the most sharply depressing scenes in African literature comes in Ayi Kewei Armah's *The Beautyful Ones Are not Yet Born*, when a policeman, manning a road block immediately after the army and police overthrow of the corrupt Nkrumah regime, points his finger to his mouth in a gesture to indicate that a bribe would be acceptable; deep-seated structural conditions are not to be altered by a simple change in government.

A further reason for the salience of corruption lies in the external connections of the third world state. At one level, many of the benefits which corruption provides are external ones, such as imported luxury consumer goods or overseas travel and education; without access to the world market in one form or another, there is usually not very much that you can do with the money, apart from passing it down the line to build up political support. At another, contacts between third world governments and the international economy provide lucrative opportunities for corruption which (though the domestic society pays for them in the end) are less immediately visible and politically unpopular than direct exactions from one's own people: government contracts, concession agreements, suppliers' credits, import licences all provide links between the domestic and international economy, controlled by state officials who may charge their own personal management fee. Finally, a regime with a shaky domestic political base may survive through the support of external powers, either indirectly through aid or directly by military intervention on its behalf, and as a result is better able to exploit its own people. While both western and Soviet blocs have supported some extremely unpleasant regimes, it is on the whole true to say that the western ones have been more corrupt in financial terms, the Soviet ones more brutal in terms of physical extermination. The external connections of the third world state are examined in a later chapter.

Several distinctions have been made between different kinds of corruption, most of which come down to the difference between parochial or distributive corruption on the one hand, and market or extractive corruption on the other. Parochial corruption is generally small in scale, fits into an existing set of values and obligations, and leads to the redistribution and exchange of benefits within a community, rather than the siphoning of resources from it. Extractive corruption is often on a large scale rests on the manipulation of state power, and maintains the life style of a privileged class of state employees and their confederates. Although a low level of petty corruption may be ascribed to digenous values which are harmless and even helpful in maintaining social solidarity, the weight of corruption falls into the second category, and can be crudely described as the means by which those with power get money. No purpose is served by the abusive moral condemnation of those who succumb to this temptation by those who have not had the chance to; but viewed as a social phenomenon, it has corrosive effects on trust in public authorities, and hence on their capacity to direct communal action towards the achievement of common goals, as well as wasting resources both through inefficiency and by directing them abroad. Even though it is a symptom quite as much as a cause, it provides the most striking indication of the failure to link society and government in a shared sense of values.

Patrons and Clients

The power and the fragility of the state, and the social, economic and political gap between those who run it and the great majority of those who are ruled by it, raise an acute problem in the relationship between political power on the one hand and popular support and participation on the other. The key political difficulty facing third world rulers is to extend their support beyond the immediate group of courtiers who have a personal stake in their survival. It is a problem which many do not solve, and which some do not seriously try to. At a minimum, survival may depend simply on their ability to maintain a force more effective than any directed against them, like Amin of Uganda's bodyguard, sustained by a weekly airlift of luxuries from the United Kingdom, before the Tanzanian invasion of 1978-9. A successful coup d'état, launched at times by forces of trivial size, often serves to show that there is no one outside the leader's entourage who is prepared to take any action to try to preserve the regime.

But if a regime is to seek support, how can it do it? The initial boost provided by anticolonial nationalism or by some equivalent triumph cannot be sustained for long. The class divisions which maintain the principal parties of western European states rarely serve the purpose in the third world, not because there are no such divisions – far from it but because the ruling class is usually so well established that class solidarity is a pointless appeal. It is only in highly developed states, such as Chile, that there is a threat to the economically dominant classes sufficient to bring them together in support of the Pinochet regime, and previously to sustain the pre-Allende Christian Democratic governments. An ideological political base in itself generally depends on the support of a class whose interests are served by the ideology, and equally on a competitive party structure through which the relevance of alternative ideologies can be made clear. This is not impossible Jamaica provides at least a partial example – but it is unusual.

The solution characteristically attempted in third world states is through some form of clientelism or patron-client relationship.[4] Clientelism is indeed the application of the principles of neo-patrimonialism to relationships between superiors and inferiors. It is, fundamentally, a relationship of exchange in which a superior (or patron) provides security for an inferior (or client), and the client in turn provides support for the patron. The form taken by this security and support may vary widely: on the one hand physical or legal protection, land or a job, some kind of economic development assistance, even religious intercession; on the other, military service, voting, economic labour power, information. Very often several of these are joined together, and the bond strengthened by some moral sanction which obliges each side to support the other. It is a kind of relationship which characterises any society in which there are sharp divisions (usually on class lines) between superiors and inferiors, but in which neither superiors nor inferiors form politically coherent class units acting together; instead, individual superiors or inferiors need the security and support which is provided by members of the other class. The most familiar arena for patron-client ties is an agrarian economy of a broadly 'feudal' type in which control of land is vested in a landowning class whose members are in constant competition with one another; each landowner needs to attract peasants to work his land, providing him both with produce and with a political-military following, while each peasant, if he is to survive, needs to find a landlord who will provide him with land and protect his right to work it. It is an inherently unequal exchange, hence liable to exploitation, but none the less meeting essential interests on both sides.

The neo-patrimonial state – indeed the modern state as a whole – provides an equally fertile breeding ground for exactly the same kind of relationship. It likewise embodies inherent inequalities, between those who control the state (or more generally, those who have the technical qualifications to do so if they get the chance) and those who do not, and also between those higher and lower within the state hierarchy. Control of the state carries with it the power to provide (or withhold) security, and to allocate benefits in the form of jobs, development projects and so forth; and where the government is under no compulsion to furnish these benefits according to public or universal criteria such as justice, efficiency and need, it may do so at its own discretion to encourage political support. By the same token, those who control the state do generally need political support, unless they can rely on a repressive apparatus which is both loyal and efficient enough to deal with any opposition. In one situation, they need it very badly: when there is an effective electoral system which gives votes to all of the adult citizens, and which awards control of the state to the party which (allowing for the workings of particular electoral systems) wins most votes. Clientelist organisation is, therefore, especially characteristic of competitive party systems, and often, therefore, of the period immediately before independence when rival parties were struggling to win control of the state; the same kind of organisation, and the attitudes to politics which go with it, then usually survive into the post-independence period.

One common way in which it works is this: political party leaders at the national level look around for local leaders who command appreciable support within their own areas. They offer the local leader (or perhaps one of his close relatives or associates) a place in the party, perhaps as a candidate in his home constituency. The local leader gets out the vote, essentially through his own contacts and authority, and delivers it to the national party. The national party in turn – assuming that it wins power – delivers benefits to its local representative, in the form either of economic allocations from the centre to the constituency, such as a road or a piped water supply, or of a purely personal payoff, or of central government support in local political conflicts. Local politics is often extremely factionalised and it is common for one village, or one chief or magnate and his following, to support one party, while their rivals go for the other one. After the election comes the settling of the scores: the successful village gets its piped water supply, the unsuccessful chief is deposed. In the process, the local leader becomes a broker between his own community and central government, passing benefits in each direction and (if he is lucky and successful) taking his share of them. Even when the period of competitive elections passes, and the central government no longer really needs the electoral support which the broker provided, he may still retain his status as a local political boss, someone who is kept on in government because he is still taken as 'representing' an area with which the regime wishes to remain associated. He may then become effectively the representative of government in that area, holding his own local court, the target of supplicants who beg him for government favours. Come a military coup and he will be out, perhaps imprisoned, condemned for corruption; his local rivals will be enthroned in his place, favouring their own villages, installing their own chiefs, praising the new government, in a general reversal of fortunes. But given new elections, or a counter-coup, the original boss may well be back again, unless he has died (or been executed) in the meantime, or so abused his position in the years of triumph that his people refuse to support him. Local level politics in third world states must constantly adapt itself to the realities of central power, but usually survives remarkably unscathed by the vicissitudes of politics at the centre.

In societies without strong local identities, clientelism may work in different ways. In Jamaica, a fairly homogenous and heavily urbanised society, the trade unions affiliated to each of the major political parties may be seen as essentially clientelist organisations formed to maintain support and provide jobs for party stalwarts. In Senegal, where the principal brokers have been the Muslim brotherhoods, these extend from the countryside into the towns, where they collect cash subscriptions from their members and adapt the benefits they provide to the urban setting. Indeed immigrants into towns are often so vulnerable that the protection provided by a patron is well worth paying for. These in turn become brokers whom political parties will seek to recruit, and who in the Latin American context, say, can be used to organise demonstrations of support for, or opposition to, the governing party or junta's policies.[5] In Brazil, the military government in power since 1964 has been able to form and manipulate political parties in this way, especially the ARENA party, and thus provide itself with at least some appearance of popular support.[6] The much greater difficulties of Argentine military regimes, reflected in their resort both to domestic political repression and to external military adventure, have to some degree been due to the fact that these resources had already been mobilised by rival (and in their way equally clientelist) civilian political movements, especially Peronism.

One of the strongest, most alluring, and at the same time most dangerous forms of clientelism is the mobilisation of ethnic identities. We have already seen how the artificiality of the colonial state, the unevenness of social and economic change and the competition for power among indigenous parties during the nationalist period, all tended to intensify ethnic awareness. From a political viewpoint, ethnicity may be seen as a means for giving a moral bond or cement to a clientelist network. The party leadership is placed under an obligation to look after the interests of its constituent race, tribe, caste or religious group; equally to the point, the leadership acquires a kind of legitimacy as the authentic representative of that group, regardless of the enormous differences of class and wealth, and in some respects of political interest, between it and its followers. Clientelism, which depends for its existence on a hierarchically ordered society in which class differences are often intense, both serves as a mechanism for maintaining ruling class interests and, at the same time, systematically inhibits the articulation of class as a source of overt political conflict.

Even when patron-client bonds are not reinforced by the dubious morality of ethnic consciousness, their strength should never be underestimated. They have a resilience, a flexibility, and a degree of rationality for the interests of both patron and client which enable them to survive even the most drastic attempts at their suppression – a point most strikingly illustrated by the role of clientelism within the elephantine *apparats* of the Soviet party and state.[7] They bear a high degree of responsibility for the astonishing rarity of revolutionary upheavals, or even of effective revolutionary movements, anywhere in the third world. For so long as people are vulnerable to political and economic circumstances, and for so long as clientelist networks offer some plausible hope at least for alleviating (though never for fully overcoming) that vulnerability, then the network offers a far less risky option than the untried dangers of revolution. At the same time, clientelism provides some kind of political structure, some mechanism for representation and participation in politics by and on behalf of people outside the central elite. It has many of the advantages, and also the defects, of the oligopolistic economic structure which in so many ways it resembles: where there is a market, in that the producers of government benefits have something to supply to consumers, and something that they want from them in return, then entrepreneurs will spring up unbidden to manage that market.

The fact that clientelism has something to offer both the patrons and the clients should not mislead one into supposing, however, that it is an inherently desirable and beneficial system. There are two main reasons why this is not so. First, it is founded on a premise of inequality between patrons and clients, and the benefits accruing to each of them from the exchange may be very uneven indeed. Clients only benefit in so far as they have anything to offer which the patrons feel a need to pay for (and cannot just exact by force). Unless there is an effective electoral system which gives real choice to clients, this may not be very much; it is much more likely to be a small sweetener to give them some kind of stake in the system, while its main benefits go elsewhere. Secondly, the particularistic or neo-patrimonial nature of the exchange carries serious defects of its own. It may serve to inten-sify ethnic conflicts, though it is equally capable of adaptation so that each group gets a slice of the cake. It leads to allocations often very different from those which would be pro-duced by 'universal' criteria of efficiency and need: the road goes to the 'wrong' place, the 'wrong' person gets the job. Itself a form of corruption, it encourages corruption in other ways: what one is looking for from government is the satisfaction of a private benefit, not of a public need. It is oriented towards the consumption of government services, but does nothing whatever to supply the means for their production: it lends itself to a form of gov-ernment by handout, in which the government itself becomes dependent on the sources of funds through which it is effectively obliged to buy support, whether these be foreign aid receipts or royalties from multinational corporations. Most of all, it supplies no way by which governments can develop the efficiency and accountability which are needed to ren-der legitimate the enormous powers of the modern state.

Clientelism is a form of political organisation which characterises several different kinds of system, of which the underdeveloped state is one of the most important. It depends ulti-mately on the vulnerability of clients, and may give way to other forms of organisation either though a decline in that vulnerability, such that the services of patrons are no longer needed, or through an increase in it, such that there is not the slightest prospect of their being effective. In the first case, which has been described from a number of both Euro-pean and non-European studies,[8] a process of economic development reduces vulnerability and makes it rational for clients to pursue their goals through other, more objectively efficient, mechanisms. In the second, a progressive descent into immiserisation and despair from which no other mechanism offers any prospect of relief may lead clients to follow, at whatever cost, some new and revolutionary path which will also be based on uni-versalistic rather than particularistic values. The great majority of third world peoples are still subsisting in the middle ground between these two extremes.

Notes

1. See, for example, F. Riggs, *Administration in Developing Countries: The Theory of Prismatic Society* (Houghton Mifflin, 1964).

2. See J.F. Medard, 'The Underdeveloped State in Tropical Africa: Political Clientelism or Neopatrimonialism?' in C. Clapham (ed.), *Private Patronage and Public Power: Political Clientelism in the Modern State* (Pinter, 1982).

3. See World Bank, *World Development Report 1981* (Oxford University Press, 1981), Table 25.

4. See C. Clapham, 'Clientelism and the State' in Clapham, *Private Patronage and Public Power*.

5. See for example the contributions by Foltz, Cornelius, Chalmers and Guasti in S.W. Schmidt *et al.* (eds.), *Friends, Followers and Factions: A Reader in Political Clientelism* (University of California Press, 1977).

6. P. Cammack, 'Clientelism and Military Government in Brazil' in Clapham, *Private Patronage and Public Power*.

7. R.H. Baker, 'Clientelism in the Post-Revolutionary State: The Soviet Union' in Clapham, ibid.

8. See the contributions by Silverman and Cornelius in Schmidt *et al.*, *Friends, Followers and Factions*.

World Markets and Political Instability within Less Developed Countries

David P. Rapkin & William P. Avery

I. INTRODUCTION

Political instability, in the form of revolution, internal war, military coups, widespread anti-government demonstrations, strikes, violence, and frequent government recourse to repression is a recurrent aspect of political life in Africa, Asia, Latin America, and the Middle East. Though usually less visible and dramatic, economic instabilities are probably as extensive among less developed countries (LDCs) as those of a political variety. This problem has been recognized and studied by economists, who generally agree that LDCs experience wider economic fluctuations in key economic variables than their more developed, industrialized counterparts. In this context, some effort has been given to measuring and attempting to explain instabilities in exports and imports, income, production, foreign and domestic investment, available foreign exchange, balance of payments, and other areas of economic activity.

Despite the frequency of political instability, and despite considerable journalistic and scholarly attention, our understanding of the causes and consequences of this phenomenon remains incomplete. Especially lacking is knowledge about the linkages between political and economic instabilities. Prior theoretical and empirical work on these linkages is scattered across disciplinary subfields, no doubt reflecting the high degree of specialization and compartmentalization that prevails in the social sciences. The present study is an attempt to fill this void by drawing together the disparate literature on these phenomena and specifying the types of linkages that may exist between them.

The major source of hypotheses concerning these relationships is the body of literature that may be loosely assembled under the rubric of 'dependency theory'. Central to most dependency approaches to the international relations of development and underdevelopment is the idea that LDCs are inordinately vulnerable to events, processes, and forces which originate in the world economy and which interact with domestic forces. Among a wide array of alleged vulnerabilities, it is frequently asserted that instabilities in international markets (for goods, capital, and other factors of production) are transmitted into and exert destabilizing effects upon the national economies of LDCs, and thus also on their class structures and political systems. In short, economic phenomena are viewed as causally prior to political behavior. Though there are a variety of case studies that posit one or another version of this transmission effect, the general proposition has yet to be subjected to systematic empirical examination. Given the uncertain state of knowledge in this area, it would be imprudent to rule out causal sequences, spirals or reciprocal relationships

Originally published in *Cooperation and Conflict*, vol. XXI, 1986. Reprinted with permission.

involving political and economic instabilities. Before these more complex kinds of relationships can be specified and tested, however, a good deal of 'brush-clearing' needs to be done in order to impose some order on the maze of variables that bear on these phenomena.

II. TYPES OF POLITICAL AND ECONOMIC INSTABILITY

This article embarks upon these preparatory tasks by delineating major categories of relationships between political and economic instabilities. The resulting categories will serve as a framework within which subsequent empirical research can be organized. Specifically, we identify two broad categories of linkage. The first involves the domestic consequences— both economic and political—that issue from the exposure of LDCs to the vicissitudes in international markets for the goods and commodities that they export and import. The second category, encompassing markets for capital, technology and other factors of production, involves different types of 'penetration' of LDCs by 'intrusive actors' that are capable of exerting (intended and/or unintended) destabilizing effects. This broad second category is further partitioned into two subtypes of intrusive actors: transnational corporations (TNCs) and international financial institutions (IFIs).[1] We recognize at the outset that these categories are not necessarily mutually exclusive; though some real-world occurrences may fall neatly into one or another category, many concrete instances represent a confluence of two or more of these linkage categories.

Linkage between political and economic instabilities thus serves as a metahypothesis or organizing, umbrella concept under which a variety of more specific relationships are hypothesized to be operative.[2] The balance of this paper describes specific relationships that have been observed within each category of linkage and discusses the conceptual and methodological problems attendant to modeling and testing these relationships. Before proceeding to this task, working definitions for the concepts of political and economic instability are necessary.

Political instability

The term political instability has been used to refer to a wide range of phenomena, from spontaneous demonstrations and protests, on the one extreme, to protracted internal war and revolution, on the other. An array of different kinds of behavior remains within these extremes, including assassinations, conspiracies, military coups, and government sanctions. One commonality that obtains across the different forms of political instability is the element of irregularity and discontinuity in the political environment. Although we emphasize the effects of external forces on political instability, this should not be taken to imply monocausal explanation. In fact, most prior theoretical and empirical studies of political instability have focused on internal causes, stressing such factors as social inequality, economic discontent, and social mobilization.[3] Midlarsky & Tanter and Gurr & Duval do include some measures of external economic ties and show that those are related to the occurrence of political instability; however, these measures are incorporated into multiple-indicator indexes and it is thus impossible to assess their independent effects.[4]

For our immediate purposes, we make one gross distinction between the various manifestations of political instability: we differentiate between destabilizing behavior on the part of the masses (e.g., political violence and turmoil of various sorts, some spontaneous and some planned) and destabilizing behavior on the part of elites (e.g., mainly, but not exclusively, the military coup). We recognize, of course, that distinctions can be made in these types, especially in different forms of mass conflict. The distinction made here is useful because certain types of economic instabilities may catalyze a mass response, while other types may trigger an elite response.

Economic instability

Perhaps the most familiar type of market-related instability affecting LDCs is export instability (typically defined as short-term fluctuations in export prices and/or earnings that stem from variations in supply and demand factors). Export instability is frequently viewed as a problem that precipitates or triggers a number of other difficulties. The following statement by Erb & Schiavo-Campos includes many of the effects that are alleged to ensue from export instabilities:

> . . . export instability affects domestic investment, consumer incomes and government revenues and expenditures; and that its consequences for less developed economies are instability of key domestic variables and retardation of growth of internal sectors. Furthermore, a planned dependence of development projects on certain projected levels of foreign exchange earnings may add an element of rigidity to internal adjustments to external variations, hampering implementation and follow-up of planned projects. At the very least, there are repercussions on the external payments sector, with implications for exchange policy, liquidity needs and programs of export diversification.[5]

Though not all these claims have been empirically substantiated, there is considerable evidence suggesting that export instability is extensive among LDCs and that it can lead to a number of other problems. The connections between export instabilities and fluctuations in international reserves, the ability to import, and the balance of payments are straightforward. Empirical connections between fluctuations and in export earnings and domestic capital formation and directly estimated components of GNP have also been demonstrated.[6]

Another market-related phenomenon that may have implications for political instability is movements in the terms of trade. Whereas export instability refers to short-term variability, the terms of trade refer to the longer-term relationship between the prices a country receives for the goods that it exports and the prices of the goods that it imports. The deterioration of the terms of trade of oil-importing LDCs that resulted from the oil price increases of 1973-74 and 1979-80 provides a vivid example of the destabilizing shocks induced by adverse terms of trade movements. As import bills mounted, balance of payments deficits ballooned, with the result that oil-importing LDCs have had no resource other than more and more loans from private and public sources in international capital markets. Servicing of the resulting ever-larger debt burdens has in turn worsened the original balance of payments disequilibria.

LDCs also enter into markets for medium and long-term capital, technology, and managerial and marketing expertise, involving them in a variety of relationships with TNCs and IFIs. These private and public actors then operate in and exert influence on the societies of host LDCs. Within the extensive literature on transnational corporations are a number of propositions about the destabilizing effects of direct foreign investment for host economies. There is wide agreement among critics of TNCs that direct foreign investment in less developed societies leads to: decapitalization of host economies, displacement of indigenous firms, increased maldistribution of income and social benefits, the transfer of limited and inappropriate technology, alteration of traditional consumer preferences, and involvement in domestic political processes. (How generally these effects obtain, however, has not been conclusively determined.)

Economic instability can also ensue from the intrusive activities of international financial institutions. For instance as a condition for approving loans, the IMF typically requires that borrowing countries adopt a package of policies designed to control inflation and to correct balance of payments disequilibria. These 'stabilization' policies are tantamount to an austerity program for major segments of the population and, as such, often serve to destabilize other facets of the domestic socio-economic system.

In sum, social, economic and political externalities (or diseconomies) may be produced by virtue of participation in the world economy. This is meant as an observational—not a pejorative—statement. We do not mean to imply that the flow of destabilizing 'diseconomies' exceeds the reverse flow of positive benefits. Determination of the net balance, which may or may not be positive for a majority of LDCs, is not our intention. Rather, we simply seek to demonstrate that systematic consideration of these linkages should improve our ability to explain the occurrence of political instability. Nor are we postulating deterministic external causes to the point of excluding or underemphasizing internal causal factors. A complete explanation of political and economic instabilities will have to account for both internal and external causes, as well as for the interaction between the two.

III. CATEGORIES OF LINKAGE

Our categorization of different types of linkage builds upon Weisskopf's distinction between 'market dependency' and 'economic power dependency'. For Weisskopf, market dependency refers to 'participation in world capitalist markets in such a way that a nation's economy is strongly affected by what is happening in the metropolitan capitalist economies', while economic power dependency denotes a situation in which 'a nation's economy is conditioned by the decision-making power of particular individuals, firms, and agencies from the capitalist metropolis'.[7] We augment Weisskopf's meaning by hypothesizing that political, as well as economic, effects result from these kinds of dependency relationships.

Market for goods and commodities, and political instability

Our conception of markets abstracts from efficiency and other explicitly economic considerations and instead focuses on the range of socio-political effects exerted by dynamic and (more-or-less) anonymous market forces. To suggest that markets generate destabilizing consequences is not to imply that these consequences are the intended result of conscious, purposive actions by particular capitalist agents, firms, organizations or states. While we acknowledge that international markets are susceptible to deliberate manipulation and distortion by capitalist actors of different sorts, we are assuming that the generation of political instability by international market forces is primarily an unintended by-product of the normal operation of world capitalism.

That the ongoing integration of contemporary LDCs into the world capitalist system serves to destabilize them in a socio-political sense should not strike the student of political economy as a new idea. Polanyi detailed how the advent of market capitalism in its North

Atlantic birthplace had shattering, often violent, effects on pre-existing social and political institutions.[8] If these kinds of effects obtained in those Western societies in which capitalism originated and has since flourished, should we not expect similar socio-political outcomes in contemporary LDCs? There is ample reason to expect politically destabilizing effects to be even stronger in the contemporary setting. Lofchie's comparison of the situation faced by today's African states with that of the early-developers of Western Europe is worth quoting at some length:

> the political environment of Western society during early industrialization was such as to insulate fledgling state institutions from the social misery generated by an incipient industrial process. A widening of the political franchise and a change of political values from laissez-faire to welfare liberalism did not occur until the industrialization process was well advanced and many of its more harsh social consequences has been ameliorated... the political burden on state institutions was lightened considerably by the fact that the basic dynamism for economic transformation was supplied by an autonomous entrepreneurial class outside the state... the stimulation of economic growth was not a governmental function. In Africa, where autonomous economic elites are largely lacking, the generation of economic growth is a state function. This means that embryonic political institutions have a twofold task to perform. They must be concerned both with economic growth and with alleviation of the human hardships created by economic change.[9]

When we add to these contrasts the fact that present day LDCs do not enjoy the luxury of technological gradualism and that the time frame within which development is expected to unfold is greatly compressed, it is no wonder that political regimes in many LDCs are unable to survive the volatilities and external shocks generated by worked markets.

What kinds of volatilities and shocks are we referring to? Why should we expect openness to international market forces to result in political instability? What are the mechanisms by which instabilities are transmitted? Openness means that the domestic economy must respond to market signals (i.e., changes in world supply, demand and/or prices) by reallocating resources and factors of production. Movement of factors from one productive sector to another is likely to engender resistance and conflict behavior from those groups that perceive themselves to be adversely affected. Failure to respond by shifting productive resources, on the other hand, will result in a loss of income and shortages of scarce foreign exchange. When faced with rapid and substantial adverse shifts in demand or price, the typical LDC, with a limited basket of export commodities, is often unable to, respond at all. In addition, the typical LDC government is highly reliant (relative to more developed countries) on export proceeds as a primary source of government revenues.[10] Unexpected shortfalls in export revenues diminish the ability of the government to reward or otherwise satisfy either elite groups (e.g., the military) or one or more mass political groups (e.g., urban workers), thereby heightening distributive conflict, either in the form of inter-group conflict or pressures on the state for redistributive measures.

Several studies of social revolution point to the international system as a reservoir of causal forces. Skocpol has stated that 'virtually all modern revolutions other than the French, Russian, and Chinese have occurred in relatively small, formerly colonial countries situated in highly vulnerable and dependent positions within the world capitalist economy and the international state system.'[11] Wolf's examination of peasant wars led him to conclude that the world market is a motor force behind revolutionary change.[12] Similarly, in his cross-national study of agrarian revolution, Paige finds agricultural exports to be 'one of the principal means by which the rural population is brought into contact with market forces and consequently a major source of economic and social change in rural areas'.[13]

In the African context, Wallerstein has argued that a situation of increasing demands on the state, coupled with export shortfalls and declining foreign financial assistance,

> needed then only a small spark to set in motion the first coup. If the job squeeze led to acute rivalry and eventually conflict, government action to contain such rivalry usually led to an accumulation of enemies to the regime. When enough such had been accumulated, as in Nigeria, there was a coup. Or if the government, facing financial crisis, sought to limit expenditure or cut back on civil service salaries, there might be a crisis and a coup (as in Togo and Dahomey in 1963). Or if the government sought to contain the growing expression of political discontent by forced unity moves which would have the effect of limiting political outlets, there might be a coup (as in Congo-Brazzaville in 1963 and Sierra Leone in 1967).... The post-coup regime, being faced with the same dilemmas, found it difficult to do better than the precoup illegitimacy of its own route to power.[14]

Similarly, Callaway & Card attribute political instability in Ghana to declining terms of trade and Young discusses the same relationship in Uganda.[15] O'Leary & Coplin's cross-national study of political instability in Africa in the 1960s revealed that stagnating economic performance, as measured in part by cumulative balances of trade, contributed to both communal and elite political instability.[16] There is also considerable evidence of the existence of similar relationships in Latin America. Dean, in a study spanning the period 1823-1966, shows that fluctuations in coup activity were related to contractions in Latin American imports and concludes, with somewhat less firm evidence, that the pattern of covariation between coups and imports was related to international trade cycles.[17] In studies of shorter and more recent time periods, both Needler and Fossum report that military coups are significantly more likely in periods of economic deterioration than in more prosperous times.[18] Fenmore & Volgy's cross-national study of Latin America over the years 1969 to 1967 reveals that export performance is a strong predictor of political instability. They conclude that this finding 'confirm(s) the importance of the international economic market for the political health of Latin America.'[19]

Also in the Latin American context, Sheahan argues that the abandonment of import substitution and the concomitant adoption of market-oriented economic policies has resulted in severe political repression. He demonstrates how emphasis on efficiency criteria—in the determination of wage rates, interest rates, exchange rates, commercial and private foreign investment policies—can lead to heightened political repression.[20]

Markets for capital, intrusive actors, and political instability

Other external factors affecting the political stability of LDCs fall under the classification of Weisskopf's economic power dependency. In this section, the emphasis shifts from economic influences emanating from world markets for goods and commodities to those influences that are more readily identified with specific actors and institutions associated with international capital markets. We argue that intrusive behavior of TNCs and certain IFIs helps shape the conditions within which political instability occurs in LDCs.[21]

Transnational Corporations. One of the principal vehicles for the ongoing incorporation of LDCs into the contemporary world economy is the transnational corporation. While there is much debate over the effects of foreign capital in less developed countries, arguments that it is exploitative and results in net negative consequences for the LDCs are common.[22]

Among the alleged negative effects, TNCs are claimed to decapitalize LDC economies by siphoning off economic surplus through excessive profit remittances, by limiting their subsidiaries to the host market, and through the use of transfer pricing and tie-in clauses. Another argument contends that TNCs, through superior competitive advantages, displace local industries or pre-empt their growth. TNCs often buy local firms, capturing an increasing share of the domestic economic base, thereby retarding indigenous industrial development. Both decapitalization and displacement are viewed as important channels through which national control over vital industry is eroded. Foreign enterprises, with their superior financial and technological resources, overwhelm national firms, often placing them in the role of suppliers for TNCs. The net outcome is what some have called the 'denationalization' of domestic industry.[23] This loss of control can create resentment toward the TNCs and impose severe constraints on state economic policy-making by hampering efforts to respond effectively to popular demands.

Critics also contend that transnational firms distort host economies through the limited transfer of technology, much of which is deemed inappropriate to typical LDC factor proportions. The TNC holds a virtual monopoly on technology, concentrates research and development operations in the home country, and maintains a factor mix that is highly capital-intensive. The control of technology increases technological dependence and enables the TNCs to protect their superior bargaining position in the local economy. Capital-intensive technology is often felt to produce higher levels of unemployment, to favor skilled labor markets, to create restricted, upper class consumer markets, and to discourage production linkages and the development of capital goods markets in the host economies.

Another argument holds that direct foreign investment worsens the distribution of income and social benefits in host LDCs. Higher wages paid by TNCs contribute to a widening gap between employees of foreign enterprises and the rest of the labor force. Interdependencies between the urban and rural sectors of the host society arc diminished, and the gap between elites and masses is increased. Development of traditional sectors is retarded; inflation and unemployment are aggravated; and the goals of full and integrated development are subverted. Mahler's cross-national study of foreign investment in LDCs provides empirical evidence that foreign capital is associated with inequalities of income and social welfare, and with higher unemployment rates.[24] And studies of political instability have long demonstrated that income inequality or relative deprivation is causally related to domestic political strife.[25] There is reason to expect, therefore, that the distributive consequences of TNCs are related to increased alienation of workers and to heightened conflict and tension between the modern and traditional sectors of the host society.

Direct foreign investment is also alleged to alter national consumer preferences through the development of markets for new and alien products. Some critics charge that this introduces foreign values into the host society and undermines the national culture. Societies which are already undergoing changes in traditional values and cultural patterns often find that the introduction of Western consumer values increases existing tensions. It is also likely that shifting consumption patterns will increase expectations for more consumer goods. The inability of the national economy to expand its capacity to meet these demands creates mass discontent and heightened pressures on already hardpressed regimes.

Finally, critics of direct foreign investment in less developed countries contend that TNCs pervert the political processes of host countries. One of the charges most frequently made is that TNCs coopt local elites, forming alliances between foreign economic interests and local interest, both public and private. Local business elites are thus integrated into the world economic system, and since they derive much of their wealth and status from linkages with that system, they are reasoned to have a vested interest in preserving these linkages.[26] This elite linkage has been depicted variously as a dependent bourgeoisie, foreign sponsored plutocracy, transnational kernel, and collaborating or comprador elites. It is plausible to hypothesize that this linkage is the source of much elite political instability—usually expressed in the form of a coup d'etat—as attempts are made to screen out groups and demands which threaten to alter the economic system from which dominant elite groups derive so many benefits. A perceptive analysis of development in Brazil by Evans argues that a 'triple alliance' among TNCs, local private enterprises and, state-owned enterprises has promoted a form of industrialization that benefits the elite but excludes the larger population from the benefits of development.[27] Moreover, there is no shortage of evidence indicating that a national elite whose power and wealth are tied to the dependent status quo may actually resist independent national growth in order to preserve their position of privilege.

International financial institutions. Another set of actors involved in the complex web of relationships between political and economic instability are international financial institutions, principally the International Monetary Fund (IMF) and, to a lesser extent, the International Bank for Reconstruction and Development (IBRD or World Bank). The IMF's role stems from its involvement in the economic policies of member LDCs which seek IMF loans to remedy balance of payments (BOP) disequilibria. A BOP deficit, which usually translates into difficulties in meeting prior debt obligations and in fulfilling ongoing import needs, is itself a form of economic instability. BOP disequilibria may be the product of adverse trends in world markets, failure to respond to market signals, mismanaged domestic economic policies, or some combination of these factors. The point is that the IMF does not trigger economic and/or political instability in LDCs that are stable and viable prior to their involvement with the IMF; rather, the IMF is drawn into the domestic affairs of LDCs which are already experiencing some measure of economic difficulty. It is at this juncture that the IMF is argued to exert destabilizing effects. In this role, the IMF should be viewed as occupying an intermediate or intervening position in a complex causal sequence.

The loans granted to LDCs suffering from BOP disequilibria are conditional on the adoption of specific economic stabilization policies by the borrowing government. The IMF (and other IFIs more generally) is guided by a free market orientation reflective of orthodox neoclassical and monetarist economic philosophy. Thus the specific policies prescribed by the IMF, which are designed to correct distortions of the price system within the prospective borrower's economy, typically include: removal of price controls and subsidies, abolition of foreign exchange and import controls, currency devaluation, greater openness toward foreign investment, and a variety of anti-inflationary measures such as reductions in public sector spending and restriction of money supply. Leverage over the policy framework within which the borrowing government is to deal with its economic problems is exercised by means of 'standby agreements' (negotiated between the IMF, the borrower, and sometimes other major creditors), with failure to implement the terms of the standby agreement resulting in suspension of undisbursed portions of the loan. The borrower also must consult with the IMF on subsequent policy decisions, thereby granting the IMF internal auditing and monitoring functions with respect to virtually the whole of its economic affairs.

Moreover, the IMF's influence over member LDCs stretches far beyond the extent suggested by the dollar amount of its loans. This extended influence derives from the IMF's informal role as an international credit rating agency. Other international lending institutions, both public and private, rely heavily on IMF approval (via the standby agreement) of borrowing countries' stabilization programs as an indicator of credit worthiness. In other words, failure to reach agreement with the IMF—reflecting either the inability or unwillingness to adopt IMF prescriptions—serves as a 'kiss of death' in international credit markets. With the amount of commercial financing increasing markedly in proportion to that provided by IFIs in recent years, the magnitude of international finance that is affected by IMF judgments exceeds by a wide margin the hard currency loans that the IMF directly allocates.

The hypothesized connection between IMF operations and political instability is based on observation of the domestic consequences of the economic policies required by the IMF. The combined domestic effects of the package of stabilization measures tend to be recessive and are frequently tantamount to a severe austerity program. Typically, government services are cut back, imports are reduced, businesses suffer a credit squeeze, prices rise, workers' wages and consumption fall, and national income distributions are skewed in the direction of greater inequality. Such developments often have serious political repercussions for LDC governments, many of which already suffer from low levels of legitimacy and have only a tenuous hold on political power. Ample evidence exists to show that LDCs are frequently placed in 'no win' situations when negotiating agreements with the IMF and that many are unable to weather the ensuing political storm. Presenting evidence from several case studies, Payer contends that:

> a government which attempts to carry out the conditions... (of) the IMF is likely to find itself voted out of office. A government which does not carry out the conditions, or make an arrangement at all, is likely to find its international credit for imports cut off, which puts it into a popularity bind of a different variety and makes a rightist coup likely.[28]

Libby's study of Ghana's economic crisis during the period 1969 to 1972 shows that the government had no choice but to negotiate an economic program within the parameters set out by the IMF.[29] The policies thus formulated constituted externally-imposed constraints on Ghana's policy-making process which, while sensible from the standpoint of abstract market criteria, were 'suicidal' in the domestic political context. Libby concludes that the IFIs:

> co-opted Ghana's policy formation process by coordinating external contacts with the government. When external assistance became crucial for the government's survival due to a serious decline in the world price of cocoa beans in mid-1971, Ghana became heavily dependent upon the IGOs and creditors. The devaluation package which the IMF, IBRD, Britain and other creditors presented as a precondition for their help was primarily designed to persuade creditor and donor governments that Ghana was deserving of further assistance . . . (The government) was placed in a dilemma of taking extreme policy measures which would have a traumatic impact upon the Ghanaian public or risking the severance of export credit and aid—which would also undermine public confidence in (the) government. Neither course was a viable option because neither took the precarious position of the government into account.[30]

The evidence from these and other cases leads to the preliminary conclusion that the IMF (and other IFIs) is yet another element in the international economic environment that can affect LDCs in a politically destabilizing manner. The thrust of the Payer and Libby arguments cited above are captured nicely in the statement of the Indian observer of the 1982 IMF-IBRD joint meeting: 'The IMF may end up causing more revolutions than Karl Marx ever dreamed of.'[31]

IV. DISCUSSION

We have adduced a number of theoretical arguments and concrete cases to demonstrate the tenability of the broad hypothesis linking political and economic instabilities. We have also delineated several linkage categories into which this metahypothesis can be disaggregated and within which its subtypes can be specified. But arguments, examples and categories are not evidence and thus leave unaddressed the questions of spatial and temporal generalizability of the relationships we have posited. Though empirical tests are beyond the scope of this paper, think it important to consider some conceptual and methodological issues that arise from the preceding analysis and which must be taken into account before appropriate empirical procedures can be designed and implemented.

Multiple linkages

Though the linkage categories have been presented separately, the reader has no doubt noticed that given instances of linkage may unfold across several categories, either sequentially, cumulatively or simultaneously. For example, as we pointed out, involvement with the IMF is invariably preceded by worsening balance of payments deficits.

Balance of trade deficits (which are often a significant component of overall BOP deficits) may derive wholly or partially from short-term volatilities or longer-term trends in those world goods/commodities markets in which a country is either a buyer or a seller. To the extent that this is the case, the relevant linkage category would be the one we described in terms of Weisskopf's concept of 'market dependency'. Another significant element in the BOP deficits of many LDCs is the 'investment income' entry, which registers the outflow of profits on direct foreign investment and interest on international debts. Direct foreign investment is of course the business of transnational corporations, and it is on this point that the 'decapitalization' thesis, whatever its empirical generality, is of crucial importance. From this perspective the instability problem stems from penetration by intrusive actors. Thus, economic instability resulting from interactions in either or both of these linkage categories can force the LDC to interact with another type of intrusive actor, international financial institutions.

The occurrence of multiple linkages is well illustrated by the case of Allende's Chile. Following his election and assumption of the presidency in 1970, Allende undertook measures designed to alter the relationships linking Chile to the world economy. Notable among these measures, which can be described as efforts at dependency reduction, were the nationalizations of the Chilean investments of a number of transnational corporations (*inter alia*, ITT, Dupont, General Motors and the major copper producers, Kennecott and Anaconda). At the same time, Chile's BOP problems were becoming acute due to the confluence of several factors: the decline of world market prices for copper, Chile's major export commodity;

large-scale outflows of repatriated profits by transnationals; and the Chilean government's profligate import policies.

Chile's economic problems, generated within several linkage categories, were severely exacerbated by the reactions of affected firms, international financial institutions, and the US government to Allende's dependency reduction measures. In a sequence of overt and covert actions that is now well known, these 'intrusive actors' mounted a concerted effort to destabilize the Chilean economy and polity. US government aid was sharply reduced, flows of capital from private banks and IFIs were severed, direct foreign investment slowed markedly, commercial credits and exports to Chile of critical industrial materials were interrupted, and resources were expended in order to undermine Allende's democratically elected government.[32] These actions culminated in 1973 with the overthrow of his government by a right-wing military coup. In sum, the case of Allende's Chile provides a useful, if extreme, example of the transmission of destabilizing effects through multiple world economy linkages.

As should be apparent, multiple linkages make it more difficult to specify the linkage metahypothesis and hence also more difficult to subject it to empirical scrutiny. Simple bivariate procedures matching various kinds of links to the world economy with measures of instability are unlikely to yield meaningful results. While the metahypothesis needs to be disaggregated in ways we have indicated, it will also have to be put back together in a manner that captures the complexity of concrete situations. Minimally, we expect that the probability of political instability increases as a function of the number of linkage categories through which different kinds of economic instabilities are transmitted into a particular LDC. With reference to sequence, it seems evident that instabilities stemming from involvement in world goods/commodities markets and from dealings with transnational corporations precede, indeed precipitate, BOP problems which in turn subject the LDC to the problems attendant on involvement with IFIs (and more recently with private banks). This chain of problems implies a definite temporal sequence around which initial modeling efforts should be structured.

Gradual and sudden effects

Another conceptual and methodological problem arises from the differential rate at which destabilizing effects unfold through time. The linkage categories encompass two distinct temporal possibilities: gradual, 'time release' effects and sudden shocks or disturbances. We would expect a long term deterioration in an LDC's term of trade or a gradual decapitalization process to result in cumulative strain on its economy and/or polity rather than in immediate and direct destabilization. Cumulative strain (or destabilization by accretion) might directly engender political instability once some 'threshold' is reached (though the level of such thresholds would be country-specific rather than universal). We believe it more probable, however, that longer-term effects of this variety serve to make a particular LDC more vulnerable to the destabilizing consequences of sudden disturbances emanating from the world economy. Short-term disturbances or shocks, such as a large increase in the price of energy imports, the unanticipated exit of a TNC in a crucial industrial sector, or the cessation of external finance, are more likely to produce precipitous changes in an LDC's economic and political processes. This distinction, while clear enough in the abstract, may often be blurred in data analysis, i.e., it might be difficult to differentiate between long and short term effects for any particular case. Since cross-sectional designs will not enable determination of these kinds of differences, some form of longitudinal design will be necessary. Interrupted time series designs should be useful in this regard; first-differenced series (registering the amount of change from one period to another) rather than absolute-value point estimates should also help in coping with this problem.

Another time-related consideration concerns the state of the world economic environment. As is well known, the capitalist world economy is prone to cyclical alternation between periods of growth and expansion and periods of stagnation and contraction. We expect the various problems confronting LDCs that we have discussed to be more acute during periods of recession in the world economy, during which demand for LDC exports, available liquidity, and flows of foreign investment are all likely to shrink significantly. This consideration places great importance on the temporal frame selected for study and implies the need to control for overall systemic conditions, i.e., location along the business cycle, since analysis of the linkage metahypothesis is likely to produce different results within periods characterized by growth than within those characterized by stagnation.

Mediating effects of domestic Political and economic context

Though we have emphasized the external-to-internal and economic-to-political directions of causation, any serious attempt to test these relationships will have to balance this emphasis with consideration of LDCs' domestic political and economic context. We have not meant to convey the impression that most LDCs would be stable and harmonious, politically and economically, were it not for the destabilizing influences absorbed through their links with the world economy. Although this impression may accurately describe the circumstances of some LDCs, most are already beset by a host of political and economic problems which often stem from internal sources. In these circumstances, an externally-generated disturbance is likely to act as a precipitant or proximate cause of instability, triggering latent political dissent that would probably erupt sooner or later in any event.

The domestic context of individual LDCs is therefore analytically crucial insofar as it mediates the strength and form of disturbances emanating from the world economic environment. Deutsch states this mediating relationship in general terms: '. . . the impact of external events upon the internal affairs of a country could be said to decline with the stability and autonomy of the internal decision-making system'.[33] More specifically, certain configurations of political and economic structures and policies can function so as to mitigate destabilizing external forces, cushioning society against their more deleterious effects. Conversely, existing structures and policies may actually intensify the external disturbance, propagating it more deeply and widely throughout the society.

While it is hence necessary to account for domestic context, such an accounting complicates the analytical task immensely. It is impossible to provide here a full discussion of domestic contextual factors. What follows is a brief description of what we consider the main elements of economic and political structure of LDCs that mediate the impact of external forces on internal stability.

Economic Context. With reference to economic structure, the major considerations are (1) the extent of reliance on international trade and foreign capital, and (2) the diversity and mobility of a country's productive resources. The greater the dependence of a country on trade (exports and/or imports as a proportion of aggregate economic activity), the larger the potential vulnerability to short-term and long-term disturbances arising in world goods/commodities markets. Similarly, the higher the share of foreign capital in a country's aggregate capital formation, the greater is its susceptibility to the kinds of instabilities associated with the presence of intrusive actors.

The diversity and mobility of productive resources refer to a number of structural features of a country's economy that bear on its ability to respond to changes in its international economic environment. Of fundamental importance is the degree of sectoral diversification; countries with a wide dispersal of economic activities across different primary and industrial sectors are in principle more flexible and resilient in the face of changing market conditions than countries in which a preponderance of aggregate economic activity is concentrated in one or a few sectors. This same consideration is relevant in the trade realm in the form of commodity concentration; those countries with a diversified basket of export commodities will be less affected by adverse price and/or demand trends for any single commodity than countries whose export earnings derive from one or a few commodities. Given diversification, shortfalls arising in the exchange of one commodity are likely to be offset by positive market trends for others. Diversification also enables the shifting of resources from one sector to another in reaction to market developments. Conversely, high commodity concentrations imply rigidity and an inability to shift factors of production in response to world market signals. Another relevant structural variable is partner concentration, which refers to the extent to which a country's exports and/or imports are concentrated across trading partners. LDCs whose exports are oriented largely toward a single national market often find their economic fortunes tied to prevailing economic conditions in that market and are also susceptible to monopsonistic manipulation of their terms of trade.

The international economic policies of LDCs, as distinct from their economic structure, also play an intervening role between external disturbances and internal stability.[34] While we cannot discuss in detail here the ramifications of different policies, the following interrelated policy areas are especially pertinent to our concerns: choice of exchange rate system; if applicable, the set of exchange (capital market) controls; and, commercial policies and tax and subsidy arrangements that alter the domestic prices of internationally traded goods.[35] Each of these policy areas necessitates a choice, in the extreme, between economic efficiency via the unfettered operation of market forces and efforts to maintain domestic economic stability by modulating (distorting) these forces. In practice, the choice is usually a matter of degree among policies reflecting different tradeoffs between the two objectives.

The major consideration in the formulation of exchange rate policy is the choice between a 'floating' rate (in which the value of a currency is determined by supply and demand factors in foreign exchange markets) and one of several 'pegged' rate schemes (in which a currency's value is fixed in relation to one or a combination of reference currencies). Floating (or flexible) rates, favored by those advocating efficiency as the dominant policy criterion, allow fluctuations in foreign exchange markets to be directly reflected in domestic price levels. Pegged rates, in contrast, are usually chosen with the intent of insulating the domestic economy from volatilities in foreign exchange markets.

Exchange controls are a means by which governments attempt to regulate the use of scarce foreign exchange. Allocation of foreign exchange by administrative decision is usually designed either to give priority to essential imports or to proscribe certain types of capital outflows. In the former case, the motivation is to avoid economic and/or political disruptions that would result from shortages of essential imports such as crucial industrial inputs or staple foods. In the latter case, the purpose of controls is to shield the domestic economy from short-term volatilities in capital markets or to arrest or avoid a deteriorating BOP position.

Tax and subsidy policies encompass a range of restrictive instruments, including tariffs, import quotas and other non-tariff barriers, variable levies, multiple (commodity-specific) exchange rates, export subsidies, and price subsidies for politically sensitive imports such as food. Again, the purpose of such policies is to insulate the domestic economy against destabilizing world market forces, primarily by trying to maintain stable domestic prices in the face of unstable world market prices.

Political Context.

A high level of economic instability may not affect political stability in a given LDC, whereas the same (or a lesser) dose of economic instability can translate into acute political instability in another. In other words, there is no necessary relationship between the two types of instability. This assertion implies that domestic political factors must play an important mediating role: they may either dampen or magnify (or not affect at all) the destabilizing external influences. While the set of potentially relevant political variables is quite large, our reading of the political instability literature suggests that the following are of critical importance: governmental legitimacy, coercive capability, tax structure, income distribution, and conflict tradition.

We expect that the degree of governmental legitimacy affects inversely the impact of economic instability. Regimes that enjoy a broad consensus among their mass publics on the appropriateness of their rule should be better able to weather the destabilizing effects of external economic disturbances. The coercive capability of a given regime may also mediate the differential effects of economic instability. Governments which possess greater coercive potential can threaten or employ repressive measures to prevent economic instability from translating into political unrest. Existing distributions of income are important in determining what segments of society bear the burdens of economic instability. The political effects of economic instability depend largely upon which groups or classes in society absorb its costs. Some groups are more intensely affected than others, but what is crucial is how important these groups in the regime's support structure, their propensities for violent dissent and their abilities to mobilize resources.

Tax structures in the LDCs can exert further mediating effects in the relationship between economic and political instability. Developing countries rely heavily upon trade-derived taxes for state revenue, much more than do the industrialized countries. The result is that the state apparatus in many LDCs is more dependent on transactions with the international economic system for tax revenue and thus less capable of insulating itself from volatilities in that system.[36] A final mediating factor is prior levels of political instability in a given LDC. For countries with a tradition of domestic conflict, economic instability will likely translate with greater certainty and rapidity into domestic political strife.

Figure 1 summarizes the categories of variables we have discussed and delineates the anticipated relationships among them. We hypothesize that influences, pressures, and constraints emanating from the world economy produce negative economic consequences (either gradual effects or sudden shocks) for LDCs which, in turn, can lead to various forms of political instability. The impact of economic instabilities on political stability, however, is refracted through the prism of a variety of existing conditions in the political and economic contexts of the affected LDCs.

Fig. 1. *World markets and domestic political instability: an outline of hypothesized relationships.*

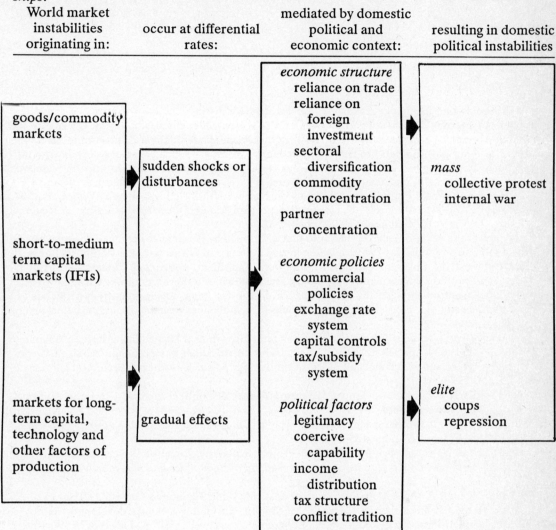

| World market instabilities originating in: | occur at differential rates: | mediated by domestic political and economic context: | resulting in domestic political instabilities |

V. CONCLUSION

This paper has attempted (1) to give specific content to the proposition that participation in the capitalist world economy renders less developed countries vulnerable to a variety of destabilizing influences, and (2) to sketch out an analytical framework within which the empirical questions raised by this proposition can be examined. The dilemmas currently faced by the majority of LDCs place all the more importance on gaining an understanding of the world political economy and the ways in which it affects its constituent parts. We believe that the foregoing discussion enhances our understanding of this question by specifying the linkages between world economy and domestic political instability, thereby providing a framework for further, more systematic scrutiny of the linkage question.

Notes

Author's note: The research on which this paper is based was supported in part by a Maude Hammond Fling Fellowship awarded to the first-named author by The Research Council of the University of Nebraska — Lincoln.

[1] We recognize that foreign governments also constitute a distinct category of intrusive actors that are capable of exerting destabilizing effects on LDCs (see our later discussion of the US role in the downfall of Allende's government in Chile). Though the means used in deliberate governmental efforts to destabilize other governments are frequently economic, we regard such behavior as explicitly political in nature. This category of intrusive actors has been well-covered in the literatures on economic sanctions and foreign aid, and thus we will not treat it here. See, however, Richard S. Olson, 'Economic Coercion in World Politics: With a Focus on North-South Relations', *World Politics*, Vol. 31, (July 1979), pp. 471-94; and Charles F. Doran, 'US Foreign Aid and the Unstable Polity: A Regional Case Study', *Orbis*, Vol. 22 (Summer 1978), pp. 435-52.

[2] Our usage of the term 'linkage' is similar to that developed by Rosenau, who defines linkage as 'any recurrent sequence of behavior that originates in one system and is reacted to in another' (James N. Rosenau, 'Toward the Study of National-International Linkages', in *Linkage Politics*, ed. by J. N. Rosenau, The Free Press, New York 1969, p. 45). Our application differs from Rosenau's, however, in that effects transmitted through any of our linkage categories need not be 'recurrent sequences of behavior', but instead may consist of one-time shocks or disturbances (see the discussion below on this distinction).

[3] See, respectively, Mancur Olson, 'Rapid Economic Growth as a Destabilizing Force', *Economic History*, Vol. 23 (1963), pp. 529-52; Charles Tilly, *From Mobilization to Revolution*, Addison-Wesley, Reading, MA 1978; and A. Oberschall, *Social Conflict and Social Movements*, Prentice Hall, Englewood Cliffs, NJ 1973.

[4] Manus Midlarsky & Raymond Tanter, 'Toward a Theory of Political Instability in Latin America', *Journal of Peace Research*, Vol. 3 (1967), pp. 209-77; and Ted R. Gurr & Raymond Duvall, 'Civil Conflict in the 1960s: A Reciprocal Theoretical System with Parameter Estimates', *Comparative Political Studies*, Vol. 6 (July 1973), pp. 135-69.

[5] Guy F. Erb & Salvatore Schiavo-Campos, 'Export Instability, Level of Development, and Economic Size of Less Developed Countries, *Oxford Bulletin of Economics and Statistics*, Vol. 31 (1969), p. 263.

[6] See Peter Kenen & C. S. Voivodes, 'Export Instability and Economic Growth', *Kyklos*, Vol. 25 (1972); and Donald J. Mathieson & Ronald I. McKinnon, 'Instability in Underdeveloped Countries: The Impact of the International Economy', in *Economic Growth*, ed. by P. A. David & M. W. Reder, Academic Press, New York 1974, pp. 315-31.

[7] Thomas E. Weisskopf, 'Dependence as an Explanation of Underdevelopment: A Critique', paper presented at the sixth annual meeting of the Latin American Studies Association, Atlanta, Georgia, March 1976, pp. 34.

[8] Karl Polanyi, *The Great Transformation*, Beacon Press, Boston, 1957.

[9] Michael F. Lofchie, 'Preface', in *The State of the Nations: Constraints on Development in Independent Africa*, ed. by M. F. Lofchie, University of California Press, Berkeley, 1971, pp. 5-6.

[10] For empirical demonstration of the close connection between trade perturbations and fluctuations in government revenues among LDCs, see Stephen D. Krasner, 'Transforming International Regimes: What the Third World Wants and Why', *International Studies Quarterly*, Vol. 25 (March 1981), pp. 134-36.

[11] Theda Skocpol, *States and Social Revolutions*, Cambridge University Press, New York 1979, p. 288.

[12] Eric R. Wolf, *Peasants' Wars in the Twentieth Century*, Harper and Row, New York 1969.

[13] Jeffrey M. Paige, *Agrarian Revolution*, The Free Press, New York 1975, p. 3.

[14] Immanuel Wallerstein, 'The Range of Choice: Constraints on the Policies of Governments of Contemporary African States', in *The State of the Nations*, ed. by M. F. Lofchie, University of California Press, Berkeley 1971, p. 30.

[15] Barbara Callaway & Emily Card, 'Political Constraints on Economic Development in Ghana', in *The State of the Nations*, pp. 6592; and M. Crawford Young, 'Agricultural Policy in Uganda: Capability and Choice', in *Ibid.*, pp. 141-64.

[16] Michael D. O'Leary & William D. Coplin, *Quantitative Techniques in Foreign Policy Analysis and Forecasting*, Praeger, New York 1975.

[17] Warren Dean, 'Latin American Golpes and Economic Fluctuations, 1823-1966', *Social Science* Vol. 51 (1970), pp. 70-80

[18] Martin C. Needler, 'Political Development and Military Intervention in Latin America', *American Political Science Review*, Vol. 60 (September 1966), pp. 616-26; and Egil Fossum, 'Factors Influencing the Occurrence of Military Coups d'Etat in Latin America', *Journal of Peace Research*, Vol. 4, No. 3 (1967), pp. 338-51. These Latin American findings are consistent with Thompson's crossnational finding that economic adversity makes coups more likely but that, in and of itself, it does not empirically account for their occurrence. Given the comprehensiveness and generality of Thompson's study, all references herein to case studies involving coups should be qualified with reference to his findings. (William R. Thompson, 'Regime Vulnerability and the Military Coup', *Comparative Policies*, Vol. 7 [July 1975], pp. 459-87.)

[19] Barton Fenmore & Thomas J. Volgy, 'Short-Term Economic Change and Political Instability in Latin America', *Western Political Quarterly*, Vol. 31, No. 4 (1978), p. 559.

[20] John Sheahan, 'Market-Oriented Economic Policies and Political Repression in Latin America', *Economic Development and Cultural Change*, Vol. 28 (January 1980), pp. 267-91.

[21] The concepts of 'economic power dependency' and 'intrusive actors' are similar in meaning to Rosenau's concept of a 'penetrated political system', which he defines as, 'one in which nonmembers of a national society participate directly and authoritatively, through actions taken jointly with the society's members, in either the allocation of its values or the mobilization of support on behalf of its goals' (James N. Rosenau, 'Pre-theories and Theories of Foreign Policy', in *Approaches to Comparative and International Politics*, ed. by R. B. Farrell, Northwestern University Press, Evanston, Ill. 1966, p. 65). Kerbo's study of political violence in Chile stresses the direct and intentional nature of efforts to destabilize the Allende government by various intrusive actors (Harold R. Kerbo, 'Foreign Involvement in the Preconditions for Political Violence: The World System and the Case of Chile', *Journal of Conflict Resolution*, Vol. 22 [September 1978], pp. 363-92). Though the distinction is not hard-and-fast, we contrast the intentionality found in the intrusive actor category with the often unintended consequences for political stability that stem from involvement in the goods/commodities market category.

[22] For a balanced overview of this debate, see Thomas J. Biersteker, *Distortion or Development? Contending Perspectives on the Multinational Corporation*, The MIT Press, Cambridge, Mass. 1978.

[23] Osvaldo Sunkel, 'Big Business and in Dependencia', *Foreign Affairs*, Vol. 50 (1972), pp. 517-31.

[24] Vincent A. Mahler, 'Mining, Agriculture, a and Manufacturing: The Impact of Foreign Investment on Social Distribution in Third World Countries', *Comparative Political Studies*, Vol. 14 (October 1981), pp. 267-97.

[25] James C. Davies, 'The J-Curve of Rising and Declining Satisfactions as a Cause of Some Great Revolutions and a Contained Rebellion', in *Violence in America*, ed. by H. Graham and T. Gurr, Signet Books, New York 1969, pp. 547-76; Ted R. Gurr, *Why Men Rebel*, Princeton University Press, Princeton, NJ 1970; and Lee Sigelman and M. Simpson, 'A Cross-national Test of the Linkage Between Economic Inequality and Political Violence', *Journal of Conflict Resolution*, Vol. 21 (March 1977), pp. 105-28.

[26] For a case study of Nigeria which illustrates how these elite linkages can be politically destabilizing, see Terisa Turner, 'Multinational Corporations and the Instability of the Nigerian State', *Review of African Political Economy*, Vol. 5 (1976), pp. 63-79. For the Philippines, see Robert B. Stauffer, 'The Political Economy of a Coup: Transnational Linkages and Philippine Political Response', *Journal of Peace Research*, Vol. 11 (1974), pp. 161- 78.

[27] Peter Evans, *Dependent Development: The Alliance of Multinational, State, and Local Capital in Brazil*, Princeton University Press, Princeton, NJ 1979.

[28] Cheryl Payer, *The Debt Trap: The IMF and the Third World*, Monthly Review Press, New York 1974.

[29] Ronald T. Libby, 'External Co-optation of a Less Developed Country's Policymaking: The Case of Ghana, 1969-1972', *World Politics*, Vol. 19 (1976), pp. 67-89.

[30] *Ibid.*, p. 88.

[31] Quoted by Clyde H. Farnsworth, 'IMF Focus: A Determination by Debtors to Cure Their Ills', *The New York Times*, September 11, 1982.

[32] For accounts of these sanctions, including their timing and coordination, see US Senate, *Covert Action in Chile, 1963-1973*, Report of Select Committee to Study Governmental Operations with Respect to Intelligence Activities, Government Printing Office, Washington 1975; Kerbo, 'Foreign Involvement in the Preconditions for Political Violence'; and Steven J. Rosen, 'The Open Door Imperative and US Foreign Policy', in *Testing Theories of Economic Imperialism*, ed. by S. J. Rosen and J. R. Kurth, Lexington Books, Lexington, Mass. 1974, pp. 117-42.

[33] Karl W. Deutsch, 'External Influences on the Internal Behavior of States', in *Approaches to Comparative and International Politics*, ed. by R. B. Farrell, Northwestern University, Evanston, Ill. 1966, p. 8.

[34] We are referring here to extant policies (i.e., those that are operative prior to the disturbance) rather than to policy responses designed to cope with the disturbance. It may often be difficult to make this distinction in an unequivocal manner; also, it is clear that the nature of the policy response may be of crucial importance. Nonetheless, the distinction is necessary, since we are focusing on contextual factors which connote vulnerability to external influences.

[35] Tyson and Kenan discuss these policy areas as elements of a transformation process that modifies the effects of external disturbances (Laura d'A. Tyson & Peter B. Kenen, 'The International Transmission of Disturbances: A Framework for Comparative Analysis', in *The Impact of International Economic Disturbances on the Soviet Union and Eastern Europe*, ed. by E. Neuberger & L. d'A. Tyson, Pergamon Press, New York 1980, pp. 33-61). Their taxonomy for the examination of the transmission of international economic disturbances into centrally planned economies is of more general application and has been most useful in the formation of the arguments presented herein.

[36] Krasner, 'Transforming International Regimes', (fn. 10).

Chapter 3
Arms and Development

Introduction

It is the objective of this chapter to illuminate two well-known paradoxes, logically ridiculous and indefensible, but so regarded only by a small number of people while being accepted as "natural" by the vast majority of us. The first is that the military expenditures of the developed north, continue to be immense while the Third World remains in poverty. The second is that average growth rates of military spending regularly outstrip growth rates government spending on non-military goods and services in the Third World, with *both* far outstripping the increase in per capita income. Tables 1 and 2 graphically demonstrate these two sets of paradoxes.

TABLE 1

World military expenditure summary, in constant price figures

Figures are in US $m., at 1980 prices and exchange-rates. Totals may not add up due to rounding.

	1976	1977	1978	1979	1980	1981	1982	1983	1984	1985	Share of 1985 total (%)
World total	**522 520**	**531 930**	**547 090**	**561 850**	**567 050**	**579 560**	**615 050**	**631 590**	**642 580**	**663 120**	*100.0*
Industrial market economies	249 924	257 241	262 841	267 683	276 957	287 383	305 116	321 625	331 619	351 870	*53.1*
Non-market economies	[183 646]	[184 858]	[192 760]	[199 248]	[199 449]	[186 265]	[190 684]	[191 057]	[195 201]	[196 451]	*29.6*
Oil-exporting countries	40 892	39 833	41 851	44 125	47 005	[51 910]	[58 195]	[57 832]	[55 768]	[54 624]	*8.2*
Rest of the world	48 057	49 999	49 634	50 793	51 635	54 007	[61 059]	[61 075]	[59 991]	[60 174]	*9.0*
with 1983 per capita GNP:											
<US $440	8 201	7 805	8 411	9 006	9 297	9 562	10 387	10 761	11 077	11 552	*1.7*
US $440–1639	12 982	13 760	12 168	11 934	11 651	12 666	13 495	14 086	13 772	14 008	*2.1*
≥US $1640	26 873	28 435	29 054	29 853	30 687	31 780	37 177	36 228	35 143	34 615	*5.2*

World military expenditure, annual rate of change

Figures are percentages, based on constant price figures (see table above).

	1976	1977	1978	1979	1980	1981	1982	1983	1984	1985
World total	**1.7**	**1.8**	**2.8**	**2.7**	**0.9**	**2.2**	**6.1**	**2.7**	**1.7**	**3.2**
Industrial market economies	−2.2	2.9	2.2	1.8	3.5	3.8	6.2	5.4	3.1	6.1
Non-market economies	[3.8]	0.7	[4.3]	[−3.9]	[−2.7]	[2.4]	[0.2]	[2.2]	[0.6]	
Oil-exporting countries	10.1	−2.6	5.1	5.4	6.5	[10.4]	[12.1]	[−0.6]	[−3.6]	[−2.1]
Rest of the world	1.0	1.6	3.2	2.7	0.9	2.0	[5.4]	[3.0]	[2.1]	[3.5]
with 1983 per capita GNP:										
<US $440	6.5	−4.8	7.8	7.1	3.2	2.9	8.6	3.6	2.9	4.3
US $440–1639	7.0	6.0	−11.6	−1.9	−2.4	8.7	6.5	4.4	−2.2	1.7
≥US $1640	11.3	5.8	2.2	2.7	2.8	3.6	17.0	−2.6	−3.0	−1.5

Source: Excerpted from Tables 11A1 and 11A2, pp. 230, 231, SPRI Yearbook 1986.

TABLE 2

Annual average percentage growth rates, 1972–82

Figures are percentages.

Region	Per capita income	Central government spending *minus* military spending	Military spending	Arms imports
South Asia	2.0	6.2	5.1	9.2
East Asia[a]	3.4	6.9	7.7	(-7.9)[b]
Latin America	1.6	6.0	12.4	13.2
Africa	0.3	6.5	7.8	18.5

[a]Including Japan.
[b]Reflecting US disengagement from Indo-China. The figure for 1976–82 is 5.6 percent.

Source: Military expenditure figures from SIPRI sources. Remaining figures from *World Military Expenditures and Arms Transfers 1972–82* (US Arms Control and Disarmament Agency (ACDA), Washington, D.C., April 1984), table 1, pp. 12–14 and table 2, pp. 53–56.

Source: SIPRI Yearbook 1985, Table 12.5, p. 452.

It is argued that the reason why little or no progress has been made to reverse these trends is that domestic structural obstacles, both systemic and subsystemic, built into the socio-political and economic systems of primarily the industrialized countries, have proven to be too strong to be overcome the logic of disarmament. For the only way in which global military expenditures can be reduced is to reduce the importance of armaments in the eyes of the governments that procure them. This, however, can only happen if the apprehended danger from abroad is perceived to be in *continuous decline* in the foreseeable future, and if the value of the armaments industry in the economic structure (especially vis-à-vis employment) can similarly be seen to be in continuous economic decline in the future. So far this has not happened.

Hence, two arms races continue apace, with but slight fluctuations in intensity: one between the First and Second Worlds, i.e., between the Soviet Socialist bloc and the Western NATO countries, and the second, among the Third World countries themselves. The latter is nurtured and fed by the former in two ways: by arms transfers, as shown in Figure 1, and by the allocation of credits by the First World countries, as shown in Table 3, both fed by the rivalry between the First and Second Worlds in attempting to prevent the influence of the other increasing in the Third World.

FIGURE 1

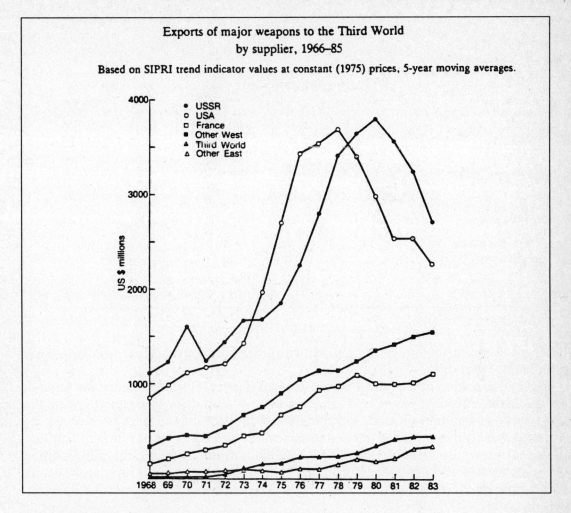

Exports of major weapons to the Third World
by supplier, 1966–85

Based on SIPRI trend indicator values at constant (1975) prices, 5-year moving averages.

• USSR
○ USA
□ France
■ Other West
▲ Third World
△ Other East

Source: SIPRI Yearbook 1986, Figure 17.2, p. 326

Arms transfers and the administrative, technical and doctrinaire relationships that accompany them have established networks of continuing relationships between the First and Third Worlds and the Second and Third worlds. One could even say that we have two global military establishments, each led by one of the superpowers. This has led to a global militarization quite divorced from the ideological rivalry between communism and western democracy, since military structures, processes, tactics and strategy have no ideological content. Any ideology that is present is there merely as a psychological wrapping to exhort or to contain the military enthusiasm. The result is that the "militarization" of the Third World, which has been abetted by the First and Second Worlds rivalry, has very little of the original ideological colour-

TABLE 3

Non-oil developing countries: alternative estimantes of arms transfer credits as a percentage of net flows (disbursements – amortization = net flows), 1972–82

Figures are in current $ millions.

	1972	1973	1974	1975	1976	1977	1978	1979	1980	1981	1982
1. Arms transfers (excl. China)	6 005	7 390	5 165	5 145	6 120	7 025	8 565	11 085	12 690	12 540	13 895
2. US gifts	2 400	3 420	1 520	1 400	190	70	130	170	340	280	290
3. Soviet gifts	490	900	520	360	760	710	1040	2540	1580	1560	1720
4. Arms to be paid for	3 115	3 070	3 125	3 385	5 170	6 245	7 395	8 375	10 770	10 700	11 886
5. Possibly paid for	165	590	615	80	15	255	870	465	500	1 165	525
6. Estimated arms transfer credits (A)	2 950	2 480	2 510	3 305	5 155	5 990	6 525	7 910	10 270	9 535	11 361
7. Net flows to non-oil developing countries (B)	8 019	10 262	16 031	20 177	24 236	28 641	34 199	39 525	41 474	46 151	43 108
8. Net flows, alternative estimate (C)	8 821	11 288	17 634	22 195	26 660	31 505	37 619	43 478	45 621	50 766	47 419
9. Estimated arms transfer credits as percentage of net flows											
A as a percentage of B	37	24	16	16	21	21	19	20	25	21	26
B as percentage of C	33	22	14	15	19	19	17	18	23	19	24

Source: SIPRI Yearbook 1985, Table 12.3, p. 449.

ing that maintains the budgetary and structural support for the Moscow-Washington armaments build-up.

The militarization of the Third World has had important social effects, not least of which is the encouragement and maintenance of authoritarian regimes with the socialization attendant on that, including belief in the value of large military establishments and armaments for the maintenance of sovereignty as paramount and fundamental values of social organization. Equally unfortunately, global militarization has also abetted the dependency of the Third World on both the First and Second and subverted the national and social objectives of economic welfare and development.

The first article in the chapter, by Jayantanuja Bandyopadhyaya, reviews the structural linkages between disarmament and development in detail, and describes the UN efforts at global disarmament to free up funds for economic development that have taken place since 1953 – with disappointing results. It then describes the military-industrial complexes in the United States and the Soviet Union and their structural characteristics which tend to counteract attempts at disarmament. The second article, by Hans-Henrik Holm, reviews the most recent attempts in the First World and within the framework of the United Nations to come to grips with the problem of armaments and their negative impact on Third World economic development. The first Brandt report, entitled *North-South,* stresses how few of the resources used for military purposes would be needed to solve the development problems of the Third World. For example, only 0.5% of one year's world military expenditures could pay for all the farm equipment needed to increase food production to a level approaching self-sufficiency in low-income countries. The second Brandt report, *Common Crisis*, laments the failure of disarmament attempts and argues that only an end to the arms race can end the "grim political and economic confusion engulfing earth's societies everywhere." Brandt emphasizes that the failure to check the arms build-up is primarily the result of the "lack of a clearly and broadly reflected awareness of the current realities and dangers." A highly publicized independent commission on disarmament and security issues headed by the late Swedish Prime Minister Olaf Palme (who also sat on the Brandt Commission), "concentrated on security and disarmament measures and argued that only through the removal of mutual suspicion and fear can security be achieved." The Palme report details the way in which relationships of conflict and tension are translated into demands for increased arms expenditures, leading to the spiralling of tensions. It also pays special attention to the economic and social consequences of military spending. The Thorsson report, commissioned directly by the United Nations, focuses specifically on the relationship between disarmament and development.

The objective of the Holm article is to critically review the ways in which the disarmament and development lobby, through its high profile members' reports, has argued for the achievement of its objective. Unfortunately, it concludes that few of the proposals are practical and that the linking of the disarmament development objectives has not moved beyond the conceptual level.

Disarmament and Development: Structural Linkages

Jayantanuja Bandyopadhyaya

Profile of UN efforts

In 1953, the UN General Assembly for the first time linked disarmament with economic development when it recommended, in Resolution 724 A(VIII), that when effective disarmament measures were implemented, a portion of the resulting savings should be used for economic assistance to the underdeveloped countries. Following the adoption of general and complete disarmament as a UN goal by the General Assembly at its fourteenth session, an attempt was made to inquire into the problems and possibilities of transferring funds from armaments to economic development on national as well as international scales. Resolution 1516(XV), adopted by the General Assembly on 15 December, 1960, requested the Secretary-General to examine:

(a) The national economic and social consequences of disarmament in countries with different economic systems and at different stages of economic development. including, in particular, the problems of replacing military expenditures with alternative private and civil expenditures so as to maintain effective demand and to absorb the human and material resources released from military uses;

(b) The possible development of structural imbalances in national economies as a result of cessation of capital investment in armament industries and the adoption of possible collective measures to prevent such imbalances, including expanded capital assistance to the underdeveloped countries;

(c) The impact of disarmament on international economic relations, including its effects on world trade and especially on the trade of underdeveloped countries;

(d) The utilization of resources released by disarmament for the purpose of economic and social development, in particular, of the underdeveloped countries.[1]

The resolution correctly emphasized the inevitable problem of structural transformation, which is central to the relationship between disarmament and development. But the political, ideological, economic and cultural prerequisites for the structural transformation necessary both at the systemic and at the subsystemic levels lay in highly sensitive areas of domestic policy, especially of the superpowers, which the UN has traditionally been shy of investigating. This, indeed, has been the basic lacuna and weakness of all UN resolutions and reports on the disarmament-development syndrome.

In pursuance of this resolution, the Secretary-General appointed a group of ten experts drawn from countries with different political and economic systems and at different stages of economic development to report on these issues. Their unanimous Report was

Originally published in *Alternatives*, vol IV, 1979. Reprinted with permission.

presented by the Secretary-General to the Economic and Social Council in February 1962.[2] It drew attention to the enormity of the arms expenditure incurred by a few states, and pointed out the large economic benefits likely to result from general disarmament, particularly for the developing countries. But on the crucial question of structural impediments the Report failed to proceed beyond platitudes. It merely expressed the opinion that:

> All the problems and difficulties of transition connected with disarmament could be met by appropriate national and international measures. There should thus be no doubt that the diversion to peaceful purpose of the resources now in military use could be accomplished to the benefit of all countries and lead to the improvement of world economic and social conditions. The achievement of general and complete disarmament would be an unqualified blessing to all mankind.

The Economic and Social Council, which commended the findings of the Report, requested the Secretary-General to transmit it to the Eighteen-Nation Disarmament Committee and to give it wide publicity. The General Assembly also endorsed the conclusions of the Report.

In December 1970, the General Assembly again requested the Secretary-General to prepare a report, with the help of consultant experts, on the economic and social consequences of the arms race and military expenditures. The report was submitted at the end of 1971. This report also dwelt at length on the magnitude and on the unwholesome consequences of the arms race, and recommended the transfer of funds from arms manufacture to economic development. But, again, like the earlier one, it did not discuss the structural issues at all.[3] The General Assembly welcomed the report and recommended that the conclusions of the Report should be taken into account in future disarmament negotiations.

At its twentyfifth session, the General Assembly asked the Secretary-General to suggest measures for establishing a link between the Disarmament Decade and the Second United Nations Development Decade, so that resources released by disarmament could be partially canalized into economic assistance for developing countries. The Secretary-General appointed a group of experts, which submitted its report in August 1972. The Group accepted the findings of the earlier studies regarding the benefits that would result from development-oriented disarmament. For the first time this Report noted the possibility of partial disarmament as a prelude to general disarmament. It envisaged a partial disarmament consisting of '(a) a comprehensive test ban; (b) a comprehensive prohibition of the possession and production of chemical weapons; (c) the complete demilitarization of the sea-bed and deep-sea environment; and (d) the elimination of all foreign bases (i.e. physical installations) and the withdrawal of all foreign troops to their own countries'.[4] It argued that if the target of 6% growth set by the Second United Nations Development Decade for the developing nations was to be achieved, official development assistance from the developed to the developing countries would have to double itself from 0.35% to 0.7% of the GNP. It felt that the partial disarmament suggested by it would release enough resources in the developed countries to make this possible.[5] But these experts also ignored the structural factors and only stated; 'We agree with the authors of earlier studies that there would be no insuperable technical difficulties in ensuring the redeployment of the released resources to peaceful uses.'[6]

In 1974, the Soviet Union moved a resolution in the General Assembly to the effect that the five permanent members of the Security Council should cut their military budgets by 10% from the 1973 level during the next financial year, and that 10% of the funds thus released should be given as economic assistance to the developing nations. The resolution was adopted with an overwhelming majority in the General Assembly. But in the Security Council, the Soviet Union alone, as mover of the resolution, supported it; China opposed the resolution, while the USA, UK and France abstained from voting. The General Assembly then set up the Special Committee on the Distribution of the Funds Released as a Result of the Reduction of Military Budgets. This Committee also requested the Secretary-General to prepare a report on the subject with the help of qualified experts.[7] This fourth Report[8] of the Secretary-General on disarmament and development was presented to the General Assembly in September 1974. It drew attention, although briefly, for the first time to some of the structural linkages between the two. It found no definite correlation between the degree of international tension and the volume of arms expenditure, and pointed out that, in fact, the 'arms race in the developed world has continued in spite of a marked relaxation of tension in recent years'.[9] The explanation, argued the Report, lay in several structural features of the linkage between disarmament and development, including the technological. It observed:

> The forces behind the intense development and exploitation of technology for military purposes cannot then be simply explained as an 'action/reaction' process in a world of increasing tension. One explanation is that modern weapons have now a very long gestation period or lead-time. It may take 10 years from the initial design to the final development of a fighter. Consequently military authorities tend to focus their attention, not on what the other side has already produced, but on possible future developments. Then again, technical and industrial teams are built up to design and develop types of military equipments; these teams are regarded as national assets which, once established, should not be allowed to disintegrate. So, when one project is completed, another project is found for them. There are also economic and bureaucratic forces at work. Firms who derive a major portion of their sales from the manufacture of armaments are obviously concerned to maintain their position. In many countries it is to be expected that a military establishment will attempt to preserve its relative share in the government programmes as a whole.'[10]

However, the Report did not go deep into the political, economic, ideological and cultural bases of the structural linkage between disarmament and development. Nor did it suggest how these built-in structural obstacles to disarmament could be removed.

With the Disarmament Decade and the Second UN Development Decade nearing their end, there is still no sign of any of the five permanent members of the Security Council, or any other major military power, reducing its military expenditure to release funds either for domestic economic development or for economic assistance to the developing countries. It was against this background that the UN Secretary-General presented his fifth and latest report on disarmament and development on the General Assembly in August 1977. The Report, prepared by a panel of experts, observed that a mere 5% of the military expenditure by the industrialized countries would have met the target of 0.7% of their GNP to enable the developing nations to achieve a 6% growth rate in the Second UN Development Decade. It lamented the fact that only the Netherlands, Norway and Sweden had met the Disarmament Decade target of 0.7% of the GNP for development assistance. The Report questioned the assumption that advances in military technology had induced technological innovations in the civilian economy. It argued that the conversion of military industries and installations to civilian ends was possible without economic dislocation or depression. It also argued that the demilitarization of so-called strategic commodities, including raw materials and sophisticated technology, would lead to their application to such sophisticated civilian sectors as electronics, propulsion systems, etc.[11]

The Report briefly discussed the problems of transition from a militarized economy to a predominantly civilian economy, and concluded that there were no insurmountable structural obstacles to this transformation:

> The possibility that localized and temporary difficulties may arise is not excluded by the fact that the overall economic effects of disarmament would be highly beneficial. Indeed, there have been cases when such difficulties did occur as a result of the discontinuation of specific military programmes. Nevertheless, it is important to note that the overall effect to be expected from disarmament is not recession but, given the necessary compensatory measures, stimulation of the economy and a decline in unemployment. . . If cuts in military expenditure are spread over a number of years and adequate compensatory steps are taken, economic disruption, even in the short term, would be minimal. We fully agree with the conclusion of the 1962 experts' report on *Economic and Social Consequences of Disarmament*, that no major instability need result from disarmament.[12]

Thus the latest report of the Secretary-General has also failed to examine the ideological, political, economic and cultural bases of the structural linkage between disarmament and development. From 1962 to 1977, all the reports of the Secretary-General have regarded it as axiomatic, without adequate consideration of the facts, that there are no serious systemic or subsystemic structural obstacles to the transformation of militarized societies into peaceful ones.

From 1953 to 1977, i.e. during a quarter century, the UN General Assembly remained preoccupied with the linkage between disarmament and development, but without achieving any tangible results. Even the studies initiated by it do not seem to have gone deep into the problem. It is in this context that the Special Session of the General Assembly on Disarmament is being held in May-June 1978, largely at the initiative of the non-aligned countries. Although the scope of the Special Session includes the whole range of disarmament issues, there are indications that the problem of linkage between disarmament and development would receive special attention. In August 1977, the Scandinavian countries submitted a working paper to the Preparatory Committee for the Special Session, proposing a major international study on armaments, disarmament and development.[13] General Assembly Resolution 32/88A dated 12 December, 1977, endorsed a recommendation by the Preparatory Committee that the General Assembly should initiate a study on the relationship between disarmament and development, the terms of reference of the study being left to be determined by the Special Session. It is obvious that any future study of this nature, in order to be more useful than the earlier ones, must probe into the deeper bases of the structural linkage between disarmament and development, both at the systemic and the subsystemic levels, and indicate the steps necessary for initiating the transformative and regenerative process.

As noted earlier, Resolution 1516(XV) of 15 December, 1960, had drawn attention to the structural link between disarmament and development. But subsequent reports of the Secretary-General, while occasionally touching upon these structural features, neither went into them deeply nor offered any suggestions regarding the process of structural adaptation and transformation. Yet, it is obvious that it is the removal of the structural obstacles to the transformative and regenerative process in the national subsystems as well as in the international system as a whole, and not a 'change of heart', that is the crux of the disarmament-development problem.

The global schism

In a fundamental sense, the problem of disarmament is one of the major facets of the structural schism in the international system between the North and the South. The political, military and economic aspects of this great schism are closely interconnected. As a matter of fact, the power gap between the North and the South may be regarded as the superstructure, and the military economic gap as the infrastructure of the 'great divide' between the developed and the developing nations. The nature and extent of this enormous global schism in terms of military expenditure and military power since 1960 would be evident from Table 1.

It would be seen from Table 1 that the share of the industrialized states in world military expenditure, in both absolute and percentage terms, has declined slightly in the Seventies, after a phenomenal rise in the Sixties. There has also been a corresponding increase, in both absolute and percentage terms, in the share of the developing nations. This trend is due to the slightly falling rate of growth of the military expenditure of the industrialized states, and an appreciably rising rate of growth of that of the developing states, as indicated in Table 2.

Table 2
Rates of growth of military expenditure, 1960-1975*
(percentage average annual increase of real expenditure)

	1960-65	1965-70	1970-75
Six main military spenders	4.2	4.6	−0.1
Other industrialized countries	6.1	6.1	4.9
Developing countries	—	8.1	14.7
World total	4.7	5.0	1.1

*Derived from the figures in Table 1.

It should be realized, however, that the rise in the military expenditure of the developing states in the Seventies is largely accounted for by the rapid increase in arms expenditure in the OPEC area. An even more significant fact is that the few states which are industrialized still account for 87.4% of world military expenditure, the developing states being responsible only for the remaining 12.6%. The same structural characteristic of the international system is highlighted by the enormous gap between the per capita military expenditure of the industrialized states and that of the developing states. Table 3 below, which shows the per capita annual military expenditure of the USA, the USSR, India and Pakistan over a number of years, illustrates the point.

The fifth report of the Secretary-General on disarmament and development noted that the annual per capita military expenditure in poor countries, such as those of Asia as a whole, was between 1% and 2% of that of the major industrialized nations.

Thus, from the military point of view, the international system is characterized by the overwhelming predominance of what we would like to call the global military establishment

Table 3
Per capita annual military expenditure ($ per head)

	1972	1973	1974	1975	1976	1977
USA	372	372	405	417	477	523
USSR	342	352– 368	432– 447	490	492	n.a.
India	4	4	4	4	5	6
Pakistan	7	9	11	10	11	11

Source: *Military Balance* (London, 1975-76), p. 76; (1976-77), p. 78; (1977-78), pp. 82-83.

(GME), consisting of the two superpowers, their industrialized allies, and China. This GME is sustained by what is generally called the 'weapons culture'. From the global point of view, therefore, disarmament primarily means a phased but drastic reduction of military expenditure by the GME until it comes close to the military expenditure of the Third World countries.

In this connection, it is necessary to refer briefly to the question of international arms transfers. The rise in global military expenditure has generally been associated with a corresponding rise in international arms transfers, as would be evident from Figure 1, the drastic rise in the Seventies being accounted for by the massive arms purchase by the OPEC.

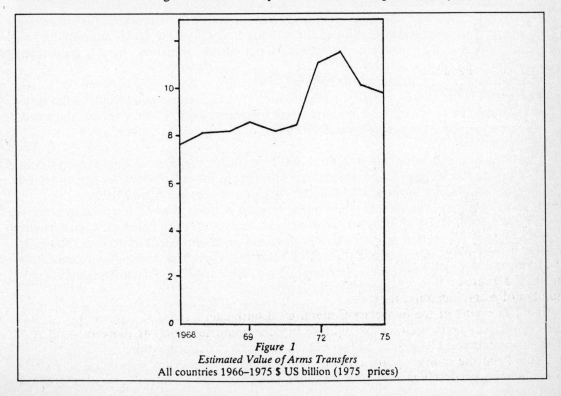

Figure 1
Estimated Value of Arms Transfers
All countries 1966–1975 $ US billion (1975 prices)

It should be remembered, however, that virtually all arms transfers originate in the GME; they are an output of the domestic structures of the states belonging to it. According to SIPRI estimates, the six major military spenders, who together account for 96-97% of all military R & D outlays,[14] are responsible for 90% of all military exports[15] and 95% of major weapons exports to the developing countries.[16] If other industrialized states are added to the list, the GME would account for practically all international arms transfers. Moreover, these arms transfers are largely the result of vigorous promotional drives on the part of the governments and manufacturers of the GME. As a major study on the subject sponsored by the International Institute for Strategic Studies, London, has observed:

> The recognition by governments that the arms trade has its uses – political, military and economic – as well as its hazards has turned some governments into salesmen as well as policeman. In three Western countries, Britain, France and the United States, government promotion of arms exports has reached a high level of sophistication and involvement. Results suggest that this is equally true of the Soviet Union, and possibly of China also.'[17]

The finding has been corroborated by the SIPRI Yearbook of World Armaments and Disarmament, 1978, in the following words:

> "For poor countries the investment in major weapons and weapon industries depends mostly on the success of sales campaigns from the producing companies and government sales agencies, and results in a drain of the scarce resources needed for civilian economic development."[18]

In other words, international arms transfers are a function of the weapons culture represented by the GME and integrally related to the domestic structures of the countries belonging to it. If a drastic reduction of the military budgets of the GME undermines the weapons culture, the problem of international arms transfers would pale into insignificance.

One structural characteristic of the wide and widening economic gap between the North and the South is the share of GNP devoted to military expenditure and to official development assistance by the developed countries over the years. Table 4 below reveals the structural link between arms expenditure and development assistance on a global scale.

Another way of highlighting this structural characteristic of the international system would be to compare the level and rate of increase of financial flows from the developed to the developing nations with those of world military expenditure, as in Figure 2 below.

Table 4 and Figure 2 show that while the developed nations as a whole spend a sizeable portion of their GNP on armaments, they are reluctant to offer the developing nations any but a negligible proportion of their GNP in the form of development assistance. Not only has the UNCTAD target of 1% of their GNP being transferred as development assistance to the less developed countries remained unfulfilled; such assistance declined from the paltry 0.40% to 0.26% of the GNP during 1962-1963.

The détente between the USA and the Soviet Union is, therefore, of very little benefit to the Third World countries from both the political and the economic points of view. Politically, it heralds a kind of condominium of the two superpowers over the rest of the world, especially the Third World countries. Arms control rather than disarmament is the accepted paradigm of the global military establishment. SALT I, the *ad hoc* understand-

Table 4

Estimates of the share of Gross National Product devoted (a) to military expenditure and (b) to official development assistance by the developed countries

		Percentage of GNP			
		1962-64	1965-67	1968-70	1971-73
(a)	To military purposes:				
	US ACDA estimate	8.7	7.9	7.7	6.6
	SIPRI estimate	7.8	7.2	7.2	5.9
(b)	To official				
	development assistance	0.40	0.35	0.29	0.26

Source:
   (a) To military purposes: *SIPRI Yearbook of World Armaments and Disarmament*, 1974, US ACDA, *World Military Expenditures and Arms Trade, 1963-1973* (US Government Printing Office, Washington D.C).
   (b) To official development assistance: OECD, *Development Cooperation, 1973 Review*, November 1973; and UNCTAD estimates. Cited in *Reduction of the Military Budgets of States permanent members of the Security Council by 10 per cent and Utilization of Part of the Funds thus Saved to Provide Assistance to Developing Countries*, Report of the Secretary-General (United Nations, New York, 1975, UN Sales No. E. 75.1.10), p.4.

ings and negotiations in connection with the proposed SALT II, and the highly discriminatory Nuclear Nonproliferation Treaty are all aimed at the consolidation of the GME, indirectly including China. Economically, it represents an attempt on the part of the industrialized and 'white' nations to preserve and enhance their material affluence as well as to perpetuate the wide economic gap between themselves and the developing 'coloured' nations.[19]

That the broad structural schism in the international system detracts from its tensile strength and makes it unstable - even explosive - is generally recognized. What is not equally emphasized is that the structural transformation of the international system can be brought about only by gradually bridging the present gap by new structural linkages. The problem of disarmament and development must, therefore, be viewed as a global one and solutions to it sought in terms of new global linkages.

In this connection, it should be noted that while reduction in military expenditure by the major military powers and the diversion of the released funds to development assistance to the Third World countries may be justified in terms of political idealism, it would be extremely difficult to operationalize these measures except in terms of the national interest

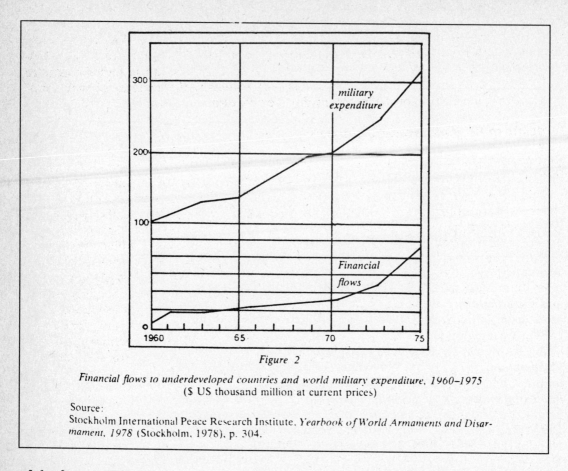

Figure 2

Financial flows to underdeveloped countries and world military expenditure, 1960–1975
(\$ US thousand million at current prices)

Source:
Stockholm International Peace Research Institute, *Yearbook of World Armaments and Disarmament, 1978* (Stockholm, 1978), p. 304.

of the former. What is necessary is to demonstrate through irrefutable economic logic that the transfer of funds from the developed to the developing nations would, in the long run, contribute to the further economic development and security of the former.

If the world is regarded as one market, as it should be in the contemporary state of technology and communications, it is easy to demonstrate that one part of it cannot develop indefinitely if the other parts remain relatively undeveloped. From Hobson to Keynes, many economists have emphasized the need for continually increasing the purchasing power of the masses in order to ensure the economic prosperity of the nation as a whole. For low purchasing power of the masses of people means low effective demand, which acts as a restraint on investment, production and employment. In the world economy as a whole, therefore, it is necessary to continually increase the purchasing power of the great majority of people living in the developing nations so as to create an ever-growing effective demand for goods and services, including those produced by the developed countries. In other words, the continued prosperity of the developed nations is functionally dependent on the rapid economic development of the less developed nations. At present, the major industrial nations are trying to overcome the problem of limited domestic effective demand

and market potentialities by resorting to an arms economy, as we shall presently try to show. But this can be neither a rational nor a long-term strategy for their further development. The correct solution, even from the purely economic point of view, lies in drastically curtailing their spiralling military budgets and using the released resources for the development of the less developed sectors of the world market. But there are structural obstacles within their present domestic politico-economic subsystems to the adoption of such a policy. To an analysis of these obstacles, therefore, we now turn.

Domestic milieus of two superpowers

In the 30s and 40s, many liberal thinkers used to regard the private manufacture of arms as the root cause of all forms of war and imperialism. In his famous two-volume treatise, Philip Noel-Baker tried to show how the armaments industries made enormous profits from the production and sale of arms, how other civilian industries were closely linked with them and how the combination of all these war-related industries exerted pressure on the economic, political and foreign policy of the government. He attributed the First World War and the failure of the post-war disarmament negotiations to the machinations of the arms merchants.[20] A few years later, Fenner Brockway and Frederic Mullally broadly supported Noel-Baker's analysis, and attributed war and imperialism to 'the existence of an elaborately organized and financially powerful vested interest devoted to the propagation of aggressive nationalism and the multiplication of armaments'.[21] Later researches have shown the causes of war to be much more complex than these authors had supposed, but there can be little doubt that they had drawn attention to a fundamental structural characteristic of the politico-economic system represented by Western capitalism.

United States of America

The economic and political power of the military-industrial complex in the USA, to which President Eisenhower was the first to draw attention, is now a well-known and established fact. This complex, consisting of the privately owned armaments industries and the civilian industries structurally related to them, depends heavily on government military contracts for its sales and profits, as would be evident from Table 5 below.

Several scholars have argued that the influence of the military-industrial complex on decision-making in the fields of defence and foreign policy has been exaggerated. Raymond Aron, for instance, has tried to show that civilians, including academics and lawyers, have often exercised a greater influence on decision-making in these fields than military leaders.[22] But Aron seems to have missed the essential point that the political parties themselves, including their academic and lawyer supporters, are dependent on the military-industrial complex, particularly for financial as well as logistic support. There is now a large volume of literature which demonstrates, with irrefutable evidence, that the political parties, the Administration, the Congress and the regulatory agencies of the government of the USA are all linked with the military-industrial complex by strong bonds of mutual interest and support.[23]

One important example of this linkage between the military-industrial complex on the one hand, and the government and the political parties, on the other, is the process of shared benefits associated with the sale of arms abroad. The State Department benefits from the political leverage it gets in foreign lands from the sale of arms to foreign govern-

Table 5

Prime military contracts awards 1960-1967 to 15 US companies
(amounts in millions of dollars)

	Name of firm	7-year total	Percentage of total sales
1.	Lockheed Aircraft	10 619	88
2.	General Dynamics	8 824	67
3.	McDonnell Douglas	7 681	75
4.	Boeing Co.	7 183	54
5.	No. American-Rockwell	6 265	57
6.	United Aircraft	5 311	57
7.	Martin-Marietta	3 682	62
8.	Grumman Aircraft	2 492	67
9.	Raytheon	2 324	55
10.	AVCO	2 295	75
11.	Ling-Temco-Vought	1 744	70
12.	Newport News Shipbuilding	1 520	90
13.	Northrop	1 434	61
14.	Thiokol	1 301	96
15.	Collins Radio	1 105	65

Source: Department of Defence, Directorate for Statistical Services,
USA; cited in Ralph Lapp, *The Weapons Culture* (Pelican Books, 1969),
Appendix II.

ments - often illegitimate and authoritarian governments in the developing nations. The Defence Department benefits from the transference of military obsolescence, which arms sales to the Third World almost inevitably involves, as well as from the enhancement of its power and prestige resulting from foreign military involvements. The military-industrial complex reaps enormous profits from government contracts. Finally, the political parties benefit from the material and moral support of the military-industrial complex.[24] This process explains why the USA has been the biggest arms merchant of the world throughout the post-war period, and why the policy of arms sales has not undergone any change whatever, irrespective of whether the Administration has been under the control of the Democrats or the Republicans. The existence of the military-industrial complex is thus probably the greatest structural impediment in the USA to any significant reduction in defence expenditure.

Another major structural characteristic of the American system is the size and political influence of the Pentagon. The enormous military establishment is an inevitable institutional link in the decision-making processes in defence and foreign policy. Since the power and prestige of this establishment depend heavily on a massive and ever-expanding weapons programme, it has always demanded, with considerable success, larger defence budgets, new and more extensive weapons systems, and greater military involvements abroad.

The military-industrial complex also influences the policies pursued by the Pentagon through the employment of retired military personnel in senior executive positions and through other well-known pressure-group tactics; it benefits from these policies in terms of contracts and profits. The political interests of the Pentagon and the economic interests of the military-industrial complex thus interact with and reinforce each other. In addition to the military-industrial complex, therefore, the Pentagon is also a major structural obstacle to any serious attempt at disarmament.[25]

Finally, mention must be made of the direct and indirect economic benefits accruing to the American nation as a whole from the manufacture and sale of arms in the short run. In the first place, some industries are directly dependent on government arms expenditure for their survival. At the end of the 50s, for example, government purchase of an overwhelmingly military nature accounted for over nine-tenths of the final demand for all aircraft and parts; about three-fifths of the demand for non-ferrous metals; more than half the demand for electronic goods and chemicals; over one-third of the demand for scientific instruments and communications equipment, and so on.[26] The broad trend has remained the same in recent years. In 1974, for example, military expenditure claimed almost half of all the scientific and engineering manpower in the USA. It accounted for almost four-fifths of all federal procurement of goods and services, and for most of the increases in such federal purchases during the preceding two decades. Large industries, catering to defence requirements and the regions in which they are located, have been leading growth areas in the US economy in the post-war period.[27] Secondly, arms expenditure has a direct effect on investment and stability in the national economy as a whole. As noted by Kidron,

It is heavily concentrated in the capital goods industries which are responsible for the big swings in the traditional business cycle. It provides a floor to the downswings and has, in the US, been deliberately used in this way. The fact that much of this capital equipment has no alternative use and is therefore normally included in the contract price for military supplies both removes the risk element from investment and provides the wherewithal to keep it at a high level.[28]

Thirdly, as is well known, arms expenditure has acceleration and multiplier effects in the short run over the economy as a whole, not only in terms of production and employment, but also in terms of technological progress and innovation. Fourthly, as Michael Kidron has argued, arms production is at present a structural offset to the apparent tendency of the rate of profit to fall in a capitalist economy, and therefore a major stabilizer of the system.[29] Finally, 'arms production has a domino effect: starting in one country, it proliferates inexorably through the system, compelling the other major economies to enter a competitive arms race, and so pulling them into the stabilizer's sphere of operations'.[30]

But economic stabilization through massive arms expenditure can at best be a short-term strategy for the Western capitalist countries led by the USA. Arms production being an infinite-gestation-lag industry, its direct as well as multiplier and acceleration effects are bound to be temporary. Moreover, the rapidly growing sophistication of military and space technology as well as the increasingly capital-intensive nature of military-space investments have been progressively undermining their links with civilian production and employment. As an OECD study observed in 1966 (on the question of the transfer of military technology to non-military uses), 'the technological requirements of defence and space are diverging from those of civilian industry which means that the possibilities of such direct transfer will tend to diminish'.[31] In the long run, therefore, astronomical defence budgets can only lead to inflation and unemployment—a trend already noticeable in the American and other Western economies.

In terms of economic theory, it should be possible to divert resources from arms expenditure to investment in civilian goods and services in a phased manner, without causing mass unemployment or any other serious economic dislocation. Various steps have, in fact, already been suggested for tackling the domestic economic consequences of a phased programme of disarmament.[32] But this possibility presupposes a great deal of state interference in the economic system, and a radical structural transformation of the entire politico-economic system. In shod, it presupposes a new American ideology. As Paul A. Samuelson has argued:

> If there is a political will, our mixed economy can rather easily keep C+I+G spending up to the level needed for full employment *without arms spending* . . . There is but one possible flaw in the story. It lies inside the realm of politics, not economics. . . Any citizenry, any time and place, that cannot *ideologically* stomach the political moves necessary to maintain healthy growth and high-capacity economic activity, can create *for itself* a problem of mass unemployment.[33]

The crucial question, therefore, is whether the political will and ideological reorientation required of the American people and the American politico-economic system would be forthcoming. The chances are that any attempt to reduce arms expenditure and divert the released funds to civilian production and to international transfers through state initiative would be strongly resisted, not only by the military-industrial complex and the Pentagon, but also by the national trade unions. except perhaps in the event of a severe economic crisis. In the light of the individualistic and anti-collectivistic traditions of the American intellectual and political culture, it also seems doubtful whether the American *people* would welcome the degree of state control that would be necessary for the structural transformation analysed above, except temporarily as a result of an economic crisis. Nothing short of a fundamental change in the cultural and ideological heritage of the American people, in the system of free enterprise and capitalism, and in the whole structure of the American politico-economic system, would seem to be adequate for the purpose of development-oriented disarmament. In essence, this change will have to take a broadly socialistic form.

The Soviet Union

Theoretically, it should be easier for the Soviet Union than for the USA to readjust its socialist economic system from armaments production to civilian production. The absence of private enterprise apparently minimizes the impediments to the shifts in production and employment which would follow from partial or general disarmament. It may, therefore, appear at first sight that there are no structural obstacles to disarmament in the Soviet domestic milieu, and that the linkage between disarmament and development is merely one of the allocation of priorities by political decision-makers.

Following this logic, it is always argued by Soviet political leaders and many socialistically inclined academics throughout the world that there are no domestic constraints on disarmament in the Soviet Union, that the only obstacle to disarmament by the Soviet Union is the external threat posed by the enormous arms build-up of the USA and other Western powers. It is claimed that as soon as the other military powers have reduced their arms expenditure, the Soviet Union would immediately do the same. As if to prove this point, the Soviet Union moved a resolution in the UN General Assembly in 1973, as noted earlier, recommending a 10% cut in military expenditure by the five permanent members of the Security Council.

But this is a rather simplistic view of the structural characteristics of the Soviet domestic milieu. The logic of a gigantic military programme like that of the USA or the USSR inexorably leads to the growth of a military-oriented industrial complex and a massive military establishment, irrespective of ideology. From all accounts. a huge military-industrial complex has come into existence in the Soviet Union also, although the structure of this complex is somewhat different from that of the USA due to the different politico-economic environment in which it operates.[34] According to Vernon V. Aspaturian, an authority on the subject:

> The physical components of the Soviet military-industrial complex consist of four distinct elements: (1) the armed forces; (2) the defence industries complex and related research and development institutions; (3) heavy industry; and (4) the conservative wing of the party apparatus. The first two components constitute the 'core' of the complex, but it is the association with heavy industry and sectors of the Party apparatus that converts the complex into a political force of some magnitude.[35]

According to one estimate, the military-industrial complex employs approximately 10 million people in the Soviet Union[36], i.e. about 5% of its population. As Aspaturian observes, one major difference between the Soviet military-industrial complex and that of the USA is that 'because of the fundamental difference in incentive structures, the relationship between the military establishment and the defence industries in the two countries is reversed'. While in the USA the military establishment often tries to please its suppliers, the defence industries, 'Soviet defence industries always strive to satisfy the military establishment, their sole client, and little incentive exists for the Soviet military to please their suppliers'. Moreover, according to David Holloway:

> The Soviet armaments complex should be seen not as a military-industrial complex in the sense of an alignment between military and industrial interests, but rather as a part of a bureaucratic complex in which various groups, coalitions and departments interact and form alliances in the pursuit of particular policies. This is not to deny that cleavages exist, but to suggest that the armaments complex should be viewed as a bureaucracy rather than as a field of interest-group activity.[37]

But, as is well known, one major point of convergence between the American and the Soviet systems is the political power of the military establishment. It inevitably depends in both countries on the maintenance and raising of the existing levels of military expenditure. The vast military establishment in the Soviet Union has therefore always demanded, like the Pentagon, a perpetual increase of military expenditure and the development of new and more extensive weapons systems. In both countries, the sophistication of nuclear technology and the enormous destructive power of the strategic weapons at their command have added to the power and influence of the respective military establishments. If anything, the military establishment in the Soviet Union is even more powerful than the Pentagon, for it plays a much more direct political role in the Soviet system and participates much more directly and actively in the decision-making of both the party and the government.[38] Roman Kolkowicz has shown that Soviet strategic elites have performed the same functions with regard to the arms race as their US counterparts in the following ways:

—they projected an adversary that was dangerous and threatening and who subscribed to the view of international politics as a zero-sum game;

—they came to adopt the language and concepts of Western strategies (although sanitized by Communist Party sensitivities);

—they argued for ultimate priority of defence at the expense of other societal objectives

—they argued that the complexity of war and politics in the nuclear context requires the attention of professionals, and that political amateurs may bring on catastrophe.[39]

The existence of the military-industrial complex, in particular of the huge military establishment, in the Soviet union must, therefore, be regarded as a serious domestic structural obstacle to disarmament. The latest report of the UN Secretary-General on the *Economic and Social Consequences of the Armaments Race and its Extremely Harmful Effects on World Peace and Security* has rightly observed:

> Wherever they occur, military-industrial or military-economic-political complexes have a self-preserving and self-reinforcing character. They are powerful, resourceful and pervasive coalitions that have developed around one common purpose: the continued expansion of the military sector, irrespective of actual military needs. In those countries where their influence is strong, such complexes are obviously an important factor in the perpetuation of the arms race. . . Disarmament efforts, if they are to be successful, will have to take account of this.[40]

One obvious manifestation of the role of the Soviet military-industrial-political complex is the major drive for arms export promotion. The Soviet Union is the second largest arms exporter of the world. All its arms exports are financed by easy credit extended by the state.[41] The main reason is that, irrespective of their ideological and structural differences, the macro-economic gains from arms exports are the same for the Soviet Union and the USA. As John Stanley and Maurice Pearton have rightly observed, arms exports enable a country to improve its balance-of-payments position, to promote employment and regional development, to extend the domestic market into the international, and to improve its relative position in the international balance of industrial power.[42] Another major national economic motive is the transference of obsolescence, resulting from the qualitative character of the arms transfers and the perpetual technological innovations associated with it, to the developing states, at a high profit. In addition, international arms transfers are used by the superpowers as a leverage in their political competition, and for manipulating national and regional politics in the Third World. The Soviet gains on all these accounts are no different from those of the USA.

Moreover, the direct as well as indirect economic consequences of the massive arms expenditure are felt as much in the USSR as in the USA, irrespective of ideological differences. The direct effects of arms expenditure on production and employment, as well as its multiplier and acceleration effects, not only on investment, output and employment in the economy as a whole, but also on technological advance and innovation, are not, and cannot be, fundamentally different in the Soviet Union from those in the USA, either in the short run or in the long run, although total state control in the former may obscure some of these effects.

But the massive arms build-up is bound to have adverse economic consequences for the Soviet Union, as for the USA, in the long run. One visible effect of the astronomical arms budget is, of course, the galloping inflation which has characterized the Soviet economy in the post-war period. While this inflation has been caused by lop-sided investment in heavy industry in general, there can be little doubt that the huge and unproductive investment in armaments has greatly aggravated it. It also appears that the spillover of technological inno-vations from the military to the civilian sector of the economy has been considerably less in the Soviet Union than in the USA, mainly on account of the virtually complete state con-trol over the economic system in the former.[43] Another important fact, as pointed out by William T. Lee, is that he massive arms programme has compelled the Soviet Union to devote approximately half of its durable output to military-space programmes, leaving only 40% for civilian durable investment and only 10% for consumption. According to Lee, this fact has been largely responsible for a decline in the rate of economic growth in the Soviet Union in recent years.[44]

In view of the virtually total state control over the economic system in the Soviet Union, it should be theoretically easier for it than for the USA to deal the potential problems of economic transformation resulting from disarmament, although problems of transitional adjustment in terms of both investment and employment are bound to arise in the Soviet economy as well. But in addition to the military establishment, the structure of Soviet domestic politics must be regarded as a major obstacle to this process of change. For it is doubtful whether the present authoritarian political structure can be internally sustained without a colossal military build-up and a giant defensive posture against a perennial exter-nal threat. Any significant reduction in military expenditure and lessening of international tension is likely to undermine irretrievably the authority of the political elite and to let loose certain centrifugal tendencies and forces within the political system that would threaten its very foundations. The perpetuation of an astronomical military budget would, therefore, seem to be a domestic political imperative for the Soviet system.

As in the case of the USA, it would be extremely difficult in the Soviet Union to reduce military expenditure substantially and to divert the released funds to national economic development as well as to international transfers without transforming the structure of the entire domestic system. But, while in the case of the USA the structural transformation would have to take a fundamentally economic and socialistic direction, in the case of the Soviet Union it would have to assume the form of a fundamentally libertarian political transformation. In any case, the domestic structures which have grown up in the USA and the Soviet Union to promote the manufacture and sale of arms, and to acelerate the inter-national arms race, cannot be expected to reverse their function and contribute to disarma-ment and development. They will have to be greatly modified or replaced by new structures for performing the new function of development-oriented disarmament.

Roles of United Nations and Third World

The structural linkages between disarmament and development, characteristics of the US politico-economic system, may be regarded as an 'ideal type' in the Weberian sense, repre-senting the Western capitalist states which permit the production of armamen by private industrial conmbines. The economic systems of these states are predominantly character-ized by private enterprise and concentration of capital, and the political systems by a form of individualist democracy. Similarly, the structural linkages between disarmament and development, characteristic of Soviet politico-economic system may be regarded as an 'ideal type' representing all major military states with a socialistic economic system and an authoritarian political structure. It can then be shown, in the light of the foregoing analysis, that a broadly democratic as well as broadly socialistic politico-economic system represents the structural prerequisites for development-oriented disarmament.

It would not, however, be rational to expect the necessary structural transformation to take place within either of the two broad 'ideal types' in the form of a sudden revolutionary upheaval. In the given circumstances, the process of change can only be slow and piece-meal. A neo-functionalist 'incremental' process of adaptation, rather than a classical functionalist 'grand design', has to be accepted as the strategic operational model. As Alva Myrdal has said in her *Game of Disarmament*, a concerted attack will have to be launched on those forces within the democratic subsystems of the US and the Soviet Union which propel the arms race in their own interests.[45] Admittedly, the task will be far from easy, particularly in the Soviet Union. But herein lies the only hope for the beginning of a process of development-oriented disarmament.

Noreover, it would be incorrect to visualize this process of structural adaptation as the outcome of the efforts of purely domestic forces, although domestic factors and forces would undoubtedly play a major role in it. The political, ideological, economic and even cultural bases of the subsystems analysed here are much too strong and rigid to permit the subsystems to be transformed by domestic forces alone. It would also be necessary for the international milieu to generate new forces and movements to act as transformative external inputs of the subsystems concerned.

This is where the United Nations comes into the picture. For it is the widest possible international platform on which the nations of the world, especially the victims of the militarism of the global military establishment, can express themselves and make their collective global influence felt. The UN resolutions on disarmament and development have not so far been respected by the major military powers, mainly because the UN has failed as a dynamic political and moral force in the international milieu, as an irresistible external input of the subsystems concerned. This, in turn, has been largely due to the relative absence of political organizations among developing nations, which constitute over two-thirds of the total membership of the UN. But today, thanks to the rapid expansion and growing importance of the non-aligned movement, as well as various regional and functional groupings among the developing nations, the Third World is fast becoming an international political force of major significance. Although the strength of the non-aligned movement derives essentially from international communication, rather than from the mobilization of military power,[46] it has a great potential for spearheading the movement of the South for greater economic and political justice from the North. Needless to say, the Third World countries, on their part, must resolve or ignore the secondary contradictions among themselves in the face of the primary contradiction between themselves and the GME and refuse to cooperate with the latter by the large-scale acceptance of its arms and ammunition. As explained earlier, the demand for disarmament and development on a global scale is an integral element of the wider demand for the restructuring of the international system, and can gather momentum and force only as a part of a global political movement of the Third World nations. Such a concerted movement, in the United Nations and outside, can alone bring transformative pressures to bear upon the reluctant militaristic subsystems form outside. If sufficiently strong, it can even perform a 'step-level function' as an external input, altering the state of the subsystems concerned, in conjunction with the domestic forces trying to undermine the weapons culture of the GME from within.

For this purpose, it would be necessary to insist that all disarmament negotiations must henceforth be conducted under the auspices of the United Nations, and in a manner that would permit the Third World countries to play a significant decision-making role. It would be equally necessary to demand that all international transfers of funds and technology from the developed to the developing nations, including those resulting from disarmament, must be made through a UN agency with Third World representation at the decision-making level, and not bilaterally through multinational corporations, or even through governments. The UN is sure to receive adequate support from the General Assembly for such moves. Only in this way can the UN initiate the process for the creation of a just world order characterized by symbiotic interdependence and collective prosperity.

This paper was presented at the International Workshop on Disarmament, New Delhi 27-31 March 1978. The author is thankful to Dr. M.S. Rajan of the Jawaharlal Nehru University, New Delhi, and to Dr. Raimo Väyrynen of the Tempere Peace Research Institute, Tempere, Finland, for their comments on the original draft.

References

[1]United Nations, *The United Nations and Disarmament, 1945-1970* (New York: United Nations, 1970), ch. 5.

[2]United Nations, *Economic and Social Consequences of Disarmament* (New York: United Nations, 1962).

[3]United Nations, *Economic and Social Consequences of the Arms Race and of Military Expenditures* (New York: United Nations, 1972).

[4] United Nations; *Disarmament and Development: Report of the Group of Experts on the Economic and Social Consequences of Disarmament* (New York: United Nations, 1973), paras. 14, 44.

[5]ibid., paras. 16, 19, 33, 44, 45.

[6]ibid., para. 8.

[7]United Nations, *The Nations and Disarmament, 1970-1975* (New York: United Nations, 1976), ch. 15.

[8]United Nations, *Reduction in military Budgets of States Permanent Members of the Security Council by 10 per cent and Utilization of Part of the Funds thus saved to Provide Assistance to Developing Countries* (New York: United Nations, 1975).

[9]ibid., para. 15.

[10]ibid., para. 16.

[11]United Nations, *Economic and Social Consequences of the Armaments Race and its Extremely Harmful Effects on World Peace and Security*, Report of the Secretary-General, 12 August 1977 (New York: United Nations, 1977).

[12]Ibid., para. 113.

[13]United Nations, *Disarmament and Development: Proposal for a United Nations Study. Finland, Denmark, Norway, Sweden: Working Paper*, 31 August 1977 (New York: United Nations, 1977).

[14]Stockholm International Peace Research Institute, *Resources Devoted to Military Research and Development* (Stockholm, 1972), p. 10.

[15]United States Arms Control and Disarmament Agency, *Arms Control Report* (Washington D.C., 1976), p. 46.

[16]Stockholm International Peace Research Institute, *Yearbook of World Armaments and Disarmament, 1976* (Stockholm, 1976), pp. 252-253.

[17] John Stanley and Maurice Pearton, *The International Trade in Arms*, published for the International Institute for Strategic Studies (London: Chatto & Windus, 1972), p. 9.

[18] Stockholm International Peace Research Institute, *Yearbook of World Armaments and Disarmament, 1978* (Stockholm, 1978), p. 253.

[19] For an analysis of the incorrect use of the terms 'white' and 'coloured' and its causes, see Jayantanuja Bandyopadhyaya, 'Racism and International Relations', *Alternatives III*, 1, 1977, pp. 19-48.

[20] Philip Noel-Baker, *The Private Manufacture of Armaments*, 2 vols. (London: Victor Golancz, London, 1938).

[21] Fenner Brockway and Frederic Mullally, *Death Pays a Dividend* (London: Victor Golancz, 1944), p. 8.

[22] Raymond Aron, *The Imperial Republic: The United States and the World, 1945-1973*, (Englewood Cliffs: Prentice-Hall, 1974), pp. 264-267.

[23] See, for instance, Morton Mintz and Jerry S. Cohen, *America Inc.: Who Owns and Operates the United States.* (New York: The Dial Press, 1971); Ralph Lapp, *The Weapons Culture* (Pelican Books, 1969); Stephen Ambrose and James A. Barber. Jr (ed). *The Military and American Society: Essays and Readings* (New York: Free Press, 1972); Murray L. Weidenbaum, *The Economics of Peacetime Defense* (New York: Praeger, 1974), Seymour Melman, *The Permanent War Economy: American Capitalism in Decline,* (New York: Simon & Schuster, 1976); Alva Myrdal, *The Game of Disarmament*, Pantheon, New York, 1976.

[24] See John Stanley and Murice Pearton (f.n. 17). See also the references in f.n. 23.

[25] See, for example, John Kenneth Galbraith, 'Characteristics of the Military-Industrial Complex', in Stephen Ambrose and James A. Barber (f.n. 23). See also the other references in the same f.n.

[26] See Michael Kidron, *Western Capitalism Since the War* (London: Weidenfeld and Nicolson, 1968), p. 40.

[27] See Murray L. Weidenbaum (f.n. 23), pp. 26-27.

[28] Michael Kidron (f.n. 26), p. 41.

[29] (f.n. 26), pp. 46-47.

[30] Michael Kidron (f.n. 26), pp. 47-48.

[31] OECD, *Government and Technical Cooperation* (Paris, 1966), p. 31.

[32] See, for example, Alva Myrdal (f.n. 23), (f.n. 11), paras. 114, 115.

[33] Paul A. Samuelson, *Economics,* (New York: McGraw-Hill, 8th edition, 1970), pp. 803-804.

[34] See William T. Lee, 'The Politico-Military-Industrial Complex of the USSR', *Journal of International Affairs 26*, 1, 1972, pp. 73-86; Vernon V. Aspaturian, 'The Soviet Military-Industrial Complex - Does it Exist?', *ibid.*, pp. 1-28; Roman Kolkowicz, 'Strategic Elites and Politics of Superpower', *ibid.*, pp. 40-59; David Holloway, 'Technology and Political Decision in Soviet Armaments Policy', *Journal of Peace Research, XI*, 4, 1974, pp. 257-273; H. Gordon Skilling and Franklin Griffiths, *Interest Groups in Soviet Politics* (Princeton, N.J.: Princeton University Press, 1971); Alva Myrdal (f.n. 23).

[35] Vernon V. Aspaturian (f.n. 34).

[36] William T. Lee (f.n. 34).

[37] David Holloway (f.n. 34).

[38] For a detailed analysis, see Vernon V. Aspaturian (f.n. 34).

[39] Roman Kolkowicz, (f.n. 34).

[40] (f.n. 11), para. 119.

[41] (f.n. 17), para. 111.

[42] (f.n. 17), p. 123.

[43] See Vernon V. Aspaturian (f.n. 34).

[44] See William T. Lee (f.n. 34). For a more detailed analysis, see William T. Lee, *The Estimation of Soviet Defense Expenditures, 1955-75: An Unconventional Approach* (New York: Praeger, 1977), particularly pp. 144-145.

[45] (f.n. 23).

[46] For a detailed analysis, see Jayantanuja Bandyopadhyaya, 'The Nonaligned Movement and International Relations', *India Quarterly*, April-June 1977.

Brandt, Palme and Thorsson: A Strategy That Does Not Work?

Hans-Henrik Holm

In the 1950s we worried about the Cold War and the danger of nuclear accidents. For the 1960s the main agenda item was development in the Third World. The economic crises of the 1970s made these problems and concerns come together, and the 1980s present us with the twin problems of militarisation and development. Exacerbated by the economic, social and political problems experienced by the North, development and peace have become foci of attention for scholars, politicians and administrators, and for the general public.

From the mid-1970s a series of international reports has addressed various aspects of this linkage. The first of these, *North-South*, under the Chairmanship of the former West German Chancellor, Willy Brandt, outlined a global strategy for survival. In Brandt's introduction it was stressed that resources used for military purposes could be used instead to solve the development problems of the Third World: for example, 0.5 per cent of one year's world military expenditure could pay for all the farm equipment needed to increase food production and approach selfsufficiency in food deficit low-income countries by 1990 [*Report of the Independent Commission on International Development Issues 1980*: 13-15]. This proposal, though not part of the report proper, is illustrative of its underlying conception. Transfer of resources from the rich countries (the industrialised West) and the surplus producing countries (OPEC) to the poor countries in the Third World is the answer.

Survival is the main theme and economic survival problems are at the centre of the report's recommendations. Survival is also the reduction of conflict. By accommodating the concerns of the Third World as expressed in their demands for a New International Economic Order (NIEO) further conflict between North and South is reduced. If Third World countries get better prices for their raw materials, better access to the markets of the industrialised countries, and a better position in international decision-making, the chances of common survival are improved. Furthermore, some of the problems that beleaguer all countries today can only be solved through concerted action. The protection of the environment, the reduction of the dangers and costs inherent in the arms race are problems that can only be dealt with by the entire international community.

These problems were described and analysed in detail in the report, but the proposals that were agreed upon as a consequence of the description of the problem were in reality very limited in scope, detail, and effect. For example, industrial restructuring in the industrialised countries is presented as one of the things that needs to be done, but the specific proposals only say that adjustment programmes should be pursued.

The report's recommendations concerning disarmament and development [*ibid*: 117-25, 284] are equally vague. They talk about the need to educate the public; the development of a more comprehensive understanding of security, including its non-military aspects; inter-

Originally published in *The IDS Bulletin*, vol. 16, no. 4, 1985. Reprinted with permission.

national agreements to prevent the proliferation of nuclear weapons; the need to build upon the process of *détente* by undertaking negotiations to get the arms race under control; an enlarged role for the United Nations; and a globally respected peace-keeping mechanism. More specifically, the report proposes an international tax on the arms trade to be used for development; disclosure by governments of their arms exports and transfers of military technology; and negotiated limits on the arms trade, especially in areas of conflict and tension.

The follow-up report, *Common Crisis*, restated many of the previous proposals, underlining that very little of what the original report advocated had been achieved: 'The North-South dialogue remains much where it was when the Commission reported. Some modest steps forward have been taken. And some backwards. Meanwhile the world economy continues its dangerous downward slide, and the desperate situation of many developing countries finds no new hope or relief' [*Brandt Commission 1983*:12]. It went on to note the complete failure of the 1982 UN Special Session on Disarmament, as well as the upsurge in world military spending [*ibid*:37-8]. In his introduction Willy Brandt was even more explicit, arguing that only an end to the arms race would provide a change to 'end the grim political and economic confusion engulfing our societies everywhere'. In his view the failure to respond to the crisis was 'not primarily the lack of technical solutions. . . but the lack of a clearly and broadly reflected awareness of the current realities and dangers, and an absence of the political will necessary to meet the real problems' [*ibid*:8].

However, another reason the reports failed to produce results was the nature of their own diagnoses and recommendations. Their basic philosophy is 'something for everybody', and they urge common action and negotiation as the way to solve problems. Common interests should motivate this type of action and the main goal of the reports was to help create a political consensus around the need for a common international effort to solve global problems.

The second Brandt report, however, gave less attention to the relationship between disarmament and development. Instead this fell within the terms of reference of a new Commission on Common Security, headed by the Swedish Social Democratic leader (now Prime Minister) Olof Palme, whose membership overlapped (in the persons of Palme himself, Shridath Ramphal and Haruki Mori) with the Brandt Commission. Whereas the latter 'concentrated its work on economic matters, the new Commission' . . . 'will seek to complement that broad overview of global issues by concentrating on security and disarmament measures that can contribute to peace in the 1980s and beyond' (*Report of the Independent Commission on Disarmament and Security Issues 1982*).

The Commission's central theme is that 'states can no longer seek security at each other's expense. . . A doctrine of common security must replace the present expedient of deterrence through armaments' [*ibid*: 139]. Much of the report is given over to discussion of nuclear disarmament, East-West relations and qualitative arms control. However, it then goes on to discuss the role that the United Nations could play in creating a collective security system which would be based on 'political agreement and partnership between the permanent members of the Security Council and the Third World countries' [*ibid*: 164] and would be primarily concerned with the resolution of Third World conflicts. Through this system it might be possible to prevent the escalation into major wars of local conflicts, border wars and ethnically based clashes. Enhancing collective security means reactivating the security system originally built into the UN Charter, the creation of a UN army, the establishment of Helsinki-type regional security accords in the Third World, etc.

The Palme report is based on a state-centric view of the world, and its basis for analysis is the traditional security dilemma. All states seek national security through the acquisition of weapons. Weapons are equated with security. Security cannot, however, be achieved at the expense of others, and cooperation is necessary. All states live in an insecure world and share a common vulnerability. No nation can escape the threat of nuclear destruction, and both developed and developing countries live under this threat. Socially and economically, states have become vulnerable too, and security must be viewed and understood in this context, according to the report.

Only through the removal of mutual suspicion and fear can security be achieved. Security is common, and to create the foundation for true national security, the international system needs to be changed, so that cooperation instead of confrontation is the basis of the system. In the words of the report: 'Neither physical nor psychological security can be achieved without the development of an international system which would outlaw war. . .' [ibid:12].

With this as the premise, the report goes on to analyse the threat of war. A major part of this analysis naturally concentrates on the nature of the East-West conflict and the specific problems and dangers in Europe. However these East-West confrontations are now being transferred to the Third World, and increased conflict is the result. The report does add that indigenous factors are a fundamental cause of Third World conflicts. Yet the North often acts in ways that make the resolution of such conflicts more difficult, and supplies the increasingly advanced weapons that make the escalation of conflict more likely [ibid:27-31].

The relationship between the East-West conflict and the conflicts in the Third World are outlined in various ways in the report. The accelerating nuclear weapons competition creates tension that in itself heightens the danger of war and therefore also puts security in the Third World at peril. Tension is also transferred to the various regions of the Third World through an intensified arms race and the policies of the superpowers. The superpowers acquire bases and military facilities on the soil of Third World countries, and they pressure these countries to play a more active supporting role in the Cold War. Increased regional tension in the Third World in turns fuels the competition between the superpowers and has adverse effects on the prospects of building mutual trust and reducing war.

After this survey of causes of war and its consequences for the Third World, the report focuses on the effects of military expenditure upon both the developed and the developing countries [ibid:Ch4]. Its analysis of this is thorough, being partly based on commissioned studies by outside researchers. To states in the Third World, the rising costs of armaments are of particular importance. The report says that the military use of scarce resources and skills in the developing countries increases 'human deprivation' and 'can jeopardise economic growth and development and thus the foundation for lasting security' [ibid:87-8]. Since the developing countries have to import a large part of their arms, the economic burden is even greater than in the developed countries. Socially, military expansion presents the developing world with 'alien lifestyles and military cultures' that in themselves have negative effects on the development process [ibid:86ff].

But the security problem in the Third World is not seen merely as a reflection of the East-West confrontation or of induced militarism. The weakness and dependency of the developing countries in itself generates military conflicts and tempts other states to achieve political goals through military intervention. It is in this connection that the report proposes a system of collective security, UN peace keeping and regional conflict-resolution. The responsibility for achieving security between states is placed with the international community and the UN. The collective security system is mainly seen in relation to the Third World. Whereas security in the East-West context has to be negotiated, security in the Third World is to be enforced through a reconstituted UN system.

Central to the analysis of the report is a perception of development as primarily an economic process and of armaments and militarisation as wasteful spending. There are relatively few attempts in the report to establish in a rigorous way the causal connections between militarisation and development. The stress is on conflict avoidance through regulation of conflicts. A new international regime is needed, and here the burdens and the benefits must be evenly distributed. 'The burden of making the world safe for all (must) be shared by all' [ibid:3].

Thus the Palme Report, just like the Brandt Report, is premised on common interests. However there is little or nothing in the report to translate the obvious common interest in avoiding nuclear destruction into a political programme that can remove the perception of mutual threats between states. States can only achieve security through cooperation, and this is a readily recognised fact. But states have other goals, and these goals often take precedence. The central problem is how political conflicts are solved, and her disarmament as such has little to offer.

The perspective of the Palme Report is illustrated very clearly in the illustration on the book cover. The world is seen from above in a projection that makes the South look much larger than it is. It is also the way that the world is presented in the official UN symbol, except that the world is turned 45 degrees. The drawing of the world is surrounded by ten hands that form a ring of cooperation between people. Cooperation is seen as the way to shield the world from war and insecurity.

Holding hands, however, does not solve conflicts of interest. Common security can only be achieved through the resolution of existing fundamental conflicts. How that is done is not addressed in the Palme report. The more than 30 proposals contained in the report have received scant attention since they were published in 1982. The only proposal that has been met with some public interest is the proposal for a battlefield-nuclear-weapon-free zone in Europe. This had been widely discussed internationally; but the prospects for its implementation seem very dim.

Of the many recommendations of the report only a minority deal with the Third World. These include broader adherence to the Non-Proliferation Treaty and greater international control over sensitive parts of the nuclear fuel-cycle. The report also proposes negotiations among supplier states to restrict the flow of arms to the Third World, particularly to regions where there are severe political tensions; and negotiations among recipients to regulate their acquisition of arms and prevent local arms races. There is little in the report, however, that directly addresses the connection between security and development, except perhaps the idea of promoting periodic Regional Conferences on Security and Cooperation à la mode Helsinki (CSCE) in the various Third World regions. These could provide a framework for cooperation, not only on security but also on economic, social and cultural issues. They could also establish the infrastructure for regional zones of peace and nuclear-weapons-free zones, both of which are endorsed by the report.

The report stresses that economic cooperation between the participating states in these regional security talks is a necessary foundation for the development of common perceptions of security interests and concerns. Economic development and cooperation is seen as a prerequisite for the attainment of security in the Third World: 'Without economic recovery there is no hope for common security — for the common prosperity which is the basis of security itself [*ibid*:96]. However, the development perspective of the report is based on very conventional thinking. The development problem in the Third World is seen as mainly a question of financial resources. Consequently, the task at hand is to divert resources From wasteful use on armaments and into productive use for development. Thus the Palme Report proposes that specific national plans are devised in the developed countries and in the rich OPEC countries to release resources from their defence budgets which can be reallocated to development assistance; and that these be complemented by reductions in the military spending of the developing countries themselves [*ibid*:172-4].

As critics of the Palme Report have pointed out, these proposals have little bearing on national policy processes. They do not address the problem of military doctrine, or of the bureaucratic and industrial interests in weapons production. There is an overall focus on multilateral measures that makes it very difficult to translate the proposals into national policies for action and change [Galtung 1984:138-45]. This underlying confidence in international negotiations and multilateral solutions channelled through the UN seems misplaced at a time when the national solutions and problems are at the forefront of leaders, attention everywhere. Because it fails to address specific interests, the impact of the Palme commission has been limited. The concentration of the report on the international and multilateral levels has in a sense made it easier to ignore its proposals at the national level of decision making. There is no need for individual governments to worry about a programme that can only be enacted when all the others have agreed to it.

The Palme Report details the economic and social consequences of military spending. But it does not adequately address how development and disarmament would be linked as political processes. The proposals do not posit a realistic way forward. One reason is that the report provides insufficient intellectual or political foundation for understanding the link between the security and development problems of individual Third World countries and the driving forces behind the East-West confrontation.

In a study prepared for the United Nations (called the Thorsson Report after Inga Thorsson, the chairperson of the expert group [United Nations 1981]) the analysis of these connections and their consequences is more centrally placed. And like the Palme Report it is based on the findings of a number of commissioned studies by outside researchers. This report stresses that previous studies had tended to refrain from coupling disarmament and development, because this might lead to a situation where neither was achieved. The report argues that this is no longer a relevant consideration. There is tremendous pressure on the scarce resources that governments control, which means that increases in expenditure in one area usually necessitate cuts in another. Increases in development assistance therefore can no longer be achieved in isolation. Furthermore, international negotiations on development issues and negotiations between superpowers on arms control are interrelated. The present Cold War situation makes it very difficult to get negotiations going on the NIEO. Consequently the two sets of problems now have to be studied together. The arms race, according to the report, directly reduces the security of the participating states, and disarmament will tend to increase their security. Development has to be seen both as a need for continuing economic growth and as an opportunity and responsibility for everybody to participate fully in the economic and social processes and their ensuing results [*ibid*: 163].

The coupling between security and development is primarily seen in terms of their mutual economic interdependence: meaning that a continuing arms race will create a vicious circle of confrontation, distrust, economic nationalism and protectionism and in the end reduce the policy options available to all parties. Besides highlighting the general negative effects which high armament expenditure has on the global economy, the report concentrates on showing the special burden that these expenditures entail for Third World countries. It cites a number of the detailed empirical studies carried out on behalf of the expert group, showing among other things that countries with high military expenditures have lower levels of investment and a greater tax burden than other countries; that military spending has limited positive spin-offs; that arms imports divert scarce foreign exchange and entail political as well as economic costs for the recipients, etc. [ibid:92-4].

On the basis of an input-output model of the world economy submitted to the expert group, the report suggests that simultaneous cuts in military spending by both the developed and the developing countries could produce substantial economic benefits [ibid:97100]. Gradual cuts in the share of military outlays relative to GNP, reducing military spending to around 65 per cent of what it would have been if the arms rice continued at the present level, would result in a world GNP 3.7 per cent higher than would otherwise have been projected. More important, on the assumption that the relatively wealthy countries transferred a fraction of the savings generated by their military cuts to development assistance, this could substantially increase the capital stock, industrial employment and per capita GNP of the poorer developing countries compared with the base (continuing arms race) level: the per capita GNP increases would range between 17 per cent (for resource-poor Latin America) and 146 per cent (for the and regions of Africa). However, as the report itself admits, the model is 'highly aggregative, somewhat static and its detailed results are dependent upon a number of explicit and implicit assumptions. Some of these can be easily questioned' [ibid:99]. Another empirical analysis of the same problem [Duchin 1982] concludes, much less optimistically, that transfers of this type would only marginally increase the standard of living of the poor countries.

The report further argues that cuts in military spending need not produce unemployment in the industrialised countries. The direct job losses would not affect a large proportion of the labour force and would be more than offset by the gains generated by increased growth — especially if the military reductions were combined with a reduction in protectionism and consequent gains in North-South trade [UN 1981]. After a discussion of the problem of conversion from military production by the major military producers (discussed in other contributions to this Bulletin) and of possible institutional mechanisms for the transfer of resources from military spending to development assistance [ibid: Ch 5 and 6], the report concludes with a number of proposals for action. These are primarily directed to states and governments asking them to carry out detailed assessments of the costs of their military activities, the possible benefits of a reallocation of military resources to other purposes and of the practicability of conversion. The report also proposes an intensified campaign for educating the public on peace and development, to be orchestrated by the UN. And it proposes that the UN should investigate the French government's proposal to create an international disarmament fund for development, financed either by a levy on armament or by a disarmament dividend financed by the budgeting savings resulting from the implementation of disarmament measures. Versions of this proposal are still under negotiation internationally (e.g. in Stockholm at the Conference on Confidence and Security-building Measures and Disarmament in Europe).

The Thorsson Report suffers from the same defects as the other reports, despite its sharper focus on the relationship between disarmament and development. It is based on a conception of security that is valid in principle, but not adhered to by most individual nation states. The report argues that security is much broader than military security, with economic and social aspects placed at the forefront. In the security policy of states the perception of threats and of the intentions of adversary states is, however, the determining factor. Defining security in the way that the Thorsson Report does may therefore be counterproductive, if the objective is to ensure an impact on state policy. The intermediate steps between common goals and short term interests need to be spelled out much more clearly.

The concept of development in the report is equally broad and hard to apply. Development is defined as sustained economic growth with the opportunity and responsibility for full participation. The result should be profound economic and social changes in society and a universal share in the benefits of economic growth. However, unless this conception of development is translated into policy it will have little relevance or impact.

In sum, the main suggestions in all three of the reports under circulation are for more studies, reports and funds to be created. Besides an appeal to everybody's long term interests there is little to motivate spending time and money on this. There is nothing in the reports on how to translate the studies into a practical strategy for change. Educating the public, governments and the international community is an impossible task unless you address interests that people and states have—here and now.

One cannot deny, however, that the three reports are of major international significance and address themselves to the long term interests of all of us. They point to many mistaken beliefs that float around in political discussion, and present a platform for discussing the interrelation between North-South and East-West problems. But they are not, nor can they be, an adequate foundation for action to change these systems. As a result of their terms of reference, they address long term global interests; which in the real world tend to be overshadowed by the short term national interests of particular states, groups and classes.

The fundamental problem of coupling such interests to common global interests is still unresolved. It is to be hoped that is where the next international report will start.

References

Brandt Commission, 1983, *Common Crisis, North-South: Cooperation for World Recovery*, Pan Books, London
Duchin, Faye, 1982, *How Much Development can Disarmament Buy?* International Studies Association, Cincinatti
Galtung, Johan, 1984, *There are Alternatives: four roads to peace and security*, Spokesman, London
Report of the Independent Commission of International Development Issues, 1980, *North-South: A Programme for Survival*, Pan Books, London
Report of the Independent Commission on Disarmament and Security Issues (under the chairmanship of Olof Palme), 1982, *Common Security: A Programme for Disarmament*, Pan Books, London
United Nations, 1981, *Study on the Relationship between Disarmament and Development, Report of the Secretary-General*, New York

PART II

DEPENDENCE AND INTERDEPENDENCE

Chapter 4

Trade Policy

Introduction

Developing countries have made significant export progress, primarily in manufactured products, over the past two decades. Whereas in the 1960s and early 1970s this growth was attributable to a relatively small number of "newly industrializing countries" (NICs), in the 1970s a second tier of developing country manufacturing exporters emerged. During this process there has been a changing pattern in comparative advantage, with the NICs increasingly exporting skill-intensive commodities and the less developed countries starting to export unskilled labour-intensive products. Within this framework trade between developing countries is likely to have an increasingly important role to play. This is already reflected by the marked shift of developing country primary commodity exports towards Third World markets, which has occurred as a direct complement to increased raw material processing activities in these countries. Meanwhile, the developed countries (and a few developing countries) have increasingly developed a trade in services as the primary growth sector of their trade.

In part as a reflection of their own export growth, developing countries constituted a buoyant market for developed country exports during 1973-80. By the end of the 1970s over one third of the industrialized countries' exports of capital goods were purchased by developing countries, compared with only about one fifth at the start of the decade. Moreover, it has been estimated that OECD trade with developing countries has typically led to a net creation of jobs, the loss of jobs, while contributing to adjustment requirements, has been more than offset by job gains. Nevertheless, the loss of jobs in the less competitive sectors has been one factor behind increasing public intervention, often bilateral, in the operation of the market. Developing country export growth has thus taken place despite a marked increase in measures affecting international trade through more-or-less formal self-restraint agreements as well as domestic subsidies. In addition, these and other national economic, manpower, industrial and regional policies have sometimes tended to delay rather than facilitate adaptation and adjustment, and have thus compounded the effects of international recession. The extension of the Multi-Fibre Arrangement, (MFA) authorizing importing countries to restrict imports from individual exporting countries, highlights one of the major outstanding problems of protectionism – the use of safeguards.

Protectionist pressures in the agricultural sector have also increased, reflecting the continuing risk of instability in agricultural markets, growing competition for outlets and the fact that trading rules established under GATT are not always applied to agriculture.

More than 60 developing countries are members of the multilateral commercial framework of the General Agreement on Trade and Tariffs (GATT). Their specific development situations and needs are partially recognized in the General Agreement, particularly in Part IV, as well as in the Framework Agreement, so that these countries are often exempted from many of the rules governing international trade. In addition, developing countries benefit from MFN (Most Favoured Nation) treatment and preferential concessions, especially GSPs, (the Generalized System of Preference Items), extended by industrial countries. Efforts to maintain the open international trading system and to reduce distortions in trade must be firmly based on the recognition of the mutual benefits from trade. Expanded trade with developing countries can make a critical contribution to the efficiency of the world economy. For the Third World, trade is the keystone in the complex of interdependent relationships among growth, export earnings, debt servicing and borrowing capacity.

For commodity dependent developing countries, "commodity problems" reflect not only the specific difficulties of producing and exporting a particular primary product but also the basic rigidities associated with underdevelopment and the difficulties of creating integrated resilient socio-economic systems. The tendency for the prices of primary products exported by developing countries to fall by more than those exported by developed countries reflects the inability of many developing countries to time sales over the cycle, as well as their limited scope to diversify away from products with a relatively low income elasticity of demand. This problem is particularly acute for the low-income developing countries, some 32 of which rely on a single non-fuel primary commodity for over one third of their exports, and face particular hardship in circumstances when commodity demand is slow, especially when First World growth rates average less than 4% per annum, an endemic situation in the 1980s. If the vulnerability of the commodity-dependent developing countries is to be reduced they must broaden their economic bases. In the initial stages their ability to do this is likely to depend on their ability to increase their scope for raw material processing (vertical integration or forward linkages) and to diversify within the primary sector (horizontal integration).

The international monetary policy of various nations has been left largely to their respective central bankers, finance ministers, and the handful of cognoscenti who can fathom the intricacies of exchange rate management, SDRs (Special Drawing Rights), and Eurodollar markets. Trade policy, however, is the stuff of domestic politics. In America, the US Constitution has accentuated political conflict over trade policy by giving Congress the power to levy tariffs and to regulate foreign commerce. Conflict within Congress and between Congress and the Executive branch is a central characteristic of American trade policy. Because congressmen are responsive to the economic concerns of their constituents, there is often pressure within Congress for a trade policy which reflects and protects special interests. Furthermore, the demands of a relatively small number of interest groups directed at Congress may snowball into national trade policy. The Smoot-Hawley tariff of 1930 is a particularly harrowing example.

Unlike Congress, which tends to link trade policy with particular domestic interests, the United States Executive often links trade policy with larger foreign policy and foreign economic goals. Since the 1930s American presidents have advocated free trade as the preferred economic policy for broad economic and strategic rea-

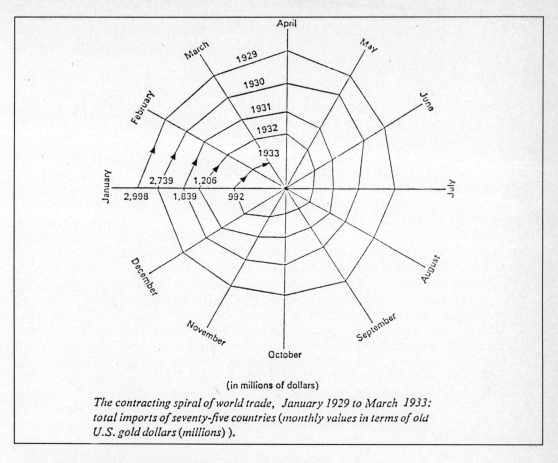

(in millions of dollars)

The contracting spiral of world trade, January 1929 to March 1933: total imports of seventy-five countries (monthly values in terms of old U.S. gold dollars (millions)).

Source: Charles P. Kindleberger, *The World in Depression 1929–1939*, Berkeley, University of California Press, Revised Ed., 1986, p. 170.

sons. However, in their efforts to carry out such a policy, presidents have been consistently constrained by Congress.

Domestic politicization has been an important constraint on international management. It is not possible in trade, as it is in the monetary system, for a small elite to manage relations.

The factors which led to the creation of a managed international monetary system after the Second World War also led to the attempt to subject trade for the first time to systemic international control.

The disintegration of world trade brought about by national protectionism in the 1930s (as shown by the Figure above) created a common interest in an open trading order among the western allies during the Second World War. Although Britain took the leadership in proposing the negotiations for both a managed international monetary system and a trade system, it was the American willingness to take the leadership role during the early post-war period in both the reconstruction of war-torn

Europe and Japan, and in establishing an orderly liberal trading system that was instrumental in bringing about the liberal economic regime of the world as we know it today. And, although the monetary system was established and operated more or less successfully for about 20 years, the trading system that came about was the result of a compromise brought about in the United States Congress. The comprehensive Havana Charter, which was to provide a framework for both a trade and tariffs regime as well as a process for industrialization and economic development of the whole of the world's economy, was blocked in the United States Senate, and thus only an interim arrangement, the General Agreement on Tariffs and Trade (GATT) was possible. Nevertheless, GATT *has* provided an orderly framework for the tremendous expansion of world trade that has taken place during the past forty years. The essence of GATT is three basic rules: 1) Most Favoured Nation treatment (MFN), which means that all members must extend the most favoured treatment for any trade partner to all trade partners (future customs unions and free trade areas are exempted from this); 2) a Multilateral Tariff Negotiation (MTN) process, meaning that tariff reductions should be negotiated on a system-wide basis rather than on a bilateral basis; and 3) an international commercial code with rules on dumping and subsidies. The MFN system has worked reasonably well, although the rights of members to form customs unions and free trade areas has meant that the European Community has established a trading system which has built a common wall of tariffs and other impediments to trade against the rest of the members of GATT, and the United States and Canada are negotiating a similar arrangement during the late 1980s. The MTN rule has been the most successful of all and has led to seven tariff reduction rounds between 1947 and 1979, which by 1987 have led to a virtual abolition of tariffs on non-agricultural products. Unfortunately, the third rule, that of an international code on dumping and subsidies, has not worked very well; important areas were left out, with the result that as tariffs were progressively reduced, and especially during the 1970s and 1980s, Non-Tariff Barriers (NTBs) in the form of "voluntary" quotas, health regulations, licencing requirements and subsidies of various kinds, including differential tax treatments, replaced the tariffs and have become even greater distorters of trade patterns than the tariff walls themselves ever were. This new protectionism by means of NTBs has been politically very attractive for all industrialized countries because it appears to conserve jobs in the intermediate manufacturing industries at a cheap political price. NTBs have become particularly attractive since the confluence of two movements beginning in the 1970s; a combination of inflation and recession and the collapse of the Bretton Woods system of fixed exchange rates led to a series of wild fluctuations in foreign exchange values of trade. Although the Tokyo round of MTN between 1973 and 1979 attempted to come to grips with the NTBs it was not very successful. Nor did it succeed in negotiating tariff reductions in agricultural goods. The eighth MTN round, instigated by the United States as all the preceding seven had been, was inaugurated in Uruguay in the fall of 1986 and is attempting to come to grips with NTBs and to negotiate a tariff regime for agricultural commodities, as well as bring the trade in services within the purview of GATT's regulations.

It should be noted that GATT's rules apply only to its members, and, since from the beginning they have related exclusively to industrial manufacturers, the Third World has not been served very well by GATT. This has led to demands for a restructuring of the whole of the world's trading arrangements and the inclusion of both the First and the Third Worlds within it. The United Nations Conference on Trade and Development (UNCTAD) has met six times since 1964 and has become a regularized negotiation-*cum*-pressure forum where the Third World "gangs up" on the First World and attempts to gain economic advantages and trade concessions from the First World. So far it has not been markedly successful; the world trading system still revolves around the main industrial countries of the West and the regime that they have developed within, or around, the rules of GATT.

The eight articles in this chapter illustrate the turmoil that the trade policy of the industrialized world is currently in. The first article by P.K. Kuruvilla emphatically states in a few words the importance of trade for Third World development. The second article, by Raymond Vernon, provides an overview of the international trade regime during the past four decades and then assesses the possibilities for change in the regime, concluding that US policy is still critical in bringing about successful rational change. American policy has consistently contained two strands: 1) a long-term commitment to the principle of open markets; and 2) a tendency to stray from that commitment in specific cases, a tendency deriving from structural features of the conflict between Congress and the Executive Branch. The third article, by Alex Ashiabor, provides an overview of the main "successes" of the Third World and UNCTAD in its negotiations with the First World, in gaining a fairer access for commodities in the First World's markets. The fourth article is an editorial article written by the editors of the IMF/World Bank quarterly journal *Finance and Development*, which reviews the current trade restrictions, factors influencing trade policies, and the implications of First World protectionism for the Third World.

Susan Strange takes a somewhat different look at protectionism by arguing that protectionism may be rational if there are "very good social reasons for it and/or if there is plenty of competition in the domestic market." She concludes that because Europe has to compete with the United States and Japan, which both have built-in advantages of various kinds, protectionism is not to be ruled out as a matter of self-preservation.

The *New York Times* article by William N. Walker demonstrates again the conflict between President and Congress in US trade policy making, referred to by William Diebold Jr. in Chapter 1, and the *Kitchener-Waterloo Record* column by Jim Romahn poignantly points to the simplicity of solutions available to the protectionist wars fought between the US and the EC, as well as Canada.

The final article, by S. J. Anjaria, an official of the IMF, provides an up-to-date overview of the main issues and prospects of the new multi-lateral trade negotiations, the so-called Uruguay round, which will determine the international trade regime into the twenty-first century, for both the First and the Third Worlds.

Trade is Better than Aid

P. K. Kuruvilla

It is impossible to exaggerate the importance of trade as an instrument of economic development to the developing countries. As the Pearson Commission on international development pointed out in the late 1960s, expanded external trade is *by far the most important of the external conditions of growth for the developing countries.* Trade is increasingly viewed by the developing countries as the most important element in their long-term strategy to industrialise themselves, to strengthen their economies, and to improve the standard of living of their people.

As far as the developing countries are concerned, notwithstanding the many negotiations that have taken place in the international political arena over the years, the developed countries are not yet making sufficient efforts to safeguard the vital economic and trading interests of the developing countries.

As seen through the eyes of the developing countries, there are many severe shortcomings of the international economic order which prevent them from exploiting the opportunities offered by international trade. These include among other things:
- tariff barriers in the developed countries affecting agricultural commodities, which constitute the bulk of exports from the developing countries;
- non-tariff barriers such as import quotas, variable levies, health and safety standards, and licensing and environmental regulations that are designed to discourage exports from developing countries and to protect inefficient domestic producers in developed countries;
- vesting of widespread discretion in the hands of officials who administer customs and foreign exchange regulations in developed countries;
- ad hoc and unpredictable ways in which important trading decisions which have far-reaching consequences for the developing countries are often arrived at in the developed countries;
- restrictions in the form of requests or demands for "voluntary" export restraint affecting certain products from the developing countries the moment they manage to penetrate the particularly sensitive markets of the developed countries;
- existence of preferential trading systems exclusively among the developed countries;
- instability of prices and demand for exports of primary products from the developing countries, mainly caused by the unwillingness of developed countries to enter into meaningful and lasting commodity agreements;
- existence of a plethora of fixed credit and exchange policies which are clearly discriminatory to the developing countries;
- artificial price supports, particularly in the agricultural sector in the developed countries, which tend to generate significant production surpluses, which are then pushed on to world markets through export subsidies, and
- systematic exclusion of developing countries from effective political management of many major matters pertaining to international trade.

Published for the first time in this volume.

If the developing countries are to succeed in improving their economic performance noticeably within a reasonable period of time, they will require significant economic concessions from the developed countries with particular emphasis on eliminating the many tariff as well as non-tariff trade restrictions facing them.

However, this is more easily said than done, especially when the developed countries have their own strong political and economic motivations for maintaining their protectionist postures. As a number of them point out, they themselves are saddled at present with major domestic economic difficulties. They are experiencing slow or stagnant economic growth, staggering trade deficits, and high levels of unemployment or underemployment due in part at least to soaring imports and shrinking exports.

They have also been pointing out that, while criticizing them for not moving towards a more liberalized external trade policy, the developing countries themselves have not hesitated to ignore their own advice and to follow protectionist policies which are hostile to the developed countries whenever it was in their own interest to do so.

From the point of view of global peace and harmony and humanitarian considerations towards the less fortunate countries and peoples, significant improvements to international trading practices are clearly needed. Moreover, given the gross inequalities in the existing distribution of the world's resources between them, it is the developed countries that have considerably more room to manoeuvre and to make concessions without necessarily receiving the benefit of full and immediate reciprocity.

It must not be forgotten that in a relative sense, the economic problems menacing the developing countries are many times more monumental than those facing the developed countries. More than 70 percent of the world's population lives in the developing countries, but they consume less than 20 percent of the world's output. The average income per head in the developing countries is less than one-tenth that of the developed countries.

For almost all the developing countries, primary products constitute a preponderant share of their exports. Since they depend mainly on the export of relatively few agricultural products, they are extremely vulnerable to variations in world market prices and in their own crop yields. In addition, for historical and other reasons, they have not had much success in increasing the volume of trade among themselves.

Without considerable increase in the flow of foreign aid or other capital imports, it is virtually impossible for developing countries to diversify their production in favor of products with greater long-term export potential or to industrialise themselves to any significant degree. Many of them do not have domestic markets large enough to provide a solid basis for their economic development and industrialisation. They also desperately need foreign exchange for repayment of loans, payment of interest and amortization and repatriation of profits.

Moreover, unlike most developed countries, even those few developing countries that are in a position to produce certain semi-manufactured products for export are often unable to find their way around the non-tariff barriers facing them through devices such as tailoring their production to particular market conditions and rules, or by investing in production or assembly facilities in other countries.

Furthermore, in recent years their economies have been ravaged by recession, depressed commodity prices, and massive debt, all leading to a sharp downturn in their trade with the rest of the world. In 1985 the export earnings of the developing countries fell 5.5 percent. Given these disturbing realities, there is little doubt that if the restrictive trade practices which have been bringing the world closer to an all-out trade war are allowed to continue unabated, the developing countries will suffer much more than the developed countries.

It is true that the latest round of multilateral trade negotiations under the auspices of the Geneva-based General Agreement on Tariffs and Trade (GATT) which was officially launched in Uruguay recently is being hailed by many observers as a welcome step towards hammering out a fresh trade liberalisation package.

It may be recalled, however, that during the last four decades or so we have already had seven similar rounds of multilateral trade negotiations under the GATT itself and apparently each one of them did succeed at least to a certain extent in establishing a few international codes of conduct aimed at progressive liberalisation of trade, but ironically the overall attitude among nations still remains profoundly protectionist.

While a trade war is being waged among major developed countries themselves, it may not be a propitious time to ease their protectionist stance against the developing countries. Moreover, the GATT itself has been plagued with problems which impede its effectiveness in reducing tariff and non-tariff barriers in international trade through reciprocal agreements and elimination of discriminatory practices among its member nations.

For instance, at its inception, the GATT was not conceived as an elaborate and effective international institution. Consequently, its constitutional structure contains only the most rudimentary outlines of necessary procedures for settling disputes and distribution of powers. Similarly, it lacks a well established and effective rule system at the international level. It is equally difficult for the institution to formulate new rules and regulations that will keep it abreast of changing international economic conditions. Also, the GATT talks generally take an inordinately long time to conclude and have a tendency to avoid topics that are perceived as too disputatious.

Furthermore, a totally uniform and non-discriminating application of certain GATT codes has been proving to be terribly detrimental to the vital interests of the developing countries because of the many innate economic inequalities between them and the developed countries.

Under these circumstances, one more routine round of negotiations alone may not make a profound difference. It may be necessary also to draw up a new and more effective set of rules of international trade and to revamp and strengthen the existing GATT mechanism in many respects. Besides, there is an acute need at the moment for a greater commitment than presently exists by every country in the world, but especially by the developed ones, to put an end to growing protectionist sentiments.

International Trade Policy in the 1980s: Prospects and Problems

Raymond Vernon

The past thirty years have seen a remarkable reduction in the trade barriers that once existed among the world's principal trading states. The tariff rates of the advanced industrialized countries, for instance, have been cut to about one-quarter of their previous levels. The import licensing schemes that were in effect in all but a few of these countries in the early 1950s have long since been dismantled. More recently, those countries have made a promising start on nontariff trade barriers in the form of a series of negotiated codes. In recent years, too, even a few of the developing countries have taken steps to reduce their import restrictions.

Yet, despite these remarkable developments, there is everywhere a sense of foreboding. There is a widespread expectation that the world is in for a period of protectionism as states respond to a reduction in their growth rates by closing their borders to foreign goods. So far, to be sure, the prospect does not seem to have materialized (at least not in any acute form), but the expectation persists. The need to understand the basis of that expectation, as well as the probability of its realization, is also strong.

U.S. POLICY

The policies of the United States are particularly critical in assessing the future. In decades past, this country served as the principal energizer and organizer of projects for the reduction of trade barriers, as in the formation of the General Agreement on Tariffs and Trade (GATT) in 1948, and in the succession, in the following decades, of giant tariff negotiation sessions. However, the future behavior of the U.S. government cannot easily be assessed without reference to the institutions and the history on which its past actions have been based.

A Style of Governance

The United States has been committed to open competitive markets and nondiscrimination among its trading partners. Its trade policies over the past thirty or forty years, when viewed as a whole, seem remarkably stable. At the same time, when viewed in detail, those policies have appeared riddled with inconsistency and contradiction. Behind this combination (stability in the large, inconsistency in detail) lies a structure of government and a philosophy of governance that are fairly unique in world societies.

Originally published in *International Studies Quarterly*, vol. 26, no. 4, Dec. 1982. Reprinted with permission.

The stable aspects of U.S. trade policy during the past fifty years have rested on a persistent American view that a world system of open competitive markets is in the country's interests, and on a related assumption that such a system could be realized under U.S. leadership. International negotiation was seen as the main instrument in the achievement of that objective; and U.S. trade policy had to be shaped in ways that would increase the chances of success of such negotiations.

The seeming inconsistencies of U.S. trade policy have been due to various factors, some of which trace back to the extraordinary diffusion of power in the U.S. system of governance. Lord Keynes, on observing U.S. governmental behaviour in the midst of World War II and under the strongest president in its modern history, was reported to have said to a U.S. delegation, "But you don't *have* a government in the ordinary sense of the word." Elaborating on the point in his memoirs, Keynes notes that "the Administration, not being in control of Congress, is not in a position to enter into commitments on anything" (quoted in Salant, 1980: 1058).

That special attribute of the U.S. system of governance has been more evident in some administrations than in others, but the roots go far back in its history (see, for instance, Epstein, 1967: 193-198; Alford, 1973: 94-122, 219-248, 309-318; Chambers, 1966: 83; and Krasner, 1978: 61-69). The extensive overlap of authority among the three main branches of the U.S. government, consciously provided for in the Constitution, explains part of the dilution of power. Anomalous government agencies, such as the "independent" International Trade Commission (ITC), have added to the pattern. The device of the congressional veto, increasingly applied in the 1970s, has accentuated the diffusion (Gilmore, 1982). And numerous "sunshine laws," buttressed by prolific rights of suit and appeal, have added to the conditional and uncertain quality that characterizes the exercise of governmental power in the United States (see, for example, Marks, 1978; Green, 1980).

The seeming incoherence in the day-to-day behaviour of the U.S. government must also be attributed in part to the character of its bureaucracy. As is not the case in Britain, France, or Japan, the U.S. public has always resisted the idea of a tightly knit professional bureaucracy. Partly as a result, American values are not offended when a new president and his cabinet bring a fresh team of high administrators into office with them (for example, Jacoby, 1973: 26-85). These administrators can be drawn from anywhere, from different professions, geographical origins, even ideologies (Heclo, 1977).

But the consequence of the curious style of U.S. governance is not always immobility, as Keynes implied. On the contrary, the loose jointed and unfocused nature of the structure allows a persistent pressure group, when allied with a resourceful politician or an energetic bureaucrat, to beat the system. U.S. bureaucrats and politicians, in sharp contrast to, say, Japanese bureaucrats and politicians, do not ordinarily feel the need to develop a broad internal consensus before they act. Indeed, given the heterogeneous aspects of the country's structure, consensus could well prove impossible. Instead, successful bureaucrats and politicians usually see the challenge as one of threading their way through the political maze, bypassing the opposition and capturing the power of government for some transitory or limited objective (Halperin, 1974: 101).

U.S. actions in the field of international trade, therefore, have been the product of two distinct processes. One of these has been based on the bedrock preferences of the country; it has created a succession of international negotiations that have served as action-forcing events to produce a fairly continuous decline in import restrictions over the past three or four decades. The other has been a succession of unilateral acts on the part of the United States, restrictive in nature, which have represented the sporadic successes of special interest group in achieving their objectives through one or another of the various avenues for political action that the system characteristically provides. The 1980s could generate either pattern of behavior; history provides some hints of which pattern is likely.

Prewar Origins, 1934-1945

One piece of conventional wisdom, less reliable than most, is that depressions have been the triggers that have led the United States in the past to apply restrictive trade measures. The facts suggest much more complex conclusions. The notorious Smoot-Hawley Tariff was formulated between 1928 and 1930, after a prolonged period of prosperity. The Trade Agreements Act was first developed in 1934, in the midst of a depression in which unemployment reached record levels of 25% in the United States, and large-scale social programs to assist the unemployed were still a novelty. It was then that the country undertook, for the first time, a long-term commitment to negotiate with other countries for the lowering of its tariffs and other import restrictions.

During the four decades after 1934, it became evident that the commitment to the policy of lowering trade barriers was deeply rooted in the body politic of the United States. In these years, the issue was repeatedly reconsidered. Although the margins of support were sometimes narrow and although new reservations and conditions were introduced with each successive commitment, the general direction of the policy remained clear (Pastor, 1980: 67-200). Moreover, the years in which some of the important renewals occurred—notably 1945, 1962, and 1974—were years of relative turmoil and stress, not years of tranquility. The 1945 debate was conducted at a time of grave national concern over the problems of transition from a wartime to a peacetime economy, the 1962 debate occurred at the end of a yearlong recession, and that of 1974 occurred in the midst of an acute bout of stagflation.

The origins of the widespread support for an open trading system in the United States are of only marginal interest today. But the movement is easily traceable to the growing confidence of the United States early in the twentieth century in its strength as an industrial power (Lefeber, 1963: 1-63; Smith, 1981: 138-157). The Wilson administration's emphasis on the open door policy, the U.S. Tariff Commission's adoption in 1923 of the nondiscrimination principle in the application of import duties, and the indignant protest of pratically all of America's leading economists to the passage of the Smoot-Hawley Tariff (New York Times, 1930) were manifestations of the pervasiveness of the open market sentiment. Yet a coalition of special interests, using its power over individual members of Congress, could briefly muster the strength to bypass the opposition. It was not until four years later, with the passage of the Trade Agreements Act of 1934, that the United States was drawn back to its basic preference for open international markets.

The Hegemonic Period, 1945-1962

The United States came out of the war with a profoundly changed perception of its place in the world economy. The conduct of the war had required the marshaling of various elite groups into the government service—business executives, labor leaders, and academics, among others. After the war ended, some of these lingered behind for a time, working in the treasury and state department or in the White House, on issues of postwar reconstruction. This group shared one common perception: They assumed that if an effective international economic system were to be restored in the world, the United States would have to take the lead in fashioning it.

In ordinary times, that concept might have provoked resistant reactions from the two groups in the political structure of the United States that traditionally constituted the backbone of the special interest organizations, namely, business organizations and labour unions. Exploiting the loose-jointed structure of the U.S. government, these groups could probably have reduced the strength and lessened the clarity of the trade policies that the government was pursuing. But many leaders of labour had been coopted into the highest councils of U.S. government, sharing the heady successes of war with other national leaders; for the time being, they were part of the Establishment, not its adversaries.[1] Besides, despite the substantial worries of business and labour over the problems of postwar readjustment, the industries that felt genuinely imperiled by the threat of foreign competition were, at the time, fairly limited in number and importance.

The widespread assumption that the United States was the indispensable leader in any movement to reestablish an effective international economic order was, of course, wholly consistent with the economic facts of the immediate postwar period. If the United States presented any problem for the international economic system at the time, it was the threat that its overbearing dynamism might prevent the achievement of an equilibrium in world trade (Kindleberger, 1950). Out of these attitudes and perceptions came the leadership of the United States in sponsoring an International Trade Organization and its offshoot, the General Agreement on Tariffs and Trade (GATT). These same forces were instrumental in generating five large-scale tariff negotiations between 1947 and 1956 that drastically reduced the world's tariff levels.[2]

The consensus among the U.S. elite during the latter 1940s, imperfect though it was, helped for a while to mask the endemic inability of the government to act consistently in the execution of major policies. But the consensus could not last for long, especially in the field of international trade.[3] The Congress, having been charged expressly by the Constitution with controlling "commerce with foreign nations. . . and with the Indian Tribes," has always been ambivalent about allowing the president to share in that power, even when international negotiation was obviously necessary to put the power effectively to work. Accordingly, throughout the period from 1948 to 1962, Congress was at pains to insist that the country's participation in the GATT had no standing in its eyes. Moreover, Congress was careful to circumscribe narrowly the president's power to alter U.S. tariff rates; that authority was doled out for periods of a few years at a time and was limited in scope by various precise formulas. As for nontariff trade barriers embodied in U.S. law, the president was given no power whatever to alter such restrictions in the pursuit of international agreements.

Where trade policy was concerned, therefore, the president was in a poor position to resist all the demands of Congress. As one special interest group after another established a support point in Congress, escape clauses were legislated on their behalf. As the years went on, these clauses grew in scope. Worse still, in an effort to head off such congressional initiatives, the president found himself adopting actions from time to time that were flatly at variance with the principles he was so earnestly proposing to other countries. In 1956, for instance, the U.S. chief executive compelled Japan to restrict "voluntarily" its exports of textiles to the U.S. market, a measure grossly inconsistent with the spirit of the GATT. Incidents of this sort were sufficiently frequent in the latter 1950s that the underlying continuities in U.S. policy could easily be missed.

Interdependence and Ambibalence After 1962

The commitment of the U.S. body politic to the concept of open markets and nondiscriminatory treatment in world trade survived the 1950s, but the support for that commitment meanwhile underwent some critical changes. By 1962, the leadership role of the United States was beginning to be questioned. The American dollar was no longer quite so impregnable. The country's exports still exceeded its imports, but the trend had grown uncertain. At the same time, high levels of foreign aid and foreign military expenditures were adding to the burden of the dollar.

More important was a decline in the relative importance of the U.S. economy. Between 1950 and 1960, U.S. exports dropped from about 50% of the exports of all advanced industrialized countries to less than 25% of the group's total. Further, the European Economic Community (EEC) was emerging as an economic unit equal to the United States in aggregate output and in exports. The possibility that European and Japanese producers might reduce the technological lead of American industry began to be realized.

To be sure, the birth of the EEC could be viewed as a logical outgrowth of U.S. postwar policy, a triumph of the country's efforts to strengthen Europe as a political and economic unit. But the EEC treaty, negotiated under French leadership in the latter 1950s, was wholly a European product. Psychologically, it drew part of its strength from being viewed by many Europeans as a counterinfluence to the United States in Europe. In matters of trade, it was based on the principle of preferences, not of nondiscrimination. It presented the prospect of an agricultural policy that would displace U.S. farm exports in favor of French and German products. Moreover, it contemplated a tariff system that would handicap any goods manufactured in the United States that might be competing for European markets against other European sellers. The brief period of U.S. hegemony over Europe, it was evident, was rapidly coming to a close.

After 1962, the continuation of trade liberalization policies by the United States, therefore, could no longer be attributed quite so strongly to the imperialist perceptions of its leadership and its related concern for the global system as a whole. Instead, continuation rested to a considerable extent on a growing perception in some quarters of the United States that a return to protectionism in world markets would harm their immediate interests. In 1950, U.S. merchandise exports had amounted to only 6.2% of the final sales of U.S. goods. By 1960, the figure had risen to 7.6%. In later years, it was destined to grow to much higher figures—for instance, to 9.1% in 1970 and 19.1% in 1980. Part of the rise, to be sure, could be attributed to the growing export of agricultural products. But with which products excluded from the export totals, the relative importance of the remaining exports still rose rapidly between 1950 and 1980, growing from 4.5% to 12.7% of final sales of U.S. goods.

Most significant of all, perhaps, was the rapid multinationalization of U.S. firms. In 1957, the foreign manufacturing affiliates of firms in the United States had recorded sales amounting to less than 6% of all the country's shipments of manufactured products; but by

1965, the figure was above 9% and in 1976, would rise to 18%.[4]

Of course, firms that develop a multinational structure cannot automatically be counted on to throw their weight against protectionism. Some multinationals prefer open markets for their international operations, especially those that have adopted a strategy of scattering the production of their required components and intermediate products across a number of different countries. Other multinationals, however, rely on high import duties or on other import restrictions to protect their foreign subsidiaries; this is particularly the case, for instance, for subsidiaries that are producing for markets in developing countries. Still, industries that have been most consistently protectionist in outlook, notably textiles and steel, have been dominated by national, not multinational, firms. Moreover, there is some direct evidence that multinational enterprises as a group tend to give greater support to a regime of open world markets than would national firms similarly situated (Hedlund and Otterbeck, 1977: 155-162; Perlmutter, forthcoming).

Nevertheless, despite the growth of multinational enterprises in the U.S. economy, individual industries in increasing number have pushed for some form of special protection for their products. The number of escape clause investigations completed by the U.S. Tariff Commission (now the U.S. International Trade Commission) reflected those increased pressures, rising from two or three per year in the 1960s to twelve in 1976 and thirteen in 1977.[5] The quickened tempo of protectionist efforts appeared also in an increase in petitions to secure countervailing, or antidumping, duties on imports, as well as in the increased number of special trade bills before the Congress.

Despite the growing obstacles, the general direction of U.S. trade policy has been maintained. However, with each renewal of the legislation that authorized the president to alter U.S. tariffs as a result of international negotiations, a succession of ingenious provisions has been added that increases the capacity of interest groups to secure special consideration (Balassa, 1978: 409-436). So far, to be sure, these provisions have not been very effectively exploited. Ironically, foreign exporters and U.S. importers associated with them have been learning how to use the loose-jointed structure of the U.S. government and its elaborate system of checks and balances in their efforts to block the initiatives of the groups seeking import restrictions. One careful study of Latin American disputes over the past fifteen years suggests that more than half of those initiatives have been blocked or substantially compromised (Odell, 1980: 207-228).

Still, domestic industries continue to look for ways to increase their ability to threaten or block foreign imports; indeed, with the enactment of the 1979 Trade Act, so many devices of this sort have been created as to raise serious questions about whether the main lines of United States trade policy can still prevail.

THE POLICIES OF OTHER COUNTRIES

The decline in the leadership position of the United States has left a vacuum. Neither the New International Economic Order of the developing countries, nor the network of trade agreements spawned by the Europeans, nor the growing strength of the Japanese offers much promise of filling the leadership role.

The Developing Countries

Throughout the past three decades, the developing countries of the world have resisted the blueprint for an open world trading system epitomized by the GATT. Instead, the developing countries have been groping for some alternative, so far not very well specified, that would curb the political and economic power of the advanced countries and more fully reflect their own interests.

Nevertheless, because the United States and other advanced industrialized countries saw themselves at first as shaping a world trading system, they were eager to include the developing countries in any global trade organization, even if the commitments of those countries, for the time being, were trivial or nonexistent. Various exemptive clauses in the GATT, when applied in combination, effectively relieved developing countries of any significant trade-liberalizing obligations. In practice, even when a developing country applied discriminatory or restrictive trade measures in obvious violation of the GATT's provisions, no serious efforts were made to enforce the agreement. At the same time, having opted out of their GATT obligations, the developing countries had no real influence over the pace and direction of negotiations in the GATT. Nevertheless, as the advanced industrialized countries progressively reduced their tariffs and other import barriers in successive rounds of negotiations, the nondiscrimination clauses of the GATT served to ensure that the liberalization measures were extended to the developing countries as well (Balassa, 1980).

The developing countries made numerous efforts to generate trade commitments among themselves that would lie alongside the network of GATT commitments. But none of these projects made much of a mark (Business International Corp., 1977; Hazlewood, 1979; Abangwu, 1975; and Ramasaran, 1978). The only trade-liberalizing undertakings sponsored by the developing countries that were successful in any substantial degree were projects that extracted special trade concessions from the advanced industrialized countries (Spero, 1981: 197-216). One such undertaking was the so-called Generalized System of Preferences sponsored by the UN Conference on Trade and Development (UNCTAD).

Still, as industries in the developing countries have grown and matured, some of these countries have shifted their trade policies toward the encouragement of exports. As part of that shift, the early propensity of most of these countries to restrict imports without limit has given way to a more eclectic approach. At the same time, however, the attachment of developing countries to the GATT continues to be tenuous and equivocal, more akin to the role of observers than of committed participants. Accordingly, when developing countries have taken steps toward trade liberalization, these have been the result mainly of their unilateral decisions, not of commitments under the GATT. For the present, there is nothing in the offing to suggest that the developing countries will prove willing to accept new obligations in world trade.

The Europeans

Europe's relationship to the GATT system has always been more ambivalent and reserved than that of the United States. The success of the first few tariff negotiations under the GATT, undertaken soon after the end of World War II, said very little about the real attitudes of Europeans toward trade liberalization. These early negotiations were being conducted at a time when the United States was helping to finance the recovery of Western Europe, and when import licensing, rather than tariffs, was the means by which most European countries controlled imports.

By the early 1960s, however, the European Economic Community had come into existence. Its six original members were in the process of creating the customs union and common agricultural policy that were the core of the arrangement. From that time forward, two things became clear. The European Community would pursue a trade policy that was much more eclectic than that of the United States, highly liberal in some sectors and highly protectionist in others. And in that context, despite the participation of its members in the GATT, it would feel free to deviate from the principle of nondiscrimination to any extent that its interests required.

As far as most European states were concerned, they had little choice during the postwar period but to maintain open borders with respect to a considerable part of their trade. Under the benign influence of the European Recovery Program following World War II, these countries had managed to develop extensive economic ties with one another, reflected in extraordinarily high levels of foreign trade. The eclectic quality in their trade policies, however, stemmed from the fact that their interest in maintaining open borders was based heavily on parochial or regional factors rather than on global considerations.

According to conventional wisdom, the survival of the Community rests mainly on a critical bargain between Germany and France (Curtis, 1965: 23, 194-200; Marjolin, 1981: 36-54). One element in that bargain is an undertaking to create a highly protected area for agricultural products, in deference to France's aspirations to displace North America from the grain markets of Europe; the other is an undertaking to follow a liberal trade policy with respect to manufactured goods, in accordance with Germany's desire to push its products in world markets. That basic element of the original bargain seems to have persisted through the decades of the 1960s and 1970s.

Another set of forces has been operation to keep the European community on a liberal trade course, namely, the intimate linkages of its members to various sets of countries outside the community. The French, for instance, have been eager to maintain close ties to three groups of countries outside the Community: the francophone states that once were French colonies or protectorates, other Mediterranean countries that might fit into the *mare nostrum* strategy that France has been interested in pursuing, and, finally, the oil-exporting countries of the Middle East. The British have had similar interests with regard to some of their own ex-colonies. And both countries, joined by Germany and the Low Countries, have been eager to encourage the peaceful democratic development of the weaker European states, notably, Spain, Portugal, Greece, and Turkey.

The upshot has been that consistency of principle has been much less important in the trade policies of the Community and its member states than in the policies of the United States. The preoccupations of the various EEC member countries have produced some specific responses, such as a national quota, or a preferential bilateral trade agreement, or a multilateral convention with developing countries. When they have decided that it was in their interest to apply restrictions on imports from any source, such as Japan or Korea, they have been quite uninhibited in choosing the form and fixing the level of the restrictions.[6] Not all of the trade measures, however, have been restrictive; some have been trade liberalizing in the sense that they have displaced internal production with the products of their outside trading partners. But throughout, the approach of these countries has been eclectic, without substantial commitment to any overall global policy.

The United States has also been indifferent to its GATT commitments from time to time; but on the whole, it has been more careful than Europe in trying to preserve the forms of adherence to these commitments.[7] Early U.S. efforts to slow down other countries' exports by demanding "voluntary" export restrictions were motivated in part by the desire to avoid a formal breach of the GATT. Moreover, U.S. authorities have generally set such restrictions at levels that were not extraordinarily restraining and have not gone to any great lengths to block some obvious channels for evasion. Although I am not aware of any systematic studies on the point, it is widely assumed that these measures have been substantially less restrictive than those of Europe.

The Japanese

Japan's heavy stake in the maintenance of open competitive markets, coupled with the country's growing economic strength, raises the possibility that Japan might assume a leadership role in protecting what is left of the principles of the GATT. But on closer examination that possibility does not appear very strong. Japan's internal political process inhibits it from taking strong initiatives in the foreign trade field. Even if those internal difficulties could be overcome, other countries would find it hard to accept Japan's leadership in any major initiative involving international trade.

Japan began the postwar era with special economic ties to the United States, a relationship first created during the six years of military occupation immediately following World War II. During the occupation, Japan faithfully played the role of the subjugated state and ward, adopting without protest a series of radical reforms imposed by the conquering state, including redistribution of the land, creation of a labor movement, renunciation of the right to rearm, and "democratization" of political processes.[8] Meanwhile, the relatively benign U.S. attitude toward Japan, which rested at first on complex cultural factors, was strengthened by the advent of the Cold War and by hostilities in Korea.

When the occupation ended, the United States continued to act as Japan's guardian and mentor for a little while longer. By 1952, the United States was sponsoring Japan's membership in various international bodies, notably including the GATT, the International Monetary Fund, and the World Bank. And in 1964, the United States promoted Japan's membership in the Organization for Economic Cooperation and Development (OECD).

Although Japan was admitted into various global organizations in the two decades following the end of the war, a number of countries continued to look on Japan's performance in world markets with special misgivings. In the 1950s, European countries were slow to end their discrimination against Japan's goods, despite Japan's adherence to the GATT (Hanabusa, 1979: 2-3). The U.S. government's pressure on Japan to restrict "voluntarily" the export of some of its textile items is well known.

Japan's early experiences, therefore, were hardly calculated to inspire confidence in the GATT system. At first, Japan's adherence to the GATT did not force any major changes in the country's own trading practices. In 1955, as part of the GATT procedures, Japan agreed to a substantial reduction in its tariff levels; but being in balance-of-payment difficulties at the time, Japan continued for some years thereafter to maintain high import restrictions and to discriminate among its trading partners. It was not until the early 1960s that Japan found itself faced with strong demands from other countries to reduce its restrictions on imports and investments.

As these pressures continued during the 1960s, Japan repeatedly pointed to three factors to justify its policies: the continued vulnerability of its economy deriving from heavy dependence on foreign raw materials and foreign markets, which required a cautions step-by-step approach to world trade; the deliberate nature of Japanese decision making, which required extensive discussion in the bureaucracy and the building of consensus between the bureaucracy, the political parties, and the affected business interests; and, finally, the ineptitude and lack of effort of foreign investors and traders in overcoming the bureaucratic and commercial barriers that remained in Japan (Tasca, 1980: 21-92; Hanabusa, 1979: 16; Japan-United States Economic Relations Group, 1981: 54-69).

Some students of the Japanese economy have stressed other factors that might account for the seeming lack of success of western traders and investors in Japan's economy. Among them was the structure of the Japanese distribution system; for example, wholesalers were often bound to their manufacturers by ties that precluded their switching to foreign sources of supply (Amiaya, 1978; Yoshino, 1975: 39). Another factor was Japan's remarkable capacity for blending public and private initiatives in ways thought to add substantially to the competitive power of the private sector.

The extensive interaction between Japan's public and private sectors has been based on a long-standing national conviction that substantial official guidance is needed to achieve the state's social objectives (MITI, 1971, 1980). That guidance is expressed in much richer and more complex interrelationships than those ordinarily encountered between the two sectors in the West.[9] For instance, under the leadership of the Ministry of International Trade and Industry (MITI), the government is in a position to inspire and support various key projects carried out by private enterprises that affect Japan's position in international trade. It does this through a wide variety of mechanisms: providing seed money for important research and development projects, providing industrial credits on favorable terms through the Japan Industrial Bank and other specialized credit institutions, organizing and financing leasing arrangements to facilitate the sale of new capital goods, organizing and financing buying consortia to reduce the cost of imported products, and, especially where the Japanese purveyors of goods of services are publicly owned enterprises, developing schedules of prices that contribute to the strength of Japan's export industries.

For the most part, the relatively naive provisions of the GATT, largely framed against a background of U.S. trade practices, are practically silent with regard to policies as complex as those pursued by the Japanese. At the same time, it has been evident that any country that can apply such policies with a high degree of efficiency is in an advantageous position in a GATT-regulated world.

By the 1970s, Japan had obviously succeeded, for the time being, in overcoming the obstacles that lay in its way for securing needed raw materials and penetrating foreign markets. Accordingly, the state was gradually becoming convinced that it must support an open competitive market system.[10] Moving at a rate that often seemed maddeningly glacial in the eyes of other governments, Japan formally suspended most of the licensing requirements and other special restrictions that had previously encumbered the importation of foreign goods and the investment of foreign capital.[11] By 1982, the government was engaged in an ambitious process of dredging out some especially resistant practices, such as the use of elaborate inspection schemes, meticulous classification systems, and forbidding health and safety requirements that were serving to block the importation of foreign products (Anonymous, 1982: 6, 10-13).

A considerable debate continues over whether a system of informal restrictions still exists in Japan that tends to reduce the liberalizing effect of the official measures. But there is no doubt that a major change in Japanese practices had in fact occurred. The movement was all the more significant because Japan continued to be the target of discriminatory trade measures, as embodied in "voluntary export agreements" or in overt import quotas on the part of several important countries, including the United States and various European states.

The oil crisis of the past decade has threatened Japan's support for an open trading system but has not reversed it. In light of Japan's perceptions of its special vulnerability with respect to raw materials, its reaction to the oil crisis was bound to be strong and singleminded. In the late 1960s, even before the crisis had surfaced, the Japanese government was already beginning to ask itself whether the country could afford to rely quite so heavily for its crude oil requirements on the foreign-owned multinational oil companies. The oil crises of 1973-1974 and 1978-1979 weakened the position of those companies and gave Japanese refiners the opportunity to deal directly with the state-owned enterprises of the oil-exporting countries (MITI, 1980: 12). This response inevitably has had implications for Japan's more general trade policies, including its adherence to what remains of the GATT system. In an effort to diversify its sources of supply, Japan has been diligently attempting to expand its trade with China and the USSR. Moreover, it has been developing government-to-government arrangements in raw materials with Mexico, Iraq, and other countries. Such arrangements implicitly encourage preferential dealings between the parties concerned.

As in the case of a number of other countries, including France and Germany, Japan thus finds itself in a position of trying to live within two quite distinctive systems of trade. So far, fortunately, the inherent contradiction between the GATT-sponsored system and the system of government-conducted trade has not reached very significant proportions. If it does, the market economies may have to consider jointly how the two systems of trade can be reconciled; otherwise, what is left of the principle of nondiscrimination in trade will be imperiled.

In any future negotiations over the direction of the world trading system, Japan is likely to support the continuation of an open trading regime, fearing that any other regime would make it the target for more flagrant discriminatory measures. But Japan's concern with the vulnerability of its economy will inhibit it from making strong commitments in any direction and hence limit its capacity to play a leadership role. At the same time, however, Japan is likely to be less passive and acquiescent in multilateral negotiations than it has been in, the past (MITI, 1980). In recent years, some Japanese commentators have questioned whether Japan should continue to follow a "tradesman's policy," that is to say, a policy of accommodating to all economic pressures without responding to any principles other than survival itself (Amaya, 1980; Sase, 1980; Nukazawa, 1980). These discussions may eventually bring Japan's role in the shaping of new international regime more into line with her economic power.[12] But for the time being, they will not overcome Japan's deep-seated sense of caution when approaching issues of international trade.

FUTURE POLICIES

Starting Assumptions

Robert Marjolin, looking back on thirty years of the evolution of Europe's Common Market, said sadly, "The time for grand designs is over, at least for a while, until circumstances change and the existing order is shaken again" (1980: 77). His observation could apply to trade policies on a global scale as well. For the present, one can only hope to protect and conserve some of the extraordinary openness in international markets that has been achieved in the past three decades. Even to achieve this modest objective, however, will be difficult.

One change that may support the objective is the great increase in the importance of foreign trade and foreign investment interests in the economies of most countries. But it will be imperiled by many countries' increased determination to reduce the impact that the increasing openness of their economies has generated and to limit the rate of adjustment demanded of their industries. In addition, there has been a change in the nature of existing barriers to trade, from relatively transparent tariffs and quotas to less visible subsidies, administrative practices, and procurement policies. Finally, there has been a weakening in the concept of unconditional most-favored-nation treatment as the norm for international trade. I assume these trends will not be reversed in the 1980s; therefore, they should be viewed as constraints in the formulation of policy for this period.

I make one other critical assumption based on the history outlined earlier. Both the United States and Japan require the action-forcing discipline of a prospective international negotiation in order to maintain an open trading system. Such pressures seem needed to focus the diverse elements in each country on a general policy that transcends narrower group interests. Otherwise, the internal political process in the United States will generate restrictive measures in response to those narrower interests, while the internal process of Japan will produce near immobility.

With these starting assumptions, policymakers in the United States and elsewhere will have to address a series of linked questions: If the content of the global trade agreements of the past no longer suffices, what is the direction in which new agreements should move? If the most-favored-nation principle is losing its force, what is to take its place? And, if the United States is no longer in a position to assert its leadership in the formulation of global trade proposals, what kind of process can be envisaged that will produce such proposals?

Scope and Substance

The direction in which global trade agreements are heading became fairly obvious in the last giant negotiating session of the GATT, the so-called Multilateral Trade Negotiations (MTN) that were completed in Geneva in 1979. With tariffs reduced to tolerable levels, the ascendant problems in the 1970s included the proliferation of public subsidies in all their obvious and subtle forms: governments' demands on selected enterprises (usually foreign owned) in their territories that the enterprises should limit their imports and increase their exports, the procurement practices of state entities, and the unilateral application of quotas by importing countries.

These problems have proven much more varied, much less transparent, and much more deeply embedded in domestic programs than the fixing of tariff rates.[13] Accordingly, both the formulation and the enforcement of agreements in these fields are much more difficult than agreements to freeze or reduce existing tariff rates. They demand more trust among the contracting parties and a better fact-finding, conciliating, and adjudicating apparatus than the 100-member GATT can be expected to provide. Not surprisingly, therefore, it has proved impossible to reach agreement on some of these subjects in the GATT context.

Even with appropriate sponsorship, one can anticipate only a limited number of countries reaching agreement on these difficult subjects. The complexity of these areas is illustrated by the supplemental negotiations that became necessary to implement the 1979 Geneva agreement on governmental procurement. Although the agreement was limited, in the first instance, to a small number of countries, Japan and the United States nevertheless found it necessary to elaborate the agreement in much greater detail for its application between them (Yoshino, 1981: 75-77). Until many other governments widen the circle by joining in—a most unlikely development—the government procurement code establishes preferential rights within a small group of countries.

The question raised by this illustration is whether or not we have reached a point at which selective discrimination may generate more open international markets than the rule of nondiscrimination could produce. In some circumstances, as the rules of the GATT recognize, this may well be the case. GATT's tolerance of customs unions, free trade areas, and similar preferential arrangements acknowledge this point; although arrangements of this sort sometimes have the effect of diverting trade from efficient outside sources to less efficient inside sources, they are justified since they reduce the level of protection among the participants themselves.

Understandably, however, some members of the GATT, including Japan and the United States, have resisted the possibility of a more uninhibited recognition of the right of GATT members to apply discriminatory trade measures, especially when these are clearly restrictive.[14] The reasons for American and Japanese hesitation are fairly evident. Even though the United States has violated the rule of nondiscrimination from time to time, it has had trouble envisaging a coherent world trading system without such a rule. From the Japanese viewpoint, the danger of legitimizing restrictive preferences and discrimination in international trade lies in Japan's risk of being the first victim. But both these arguments have been losing their force as preferential arrangements have been proliferating under other names. In a world of second-best choices, international agreements based on the principle of nondiscrimination may no longer be possible on any significant scale; the question then is whether or not international agreements with preferential provisions can be made to produce results that are superior to inaction.

The possibilities for using preferential agreements as action-forcing occasions for trade liberalization are illustrated by the various liberalizing codes that were adopted in the 1979 GATT agreements. But the possibilities are illustrated also by the 1981 imbroglio over Japanese exports of automobiles to the United States. Predictably, the preference of the United States has been to cheat on the GATT's rule of nondiscrimination by forcing Japan to restrain "voluntarily" its exports to the U.S. market. If, instead, the U.S. restrictions on Japanese cars were forthrightly acknowledged, there would also be the possibility of acknowledging Japan's right to preferential compensation. For instance, one could envisage a bilateral agreement between the United States and Japan that imposed a temporary restraint on U.S. imports of Japanese cars but that was offset by a temporary preference in the importation of other Japanese manufactured products.

The introduction of extensive preferential provisions in bilateral and multilateral trade agreements among the advanced industrialized countries in the GATT would force a reexamination of various other aspects of the GATT structure, including the smoldering issue of "graduation." This is the question of whether or not the "newly industrializing countries" of the GATT, such as Brazil, India, and Korea, should now be obliged to assume some of the agreement's obligations in addition to being entitled to its rights (Frank, 1979). It is worth noting that if any group of GATT countries enters into preferential agreements that the developing countries chose not to join, the developing countries will find themselves disadvantaged in the first instance. At the same time, however, if preferential agreements were more widely legitimated, Brazil might still hope for access to the markets of the advanced countries through bilateral agreements. For example, if Brazil failed to adhere to a GATT code, the United States might still exchange equivalent rights and obligations with Brazil in a bilateral agreement.

There should be no illusions about the pattern of trade relations that would emerge from agreements of the sort just described. At times, preferential measures that are liberalizing in nature can be made to endure for a while: Witness the twenty-year record of the European Economic Community. But by and large, preferential measures of trade liberalization that are based on agreements among a limited group of countries risk being restrictive. All that can be said in favor of such measures is that they are superior to the alternative, when the alternative appears to be unilateral measures of restriction. Eventually, a return to a global approach in the development of international trade relations will be indispensable. Meanwhile, the problem is to stem or reverse the threat that inertia, accompanied by piecemeal measures of restriction imposed unilaterally by individual countries, may sharply reduce the openness of international markets.

THE INSTITUTIONAL CHALLENGE

The proposals sketched out above have some profound implications for the U.S. approach to international negotiations on trade matters. One important question is how to keep the GATT itself from moldering away, once the decline of the nondiscrimination principle is so explicitly recognized. Even with that critical principle in eclipse, the GATT organization would still have major importance by performing some of its traditional functions. It could continue, for example, to provide a forum in which quarreling countries could let off steam over their unsettled trade disputes and could bring in third parties to help compromise such disputes. And it could provide a ready-made structure for launching large trade initiatives once the time was ripe again for moves of that sort.

Another major issue is internal, namely, the question of the relationship between Congress and the executive branch in negotiating new trade agreements. Even more than in the past, U.S. participation in any international agreement will depend on the willingness of Congress to make the necessary changes in the country's legislation. Some of these changes will consist of amendments to existing trade legislation, which in its present form grants paralyzing powers of litigation and appeal to special interest groups. Other changes will involve new legislation bearing on subsidies, procurement, and other matters.

The needed response, in this instance, is already suggested by experience. In grappling with this same problem, the Trade Act of 1974 incorporated an approach that responded realistically to the existing distribution of powers. In an innovation that was almost revolutionary in nature, ten members of Congress were included as official advisers on a U.S. team charged with the negotiating trade agreements. In return, Congress agreed at the outset to tie its own hands in the procedures to be followed when ratifying any subsequent agreement. Congressional deliberations were to be completed within sixty days after receiving the agreements, and substantive amendments to the agreements were the barred.[15] Since questions of trade policy are inseparable from those of domestic policy, such an explicit sharing of power between Congress and the executive branch seems inescapable.

Equally important is the relationship of the U.S. government to special interest groups that influence trade legislation. Until a few years ago, hundreds of trade association staffs that inhabited the corridors of Washington's Capitol Hill confined their activities almost entirely to attempting to block imports. The promotion of exports first became an issue as the result of a provision of the 1974 trade Act, which authorized the president to retaliate against foreign governments that imposed "unjustifiable or unreasonable" barriers against United States exports (sec. 301). It would be a small added step for these interest groups to widen their export-promoting activities; instead of limiting themselves to acting as watchdogs over the "unjustifiable and unreasonable" provision and other restrictive provisions of U.S. legislation, they might conceivably become the galvanizing force for new initiatives to negotiate for the reduction of barriers to U.S. exports. Given the increased importance of exports for the U.S. economy, perhaps that change in perspective can be achieved.

From the U.S. viewpoint, the changes in policy and practice that are proposed here are fairly considerable. The probability that such changes can be achieved is not high, but the alternative is sufficiently threatening to national interests to justify the effort.

Notes

[1] The behavior of business and labor organizations in this period deserves extended analysis that space limitations prevent. In both cases, the leadership for a time took positions that were measurably different from those of their rank and file.

[2] Historians have observed the striking similarities between the U.S. position during this postwar interlude and the position of the United Kingdom a century earlier (see Semmel, 1970; also Smith, 1981).

[3] The paternalistic attitudes of the U.S. leadership, as well as the early signs of an unraveling of the consensus, are reflected vividly in Commission on Foreign Economic Policy (1954).

[4] Calculated from various published studies of the U.S. Department of Commerce. For evidence of the link between multinational structure and international transactions see Vernon (1971: 16).

[5] From annual reports of the U.S. Tariff Commission and the U.S. International Trade Commission.

[6] for a description of measures taken in the 1950s and early 1960s, see GATT (1966: 79-84). For later periods, see Hanabusa (1979: 3).

[7] For a revealing indication of important if sometimes subtle differences in the approaches to the Europeans and the United States, see Perlow (1981: 93-133).

[8] The strong cultural factors that allowed the United States and Japan comfortably to assume their respective roles are nicely summarized in Destler (1976: 114-119).

[9] For illustrations of the depth and complexity of these relationships, see Johnson (1978: 125-133) and Caldwell (1981).

[10] Numerous studies exist on trade disputes between Japan and other countries, analyzing such disputes from the differing viewpoints of the various disputants. In addition to Tasca (1980) and Hanabusa

(1979), see, for instance, Weil and Glick (1979) and U.S. Controller-General (1980).

[11] The relatively unrestrictive character of Japan's formal system of trade restrictions is suggested by data in Cao (1980: 97).

[12] Illustrations of the new quality of Japanese participation in global economic issues are found, for instance, in numerous documents of the Tripartite Commission, and in the Wise Men's Report, cited above, where Japanese contributors have been increasingly explicit in their stated preferences. See also Hosomi (1978) and Tanaka (1980).

[13] For a description of export credit programs illustrative for these points, see *The Economist* (1981: 78).

[14] The question has been debated repeatedly in the GATT and was the center of an inconclusive negotiation in the recently completed MTN agreements. See Merciai (1981).

[15] "Trade Act of 1974," Public Law 93-618, 93d Cong., H.R. 10710, January 1975. See also Winham (1979).

References

ABANGWU, G.C. (1975) "Systems approach to regional integration." J. of Common Market Studies 13, 1/2: 116-133.

ALFORD, R.A. (1973) Party and Society: The Anglo-American Democracies. Chicago: Rand McNally.

AMAYA, N. (1980) "Grumblings of a shop-clerk of Japan, a tradesman's country." Translated from Bungei Shunju (March).

— (1978) "Japan's system of distribution under scrutiny." World Economy 1 (April): 219-326.

Anonymous (1982) "Government making all-out effort to remove non-tariff barriers." J. of Japanese Trade and Industry 1, 2.

BALASSA, B. (1980) "The Tokyo Round and the developing countries." World Bank Staff Working Paper No. 370. Washington, DC: World Bank.

— (1978) "The 'new protectionism' and the international economy." J. of World Trade Law 12: 409-436.

Business International Corp. (1977) Operating in Latin America's Integrating Markets: ANCOM, CACM, CARICOM, LAFTA. New York: BIC.

CALDWELL, M.A. (1981) "Petroleum politics in Japan: state and industry in a changing political context." Ph.D. Dissertation, University of Wisconsin. Ann Arbor, MI: University Microfilms.

CAO, A. D. (1980) "Non-tariff barriers to U.S. manufactured exports." Columbia J. of World Business 15 (Summer): 93-102.

CHAMBERS, W. N. (1966) "Parties and nation building in America," in J. LaPalombara and M. Weiner (eds.) Political Parties and Political Development. Princeton: Princeton Univ. Press.

Commission on Economic Foreign Policy (1954) Report to the President and the Congress. Washington, DC: Government Printing Office.

CURTIS, M. (1965) Western European Integration. New York: Harper & Row.

DESTLER, I. M. [ed.] (1976) Managing on Alliance. Washington, DC: Brookings Institution.

The Economist (1981) "The high cost of export credit." (February 14): 78

EPSTEIN, L. D. (1967) Political Parties in Western Democracies. New York: Praeger.

FRAN K, I. (1979) "The 'graduation' issue for IDCs." J. of World Trade Law 13: 289-302.

GATT (1966) A Study of Cotton Textiles. Geneva: GATT (March).

GILMORE, R. (1982) "The congressional veto: typing down the executive branch." J. of Policy Analysis and Management 2 (Fall).

GREEN, C. J. (1980) "Legal protectionism in the United States and United States-Japan economic relations." Report to the Advisory Group on United States-Japan Economic Relations (July). (unpublished)

HALPERIN, M. M. (1974) Bureaucratic Politics and Foreign Policy. Washington, DC: Brookings Institution.

HANABUSA, M. (1979) Trade Problems Between Japan and Western Europe. New York: Praeger.

HAZLEWOOD, A. (1979) "The end of East African community: what are the lessons for regional integration schemes?" Common Market Studies 18 September: 40-58.

HECLO, H. (1977) A Government of Strangers: Executive Politics in Washington. Washington, DC: Brookings Institution.

HEDLUND, G. and OTTERBECK, L. (1977) The Multinational Corporation, the Nation-State and Trade Unions: A European Perspective. Kent, OH: Kent Univ. Press.

HOSOMI, T. (1978) "Japan's changing perception of her role in the world economy." World Economy 1 January: 135-148.

JACOBY, H. (1973) The Bureaucratization of the World." Berkeley: University of California Press.

Japan-U.S. Economic Relations Group (1981) Report (The Wise Men's Report"). Tokyo and Washington, D.C. (January).

JOHNSON, C. (1978) Japan's Public Policy Companies. Washington, DC: AEI.

KINDLEBERGER, C. P. (1950) The Dollar Shortage. New York: John Wiley.

KRASNER, S. D. (1978) Defending the National Interest. Princeton: Princeton Univ. Press.

LEFEBER, W. (1963) The New Empire: An Interpretation of American Expansion 1860 1898. Ithaca, NY: Cornell Univ. Press.

MARJOLIN, R. (1981) "Europe in search of its identity," in Council Papers on International Affairs. New York: Council on Foreign Relations.

MARKS, M. J. (1978) "Remedies to 'unfair' trade." World Economy I (January): 223 236.

MERCIAI, P. (1981) "Safeguard measures in GATT." J. of World Trade Law 15 (January-February): 41-66.

Ministry of International Trade and Industry [MITI] (1988) "The vision of MITI policies in the 1980s." March 18. MITI Information Service.

— (1971) "Trade and industrial policies for the 1970s: a report by the industry Structure Council." MITI Information Service.

New York Times (1930) ". . . 1028 Economists Ask Hoover to Veto Pending Tariff Bill." (May 5): 1.

NUKAZAWA, K. (1980) "Whither Japan's foreign economic policy? Straws in the wind." World Economy 1 (February): 467-480.

ODELL, J. S. (1980) "Latin American trade negotiations with the U.S." Int. Organization 34 (Spring): 207-228.

PASTOR, R. A. (1980) Congress and the Politics of United States Foreign Policy 1929-1976. Berkeley: Univ. of California Press.

PERLMUTTER, H. V. (forthcoming) "The multinational firm and the future." Annals of the American Academy of Political and Social Sciences.

PERLOW, G. H. (1981) "The multilateral supervision of international trade: has the textiles experiment worked?" Amer. J. of Int. Law 75: 93-133.

RAMSARAN, R. (1978) "CARICOM: The Integration Process in Crisis." J. of World Trade Law 12, 3: 208-217.

SALANT, W. (1980) "The collected writings of John Maynard Keynes." J. of Economic Literature 18, 3: 1056-1062.

SASE, M. (1980) "Rejection of 'tradesman's nation' argument." Translated from Bungei Shunju (April).

SEMMEL, B. (1970) The Rise of Free Trade Imperialism. Cambridge: Cambridge Univ. Press.

SMITH, T. (1981) The Pattern of Imperialism. New York: Cambridge Univ. Press.

SPERO, J. (1981) The Politics of International Economic Relations. New York: St. Martin's.

TANAKA, N. (1980) "The increasingly complex Japan-U.S. relationship." Econ Eye 1 (September): 23-25.

TASCA, D. [ed.] (1980) U.S.-Japanese Economic Relations: Cooperation, Competition. and Confrontation. Elmsford, NY: Pergamon.

U.S. Comptroller General (1980) "U.S.-Japan trade: issues and problems." Report of the Comptroller General of the United States, September 20. Washington, DC: General Accounting Office.

U.S. Department of Commerce (1955) Business Statistics 1955. Washington, DC: Government Printing Office.

U.S. Office of the President (1981) Economic Report of the President. Washington, DC: Government Printing Office.

VERNON, R. (1971) Sovereignty at Bay. New York: Basic Books.

WEIL, F. A. and N. D. GLICK (1979) "Japan—is the market open?" Law and Policy in Int. Business 11, 3: 894-902.

WINHAM, G. R. (1979) "Robert Strauss, the MIN, and the control of factions." Presented at the 75th Meeting of the American Political Science Association (August/September).

YOSHIMINE, T. (1981) "Settlement finally reached for NTT procurement issue." Business Japan 3: 75-77.

YOSHINO, M. (1975) Marketing in Japan: A Management Guide. New York: Praeger.

International Commodity Policy in the UN System: Two Decades of Experience

Alex Ashiabor

The Pre-UNCTAD Period

International trade in primary commodities has been a subject of concern to governments since colonial times. However, it was not until the early decades of this century that efforts to evolve an international policy among governments on a cooperative basis began to receive serious attention. Early attempts at international cooperation in trade in primary products included the World Economic Conference in Geneva in 1927, which recommended in its Final Report, among other things, the establishment of international commodity agreements (ICAs) whose object was limited to rationalisation of production and reduction of costs, and the more efficient use of existing equipment [Gordon-Ashworth 1984].

Subsequently, against a background of deepening crisis, declining world trade and a collapse in commodity prices, a sub-committee of the League of Nations Monetary and Economic Conference meeting in London in 1932 and 1933 addressed the question of ICAs as a potential solution to the commodity price crisis. It recommended that their main object should be to attenuate excessive price fluctuations and improve the incomes of producers by raising the export prices of commodities to "reasonable" and "fair and remunerative" levels. The appropriate price levels were to be determined by International Commodity Organisations (ICOs) consisting of consumers and producers, and strong domestic measures were to be used to support the international agreements. Even at this early stage, stock control or quota systems and buffer stocks were regarded as essential instruments to regulate periodic instabilities in international commodity trade.

These budding ideas for widespread cooperation in trade in primary commodities fell casualty to the overall collapse of international cooperation and the beggar-my-neighbour policies of the inter-war years. Only a few ICAs were established (for tin, wheat, tea, sugar and rubber). Second World War brought renewed interest. Two dimensions to international commodity policy emerged during this period. The first was the conclusion by the 1943 United Nations Conference on Food and Agriculture that ICAs were a suitable means of promoting world economic growth. This conclusion clearly linked international action in the area of trade in primary commodities with development.

The second was the concept of a unified approach to international commodity price stabilisation advocated by Keynes (1974).[1] Influenced by conditions which prevailed in 1919-20 and opposed to the producer cartels and ICAs of the 1930s, he proposed a comprehensive plan for international action over a range of commodities, to be administered by a general

Originally published in the *IDS Bulletin*, vol. 15, no. 3, 1984. Reprinted with permission.

council for commodity controls on which producers and consumers would be equally represented. Buffer stocks managed by the general council would be financed by an "international clearing union". The case for the use of internationally financed buffer stocks rested on Keynes' perceived divergence of private and public interest in holding stocks for long periods for the purpose of stabilising commodity prices. These proposals were in essence the same as the Common Fund which was eventually included as an essential part of UNCTAD's Integrated Programme for Commodities (IPC), 30 years later.

Even before the end of the Second World War, governments were expressing interest in international commodity regulation, and references in the Atlantic Charter of 1941 and the UN Charter of 1945 are evidence of this. The Havana Conference of 1947-48 led to the Havana Charter, which recommended inter alia the formation of an International Trade Organisation. Although the Charter disapproved of restrictive practices and cartels of any kind, it recognised that ICAs could be employed to stabilise prices around trend, ensure reasonable and stable incomes for producers and correct adverse situations resulting from "burdensome surpluses". Since international measures of commodity control were to be the exception rather than the rule, it was provided that ICAs should run for not more than five years, to allow periodic reviews at the end of the life of each agreement. Also, to avoid cartelisation, producers and consumers were to be represented on an equal basis.

Establishment of UNCTAD

For various reasons the International Trade Organisation (ITO) as proposed in the Havana Charter was never established [Brown 1980:5]. In the United States for instance, protectionists and firms, especially the large oil companies, opposed it for fear that they might become targets of international scrutiny. In its absence, the Economic and Social Council of the UN (ECOSOC) established in 1947 an Interim Coordination Committee for International Commodity Agreements (ICCICA) to coordinate international efforts towards establishing commodity control schemes along the principles of the Charter. Although a number of commodity stabilisation agreements -for coffee, sugar, tin and wheat — were concluded under the aegis of the ICCICA, the machinery was inadequate. Pressure in the General Assembly in response to these and other failures of the existing international institutional machinery led to the creation of UNCTAD in 1964. The General Assembly transferred, among other things, the functions of the ICCICA to UNCTAD which was mandated as the agency within the UN system responsible for formulating international commodity policy, including ICAs.

The Early Years

From the inter-war years to the early post-Second World War period, the main elements of international policy on commodity trade and development had been enunciated in various forums, albeit in an uncoordinated way. Dr Prebisch's report to UNCTAD I as its first Secretary-General [UNCTAD 1964] was an important milestone. In his report Prebisch not only established the links between trade in primary commodities and development, but also provided a theoretical framework (in its essentials the same as the views put forward simultaneously elsewhere by Hans Singer).[2] He argued, contrary to the conventional wisdom of the time, that there was not only a tendency for the terms of trade of primary products to deteriorate vis-à-vis manufactured products, but that this phenomenon was due to inherent structural differences between the economies of the developing and the developed countries. He also observed that technological innovation was an important factor in extending the frontiers of diminishing returns and *per capita* productivity beyond the constraints recognised by earlier theorists. This could of course apply to both primary and manufactured products. The significant difference is that the strong bargaining power of labour in the industrialised countries, which predominantly produce manufactured goods, leads a greater share of the increase in productivity in manufacturing industry than in primary production to be appropriated by labour. In the labour surplus primary product-based economies of developing countries, the bargaining power of unions is weak and producers fail to influence the market. Consequently, the benefits of increased productivity are passed on to the consumer in developed countries in the form of lower export prices. The tendency towards inferior terms of trade for primary commodities is further perpetuated by two factors. On the supply side, if the market clearing process tends to raise prices, excess supplies of labour are attracted to the sector to increase production, thereby further depressing the price. On the demand side, low income elasticities of demand for many primary products are an important contributory factor. The Prebisch-Singer argument, with refinements and additions from others (especially Lewis 1953] was a major breakthrough in the analysis of these relationships [Spraos 1982]. It provided the basis for proposals for structural diversification of productive capacities through increased processing of primary products in developing countries and enhanced access of those products to the markets of the developed countries.

The period between UNCTAD I and UNCTAD IV (1964-76) was a difficult one. The final act UNCTAD I outlined a set of new principles and a global framework for development, but the developed market economy countries expressed reservations on a number of critical issues. Twelve countries opposed the recommendation on price stabilisation agreements for primary commodities, while most others abstained. A large number abstained from a recommendation to developed countries to modify their price support policies for primary production, and the United States opposed recommendations on disposal of stocks of primary commodities held by developed countries.

At UNCTAD II, held at New Delhi in 1968, discussion was focussed on a comprehensive analysis of the commodity problem presented by the UNCTAD secretariat [UNCTAD 1968a]. The Conference agreed that the difficulties faced by some 19 problem commodities should be considered in the relevant specialised bodies.[3]

However, by the time of UNCTAD III, held at Santiago de Chile in 1972, no noticeable progress had been achieved in these fora. It is significant to note, however, that the Conference entrusted an important role to the World Bank to support price stabilisation agreements in certain commodities in accordance with previously accepted principles. Specifically, the Conference recommended that the World Bank make price stabilisation an object of its loan policies and encourage the conclusion of such agreements, give priority in its lending policy to agro-industrial projects and promote local processing. The Bank was also requested to pay particular attention to the implications of loan proposals submitted to it in the light of their effects on export earnings and their implications for the terms of trade of the country concerned. It was urged further to provide direct financing to international agencies whose object was to stabilise prices of raw materials in accordance with the provisions of the individual ICAs, particularly where prefinancing, stabilisation over the long-term and direct assistance for diversification, adjustment or improvement of production was required. There is little evidence that the World Bank took any serious notice of this recommendation. What would have been an important step forward in providing substantive support for international commodity policy through appropriate lending by the World Bank was thus successfully blocked. On the contrary, international financial institutions and bilateral donors proceeded to encourage supply expansion of primary products, thereby contributing to the current conditions of structural over-supply in some commodities [de Silva 1983].

The Integrated Programme for Commodities

The next stage in the evolution of UNCTAD commodity policy is set against the background of the emergence of OPEC in 1973 as a major determinant in international economic relations and the adoption by the United Nations of the principles of the New International Economic Order (NIEO). At UNCTAD IV in 1976 the Integrated Programme for Commodities was launched. This new approach, while recognising the importance of dealing with specific problems of commodities on a case-by-case basis, brought into sharper focus the common difficulties facing all commodities and in which all developing countries exporting primary commodities had a common interest. It sought to depart from the fragmented approach of the past and to present problems of international commodity trade and development within an integrated framework of problems, principles, objectives and instruments. Commodity problems were thus presented as a single complex whole, affecting the interests of all developing and developed countries and transcending the specific trading problems of individual commodities.

The Integrated Programme included a number of elements which fall into two broad groups: those directed towards reducing the short-term instability of commodity markets, and those concerned with improving the longer-term structures of those markets. The short-term problem was to be tackled by a dual set of negotiations. First, it had been agreed at UNCTAD IV to enter into negotiations for the establishment of a Common Fund to finance international buffer stocks, or internationally coordinated national stocks, within the framework of international commodity agreements. Second, negotiations were to be launched on a wide range of commodities in order to establish new commodity agreements designed to reduce market instability. These two elements were closely interrelated, since it was envisaged that the Common Fund, by providing as assured source of finance, would act as a catalyst in promoting the speedy conclusion of commodity agreements.

The Common Fund

The nature, structure and method of operation of the proposed Common Fund came under intensive discussion in the four years of negotiation which followed the UNCTAD IV resolution. A major difference of viewpoint emerged concerning the nature and type of finance to be provided by the Fund. The developing countries pressed for a strong financial institution with adequate resources so that it could discharge its functions effectively. On this view (the "source of finance" model), the Fund would be the sole, or the main, source of finance for buffer stock operations. The Fund's resources would come from government contributions and from government-guaranteed loans. This would provide a strong capital base, maximise its credit rating for borrowing, and encourage the establishment of price-stabilising commodity agreements. Reservations were, however, expressed by some governments on the size of contributions.

The developed countries, on the other hand, discouraged the idea of a strong Common Fund, not only because of the size of direct contributions, but also because of their traditional aversion to intervention in the international commodity markets. They proposed instead that the Common Fund should be financed by deposits of surplus cash balances held by individual International Commodity Organisations (ICOs), the latter continuing to be responsible for their own financial requirements (the "pool of finance" model). Though this proposal involves a lower incidence on governments as sources of finance, it offers no particular advantage to ICOs, and thus could not be expected to have the catalytic effect that had originally been envisaged. Moreover, commodities not amenable to stocking would be denied assistance, whereas a Fund with its own resources would be capable of market intervention in emergency situations.

After prolonged negotiations, an agreement was reached in June 1980 establishing a Common Fund, essentially on the "pool of finance" model. In addition to assisting ICOs in financing buffer stock operations (the First Account), the Fund is also empowered to help finance longer-term development in the commodities field (through its Second Account), a function which had not been envisaged in the original concept.

As a response to the call for structural change, there was a novel attempt in the design of the voting structure of the new Common Fund to shift the dominant voting power of the developed market economy countries in favour of the developing countries. The latter have been in a disadvantaged position on the policy boards of the Bretton Woods institutions. It was felt that the Common Fund should depart from the existing form, creating for the first time a financial institution in which developing countries would have a major voice.

Though the final provisions remain a far cry from the original proposals, the agreement represents an important new instrument of international commodity policy. For the first time the international community has agreed to establish a financial institution specifically designed to promote trade in primary commodities, and to serve the interests of the developing countries in particular. There is some reservation among countries, however, that the Common Fund may not be very effective because of the heavy dilution of the original concept during negotiations. Those who argue this way point to the reduced capital, and the later tendencies to place greater emphasis on developmental measures as against buffer stock financing, which was the original purpose. On the other hand, the Common Fund must be viewed as an organic institution capable of adapting to an evolving environment. The dramatic changes in the capital resources of the IBRD and IDA and evolution of policy in the IMF are a source of encouragement. There is no reason why the Common Fund, when it comes into operation, should not expand its resources as and when considered necessary by its member states.

Individual Commodity Negotiations

Though consultations and negotiations on the need for price-stabilising agreements on a wide range of commodities have been in progress since UNCTAD IV, results have been generally disappointing. Only one new price-stabilising agreement, for natural rubber, has been negotiated, while two additional agreements, for jute and tropical timber, do not include price-stabilisation provisions. Many factors are involved in this slow progress. The fact that the Common Fund is not yet operational may well have acted as a disincentive. Then there are the inevitable conflicts of perceived interest between exporters and importers about price ranges, and among exporters about market shares. There is also the underlying problem, mentioned earlier, of the aversion of the developed countries to market intervention. But the failures of the international community to provide a "safety net" for commodity price support has already had drastically adverse consequences for developing countries heavily dependent on commodity exports.

The Proposal for a Compensatory Financing Facility

One other complementary element of the IPC consists of proposals on compensatory financing for developing countries suffering export earnings shortfalls. This idea is not new. The Secretariat's analysis at UNCTAD II[4] had shown the effects of short-term price fluctuations on export earnings and economic growth, on the incomes of individual producers in producing countries, and on the longer-term growth of demand and supply of the commodities concerned. Also, an instrument directed towards price stabilisation will not necessarily always or fully obviate the need for earnings stabilisation. For instance, sudden changes in supply conditions — say, a bumper crop or a drought — can cause serious fluctuations in export earnings. To attack the negative effects of export earnings instability, such as the disruptions to mechanisms for economic development planning, debt servicing capacity, external borrowing programmes or credit ratings of developing countries, erratic investment responses which in turn could exacerbate instability in the future, a programme of export earnings compensation measures was proposed as a major element of the IPC, additional to the existing Compensatory Financing Facility of the IMF and the EEC's STABEX scheme. Although the IMF's compensatory financing and buffer stock financing facilities have some general commodity orientation, they are predicated on balance of payments needs, and do not address the problems of the commodity sector as a central object of policy. The STABEX facility attempted to meet this void but also lacks the integrated policy approach. The UNCTAD proposal attempts to fill this gap in the two facilities through a commodity-specific compensatory financing facility with a commodity focus and an integrated approach. This is particularly important for commodities where long-term structural problems are indicated.

This issue, first articulated in Nairobi, was further expanded at UNCTAD V, held in Manila in 1979, but was received with extreme suspicion by the developed countries. Some member countries felt the proposal went beyond UNCTAD's basic mandate, straying, as it were, into the IMF's territory. After further intensive negotiations at UNCTAD VI, the developed countries grudgingly agreed that an expert group be set up by the Secretary-General of UNCTAD to study the need for such a facility and, without prejudice to any final outcome, make proposals on it, taking into account, amongst other things, existing facilities.

Processing, Marketing and Distribution

The second complementary element of the IPC relates to proposals on processing, marketing and distribution of primary products of developing countries. To respond to the problem of the secular decline in demand for primary commodities, the IPC called for a programme to support the efforts of developing countries in the increased processing of their products. This was to be supported by efforts to remove barriers to the access of developing countries' processed commodities to developed country markets as well as to increase their share in the distribution and marketing of these products. These latter aspects of the IPC were further elaborated at UNCTAD V. This approach is seen not only as a means of promoting structural change in developing countries but also of countering both the long-term decline in the global significance of primary commodities in international trade and the highly organised control by transnational corporations over the channels of distribution of primary products in their processed or unprocessed forms.

The proposal caused considerable concern among the developed market-economy countries. Moreover, the international economic environment of 1980-82 was not the most ideal for demands on developed countries to reduce or restrain productive capacity in certain products in favour of similar ones from developing countries. Even more difficult to accommodate at this time was the demand that investment in productive capacity in the processing of certain commodities should be diverted from developed to developing countries. But this is not to deny that the proposal has some basic merits. It is only to say that the merits are not as self-evident to the developed countries as the presentation so far seems to suggest.

Typically, the developed countries have resisted attempts by the developing countries to move the proposals to the negotiating stage, calling again for a commodity-by-commodity approach, arguing that the problems differed for each commodity. The developing countries, while acknowledging this, insisted nevertheless that the problems of increased processing and barriers to markets were common to many commodities. As a compromise, the UNCTAD Secretariat was again requested to elaborate the elements of the frameworks for cooperation in processing, marketing and distribution of processed and semi-processed commodities from the developing countries.[5]

A Missing Link: self-reliance and domestic policies

The NIEO principle of self-reliance has been interpreted as group self-reliance, and has, therefore, been dealt with in the context of the South-South debate or within the context of regional groupings and programmes such as the Lagos Plan of Action and the Caracas Programme. Discussions on international commodity policy and its relationship to development have avoided the issue of domestic policies, even in relation to commodities. One reason for this is that domestic policy is seen as the sovereign prerogative of states and as an inappropriate subject of international discussion or negotiation. A second reason is the fear that this approach might be used to influence the chosen socioeconomic systems of sovereign states. This latter point is a particularly sensitive one.

Granted that countries should retain the sovereign right to determine their own systems, it is not at all clear that by discussing domestic policies one will necessarily always seek to change the basic system. Such influences, if they occur, should be resisted if judged by the sovereign authorities to be undesirable. On the other hand, one cannot deny that domestic policies should be directed in such a way as not to frustrate the aims of international commodity policy. Questions of consistency between overall domestic policy and sectoral or global policies on commodities in structural over-supply and access to markets of developed countries are not issues which can easily be set aside. Besides, by avoiding a discussion, the opportunity is lost for proposing alternative policy options to some of those currently offered.

Conclusion

In their efforts to achieve structural change through increased processing, marketing and distribution of their primary products, domestic policies provide an important policy environment which can contribute in an important way to their success or failure. A major dimension could be added to the evolutionary process with the acceptance of suitable domestic policies as an essential underpinning for the various elements of the IPC.

References

Brown. C. P., 1980. *The Political and Social Economy of Commodity Control*, Macmillan, London
de Silva. L., 1983, "Commodity export policy and technical assistance", *Development Policy Review*, vol 1 no 1
Gordon-Ashworth, F., 1984, *International Commodity Control: a contemporary history and appraisal*, Croom Helm, London
Keynes, J. M., 1974, "International control of raw materials". *Journal of International Economics*, 4
Lewis, W. A., 1953, "World production, prices and trade 1870-1960", *Manchester School of Economic and Social Studies*, vol 20
Spraos, J., 1982, "Deteriorating terms of trade". *Trade and Development*, no 4, winter
UNCTAD, 1964, *Report of the Secretary-General: towards a new trade policy for development*, Geneva
—1968a, Document TD/8/Suppl. 1, Geneva
—1968b, *Proceedings of UNCTAD II, New Delhi*, vol 2, Geneva

Notes

[1] Keynes' views are set out in a memorandum of 1942, recently rediscovered in his papers and reprinted in Keynes [1974:299-315].
[2] Spraos [1982] reviews the contributions made by Singer, Emanuel Lewis and others as well as Prebisch.
[3] Resolution 16(II) listed cocoa, sugar, oils, oilseed and fats, natural rubber, hard fibres, jute and allied fibres, bananas, citrus fruits, tea, wine, iron ore, tobacco tungsten, cotton, manganese ore, mica, pepper, shellac and phosphates.
[4] Adopted in UNCTAD Resolution 156(VI).
[5] The centrally planned economy countries of Europe abstained on this proposal.

Protectionism

S. J. Anjaria, Z. Iqbal, N. Kirmani & L. L. Perez

For much of the period from the end of World War II to 1973, world trade grew rapidly, aided by significant liberalization achieved in successive rounds of multilateral trade negotiations. The world economy became increasingly integrated as the growth of trade outpaced production. Since 1973, although export performance has differed widely between and within broad country groupings, global trade volumes have been erratic, growth has slowed considerably, and the pace of integration has stabilized. By 1981, when output rose by only 1 per cent, world trade had stagnated.

A major problem currently facing the world economy is a substantial underutilization of resources. The unemployment rate in seven major industrial countries, which averaged just over 3 per cent in 1963-72, exceeded 6 1/2 per cent in 1981, and further increased in 1982. Capacity utilization is generally low, and employment opportunities have been eroded severely in some industrial sectors.

In 1981-82, restrictive actions on trade became more widespread in both the industrial and the agricultural sectors. The measures affecting trade in industrial products have been recognized, in principle, as being exceptions from the existing liberal framework of the General Agreement on Tariffs and Trade (GATT), to be applied temporarily. For legal and historical reasons, GATT rules have not applied equally rigorously to agricultural trade. Policymakers continue to recognize the need to overcome structural rigidities and to encourage goods to be exchanged on the basis of comparative costs. Not surprisingly, however, there is little agreement on specific measures to encourage structural adjustment. Agricultural protection has again become a debated issue—both in the protecting countries, because of its economic and budgetary costs, and in the competitive exporting countries, because of the burden of adjustment it imposes on their agricultural sectors. But the central problem of international trade policy persists—the urgent need for structural change remains greater than the adjustment that is under way.

The rise in protectionist pressures is worrisome, because the likelihood of chain reactions toward more protectionism generated by individual restrictive actions is greatest in a setting of slow economic growth and highly interdependent economies. Two broad developments are of particular concern. First, with the conclusion of the Tokyo Round of Multilateral Trade Negotiations (MTN) in 1979, the momentum toward trade liberalization that had been sustained for three decades appeared to have been dissipated. Protectionist pressures and protective actions that were taken or intensified since the conclusion of the Tokyo Round affect sectors accounting for more than one fifth of world trade in manufactures, including iron and steel, automobiles, textiles, and clothing. In addition, industrial countries apply restrictions at the border or use other measures that affect or distort trade in temperate zone agricultural products that account for one third of international trade in agriculture, including sugar. Apart from the increase in the number of restrictive actions,

Originally published in *Finance and Development*, vol. 20, no. 1, 1983. Reprinted with permission.

domestic and export subsidies have also increased in recent years in many major trading nations.

A second cause for concern is that there appears to have been a perceptible shift in the attitude of policymakers, who seem to be increasingly preoccupied with bilateral trade balances. Bilateral approaches also reflect a concern that foreign competitors are receiving an undue advantage as a result of their domestic policies and institutional arrangements. In addition, efforts to protect particular sectors have become more entrenched, jeopardizing the prospects for developing and strengthening the rules of general application that constitute the multilateral trading system. This shift could bring about greater international acceptance of existing sectoral restrictions or lead to further regulation of international trade flows; at worst, it could lead to balancing trade flows, bilaterally or sectorally, at progressively lower levels. Political and strategic considerations also appear to have influenced trade policy in several recent instances.

Factors in trade policies

Protectionist pressures tend to increase during periods of cyclical downturns in economic activity and the associated rise in unemployment, as industries and workers seek government action to insulate sectors of the economy from import competition. The groups threatened by import competition tend to be the traditional industries, where political influence is relatively well developed. On the other hand, those hurt by protectionist policies, including consumers and taxpayers, generally do not influence policy as actively. Pressures become particularly acute when recessionary conditions spread worldwide—as they did for example, in 1974-75 and as they have since 1980—and the possibilities for maintaining employment through increased export activity diminish. Furthermore, protection granted through restraints on imports and subsidies for exports during periods of rising unemployment is, in practice, difficult to dismantle speedily when economic activity improves. Unless the recovery is sustained over relatively long periods, there is a tendency for protection to persist when the need for it has passed.

Protectionist pressures are also closely related to underlying structural rigidities; such constraints had become increasingly apparent after 1974-75 in several industrial countries. They have been manifested as: (1) successive rounds of inflation over the last two decades, each beginning at a higher level; (2) high and growing unemployment, particularly of semi-skilled laborers in traditional industries, who are difficult to retrain and relocate; and (3) sluggish private investment. The Organization for Economic Cooperation and Development (OECD), in 1978, adopted guidelines on positive adjustment that emphasized the importance of pursuing policies consistent with efficient resource allocation. Commitment to this principle was renewed by governments in the OECD Declaration on Trade Policy, adopted June 4, 1980.

In addition to the OECD initiatives, recent discussions at the GATT and the United Nations Conference on Trade and Development (UNCTAD) have focused on the general policy issues relating to structural adjustment. The practical difficulties of adopting more positive adjustment policies were compounded by the cyclical downturn that began in 1980. The problems ensuing from structural rigidities in many major trading nations have been made worse, too, by the rapid emergence of the newly industrializing countries as competitors in a wide range of sectors.

The recent pressures for protection have sometimes been attributed to exchange rate developments. Some exchange rates have continued to diverge from levels consistent with the underlying economic fundamentals. The effects of these on trade have at times encouraged protectionist forces in countries experiencing trade deficits to demand bilateral restrictions. Moreover, increased exchange rate instability is said to have impeded rational long-run policymaking by business. Finally, it is sometimes contended that trade liberalization is less important under a floating exchange rate system than under fixed exchange rates because the effects of arduously negotiated tariff concessions are likely to be swamped by large exchange rate changes.

The importance of exchange rates that reflect economic fundamentals has long been recognized and is central to Fund surveillance over members' exchange rate policies. However, protectionism is not a viable solution to the problems arising from inappropriate exchange rate levels or exchange rate instability. Protectionist measures have direct, industry-specific effects on resource allocation. Exchange rate changes and trade liberalization do not offset each other. Protectionism is likely to lead to a misallocation of resources, to slow the pace of necessary structural adjustment, and to invite retaliation in other countries. Indeed, protectionist measures tend to perpetuate inappropriate exchange rate levels.

Industrial trade policies

The loss of dynamism in world trade has been particularly marked in the case of manufactured products, which make up 55 per cent of world trade and 70 per cent of trade among industrial countries. The growth of world exports of manufactures decelerated from 11 per cent annually during 1963-73 to 5 per cent during 1974-80 and further to 3 per cent in 1981. In 1981-82, a few existing import restrictions were liberalized, but the main trend was toward increased protection that affected not only historically protected industries but also new sectors.

An important set of recent protectionist actions has been in the automobile sector, which accounts for 8 per cent of total world trade in manufactures. In 1981, bilateral limitations or other forms of restraints were introduced on Japanese exports to several industrial countries, including the United States, that together account for two thirds of Japan's exports of automobiles. Combined with previous restrictions, the measures now affect virtually all Japanese exports of automobiles to industrial countries. The spread of protection in this important sector is symptomatic of the problems of structural adjustment in the industrial countries.

International trade in iron and steel accounts for 4 per cent of world trade and has been growing relatively rapidly despite restrictions imposed periodically by one or more industrial countries since the 1960s. Since early 1981, pressures for protection have remained high. In October last year, a new restraint arrangement covering the European Community's steel exports to the United States was concluded. Given the persistence of trade and adjustment problems in this sector and the increasing inroads that competitive developing country suppliers have recently made in the markets of the industrial countries, it would not be surprising if suggestions for negotiating still wider restrictions on steel continued to surface from time to time.

Trade restrictions in the textile and clothing sector, which constitutes about 5 per cent of world trade, also raise difficult issues of trade policy. In December 1981, the Multifiber

Arrangement, which authorizes importing countries to restrict imports from individual exporting countries, was extended by a protocol of extension to July 1986 (MFA III). Although it is still too early to judge the effect of MFA III on the export prospects of developing countries, indications are that it may be used by some importing countries to restrict exports of "dominant"—that is, efficient—developing country suppliers more severely than those of other countries. At the expiration of MFA III, multilaterally negotiated restrictions in textiles and clothing will have been applied for nearly 25 years. During this period, they have become progressively more complex and comprehensive. In other industrial sectors that have been subject to protectionist pressures in recent years, such as footwear, petrochemicals, shipbuilding, and electronics, the picture is somewhat mixed.

Sectoral pressures for protection in North America and Europe have commonly arisen with respect to the industrial performance of Japan. The flexibility of the Japanese economy and its ability to shift resources rapidly to more promising lines have been generally recognized. Nevertheless, pressures in North America and Europe have increased to address alleged specific problems in their bilateral trade with Japan. In late 1981 and early 1982, Japan announced measures to facilitate imports and streamline import procedures and to deal more effectively with complaints from abroad through the establishment of a trade ombudsman's office. The measures included the elimination and reduction of some tariffs, and the simplification and relaxation of certain procedures and standards perceived as nontariff barriers.

Agricultural trade policies

In the agricultural sector, the major trading nations pursue the following objectives in varying degrees, though they are not necessarily mutually consistent: selfsufficiency or security of supplies in food; parity or fair income for the domestic farm sector; market stabilization; and reasonable prices to the consumer. In addition, agricultural policies also take account of social, regional development, environmental, and health considerations. Agricultural production is inherently subject to the vagaries of the weather, which can bring about sharp variations in supplies. These factors, combined with generally low short-term demand and supply price elasticities, tend to produce relatively wide price fluctuations.

International trade policy in the agricultural sector is often designed to achieve the main objective of income support for domestic farmers through a variety of measures, including import quotas, tariffs, variable import levies, and export subsidies, and is often designed to mitigate the extent of market fluctuations. Market developments are also related to policies on food security and food aid, and they are influenced by preferential access commitments undertaken by some industrial countries. In addition, international agreements exist for sugar, dairy products, grains, and meat, but only the sugar and dairy products agreements contain pricing and other economic provisions.

The Fund's study focused on the five principal agricultural commodities produced in temperate zones—dairy products, fats and oils, grains, meats, and sugar.

While the specific means of protection vary from product to product, virtually all major industrial countries protect their domestic agricultural sectors to a considerable extent. In the fats and oils sector, protection is relatively low. In the other sectors, high domestic price supports often encourage production that cannot be absorbed at prevailing prices; this

World production and exports, 1963-81

	1963	1973	1975	1977	1979	1980	1981
				In per cent			
Growth of world							
commodity output	5.4	8.7	−1.1	4.6	2.8	1.4	1.3
				In billions of current U.S. dollars			
World exports	154	574	873	1,125	1,635	1,985	1,970
Of which				In per cent of world exports			
Agricultural products	29.2	21.1	17.2	16.7	16.0	15.0	14.7
Minerals[1]	16.9	16.7	23.7	23.6	24.5	28.5	27.4
Manufactures	53.2	60.5	57.4	57.6	57.8	55.2	56.1
Growth of volume of				In per cent			
world exports	7.1	11.1	-2.9	4.3	5.6	1.7	—

Source: GATT, *International Trade, 1981/82.*
—Indicates zero.
[1]Including fuels and nonferrous metals.

obliges the disposal of stocks in international markets, displacing more efficient producers.

An indication of the extent to which industrial countries' agricultural sectors are insulated is given by the generally low ratio of international trade to global production. This insulation of domestic markets produces a considerable divergence in domestic wholesale prices among countries. A comparison of nominal protection coefficients, that is, the ratio of domestic wholesale to "international" price, for selected agricultural commodities in the three major industrial areas—the European Community, Japan, and the United States—is illustrative of the degree of agricultural protection, although subject to the many qualifications outlined in the study on which this article is based. The nominal protection coefficients are well above unity, reflecting positive protection, in both the European Community and Japan, the major importing countries for the commodities concerned. For the United States, the ratios have generally remained, or have come down to, around or below unity.

Although trade policies and market conditions for each of the main temperate zone products differ, a broad generalization that emerges from the survey of agriculture is that national policies have given an unequivocal priority to the achievement of domestic social and political objectives, to the detriment of trade liberalization. In the few products where international trade has remained relatively free, such as cereal substitutes, the liberal stance of policies is increasingly in jeopardy. Long-term trade agreements that involve elements of market organization could become increasingly important in the future. Currently, such agreements reportedly cover principally grains (accounting for at least 15 per cent of international grain trade), beef, soybeans, and dairy products.

The economic effects of agricultural protection can take the form of overproduction and underconsumption of agricultural output in the protecting country, as well as distortions in the allocation of resources between agriculture and other sectors. Large exportable surpluses may develop that may be disposed of in the international market through export subsidization, imposing costs on consumers or taxpayers in the protecting country and on efficient producers abroad.

According to some studies, including a recent report by the OECD Secretariat, reform of agricultural policies might not provoke the massive structural dislocations that are sometimes feared. Moreover, even a relatively small reduction in surpluses in the traditional importing countries would bring about a significant improvement in conditions of access for the traditionally efficient suppliers of agricultural products such as dairy products and meat. In spite of the somewhat higher rate of growth of world agricultural trade since 1973, the proportion of total production entering trade is still generally small. More open agricultural trade policies may reduce market instability and possibly raise the average level of free international market prices for certain commodities, while lowering high consumer prices in certain countries. Even so, the establishment of more liberal international trading conditions in agriculture is still not generally accepted as a priority. In the absence of new policy initiatives to promote reform of agricultural trade policies, an intensification of restrictions through a proliferation of bilateral arrangements cannot be ruled out; this would pose serious consequences for efficient producers.

Implications for LDCs

In the aggregate, non-oil developing countries' exports have since 1973 grown rather well, but within this group there have been wide disparities in export performance. Non-oil developing countries' export performance and growth rates depend on a number of factors in addition to the stance of trade policies in the industrial countries. Among such factors, analyzed in a recent study by Goldstein and Khan (*Effects of Slowdown in Industrial Countries on Growth in Non-Oil Developing Countries*, IMF Occasional paper No. 12), are the rate of economic growth of the industrial countries; the stance and general orientation of the developing countries, own economic policies (including their trade policies, which are not discussed here); the scope of demand and production linkages between their export and domestic sectors; and the quantity and efficiency of physical and financial capital available in these countries. The observed variations in the developing countries' export and growth performance must therefore be assessed with reference to the sensitivity of their existing production and trade patterns to the interaction of these factors. In the past three years, in particular, the impact of the economic slowdown in industrial countries on the export performance of many developing countries has been marked.

Although there are obvious and important differences in export and growth performance among the developing countries, there is little doubt that protectionism in the major trading nations has hampered developing countries' efforts to specialize in production in accordance with their comparative advantage. The MTN most-favored-nation tariff reductions on industrial products exported by developing countries were, on average, less deep than the overall cut. Tariff escalation—increasing normal protection by stage of processing—on products of export interest to developing countries remains a problem, and it has received increased attention recently in the GATT and elsewhere. The incidence of nontariff barriers is frequently higher in sectors where developing countries have a comparative advantage; the imposition of nontariff barriers on agricultural commodities produced in both industrial and developing countries is widespread; and in textiles and clothing, restrictions are applied to exports from developing countries, while those from other countries that account for a significant portion of world export are generally unrestricted.

During the MTN and subsequently, considerable controversy has arisen on the concept of "graduation." The enabling clause agreed in the MTN states that, with the progressive development in their economies and improvement in their trade situation, developing countries would be expected to participate more fully in the framework of rights and obligations under the GATT. Attempts to apply this clause have, however, generated trade frictions, and the precise criteria for what constitutes "development" and "improvement in trade situation" are—and probably will remain—controversial issues. If successful efforts by more advanced developing countries to pursue export-oriented development strategies are frustrated by selective protection, export diversification of other developing countries and their greater integration in the world economy may well be hindered. Inward-looking bilateral and regional approaches to trade policy could be encouraged, and these would be contrary to the interests of all countries.

The existing structure of protection and the tendency of major trading nations to approach trade issues on a bilateral or sectoral basis also have detrimental effects on developing countries' longer-term prospects for increasing exports. Even in sectors where access to major markets is relatively liberal, these approaches generate uncertainty about future continued access. If major trading nations avoid pressures for structural change by applying policies that necessitate or validate restrictions or perpetuate trade distortions, longer-term investment planning becomes more uncertain. This can occur even if individual trade restrictions are not directed specifically at imports from developing countries.

Several developing countries, including some newly industrializing ones, have recently begun to rationalize and simplify their import regimes, as well as to reduce import restrictions and their reliance on export subsidies. These efforts would be greatly discouraged if it appeared that open, multilateral approaches to trade problems were to be abandoned by the major trading nations. Experience indicates that when restrictions, such as those in the agricultural and textile and clothing sectors, become entrenched, the relatively smaller trading nations are obliged to seek the best possible accommodation of their commercial interests in order to avoid the loss of markets. This further weakens the basis for the pursuit of more fundamental liberalization or reform of trade policies deriving from multilateral rules of general application.

Protectionism—Why Not?

Susan Strange

We seem to be surrounded these days by important people who tell us that protectionism is a terrible thing, and that the creeping tide of trade restrictions must be turned back if we are ever to escape from world recession. At the April Summit of Heads of State, all seven were agreed (so we were told) that one of the most important challenges facing the industrial countries is to find ways to stop the growth of protectionism. Here in London, the Commonwealth Secretariat produced a report in 1982 called "Protectionism—threat to international order-impact on developing countries". In April this year, the organisation's Secretary-General followed up with a memorandum on development prospects which declared that "the central problem is the increase in protectionist pressures and measures—especially in major economies—over the last decade".[1]

President Reagan was most anxious that the Summit meeting should set a date for new multilateral trade talks. It did not because President Mitterrand said he thought monetary reform was more important and he would not agree to setting a date for trade talks. The Americans are backed by the secretariat of GATT (General Agreement on Trade and Tariffs).

Their last report concluded its introductory chapter by declaring that

> 'When discrimination in international trade becomes acceptable, the general level of protection *cannot but rise*. Indeed [it went on] there is *no way* of maintaining an international trade *system* in the full sense of the word, referring to regularity, orderliness and predictability, without the most-favoured-nation commitment. If the system was to be maintained, [it ended], parties to the GATT would have to indicate in some binding manner their willingness to return to the nondiscriminatory trading system embodied in the General Agreement.[2]'

The same message has come not only from the GATT secretariat in Geneva but also from UNCTAD (United Nations Conference on Trade and Development).

The Indian delegate, speaking for the Group of 77 in March this year said he thought the most immediate concern of the Trade and Development Board should be the trading system. Here, "the supreme task was to restore confidence in the system by implementing commitments already undertaken on standstill and roll-back of protectionism and on increasing the access of developing countries to the markets of the developed countries."[3]

On all sides we are told that, if the creeping tide of protectionist measures is not turned, things will get progressively worse; that trade disputes will become trade wars, possibly breaking up the western alliance even if they do not lead (as it is said of the 1930s) to some-

From the August/September 1985 issue of *The World Today*, published monthly by the Royal Institute of International Affairs, 10 St. James Sq., London SW1Y 4LE, U.K. Student discounts for subscriptions.

thing much worse still. Already, some people are pointing to the American Congress voting $2 bn to help American grain exporters undercut the French in the Algerian market. The downward slide to economic perdition, they say, is already beginning.

In short, there are at present many distinguished people—economists and academics as well as officials—all saying more or less the same thing: 'If we don't do something about the "new protectionism", the world economy will never recover, developing countries will never develop, things will go from bad to worse'.

I believe this to be a great myth; it is a piece of conventional wisdom that asks to be challenged. I shall argue that world trade is not seriously jeopardised by protectionism and that behind the conventional unwisdom there is a coalition of vested interests with particular reasons for going on at such tedious length about the dangers of protectionism.

What I do believe is that the real weakness of the world economy lies elsewhere, and results from 10-15 years of monetary mismanagement and financial uncertainty. It is the instability of the banking system; the unpredictability of perverse exchange rates; interest rates far too high for productive investment as distinct from speculative investment; a volatile and uncertain market for oil; and the shrinkage of the less developed countries' (LDCs) purchasing power in the aftermath of debt repayment problems that is the real trouble.

The wringing of hands over protectionism only serves to distract our attention from these real problems.

I also believe that there is little danger of protectionism spreading like some kind of infectious disease and that the general outlook for world trade is not too bad.

The facts

The GATT report for 1983-84 noted that the volume of world trade in that year was at an all-time high. In the first half of 1984, it actually increased by 9 per cent. This was nearly double the rise in world production in 1984. Despite the drop in the volume of trade in oil (8 per cent) and other minerals, trade in manufactures rose 4 per cent. The overall rise in trade in the period covered by the report was 2 per cent, more than making good the relatively small fall in trade experienced in 1982-83. In short, we were back to 1980-81, despite the weak oil market, and despite the continued problems of debtor countries. World trade in manufactures, indeed, which suffered a rather milder hiccup in 1981-82 than it suffered in 1974-75 was back again on the upward trend which, if continued, will be double its 1973 level well before the end of the 1980s.

From the way the Commonwealth Secretariat and some champions of the Group of 77 talk, one would think that the LDCs were the chief victims of trade policies. So it is rather surprising to see from the GATT figures that LDC exports of manufactures rose by 9 per cent, more than twice the overall figure. That was in terms of volume; by value, and largely because of the rising dollar, they rose by 15 per cent. Some victims!

Particular attention is given in such circles, as I have quoted, to the infamous Multi-Fibre Agreement and the restrictions it has put on LDC exports of textiles and clothes. The record suggests, however, that it has not been very effective. "Of the two main areas of supply", says GATT, "exports from industrial countries declined, while those from developing countries increased". The latter now take 25 per cent of the world market for textiles and 42 per cent of that in clothing. In 1983, textile "imports from developing countries increased faster than total imports" into the United States and were up 14 1/2 per cent on 1982. As an exporter, Hong Kong increased the volume of its textile exports by 30 per cent, of its exports of clothes by 6 1/2 per cent. The colony's overall clothing trade surplus went up from $1.27 bn in 1973 to $3.51 bn in 1983. South Korea's record is similar. Its exports of textiles and clothes to the United States in the thick of the world recession rose steadily from $162m in 1981 to $260m in 1983. Its exports to Japan were nearly three times as great in 1983 as they had been in 1980.

In automotive and electronic manufactures the story for the exports from LDCs is the same. It also shows that Voluntary Export Restriction (VER) agreements are not entirely effective. Japan—the object of both American and European protectionism—increased its exports of cars and automotive parts by 9 1/2 per cent. "Despite the various import restrictions", says the same GATT report, "the rapidly expanding North American market took one half of these exports, or 19 per cent more than in the preceding year." Its share of world exports of automobile parts is worth nearly $6 bn: it rose in 1983 by 27 per cent. And Mexico and Brazil (not to mention other newly industrialised countries like Spain and South Korea) are rapidly increasing their market shares. Mexican and Brazilian exports of parts to North America rose by 45 per cent in 1983 to $1 1/2 bn.

In electronic products, trade is booming: up 13 per cent despite the large number of bilateral "voluntary" export restraint agreements. Most of the growth is in Japanese export to the United States, but seven Asian countries are also busy expanding their exports of electronic components and semimanufactures.

We can conclude from these facts that protectionism is no great threat to the prosperity of the international system. It may well be that, without the protectionism we have, the shift of manufacturing industry from North to South would have been even greater and even faster. No-one knows. What is clear is that it has not been bad enough either to stop the growth of world trade or to stop the growth of LDCs' exports of manufactures. In dollar value, LDCs' exports of manufactures are now five times what they were in 1973 while trade in manufactures is three times what it was in 1973 and LDC exports of primary products are only three times what they were in 1973 (in dollar value, that is).

It should be added that we do not know for sure that there has been a net increase in protectionism. It is true that there has been an increase in trade restrictions—but there has also been an increase in opportunities, opportunities opened up by bilateral agreements, by tariff liberalisation in the past and by joint production arrangements and so forth. We do not really know what the net figure is or how to measure it.

Secondly, there is the question of efficiency. Predictably, the International Monetary Fund (IMF) joins the general cacophony of voices about "the new protectionism" —indeed it was one of their staff who first coined the phrase. The IMF says that counter-trade, which is a kind of bilateral trade, adds 12-15 per cent to transaction costs in international trade. Yet if you spread that 15 per cent over all the transaction costs for an export industry or for an importing company, the difference in average transaction costs may be much less, while the marginal benefit both to the company and to the exporting country may be rather more than 15 per cent. The fact is that some trade in certain circumstances may be better than no trade, even at some increased cost.

How, them, are we to explain all the weeping and wailing and gnashing of teeth that has been going on about the new protectionism?

The explanations

The first point is that people do not look at the facts. They do not actually read the GATT report. They rely on tribal memories, and tribal memories are often more based on tribal myths than on historical facts. The facts are that the 1980s are very different from the 1930s and that most of the tribal memories of the 1930s are wrong. It is true that from 1929 to 1933 there was a drop in world trade of the order of 26 per cent. The drop this time was only 2 per cent. What was the same was that the cause of the slump, of the slow growth and the unemployment was the lack of purchasing power due to sudden shrinkage of credit. After the Wall Street crash in 1929, the world economy suffered from a sudden sharp shrinkage of American credit and of British credit. That then brought about shrinkage of trade from people who no longer had the purchasing power to buy imports. All over the world, governments responded with protectionism. But protectionism was only the response to the financial disorder. And when economic historians got around to writing at the end of the 1930s about the world depression, most of them said that the increase in tariffs had made very little difference, and that some parts of world trade had gone on increasing and others had not. But by the time they were writing that sort of stuff, everyone was engaged in the Second World War and their conclusions were ignored.

So why, in contrast to the 1930s, has trade held up so well this time? There must be an explanation for the difference between that 26 per cent figure and the 2 per cent figure. And why is it that protectionism has been so ineffective?

There are two answers. One is the internationalisation of production. Big companies have to produce for a world market. It was Professor Fred Meyer, of Exeter University, who got the answer when he said that one had really to look at changing technology, because in most sectors of the world economy the new plant that a company put in was going to be more expensive and was going to be obsolete faster than the plant it was replacing. This had happened so often since the Second World War that it was increasingly impossible for any company to make a profit out of a purely national market. It needed an international market in order to get the returns back fast enough to be ahead with the next new process or plant. The way, to get market access to other national markets in order to sell on the world market is very often to negotiate a joint production arrangement.

The second reason why trade has held up so well is, simply, bilateralism. Now 'bilateralism' is a dirty word with most international organisations. Yet the fact is that there was a lot of bilateralism in the 1930s and one of the reasons for the admittedly slow recovery of trade in the late 1930s lay with the bilateral agreements that the Latin Americans made, the Germans made, the Americans made. Everybody was up to it. It only got such a bad name because Dr Hjalmar Schacht used it exploitatively, in southern-eastern Europe in conjunction with the political intimidation of his boss, Adolf Hitler. Yet, bilateralism was trade-creating then and so it is now. Some bilateralism is state-to-state, as with the recent French-Soviet agreement. Some of it is between state enterprises and foreign companies, and some of it is between companies. One of the commonest and fastest-growing forms of bilateralism is known as counter-trade. The GATT estimates that counter-trade only accounts for 8 per cent of world trade. But the United States Department of Commerce says it is already something like 20-30 per cent; it reckons that it will rise to 50 per cent of world trade by the end of the 1990s. Certainly, 88 countries are engaged in counter-trade today instead of only 13 in 1972.

The third reason why we hear so much weeping and wailing about protectionism is that there is a lot of vested interest in perpetuating the conventional myths about it. One of these vested interests is certainly the GATT secretariat, which has come to a dead-end. It had a ministerial meeting in November 1982, which was a fiasco; the French predicted correctly that it would be so and nothing much has changed since then. I am not sure that it will. Indeed, if GATT were to close down, all its people given a golden handshake to go away, nothing much would happen to world trade. Secondly, the United States government has a vested interest in insisting loudly but in a very hypocritical way, on the importance of liberalising trade. It is interested in only two things.

It is interested in the liberalisation of trade in agriculture because it does not like the EEC's Common Agricultural Policy (CAP) amid it is interested most of all in liberalisation of trade in services. The figure for American exports in services continues to rise at a meteoric rate and the United States government is keen to see that it should continue to rise, in order to make up for the increasing failure of American industry to sell its manufactures. But manufactures are not nearly as profitable as trade in services. And so the Americans pretended that there was once a multilateral system for the regulation of world trade. As GATT says, such a system implies regularity, order and defined rules. In those terms, there never was a system. The United States kept on changing the rules to suit itself. There was no golden age of the GATT to get back to. It is a great illusion to believe there was—an illusion shared by many liberal economists. Some are much tempted to get very emotional, not to say evangelical about problems of trade. Politicians, they say, are a rotten, spineless lot who give in to political pressures and if it were not for them everything would be fine. Academic economists find it much easier to tell students that this explains any tendency by governments to protectionism and to explain the world economic recession in these simple, moralistic terms. It would be much more difficult to explain the complications of the world financial system, to which none of them (and no politician either) has a simple or an easy answer. That is why I think they are 'clerical traitors'.

But does protectionism matter? It is clear that it does not matter to the world economy. However, it may matter—and it probably does—to individual states in some economic stores. That it does is a further, third reason why we need not stay awake at night worrying about protectionism as a major problem of international economic relations. Like corporations, enough states are realising that they will not be able to survive unless they can compete in world markets. They cannot afford too many inefficient, uncompetitive manufacturing industries or service sectors, especially where trade is growing and where, therefore, they must liberalise in order to survive.

The South Koreans are saying that they are not going to make the same mistake as the Japanese. They are going to open up the domestic market to make sure the Korean corporations and enterprises stay competitive at home in order to stay competitive on the world market. The Brazilians are now designing their arms industry for a world market from the very beginning. Regardless of what the Brazilian army or air force wants, they are selling tanks and aircraft designed specially for war in the Middle East and making sure that there is competition in the industry. Even the Australians who have been habitually protectionist have adapted policy to this imperative. Despite the unions, the Prime Minister, Robert

Hawke, has said that Australia must liberalise its restrictions on automobile imports in order to make its own domestic producers more competitive.

The conclusions

The policy implication of this analysis is that we in Europe should follow the example of the United States. Just as the United States has been, we should be pragmatic about protectionism. We should not be the prisoners of somebody else's ideology. In certain sectors, the United States has always been highly protectionist. Look at meat, at wool, at shipping and shipbuilding, steal and textiles. There are lots of other sectors where the United States has not been consistently protectionist, but where it is a mixed picture. The United States has also used government procurement very effectively in some newer industries, particularly in computers and integrated circuits. American companies would not be nearly so far ahead of everybody else if they had not started with the security of very large, no-risk government contracts. In short, the United States has felt free to be inconsistent about trade policy and to change its mind. Europe, too, should be pragmatic about protectionism. There are two good grounds for protectionism.

One is on social grounds where the state may be acting quite rationally if, in seeking that to maintain social cohesion, it finds it better to give some protection to a threatened domestic sector, whether it is agriculture or textiles, rather than to have an expensive, disruptive riot to cope with or to nurture a disaffected minority that may disrupt, if not destroy, the state. For all the faults of the European Community's Common Agricultural Policy (CAP), it appears rather more rational when compared with the policies of the United States as they have affected American farmers in recent years. They have been sold up in large numbers because the banks foreclosed on them. By comparison with the uncertainties of American agricultural policy, the CAP seems less wasteful in social as well as financial terms.

Second, there is sometimes a strong case for protection in the form of preferential government procurement. To many liberal economists, preferential procurement is a kind of protectionism. But the American experience suggests that it may be a rather more efficient and more easily controlled kind of policy. The advantages of preferential procurement for one's own corporations are plain enough. Only last April, the head of Philips, Mr Wisse Dekker, warned European governments of the need to get their act together and to provide a truly common market, a common procurement and a common research and development policy. If they failed to do so, he said, some of the big companies like Siemens and Phillips would increasingly invest their money elsewhere and move their operations elsewhere.

To sum up, from the point of view of national policy pragmatism is the watch-word. Protectionism is rational if there are very good social reasons for it and/or if there is plenty of competition in the domestic market. If there is concentration in an industry or it is ridden by cartel agreements over prices, it may be dangerous in the long-term national interest to go in for too much protectionism. But preferential procurement is probably highly necessary in certain high-technology sectors such as biotechnology, lasers, communications systems, electronics, informatics. In all these, Europe has to compete with the United States which has the advantage of a tremendously large defence budget. It also has to compete with Japan, with its immense concentration of corporate and state purchasing power and a large, highly impervious national economy. Since in Europe we cannot imitate Japan, we surely need to take a leaf out of America's book. Narrow nationalism here is probably the great danger to the European economies, not protectionism.

[1] *Development Prospects, Policy Options and Negotiations*, (London: Commonwealth Secretariat, April 1985), p. 26.

[2] "International Trade", 1983/4, pages 20 and 22.

[3] UNCTAD *Bulletin*, April 1985, p. 7.

Trade Does Not Need Scapegoats

William N. Walker

As the U.S. Congress returns to work, the word on everyone's lips (after Iranscam) is "trade." There is much indignation about unfair trade practices and brave talk of forcing president Ronald Reagan to get tough with other trading nations. The reason, of course, is the estimated U.S. trade deficit of $170-billion for fiscal 1986. Before the subject becomes entirely obscured in the clouds of rhetoric, however, it may be useful to set out a few benchmarks.

The first is that trade measures don't have much to do with the size of the trade deficit. For that, we have to look to factors like the size of the budget deficit, the impact of exchange rates and the pace of growth rates in the United States and abroad.

Second, a large part of the trade imbalance is a direct result of actions we have taken in the past, continue to follow today and seem unlikely to change; bashing foreigners may be fun, but we could accomplish more by bashing ourselves.

Third, fairness is in the eyes of the beholder and before we accuse too many other countries of unfairness we should recognize that some of our own practices are not above reproach.

In 1981, the United States enjoyed a $11-billion trade surplus with the European Community. By 1983, we suffered a $22-billion deficit. Similarly, in 1981 developing countries accounted for nearly 58 per cent of our merchandise exports; by 1985, that share had dwindled to 34 per cent, a decline or $17-billion. But what happened during those intervening four years to devastate our trade balance with the European Community and our sales to developing countries had nothing much to do with the trade policies in these places. The foreign trading practices that we rail against today are not very different from the trade measures that were in effect in 1981. Indeed, access to Japanese markets today is clearly easier than it was five years ago when our bilateral deficit was less than half the current level.

The major changes that occurred during the interim were the debt crisis, which throttled developing-country imports, and the large-scale devaluation of the world's currencies against the dollar, which made U.S. exports uncompetitive and sucked in the world's exports. So, if trade measures did not get us into the dilemma in the first place, trade legislation seems unlikely to get us out of it. Moreover, we already have it within our grasp to shrink the trade deficit sharply, but we have not acted. We forbid the export of Alaskan crude oil and limit the export of logs cut on federal land, which, together, could be worth as much as $20-billion. We handcuff U.S. exporters by imposing restrictive export controls on, high-tech products. Exports of oil-drilling equipment to the Soviet Union are banned. And not until last November did we allow exports of drugs that were perfectly legal in the market of destination but which the Food and Drug Administration had not gotten around to approving in the United States.

The most egregious self-inflicted wound is in the telecommunications industry, where the United States unilaterally dismantled the Bell System, deregulated the industry, forbade the operating companies to produce equipment and invited the rest of the world to come in and exploit our market — without getting anything in return.

Advocates of the level playing field seem to assume that only foreigners engage in field-tilting. But we impose restraints of one kind or another on imports of meat, sugar, rice, peanuts, tobacco, dairy products, textiles, apparel, motorcycles, automobiles, machine tools, semiconductors and steel. Concern is voiced about growing South Korean penetration of the U.S. market, but nearly 45 per cent of South Korea's exports to the United States are already subject to restraint.

Trade invites mischievous legislation. Foreigners, after all, don't vote; the temptation is, therefore, strong to get in a few licks. There are lots of reasons why that would be bad policy. Among other things, imposing barriers in the United States can provoke retaliation.

A recent Canadian decision to impose a 67 per cent punitive duty on U.S. corn exports was hardly unrelated to earlier U.S. actions to penalize Canadian lumber and shingle exports. Similarly, the United States and the European Community are threatening each other with retaliation and counterretaliation for what each believes is commercial misbehavior by the other.

Probably the best reason to oppose belligerent trade legislation is that it would not do anything to solve the trade deficit—supposedly the object of the exercise. So, as Congress gets down to the business of drafting trade legislation, we should encourage it to avoid seeking scapegoats: don't blame someone else for a series of problems that were brought about largely by our own actions and that we can solve only by ourselves.

A Sensible Way to Ease Trade Wars

Jim Romahn

One of the ideas being floated among farmers interested in trade talks is to limit countervailing duties to the net difference in subsidies.

It takes a lot of background to understand the proposal.

Countervailing duties can be imposed on imports if the local industry — not the government, but the industry — can make a convincing case that the imported products are subsidized.

That's enough to persuade the federal government to impose a temporary countervailing duty, which is what Canada has imposed against U.S. corn. The next step is to prove that the subsidized imports are causing injury. Once that's proven, the temporary countervailing duty can become permanent, which is what Canada has imposed against beef from the European Economic Community and the U.S. has imposed against hogs from Canada.

When farmers draft their petition for a countervailing duty, they tally all of the subsidies of the foreign competitors enjoy; they concede nothing for similar subsidies they receive from their own governments.

This is not fair, but it's the way the system works.

Canada can subsidize its domestic farmers to the hilt, yet those same farmers can ding their foreign competitors with a countervailing duty. The same can and has been done by U.S. farmers. It's simply a matter of farmers getting off their duffs and making a convincing case for a countervailing duty.

Eventually we might end up with countervailing duties on every farm commodity in every one of the 91 nations that are members of the General Agreement on Tariffs and Trade.

But it will be the poorest farmers in the poorest nations that will suffer the most because they're the least organized to plead for countervailing duties and because their politicians have the least bargaining power when it comes to irritating the big, rich nations by hitting their subsidized exports with duties.

This is a fool's game.

And it explains the thinking behind the proposal to limit countervailing duties to the net difference in subsidies between two countries.

For example, now that the Ontario Corn Producers Association has persuaded Revenue Canada that the U.S. subsidies amount to more than $1.04 a bushel, U.S. corn producers might tally Canadian subsidies and convince the International Trade Commission that ours come to, say, $1 a bushel.

Once there's agreement on those tallies, the two governments might settle for a Canadian countervailing duty of four cents a bushel — the net difference between the U.S. and Canadian subsidies.

Originally published in the Kitchener–Waterloo *Record*, Jan. 1987. © 1987 Kitchener–Waterloo *Record*; reprinted with permission.

This type of proposal seems so sensible that it stands some chance of making it into the trade talks now underway between Canada and the U.S., then later into the negotiations towards a new General Agreement on Tariffs and Trade embracing all 91 trading partners.

Progress is possible on a few related issues, such as definitions of the types of subsidies that can be countervailed and some agreement on the procedures each country should follow in dealing with countervailing duties.

There might even be agreement on new ways to settle disputes. As matters stand now, the U.S. countervailing duties on pork and hogs are heading into an American court in New York City and the Canadian countervailing duties on Irish and Danish beef are heading into a GATT tribunal in Europe.

Even if there's agreement on all of these things, it will still take years of patient effort to translate these type of agreements into practical changes in international subsidies, countervailing duties and trade. For example, if we could miraculously strike this type of deal with the U.S. tomorrow, the corn and hog industries still face a prolonged round of research and negotiation before they could reach agreement on the net subsidy differences and appropriate countervailing duty.

But the process itself might help farmers to recognize some of the folly and futility of subsidies and supply management. They might even gladly divert more of their energies to the things that really matter, such as marketing superior products at competitive prices.

A New Round of Global Trade Negotiations

S.J. Anjaria

Since 1947, seven rounds of global trade negotiations under the auspices of the General Agreement on Tariffs and Trade (see note on GATT on p. 202) have codified the rules for international trade while further opening trade regimes. In late January 1986, the 90 member countries (known as the contracting parties) of the GATT took initial steps toward yet another round of multilateral trade negotiations, which may be formally launched in September 1986. The results of this round are likely to be implemented during most of the 1990s. The number and technical complexity of the specific issues that are likely to be raised in the new round is quite impressive. Some are perennial topics, others are being raised for the first time (see box on major areas of negotiation). Rather than attempting to review the detail each of the specific areas for negotiation at this early state, this article will identify and explain the basic issues that are likely to shape the discussions.

The four main elements of the global trading system likely to be at issue in the new round are: (1) nondiscrimination; (2) the distinction between "border" measures (such as taxes on international trade) and "nonborder" or domestic measures such as subsidies; (3) evolving trade relations between developed and developing countries; and (4) the future role of a strengthened GATT. With the growing importance of international trade, the economic difficulties of the past decade, and the shifts in relative positions of the major trading nations, it is not surprising that such fundamental matters should be at stake. A closer look at each topic illustrates the breadth of specific trade issues subsumed by each of these subjects.

The process of negotiation itself will bring these subjects into sharper focus. However, the ultimate outcome of the negotiations is not the only element that will determine the climate of international trade relations in the coming decade: also crucial will be the relative priorities and the sequence in which the issues are addressed. Thus one of the first important steps governments could take to encourage a useful outcome is to eschew new protectionist measures while the negotiations are in progress. Such a "standstill" was regarded as a normal feature of the Dillon and Kennedy Rounds, but it proved difficult to enforce during the Tokyo Round. The GATT Ministerial meeting of 1982 endorsed—but failed to enforce—a standstill on new restrictions and a "rollback" of existing ones. Some unwinding of recent protectionist measures would also aid in creating open trading conditions. Although proposals for a standstill and rollback have featured prominently in the preparations toward a new round, and some countries were initially reluctant to agree to a new round until these were effectively in place, there remain uncertainties about how such a scheme will be implemented in practice. In particular, it was still unclear, at the time of writing, if a standstill and rollback would cover all measures, or only measures that are inconsistent with GATT principles.

Originally published in *Finance and Development*, vol. 22, no. 2, June 1986. Reprinted with permission.

Nondiscrimination

A cornerstone of international trade rules is the principle of nondiscrimination, or "most-favored-nation" treatment. Nondiscrimination allows international exchanges to take place on the basis of price competitiveness and comparative advantage rather than on the basis of political or economic weight. The principle thus safeguards the interests of smaller trading nations.

As a principle of international trade behavior, nondiscrimination is widely supported. In practice, however, it is sometimes not adhered to, even by the major trading nations. This is especially so when countries impose nontariff trade barriers, particularly quantitative restrictions on imports. Faced with a choice between nondiscriminatory restrictions and selective restrictions, policymakers are often tempted to opt for the latter. Once introduced, these restrictions are difficult to dismantle or convert to nondiscriminatory barriers.

There are two obvious ways to deal with this discrepancy between principle and practice. One is to allow legally a degree of selectivity or discrimination, under strictly defined conditions, thus encouraging greater adherence by the world trading community to the established rules. The other is to strictly enforce adherence to the rule of nondiscrimination as originally agreed by GATT members.

An examination of these options began even before the launching of the Tokyo Round of trade negotiations in September 1973, but no consensus has emerged. The difficulty of enforcing the principle of nondiscrimination is reflected in the continuing debate on the scope and applicability of "safeguard provisions." These provisions allow a GATT member to impose temporary nondiscriminatory import restrictions to safeguard the position of a domestic industry injured by import competition. The growing degree of bilateral management of trade in some sectors has, in turn, raised more general doubts about the effectiveness of the multilateral trading system. The developing countries, and some industrial countries, have questioned whether the major trading nations can legitimately expect to improve the overall functioning of multilateral trade rules without bringing their own trade policies into strict conformity with the GATT principle of nondiscrimination. On the other hand, some observers have emphasized that the GATT already explicitly authorizes departures from the principle of nondiscrimination—for example, for customs unions, free trade areas, and preferential arrangements such as the Generalized System of Preferences. According to these observers, the GATT system can be realistically strengthened only by allowing further, but well-defined, departures from the nondiscrimination principle.

"Border" and "nonborder" measures

Much of the international effort to preserve and improve upon the openness of world trade has focused traditionally on tariffs, quantitative import or export restrictions, and export subsidies—all measures applied at the border. GATT rules do contain several provisions relating to "nonborder"—or domestic—measures and practices, since such measures may offset the effects of liberal border measures. For example, under GATT rules generally, an export subsidy is a border measure that is frowned upon, while domestic subsidies are accepted as internal measures. Although subject to countervailing duties by trading partners in certain circumstances, domestic subsidies are often regarded as less directly harmful to international trade than export subsidies.

The somewhat artificial nature of the distinction between border and nonborder measures, in terms of their impact on international trade and welfare, has recently come to be emphasized. One commentator (Richard Blackhurst, writing in *The World Economy*, December 1981) suggested that as the traditional distinction between a country's domestic and foreign economic policies breaks down, governments may increasingly need to discuss internal policies with their trading partners. For example, signatories of the Tokyo Round code on subsidies agreed explicitly, when drawing up their subsidy policies, to take into account not only their internal effects but also, as far as practicable, their possible adverse effects on trade.

Underlying the difficulties in developing rules of international cooperation on nonborder measures and practices is the conceptual problem of shifting from what Blackhurst calls a "measure-based" system of trade rules to one that relies rather more on "effect-based" rules. Under the former, only the practices and restrictions that directly affect trade flows would be subject to international rules. Under effect-based rules, it can be argued that any domestic policy action that affects trade flows is, in principle, a "trade measure." Although there may be sound economic justification for emphasizing the development of an effect-based set of rules, it remains to be seen whether governments consider this a realistic negotiating objective in the new round. The concept of effect-based rules was introduced in the Tokyo round code on subsidies, which proved to be relatively ineffective in comparison with the more conventional measure-based rules.

The complexity and importance of this issue is illustrated by the recent debate in the United States on "foreign industrial targeting." A study completed in 1985 by the US International Trade Commission defined industrial targeting as "coordinated government actions that direct productive resources to give domestic producers in selected nonagricultural industries a competitive advantage." Examples of targeting techniques in the ITC study include: use of protection to foster the development of specific domestic sectors or industries, tax policies, financial assistance, science and technology assistance, and exemptions from laws governing cartels and mergers. Critics of targeting practices are concerned about their effects on US competitiveness and exports, and have suggested that US trade laws should be broadened to include remedies for local producers injured by the targeting practices of countries that compete with US producers in the home or third markets. As yet, the views of these critics are not accepted generally.

The distinction between border and nonborder measures is blurred in the increased international concern with so-called unfair trade practices. This concern has traditionally been particularly acute in the United States, but it has recently spread to the European Community and some developing countries. In the new round, the basic issue will, in all likelihood, not be the classification of trade practices into "fair" and "unfair" categories, but their definition and the levels of use that would trigger actions to compensate domestic producers in the importing countries. Examples of such rules include the current ones allowing antidumping measures and countervailing duties: not all dumping or subsidization triggers compensatory action in favor of injured local industries, but only that which leads to demonstrable injury. The range of trade practices considered "unfair" or undesirable may well be expanded as discussions proceed (for example, by considering certain natural resource pricing policies as subject to countervailing duty) or by allowing for newer forms of compensatory action. For example, a "countervailing subsidy" has been suggested by

Gary Hufbauer and Joame Shelton Erb ("Subsidies in International Trade," Institute for International Economics, Washington DC, 1984) to offset the effects of subsidization by a competing supplying country in a third market. It will be interesting to see if any of these newer suggestions are taken up in the new trade round.

North-South trade relations

Another important element of the present framework is the set of rules and practices that serve as benchmarks for determining trade relations between developed and developing countries. GATT rules have come to accept, especially since the addition of Part IV in 1966 to the text of the General Agreement, that the world trading system should provide for preferential treatment of developing countries. The critical issue is whether the general expansion of world trade, and the growth and adjustment efforts of developing countries in particular, call for more, or less, preferential treatment in trade policy. The new round will, it is hoped, provide guidance on whether all countries that receive preferential treatment will continue to do so, and on whether some developing countries will "contribute" to the negotiations by offering new concessions to their main trading partners.

There is little ambiguity about the legal form of preferential rules. The General Agreement allows developing countries to pursue protective trade policies (for infant industry or development purposes, for example). Further, it includes more lenient treatment of developing countries in the application of rules than industrial countries. For example, the GATT stipulates that a developing country should consult with the Contracting Parties on its balance of payments restrictions under Article XVIII only once every two years; industrial countries invoking similar restrictions are expected to consult under Article XII provisions every year. The developing country consultations may be held under simplified procedures. Similarly, the GATT allows developing countries to subsidize exports of manufactures to a greater degree than industrial countries. Under Part IV of the GATT, developed countries undertake to strive to reduce trade barriers affecting developing countries and to refrain from establishing new ones. Following an understanding reached in the GATT in 1979, developed countries' trade preferences, under the GSP, in favor of developing countries no longer require a waiver of the most-favored-nation provision.

The controversy centers, in fact, on the implementation and the effects of these rules. Developing countries have benefited from GSP trade preferences and the reduction of trade barriers in important sectors such as tropical products. But in some sectors trade restrictions place a special burden on these countries: import tariffs on some developing country exports such as processed agricultural products, textiles, and clothing are often higher than the average tariff for manufactured goods generally in industrial countries. Further, the nontariff restrictions authorized under the Multifiber Arrangement (MFA) of 1974 apply mainly to developing countries' exports. At the conclusion of the Tokyo Round, GATT members agreed that with the "progressive development of their economies" developing countries would be better placed to participate more fully in the framework of rights and obligations under the General Agreement. But, perhaps because of the potential for controversy, the way in which a developing country's trade policy should be adapted as its economy grows and matures has been insufficiently discussed. A statement made by India on behalf of a group of 23 developing countries in mid-1985 proposed that GATT members should establish techniques and modalities "to concretely quantify" the application of the GATT provisions on special and more favorable treatment for developing countries, but this suggestion has not been pursued.

In a recent study, the GATT Secretariat identified trade policies in both developed and developing countries that their trading partners considered impediments to trade expansion. The study suggested that a logical first step in any initiative to promote trade liberalization would be a rollback of recent restrictions by developed countries on exports from developing countries. Developing countries, in turn, could take steps to simplify their import regimes, make them more transparent or visible, stabilize levels of protection, or progressively lower excessive protection. How these objectives are to be achieved is likely to be a matter of negotiation.

An important aspect of future trade policy reform in developing countries would be whether and how their liberalization measures could be "bound" or made permanent within the GATT rules, bearing in mind that GATT currently allows for some flexibility on the "permanence" of their trade measures. The GATT study noted, for example, that developing countries can obtain time-bound exemptions from certain GATT commitments, or stagger the implementation of their trade measures. Commitments on trade restrictions for development purposes can be revised or temporarily suspended in certain circumstances.

While developing countries will probably wish to retain this flexibility, an important question is the degree to which their trading partners will expect them to adapt their trade regimes as a result of the new trade round. Many developing countries rely simultaneously on high tariffs as well as complex and restrictive nontariff barriers. Adherence to GATT rules is relatively straightforward on tariff matters. Nontariff barriers—particularly quantitative restrictions—are, with specific exceptions, outlawed under GATT rules in any case. Understandings on their treatment will need to be reached.

Role of the GATT

A guiding element in the discussions during the new trade round will be the question of how the role of the GATT and its Secretariat could be strengthened. Although the plans to establish an International Trade Organization after World War II failed and the GATT came into existence only by virtue of a Protocol of Provisional Application, the contractual rights and obligations of members embodied in the General Agreement have provided a substantial degree of order in world trade relations. GATT members have benefited from a neutral forum and set of rules to which national authorities could resort, if needed, to fortify themselves against pressures from domestic protectionist lobbies.

Increasing bilateral, sector-specific restrictions have led to discussions on how to strengthen GATT procedures and principles. The results of such discussions would be particularly important if it were decided during the trade round, for example, that selective (discriminatory) safeguards would be allowed in future under certain conditions monitored and enforced by the GATT. A particular feature of the recent growth of bilateral measures is that the international interest is not taken into account in negotiations between the exporting country and the importing country. A greater GATT role in such surveillance (under a more transparent set of national trade policies) would increase national governments' accountability for their trade and trade-related actions not only toward their trading partners but also for the international trading system. More immediately, for a new standstill and rollback to be effective, many consider a strong GATT monitoring mechanism necessary.

Prospects

Each of the successive rounds of trade negotiations so far has dealt with increasingly complex issues, and has taken longer to complete, and the forthcoming eighth round is unlikely to be an exception from this trend. Some of the broad issues discussed above were addressed to some extent by the Tokyo Round, the last set of international trade negotiations, that ended in 1979. However, none of the main issues to be discussed is likely to be resolved easily.

The rise in protectionist pressures and barriers in the past several years has enhanced awareness of the need to resist the spread of restrictions and to seek trade liberalization (see box on the Leutwiler Group). The prospective launching of a new trade round is a signal of governments' intention to strengthen and improve the open trading system. Once the negotiating process is fully engaged, a critical issue for governments will be how to accelerate the process of liberalization in a way that would promote the interests of all countries in a balanced way. The sense of realism and political will that participating countries bring to bear on the new round will determine its outcome.

APPENDICES

What is GATT?

The General Agreement on Tariffs and Trade, or GATT, is the multilateral treaty that provides and monitors a global system of rights and obligations governing international trade that are voluntarily accepted by its member countries. GATT emerged out of an international conference in 1947, and its secretariat began operating in Geneva in January 1948.

Today, 90 countries are full signatories (or contracting parties) of the General Agreement; one country applies the Agreement provisionally, and 31 other countries apply GATT rules *de facto* while benefiting from treatment under GATT rules by signatories of the General Agreement. While altogether 122 countries operate under GATT rules, most of the remaining nations benefit from these rules under the umbrella of the most-favored-nation rule. Some major trading nations, notably the Soviet Union and some oil-producing countries, are not members of GATT.

The basic purpose of GATT is to foster fair and free international trade among its members, on the basis of reciprocity and nondiscrimination. GATT offers a forum for review of trading arrangements and practices to ensure that they are in accord with the principles outlined in the General Agreement, and for arbitration and adjudication of trade disputes. It also provides a means of surveillance of international trade.

Likely Major Areas of Negotiation of Uruguay Round

The mandate for the negotiations that is expected to be adopted by ministers before the end of this year will both identify the specific matters to be taken up in the new round and determine the broad interrelationships among the various items on the negotiating agenda. While it is premature to predict precisely which issues will be included or excluded, discussions in the GATT and other fora in the past several years have clearly identified several specific areas (some old, some new) where at least some countries or groups of countries would intend to press for liberalization and strengthened trading rules.

Sectoral issues

Agriculture. Trade in agriculture has, from the inception of the GATT, been subject to looser discipline than nonagricultural trade. This is regarded by the relatively more efficient agricultural producers as a fundamental imbalance in the rights and obligations under the GATT. In the recent past, considerable progress has been made in GATT discussions toward defining a framework for lowering agricultural protection in the new round of negotiations. Will governments be prepared to modify domestic farm support programs?

Textiles and clothing. For nearly three decades, trade in textiles and clothing has been subject to special restrictions, which have the effect of undermining basic GATT principles. The Multifiber Arrangement (MFA), initially negotiated in 1974 and renewed twice (most recently in 1982), is scheduled to expire in July 1986. Decisions in this sector will be crucially important for the new round. The MFA, like its predecessors the Long-term Arrangement on Cotton Textiles (1962-73) and the Short-term Arrangement (1961-62), was based on the principle that industrial countries, which are the main importers in this sector, need special protection against "market disruption" by lower-cost (usually developing country) suppliers. Thus, the nondiscrimination principle of the GATT was breached in a major way. Further, discrimination against developing countries hindered the expansion of their exports of textiles and clothing during a period when they were faced with the need to pursue strong adjustment policies. This in turn accentuated tensions in North-South trade relations. Will GATT members agree to bring MFA into conformity with GATT rules?

Tropical products. During the Tokyo Round, industrial countries agreed to concessions on tariff and nontariff barriers on tropical products, which are mainly exported by developing countries. In November 1982, the Contracting Parties agreed to carry out "consultations and appropriate negotiations" aimed at further liberalization of trade in tropical products. Since then however, little progress has been made in lowering trade barriers in this sector. Tariff escalation on processed tropical products remains a problem for developing countries. This sector will therefore feature importantly in the new round.

Natural resource products. At the initiative of certain developed and developing countries with a particular interest in trade in natural resource products, the Contracting Parties, in November 1982 agreed that tariffs and nontariff barriers affecting nonferrous metals and minerals, forestry products, and fish and fisheries products should be examined with a view to developing appropriate solutions. The subsequent examinations have focused in particular on nonferrous metals and minerals, and fisheries. Controversies on product coverage have held back the discussions on forestry products. These issues may be taken up in the new round as well, provided there is sufficient support for the concept of sector-by-sector negotiations, about which some countries have reservations because they can lead to uneven trade liberalization and market fragmentation.

Services. Ever since the idea of a new negotiating round was put forward several years ago the question of whether, and how, trade in services should be incorporated in the negotiations—and in the GATT itself—has remained very controversial. The question of services has been discussed most recently at the meetings of the GATT Preparatory Committee. If rules on trade in services were to be negotiated in the context of the new round, this would be potentially one of the most far-reaching extensions of international surveillance over national policies since the establishment of the General Agreement. For this reason, the scope and modalities of discussions on services are expected to be intensely debated

Other principal areas

Safeguards. Safeguards are the GATT provisions that entitle a member to impose emergency protection on imports when a domestic industry is threatened by import competition. The issue of safeguards and the proliferation of safeguard-type measures, at the head of any listing of critical trade policy concerns is likely once again to dominate the new round of trade negotiations, as is evident from the accompanying main article.

Although safeguards were extensively discussed in the Tokyo Round, no agreement was reached, in part because an important body of opinion among the GATT membership believed that an impasse on this question was preferable to the alternative of international acceptance of discriminatory restrictions. The talks on safeguards were continued (unsuccessfully) after the Tokyo Round. There is wide agreement that without a generally acceptable resolution of the matter of safeguards, it would be difficult to claim final success in the new round of trade negotiations.

Quantitative restrictions and other nontariff measures. The problem of quantitative import restrictions partly overlaps the question of safeguards which may take the form of quantitative restrictions. It also goes beyond safeguards, since some existing quantitative restrictions were not applied in response to injurious import competition, but were inherited from the early postwar period. An important aspect of nontariff barriers is whether or not measures inconsistent with the GATT will be removed unilaterally, without reciprocal concessions by trading partners.

Nontariff measures other than quantitative restrictions cover a vast field, and the difficulties of dealing effectively with such trade barriers or distortions are even greater. This is because national health or safety standards, licensing procedures, and the like are often designed for legitimate purposes of public policy and only incidentally have a trade restrictive effect. The distinction between border and nonborder measures (referred to in the accompanying main article) is particularly relevant here.

The Tokyo Round codes, which also deal with several types of nontariff measures, will themselves be reviewed and possibly amended or reinterpreted in the course of the new round. Codes such as those on subsidies and government procurement could, if reinforced, have a very important influence on the openness of markets and the avoidance of protectionism in the future.

Tariffs. Despite the growing relative importance and complexity of nontariff barriers, tariffs often constitute an important remaining obstacle to trade expansion. In the previous two trade rounds, tariffs of the major industrial countries were reduced by the application of an across-the-board formula (for example, a one third cut, in the Tokyo Round). Although exceptions were permitted—leading to a significant remaining tariff level in some important sectors such as textiles—this method of reduction was generally thought to be more comprehensive and effective than the old item-by-item method. In the new round, decisions will first need to be taken on the appropriate method of tariff negotiations. Another issue will be tariff "bindings" particularly by developing countries and some smaller industrial countries which at present have agreed to bind a relatively small proportion of their tariffs and thus retain substantial freedom to unilaterally increase protection to domestic industries.

Other areas. The above list by no means exhausts the extremely wide range of issues and problems that could arise in the negotiating context. Some other issues of considerable importance include: GATT dispute settlement procedures; trade related investment measures; counterfeit goods; export of domestically-prohibited goods; and possible reform of specific GATT provisions such as Article XXIV on customs unions and free trade areas. Decisions of considerable technical and political difficulty will be required not only in defining the specific areas for negotiation, but also in ensuring that the new round moves forward in a balanced and mutually reinforcing way.

Previous trade negotiations

Since the Second World War there have been seven rounds of multilateral trade negotiations:
1. Geneva negotiations, 1947
2. Annecy negotiations, 1949
3. Torquay negotiations, 1950-51
4. Geneva negotiations, 1955-56
5. Geneva negotiations ("Dillon Round"), 1959-62
6. Geneva negotiations ("Kennedy Round"), 1963-67
7. Geneva negotiations ("Tokyo Round"), 1973-79

The first six rounds were concerned almost exclusively with multilateral reduction of tariffs. With the successful and progressive lowering of tariffs, nontariff barriers to trade became the subject of greater concern. The Tokyo Round was a comprehensive effort to deal with tariff and nontariff measures. In addition to tariff reductions of about one third in the major industrial markets, the Tokyo Round produced a series of new or reinforced codes dealing with a variety of nontariff practices, including codes on subsidies and countervailing duties, technical barriers to trade, import licensing procedures, antidumping, government procurement, and customs valuation. In addition, agreements dealing with dairy products, meat, and civil aircraft were also reached.

"Leutwiler Group"

In November 1983, the Director-General of the GATT appointed an independent study group on the international trading system. The group, headed by Dr. Fritz Leutwiler of Switzerland, consisted of seven distinguished persons from developed and developing countries, participating in their personal capacities. In March 1985, the group, generally referred to as the "Leutwiler Group" issued a report entitled "Trade Policies for a Better

Future: Proposals for Action." The report, containing 15 principal recommendations, sum-marized below, indicates the scope of potential trade policy reform that governments may need to address in the coming years:

1. Open formulation and monitoring of trade policy and actions; analysis of the costs and benefits of trade policy actions through a "protection balance sheet."

2. Clearer and fairer rules for agricultural trade, with no special treatment for particular countries or commodities.

3. A timetable and procedures to bring into conformity with GATT rules in all countries all measures which are currently inconsistent with the GATT, including voluntary export restraints and discriminatory import restrictions.

4. Trade in textiles and clothing should be fully subject to ordinary GATT rules.

5. Rules on subsidies need to be revised, clarified, and made more effective.

6. Improvement and vigorous application of GATT codes governing nontariff distortions of trade.

7. Clarify and tighten rules permitting customs unions and free-trade areas to prevent their distortion and abuse.

8. Regular oversight or surveillance of country trade policies and actions by the GATT Secretariat which should collect and publish information.

9. Greater scrutiny and limitations on application of emergency "safeguard" protection for particular industries which should continue to be nondiscriminatory.

10. Greater integration of developing countries into the trading system, with all the accompanying rights and responsibilities.

11. Expansion of trade in services, and discussion of multilateral rules for this sector.

12. GATT's dispute settlement procedures should be reinforced by building up a perma-nent roster of nongovernmental experts to examine disputes, and by improving the imple-mentation of panel recommendations.

13. A new round of GATT negotiation should be launched to strengthen the multilateral trading system and further open world markets.

14. Establishment of a permanent Ministerial-level body in GATT to ensure high-level attention to trade issues.

15. A satisfactory resolution of the world debt problem, adequate flows of development finance, better international coordination of macroeconomic policies, and greater consis-tency between trade and financial policies.

Chapter 5

Investment, Industrialization and Development

Introduction

With thirty years of development experience completed, it is now possible to attempt some tentative conclusions. The developing world entered the 1980s with mounting debts, disappointing economic growth, increasing populations, food scarcities and rising energy costs. Much development planning has had mediocre results because the concept of the wholeness of a country's economy had been disregarded. Industrialization alone cannot solve economic backwardness and poverty, for it is but one form of development and its advance is closely related to that of the other sectors of the economy. Infatuation with industrialization can bring dire results as shown by the recent histories of Argentina and Yugoslavia, whose agricultural production withered away as programs of over-industrialization ignored the agrarian sector. In 1950, a year in which Yugoslavia suffered famine, it was discovered that only 70% of the usable land was being cultivated because low-price ceilings relative to industrial products and heavy taxation had removed incentives from agriculture. There is no hope of success for any country if economic advance is one-sided, yet this is precisely what has been happening in many developing countries during the recent past. Only at the end of the 1970s was it coming to be realized that even moderate industrialization contains a multiplier element that works adversely against the agrarian sector; for example, policies furthering import-substituting industries penalize agriculture but boost the urban-industrial centres. They thus compound the distortion of the economy, since it is these cities that hold the rulers, planners and administrators. Unfortunately, the town-dwellers often have little understanding of rural ways and rural requirements and are all too conscious that it is the town that exhibits progress and modernization. Almost everywhere in the Third World the agricultural sector has suffered neglect and has seen its most active and virile members move to the cities. Production has fallen and country after country now spends scarce resources on importing food for its urban masses.

The second major realization of the end of the 1970s concerns the dynamic but often obstructionist character of demographic factors. Again and again in South-East Asia material gains are cancelled out by unexpectedly high rates of population increase. It seems that Asia, for example, can abolish poverty or she can increase her numbers, but it is becoming clear that she cannot do both simultaneously. At the moment too many of the fruits of development are wasted in supporting more people in poverty instead of being used to abolish poverty. The whole problem of development, and particularly the furthering of industrialization, becomes more and more intractable with soaring population totals.

According to UN statistics the populations of cities in underdeveloped countries are growing at an average of 3.5% annually. The average for all cities is 2.5%. The experts predict that 15 cities in the Third World will grow to between 11 and 26 million residents by 2000—populations greater than those of all but the five largest cities today. These increases in size will create enormous pressures for social services and for economic opportunities.[1]

These figures also support the conclusion that present-day conditions necessitate planned development. The developing countries need to do in a relatively brief period what took the richer countries several generations. The need to plan, to mobilize resources and deploy them effectively and economically, cuts across ideology; it is a matter of simple common sense.

The fourth conclusion is that there can be no hope of successful industrialization without the establishment of a firm foundation both in social services and public utilities, for the infrastructure concerns humans as well as material resources.

The example of Hong Kong suggests that something more than large doses of capital will be required for successful industrialization. Increasingly "trade as well as aid" must become a world slogan. Poor countries overpopulated in relation to their primary resources must turn to industry for succour, but industrialization cannot be effective if overseas markets are closed to their products. Trade is a two-way process where exchange of both primary and secondary products in the world as a whole must increase together. Growing incomes everywhere create greater demand; world trade may well grow faster than ever, for food and raw materials, as well as capital goods and more high-tech manufactures, will be urgently needed by the overpopulated newly industrializing countries. Although degrees of "comparative advantage" will play a very important part in determining patterns of specialization, it is clear that the simpler manufactures, i.e. intermediate technology products, will be made increasingly in the Third World.

Fifth, the struggle for betterment by the developing countries has now gone on long enough for paths to be evaluated and lessons to be learned. What is becoming disturbingly clear is that while economic growth has been taking place in Third World nations (according to indicators such as GNP, per capita income, etc.), the mass of the population in many of these countries seems to have received few benefits. Economic growth alone is not development; social improvement in terms of education, health and welfare is an integral part of the "modernization" process. Another conclusion is that there can be little prospect of successful economic development without harmony among countries. Further, it is clear that substantial help from the more developed countries has become a *sine qua non*.

The calls for aid from the developed world, already of massive proportions, will continue to increase at an accelerating rate. A new and formidable problem has become apparent: the growing indebtedness of Third World countries. According to World Bank estimates the international debts of about 100 developing countries amounted to US $33 billion in 1964, to $80 billion in 1971, US $370 billion in 1980, and US $711 billion in 1985. Many developing countries are now using more than one half of their foreign exchange earnings merely to service their debts; this figure is rising sharply. In fact, the ratio of debt to exports has risen from 90.1 in 1980 to 135.7 in 1985. This is a major issue that must be tackled quickly by the world community, particularly since it is coming to be realized that the speed of development is far slower than the optimistic forecasts of one and two decades ago. The idea of "development in a decade" is giving way to "development in a half-century". Figures show that even during the first Development Decade (1960-69)—a period of unprecedented growth—the gap between rich and poor nations' incomes widened. The rich countries maintained rates of growth of 5-6% a year; the developing countries had rates of about 4%. This meant, for example, that each year the United States added to its national income the equivalent of the entire national income of the African continent—some US $30 billion.

While there are unlikely to be dramatic effects in the future such as those created by the alliance of the oil-producing states, nevertheless a changing relationship between the Third World and the industrial countries began to evolve during the 1970s. Further changes in the economic relations between rich and poor are inevitable, with the era of cheap food and cheap commodities passing for the advanced countries, and with a diminution of the "poor relation" status that so far has been the lot of the developing nations.

Although so far we have not even mentioned investment, the articles in this chapter in fact deal with investment, for investment flows from the First World to the Third World, whether multilateral, or public or private, are heavily industry development-oriented. This, of course, is especially the case with private investment. The excerpt from the IMF Occasional Paper 33 discusses the role of foreign direct investment in development. It focuses specifically on the costs and benefits of foreign direct investment (FDI) by examining the transfer of resources and the impact of this on the developing countries. There is considerable controversy about the relative costs and benefits of FDI on developing countries. The principal argument in favour is that the capital, technological and managerial resources generally increase the real domestic income of a host country. Evidence of this is found in higher tax revenues and labour incomes, and/or lower prices. On the negative side, there is concern that the activities of the TNCs, which are the primary investors, will have adverse consequences for the host country's development priorities. In general, many of the costs and benefits of FDI are greatly affected by the macroeconomic policies of the host country, e.g., the relative price level in the host country and the degree of cooperation between the host country strategy for development and foreign investors. The excerpt concludes that the costs and benefits of FDI depend on particular circumstances for each country and each project. The distribution of gains will depend on the bargaining positions of both the direct investor and the host country.

The Goldsborough article deals with macroeconomic aspects of direct investment, in particular with its role in capital transfers and adjustments. It examines some of the causes and consequences of the decline in the relative importance of direct investments since the early 1970s and discusses the conditions and modifications in policies in both lending and borrowing countries that might encourage larger flows of FDI.

The Shihata article discusses ways of increasing private capital flows to Third World countries. Because of the decline in foreign direct investment of both a medium and long-term nature, as well as a decline in official development assistance (ODA) there definitely is a need to create a more favourable investment climate in the Third World. Shihata argues that these declines are due in part to the prevailing presumption that investing in developing countries usually entails greater non-commercial risks, mostly of a political nature, than is the case with investments in the First World. Given the negative result which comes about as a result of a debtor country's dependence on external borrowing, LDCs have come to realize the positive aspects of foreign direct investments, under appropriate conditions. It is in this context that Shihata examines the World Bank's proposal to establish a Multilateral Investment Guarantee Agency, which would guarantee the foreign investor against political risks.

The Landell-Mills article examines the role of Development Finance Corporations (DFCs), more commonly called Development Banks. In the past these corporations were established in countries where commercial banks had inadequate resources to provide either the longer-term financing needed for development projects or short-term loans to potential growth firms in the high-risk category. Landell-Mills' article looks at the experience of the World Bank with two of its most successful DFC borrowers during the 1970s—the Korean Development Finance Corporation and the Industrial Credit and Investment Corporation, India, to demonstrate the ability of these to adapt to environments not normally conducive to long-term investment. The final article in this chapter, by Burki and Ayres, turns to official development aid (ODA), pure and simple. Although this form of assistance, also known as concessional flows or more commonly, aid, forms but a small part of the financial help flowing to the Third World for industrial investment development purposes, it is one that probably engenders more debate than do private flows, for the simple reason that national appropriations by donors are made on political bases and come from taxpayers' pockets. The authors discuss the ongoing debate by examining four inter-related issues: the effectiveness of aid; the support for aid in donor countries; the volume of ODA; and the overall effectiveness of aid. This debate has emerged in response to the growing politicization of aid, in particular the frequent linking of aid to a country's foreign policy—both the donor's and the recipient's. The end result of such practices is that poor countries, lacking a central place in a donor's political strategy, receive considerably less aid than countries that are more visible and politically important to a donor's foreign policy. This discussion is continued in the Introduction to Chapter 12: The North Views the South.

---

[1] "Urban Growth Called Danger to Stability of Poor Nations", *N.Y. Times*, 8 February 1987

The Role of Foreign Direct Investment in Development

The International Monetary Fund

There is considerable controversy about the relative costs and benefits of foreign direct investment to developing countries. The principal argument in its favor is that the package of capital and technological and managerial resources generally increases the real domestic income of the host country by more than the profits returned to the investor. This increase is manifested in higher tax revenues, higher labor incomes, or lower prices. Moreover, since profits are earned only when the investment earns a positive return, part of the risk is borne by the foreign investor. Nevertheless, the association of direct investment with some degree of overseas managerial control, and generally with large transnational companies, can have wide-ranging effects on the economy of the host developing country. Concern that some of the activities of the enterprise might have adverse consequences for a country's development prospects may lead to the adoption of restrictive policies toward foreign direct investment. This concern has been reinforced by dissatisfaction with some of the results of earlier investments.

In assessing the overall effects of direct investment, however, it is relevant that many of the principal benefits and costs can be substantially affected by the economic policies of the host country. In particular, the types of investment projects chosen will depend on relative prices in the host country; if these are inappropriate, the investment will also be inappropriate and of less benefit to the economy. The foreign investors themselves can also help to ensure that the direct investment process is mutually beneficial by cooperating with a host country's chosen development strategy and showing willingness, where necessary, to consider alternative arrangements, such as joint ventures and minority equity participation.

Transfer of Resources

There are wide variations in the extent to which different developing countries have relied on direct investment. Such inflows have made an important contribution to total capital formation in only a few developing countries since 1973, as many countries turned to overseas borrowing as a source of foreign savings. Between 1979 and 1981, direct investment inflows represented about 25 percent and 11 percent of total fixed capital formation in Singapore and Malaysia, respectively; around 5 percent in Chile and the Philippines; only about 1.5 percent in Brazil, Indonesia, and Mexico; while they were negligible in India, Korea, and Nigeria. However, these measures understate the contribution of foreign-owned enterprises to gross capital formation. Reinvested earnings are not recorded for some developing countries; in addition, the depreciation funds of direct investment enter-

Originally published as Chapter III of *Foreign Private Investment in Developing Countries*, IMF Occasional Paper no. 33, 1985.

prises, which are not included in the definition of direct investment, finance a substantial proportion of their gross capital expenditures.

There are major differences among countries in the degree to which direct investment can be substituted for other forms of foreign capital inflow. . . . The differences in substitutability are the result both of variations in economic structure that affect countries' attractiveness to investors, and differences in the underlying macroeconomic causes of the need for capital inflows. Countries with small internal markets, few natural resources, a relatively underdeveloped infrastructure, and limited possibilities for manufactured exports may not be able to attract substantial direct investment, even with liberal regulations and generous incentives. Such countries are also generally not able to borrow significantly on commercial terms, and must rely primarily on concessional borrowing. Consequently, the possibilities for substitution between overseas commercial borrowing and direct investment mainly concern countries that are larger, better-endowed with natural resources, or that have a more developed industrial sector. Countries that already have a substantial amount of foreign-affiliated investment will also generally find it easier to influence the future composition of capital inflows, since they can also influence direct investment through the financial structure of existing subsidiaries of foreign companies, and in particular the amount of borrowing from domestic sources and from third parties abroad. But . . . direct investment has tended to be even more concentrated in a few countries than has external borrowing.

The macroeconomic causes of capital inflows can also have a large influence on the degree of substitutability between direct investment and commercial borrowing as sources of foreign capital. In countries with well-integrated capital markets, the particular sources of macroeconomic imbalance would have only a limited impact on the composition of capital inflows. However, most developing countries have fragmented domestic capital markets, and for them the causes of capital inflows are of greater significance. Three types of factors lead to a need for increased capital inflows, presenting varying possibilities for substitution between direct investment and external borrowing.

First, aggregate demand may increase relative to aggregate supply because of increased expenditure on investment projects that are regarded as financially viable. If such investment takes place in the private sector, then the potential for substitution is high, provided the tax and regulatory frameworks are suitable for direct investment. If the investment is undertaken mainly by state enterprises, then in many countries the potential for substitution is lower because of institutional barriers to the participation of foreign direct investment. Nevertheless, there could still be substantial possibilities for the participation of foreign equity through various forms of joint venture arrangements with the relevant state enterprises, provided these were consistent with the host country's overall development orientation. Such arrangements are common in mineral exploration and development, where much of the risk is borne by foreign equity capital operating in partnership with public corporations, but are also evident in many other sectors. Brazil has encouraged joint ventures involving a combination of state and both local and foreign private equity capital, particularly in the petrochemical industry. The experience of China, which at present uses foreign direct investment more than overseas commercial borrowing, demonstrates that a system of state enterprises need not be a barrier to substitution between different forms of foreign capital. One policy measure that has frequently reduced such substitutability has been the provision of government guarantees on overseas commercial bank borrowing by state enterprises. These lower the cost of commercial borrowing to the enterprise, since the government assumes part of the lender's risk, so it becomes relatively more attractive to the state enterprise than foreign equity participation.

Second, aggregate demand may rise relative to aggregate supply because of increased expenditure on consumption or on investment projects that are regarded as not financially viable, including infrastructure projects that might have high overall economic returns but that do not generate any revenue directly. Such excess demand frequently takes the form of larger fiscal deficits as government expenditure on subsidies, higher wage bills, or social infrastructure rises. In this situation, the possibilities for substituting foreign direct investment for overseas borrowing, which is usually undertaken directly by a government or central bank, are lower. There are no additional investment projects that would be attractive to direct investors. In principle, higher domestic borrowing by the government could drive up domestic interest rates, and lead to greater inflows of direct investment, in part by reducing domestic borrowing by transnational companies. In practice, however, such indirect effects on foreign capital flows are limited because capital markets are fragmented, and flexible interest rate policies do not exist in many developing countries.

Finally, part of the external borrowing of some developing countries has been used not to finance an increase in aggregate domestic expenditures, but to offset an outflow of private residents' capital. The possibilities for substituting direct investment for such borrowing are generally low, especially since the inappropriate exchange and interest rate policies that are often the cause of such capital flight are also likely to discourage direct investment.

Therefore, the extent to which different developing countries could have substituted foreign direct investment for part of their external borrowing over the last decade would have depended on how they used it. A significant proportion of the borrowing that took place immediately after the two large increases in oil prices was for short-term balance of payments support, for which the possibilities for substitution were probably quite low. However, the scope for switching between types of capital inflow probably increases with the length of the period after the initial external imbalance. In this regard, evidence presented in the Fund's *World Economic Outlook* for 1983 suggested that, for most of the largest borrowers among non-oil developing countries, the increase in external debt during the last decade was associated with a higher rate of investment and was not used primarily to finance consumption.[1] However, part of the higher investment must have been in infrastructural projects of a sort that would not have attracted foreign direct investment.

Technology transfers (including managerial and marketing expertise) are more difficult to measure than capital flows but . . . a substantial proportion of such transfers took place between overseas parent companies and their subsidiaries. Once again, however, the importance of such intrafirm technology transfers relative to transfers between unrelated parties varied substantially among developing countries and across industries. In Korea, where direct investment was regulated and channeled into particular sectors, some three quarters of all overseas licensing agreements between 1973 and 1980 were concluded by locally-owned firms; in Singapore, however where there were relatively few restrictions on direct investment, most licensing agreements were entered into by firms that were at least partly foreign owned.[2] In industries with new or highly firm-specific technologies (such as the electronics industry), most transfers were between a parent company and its fully- or majority-owned affiliates, since there was concern with retaining close control of the technology involved. In many other industries, however, technology transfers through various licensing agreements grew more rapidly than the transfer of technology through direct investment.

Impact on Host Developing Countries

The overall economic impact of enterprises established through direct investment goes well beyond the direct transfer of capital and technology that they entail. Since these enterprises also borrow in the host country and from third parties abroad, they affect a share of total resources that is much larger than the recorded inflow of direct investment. Moreover, direct investment is often concentrated in import-substituting or export industries, so that the foreign trade performance of enterprises based on direct investment can have a significant impact on their host's balance of payments. Consequently, the achievement of development objectives can be significantly affected by the actions of foreign-controlled affiliates and their parent companies. Many developing countries have been concerned by the loss of local autonomy that this might imply. Moreover, substantial foreign ownership of major sectors of the economy has frequently been regarded as involving a weakening of indigenous industry and the growth of oligopolistic market structures which impose welfare costs on the population. In addition, it has been argued that foreign-controlled firms may adopt overly capital-intensive production techniques (which are available, but inappropriate), make insufficient transfers of technology at too high a cost (to retain technological advantage), set artificially high transfer prices (to extract excessive profits), and exert strain on the balance of payments (because, as part of an enterprise with multinational production facilities, they may be less able than firms under domestic control to expand exports and may be overly dependent on imports).

There can also be many indirect effects of foreign investment that are beneficial to the host country's economy. Such investment may contribute longer-term advantages in terms of improved productivity and international competitiveness. The presence of efficient firms that are competitive on world markets can provide a potentially important channel for transferring to host countries technological and managerial skills. This can take place within a particular industry, where suppliers of inputs to the foreign affiliate, domestic users of the affiliate's output, and its competitors may all be induced to adopt more efficient techniques. It can also occur more generally within the economy, through an eventual improvement in the level of training and experience of the labor force and through the possible encouragement of various financial and technical support industries that can lower all industrial costs.

Judgments on the permissible degree of foreign ownership and control involve broader political as well as economic considerations. Nor are such issues confined to developing countries, since groups in some industrial countries have also been apprehensive about the growth of foreign direct investment within their borders. Each host country, therefore, must determine the appropriate level of foreign participation in particular sectors in the light of its needs and objectives. It should be borne in mind, however, that many of the costs and benefits associated with direct investment can be strongly influenced by the host country's economic policies. The attitudes and policies of transnational companies can also play an important role in ensuring that the direct investment process is one of mutual benefit.

Foreign direct capital can have complex and wide-ranging effects on indigenous enterprises and the level of competition in a developing country. It can stimulate local entrepreneurship by providing increased competition and opportunities for subcontracting by local suppliers; it can also, however, reduce the number of locally-owned firms, either by takeover or because such firms are not able to compete with the greater resources of foreign-controlled subsidiaries. It is estimated, for instance, that around one third of foreign subsidiaries in developing countries were established through the acquisition of existing enterprises.[3] Whether such takeovers reduce overall competition would depend partly on the competitiveness of other firms in the industry. The policies of the host country also play an important role; the welfare costs of excessive market concentration are greater, for instance, when the domestic market is also insulated against competition from imports.

Because of the nature of technological information, it is transferred in a highly imperfect market in which it is often difficult to fix an exact price. Developing countries are frequently in a weak bargaining position in these markets, especially if they lack specialized manpower that can help determine the likely contribution of proposed technology transfers. This can be particularly so when the technology is transferred as one element of a package of resources provided by direct investment, since the exact cost of such technology is frequently unclear. Some developing countries have attempted to strengthen their bargaining positions by imposing limits on royalty payments (as a fixed percentage of total sales receipts, for instance) or by establishing vetting procedures for all technology contracts. The increased willingness of some transnational corporations to consider alternative forms of technology transfer——including licensing, franchising, and subcontracting—may help lower the costs of these transfers, especially for host countries that may not need other elements of a direct investment package, such as managerial or marketing skills.

It is frequently argued that since the technology transferred to developing countries through direct investment is generally developed for industrial countries, it involves overly capital-intensive techniques, especially since multinational enterprises conduct little research and development in most developing countries. There is some evidence that, in many developing countries, average capital-labor ratios of foreign subsidiaries in manufacturing are higher than those of local firms. However, this appears to be largely due to their greater concentration in industries with high capital requirements; differences in capital intensity between foreign- and locally-owned firms within the same industry are less clearcut. In any event, host country governments can significantly influence the choice of production techniques. A number of frequently adopted policies encourage the substitution of capital for labor; these include overvalued exchange rates that reduce the cost of imported capital equipment, administered interest rates below current rates of inflation, and various fiscal incentives for investment that reduce the cost of capital.

The external trade of foreign-controlled companies may be less responsive to shifts in relative competitiveness between the host country and its trading partners because much of it consists of intrafirm transactions. There are indications that such intrafirm trade between industrial countries is less sensitive to relative price changes than trade between independent producers, who are unconcerned with the effects of their actions on the profitability of other affiliates.[4] Although intrafirm trade is generally less important for developing than for industrial countries, it plays a major role in certain developing countries, particularly those with substantial exports from technology-intensive industries. In recent years, trade between related parties (parties of which one owns 5 percent or more of the voting stock of the other) accounted for only around one quarter of manufactured imports into the United States from all developing countries, compared with over one half of such imports from industrial countries. However, related-party trade accounted for around three quarters of manufacturing exports to the United States from Malaysia, Mexico, and Singapore, over one third of such exports from Brazil, but less than one tenth of those from Argentina and India.[5]

The transfer prices used in such intrafirm transactions can diverge from the equivalent "arm's length" market price that would be set in trade between unrelated parties. Although under- or over-invoicing to shift profits for tax purposes, or to evade foreign trade taxes or exchange controls, is a problem for all foreign trade, the opportunities for such actions are clearly greater in intrafirm trade. This places a correspondingly greater burden on the monitoring ability of customs services, especially for highly differentiated products (such as pharmaceuticals) or for specialized intermediate components for which there is often no ascertainable arm's length price.

As has already been mentioned, an inappropriate set of policies can significantly increase the costs and reduce the benefits of foreign direct investment in the host country. For example, much of the initial inflow of direct investment into the manufacturing industries of developing countries, particularly in Latin America, was to establish import-substituting production, and was encouraged by high tariff barriers and quantitative restrictions on imports. The results of such investment were frequently disappointing; costs of production were high, value added at international prices and exports were low, and dependence on imported intermediate inputs was significant. At the same time, import restrictions contributed to an overvalued exchange rate that, together with fiscal incentives granted to attract direct investment, increased the real resource costs of profits earned on the investment. Disappointed with these results, host developing countries frequently attempted to increase their net benefits by imposing more detailed regulations on direct investment, including requirements for a minimum level of exports or local value added. Nevertheless, such regulations were generally less effective than more open exchange and trade policies would have been. The effects of more open trade policies were apparent in Singapore and Korea, where affiliates of multinational companies were responsible for some 90 percent and 27 percent, respectively, of total manufactured exports in the late 1970s, even though their share of total manufacturing sales in these countries was much smaller (around 30 percent and 10 percent, respectively).[6]

Transnational corporations can help reduce developing countries' concerns about foreign economic influence by respecting the economic and social objectives and priorities of host governments and by signalling their willingness to abide by generally acceptable standards of behavior in such areas as transfer pricing, restrictive business practices for both domestic and international trade, and the transfer of technology. International codes of conduct, such as the code established under the auspices of the Organization for Economic Cooperation and Development (OECD) or the more comprehensive code still being discussed under the auspices of the United Nations, may help to reduce potential areas of conflict in this area by setting guidelines for the responsibilities of both investing companies and host governments.[7] The growing diversity of sources of foreign direct investment, and an increased willingness by many investors to consider arrangements other than wholly- or majority-owned affiliates, may also help reduce concerns prevalent in host countries about loss of local autonomy.

Thus, although the overall costs and benefits derived from specific direct investments depend on the particular circumstances of each country and each project, it is evident that direct investment can be of mutual advantage to the host country and the foreign investor. Moreover, its net benefits can be strongly influenced by the host country's economic policies. The distribution of any net gains will depend, in part, on the relative bargaining position of the direct investor and the host country, but there are clearly opportunities for mutual advantage through policies that can both increase the attractiveness of a country to potential investors and increase the likely benefits that the country receives from such investment.

References

[1] *World Economic Outlook*, Occasional Paper No. 21 (Washington, May 1983), Appendix A. Supplementary Note 7, pp. 140-44.

[2] Bohn-Young Koo, "New Forms of Foreign Investment in Korea" and Pang Eng Fong, "Foreign Indirect Investment in Singapore" in Charles Oman, *New Forms of International Investment in Developing Countries*, Organization for Economic Cooperation and Development (Paris: OECD, 1984).

[3] R. Vernon, *Storm Over the Multinationals; the Real Issues* (Cambridge, Massachusetts: Harvard University Press, 1977), p. 72. based on data from the Harvard Multinational Enterprise Project.

[4] David J. Goldsbrough, "International Trade of Multinational Corporations and its Responsiveness to Changes in Aggregate Demand and Relative Prices," *Staff Papers*, International Monetary Fund (Washington), Vol. 28 (September 1981).

[5] G. K. Helleiner, *Intra-Firm Trade and the Developing Countries* (New York: St. Martin's Press, 1981).

[6] Oman, op. cit.

[7] Organization for Economic Cooperation and Development, *Declaration by the Governments of OECD Member Countries and Decisions of the OECD Council: On Guidelines for Multinational Enterprises, National Treatment, International Investment Incentives and Disincentives, and Consultation Procedures* (Paris: OECD, 1976); *Declaration by the Governments of OECD Member Countries and Decisions of the OECD Council: On International Investment and Multinational Enterprises* (Paris: OECD, 1984).

Foreign Direct Investment in Developing Countries:
Trends, Policy Issues and Prospects

David Goldsbrough

The relative importance of direct investment in the capital flows to developing countries has been declining since the early 1970s. While direct investment continued to increase in absolute terms, bank credit has become a much more dominant factor in private capital flows. Some observers have argued that this shift in the composition of private capital flows has increased the vulnerability of the developing countries to external payments difficulties. Moreover, with relatively slow growth in bank lending to these countries in prospect for the medium term, other sources of external financing, including direct investment, will be required if the pace of development is to improve. With these considerations in mind, this article examines some of the causes and consequences of the decline in the relative importance of direct investment since the early 1970s and discusses the conditions and modifications in policies in both lending and borrowing countries that might encourage larger flows of such investment. Direct investment also involves the transfer of a package of resources, including technological and managerial expertise in addition to capital; these may have an even greater impact than capital flows on a recipient country's production capabilities. However, this article is concerned with the macroeconomic aspects of direct investment, in particular with its role in capital transfers and adjustment.

Direct investment refers to investment made to acquire a lasting interest and an effective voice in the management of an enterprise. Many countries set a minimum proportion (generally between 10 and 25 percent) of foreign ownership of the voting stock as evidence of direct investment. In principle, all capital flows provided by direct investors, including equity capital, reinvested earnings, and net lending, are classified as direct investment.

Trends in investment

Net inflows of foreign direct investment into developing countries generally increased throughout the 1960s and 1970s. Direct investment flows from industrial to developing countries rose from an average of under $2 billion a year during the early 1960s to an average of around $13 billion a year during 1979-81. However, their share in total capital inflows declined substantially as external borrowing, particularly from commercial banks, grew rapidly.

Although the rapid expansion of commercial bank lending was already underway before the first large oil price increase of 1973-74, that event accelerated the decline in relative importance of direct investment flows, especially for the non-oil developing countries,

Originally published in *Finance and Development*, vol. 22, no. 1, 1986. Reprinted with permission.

which financed most of their larger current account deficits by external borrowing. In 1973, direct investment flows financed some 20 percent of the combined current account deficit and net accumulation of reserves of non-oil developing countries, compared with an average of only about 12 percent in later years (see chart). Nevertheless, these inflows continued to increase in real terms-at an average annual rate of about 3 percent in terms of constant prices—to an average of about $10.5 billion during 1979-81, but declined during the recession of 1982 and 1983.

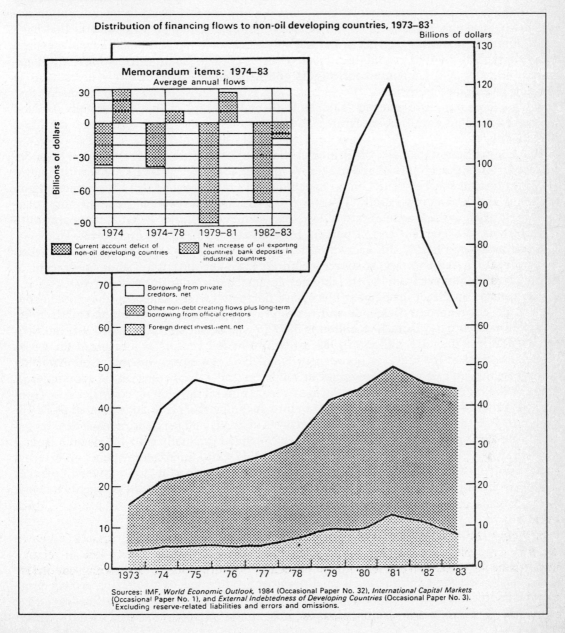

Distribution of financing flows to non-oil developing countries, 1973–83[1]

Billions of dollars

Memorandum items: 1974–83
Average annual flows

Billions of dollars

Current account deficit of non-oil developing countries

Net increase of oil exporting countries' bank deposits in industrial countries

Borrowing from private creditors, net

Other non-debt creating flows plus long-term borrowing from official creditors

Foreign direct investment, net

Sources: IMF, *World Economic Outlook,* 1984 (Occasional Paper No. 32), *International Capital Markets* (Occasional Paper No. 1), and *External Indebtedness of Developing Countries* (Occasional Paper No. 3).
[1] Excluding reserve-related liabilities and errors and omissions.

As a consequence of the shift in the composition of financing, the structure of the external liabilities of these countries changed significantly. The share of direct investment in total gross external liabilities (total external debt plus stock of foreign direct investment) of non-oil developing countries declined from an estimated 26.5 percent in 1973 to 17 percent in 1983, while the share of public and publicly guaranteed debt to private financial institutions rose from 10 percent to 25 percent (see table).

These global trends mask a wide diversity of experience in individual countries, resulting from differences in both economic environment and policies toward foreign direct investment. Much of this investment is concentrated in a small number of countries that have large domestic markets, are rich in natural resources, or have significant advantages as a base for export-oriented production. Five countries (Brazil, South Africa, Mexico, Singapore, and Malaysia) accounted for almost one half of the stock of direct investment in non-oil developing countries at the end of 1983. Nevertheless, some other countries that also have large domestic markets (such as India and Turkey) or that successfully pursued an export-oriented development strategy (such as Korea) were much less reliant on direct investment.

The United States has been the principal source of private direct investment in developing countries, although it declined in relative importance in recent years along with the two other traditional sources—the United Kingdom and France—while direct investment from Germany and Japan grew rapidly. The stock of U.S. direct investment in developing countries grew at an average annual rate of less than 10 percent during 1970-82, compared with growth rates of 17 percent and 21 percent for Germany and Japan, respectively. However, in 1982 the United States still accounted for almost half of the total stock of such investment. Together, the five largest source countries have accounted for some 85 percent of direct investment flows from industrial to developing countries during recent years.

The returns on direct investment flows have fluctuated with changes in the global economy. Total net recorded dividends and net interest payments by developing countries on direct investment rose from $9.5 billion in 1973 to a peak of $26.5 billion in 1981, but then declined to less than $18 billion in 1983, when profits fell sharply as a result of the world recession. Most of the increase between 1973 and 1981 came from the major oil exporting countries; the later decline reflected lower oil prices and a weakening of the economies of some of the oil exporting countries. Payments from non-oil developing countries rose from $3.5 billion in 1973 to $9.5 billion in 1981, before declining sharply to an estimated $6.25 billion in 1983. Expressed as a percentage of exports of goods and services, non-oil developing countries' total payments on direct investment declined gradually over the decade from 3 percent in 1973 to less than 1.5 percent in 1983. Meanwhile, interest payments on external debt rose from some 6 percent of exports of goods and services in 1973 to over 13 percent in 1983, reflecting the increased emphasis on financing of the balance of payments through debt.

Changes in financial markets

Structural changes in the financial system were already underway by the late 1960s as major banks increased their international operations and, attracted by promising growth prospects, greatly increased their lending to some of the more rapidly industrializing developing countries. This trend was continued after 1973, as the relatively risk-averse asset preferences of oil exporting countries led them to hold many of their assets in the form of liquid bank deposits. Together with the greatly increased demand for medium- and longer-term financing by developing countries, this provided banks with the opportunity to expand their role as international financial intermediaries. To indicate the magnitudes involved, the cumulative current account deficits of non-oil developing countries over 1974—83 amounted to $588 billion, while net borrowing from banks by these countries was $216 billion and the net inflow of direct investment $82 billion (also see chart). Much of the new bank lending was either to, or guaranteed by, governments and was encouraged by the view that the risks associated with such lending were relatively low in comparison to normal commercial lending.

In contrast, there was much less scope for large immediate increases in direct investment, which depended on the identification of individual opportunities for profitable investment and was influenced by a wide range of institutional restraints that could not be altered quickly. A considerable part of the external borrowing was undertaken by governments to finance balance of payments or fiscal deficits and it might have been difficult for foreign equity capital, which is more directly associated with private enterprise investment, to substitute for a substantial proportion of such borrowing, at least in the short term. This is because most developing countries have limited and fragmented capital markets, which means that the particular causes of a macroeconomic imbalance have a strong influence on the composition of capital inflows. Even so, longer-term possibilities for substitution between direct investment and borrowing from commercial banks as sources of capital inflows can still be significant, especially for countries with substantial domestic markets or natural resource endowments; these countries were often among the larger borrowers from commercial banks. In this regard, restrictive policies adopted by many developing countries toward foreign direct investment also seem to have contributed to a greater reliance on bank credit.

Host country policies

Most developing countries combine some degree of regulation and control of direct investment, aimed at improving net benefits to the host country, with various incentives designed to attract such investment. In general, during the 1960s and much of the 1970s there was a trend toward greater restrictions. Increased availability of alternative external financing, disappointment with some of the results of direct investment, and growing nationalist sentiment in many countries all contributed to this trend.

Although the combination of policies chosen depends to a large extent on a country's development strategy and market philosophy, the underlying attractiveness of a country as an investment location is also important since this affects its relative bargaining strength vis-à-vis potential direct investors. A number of countries (particularly in Africa and the Caribbean) were unable to attract significant inflows of direct investment despite offering substantial incentives, because of their small domestic markets and limited natural resources. However, a few territories and countries with relatively small domestic markets (including Hong Kong, Singapore, and, to some extent, Malaysia) that pursued open economic policies and maintained few restrictions on foreign investment were able to attract substantial export-oriented direct investment, while generally offering only moderate incentives. Many other countries imposed a number of restrictions or specific performance requirements on such investment, as they sought to extract greater benefits.

Restrictions and regulations often acted as a barrier to the entry of new investment, but they were sometimes offset by a country's attractive location, especially if they were not too complex or subject to sudden and frequent changes. The provision of a stable economic environment and the adoption of appropriate financial and exchange rate policies are probably at least as important for encouraging foreign investment and for increasing the flow of new benefits to the host country as are policies related specifically to such investment.

Recent trends in a number of countries indicate a liberalization of policies in order to attract more foreign investment. Some countries (including Egypt, Jamaica, the Philippines, and Turkey) shifted from policies that emphasized detailed control of direct investment to much more flexible arrangements, while more gradual policy changes took place in other countries (including Korea, Mexico, Morocco, and Pakistan). The policies of some centrally planned economies toward foreign direct investment were also modified in recent years. One of the greatest changes took place in China, which now encourages investment through either joint ventures or wholly foreign-owned enterprises, and has liberalized regulations governing the purchase of inputs and the sale of a proportion of output on the domestic market.

Foreign direct investment and external debt in developing countries, 1973—83

	Stock of foreign direct investment[1] (in billions of dollars)		Total outstanding external debt[2]	Share of foreign direct investment in total gross external liabilities[3] (in percent)
	1973	1983 (Estimate)	1983	1983
Seven major borrowers	**20.0**	**59.6**	**350.1**	**14.5**
Argentina	2.5	5.8	44.4	11.6
Brazil	7.5	24.6	88.0	21.8
Indonesia	1.7	6.8	30.4	18.3
Korea	0.7	1.8	38.9	4.4
Mexico	3.1	13.6	89.4	13.2
Philippines	0.9	2.7	23.9	10.9
Venezuela	3.6	4.3	35.1	10.9
Non-oil developing countries	**47.0**	**140.9**	**685.5**	**17.0**

Source: Fund staff estimates

[1] The 1983 end of year stock figures equal the estimated book value of the stock of direct investment from industrial countries at the end of 1978 plus total direct investment flows during 1979-83.

[2] End of year. Includes short-term debt, but not reserve-related liabilities.

[3] Total gross external liabilities are defined as stock of foreign direct investment plus total outstanding external debt.

Industrial country policies

At present, most industrial countries maintain relatively few restrictions on capital outflows and provide some encouragement for direct investment in developing countries, through guarantee and insurance schemes and various forms of official financial support. The decline in the relative importance of direct investment in total capital flows to developing countries during the 1970s was not due to any major change in such policies. Nevertheless, the protectionist trade measures adopted in recent years could have discouraged direct investment since they reduced opportunities for profitable investment in export sectors where developing countries have demonstrated a comparative advantage.

Most industrial countries provide insurance for new direct investment in developing countries, generally with coverage of noncommercial risks such as expropriation, losses due to war, and inconvertibility of dividend and capital transfers. However, with the exception of Japanese and Austrian direct investment, more than half of which is covered by such insurance, existing official arrangements cover only a small fraction—generally less than 10 percent—of industrial countries' total direct investment in developing countries. The World Bank is exploring a multilateral investment insurance scheme that would build upon and complement existing national and private schemes

Effects on external adjustment

The shift in the composition of capital inflows into developing countries, toward more bank credit and less direct investment, is likely to have increased these countries' vulnerability to various economic disturbances. This is because, unlike debt, an equity investment requires no service payments unless it earns a positive return. In this sense, the greater the share of direct investment in a country's portfolio of external liabilities, the greater is the share of risk associated with economic disturbances that is borne by foreign investors. In addition, since direct investment can be sensitive to changes in a host country's relative competitiveness, as well as to its interest rate and credit policies, a higher proportion of such investment in total capital flows can increase the responsiveness of such flows to a country's adjustment policies.

Because of the greater risk associated with equity investment generally, returns on such investments usually need to be higher than those on external debt. The combination of risk and return that a country is willing to accept is determined not only by individual preferences within the country but also by the costs associated with maintaining service payments on foreign liabilities when economic conditions deteriorate. These costs generally result from the need to restore a sustainable current account position either by reducing aggregate expenditures or by switching resources from nontraded to traded sectors.

There is some evidence that total returns on equity investment are more correlated with a country's ability to service its external liabilities than are interest payments on external debt. For a group of non-oil developing countries for which sufficiently long time series are available on reinvested earnings, the estimated annual rate of return on direct investment was positively associated with the annual rate of growth of GDP; there was a similar, although much weaker, association with the rate of growth of exports. By contrast, there was little association between these countries' rates of growth of GDP or exports and the average interest rate paid on their outstanding external debt. The contrast in movements in rates of return and interest rates was particularly marked during the recent recession.

In light of the relationships described above, the process of adjustment to economic disturbances should be easier in a country with a large proportion of direct investment in total external liabilities. For 28 developing countries that rescheduled part of their external debt during 1983, the stock of direct investment accounted for an average of only 14 percent of their total external liabilities (i.e., direct investment plus external debt) at end-1983, compared with an average of 24 percent for those 49 developing countries with available data that did not reschedule debt.

However, the way in which variations in profits affect current account adjustment also depends on their distribution between remitted dividends and reinvested earnings, since this influences the immediate foreign exchange outflow. The share of earnings that are reinvested fluctuates substantially with changes in economic conditions. For example, there are indications that—at least during the recent recession-remitted dividends declined much less than did reinvested earnings, particularly for direct investment in the manufacturing sectors of developing countries.

Prospects and policies

The financing pattern that supported the upsurge in current account deficits of developing countries through 1981 is unlikely to be repeated. In particular, new net lending through the international banking system is likely to be much more constrained in the future, so that foreign direct investment will probably be needed to contribute a greater share of future capital inflows. New net bank lending to countries with heavy principal payments on rescheduled debt is likely to be particularly constrained. These countries could find it advantageous to encourage a greater inflow of direct investment so as to maintain resource inflows sufficient to support an adequate growth rate, as well as to reduce vulnerability to any future deterioration in economic conditions. There are, of course, many other factors which will affect these countries' overall growth prospects; for example, higher domestic savings rates could help achieve higher growth rates without increased reliance on foreign financing.

The scope and need for an increased role for such investment can be illustrated in the context of the medium-term scenario for developing countries prepared for the Fund's 1984 World Economic Outlook. Over the period of the scenario, 1986-90, foreign direct investment flows to non-oil developing countries are assumed to increase by around 5 percent per annum in real terms. However, the volume of direct investment inflows would only reach the peak level achieved in 1981 by around 1988 because much of the growth would simply represent a recovery from the downturn in direct investment that occurred in 1982 and 1983.

Such growth in direct investment flows appears achievable for the group of non-oil developing countries as a whole—though not necessarily for each country—provided that the generally more encouraging policies of recent years toward direct investment are maintained and that the improvements in the world economic environment assumed in the medium-term scenario are achieved. If the exposure of international commercial banks evolves as assumed in the "base" scenario (i.e., with total exposure unchanged in real terms, except for trade-related credits, which increase in line with imports), the share of direct investment in total financing of the combined current account deficit and reserve accumulation of non-oil developing countries would rise moderately, to around 15 percent in 1988-90 compared with some 11 percent during 1979-81. A more substantial liberalization of policies toward foreign private investment could lead to much greater inflows.

Many of the more heavily indebted countries will need to make more substantial changes in policies toward direct investment if they are to achieve the level of inflows consistent with the growth prospects of the "base" scenario. This will be especially so if, as seems likely, new bank lending to countries with a large volume of rescheduled debt expands less rapidly than lending to countries with a lesser debt burden.

Increasing Private Capital Flows to LDCs: An examination of the proposed multilateral investment guarantee agency

Ibrahim F. I. Shihata

The share of developing countries in foreign direct investment is small, perhaps less than 30 percent of the total. The volume of this small share has also declined in recent years from more than $17 billion in 1981, according to the highest estimates, to some $10 billion in 1983. The higher financial returns that an investor often receives from investing in developing rather than developed countries have not changed this picture, due in part to the prevailing perceptions that investing in developing countries usually entails greater noncommercial risks. So important are these perceptions that quite often even investors from developing countries, when given the choice, tend to invest in developed countries despite awareness of the smaller profits and more complex regulatory requirements often encountered there.

The effects of this decline in the volume of foreign investment and the continued problem of capital flight have been aggravated by the serious fall in commercial bank lending to developing countries as a group (net transfers—a concept used by the World Bank to denote net flows less interest payments—dropped from $16 billion in 1981 to –$21 billion in 1983) and by a decline in official development assistance. More than at any previous time, there seems to be a need to improve the investment climate in developing countries and stimulate greater commercial flows to them. In addition, there has been a growing realization among developing countries that foreign private investment, under appropriate conditions and safeguards, can produce net gains. The complex relationship between investors and their hosts has become more balanced with the growing importance of developing countries in the world economy and the evolution of substantive and procedural rules for the treatment of foreign investment. It is in this context that the Bank has revived its proposal to establish a multilateral investment guarantee agency.

Governmental guarantees against noncommercial risks in foreign countries are not new; their origins lie in the export credit schemes that European countries adopted in the 1920s. The United States established a national program in 1948, guaranteeing U.S. investments in Western Europe against restrictions on the conversion of currencies (transfer risk), and gradually expanded it to cover investments in developing countries against all political risks. Similar programs have now been adopted by other industrial countries and some semi-industrial countries, with many of them combining these programs with their previously established systems of export credit insurance.

Originally published in *Finance and Development*, vol. 22, no. 1, 1985. Reprinted with permission.

In the late 1950s a proposal was made to establish an international agency that would insure foreign investors against noncommercial risks. Although the Bank, at the request of the OECD's Development Assistance Committee, assumed responsibility for the matter in 1961 and produced a number of elaborate studies and draft conventions in the late 1960s and early 1970s, the establishment of such a multilateral agency did not materialize.

Citing the need "to improve the investment climate—for potential investors and potential recipients alike," A. W. Clausen, the President of the Bank, took the initiative to revive the proposal in his first address to the Fund-Bank Annual Meetings in 1981. As a result of detailed studies undertaken by the Bank and informal discussions by its Executive Directors, the management of the Bank formulated a new plan. This version differs in many respects from previous proposals in which the agency would have no share capital and would have conducted operations exclusively on behalf of sponsoring member countries. The new features—which include a primary reliance upon share capital, a willingness to leverage this capital, and a greater role for the host countries—should give the agency broader scope in which to operate and greater flexibility, thus making it of particular interest to developing countries. The Bank is currently in consultation with members prior to a formal presentation of this proposal to its Executive Board.

Nature and scope

The basic objective of the proposed new multilateral agency is to encourage greater flows of resources to productive enterprises in developing member countries by guaranteeing foreign investments against noncommercial risks. The agency would, in addition, furnish information on investment opportunities, prepare studies, give advice to its members on formulating and implementing policies toward foreign investment, and cooperate with other international organizations engaged in related areas. The agency's operations would be broadly delineated in its convention, elaborated in its policy rules, and more precisely defined in its contracts of guarantee. This would permit it sufficient flexibility to adjust coverage to changes in investment arrangements and gradually expand operations as it built up financial reserves and gained experience.

Covered risks would encompass noncommercial events that affect an investor's rights, including the three traditionally recognized political risks: (1) the transfer risk resulting from host government restrictions and delays in converting and transferring local currency; (2) the risk of loss resulting from host government action or omission depriving investors of control over or substantial benefits from investments; and (3) the risk of loss resulting from armed conflict or civil unrest. (Other specific noncommercial risks may also be covered under the joint request of the investor and the host country.) General nondiscriminatory measures, such as those normally taken by states to regulate economic activity, are, however, not included unless they result in breach of legal commitments. In all cases, guarantees would be confined to measures introduced or events occurring after a contract had been concluded. Transfer risk seems the obvious candidate for wide coverage; under present circumstances it is the most relevant from the viewpoint of investors, and probably least likely to evoke political objections from the host countries.

Although the agency would focus primarily on direct investment, eligible investments could include any other transfer of assets, in monetary or nonmonetary form, for productive purposes. The scope of eligible investments could be expanded as the agency's resources increase and it becomes better able to develop its risk-measurement rules. At the outset the investment covered might include equity participation and equity-type loans; eventually it could also encompass profit-sharing, service, management and turnkey contracts, arrangements concerning industrial property rights, international leasing arrangements, and arrangements for the transfer of know-how and technology. It might even cover straight project loans, portfolio investments, and some forms of export credits. Coverage would be limited to long- and medium-term arrangements that involve productive new investments, including new transfers of foreign exchange to modernize, expand, or develop existing enterprises. Reinvested earnings, which could otherwise be transferred abroad, could also be deemed new investments.

The agency would charge premiums and fees for its services, the structure and level of premiums to be determined by its board. Revenues would be allocated, in order of priority, to (1) cover administrative expenses; (2) pay claims of insured investors; and (3) a reserve fund. Initially, however, the agency would have to rely on its members in meeting its administrative expenditures and paying whatever claims might arise under contracts of guarantee.

There would eventually be separate windows for two types of operations: guarantees issued on the basis of the agency's own capital and reserves, and guarantees issued for investments sponsored by members. The latter would be issued by the agency on behalf of the sponsoring members who would carry the ultimate financial burden of the sponsored guarantees on a *pro rata* basis. The proposed $1 billion initial capital would be subscribed by all members, with only a small portion (10 percent) paid in and the remainder kept under call to meet obligations that could not otherwise be met through paid-in capital and retained earnings. The agency's operations would be financed through its capital and reserves until it reaches the ceilings designated by its board. Such ceilings would include a general limitation of up to five times capital and reserves, as well as country ceilings related to the volume of investments originated from or carried out in one member country. Once a ceiling is reached, the agency could start the second window operations based on sponsorship; here the agency basically would act as the agent of the sponsoring countries and hold a separate sponsorship fund. This would receive the premiums of sponsored guarantees and pay for administrative costs and claims resulting from them, complemented in this respect by calls on sponsoring members.

Additionality

One basic concern raised about the proposed agency is whether it would, in fact, increase investment flows. Additional flows would result when guarantees attract investments that would not have taken place otherwise. Although it is impossible to quantify potential additional investments, there are strong indications that multilateral guarantees would encourage otherwise hesitant investors by providing a better investment climate.

Investors' calculations to maximize profitability usually involve two components, risk and return. Any perceived improvement in the risk profile could lower the rate of return required by the investor to undertake the investment ("hurdle rate"). If noncommercial risk is associated with an investment, an investor can expect to reduce this hurdle rate in return for a guarantee that diminishes risk. As the premium that the investor would pay for such a guarantee would reduce the return from the investment, additionality could ensue whenever the reduction in the hurdle rate exceeded the premium.

Concern over noncommercial risks has been reflected in the creation of national investment guarantee schemes and underscored by the rapid growth of the private political risk insurance market and the political risk analysis profession over the last decade. A study for the U.S. Overseas Private Investment Corporation concluded that in about 25 percent of the cases it examined, investments would not have taken place without a guarantee; in 18 percent, investments would have proceeded without a guarantee; and in the remaining 57 percent, there was no decisive evidence, a guarantee did appear essential in many instances.

"Qualitative additionality" can also occur when a guarantee offered by an international agency, even if not essential for the investment to be undertaken, has an impact on the structure of the investment. This would be the case when, as a result of the agency's evaluation, investments are made for longer periods of time or with greater benefits to the host country. It may also ensue from changes in the mix of foreign investors: if a guarantee plays a larger role for small- and medium-sized investors than for large transnational corporations, host countries might be able to gain more technology adapted to their needs and more labor-intensive investments.

Some developing countries could also benefit as home countries of investments, since an agency would accord their nationals investing abroad protection that is lacking at present. This aspect is gaining importance with increased investment flows among developing countries.

Links to national programs

With all DAC member countries operating their own national investment guarantee programs, is an international agency necessary and would it increase effectiveness? If is estimated that less than 20 percent of net investment flows from DAC member countries to developing countries was guaranteed under national programs during 1977-1981. According to OECD sources, only an estimated 9 percent of the existing stock of investments was covered at the end of 1981. The various national programs are utilized in different degrees, varying from more than 50 percent (Japan, Austria and, possibly, Korea) to less than 5 percent (most European programs). The small percentage of coverage by national agencies cannot be taken as evidence of the lack of need for guarantees. Recent contacts with investors prove the contrary; there is a potential demand for investment guarantees that is not met by the national programs, due mainly to constraints inherent in the national approach to investment insurance (lack of risk diversification, emphasis on nationality and national interests, and limited financial and appraisal capacities).

The proposed agency would complement national programs rather than compete with them. It would be designed to enhance risk diversification, contribute additional appraisal capacity, and overcome gaps resulting from different terms, conditions, and administrative practices of the various national agencies. To achieve this complementary role, it would focus on the following operations:

• Guarantee, or co-guarantee with national agencies, investments in countries where the national agency is already heavily exposed.

• Guarantee investments from member countries that do not have a national investment guarantee program.

- Guarantee investments that, though sound, are not eligible for a national guarantee.
- Guarantee types of investments (e.g., service contracts) or risks (e.g., breach of host government undertakings) not covered under the respective national programs.
- Co-guarantee large investments with national agencies, thus mitigating risk concentrations for both the national and the multilateral agency.
- Guarantee, or co-guarantee with national agencies, multinationally financed investments, permitting uniform protection to all co-investors.
- Guarantee low-risk projects in high-risk countries (most national investment guarantee administrations are not fully equipped to assess risks on the basis of project-related criteria).
- Provide reinsurance of national investment guarantee agencies, in particular of branches of large investments and part of large host country exposures. In this way the agency could enhance its own risk diversification and that of the reinsured national agencies.

Financial viability

The agency must become self-sustaining over the medium term. Administrative expenses and claims would have to be met through premium revenues and returns on invested reserves. The experience of national investment guarantee programs of OECD countries sustains this expectation: as of December 1983, their aggregate net payments on claims (claims not recovered from host countries) amounted to just 16.4 percent of their aggregate premium revenues. The dramatic expansion of private political risk underwriting over the last decade also indicates that it has been a profitable business.

Nonetheless, the agency might not quickly become self-sufficient, as the term is understood in insurance economics, because political risks cannot be readily calculated by conventional actuarial criteria. The proposed financial structure would ensure that claims would be paid even if losses exceeded premium revenues. These would be met through calls on shareholders or sponsors, as the case may be.

Obviously, the agency's ability to pay claims without recourse to such calls would largely depend on its premium structure. While a variation of premiums according to actual loss potential would serve the financial interests of the agency, differentiation by host countries might give rise to political difficulties. To reconcile these two aspects, the agency could differentiate by project rather than by host country. This would follow the practice of all major private U.S. political risk insurers and the Overseas Private Investment Corporation. Private insurers in the United States, for example, have quoted premiums ranging from 0.75 to 7 percent per annum for investments in the same host country. OPIC considers 12 different factors to rate expropriation risks and another 11 factors to rate armed conflict risks. Aspects such as the host government's attitude toward the guaranteed investment are also considered. While the transfer risk is normally associated with the foreign exchange liquidity of the host country, investments generating export revenues might not be affected by the general balance of payments problems of a host country. Premiums would reflect a variety of considerations and most differences would relate to economic rather than political factors.

Voting arrangements

Most international financial institutions, such as the World Bank, are donor agencies that transfer funds on their own account to developing countries. The proposed agency would, by contrast, only guarantee investments made by third parties in developing member countries. It would emphasize the importance of stable investment conditions rather than provide financial intermediation. As a consequence, its proposed voting structure differs from that of a typical financial institution where voting is primarily linked to capital contributions. Voting in this context would reflect an emphasis on building mutual confidence and policy cooperation within the agency.

The proposed allocation of equal voting power to home and host countries as groups is intended to reflect the focus on policy cooperation between host and home countries. A requirement of special majorities for decisions of particular financial significance would provide an advantage to larger contributors, reflecting the financial nature of the agency.

A distinction between home and host countries as groups would be confined to the allotment of voting rights. Votes would not be cast in groups but by individual governors or directors according to the merits of each case; in effect, it is expected that decisions would be taken by consensus in most cases. Home and host countries have a common interest in a well-balanced voting structure, since such a structure would ensure the agency's credibility and success.

Relations with host countries

Since the agency would underwrite only investments specifically approved by the host country for that purpose, any involvement or potential for a dispute with a host country would be confined to investments guaranteed by the agency with the full consent of the host country. Where the agency compensated an investor under the contract of guarantee, it would assume only the substantive rights that the investor had acquired. Subrogation, assumption of the legal rights of the compensated investor to collect damages, could thus achieve nothing more than the assignment of an existing claim from the investor to the agency.

Host country approval could eventually result in international arbitration of a dispute between the agency and a member country. The jurisdiction would be limited to disputes between the agency and a member state related to a guaranteed investment. It would not endow a private investor with procedural rights under international law.

The convention establishing the agency would not include substantive rules with respect to the treatment of guaranteed investments. Any bilateral agreement between a member and the agency would be concluded by mutual consent and no member would be under obligation to enter into such an agreement. The convention could not conflict with the Code of Conduct of Transnational Corporations currently under negotiation within the framework of the United Nations, nor could it conflict with bilateral investment protection treaties whereby the contracting parties give reciprocal assurances on the treatment of the investments of the nationals of a party in the territory of the other. In particular, a multilateral guarantee would not affect the validity of an investment protection treaty; it would add to it.

Multilateral guarantees, though normally available for foreign investment only, would not in themselves discriminate against domestic investment, since they would protect only existing rights rather than create new rights for the investor vis-à-vis the host country. A transfer risk occurs because a foreign investor must rely on the ability to repatriate invested capital. In an expropriation, the guarantee would assure the investor only adequate compensation in a foreign currency; it would not protect against host governmental actions as such. Foreign investment would remain subject to host governmental regulation, as would domestic investment.

The agency and the Bank

As proposed, the Bank would not have an institutional stake in the agency or assume responsibility for its operations. Although the agency would presumably enter into a cooperative agreement with the Bank to benefit from its service and cut down its own costs, the only direct role envisaged for the Bank is that its President would act as chairman of the agency's board of directors. The interests of Bank members that do not wish to join the agency would not be affected. The initiative to create a multilateral agency has, nonetheless, been taken by the Bank's management; it is being discussed by the Bank's Board, and its various aspects are being studied by Bank staff. This is consistent with the Bank's role as a catalyst in the promotion of foreign investment.

The experience of several national investment guarantee schemes in developed countries should point to the need for a multilateral agency to support and supplement their work through reinsurance and co-insurance activities and the provision of insurance where protection by national schemes is unavailable or inefficient. It is hoped that the mutual interests involved would enable the Bank to bring the proposed agency to fruition in the near future. Although not a substitute for concessional flows or for new lending by commercial banks, foreign direct investment from developed as well as from capital-exporting developing countries should be encouraged to promote development efforts. An adequate financial protection provided through a multilateral agency may well prove to be the most timely step required in this direction.

APPENDIX

Salient features of the proposed multilateral investment guarantee agency

Membership*: open to all Bank members and Switzerland*
Entry into force*: when 15 (10 developing) countries join and furnish part of initial capital subscriptions*
Organization*: council of governors, board of directors, and president and staff. Council delegates general authority to board, but retains vote on admission, changes in capitalization, amendments, and suspension or liquidation of operations. President has responsibility for ordinary business.*
Subscribed capital*: share capital, initially $1 billion, is open-ended and increased with new membership. Individual subscriptions negotiated on the basis of ability to pay.*
Sponsorship*: in addition to operations based on share capital and reserves, members may sponsor investments for guarantee, incurring loss-sharing liability for them on pro rata basis with other sponsoring members.*
Relationship with national agencies*: cooperative arrangements using their administrative support, facilitating communication between them.*
Relationship with private risk insurers*: cooperative arrangement to leverage underwriting capacity, diversify risks, maximize administrative efficiency. Reinsures some of its portfolio with private insurers and co-insures large investments.*
Payment of claims*: investor first required to seek administrative remedies in host country. Agency assesses claims, provides for prompt payment. Disputes submitted to arbitration, unless the parties agree on other methods.*
Voting*: Members classified for voting purposes only as home or host countries; each group allotted the same number of votes. Important decisions require approval by a special majority.*

The Role of Development Finance Corporations: Experiences in India and Korea

Joslin Landell-Mills

Development finance corporation is the World Bank's name for an institution more commonly known as a development bank. Originally designed to complement existing financial arrangements, these corporations have generally been established in developing countries where commercial banks are not able to provide either the longer-term financing needed for development projects or short-term loans to unproven entities that nevertheless have the potential to contribute to growth. Commercial banks in these countries traditionally finance inventories in urban trade and industry. Their loans are generally short term; the borrowers' inventories form collateral; and the recipients of the funds typically have an established financial record. Because these banks are usually risk averse, and do not have the capacity to evaluate longer-term or unusual projects submitted by unproven borrowers, commercial bankers neglect the investment opportunities that could be profitable beyond the short term. DFCs were conceived to meet several needs—to make the long-term loans or equity investment required by a nascent industrial sector; to strengthen national development strategies by investing in rural areas or by improving project appraisal methods; and, no less important, to mobilize long-term investment resources.

This article looks at the Bank's experience with two of its most successful DFC borrowers during the 1970s—the Korean Development Finance Corporation and the Industrial Credit and Investment Corporation, India—to illustrate how effectively such institutions could be adapted to different conditions in an economic environment not always conducive to long-term investment. The Bank has been lending to DFCs since the 1950s, when inadequate long-term credit was widely recognized as a primary constraint on the growth of the private industrial sector in the developing world. The investments suitable for promoting each individual project in the sector were relatively small—and therefore too expensive in terms of cost and staff time—for direct Bank loans. The Bank viewed DFCs as a way of financing a broader cross-section of enterprises than it would otherwise be able to reach. It also saw DFCs as potential catalysts for local development initiatives; through their work with raising resources and stimulating local entrepreneurs it was hoped that they would become a source of innovative solutions to local constraints.

The main contribution that KDFC and ICICI made during the 1970s to working out new solutions to investment problems was probably to instill the discipline of systematic project design and evaluation among their clients. KDFC also introduced novel features in its project design to advance broader development objectives: it attempted to diversify the domestic financial system by introducing instruments to promote resource mobilization, and it expanded its activities in the industrial sector. These activities were particularly appropriate in a country such as Korea, where the financial sector needed to become more flexible and

Originally published in *Finance and Development*, March, 1985. Reprinted with permission.

sophisticated to sustain growth in its already very highly developed industrial sector. In India, however, a major constraint on growth in the 1970s was limited purchasing power in the rural areas, and ICICI, while remaining financially profitable, emphasized the promotion of productive industrial enterprise in backward areas. It developed a sophisticated approach toward the economic evaluation of these projects, which in general achieved high economic returns in difficult growth conditions.

Flexibility

It is difficult, of course, to draw general conclusions from the individual experiences reviewed below. Many external and often unique factors affected the performance of these DFCs and could have been crucial in their success. KDFC, for instance, provided scarce foreign exchange to Korea's industrial sector at a time when this was growing at an average annual rate of 14 percent. In addition, both KDFC and ICICI were particularly well-managed and efficient compared with other DFCs, and were able to train and retain staff because there was a steady supply of skilled people within the country available to competing institutions. Few other developing countries are so fortunate. Both ICICI and KDFC, too, formed part of a relatively well-developed financial system, in which they were able to find a role for themselves; they did not encounter the operational problems of DFCs in countries with less mature financial sectors. However, a large part of their effectiveness must be attributed to their own efforts.

In particular, both have demonstrated a consistent ability to adapt to fit the investment needs of the time. Since the early 1980s, like all other financial institutions, DFCs have been affected by a deteriorating economic environment. Largely because of the increasing levels of financial distress experienced by the industrial corporate sector in many developing countries, there has been a marked deterioration in the quality of most DFCs' portfolios. KDFC—which became the Korea Long-term Credit Bank in 1980—and ICICI have faced the same problems, but their difficulties have not been so acute. During the latter part of the 1970s both corporations faced falling demand for foreign exchange and an increasing call for domestic currency loans, as more firms needed domestically produced equipment. ICICI was able to respond, and its domestic currency lending became an increasingly important part of its portfolio. KDFC was initially precluded by its charter from mobilizing domestic currency resources (except in the form of equity), but since its transformation into a long-term credit bank, it can issue long-term domestic currency debentures and accept domestic currency deposits from corporate borrowers. The share of domestic currency loans in its total loan portfolio has risen substantially. Both corporations have changed materially since 1980, as the need has grown to diversify their sources of funds and the scope of their operations.

In spite of their different functions, and the differing economic environments in which they were pursued, the two DFCs discussed demonstrate some important common features which have a bearing on how institutions such as these can continue to play a role in the development process. The Bank first supported DFCs as a way of reaching the small entrepreneur and providing what was then the industrial sector's most scarce and most needed resource—foreign exchange—a resource that DFCs supported by the Bank had privileged access to. But as their domestic capital goods sectors grew, many of the inputs needed by borrowers began to be produced locally, and both ICICI and KDFC were able to expand their domestic currency borrowing and lending. This flexibility was an important factor in their capacity to maintain a high level of operations (and profitability) since the 1970s.

The Industrial Credit and Investment Corporation of India

The Industrial Credit and Investment Corporation of India has had a relationship with the Bank for many years; the Bank was involved in its creation in 1955. The Bank's experience with it, as well as with KDFC, provides a practical example of how DFCs can function effectively in contrasting environments.

ICICI allocates resources to viable projects in the industrial sector. These may be privately owned or have joint government ownership. During the 1970s, the Bank granted loans to the Corporation to support its financing particularly of private productive enterprises in backward areas. This emphasis was echoed later in a shift in the government's priorities toward the development of small-scale, labor-intensive enterprises.

Between 1972 and 1978, industrial production in India was growing at about 5 percent a year, with a sharp increase in 1975-76, followed by a decline in 1977-78. Industrial investment remained fairly stable at 1973 levels, while private sector investment fell after 1975. However, ICICI was able to maintain a steady annual disbursement rate of 14 percent, in concordance with projections. In terms of its contribution to total investment in India, its disbursements fell as a share of investments made by all financial institutions—from a high of about 18 percent in fiscal year 1973 to about 11 percent in fiscal year 1977. But its lending is mainly directed to the industrial sector, and here its share more than doubled over the period—to reach over 10 percent in fiscal year 1977. This is primarily the result of the combination of its own high disbursement rates and sluggish national investment.

ICICI did not engage in activities in securities and capital markets in a major way, but it promoted new enterprises by underwriting or direct subscription—providing, on average, almost 13 percent of disbursements in these activities by all financial institutions during the 1970s.

Financially, the Corporation's performance was better than expected. Net profits as a percent of equity were, on average, 12 percent between 1971 and 1977, while they were projected to be about 10 percent. It increased its lending and dividend rates in line with its profits and was able to redeem some debts two years ahead of schedule in 1975. In general, its debt/equity ratio was kept within its contractual limits. However, total arrears increased almost threefold during these years, mainly because of some 35 problem companies—in the metals and electrical equipment sectors—which were badly affected by the oil crisis and the subsequent business recession in India. But these problems were manageable and did not have a serious impact on the Corporation's portfolio. Its profitability also testifies to its capacity for sound project evaluation. Consistent with its emphasis on development work, ICICI was the first DFC associated with the Bank to use systematically advanced economic evaluation methodology. It has a particularly good record in appraising large-scale complex projects.

It was also able to diversify its sources of foreign exchange somewhat, and was successful in raising domestic currency by obtaining a government guarantee on two 15-year bond issues. ICICI has always accounted for the bulk of foreign exchange disbursements made by India's financial institutions, but during the 1970s the share of its rupee disbursements rose from being about 28 percent of its total investments to represent almost 76 percent by fiscal year 1978. This increase was due mainly to the fact that more domestic goods were available to local enterprises, and also that they had alternative sources of foreign exchange.

The efforts made by ICICI to increase its promotion of projects, particularly in backward areas, led lending to these regions to increase by almost 30 percent of its total approvals between 1955-70 and 1974-76, some 6 percent of the total financing going to new entrepreneurs. Out of the 392 projects financed during the 1970s, 60 were new, and 63 were in backward areas. However, ICICI does not lend to small-scale enterprises; these are financed by institutions specifically catering to them.

Economic conditions in the 1970s in India were not particularly conducive to profitable long-term investments: growth in industrial production was sluggish; investment rates were low; and general conditions were not such as to promote enterprise. ICICI's problems with arrears, implementation delays, and cost overruns reflected those conditions. Furthermore, it was not easy for ICICI to diversify its sources of foreign funds. In spite of these disadvantages, ICICI's profitability was high, its investment levels well above average for similar national institutions, and its efforts to promote industrial enterprise in backward areas were sustained and sustainable.

The Korean Development Finance Corporation

The Korean Development Finance Corporation was established in 1967 as a privately owned corporation to accelerate industrial growth by providing long-term finance to private manufacturing enterprises. Until 1980, when it became Korea's first long-term credit bank and was authorized to expand its domestic currency lending, KDFC dealt almost exclusively in foreign currency long-term loans, and investments. During the decade that followed its creation, the Korean economy was growing at about 10 percent a year, and the export-oriented manufacturing sector at 18 percent a year, supported by an annual gross capital investment of about 12 percent a year in real terms. Commercial banks were, and continue to be, the principal institutional source of funds to the private sector; KDFC was a major provider of long-term foreign exchange financing to medium- and large-scale private enterprise that did not receive government funds.

During the 1970s, the Bank made five loans to KDFC to meet the corporation's foreign currency requirements over the period. The Bank's experience with these loans provides a useful illustration of the ways in which KDFC was able to experiment with promoting manufacturing, albeit in a booming economic environment, and remain financially profitable. Each loan had a slightly different emphasis; the first ones aimed primarily to ensure efficient allocation of scarce foreign resources to private business and to strengthen the institutional side of KDFC, particularly its economic analysis. With institutional strengthening achieved, the next loans stressed the Corporation's development potential—to expand export-oriented enterprises, to deepen and strengthen the financial system, and to promote small entrepreneurs in the business of producing machinery and agro-industrial products in less developed areas.

Between 1971 and 1979, the corporation used its Bank funds to invest in 146 projects (108 of these investments were for the expansion and modernization of existing firms). Few had cost overruns, and most were completed on time. In their first year of operation, 42 had losses and 24 of these ran at a loss in their second year, but by 1979 most were financially sound and none were in arrears. These projects created a total of 12,950 jobs, and generated returns and exports well above estimates. The export-oriented textile industry received 20 percent of the loans made, and, in line with government priorities, machinery, deep sea fishing, and marine transport received significant shares.

The success of its lending to projects reflected the Corporation's sound appraisal and evaluation capacity. This is also evident in its ability to raise foreign resources; between 1969 and 1979 it mobilized $561 million, about 79 percent from official sources, although its reliance on these is rapidly decreasing. KDFC's net income rose by 25 percent annually between 1971 and 1979, and paid a return on equity of about 17 percent a year (although the effective rate is much lower given the 6.5 percent devaluation of the won against the dollar over the same period). It should also be noted that KDFC was able to increase its share capital through offerings in the market during this period. Perhaps the greatest achievement of the Corporation in terms of efficiency was to reduce its operational expenses from 2.4 percent of assets in 1971 to 0.9 percent in 1979.

Profitable operation is clearly a *sine qua non* for an enterprise's existence, but to perform its proper function, a development finance company has to play more than a financial role. After 1975, KDFC had a developmental strategy which it pursued in an innovative and highly successful way. To draw more enterprises into the financial net, KDFC helped to establish a leasing company to purchase foreign and domestic manufactured equipment and lease it to firms that could not otherwise afford it. The Corporation also cooperated with some of Korea's regional commercial banks to increase the funds—particularly in foreign currency—available to small enterprises in rural areas. To promote technology development, it helped to found a firm that assists ventures using technical patents and processes developed by another company supported by KDFC. To diversify the financial system, it helped to establish an institution to handle short-term credit transactions—an innovation that led to the establishment of 15 other short-term financing companies between 1973 and 1979. By the end of 1979, these companies had mobilized 765 billion won (about $1.6 billion) in discounted notes.

Although KDFC only accounted for 23 percent of total fixed investment in Korea's manufacturing sector between 1971-78, it created 44,600 new jobs out of a total of 1.7 million in that sector. Its ability to innovate in the financial sector, and its efficient operation clearly had a greater impact than the size of its investments would indicate.

A Fresh Look at Development Aid

Shahid Javed Burki & Robert L. Ayres

There has been considerable rethinking of development strategies in recent years, prompted in part by the great divergence in the performance of developing countries over the last 30 years. Developing countries today are characterized by considerably more diversity than they showed in the mid-1950s, which suggests that universal prescriptions are less valid now than they were when the discipline of development economics was in its infancy. The debate over approaches to development includes a number of new and some perennial issues, such as the respective roles of the public and private sectors, encouragement of greater export orientation in developing economies, new approaches to poverty alleviation, and the harmonization of economic stabilization and growth policies. It is only natural that the intellectual ferment about alternative development strategies should also include debate about the role of official development assistance (ODA) (also known as concessional flows or, more commonly, as aid). This is because aid has played a central role in the development of many nations-including middle-income countries, such as Colombia and the Republic of Korea, that have "graduated" from concessional assistance, and low-income countries, such as those of sub-Saharan Africa that still depend heavily upon it for sizable proportions of their investment resources.

The aid debate of the early 1980s has had several prominent themes. One is the effectiveness of aid. A number of donor governments as well as academic and journalistic observers have been taking a harder look at how effectively aid has contributed to development. A second theme is the support for aid in donor countries. There is a perception in some quarters that such support has declined among both the general public and political leaders. This situation is often summed up in the phrase "aid fatigue." A third issue is the volume of aid: how much is required to meet the developmental needs of recipients? What are those needs? These themes are seen to be interrelated in a number of complex and important ways. For example, a demonstration of aid's effectiveness might serve to increase public support for it and thereby contribute to increases in its volume.

The early 1980s have also witnessed the increasing politicization of aid and the increased mixing of aid with the foreign policy and commercial objectives of donors. The bilateral aid programs of a number of donors have become increasingly concentrated on countries of geopolitical interest. One unfortunate consequence of this tendency is that poor countries lacking a central place in donors' larger foreign policy concerns receive a disproportionately small amount of aid. (See Tables 1 and 2.)

Moreover, aid volume, after growing at an annual average rate of about 6 percent in real terms during the 1970s, began to stagnate after 1980, and even declined in real terms from 1981 to 1983. At the same time, most developing countries were confronting an external environment that had become grim and inhospitable to development as a consequence of the most severe global recession since the 1930s compounded by increases in oil prices,

Originally published in *Finance and Development*, vol. 22, no. 1, 1986. Reprinted with permission.

Table 1

Changes in distribution of ODA, 1975-83

(in millions of US dollars)

Country group	1975		1980		1983	
	Amount	Percent	Amount	Percent	Amount	Percent
Low-income	6,627.7	41.7	9,773.7	38.3	9,865.8	41.5
Africa	2,097.0	13.2	4,626.1	17.4	4,326.0	18.2
India	1,708.6	10.7	1,127.1	8.0	1,720.0	7.2
China	0.0	0.0	66.1	0.2	663.2	2.8
Other	2,822.1	17.7	3,954.4	14.9	3,156.6	13.3
Middle-income	9,226.8	58.0	15,544.4	58.6	13,715.0	57.7
High-income	49.3	0.3	203.5	0.8	169.7	0.7
Total	**15,903.8**	**100.0**	**25,521.6**	**100.0**	**23,750.5**	**100.0**

Source: The data on aid flows are from: OECD, *Geographical Distribution of Financial Flows to Developing Countries* (Paris, various issues). The country classifications are derived from the World Bank, *World Development Report 1985* (New York, Oxford University Press, 1985).

Note: Low-Income countries are those with 1983 GNP per capita of $400 or less.

Middle-income countries are those with 1983 GNP per capita between $400 and $6,850, excluding three industrial market economies (Italy, Ireland, and Spain) and one oil exporter (Oman). These exceptions are included in the high-income group.

interest rates, and debt-servicing difficulties. Growth rates slowed in most countries (and even turned negative in some).

These various circumstances persuaded some governments to begin to seek a new political consensus on the relationship between developed and developing countries, including the role of aid. This in turn resulted in the creation of several task forces of the Development Committee (the Joint Ministerial Committee of the Boards of Governors of the Bank and the Fund on the Transfer of Real Resources to Developing Countries): one studied issues of private direct investment in developing countries, another the role of nonconcessional flows. Several years ago three members of the Committee—Canada, the Netherlands, and the Nordic constituency—urged the creation of a Task Force on Concessional Flows. The Task Force was officially established at the May 1982 meeting of the Development Committee in Helsinki to study and assess the flows of short- and long-term ODA, their use, and their effectiveness, with a view to enhancing the quality and volume of such aid. (Its membership and methods of operation are detailed below.) The Task Force concluded its work with the presentation of its final report at the Committee's meeting in Seoul in October 1985. The report contributes to the current debate about development strategies and the role that aid plays in them.

The Task Force took a decision at its first meeting, in October 1982, that influenced all its subsequent work. It decided that the major issues about aid could most fruitfully be approached in a systemic manner, that is, in a way that examined the relationships between the effectiveness of aid, political support for aid, and the volume of aid flows. While the Task Force carried out separate investigations in each of these areas, it called frequent attention to the links between them. It gave particular attention to the link between the vol-

Table 2
Ranking of 25 major recipients of aid, 1973-83

By total cumulative ODA receipts (In millions of US dollars)		By average annual ODA receipts per capita (In US dollars)	
1. Egypt	17,750.9	1. Jordan	209.87
2. India	16,789.6	2. Israel	185.53
3. Syrian Arab Republic	10,193.9	3. Oman	118.06
4. Bangladesh	10,185.1	4. Syrian Arab Republic	97.55
5. Pakistan	8.364.1	5. Mauritania	95.71
6. Israel	8,163.4	6. Papua New Guinea	92.28
7. Indonesia	8,086.8	7. Lebanon	56.17
8. Jordan	7,156.7	8. Somalia	54.27
9. Sudan	4,972.5	9. Yemen, People's Dem. Rep.	45.38
10. Tanzania	4,817.4	10. Jamaica	41.86
11. Morocco	4,026.4	11. Congo, People's Rep.	41.63
12. Turkey	3,978.7	12. Lesotho	40.98
13. Viet Nam	3,386.8	13. Egypt	36.43
14. Zaïre	3,199.6	14. Senegal	36.24
15. Papua New Guinea	3,246.7	15. Yemen Arab Republic	35.37
16. Kenya	2,993.8	16. Nicaragua	33.22
17. Sri Lanka	2,965.0	17. Tunisia	31.45
18. Yemen Arab Republic	2,918.4	18. Liberia	30.49
19. Philippines	2,884.6	19. Central African Republic	27.64
20. Thailand	2,822.8	20. Zambia	27.36
21. Somalia	2,686.4	21. Costa Rica	27.19
22. Senegal	2,392.1	22. Niger	26.13
23. Tunisia	2,318.0	23. Togo	24.94
24. Burma	2,218.9	24. Mali	22.86
25. Korea, Rep. of	2,051.1	25. Burkina Faso	22.76

Source: OECD, *Geographical Distribution of Financial Flows to Developing Countries* (Paris, various issues).

ume and the effectiveness of aid. This article presents the principal findings of the Task Force and its analysis of the conditions that govern aid flows and their effectiveness.

Effectiveness of aid

The Task Force investigated the subject of aid effectiveness by carrying out a systematic review of four central aspects of concessional aid: its contributions to (1) economic growth of recipient countries; (2) poverty alleviation, particularly in the poorest countries; (3) improved policies and institutions through "policy dialogue" and the provision of technical assistance; and (4) enhanced market forces and development of the private sector. (For a detailed discussion of aid effectiveness, see the article by Robert Cassen in this issue.)

The most important conclusion reached by the Task Force in this area was that aid has been productive and helpful to development; without it, a number of countries would not have been able to graduate from the ranks of poor to middle-income nations, and the countries that remain poor would have been still poorer. In some cases, aid has been spectacularly successful—for example, the "Green Revolution" in South Asian agriculture was greatly facilitated by aid for agricultural research, credit, and improvements in infrastructure. In sub-Saharan Africa, where much aid has been legitimately criticized for not achieving fully its intended objectives, aid nevertheless has contributed significantly to the development of basic infrastructure-roads, dams, ports, and telecommunications facilities. A good example is the development of a national road network in Malawi, financed by aid. Educational development in sub-Saharan Africa has also been greatly stimulated by aid.

The Task Force recognized, however, that in some situations aid has been much less effective. In general it has had a better record in Asia than in Africa. For example, despite the commitment of large amounts of aid to African agriculture, food output per capita declined in 23 out of 33 countries in the region between 1975 and 1982 (based on most recent data available; there were no data for six other countries). This was a major reason for the stagnation (and even decline in some countries) in overall growth of per capita income. Even though the many reasons for retarded development in sub-Saharan Africa do not include aid as the main factor, aid donors could have done better—in encouraging more appropriate technical packages for rainfed agriculture, for example, or in displaying greater awareness of local conditions affecting production and employment.

Examination of the successes and failures of aid led the Task Force to conclude that there is considerable room for increasing the effectiveness of aid, both in how recipients use it and how donors supply it. For example, countries that receive aid need to devote greater attention to domestic resource mobilization so that aid resources complement local efforts rather than substitute for them The effectiveness of both internal and external resources can be negated by bad policies, such as official pricing policies that act as disincentives to private producers or artificially overvalued currencies that discourage exports. Where macroeconomic policies are not designed to support long-term development, aid will be less productive.

But donors need to undertake reforms as well. Most important, they should display a greater awareness of the impact of their economic policies on the development prospects of recipient countries. Donors' non-aid policies (on trade, for example) can have an indirect but substantial impact on the effectiveness of aid. Certain policies, such as the practice of "tying" aid to the purchase of goods and services in the donor country, reduce the contribution to development that aid can make. Donors also need to learn more from their own experience and those of other donors. In many cases donors have deliberately promoted "white elephants" based on noneconomic factors.

The importance to aid effectiveness of supportive recipient and donor policies underscores the need to coordinate development and aid more closely. Coordination must take several forms—between donors, between donors and recipients, and within various development agencies and departments working in recipient countries. The mechanisms for achieving this include consultative groups and aid consortia, greater coordination by central agencies within recipient countries, and better coordination in the field among aid donors.

One of the more important conclusions about aid effectiveness reached by the Task Force concerned the inadequacy of existing efforts at "learning by doing." Transfer of information about successes and failures has not been adequate or effective within most aid agencies, and it has been even less effective between them. Individual donor agencies can improve the efficiency of the learning process in a number of ways, such as making information about their project and program experiences more available to others and ensuring that the relevant lessons are incorporated in new projects. Some agencies have done well, but in many cases improvements are still needed.

Support for aid

The Task Force directly addressed the question of whether the slowdown in the rate of increase of aid flows was the consequence of a weakening in the support for aid in donor countries. The available evidence suggests that levels of public support for the general concept of development assistance are high in most donor countries and have not changed much in recent years. The majority of people—in some countries more than 75 percent of people surveyed—say they are "in favor" of aid as a matter of principle. But this support for aid at a somewhat abstract level is subject to a number of qualifications. It varies across countries and even within the same country at different times. In most countries, furthermore, support is not well articulated; it is rather general and diffuse. Support is less apparent when the public is asked about its preferences on aiding specific countries or funding specific initiatives. Moreover, while the public tends to support aid in principle, most of the public does not hold strong views on the subject: the opinion polls in several industrial countries suggest that aid ranks low in the scale of the public's priorities when compared to other more immediate or local concerns. Expressions of support for aid are greater when the appeal is phrased in terms of humanitarian concern or the alleviation of world poverty and hunger. In a 1979 poll in the United States, for example, 77 percent of the respondents were in favor of maintaining or increasing "aid to combat hunger", but support dropped to 49 percent when put in terms of "economic aid" to developing countries.

The recent public attention and response to the drought and famine in sub-Saharan Africa are a particularly vivid demonstration of this. The Task Force was encouraged by its finding that the public has a generally positive attitude toward aid, since this would appear to facilitate efforts to increase aid volume.

A key issue deserving greater attention therefore, is how to convert the reservoir of good will that exists for emergency and relief aid into support for long-term development assistance efforts. This is where the role of political leadership becomes critical. In a number of instances, governments have asserted the importance of aid and increased its volume. Four Nordic countries—Denmark, the Netherlands, Norway, and Sweden—have exceeded the 0.7 percent target of ODA as a proportion of GNP set by the United Nations in 1970. In order to achieve this, the governments have carried out well-conceived programs to educate the public about the importance of aid. The Japanese Government doubled aid between 1977 and 1981, and then doubled it again from 1981 to 1985. The first decision seemed to run ahead of public opinion but the Government's commitment has since helped to foster a positive public attitude toward aid. In Italy, too, a dramatic increase in aid has been achieved in recent years, largely because of the efforts of political leaders.

Since maintaining and strengthening support for aid can be assisted by more effective communication of its role in the development process and the successes that aid has achieved, the Task Force stressed the important role of development education programs and nongovernmental organizations in donor countries. There is a special need for continuing and enhancing the development education role of nongovernmental organizations, especially those engaged in development work overseas. The Task Force called upon both bilateral and multilateral aid agencies to work closely with these organizations in providing a better understanding of development problems and the role of aid in alleviating them.

Volume of aid

The Task Force addressed the subject of aid volume from two perspectives: need and supply. It eschewed the conventional method of estimating aid needs by determining a priori the rate of growth for aid recipients, the resources needed to generate these rates, the proportion that could be met from domestic sources, and the proportion that had to be obtained from outside (foreign savings). This method of treating aid flows as a residual is not satisfactory, since it assumes domestic savings as fixed. Instead of adopting this excessively mechanistic approach, the Task Force carried out a more qualitative assessment. It identified four key areas where concessional assistance is urgently needed: (1) tackling the fundamental problems of poverty, particularly in the poorest countries; (2) helping a number of countries complete needed structural adjustments of their economies; (3) sustaining investment and growth in those low-income countries that have pursued effective policies and have succeeded in establishing development momentum; and (4) responding to emergencies.

Based on such a qualitative assessment, the Task Force believed that the currently projected growth in ODA—estimated by DAC at about 2 percent a year in real terms over 1985-90—would be insufficient to meet these needs. Accordingly, the Task Force urged all concerned in both developing and developed countries to help ODA recipients cope with increased needs for resources by one or more of the following options:

- Increasing the effectiveness of official aid;
- Changing present country allocations of ODA;
- Concentrating expected increments in ODA on low-income countries;
- Combining ODA with less concessional flows, mainly other nonconcessional official flows in ways that would result in a higher overall volume of external resources; and
- Supplementing ODA flows by encouraging one or more of the following: increased flows of voluntary contributions; contributions of ODA from new donors; earnings from trade; and foreign private investment.

Each of the "coping mechanisms" has some potential for helping recipients as follows:

Improvements in the efficiency of capital utilization. This could ensure that a given amount of aid goes further toward promoting development. There is particular scope for improvement in the low-income countries of sub-Saharan Africa where evidence shows declining rates of return on all investments including aid in recent years.

Reallocation of ODA. Redirecting aid, particularly from middle- to low-income countries, would be highly desirable on development grounds and would help to stretch ODA to the latter group. Currently, low-income countries receive only about 40 percent of ODA, with the remainder going to middle-income countries (if low-income countries are defined, as they are by the World Bank, as those with GNP per capita of less than $400 in 1983). Indeed, the share of upper middle-income countries in total ODA has lately been about as high as the share of low-income Africa, and the per capita aid receipts of a number of middle-income countries are extremely high. Even without substantial increases in aid volume, reallocation could ensure the greater concentration of ODA on countries that need it most.

Directing all increases in aid for the rest of the 1980s to the low-income countries. This could do much to close the gap between need and supplies. Even if total ODA grows at only 2 percent a year in real terms, concentration of the increment on low-income countries would boost their receipts by about 8 percent a year.

Combining ODA with less concessional flows. This is another possibility, although not for the poorest and least creditworthy. If the legitimate needs for aid of countries such as China, India, Pakistan, and Sri Lanka (the so-called "Asian blend" countries that have access to the commercial market official nonconcessional flows, and ODA finances) cannot be entirely met from budgetary sources, it is important that they obtain additional official transfers of a nonconcessional nature and not be left to the commercial market alone. To act as a reasonable substitute for ODA, however, the rates and maturities of such flows would need to be improved and their volume significantly increased.

Grants from private voluntary organizations. For overseas development activities in 1984 these were estimated at $2.5 billion equal to about 9 percent of ODA. The idea of increasing the role of nongovernmental and private voluntary organizations in transferring resources for development is very attractive. In some DAC countries, new tax incentives might help to raise the receipts of such organizations. The DAC is currently exploring new forms of cofinancing between official aid agencies and nongovernmental organizations.

New donors. This term covers some (mostly upper middle-income) countries that long ago stopped receiving new disbursements of ODA. They include Argentina, Brazil, Colombia, Israel, Korea, Mexico, and Venezuela, as well as (among OECD countries) Greece, Ireland, Luxembourg, Portugal, and Spain. It is important to establish the principle that those who have benefited from aid in the past should begin to act as donors themselves, even in a small way. Eventually, ODA from such new donors may grow into sizable amounts.

All countries should enhance trading opportunities for the developing world. In light of the uncertain supply outlook for ODA, increased exports would help close the resources gap. Industrial countries need to resist increasing pressures for protectionism; developing countries need to restructure their economies, investing more in those tradable goods in which they have a comparative advantage and taking care to avoid sustained overvaluation of their currencies.

Direct foreign investment. Both direct and portfolio investment have the potential to satisfy a higher proportion of the financial needs of developing countries than in the past. The contribution that direct investment makes to development, however, depends significantly on the policy framework in which it takes place. Many developing countries have recently undertaken policy reforms that give more scope for private sector activities. They have also become more receptive to foreign direct investment since lending by commercial banks has declined.

Table 3
Ranking of 17 largest DAC donors of aid, 1984[1]

Volume of aid (In millions of US dollars)		Share		Percent of GNP	
	Amount	(Percent)			
1. United States	8,698	30.4	1. Netherlands		1.02
2. Japan	4,319	15.1	2. Norway		0.99
3. France	3,790	13.2	3. Denmark		0.85
4. Germany	2,782	9.7	4. Sweden		0.80
5. Canada	1,625	5.7	5. France		0.77
6. United Kingdom	1,432	5.0	6. Belgium		0.56
7. Netherlands	1,268	4.4	7. Canada		0.50
8. Italy	1,105	3.9	8. Germany		0.45
9. Australia	773	2.7	9. Australia		0.45
10. Sweden	741	2.6	10. Finland		0.36
11. Norway	526	1.8	11. Japan		0.35
12. Denmark	449	1.6	12. United Kingdom		0.33
13. Belgium	434	1.5	13. Italy		0.32
14. Switzerland	286	1.0	14. Switzerland		0.30
15. Austria	181	0.6	15. Austria		0.28
16. Finland	178	0.6	16. New Zealand		0.27
17. New Zealand	59	0.2	17. United States		0.24
Total	**28,647**	**100.0**			

Source: OECD Press Release (Press/A(85)44), June 18, 1985.
[1] Preliminary estimates.

Limitations

While these various coping mechanisms have some potential (some more than others) for helping developing countries face the prospective shortage of aid, they have a number of serious limitations as well. For example, there are clear limits to the extent to which increased aid effectiveness can substitute for increases in volume: gains stemming from the more effective use of aid will be gradual and incremental; they are a necessary, but not sufficient, response to the needs of developing countries.

Similarly, reallocation of ODA to low-income countries is highly desirable and would make a major contribution to meeting their needs even if total ODA were not to increase by much. But the scope for such reallocation appears to be limited for a number of reasons: some donors have already gone quite far in this direction; a reduction of ODA flows to lower middle-income countries could have severe disruptive effects; and some donors' ODA allocations to middle-income countries are based in large measure on political, strategic, historical, or commercial reasons, which are not easy to adjust. The possibilities for reallocation within the group of low-income countries are also limited. Further reductions of aid to members of this group—and particularly to the largest among them, India and China—could have a negative impact on their fragile creditworthiness.

The Task Force's review of the other coping mechanisms led to generally similar conclusions. For example, the Task Force found limited possibilities among the various schemes for blending highly concessional ODA with nonconcessional flows. How much "additionality" (in the total flow of resources) would result from such schemes was deemed open to considerable question. While private voluntary organizations now play an important role all over the world in providing development services, there are inherent limitations on their financial resources. Opportunities for significantly expanding private flows and earnings from trade seem mainly limited to middle-income countries and only a few low-income countries at present. Whereas expansion in world trade in the 1960s and 1970s was of tremendous benefit to the countries that graduated during this period from being aid receivers to aid givers, it appears that trade in the foreseeable future will make a smaller contribution to the growth of developing economies. Most poor countries are commodity exporters and, despite recovery in industrial countries, commodity prices have continued to decline.

These considerations brought the Task Force to its main conclusion about aid volume: that "no single one of the measures considered, nor any combination of them, will cope adequately with the challenge of development in the low-income countries. Since there is no escaping the need for predominant reliance on traditional, appropriated concessional assistance, donor governments should exert redoubled efforts to increase the supply of ODA as a matter of urgency." The Task Force found the need for an increase in ODA volume "known and unmistakable" and urged each donor to adopt the most effective means at its disposal to increase the volume of aid. Donors that have not yet reached the international ODA target of 0.7 percent of GNP were urged to do so or, alternatively, to set their own national targets for increasing aid.

Conclusion

The main contribution made by the Task Force on Concessional Flows was to underscore the important links that exist between the effectiveness of aid, political support for aid, and the volume of aid flows. While there is no question that revival of growth in poor countries will only become possible if they have access to flows of concessional assistance larger than those currently anticipated by the DAC and the sum indicated by the turn of events affecting OPEC, the amounts needed will materialize only if the recipients can continue to demonstrate that they can use them effectively. Financial stringencies in donor countries and economic difficulties in some of them threaten aid budgets. If aid levels are to be maintained or increased, the public must not only continue to support aid in the face of tight finances but also such support needs to grow. The increase in this support will in turn depend on both a convincing demonstration of the aid needs of recipients and on their effective utilization of aid.

It was for these reasons that the Development Committee in its meeting in Seoul decided to keep the subjects studied by the Task Force on its agenda for some time to come. Urging that the report and its suggestions be taken into account by all governments concerned, the Committee called upon the World Bank to take the lead in following up on the Task Force's conclusions and to report to future Development Committee meetings on progress achieved.

Operations of the Task Force on Concessional Flows

Established in May 1982, the Task Force on Concessional Flows comprised governmental representatives from a diverse group of industrial and developing countries. The countries represented were Belgium, Canada, China, Costa Rica, the Dominican Republic, the Federal Republic of Germany, Finland, France, India, Indonesia, Italy, Japan, Kuwait, the Netherlands, Saudi Arabia, Senegal, Tanzania, the United Kingdom, and the United States. Belgium and Italy shared representation, alternating attendance at meetings. Professor John P. Lewis of the Woodrow Wilson School of Public and International Affairs at Princeton University was the Chairman. The work of the Task Force was carried out in a series of eight meetings from October 1982 to August 1985. Between meetings the Secretariat, provided by the World Bank's International Relations Department, prepared issues papers and other supporting documentation for the members, consideration.

To assist its work on the effectiveness of aid, the Task Force engaged a team of independent consultants, under the guidance of Professor Robert Cassen of the Institute of Development Studies, University of Sussex, to carry out a number of studies financed by contributions from some of the member governments themselves. The consultants examined and effectiveness in seven countries—Bangladesh, Colombia, India, Kenya, Korea, Malawi, and Mali—and in a number of sectors. The Task Force's judgments about the effectiveness of aid were assisted by, but not limited to, the consultants' inquiries.

In the area of aid volume the Task Force reviewed the work of a study group of Dutch and Nordic experts established under its auspices to look at the possibilities for raising concessional resources by various "non-traditional" means—for example, seabed royalties and international taxes—that would not impose claims on donors' national budgets. It concluded that "at the present time, there is no real scope for increasing ODA by such means."

The Task Force also commissioned two consultants' studies on the support for aid. One, prepared under the auspices of the Overseas Development Council, in Washington, DC, analyzed support in the United States and Canada; the other, prepared under the auspices of the Overseas Development Institute in London, analyzed support in Europe. In addition, donor-country members of the Task Force contributed papers on the nature of the support for aid in their respective countries.

Chapter 6

Transnational Corporations and North-South Relations

Introduction

The emergence of Transnational Corporations (TNCs)[1] on the world scene signifies the beginning of a new international situation with multiple ramifications. The TNCs' command over economic resources and their enviable possession of managerial skills and technology provide them with a unique opportunity not only to influence the process of socio-economic development in host countries, but also to imprint patterns of international relationships on host economies. Moreover, whenever the socio-economic environments provoke such corporations they lose no time in becoming "extra-economic" and act politically until they get their way. And, because of their vast economic resources crossing many boundaries, they usually get what they want.

Different opinions have been expressed about the activities and objectives of TNCs. While many people in the developed countries regard the TNCs as effective instruments of "world welfare", they are decried by both socialists and Marxist–Leninists as dangerous agents of imperialism. The size, ubiquitous presence and the activities of the TNCs have evoked serious concern throughout the smaller countries of the world, but especially in the Third World. Many view these corporations "as old wine in new bottles", that is, as a modern, economic form of colonialism—neo-colonialism.

Their capacity to influence political decisions, patterns of consumption, changes in culture, the direction of production and trade, the structure of social class and even the transformation of the politico-economic structure has aroused genuine concern among more than two thirds of the world population. This apprehension led Asian, African and Latin American members of the United Nations not only to force the UN to to make a study of the "Impact of the Multinational Corporations on Development and International Relations," but also to keep a constant vigil over the activities of these corporations by establishing the UN Centre on Transnational Corporations.

In light of the above, three topics stand out as deserving of particular attention: the pattern of dominance, the economic implications, and the social effects of TNCs in the countries of the Third World.

The influence of TNCs based in the US, France, the Federal Republic of Germany, Japan and Canada—the home countries of the vast majority of TNCs—has increased considerably in the Third World during the past three decades. The increasing number of their affiliates in the developing countries, the rising tempo of investment, their growing share in production and ownership of means of production and distribution; these are the visible symptoms of their importance.

Of the approximately 550 large transnational corporations in the world which control about 80% of all transnational subsidiaries, 250 are US based, 250 are from Europe, Japan, Canada and the rest of the OECD countries, and approximately 50 are based in the Third World itself, some of them joint ventures with First World corporations. The total of TNCs (i.e., firms which are headquartered in one country and pursue business activities in one or more other countries) has been estimated at 10,000, controlling 90,000 subsidiaries. The total of US direct investment abroad increased from $11.8 billion in 1950, of which 37% ($4.4 billion) was invested in the Third World; to $32 billion in 1960, of which $10.9 billion (34%) was in the Third World; to $78.1 billion in 1970, with $21.3 billion (27%) in the Third World; to $213.5 billion in 1980, with $52.7 billion (25%) in the Third World; and to $232.7 billion in 1985, with $54.5 billion (23%) in the Third World. (See David H. Blake and Robert S. Walters, *The Politics of Global Economic Relations*, Prentice-Hall: Englewood Cliffs, NJ, 3rd edition, 1987, Table on p. 93.)

It is clear that while US investment in the Third World in nominal dollars increased twelve-fold from $4.4 billion to $54.5 billion in 35 years, its share decreased steadily, from two fifths (37%) to less than a quarter (23%) during this period. Hence, although the relative importance of US investment (most by TNCs) in the Third World countries is large and influential , to American investors the Third World is of decreasing interest. Most American foreign investment—three quarters—goes to Canada and the European Community, both equally developed and post-industrial, and therefore compatible with American business.

The sectoral role of direct foreign investment in the developing countries is yet another visible feature of the TNCs. They have invested extensively in mining and smelting, petroleum, manufacturing, public utilities, trade, and services such as banking. These investments in the Third World accounted for about 33% of the total direct investment made by transnationals in the world. However, compared to this one third share of direct foreign investment in the developing countries, the total of TNC's contributions to world exports and world domestic product do not exceed 25% and 16%, respectively.

The concentration of direct foreign investment has been very tangible in a few developing countries. For instance, Argentina, Brazil, India, Mexico, Nigeria, Venezuela and certain Caribbean islands account for 43% of the total direct foreign investment in the developing countries. This investment is concentrated in petroleum, mining and smelting, and manufacturing. The study of patterns of investment in different regions reveals that more than 90% of the total investment in the Middle East is in petroleum, whereas in South Asia and Central America the manufacturing sector accounts for the major share in the investment of TNCs.

It should also be mentioned that the character of the transnational corporation has changed twice over the past two decades. Originally the transnational corporation usually had subsidiary firms in various host countries. Then the controlling structure was reorganized so that the subsidiaries came under the international division of the parent company which then ran the subsidiaries as a separate profit-making set. The

the current general arrangement is for the worldwide activities of the TNC to be integrated. This means that the control of the overseas firms and subsidiaries is centralized at head office, along with control of national operations. In fact, the transnational corporation today operates according to the rule of efficiency and least cost production for various products and components, all organized to maximize the profitability of the corporation as a whole. This, of course, means that local firms, subsidiaries, branches, and factories, whether they be physically located in various parts of the home country or in various host countries, have little local autonomy.

Aside from the erosion of local autonomy they represent, the TNCs have also been criticised for paying lower wages and following less stringent safety and pollution controls in Third World countries than they do in their home countries (though these are often still higher than local standards); for contributing to disruptive changes in the nature of Third World economies; and in some cases for helping to prop up corrupt or reactionary Third World governments.

However, whatever the negative aspects and costs of transnationals in host countries may be, they do bring significant benefits with them. Among these are industrialization, the transfer of technology and technological culture as well as a significant increase in employment and in the provision of cash flows into (as well as out of) the host country. During the early 1980s the hitherto negative attitudes of Third World host countries towards the TNCs changed rapidly to a welcoming approach. The first article by Lall describes this change. Lall's second article deals with the rise of transnational corporations based in the Third World—a new and growing phenomenon. The final article, by Maule and Vanderwal, evaluates the various international regulatory activities which attempt to control foreign investment, particularly in Third World countries.

---

[1] The term Transnational Corporation was coined by the UN and is interchangeable with the older term Multinational Corporation (MNC).

Transnationals and the Third World: Changing Perceptions

Sanjaya Lall

Introduction

In February 1975 I wrote in the National Westminster Bank Quarterly Review an article entitled, 'Multinationals and Development: a New Look'. The summary is quoted below:

'To sum up, it is the intrinsic nature of the MNC combined with the peculiar socio-economic-political structure of LDCs that produces a pattern of 'dependence'. Possibly this dependence will lead to industrialization and growth in GNP; certainly it will lead to the benefits being shared extremely unequally, and even to increased misery for the bulk of the populations of developing countries. It would, however, be possible to conceive of MNC investment benefiting the whole population of poor countries if the governments of the latter were capable and desirous of providing a different kind of development. It often happens, unfortunately, that the attitudes of the MNCs and the governments of their home countries work against this: pressures for 'free enterprise' and conservative laissez-faire policies are not always in the best interests of the poor. The growing power of MNCs may not augur well for the poor unless governments show a better understanding of the development process.'

The summary reflected the climate of thinking prevalent in less-developed countries at the time. After several years of research on the subject I find that the general climate in developing countries seems to be changing.

As with many topics of intellectual debate, that of transnational companies (TNCs) and economic development has undergone changes in fashion. The early development literature saw direct foreign investment mainly as a means of transferring investable resources to countries which had little domestic savings and even less foreign exchange resources. Over time there was growing awareness of the other attributes of the investors—advanced technology, sophisticated marketing, complex organizations and all the good and bad characteristics of enormous size. The benefits that this could bring developing economics, with their pressing needs for all the knowledge and skills that TNCs possess, were obvious. The costs that may be associated with TNC presence also became apparent. At the crudest level, TNCs were 'agents of imperialism', and took out more money than they put in. At more subtle levels, they transferred inappropriate technologies and consumption patterns, did not export enough or pay due taxes, suppressed local technological development and the growth of indigenous enterprises, corrupted the local elite and generally launched the Third World on a dead-end route of 'dependent capitalism'.

Originally published in *National Westminster Bank Quarterly Review*, May 1984. Reprinted with permission.

The fashion has changed again in the past few years. TNCs are regarded, if not exactly with longing, with a mixture of cautious welcome and pragmatic hard-headedness by many developing countries. Several factors account for this change in attitude. First, the economic realities of recession, protectionism and growing competition have forced many governments to look abroad for all possible sources of financial and other assistance. The quick relief offered by commercial bank lending has, equally quickly, raised problems of its own. Second, the growing industrial capabilities of many developing countries (the NICs) have both induced them to look to TNCs for the more advanced technologies and skills they need and also given them greater confidence to get these by direct investment (and to set up TNCs of their own). Third, the passage of time has itself soothed some of the greatest fears about TNCs —the companies concerned have turned out to be less bad than feared (or their attractions greater than expected) and the alternatives have, in many cases, turned out to be more difficult and costly. Finally, within the academic field, greater research and empirical experience have also served to tone down the strongest of the criticisms of TNCs in the Third World.

This is not to argue that the Third World will, or should, move towards complete *laissez faire* on international investments. Legitimate grounds remain to regulate TNCs and to seek international co-operation on Codes of Conduct. But these grounds are much more limited than was perceived, say, a decade ago. An application of the old perceptions, by means of harsh and restrictive measures, may well prove counterproductive to the developing countries. In this article I want to discuss some of the main areas of economic concern about TNCs.

Recent trends

We are fortunate that the UN centre on TNCs has recently published its third survey of TNCs in world development. It states that in current US dollars, the flow of foreign direct investment from developed to developing countries rose from $3.7 billion in 1970 to $14.5 billion in 1981 (Table 1). The United States remained by far the major investor throughout this period. The United Kingdom, West Germany and Japan vied for second place, each showing sharp fluctuations in their annual investments in the developing world. The Third World has always figured prominently in Japanese foreign investments, and its growing size indicates the overall rise in Japanese activity abroad. The United Kingdom has also been a relatively large investor in the Third World by Western standards, while West Germany has concentrated more on the developed countries.

Foreign investment in the Third World is highly concentrated by destination. As Table II shows, high income developing countries (with over $1,000 *per capita* GNP) accounted for nearly 60 per cent of the stock of foreign direct investment by end-1978 and also took the lion's share of fresh inflows in 1978-80. As the *Third Survey* states, 'Low income developing countries (considered as those with an annual *per capita* GNP of less than $380 in 1979 but excluding the socialist countries of Asia) accounted for almost 60 per cent of the population of the same group of developing countries, but received less than 5 per cent of the flow of foreign direct investment in 1978-80 compared with 14 per cent in 1970-72.' (p.28)

The countries which pushed up their shares in the 1970s were the tax-haven countries and the oil-importing newly industrializing countries (NICs). Among the NICs, the largest recipients were Brazil (with an accumulated stock of over $14 billion), Mexico (about $7

Table I
Flows of foreign direct investment from developed market economies to developing countries by major home country, 1970–81
In millions of US dollars

Country	1970	1971	1972	1973	1974	1975	1976	1977	1978	1979	1980	1981
Australia	106.2	48.0	101.7	104.0	117.1	48.3	74.7	84.3	68.1	112.8	136.4	n.a.
Austria	4.6	−0.1	4.2	4.7	8.3	6.8	32.9	18.4	19.9	12.9	20.0	31.5
Belgium	45.7	28.5	57.7	48.3	49.5	68.8	235.8	69.5	137.8	253.8	198.2	123.1
Canada	64.2	76.0	176.0	125.0	193.0	300.0	430.0	390.0	558.0	−100.0	400.0	700.0
Denmark	8.4	24.7	9.5	16.1	26.3	30.4	30.0	n.a.	76.5	65.6	79.3	66.0
Finland	0.8	0.8	0.7	0.1	0.3	2.6	0.5	2.0	6.1	15.4	26.5	17.4
France	235.2	170.4	230.6	287.1	239.4	274.2	245.5	264.7	413.4	681.2	899.5	1,137.0
Germany, Fed. Rep. of	317.5	358.1	601.2	786.6	701.3	815.9	765.4	846.0	1,025.1	817.7	1,578.9	1,351.8
Italy	123.4	213.7	280.1	245.6	99.9	150.1	212.9	162.2	71.1	454.9	316.0	131.8
Japan	261.5	222.4	204.0	1,301.1	705.4	222.7	1,084.2	724.4	1,318.3	690.6	906.0	2,426.1
Netherlands	183.2	130.2	321.3	88.5	241.9	228.5	244.7	485.7	443.5	167.4	135.3	353.9
New Zealand	n.a	n.a	−1.9	0.9	3.3	0.8	0.6	9.3	10.5	7.1	23.5	15.4
Norway	18.9	10.6	6.8	14.4	14.9	16.8	42.7	15.7	30.2	7.8	9.0	8.2
Sweden	36.5	40.1	41.9	21.9	49.0	82.2	125.0	126.3	115.0	127.4	90.1	85.5
Switzerland	55.4	65.7	73.1	80.5	128.0	208.2	226.1	211.3	174.1	415.9	352.8	340.0
United Kingdom	340.6	233.2	390.7	698.8	718.7	796.5	986.3	1,178.2	820.0	1,028.7	1,231.0.	1,216.8
United States	1,888.0	2,010.0	1,976.0	2,887.0	3,788.0	7,241.0	3,119.0	4,866.0	5,619.0	7,986.0	3,367.0	6,475.0
Total	3,690.1	3,632.3	4,473.6	6,710.6	7,084.3	10,493.8	7,856.3	9,454.0	10,906.6	12,745.2	9,769.5	14,479.5

Source: UN Centre on Transnational Corporations, Transnational Corporations in World Development: Third Survey, New York, 1983, Table II. 12 of statistical annex.

Table II
Distribution of foreign direct investment and other resource flows from OECD countries among groups of developing countries, 1978–80
(Percentage)

	Gross national product 1979	Stock of foreign direct investment end-1978	Flows from OECD countries Annual average, 1978–80		
			Foreign direct investment	Bank loans	All resources
Total developing market economies	100.0	100.0	100.0	100.0	100.0
By income group					
Less than $380 *per capita* GNP	16.9	13.5	3.1	1.4	16.8
$380–$1,000 *per capita* GNP	14.7	13.5	8.7	11.4	19.4
Above $1,000 *per capita* GNP	68.0	58.2	49.5	86.8	50.2
Of which: tax havens	0.3	14.2	14.8	0.2	3.6
No *per capita* GNP data	0.0	0.6	23.7	0.0	26.1
By region					
Europe	3.0	0.4	1.7	6.4	3.7
West Asia	14.6	3.2	−2.6	3.4	11.5
South Asia	9.9	5.0	4.7	13.0	8.5
South and East Asia	13.9	22.1	18.7	12.3	12.5
Socialist Asia	13.7	0.0	0.1	0.2	0.8
Latin America	30.7	56.7	64.4	62.7	33.7
Africa	14.1	12.4	13.1	13.7	29.4
Unallocated	0.0	0.0	7.9	0.0	16.9
Other country groups					
Least developed countries	2.9	1.5	0.4	0.6	9.0
Oil exporting countries	21.8	16.6	10.7	12.2	13.4
Newly industrializing countries	27.1	33.7	40.1	56.9	20.1
Tax havens	0.3	14.2	16.0	0.2	3.6

billion), Argentina and Venezuela (between $3 and $4 billion each), Malaysia (about $4 billion), Singapore (about $2 billion), Hong Kong (between $2-3 billion), and South Korea (about $2 billion). Taiwan is not reported in UN statistics, but may be taken to have a somewhat higher stock than Korea. India has a fair accumulated stock (about $2.5 billion) but has received virtually no new foreign investments in the past thirteen years.

The large Latin American countries, with Brazil in the lead, have been the most favoured destinations for developed-country investments in the past decade and a half. Brazil and Mexico by themselves account for roughly 40 per cent of total direct investments in the Third World. The poorer countries, while holding the great mass of the Third World's population, receive very little of TNC investment.

There are several reasons for this. Most of direct investment is directed at the home markets of the receiving countries: thus, the richer the country, and the larger the market, the more will (government policies being equal) it receive of TNC investment. Furthermore, since TNCs are strongest in sectors requiring advanced technologies, sophisticated skills and large scale operations, larger markets with more complex industrial structures are cumulatively more attractive to TNCs. Even export-oriented foreign investments, which may be expected to go mainly to the lowest wage areas, go predominantly to the better-off countries. Why? Export-oriented operations require excellent infrastructure, a relatively skilled workforce with a certain industrial discipline, and stable political regimes. Many of these attributes are possessed by some NICs, and serve to compensate for relatively high wage rates.

Economic factors in determining foreign investment flows are generally overwhelmed by political and policy factors. Many countries have imposed such strict conditions on TNC entry that they have effectively kept new inflows out, though ostensibly they permit foreign investments (India is the best example); others may have welcomed inflows but their own instability has deterred prospective investors; and yet others deliberately keep TNCs out for ideological reasons. The UN *Third Survey* notes, however, that the large developing countries which have historically attracted most of TNC investment have shown two distinct phases in their policies in the past decade. To quote:

'In the early 1970s, fortified by their strengthened bargaining position as the centres of economic growth and as recipients of investments by transnational corporations in the developing world, most of these countries introduced rigorous regulatory regimes for foreign investment and technology. The basic objective of such regimes was not to discourage foreign investment or diminish the flow of foreign resources, but to regulate them. These regulations provided *inter alia* for the screening and registration of foreign investment; the prohibition or restriction of foreign participation in specified sectors; the control of take-overs; the restriction of foreign capital to minority holdings in certain sectors; specific regulation of technology agreements; the prohibition of restrictive business practices; and performance requirements for subsidiaries of transnational corporations, such as requirements relating to exports and integration with the domestic economy. However, since the mid-1970s, many of these countries have initiated policies and strategies that depart in certain significant respects from these earlier regimes. These new policies on the whole portray a more flexible and pragmatic approach aimed at facilitating and speeding up foreign investment inflows'. (pp. 56-7)

Transfer of technology

In the highly imperfect international market for the sale of technology, it has long been the convention to regard TNC entry as a particularly costly means of transferring technology to Third World countries. Apart from the questions of appropriateness and local technological development, it has been felt that the host country would do better to 'unbundle' the package which TNCs bring, and to buy the technological element on its own. This would provide cheaper technology, not under control of the TNC (which may prevent its dissemination within the host country and its utilization for export activity) and more amenable to local adaptation and subsequent development.

In certain circumstances, this analysis is valid. In simple industries, with relatively stable technologies and/or undifferentiated products, a developing country with some industrial experience may indeed do better by licensing (or copying) foreign technologies. A large part of the industrial success of countries like Korea, Taiwan and Hong Kong is attributable to local firms buying or copying foreign technologies rather than to the entry of foreign affiliates. Their initial spurt was based upon labour-intensive activities in mature technologies which are not the main stamping grounds of TNCs.

In more complex areas of industry, however, the cost advantage of licensing technologies is not so obvious for several reasons. First, some leading-edge technologies are simply not available on license. Second, the transfer may be less efficient, slower and less continuous under a series of licensing agreements than with an affiliate. Third, a licensee may be subjected to greater 'restrictive business practices' than a subsidiary, simply because the parent company appropriates a greater proportion of profits in the latter case than the former. The case for buying technology outright is often grounded on the historical experience of Japan, but we must bear in mind that by the time Japan was buying advanced technologies it already had a century of industrial experience, a highly trained workforce, considerable technical and scientific manpower, a specific and finely-tuned technology policy and a highly efficient industrial structure. Without these assets, developing countries should think very carefully about going it alone' in complex industries—after all, few countries have shown the capability to 'do a Japan' in recent years. Even Korea has realized its technological limitations and is actively seeking to promote foreign investment.

Technology never comes cheap. It is not, and cannot be, a 'public good' which can be made freely available to all possible users. As long as its creation is risky and expensive, and its utilization a source of income, buyers must accept that innovators must necessarily appropriate substantial benefits if they are to innovate at all. Furthermore, it is common—and quite wrong—to think that technology transfer is costless: every new application of a given technology requires adaptive engineering work. The costs entailed are usually higher in less industrialized countries, where the absorptive capacity for new technologies is weak. Add to this the consideration that no industrial technology is static. All technologies change, some faster than others, and some at greater cost than others: but any industrializing country must have the wherewithal to keep abreast of technological frontiers. Given these facts, it must be accepted that TNC investment can promote efficient technology transfer to developing countries in a variety of circumstances. Where the line is drawn between autonomy and 'dependence' (on TNCs) must be a very pragmatic issue.

It would appear that the industrialization experience of leading developing economies has made them pragmatic in this precise sense. Their growing need for more advanced technologies, the realization of their own technological handicaps and the accelerating pace of technological change in several industries, have led even those NICs averse to TNC entry (Korea among the dynamic ones, India among the laggards) to believe they they must be more liberal. They impose certain requirements on entrants, of course, to ensure that valuable technology enters the country, but earlier concerns about restrictive practices, excessive profits, secrecy etc., seem far more muted.

Appropriateness of technology

The debate over the 'appropriateness' of imported technologies for Third World conditions continues—but it is now largely academic. Most policy makers in the industrializing Third World have opted for modern technologies in much of manufacturing industry (by 'modern' is not necessarily meant the kind of state-of-art, automated, large-scale technologies in use in the advanced industrial countries, but some version of the technologies used there recently, without major changes in its main features). Some countries have sought to preserve traditional technologies in a few activities where these exist—food processing, textiles, simple consumer goods—but these are also on the way out. Their lack of commercial competitiveness has rendered them a burden on the state. Only a few (for example, carpets, ethnic handicrafts) have proved viable on their own, and these have grown into important export products.

In large areas of industry, especially the complex sectors (making consumer durables and producer goods) which come in the later stages of development, the issue of finding intermediate or 'appropriate' technologies—significantly different in their labour usage, skill requirements, etc.,—has slid into policy oblivion. There may be many reasons for this. While 'appropriateness' of technology is, by definition, a good thing, the commercial competitiveness of alternative, highly labour-intensive technologies has not been established. Truly appropriate technology does not exist (outside the traditional sectors), and its development (if at all possible) would be extremely expensive. Technological progress in the advanced world continues to produce more efficient products and processes, whose deployment would raise productivity in developing as well as developed economies, generally regardless of different factor prices. Some analysts feel that there is a natural trajectory of scientific advance, and that it would be unrealistic to expect it to go in a completely different direction to suit different factor endowments. Finally, there is an intrinsic and complex interlinkage between different forms of technological advance (the pervasiveness of micro-electronic revolution is an excellent example). Thus, developing countries can create unfavourable repercussions on technological progress in sectors they wish to promote by keeping out new technologies in sectors they do not wish to promote. In sum, the pervasiveness of technological change along a certain historical trajectory in practice renders appropriate technologies largely irrelevant.

If this argument is accepted, much of the blame which has been laid on TNCs for spearheading the transplantation of over-capital-intensive technologies in developing countries has been misplaced. This is being increasingly accepted in the study of TNCs. Third World policy makers have never been enamoured of the idea of using intermediate technologies in their fledgling industries. Thus, in general there is a more favourable attitude to technology transfer by TNCs.

The appropriateness debate has been conducted at a fairly high level of abstraction, taking as a premise that TNCs in fact transfer unadapted technologies from developed to developing countries. At the micro-level, this premise is unfounded. Every new application of a technology entails considerable adaptive effort. The core process may not be significantly altered, but changes in scale, inputs, outputs, automation etc., may constitute between 10-60 per cent of total project costs. Product ranges of TNCs in developing countries are very different from those in advanced countries, and new products are developed specifically for developing country conditions. There is no evidence that TNCs lag behind local firms in generating 'appropriate' technology in this limited sense.

Local technological development

One major cause for concern about TNC entry into developing countries continues to be the effect that this may have on the development of local technological capabilities. Even if it is admitted that TNCs transfer the best production technology, they do not transfer the capability to generate new technology to affiliates in the Third World. They transfer 'know-how' (production engineering) and not 'know-why' (basic design, research and development).

By contrast, local firms which license foreign technologies or develop their own (by imitation) generally develop greater know-why simply in order to absorb and adapt foreign technologies. They cannot rely on a continuous flow of basic design knowledge from a foreign parent, and they may wish, as a conscious strategy, to develop technological autonomy over time.

There is a subtle addition to this argument. A large TNC presence may inhibit local firms from investing in their own know-why development because their learning process is not protected. If TNCs are kept out, local firms have a protected period to develop their know-why without the severe competition of imported technology by TNCs.

There is a great deal of power in these arguments. It does not make economic sense for TNCs to set up research and development centres in most Third World countries, though some larger countries *have* attracted R & D activity by some firms. The competitive advantage of being transnational rests to a large extent on centralizing activities like R & D which enjoy tremendous economies of scale, and which have vital linkages with the sophisticated scientific infrastructures of the developed countries. On the other hand, as the NICs develop advanced skills and accumulate industrial experience, their ability efficiently to undertake know-why activity grows. There is thus a strong possibility that these capabilities outrun the willingness of the TNCs to shift research activity to them.

The Japanese case often lies in the background to these discussions. A conscious strategy to develop indigenous know-why, based on massive injections of imported technology, can pay handsome dividends in certain circumstances.

Given the dangers of generalising the developing countries from the Japanese example, a valid case still remains for policy intervention in this sphere. Private interests (of TNCs) can diverge seriously from social ones where the dynamic comparative advantage of technological activity is shifting in favour of the NICs.

Some important qualifications, however, must be noted:

☐ The promotion of local technology may not necessarily involve excluding TNCs. There are several 'easy' industries where TNCs are not active in any case, and developing countries can go a long way on their own steam. At the other extreme, TNCs may be necessary in high technology industries where it simply does not make sense to set up indigenous R & D activity. In between, TNCs may be persuaded or cajoled into transferring a greater amount of R & D work than they would do without intervention. Several NICs and developed countries have in fact done this, with some success.

☐ A policy of excluding TNCs may have detrimental effects on local know-how. The protection of local enterprises from foreign competition may induce inefficiency in production. The case of India illustrates how a highly protected environment, while generating local know-why, also leads to gross inefficiencies in the application of technology.

☐ The protection of local learning may easily be carried to the extent that local technologies become outdated and uncompetitive. Two factors may be responsible and need highlighting. First, it is tempting to keep out foreign technology in every form in order to achieve self-reliance. This is dangerous, since developing countries do not have the capability even to keep up with changes in a technology they have assimilated. Such are the scientific and financial requirements of technical progress that even imitation is a very complex, risky and expensive task. Thus, in India we find that local innovation has led to assimilation and minor adaptations of imported technologies, but has left even the most dynamic enterprises well behind world frontiers (and behind more liberal NICs, its competitors in world markets). Second, once a protectionist strategy is launched, and imports as well as TNCs excluded, the competitive spur to innovation is blunted. Vested interests in outdated, inefficient technologies grow, and the potential abilities of the country are not fully exploited.

The correct strategy then must be a judicious and careful blend of permitting TNC entry, licensing and stimulation of local technological effort. The stress must always be—as it was in Japan—to keep up with the best practice technology and to achieving production efficiency which enables local producers (regardless of their origin) to compete in world markets. This objective will necessitate TNC presence in some cases, but not in others.

Product choice

It is not true that TNCs introduce exactly the same products, made to same specifications, in every country in which they operate. Where local market conditions require adaptations (say, to the storage properties of medicines, the ruggedness of vehicles, the degree of automation of equipment), such adaptations are made. Where income levels preclude sophisticated, high performance products, these are not introduced.

Where local tastes, climate, religion etc., call for specific products, these are innovated and marketed (this is more relevant in the case of large countries than small ones). Thus, while the product range of TNCs will certainly be broadly similar between a developed and developing country, the precise nature and models of products will often be quite different. Local needs will be catered to. If the resulting consumption patterns are considered inappropriate, the 'fault' lies with the pattern of income distribution and the nature of technical change in the developed world, rather than the operations of profit-seeking TNCs.

To some extent new products will replace old ones, and so throw traditional producers out of business. While this creates adjustment problems—in the Third World these may be serious and painful—it is the very essence of economic growth that structural change should occur. Needless to say, local enterprises play a role here along with TNCs: there is nothing peculiarly transnational about introducing new products and technologies. Whether the new products which are introduced successfully into Third World markets are actually desirable is a hotly contested point. Barring obvious aberrations like the infant-food case, where a new product was clearly inferior to traditional mother's milk for low-income consumers, in general it seems fair to say that consumers are the best judge of their own welfare. Persuasive advertising by TNCs (and large local firms) can instead in some cases and for some periods, but over the long term consumer welfare is better measured by private decision-making than by arbitrary judgments made over the entire range of industrial products by a bureaucracy.

Different developing countries have adopted widely differing policies in respect of new product introduction by TNCs and local firms. The general trend is a mixed one, a compromise between selling the latest and best and protecting traditional producers (and, in some cases, cultural and social norms). With the speeding of technological change and of information transmission across national boundaries, most developing countries are growing more relaxed about the process of product introduction. This is particularly the case with electronic-related products, where technological lags can be harmful to industry and where consumer demand for new 'goodies' is growing apace. India presents the usual muddled paradox here: the government is eager to utilize electronics in industry, but its policy of restricting TNCs and continuous technology inflows, in order to promote indigenous technology, have set electronics application back by several years. The result shows up not just in the backward state of information/data processing and transmission, but in lags in other manufacturing industries which are increasingly using electronics in their products and processes. Harking back to what was said earlier about the close inter-linkages between different forms of technical progress, the policy of holding back the technological upgrading of one product (or set of products, based upon micro-electronics) will affect, in subtle ways, the progress of other sectors. Thus, a newly-industrializing country wishing to participate in the international community, expanding its industrial prowess and trading strength, must tread very carefully in intervening in market-determined product introduction. Whether or not TNCs are involved, intervention should be exceptional.

Transfer pricing

This has been one of the most sensitive areas of TNC regulation, and will continue to be so as long as firm-specific products are traded across countries. However, the flurry of policy interest which had been aroused in the early 1970s has died down, at least in the Third World. Recently interest has been aroused by the US proposal to impose unitary taxation (unitary taxation means that the multinationals are taxed on a portion of their worldwide profits without reference to the profit gained in a particular state) on foreign TNCs. What are the main reasons for this development?

First, part of the early anxiety had been based upon misconceptions about what the phenomenon was all about. Most of the evidence came from one industry, pharmaceuticals, and involved the comparison of prices charged on intra-firm transactions with what would be charged by a non-patent observing imitator. The price differences were enormous, leading analysts to believe that the impact of the practice was huge; furthermore, it was felt that the pharmaceutical industry was representative of all sectors inhabited by TNCs. More reasoned analysis showed that the initial basis for assessing transfer prices was wrong—an innovating firm *had* to charge much more than an imitating one. By choosing an imitator's price as the reference point, the host country was in effect asserting that it wanted to opt out of the innovation process. It was this consideration which led the UK authorities to reverse their earlier policy on transfer prices charged by Hoffman La Roche. The pharmaceutical industry case seems exceptional. Few examples of gross misuse of transfer prices have surfaced from other sectors; indeed, there are few other industries where highly firm-specific innovatory products can be copied easily and so provide a ready basis for comparison.

Second, the other factors which made Third World countries seek TNC investment more eagerly also made them more willing to accept the potential abuse of transfer pricing as a necessary cost of having TNCs. All possible regulations which could be applied to transfer prices were cumbersome and possibly unfair to TNCs (such as unitary taxation). Thus, an otherwise welcoming posture to TNC entry could be outweighed by a strict policy of transfer-pricing control.

Third, some developing countries which had adopted very liberal policies on TNCs, with no regulation on transfer-pricing and relatively attractive tax rates, did not seem to suffer from the problem. For instance, Singapore felt that it probably gained from transfer pricing rather than losing, even though it was not a tax-haven country. This allayed fears that transfer-pricing was bound to be used to exploit the Third World, regardless of tax-tariff considerations.

Over time, as a consequence of practical difficulties and the desire to attract TNCs, Third World countries gradually downgraded the priority they had once attached to transfer pricing. This does not imply that a transfer-pricing problem does not exist. Clearly, as long as arbitrary prices can be attached to intra-firm transactions, and there are reasons for preferring to show profits in one country rather than another, TNCs will be tempted to use the instrument. They may do so discreetly and within narrow limits, but even this may be sufficient to pose a serious fiscal problem to the host country. For reasons given, developing countries may be unwilling to take strict measures on their own. This is then a prime candidate for multilateral action—on the exchange of information and on harmonization of policies—and so a very important constituent of any Code of Conduct that may evolve.

Export performance

Apart from the transfer of advanced technologies, it is the prospect of increased exports of manufactured goods that leads developing countries to seek TNCs. The NICs which have relied heavily on TNCs have gained substantially by way of increased exports. Over 90 per cent of Singapore's manufactured exports come from TNC subsidiaries and joint ventures; in Korea, Taiwan, Brazil and Mexico it is between a third and a half. For others, there are also benefits, though on a lesser scale. A large number of developing host countries have set up export-processing zones, and those in South East Asia have had some measure of success. On the other hand, in the present recessionary climate, with shrinking or stagnant world trade, growing protectionism and fierce international competition, not many developing countries can expect even TNCs to boost their export earnings substantially.

Many Third World countries have not gained much export earnings via TNC activity. Some have the wrong location. Some do not have the requisite materials, skills or infrastructure, and so are too high-cost. Some are too unstable for TNCs to commit themselves to world-wide sourcing from them. And some are too restrictive to permit efficient TNC operation in world markets. Even if world trade were to start booming again, these countries could not hope for much on this score.

The realization of this seems to be seeping into the minds of policy makers, and even the most restrictive among them (for example, India) have started to liberalize on export-oriented ventures as a special case. This may not be enough. TNCs have practically the whole world to choose from for locating export-oriented investments, and will not go to countries which have cumbersome procedures, inadequate infrastructure and a troublesome workforce—even if they had low wages. The most dynamic of export-oriented industries, semi-conductor assembly, is shifting back to the industrial world because of automation. No other comparable activity, based primarily on cheap labour, has made an appearance.

I expect, therefore, that export-oriented operations by TNCs will continue to grow mainly in those NICs where TNCs have been well-established for a long time. Here the TNCs will move into more complex, scale-intensive activities as they rationalize their global production to meet intensifying competition, such as in the automobile industry. Other countries will naturally try to emulate the successful ones, but will not be able to reap the same benefits. There is a circle of cumulative causation which leaves out countries that chose to ignore TNCs in the beginning.

In terms of changing perceptions of TNCs, the implications are obvious. When the world economy picks up again, and protectionist pressures recede in the developed world, TNCs will play a significant role in expanding sophisticated exports from the NICs. This will make them all the more attractive to countries which have not been able to succeed in export markets. The experience of TNC exports during the past decade has contributed greatly to the increased desirability of TNCs to the Third World. Whether the feeling is requited is quite a different matter.

Local enterprises

Local enterprises in the NICs have withstood the challenge of TNCs. In sectors where TNCs are not particularly active, they have grown, flourished in export markets and set up their own transnational operations. In sectors where they compete more directly, they have flourished only when given substantial protection by their governments, either in the form of state ownership or by keeping TNC competition out (or both). A major development which has defused the issue of TNC versus local firms has been the growth of joint ventures between the two. Third World governments have forced the pace (sometimes at the cost of scaring off high-tech TNCs) and TNCs have learnt to compromise.

The fact that Third World firms have themselves emerged as TNCs has placed the NICs in a somewhat awkward position. The international posture of the more anti-TNC among them has had to be modified, in practice if not in rhetoric. Some countries find themselves being accused of 'sub-imperialism', and their TNCs of using exploitative business strategies. An interesting new development, still in its infancy, is joint-ventures between developed and developing country TNCs in third countries. This sort of international investment has a great potential for future growth and forces developing countries to adopt a much more pragmatic attitude to TNCs.

Conclusions

This article has touched upon some areas of long-standing concern in the Third World about the impact of TNCs. For a variety of reasons, developing host countries have adopted more welcoming—or at least less mistrustful—attitudes to TNCs.

This change in attitudes may not lead either to substantial increases in international investment flows to the Third World or to particular countries realizing significantly greater benefits from their presence. Experience shows that TNCs are very selective in the countries they seek to invest in. By their very nature, their contribution is limited to industries which offer advantages to high technology, large size and sophisticated product marketing. Thus, a large number of developing countries fall below the skill, size, income or location threshold above which the benefits of TNC operations become noticeable.

More liberal attitudes to TNCs do not indicate that controls need not be exercised on their operations. In the highly concentrated and imperfect markets in which TNCs flourish, and in the sphere of economic decision-making on a scale which has powerful political repercussions, government intervention can often increase the benefits derived by the host country and maintain the integrity of the local government. Transfer-pricing is an obvious case where regulation, backed by international co-operative measures, can be useful. The realization of other benefits of TNC presence—technology transfer, increased exports, and the like—require more efficient macro-economic policies and subtle negotiations rather than strict regulations or international Codes of Conduct. This understanding is now seeping into the traditionally hostile countries of the Third World. It remains to be seen whether it will be translated into practical policy making.

The Rise of Multinationals from the Third World

Sanjaya Lall

Introduction: the background

The internationalisation of economic activity has taken many new and dynamic forms in recent years, of which perhaps the most dynamic and least expected has been the emergence of multinationals from less developed countries. Not that the phenomenon is particularly new. The first recorded instance of a Third World multinational investing abroad dates back to 1890, when an Argentine textile manufacturer, Alpargatas, set up an affiliate in Uruguay, and followed it up in 1907 with a similar plant in Brazil. But Argentina is a very unusual case in many ways. At the turn of the century it was the most highly industrialised of the LDCs. Waves of immigrants from Europe who were skilled technicians and entrepreneurs had given it a diverse and sophisticated industrial base. By the time the Great Depression struck, three giant firms, Alpargatas in textiles, Siam di Tella in mechanical engineering, and Bunge y Born in grain trading, finance and miscellaneous manufacturing activities, were already well established in several Latin American countries.

But these are unusual cases from an unusual country. They did not herald the growth of Argentine industry as a leading force in Third World industrialisation or multinationalisation. In the past quarter-century, the pace of Argentina's economic growth faltered for numerous political and economic reasons. It has now become a relatively stagnant (if technologically advanced) industrial and trading nation in the community of "newly industrialising countries". Of its early multinationals, Alpargatas has been reduced to a tiny shareholder in its major affiliate in Brazil, Siam di Tella has gone into government ownership because of sustained losses, and Bunge y Born has effectively shifted out of Argentina to its major base in Brazil (where it controls over 50 firms with total sales of over $1.5 billion). These multinationals have not really been "multinational corporations" in the normal sense of the term, with the parent company supplying technology and skills to its affiliates, making strategic decisions and exercising corporate control, for many decades now. After the initial injection of capital and know-how, the different branches have gone their different ways. And, given the prolonged crisis in their original home country, the affiliates have tended to grow faster and larger than their parents. The participation this entails thus resembles a portfolio rather than a direct foreign investment.

These cases apart, the real growth of Third World direct investments started in the 1960s and gained momentum in the 1970s. By now a larger number of developing countries— between 30 and 50—can claim to have at least some companies which have direct investments abroad. It is difficult to quantify the total amounts of investment involved with any accuracy, because many countries do not collect data on their overseas direct investments.

Originally published in *Third World Quarterly*, vol. 5, no. 3, 1983. © *Third World Quarterly*; reprinted with permission.

In any case, many such investments are undertaken without the knowledge of the authorities, in order to bypass foreign exchange and other regulations. And, for countries which do keep records of foreign investments, it is impossible to separate out direct investments by national companies from those made by affiliates of foreign firms or by "expatriate" firms (for instance, British firms headquartered in Hong Kong). Needless to say, I exclude portfolio-type investments by oil-rich developing countries, even when these involve buying shares in manufacturing firms abroad, from the category of "Third World MNCs".

Despite these problems in assessing the value of foreign investments by Third World enterprises, a number of studies in recent years enable us to identify which countries are the leading exporters of private capital and what their areas of specialisation are.

The largest investor in the Third World is Hong Kong, with over $2 billion worth of equity held abroad (including some in the People's Republic of China). A substantial proportion of this is, however, accounted for by British "expatriate" firms such as Jardine Matheson, which have investments all over the world in a variety of manufacturing, real estate, trading, banking and other activities. However, indigenous Chinese enterprises are also very aggressive investors abroad—a very rough estimate (by professor Edward Chen[1] of the University of Hong Kong) puts their foreign capital stake at $600-800 million.

This estimate makes Hong Kong a slightly smaller indigenous investor than Brazil, whose overseas capital stock (excluding banking) was estimated at over £1 billion in 1980.[2] There are interesting differences between these countries which I will touch on later, but one worth noting now is that a major part of Brazilian overseas investment is accounted for by the giant state-owned enterprise, Petrobras. Hong Kong overseas investment, by contrast, is entirely by private enterprises, and by enterprises which are not very large even by Third World standards.

A capital exporting developing country which is almost as important as Brazil is Singapore—though its investments are highly concentrated in contiguous Malaysia (of which it was historically part). As with Hong Kong, it is relatively small Chinese entrepreneurs who account for its indigenous multinationals. However, Singaporean enterprises are less dynamic in the international field than their Hong Kong counterparts, in terms of the amount, spread and diversity of activity. This may be somewhat surprising at first sight. Singaporean industry is generally more skill-based, high technology and capital-intensive than Hong Kong's, and so may be expected to have a relatively greater foreign presence. However, over three-quarters of Singapore's industrial output, and over 90 per cent of its manufactured exports, come from foreign-controlled enterprises, as compared to under one-quarter for Hong Kong. The weaker position of indigenous enterprise in Singapore thus undoubtedly reflects itself in its lower international profile vis-à-vis Hong Kong.

There is, then, a whole group of middle-income countries which have foreign investments of around $50-100 million each—South Korea, Taiwan, Argentina (excluding its early investments), Mexico and Venezuela. Thus, the group of NICs (newly industrialising countries) are all involved in international production, and they lead the Third World in this activity. Smaller and less industrialised countries in Latin America and Asia are also foreign investors, but their activity is more sporadic and less firmly grounded in domestic industrial expertise.

A country which is a relatively large foreign investor but does not fit into the broad pattern of high per capita income associated with overseas investment is India. With income levels far lower than the NICs, India now has foreign equity of over $100 million. Even more surprisingly, India's direct investment overseas has far surpassed the inflow of new foreign capital in the 1970s—certainly not a pattern common to developing countries. There are other features of interest in India's overseas investment which will be remarked on later.

To sum up this introduction, therefore, we note that the emergence of Third World multinationals is a real and growing phenomenon. It encompasses a large range of countries, but is spearheaded by the NICs (and India). The amounts involved are still small; probably the entire stock of Third World direct foreign equity (excluding portfolio investments by oil-rich countries) is not more than $10 billion. The great bulk of this investment is directed to other developing countries, though a few investments in manufacturing (and several in distribution, banking, and hotels) have been made in the developed world. This geographical distribution is entirely to be expected. Third World enterprises do not have the wherewithal to compete with developed country firms on their home ground. What is of interest, however, is that they do compete with them in other developing countries. How has this become possible? The next two sections attempt to answer this question.

The Nature of Industrial MNCs from Developing Countries

Much has been written recently about the specific advantages that Third World firms may have in investing abroad and competing both with local firms and the host countries and with affiliates of MNCs from the developed countries. As this discussion has really focused on manufacturing investments, we also confine ourselves to this. Before reviewing the current state of knowledge, however, we should form some idea of the pattern of Third World foreign investments.

There are marked differences between the major Third World capital exporting countries, as far as the share of manufacturing in total investment is concerned, and, also, in the sorts of manufacturing industries in which different countries reveal their strengths.

Thus, over 95 per cent of Brazil's overseas capital is invested in oil exploration, construction and agricultural activities. About 70 per cent of Korean foreign investment is in trading and natural resources based activities. About half of Argentine investment is in non-manufacturing. A significant but unknown proportion of Hong Kong and Singapore investments is in the service sectors. And about 5 per cent of Indian foreign investments is in hotels, banks, insurance and trading ventures.

In terms of manufacturing industry alone, the major Third World investors are Hong Kong, Singapore, India and Argentina. The other NICs such as South Korea, Taiwan, Brazil and Mexico have relatively few manufacturing investments overseas. The first two and Hong Kong have started to follow the early Japanese pattern of resource-scarce economies investing abroad in the development of natural resources. Brazil's absence in the field of industrial investments is very unexpected, since it is by far the most individualised LDC—the explanation may be partly in the locational advantage of producing in Brazil, and partly in the dominant role of foreign MNCs in most advanced industries.

The four leading Third World industrial investors show quite different patterns of manufacturing activity abroad. The differences arise both in the nature of activity undertaken as well as the extent of indigenous embodied (capital goods) and disembodied (know-how, managerial skills, marketing, and so on) technologies involved in overseas ventures. They reflect the size of the capital exporting economy, the diversity of its industrial base (in particular, the development of the capital goods sector) and its level of indigenous technological development.

Hong Kong invests abroad mainly in the simpler of its major export products—textiles, garments, plastic goods, and simple consumer electronics. Those of its export products demanding more intensive use of skills and marketing—toys, fashion garments, watches, and the like—do not figure largely in its overseas investments. Essentially, the overseas affiliates transfer the production of relatively standardised products with well-diffused technologies. These face increasingly severe competition from new entrants into world trade and industry, which enjoy the advantage of lower labour and land costs. Thus, Hong Kong enterprises are forced to locate in those very countries in order to take advantage of lower production costs. This shift is further encouraged by protectionist policies in Hong Kong's major markets, which allocate quotas for textiles and garments by country—once the home quota is filled, exports can only take place by producing in other countries with unfilled quotas (and less competitive local manufacturers). Products which require greater design, marketing and entrepreneurial skills are kept in Hong Kong because these skills are more difficult to transfer abroad, and also because protectionist and competitive pressure are relatively less on these products.

Hong Kong's direct investments are unusual in that they tend to be export-oriented rather than import-substituting, and they contain relatively little embodied technology from the home country. Hong Kong investors source their equipment worldwide (for second-hand as well as new machines), and have very limited capabilities to design and manufacture capital goods at home. Though some minor modifications are often made to machines sent to overseas affiliates, the basic production technology is imported. The technological contribution of Hong Kong investors is thus that of efficient production engineering (know-how), rather than basic equipment or plant design and manufacture (know-why). Since this is unlikely to provide a special competitive edge in international markets, their monopolistic advantages must lie elsewhere, in good management and intimate knowledge of export markets.

Much less is known about Singapore multinationals. In terms of their marketing strategy they seem to be very different from their Hong Kong counterparts. They specialise in import-substituting or ethnic (Chinese) products. Despite even greater cost pressures than Hong Kong, major export activities have not been transferred abroad by local firms. The overwhelming significance of developed country MNCs in Singapore's industry has meant that higher wages and rentals have led to rapid upgrading of local manufacturing activities, with older, more labour-intensive products being phased out and transferred to cheaper locations by these MNCs rather than local ones.

In technological terms, Singapore's foreign investors are similar to those from Hong Kong. Singapore is into "heavier" and technologically more advanced industry than Hong Kong, but it does not have a diverse capital goods base to serve local manufacturing industry. Its foreign investors rely, in consequence, on imported technology and essentially complement it with their entrepreneurial and managerial skills. The ethnic factor gives them a strong additional advantage in countries where the local Chinese community is well entrenched in commerce and distribution.

Argentina's manufacturing investments are firmly rooted in local technology and capital goods, and the products are directed mainly at import substitution in the host country markets. Given Argentina's strong base in food products and engineering, the majority of its overseas activities are in these two sectors, supplemented by an unusually active and dynamic (but not truly innovative) indigenous pharmaceutical industry.

Indian manufacturing MNCs are rather similar to those of Argentina, in terms of the high indigenous technological content and the main emphasis on import-substitution in the host economies. There are, however, noteworthy differences also. Indian investments are spread over a much broader spectrum of activity than those of Argentina. Indeed, they are the most diverse in terms of the range of technologies spanned in the whole Third World. The largest sector is textiles and yarn, accounting for a quarter of total capital held abroad. This is followed by paper and pulp, engineering of various types, food-processing, and chemicals. In these broad categories, there are individual investments which are unexpected if one believes that Third World MNCs are confined to labour-intensive, small-scale, low-technology activities. The largest pulp and paper mill in less-developed Africa is an Indian venture; Indian firms are assembling their trucks in Malaysia and jeeps in Greece; one firm makes precision tools for the electronics industry, mainly for export, in Singapore, while another manufactures mini computers there; two of the newest rayon plants in Indonesia have Indian participation; Malaysia's largest integrated palm-oil fractionation facility is controlled by an Indian firm, as is Thailand's sophisticated carbon black plant: an Indian public sector firm has taken a share in a machine-tool manufacturing venture in Nigeria; and so on.

Indian industrial investors abroad are required to contribute their equity in the form of plant and equipment from India. This ensures that the manufacturing technology used (or a major part of it) has been transferred from India. Most of the technologies have, of course, been imported by India in the first place, but over time they have been assimilated and adopted to Indian conditions, and occasionally changed in significant ways to perform better in those conditions than developed country technologies.

India is also engaged in other forms of overseas activity which involve the transfer of its technology but which do not entail direct investment. It has exported over $2 billion worth of industrial turnkey projects, about $125 million of consultancy services (about half of which are directly for manufacturing activity), and a large number of low-value services for management, trouble-shooting, know-how and various technical matters. In fact, it appears that, as for as manufacturing industry goes, India is the largest exporter of technology in the Third World.

This surprises most observers. Although it is well known that India has a major industrial sector, it is also regarded as having the worst growth and export performance in the group of NICs. In the two decades when the other new industrialisers recorded high rates of growth and rapidly expanded their share of world industrial trade, India has had a variable but generally poor rate of growth and steadily lost its share of world markets. A number of studies have shown that Indian industry is, broadly speaking, highly protected, high cost, and technologically obsolete; few plants reap proper economies of scale; there is little attention paid to product quality and marketing in the consumer goods sector; and there is little evidence of major technological innovation. Indian firms remain highly inward-looking and resistant to any attempt at genuine liberalisation of the economy.

The fact that India is simultaneously able to export more technology than richer, more export-oriented and more efficient NICs raises something of a paradox. The explanations are complex and need much further research. However, I believe they lie partly in the nature of the highly interventionist and inward-looking nature of the policy regime which has itself led to poor overall economic performance, and partly in the nature of the technical effort which has been undertaken in India. The import-substitution regime has spawned a highly diverse capital goods industry, parts of which have developed basic design capability and in a few cases (where scale economies are not crippling), are competitive abroad. The government has severely restricted the entry of foreign MNCs and controlled the inflow of technology via licensing, so forcing local firms to develop their own technological base. At the same time, excessive regulation at home has forced firms to look for diversification abroad. Diversification by exporting has been difficult because of high cost inputs at home, small scales of production, infrastructural failures, and technological lags. Thus, technology exports and direct investment have appeared as a logical means of escape.

Technological lags have not prevented the sale of Indian technologies overseas because many other developing countries deliberately opt for somewhat older and simpler technologies. In many process industries, technological lags take the form of smaller-sized plants rather than very different products or processes; here the competitive disadvantage of Indian firms in the Third World markets is minimal or non-existent. Of course, this leaves out a large number of modern industrial technologies where Indian firms are uncompetitive.

There are, therefore, interesting differences between developing countries in the nature of their foreign investment which can be traced to the nature of the economy and home government policies. Small open economies basically export production know-how and efficient management and marketing. Larger, more closed economies export some basic technology and capital goods as well as production know-how, but their technologies may be somewhat outdated and their marketing skills relatively less developed. There are also several cases where Third World MNCs provide technologies practically identical with that provided by developed countries. Let us now specifically compare the old and new multinationals.

The Competitive Edge of Third World MNCs

The prevalent view of Third World multinationals, as characterised by a forthcoming work on the subject (which synthesises the findings of a major research effort undertaken at the Harvard Business School [3]), is that their competitive edge lies in small-scale, labour-intensive technologies; in manufacturing undifferentiated, price-competitive products; and, in possessing cheap, skilled management which is particularly adept at setting up and running enterprises in the primitive environments of less-developed countries.

There is a great deal of validity in this portrayal of Third World MNCs. We certainly can find numerous examples of investors who have mastered technologies no longer in use in developed countries, or adapted them to the conditions prevalent in less-developed ones. Their scale of operations is often fairly small, and many of their products are unbranded, or sold mainly because of their cheapness; their managers and technicians are certainly paid less than their expatriate counterparts from the rich countries.

However, it would be unwise to generalise from these observations that small scale, low technology, labour-intensity and cheap management are distinct   a sources of competitive advantage vis-à-vis the developed country MNCs. Our own cross-national researches suggest that there are sufficient exceptions to lead us to question the rule itself. Thus, there are several cases of Indian overseas investment which have undertaken in direct competition with other MNCs, and where the scale and technology are practically indistinguishable. Even where technologies have been adapted or descaled, Western MNCs have already undertaken similar adaptations in the home countries of the Third World MNC and in LDCs in which they have long established operations. There seems to be little a priori reason to argue that a local firm has a specific advantage in transferring its adaptations over a Western MNC with similar, but even broader, experience of adapting technologies.

Cheaper skilled manpower also does not appear to give a very substantial cost advantage to Third World MNCs. Most Indian investors, for instance, tend to keep only two to three managers in their affiliates once they have been fully established. The edge that this can give to an affiliate with substantial sales is really very marginal.

These findings do not lead us to a very clear or strong theory of monopolistic advantages possessed by Third World MNCs. It would appear that the advantage varies greatly from case to case—in some it is a unique set of minor innovations to the product or process which it is difficult for other firms to copy (our researches have never, however, turned up an instance where technologies were made more labour-intensive); in others, it is a strong base in marketing a particular product (not necessarily involving a highly advertised brand name); in yet others, it is imply historical accident—they happen to be first in a particular location and so preempt the market. In many ways, Third World MNCs do not differ much from MNCs from the developed countries.

This must not be interpreted to mean that the two are substitutes. Developed country MNCs can do most things which Third World MNCs can, but certainly not vice versa. Third World MNCs may be able to reproduce efficiently certain technologies possessed by developed countries, but they cannot match them on the frontiers of innovation. Their capabilities rest very firmly on the conditioning and experience of their home countries, and their small size and lack of massive technological resources necessarily mean that they cannot compete in fast-moving, very large-scale technologies, or in products which are geared primarily to very high incomes or sophisticated tastes (though Hong Kong firms are beginning to attack high fashion markets).

All this means that Third World MNCs have much smaller "proprietary assets" to protect when they go abroad. This is why it is universally observed that they are more prone to enter into joint ventures with local firms than developed country firms. Increasingly, they are also eager (and sometimes able) to enter into joint ventures with developed country MNCs, an ideal arrangement for them to gain access to advanced technologies and well-known brand names.

The absence of strong proprietary advantages has been taken by Wells to imply that individual Third World MNCs will not last long in the competitive jungle of international production. Third World foreign investments will probably continue, but with individual firms withdrawing from abroad and being replaced by new aspirants. I am not so pessimistic, for several reasons. First, some Third World MNCs do possess unique technological advantages. These may well be based on "minor" innovations, but they are derived from peculiar challenges (mainly of finding the right materials and components in their home economies) faced by that particular firm and are costly for other firms to reproduce. Second, there are many technologies which do not change very rapidly, where it is possible for Third World firms to keep up with world frontiers entirely by their own efforts. Third, the fact of "being first" in a particular market gives the entrant an advantage over others, and this may be exploited by Third World firms in several small markets which the larger MNCs do not bother with. Finally, Third World MNCs can always replenish their technological stock, where their own efforts are inadequate, by licensing technologies from developed countries or entering into joint ventures with their MNCs. In other words, they can become complements to, rather than competitors of, developed country MNCs where their own technologies are uncompetitive, but they are able to set up and manage the production process efficiently.

Some of the arguments advanced about the ultimate demise of Third World MNCs have a familiar ring about them. The same was said of developing country exporters when they started to enter new and sophisticated areas of production (and, earlier, of "cheap, shoddy Japanese goods"). But the new producers are still there, and moving from strength to strength, forcing the advanced countries to adjust to evolving patterns of comparative advantage. Foreign investment is simply another facet of the competitive edge which is first exploited in export markets, and recent history gives us little reason to expect it to be a transient phenomenon. Third World MNCs are here to stay, and they will graduate to First World MNCs as their home countries grow into major industrial powers.

A final note on a new form of overseas investment by some NICs which is also expected to grow in the future: the taking of equity shares in some high technology firms in developed countries in order to obtain direct access to their technology. Hong Kong, Taiwan and Korea have already undertaken investments of this sort. It is not yet known how effective they have been in transferring the basic technology to their home countries, but in principle there is no reason why small, specialised producers (without strong international interests) in the developed countries should resist the offer of equity participation from the NICs. Even large firms, facing financial difficulties in the current recession, may look to the new giant corporations in the NICs for cooperation. Of course, given the nature of the innovation process, the newest and most valuable technologies may not be given even to equity shareholders who might become strong rivals. But there is, as I have said, little known about this particular mode of technology transfer, and it is a promising area for future research.

This paper draws upon research being directed by the author on multinationals from India, Hong Kong, Argentina and Brazil for the Institute for Research and Information on Multinationals, Paris.

[1] This finding is part of the IRM project on Third World multinationals.
[2] *ibid*.
[3] L T Wells Jr, *Third World Multinationals*, Cambridge, Mass: MIT Press(forthcoming). I am grateful to Professor Wells for sending me his manuscript prior to publication.

International Regulation of Foreign Investment

Christopher J. Maule & Andrew Vanderwal

Pressure for the development of international investment codes grew in the early 1970s. Initiatives were taken by developing countries individually and through the United Nations and regional organizations, as well as by labor and business organizations. Two related antecedent events were the US government's voluntary balance of payments guidelines in the 1960s, which affected outward investment flows and the repatriation of earnings and capital, followed by the passage of the Canadian government's *Principles of Good Corporate Behavior for Foreign Investors*.

Revelations that multinational enterprises (MNE) were engaging at times in conduct that was clearly detrimental to the interests of some of the countries in which they operated led to mounting pressure for the international regulation of MNEs. An investigation of transfer pricing in the sale of drugs led to Hoffman-La Roche paying $30 million to the British National Health Service. During their Watergate investigations the US Securities and Exchange Commission (SEC) found that corporations frequently used funds set up outside corporate financial accountability to bribe foreign governments or officials, and to make legal and illegal political contributions in host countries. The resulting US pressure to regulate US corporations led these firms to attempt to internationalize any debate on regulation, in the hope that an international forum would be less discriminatory by including all MNEs.

During the mid-1970s numerous cases of high ranking public officials accepting bribes offered by US corporations severely embarrassed governments around the world. Implicated for taking a series of bribes from the US Lockheed Aircraft Corporation, Prince Bernhard of The Netherlands abdicated all public posts in 1977, and escaped prosecution only by virtue of being the husband of the country's Queen. A major bribery scandal also emerged in Canada concerning the efforts of a crown corporation, Atomic Energy of Canada Ltd. (AECL), to sell a CANDU reactor to Argentina. AECL deposited $ US2.5 million into a Swiss bank account in 1974, to act as a payment to an undisclosed agent who would facilitate the Argentine sale. These incidents underlined the need for guidelines for the international commercial activities of both private and government controlled corporations.

Multinationals on the loose

A number of further considerations served to increase the momentum for developing a regulatory framework. The currency exchange instability in the early 1970s, at a time when attempts were being made to maintain the fixed exchange regime, raised the issue of the damaging role MNEs can play in currency speculation. Additionally, US labor organizations protested what they saw as an export of jobs through the foreign investments of US

First published in *International Perspectives*, November/December 1985. Reprinted with permission.

MNEs, while European labor organizations were growing increasingly concerned over the effectiveness of collective bargaining on a national scale with firms that operated globally. At the same time, developing countries were discussing the need for a new international economic order (NIEO) that would redress economic disparities in the world. Developing countries exerted pressure through the UN for the international regulation of MNEs as part of their greater efforts to bring about a NIEO. Provided that their actions could be regulated, MNEs were to play an important role in this new order by becoming a vehicle to transfer resources to the Third World.

An early initiative for the international regulation of MNEs was the 1970 request by the International Confederation of Free Trade Unions (ICFTU) to the UN to develop a code of conduct for MNEs. In 1972 the UN responded by establishing a Group of Eminent Persons (GEP) — including John J. Deutsch from Canada — to prepare a report on MNEs. Impetus to UN initiatives was given by a debate in the UN's Economic and Social Council (ECOSOC), brought about by charges that the US-owned International Telephone and Telegraph (ITT) had interfered in Chile's domestic political process. At the same time, the business-based International Chamber of Commerce (ICC) issued guidelines for international investment, and the UN-related International Labor Organization (ILO) convened a tripartite meeting of experts on MNEs with representation from labor, business and governments.

UN involvement

The UN GEP reported in 1974 and proposed that a Commission on (not *for*) Transnational Corporations (TNCs) and a Center on TNCs be established, and a noncompulsory code of conduct on TNCs (the new name to be used for MNEs, but it has never caught on outside the UN) be developed. Since its creation by ECOSOC in December 1974 the Commission on TNCs has given priority to the development of a comprehensive international code of conduct for TNCs. The Center on TNCs was established in November 1975, and has served both to gather and to generate data on international business and to provide technical advice to member countries in their relations with TNCs.

In 1975 revelations of illicit payments by MNEs led the UN General Assembly to condemn corrupt practices and to request the ECOSOC to develop guidelines on corrupt payments. By 1977 the ILO had adopted a Tripartite Declaration of Principles Concerning Multinational Enterprises and Social Policy. Although the US had terminated its membership in the ILO earlier in the same year, their representatives had taken part in discussions leading to the Declaration and appeared to be in agreement with most of the provisions. UN activity picked up in 1978 with ECOSOC publishing a draft Code of Conduct on TNCs, and with the United Nations Conference on Trade and Development (UNCTAD) publishing a Code of Conduct on the Transfer of Technology. UNCTAD also organized discussions on a UN code dealing with restrictive business practices.

Regional action

Throughout this period the ICC remained active as did the Organization for Economic Cooperation and Development (OECD), the latter representing the developed country viewpoint on regulation of international investment. Partly as a reaction to UN-related

List 1

Chronology of selected events concerning Codes of Conduct for foreign investment and multinational enterprises, 1960-1980

1960	US government introduces voluntary and then mandatory controls on capital outflow and repatriation of earnings.
	Canadian government introduces "Some Guiding Principles of Good Corporate Behavior for Subsidiaries in Canada of Foreign Companies" (known as the Winters guidelines).
	ICFTU adopts resolution on MNCs and conglomerates.
1970	ICFTU requests UN to adopt a Code for MNCs.
	ANCOM adopts Decision 24 relating to the treatment of foreign capital.
1971	ICFTU hosts a major conference on MNCs.
1972	Chile charges International Telephone and Telegraph with interference in domestic political processes.
	UN appoints Group of Eminent Persons to report on MNCs.
	ILO convenes a Tripartite Meeting of Experts on MNCs.
	ICC issues Guidelines for International Investment.
1973	EEC Commission submits a communication to the Council of the Community on the subject of MNCs.
1974	UN-ECOSOC Report of the GEP proposes a Commission on TNCs and a center on TNCs be established, and a non-compulsory code of conduct for TNCs be developed.
	UNCTAD initiates discussion of a UN Code for Restrictive Business Practices.
1975	UN General Assembly condemns corrupt practices and asks for Guidelines on this issue.
	OAS adopts three guidelines on MNCs and fails to reach agreement on seven others.
	ICFTU issues a Charter of Trade Union Demands for the Control of MNCs which is adopted at a convention.
1975	US Senate Committee on Foreign Relations' Subcommittee on Multinational Corporations (Church Committee) issues a report on *Multinational Oil Corporations* and *US Foreign Policy* (one of the reports on MNCs resulting from hearings conducted over several months).
1976	EEC Parliament approves a fifty-four section Draft Code of Principles on MNEs and governments.
	OECD adopts five instruments including Guidelines for MNEs, national treatment of foreign investment, end international incentive and disincentives for investment.
	UNCTAD issues proposals for a UN code on the transfer of technology.
1977	ILO adopts the Tripartite Declaration of Principles Concerning Multinational Enterprises and Social Policy.
	EEC approves a Code for Companies with interests in South Africa.
	ICC proposes stringent national laws proscribing bribery and corruption.
	UN ECOSOC's Commission on TNCs establishes an intergovernmental working group to develop a Code of Conduct.
	UN ECOSOC adopts a resolution requesting research into institutional and legal arrangements in national consumer protection.
1978	PBEC adopts the second issue of the Pacific Basin Charter on International investments.
1980	UNCTAD's Restrictive Business Practices Code is unanimously adopted by the General Assembly.

activity, the OECD in 1976 passed a Declaration which included Guidelines for MNEs, as well as statements on the national treatment of foreign investment, and on incentives and disincentives for international investment. This has become the most influential initiative in effect, although it is neither mandatory nor agreed to by developing countries.

Other regional organizations which have been actively engaged in debate on international investment issues are the European Economic Community (EEC), the Council of Europe, the Organization of American States (OAS), the Andean Common Market (ANCOM) and the Pacific Basin Economic Council (PBEC). A chronological listing of these developments is shown in List 1. The role of the UN should be recognized both in terms of the initiatives taken by its own bodies, and by the impact which their discussions have had in other governmental, business and labor organizations. Often many of the same issues were being discussed more or less simultaneously in different settings, at times even with the same persons involved.

Codes today

There are presently two categories of codes: those agreed to and those still under discussion. The main codes and their current status are shown in List 2, with the UNrelated international codes separated from other codes of a more regional focus. This does not mean that the UN codes are necessarily more effective. In fact the actions of the OECD and the ICC probably have the greatest influence on foreign investors and capital exporting countries, in much the same way that the arbitration facilities of the ICC are used far more extensively than those of the World Bank's associated International Centre for the Settlement of Investment Disputes (ICSID). The latter has greater official government status but few users, while the procedures of the ICC have gained the respect of both host governments and investors.

The main issues addressed by these eleven existing and proposed codes are shown in List 3. The UN Code of Conduct on TNCs is the most comprehensive and the wording of the issues reflects the interests of the developing countries which have the majority voting representation in most UN bodies. The OECD Guidelines, reflecting the viewpoint of the Western industrialized and capital-exporting countries, stress the obligations of both corporations and host governments in dealing with foreign investment. At the insistence of developed countries, the proposed UN Code also contains a section on the treatment of MNEs by host countries, but this has been a source of considerable controversy due to opposition by developing and socialist countries.

UN initiatives

There are in addition a number of other UN initiatives which tend to be more specialized but which are of importance to corporations and to government policy makers. The most prominent of these initiatives are shown in List 4. The renegotiation of the Paris Convention on Industrial Property under the auspices of the World Intellectual Property Organization (WIPO) was undertaken at the suggestion of developing countries. The initiative represents part of a greater effort by developing countries to facilitate the transfer of the control of technology to their countries, in this case through the ultimate reduction in the monopoly rights of patent protection. In another specialized initiative, the World Health Assembly (WHA) negotiated and adopted the Code on Marketing Breast-milk Substitutes due to allegations that Nestlé, in particular, was promoting the use of inappropriate and hazardous infant formula in developing countries.

Although not elaborated upon in this article, specific investment issues are also addressed by the policies of individual governments, such as the Canadian government's Code for companies operating in South Africa. Some of these country initiatives are dealt with in the comprehensive UN Code on TNCs. Additionally, many bilateral treaties relat-

List 2

Principal international and regional Codes of Conduct for foreign investment and multinational enterprises.			
UN-related Codes		**Date Initiated**	**Current Status**
UN-ECOSOC	Code of Conduct on TNCs	1977	Under negotiation
UN-ECOSOC	Corrupt Practices Code	1976	Not implemented
UNCTAD	Restrictive business practices	1974	Adopted Dec. 5, 1980
UNCTAD	Technology transfer	1976	Under negotiation
ILO	Tripartite Declaration	1972	Adopted Nov. 1977
Other Codes			
OECD	Declaration, including Guidelines for MNEs	1975	Adopted June 21, 1976
EEC	Draft Code of Principles	1974	Not implemented
EEC	South Africa Code	1977	Adopted Sept. 20, 1977
OAS	Guidelines for Foreign Investment	1974	Adopted Jan. 1975
ANCOM	Common Treatment of Foreign Capital Code	1969	Adopted Dec. 1970
PBEC	Pacific Basin Charter on International Investments	1972	Adopted (Second Issue) May 7, 1978

ing to international investment issues, such as double taxation and the applicable law in dispute settlement, find expression in both regional and international codes.

List 3

Issues treated by principal international and regional Codes of Conduct

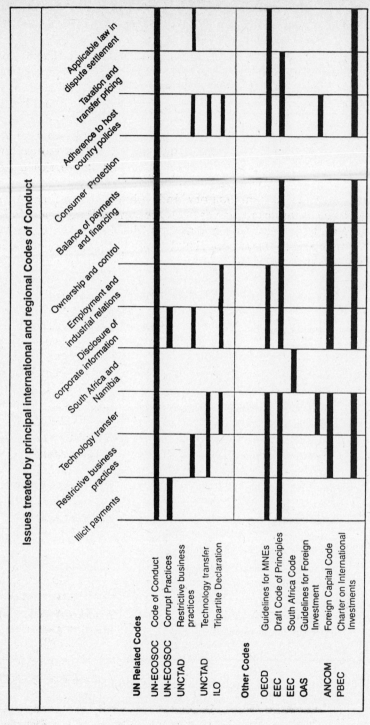

Voluntary versus mandatory

An important consideration in the eleven major codes mentioned in Lists 2 and 3 is the effectiveness of voluntary as opposed to mandatory codes. Developing countries argue in favor of implementing codes of conduct in the form of a legally binding multilateral agreement such as a convention or treaty. Signatories would then be obliged to enforce the codes domestically and an international enforcement arm could be established, under the auspices of an existing institution, to reinforce national regulation and to deal with those aspects of MNE global activity that any one state would have difficulty controlling. Developed countries are strongly opposed to the creation of instant international law on this issue and argue for voluntary codes of conduct.

Ultimately the distinction between mandatory and voluntary forms of implementing codes of conduct may not be as important as has been presumed. Treaties and international conventions are an important but not sole means by which binding international law is created. The four main sources of international law listed in Article 38(1) of the Statute of the International Court are treaties, custom, general principles of law and judicial decisions and teachings. Treaties and international custom as evidenced by the practice of states have proven to be the most important sources in practice.

Even when specifying their own voluntary nature, codes may over time become binding. This can occur as the practice of states in encouraging compliance to the codes, and engaging in follow-up procedures to the codes, can give rise to the status of customary international law. However, just as state practice in applying the codes became an international custom, so can state practice in not applying the codes. The evolution from a voluntary to a binding code may result from circumstances wherein state practice causes certain provisions of a particular code to become binding, while other provisions remain voluntary.

There are a number of major outstanding issues common to both the ongoing negotiations of the UNECOSOC's Code of Conduct on TNCs and UNCTAD's Transfer of Technology Code. These issues include the extent to which principles of international law prescribe standards for the treatment of MNEs. This is a fundamental question that cuts across many disputed provisions in the proposed codes. Many developing countries deny the validity of using principles of law, as these principles were developed prior to their independence, and thus are biased in favor of the developed industrialized countries.

Your law or mine?

A related outstanding issue concerns which country's laws will apply in the settlement of disputes. Competing and often conflicting claims to jurisdiction have frequently been advanced by home and host governments. Developing countries maintain that disputes concerning MNE activity within their borders be subject to their exclusive jurisdiction, and be settled in the national courts of the host country. Proposals to refer disputes involving MNEs to an international forum are resisted by developing countries, as it removes the settlement of the dispute from their jurisdiction, and implies a lack of confidence and credibility in the laws and courts of developing countries.

The attempt to implement the UN-ECOSOC Code on Corrupt Practices appears to have been abandoned due to a lack of real interest in the code outside the US. During the 1970s

List 4

Specialized UN initiatives relating to international corporate activity		
Organization	**Code**	**Current Status**
UN-ECOSOC	International Guidelines for Consumer Protection	Under Negotiation
WHA	Code on Marketing Breast-Milk Substitutes	Adopted May 21,1981
UN General Assembly	Resolution on Use of Harmful Products	Adopted Dec. 1982
UN Environment Program	Exchange of Information on International Potentially Harmful Chemicals	Implemented 1985 Trade in
WIPO	Renegotiation of Paris Convention on Industrial Property	Under Negotiation
UN-ECOSOC	International Standards of Accounting and Reporting	Under Negotiation
ILO	Convention on Termination of Employment at the Initiative of the Employer	Approved by ILO in 1982
UNCTAD	Convention on a Code of Conduct for Liner Conferences	Adopted 1983

the US had implemented national legislation restricting the use of illicit payments abroad, and was eager to have MNCs from other countries operate under the same set of constraints. Realizing the importance of this code to the US, developing countries used the code as a bargaining tool in attempts to obtain concessions on issues of importance to themselves. Many developing countries have also been reluctant to pursue a binding code on illicit payments. As countries with inadequate public revenue to pay for their own bureaucracies, they have often tacitly condoned illicit payments as a means by which to remunerate civil servants. With US MNEs operating under the constraint of US national legislation on illicit payments, other developed home countries to MNCs had little incentive to remove the advantage this provided their own firms. For all these reasons, vigorous US efforts to have the code implemented have failed.

By pressuring for codes of conduct in the UN, developing countries are hastening and shaping the evolutionary process of change in international law. The adoption and implementation of codes are an important source of customary international law, and can take precedence over more than a hundred years of case law on the rights of foreign investors. Developed countries strive to ensure that the codes result in a source of customary international law that will not accidentally restrict many potential global benefits of MNE activity. Such a development could occur if the practice of states in implementing restrictive codes resulted in a harsh investment climate and a reduction of beneficial MNE investment.

Canadian concerns

Canada's interest in these codes has recently broadened because its role as a host country to foreign investment has become complemented by its role as a capital exporting country. Our traditional concern as a host country to direct foreign investment is rapidly being superseded by the concerns of being a home country to such investment. Canadian direct investment abroad increased from 1981 to 1984 by about one-third to $41.4 billion. Investment abroad is now about half the value of the investment in Canada compared with about one-fifth a decade earlier. Not only will Canada have to take a consistent stand on its policy to inward and outward investment, but future multilateral trade negotiations will need to recognize the role played by investment as a substitute to trade, and the ways in which investment codes can influence the interrelationship between trade and investment.

Chapter 7
The Monetary System in Crisis

Introduction

Over the last decade and a half there has been an extremely rapid development in the degree of interdependence in the financial markets and monetary systems of the world. The expansion of world trade created the need for an expanded and more sophisticated financial system. The growth of international investment and the financial requirements of multinational firms presented new demands for financial services. The progressive liberalization of capital movements, combined somewhat paradoxically with the application in some major countries of restrictions and regulations on domestic financial institutions and capital markets, has created a large "offshore" international financial market. Institutional change has been particularly rapid in the banking sector, which has become both internationalized and integrated as a result of deregulation and of the evolution of new communications and information processing technology.

In the 1970s the two oil-price shocks exerted a profound influence on the development of the financial system, producing quantum leaps in the demand for balance-of-payments financing and development capital on the one hand and for placing various kinds of financial assets on the other. The emergence in the mid-1970s of major balance-of-payments disequilibria and of increasing disparities in real economic performance and in inflation rates among the major industrial countries created new pressures on international adjustment mechanisms and led to major changes in the international monetary system itself.

The international capital markets have mobilized financial resources for many developing countries on a scale that would have been impossible for political processes to achieve. Developing countries clearly place a high value on the efficient operation of the capital markets and the independence which direct access to these markets provides them. Improving and underpinning the private capital markets and the associated institutional structure therefore remains a major element in the further evolution of a mutually beneficial international economic system.

It remains clear, however, that the sharp increase in bank lending has also generated new problems and that in the case of most of the less advanced developing countries market processes cannot provide means of obtaining their fundamental development needs. At the stages of development which most of Third World countries are currently in, there are large requirements for investment in human capital and social infrastructure. But when public finance systems are themselves relatively underdeveloped, governments are not able to generate financial surpluses adequate to meet the difference between social returns and private returns. Nor is the economic structure sufficiently developed to sustain an external debt-servicing capacity. Hence, concessional aid will remain critical, and cannot be replaced by private commercial financial flows.

The developing countries, in parallel with their increasing integration into the world economy, have participated in and been affected by the rapid transformation of the international financial system. A few advanced developing countries have become sites of significant international financial centers. More important, developing countries have come to play a significant role in the structure of the international financial system, with the oil surplus countries becoming major suppliers of lendable funds and owners of financial assets while middle and high-income developing countries, including other oil exporters, have collectively been the most rapidly-expanding absorbers of investment capital. Most low-income countries have remained outside these developments; their continuing and increasing dependence on external financing has been accommodated to some extent by expanded aid flows.

With the increase in the size of international financial flows, their structure has also changed. Whereas in the 1960s official concessional aid and direct investment formed the major financing flows, after 1973 there was a major shift to private capital financing (bank lending) and, on the part of the surplus countries, investment of reserve assets. The volume of concessional aid and direct investment continued to grow, both in absolute terms and as a proportion of GNP, but the much faster growth of short-term private capital flows and of reserve assets accumulation produced a marked change in the structure of external financing.

An important feature of international development cooperation has been the rapid evolution and strengthening of the system of multilateral development lending institutions, both as intermediaries of market capital to middle-income developing countries and as a source of concessional development finance for low-income countries. The future level and orientation of the operations of these institutions is one of the most critical problems on the international finance agenda.

The main problem in non-concessional financing is the outlook for international bank lending. The constraints here are not so much the ability of the banks to fund increased lending, but whether current developments, including recession conditions, still high interest rates, sharply reduced oil receipts and an increased awareness of political risks, might lead to a continuing deceleration in international bank lending to developing country borrowers. The decline in bank lending since mid-1982 in part reflects an adjustment of the rather large lending levels in recent years to a small number of major borrowers in Latin America. As world economic recovery proceeds and the acute debt servicing problems of some of the major debtors are overcome and business confidence is re-established, the banking system can be expected to respond positively to market opportunities, although it seems likely that the experience of 1982/83 will lead both creditors and borrowers to be more selective in large-scale use of loans at floating interest rates.

In general the overall level of market-determined non-concessional lending to developing countries in the future will depend on perceptions of the overall economic outlook and the specific conditions in each country, including the success of its adjustment policies, rather than on the need for placing assets in revenue-producing loans, as was the case in the late 1970s. Although direct foreign investment in developing countries has declined in relative importance as a financing flow to developing countries, in real terms direct investment flows have increased more rapidly since 1972/73 than during the 1950s and 1960s. There is some evidence of an emerging trend towards what might be called a new division of responsibilities among the three major groups involved in direct investment in developing countries - that is, the multinational firms, the international financial organizations and major public and private enterprises in developing countries.

There are a number of other institutional developments which could assist the flow of direct investment, particularly to those developing countries which have not so far proved to be attractive locations for international firms. These measures include the expanded use of "facilitating agencies" such as the International Finance corporation (IFC). The push to set up a multilateral guarantee system and, finally, the efforts made in recent years to put in place a network of bilateral investment treaties between developing countries and a number of OECD countries have been gaining in momentum.

The International Monetary Fund is now playing an increasingly important role in the adjustment and the financing of balance-of-payments deficits. Quotas, the major source of Fund financial resources, have increased substantially and a special facility was put into place, as a short-term measure, following the first oil-price shock, adding important resources to the Fund's liquidity. After each of the two oil shocks, special measures were taken to assist low-income Fund members. Normal Fund facilities have also undergone important changes, with payback periods being lengthened and access to Fund resources being enlarged in relation to a member's quota. The terms of the Fund's conditionality have also been modified to provide wider scope for tailoring country programmes to specific economic and social conditions. Since late in 1982, the Fund has been playing a key role in the new pattern of relationships between developing country governments, major industrial country authorities, commercial banks and the Fund itself, to cope with the increased number of "problem" countries.

A new player, the World Bank, has joined the Third World debt management team. The World Bank's new president, Barber Conable, an activist during his years as a member of the US House of Representatives, believes that the Bank must help solve the debt crisis in order to carry on its basic development work. "Unless [the debt] is dealt with in some rational way, it will not permit us to sustain development," he told a group of reporters as he discussed his first six months as head of the World Bank. Mr. Conable's approach is partially an implementation of US Treasury Secretary James Baker's proposal in the fall of 1985 to provide the development banks with more funds to assist countries towards growth-oriented policies, with the World Bank given a greater role in this effort. The proposal was based on the belief that Third World debtor countries had tightened their belts sufficiently since the debt crisis emerged in 1982, and that there would be little real progress unless their economies could be made to flourish. Hence, there are now four major players attempting to control and reduce the Third World's debt problems: the International Monetary Fund, which continues to approve economic packages tailored for each country, the Paris Club, consisting of creditor governments and guarantor governments, the London Club, consisting of a consortium of commercial banks which have uninsured loans to Third World countries, and the World Bank, which is in the business of providing new loans to debtor governments. The role of the Bank could become crucial if Mr. Conable's activist philosophy succeeds - for in giving new loans to debtor governments, he makes it clear that he expects both the creditor governments and the commercial banks to financially back the countries that the World Bank makes new loans to. The International Monetary Fund cooperates directly with the Bank in formulating its packages of assistance to these countries.

The articles in this chapter demonstrate the diversity of the problem as well as the complexity of attempts to solve the debt problem for the Third World. The first article, by Toivo Miljan, uses a conceptual framework to demonstrate how the international monetary system got into its current difficulties. The second article, by Wood and Mmuya, provides an overview of the problems faced by the poorest members of the world economy, the countries of the so-called Fourth World, which are given short-thrift both in the newspapers of the First World and in serious debt management discussions, but which probably suffer more than the largest creditors and whose debt crisis may be endemic. In the third article, Richard Swedberg examines in detail the main ideological tenet of the World Bank—the doctrine of neutrality—and concludes that the real function of this doctrine is to provide an ideological smokescreen for the powerful Western nations to intervene in favour of free trade and capitalism in the domestic affairs of Third World countries. According to Swedberg politics cannot be kept out of the IMF or the World Bank; decisions cannot be made on neutral, economic grounds. The Amuzegar article takes issue with the critics of the IMF, including sentiments expressed in the preceding article, and answers charges that the IMF is a highly-rigid, single-minded, biased institution dominated by a cabal of industrial countries which follows narrow, free market approaches in total disregard of the crippling effects of its adjustment policies on growth. The brief excerpts from the World Debt Tables Annual 1985-86 outline the involvement of the Paris and the London Clubs in debt renegotiations and provide a statistical overview of debt problems of the Third World, and a brief description of the changing world financial markets. The speech by US Secretary of the Treasury James A. Baker III outlines current American leadership roles in the attempt to come to grips with the debilitating drain of indebtedness on the international system and the necessity of providing funding for growth. The final article by Bloch is at first glance a whimsical essay about the "near future" after the debt crisis has brought about the near collapse of the international monetary and economic system as we know it today. The point of the article is that the debt reschedulings and the servicing thereof, which form by far the largest component of First-Third World financial flows currently, could very well lead to both economic and political disasters of a revolutionary character if we do not resolve the problem soon.

The International Monetary System and Interdependence

Toivo Miljan

1. Conflict of Models: Sovereignty Model and the Complex Interdependence Model

Although economic factors have clearly had a greater impact on international relations during the past three decades than the use of force has, political scientists for some reason are still wedded to varieties of power politics frameworks, including conflict analysis models, for analyzing international relations. The result is that there is a general tendency to analyze the international system and its components in terms of power politics concepts such as military capability, prestige and sovereignty, including the maintenance, expansion, and defence thereof. Concern with these factors is generally labelled *high politics*, wording which is meant to emphasize the indivisibility of the core values of a state. Concerns relating to economic factors are labelled either *welfare politics* or *low politics*, wording intended to de-emphasize the relative importance of economic concerns. However, despite the linguistic separation of economic and "high" politics the tendency is to subordinate the economic to the high politics and to treat the economic as a support for high politics, or as a substitute for it when high politics proper appears to be absent. The central factor which leads to a confusion between high politics and the politics of economics is the concept of sovereignty. Sovereignty implies independence and the right to exercise the authority of the state within the territory of a state absolutely and without the necessity of regard for anything outside the borders of the territory of the "sovereign state." In other words, sovereign independence is the foundation of the concept of power politics.

This conceptualization of the world is unfortunately a false one since relatively little in the post-war world of conflict relationships operate with any regard, much less with due regard, to sovereign independence of the authority of the state within territorial boundaries. In the economic realm the opposite of sovereign independence, *complex interdependence*, is the rule of relationships among states and among systems across inter-state boundaries.

In the sovereignty model (Figure 1) there is the legal fiction that states in the international system are equal and the political fiction that each government in each state is in total control of the activities of the component social-economic-political clusters of relationships within the State, and that it either acts as the only channel of relations with other States or controls all relations between its own "subsystems" and those of another State by dealing directly with the government of that other state which is similarly in total control. Indeed, this kind of conceptualization lies behind the term "interstate relations".

Published for the first time in this volume.

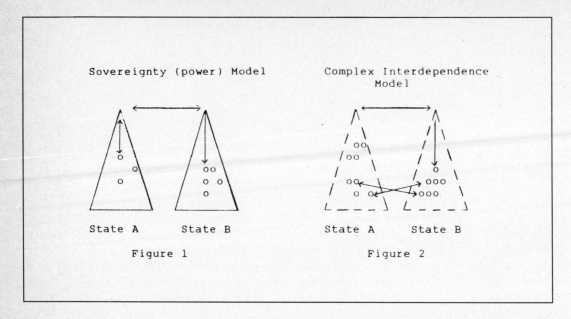

Sovereignty (power) Model

State A   State B

Figure 1

Complex Interdependence Model

State A   State B

Figure 2

Clearly, the conceptualization behind the term "interstate relations" is today a gross oversimplification, even in military relations, and patent nonsense as a description of economic relations. Today, instead of interstate relations in economic matters we have "transgovernmental" relations, which term implies that states do not act coherently as authoritative allocators of values and that relations among States are often channeled directly between the clusters of systems within their territorial boundaries without regard for the authority of the State apparatus and its government. In addition during the 1970s it has become clear that even in relations among States governments are not the only primary actors—there are, for example, intergovernmental organizations and transnational corporations. Hence a third concept must be added, that of "transnational" relations. Any model that purports to analyze economic relations among states today must then include the concept of *interstate relations, transgovernmental relations* and *transnational relations*. This model may be labelled the *complex interdependence model*. In addition to multiple channels of relationships the complex interdependence model also accepts the fact that there are multiple issues in the international economic system and that these issues simply cannot be structured hierarchically. This also means that the distinction between what is domestic and what is foreign is often blurred, and that at the governmental level many ministries are involved with both domestic and foreign matters directly without the blessings or the benefits of the foreign office. In a federal country like Canada this means that provincial ministries are engaged directly in what in the power model is considered to be the exclusive realm of the federal foreign office. It also means that corporations, voluntary associations such as churches and labour unions, and interest organizations, not only become involved in "relations" across national boundaries but become active participants in the political systems of other states through lobbying and public opinion consciousness-raising activities. Indeed, governments, both federal and provincial, may become involved as well, as demonstrated by the acid rain lobbying of Canadians in the United States. Finally, in the complex interdependence model the mainstay of the power model, military capability, is irrelevant. This, however, does not mean that military questions may not enter into a relationship of complex interdependence through the back door. "Military force could, for instance, be irrelevant to resolving disagreements in economic issues among members of an alliance, yet at the same time be very important for that alliance's political and military relations with a rival bloc."[1]

Although the difference between the ideal types of the power or sovereignty model and the complex interdependence model is clear, in the real world money enters the scene and confuses the picture. For, without money nothing can be done—either on the economic or on the high politics plane of relations. But the question is, how does money confuse the issue? Does money transform the complex interdependence model into the power model, or does it necessarily subordinate complex interdependence to power? The short answer to these questions is clearly "No". Nevertheless, those who do not bother going through the complex technical details of money sometimes misunderstand the role played by what are called "Top Currency States" and assume that enough money is always a substitute and/or a means for conducting power politics. Money does of course in certain cases lead to domination, but domination within the interdependence model framework and not in the power politics framework. Moreover, domination fluctuates in the interdependence framework, as demonstrated by the history of economic relations of such top currency states as the United States and Britain during the past half century. Susan Strange puts this condition, which she calls the "top currency syndrome", the cause of domination by top currency states, very clearly in a short paragraph:

The top currency state seems inclined to develop a strong political/economic ideology that asserts a) that [its] domestic and international interests are coincident if not identical, and b) that a prime aim of the state should be to persuade others that their national economic interests coincide with a maximum development and extension of the international economy. The top currency state characteristically does all it can to propagate this ideology and to use it to enlist the support of others for whatever measures of international cooperation and support it thinks are needed to protect, defend and stabilize the international economic system . . . the opinions of foreigners who put national economic interest before the general welfare are regarded as simply unregenerate and perverse. Indeed, a high moral tone quickly creeps in, and what I would describe as a top currency syndrome is distinguished by an obstinate and to others inevitably an objectional, tendency to self-righteousness.[2]

Clearly the clashes between the United States and Canada, the United States and Europe, and the United States and the Third World over money, capital flows, and other economic relations facilitated by money, which have often been regarded as reflections of a desire on the part of the United States to play power politics, may be better understood as expressions of the top currency syndrome operating within complex interdependence.

II. The International Monetary Regime

To demonstrate that the top currency syndrome is not to be analyzed within the power politics framework but within the complex interdependence model approach we must understand the technical operation of the international monetary system.

The basic link between the political and the economic systems in international economic relations as well as the links between the domestic and foreign components of economic policy are to be found in the operation of the balance of payments adjustments and the conduct of international monetary relations.[3] A country's balance of payments consists of the sum of all public and private transactions across the national boundary and includes such specific components as trade (exports and imports), services (shipping, insurance, financial transaction fees etc), capital flows (foreign investment in stocks, bonds and direct acquisition of firms) tourism, and government expenditures abroad (support of diplomatic representation, foreign aid and military expenditures abroad). The balance of payments is calculated by subtracting the monetary value of all outflows from all inflows in these components. Normally the States attempt to either keep a surplus of financial inflows over financial outflows or to maintain an equilibrium between them. Naturally, it is not possible for most countries to have either a consistent surplus every year or to maintain an equilibrium from year to year. However, in the medium to the long-term countries that have a policy of equilibrium balance the outflows and the inflows.

But there are countries that for a variety of reasons tend to run chronic imbalances and consequently find it necessary to find ways and means to adjust these financial flows to restore equilibrium. Those countries that tend to persistently run surpluses are under very little pressure to restore equilibrium for, after all, they are enjoying the enviable position of earning more than they spend abroad. In contrast, those countries which run negative balances of payments soon find themselves under tremendous pressure to apply policies to reduce the deficit and eventually return the balance of payment to an equilibrium position, for neither an individual nor a country can persistently live beyond its means.

Essentially, there are three main types of measures that can be taken to adjust the deficit payment position of a state—*internal adjustment* measures, *external adjustment* measures, and measures to *increase liquidity*. While the measures themselves are technical-economic, the considerations leading to their application and their implementation usually have a significant political impact at home and abroad. In fact, a combination of financial policies by a number of important countries led to the Great Depression and created the conditions which led to the establishment of the post-war trading system and the Bretton Woods monetary regime, which in turn not only profoundly affected the political makeup of the post-war world but created it. And, as implied above in Susan Strange's quotation, much of the turmoil of the past decade is due to the political impact of the application of various techniques of adjustment by both middle states and top currency states.

II.1 Internal Adjustment Measures

The objective of these is to decrease purchases abroad by reducing public and private domestic and foreign expenditures. Specific measures that may be used are often described as deflationary policies, the objective of which is to reduce the disposable income available to individuals, business firms and government offices for purchases both domestically and abroad. Hence, interest rates and/or taxes are raised to reduce the level of spending by both business and private individuals, and government expenditures are reduced by cutting government programmes both at home and abroad. The result of deflationary policies should be an improvement in the balance of payments as financial flows abroad are reduced as a result of less money available for imports, foreign investment, travel, foreign aid, and military and diplomatic activities abroad.

II.2 External Adjustment Measures

The objective of these measures is to restore balance of payments equilibrium to a country with payments deficits by directly altering the conditions (terms of exchange) under which foreign economic transactions are carried out. Some specific measures that may be applied are new or increased tariffs and/or quotas, with the objective of reducing and/or limiting imports; tax incentives are often extended to domestic businesses with the objective of encouraging exports; foreign exchange and other controls may be applied to reduce the flow of investment funds abroad, firms with foreign subsidiaries are sometimes encouraged to increase the rate of profit flows from abroad. However, the most general and blanket external adjustment measure, used with increasing frequency during the 1970s since the destruction of the Bretton Woods regime is the *devaluation of currencies* by countries relative to foreign currencies. The effect of a devaluation is felt across the national economy as the acquisition of foreign goods, services and capital become more expensive and conversely foreigners are encouraged to purchase goods, services and capital in the devaluing country because all of these became cheaper to them. The overall impact of external adjustment measures is to reduce financial outflows and to increase inflows to reduce, and even eliminate, the balance of payments deficit.

II.3 Measures to Increase Liquidity

The concept of liquidity may be defined most clearly, although crudely, as the value of the financial reserves held by a country and/or the international system which can easily be converted into a currency or currencies. Such reserves exist in the form of gold holdings and holdings of foreign exchange from past balance of payment surpluses held by individual countries. Lately a special kind of substitute for gold, the SDR or Special Drawing Rights, has been added to the international system and may be held as an easily convertible (liquid) reserve asset. Clearly, states which have sufficient liquid assets can easily cover their balance of payments deficit without resort to harsh internal or external adjustment measures. However, almost no state is in a position to meet chronic deficits for any length of time by continuing to draw on its reserves. Hence, states in deficit positions for any length of time require additional liquidity. Liquidity can be increased by borrowing from abroad, either from other State's governments, from a variety of interstate or more correctly intergovernmental banks, or from international commercial banks. Such borrowings, however, depends on the credit-worthiness of the State and its government in the eyes of the major lending institutions and lending governments. Clearly again, no State can hope to maintain credit-worthiness if it is in chronic need of borrowing to increase its liquidity to cover its balance of payment deficit. According to any and all theories of accounting practice, to all theories of money, and to supply and demand economic theories, liquidity can play only a limited and short-run role in financing balance of payments deficits. Hence, persistent deficits in balance of payments can only be handled by means of internal and external measures, usually in some combination.

II.4 Economic and Political Impact of Measures

The relative economic and political impacts of internal and external measures are consider-able. The internal deflationary measures all create economic squeezes which drive firms out of business and increase unemployment. Reducing government programmes requires the political decision of determining which policy goals to sacrifice. Often the choice is among different welfare policies, education policies defence policies, and foreign aid policies. Clearly, although technically reducing a deficit and restoring equilibrium to balance of pay-ments is an economic problem, the choice of means as well as the determination of whom the specific measures will affect is a political one. But it must also be noted that although internal measures of adjustment fall most heavily on the electorate, business and govern-ments of the adjusting State, in case of major States such measures have important conse-quences abroad as well. Deflationary policies applied by such States as the United States and Germany, for example, will lead to economic downturns in Canada, Western Europe and the world at large because of the importance of the United States as a market for Cana-dian goods, Germany as a market for West European goods and the United States as the premier market in world trade. In contrast to internal measures, external adjustment mea-sures victimize foreigners primarily—citizens and workers, businesses and governments abroad rather than those of the country employing external adjustment measures. Unfortu-nately the applying State does not escape the economic (and even the political impact) since nearly all of these measures, but in particular devaluation, will lead to increased domestic inflation and inefficient internal production of goods at the expense of "world class" manufacturing (and even services) both at home and internationally. Moreover, all external adjustment mechanisms distort the international economic system and cause vary-ing degrees of retaliation, which leads to even greater distortion. Nevertheless, because politically the external measures are often easier to apply than internal ones—particularly by democratic governments which are held responsible for their economic well-being by their electorates—internal measures tend to be applied either sparingly or only after the external ones have not worked. The result, fortunately, is the protectionist tendency of the past decade which has led to severe international political conflicts and a reduction in the level of welfare across the world. Similarly, because the world was awash with excess liquidity as a result of the tremendous inflation unleashed by the war in Vietnam, which pumped American dollars into the international market at unconscionable rate, and OPEC's success in jacking the oil price from less than US $3 a barrel in 1972 to US $28 in 1978, countries (including governments and business organizations) found it easy to finance deficits through increasing liquidity by means of public and private borrowing abroad.

III. The Triangle of Conflict

To the dispassionate observer, even after only a cursory overview, it is clear that the three sets of measures—internal, external and liquidity—are not competitive but must be applied judiciously in combination for maximum positive economic and political effect. However, history shows that each has its ideological exponents. Richard N. Cooper has devised a tri-angle that illustrates the relative positions of the three sets of ideologies and the actions advocated by them in relation to the three types of adjustment measures open to them. As he puts it, most analysts and decision-makers want States to "avoid extreme forms of each of the three categories of action."[4] But analysts and politicians, even under the most propitious of circumstances, differ as to which side of the triangle they prefer. And the past decade has demonstrated that politicians and even analysts sometimes (and some consistently) pursue one or other extreme of the points of the triangle.

Nevertheless, whatever the actual policies pursued by different actors, the triangle demonstrates that central bankers, commercial bankers, and finance ministers typically insist upon the need for,

discipline and rely upon [a judicious mixture of] external and internal adjustment measures to eliminate the root causes of a State's payments deficits. They desire to see states located away from the liberal liquidity position in the triangle . . . [5]

In contrast, free traders (also known as classical liberal economists and proponents of the laissez faire theory of economic change) are opposed to any external measures since they do not wish to interrupt the free exchange of goods, services and capital across State boundaries; hence, they prefer a judicious fixture of internal measures and liquidity to restore balance of payments deficits. The third side of the triangle is occupied by radicals (including nationalists, and all those who believe that States have the right to pursue particular inward looking national goals autonomously, such as the satisfaction of internal social needs, full employment and equitability of welfare; hence, they shy away from application of rigorous internal measures and tend to employ various mixtures of external measures and increased liquidity to meet balance of payments deficits.

In addition to the above ideological positions, decision-makers (both public and private) in States on the opposite sides of the balance of payments equilibrium tend towards diametrically opposed measures for balancing payments; hence, States with persistent payments surpluses tend to universalize their particular position and argue that States with deficits should apply internal measures exclusively and, decision-makers in States with chronic payment deficits tend to argue that they should be given access to increased liquidity and that external measures should be used to force States with payments surpluses to share the burden of equalizing the deficit States' balances of payments.

The Cooper diagram is doubly useful in that it also permits us to position States in various parts of the triangle depending on their particular balance of payments conditions, size of reserves, and political-economic ideology. Similarly, non-governmental actors, such as banks and transnational corporations can be placed in the diagram, with the result that one can get a very good overview of not only the relative positions of different actors in the international economic system but also of conflicts, likely conflicts and possible outcomes of these. As a brief example one need but mention the supply side theories of the Reagan White House, the persistent emphasis on internal measures by all the governors of the Bank of Canada, emphasis on protectionism by nationalists and trade unionists nearly everywhere, the demand for increased world liquidity by chronic deficit States and corporations everywhere, and the demand for free trade and removal of all tariffs, quotas and non-tariff barriers by transnational corporations.

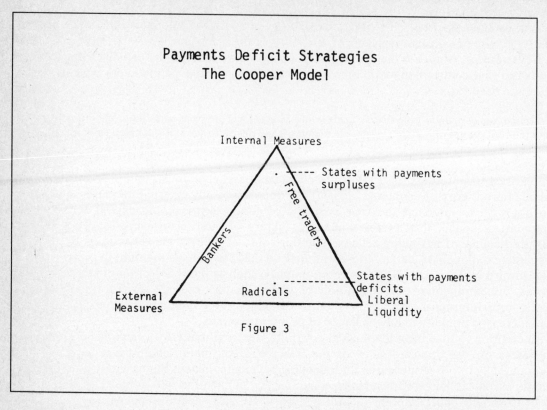

Payments Deficit Strategies
The Cooper Model

Figure 3

IV. International Monetary Regimes: From Bretton Woods to Conflict of Syndromes

Clearly, an international system composed of actors pulling in different directions depending on their ideological and balance of payments conditions, becomes one of erratic conflict and cooperation without some generally agreed rules regulating behaviour. Accordingly, as a result of the decade of increasing chaos initiated by the failure of the Kredit-Anstalt of Vienna in 1931—which according to some analysts was one of the main indirect causes of the Second World War—the victorious powers initiated discussions among themselves during the closing stages of the war to establish a monetary and a trading regime for the post-war world. The Bretton Woods discussions of 1944 led to the establishment of the International Monetary Fund. The Fund was to be the guardian of the British and American interpretation of the modern laissez-faire international economic order (all American administrations from FDR's onwards first have been free traders) in which rules would encourage and guarantee free flow of capital. This, in turn, would encourage and maintain the free flow of international trade. The Bretton Woods international monetary regime consisted of two sets of institutions, both operated by the IMF. The first, which lasted in various forms until it was destroyed in the aftermath of the Nixon shock of 14 August 1972, consisted of a set of three fixed rules; an agreement by all state members to adhere to fixed exchange rates fluctuating within a very narrow band of parity (at first 1% and later as much as 2 1/2%) with approval to be granted by all members for any revaluations or devaluations outside the narrow float band. All currencies were to be freely convertible without any restrictions whatever, and all members were to pursue the precepts of free trade. The second "institution" of the Bretton Woods system was a central bank credit function operated by the International Monetary Fund. The IMF provided loans to its members to assist them in short-term balance of payments deficit adjustments. The objective was, and is, to increase international liquidity temporarily to prevent States from having to disrupt internal social and economic policies or raise barriers to international trade and possibly create retaliatory spirals of action which would lead to a downturn of international economic exchanges. In other words, the IMF, through the first set of rules prevented easy and autonomous resort to devaluation and through the second provided an alternative to applying either excessive internal or external measures of adjustment while limiting the tendency of any State to become dependent on ever-increasing liquidity.

The objective of the IMF was to act as a moderating influence of the total community upon each member and to assist members in temporary difficulties to overcome them with help from a collective pool of funds. Unfortunately, the original collective action approach of the system broke down after only two years because of the destruction brought by the Second World War in Europe, which led to enormous demands for reconstruction capital requiring enormous amounts of deficit capital borrowing. Luckily the United States, with the strongest economy in the world, was able to step into the breach and as a result of having turned its back on the "Fortress America" insularity of the 1930s felt ideologically obligated to help the reconstruction of Europe and Japan by applying two measures, one inconsistent with the concepts of the Bretton Woods regime, but the other fully consistent. First, the United States opened its borders wide to trade goods from Europe and Japan, and second it poured large amounts of capital, economic aid and military assistance and personnel maintenance funds abroad to both Japan and Europe, with the result that the United States ran a chronic balance of payments deficit. But as a result of this the United States encouraged a free trade-oriented international system, while the IMF was able to act as the formal moderator and maintained a collective approach to adjustments. Unfortunately, the result of this American largesse was the development of an excessive American top currency syndrome:

The universal utility of the top international currency is a medium which change gives the top currency nation the unique privilege of enjoying international support, or at least tolerance, for running persistent balance of payments deficit without having to adopt significant adjustment measures to restore a payment equilibrium. Deficits for the top currency state pump money into the international economy that can be used by other countries for international transactions. Thus the top currency nation can enhance its economic-political-military posture abroad at levels of expenditures that exceed its international earnings for years on end—no other nation in the international system can behave in such a fashion. Charles de Gaulle pointed to this fact with frustration as America's "exorbitant privilege".[6]

As the 1960s wore on the American dollar became grossly overvalued and no longer as important in maintaining the support base for the Bretton Woods regime since other currencies, particularly the German and the Japanese, had reached at least secondary status as top currencies as a result of the miracles of economic reconstruction that took place in their economies. Unfortunately, the United States, as a result of its top currency syndrome, was simply unable to make the internal political adjustment to devalue its currency. In addition, the Vietnam war pumped additional excesses of American dollars into the international system and out of the direct control of the United States, with the result that American dollars in the Eurocurrency market—not in control of either the American or any other government—increased from US $2.8 billion in 1964 to 284 billion in 1974 and 818 billion in 1979. Thus, by 1972 there was an enormous excess of liquidity in the international system not under the control of any government or the IMF. Moreover, a revolution had taken place beginning in the early 1960s in international banking practices, with the result that by the early 1970s commercial banks had set up enormous consortia[7] and were lending money—largely outside the control of the governments of the IMF States—to commercial firms across State boundaries and to governments of States, including Third World governments. Clearly the Bretton Woods regime, which depended on a collective acceptance of the rules by all member governments, was no longer in control of the international monetary system.

Three other developments destroyed the Bretton Woods regime utterly. The first was the run on the American dollar, fundamentally because it was overvalued and the United States government had consistently maintained a policy of free convertibility of dollars to gold. Since the United States did not have enough gold to purchase the dollars that many governments (especially the French) wanted to sell, President Nixon was forced to end gold convertibility and effectively devalue the dollar by 10%. Since this was a unilateral action in flagrant disregard of IMF rules and since the United States was the primary financial supporter of the IMF, at one stroke the first set of Bretton Woods rules were shown to be "inoperative". The result was that although serious attempts were made to reinstate the rules over the next three years the rules in fact had to be abandoned and the IMF has been searching for ways to reestablish the rules ever since. Unfortunately, the second and third developments during the 1970s prevented this and led to increased reliance on ideological and positional conflict and cooperation in international and financial transactions.

The second development was the tenfold increase in the price of oil between 1972 and 1978. This transferred enormous amounts of cash to a few thinly populated Arab countries which recycled these "petro dollars" mainly through commercial banks and thus added enormously to the excess liquidity in the Eurodollar market.

The third development in the 1970s which prevented a return to generally accepted rules and which continues today as the primary block to such agreement, was the rise of the Third World States to political consciousness as a result of their admission to the United Nations and the pursuit of economic opportunities in their economies by transnational corporations. The problem of the Third World, which continues to plague us today, was created in equal measure by politics and excess liquidity. While it is easy to understand the political demands of the Group of 77 for equitable treatment in the international financial and trading system dominated by no more than two dozen Western States, not many realize that the political demands made by the Third World are backed up by an economic dilemma created in no small measure by the Western World itself during the 1970s. It is the product of the excess liquidity in the hands of the commercial banks, particularly the Eurocurrency market not controlled by any government, that, in search of profits, abandoned its normal cautious banking practices and became excessively entrepreneurial in lending enormous sums of money to both governments and corporations (both local and transnational) in the Third World without assurance of adequate assets to back up the loans. The result is that in the current economic recession a large number of leading Third World countries' governments, and public and private enterprises, are over-exposed and need increased liquidity to meet their international obligations. Most internationally active commercial banks in the Western world are creditors of these Third World governments and enterprises. The result is that we have today a curious situation that might be labelled the Radical Liquidity syndrome, where Third World countries and Western banks are all clamouring for increased liquidity provisions by First World governments; the demand of the G77 to double the governmentally underwritten assets of the IMF is supported by the creditor banks of the West. Thus the currently ongoing battle of ideologies and balance of payments positions is distorted by the radical liquidity syndrome.

V. A Summing Up

One may conclude from this overview that no state that is at all involved in international trade, tourism and with international financial movements has much freedom to make decisions independently on the basis of sovereignty in financial matters. This includes the small and powerless states, the debtor states and the creditor states, and the large top currency states as well. Every state in the international economic system has been affected by the activities of the largest states and of the international commercial banks during the 1970s. At the beginning of 1987, 107 developing nations owed US $1010 billion to foreign creditors, and of these 8 Latin American countries owe nearly US $380 billion or about 38% of the total. Of the total over $500 billion is owed to commercial banks, including American banks. Although newly created liquidity by means of new commercial loans, large government aid packages and rescheduling some of the debt by the International Monetary Fund and other multilateral intergovernmental banks, has eased the current international debt crisis the problem is far from solved. "This is a situation requiring almost continuous nervous tension on the part of everyone involved . . . ."[8]

The problem referred to is that should one of the major debtors, such as Mexico, owing US $98 billion, or Brazil with US $108 billion, or Argentina with US $53 billion, default on its debt a number of large commercial banks would become insolvent which would lead to a domino effect exactly like that created by the collapse of the Kredit-Anstalt in 1931. The ensuing financial chaos would bring all financial and trade transactions to a virtual standstill and affect directly and severely all of the world's economies very quickly. The fact that the Reagan Administration, which has been arguing for very strong deflationary policies to be followed by all debtor countries, agreed to an increase of 60% of the IMFs assets to increase the liquidity available to Third World borrowers, shows how seriously the United States, still the premier top currency state, regards the impact of a possible default by Third World countries.

The second fact that the above overview forces us to consider is the curious situation in which the Third World debtor states are forcing the dominant states in the system of complex interdependence to not only pay attention to them but also to satisfy some of their demands. In fact, we might even characterize the Third Energy shock (the collapse of petroleum prices in 1981-82) and its aftermath as the era of the Radical Syndrome in international financial negotiations, where Third World states demand radical increases in liquidity and one-sided protectionism for their industries while demanding free access to First World markets. The argument for the latter is not a free trade argument but a preferential treatment argument—an international affirmative action—to right past wrongs and to give the Third World a greater role in international trade, as well as to assist in adjusting its balance of payments deficits.

Third, the radical syndrome demands have led to a reaction by the First World to increasingly protect its industries from competition not only from the Third World but from each other. In other words, there is a Protectionist Syndrome in the First World. It should, however, be noted that as in the past the American Administration does not support protectionism in any form. Indeed the Smoot-Hawley Tariff Act was passed in 1934 over the objection of the American Administration and the most serious post-war attack on free trade, the Burke-Hartke Bill, was fought to defeat by the Nixon and Ford Administrations. Nevertheless, the American Administration cannot win every battle against a Congress that is increasingly protectionist. Moreover, the publics in Japan, Europe and Canada have all fallen increasingly under the spell of the Protectionist Syndrome—all because of a recession initiated by a too rapid and uncontrolled expansion of international liquidity and the lending of funds without demand for adequate collateral reserves.

The fourth factor to be noted is that there is also a Deflationary Syndrome, initiated by the American and British Administrations, that was subsequently copied by every member of the OECD, and which is in direct conflict with both the Radical and Protectionist syndromes.

VI. The Prognosis

Thus, it is clear that we have a series of conflicts over money and other international economic exchanges which is affecting the wellbeing of all people within the world monetary economy (including the Second World). And, unless rules are reestablished for the monetary system the crisis will continue to fluctuate or even worsen. Perhaps it is not surprising that most Third World political decision-makers as well as economic experts whatever their ideological persuasion generally agree that the engine of growth theory is still valid. The blue ribbon Committee for Development Planning of the United Nations in its last report titled *World Economic Recovery—the priority of international monetary and financial cooperation*[9] makes it very clear that the world economy will only recover if the United States plus West Germany, and the European Community generally, and Japan put their houses in order and create conditions in which they will begin buying abroad again. At the same time they are also demanding judicious increases in government created liquidity for Third World governments. Although we have no quarrel with the engine of growth argument the demand for yet greater increases of government sponsored liquidity flies in the face of all supply and demand economic theory and will lead to yet another round of inflation-deflation and a continuing crisis.

There seem to be only two possible ways of dealing with the current crisis and establishing a foundation for a rational self-regulating system in the near future for the complex interdependent system of finance. It appears that the only rational interim solution is to create a Felix Rohatyn type of MAC (Municipal Assistance Corporation) which saved New York City from bankruptcy in the 1970s. Peter B. Kenen of Princeton argues that an International Debt Discount Corporation should be set up by governments of the First World states:

They would subscribe to the capital of the debt corporation but would not have to put up cash if the IDDC did its job properly. The corporation would issue long-term bonds to banks in exchange for the debts of developing countries . . . at a discount . . ., say ninety cents on the dollar [the IDDC] would reschedule the debts of developing countries on a one-time, long-term basis, using five cents of the ten cents extracted from banks for modest debt relief, charging lower interest rates for granting grace periods.

In other words, the short-term debt (the bulk of the US $720 billion) would be rolled over into long-term debt. For this to work, however, any new liquidity provided to the Third World must be strictly controlled. As Kenen puts it, "the IDDC must not be permitted to discount new debts acquired by the banks, and banks must be supervised more strictly than heretofore.[10]

For the international system to return to equilibrium a new national monetary regime has to be created with fixed exchange rates, a commitment to free trade and, as a departure from the Bretton Woods system and in recognition of the changed world of complex interdependence, mandatory participation by non-governmental institutions, such as the international commercial banks, in the International Monetary Funds' controlling organ. For, without representation it is not possible to demand acquiescence to the rules. And, whatever power theorists may argue the fact is that no government will ever be able to directly control the enormous and growing Eurocurrency market.

But what of sovereignty in this new international monetary regime? In practice it would not be relevant as States would be required to operate on rational grounds in mutual interests and keep away from the extremes of the triangle, but particularly the protectionist and excess liquidity corners.

Notes

[1] Robert O. Keohane and Joseph F. Nye, *Power and Interdependence*, Boston 1977, p. 25.

[2] "The Politics of International Currencies", *World Politics*, 23, No. 2 (January 1971), p. 229.

[3] See an excellent discussion of this in David H. Blake and Robert S. Walters, *The Politics of Global Economic Relations* (second edition), Prentice-Hall: Englewood Cliffs N.J., 1983, pp. 51-60. This section is based on pp. 51-4.

[4] Richard N. Cooper, *The Economics of Interdependence*, New York: 1968, p. 19.

[5] Blake and Walters, ibid., p. 54.

[6] Blake and Walters, Ibid., p. 59.

[7] Between 1964 and 1971 over 3/4 of all the largest commercial banks in the world established transnational banking syndicates.

[8] Robert V. Roosa, partner at Brown Brothers, Harriman and Company Investment Bankers, cited in Kenneth N. Gilpin "The Maze of Latin Americas Debt" *New York Times*, 13 March 1983.

[9] UN publication sales No. E82 II C3.

[10] Peter B. Kenen "A Bailout Plan for Banks", *New York Times*, 6 March 1983.

The Debt Crisis in the Fourth World: Implications for North-South Relations

Robert E. Wood & Max Mmuya

The debt crisis has been widely perceived in the West as basically the problem of a few, relatively wealthy countries. From the standpoint of a creditor, such an assessment is accurate. Of the 20 most heavily indebted less-developed countries (LDCs), owing over two-thirds of total LDC debt, only one (India) is currently classified by the World Bank as a "low-income country". Indeed, three countries alone—Mexico, Brazil and Argentina-account for almost one-half of the LDC debt to commercial banks, prompting some bankers to refer smugly to the debt crisis as their "MBA problem". It is probably true that only a default by these three countries, and perhaps by South Korea (the fourth largest debtor) as well, could seriously threaten the viability of the commercial banks and, by extension, the world economy. However, to consider the debt problematique in such a narrow fashion is not only morally and politically repugnant, but also very short-sighted because it obscures the existence of long-term processes of structural change that have direct implications for the rest of the world.

Our basic thesis in this article is that the debt crisis has penetrated deeply into the poorest countries of the Third World, collectively known as the "Fourth World". Indeed, the debt problems of the Mexicos and the Brazils are very likely more tractable than the debt crisis in Fourth World countries. That the West is so preoccupied with "MBA debt" reflects a very short-sighted and callous perspective of the debt problem which explicitly values profits over human lives. As South magazine put it in mid-1984, "The world is so concerned with Brazil and Mexico that Tanzania could disappear without anybody noticing it."[1] Yet, with nearly half of the world's population living in the Fourth World, the long-term effects and human dimensions of the debt crisis cannot and should not be ignored.

In this article, we first document the existence of a debt crisis in the Fourth World. We show that Fourth World debt has increased rapidly in size and worsened in structure, so that debt service on past "aid" has increasingly offset new aid, accounted for a substantial proportion of current account deficits, and resulted in a spate of both renegotiations and emergency, high-conditionality drawings from the International Monetary Fund (IMF). Secondly, we describe how the responses to the debt crisis, which have been largely orchestrated by the creditor countries and banks, have produced an altered international environment which reflects and compounds the South's weakened position in the world economy. Finally, in briefly examining the consequences of these changes for South-South relations, we argue that although their immediate impact weakened the solidarity and bargaining position of the South, the long-term effects of the debt crisis remain uncertain, because of potential contradictions in the North's strategy.

Originally published in *Alternatives*, vol. XI, no. 3, 1986. Reprinted with permission.

At the outset, we want to emphasize that our use of the term "Fourth World" is in no way intended to deny what Irving Louis Horowitz has called the "essential integrity and autonomy of the Third World".[2] Indeed, our focusing on the Fourth World is intended to demonstrate the universality of the debt crisis across the Third World. While the poorest countries face special problems, the most basic sources of the debt crisis are rooted in the structure of the world economy, and apply to all Third World countries.

Given this underlying unity, it is not surprising that there is no agreement in the literature on the definition of "Fourth World". The term has been applied alternatively to countries designated as "least developed" (LLDCs) by the United Nations; to a broader set of "low-income countries" (LICs) variously defined; and more generally to all of the Third World save a politically-defined sub-set of "sub-imperialist" countries.[3] The problem with the LLDC category is that it excludes countries such as India and Pakistan, thereby distorting the extent of the "absolute poor" as defined by the World Bank. Hence, it seems more appropriate to use the broader LIC category. But how much broader? The World Bank's *World Development Report 1984* defined $410 per capita income as the cut-off point, while the Organization for Economic Co-operation and Development (OECD) sets the cut-off at $600, resulting in a considerably expanded list.[4] For the sake of convenience, we have adopted the World Bank list of 34 LICs, excluding however, the state socialist countries and two others for which few data are available.[5] The 27 remaining countries constitute, therefore, our population of the Fourth World, or low-income countries. When our data are based on the OECD's broader classification, we shall take note of it. The most significant additions on the larger OECD list, from the point of view of debt, are Bolivia, Egypt, Indonesia, Sudan and Zambia.

Changing structure of Fourth World debt

Table 1 provides data on the growth of debt and debt service in the 27 low-income, or Fourth World, countries. Total debt in 1982 was about $57.1 billion, four times what it had been in 1970. Aggregated together, the debt of the Fourth World is surpassed in the Third World only by Mexico and Brazil, although it accounts for only a little more than 10 per cent of total LDC debt. Fourth World debt has grown somewhat faster than that of the major borrowers, but the extraordinary individual increases—e.g., the 99-fold increase in Nepal's debt between 1970 and 1982—are actually statistical artifacts attributable to low starting points. Debt service has increased more slowly than disbursed debt, reflecting its concessional terms. But Fourth World debt service still came to over $3.3 billion in 1982, a figure exceeding World Bank disbursements to all low-income countries in that year. It would have been substantially more except for extensive debt reschedulings in 1979-82, to be discussed below.

Table 2 allows us to examine the changing structure of both Fourth World debt and debt service. Between 1973 and 1982, the average proportion of debt owed to bilateral creditors declined from 55.6 per cent to 41.7 per cent. Debt service to bilateral creditors amounted to less than half of total debt service in all but seven countries in 1982. In contrast, for all countries except one, debt to multilateral institutions increased substantially, from an average of 23.5 per cent of total debt in 1973 to 41.3 per cent in 1982. While the average proportion of total debt service going to bilateral creditors declined from 49.6 per cent to 33.8 per cent, the average proportion going to multilateral creditors rose from 13.7 per cent to 29.8 per cent.

Table 1. Disbursed debt and debt service of Fourth World countries, 1970 and 1982 ($ millions)

Country	1970 debt	1970 amortization	1970 interest	1982 debt	1982 amortization	1982 interest	Ratio: 1982/ 1970 debt	Ratio: 1982/1970 debt service
Bangladesh	na	na	na	4353	63	48	na	na
Benin	41	1	—	556	19	28	13.6	47.0
Burma	101	18	3	1960	68	52	19.4	10.9
Burundi	7	—	—	201	3	2	28.7	—
Central African Rep.	24	2	1	222	2	2	9.3	1.3
Chad	32	2	—	189	—	—	5.9	—
Ethiopia	169	15	6	875	33	22	5.2	2.6
Ghana	489	12	12	1116	38	27	2.3	2.7
Guinea	314	10	4	1230	55	24	3.9	5.6
Haiti	40	4	—	405	11	8	10.1	4.8
India	7940	307	189	19487	675	476	2.5	2.3
Kenya	316	16	12	2359	178	147	7.5	11.6
Madagascar	93	5	2	1565	70	42	16.8	16.0
Malawi	122	3	3	692	33	32	5.7	9.2
Mali	238	—	—	822	3	5	3.5	—
Nepal	3	2	—	297	3	3	99.0	3.0
Niger	32	1	1	603	66	44	18.8	55.0
Pakistan	3059	114	76	9178	326	213	3.0	2.8
Rwanda	2	—	—	189	3	2	94.5	—
Sierra Leone	59	10	2	370	8	2	6.3	0.8
Somalia	77	—	—	944	9	10	12.3	—
Sri Lanka	317	27	12	1969	68	68	6.2	3.5
Tanzania	248	10	6	1659	20	33	6.7	3.3
Togo	40	2	1	819	11	22	20.5	11.0
Uganda	138	4	4	587	57	10	4.3	8.4
Upper Volta	21	2	—	335	13	7	16.0	10.0
Zaire	311	28	9	4087	65	72	13.1	3.7
Total	14233	595	343	57069	1900	1401	4.0	3.5

Source: *World Development Report*, pp. 246-249.

The fact that an increasing proportion of Fourth World debt is owed to multilateral creditors has a special significance. Multilateral institutions claim a "preferred creditor status" and uniformly refuse to reschedule debt service on their loans. And given the ability of these institutions to determine the availability of other sources of financing as well, no country has ever dared to default. By 1982, over one-third of aggregate Fourth World debt has been "locked in" with this method, removed from even the possibility of renegotiation in times of difficulty. The phenomenon has proved to be a severe constraint for several Fourth World countries. Almost three-fifths of Tanzania's current debt service, for example, goes to multilateral institutions. The leeway for renegotiations is therefore very small, and the very limited relief available from the rescheduling of debt to bilateral creditors would hardly compensate for the political costs of such an agreement.

The data in Table 2 suggest that Fourth World debt to private creditors has greater significance than is commonly recognized. While commercial bank claims on low-income countries constituted only 1 per cent of their total net claims in 1982,[6] a significant proportion of Fourth World debt has been owed to private creditors for some time. Even in 1973, before the OPEC-induced expansion of Euromarket lending to the Third World, the 27 Fourth World countries owed on average 20.7 per cent of their debt to private creditors and paid to them on average 37.8 per cent of their debt service. These figures had actually declined slightly by 1982, to 17.0 per cent and 36.4 per cent respectively, but debt service to private creditors was still the largest category of debt service for almost half of all Fourth World countries in that year.

Table 2. Components of disbursed debt and debt service of Fourth World countries, 1973 and 1982 (per cent)

| Country | Percent of total debt | | | | | | Percent of debt service | | | | | |
| | 1973 | | | 1982 | | | 1973 | | | 1982 | | |
	bilat.	multi.	priv.	bilat.	multi.	priv.	bilat.	multi.	priv.	bilat.	multi.	priv.
Bangladesh	47.7	26.2	26.1	53.5	43.1	3.4	51.0	3.9	45.1	55.5	25.0	19.5
Benin	51.1	22.4	26.5	18.2	27.3	54.5	4.3	47.8	47.9	9.7	8.8	81.5
Burma	76.8	3.0	20.7	55.3	25.4	19.3	25.6	9.5	64.9	33.3	4.2	62.5
Burundi	30.8	55.1	14.1	36.9	60.8	2.3	0.0	55.6	44.4	32.0	24.5	43.5
Central African Rep.	36.8	14.7	48.5	40.1	32.2	27.7	52.2	0.0	47.8	60.9	19.6	19.5
Chad	43.0	26.7	30.3	36.0	50.9	13.1	87.9	0.0	12.1	0.0	100.0	0.0
Ethiopia	49.3	44.0	6.7	40.2	50.4	9.4	38.9	36.2	24.9	39.5	23.8	36.7
Ghana	55.1	9.9	35.0	49.5	36.4	15.1	71.1	21.1	7.8	57.0	34.4	8.6
Guinea	74.0	12.0	14.0	69.2	15.8	15.0	41.5	26.8	31.7	66.8	14.9	18.3
Haiti	73.2	1.0	25.8	28.9	50.1	21.0	56.9	0.0	43.1	26.2	11.2	62.6
India	74.4	23.0	2.6	47.1	46.5	6.4	70.8	15.4	13.8	62.3	21.8	15.9
Kenya	50.8	25.8	23.4	27.4	39.8	32.8	53.7	12.3	34.0	11.4	18.4	70.2
Madagascar	55.4	33.3	11.3	44.3	19.8	35.9	82.5	6.7	10.8	18.6	4.6	76.8
Malawi	58.7	23.0	18.3	22.3	49.1	28.6	51.8	4.5	43.7	12.8	15.6	71.6
Mali	89.8	7.9	2.3	63.2	35.1	1.7	94.1	5.9	0.0	45.7	46.9	7.4
Nepal	28.4	70.6	1.0	11.0	88.6	0.4	80.0	20.0	0.0	28.3	71.7	0.0
Niger	70.2	24.3	0.5	32.1	32.6	35.3	88.5	3.8	7.7	12.7	26.8	60.5
Pakistan	76.4	17.6	6.0	63.8	31.8	4.4	36.8	32.6	30.6	52.6	20.0	27.4
Rwanda	18.7	46.3	35.0	29.1	70.9	0.0	0.0	0.0	100.0	28.3	71.7	0.0
Sierra Leone	37.0	23.2	39.8	31.9	47.7	20.4	24.8	7.8	67.4	22.9	7.4	69.7
Somalia	83.4	13.7	2.9	60.8	32.9	6.3	83.3	4.2	12.5	17.2	73.7	9.1
Sri Lanka	69.2	17.7	13.1	49.0	32.9	18.1	52.8	8.8	38.4	34.1	9.0	56.9
Tanzania	64.5	20.3	15.3	44.4	47.8	7.8	23.5	8.5	68.0	26.0	58.1	15.9
Togo	43.3	12.7	44.0	44.1	26.5	29.4	45.5	0.0	54.5	46.6	10.1	43.3
Uganda	65.6	23.9	10.5	42.1	45.4	12.5	24.3	4.4	71.3	51.7	29.2	19.1
Upper Volta	65.0	31.0	4.0	29.5	62.5	8.0	87.1	32.3	9.6	30.0	36.5	33.5
Zaire	13.7	5.4	80.9	56.7	12.9	30.4	9.4	1.2	89.4	31.8	15.3	52.9
Average	55.6	23.5	20.7	41.7	41.3	17.0	49.6	13.7	37.8	33.8	29.8	36.4

Source: World Bank, *World Debt Tables* 1983-1984 edition.

More than with bilateral debt, there is an enormous range in the importance of debt to private creditors, with no obvious relationship to standard market measures of creditworthiness. Certainly much of the money borrowed was wasted by some of the big debtors, such as Zaire. It is nonetheless instructive to speculate on why such a large number of Fourth World countries have engaged in this kind of costly borrowing—labeled "excessive" by the OECD[7]—when access to concessional aid financing has been relatively unproblematic. The reason, we suspect, lies in the norms of aid allocation: specifically, the near-universal practice of withholding aid for projects deemed appropriate for foreign private investment, a practice which has resulted in a very small proportion of aid allocated for direct industrial projects (about 5 per cent in 1980).[8] For governments wishing to establish state industrial enterprises, relatively unconditional (in terms of end use and ownership) commercial bank financing and suppliers' credit have constituted the only major external financing available and a portion of Fourth World debt to private creditors undoubtedly reflects these priorities and constraints.

Debt and resource transfers

The burden of debt is generally measured by the debt service ratio: the proportion of export earnings offset by debt service. To some degree, use of this particular measure reflects the creditors' preoccupation with the question of whether debts will be repaid—which is clearly a different issue from the impact of debt on debtor nations. For low-income countries, the threshold at which debt service begins to cut into basic development expenditures and levels of popular consumption is considerably lower than in better-off LDCs. Indeed, amounts of debt which would attract little attention elsewhere may be sufficient to force Fourth World debtors into debt renegotiations and/or high conditionality borrowing from the IMF, with the attendant consequences.

Data on debt service ratios are available for only 19 LICs in 1982. Five had debt service ratios under 5 per cent, nine between 5 per cent and 10 per cent, and five over 20 per cent, the last figure being the usual upper limit of acceptable debt servicing for years. Weighted by population, the average ratio for LICs other than India is reported by the World Bank to have been 9.9 per cent in 1982, slightly less if India is included. It should be noted that the average increases substantially if a wider definition of low-income countries is used. The OECD, using the higher income cut-off discussed earlier, reports that between 1970 and 1982, the debt service ratio of LICs almost doubled, to 23 per cent.[9]

In addition, debt service ratios would have been much higher if not for the widespread rescheduling of debt between 1979 and 1983. When this debt and IMF loans taken out in the early 1980s become payable, Fourth World debt service ratios in the next several years will drastically increase, particularly in low-income Africa. Between 1970 and 1980, low-income African countries paid an average of $1.2 billion annually in external debt service. This increased to $1.5 billion in 1981 and $1.7 billion in 1982. Between 1985 and 1987, however, these African countries will be expected to pay $9.5 billion in debt service on past loans alone, almost $3.2 billion a year.[10] With their debt service ratio already at 16 per cent in 1982, this increase could double it. Furthermore, debt service ratios have been kept down partly by non-payment of debt. This accumulation of arrears is extensive—as many as 40 LICs were in arrears in 1982.[11] The World Bank recently warned:

When Africa's arrears are taken into account, its debt service outlook is even more dismal. Servicing obligations in 1984 would jump about 30% if all arrears were paid in that year. Unless corrective measures are taken, the external resource position of sub-Saharan Africa is likely to become disastrous in the next few years.[12]

The World Bank refrained from adding that future financing will be affected if arrears continue to accumulate. Thus, a strict application of this policy had led the Bank to cut off all further funding on 43 projects when Tanzania fell into arrears in 1982. The country had to come up with $15 million to receive new aid.[13] Other organizations have been equally inflexible: USAID is phasing out its aid program in Tanzania because of arrears; and failure to reduce arrears was an important reason why the one agreement Tanzania was able to reach with the IMF in recent years was cancelled. Tanzanian arrears amounted to over $300 million in 1983, about two-thirds of a year's export earnings.[14]

Compounding this bleak scenario is the current trend of declining net resource transfers to the Fourth World. Between 1980 and 1982, the proportion of new loan disbursements offset by debt service increased sharply. In terms of aggregate Fourth World debt, debt service as a proportion of new loan disbursements increased from 36.4 per cent in 1980 to 45.7 per cent in 1982; or, put differently, during this period the ratio of debt service to new disbursements increased for 23 of the 27 Fourth World countries. Since the aggregate figures are strongly affected by changes in the situation of the largest debtors, it is useful also to consider the average proportion for the 27 countries, which rose from 29.5 per cent in 1980 to 52.6 per cent in 1982. In other words, the average Fourth World country paid out over half of its new loan disbursements as debt service on past loans in 1982.[15]

The increase in the proportion of debt service from new loan disbursements between 1980 and 1982 resulted primarily from a decline in disbursements, rather than from the relatively modest increase in debt service costs in these two years. New loan disbursements for the Fourth World declined by over $1.4 billion between 1980 and 1982. This contrasts sharply with the situation of the major "middle-income" borrowers, whose debt service costs skyrocketed in response to increases in the variable interest rates on their loans.

Even so, the twin problems of rising debt service and declining disbursements affected the low-income African countries particularly hard. In 1978, their net transfer on loan disbursements came to $1.8 billion, with debt service accounting for 38 per cent of new disbursements. By 1982, net transfers had declined to $1.3 billion, and debt service took up to 48 per cent of new disbursements. Estimates for 1983 indicate a decline to $1.1 billion in net transfers and an increase of debt service's share of new disbursements to 66 per cent. Indeed, low-income African countries had negative net transfers in 1982 with the IBRD (the hard loan window of the World Bank), private suppliers, and commercial banks amounting all in all to $167 million.[16] Low-income Asian countries fared somewhat better, maintaining positive levels of net transfers with all categories of creditors in 1982, although the proportion of new loan disbursements offset by debt service increased to 42.7 per cent in 1982.[17]

* * *

South-South relations

In the context of the international political economy, "adjustment" is largely a response of the weak. To be sure, IMF and World Bank officials often make pious pronouncements about the need for all countries, including the advanced capitalist ones, to adjust. The Managing Director of the IMF, Jacques Larosiere, has even gone so far as to call on the industrialized countries to "face up to the formidable structural problems they themselves are confronting".[18] But the reality is that the IMF and the World Bank have virtually no leverage against them. Surplus countries are under no compulsion to adjust and, in any event, industrial countries with deficits can always locate other sources of financing if necessary. Behind the technocratic language of "distortions" and "inefficiencies" and homilies about "living beyond one's means" are the realities of international power, which make "adjustment" primarily a matter of the weak adapting to a situation created by the strong.

This fact both defines the fundamental structural unity of the South and makes the realization of political unity difficult. Structural adjustment necessarily pits Third World countries against each other and, since they are in the weakest bargaining position, threatens Fourth World countries most seriously. As Gamani Corea, who was unceremoniously dumped from his post as Secretary General of UNCTAD in December 1984 after the Group of 77 was unable to agree on a successor and the United States refused to allow his term to be extended, observed: "In the present crisis—debt burden, contraction of resources, and slow or failing growth—these [Group of 77] countries have become vulnerable, and forced to look for bilateral solutions. This has not increased the group's negotiating power or even the will to negotiate, or its unity."[19]

Whether stronger Group of 77 unity in the past would have elicited serious concessions from the North remains moot. But it is one of the ironies of the situation that some of the strategies pursued in the past by these countries to reduce their dependence on the North actually exacerbated the problem. We have seen how one motive behind the accumulation of debt to commercial banks was to avoid the conditionality of the official institutions. And for the Fourth World countries, where this was a limited option at best, even a program of self-reliance could result in its opposite.

Tanzania's proclaimed strategy of self-reliance, dating to the Arusha Declaration of 1967, had made it a particularly attractive country for aid agencies to lend money to. Some were attracted by the possibilities of new forms of social experimentation, others by the useful moral cover provided for the less savory uses of aid elsewhere.[20] In any event, the result was massively-increased debt: $2.5 billion (disbursed and undisbursed) in 1982.[21] Yet even if aid projects, often conceived by the aid agencies themselves, were complete failures, Tanzania was expected to pay for them, or alternatively to face the consequences.

Implicit in the common assertion that debtor countries have no choice but to adjust is the political demand that the claims of external creditors take precedence over domestic needs. Since these claims, ultimately, can be serviced only by radically expanded trade surpluses, the domestic impact is usually some combination of reduced social spending (whether through cutbacks on programs or the imposition of user fees) and the reallocation of resources to the export sector. And because the exports of Fourth World countries are overwhelmingly agricultural, such measures entail shifting resources out of domestic food production, thence increasing significantly the likelihood of malnutrition and hunger. Domestic deflation has to be particularly severe for a trade surplus to be created, in any case, since the IMF and the World Bank are ideologically opposed to import controls.

At the international level, such a strategy pits Third World countries increasingly against each other, as they compete for scarce markets. In its recent report on Africa, the World Bank called on sub-Saharan African countries to endeavor to "increase their share" of the world market for export crops,[22] but it neglects to mention that another part of the (also indebted) Third World would have to decrease its share, or to specify which part that would be. One area in which this increased competition has taken its toll is the various commodity agreements negotiated in recent years. The desperation induced by the debt crisis has led to increased cheating by producer countries. According to one account of the International Coffee Organization, which includes several Fourth World countries:

Over the last year, crushing foreign debt obligations and shortages of hard currency have led some coffee producers to sell portions of their surplus coffee at discount rates in violation of the agreements. . . To date, the International Coffee Organization has been unable to come up with an effective method of tightening control over illicit coffee shipments. Analysts believe the problem is increasing, and note that the amount of coffee exported to countries outside the agreement is running 24 per cent higher than last year. . .[23]

The disarray in the ranks might be even more severe. On the few occasions where the debt crisis and adjustment strategies have produced Southern cooperation, it has been more to maintain the system than to challenge it. A case in point is the extraordinary spectacle of Mexico, Brazil, Colombia and Venezuela—all deeply indebted themselves—coming up with a $300 million loan in March 1984 (supplemented with another $100 million from US commercial banks) to help Argentina keep up its interest payments rather than take the risk that a technical default by Argentina would worsen their own position in international financial markets. While the loan may have enabled Argentina to stretch out its negotiations with the IMF, that the other major debtors were not interested in rocking the boat was definitely not lost on Argentina: it came to terms with the IMF six months later.

A similar scenario was played out on a larger scale with the Cartagena conference of eleven Latin American debtors in June 1984. The Western media had been full of ruminations on the likelihood of a debtors' cartel, and the preparations for the conference were greeted with feverish maneuvering by the major creditor countries and institutions. Within debtor countries, a wide range of proposals circulated, including the idea of a debtors' commission which would renegotiate debt collectively, and placing ceilings on the proportion of export earnings which would be allowed for debt service.[24] A wide range of proposals also circulated within the creditor countries, albeit of a much more limited nature. The two main plans involved the assumption of debts at a discounted rate by a multilateral institution and the capitalization of interest above a certain level. At the last minute, however, the economic summit meeting in London of leaders from the major advanced capitalist countries endorsed the *only* reform which was actually implemented: multi-year rescheduling for a few particularly cooperative major borrowers (first Mexico and Brazil, then Venezuela and the previously recalcitrant Argentina). As with the institution of two-tiered IMF access, this measure was very successful in dividing debtor countries, not only along the axis of resistance versus compliance but also along an axis of unequal power of debt. And as before, fourth world countries simply could not win: no matter how compliant, they are unlikely to receive the relatively privileged treatment afforded the really big debtors; and no matter how intransigent, by themselves, their efforts are in vain. As one West African official commented, "We just don't owe enough money for anyone to be frightened by us."[25]

What is really significant about the Cartagena conference, therefore, is its unambiguous demonstration that the political basis for a coordinated radical debt strategy does not exist. The Colombian Finance Minister had announced even before the conference issued its communiqué that: "There will not be a debtors' club. There will not be a moratorium on debt payment, there are no schemes for collective negotiation, there isn't any kind of break with the financial organizations."[26] While the Cartagena group has continued to call attention to the seriousness of the debt crisis, it has failed to expand beyond its core of Latin American debtors or to entertain seriously proposals for the kinds of political mechanisms which would be necessary to achieve even its limited objectives.

All this aside, it must be said of the Cartagena conference that it represents an important step forward in the politicization of the debt crisis. Its failure to advance Southern unity in the short run attests to the enormous constraints imposed by the altered international circumstances of the South discussed in the previous section. The existence of a *de facto* creditors' cartel threatening dire consequences for any country that defaults or repudiates its debt, sharply increased coordination and centralization of capital flows, the increased dominance of the IMF and the World Bank and their basic agreement on the structural adjustment agenda, and selective mechanisms of cooptation, all have contributed to offset the potentially unifying nature of the debt crisis. And since its economic position is weakest, the Fourth World has been the biggest loser.

But there is one fairly widespread and relatively successful strategy within the South dealing with debt crisis which offers hope for new forms of solidarity. It involves some innovative trade relations, or "countertrade", based usually on some mechanism of barter. The two most important forms of countertrade are direct barter of commodities and "counterpurchase", in which suppliers of imports accept an obligation to buy an equivalent value of exports from the importing country. Over 80 countries are now engaged in countertrade, with estimates of the proportion of world trade it accounts for ranging from 8 per cent to 30 per cent.[27] For obvious reasons, the advanced capitalist countries, along with the IMF and the World Bank, oppose countertrade on principle. This is despite the fact that the bulk of countertrade, mainly in the form of counterpurchase agreements, is between the South and Western suppliers fearful of otherwise losing desirable markets. Nonetheless, with roughly 29 per cent of countertrade being conducted among Southern countries, this is an important and growing mechanism of economic interdependence and self-reliance.[28] Such a feature is especially attractive because earlier forms of South-South trade were generally transacted in dollars, with the result that commerce suffered and many bills went unpaid when the debt crisis emerged. What foreign exchange there was available had to be used to service debt rather than settle accounts with other LDCs. By bartering rather than using dollars or any convertible currency as the medium of exchange, countertrade insulates the South from economic fluctuations in the North. It thus represents a step forward toward greater Southern autonomy and self-reliance.

It is important to emphasize that while the debt crisis has weakened Southern unity in some ways, it has by no means eliminated it. For all its diversity and distress, the South has continued to demonstrate an ability to formulate and articulate common positions and proposals in a variety of international fora. In addition, it has resisted efforts by Northern countries, particularly the United States, to link debt relief with foreign policy positions: for example, supporting the US campaign against Nicaragua. Thus, despite bilateral conflicts within the South, such as the Iran-Iraq war, there appears to be a political basis for ideological tolerance and common interests that could sustain a renewed and more aggressive Southern solidarity in the future.

Conclusion: The continuing debt crisis

After a great deal of alarm about the imminent collapse of the international financial system in 1982 and 1983, the debt crisis has receded from view in the mass media. As early as April 1983 even, the Wall Street Journal had declared that there was no longer any crisis. The New York Times was more cautious, waiting for nearly two more years before joining the growing consensus with an article entitled "Debt Crisis Called All but Over".[29] Even the IMF shared these sentiments. Shortly after the New York Times piece appeared, the IMF managing director, in a reference to the catastrophic predictions surrounding the debt crisis earlier on, observed that "the grim scenario was not played out".[30]

In reality, however, this is only the beginning. Third World countries will be paying about $100 billion in debt service annually for the foreseeable future. Net resource transfers for many countries will be negative; indeed, Latin America paid out some $16 billion more than what it took in for 1983, and suffered approximately the same deficit in 1984. Similarly, Fourth World African countries, as we have seen, are running negative balances with several sources of finance. Clearly, debt and associated issues will remain at the center of North-South relations for years to come.

Indeed, there are reasons to believe that the debt problem is likely to become even more acute. Three separate but related sets of considerations are especially pertinent in this regard: political developments within debtor countries; the likelihood that the assumptions underlying the adjustment programs of the IMF and the World Bank are not viable; and the ways in which the management of the debt crisis to date may itself constitute an obstacle to the management of future crises. In this concluding section, we briefly take up each of these points.

South-South political initiatives have indeed been limited, but there are more profound domestic transformations taking place within individual countries. In Latin America, especially, the debt crisis and its aftermath have helped to discredit authoritarian military regimes and strengthened long-standing democratic forces. Indeed, elected presidents have assumed office in nine Latin American countries since 1980, albeit that economic difficulties were not always the main reason for the military returning to their barracks. Still, while new governments have almost always sought to reassure foreign creditors as one of their first acts, democratization has invariably engendered a more assertive stance on the debt issue. "The politics of debt," a New York Times columnist has observed, "is rapidly becoming the dominant politics of Brazil,"[31] a statement increasingly applicable to the rest of the Third World if, as seems likely, democratization continues and current efforts to contain the crisis fail.

And that IMF agreements have usually been very inflexible has not helped its cause. The most orthodox agreements have been negotiated with Western-oriented military regimes, such as the Philippines, so that the unfavorable comparison with terms obtained by other, more democratic countries has strengthened opposition forces in those countries. Riots erupted after drastic IMF-dictated price increases in basic commodities went into effect in the Dominican Republic and Brazil in 1984, as well as in Jamaica in January 1985. However, the issue goes deeper than even the political viability of austerity measures. Many observers have argued for years that the export-oriented development model promoted by the World Bank and the IMF requires a high level of political repression to keep down labor costs and to maintain the "stable investment climate" multinational corporations insist on.[32] In this sense, there is a more natural fit between the IMF and the World Bank and authoritarian governments than democratic governments. Concomitantly, however, the demands and costs of adjustment to the debt crisis have been very extensive, going beyond the capabilities of many authoritarian regimes. At work is a dynamic process: debt-related problems undermining the credibility of authoritarian governments which have been its staunchest supporters, and the resulting propensity toward democratization encouraging more militant bargaining postures. This phenomenon is most clearly manifested in the official positions of Bolivia, Nicaragua, and Peru who have for all intents and purposes defaulted.

Increasingly, the basic theoretical underpinnings of the structural adjustment model, as defined by the World Bank and the IMF, are being called into question. Given current trends in the world economy and incipient contradictions in the management of the debt crisis to date, it is difficult to imagine where and how it might work successfully. IMF Managing Director Larosiere has stated on numerous occasions that the success of the structural adjustment strategy depends on restored and steady growth in the advanced capitalist countries, adequate financing (both concessional and nonconcessional) for the Third World, avoidance of protectionism, and expanded markets for Third World exports. All these caveats remain problematic. What economic recovery experienced thus far, has been geographically limited and largely fueled by enormous deficit spending by the United States. Such "an unprecedented absorption of global savings"[33] in turn has kept real interest rates at record levels, increasing the debt-service burden of the Third World. Moreover, the US GNP annual growth rate fell sharply to 1.3 per cent during the first quarter of 1985, raising doubts about both the stability and duration of world economic recovery.[34]

Levels of concessional financing have been declining since 1981, with the balance between more concessional and less concessional aid flows shifting decisively towards the latter. The International Development Association (IDA), an important source of Fourth World financing, was re-funded in 1983 at only 60 per cent of its previous level in real terms. And despite all sorts of new inducements, new international flows of private direct investment are unsubstantial. The level of commercial bank lending to the Third World remains low, and virtually excludes the Fourth World. This reluctance to lend to the low-income countries is ironic. After all, the successful opposition of the United States to an expansion of World Bank quotas was predicated in part on fostering reliance on private financing.

Further, despite the hopeful claim in the IMF *Annual Report 1983* that "conditions should be propitious" for a serious attack on protectionism in the industrial countries, it continues to rise and limit the access of Third World exports.[35] The proportion of products restricted by tariffs and other barriers grew from 20 per cent of total consumption of manufactured goods in the United States and Europe in 1980 to 30 per cent in 1983, and kept climbing in 1984.[36] While the IMF is powerless to apply more than moral suasion to the industrial countries, it recognizes the threat posed to its structural adjustment programs and has warned that "restrictions against the exports of developing countries penalize most severely those countries that have adopted the outward-looking growth strategies and the liberalization of their domestic economies advocated by the Fund".[37] Even without protectionism, however, it is unlikely that the demand for Third World products will grow as rapidly as in previous booms;[38] the terms of trade for virtually all Third World countries have remained far below 1980 levels.

For the Fourth World, the premises of the structural adjustment model seem especially unsuitable and might actually engender adverse effects if imposed. Fourth World markets are small, and provide it with little leverage. Its commodity prices continue to be weak, so that its terms of trade are very likely to deteriorate further. Also, the Fourth World will conceivably remain shut-off from commercial financing while having to accept harder terms on the declining amount of aid it will receive. Some countries, most notably India, are already being "graduated" from more to less concessional sources of aid financing. In contrast to these structural deficiencies, the terms of trade for the newly-industrializing countries are improving. Clearly, the ability of Fourth World countries to compete with other Third World countries for scarce foreign markets is likely to remain limited.

Such pessimism is borne out by preliminary evidence which indicates that IMF-sponsored programs are not doing well in low-income countries. A recent study of adjustment programs in Africa since 1980 by the IMF itself found that economic growth targets were met in only 20 per cent of the 23 cases examined. In 60 per cent of the cases, economic growth rates either stagnated or declined. Further, inflation and the status of the current accounts failed to improve in about half the cases.[39]

In addition, there are potential contradictions built into the mechanisms by which the debt crisis has been managed. The most obvious contradiction is that problems of debt have been dealt with by the accumulation of more debt. As we have seen, new borrowing is used increasingly to service old, overdue debts. In 1983, less developed countries as a whole increased their debt by an estimated $68 billion, an 8.8 per cent increase. In 1984, a further $52 billion was added; and in 1985, it is estimated that LDC debt will increase by $75 billion, an 8.4 per cent increase. While this rate of increase is lower than in the early 1980s, it surpasses in absolute amount the $73 billion increase in 1982, the year when the debt crisis broke out formally. More important, even as these increases in debt paper over the immediate crisis, unless there are radical and far-reaching strategies to reform the world economy, the corresponding increases in the debt servicing burden will trigger more extensive and devastating debt crises in future.[40]

Another set of contradictions stem from the required simultaneity of adjustment, whereby practically all Third World countries are expected to deflate their economies, slash imports, and increase exports together. As many critics have pointed out, all these countries cannot reduce imports and expand exports in unison. One European official observed thus of the IMF: "The IMF was not set up to deal with the world as a system, and it does not treat the effects of its policies globally."[41] So far, almost all of the improvements in the current accounts of the Third World have been brought about by drastic reductions in imports. This not only reduces the opportunities for export expansion by other countries, it also means a drastic decline in domestic investment—for example, almost 50 per cent of industrial investment in Latin America.

Similarly problematic is the increased linkage of previously separate financial flows to the multilateral institutions. While this linkage gives those institutions, particularly the World Bank, great power, it also imparts a structural rigidity to the system. With more bilateral aid, commercial bank credits, and private investment brought under the "preferred creditor" umbrella of the multilateral institutions, the capacity for flexible response in terms of future economic downturns and debt crises is undermined, since an increasing proportion of capital flows lies outside the realm of potential renegotiation. In addition, because of cross-default clauses which make a default against one creditor a default against all, the seriousness of debt servicing difficulties could escalate very quickly in future. Thus, default against the multilateral institutions by the South now, hitherto unimaginable, would not only threaten their access to financing in private capital markets but would also shake the basic foundations of international finance much more seriously than in 1982-83.

Despite the tenuousness of the structural adjustment strategy and all these contradictions in debt crisis management, Third World countries are expected to assume that somehow the conditions for successful adjustment will materialize. Fritz Leutwiler, president of the Bank for International Settlements, announced in June 1984 that the Western central banks had developed a contingency plan to deal with the possibility of massive default by the South.[42] However, the aid institutions actively oppose any form of contingency planning on the part of Third World countries in case the premises of such externally-oriented development prove to be false. Instead, Third World countries are told to eschew proposals for international delinking and to endeavor to ride "the world economy rollercoaster" more efficiently.[43]

The onset of the debt crisis led to widespread speculation on what Nyerere has called the "power of debt".[44] To date, debt has proven more of a force for disunity than unity, for subordination and co-optation than power. Still, a combination of necessity and opportunity may yet lead the South to mount a more united and sustained challenge to the current state of North-South negotiations. The South, and the Fourth World in particular, cannot expect the North to bail it out of the debt crisis. It is imperative that they find new and imaginative ways to deal collectively with this problem so that the full destructive impact of the crisis may still be averted.

Notes and references

[1] Editorial, 'If wishes were horses. . .', *South*, 46, August 1984, p. 10.

[2] Irving Louis Horowitz, *Beyond Empire and Revolution* (New York: Oxford University Press, 1982), p. vii.

3. All three of these approaches are described in Ankie M. Hoogvelt, *The Third World in Global Development* (London: Macmillan, 1982). For a descriptive survey of the fourth World, see Irving Louis Horowitz, *'Three Worlds of Development Plus One'*, in Horowitz (note 2), pp. xiii-xxvii. For the LLDC concept, see Thomas G. Weiss and Anthony Jennings, *More for the Least? Prospects for the Poorest Countries in the Eighties* (Lexington, MA: D.C. Heath, 1983), pp. 1-10.

4. World Bank, *World Development Report* 1984 (New York: Oxford University Press, 1984), p. 218; and Organization for Economic Co-operation and Development, *External Debt of Developing Countries: 1983 Survey* (Paris: OECD, 1983), p. 223.

5. Those excluded are China, Vietnam, Kampuchea, Laos PDR, Mozambique, Afghanistan and Bhutan. The World Bank's list excludes countries with populations under one million.

6. In Richard Williams et al., *International Capital Markets: Developments and Prospects, 1983* (Washington, DC: IMF, 1983), p. 70.

7. OECD, *External Debt of Developing Countries: 1982 Survey* (Paris: OECD, 1982), pp. 15-16.

8. For further discussion of this point, see Robert E. Wood, 'Foreign Aid and the Capitalist State in Underdeveloped Countries', *Politics and Society*, 10: 1, Fall 1980, pp. 1-34.

9. OECD (note 7), p. 15.

10. World Bank, *Toward Sustained Development in Sub-Saharan Africa: A Joint Program of Action* (Washington: World Bank, 1984), p. 12.

11. Darrell Delamaide, *Debt Shock: The Full Story of the World Credit Crisis* (Garden City, NY: Doubleday, 1984), p. 40.

12. World Bank (note 10), p. 13.

13. Delamaide (note 11), p. 41; and World Bank, Tanzania: Agricultural Sector, *Report No. 4052-TA*, (Washington: World Bank, 1983), p. 6.

14. Cheryl Pyer, 'Tanzania and the World Bank', *Third World Quarterly*, 5:4, October 1983, p. 800: and Reginald Herbolt Green, 'Political-Economic Adjustment and IMF Conditional ity: Tanzania, 1974-81', in: John Williamson (ed.), IMF Conditionality (Washington: Institute for International Economics, 1983), p. 359.

15. Calculated from data in World Bank, *World Debt Tables 1983-1984 edition* (Washington: World Bank, 1984).

16. World Bank, *Debt and the Developing World: Current Trends and Prospects* (Washington: World Bank, 1984), pp. ix, 6-7.

17. Ibid., pp. 10-11.

18. *IMF Survey*, 13 June 1983, p. 166.

19. Quote in C. Raghavan, 'Corea bows out with a broadside—and a plea for unity', *South*, 53, March 1985, p. 62.

20. See the following good background sources: John Loxley, 'Monetary Institutions and Class Struggle in Tanzania', in: Bismarck U. Mwansasu and Cranford Pratt (eds.), *Towards Socialism in Tanzania* (Toronto: Toronto University Press, 1979), pp. 79-84; Idrian N. Resnick, *The Long Transition: Building Socialism in Tanzania* (New York: Monthly Review Press, 1981), pp. 126-134; and Andrew Coulson, *Tanzania: A Political Economy* (Oxford: Clarendon Press, 1982), p. 315.

21. World Bank (note 15), p. 82.

22. World Bank (note 10), p. 11.

23. Stephen Kinzer, 'Cracks in the World Coffee Pact', *New York Times*, 18 July 1983, p. D7.

24. In a best-selling book, Brazilian economist Celso Furtado attacked the policies of the IMF and argued that sovereign borrowers had the right to declare payments moratoria and inform creditors and the new conditions they were offering unilaterally. He urged this course of action for Brazil, but warned Brazilians to be prepared to face the consequences of "a long period of financial abstinence on the international financial market". Celso Furtado, *No to Recession and Unemployment: An Examination of the Brazilian Economic Crisis* (London: Third World Foundation, 1984), p. 23.

25. Quote in Clifford D. May, 'Africa's Debts Appear More Troublesome Than Others', *New York Times*, 1 July 1984, p. E3.

26. Robert A. Liff, '11 Latin American Debtors Agree to Continue Lobbying', *Philadelphia Inquirer*, 23 June 1984, p. 11D.

27. *South*, 53, March 1985, pp. 55, 57.

28. Ibid., p. 60.

29. 'What Debt Crisis?' *Wall Street Journal*, 20 April 1983, p. 28: and Nicholas D. Kristof, 'Debt Crisis Called All but Over', *New York Times*, 4 February 1985, p. D1.

30. *IMF Survey*, 18 February 1985, p. 51.

31. Alan Riding, 'The New Crisis for Latin Debt', *New York Times*, 11 March 1984, p. 8F.

32. Bello (note 38); and Cheryl Payer, *The World Bank: A Critical Analysis* (New York: Monthly Review Press, 1983).

33. *IMF Survey*, 23 April 1984, p. 123.

34. Michael Quint, 'Rates Fall Sharply on G.N.P. Data', *New York Times*, 19 April 1985, p. D1.

35. IMF, *Annual Report 1984* (Washington: IMF, 1984), p. 33.

36. *IMF Survey*, 18 February 1985, p. 50; and 15 April 1985, pp. 114-115.

37. IMF, *Annual Report 1983* (Washington: IMF, 1983), p. 2.

38. See Albert Fishlow, 'The Debt Crisis: Round Two Ahead?' in: Richard E. Feinberg and Valeriana Kallab (eds.), *Adjustment Crisis in the Third World* (New Brunswick, NJ: Transaction Books, 1984), pp. 40-45.

39. *IMF Survey*, 15 April 1985, p. 126.
40. *IMF Survey*, 18 March 1985, p. 88.
41. *Business Week*, 21 february 1983, p. 112.
42. Paul Lewis, 'A "Cartel" of Debtors Ruled Out', *New York Times*, 19 June 1984, p. D19.
43. World Bank (note 4), p. 44.
44. See interview in *South*, 46, August 1984, p. 36.

The Doctrine of Economic Neutrality of the IMF and the World Bank

Richard Swedberg

Our ideology is economics... We should not address political questions and we don't.
— A. W. Clausen, President of the World Bank, 1982

1. Introduction

After World War II there was a tremendous desire to avoid war in the future, and a great hope that the newly founded UN would create a world without armed conflict. This optimism also extended to two organizations, which were connected to the UN if not subordinate to it: the World Bank (IBRD) and the International Monetary Fund (IMF). The task of these two organizations was primarily to take care of the 'economic' as opposed to the 'political' dimensions of the post-war world. According to their statutes, they had to be politically neutral and only take economic considerations into account when reaching their decision.[1]

Today, nearly half a century later, it is common to hear accusations that the Bank and the Fund are not neutral; that they interfere in political matters and even have become tools of imperialism (e.g. Payer 1974, 1982). IMF and IBRD deny these charges vehemently and refer to their legal obligations to remain politically neutral and exclusively base their decisions on economic grounds (see e.g. Gold 1983).

Who is then correct—the Bank and the Fund or their critics? This is the question we shall attempt to address in this article. We shall go about it by looking at the forces which threaten what can be called the doctrine of economic neutrality from inside as well as from outside the two organizations (Sections 2-3). A presentation then follows of some cases where the IMF and the IBRD have unambiguously interfered in political situations (Section 4). The article ends with a suggestion that the doctrine of economic neutrality is used by certain political actors as an ideological shield for their own interests.

2. Political pressures inside the IMF and the World Bank

By virtue of their origin—the US vision during World War II of an international economy without currency blocks and protective tariffs—it can be argued that the IMF and the World Bank were biased from the beginning (e.g. Block 1977). This is true up to a point. There exist, however, several additional factors which have made these two organizations extra sensitive to political forces and hence less 'economically neutral'. These factors can conveniently be divided into two categories of political factors concerning the Fund and the Bank: those that come from inside these organizations and those that come from the outside.

Originally published in Journal of Peace Research, vol. 23, no. 4, 1986; reprinted with permission.

In this section we shall look at the first of these two categories, political pressures from inside the Fund and the Bank. Already at Bretton Woods and Savannah in 1944-46, the US systematically opposed all of Keynes' proposals to insure a minimum of independence and neutrality for these two institutions. The US, in other words, was from the beginning convinced of the necessity of having firm, political control of the IMF and the World Bank. The two major features of this control were to be the weighted voting system and the political appointments of the decision-makers inside the Fund and the Bank.

The weighted voting system, it should be noted, was not by itself seen as 'political' at Bretton Woods and Savannah. The reason for this is intimately connected with the concept of political democracy in the Western countries, according to which equality is something that belongs to the political realm and has nothing to do with the economy (e.g. Schmitt 1976). In the US planning during World War II, this way of thinking was clearly expressed in the division of labor between, on the one hand, the UN and, on the other, the IMF and the World Bank. The UN was viewed as a 'political' organ and hence one vote-one country was the rule; the IMF and the World Bank, however, were seen as purely 'economic' organs, and here a country's voting strength reflected its economic power (e.g. US House of Representatives, 1945, p. 28).

The US share of the vote was originally 36% in the IMF and 27.2% in the World Bank (Mason & Asher 1973, p. 30). Over the years the US vote has tended to decline, reflecting among other things the fact that Europe and Japan have emerged as major economic powers. It should also be noted that a complicated set of veto rules exists in the IMF and the World Bank that considerably strengthens the power of the US and Europe in key questions. The Soviet Union signed the Bretton Woods agreement and would probably have received about 10% of the vote if it had not been forced out of the Fund and the Bank before its vote was decided (Gardner 1969, p. 295; Horsefield 1969a: 117; Gold 1974, pp. 113-137). The third world has traditionally had a minority vote in the two organizations. Over the years its vote has increased, but not enough to even remotely challenge the power of US-Europe-Japan.

Keynes' struggle in 1946 at Savannah to fight off the US proposal to 'politicize' the Fund did not include the weighted voting system. He accepted, it seems, the economic inequality of the various nations in the IMF and the World Bank as inevitable (Harrod 1951, p. 631). He did not, however, find it suitable that the political organs in the various countries should have direct political control of the international economy via the IMF and the World Bank. The world economy, he felt, should rather be regulated in a more anonymous and automatic way—it should, as far as possible, operate like the market in classical economic theory.

The US disagreed with Keynes and instituted a series of mechanisms that politicized the Fund and the Bank by tying the weighted voting system directly to the political institutions of the member countries. A brief glance at the position of the executive directors, the governors and the managing director (IMF) and the president (IBRD) illustrates how this works. The key to the political influence over the alleged 'neutral' decisions of the Fund and the Bank is the powerful board of executive directors (e.g. Strange 1974). The board takes decisions on the specific loans and is continuously in session. The executive director is a full-time political appointee and votes on instructions by his or her government (e.g. Horsefield 1969a, p. 133). He or she is not, in other words, the independent civil servant as Keynes wanted. In the US, which is still the most powerful country in the Fund as well as in the Bank, the executive director is ordered by law to clear his or her decisions with the Secretary of the Treasury. There exists a similar legal obligation for the executive director from the Federal Republic of Germany. In other countries the situation is less formalized but essentially the same.

About a fourth of the executive directors are appointed and only represent one country (the US, France, Great Britain, West Germany and—for the Fund—Saudi Arabia). The rest are elected and speak, as a rule, for a group of countries. IMF's executive director for Spain, for example, represents Spain, the Central American nations, Mexico, and Venezuela.

The board of governors makes, according to the articles of agreements, the most important decisions at the IMF and the World Bank, such as the change of quotas and the expulsion of members. The board, however, meets only once a year and is, according to an authority like Susan Strange (1974, pp. 283f.), without any practical importance, since the most important decisions concerning the international economy are taken elsewhere. Governors are customarily ministers of finance or heads of central banks. While the official writings of the Fund describe the status of the executive director as a 'subtle one', the board of governors is openly labelled 'political' (e.g. Gold 1979, pp. 239, 241).

The managing director of the IMF and the president of IBRD owe allegiance exclusively to their respective organizations according to the articles of agreements. In reality, however, the US has chosen all managing directors and presidents till now, and to whom these officials owe their allegiance in reality is a more complicated question than the statutes make out (e.g. Payer 1982, p. 39). As a rule, it can be said that no managing director or president can make a major decision of any kind without clearance from the US and—today—also from the major European nations and Japan. He or she can, however, initiate changes and hope that they will be cleared by the most powerful member countries.

By tradition the president of the World Bank is a US citizen, while the managing director of the IMF is a European. This goes back to the situation in the 1940s when the US decided that the president of IBRD had to be a US citizen in order to appease Wall Street, but that it would be undiplomatic to also have a US citizen as head of the IMF (the deputy to the managing director, however, is always an American). The president of IBRD is usually a banker and has more power over the executive directors than the managing director of the Fund (Mason & Asher 1973, p. 738). During the first years of the Bank's existence, the US executive director had so much power that no-one was willing to take the position as head of the IBRD; the remedy was to invest the power of the president with that of the US executive director (Mason & Asher 1973, pp. 48f; Nissen 1974, pp. 48f.).

In conclusion, it can be noted that the weighted voting system in combination with political appointments to the highest positions in the Bank and the Fund have seriously endangered the 'economic neutrality' of these two organizations. It can be added that the political pressure system inside the Fund and the Bank has also been used to politicize these organizations from another direction. This is especially the case in the US, where human rights activists have tried to stop the US from approving loans to countries were gross violations of human rights occur. In 1983 progressive forces in the US—in combination with some rightwing forces in the Congress—tried to block the contribution to the IMF. The effort failed, but a law is now on the books which says that the US representative to the IMF must vote 'no' on certain loans to South Africa.

3. Political pressures from outside the IMF and the World Bank

It is not only from inside the Fund and the Bank that there exist political pressures that endanger the specious neutrality doctrine. There also exist political forces outside these two organizations which put pressure on the Fund and the Bank. The US and some West European countries have thus forced the IMF and the World Bank to follow their wishes at every critical juncture in international economic affairs. In these cases, the Fund and the Bank have simply been told what to do through political channels outside the organizations themselves.

Many times, then, the Fund and the Bank have simply been bypassed or ordered around in matters which, according to the Bretton Woods rules, belong to their sphere of action. If one looks closely at these instances, a clear pattern emerges. The US made the key monetary decisions till around 1960. Since then, the power to decide has resided in a coalition of US-Europe-Japan. A few cases will illustrate.

'The architects of the Fund and the Bank', Richard Gardner (1969, p. 287) notes 'expected these institutions to play a significant part during the transition period (after World War II) in leading the world back to nondiscriminatory currency practices'. In reality, however, the very opposite happened. The US decided that the economic reconstruction of Western Europe must have first priority and that the Fund and the Bank were unsuitable for this task (Strange 1974, p. 270). The decision to administer the Marshall Plan through channels separate from IMF-IBRD was taken in 1947, a year which in Gardner's phrase constituted the 'end of Bretton Woods' (1969, p. 287). 'With the beginning of the European Recovery Programme', Gardner (1969, pp. 304f.) states, 'the Fund practically ceased exchange operations and the Bank left the field of reconstruction lending'. Bilateral trading and currency restrictions were encouraged and actually came to surpass their pre-war level. According to the IMF in 1949, 'dependence on bilateral trade and inconvertible currencies is (today) far greater than before the war' (Gardner 1969, p. 298).

The IMF and the IBRD's activities during these first years of existence were definitely minor. During 1947-1955 the IMF, like the Bank, did very little business (Krasner 1968, pp. 673f.; Mason and Asher 1973, p. 198). And whatever loans were granted, were done so only on condition that the US approved. Till 1960, according to Brian Tew (as cited in Strange 1974, p. 229), 'no drawing was approved by the Executive Board without it being made clear in advance that the US authorities were in agreement'. The US power during these years, it should be noticed, not only depended on its superior voting power but also on the fact that the dollar was the only currency that carried weight in international affairs. In the early years of the Bank, Asher (1962, p. 697) writes, it operated 'almost exclusively on United States resources'. In the IMF the situation was the same; until 1960, 87% of all drawings were made in dollars (Strange 1976, p. 104).

The US, as we have seen, was not willing to totally write off the IMF and the IBRD. In addition to administrating a few loans, the Fund and the Bank were also used to humble the Soviet Union and its satellites. The US decision to utilize the IMF and the IBRD in the Cold War—and thus to 'politicize' them in Gardner's (1969, p. 296) opinion—first resulted in the blocking of Soviet membership. A few years later Poland and Czechoslovakia were barred from the IMF and the IBRD on US initiative (Sohn 1964, p. 1405; Mason & Asher 1973, p. 169f.). A further move to politicize the Fund took place in the early 1950s, when the US forced the IMF to accept restrictions on trade in currencies used by enemies of the

US. In the Funds formulation, the restrictions were needed 'for the preservation of national or international security' (Horsefield 1969a, p. 275f., 1969b, p. 257).

Toward the end of the 1950s US monetary policy started to change. Europe was well on its way to economic independence, and the reconstruction phase was over. The US balance of payments situation was worsening, and in 1958 the US gold reserves were for the first time less than the outstanding liabilities in foreign countries (Strange 1976, p. 33). The US responded to this development in various ways; one was to increase the use of 'tied aid', another to reactivate the Fund and the Bank (Payer 1974, p. 27f.). The IMF and the IBRD, it was realized, had two major advantages for the US: they were cheap, and they had the reputation of being 'neutral'.

Neither the Fund nor the Bank, however, were to remain as docile to US interests as they had been during the early post-war period. In the 1960s Europe's economy was fully restored, and since 1958 the key European currencies were convertible. Coupled with the US balance of payments deficit, which was getting worse every year, a shift in the power structure of international finance was inevitable.

The replacement of US hegemony with a coalition of US-Europe-Japan did not mean that the IMF and the World Bank were suddenly 'politicized', as many students of international finance have suggested (e.g. Aubrey 1969, p. 14; Russell 1973, p. 434; Krause & Nye 1975, p. 323). Rather, the political pressures from outside the Fund and the Bank continued with unabated force. The only novelty was that the Fund and the Bank from now on were bypassed by a combination of states rather than by just one.

Gone were the days when the US president could simply pick up the phone and announce his decision to the heads of the Fund and the Bank. This still happened, as is clear from 1971, when Pierre-Paul Schweitzer, the managing director of the IMF and no favorite of the US, was informed of Nixon's decision to devalue the dollar just before it was to be announced on national television (e.g. Mayer 1981, p. 168). In most financial matters of international importance, however, decisions from now on had to be reached through negotiations between the major Western powers. The institutional form chosen for these negotiations were often small clubs or forums, which either already existed—the Bank for International Settlements (BIS) being one case—or which were quickly put together. There were several advantages to these clubs in comparison to the IMF. They were, for instance, suitably small and not filled with troublesome third world delegates. The clubs were also very flexible and had few formal rules; they were secretive and totally unknown to the public. The *Financial Times* noted, for example, on November 23, 1983 with regard to the thirty year-old Paris Club that 'the club's inner workings (still) remain a mystery'.

Apart from the Paris Club, which specializes in reschedulings of public debts, the most important group is the Group of Ten (G-10). It was formed in 1961 by the major Western countries to provide resources for international monetary stabilization. This was a matter that properly belonged to the Fund, and it was actually the Fund that had come up with the idea that more resources were needed. The IMF, however, was quickly pushed aside and all the key decisions were taken inside the G-10. Eventually the Fund succeeded in having some joint meetings with the G-10, but it is generally understood that the first 'General Arrangements to Borrow' (GAB) was a product of the G-10 and not the Fund (e.g. Strange 1976, p. 1112). The GAB meant that the Fund now had more resources to dispose over. None of this money, however, could be lent to states which were not members of the G-10.

The voting system in matters concerning the GAB is also rigged in such a way that the EEC states can veto a US request for money.

Apart from the GAB, the G-10 has another major accomplishment to its name, namely the creation of Special Drawing Rights (SDRs) in 1969. The key issue that the G-10 resolved in this case—and which again belonged to the domain of the Fund—was how to increase international liquidity in a way that was both cheap and efficient.

The G-10 had originally planned to split the first batch of the new international currency exclusively among its own members. This naturally offended third world countries, which argued that if any new monetary resources were to be created, they needed them the most. The IMF took a cautious middle position, which was the one finally agreed upon. The SDRs were split among all the members of the Fund according to their quotas. According to the IMF's managing director, all the final decisions concerning the SDRs were taken by the G-10 (Schweitzer 1976, p. 215).

The World Bank, like the Fund, has often been exposed to strong outside political forces. In the mid-1950s the Bank was, for example, reactivated through a decision by the US. In 1956 the International Finance Corporation (IFC), a World Bank subsidiary that specializes in loans to private companies without government guarantees, was created on special demand by the US (e.g. Mason & Asher 1973, pp. 345-350). A few years later—also this time on US initiative—another member of the World Bank group was founded, the International Development Association (IDA) (Strange 1976, pp. 102-103). IDA's main function is to grant loans to poor countries at rates which are considerably lower than the current market rate. It was not, however, created for altruistic reasons. According to IBRD President Black (Mason & Asher 1973, p. 386), the main purpose of the IDA was to 'offset the urge (among third world countries) for SUNFED' (SUNFED was a UN-sponsored soft-loan agency). In 1968 McNamara became president of the Bank and quickly expanded its activities. Though there exist several accounts of the Bank under McNamara, it is not, to my knowledge, known who made the decision to suddenly increase the role of the Bank. A reasonable guess is that it was the US government.

The 1970s and 1980s have been the most tumultuous decades in international finance since the 1930s. In 1971 and 1973 the dollar was devalued. During the early 1970s the link between gold and the dollar was broken and floating exchange rates introduced. In 1973-74 and 1979-80 oil prices were raised to record levels. The Eurocurrency market, born in the 1960s, quickly expanded with the flood of OPEC money. Private banks became truly international in the 1970s and played a key role in recycling the petrodollars. Third world countries, as a result, ran up enormous debts to the private banks. Many of these countries are, as every newspaper reader knows, paying dearly for these loans today.

In some of the events during the 1970s and 1980s—the devaluation of the dollar and the introduction of floating exchange rates being the two most obvious cases—the Fund simply had to go along with decisions made by the US and the European powers. In other events, the element of direct political intervention seems rather small. This is especially true for the growth of the Eurocurrency market and the recycling of petrodollars. It should however by noted that very little is known about the political dimension of these events. Here, as in so many other areas of the international economy, the level of knowledge is low (e.g. Strange 1972).

4. Political pressures by the IMF and the World Bank

In many cases the IMF and the IBRD have been fairly passive targets for the power policies of a few Western countries which, as we have seen, have exerted political pressure on the Fund and the Bank from inside these two organizations as well as from the outside. The IMF and the World Bank, however, have considerable power of their own, and it is to the political dimension of this power that we now shall turn.

The only countries that the Fund and the Bank have power over are third world countries. 'The IMF', Krause & Nye (1975, p. 338) note, 'have exercised authority primarily in relation to weaker countries, it has been a follower rather than a leader...' The situation is the same with the World Bank, whose loans have gone nearly exclusively to third world countries (World Bank 1983, pp. 218-220).

The political pressures that the IMF and the World Bank have exerted on third world countries have sometimes been openly political. At other times—and more frequently—the political pressures have been more hidden, often disguised as motivated exclusively on economic grounds. The unambiguously political decisions by the IMF and the Bank will in this article be seen as examples of 'direct political pressure', while the term 'indirect political pressure' will be used for typical cases of IMF 'conditionality' and World Bank 'leverage'.

4.1 Direct political pressure

The Fund and the Bank naturally do not acknowledge that they exert any kind of political pressure; their ideology of economic neutrality forbids that. In several typical cases, however, the IMF and the World Bank have interfered in such an obvious way with the political machinery of a debtor country that their decisions can be called openly political. These cases are the following: (1) loans to the government side in civil wars (*'civil war loans'*); (2) cutoffs of lending to socialist and/or nationalist countries followed by loans to the right-wing leaders that topple these governments (*'destabilizing non-lending'*); (3) loans in violations of UN resolutions (*'loans in contradiction to international conventions'*); (4) loans that become major issues in elections (*'political campaign loans'*); and (5) situations where the IMF and the World Bank practically take over the economy of a country (*'trusteeship loans'*).

'Civil war loans' are political in the fairly obvious sense that they interfere in a struggle waged exclusively over the political power of a country. Experiences from two world wars are unambiguous in showing that 'economic' questions become 'political' matters of highest priority when a country is involved in a war against an outside enemy. In a civil war situation the element of politization is even stronger. The IMF and the World Bank have several times supplied money to the government side in civil wars. Two examples are Indochina in the 1970s (Payer 1974) and El Salvador in the 1980s (Morrell & Biddle 1983). There also exist a series of situations which are close to civil wars though they do not involve the whole of the population. The 'dirty war' in Argentina in 1976-1979 and the Indonesian invasion of East Timor (1975-) are examples—in both cases the IMF and the World Bank supplied the government with huge resources.

'Destabilizing non-lending' means that the IMF and the World Bank cut off loans to a country at the same time as another nation is trying to slowly overthrow its government.

Destabilization often occurs when a government is trying to free its country from outside economic control. Usually, the non-lending phase is followed by a flood of loans to the right-wing clique that finally topples the socialist/nationalist government and switches to a policy that welcomes foreign investments. Cheryl Payer, author of the most astute study of the IMF's relationship to third world countries, writes:

In Indonesia, Brazil, and Argentina the military seize power from elected governments or popular rulers. Within a few weeks of the coup a mission from the International Monetary Fund arrives in each country to advise the new rulers on the reorganization of their economy (Payer 1974, p.ix).

Another example of 'destabilizing non-lending' is Chile in the 1970s. Here the World Bank cut off all lending to the Allende government only to start pouring money into the country when the legal government was toppled in a fascist coup (e.g. Petras & Morley 1975, pp. 144, 165-167). The Fund and the Bank's lending to Honduras in the 1980s is a further example of destabilization, Nicaragua being the target.

Finally, in one case—Jamaica in 1977-1979—the IMF did most of the destabilizing itself. The conditions demanded by the Fund, two Jamaican scholars and politicians note, 'completely undermined its (that is, the Manley government's) popularity and alienated its most important source of political support' (Girvan & Bernal 1982, p. 35). The result was the loss in the 1980 election of Manley to Seaga.

The first loans in violation of UN resolutions ('*loans in contradiction to international conventions*') were IBRD loans to Portugal and South Africa in the 1960s (Bleicher 1970). The World Bank claimed that it was forbidden by its statues to deny loans on 'political' grounds to these countries and went ahead despite strong protests from the international community. The IMF loan of USD 1.1 bn to South Africa in the fall of 1982 was also in contradiction to international conventions (e.g. Morrell 1983). '*Political campaign loans*' are loans given by the IMF and the World Bank which become major issues in critical elections in the debtor country. Typically the two major political parties split over the issue of the loan and the hardship it entails. In some cases, the opposition to the loan is very seriously intended, as was the case in Jamaica in 1980 when Manley campaigned directly against the IMF (Girvan & Bernal 1982). In other cases, the opposition to the IMF is more of a campaign ploy or just impossible to maintain under pressure:

In the Philippines, Columbia, and Ceylon, candidates for the post of President or Prime Minister campaign for election on a platform of opposition to the IMF. Months, or even weeks, after the election is won, the same leaders forget their campaign promises and come to terms with the IMF—having found out that it is as impossible to live without it as to live with it (Payer 1974, p. ix).

An extreme form of political pressure by the IMF and the World Bank is exerted in the case of the so-called '*trusteeship loans*'. Here the Fund and the Bank more or less take over the economic running of a country. This is typically done by having all the key positions in the government filled with IMF/IBRD staff or with people who are very close to these institutions. Sid-Ahmed (1978, p. 178) notes that the IMF in the late 1970s succeeded in 'imposing a genuine protectorate on Zaire, by the appointment to the key posts in the economy and finances of representatives of the Fund'. In 1981 in the Philippines, another study tells us, 'the mechanism for the virtual direct rule of the World Bank was set in place: a cabinet dominated by technocrats and headed by the Bank's most reliable agent, Prime Minister

Cesar Virata' (Bello, Kinley & Elinson 1982, p. 64). In Haiti, the IMF tried in 1982 to break the monopoly on political and economic power by various sections of the Duvalier clan by appointing the minister of finance. This attempt, however, failed (Bello 1982, pp. 13-16).

4.2 Indirect political pressure

The term 'indirect political pressure', as noted earlier, can be applied to many cases of World Bank 'leverage' and IMF 'conditionality'. In typical cases of 'indirect political pressure', the Fund and Bank attach conditions to their loans which formally fall within the area of 'economics' and seem to have little to do with the political steering of a country. In reality, however, these conditions have important consequences for the politics of the debtor country—even if their political impact is more muted than in the case of 'direct political pressure'.

The ultimate purpose of the indirect political pressures by the bank and the Fund is, however, the same as that of the direct political pressures, namely to integrate the debtor country into the worldwide economic system that the US constructed just after World War II. This system, everybody from Hull to Keynes agreed, could only operate effectively if a new kind of free trade was instituted. As few currency restrictions as possible, low tariffs, and open doors to foreign investments—these were the main traits of the system constructed at Bretton Woods, and these are ultimately the goals of the indirect political pressures as well as the direct political pressures by the Fund and the Bank.

4.2.1 IMF conditionality

IMF's main task, according to its articles of agreement, is to guarantee a smoothly functioning and open international monetary system. This task has often collided with third world countries' desire to protect themselves against international capital in order to build up viable economies. In some cases the IMF has consequently gone about its task at the expense of third world. It has forced its will on reluctant countries through the conditions it attaches to its loans ('conditionality').

The history of conditionality is, briefly stated, the following (Strange 1976, pp. 92-97; Sid-Ahmed 1982). In 1952 it was formally decided that conditions should be attached to the drawings beyond the 'gold tranche' or the amount in gold—25 per cent of a country's quota—that it had to pay to become a member of the Fund. Conditionality was thus attached to the higher credit tranches (eventually 'low conditionality' to tranche number two — the 'first credit tranch', and 'high conditionality' or conditionality which entails a 'stabilization program' to tranches number three to five; all tranches being the same amount as the 'gold tranche', which today is called the 'reserve tranche'). A few years later it was formally decided that the borrowing country should enumerate the conditions that the Fund wants it to follow in a so-called 'letter of intent', which as a rule is not published. In the 1960s and 1970s the Fund instituted a series of new facilities with varying degree of conditionality. These are 'the compensatory financing facility' (1963; extended in 1966 and 1975), 'the buffer-stock facility' (1969), 'the extended fund facility' (1974), 'the oil facility' (1974-76), and 'the supplementary financing facility' or 'the Witteveen facility' (1979). How much a country can borrow from these facilities is calculated in a fairly complicated manner (see e.g. Sid-Ahmed 1982, p. 126). Only 'the extended facility' and 'the supplementary financing facility' carry 'high conditionality'; the others are 'low conditionality' facilities.

In the 1950s and 1960s conditionality (that is, 'high conditionality') was mainly attached to loans to Latin America. In the 1970s and 1980s, however, conditionality has spread to third world countries in general. There are mainly three reasons for this development. First, the ever more active debt-rescheduling institutions like the Paris Club usually attach IMF conditionality to their loans. Second, the Fund itself has under the impact of the present debt crisis expanded its lending considerably to third world countries. And third, international banks have started to include IMF clauses in their loans. For a long time now, it should also be noted, so much importance is attached to a country's relationship to the IMF that if it reneges on a loan to the Fund, it will be cut off from the whole international money market. Some of the Fund's power thus resides in the fact that its 'seal of approval' is needed even when its money is not.

IMF conditionality typically contains various prescriptions for how the debtor country must improve its balance of payments. In itself, it should be noticed, this means that the borrowing country's 'economic sovereignty' is limited by the Fund. That the Fund makes 'political' demands when it restructures a country's balance of payments has been verified by IMF's managing director Pierre-Paul Schweitzer (1976, p. 208):

The problems involved (in managing the international monetary system) are of course of a highly political nature. The balance of payments and exchange rates affect the economy and social life of a country. The domestic policies which have to be pursued in order to achieve certain objectives are at the core of each country's political life...

Any agreement on monetary co-operation would of course entail a limitation to some degree of the participating countries' 'economic sovereignty'. What should be understood about the Fund, however, is that some countries do not need to follow its prescriptions, and that these prescriptions are politically biased in certain directions. The *Financial Times* recently noted that

if the US were being examined by the IMF in the rigorous way that the Reagan administration believes should apply to developing countries, the US would receive an adverse report. In a couple of years it might not even (apart from its political clout) qualify for IMF assistance (*FT*, December 1, 1983, p. 19).

That the Fund's conditions are politically biased in certain directions becomes quite apparent if one takes a close look at them. Usually, IMF conditionality involves the following items:

(1) abolition or liberalization of foreign exchange and import controls.
(2) Devaluation of the exchange rate.
(3) Domestic anti-inflationary programmes, including: (a) control of bank credit; higher interest rates and perhaps higher reserve requirements; (b) control of government deficit; curbs on spending; increases in taxes and in prices charged by public enterprises; abolition of consumer subsidies (c) control of wage rises, so far as within the government's power;
(4) Greater hospitality to foreign investment (Payer 1974, p. 33).

A third world country which follows these prescriptions has great difficulty in constructing a strong industrial base of its own, since it is not allowed any protection against foreign capital. The country is also likely to have little control over its own raw materials, and nationalizations, as mentioned before, are frowned upon. The IMF is also hostile to labor movements and large public sectors. In brief, a country that follows IMF's advice is likely to lose quite a bit in economic and political independence.

Through the use of conditionality, the Fund can be said to exert indirect and undue political pressure by constantly demanding changes that only fit a certain type of society: a capitalist society with a weak labor movement and the doors open to foreign economic interests. We can also note that the implicit virtue of 'economic neutrality' here turns into its opposite: the IMF decision to be 'non-political' means that any regime—however oppressive and murderous—qualifies for support as long as it supports private foreign investments, low tariffs and so on. By not facing the question of what is 'political' in a direct manner, the Fund thus runs the risk of becoming politically naive.

4.2.2 World Bank 'leverage'

The concept of 'letter of intent' can be found not only in the IMF but also in the World Bank. Some conditions are set out in the specific loan agreement, which is public and published as a treaty by the UN (Payer 1982, pp. 7f.). Additional conditions, however, are secret and either made orally or set out in a letter of intent (Mason & Asher 1973, pp. 420, 433-435). According to a secret memorandum, it can be added, the World Bank does not give loans to a country which reneges on its international debt, expropriates foreign property without 'adequate' compensation or fails to honor its agreements with foreign companies (Hayter 1971, p. 31; Mason & Asher 1973, pp. 337f.).

At first glance, World Bank 'leverage' looks quite different from IMF 'conditionality'. This, however, is more apparent than real, and the Bank tends to set conditions which are quite similar to those of the Fund. In some loans the Bank uses an IMF clause (Mason & Asher 1973, p. 543). The Bank has also started to dispense so-called 'structural adjustment loans', which are very similar to ordinary balance of payments loans. Like IMF 'conditionality', World Bank 'leverage' is exclusively directed at third world countries since these are practically the only ones that today receive loans from the IBRD.

World Bank 'leverage' varies with the scope of the program and the dispensing agency. IDA grants, for instance, enable the Bank to exert more 'leverage', since these have considerably lower interest rates than loans from the IBRD or the IFC (Mason & Asher 1973, p. 429). World Bank loans can also be differentiated according to scope. The loan can be limited to a specific project, say a dam. But it can also cover a sector of the economy—the road system, for instance—or the country as a whole. Each of these cases has naturally very different political implications. As a rule, the broader the scope of the loan, the more room there is for political considerations. 'Country leverage' is thus potentially more political in nature than 'sector leverage' and 'project leverage'.

Albert O. Hirschman pays much attention to 'project leverage' in *Development Projects Observed* (1967). He shows that the Bank's idea of having non-political 'autonomous agencies' administering 'neutral' projects is quite unrealistic. Any project, Hirschman observes, is apt to have a political dimension. *Development Projects Observed* contains subtle typology of the different social and political implications that various projects entail.

Site-bound projects like mines and ports, for example, are unlikely to cause political rivalry between different local groups since there is usually only one place where a mine or a port can be located. A railway is potentially of more interest to a corrupt government official than a highway, since the former generates an income that can be siphoned off, and so on.

Mason and Asher, the two semi-official historians of the World Bank, also discern a political dimension to 'country' and 'sector leverage'. They write:

In the typical case... the Bank finds itself supporting certain elements in the government against others. This is but inevitable if the proposed policy changes are macroeconomic, and it is usually true if what is involved are changes in broad sectorial policies. Changes in monetary and fiscal policy affect the distribution of income; devaluation or changes in tariff rates benefit some to the disadvantage of others. Usually the various interests enjoy some form of political representation, and consequently the proposed policy changes become a matter of intra-governmental debate (Mason & Asher 1973, p. 434).

There is of course an important truth to this kind of analysis: no project can be 'politically neutral'; it always benefits some group in society. There exists, however, a further aspect of World Bank leverage besides the ones highlighted by Hirschman and Mason-Asher, namely that the policies it pushes for entail a specific form of national economic development.

'Leverage' is thus used by the World Bank to open up third world countries to foreign investments and to protect those investments against nationalization. This means that the Bank, like the Fund, in practice discourages third world countries from protecting their own economies and slowly building up a sound basis for national independence. A constant theme throughout the Bank's existence has been to discourage government control over the economy. The 'autonomous agencies' that the IBRD is so fond of constitute, for instance, one way of diminishing the political power of a country's elite. The Bank's demand for a small government budget and its hostility to 'overambitious' government investment schemes are some others. Many other consequences follow from the central aim of diminishing the economic power of the local government and safeguarding the interests of foreign investors. The trade-union movement, for example, is weakened by the massive government layoffs demanded by the Bank. The IBRD is not too fond of either decent minimum wages or of labor law legislation.

Every loan that the Bank grants, it should be noted, must according to IBRD's articles of agreement facilitate foreign investment in the country. The Bank's liberal attitude to foreign companies willing to invest in third world countries sharply contrasts with its hostility to all forms of government investments that do not favor outside economic interests. The Bank, for example, has supported the creation of free trade zones, which are of dubious value to the country that houses them and usually pose grave threats to the trade union movement (Payer 1982, p. 156).

5. Concluding remarks: The functional role of the doctrine of economic neutrality

We ask a lot of questions and attach a lot of conditions to our loans. I need hardly say that we would never get away with this if we did not bend every effort to render the language of economics as morally antiseptic as the language the weather forecaster uses in giving tomorrow's prediction. We look on ourselves as technicians or artisans.
—Eugene Black, President of the World Bank, 1962

In a certain sense no institutions which have come into existence as a result of deliberate political actions—as the Fund and the Bank have—can be said to be 'neutral'. Regardless of this argument, however, the capacity for 'economic neutrality' in the IMF and the World Bank has been threatened in mainly three ways: (1) through political pressures inside these institutions by the major Western countries; (2) through political pressures from outside the IMF-IBRD by these same countries; and (3) through the political pressures that the Fund and the Bank themselves have exerted on third world countries. The myth of 'economic neutrality' is, however, still actively maintained and even fiercely defended by the IMF and the IBRD (e.g. Bleicher 1970; Gold 1983). What are the reasons for this?

One reason is no doubt that the doctrine of economic neutrality is advantageous to IMF-IBRD's own interests as organizations. The more independent the Fund and the Bank are, the more powerful its officials will become. IMF and World Bank officials, as a consequence, have often tried to present their organizations as neutral and non-political. Susan Strange (1975, p. 24), when writing her history of international economic relations in the 1960s, quickly noticed that Fund officials 'have usually tended to avoid nasty political questions' and 'pretend (that) they do not exist'. Mason & Asher (1973, p. 477), in their history of the World Bank, also came to the conclusion that the IBRD preferred to avoid political questions: 'the Bank has rarely inquired in making a loan what the consequences are likely to be for income distribution, the political power of vested interests or the stability of a particular government'.

A second reason for the doctrine of economic neutrality being alive today and actively maintained is, no doubt, that some third world leaders prefer to hide behind its shield when it comes to announcing austerity measures. These can now much easier be presented as being instituted for neutral, non-political reasons. These leaders also know that when the World Bank and the IMF advance funds, these can be used to boost the economy for the moment—even if the economic future of the country is damaged in the long run (Payer 1974). In addition, loans corruption, weapon buying and similar uses.

In the final analysis, however, it matters little that the IMF and the World Bank want to be seen as 'neutral' and that some third world leaders believe or pretend to believe them. The doctrine of economic neutrality stands or falls according to what the most powerful Western nations can get out of it. Till now this doctrine has served them well, mainly by allowing these countries to intervene politically and economically in the third world in a way that is fairly inconspicuous. The IMF and the World Bank, in other words, can set demands that a single state could not do without being accused of interfering politically with another (e.g. Vaubel 1983, p. 299). When the US revived the Fund in the 1950s Per Jacobsson, IMF's managing director, understood that this was a good selling-point. As he put it in 1958: 'Since monetary discipline is exerted by changes in fiscal and credit policies, it would be politically difficult for the American authorities to try to exert direct influence—there could easily be accusations of dollar diplomacy' (Mason & Asher 1973, p. 543).

Twenty-five years later Paul Volcker (1983, p. 19) emphasized the same point when he appealed to the US Congress to pass an IMF authorization bill: '(the IMF) has legitimacy, as the agreed and politically neutral international vehicle for evaluating national economic programs'. The doctrine of economic neutrality, in brief, is still around because it serves the interests of some very powerful nations.

Notes

1. The doctrine of economic neutrality rests on a legal foundation as expressed in the articles of agreements of the Fund and the Bank. For the exact wording of the relevant passages as well as the historical context of the doctrine, see Swedberg (1985), pp. 1-12, 41-43.

References

Asher, Robert E. 1962. 'Multilateral versus Bilateral Aid: An Old Controversy Revisited', *International Organization*, vol. 16, no. 4, pp. 697-719.

Aubrey, Henry G. 1969. *Behind the Veil of International Money*. Princeton: Princeton University Press.

Bello, Walden 1982. 'Haiti: IMF or Duvalier—Choice Between Two Evils', *CounterSpy*, vol. 7, no. 2, pp. 13-16.

Bello, Walden, David Kinley & Elaine Elinson 1982. *Development Debacle: The World Bank in the Philippines*. San Francisco: Institute for Food and Development.

Bleicher, Samuel A. 1970. 'UN v IBRD: A Dilemma of Functionalism', *International Organization*, vol. 24, no. 1, pp. 31-47.

Block, Fred L. 1977. *The Origins of International Economic Disorder: A Study of United States International Monetary Policy from World War II to the Present*. Berkeley: University of California Press.

Gardner, Richard N. 1969. *Sterling-Dollar Diplomacy: The Origins and the Prospects of Our International Economic Order*. New expanded ed. New York: McGraw-Hill.

Girvan, Norman & Richard Bernal 1982. 'The IMF and the Foreclosure of Development Options: The Case of Jamaica', *Monthly Review*, vol. 33, no. 9, pp. 34-48.

Gold, Joseph 1969. *Membership and Non-Membership in the International Monetary Fund: A Study in International Law and Organization*. Washington, D.C. IMF.

Gold, Joseph 1983. 'Political Considerations Are Prohibited by Articles of Agreement when the Fund Considers Requests for Use of Resources', *IMF Survey*, May 23, pp. 146–148.

Harrod, R. F. 1951. *The Life of John Maynard Keynes*. London: Macmillan.

Hayter, Teresa 1971. *Aid as Imperialism*. Harmondsworth: Penguin.

Hirschman, Albert O. 1967. *Development Projects Observed*. Washington, D.C.: Brookings.

Horsefield, J. Keith 1969a. *The International Monetary Fund 1945–1965: Twenty Years of International Monetary Cooperation. Volume I: Chronicle*. Washington, D.C.: IMF.

Horsefield, J. Keith 1969b. *The International Monetary Fund 1945–1965: Twenty Years of International Monetary Cooperation – Volume III: Documents*. Washington, D.C.: IMF.

Krasner, Stephen D. 1968. 'The International Monetary Fund and the Third World', *International Organization*, vol. 22, no. 3, pp. 670–688.

Krause, Lawrence B. & Joseph S. Nye 1975. 'Reflections on the Economics and Politics of International Economic Organizations', pp. 323–342 in Fred Bergsten & Lawrence B. Krause eds. *World Politics and International Organizations*. Washington, D.C.: Brookings.

Mason, Edward S. & Robert E. Asher 1973. *The World Bank Since Bretton Woods*. Washington, D.C.: Brookings.

Mayer, Martin 1981. *The Fate of the Dollar*. New York: Signet.

Morrell, Jim 1983. *A Billion Dollars for South Africa*. Washington, D.C.: International Policy Report.

Morrell, Jim & William Jesse Biddle 1983. *Central America. The Financial War*. Washington, D.C.: International Policy Report.

Nissen, Bruce 1974. 'Building the World Bank', pp.35–60 in Steve Weissman, ed. *The Trojan Horse: A Radical Look at Foreign Aid*. San Francisco: Ramparts Press.

Payer, Cheryl 1974. *The Debt Trap: The International Monetary Fund and the Third World.* New York: Monthly Review Press.

Payer, Cheryl 1982. *The World Bank: A Critical Analysis.* New York: Monthly Review Press.

Petras, James & Morriss Morley 1975. *The United States and Chile: Imperialism and the Overthrow of the Allende Government.* New York: Monthly Review Press.

Schmitt, Carl 1976. *The Concept of the Political.* New Brunswick: Rutgers University Press.

Schweitzer, Pierre-Paul 1976. 'The International Monetary System', *International Affairs (England)*, vol. 52, no. 2, pp. 208–218.

Sid-Ahmed, Abdelkader 1982. 'The Conditionality of Drawings on the International Monetary Fund', pp. 111–184 in J. C. Sanchez Arnau, ed. *Debt and Development.* New York: Praeger.

Sohn, Louis B. 1964. 'Expulsion of Forced Withdrawal from an International Organization?' *Harvard Law Review* vol. 77, no. 8, pp. 1381–1425.

Strange, Susan 1972. 'International Economic Relation, I. The Need for an Interdisciplinary Approach', in Andrew Shonfield, ed. *The Anatomy of Influence: Decision Making in International Organizations.* New Haven: Yale University Press.

Strange, Susan 1974. 'IMF: Monetary Managers', pp. 263–297 in Robert W. Cox & Harold K. Jacobson, eds. *The Anatomy of Influence: Decision Making in International Organizations.* New Haven: Yale University Press.

Strange, Susan 1976. *International Monetary Relations*, volume 2 of Andrew Shonfield, ed. *International Economic Relations of the Western World 1959–1971.* London, Oxford University Press.

Swedberg, Richard 1985. *The Doctrine of Economic Neutrality of the IMF and the World Bank: A Case Study in Economic Sociology.* Uppsala: Department of Sociology Research report Series 1985:3.

US House of Representatives, Committee on Banking and Currency 1945. *Participation of the United States in the International Monetary Fund and the International Bank for Reconstruction and Development.* Washington, D.C.: US Government Printing Office.

Vaubel, Roland 1983. 'The Moral Hazard of IMF Lending', *The World Economy*, vol. 6, no. 3, pp. 291–303.

Volcker, Paul A. 1983. 'How Serious is US Bank Exposure?' *Challenge, May-June, pp. 11–19.*

World Bank 1983. *The World Bank Annual Report 1983.* Washington, D.C.: The World Bank.

The IMF Under Fire

Jahangir Amuzegar

The global economic challenges of the 1980s—the colossal debt overhang, wild swings in exchange rates, and continued imbalances in external payments—have presented the International Monetary Fund (IMF) with the immense task of devising orderly and effective solutions. And they have focused unprecedented attention on the organization. Thrown suddenly and inadvertently into the epicenter of the world economic crises after the 1973-1974 oil price shocks, the IMF has gradually, and erroneously, come to be seen as the world's master economic trouble-shooter. A limited-purpose organization, conceived in 1944 to deal with 1930s-style exchange and payments problems, the Fund has recently been pushed by circumstances into becoming a superagency in charge of the global debt and development problems of the 1970s and 1980s—tasks for which it has neither adequate expertise nor sufficient resources.

The IMF still enjoys the support and respect of many multinational economic organizations, bankers, business leaders, government officials, and academics in both industrialized and developing countries. But misconceptions and unrealistic expectations have prompted harsh and often distorted criticisms from other quarters, especially the media.

Initially confined to some left-leaning fringe elements in the Third World, recent attacks on the Fund have been echoed by a curious coalition—including some U.N. agencies—that defies both North-South and Left-Right divides.

Critics from the less developed countries (LDCs) and their supporters paint the IMF as a highly rigid, single-minded, biased institution dominated by a cabal of industrial countries. These critics accuse the Fund of following a narrow, free-market approach to external imbalances and contend that the Fund shows little or no concern that its adjustment policies often cripple economic growth and further skew income distribution in Third World countries. They also think that the IMF is cruelly indifferent to the social and political consequences of its stabilization programs.

Fund detractors in industrialized countries criticize the IMF for being insufficiently market-oriented; for helping noncapitalist and anti-Western countries; and for progressively evolving into a softheaded foreign-aid agency.

Some observers from both sides of the North-South divide claim that Fund-supported adjustment programs, by checking demand in many countries simultaneously, give a deflationary bias to the world economy as a whole.

Some skeptics see no useful role for the IMF under the present world economic order. A few believe that the Fund's existence blocks the Third World's economic interests; others argue that, in a world of floating exchange rates, the IMF—which was devised to ensure currency stability—has no part left to play. A hodgepodge of consumerists, religious activists, and neoliberals oppose the Fund because the IMF allegedly bails out big multinational banks, favors the rich, helps big business, and supports dictatorial regimes. Some old-line conservatives and free-market ideologues disapprove of the IMF because they generally oppose public intervention of any kind in the economy. And monetarist critics of the U.S. Federal Reserve Bank would like to dismantle anything that seems like an international central bank.

Originally published in Third World Quarterly, vol. 5, no. 2, 1983; reprinted with permission.

There are Western analysts who believe that Fund programs and facilities—increasingly tailored for and used by the LDCs—no longer benefit industrialized countries. Other radical critics, such as the political economist Cheryl Payer, believe that only a radical restructuring of the international economic system will solve today's international economic problems. They believe that Fund assistance frustrates the very type of economic discipline and financial autonomy LDCs need to break out of "imperialism's grip."[1]

Many analysts, by contrast, urge major reforms of the Fund. Some conservatives want the IMF to be stricter with borrowing countries. Their liberal counterparts emphasize creating a more Third World-oriented Fund.

Five aspects of the relationship between the IMF and its LDC clients dominate the debate over the organization: the Fund's philosophy and principal objectives; its approach to economic stabilization in deficit countries; the conditions attached to the use of Fund resources; the costs of domestic economic adjustment; and the IMF's alleged biases in the application of its policies and programs.

Critics accuse the IMF of deviating from its principles and objectives as contained in its Articles of Agreement. They include a call for "the promotion and maintenance of high levels of employment and real income." The Fund, they argue, favors internal and external stability in deficit member countries at the expense of economic growth and full employment. Most LDC-oriented critics would like to see the IMF facilitate capital flows and encourage stabilization and expansion of trade in the primary commodities that many Third World countries depend on for export earnings. Many also would like to see more IMF control over the creation, distribution, and management of global liquidity, and more Fund authority over worldwide capital flows, the domestic policies of reserve-currency countries, and external debt issues. The positions taken by the Third World blocs in the United Nations Conference on Trade and Development, the U.N. General Assembly, and the Fund's Interim Committee and its annual meetings point in the same direction.

These critics argue that at its birth, the Fund was expected to deal with problems of the developed countries. Since no major industrial country currently uses Fund resources or is expected to tap them in the near future, the Fund should now cater to its new, Third World, clientele.

The Fund staff rejects allegations of a vested interest in restoring external balances at the expense of other objectives such as employment and growth. The IMF maintains that its stabilization programs are designed to ensure domestic price stability and a sustainable external balance, and are, in fact, the very ingredients of increased domestic production, more jobs, and larger incomes. By improving the allocation and use of internal resources like capital and labor, Fund programs help a country increase its productive capacity over the long term.

Additionally, the Fund has adapted its role and its policies to the perceived needs of its LDC membership by developing special facilities such as the buffer stock financing facility, the extended fund facility, the subsidy account, the supplementary financing facility, the cereal imports facility, the Trust Fund, and the latest structural adjustment facility.

Defining Responsibilities

The debate here seems largely a matter of nuance and emphasis rather than basic philosophy. The Fund's argument is that, within the Bretton Woods framework for postwar stability and development, its global task has been to serve as a monetary and financial agency, dealing with short-term gaps in external payments, exchange fluctuations, and capital flows. Its added responsibility for economic expansion and larger productive capacity in the Third World, the IMF emphasizes, must be achieved by encouraging balanced growth in international trade and by evening out short-term capital movements, not by dispensing aid.

Economic stabilization under the IMF's standard "monetarist" model sees short-term external balance as a precondition for longterm growth. But many liberal critics insist that IMF programs must speed up economic growth and thereby achieve a viable balance of payments by stimulating supply instead of reducing demand. They believe that growth is a condition for adjustment.

According to these critics, the Fund's model subverts LDCs' development strategy in many ways. Essentially, they claim that the IMF view blames inflation on excess aggregate demand while the real culprits are structural bottlenecks in the agricultural, foreign trade, and public sectors; supply shortages due to unused capacity; and other nonmonetary problems common in developing countries. Thus combating inflation and external imbalances by choking off demand—by devaluing currency, reducing credit subsidies and imports, and raising taxes—results in depressing the economy instead. Economic stability requires removing supply bottlenecks by reallocating investment, cutting taxes, and somehow restraining prices and wages.

But the record of the IMF shows that as the nature and causes of the initial problems differ widely in different countries, so do the Fund's policy recommendations. A 1986 Fund staff study, *Fund-Supported Adjustment Programs and Economic Growth*, by Mohsin S. Kahn and Malcolm D. Knight, reiterates that Fund-supported adjustment programs comprise three distinct features: demand-side policies aimed at cooling an overheated economy, supply-side measures designed to expand domestic output, and exchange-rate incentives to improve a country's external competitiveness. For example, IMF programs in Gabon, Panama, Peru, and South Korea during the late 1970s and early 1980s did emphasize demand restraint. But similar programs in Burma and Sri Lanka encouraged an increase in the rate of public investment and the liberalization of imports. In Gabon, Panama, Peru, South Korea, and Sri Lanka, the objective was to increase supply by using excess capacity, improving external competitiveness, or boosting private or public investment.

According to a 1985 Fund report, *Adjustment Programs in Africa*, IMF staff members Justin B. Zulu and Saleh M. Nsouli show that IMF programs in 21 African countries strove to tailor each country's adjustment policies to that country's specific circumstances. While most programs aimed at increasing growth, reducing inflation, and improving balance of payments, considerable flexibility was shown with regard to budgetary deficits, credit expansion, inflation rates, and import volume. According to the same study, all stabilization programs in recent years have emphasized both supply- and demand-oriented policies. The former, addressing exchange rates, prices, interest rates, investment incentives, and efficiency of public enterprises, have all been conducive to growth.

A review of some 94 Fund-supported programs in 64 countries during the 1980-1984 period, prepared by Charles A. Sisson and published in the March 1986 issue of *Finance and Development*, shows a distinct variety of approaches to the adjustment problem and a wide range of policy measures. Although nearly all programs contained limits on credit expansion and government current expenditures, only 55 per cent included measures related to currency values and external trade liberalization; 41 per cent required a cap on or reduction in consumer subsidies; and a mere 25 per cent dealt with budgetary transfers to nonfinancial public enterprises. Even some of the Fund's more knowledgeable critics, such as the economist Graham Bird, clearly admit that "it is far too simplistic and inaccurate to claim that the Fund is a doctrinaire monetarist institution."[2]

Critics who concede that the Fund's primary objective is restoring short-term external balance still assail its approach to adjustment. They maintain that the Fund perceives LDC balance-of-payments deficits, foreign-exchange shortages, budgetary gaps, supply crunches, declining rates of productivity, inflation, and black markets to be largely of domestic origin—the result of economic mismanagement, overspending, exorbitant social welfare programs, and price controls. Domestic inflation and balance-of-payments deficits, in turn, are allegedly traced by the Fund to excessive consumption, insufficient investment, excessive import levels reflecting increased aggregate demand and caused by large budget gaps and loose credit, and anemic export earnings due to domestic inflation and overvalued currencies.

These critics maintain that LDC external imbalances are in fact frequently caused by a host of other external factors beyond LDC control that have nothing to do with domestic waste or inflation: oil prices, artificially stimulated rapid growth through easy credit, world-wide inflation, declining demand for commodities, deteriorating terms of trade and protectionism, rising real rates of interest on foreign debt, and poor harvests. The Fund is thus blamed for believing that deficits—no matter how they are caused—call for adjustment, and that adjustment must focus on the deficits, whether temporary or persistent.

The Fund is also often accused of identifying the adjustment's success with improvements in the trade or current account balance—an interpretation that the critics see not only as tautological but also as harmfully misleading. For improvements in the trade balance, they argue, result overwhelmingly from cuts in imports, not necessarily in big increases in exports. Such drastic and unsustainable cuts in foreign purchases not only limit LDCs' current and future output levels, they also hurt LDC trading partners, who end up losing markets. The real adjustment, say the critics, must be structural, involving such permanent changes as a shift in the composition of production and demand to boost export earnings and reduce dependence on imports.

The Fund's critics are right in claiming that it always insists on adjustment regardless of the nature or origin of the external balance. But the Fund also has an equally valid position in arguing that the need for adjustment is a pragmatic necessity, not the reflection of any dogma. In the March 1986 issue of *Finance and Development*, IMF Managing Director Jacques de Larosière observes that countries with soaring inflation, enormous fiscal deficits, huge and wasteful public sectors, money-losing public enterprises, distorted exchange rates, and low interest rates are unlikely to mobilize domestic savings or attract foreign investment, and are bound to crowd out domestic resources in a way that will hurt growth. Without adjustment, writes Fund staff member Wanda Tseng, external and internal imbalances eventually will deplete the country's international reserves, erode its international creditworthiness, dry up access to foreign funds, and result in the stoppage of needed imports.[3]

With regard to the origin of external deficits, Fund critics seem bent on constructing a general thesis out of isolated cases. Some, but not all, balance-of-payments gaps are clearly caused by factors outside a country's control. In the case of Jamaica, for example, even one of the Fund's most astute critics admits that during the 1972-1980 period domestic policies and structural factors were the prime culprits behind the excess demand and the worsening payments position. Nor was imported inflation found to be a "major cause" of the island's deteriorating economy. In general, the authorities declined to adopt unpopular adjustment measures necessitated by their own profligate fiscal and monetary policies. Another IMF critic attributed Indonesia's 1965-1966 crisis mainly to hyperinflation between 1962 and 1966 resulting from government deficit financing. Even in Kenya between 1974 and 1981, where major external factors—mainly the two oil shocks—were at work, domestic monetary forces and the mismanagement of the coffee and tea boom had to bear their share of responsibility.[4]

The critics, however, seem to have a strong point in arguing that, for most of the deficit-ridden LDCs, the external shocks of the 1970s and the early 1980s almost totally altered the fundamental assumptions on which their medium-term economic planning was based. A completely different type and direction of adjustment was required for many of these countries, such as a much bigger shot of capital and much more stimulation of supply, instead of routine belt tightening.

IMF Biases

A much stronger and more vituperative attack is aimed at the Fund's conditions for making its resources available. The main condition—a "viable" payments position—is defined as a current account deficit that can be sustained by capital inflows on terms compatible with a country's development prospects without resorting to restrictions on trade and payments, which add to rather than correct the existing distortions.

Almost all critics agree on the need for some conditionality. The quarrel, then, is about the types of conditions needed. At the macroeconomic level, the IMF's "draconian" approach and "shock treatment" are blamed for hindering economic growth, raising unemployment, lowering the already low Third World standards of living, ravaging the poorest of the poor, and seriously undermining the country's capacity for realistic adjustment.[5] Even in countries committed to adjustment and stabilization, the critics point out, formidable constraints—internal political friction, inadequate central financial control mechanisms, pressure groups or broader public resistance, and bureaucratic inefficiencies—make Fund measures hard to swallow.

Fund-prescribed microeconomic remedies are considered by the critics particularly ill-conceived, if not downright harmful. Devaluation is regarded as inherently regressive because it raises the costs of essential imports, leaves untouched exports subject to extremely low supply elasticities, and adds to domestic inflation. Higher interest rates are judged irrelevant in the context of Third World economies because so much credit goes to the public sector, because private savers are usually few and insignificant, and because capital flight has little to do with interest-rate differentials. Reduced real wages, lower subsidies for the poor, and cutbacks on other social welfare programs are regarded as the nemeses of sociopolitical stability. Credit restrictions are thought to reduce employment rather than inflation.

The IMF responds by arguing that conditions are neither rigid nor inflexible and that they are designed jointly with the member country. IMF conditions are applied flexibly as well, with varying socioeconomic circumstances taken into account. The periodic review of

Fund programs confirms the agency's interest in ensuring sufficient flexibility. Further, the IMF's approach to balance of payments does not work only through demand deflation and real-income reduction. The relationship between monetary factors and external imbalances is important, but the IMF approach embraces all aspects of economic policies, bearing on both demand and supply conditions. Finally, although restoring the external balance is admittedly a Fund objective, it is not the sole purpose of adjustment. The IMF believes that adjustment ultimately encourages high employment and long-term growth by balancing aggregate demand and supply better.

Fund programs are also often blamed for their allegedly high social and economic costs. The critics argue that, despite its best efforts, the IMF can hardly avoid politics. National strikes, riots, political upheavals, and social unrest in Argentina, Bolivia, Brazil, the Dominican Republic, Ecuador, Egypt, Haiti, Liberia, Peru, Sudan, and elsewhere have been attributed directly or indirectly to the implementation of austerity measures advocated by the IMF.

The companion charge of undermining national sovereignty and political democracy in Third World countries follows from the social frictions and imbalances that austerity allegedly brings. LDC governments add that the Fund does not quite appreciate the political risks involved in applying the IMF recipe.

Conditionality is also thought to undermine fair income redistribution. The argument maintains that the Fund's adjustment programs almost always require a cut in both public and private consumption, in order to transfer resources to investment and the export sector. Critics frequently argue that the heaviest and most immediate burdens of adjustment are likely to be passed by the upper and middle classes to the poor. The Fund's alleged insistence on reducing or eliminating food and other consumer subsidies is further attacked on the ground that these policies are in fact a rational means of internal income redistribution in countries lacking an effectively progressive tax system or adequate social security schemes.

Fund supporters argue that blaming the IMF for fomenting political unrest merely confuses cause and effect. Many countries do not come to the IMF until the seeds of political turmoil are firmly rooted in their soil. Indeed, economics-related civil disturbances are hardly unknown in countries without Fund programs—witness Iran, Nigeria, South Africa, and Tunisia. And scores of countries adjusting with the IMF's assistance have been remarkably stable. Of the 67 countries that carried a stabilization program at some period between 1980 and 1983, critics can single out only the 10 mentioned previously as having experienced serious turmoil—not all of it Fund-related. Nevertheless, the unrest that can be blamed on the IMF must be considered a minus for adjustment policies.

Finally, the Fund is charged with harboring biases toward capitalism and against government planning and economic intervention. Worse, it is called an agent of neocolonialization for the West. More moderate critics accuse the Fund of an ideological slant that results in the scrapping of public enterprises, the abandonment of price controls, the reduction of food subsidies and free medical and educational facilities, and the elimination of social services from already deprived populations.

The Fund is also alleged to discriminate in its treatment of poor and rich members. LDC supporters claim that the Fund opposes as distortions of the free market such policies as exchange restrictions, wage-price controls, rationing, and subsidies when pursued by the developing countries. Yet the IMF is virtually impotent in the fight against similar practices by its industrial members. Critics additionally see a perceived asymmetry in treatment between reserve-currency centers (and surplus countries) on the one hand and the rest of the world on the other. This asymmetry is considered not only inconsistent in itself, but also crucial in shifting the onus of adjusting external imbalances to deficit LDCs. Reserve-currency countries like the United States, it is alleged, cannot be pressured by the IMF to adjust, and can continue their profligate ways year after year.

Finally, critics see an IMF political bias that is reflected in sympathy and leniency toward regimes pivotal to the economic, military, strategic, or geopolitical interests of the United States or other major Fund shareholders, and toward countries with international economic clout because of enormous debts that threaten the global monetary system.[6] To prove this political bias, critics such as staff members of the Center for International Policy claim that proposed IMF loans to "countries from the wrong side of the track," including Grenada before the U.S. invasion, Nicaragua, and Vietnam, have been vetoed by major shareholders for "technical reasons." Credit for others, such as El Salvador and South Africa, is routinely approved.

Yet Fund members today include countries with distinctly nonmarket philosophies. Any penchant toward the market simply reflects the belief that market allocations are more efficient. On the question of discriminatory treatment of the poor, the dividing line is not poverty but the balance-of-payments situation. Surplus or reserve countries may indeed escape the Fund's strict discipline. After all, they have no need for Fund resources. But this is a choice open also to poor countries, which can decide not to approach the IMF. Further, some of the rich deficit countries that have drawn on the Fund in the past, such as Great Britain, France, and Italy, have been similarly treated.

It is no secret that the IMF statutes and covenants expect the Fund to promote a world of free markets, free trade, and unitary exchange rates under a multilateral payments system. To allow any different course of action would place the IMF in violation of its legal mandate.

Yet not only do such centrally planned economies as China, Hungary, Romania, and Yugoslavia enjoy full IMF membership and make ample use of its resources without any encumbrances or impositions, but some left-of-center governments, in fact, have in the past benefited more from Fund assistance than supposedly favored regimes. By one key measure, Jamaica, under then Prime Minister Michael Manley's democratic socialist regime in 1979, was the world's largest recipient of Fund resources, receiving 360 per cent of its quota compared with only 64 per cent for other developing countries.[7]

The Fund adamantly maintains that its Articles of Agreement specifically prohibit political considerations for the use of its resources. Yet the charges of political bias deserve closer scrutiny. The Fund's ability to maintain absolute neutrality is, to be sure, affected by the interests of influential member governments, by the decisions of the executive board to grant or deny loans to a given country, and by the evaluation reports and recommendations of staff missions on a country's underlying economic conditions.

Major shareholding governments obviously have political, strategic, and economic interests in their own zones of influence or involvement and do not wish to separate economic from political and other considerations. The U.S. Congress, for example, explicitly requires that the American executive director at the Fund vote in a prescribed manner in regard to certain countries and regimes. Other major governments may have similar predilections, but are not quite prepared to legislate them.

The executive board has a mixed position. Its members are appointed or elected by developed or developing member governments, to whom they are beholden. They, too, cannot be purely apolitical robots. They lobby for their views among their colleagues; they try to win over management and staff; and they endeavor to protect the political and other interests of their constituencies. At the same time, board members are required and expected to uphold the Fund's basic objectives and to ensure the proper functioning of the international monetary system. In neither of these two capacities can the executive directors as a whole be found to be practicing a distinct, or immutable, political bias. The burden of proof is still on the critics to show that many IMF decisions are made deliberately according to political considerations. Significantly, the IMF staff has never been accused of partisan political bias.

The issue of inherent bias against the poor is more intractable. In general, allegations that the Fund's reluctance to suggest specific national redistributive priorities is of no help to the poor and the powerless may have a certain moral validity. It is also true that the objective of better income distribution, or at least of proportionate sacrifices, is not explicitly included in a country's letter of intent as a condition for Fund assistance. But claims that the IMF is indifferent to such factors are grossly unfair.

More important, the critics' ardent contention that the cost of adjustment is always borne disproportionately by the poor has seldom been supported by any statistical evidence. Rather, there is usually an a priori presumption that Fund programs aggravate income inequities because the rich and the strong see to it that they avoid the effects of the stabilization measures. The arguments have been at best theoretical, and usually anecdotal. The countless books, articles, speeches, and statements critical of the Fund contain not a single piece of empirical information or statistical data showing that Fund-supported programs have, in a clear and convincing manner, aggravated internal income-distribution patterns.

Moreover, the impact of IMF programs on income distribution essentially depends on how the program is implemented by national authorities. In the Fund's view, any other approach would entangle the IMF directly in microeconomic policy measures closely related to a country's social and political choices. Such involvement probably would be vehemently resisted by most countries, and would also violate the Fund's own mandate and guidelines.

In addition, the Fund believes that changes in income distribution as such cannot be performance criteria in adjustment programs because this area is so difficult to quantify. The numbers can be affected by methods of classifying income recipients. Further, few programs last long enough to allow a comprehensive study of their distributional implications, particularly where necessary information on consumption, government transfers, non-monetary sources of income, and personal income levels is inadequate or unreliable—as is generally the case in developing countries. Finally, the Fund maintains that any given domestic distributional system is the product of deep-rooted economic, social, political, and cultural phenomena going back decades, if not centuries. Fund programs, being of relatively limited scope and duration, cannot be expected to make much of a dent in the system.

In the absence of clear-cut evidence and good data, theoretical arguments do assume importance. In the short run, stabilization programs can worsen income distribution. But the story scarcely ends there. The distributional outcome of a cut in government outlays, for example, depends on where the specific reductions are made. A reduction of food subsidies to urban workers could help the rural poor by raising farm prices. A tax on urban services and amenities could likewise redistribute income from workers in modern industries—a minority in the labor force—to the rural poor. Moreover, a reduction in inflation itself tends to favor poorer groups because they can rarely adjust their incomes to rising prices.

A forthcoming IMF study, *Fund-Supported Programs, Fiscal Policy, and Income Distribution*, concludes, after presenting some case studies, that Fund programs have not been directed against the poor; often, in fact, policies have been designed to protect low-income groups as much as possible. Even when total consumption has been reduced through prudent demand-management policies, high-income groups probably have been hit hardest. The elimination of large general subsidy programs has inflicted some hardships on the population as a whole, including the poor. But the study calls such programs "inefficient and ineffective" mechanisms for redistributing incomes.

Some Success Stories

Some Fund detractors are quick to denigrate the IMF's achievements in the Third World and cite Mexico's current crisis in particular as a blatant example of the failure of the adjustment formula. More moderate critics admit that Fund programs have succeeded in improving the balance of payments in several countries. But they contend that other significant benefits have not followed.

Yet the overall track record of IMF programs shows some noteworthy accomplishments. An independent 1984 study by the German Federal Parliament, *The Conditionality Policy of the IMF*, shows that although the current account deficits of all non-oil-developing countries (NODCs) tended to expand between 1970 and 1980, most Fund-assisted countries managed to close those gaps perceptibly. The inflation rate for all NODCs increased during that period, while the tempo in countries with adjustment programs was slower. Countries undergoing adjustment experienced sharper decreases in short-term growth than the group as a whole, but their long-term expansion rates were above average. Finally, the report noted, the increase in real consumption in program countries was only slightly less on average—4.3 per cent as opposed to 4.7 per cent annually—than in the whole group.

According to the aforementioned 1985 IMF study of the 21 African countries where the IMF had an ongoing program from 1981 to 1983, economic growth targets were achieved in about one-fifth of the countries, inflation targets were reached in roughly one-half of the cases, and the balance-of-payments goals were reached in about two-fifths of these states.

At first glance, improvements under Fund-supported programs may show that the IMF's advice is often better suited to containing inflation and rectifying external imbalances than to fostering growth. But some short-term consolidation in the growth tempo may in fact be necessary for longer-term expansion. And although the success stories may not be numerous or seem spectacular or even truly impressive to the hostile critics, they nonetheless tend to contradict the allegations that Fund programs bring few, if any, benefits to LDCs. Moreover, these detractors frequently fail to ask where these countries would be without the IMF.

Still, it is disturbing that, despite its valiant rescue efforts across the Third World, the IMF is hard pressed to show more than a few clearly viable programs out of the roughly three dozen under its wing. Why haven't the programs done better?

One answer is that the IMF's latest perennial clients have been among either the poorest LDCs with large balance-of-payments disequilibriums, or the newly industrializing countries with gargantuan external debts. Adjustment has been made more difficult by outside factors such as high energy costs, high interest rates, world recessions, and protectionism.

Second, IMF programs often bring some concealed problems into the open, making partial success look like a setback and partial recovery like a retrogression. In a country living beyond its means, the real causes of payments difficulties—such as overvalued currencies, artificially low prices, and virtual rationing, as evidenced by shortages and black markets—are rarely acknowledged. When Fund programs begin to remove some of the existing distortions and dislocations through cost-price adjustments, the economic weaknesses that these policies hid or suppressed begin to emerge for all to see.

Third, the worse a country's problems, the harder it will be for IMF programs to succeed. The host government's cooperation is crucial as well. A 1984 Fund study showed a 'striking" correlation between the success of IMF programs and the observance of policy measures by the governments concerned.[8]

Fourth, most of the Fund-assisted countries that have been less than successful are those that had long postponed adjustment efforts. As stabilization is delayed, distortions become solidified, and rectification becomes correspondingly costlier and more painful. It literally pays economically, socially, and politically to go to the IMF early.

In no other North-South debate has the so-called dialogue of the deaf been so evident as in that over the IMF. The biggest reason for the critcs' persistence is surely the Fund's patchy track record. The increasing number of cases where disbursement of standby credits has been suspended because of noncompliance with Fund criteria, and the growing number of members declared ineligible for further assistance because of long overdue financial obligations, show that the path of the Fund-supported programs has been neither short nor smooth.

Indeed, in spite of prolonged use of Fund programs by certain members, economic imbalances persist for many internal and external reasons. Fund successes in other countries also have often been temporary.

But if the IMF cannot or will not influence domestic priorities, such as the size of military budgets or the pattern of income distribution, that have a major impact on the economy, why, the critics ask, impose an austerity program that skirts these problems? The same question is prompted by the IMF's inability to do much about external problems, such as protectionism or foreign recessions, that lie beyond the control of deficit LDCs and that can often make or break a country's prospects. If the IMF's conditional assistance produces no more than certain short-term improvements in the country's external balances and some temporary reductions in the rate of inflation at the cost of growth, full employment, social welfare, and self-reliance, is it worth the attendant sacrifices?

Convincing answers to these questions are not easy to come by because all these critical inquiries seem to miss two crucial points. First, what other choices do LDCs facing deteriorating debt and development problems have? Second, putting aside the merits of the critic's arguments or of the Fund's defense, are there other practical and effective policies that the IMF, as presently constituted, can pursue?

Debt-strapped countries incapable of paying their external bills and unable or unwilling to adopt Fund-supported adjustment programs have three alternatives: repudiate external debt altogether and seek to start afresh; seek bilateral accommodations with bondholders; or go it alone.

An outright repudiation, or even a debt moratorium, obviously, would release resources for more urgent outlays. But it might close off larger and more valuable access to foreign reserves, assets, credits, markets, and technology. For this reason, even the poorest African countries assembled for the July 1985 Organization of African Unity summit refused to endorse any suggestion of wholesale default. Nor did Cuban Premier Fidel Castro's similar proposal for Latin America attract any takers.

The second alternative is appealing, but except for a very few lucky and resourceful countries, foreign creditors usually ask LDC debtors to accept the Fund's discipline before engaging in debt renegotiations or extending new credits. The consequences of doing nothing, the third alternative, would be further economic deterioration and perhaps a need for stricter adjustment efforts. In the Fund's view the costs of nonadjustment by any measure will probably greatly exceed those of adjustment.

The IMF, in its turn, can adapt to external realities and the critics' challenges in four ways: by increasing its resources and expanding both the scope and the number of its special LDC facilities to serve its Third World members better; by revising its rules and statutes to become more adjustment-oriented toward its developed members and comparatively more finance-directed toward LDCs; by abdicating its structural adjustment role in the LDC economies in favor of the World Bank; or by doing nothing.

A Fund with twice as much liquidity could accommodate its LDC members with less painful adjustment programs. The Fund also could revise its rules to improve more decisively its role in overseeing the exchange-rate system, its surveillance capabilities over the surplus and reserve-currency countries, and its management of international liquidity.

The Fund staff has already recommended improvements in the design of adjustment measures in favor of low-income groups. These include exchange-rate changes that provide adequate incentives for the agricultural sector dominated by small farmers, greater access to domestic credit markets, taxation of global income, expansion of tax bases, replacement of quotas by tariffs, and the provision of basic skills and vocational training for unemployables.[9]

In addition, the Fund could get out of medium-term or Extended Facility financing—activity that may duplicate the World Bank's structural adjustment loans. This step would free the Fund to concentrate on its exchange-related functions and operations.

The fourth alternative—and perhaps the easiest—is for the Fund to do nothing. But the status quo includes the current and thorny problem of the repayment of the Fund's past loans, some of which are now technically in default. Without fresh efforts and initiatives, the number of countries in arrears will steadily rise. Further, the continued attacks on the Fund, if not properly dealt with, may further tarnish and distort the Fund's image, discourage some member governments from seeking badly needed IMF help because of domestic political opposition, and weaken and erode world public support for the Fund's surveillance, guidance, and assistance.

Meanwhile, the difficulty for the IMF in adopting any of the first three alternatives remains its members' inability to agree on either the need for fundamental revision of the current trade and exchange regime or the nature of critical procedural changes in the system's implementation. Most developed countries repeatedly have rejected such basic Third World proposals as a system of target zones for keeping major currencies in leash, a doubling of IMF quotas, larger LDC access to Fund resources, periodic issues of the Special Drawing Rights (SDRs), the IMF's reserve currency, a link between SDRs and development finance, a grant to LDCs of 50 per cent of the vote on all Fund decisions, the reactivation of the Trust Fund for fresh lending to poorer countries, and the establishment of a new interest-rate facility.

And the LDCs deem unacceptable such rich country suggestions as giving greater publicity to the outcome of Fund consultations with members, extending the techniques of enhanced surveillance, assuring that commercial banks continue to play a big role in providing international reserves, and increasing World Bank-IMF collaboration in the design of conditionality.

No realistic compromise is yet in sight, except for possible elaboration of the Baker plan. Memories of the past create the uneasy feeling that, without a major new financial crisis, the Fund's principal shareholders and their bankers may not have enough incentive to accommodate poorer countries. Some concerned observers actually believe that such a crisis is already on the horizon. Averting disaster requires genuine debtor-creditor cooperation—no matter which side has a more valid position or better arguments.

Any new initiative must synthesize the positions of the two groups. The chances of reaching this consensus, in turn, would be greatly enhanced if the sparring partners could agree upon several fundamental postulates. First, LDC debtors must admit that the bulk of their credit needs must be reasonably conditioned. The debtors must also be willing, in exchange for fresh inflows of foreign credit, management, and technology, to adopt certain genuine domestic economic reforms.

The industrialized creditors must accept the fact that no matter how economically necessary adjustment conditions are, they must be politically palatable and operationally feasible and must offer a clear promise of growth in addition to economic stability. Also needed are improvements in the workings of the international exchange system, a multilateral trading regime where the handicaps of different players are properly reckoned with, and a system of resource transfers based on both country needs and global competitiveness. Such measures as multi-year reschedulings of debts, the reduction of interest rates, or some eventual debt write-offs might be part of the solution.

Serious North-South negotiations in the framework of the forthcoming meetings of the Fund's Interim Committee and the joint Bank/Fund Development Committee—or a new global monetary conference—may offer new possibilities for such an approach. Without them, the expectations of critics and the Fund's capacity to meet these expectations will remain far apart. The persistence and poignancy of the attacks on the Fund—and eventually on the World Bank, once its inevitable conditionality begins to bite—will further damage the prestige and influence of both organizations at a time when their involvement in the Third World is more necessary than ever to ensure global economic stability and growth.

Notes

[1] See, for example, Cheryl Payer, *The Debt Trap* (New York: Monthly Review Press, 1975).

[2] Graham Bird, "Relationship, Resource Uses, and the Conditionality Debate," in The Quest for Economic Stabilization ed. Tony Killick (New York: St. Martin's Press, 1984), 179.

[3] Wanda Tseng, "The Effects of Adjustment," *Finance and Development*, December 1984, 2-5.

[4] Jennifer Sharpley, "Jamaica, 1972-80," Mary Sutton, "Indonesia, 1966-70," and Tony Killick, "Kenya, 1975-81," in *The IMF and Stabilization* ed. Tony Killick (New York: St. Martin's Press, 1984).

[5] See Chuck Lane, "Dunning Democracy," *The New Republic*, 4 June 1984, 9-12; and Richard E. Feinberg and Valeriana Kallab, eds., *Adjustment Crisis in the Third World* (Washington, D.C.: Overseas Development Council, 1984).

[6] See, for example, Amir Jamal, "Power and the Third World Struggle for Equilibrium," in *Banking on Poverty: The Global Impact of the IMF and World Bank* ed. Jill Torrie (Toronto: Between The Lines, 1983); and Ismaïl-Sabri Abdalla, "The Inadequacy and Loss of Legitimacy of the IMF," *Development Dialogue*, 1980, no. 2: 25-53.

[7] Sharpley, "Jamaica, 1972-80," in *IMF and Stabilization*, 160.

[8] Justin R. Zulu and Saleh M. Nsouli, "Adjustment Programs in Africa," *Finance and Development*, March 1984, 7.

[9] Charles A. Sisson, "Fund-Supported Programs and Income Distribution in LDCs," *Finance and Development* March 1986, 36.

Third World Debt

The World Bank publishes annually in March *World Debt Tables, External Debt of Developing Countries*, which provides an overview of the debt situation of 107 reporting countries, evaluations of developments in the global economy, trends in lending to developing countries and problems of, and proposals for managing the debt problem. In addition there are detailed statistical tables showing the debt situation for each reporting country.

We reproduce here three excerpts from the 1985-86 edition. First a table of the debt renegotiations between 1975 and 1985, which shows a detailed break-down between official government and private debt rollovers. The Paris Club consists of creditor governments meeting to collectively renegotiate official debts and credits owed to them by Third World debtor countries. The "Club" has been meeting and negotiating debts since 1956. Commercial banks also meet and collectively negotiate reschedulings of debts owed to them by Third World governments in what has come to be called the London Club. The London Club reschedulings typically consolidate repayments ranging from six to nine years, including two to four years grace. Interest charges vary from a margin of 1 7/8 to 2 1/2 points over the London Inter Bank Offering Rate or LIBOR (the preferential rate at which banks lend to each other). The rescheduling is normally accompanied by a commission of 1 1/4 to 1 1/2 %. It should be emphasized that both the London and Paris Club debt reschedulings involve short-term debts; hence the need for frequent negotiations.

The second excerpt, "The Changing Character of Financial Markets" demonstrates the fluidity and rapidity of change in world finances that is currently taking place. It also shows that the Third World share is relatively small, except in syndicated lendings (Paris and London Clubs).

The third excerpt, "Debt Service and Growth", illustrates the difficulties of managing debt repayments for 17 of the most heavily indebted countries.

Multilateral Debt Renegotiations, 1975–85
(U.S.$ Millions)

	Number of Renegotiations 1975-85	1975-81		1982		1983		1984		1985		
Country		Paris Club	Commercial Bank	Paris Club	Commercial Bank	Paris Club	Commercial Bank	Paris Club	Commercial Bank Signed	Paris Club	Commercial Bank Signed	Commercial Bank Agreed In Principle
1. Argentina	3		970							(2,000)	(16,600)	
2. Bolivia	2		444									(536)
3. Brazil	3					(3,478)	(4,532)		(5,350)			
4. Central African Republic	3	55				(13)		(14)				
5. Chile	4	216					(3,400)	(176)[c]			(6,000)	
6. Costa Rica	4					97	1,240			(166)	(299)	
7. Dominican Republic	3						497			(296)		(787)
8. Ecuador	5					(200)	(1,835)		(590)	(400)	(4,475)	
9. Equatorial Guinea	1									(29)		
10. Gabon	1	105[a]										
11. Guyana	3		29		14							(27)[f]
12. Honduras	1											(220)
13. India	3	436[b]										
14. Ivory Coast	3							(218)		(229)	(558)	
15. Jamaica	6		229					(106)	(164)	(70)	(193)	
16. Liberia	6	55			27	18		(17)				(71)
17. Madagascar	6	142		103				(146)	(195)	(135)		(78)
18. Malawi	3			24		(30)	59					
19. Mauritania	1									(77)		
20. Mexico	3					1,550[c]	(23,625)				48,725[d]	
21. Morocco	4					1,225	475			(1,000)		(530)
22. Mozambique	1							(200)				
23. Nicaragua	4		770		102				(145)			
24. Niger	4					33		(39)	28	(32)		
25. Nigeria	2						2,006	(924)[c]				
26. Panama	2									(15)	(603)	
27. Pakistan	1	263[b]										
28. Peru	6	478	821			(450)	(380)	(1,000)	(936)			(1,415)
29. Philippines	2										(5,567)	
30. Romania	4			(234)	(1,598)	(195)	(567)					
31. Senegal	6	77		84		64			(97)	(105)	(22)	
32. Sierra Leone	4	68						88		(142)		(25)
33. Somalia	1									(142)		
34. Sudan	6	373	638	174		502		(179)			(230)	
35. Togo	7	262	68			114	74	(51)		(22)		
36. Turkey	5	4,696[b]	5,740		(22)							
37. Uganda	2	(56)		(22)								
38. Uruguay	2						(815)					(2,000)
39. Venezuela	1											(20,750)
40. Yugoslavia	6					(988)[d]	(1,586)	(750)[c]	(1,246)	(625)[c]	(3,605)	
41. Zaire	7	2,168	402			(1,317)				(383)		
42. Zambia	3					(285)		(164)	(74)			
Total	144	9,450	10,111	641	1,741	10,559	41,091	3,894	8,813	5,916	86,877	26,439

Note: Data cover arrangements formally completed in 1975-85 plus commercial bank reschedulings agreed in principle but not completed in 1985. Figures indicate renegotiated amounts as reported by the countries or, if in parenthesis, as estimated by staff members. Cuba and Poland, which also renegotiated debt-service payments with official creditors and commercial banks, are not members of the World Bank and therefore are excluded from this table.

a. Denotes an agreement of a special task force.

b. Denotes an aid consortium agreement.

c. Technically this was an agreement of a creditor group meeting, not a Paris Club.

d. Includes debt of $23,625 million previously rescheduled in 1983.

e. Denotes an agreement with suppliers on uninsured short-term trade arrears. Amount includes only promissory notes issued through 1985.

f. Denotes agreements deferred until negotiations with the IMF are finalized. Amount includes principal due from April 1983 through July 1985.

Source: World Bank, *World Debt Tables, 1985-86*, Washington DC, 1986, pp. xiv-xv. Reprinted with permission.

The Changing Character of Financial Markets

Pronounced changes have reshaped the character of international capital markets since 1982. Commercial banks now play a less direct role as intermediaries in lending, while the flow of funds through international security markets has increased. The dramatic speed and scale of these changes are shown in the table below.

Events since 1982 essentially comprise a second stage in the deregulation of the international financial markets, the first having begun in the 1970s with the rapid increase in private international capital movements. Deregulation in the 1970s was largely an "offshore" phenomenon. Banks were allowed to accept international deposits and to lend abroad under minimum regulation. By contrast, domestic financial and credit markets, and access to them, remained closely regulated. As a result, a large share of private international investment was attracted into the banking system, stimulating the growth of syndicated lending in order to spread risk and exposure. Deregulation of offshore markets in the 1970s thus facilitated lending to developing countries, which was limited only by the intermediation risk banks were willing to bear—no serious constraint before 1982.

In the 1980s, deregulation has come "onshore" to domestic credit and financial markets. Nowhere has this movement proceeded as fast and as far as in the United States, but it is general. At the same time, investors' preferences have changed, turning away from bank deposits toward marketable instruments. Deregulation abetted the transformation, as access to the major securities' markets of the world opened to overseas investors after a series of fiscal changes, including the abolition of interest withholding taxes in mid-1984 by the United States, followed by others. Parallel changes broadened borrowers' access, especially to the bond markets of the two largest balance-of-payments surplus countries, Japan and the Federal Republic of Germany.

New funding techniques, including financial futures trading and swaps and a fast-changing array of investment instruments, have revolutionized international security dealing. Commercial banks have played an active role in promoting these changes. Pushed by increased competition for their traditional business concerned with increasing both their profits and their own funds rations, they have aggressively moved to off-balance sheet assets and other commission-generating business. Particularly important among the new techniques are various forms of note issuance facilities, which offer fees and commissions to the banks, highly liquid assets to investors, and medium-term lending to borrowers.

The full significance of this transformation of financial markets will take many years to emerge. The new techniques may prove no more devoid of risk than the euroloans of the 1970s, which had seemed to shift all risks to the borrowers. Nevertheless, in the long run, developing countries should benefit from the greater liberalization and integration of domestic and international financial markets. A more diversified flow of investment capital, from a wider range of sources and in a variety of new forms, should help stabilize their external financing. For the time being, however, access is restricted. Among developing economies, only Algeria, China, Greece, Hong Kong, Hungary, India, the Republic of Korea, Malaysia, Portugal, and Thailand were notably successful issuers in the capital markets in 1984-85.

The Changing Use of Financial Instruments, 1982-85
(U.S.$ Billions)

Year	Syndicated Lending[a] Total	To Developing Countries[b]	Fixed Rate Bonds Total	To Developing Countries[b]	Floating Rate Notes Total	To Developing Countries[b]	Note Issuance Facilities Total	To Developing Countries[b]
1982	98.2	40.5	60.4	2.2	15.3	1.9	5.4	1.8
1983	67.2	32.2	57.6	0.8	19.5	1.8	9.5	0.7
1984	57.0	22.8	73.3	1.0	38.2	2.6	28.8	6.2
1985[c]	32.9	13.8	78.2	1.4	43.0	4.2	27.4	2.5

Note: All data exclude merger-related standbys and renegotiations.
a. Includes "new money" arranged under reschedulings of 1983, 14.3; 1984, 11.1; 1985, 5.0.
b. Classification of developing countries does not conform exactly to that in the *World Debt Tables*.
c. First nine months only.
Source: OECD, *Financial Market Trends*, October 1985.
Source: World Bank, *World Debt Tables, 1985-86*, Washington, DC, 1986, p. xix. Reprinted with permission.

Debt Service and Growth: Seventeen Heavily Indebted Countries

The table below illustrates the experience, since 1980, of seventeen heavily indebted countries. These countries account for nearly half of all developing countries' debts: $446 billion out of $950 billion at the end of 1985. Of this amount, they owed over 80 percent ($360 billion) to private creditors, mostly at variable interest rates. For the four largest borrowers in this group, total debt and the share owed to private creditors were $291 billion and 88 percent, respectively.

In 1982, in the wake of Mexico's difficulties, most of the other countries in this group failed to meet scheduled debt-service payments. Voluntary lending to them dried up, resulting in a striking reversal of their financial relationship with their creditors. In 1980, their receipts of resource inflows from long-term loan disbursements exceeded their debt-service payments on those loans by about $9 billion; in 1984, they paid $20 billion more to lenders in debt service than they received in new long-term loans, despite reschedulings and the accumulation of arrears. This turnabout required a shift in their trade balances from a surplus of $4 billion in 1980 to one of around $42 billion in 1984. Had these countries' imports merely stabilized rather than fallen, the growth of world trade in 1982-84 would have been one-third faster.

To engineer such a radical shift in net resource flows in so short a time required sharply reduced expenditures—in both consumption and investment. It entailed much immediate loss of income, as the overall reduction in expenditures and incomes was generally a multiple of the needed increase in the net surplus. Effective expenditure-switching measures take time to implement and to produce results. Their success has been limited by the deteriorating global environment in 1985 and by the cumulative effects of lower investment, down more than a third in four years.

This pattern is not sustainable. Quite apart from the effect that large trade surpluses have on protectionist pressures in the creditor countries, the highly indebted countries cannot run continued surpluses of this magnitude and simultaneously establish the conditions for the growth needed to secure debt-servicing capacity in the longer term. Investment must be increased, at the same time allowing for a gradual elimination of some of the cuts imposed upon consumption in the past few years. For that, the debtor countries need either to devote a lower proportion of their domestic savings to debt service or get more foreign savings to complement them.

As holders of close to three-quarters of these countries' debt, commercial banks must find most of the external finance required to supplement the countries' own savings. But so long as debt service continues to absorb such a large share of the indebted countries' resources, voluntary new lending will not amount to much. The solution lies in resumed growth, which will gradually lighten the relative weight of debt servicing. Growth, in turn, will not occur without a collective effort by banks, bilateral and multilateral agencies, and creditor governments to extend new financing, accompanied by heightened efforts to improve economic policies by the countries themselves.

Seventeen Heavily Indebted Countries

Country	Debt Outstanding, 1985[a] Total (U.S.$ bn)	Of Which Private Source (percent)	Debt Service, 1985-87[b] (U.S.$ billion) Total	Of Which Interest	Debt Ratios 1985 (percent) DOD/GNP	Interest/XGS[c]	Trade Balance, 1984[d] (U.S.$ billion) Total	Change from 1980	Average Annual Growth Rates, 1980-84[d] (percent) GDP	Exports	Imports	Investment	Per Capita Consumption
Argentina	50.8	86.8	20.4	12.7	71.9	25.4	3.9	5.3	-1.6	3.6	-14.7	-16.8	-2.7
Bolivia	4.0	39.3	1.6	0.6	121.1	43.0	0.3	0.1	-4.7	-1.7	-15.8	-22.1	-7.8
Brazil	107.3	84.2	39.7	28.0	49.7	38.2	13.1	15.9	0.1	10.8	7.3	-8.6	-1.2
Chile	21.0	87.2	9.2	5.0	126.9	42.9	0.3	1.1	-1.4	0.7	-4.2	-11.6	-2.1
Columbia	11.3	57.5	6.4	2.5	36.8	16.4	0.3	0.6	1.8	0.8	2.4	2.4	-0.1
Ecuador[c]	8.5	73.8	3.4	2.1	91.5	24.8	1.1	0.8	1.1	2.6	-13.7	-16.9	-2.3
Ivory Coast	8.0	64.1	4.0	1.4	135.4	18.4	1.3	0.9	-2.3	1.3	-8.8	-19.5	-6.6
Jamaica	3.4	24.0	1.3	0.5	238.5	12.5	-0.3	-0.2	1.3	-2.5	-2.1	9.5	-1.4
Mexico	99.0	89.1	44.4	27.2	60.9	34.1	12.8	15.6	1.3	10.5	-14.5	-10.1	-1.4
Morocco	14.0	39.1	6.0	2.4	111.4	12.7	-1.4	-0.1	2.5	4.1	-1.0	-2.7	-0.2
Nigeria	19.3	88.2	9.1	3.1	22.9	12.1	3.0	-8.2	-4.7	-13.3	-12.1	-19.3	-4.3
Peru	13.4	60.7	5.2	3.1	97.9	7.9	1.0	0.2	-0.7	-0.6	-10.8	-5.3	-3.7
Philippines	24.8	67.8	9.5	4.9	76.1	12.3	-0.7	1.3	0.8	3.6	-4.8	-12.4	0.0
Uruguay	3.6	82.1	1.4	0.8	72.7	21.8	0.2	0.8	-3.7	2.2	-11.3	-20.2	-4.7
Venezuela[e]	33.6	99.5	17.8	7.8	73.3	10.4	8.0	-0.2	-1.8	-3.8	-19.3	-15.6	-6.4
Yugoslavia[f]	19.6	64.0	13.6	4.0	44.1	12.4	-1.2	3.7	0.6	-0.6	-8.1	-2.9	-0.5
Total	445.9	80.8	194.9	106.9	58.8	23.5	41.6	37.8	-0.3	1.8	-9.2	-9.7	-1.8

a. Estimated total external liabilities, including the use of IMF credit.

b. Debt service is based on known long-term debt and terms at end-1984. It does not take into account new loans contracted or debt reschedulings signed after that date.

c. Based on estimated interest actually paid on total external liabilities in 1985.

d. Latest year for which data are available. Growth rates are computed from time series in constant prices, using beginning- and end-period values.

e. The merchandise trade balance for 1984 is not available; the value shown is for 1983.

f. Average annual growth rates are for 1980-83, except for GDP which is for 1980-84.

Source: World Bank, *World Debt Tables, 1985-86*, Washington, DC, 1986, p. xxv. Reprinted with permission.

Leadership and Cooperation

James A. Baker, III

The problems of trade and debt can be dealt with only in a healthy world economic environment. To create such an environment, we have sought to advance a strengthened framework for international economic cooperation and balanced growth.

Our leadership has taken a form different from that of recent historical experience. The recent model has been one of national dominance in an international economic system—as represented by the United States in the aftermath of World War II, or by Britain in the latter half of the 19th century. Our new leadership is more in the manner of an architect and builder, patiently but tenaciously pursuing a vision of economic growth and prosperity—trying to persuade others what may be accomplished while contributing our fair share.

Over the course of the last 15 months, we have made some headway:

- In September, 1985, the G-5 nations agreed to measures to achieve exchange rates better reflecting economic fundamentals. The currency adjustments that followed should help rectify major trade imbalances among our countries.

- In March, 1986, the G-5 nations coordinated a reduction in central bank discount rates to promote more rapid global growth.

- In April, the G-5 nations, absent Germany, implemented a second round of discount rate cuts.

- In May, the seven leaders of the industrialized nations meeting at the Tokyo Summit agreed to new arrangements for closer policy coordination.

- In September, the G-7 Finance Ministers conducted the first multilateral surveillance exercise under the Tokyo Summit accord.

- In October, within about a month of our G-7 review, the United States and Japan announced a set of mutually reinforcing actions, including an economic stimulus package and another discount rate cut to promote Japanese growth and reduce external imbalances; we also agreed that the yen-dollar rate realignment since the plaza Accord was broadly consistent with the present underlying fundamentals.

These 6 steps are only a start. We need to build on them while keeping our expectations within reasonable bounds.

Text of the speech given be the Secretary of the Treasury to the US Congressional Summit on Trade and Debt, New York, December 4, 1986.

Developing Nations' Debt: 3 Conceptual Approaches to the Problem

The program for Sustained Growth seeks to solve the debt problems of developing nations in a way that is also comprehensive, realistic, and cooperative. But there are 2 competing conceptual approaches that warrant attention. In explaining why we have rejected these alternatives, perhaps I can further explain what we are about.

The first alternative is characterized by significant debt forgiveness across-the-board for debtor developing nations.

Such a debt write-off will preclude the debtors from gaining access to credit markets for years to come—including vital trade finance. Moreover, this alternative overlooks that the problem is not the level of debt, but the ability to service it. The fact of the matter is that the investments in many developing nations are not earning their way. So a big part of the solution must be to improve the productivity of investments.

Both the debtor nations and the lending institutions would be damaged severely by this counterproductive approach. The internal funds that would be saved by reducing debt service would fall far short of the developing nations' needs. Having forced losses on commercial banks, it would be naive to think that future loans would be forthcoming. External capital would be available only at prohibitive prices, if at all. The losses to lending institutions could lead to a serious reduction of capital, possibly producing a credit contraction endangering borrowers at home and abroad.

An across-the-board reduction would forgo the benefits of case-by-case actions to secure critical economic policy changes within debtor nations. These policy changes are fundamental to debtors' abilities to generate earning power for investment and achieve sustainable growth.

In addition, it is inappropriate for the government unilaterally to force private financial institutions to sustain losses. Any adjustment in debt that may occur should be negotiated in the context of policy reforms. And such proposals would substantially reduce tax revenues at a time of budgetary restraint.

The second conceptual alternative is what I describe as the "Marshall Plan" model. It envisions great infusions of funds into debtor nations—whether from nations with trade surpluses or a new international body.

The notion of additional capital transfers is appealing. But the parallel to Europe after World War II is not apt. For all of the destruction of 1945, Europe retained the infrastructure of an economy that could put capital to work quickly and efficiently. Perhaps most important, Europe had tremendous experience with the operations of a market exchange system.

Once Europe moved painfully beyond assuring basic survival, capital and security became the only missing components. The United States supplied external security and start-up capital. Soon private capital followed or was retained—because the potential for a good return on it was evident.

In contrast, the prognosis for returns on investment in developing debtor nations is not so evident today—unless some new investment is combined with vital market-oriented policy changes. Without these reforms it is unrealistic to assume that many debtors can either attract or effectively use great infusions of Japanese, German, or American private capital: The risk-return calculation will not send the right signal yet. Nor will public funds alone supply the investment necessary for sustained growth. And public lenders acting outside the private incentive structure may not be able to achieve the fundamental shift to enhanced reliance on markets and private initiative.

Our efforts have been directed at a middle course between these two alternatives. We want to achieve structural policy changes that will make debtor nations more hospitable for future investment—both domestic and foreign. We are spurring the creation of the economic infrastructure for sustained growth in a competitive international environment.

It's plain to see that we are not talking about a "quick-fix" of the debt burden. Lasting economic hope for the developing nations requires major, durable reforms. These improvements in economic climate will not take place overnight. As much as we would like to accelerate their progress, we must acknowledge the constraints posed by politics, history, culture and sociology—as well as by the local economies. Each nation's limitations and potentialities are different—and approaches to address them must differ as well.

Under this strategy, the debt burden takes on a different face. It, too, is a limitation—but not the sole problem. Indeed, generalized debt relief may be counterproductive, because it could not be employed as an incentive linked to the achievement of individually tailored and timed domestic reforms.

Some incremental public and private funding is of course necessary while nations undertake basic economic policy improvements. But this transitional funding must be tied to the achievement of structural reforms that will improve the debtor nations' ability to service their debt. With time, and at different paces, these countries can create risk-return profiles to attract totally voluntary private capital.

Status of the Program for Sustained Growth

Many debtors are already taking important steps toward increasing savings and investment, improving their economic efficiency, and encouraging the return of flight capital and privatization of public enterprises.

The International Monetary Fund and the World Bank have an important role to play in this process. They can assist by promoting adjustment policies and longer-term structural changes within the debtor countries. The IMF has established formal programs or letters of intent for such programs with nine of the major debtors and set up enhanced surveillance programs with three others. By the end of this year, all the major debtors except Brazil and Peru will have entered into formal programs or surveillance agreements with the Fund.

The World Bank is supporting a range of market-oriented policy changes in developing countries with medium and shorter-term adjustment loans. To date, it has negotiated $3.7 billion in new policy-based loans with 10 of the 15 major debtors, and it has discussions underway with these nations for an additional $5 billion in lending.

Commercial banks are also gradually moving to support the comprehensive adjustment programs of the debtor countries. The recently completed loan agreement with Mexico combines several innovative approaches by both commercial lenders and international institutions. The arrangement of this loan represents a major achievement against the long odds of a dramatic drop in oil prices, a horrendous earthquake, and resultant financial and social problems.

An agreement has also just been reached for a $320 million commercial bank loan to Nigeria. A number of other financing packages are anticipated for Argentina, Chile, and Morocco (as their IMF/World Bank negotiations are concluded). Since October 1985, over $75 billion in debt reschedulings have been negotiated with commercial banks.

This is a start—a good one. We hope for further progress, but realistically recognize it must be gradual and will vary among nations. The prize is great: a new international economic marketplace creating prosperity through active commerce, investment, and entrepreneurial vigor.

Encouraging Equity Investments

There has been much attention given recently to the possibilities for increasing the share of equity investment in developing nations, whether through debt-equity swaps or other means. We have welcomed this interest. When we unveiled our initiative in Seoul, we pointed out that equity investment is particularly beneficial because it has a degree of permanence and can have a compounding effect on growth.

Indeed, given our strategy of seeking policy reforms to encourage investment, we envision that some day developing nations will be able to offer numerous attractive risk-return combinations for the equity investor. For now, I expect the risk-return match remains too unappealing to transform most investments from debt into equity. At the margin, however, there is much business to be done.

Roughly $2.5 to 3.0 billion of debt conversions have taken place over the last 2 years— some into equity, others into local currency instruments. The process in Chile provides an outstanding example of how smoothly debt conversions can proceed. The corporate sector has benefited from recapitalization, local capital and money markets have been strengthened and deepened by foreign investor participation, and portfolio and direct investment has been drawn by new opportunities. Chile is well on its way to converting $2 billion of its $19 billion of foreign debt to equity by early next year.

Mexico also appears to offer fertile ground. A U.S. auto manufacturer recently converted over $100 million of outstanding Mexican debt into equity shares of its Mexican subsidiary. Most of the Proceeds will be used for new plant and equipment, although the subsidiary used a portion to pay off high-cost local credits from Mexican banks.

There are ample opportunities for innovation. A new debt/equity swap structure—being tried in the Philippines—invites creditor banks to pool loan claims in a debtor country and then exchange them for shares in a newly established closed-end mutual fund. That fund will convert loans into equity claims on local enterprises with good profit prospects.

I expect we have only begun to see what useful exchanges can be arranged by investment and commercial banks. We urge more creativity and variety. The range of specialized needs among nations will parallel, on a smaller scale, the particularized reform and lending packages on which most debtors will have to rely for a time. And I am confident the quality of both financing ventures will improve.

A Perspective on Trade

This group is well aware of the myriad linkages between debt and trade, as well as of their common connection to growth. But the bonds do not necessarily form the basis of some grand policy that will correct all problems. Instead, we need specialized prescriptive actions on a number of fronts. We should recognize the interconnections, but not search endlessly for an all-embracing "solution."

Our trade policies reflect our commitment to the realistic, cooperative, and comprehensive approach:

- In concert with some nations, we have moved toward exchange rates that should help correct trade imbalances, and we are pursuing that end with more nations.

- We are working with our industrialized partners to coordinate actions to achieve more rapid and balanced global growth.

- In Uruguay, our GATT negotiators pressed successfully for a new round with updated rules to encompass agriculture, services, investment, and intellectual property rights.

- We are pursuing key bilateral talks with Japan in the MOSS negotiations and with Canada in the free trade area negotiations.

- We have attacked unfair trade practices aggressively. President Reagan is the first President to initiate Section 301 cases. Our active enforcement has produced results with a number of countries.

- And we have insisted on trade liberalization reforms in developing nations as part of our debt strategy.

An effective and comprehensive trade policy must also be concerned with improvements at home:

- It's debatable whether there is a link between the Federal deficit and the trade deficit, but it is reasonable to be concerned about the Federal deficit in any event. Most outside economists, the CBO, and others believe the deficit is now moving in the right direction. Even if you assume pessimistic economic forecasts and we miss the Gramm-Rudman-Hollings targets, Congress has put measures in place to lower the 1986 fiscal year deficit of $221 billion to roughly $170 billion in FY 1987—or to about 3.7 percent of our GNP. This will bring our public sector deficit-to-GNP ratio down to among the lowest in the Summit country group.

- We also have sought to ameliorate costly legal restraints through reforms of anti-trust and product liability laws.

- Finally, we need a thorough examination of the basis of our competitiveness, including scrutiny of some subjects that may be sensitive: the state of our educational system; the structure and management of businesses; restraints to competition; the opportunities for working men and women to profit from their employers' success; the causes of our low savings rate; our ability to enhance productivity; our commitment to R&D in different institutions—and this list goes on.

These are major challenges. To be effective, we will need to broaden the base of support for renewed competitiveness. There are many places to recruit. "Neo-liberals," traditional market-oriented conservatives, supply-siders, and many others know that protectionist proposals, however dressed up, are nothing more than government guardianship for the established few at the expense of the many who are striving. These groups can help us make government, business, and labor more competitive.

So I am convinced that working in good faith and in a bipartisan way with the new leaders of the 100th Congress—men like Jim Wright, Bob Byrd, Lloyd Bentsen, and Dan Rostenkowski, among others—we can craft responsible legislation that will enhance America's international competitiveness without resorting to protectionism.

Problem Debtors at Home

We know that a competitive United States needs to be alert to the problems of debtors and lenders at home. Treasury has been attentive to domestic financial challenges. These policies are part of our set of initiatives to support self-help reforms for the various systems that channel credit to borrowers.

At the beginning of this year, the Treasury outlined a comprehensive program to help the $1 trillion savings and loan industry and its depleted deposit insurance fund, FSLIC. The keystone of this proposal is a bill to recapitalize FSLIC's modest reserves, so that FSLIC can devote about $25 billion over five years to handle the hundreds of so-called "brain-dead" insolvent S&Ls still operating. Although delay will add to the cost of resolution, the Congress failed to pass this recapitalization legislation (passed separately by both the House and Senate) because the bill was tied to controversial items. We hope for action early next year to safeguard about $800 billion of Americans' deposits in S&Ls.

An important feature of the FSLIC recapitalization is its reliance on funds from the industry itself, through the Federal Home Loan Banks and the capitalization of future insurance assessments. By stressing self-help, we hope to increase the industry's receptivity to complementary actions that will enhance its long-run health. In addition to strengthening FSLIC, we must:

- attract more capital and management expertise—in part through making acquisitions of failing S&Ls more attractive to more businesses—both to strengthen troubled S&Ls and lower FSLIC's resolution costs;

- require financial reporting in accord with generally accepted accounting rules and establish higher capital standards; and

- match new profit-making authorities with appropriate supervision.

At the end of 1985, the Treasury also designed, with the Agriculture Committees, a reform package to steady the $70-plus billion Farm Credit System—so it could try to save itself. The FCS has suffered from, and continues to struggle with, the legacy of poor lending and business practices, exacerbated by a weak farm economy in some regions. The 1985 legislation changed the FCS's regulator, the Farm Credit Administration, from a partner and cheerleader into an independent supervisor. It also created a central Capital Corporation empowered to transfer the billions of dollars of the FCS's earned surplus to local FCS lenders. And the Act included a possibility of future government help, subject to appropriations, if FCS's truly best efforts at self-reliance turn out to be insufficient.

The FCS has absorbed billions of dollars of losses and is not out of the woods yet. Yet our actions have kept the market open to its debt at attractive spreads to Treasuries. We are giving the FCS an opportunity to use its new self-help tools. Our past efforts, and those we may need to take in the future, will aim to make FCS an independent, business-like operation, not a ward of the government.

We also have devoted attention to the problems of commercial banks heavily involved with agricultural and energy loans. In 1986, we brought the banking regulators together on a capital forbearance policy for basically sound energy and agricultural banks with a large amount of problem loans. We developed an emergency acquisitions bill with the bank regulators to ease restrictions on out-of-state purchasers of failing banks. If a bank is going to fail, the community it serves and the financial system are helped if it can be reopened as part of another bank. This legislation died in the waning hours of the 99th Congress.

We will keep at these problems in 1987. And we are reviewing other financial developments to assess their effects on systemic efficiency, competition, service, and safety. We hope the new Congress will work with us to rectify financial problems at home in a fashion congruent with the reforms the U.S. seeks overseas.

Conclusion

Last October the United States proposed a partnership among the developing nations, the international financial institutions, and the commercial lenders. We promoted mutual incentives for joint and comprehensive action on the problems of slow growth, weak investment prospects, and burdensome debt payments.

Problems still persist. Debtors will have to take the difficult steps to improve the environment for investment. They must enhance economic freedom to gain its profits. But the developed countries can do much to help this transition.

Our governments can adopt policies that bolster a growing world economy and an open trading system. We need to offer a set of tailored measures and opportunities to integrate the developing nations into a competitive, productive world market. And private parties can contribute many of the ideas, arrangements, and capital—specifically designed to serve particular needs.

This is not a time to call retreat from our responsibilities and fortune. The cost would be great to people around the globe—and to our children as well. We have a chance to offer practical leadership. I'm sure we will.

Society and Business after the Great Reshedulings:

A Futuristic Essay

Henry S. Bloch

Historically, most of the nations of Europe defaulted at one time or another, as have some American states and cities. In the 1980s the problem of indebtedness is primarily the indebtedness of the developing nations, the South, to the developed nations, the North. As the needs of the North have undergone a major change, so the newly industrialized countries (NICs), who as a group constitute the major debtors, have also been forced to change.[1] It is difficult to adapt to a changing world as long as world trade remains sluggish and hampered by barriers.

The financial disaster in debtor nations is both visible and enormous. While bankers must look at the rescheduling process as a major accounting problem, the idea is to delay write-offs as long as possible and to space them as much as permissible in order to avoid crises of confidence. Thus, the reality of payment expectations conflicts with the balance sheet appearance and the damage to the lender is not always immediately and not always entirely visible. Cosmetics cover some of the scars some of the time. Meanwhile, capital ratios of banks are improved and reserves against losses are shored up. The events of the 1970s and 1980s reduce the availability of external loan financing; hence the general austerity situation which has been introduced in debtor countries as the result of rescheduling will not be short-lived even if specific austerity measures by governments will be mitigated.

The state's capacity as borrower and lender will be weakened. Government guarantees against losses and low interest loans will become rare. A certain dogmatism will give way to pragmatism. While domestic loan and equity financing, both public and private, will have to play the primary role, foreign equity investment will be more favorably received than in the past.

Foreign equity investment will enter, however, only if it receives rewards commensurate with risk and if the possibility exists to transfer dividends and interest, and eventually to divest. At present the cheapness of assets is the principal element of attraction and these other conditions have not yet been fulfilled. Therefore, the few countries with a significant private sector and industrial base will be the countries that "take off" in the post-industrial age.[2]

The social consequences of austerity will be serious. One of the great social weaknesses in developing nations is the enormous gap between rich and poor. Many of the rich, evading exchange controls, have expatriated their capital and often themselves. Whenever there are cheap assets and misery, some will seize opportunities for enrichment. These will be the *nouveaux riches*.

Published by permission of the *Journal of International Affairs* and the trustees of Columbia University in the City of New York. Originally published in *Journal of International Affairs*, vol. 38, no. 1, Summer 1984.

Even the middle classes, which can be a stabilizing element, will suffer. Their base in developing countries will be eroded by emigration and the "déclassement" of the lower middle class, which has fewer assets. Fragile political structures in developing countries will be more threatened by continued economic decline. This essay will address the broader impacts of the Great Reschedulings on business and society.

Financial Flows in the Post-Industrial Age

In the 1970s and 1980s the world's industrial structure shifted as a result of technological change, changes in labor and energy costs, and the replacement of heavy basic materials such as steel and copper with lighter ones. These technologies and social changes have aggravated the structural problems of the developing countries, further complicating their attempts to increase exports. The developing nations were caught in a world recession cum inflation, which has had a particularly negative effect on their cost of money and exports, while making their imports more expensive.

As a result of the changes produced by the technological revolution, Japan and the United States emerged as the leading industrialized nations, with Europe trailing, and the developing nations far to the rear. Recent developments in the Pacific Rim show that it is possible for individual NICs to buck this trend, but it requires enlightened leadership in industry, highly developed manpower and, yes, a fairly flexible free enterprise system.

There is no likelihood in the 1980s of a massive capital inflow or heavy domestic investment in developing countries. The more difficult the situation, the lower the level of domestic investment and the higher the volume of capital flight. The gap between developing and developed nations will continue to increase. Even if the world economy grows at a sharply greater rate, massive capital investment in the developing nations will not be produced. It is precisely this insufficiency of capital investment that is retarding the European recovery in general, and the French economy in particular. As of this writing, even the American recovery is not producing what Federal Reserve Chairman Paul Volcker considers an adequate level of capital investment. How, then, can the required new capital investment be secured for the developing nations?

The financial transfers from industrialized to developing nations are not going to be sufficient for sustained growth. Domestic savings cannot fulfill the need for meaningful development. The conclusion is that in most developing nations there will be a period of slower growth than in the past two decades. The reduction of available capital imposes new roles on both the state and the private sector.

The State as Financier

Historically, governments in many developing nations have acted as the principal financiers of economic development. They were not only borrowers themselves but acted also as a conduit for loans to private enterprise. This happened in part, because governments in developing nations had easier access to foreign loans than did private enterprise. Many of the lenders assumed that sovereign risk was better than non-sovereign risk. Lenders relied on the concept, not necessarily wrong, that the state had greater access to financial resources than the private institutions. This became evident in Mexico when the United States made $3 billion available to the central bank of Mexico under a swap agreement in the form of $1 billion in Commodity Credit Corporation credits, $1 billion advance purchase of petroleum for the Strategic Reserve, and $1 billion in U.S. Treasury credit which was combined with International Monetary Fund (IMF) assistance of close to $1 billion.[3] Using the state to guarantee financial resources led to a lack of financial analysis when the purpose of lending to governments was to make a given project or enterprise financially viable. Inadequate financial analysis was sometimes also due to the fact that the real purpose of the loan was camouflaged. An example is Fundidora de Monterrey, a Mexican steel company that defaulted in 1981. At that time the Mexican government obtained a loan which in turn was used to bail out a company which, for all intents and purposes, was bankrupt.

Austerity and Society

Where debts were rescheduled, austerity programs were implemented in varying degrees, more or less following the guidelines prescribed in IMF stand-by arrangements. There still is widespread resistance by governments to the entirety of IMF demands. The reasons are socio-political. In March 1984, both Argentina and Rumania cancelled their IMF Agreements because the conditions were too harsh. In Egypt, the IMF backed down after street demonstrations erupted under Sadat following the implementation of IMF conditions for stand-by arrangements.

What is the situation now in those countries, mainly in Latin America, where austerity programs have been introduced? In Mexico, Brazil, Argentina, Chile and the Philippines, there is a large, powerful and politically articulate urban middle class which made great gains in the 1960s and 1970s. In Brazil, Mexico and in all newly industrialized countries, the middle class as a group is a large minority. The middle class is a phenomenon which has become significant only in the last decades — hence it is an emerging middle class.

Collective proletarian memories linger on in all the developing nations where there is poverty in workers' families and where much of middle class life is often only one step from misery. The ill-developed safety net of social benefits has resulted in a contradiction between the appearance of middle class life and reality. While fragile and vulnerable, the middle class is a major factor in developing nations and especially in NICs. The relatively greater economic fragility of the middle classes in developing nations makes proletarianization in times of economic distress a real danger. Will there be a large number of dispossessed as a result of austerity? If so, how will these dispossessed, deprived middle class persons react to the political turmoil unavoidable during periods of changing regimes, and compounded by prolonged austerity? Would this class voluntarily allow privileges and putative claims to be taken away? Would it, in the interest of possible future benefits, accept an austerity program in spite of strong resistance by parts of the population?

In Marxist terms, most developing nations have a *Lumpenproletariat*. No classic working class proletariat exists, however, that can stop the functioning of nations. The unions in some countries can, but are they a classic proletariat as Karl Marx observed it in the 19th century, or are they privileged in a society where the majority of the population is poorer than the unionized workers?

Is it a mitigating factor that in most developing countries the middle class has experienced a greater decline in real income than the poorer strata? On one hand, the middle class is politically more articulate and better able to resist. On the other hand, they also have a better understanding than the uneducated of why there is a need for governments to engage in austerity programs.

The middle class has an interest in the existing social order. They read the papers and think in a longer term than the poor who are literally forced to live from day to day. Above all, the middle class fears revolution, while the poor, the dispossessed, have little to lose.

Although many of the more affluent members of the middle class sabotage government programs with capital flight, dislike austerity, talk against it and write against it, the middle class so far does not militantly or effectively oppose austerity measures. In fact, austerity measures taken so far have been met with a remarkably weak reaction. The severe fall in social and economic well-being, particularly in Brazil and Mexico, may still, however, provoke sharp reactions by the majority of all classes. There is considerable apprehension, quite openly articulated, about further concessions if the general economic situation does not improve.

Perhaps the European model may serve as an illustrative example. In some countries unemployment is extremely high—20 percent in Belgium, 18 percent in Holland—and the unemployed are given a stake in the status quo with high benefits. This teaches one caveat: to maintain political stability, do not cut aid to the poor too deeply. In most developing countries, aid to the poor takes the form of bread subsidies and other subsidies for basic foodstuffs. This is particularly relevant in the highly inflationary situation that prevails in many developing nations. It is precisely in the category of subsidies for staple foods that austerity measures can create wounds difficult to heal and provide the litmus test for a developing country's regime. In Lima, a Marxist mayor was elected in November 1983 on the simple promise to provide free milk for children.[4]

In many of the developing nations, the middle class has a large representation in public sector employment where budget cuts are ferocious and will probably become even more so. One question is whether an intellectual proletariat will emerge. This does not seem likely, because revolutionary movements have lost credibility among the more educated public servants and intellectuals since they also have been engulfed by the middle class — the bourgeoisie.[5]

As appointments in the public sector become more scarce and less lucrative, the younger offspring of the bourgeois families will increasingly seek entry jobs in business and the private sector. Those who cannot get jobs—but who possess some capital and a modicum of initiative —will often become small entrepreneurs. Whether or not this is meaningful in enlarging the entrepreneurial stratum has not been ascertained.

Emigration has provided a safety valve for ambitious middle class persons who can establish themselves in more favorable economic climates. This is part of the middle class reaction to austerity and it is, indeed, harmful to the developing nations. As the expectations of the majority of the population—the poor and middle classes—remain unfulfilled, and as it becomes increasingly evident that debt service will continue to take its toll of social well-being, there will be resistance. There may be declarations of moratoria. That might not be the worst of all solutions, depending upon timing and particularly the mutuality of the arrangement.

Austerity and Business

Make no mistake about it: in its present form, stale capitalism has failed in all "rescheduling" countries.[6] On the whole the existing concepts of the state as capitalist, producer, trader and financier are questioned, as is the theory of unfettered free enterprise. The disastrous results of a laissez-faire economy in the case of Chile have become unfairly symbolic of the failure of the Milton Friedman formula. There are, of course, possible forms of public enterprise which do business on a fairly conservative debt/equity ratio basis according to commercial principles. They have been tested with uneven success in Latin America and somewhat more effectively in Europe.[7] Many, though not all of the older Latin state enterprises have been badly hit by the debt crisis. It is too early to assess the state takeover of commercial banking by Mexico—directly in the wake of payment difficulties and capital flight—in terms of efficiency. So far, Mexico has been successful in this activity and as it did guarantee the debt of these banks, the rumble of outrage by foreign bankers has died down.

Developing nations were bled more severely by high interest rates than they would have been by even a very large percentage of foreign ownership. The axiom stressing that interest and principal on debt have to be paid regardless of whether there are profits or losses, but that dividends and other business earnings have to be paid only when there are profits has only occasionally been emphasized in developing nations.[8] It should now have become clear that nonpayment of interest and principal of loan capital leads to considerable infringements on sovereignty and to political confrontation. Equity investment can confer certain immediate powers to the foreign investors, but payment is not expected if there are no earnings.

Most Latin American intellectuals and some politicians are ideologues. Many are followers of the essentially social democratic system of economic programming —what the French call indicative planning—which Raúl Prebisch propagated brilliantly through the United Nations Economic Commission for Latin America (ECLA). A few of these intellectuals are Marxist on the Cuban model. There are not many disciples of Milton Friedman.

As a result of the purist models having failed to live up to expectations, a period of pragmatism is now emerging. This pragmatism must include continued controls and state ownership, but the state must also provide opportunities to entrepreneurs. A form of mixed-economy will continue to prevail. Political sophistication on the part of business requires living with controls. Financial sophistication on the part of government requires understanding the limits of regulation and of debt. Politically, old labels are not dead. The new social democracy is simply more pragmatic than old social democracy. Neo-liberals and neo-conservatives are essentially more pragmatic than old-style liberals and conservatives. Pragmatism is not suited to the temper and mental makeup of the *Cepalinos* (the teams of *Comisión para América Latina*) and the Oxbridge or Paris trained technocrats. Nor does it come easily to the Chicago business school students steeped in Friedmania.

Pragmatism is, however, no problem for the MBAs from most other American schools, unburdened by *Weltanschauung* or ideology. Quite a few of these students will return to the developing nations and bring their gospel of profits and net worth. A pragmatic approach may even work if governments possess enough compassion to compensate for what the new breed may lack in this realm, if only to avoid discontent and disorders. Large-scale unemployment will remain endemic for a long time to come and the challenge, therefore, will be how to feed these people.

Pragmatism does not mean a return to the halcyon days of the United Fruit Company in Central America, or to the old-style copper companies in Chile, or Rio Tinto in Bolivia. As the elementary truth is emphasized that reward for equity will be paid only if the cash flow permits it, investors in general and even major multinationals may find a less hostile climate than in the past. While the climate may be more friendly, the multinational companies are now more cautious and frequently coexist peacefully with the state.[9] Dividends and interest, however, are difficult to remit, and many of these companies are hurt by their creditors' insolvency in countries forced into economic decline.

Private enterprises are often indebted to foreign banks, to their own domestic banks and to the government. Declining currency values and galloping inflation make it attractive for domestic and foreign investors to have a high debt-equity ratio because their loans are repaid with cheapened currency. This contributed to the debt crisis and widespread failures of private business indeed preceded the governments' debt reschedulings. On one hand, the need for disclosure was limited and the toboggan slide toward insolvency was exacerbated (for example, the Grupo Alfa in Mexico). On the other hand, the state was always there with subsidies, loans and other means of support until the house of cards collapsed.

A friendly investment climate, however, means not only the regulatory environment but also the societal environment. While it is one thing to ask firms to adapt themselves to a flexible regulatory environment, provided the regulations are intelligently implemented, it is another to ask them to adapt themselves to corrupt societies. The latter do not appeal to "desirable" investors. In the future, the state will have to allow profits, and profits should be commensurate with risk. The state, however, should not be obliged to underwrite losses.

Venture Capital Financing

Economically, without a doubt, there is a forceful argument, that foreign equity investment is preferable, *en principe*, to foreign loans. There is even the possibility that some of the private sector debt and even some of the state enterprise debt might eventually be converted into equity capital. Such investment will be regarded as high risk, and high risk investment requires high reward. In fact, such investment will be perceived by some as a form of venture capital. In rare instances in Europe, even the state has acted as a venture capitalist in partnership with private enterprise.[10]

In addition to established multinational corporations, in addition to banks which are not risk-averse, specialists in high risk, especially venture bankers, may eventually turn to the developing nations. Some different species of domestic venture banking firms will arise in those countries. It is irrelevant whether the species will be similar to those in the United States or different, the U.S. form is not necessarily applicable. It is not the form but the substance of the formula which is relevant. Note also that venture bankers have not yet become truly multinational and that multinational venture banking has first to be tested in the developed world before there will be expansion into the developing nations.

Having become very effective in the United States especially since the 1960s, the American form of venture capital has not shown itself suitable for export. Whatever venture capital financing has taken place in Japan or Europe has taken a different form from that used in the United States. Yet the principles are the same and must be the same in developing nations: professional identification of investment targets, strict financial, technical and economic analysis, the use of effective business plans, professional monitoring of investment, the combination of skill and judgement with the injection of capital, reward commensurate with risk, and the possibility of divestment after a decent interval.

In most developing nations, what is awkwardly called "country risk" will be perceived to add a major element to business risk. The domestic financier in a developing nation has often used his ingenuity in transferring funds abroad and therefore measures his investment at home against his foreign investments.

One clearly visible emerging phenomenon is that assets in Mexico, Brazil and a number of other NICs are very, very, cheap. Even in some of the Pacific Rim countries, there has been—for good reason—a collapse in the value of assets. In many of these countries, assets are cheap because the cash flow they generate is not necessarily freely transferable and convertible. Until divestment possibilities exist, foreign investment will remain difficult to come by.

Conclusion

The reschedulings per se are not major events in the course of world history. But they are significant rites of passage in the financial history of borrowers and lenders. The causes which underlie the reschedulings are more than maladjustments in the international financial system. They are deeply rooted in post-World War II economic development patterns and the use of financial tools to achieve them. The effects of the reschedulings have already accelerated the slowdown of economic growth in the debtor nations which in turn affects sociopolitical structures and processes. Part of the issue was dramatically stated in a recent paper:

There is a risk that these democratic governments will collapse, of course—possibly to be replaced by others prepared to take radical steps such as repudiation of their debts. But an even more basic threat is that the promising trend to greater democracy in the area—an intricate and delicate process of political institutionalization now under way—may be aborted, with the crushing of social expectations that were generated during the 1970s, as South America moved toward middle-class status in the international system.[11]

Wherever an austerity program continues for a long time without capital inflow and with a low level of imports, there will be trouble. Few countries other than Mexico will be able to manage it as Mexico has until now. The probable assumption is that Mexico and other countries that have used the first austerity shock to initiate a harsh policy of controls, will relax some controls after establishing financial credibility and taking certain irreversible steps in cutting the public's expectation spiral. There will, however, be a long period of pervasive regulations and either state ownership or fairly rigid control of banking and credit.

Can we assume that adaptation to lower standards of living may be accomplished without threats to the social and political fabric? It is true that a drop in well-being after rising expectations creates tensions, but is it also true that an improvement after periods of near-despair relaxes tensions?

Several queries are still unanswered: Will conditions allow for improvement before too much damage is done? Can controls be relaxed in time to prevent explosions caused by tension? The vicious circle turns as follows: austerity relaxed too early or austerity coming too late causes economic harm and foreign credit remains unobtainable. Here is the dichotomy: whether to satisfy requirements of sound financing or risk the possibility of popular domestic resistance. This is the devil's alternative each government must face in its own sociopolitical setting.

Once the Great Reschedulings have become more relaxed through sharp reductions in the debt service burdens, some countries may resume their take-off. It may be the Pacific nations, eventually it might be Brazil and Mexico. It is not likely to be Zaire or Nigeria.

This is a dark age for development and it will continue for some time to come. The banks have two options: to lend in order to service the debt, or, eventually, to forgive a large part of principal or interest. The Argentinian challenge of April 1984 and its resolution is a symptom of things to come. The status quo is gone.

Post Script [Editor]. On Friday 20 February 1987 Brazil suspended most payments of its huge foreign debt, which stood at US $108 billion. Earlier in February Ecuador had suspended payments on its US $9 billion debt and warned that without new commercial credits it could suspend payments on its US $53 billion foreign debt. Of the total Latin American foreign debt in February 1987 of US $380 billion, Brazil, Mexico and Argentina owed two-thirds.

Notes

While the thinking in this article is entirely my own, it was stimulated by discussions over the years with my friends and partners Lionel I. Pincus and John L. Vogelstein. Neither of them necessarily shares my opinions.

[1] On changes in the United States, see Claire P. Doblin, Working Paper "Patterns of Industrial Change in the U.S.A. Since 1960: a Preliminary Summary" (Laxenburg, Austria: International Institute for Applied Systems Analysis, November 1983).

[2] For "take-offs" in development see Walt W. Rostow, *The Economics of Take-Off Into Sustained Growth* and *The Stages of Economic Growth* (New York: St. Martins's Press, 1963 and 1971, respectively).

[3] Susan Kaufman Purcell, "War and Debt in South America" in *Foreign Affairs, America and the World 1982* 61, no. 3, 669. She states that "it is to the credit of the Reagan Administration (and particularly Federal Reserve Chairman Paul Volcker) that it puts its ideological preferences for private sector solutions to economic problems aside. . . ."

[4] Riordan Roett, "Democracy and Debt in South America," in *Foreign Affairs, America and the World 1983* 62, no. 3, 701.

[5] One country where there is something approximating an intellectual proletariat is India—which, however, does not fall into the category of the countries discussed in this paper.

[6] I define state capitalism as a system where the state enterprises are economically powerful, function on a theoretically profitable basis, and where much of private enterprise is subsidized by the state in one form or another. In contrast to socialism, the state bears many of the risks of the private sector.

[7] See a brilliant analysis by Henri Neuman in *Traité d'Économie Financière—De l'Épargne à l'Emploi* (Paris: Presses Universitaires de France, 1980).

[8] This point was highlighted by the author in a series of lectures on "las inversiones en el mundo desarrollado" at the University of Chile in the summer of 1959.

[9] The Brazilian model is particularly interesting. See Joseph La Palombara and Stephen Blank, "Multinational Corporations in the Developing Countries," *Journal of International Affairs*, Spring-Summer 1980, 119-36.

[10] An example is the Société Nationale d'Investissement in Belgium.

[11] Roett, 696-697.

Chapter 8

Hunger, Agricultural Policies, and Agribusiness

Introduction

Although great strides have been made since 1948 when the world community first turned its attention to the problem of hunger and nutrition in the Third World by establishing the Food and Agricultural Organization, hunger is still very much with us at the end of the century. In fact, the contrast between plenty and starvation is perhaps more vivid now than at the end of the Second World War, for large parts of the world enjoy unprecedentedly large yields of agricultural commodities while yet others are swept by periodic famines; in still other areas hunger and plenty exist side by side with millions of children crippled by malnourishment. To be sure, great strides have been made; the high-yielding varieties of rice and other grains brought about the green revolution in Asia, which has effectively removed that continent from the food-deficit list, and myriads of irrigation and land-reform and distribution assistance programs have been implemented. Still, even in the areas of food sufficiency in normal crop-yield years, underlying problems remain. These include the need for rural land reform, the need for modernization of agricultural practices using indigenous and culturally acceptable techniques, and regional imbalances in agricultural development and progress. It is also necessary to modernize the woman's role in agriculture and in rural education, for without upgrading her role the cultural developments necessary to increase concepts of hygiene, health and nutrition and thus to wean the subsistence farmer from his tried-and-true methods toward higher yielding and more efficient agricultural practices, may never come about.

Africa has become a special problem during the past two decades, primarily because of incessant internal warfare, internal political misappropriation of development programs and external political neglect by the First World. This has led to a situation where Africa is several times more dependent on food from the United States and Canada than she was 20 years ago—this even under normal crop years where there is no drought!

The problem of food security, however, is not restricted to Africa. Solving it will entail the development of a world-wide network of financial support to provide buffer stocks of food commodities to prevent starvation in crop failures and low-yield cycle years. The achievement of food security for the Third World's population also requires the elevation of agriculture from its neglected position on the political agendas in many Third World countries, and the depoliticization and consequent rationalization of food production, subsidization and protection against Third World competition on the part of the European Community and the United States. Unfortunately thus far there is little evidence that the 2-8% of the First World's population that is engaged in agriculture is willing to give up its stranglehold on national agricultural policy in the EC or North America.

The articles in this chapter introduce the reader to most of the political problems that severely cripple the Third World's ability to grow sufficient food to adequately and nutritiously feed its population—in short, to reach the standard of nutrition of Europe and North America. and Canada.

The first article, by Alexander King, provides a general overview of the geographical, climatic, demographic and political problems of Third World food production and concludes with a set of recommendations for governments, international organizations, universities and research institutes. Charles Weitz in his article reviews the development of the FAO program since its beginning and evaluates the role of the multinational corporations (transnational corporations) in the agribusiness sector, concluding that although agribusiness has played a large role in development and has made many positive contributions, the political institutions and concepts necessary to manage the complex transnational corporations in the changing interdependent world economic system have failed and are inadequate. Hence, "we are attempting today to manage the new international mechanisms of the MNCs with 19th century political institutions." Anandarup Ray, in his article, focuses on trade and pricing policies in both the First and the Third Worlds and outlines an answer to the question "If agricultural trade and domestic policies were liberalized throughout the world, could one expect substantial gains for the world economy in general and for developing countries in particular?"

The final article, by Theodore Cohn, is different in its approach for it specifically discusses the relationship between agribusiness and nutrition, using several examples of misuse of commercial success at the expense of Third World nutritional requirements, notably the Nestle Baby Formula case.

Food Crises – Perils and Promise

Alexander King

Is There a Food Crisis or a Series of Crises?

In addition to overproduction of food coexisting with hunger and starvation, there are many associate related problem areas, some of which threaten to become critical, either locally or generally. For example, there is the fuelwood crisis, especially in Africa where 90% of wood used is for cooking of food and other energy purposes and where the number of hours spent by women going far afield to collect wood has increased enormously, while in the cities its cost is often greater than the price of the food to be cooked. Then again, there is the menace of desertification, with the Sahara, for example swallowing up an extra 3.7 million acres every year. Other related matters include insufficiency of infrastructure and lack of transportation, the vicissitudes of climate, too rapid population growth with the threat of numbers shooting ahead of the food production to support them, insufficient understanding of nutritional needs and their relation to health, high energy costs with their impact on the use of fertilizers, deforestation, erosion and the depletion of resources. To these and many other factors has to be added confusion over farm subsidies, price support and agricultural policies in USA and Europe.

The core problem is to resolve the dilemma of the co-existence of overproduction and hunger. This is essentially a question of economics, politics and logistics, to which technology is only marginally relevant. Technological advances can greatly increase the quantity and quality of food, but it cannot ensure that it reaches the hungry. For decades there has been sufficient food in the world to feed everyone, but with millions lacking the minimum requirements for a reasonable existence this disparity shows no sign of shrinking as world food production grows. Producing more food is just not enough. Even in India which has moved dramatically to a position of food surplus, there is little evidence of major improvement in meeting the basic need of the masses. The hungry are the poor who have few means of buying the food which exists. The real problem is the abolition of world poverty and the distribution of wealth.

General and Regional Prospects

The success of agricultural production since the end of World War II has been phenomenal. In 1950 world grain production was 623 million tons and this increased to about 1.5 billion tons by 1983, an astonishing addition of about 900 million tons per annum, providing a comfortable margin over the population increase of the period. Especially important has been the hybridization of corn and the dwarfing of wheat and rice varieties which have been at the heart of the Green Revolution and also an impressive increase in areas under irriga-

Published for the first time in this volume.

tion in some countries. Before 1950 increase in food output resulted mainly from extension of land under cultivation, but after that date, new, fertile lands became scarce, while at the same time cheap chemical fertilizers became generally available. Agriculture has become increasingly energy-intensive. It takes approximately a ton of oil to produce a ton of nitrogenous fertilizer and petroleum energy is also required for the manufacture of pesticides and weed-killers as well as for tillage and irrigation. During the period 1950-1983 the average consumption of fertilizer per inhabitant of the planet rose from 5kg to 25kg, while at the same time, the area per capita of harvested cereals dropped from 0.24 to 0.15 hectares. Thus, in a crude sense, the great increase in world food production represents the conversion of oil to edible cereals via more efficient photosynthesis and also a partial replacement of land by oil.

The 1973 jump in oil prices has, not surprisingly, had a large impact on food production especially in the developing countries. On the supply side, rising oil prices have raised costs of production considerably, while demand has been reduced by the general economic slowdown. The high oil cost has been only one factor in inhibiting the growth of food in many countries. The loss of topsoil through erosion is widespread and threatening for the security of future food supplies. Scarcity of water is also beginning to influence food prospects. The post-war increase in irrigation has slowed down as dam building projects become less favourable and more costly, as reservoirs become silted up and water tables fall. In the Third World, also, indebtedness and economic difficulties, local wars and armament building have resulted in a heavy underinvestment in agriculture which is seldom seen by the politicians as a priority sector.

A particular feature of the situation is the dominance of the world grain trade by North America. The United States and Canada together account for 70% of exported grain, which gives the region a strong strategic role in the world food economy. This dominance relates not only to cereals for human consumption, but also to feed grains and soya beans. For years, the United States has made up for deficits in the Soviet Union and has been generous in the provision of food aid to countries facing famine, at times amounting to 25% of the U.S. harvest.

In general, there has been an extraordinary growth in cereal shipments from developed to developing countries. They increased fivefold from the early 1960s until the late 1970s and are expected to increase greatly again by the end of the century, although the balance between the demand for imports and the supply of exports is notoriously unpredictable. In the 1960s, there was widespread doubt as to whether the ever-increasing demand for imports could be met, particularly in Asia. There were crises of very low cereal stocks in the mid 1960s and again in the mid 1970s. Today, only a decade later, the concern is exactly the opposite with rapidly growing developed country surpluses, the problem is to find adequate export markets. Expansion of domestic markets is unlikely in the grain exporting nations where increase in per-capita food consumption has virtually ceased. Another feature is the emergence of the European Community as a major and rapidly growing exporter of cereals, with exports estimated to rise to 25 million tons by the 1990s.

The dependence of the Third World, and to some extent the Soviet Union, on imported food carries many risks. First, the dominant exporters, USA and Canada, belong to a single climatic zone and in a poor year with low reserves, a small fluctuation in the exportable grain surplus can disturb food prices throughout the world. Their use of food dominance for political purposes can also be serious. One has only to cite the embargo of exports to the Soviet Union or the denying of food aid to Third World countries whose policies are deemed to be incompatible with United Slates interests. It is to be noted also, although this may be a distant shadow, that there is currently a debate in the United States concerning the need to conserve the resource base of the country for its own purposes by ceasing to "mine" the topsoil and the cultivation of unsuitable lands to meet the ever-growing demands for food from the world outside. Indeed, it would appear wise to accept policies favouring long-term world interest which would reduce pressures on American soils in order to ensure *sustained* fertility and hence export availability in the future. For these and other reasons it would seem advisable that a main thrust should be towards the production of as much food as possible as close as possible to where it is to be consumed. Paradoxically this does not run counter to American interests in food exports to the developing countries, because the growth of markets in these countries is not just a function of their overall growth rate, but also of the extent to which lower income people who spend much of their additional income on food, share in the general growth. We turn now to some regional considerations. The changed situation in Asia is remarkably encouraging. Both food production and yield growth have increased considerably, reflecting the success of modern high-yield varieties and the systems which made them possible. These systems have now been institutionalized and further growth is to be expected as existing success encourages territorial extension, further investment in irrigation and more double cropping. Prospects for the year 2000 estimate a net surplus for Asia of 50 million tons. In Latin America increased demand is expected more or less to keep up with improved production, leaving a gap of about 10 million tons.

The main deficit areas will be North Africa/Middle East, where a net food deficit of about 60 million tons is to be expected at the turn of the century. In the Middle East the situation is difficult as a result of a large population increase and the extent of arid land difficult to render more productive. However, with the continuation of oil revenues, the region as a whole should get by with imports for a number of decades at least. The real danger region is Africa south of the Sahara, to which we shall devote more detailed attention.

Food for Africa

The recent conditions of drought and famine have naturally focussed attention on the need for emergency aid, but there is still insufficient attention paid to the need for fundamental improvements in food production to prevent periodic recurrences, possibly on an increasing scale as the struggle for survival in each famine tends to erode the resource base. The African situation with regard to agricultural improvement is inherently more intractable than was that of Asia.

First, the political circumstances are more difficult with black Africa balkanized into many states with unsatisfactory boundaries, often with little respect for tribal cohesion and with frequent conflicts, wars and coups d'etat.

A further difficulty, derived from the colonial period, is the lack of infrastructure. In many cases, road and rail communication is restricted to networks linking inland capitals and mining centres with ports on the coast making country-to-country communication very difficult. During the recent famine there was much food in other African countries, but it could not be transported. Moreover most national policies, dominated by the cities, have paid little attention to food production other than for export crops which bring in foreign currency.

Conditions for agricultural improvement are much more difficult than in Asia with its young soils. African agriculture is dominated by old soils, for the most part fragile and lacking in nutrients, a matter often overlooked by those seeking to transplant European agricultural methods to Africa. A further obstacle is that there is much less irrigation than in Asia and that the prospects for adequate water control are remote.

The challenges faced in increasing Africa's food production are formidable, but there is no cause for despair. Africa can approach self-sufficiency in food, but only if a number of tough decisions are taken and a large number of individual issues faced.

It appears that the productivity of labour in Africa is lower than that in Asian agriculture and is constrained by the extreme seasonality of labour demand. Much research is required as to how best to raise this productivity, both at the human level, by upgrading the quality of labour and by technological innovations to increase yields, by changed crop/labour profiles, by the provision of low interest capital, by pricing reforms which provide incentives, and so on.

A particular feature of African agriculture is the large extent to which it depends on the work of women. It is estimated that 65% of agricultural work of the continent is carried out by women; hence great benefits would accrue from an improvement of their life conditions, better educational facilities and the opening up of credit facilities especially designed for enterprising African women.

The need for technological innovation in African agriculture is evident, but is much more difficult than was the case in Asia with its more amenable soils. Any simple copy of the classical Green Revolution methods is unlikely to succeed and much attention will have to be given to the selection of those regions where a food production breakthrough is most likely to occur. The need for this is well appreciated, but the technical criteria for choice are not well developed and there will be many difficult political problems in the adoption of what will appear as specially favoured areas.

In general the need to intensify research on all aspects of agriculture in Africa is great. In the colonial period research was almost entirely centred on plantation crops such as palm oil and coffee and, in the immediately post-colonial years the research community was obsessed by European and North American agricultural practices, with relatively little attention paid to indigenous African plants which form the staple diet of the rural communities. Urban consumers, recipients of most of the imported food of recent years have acquired a taste for wheat and rice and are increasingly uninterested in the traditional foods. Some regions, especially those which have suffered famine and received massive food aid, are tending in the same direction. This, together with the low price of imported grains is producing a strong disincentive to improvement by the peasant farmers. The changed food habits of the cities, combined with increased use of kerosene for cooking in face of fuelwood cost and scarcity is making the large cities of Africa extremely vulnerable to disruption of supplies or economic collapse. As Lester Brown puts it, they are living "from ship to mouth".

The fragility and low nutrient content of African soils, while obviously calling for greater use of fertilizers, have need of a much deeper understanding of the various equilibria if sustainability is to be achieved and yields improved. Agricultural research has to be reoriented, not only towards the breeding of higher yielding and more nutritional traditional crops such as millet, sorghum and other dryland crops as well as roots and tubers, but towards understanding of the various ecological factors in relation to socio-economic realities.

This stress on the need for the introduction of new technologies and for higher labour productivity is in no way a call for large scale farming. The need to ensure food security in rural areas is paramount and this is only likely to be achieved by improving the means at the disposal of the small farmer, including better education, access to rural, low-interest credit schemes, access to advice, improved infrastructure and substantial improvements of the market mechanisms which, in Africa, whittle away so much of the farmers profits.

It is too often assumed that peasant farming is inherently inefficient. This is an uninformed judgement. Agreed, small farmers are not marked by their eagerness to adopt new technologies, but in the struggle for survival they must necessarily be cautious. A new, high-yielding strain of maize requires water, fertilizers and pesticides, the farmer knows that if any of these is missing he may well get a lower yield than with the traditional varieties he knows so well. If he is to accept an innovation he must have the credit and the knowledge to ensure that all the elements for success are there. Peasant farmers, in the Sahel, for instance, have had generations of experience of how to survive the periodic droughts that have plagued the region for centuries. There is need to build on this experience and there is no reason why it should not assimilate new and appropriate innovation. Indeed, it is necessary to do so as the land has to support many more people than formerly.

Up till now governments have left the small farmers to their own devices, concentrating on the more politically influential urban sector or on large scale cash-crop ventures. The immediate need is to make more resources available to small-scale farming and to encourage, by the injection of credit and other means, increases in its yields and productivity.

The Club of Rome has recently published a report, *The Barefoot Revolution* which describes, from a field study in 19 countries of the Third World, how groups of villagers and small farmers have spontaneously come together in attempts to improve their conditions of life. Some of these NGOs are concentrating on agricultural improvement or irrigation, others on education and training, or on health and hygiene or on a mixture of all these. Success is mixed, of course, but it is estimated that this "grass roots" movement is already beginning to touch the lives of some 100 million people.

An interesting feature of this movement which is apparently as yet politically uncaptured, is that in many instances it represents harmonious cooperation between the new NGOs of the South and the development NGOs of the North. Many of the NGOs of North America and Europe, already well known for their humanitarian and emergency aid operations are aware that it is more important to help to ensure that famines will not continue to arise. Drought, as a natural phenomenon cannot be prevented, but famine is largely man-made and can be avoided. The northern NGOs are in a much better position than are governments to adopt a participative approach to technological innovation at the grass roots and it is strongly to be hoped that governments' both in the developed and in the Third World countries will lend support to this hopeful approach, despite the fact that it is inherently undramatic and with little political appeal.

Population Growth

Very rapid world population growth is the most dangerous problem of the contemporary world, second only to the menace of nuclear annihilation. Although recent years have seen some diminution of fertility rates in a number of developing countries, high rates of demographic increase will continue well into the next century. To give a facile illustration of the present situation, a population of the size of Grenada is being launched on to the planet twice daily. By the year 2000, the world population will have crossed the 6 billion threshold as compared with about 1.8 billion at the beginning of the century. In terms of sheer numbers, population will be growing faster in the year 2000 than it is today with 100 million extra people added each year as compared with 75 million in 1975. The vast majority of the new inhabitants will be born in the already overpopulated and often hungry countries of the Third World and there, about half the population at the end of the century will be under 15 years old. Many of the developed countries will have stabilized their populations by then, or be increasingly only slowly. Indeed the total *increase* in the combined populations of North America, Europe and the Soviet Union will be less than the then populations of Nigeria or Bangladesh by 2000.

Demographic growth will thus be very different in the various regions of the world. In Europe the increase until the end of the century is estimated at about 7%, as compared with 17-18% in North America and the Soviet Union where it will be mainly in the Asian republics. It is expected to be 24% in East Asia, 55% in South East Asia, 65% in Latin America and 75% in Africa.

The consequences of rapid population growth are numerous, with its influence on food production needs the most obvious. While it will provide a greatly increased workforce, those countries where demographic growth is fast include many where unemployment and underemployment are now acute. It is estimated that there will be need to create more than a billion new jobs in the Third World before the end of the century. Other burdens arising from the increased numbers include the provision of housing and a vast increase in educational expenditure. Political problems will also arise due to population pressures and extensive waves of emigration are to be expected.

Once again, in population Africa is the crisis area. Some of the projections are staggering. Nigeria, for example is expected to have 169 million inhabitants by the year 2000 and to level off eventually at an unthinkable 618 million. With population increasing at about 3.1% per annum, food production was, in the years preceding the present drought, increasing at around 1.6%, while in those countries where food shortages are now worst, production per capita has fallen on an average by 2% per annum over the last decade. Malnutrition and the diseases which accompany it, is now the condition of 100 million individuals. There is an obvious need for the population problems of Africa to be taken seriously by governments.

Some Long Term Considerations

In the trends and estimates just quoted, there is the implicit assumption of a constant environment, politically and physically with no major event external to the food system (such as a nuclear bomb disturbing the smooth projection curves). It is, of course, impossible to allow for the statistically improbable, but nevertheless important to take a look at a few trends in very different fields, which may impact on food supply or demand and which could affect sustainability. The first and most directly related to agriculture is degradation and erosion of the soil. Soil erosion is a natural process, but when its rate exceeds that of new soil formation, there is a decline in the productivity of the land. It is estimated that this is the situation in 35% of the world's cropland, a very serious fact in face of large population increase. This phenomenon is very marked in the breadbasket of North America where enormous amounts of topsoil are annually blown away.

We shall not labour further the African tragedy, where the advance of the desert, assisted by the emergency cropping of unsuitable land, is a growing menace. The situation is difficult also in Asia, especially on the slopes of the Himalayas where population pressure has denuded the trees for fuelwood causing brutal erosion and the silting up of rivers hundreds of miles downstream with flooding consequences. Another aspect of soil deterioration has been the clearing of large areas of tropical forest to make way for agriculture. This has often proved to be a failure because, paradoxically, the most luxuriant forests seem to grow on nutrient-poor land, so that after a few years of good crops, very low productivity persists.

A second long term threat is that of fundamental climatic change. The possibility of significant warming up of the earth's surface through the "greenhouse effect" has been recognized for a couple of decades, but it has been a matter of great controversy among the climatologists. There now seems to be a consensus that the danger is real, as expressed in the 1985 Villach declaration of the International Council of Scientific Unions. The effect is caused by an increase in the concentration of carbon dioxide in the atmosphere due to the combustion of fossil fuels and also to an accumulation of other gases such as methane. It is suggested that in about forty years average surface temperature will increase by between 1.5 and 4.5 degrees Celsius, with a much greater effect at high latitudes than at the equator. This would fundamentally alter the thermal gradients of the world and cause very great but as yet unpredictable changes in climate throughout the world, completely changing present patterns of food production. It would also cause a considerable rise in the level of the sea. The effect would be virtually irreversible; if the burning of oil and coal were to be stopped when the warming became acute, it is calculated that it might take 900 years for the present carbon dioxide levels to be reestablished

While there are tremendous uncertainties in all this, it must be taken seriously, with constant monitoring of atmospheric CO_2. It is quite unrealistic to expect governments with their short time horizons to prohibit the burning of coal and oil, even were the certainty of the happening greater, but much useful preparatory work could be done to buffer the effect of temperature rise, through conventional plant breeding as well as genetic engineering, so as to give a greater range of potential crops to meet radically changed climatic environments.

This brings us to the third factor, the question of energy availability after the turn of the century. Food, with its calorie product is perhaps the most fundamental of all energy sources available to humanity and is, of course, stored solar energy. The world agricultural system is thus a sub-system within the total energy system and an element in the long term energy problem. At present most national and international considerations of energy are essentially on a short term basis, concentrating on matters such as petroleum price fluctuations and the dangers of nuclear energy generation. The long term aspects are given insufficient attention. For example, the recent lowering of oil prices had an immediate effect in diminishing the resources to support research on alternative energy sources. Yet it takes upward of 40 years to establish a new energy system on a significant scale. Oil is, of course, an unrenewable resource and we shall have burnt up this accumulated resource of the stored solar energy of millions of years through two short centuries. In a number of oil producing countries, including the United States the time is not far off when the *energy cost* of petroleum exploration and recovery will be as great as the *energy content* of the product. On the other hand, Saudi Arabia's reserves would last for almost 100 years at the present rate of extraction. The present oil glut is real and will continue for some time, but by the mid 1990s the world will witness a race between efforts to develop alternatives and the steady depletion of world petroleum reserves. Efficiency and conservation efforts in the industrialized countries can make great savings, but, at the same time the demand for oil in the Third World is expected to rise 50% between 1980 and 1995. The use of coal, reserves of which are still high, is often proposed as the alternative to oil, but the greenhouse effect and acid rain may well dampen this prospect.

To sum up, it would seem that there may be many difficult, if distant problems for the production of food, although it is theoretically possible to support a population many times that of today. Many of these may stem from developments outside agriculture as such. There is a human tendency, individual and collective, to put off facing up to difficulties as long as possible, but at the same time we know that the longer we delay, the more intractable the problems will have become. The long term sounds distant, but the lead time in analysis, research, development and implantation of widespread reforms and new systems is very long and a start needs to be made now. Neglect of long term but fundamental issues is one of the most obvious weaknesses of the political system.

The Needs

For Governments and International Organizations

- A new approach to the settlement of the Third World country debts possibly in the form of some Marshall Plan type scheme, accepting interest and repayments in local currency utilisable for new development.

- Reduction in the sale of armaments to poor countries.

- For developing country governments, higher priority to agriculture, more emphasis on rural development and the grass roots approach.

- A longer horizon for plans and policies.

- Stabilization of commodity prices and prevention of excessive fluctuations in the price of oil.

All in all there is urgent need for the harmonization of policies between developed and developing countries, new approach to the monetary and credit systems—in fact some sort of New International Economic Order, although not necessarily of the type discussed by the United Nations some years ago.

For the Private Sector

The importance of industry in food production will continue to be great in all its directions of today. But industry itself is in revolution as a result of the advanced technologies such as microelectronics, which will make possible a higher degree of decentralization and profitable manufacture and operation in smaller units. In the developing countries this should mitigate against excessive concentration in industrial regions and enable the growth of small-unit, although not necessarily small scale manufacture in rural areas, thus diminishing the rural-urban distinction and bringing amenities and cash income to the countryside.

There will be need for better industry-government understanding in countries of all types, a matter difficult for the multinationals because of their multiple capitalization and domiciles. It is likely, however, that there will be continuing need for companies to create and maintain an image of social responsibility and, as in the case of governments, to take a longer term view. They will have to balance the need for next year's profits with further off needs for survival

Much is to be hoped from the development of the Non-Governmental Organizations (NGOs) which showed up well in the recent Sahel crisis as being more flexible, less bureaucratic and more responsive to local needs than were governments and (still more obviously) international organizations. There is considerable need however, for more coherence in the work of the NGOs and better coordination between their actions. The growing and benevolent relationship between NGOs of the North and those of the South needs extension and much subtle understanding in its operation. Governments could with great benefit make much more use of the NGOs in the implementation of their aid policies. This applies with even greater force to the international organizations, many of which might abandon much of their inhouse research and other activities to work in cooperation with the NGOs. Agriculture has already set a good example in this direction.

For Universities and Research Institutes

For research—as usual the sky's the limit. The whole business of supplying food, nutritionally well balanced and in sufficient quantity to every one of the 6 billion inhabitants of the planet at the end of the century requires an enormous increase in knowledge, new methods and increased understanding as to conditions, needs and human behaviour. Throughout this paper, research challenges are implicit everywhere and I shall only list here a very few of the most obvious. These are:

- general research and plant-breeding on tropical crops, the preservation of gene pools;

- genetic engineering of varieties to provide adaptation to climatic change;

- tissue culture;

- nitrogen fixation in non-legumes;

- the breeding of improved fast-growing trees;

- research on climatic change and its consequences for food production;

- regional and local consequences of probable rises in sea level;

- development of halophytes and climate defensive crops;

- research on low energy-intensive agriculture;

- non-agricultural food production methods, bearing in mind energy constraints;

- conservation of arid lands and the greening of the desert;

- anthropological research and sociological studies of food habits and how to introduce nutritional improvements;

One aspect of the required research is particularly important. Each item is part of the general mosaic of development and even political factors. Hence there is need for a much higher degree of interdisciplinary communication than at present. Universities have a particular responsibility for evolving new approaches to interdisciplinary and multidisciplinary research in view of their importance for the solution of the food problem and indeed nearly all the issues of the contemporary world.

The challenge is great; the promise is good, but the problems are enormous. Their solution demands a concerted attack by all nations, rich and poor. An immediate requirement is a general public awareness of the importance and complexity of the issues. Public response to the tragedy of the Sahel was heartening, but it must be sustained in the knowledge that the future of all the inhabitants of the world is at stake, so as to build a basis of enlightened and common self-interest in solving the problems. Finally I have to repeat my plea for a longer term vision and concern.

To End Hunger: Four Decades of International Effort

Charles Weitz

It has been observed that sex and hunger are the two biological finalities which govern man's social life. So let us keep firmly before us the picture of 500 million fellow humans suffering each day from hunger and malnutrition as we consider the international institutional approaches to food production and agriculture during the past four decades. Indeed, the Food and Agriculture Organization of the United Nations (FAO) estimate of 500 million is a low estimate; the World Bank says 800 million live in absolute poverty, a condition including insufficient nourishment. Many reputable groups, including NGOs of high standing, put the poverty-misery figure at one billion—a quarter of the population.

The greatest tragedy of these figures is that, as a percentage of total population, they have changed little since the FAO did its first World Food Survey more than three decades ago. Poverty, hunger and malnutrition still occupy relatively as large a place in the world economy as they did when first measured. This alone is a monument to the failure of governments and people to act.

And the paradox of this situation is that there is no reason for the condition. When it called the First World Food Congress in 1963, the FAO said clearly that the world, with the science and technology then known, had enough knowledge to ensure mankind's freedom from hunger. Successive world congresses and conferences, national study groups and experts have repeated this contention. Hunger and malnutrition can be eliminated; the world can produce sufficient food and fiber.

This also at a time of record world food production! Favourable weather in 1981 produced very good crops so world food production rose by some 2.9% with grain production increasing by 7% to just over 1,500 million tons. 1982 was also a good year but it failed to show the increase of 1981; grain production figures are at about the same levels as 1981 but because of falling demand brought on by a world-wide recession, trade figures and consumption will be down. Thus carry-over stocks are expected to rise by 4% to a level of 22-23% of production, well above the FAO norm of 18% required as a "safe" level. One half of this total reserve is held in one country.[1]

However, these favourable overall statistics mask real differences and real problems. In 69 countries classified as food aid priority countries—generally the food deficit countries—per capita food production was down by 3%, and taking the least developed countries as a whole, per capita food production was down by over 2%. The long term trend is particularly disquieting; the picture for Africa is especially bleak, where both on an absolute and a per capita basis food production has been declining over a significant period of time. Food deficits continue to grow in the low income countries; their absolute need to import food has risen to over 100 million tons—a doubling in ten years—requiring the use of billions of

Based on a 1983 conference paper, this article is published here for the first time.

scarce and hard-earned foreign exchange dollars which would otherwise have been available for infrastructure and development priorities. Production is not meeting demand and these countries are moving from self sufficiency toward dependency and increased vulnerability.

At the same time FAO's foodcrop report of mid-January 1983 listed 24 countries, of which 17 were in Africa, as suffering from abnormal food shortages. These areas (and the number has remained largely unchanged over more than 6 months) sharply and dramatically increase the numbers suffering from hunger and malnutrition and place an increased burden on the World Food Programme and other emergency feeding and relief agencies. Along with the 24 countries suffering from abnormal food shortages, FAO in its global information and early warning system report identifies 26 countries which in January were suffering from unfavourable crop conditions; of these 26, 10 are those already suffering from abnormal food shortages. And among the unfavourable crop countries there are such important producers as Australia, Bangladesh, Ethiopia, Ghana, India, Sri Lanka, Sudan.[2]

Let us now review what is agreed about food and agriculture and the responses of the world to these known and agreed policies and programmes. The remarkable feature of all this is the length of time over which there has been a wide measure of agreement, and a lack of any serious divergence of views about what must be done. It has been tritely observed that if only the hungry could eat paper, there would be no hunger and malnutrition.

The first crack at the problem came from John Boyd Orr, later Lord Boyd Orr, elected first Director General of FAO after its creation by the Quebec City Conference in October 1945. With clear foresight, Boyd Orr outlined a four-part plan for the role of the newly created FAO which, while perhaps deficient in detail and based on the world politics of only the then 50-plus independent states, was nonetheless in broad outline the same as all subsequent programmes of action. But whatever the emotional orgies were which had seized governments at the close of World War II and caused them to write such lofty sentiments in the preambles to the charters of the UN organizations, governments were not about to endow their fledglings with either authority or resources to fulfill the noble goals. Boyd Orr's four major proposals were met with total resistance and his initial two-year contract was not renewed. FAO's head then became an American technician who saw FAO's role primarily as a technical one. A reflection of the effects of this leadership was that by the mid-1950s when the UN System was fully into development assistance, FAO was not only the smallest of the principal UN agencies but was ill-equipped for a significant development role.

FAO'S fourth Director General was different, however. An outstanding Indian diplomat, B.R. Sen had also been food commissioner in Bengal during the 1942/43 famine and had seen two to three million of his countrymen die from lack of food. He too saw the world dimensions and policy issues that Boyd Orr had seen, but by his time (1957) member nations in the UN numbered around 100 and the issues of underdevelopment and poverty were emerging as key questions. Despite the fact that virtually no one in those days could foresee the end of American surpluses, Sen could; he began to refashion FAO into a development agency and began a painful and slow struggle to bring peoples and governments to recognize the growing dimensions of the world food, agricultural and development problems facing them. Through a Freedom From Hunger Campaign launched in 1960, Sen forced debate and concern for the issues of underdevelopment, hunger, malnutrition, population, and transfer of technology and resources. From the beginning FAO highlighted population growth as a concern—long before the rest of the UN System would even discuss it. Through an Indicative Plan for Agricultural Development, FAO launched a first effort to do a total global perspective of the technical and economic issues—and through its First (1963) and Second (1970) World Food Congresses, FAO assembled on a world basis, people—these were not intergovernmental conferences even though governments attended—to examine and explore issues and to propose action. In both Congresses FAO said the world had the science and technology it needed to solve the world food problems; in detailed recommendations from both Congresses it spelled out the actions needed. The policies and programmes of action of both Congresses were remarkably similar, and even more remarkable was their policy overlap with the Boyd Orr outline of 1945/46.

But it took rising populations, rising consumption and demand, falling reserves, drought and the megadeaths of the Sahel, Bihar, and East African famines of 1971/73 to move governments to action. The mounting "extra deaths" as the statisticians so deftly classified them and the drop in the world food reserves to less than a one month supply (data were poor but estimates claimed reserves as low as a 23 day supply) jolted governments into mutual recognition of need. And as part of his maiden speech just days after his elevation to US Secretary of State, Henry Kissinger proposed before the General Assembly of the UN in September 1973, that the UN call a World Food Conference. Through twenty-two conference resolutions agreed to unanimously (with minor exceptions) there was spelled out in detail the policies and programmes needed to overcome world hunger. The WFSC even attempted to assign priorities both in terms of actions needed and areas for attention. It also budgeted the package. Its recommendations, some of which have been accepted, are still the norms of today. And it should be noted that once again, except for detail and matters changed by circumstances, their recommendations were not different from the two Food Congresses or Boyd Orr. We shall not examine the 22 resolutions for technical content, but look at major policy groupings only.

The World Food Conference did not end the inquiry. The US National Academy of Sciences has had a full-scale study; President Jimmy Carter set up a US Presidential Commission on World Hunger; library shelves contain many books, relevant and irrelevant; the World Watch Institute has produced some excellent monographs and two books; and a major section of the report of the World Bank-financed Independent Commission on International Development Issues headed by Willy Brandt concerns itself with world hunger issues.[3]

Like the US Presidential Commission, the World Bank report identified hunger, malnutrition and poverty as critical destabilizing issues which threaten peace and security. Both identify the problem not only in human terms of stunted lives, disease, misery, ill health and early death, but as a major stumbling block to adequate general development and as a potential contributor to political unrest, civil war, and external aggression. FAO's current Director General, Deouard Saouma has said it this way—"Hunger may destabilize regimes, make or break alliances, fan conflicts. Therefore, it is above all a political problem . . . As long as hunger is rife, peace and stability are not possible. The choice is between a society of solidarity and a society of conflict. . .".

What is the score today? Judged by the unchanging statistics of hunger and malnutrition, dismal. Third World countries per capita production falls; they are becoming increasingly dependent on imported food; terms of trade continue to deteriorate, and access to markets is becoming less secure. Deterioration in the terms of trade is progressively impoverishing

Third World countries—virtually dispossessing them of their only wealth. Real prices for a range of products—jute, tea, rubber, bananas, mais, palm oil and others—have declined in the past two decades. The real prices of tea and jute are only about 1/3 of their value of 20 years ago; the export value of bananas has declined 20% in the past ten years. Third World foreign exchange revenue from agricultural exports decreased by more than 3% in 1980 and the decline continued through 1981 to reach the lowest level since the early 1970s.

The bulk of the recommendations for action of the World Food Conference deal obviously with technical matters—soil erosion, water and irrigation, fertilizers, insecticides, seeds, machinery, education, credit, marketing, roads, etc. The underlying direction was to employ these elements through increased resources—from the budgets of the Third World countries and from external assistance. Both sources are indispensable and neither will function without the other. The evidence is not reassuring. A number of Third World countries have substantially altered development priorities and where these shifts have been radical as in the case of India, for example, results are clearly visible. From one of the "disaster" areas of the 1950s and 1960s India now has a grain reserve and a small export capability; true, 200 million Indians still live below the "poverty line" as defined by its Planning Commission, but India has stimulated its domestic rural economy, has a margin of reserve and thus the opportunity to deal with distribution-equity. A number of other countries with a significant shift in development priorities have achieved similar results. But too few by far.

The lack of understanding on the part of Third World leaders is nowhere better illustrated than in the so-called Strategies for Development of the 1st, 2nd, and 3rd UN Development Decades. The key motor function of agricultural and rural development was so little understood when the First Strategy was written for the 1960s that agriculture occupied only a few lines. By DD II (the 1970s) agriculture had come to require a section of the Strategy (written at the end of the 1960s) but still only paragraphs compared to pages for industry, transportation, communications, et al. It is only now that the Third Strategy assigns a realistic role to agriculture. In turn, this lack of understanding was reflected in national budgets where agriculture and rural development was assigned a lesser role—the "failed" profession it is called in Africa, where the Minister of Agriculture is assigned a low seat at the cabinet table, perhaps only outranking the Minister for Posts and Telegraph.

Equally, external assistance has failed to keep pace with either the aid level recommended by the WFC or extrapolated by FAO's *Agriculture Toward 2000*, (C 79/24 July 1979, Twentieth Session, Conference of the Food and Agriculture Organization, Rome) its major contribution to the development debate, which outlines three alternative growth scenarios to the end of the century. The WFC said external assistance had to rise from its then current level of about 3 to 4 billion dollars to levels of 7-10 billion dollars annually. The FAO study projects, on the most optimistic growth assumptions (which would still leave substantial hunger and malnutrition by the year 2000) needs for about 12.5 billion dollars in external assistance by 1990. Both figures are 1975 prices. With few exceptions the OECD countries achieve only about one half the agreed level of Official Development Assistance—0.70% of their GNP. Total commitments reached barely $5 billion in 1981, expressed in 1975 prices. Aid levels continue to fall as governments mistakenly attempt to solve domestic problems by slashing "foreign aid" as if the health of the world economy had no effect on the domestic economy. Terms of assistance are hardening and assistance channeled through multilateral agencies is down, affecting the International Fund for Agricultural Development, the World Food Programme, and particularly hard the United Nations Development Programme, the main funding source of the UN System for direct development assistance. There is major disarray today and signs for the future are discouraging. How is work to proceed without adequate resources?

One cannot leave the resources point without underlining the madness of the world's expenditures for war, titled "national defense." These funds, which now exceed $500 billion a year,[4] provide neither defense nor security; neither the rich nor the poor are immune to this obscene use of resources. But it is hard to accept that the rich can reach barely half of a modest UN agreed aid target of 0.70% when 5 to 6% of national income can go for weapons of mass destruction. Mrs. Ghandi reminded (The Frank McDougall Memorial Lecture—Twenty-first Session of the Conference of FAO, Rome, November 1981) the FAO Conference that the money spent on just one intercontinental ballistic missile could be used to plant 200 million trees, irrigate 1 million hectares of land, or build 6,500 health care centers. FAO, whose role, theoretically, is critical to international cooperation and action in food and agricultural development, has had funds for its regular budget from the Organization's inception in 1945 to date which equal about half the cost of one Trident nuclear submarine!

And what of the other recommendations of the WFC for achieving world food security—declared as a goal by the noble Declaration of Conference and reaffirmed since by world leaders meeting in Ottawa, Cancun, and Versailles?

A *World Food Council* has been set up and functions; but one may well ask whether creating more international machinery to consider the issues, no matter how well studied and presented at the ministerial level by a handful of governments, will add one ton of wheat or maise or relieve the suffering of one malnourished person.

The International Fund for Agricultural Development (*IFAD*), the first multilateral capital funding mechanism strictly for agriculture, has been created and initially funded; it works, but its $1 billion initial capital is committed and is totally inadequate to IFAD's task. There is now difficulty with replenishment funding.

The International Monetary Fund (*IMF*) does now have a food facility providing some relief for balance of payment difficulties for food imports, but improvements are required.

The International Fund for Emergency Relief (*IFER*) has achieved its 500,000 ton level recommended by the WFC but as outlined by the WFC it is not on a fully multilateral basis nor is it ensured of continuing resources.

A new *international grains agreement* to ensure market stability and a world security reserve is at a negotiating impasse; there are no prospects for action. Linked with this, FAO's modest proposals for voluntary national reserve systems and regional arrangements lag for lack of funding and could only be a stop-gap for international machinery in any event.

The *Food Aid Convention* has provided a safety net higher than the pre-1973 levels but substantially below the 10 million ton target set by the WFC; pledge levels are falling here too.

FAO's Global Information and Early Warning System is in place and functioning, it remains dependent on reliable national data systems of which there are too few.

There is no formal *stock policy at the global level*; there is not even agreement internationally as to the desirable level of stocks. The idea of measuring the adequacy of world stocks in the light of estimated safe levels required for world security is accepted and there is an improved framework of information on which governments can take individual stock holding decisions.

There is no mechanism for *reducing price fluctuations* or for guaranteeing the access of low income, food deficit countries to needed supplies. UNCTAD's work on the *Integrated Programme of Commodities* has marked time since 1976; the *Common Fund* has not yet been set up.

On the whole it is a dismal record for more than 30 years of international negotiation.

Let us now turn to agribusiness—or, in other words, the multinational corporations and agricultural development. Since volumes have been written on this topic and the UN Commission on Transnational Corporations has been debating the subject since the 1970s we can here only identify highspots for discussion. As beauty lies in the eye of the beholder, so the good or evil of the MNC lies in the mind of the speaker.

Let us be clear on a number of things. While transportation and communications have enabled the transnationals to grow and expand into the concept of the Global Market, the actual phenomenon is not new. Popes and emperors have run organizations as large and all pervasive as today's MNCs. The East India Company, the Massachusetts Bay Colony were 18th century examples, and the 19th century saw the emergence of MNCs for copper and bananas, while such family names as Singer Sewing Machine Company and Quaker Oats were leaders, followed by the Eastmans, CocaCola, National Cash Register and others who pioneered the multinational approach in this century.

Second, while the method of operating away from one's national base is not new, it is the revolution of transportation and communications which has permitted the MNC managers to free themselves from the fixed-place mentality to think, move and act on a truly multinational level. Indeed many can be quoted saying they see themselves existing separately from specific national ties; they do not see their corporations as American, Swiss or Dutch, but as world concerns. They regard national boundaries as historical accidents, artificial lines made by the caprices of history which may be to the advantage or disadvantage of the MNC. This is a factor of some significance, for no national leader, no matter how far thinking, is free to conceive and act internationally; each is bound by the cultural and political constraints of the nation-state.

Third, while the bulk of the multinationals (about 1000 in number) are American there are giants elsewhere: Royal Dutch Shell and Unilever started as multinationals, and names such as Nestle, Saint Goben, Volkswagen, Brown Boven, Philips, Imperial Chemicals Ltd. and Hoffman-LaRoche are also to be kept in mind.

Fourth, the MNCs have changed from typically extractive groups into manufacturing and marketing complexes with managerial arrangements and companion banking and financial services on truly global bases.

Fifth, the MNCs are an industrial power ranking only third in size and clout behind the USA and the USSR. The turnover, or product value, of many exceeds the GNP of most small and many middle-size nations.

Sixth and finally, there is nothing inherently evil about a MNC. Neither does it exist to do good. It exists to make money. In the agribusiness field the MNC does not exist to grow food or improve nutrition; it exists to make money. There is no other function for a MNC and any attempt to ascribe moral values, virtue or vice to MNCs is to miss the point. If one accepts the premise that making money is an evil or socially unacceptable, then all forms of capitalist business and industry must be classified as evil, not just MNCs. The MNC cannot be separated from or treated differently than any other form of business.

To appreciate the role of MNCs one must weigh other data. Of the 1,000 MNCs over half the "foreign" (or non-headquarter's country) investment estimated at $175/200 billion is held by U.S. companies. Actually there is no reliable data, but intelligent guesses are that offshore investments in agriculturally related industries approximate $25/35 billion, but the bulk of this is in other developed countries. Holdings in Third World countries may be in the order of $10-15 billion. Perhaps this figure seems large, but compared with Third World national budgets, or with military and/or foreign assistance transfers it is not overwhelming.

Of the 1,000 MNCs there are about 200 in the agricultural sector providing inputs such as machinery and equipment, fertilizers, insecticides, seeds, etc.; producers of bananas, fruits, vegetables, oils and fibers; and the processor/distributor group. Here there are some interesting observations to be made. Only five MNCs handle virtually all of the international trade in grains. The bulk of the banana trade is controlled by five firms. Beef and pork in international trade is processed and shipped by fewer than six countries. Fruit and vegetable processing is contracted for (thus controlling to a great extent production) by between eight and ten companies. For coffee, the export value of which was $10.4 billion in 1984, trading is dominated by the oligopolies. Cocoa, the production of which is primarily in the hands of three countries—although Brazil and Malaysia are becoming important producers—is traded within the control of six companies with 70% of all world processing in the hands of nine firms. Eight major companies dominate the international seed business while there are only three giants in the field of agricultural machinery and equipment.

The processing of agricultural products must rank as the world's number one manufacturing business with an estimated aggregate total of more than $700 billion annually, not including processing done outside the money economy. But for our purposes we need to note that approximately 90% of the value added in processing takes place in the developed countries.

There is little purpose taking time to illustrate the problems of the MNCs—a litany of woe. Stories are all too easy to come by and whole books, such as *Global Reach* by Barnett and Muller, have been devoted to them, along with volumes of summary records of the Commission on Transnationals of the United Nations.[5]

It is more useful to illustrate a few pluses and minuses and indicate the current state of the art with a few observations in conclusion. The Third World countries need capital, technology, managerial and organizational know-how, and access to markets. The MNCs sell all these things—so what is the price? What is the balance sheet?

On a positive note, a major part of the investments made in countries (Third World or other) represents a net positive transfer of resources that would not otherwise have occurred. Land improvement, roads, utilities, buildings, and machinery all remain usually and thus are an increase in the capital structure. On the negative side, the movement of an MNC into a country usually is accompanied by a stifling of competition and absorption of local industries in the same field, a destruction of local industries which usually are more labour extensive. Capital gains and surpluses are usually exported.

Another positive element is that outside firms will bring new or substantially revitalized agricultural resources into use. They will create new employment to operate the production and/or processing facilities, will provide new taxable property and income and will provide a new source of revenue and foreign exchange for the nation. Negatively, this may not happen. Land used for domestic food production may disappear; net employment may well decrease as most MNCs seek labour saving work methods and at the same time do the least allowed by custom or law for the well-being and welfare of employees and families. And if there are no, or incomplete, tax and capital laws, the incoming MNC may escape the payment of most taxes and export all gains and capital. As a footnote, one must observe, however, that growing evidence that native capital—the rising entrepreneurial class of developing countries—behaves no differently than does capital in the developed world. Sometimes, because of its closeness to local politicians and bureaucrats, it exploits even more.

The introduction of new science and technology usually is seen as a net positive benefit in the modernization of the less developed country. Unfortunately, the technology is not always appropriate and therefore has negative effects; and equally often the technology is so tightly held in secrecy by the MNC that it remains unavailable to the local economy, beneficial or not.

Finally, one must examine the internal political consequences of MNCs. At one extreme, of course, there are the banana republics where there is virtually total subversion of the country, its political, social, cultural and economic institutions. Equally, a dispassionate study of a model country usually held up for plaudits, such as Kenya—a study tracing the influence of "outside" forces starting in the 19th century, leading up to and through the independence struggle and into post independence patterns of domestic and foreign relations through the 1970s—is not reassuring. While certainly native Kenyans are no longer segregated to Native Reserves, nonetheless there is strong evidence that through financial control, the banking system, patent and technology control, "joint" partnership ventures to provide a veneer of Africanization, the judicious placing of key officials from ruling tribes and families on boards and rewarding positions of the great firms, "foreign" control of Kenya is still pervasive. And there is evidence also that the Kenyan elite has little motivation to transform this state of affairs into one more responsive to the needs of the native population and their welfare. This strengthening of the elites of Third World countries seems to be one of the most pernicious spin-offs of rapid industrialization with the help of outside capital and management. Thus far the masses in the Third World seem to have been largely untouched by three decades of independence and development.

Before concluding with a few observations on both transnationals and the world food situation I would like to illustrate the one attempt made within the UN System to deal directly with multinationals.

The boldest and most direct approach of the UN System toward work with the MNCs was the initiative taken by B.R. Sen of FAO within the framework of his Freedom From Hunger Campaign. In 1965 Sen proposed an open association between the governments of FAO, the staff of FAO, and the MNCs in an effort to mobilize the intellectual and material resources of the MNCs to meet the challenge of world hunger. Sen, as an Indian, had no illusions about MNCs but believed they were safer inside than outside and that there was no chance to try to direct the resources of industry into channels FAO believed most needed for development unless there was a direct and responsible partnership. With the financial backing and intellectual leadership of 19 industrial leaders who responded to Sen's invitation, an Industry Cooperative Programme (ICP) was set up. It remained inside FAO but was financially dependent on resources put up by the industries. Its success, despite many problems, led to its expansion to a membership of more than 100 of the world's leading agribusinesses; ICP shared technical information with FAO, loaned specialists for missions, undertook investigations of projects for investment, loaned specialists for technical working parties on such subjects as the residual toxic effects of certain pesticides, etc.

But a change of leadership in FAO, perhaps less investment response from industry than might have been hoped for, and no doubt the hostile attitude of governments growing out of the TNC debates and actions at the UN, spelled the end of ICP. It was eliminated from FAO in 1978. A revised programme was reestablished in 1979 as an Industry Council for Development in New York where with the encouragement of the Secretary-General of the UN it keeps links to the UN System as a whole through the UNDP. It is once again a growing institution but the new format and relations with the UN cannot yet be fully evaluated. With the demise of the ICP, I feel the UN System lost a valuable practical laboratory for experimentation. The nature and power of MNCs cannot be ignored. Development is not an affair exclusively for governments; nor will MNCs be controlled by jawboning.

If the United Nations agencies have a future role in world development then they must learn to deal with the MNCs, and that cannot be done without meaningful relationships.

Everywhere today there appears to be a growing mood of mutual regard in the intense transnational debate which erupted with such fury in the UN in the 1970s on the heels of ITTs role in the overthrow of the Allende government in Chile. There was harsh rhetoric and uncompromising hostility in the early days of the UN debate. According to Algeria, MNCs were "a quasi-permanent source of tension" between North and South. But as the debate continued it appeared that the issues were more complex than first described and the interests of the parties less divergent than originally thought. And the hard times of the 1980s have further softened the rhetoric. Some of the most doctrinaire countries—China, Algeria, Guinea, India—appear to be modifying doctrine to search for accommodation; many leaders today are looking for a way to avoid the heavyhandedness of central planning and the human costs of the free market—a pragmatic alliance between public planning and private enterprise. Certainly the debate is not over; certainly the Code of Conduct for TNCs which Third World countries want the UN to enact is not yet ready to emerge. But the debate today is more even-handed. Such thorny chestnuts as the issue of the socialist state enterprises, which the USSR and associated states had managed to keep out of the debate in the early years in the original all-out attack on the West, have now been included in the draft code by the Third World right along with the private enterprise firms, much to the discomfort of the Socialist Bloc. So there is movement.

On what note can we end? Agribusiness has played a large role in development both in the developed and in the underdeveloped areas. It has not been without a bloodied and strife-ridden record. Nor has it been without positive contributions, improved productivity, new developments and horizons. What must be most conspicuous is that our political institutions and concepts have largely failed to keep pace with the changing interdependence of the world economic system, so we are attempting today to describe and "manage" the new international mechanisms of the MNCs with, at the very best, 19th century political institutions. The Genie will not be put back into the bottle; attempts to carve it up, cut it into pieces theoretically manageable by a nation-state, will only result in its transforming itself and regrowing in another form and shape. Nor is the United Nations System, with its total lack of authority regarding the actions of its member states, the answer. Yet the UN System can have a powerful moral influence and it can, by example and continued pressure and exposure, achieve some degree of conformity to internationally agreed rules or codes of conduct. The World Health Organization infant feeding formula battle is an excellent example. This lacks the force of law and there are no mechanisms to ensure conformity with the Code either by the offending MNCs or by the countries which have to date permitted the MNC violation of their own mothers and children. But there has been notable progress under the Code and more can be expected.

We still lack, however, the courage to think multinationally and to free our minds to deal with issues which have international dimensions. Such issues are an integral part of our daily life and will grow in number and complexity as world population reaches and passes the 8 billion level and as the biological resources of the planet become increasingly scarce and threatened by mankind's uncontrolled rapaciousness. We have time, but precious little time, to think and act at the level needed.

No need is greater than to ensure mankind's freedom from hunger. Two decades ago, on the 14th of March 1963, a group of distinguished world leaders, including 11 Nobel Laureates, met in a Special Assembly in FAO headquarters in Rome and wrote a Manifesto on Man's Right to Freedom from Hunger. In a passionate few hundred words these leaders appealed for common sense and action to ensure man's first fundamental right. That message is just as urgent and worthy of our attention and action as it was when written two decades ago. We must heed it!

Notes

[1] Record production continued – the 1986 cereal production levels are excellent, equal to 1985's and will probably be at a total of 1,858 million tons. However, cereal trade is likely to be at the lowest level in eight years and stocks will reach an unprecedented level of 448 million tons; the bulk will continue to be held by one country.

[2] At the end of 1986 only ten countries, six of them in Africa, were suffering from abnormal food shortages; some nine countries were listed as having unfavourable current crop prospects, including three already with abnormal shortages, Angola, Ethiopia and Mozambique.

[3] (1) National Research Council (1975) "Population and Food: Crucial Issues" *Report of the Committee on World Food, Health and Population*, Division of Biological Sciences, Assembly of Life Sciences, Washington, D.C. National Academy of Sciences. (2) The Presidential Commission on World Hunger. "Overcoming World Hunger: The Challenge Ahead" Library of Congress Catalog No. 80-600057, Washington, D.C. March 1980. (3) Of the more than 70 papers of the Worldwatch Institute (Washington, D.C.) some 24 have dealt directly with food, nutrition, forestry, water, and population. The numbers and titles can be obtained from the Worldwatch Institute. The books are: *The Twenty Ninth Day* Lester R. Brown, W.W. Norton and Co., New York 1978 and *Building a Sustainable Society* Lester R. Brown, W.W. Norton and Co., New York 1981. (4) *North-South – A Program for Survival* The Report of the Independent Commission on International Development Issues under the Chairmanship of Willy Brandt Commission 1983. Pan Books, London 1983.

[4] According to Dr. Lager Sicard, writing in the 11th edition of *World Military and Social Expenditures 1986* (World Priorities Inc., Washington, D.C., 1986) global military expenditures had risen to $900 billion in 1986.

[5] Richard J. Barnet and Ronald E. Mehter, *Global Reach*, Simon and Schuster, New York, 1974.

Trade and Pricing Policies in World Agriculture

Anandarup Ray

Even a casual look at agricultural policies around the world reveals many surprising anomalies. In the United States, for example, the government pays farmers not to grow cereals; in the European Community, farmers are paid to grow more. In Japan, rice farmers receive three times the world price for their crop. In 1985, farmers in the EC received 18¢ a pound for sugar that was then sold on the world markets for 5¢ a pound; at the same time, the EC imported sugar at 18¢ a pound. Canadian farmers pay up to eight times the price of a cow for the right to sell that cow's milk at the government's support price.

In contrast to industrial market economies, developing countries tend to tax agriculture—even those low-income countries that depend critically on agriculture for their economic growth. Some pay their producers no more than half the world price for grains and then spend scarce foreign exchange to import food. Many have raised nominal producer prices but followed macroeconomic and exchange rate policies that left real producer prices unchanged or lower than before. Many have set up complex systems of producer taxation, and then established equally complex and frequently ineffectual systems of subsidies for inputs to offset that taxation. Many subsidize consumers to help the poor, but end up reducing the incomes of farmers who are much poorer than many of the urban consumers who benefit from the subsidies. Most developing countries pronounce self-sufficiency in food as an important objective, while taxing farmers and subsidizing consumers and thus increasing their dependence upon imported food. And in periods of economic adjustment, when shortages of foreign exchange make export promotion urgent, many have increased taxes on agricultural exports and cut producer support programs, while relying on unrestricted food imports to satisfy urban consumers.

These examples raise many questions. What are the typical agricultural policies of developing and industrial countries? Are they efficient? How well do they serve the objectives of economic growth, the elimination of hunger, and the alleviation of poverty? How do these countries' agricultural policies affect each other? Even if the external environment facing developing countries is a difficult one, are they making the most of it or are they making matters worse through domestic policy mistakes? If agricultural trade and domestic policies were liberalized throughout the world, could one expect substantial gains for the world economy in general and for developing countries in particular? This article outlines some answers to these questions, drawing on the discussion in the Bank's 1986 *World Development Report*.

Originally published in *Finance and Development*, vol. 22, no. 3, September 1986. Reprinted with permission.

Policies in developing countries

Agriculture is the basic economic activity of the world's poorest countries. It employs 70 to 80 percent of the labor force in low-income developing countries and 40 to 50 percent in middle-income developing ones. It is also a main source of gross domestic product accounting for 35 to 40 percent of GDP in low-income developing countries. Agriculture's share of national income generally declines as real per capita incomes rise, because people spend a decreasing percentage of their incomes on food as their incomes increase. Almost all of today's industrial nations had roughly the same percentage of their labor forces engaged in agriculture in the nineteenth century that the low-income developing countries have now. The farmers of the industrial countries have also steadily increased the productivity of their land and labor so that an ever-decreasing share of their country's resources is needed to grow food for the rest of the population. In most of the industrial economies a farm family produces enough food for itself and as many as 50 others. In the low-income developing countries, on the other hand, a farm family provides enough food for itself and only two other people.

Although the share of agriculture in national income declines over the long term, this trend should occur naturally: neglecting agriculture and forcing its share to go down faster depresses economic growth. The experience of decades suggests that a healthy agricultural sector is essential to overall growth.

Agriculture also plays an important role in short-term economic adjustment for the many countries whose exports are largely agricultural. For these countries, improvements in the balance of payments depend heavily on the foreign exchange that can be earned by agriculture. Because agriculture accounts for large shares of incomes and export earnings in so many developing countries, success there will strongly influence the course of their economies for many years to come.

Many governments have promoted agriculture by making substantial investments in rural infrastructure, in expanding irrigation and flood control, and in strengthening agricultural research and extension services. Other programs have helped to raise productivity through better farm management and improved health, nutrition, and education.

Public spending on these types of services has been extremely helpful in many cases. For example, expansion in irrigated areas and the development of new varieties of wheat and rice have been major factors behind the growth of agricultural production in Asia and South America—two regions in which per capita food production easily exceeded population growth during the last 15 years. Yet the provision of essential public services in rural areas is but one of many elements of economic policy that determine growth in agricultural output and rural incomes. Overall, policies in developing countries have been biased against agriculture.

Developing countries pursue a wide range of agricultural policies, but in many, economy-wide policies have limited the growth of agricultural production and hampered efforts to reduce rural poverty. Sector-specific pricing and tax policies have also often resulted in substantial discrimination against agriculture. Discriminatory policies have been particularly serious in sub-Saharan Africa, the only region in the developing world that has failed to expand food production sufficiently to match population growth. A reversal of that trend, as well as expansion of agricultural exports, will be necessary if the countries in that region are to cope successfully with the current problems of high indebtedness and attain positive rates of per capita economic growth over the medium term.

Economy-wide policies. Trade, exchange rate, and macroeconomic policies have a significant influence on agriculture in all developing countries. Given their importance, a companion article by Chhibber and Wilton discusses the issues in some detail. The most important points are:

• Much of the bias against agriculture in developing countries arises from policies to promote industry behind high trade barriers. Inward-looking industrialization strategies accelerate the shift of resources out of agriculture by lowering its profitability vis-à-vis the industrial sector. Agricultural exports suffer, as do agricultural products that compete with imports. This is not just because their domestic prices become lower relative to the prices of protected industrial products but also because the costs of the industrial inputs used by farmers increase. Moreover, protectionist policies result in an appreciation of the real exchange rate. As a result, traded agricultural goods also become less profitable than non-traded goods.

• During the last 15 years the bias against agriculture has often been intensified by the way developing countries have responded to changing economic circumstances. For example, when expansionary monetary and fiscal policies have led to higher inflation at home than abroad, governments have often failed to adjust exchange rates, relying instead on increased protection against imports by means of quotas, exchange controls, and licensing. In such situations the currency becomes overvalued and the bias against agriculture deepens, since the benefits of increased protection usually accrue to industry. Typically, imported foods are exempted from such measures in order to keep urban food prices low. Food imports, in short, are implicitly subsidized. Furthermore, in trying to reduce fiscal deficits in such situations countries are apt to increase taxes on agricultural exports.

• When capital inflows from abroad or sharp increases in the world prices of key exports cause the real exchange rate to appreciate, countries typically react with expansionary monetary and fiscal policies. These then lead to inflation and augment the appreciation of the real exchange rate that was caused by the favorable change in the external terms of trade. The effects of this reaction continue even after the boom ends, because by then commitments to large investment programs or to large recurrent costs have already been made.

The differential protection of industry and currency overvaluation imply an implicit taxation of agriculture, which can often—as explained in the next article—outweigh the effects of sectoral policies. But the latter have also been extremely important sources of bias against agriculture.

Sectoral policies. Farmers effectively face many sectoral taxes and subsidies apart from conventional trade duties and subsidies. Examples are quotas, domestic sales taxes, and pricing policies of public marketing agencies. The net effects of the various policies can be captured by measuring the differences between farm-gate prices and border prices, at official exchange rates, after adjustments for internal transport and marketing margins. These net effects are additional to the implicit effects of currency overvaluations.

Many developing countries tax export crops—many raw materials and beverages—at high rates. Tax rates of 50 percent or more have been common many countries, especially in Africa. Most of this taxation results from the policies of export marketing boards with statutory monopoly powers. A few years ago, the farm price for coffee in Togo was only one third of the international price; cotton and groundnut farmers in Mali received only half the international prices; and in Cameroon and Ghana cocoa producers received less than half this price. Asian and South American countries frequently tax their exports not only of raw materials and beverages but also of grains.

Some agricultural import substitutes—especially wheat, dairy products, and livestock—are protected in a few developing countries. But in most cases, the domestic producers of import substitutes receive less than import prices, adjusted for internal marketing costs. Taxation rates on import substitutes have often been excessive. For example, Tanzania's official price for maize has been only about 25 percent of the import price in some years, while in Cameroon and Ghana, rice producers have received only about half the import parity prices.

Typically, the most important reason for taxing agricultural output is to raise revenue or control the costs of other public programs. Although most parastatal export marketing boards were originally required to use their funds to assist farmers, many have become *de facto* taxation agencies for financing public spending elsewhere. The most important reason for taxing import-competing crops is to control the costs of urban food subsidy programs.

Raising revenue through export taxes may be self-defeating. First the rates of taxation often seen are likely to generate less, rather than more, revenue than lower rates, because of their effect on incentives to produce. Second, the real national income sacrificed in the process of taxation escalates rapidly as the tax rate increases. Assuming conservatively that a country's exports of a commodity rise in exact proportion to the commodity's international price, getting the last dollar of tax revenue will cost only 5.6 cents if the export tax is 5 percent. If, however, the rate is 40 percent, the last dollar of tax revenue will cost two dollars to obtain. And indeed, beyond 50 percent total revenue will decrease when the tax rate is increased so that it would be pointless to increase the tax further. If export taxes must be used, much lower rates are desirable.

Similarly, where import-competing food crops are taxed, excessive rates depress domestic supplies and cause a high dependence on imports. The priority should rather be to lower the costs of food subsidy programs to levels the country can easily afford and to target them better to reach the poorest income groups.

Among the other reasons for high taxation of export crops in developing countries are: promotion of agroindustries by lowering the costs of their exportable agricultural inputs; promotion of food production by diverting resources from export crops; and the exploitation of perceived monopoly powers in world markets. Upon close examination of cross-country comparisons, these reasons appear to be untenable. In the case of agroindustries, for example, taxes or quotas on their raw material inputs have imposed high economic losses in countries as diverse as Brazil, Ghana, and Tanzania.

As shown by detailed studies in Argentina and Chile, excessive rates of sectoral taxation, when combined with the taxation implicit in persistent overvaluations of the exchange rate, can have extremely harmful effects on economic and agricultural growth. If discrimination against agriculture is sustained for some time, farmers and private capital move out of farming altogether. Farms then deteriorate, and migration to cities becomes excessive. Those who remain on the land find it less profitable to use input-intensive methods. As in Africa, this inhibits technical progress and hastens soil degradation.

It is often argued that the generous subsidies that many developing countries provide on such farm inputs as chemical fertilizers, machinery, seeds, pesticides, and credit offset the bias against agriculture caused by the heavy taxation of farm outputs. This, however, is not true. It is extremely difficult to implement such subsidies in an equitable and efficient manner. The availability of credit and modern inputs is often jeopardized by the budgetary costs of the subsidies and of the inefficiency of public distribution systems. The main beneficiaries of these types of subsidies are typically larger and relatively affluent farmers. In addition, input subsidies cause distortions in the choice of crops and farming techniques, often compounding rather than offsetting the adverse effects of output taxes.

Neither does the widespread intervention by the government in the marketing of agricultural products help to offset the effects of taxation. Such intervention has in practice tended to be inefficient. The experience in many developing countries suggests that better results can be achieved through greater reliance on private markets. The losses of marketing parastatals are often extremely large, in some cases reaching 1 or 2 percent of national income. Public monopolies impose high costs, even when farmers are able to bypass official channels and sell in parallel markets.

Public marketing agencies are often required to stabilize consumer and producer prices, in addition to carrying out other functions. Partly because of multiple and often conflicting objectives, efficient and profitable price stabilization schemes are hard to find in developing countries. The methods typically used for price stabilization can increase the economic costs of price fluctuations in world markets; they frequently result in excessively large buffer stocks, erratic changes in "floor" and "ceiling" prices, and high budgetary subsidies. In addition public stabilization schemes displace private sector operations. Crowding out becomes especially serious when public agencies try to impose the same price across different regions of the country and across different seasons.

Regardless of their original motivation, both economy-wide and agricultural policies in developing countries have evolved in ways that discourage growth of agricultural output and rural incomes. There is great scope for improving policies and performance. In recognition of this, several countries, notably China and Turkey, have undertaken broad programs of reform. Many others—including countries in Africa—are changing their policies more gradually, to make programs for urban food subsidies more efficient to curtail or eliminate farm input subsidies, to reduce state intervention in marketing, and to improve farm output prices. Policy reforms of this type, along with better economy-wide policies and more expenditures on rural infrastructure, offer developing countries their best chance of promoting growth in agriculture and in the wider economy, thereby facilitating sustained progress toward food security—the eradication of poverty, malnutrition, and the periodic occurrence of famines.

Policies in industrial countries

The main objectives of agricultural policies in industrial countries are to stabilize and increase farmers' incomes and slow the migration of people out of the agricultural sector. Underlying these objectives are the social and political aims of stable food prices and self-sufficiency in food production, which go hand in hand with such other goals as preventing environmental damage to the countryside and preserving the traditional farming unit, usually the family farm.

A variety of measures are used to support farm incomes at levels higher than would result from free trade. Apart from import tariffs and quotas, variable import levies are often used—particularly in the EC—to maintain high and stable domestic producer prices. If protection creates excess supplies, the excess is ultimately disposed of in world markets through subsidized sales or as food aid. Export restitutions are the exporter's equivalent of variable import levies, permitting domestic prices to be independent of world prices. State-controlled marketing boards, direct payments to producers, and subsidies on inputs and credit are also widely used to aid farmers. When farmers produce too much, several countries use acreage controls to keep down surpluses.

On average, producer prices in industrial market economies are about 40 percent above comparable world prices, but there is considerable variation in protection rates by commodity and country. The average protection rate during 1980-82 in Japan, for example, was about 144 percent and in the EC about 84 percent. By contrast, there is hardly any protection in New Zealand. Among commodities, the most protected items are sugar, dairy products, rice, and beef.

While protection rates tend to vary from year to year, the general trend has been sharply upward. Average protection rates in the mid-1950s were about 40 percent in Japan and only 16 percent in the EC. Agricultural protection in industrial countries in agriculture has never been higher—even compared to the 1930s. Moreover, those developing economies which have grown fast have begun to emulate the agricultural policies of industrial countries. For example, the Republic of Korea was taxing farmers in the mid-1950s, albeit at a rate much lower than typical in low-income countries today, but by the early 1980s its average agricultural protection rate had reached 166 percent.

Excessive support of farmers over such a long period has predictably increased yields and production just as the excessive and sustained taxation of farmers in some parts of the developing world has produced the opposite effect. For example, the EC is now a large exporter of grains, although it was an importer when it initiated its Common Agricultural Policy. Thanks to its farm support policies, it is now second only to the United States as an agricultural exporter. It has captured large shares of world markets-especially in wheat and wheat flour, sugar, beef, and butter.

Support to farmers is wasteful and depresses national incomes; consumers and taxpayers always lose more than farmers gain. The 1986 *World Development Report* provides various estimates of the losses, drawing on the existing literature. It also presents the results of a special study done for the *Report*, which indicates that consumers and taxpayers in the OECD countries lose about $104 billion each year in order to support a sector of the economy that contributes only small shares of national income and employment. Farmers do gain, but by much less.

The gains that farmers realize from these support policies get capitalized in terms of higher land values. Moreover, policies to protect farmers have also become less necessary as farming has become more and more a part-time occupation. In the United States, net farm income as a proportion of farmers' total income fell from 58 percent in 1960 to 36 percent in 1982. In Japan, where small-scale farming is dominant, farm households derived 75 percent of their income from nonfarm sources in 1980. The families of part-time farmers with permanent jobs outside farming were about 25 percent better off than families with one or more full-time farm workers.

As in developing countries, many governments in industrial countries are considering agricultural policy reforms. It has become clear that without policy changes to reduce protection, domestic costs will continue to rise in the years ahead, whatever means are chosen for handling growing excess supplies. For example:

- Adding to stocks, as the EC and the United States have been doing for cereals and dairy products, will become increasingly costly and eventually unsustainable as stocks grow larger in relation to annual domestic use or the available storage capacity.
- Restricting output through direct intervention, such as the milk quotas in the EC or acreage restriction programs in the United States, is unattractive, economically and politically. Compulsory measures are unpopular with producers. If compliance with such measures is voluntary, US experience indicates that the budgetary and economic costs of obtaining even a modest reduction in output are great.
- Encouraging consumption domestically or abroad via subsidies will require even more budgetary outlays.

Consequences and priorities

As is clear from this discussion, industrial and developing countries tend to follow exactly opposite policies. Industrial countries produce too much, and developing countries produce too little. The patterns of world agricultural production and exports would change in favor of developing countries if both groups of countries followed efficient policies.

Just as a country gains by allocating its resources to where they can be most productive, the world as a whole would certainly gain if more were produced in developing countries for both domestic use and exports. This would require much freer trade and liberal domestic policies in all countries.

It is extremely difficult to make confident estimates of just how much the world might gain with such policies. Nonetheless, a review of the literature and the background work for the *World Development Report* suggest that the gains would indeed be very substantial. If industrial market economies and developing countries were simultaneously to liberalize their domestic policies and remove trade barriers, in temperate-zone products alone, industrial market economies would gain by about $46 billion annually and developing countries by about $18 billion. These estimated gains to the developing countries represent a large portion of their annual receipts of official development aid. If tropical-zone and processed agricultural products were also taken into account the potential gains would probably be much larger.

Another benefit would be the savings and convenience that would result from a higher degree of stability in world prices. Free trade allows supply fluctuations in different parts of the world to offset each other. Insular policies, on the other hand, increase the variability of prices. Policies in both industrial and developing countries have been important factors behind the high volatility of world market prices of agricultural commodities, especially sugar. In the case of wheat, for example, studies have indicated that the amplitude of international price fluctuations would be reduced by 33 to 48 percent if free trade policies were instituted.

The difficulties of coordinating domestic and trade policies in various countries have thus far prevented the multilateral liberalization of agricultural trade. Various ad hoc measures have been proposed or undertaken to increase the benefits that developing countries receive from commodity trade. Examples are international commodity agreements, compensatory financing mechanisms, special trade preferences, and food aid.

The results of some of these measures have, however, fallen short of expectations. The commodity agreements have had very little success in stabilizing prices, and only two—for coffee and rubber—are currently active. Trade preference schemes have provided only small transfers to developing countries and have not significantly increased their agricultural exports. On the other hand, compensatory financing schemes have provided valuable assistance despite the fact that their operations have remained limited in scale. Food aid has also been helpful, especially for famine relief. Getting the right commodities to the people most in need, without retarding the growth of agricultural production in recipient countries, has, however, proved to be difficult.

In any case, the potential benefits of these measures fall far short of what could be achieved through agricultural trade liberalization. Progress toward liberalization of domestic and trade policies in a coordinated manner should clearly have priority on the current agenda of the world community. The prospective GATT multilateral trade negotiations are the most promising way of achieving such liberalization at present.

Agribusiness, Development and Nutrition

Theodore Cohn

The intimate and complex interrelationships of agribusiness, development and nutrition have received surprisingly little attention, despite the large volume of literature written on each of these issues. In many studies of development, for example, nutritional matters are of only peripheral concern: and books on nutrition rarely examine the implications for development. This is particularly unfortunate since a vicious circle often exists in less-developed countries (LDCs), with underdevelopment contributing to malnutrition and vice versa.

The growing presence of multinational agribusiness in the Third World has been recognized, but the literature on this subject tends to be extremely polarized. The pervasive conflict between proponents and critics of multinational enterprises (MNEs) was characterized by a 1981 *New York Times* article on the Nestle baby-formula controversy as "a battle in which politics and money, not science have come to dominate."[1] Issues of development and nutrition are therefore frequently treated as secondary in studies of agribusiness.

Linkages between agribusiness and development are, of course, examined in some studies. For example, in *A Plough in Field Arable* Sarah Potts Voll discusses the effects of technology transfer by multinational enterprises on agricultural development in LDCs.[2] Other writings, such as those concerning efforts to market high-protein, low-cost foodstuffs, discuss the effects of agribusiness on nutrition. However, there are extremely few studies that examine the relationship of agribusiness with *both* development and nutrition.

In this paper, we discuss some reasons for deficiencies in literature, and then examine the important linkages among agribusiness, nutrition and development by focusing on two major issues: 1) the involvement of multinational agribusiness in contract farming, and 2) the role of agribusiness in the marketing of baby formula.

1. Studies of Nutrition and Development

The United Nations Food and Agriculture Organization (FAO) has defined malnutrition as "the physical effects on the human being of a dietary intake inadequate in quantity and/or quality."[3] Protein-calorie malnutrition (PCM) is the term used to describe the most severe and widespread nutritional deficiencies, especially among the most vulnerable groups (children to 2 years, and pregnant and nursing mothers). Symptoms can range from retardation of growth and development, to susceptibility to infections, diseases, and death. Also prevalent in many LDCs are iron-deficiency anemia and vitamin A deficiency. Severe shortages of vitamin A are a common cause of partial or total blindness.

Published for the first time in this volume.

Malnutrition has been described by the FAO as "the biggest single contributor to child mortality in the developing countries."[4] Children under five years are most severely affected, with reports in the 1970s that 10 million of them were suffering from severe malnutrition, 80 million from a moderate form, and 120 million from less obvious minor forms. "About 50 per cent of all young children in the developing world" were therefore described as being "inadequately nourished."[5] Yet, the malnutrition problem has often been virtually ignored in studies of development.

In his important book, *The Nutrition Factor*, Alan Berg discusses some of the reasons for this inattention to nutritional issues. Malnutrition was traditionally considered to be a welfare rather than a development problem. Although it is associated with more deaths and disease than famines, malnutrition draws less attention because it is more unobtrusive and insidious—i.e., "it lacks drama."[6]

Inadequate attention to the complex interaction between nutrition and development contributes to the tendency to view global food problems simply in terms of aggregate food availability. Thus, the 1974 World Food Conference has been severely criticized for reinforcing the impression that all would be well "if a country could increase its agricultural production and/or its food imports."[7] Unfortunately, however, there is no assurance that the poor in low-income countries will be better nourished if national food availability increases. Nutritional conditions also depend upon the development process in LDCs, and the resultant importance given to distribution of income and resources. The nutritional problem is not simply one of food supply, but also of the relationship of people to the land and of inadequate effective demand, or the inability of the poor to purchase food. Thus, Alan Berg found that malnutrition was far more extensive in Mexico, with a per capita income of $530 per year very unevenly distributed, than in Taiwan with a more evenly distributed income of $270 per year.

Recognition has gradually increased that problems of malnutrition and underdevelopment are intimately related. Indeed, they frequently form a vicious cycle with malnutrition detracting from development efforts, and with nutrition in turn dependent upon environmental conditions:

Protein-calorie (energy) malnutrition is now generally viewed as a broader ecological problem which is in part due to the inadequate availability of food or specific nutrients, but which is also a function of generalized poverty, deficient social organization, poor environmental sanitation, and ignorance of proper feeding and care of the child.[8]

2. Studies of Agribusiness and the Third World

The term "agribusiness" was first used by John Davis and Ray Goldberg of the Harvard University Business School to analyze the interrelated functions of business and agriculture.[9] Agribusiness is a broad-ranging concept, defined by Goldberg and Davis as an integrated food system extending from farm inputs to farm production, to processing and retailing (or marketing).

Unfortunately, the general theoretical literature on multinational enterprises has contributed little to our understanding of the behaviour and role of multinational agribusiness firms in LDCs:

Because overseas investments in the last three decades have flowed primarily toward the developed countries and almost entirely into manufacturing, the literature on multinational enterprises reflects this situation, resulting in few studies on MNEs and agriculture in the Third World. Some of the published observations are apt, but most, unfortunately, are irrelevant. A few are actually misleading.[10]

In recent years, however, there has been an aggressive push for expansion by multinational agribusiness, in production contracting with Third World farmers and in marketing of agricultural inputs and food products in LDCs. Contract farming has become increasingly popular for the production and export of high-quality horticultural goods to industrial states; and, conversely, as developed-country markets for some manufactured food products have become "saturated," there has been some shift in retailing towards the Third World.

The limited usefulness of the general MNE literature for studying these changes may partly account for the lack of objective analyses of the behaviour of multinational agribusiness firms. Most authors tend to be either strongly critical of, or strongly favourable to, their role in the Third World, with few studies discussing *both* positive and negative effects. This polarization of opinions also stems from widely divergent views concerning the acceptability of "profit" as a primary motivation. In a survey of agribusiness executives conducted by the Conference Board in the United States (an independent business research organization), respondents indicated that MNEs in the Third World require

First, *a market*. People with neither money nor goods with which to satisfy their need for food do not constitute a 'market' to which commercial efforts can respond. A company can respond to those who have money, or something else of marketable value—be they governments or individuals. Market, from the business viewpoint, is demand for a product or service expressed in monetary units.[11]

Since the largest proportion of peoples in LDCs lack effective demand (or demand backed by purchasing power), multinational agribusiness firms do not emphasize production and marketing for the poorest and most malnourished in the Third World. Instead, production and retailing are oriented to international markets (e.g., cash crops) and to high or middle-income groups in LDCs. This is regarded by many critics as a fatal flaw of MNEs, in view of the scope and severity of malnutrition. Even if MNEs can contribute to increases in agricultural production, the Third World poor do not benefit, and may even suffer as a result. A considerable amount of literature, for example, focuses on the fact that wealthier farmers reap the advantages of agribusiness inputs (fertilizer, pesticides, etc.), contributing to a widening gap with the more numerous impoverished peasants. It is also frequently maintained that food products marketed by multinational agribusiness are inaccessible to, or inappropriate for the poorest groups and might even contribute to a decline in nutritional conditions.

Despite some validity in many of the arguments presented, the critical literature is so preoccupied with citing negative examples that the positive strengths of multinational agribusiness are frequently ignored. A zero-sum game approach is taken, i.e., that the gains for international capital represent losses for the needy in LDCs. A research specialist for Abbott Laboratories, who studies infant nutrition in the Third World, has pointed out that

to characterize all of the business enterprise as solely money-hungry, competitive and insensitive to social problems, may reveal more about the bias of the observer than an understanding of the modern enterprise. The private sector has over and over again revealed its capacity to solve problems, to adapt to circumstances, and to produce goods and services that make life more tolerable.[12]

Furthermore, transnational agribusiness performs certain essential marketing and other functions, and will continue to do so, indicating that LDCs "cannot afford not to deal with [them]."[13]

Little attention has been devoted to utilizing the abilities of agribusiness firms, while ensuring that MNEs do not impose an unacceptable model for agricultural development and food marketing on Third World countries. The role of governments, and of international and nongovernmental organizations in cooperating with some of the more responsible MNEs, while circumscribing their role, and determining when they are/are not performing a necessary function, requires further study. For example, it would be useful to examine the extent to which behaviour of multinationals can—in the long term—be altered by voluntary codes of behaviour such as the code for marketing of baby foods adopted by the World Health Assembly in May 1981.

The strong advocacy-nature of much literature on agribusiness MNEs (whether pro- or con-) has often diverted attention from the basic issues of Third-World malnutrition, and has led to attaching simplistic labels to many individuals and groups. Although the serious harm done by marketing techniques of some baby formula companies should not be underestimated, one can nevertheless understand Margaret Mead's frustration with being forced onto one side or the other on this issue:

It's possible to give a context to breastfeeding which will see our babies and our mothers properly cared for. . . Crusaders in a different crusade are turning it into another piece of ideology, so if you are against Transnationals, you are for breastfeeding, but if you are for supplementary feeding and weaning food you are for Transnationals. . . .(that's) nonsense. We want to enlist these companies on the side of sensible supplementation of breastfeeding.[14]

3. Studies of Agribusiness, Development and Nutrition

As discussed, some of the literature on agribusiness goes beyond polemics, and provides analyses of the relationship between agribusiness and development, or between agribusiness and nutrition. However, there are few studies that analyze the relationship of agribusiness with *both* development and nutrition. A major reason for this deficiency is that certain stages of the agribusiness chain – e.g., technology transfer and provision of agricultural inputs – are more directly linked with development than with nutrition; while the marketing stage is more directly connected with nutrition. Depending on the stage of agribusiness an analyst focuses upon there is thus a tendency to emphasize relationships with *either* development *or* nutrition.

It is necessary, however, to better understand the interrelationships of all three issues. Studies of the multinational seed industry, for example, tend to focus more heavily on MNE effects on agricultural development. Yet, Pat Mooney maintains that multinational agribusiness and agrochemical companies have a "YUP" bias which emphasizes breeding for "yield, uniformity, and processing." The YUP bias is designed to increase the profitability of the company and may involve promotion of food products that are nutritionally inferior.[15]

For a more objective analysis of agribusiness, the discussion that follows draws on a variety of perspectives ranging from the business school economists to the dependencia and Marxist theorists. Interrelationships of agribusiness, nutrition and development are also examined by focusing on the agribusiness role concerning two issues: 1) agricultural production—what to produce and for whom, and 2) food marketing—the baby formula controversy. Since the formula marketing controversy provides an unusually good illustration of linkages between agribusiness and nutrition, and of polarized attitudes concerning MNEs, the marketing issue is given particular attention.

4. Agricultural Production—What to Produce and for Whom

As discussed, it is simplistic to assume that nutritional conditions depend solely (or even primarily) on the level of agricultural production and/or food imports in an LDC. Decisions concerning what agricultural commodities to produce, and for which individuals, have major implications for both nutrition and development. Agricultural exports provide a vital source of foreign exchange, but may compete with domestic food production for land, capital, labour, research facilities, and government services. If production of food staples consumed by the poorer segments of the population is given lower priority, malnutrition can obviously result.

Multinational agribusiness normally has been associated with production of cash crops for export and of foodstuffs for higher income groups in LDCs. In recent years, however, MNEs have become less involved in direct agricultural productions through ownership, while retaining control of the more profitable and less risky aspects of the production process. These include provision of inputs, processing, transport, marketing, and distribution.

Large-scale plantations have become more difficult to maintain in LDCs, particularly with the threat of nationalization or moves to promote smallholder agriculture. Furthermore, it is the direct producers that are affected most by poor harvests and price fluctuations on international markets. Direct production has also become less profitable with state regulation of wages and conditions of employment; and the costs of agricultural production have accounted for a decreasing percentage of the end-product price.[16] Agribusiness firms have therefore viewed "contract farming" increasingly as a preferred alternative to direct production. In this relationship an indigenous grower is committed to planting, harvesting, and delivering a specified product on a specific date to a contracting processor. Although the grower sustains major risks and responsibilities, he also derives some benefits such as assistance from agribusiness firms in technology and marketing.

One approach to the role of agribusiness in production contracting is typified by J. David Morrissy's study *Agricultural Modernization through Production Contracting*. Morrissy applies the agribusiness coordination model developed at the Harvard Business School to assess the role of the fruit and vegetable processor in Mexico and Central America. A largely unstated premise pervasive in the book is that agribusiness is highly beneficial for developing countries. Although the author does not claim to be writing a social study, the question arises whether the social implications of his systems analysis can be ignored. Morrissy's "system" is the fruit and vegetable processing industry in Mexico and Central America, and virtually no effort is made to relate this system to the peoples and social settings in which they reside. Thus, Third-World peoples in this study are largely viewed as factors of production, and both nutritional and development issues are entirely peripheral.

A prime example is Morrissy's discussion of Mexico's positive balance of trade in fruits and vegetables:

Foreign trade statistics suggest measures of a country's food processing self-sufficiency. . . Mexico imports $2.7 million of processed fruits and vegetables. . . Exports of fruits and vegetables are more substantial, amounting to over $26 million. . .

In summary, Mexico has performed well as a fruit and vegetable processing system. It has developed an integral chain of components that operate efficiently enough to make the country fairly self-sufficient as well as able to compete in world markets.[17]

Morrissy's discussion of "self-sufficiency" is limited to the fruit and vegetable system: the implications of emphasis on horticultural exports for self-sufficiency in basic foodstuffs and for nutritional conditions in Mexico are not even considered. The effects of contract agriculture on the indigenous food system are also beyond the scope of his study. Questions pertaining to whether or not contract farming undermines basic food production through the price mechanism (inducing farmers to shift away from cultivation of staples) and through the strictures of long-term contractual relations are simply not addressed.[18]

Yet, data of the National Food Survey indicate that in 1974 (the year Morrissy's book was published) millions of Mexicans were seriously malnourished. Mexico's nutritional problems have clearly been exacerbated by the relative decline of basic food crops (beans, maize, rice, wheat and some oats) from 78.8 percent of total cultivation in 1940 to 57.0 percent in 1980. The best northern lands, and many of the prime areas in central and southern Mexico have been increasingly dedicated to export agriculture. In the irrigation districts, two crop types have increased in importance: export fruits and vegetables, and fodder for animals. Basic foodstuffs have by contrast been more frequently subject to the uncertainties of rainfed agriculture. A division of labour has resulted where Mexico exports luxury food products to the United States, while becoming increasingly dependent on its northern neighbour for imports of basic foodstuffs.[19]

Additional examples abound in the literature critical of agribusiness emphasis on production for export and for the privileged classes in LDCs. Some of the cases cited include the following:

1) In a region of the Dominican Republic, land was diverted from the production of basic foodstuffs to sugarcane acreage "to meet the demands of Gulf & Western Industries, Inc., a U.S. multinational."[20] When peasants in the area seized some land reserved for sugarcane in 1974 and planted beans and other food staples, the army dislodged them and destroyed their crops.

2) Land in an area of Colombia was diverted from pulses (e.g., dry beans) for human consumption to production of soybeans and sorghum grown for animal feed. This was associated with the interest of Purina Colombiana, a subsidiary of the feed company Ralston Purina, in developing a local poultry industry. Unlike pulses which are accessible to the poor in LDCs, poultry and eggs are relatively high-priced foods available to the middle and upper classes. Intensive poultry production has also become increasingly popular in many African countries. In 1974, for example, a subsidiary of British American Tobacco invested in a new poultry business in Kenya.

3) At the height of the Sahelian drought of the late 1960s and early 1970gs, Senegal was exporting fresh vegetables to Europe and 55 percent of its arable land was producing groundnuts for export.

4) International organizations such as the World Bank and FAO have sometimes promoted and facilitated agribusiness involvement in export agriculture. In 1975, for example, the FAO's Industrial Cooperative Program was involved in a two billion dollar tsetse fly eradication program in Africa to improve conditions for production of beef on the continent.[21]

Although the critical literature points to some potentially damaging effects of agribusiness on production of food staples, discussion of nutritional and development problems has often been secondary to strident criticism of MNEs. Thus, much of the literature

has been premised on the dependency school and implies that international agribusiness, international financial institutions (especially the World Bank), a dependent comprador state, and the rich farmers in the Third World countries are engaged in a 'conspiracy.' Such conspiracies lead to dependent capitalist development necessarily marginalising and emmiserating the rural poor.[22]

As a result, the dilemma confronting LDCs in finding a suitable balance between production for export and for domestic consumption, the relationship between multinational and indigenous agribusiness in LDCs, and the effects of these issues on nutrition in the Third World have rarely been objectively examined.

Although efforts to promote food self-sufficiency are laudable, it is also necessary to sustain a reasonable level of cash crop exports, and export promotion cannot be dismissed as nothing more than an agribusiness-instigated "conspiracy." For example, the Tanzanian government has received considerable praise for providing incentives to peasants for growing food staples. Unfortunately, however, insufficient attention was given to the decline in revenue derived from cash crops. As a result, the volume of cash crops exported decreased precipitously from 404,000 tons in 1973 to 279,000 tons in 1978. This contributed to a foreign exchange crisis for Tanzania in 1979, which was compounded by the costs of fuel imports and of ousting Idi Amin from Uganda.[23]

It also cannot be assumed that export agriculture and basic food production must *necessarily* be in competition. Kenya is the largest tea producer in Africa and the third largest tea exporting country in the world. Multinational tea companies have been closely involved with development of a smallholder tea program in the country. Yet, very little of farmers' land is devoted to tea, and their income from tea production is often spent on increasing productivity of food crops: i.e., there is no evidence that basic food production is being marginalized as a result. In contrast, sugar production in Kenya has been somewhat more competitive with food production, but even in this case the effects have not been highly detrimental and have been limited to the smallest sugar farmers.[24] At the least, these diverse findings indicate the need for more case-by-case studies rather than broad generalizations concerning the relationship between production for export versus domestic consumption.

Although the dependency theorists examine national as well as multinational agribusiness, they perceive "the national bourgeoisie and the apparatus of the peripheral state. . .as instruments in the hands of, and controlled by, international capital."[25] Indigenous agribusiness in the Third World certainly is dependent on multinational enterprises for certain functions, such as export marketing and distribution. Pricing powers of LDC producers can also be limited because export-quality foodstuffs are often too expensive for the domestic LDC market. Nevertheless, dependency models of the multinational-national agribusiness relationship tend to underestimate the diversity of linkages that can exist in varying situations. The issue of Mexican fruit and vegetable producers provides an example of a relationship receiving too little attention in the critical literature.

American agribusiness was responsible for development of Mexico's fruit and vegetable industry, but Mexicans gradually gained control of the production and distribution phases for several reasons. Some of the largest Mexican producers originally came from the

United States to produce for export to the American market. Most of them married Mexican women and became citizens of that country. Also, the major Mexican producers were extremely successful financially and wished to expand their role through forward integration. By 1979, about half of the distributorships in Arizona (the gateway to the American market) were subsidiaries of Mexican producer firms.[26]

Alliance behaviour in the fruit and vegetable industry has been extremely interesting, with Mexican producers joining with U.S. business and consumer interests against Florida producers who want to limit Mexican competition. David Mares concludes that

it becomes misleading to view this commodity system as simply another manifestation of the expansion of capital North to South; rather the *binational* character of the industry should be stressed, U.S. *and* Mexican companies work together as part of an agribusiness commodity system.

This binational characteristic leads to transnational relations among the various components of the system based upon their mutual interdependence.[27]

The term "interdependence" can of course "subtly. . .(obscure) the inequalities of national capability" (e.g., between the United States and Mexico), and some analysts would disagree with Mares' conclusions.[28] Steven Sanderson, for example, maintains that Mexican vegetable producers for the American market have no immediate pricing power, and also do not have a domestic spillover market, because export produce is expensive and is not sold in the basic Mexican market. One could argue therefore that Mexican producers are more dependent on American agribusiness interests than David Mares implies. Nevertheless, this example does point to the failure to examine the variety of relationships that exist in different LDCs between national and international agribusiness. The dependency literature has simply been too preoccupied with criticism of MNEs to recognize the diverse effects of agribusiness, in different LDCs and for different commodities, on nutrition and development.

5. Food Marketing—The Baby Formula Controversy

Similar to the production issue, discussion of agribusiness and food marketing has frequently been marked more by positions of advocacy and polarization of groups than by objective analysis of the issues. The infant baby formula controversy which led to a boycott of Nestle products on July 4, 1977 provides an important case study that demonstrates these phenomena. In view of unethical tactics of a number of baby food companies, and the corporate strength of companies such as Nestle, it is understandable that critics had to join forces if marketing practices contributing to malnutrition were to be altered. Nevertheless, in the confrontational atmosphere that prevailed throughout the 1970s the real issues of malnutrition and development were often submerged in an atmosphere marked by politicization, militancy, and ideology. Thus, we earlier quoted a 1981 article in the *New York Times* that characterized the Nestle baby-food controversy as "a battle in which politics and money, not science, have come to dominate."[29]

The marketing of baby foods was controversial long before Nestle became involved in the Third World. Pediatricians had warned against feeding sweetened condensed milk (SCM) to babies as early as 1872. Yet, there are reports of infant malnutrition and death from improper use of SCM among the industrial poor in Britain in the early 1900s. It is frequently argued in the literature that LDCs now have problems similar to those of industrial countries about eighty years earlier.

The complex issues surrounding the infant formula debate in the Third World can be divided into three different phases: 1) The first phase covered the period from the late 1960s to the mid-1970s, and focused primarily on scientific issues. 2) The second extended from the mid-1970s to the adoption of the World Health Organization (WHO) code in 1981, and was marked by advocacy and antagonism. 3) The third, on-going phase seems to be marked by a modicum of consensus, allowing a return to scientific questions and research.

Before discussing these phases of the baby-formula controversy, it is necessary to provide some background on the current state of scientific research.[30]

A. Scientific research on breast versus bottle feeding

A fairly strong consensus has emerged among nutritionists and doctors on a number of issues related to breast versus bottle feeding:

1) Among lower socioeconomic groups in LDCs, breast milk is preferable to bottle feeding, and may be important for infant survival. Breast milk provides an inexpensive and necessary source of protein and calories, and a certain amount of immunological protection. Recent research findings concerning chemical contamination of breast milk have not altered the basic agreement on this issue.

2) The need for formula exists, in some cases as a substitute for breast milk, and more frequently as a supplement. Breast feeding is simply not always possible, or sufficient.

3) Despite some exceptions, it is agreed that many baby formulas are nutritious and safe products when used properly. Until the late 1950s, formula was essentially diluted cow's milk with sugar. Today, it is as "humanized" as much as possible, by changing the fat content, and adding nutrients and fortification. However, the compositions remain different, and human milk is superior in terms of anti-infective and immunologically-active substances.

4) In LDCs, formula is often used improperly for economic, sanitary, and educational reasons. Numerous studies show that formula is too expensive for the poor, and is over-diluted as a result. Requisite sanitary conditions for preparation of the product (e.g., clean water) are also frequently unavailable. Improper use can cause infant malnutrition, illness, and death.

5) Advertising and promotion by formula companies has sometimes encouraged the use of products when they are neither appropriate nor necessary. Many questionable marketing tactics have been employed, including the use of hospitals, physicians, and women dressed like nurses ("milk nurses") to promote the distribution of products.

6) Company promotion methods are not the sole cause for the use/misuse of formulas among lower socio-economic groups. Other factors include the role of government and health personnel, elite example, food aid, cultural bias, modernization, and the increased tendency for mothers to seek employment.

B. Phase 1: The late 1960s to mid-1970s

Beginning in the 1960s, doctors and other specialists observed several simultaneous trends among mothers and infants in the Third World: an increase in infant malnutrition, a decline in breastfeeding accompanied by a rise in bottlefeeding, and an increase in advertising of manufactured infant formula. In many cases it was found that poor mothers prepared formula with contaminated water at heavily diluted strength, and used unhygienic (non-sterilized) bottles and equipment. Bottle-fed babies were found to suffer more than breast-fed babies from undernourishment, infections, diarrhea, gastroenteritis, and death.

The breastfeeding-bottlefeeding debate began with anthropologists and sociologists such as Margaret Mead and Dana Raphael, who examined underlying causes of the decline in breastfeeding, and possible ways to reverse this trend. Pediatricians, nutritionists and economists contributed their respective arguments. Dr D.B. Jeliffe is generally credited with raising the initial alarm in the health sciences as a result of his 1968-71 findings of deteriorating infant health in the Caribbean, and he coined the famous phrase "commerciogenic malnutrition" to describe the dangers inherent in aggressive advertising of baby formula.

In response to the growing debate, the Protein Advisory Group (PAG) of the United Nations Secretariat from 1969 began a serious dialogue with eminent pediatricians and executives of the baby food industries. Issues discussed included advertising codes for government and industry, and development of inexpensive weaning foods. Although the formula companies were certainly eager to pursue their inherent goal of good profits from good markets, and were fully capable of using questionable marketing tactics, they did not refuse cooperation. Indeed, cooperation seemed to be far more apparent than confrontation during this period.

C. Phase 2: The mid-1970s to 1981

During the 1970s, the baby formula issue was marked by increased confrontation, a higher profile with the general public, and a greater tendency to target the baby food companies (particularly Nestle) in monocausal fashion as responsible for infant malnutrition.

A number of companies (multinational and indigenous) manufacture infant formula, and sell and distribute it in LDCs. Nestle was nevertheless considered the main protagonist because of its dominant presence in the Third World. Also, its Swiss headquarters placed Nestle beyond the reach of the shareholder resolution campaign in the United States challenging corporations to accept social responsibility for their actions. Nestle Alimentaria is the second largest food firm in the world after Unilever, and accounts for about one-third of the global baby food market. Similar to the case of contract farming, Nestle avoids some of the risks borne by producers; it owns no cows or land, but supplies or controls inputs and outputs. Its baby food sales in 1981 amounted to about 300 to 400 million dollars, and it distributes formula in 140 countries. In the Third World, Latin America is by far its most important area, followed by Asia and Africa.[31]

A Nestle annual report in the 1970s explained why LDCs were considered a significant market growth area for baby food companies:

. . .the continued decline in birth rate, particularly in countries with a high standard of living, retarded the growth of the market. This resulted in considerably increased competition. . . In the developing countries our own products continue to sell well thanks to the growth of population and improved living standards.[32]

The increasing popularity of a return to breastfeeding in industrial countries also encouraged MNEs to intensify marketing efforts in the Third World.

While the earlier debate concerning baby formula was largely confined to specialists, the second phase of the debate effectively began when a British periodical, *The New Internationalist*, raised the alarm before the general public in August 1973.[33] The publication's cover seemed to assert, in word and pictorial image, that Nestle's lactogen had been a principal cause of a baby's death. The image took hold among numerous individuals and groups, and each public discussion seemed to go beyond the previous one in condemning the formula industry.

A report entitled "The Baby Killer" was published by a British charity organization, War on Want, in 1974. It clearly indicated that the industry was primarily responsible for misuse of its products. The Third World Action Group in Bern, Switzerland then translated this Report into German and sharpened its tone, as evident from the new title "Nestle Kills Babies." As a result, Nestle sued the Action Group for libel in July 1974. Before, during, and after the court case, publications and interested groups multiplied.[34]

Nestle eventually dropped three of its original four counts of complaint against the Bern group, after vainly seeking a settlement out of court. It eventually won, technically, on the remaining claim that the accusation "Nestle Kills Babies" amounted to libel. Both sides felt, however, that judicial "obiter dicta" on Nestle's promotion practices in effect condemned the company and exonerated the critics.[35] After the libel case, the Infant Formula Action Coalition (INFACT) was formed in Minneapolis, Minnesota in 1977 and organized a boycott of Nestle products. By 1978, over sixty groups and well-known individuals were supporting the boycott.

The rhetoric on both sides during the final years of the 1970s was vicious, and both endeavoured to influence public opinion with wide-ranging accusations. Although protest groups raised important and valid objections to Nestle's marketing techniques, it is evident that the issues of malnutrition and development were sometimes exceedingly peripheral to the discussion. Some critics were encouraged by the nature of the baby formula controversy to perceive the issue in rather simplistic terms of "right versus wrong" and "good versus evil." Nestle and other baby food products represented the antithesis to all that was desirable and natural; products designed and used to replace the natural process of breastfeeding. Formula and mother's milk appeared as the losing and winning alternatives in a zero-sum equation. Other critics viewed the issue as resulting from the evils of capitalism, and argued for the need to organize opposing forces. One of the directors of INFACT, for example, stated that:

It's not just babies, it's not just multinational companies, it's class conflict and class struggle. . . ultimately. . .we're [seeking] a larger very class-wide, very class-conscious campaign, and reasserting our power in this country, our power in this world.[36]

The infant formula controversy was also perceived as a sexual discrimination issue, with each side claiming that the other denies free choice to women. Thus, an opponent of the boycott against Nestle maintained that the boycott is the 'worst kind of putdown for women,' as it is based on the assumption that women can be dictated to about feeding their children.[37]

In marked contrast, Nestle critics considered company advertising and promotion to be part of "an insidious propaganda machine for a male supremacist society."[38]

The negative attitudes of critics were reinforced by their tendency to focus on agribusiness linkages with nutrition, but not with broader development issues. They often seemed to ignore the fact that the shift from bottle to breastfeeding cannot be attributed solely to advertising practices of multinationals. The development process itself contributes to an increase in the real and/or perceived need for alternatives to breastfeeding. In urban settings, more women are working outside of the home and are less available to their babies. "Demonstration effects" or "elite example" also accompany the development process, and contribute to a perceived need of some women in lower socio-economic groups for bottlefeeding. Food aid in such products as dried skim milk further strengthens the view that bottle feeding is desirable. In addition, a small percentage of women are unable to breastfeed, or must rely on feeding supplements, for a variety of reasons. For women desiring or in need of feeding supplements, agribusiness firms have often been able to provide acceptable, reliable and nutritious products. As discussed, baby formulas have been gradually improved by altering the fat content and adding nutrients and fortification, even though human milk continues to be superior.

Critics are correct in asserting that agribusiness "success" is defined in terms of commercial survival in the market rather than in terms of benefitting the LDC poor. However, it is naive to assume that replacement of multinational firms with government distribution and marketing networks will necessarily "solve" the nutritional and development problems. If an LDC government were, for example, to "take over" marketing of baby formula, a subsidized price might prevent its overdilution by poorer socio-economic groups: but preparation of formula in unsanitary conditions (because of inadequate education and lack of facilities) would continue in countries suffering from underdevelopment.

When circumstances are favourable, LDC governments can clearly perform some functions more effectively than foreign companies. The use of an "Incaparina"-type product by the Indian government is a prime example. Incaparina is a manufactured food of "predominantly vegetable protein origin having a nutritional value similar to that of milk and suitable for the mixed feeding of infants and young children."[39] It was introduced by the Institute of Nutrition of Central America and Panama over twenty years ago. Whereas Incaparina marketed by private firms has been inaccessible to the LDC poor, in India an Incaparina-type formula called Bal-Ahar is supplied by the government without cost and is important in nutritional programs.

In other circumstances, however, it might be best to explore various types of government-industry cooperation, where the expertise and creativity of industry can be utilized while the LDC government establishes the development and nutritional objectives. In cases where LDC resources for providing subsidies are limited, or where political instability of a subsidy over time is likely, greater dependence on private industry might be advisable. Many critical analyses of agribusiness involvement in marketing simply do not examine the variety of roles that MNEs can or should play in food marketing, depending on the product, the target group, and the development process in a particular LDC.

It is not only the critics of Nestle who can be faulted for inattention to development and also often to nutritional concerns. Nestle's reaction to its detractors often seemed to confirm that profit was its one and only objective. Instead of focusing on serious policy reformulation, the company attempted to silence its critics with claims that they were threatening the principles of free enterprise and competitive marketing. In 1978, Nestle employed several major consulting firms and distributed over 300,000 information kits to community leaders, and by 1979 the company had fifteen staff members working in the United States on boycott issues.[40]

Although confrontation predominated in the latter 1970s, it would be incorrect to imply that cooperation was totally absent during this period. Social scientists of the Dana Raphael and PAG-type founded the Human Lactation Center in Westport, Connecticut in 1975 and held a major conference on infant feeding with industry and its critics in 1977. The conference proceedings show a markedly higher degree of cooperative spirit than the publications surrounding the boycott campaign, and also a clearer focus on nutrition and development. Issues discussed included development of low-cost, protein-rich, local-resource weaning foods for the poor; the contributory role of baby food companies, the medical profession, and international food aid in the decline of breastfeeding; the state of research and problems of infant feeding; and the scope for cooperation in the future.[41]

It was also in the 1970s that international organizations became actively involved in developing a code of behaviour for baby food companies. A meeting in Geneva in October, 1979, jointly sponsored by WHO and UNICEF, issued a number of recommendations and also resolved to draft an international marketing code for submission to the World Health Assembly. Reactions to the WHO/UNICEF recommendations demonstrated the extent to which polarization had occurred. Nestle felt that the recommendations did not in any way restrict its commercial activities, and claimed to be honouring earlier agreements on promotional restraint.[42] Many critics, in contrast, were dissatisfied that the 1979 meeting had resulted only in recommendations, and felt that industry promises to curb promotion were not enough.

From the October 1979 WHO/UNICEF meeting to the World Health Assembly of 1981, the UN code went through four drafts under bitter recriminations from both sides, and the Nestle boycott continued. When the final draft was submitted to the World Health Assembly, the United States was the only country of 155 that voted against it. The American "no" vote was based on the view that the code violated U.S. antitrust law and constitutional rights of free speech. However, some high-level officials of the Agency for International Development (AID) resigned in protest, charging the Reagan Administration with being "swayed by the self-interest arguments of the infant formula lobby;" and both houses of the U.S. Congress passed motions of concern.[43]

The UN Code of May 1981 is a non-binding recommendation urging national governments to ban all direct advertising of milk, nonmilk products, bottles and accessories, and to control the behaviour of baby food companies in a variety of areas (e.g., banning free sample distribution to mothers). The Code further requires companies to improve their information and labelling so that the benefits of breastfeeding and the hazard of improper and unnecessary bottle feeding are clearly indicated.

D. Phase 3: 1981 to the present

Judging by the rhetoric, the 1981 WHO Code changed little in the two sides' positions. To some it was "an anti-market" instrument shaped by "the self-anointed custodians of rectitude," while to others it was a means to protect "the victims of exploitation of multinationals."[44] Many critics were disappointed that the Code had not led to outright regulation. The *New Internationalist*, for example, suggested that Nestle should treat the Code as binding and stop all promotion, but Nestle disagreed. Indeed, Nestle responded to a post-WHO Code enquiry from the *New Internationalist*, maintaining that

there is no scientific evidence that demonstrates a cause-and-effect relationship between marketing practices for infant formula and infant malnutrition in the Third World.[45]

Despite the rhetoric, it appears that the companies have reduced promotion and advertising in response to the Code. There are of course differing assessments concerning *the degree* to which behaviour has changed. The *Journal of Advertising* found in early 1982 that "Advertising over most of the world has stopped."[46] In support of this view, Nestle adopted new guidelines in March 1982, restricting formula distribution to the medical profession and undertaking to rewrite all educational materials and labels over the next year. It also created an "ethics audit committee" from members of the medical profession and clergy, headed by former Senator Edmund Muskie. In the view of some critics, however, Nestle was still pushing formula but through new marketing tricks. Nestle's 1982 guidelines involving the limiting of sample distribution to doctors were greeted with skeptical questions such as who would safeguard restraint by the medical profession.

Although some critics did not feel that Nestle was complying with the Code, the boycott coalition reached an agreement with the company in January, 1984 on several further modifications to its market and promotion practices. The boycott was then suspended for a six-month monitoring period, and subsequently was repealed completely. A December, 1984 report on Nestle's operations noted a market investment shift away from LDCs and into the United States, culminating in Nestle's acquisition of Carnation Company. The report pointed out a temporal coincidence: at the same time that Nestle agreed voluntarily with new marketing practices regarding infant formula, it began "cutting its Third World ties in line with its search for lower-risk investments."[47]

Interestingly, those critics of artificial feeding who had investigated the mother-child dyad in the "first phase" of the baby formula issue, were also those who tried to regain a scientific perspective on the heated formula controversy that had developed in the second phase. From the beginning, most of the support for more research and for cooperation with the industry to improve infant nutrition had come from this group.

5. Conclusion

Some tentative conclusions can be drawn based upon the two case studies concerning contract production and marketing of baby formula:

1. Multinational agribusiness seemed particularly adept at decreasing its risks and maximizing its profits. This was true in both the production case, where the product was exported from LDCs to industrial states, and also in the marketing case, where the product moved essentially in the opposite direction. In both cases, business in industrial states tended to profit more than business in LDCs; and higher income groups in LDCs received more benefits than lower-income groups. The case studies highlight the inadequacy of trickle-down theories, and the need to view development as something more than aggregate economic growth.

2. In both cases agribusiness contributed to displacement of LDC products: in the production case, of staple foods; and in the marketing case, of mother's milk. In both instances lower socio-economic strata in LDCs were most at risk. If displacement of LDC products is to occur, it is necessary to insure that the situation of the poorest groups does not deteriorate in the process.

3. In both cases the literature was characterized by simplistic interpretations and solutions, and was either highly supportive or highly critical of multinational agribusiness. The polarization of opinions contributed to studies marked by advocacy and politicization, in which development and nutritional issues often seemed to be peripheral.

4. Some discussion of agribusiness involvement with contract production, and with marketing of formula drew linkages between agribusiness and nutrition *or* development. However, only rarely were the interrelationships of all three issues considered. Critics of Nestle, for example, frequently pointed to the effects of formula companies on Third World nutrition, but broader development issues were sometimes totally ignored.

Examination of the two case studies in this paper provides us with some preliminary conclusions regarding the interrelationships of agribusiness, nutrition, and development. Further studies are necessary in all stages of agribusiness if the complexity of relationships is to be better understood. For example, it is necessary to extend the analysis to agribusiness control of inputs such as seeds, fertilizer, and pesticides. Similar to production and marketing, agricultural input issues have also been characterized by polarization into pro- and anti-MNE groups.

In discussion of the seed industry, for example, Pat Mooney argues that the genetic base of the world's food supply is disappearing, and that restrictive varietal legislation (or plant breeders' rights legislation) is permitting agribusiness to gain control of a vital part of the global food system. Mooney warns that Third World farmers are becoming increasingly dependent for new seeds and chemicals on Western multinationals that are interested in patents and profits and not in development and nutrition. As discussed, Mooney refers to the "YUP" bias of multinational agribusiness and agrochemical companies, which emphasizes breeding for "yield, uniformity, and processing." The YUP bias is designed to increase the profitability of companies and may involve promotion of nutritionally-inferior food products.[48]

In sharp reaction to the criticisms of Pat Mooney in Canada (and of C. Fowler in the United States), the Canadian Seed Trade Association has published a study arguing that "The problem is not one of greedy industries selfishly withholding their products from the Third World," and that

Plant Breeders' Rights in the developed world have helped the diversity, productivity, disease and pest resistance and usefulness of many crops. The Third World is free to benefit from these advances, and lacks only the means of transferring the technology. Those who sincerely have the interests of the Third World at heart will not waste their time protesting the existence of improved plant varieties and the system which produces them.[49]

It is evident that literature on all stages of agribusiness, from farm inputs to farm production, to processing and retailing has often been premised on extremely positive or extremely negative assumptions about MNEs as a starting point. If our knowledge of the effects of agribusiness on development and nutrition is to be enhanced, it will be necessary to develop and maintain higher standards of objectivity in analysis.

414

Footnotes
The research assistance of Inge Bailey is sincerely appreciated.
[1] Stephen Soloman, "The Controversy over Infant Formula," *The New York Times Magazine*, December 6, 1981, pp. 92-106.
[2] Sarah Potts Voll, *A Plough in Field Arable - Western Agribusiness in Third World Agriculture* (Hanover, New Hampshire: University Press of New England, 1980).
[3] "The Food Situation and the Child - An Overview," *Food and Nutrition*, Vol. 5, no. 1 (1979), p. 4.
[4] FAO, *Lives in Peril: Protein and the Child* (Rome: FAO, 1970), p. 25. Quoted in Alan Berg, *The Nutrition Factor* (Washington, D.C.: The Brookings Institution, 1973), p. 4.
[5] "Malnutrition, Population and Development: The Vital Links," *People*, Vol. 3, no. 1 (1976), pp. 3-4.
Data on global malnutrition are only approximations, because of different methods used in various population surveys in Third World regions.
[6] Berg, p. 2.
[7] F. James Levinson, "Nutrition is More than Agriculture," in Dana Raphael, ed., *Breastfeeding and Food Policy in a Hungry World* (New York: Academy Press, 1979), p. 241.
[8] Drs. Sue Kimm and Gonzalo Donoso, "Control of ProteinCalorie Malnutrition," in Jean Mayer and Johanna T. Dwyer, eds., *Food and Nutrition Policy in a Changing World* (New York: Oxford University Press, 1979), p. 157.
[9] The term was apparently first mentioned in a paper presented by Davis at the Boston Conference on Distribution in October 1955. See John H. Davis and Ray A. Goldberg, *A Concept of Agribusiness* (Boston: Harvard University, Graduate School of Business Administration, 1957), p. 2.
[10] Voll, p. 15.
[11] Douglas N. Ross, *Partners in Agroeconomic Development*, Conference Board Report no. 711 (New York: The Conference Board, Inc., 1977), p. 15.
[12] Tom McCollough, "A Perspective on the Impact of Infant Formula in Developing Nations: Future Goals and Policies," in Raphael, p. 135.
[13] Gonzalo Arroyo, "The Industrialization of Agriculture," *International Development Review*, Vol. 21, no. 2 (1979), p. 7.
[14] Margaret Mead, "Family Contexts of Breastfeeding," in Raphael, p. 10.
[15] Pat Mooney, *Seeds of the Earth - A Private or Public Resource?* (Ottawa: Canadian Council for International Co-operation, 1979), pp. 82-84.
[16] Mogens Buch-Hansen and Henrik Secher Marcussen, "Contract Farming and the Peasantry: Cases from Western Kenya," *Review of African Political Economy*, No. 23, January/April 1982, pp. 16-18.
[17] J. David Morrissy, *Agricultural Modernization through Production Contracting* (New York: Praeger Publishers, 1974), pp. 23-24.
[18] A more radical critique of Morrissy and the Harvard Business School approach is found in Ernest Feder, "How Agribusiness Operates in Underdeveloped Agricultures: Harvard Business School Myths and Reality," *Development and Change*, Vol. 7, 1976, pp. 413-43.
[19] Steven E. Sanderson, *Trade Aspects of the Internationalization of Mexican Agriculture: Consequences for Mexico's Food Crisis*, (La Jolla: University of California, San Diego, Monograph 10, 1983), pp. 4 and 35-38.
[20] Robert J. Ledogar, *Hungry for Profits* (New York: IDOC/North America, 1975), p. 74.
[21] Barbara Dinham and Colin Hines, *Agribusiness in Africa* (London: Earth Resources Research Ltd., 1983), pp. 14, 41, and 109.
[22] Buch-Hansen and Marcussen, p. 35.
[23] Dinham and Hines, p. 126.
[24] Buch-Hansen and Marcussen, pp. 23-35.

[25] *Ibid.*, p. 14.

[26] David R. Mares, "Agricultural Trade: Domestic Interests and Transnational Relations," in Jorge I. Dominguez, ed., *Mexico's Political Economy* (Beverly Hills: Sage Publications, 1982), pp. 84-86.

[27] *Ibid.*, pp. 86-87.

[28] Kenneth N. Waltz, "The Myth of National Interdependence," in Charles P. Kindleberger, ed., *The International Corporation* (Cambridge, Massachusetts: M.I.T. Press, 1970), p. 220.

Mexican scholars have written extensively on the country's dependence on multinational agribusiness. For example, see Ruth Rama, "El papal de las empresas transnacionales en la agricultura Mexicana," *Comercio Exterior*, Vol. 34, Noviembre de 1984, pp. 1083-95.

[29] Soloman, pp. 92-106.

[30] Excellent sources on scientific research in this area are the earlier cited books edited by Dana Raphael (footnote 7), and by Jean Mayer and Johanna T. Dwyer (footnote 8).

[31] See Susan George, "Nestle Alimentaria SA: The Limits to Public Relations," *Economic and Political Weekly*, Vol. 13, no. 37, (1978), pp. 1591-1602.

[32] Quoted in Mike Muller, *The Baby Killer* (London: War on Want, 1974), p. 13.

[33] John A. Sparks, "Viewpoint: The Baby Milk Controversy," *Food Policy*, Vol. 5 (August, 1980), p. 220.

[34] See, Jane Cottingham, ed., *Bottle Babies* (Switzerland: ISIS-Women's International Information and Communication Service, March, 1976).

[35] George, pp. 1592-96.

[36] Quoted in James Grant, "Nestle Crunch: The Campaign Against Instant Formula Reeks of Sophistry," *Barrow's National Business and Financial Weekly*, Vol. 59 (July 16, 1979), p. 7.

[37] Jennifer Halpern, "Spirit of Cooperation Needed," *Food Policy*, Vol. 7 (February, 1982), p. 89.

[38] Quoted in Jane Cottingham, ed., p. 23.

[39] Nevin S. Scrimshaw, "A Look at the Incaparina Experience in Guatemala," *Food and Nutrition Bulletin*, Vol. 2 (April, 1980), p. 1.

[40] See Herman Nickel, "The Corporation Haters," *Fortune*, June 16, 1980, pp. 126-36; Douglas Clement, "Nestle's Latest Killing in the Bottle Baby Market," *Business and Society Review*, no. 26 (Summer 1978), pp. 60-65; "Social Issues: A Boycott over Infant Formula," *Business Week* (April 23, 1979), pp. 137 & 140; and Bill Beaver and Fred Silvester, "The Gall in Mother's Milk: The Infant Formula Controversy and the WHO Marketing Code," *Journal of Advertising*, Vol. 1 (January/March 1982), pp. 1-10.

[41] See Raphael.

[42] Andy Chetley, "A Rejoinder," *Food Policy*, Vol. 5 (August 1980), p. 227.

[43] See Robert Reinhold, "Furor Over: Baby Formulas - Where, When and How," *New York Times*, May 24, 1981, Section IV, p. 9; *Food Policy*, Vol. 7 (February, 1982), p. 86; and "Nestle Puts Curbs on Marketing, Infant Formula Policy at Issue," *New York Times*, October 14, 1983, Section IV, p. 16.

[44] See Beaver and Silvester; Nickel; Ernest W. Lefever, "Politics and Baby Formula in the Third World," *The Wall Street Journal*, January 14, 1981, p. 26; Andre McNicoll, "Different Ideologies; Different Diagnoses," *Maclean's*, February 16, 1981, p. 20; and "Battling the Baby Bottle," *The Wall Street Journal*, May 4, 1981, p. 25.

[45] "Nestle Replies. . .," *New Internationalist*, Issue. no. 110 (April, 1982), p. 19.

[46] Beaver and Silvester, p. 8.

[47] John Taghabue, "Nestle Shifts Investments to U.S.," *Globe and Mail*, December 3, 1984, p. B7.

[48] Mooney, pp. 82-84.

[49] The Canadian Seed Trade Association, *Seeds for a Hungry World - The Role and Rights of Modern Plant Breeders* (Ottawa, Ontario: C.S.T.A., 1984), p. 84.

PART III
THE REGIONS

Chapter 9

Latin America:
Focus on Debt and Democracy

Introduction

In terms of magnitude and therefore in terms of potential impact on the international monetary system the debt crisis of the 1980s is in fact a Latin American problem. Moreover, two-thirds of this debt comes from commercial banks, which means short maturities and commercial interest rates. Because of the general economic downturn caused by the sharp recession of 1981-2 and rising protectionism in the First World, earnings from exports to service the debt are relatively small in relation to the debt service demands. The debt itself was built up during the boom years of the 1970s, fuelled especially by the eagerness of the First World commercial banks to recycle petro-dollars after the second oil shock in 1978 to booming Third World countries such as Argentina, Brazil, Chile, Mexico and Venezuela. These five countries carry 80% of the Latin American debt burden.

The debt became a serious problem as a result of the high interest rates that came with the recession of 1981-2. Five years later rates are only now returning to normal historic levels. The debt service of the five Latin American countries mentioned averages 40% of export earnings and in some cases exceeds 50%. The problem is not so much the size of the debt, or the debt servicing/export earnings ratios, as it is the continued unwillingness of the First World's banking community to continue lending to Latin America as long as the debt overhang persists. The Paris and the London Clubs do no more than renegotiate and roll over old debt, which thus simply grows as interest payments are deferred and become capitalized. Table 1 demonstrates the relationships of debt in low-income Africa and the major borrowers, principally the Latin American ones mentioned. The last line in the first bloc of statistics shows the tremendous decline in net long-term capital flows to the Third World, especially the heavily indebted countries. By 1984, net transfers of funds to the Third World were negative and had risen to a net outflow of US $29 billion in 1986, as contrasted with a net inflow of $35.2 billion, a scant five years earlier in 1981.

Clearly the debt overhang is reducing the ability of many heavily-indebted countries that are undertaking economic reforms to increase investment and stimulate growth. The drop in the price of oil has worsened the situation for the major debtors (especially Mexico and Venezuela in Latin America), that depend heavily on crude oil exports. And, any lowering of immediate export earnings weakens a country's ability to attract additional commercial capital.

The IMF, of course, plays an important role in assisting all Third World countries with foreign exchange difficulties; however, there are costs associated with this. Table 2 shows the different ways in which eleven countries facing the debt crisis adapted to it. "It shows the maximum real exchange rate devaluation achieved by each country as it adjusted to the crisis (Column 3). It also shows a contemporane-

Table 1
Public and Private Long-Term Debt and Financial Flows, 1980-86

Long-Term Debt and Financial Flows	1980	1981	1982	1983	1984	1985ᵃ	1986ᵃ
All Developing Countriesᵇ							
Debt Disbursed and Outstanding	429.6	493.6	551.2	630.2	673.4	730.9	775.0
Disbursements	102.8	122.8	115.8	96.5	88.3	81.7	72.0
(From Private Creditors)	74.6	91.3	83.9	63.9	56.1	52.1	41.0
Debt Service	74.2	87.6	97.4	90.8	99.0	108.0	101.0
Principal Repayments	42.0	46.5	48.8	44.0	46.3	53.5ᶜ	51.0
Interest	32.2	41.1	48.6	46.8	52.7	54.5	50.0
Net Transfers	28.7	35.2	18.4	5.7	−10.7	−26.3	−29.0
Highly Indebted Countriesᵈ							
Debt Disbursed and Outstanding	204.1	244.4	276.5	329.2	354.0	367.6	382.0
Disbursements	53.2	69.5	60.1	39.7	32.3	22.4	21.0
(From Private Creditors)	46.0	60.9	50.9	29.7	22.5	13.6	12.0
Debt Service	44.4	51.5	56.6	48.2	51.6	50.1	47.0
Principal Repayments	24.6	26.1	25.8	19.1	18.4	17.1	16.0
Interest	19.8	25.4	30.8	29.1	33.3	33.0	31.0
Net Transfers	8.8	18.0	3.5	−8.5	−19.4	−27.7	−26.0
Low-Income Africaᵉ							
Debt Disbursed and Outstanding	26.3	28.7	30.7	33.3	34.0	37.3	40.5
Disbursements	5.4	4.8	4.1	3.9	3.1	3.0	2.8
(From Private Creditors)	2.1	1.5	1.2	0.7	0.4	0.4	0.3
Debt Service	2.2	2.0	1.8	1.7	2.1	2.2	2.0
Principal Repayments	1.3	1.2	1.1	1.0	1.2	1.3	1.2
Interest	0.9	0.8	0.7	0.8	0.9	0.9	0.8
Net Transfers (US$ Billions)	3.3	2.7	2.3	2.1	1.0	0.8	0.8

Source: World Bank, *Developing Country Debt*; Implementing the Consensus, Washington, DC, 1987, p. xiii.

ous rise in the consumer price index (Column 4). Since devaluation of the nominal exchange rate increases the internal prices of tradeable goods, it is almost inevitable that a large devaluation will entail a rise in the general price index. (Otherwise, a major fall in the prices of non-tradeable goods would be required.) The policy challenge is to limit this price rise. The figures in Column 5 can be taken as an index of how successfully different countries met this challenge. Venezuela, the Philippines, Uruguay and Chile were the most successful; Argentina, Bolivia, Peru and Brazil saw inflation increase more than might be expected from the extent of the real devaluations."[1]

The Bank for International Settlements (BIS) reported in early 1987 that although international bank lending grew at an exceptionally fast pace during the third quarter of 1986, leading to a US $167 billion expansion in lending (to $3 trillion), the largest quarterly increase recorded, virtually none of the increase went to the developing world.

Bank lending to developing countries remains very sluggish. Apart from lending to members of the Organization of Petroleum Exporting Countries it rose only $200 million in a quarter and fell by $4.6 billion over the first nine months of the year. "There were still hardly any signs of spontaneous new lending to problem debtor countries, which in some cases sharply reduced their official reserves held in the form of deposits with the reporting banks," the BIS said.[2] Hence, the new program of World Bank support for capital financing intended to generate confidence in commercial banks appears to be the only hope for regenerating capital development flows to the Third World. At the end of 1986 a special cooperative effort between the IMF and the World Bank saw the World Bank extend U.S. $2 billion in new loans

Table 2

Real devaluation and inflation in countries that faced a debt crisis

Country	Time periods being compared (year and quarter)		Ratio of real exchange rate[a] (3)	Ratio of CPI[b] (4)	Inflation relative to real devaluation[c] (5)
	Precrisis trough (1)	Postcrisis peak (2)			
Argentina	1980 IV	1984 I	2.57	53.34	20.75
Bolivia	1982 III	1984 II	1.59	18.83	11.85
Brazil	1982 III	1984 III	1.48	7.23	4.89
Chile	1982 I	1984 III	1.45	1.61	1.11
Mexico	1981 IV	1983 III	1.50	3.13	2.08
Peru	1982 I	1984 III	1.11	5.86	5.28
Philippines	1982 III	1983 IV	1.36	1.19	0.87
Portugal	1979 III	1983 III	1.48	2.15	1.45
Turkey	1979 IV	1984 II	1.92	5.65	2.94
Uruguay	1982 III	1984 II	2.00	2.09	1.05
Venezuela	1983 II	1984 II	1.74	1.11	0.64

a. Measured from peak to trough.
b. Consumer price index at peak divided by consumer price index at trough.
c. Column (4) divided by column (5).

Source: *World Development Report*, p. 35.

over the next two years to Argentina. The new President of the World Bank, Barber Conable, made clear in his remarks that he expected the commercial banks and others, such as the Paris Club, to financially back Argentina. "Successful implementation of Argentina's program will also need substantial additional financing from its commercial creditor banks and all other creditors. Mr. Conable expressed confidence that the medium-term framework will elicit their full cooperation," said the Bank in a public statement.[3]

However, the question of new capital financing for the Latin American countries is not one that concerns merely the creditor banks; it concerns the political world as well. As Riordan Roett so eloquently puts it,

"But it may be even more important to understand the social costs for Latin America, and especially South America, of the current economic downturn there—and the probable future social price for the people of the continent. If these social costs should lead to political changes that bring in radical governments unwilling to continue the regressive policies required by the IMF and the banks, then and then only might there be not only moratorium but outright debt repudiation—first in one country and then perhaps in others. And even if such repudiation were avoided, so that debt payments continued on an agreed schedule, financial 'victory' could be at the price of eventual political defeat."[4]

The three articles in this chapter illustrate various aspects of the Latin American debt problem, Wiesner describes the internal and external sources of the Latin American debt crisis, arguing that first, following the emergence of external imbalances that required internal adjustment measures, countries sought to avoid reducing total public and private expenditure to the level of available resources for internal political reasons; and second, loans from international commercial banks and other lenders, both public and private, expanded at an extremely rapid rate. Although these factors are closely inter-related, he argues that for purposes of analysis a clear distinction must be drawn between the domestic macro-economic policy sources and the external, international commercial bank financing ones. Doran surveys Latin American leaders' pronouncements that they should engage in some collective action aimed at easing the conditions imposed on them by the IMF and the creditors to increase their bargaining power. The leaders of the main Latin American countries have made it clear at a series of meetings held to discuss common strategy on the debt question that the problem is no longer merely a financial one but one that is primarily political. These discussions resulted in the formation of the eleven-member Cartagena group, whose aim is to establish a political dialogue among the main actors in the debt drama. So far, the group has had no success.

The final article by Riordan Roett has already been referred to and concentrates on the problem of the impact of the debt overhang on the political systems of all Latin American countries. He argues that turbulence and increased protest are increasing everywhere in Latin America and that the United States must take several strong positions to avert disaster: first, it must stand four square in defence of free trade and against protectionist pressures; second, it must seriously consider a joint effort by the United States, Western Europe and Japan to actively encourage imports from South America to enable the latter to earn the foreign exchange requirements to service its debt; third, the United States should emphasize greater lending facilities for the World Bank, the Inter-American Development Bank and other multilateral agencies; fourth, the United States should take the lead in strongly and publicly encouraging private commercial banks to reduce the terms of their loans to South America; and fifth, the United States needs to continue providing federal government support through emergency credits and financing as needed.

It is interesting to note that in October 1985, Treasury Secretary James Baker proposed variants of the second and third proposals of Roett's.[5]

Notes

[1] *World Development Report*, 1986, p. 34-5

[2] *Globe and Mail*, 13 January 1987

[3] *Globe and Mail*, 22 January 1987

[4] "Democracy and Debt in South America: A Continent's Dilemma", *Foreign Affairs*, Winter, 1983, p. 699. [see pp. 441-442 in this book]

[5] See the Baker article in Chapter 7

Domestic and External Causes of the Latin American Debt Crisis

Eduardo Wiesner

A careful analysis of economic data and the policies that most Latin American countries followed over the past five or six years clearly shows that the region's external debt crisis stems from two basic sets of causes. First, following the emergence of external imbalances that required internal adjustment measures, countries sought to avoid reducing total public and private expenditure to the level of available resources; and second, loans from international commercial banks and other lenders—both public and private—expanded at an extremely rapid rate. These factors are closely interrelated, but for purposes of analysis a clear distinction must be drawn between the first set of causes, originating domestically from national economic policies, and the second, of external origin and related primarily to international commercial bank financing.

Gravity of the debt problem

Before analyzing the factors mentioned above, it is important to recognize the scope and magnitude of the Latin American debt problem, and the fact that it is not a temporary crisis linked to a particular phase of the business cycle. On the contrary, it will take many years before most of the countries return to a normal situation in which markets resume their role as principal regulators of financial flows and international trade.

There is no single criterion by which to measure external debt or determine whether a given level of indebtedness may be considered excessive or reasonable, and there are considerable problems of definition and measurement. Nevertheless, in the case of Latin America, even though the gravity of the debt problems was not uniform among all countries, it seems abundantly clear that we have been faced with an unprecedented crisis, regardless of the indicator used. For instance, in 1983 the stock of external debt was equivalent to 120 percent of GDP in Costa Rica, 103 percent in Chile, 76 percent in peru, 66 percent in Argentina, 63 percent in Uruguay, 47 percent in Venezuela, and 44 percent in both Mexico and Brazil.

It may be argued that it is not the size of the debt, either in absolute terms or relative to GDP, that matters but whether it can be serviced; this would imply a comparison of debt-service obligations (payments of principal and interest) with exports of goods and services. The resulting picture is no less dramatic: Brazil, for instance, would have required 89 percent of its exports of goods and services in 1982 to service its external debt; Argentina, 68 percent; Ecuador, 69 percent; Chile, 65 percent; and Mexico, 57 percent. Even if the assumption is made that debt principal is not normally repaid, but refinanced, the situation would still be very serious. In 1983 Argentina would have needed to earmark 54 percent of

Originally published in *Finance and Development*, vol. 21, no. 1, March 1985. Reprinted with permission.

its exports of goods and services to pay the interest on its external debt; Brazil would have required 40 percent; Mexico, 35 percent; and Chile and Peru, about 33 percent.

Countries cannot suspend their imports or reduce them below a minimum consistent with the effective operation of their economies. In view of this the above-mentioned debt-service ratios explain why the situation had become unsustainable by late 1982. On the one hand, the commercial banks saw that they could not go on lending large amounts for ever-shorter periods. On the other hand, the countries were unable to meet their import payments as they had suffered large losses in their international reserves and were falling behind in their external payments. When commercial bank credit was suspended, the lack of confidence in domestic currencies precipitated exchange crises, and the gravity of the situation became clear. Latin America's worst economic crisis of the century had begun.

Domestic causes

The domestic causes of the debt crisis may be traced to the growing fiscal deficits that most countries incurred between 1978 and 1982 and the expansionary monetary and credit policies that were largely used to finance them. While other factors also contributed to the inconsistency of economic policies, the primary factor was a level of public—as well as private—expenditures that exceeded currently available resources or resources that could have been regarded as stable in the medium term. Thus, between 1978 and 1982 the ratio of fiscal deficit to GDP more than doubled in the three main debtor countries, Argentina, Brazil, and Mexico.

How were those deficits financed? And what were the comparative effects of the different means of financing? Generally speaking, a fiscal deficit can be financed in one of two ways, external credit (borrowing abroad or use of international reserves), and domestic credit. But—and this is of fundamental importance—there is a close and inseparable interdependence between internal and external credit: in the final analysis, the former determines the pattern of external financing.

Domestic credit for the public sector basically has two main sources: the central bank and the private sector. Opting for financing from the private financial system has important consequences—an upward pressure on interest rates as the government attempts to place its securities and, as a corollary of this, a decline in private investment as projects yielding less than the now higher interest rate cease to be profitable (the phenomenon known as "crowding out").

This problem of high interest rates is a delicate one, not only because of its effect on investment or, more accurately, on the distribution of investment between the public and private sectors, but also because high interest rates tend to become a difficult political problem as the monetary authorities are pressured to lower them. The basic problem is not the level of interest rates, as such, but the consistency of economic policies. Resources are finite, and one cannot at the same time increase private investment and use private savings to finance major public sector investments or higher current expenditure by the public sector.

The other source of domestic financing is central bank credit. In theory, this has the advantage that the interest rate paid by the public sector can be lower than what would have to be paid if bonds were to be placed with the private sector. But this presumed advantage is neither real nor permanent and implies even greater problems and risks than a short-run increase in interest rates. Although interest rates may initially tend not to rise because of the unanticipated excess liquidity, the public will soon realize that the situation is not sustainable. If the public is not willing demand or hold the additional liquidity, it will proceed to "mop it up" by exchanging domestic financial assets for real assets-domestic or imported—or for external financial assets. The excess liquidity will inevitably lead to higher inflation, increased external borrowing or greater losses of international reserves, or a combination of both. These, in turn, will lead to a devaluation of the currency.

This is the previously mentioned monetary link between a fiscal deficit financed with domestic credit and its impact on the balance of payments. Within this context, a loss of international reserves is equivalent to an increase in the external debt, or it can be viewed as a temporary substitute for either higher inflation or a devaluation of the exchange rate. Statistical data for the countries under study tend to lend support to the linkages outlined above: the fiscal deficits of most countries had, as their counterparts, first an expansion of domestic credit followed by a series of mounting deficits in the current account of the balance of payments; these deficits, in turn, were the counterpart of the external debt or of losses of international reserves.

Admittedly, the numerous factors at work make it impossible to predict, in all cases and with mathematical precision, the precise relationship between the fiscal deficit and monetary and credit policy, on the one hand, and the balance of payments, on the other; but the direction and closeness of the relationship is unquestionable. For instance, the current account deficit of the balance of payments will vary according to the degree of the economy's openness to international trade, with smaller deficits where import restrictions are severe and larger deficits where the restrictions are milder. On the other hand, there will be higher inflation in the first case and lower inflation and greater economic efficiency in the second. In both cases the adjustment will bring aggregate expenditure to the level of the resources available—unless it is possible to postpone it. And this brings us to the second set of causes of Latin America's external debt problem, namely, financing by international commercial banks.

External factors

The external factors underlying the debt crisis may be classified into three groups. The first includes those that precipitated the 1982 crisis: the rapid rise in real interest rates in international financial markets, the world recession, and the difficulties in expanding export markets. These factors precipitated the crisis and certainly aggravated it, but, important though they were (and continue to be), they did not produce the crisis. Had external debt levels not been what they were, these developments could not in themselves have brought on a crisis, although they could have created serious problems. As it happened, they coincided with a situation that was already precarious.

The second group includes factors of a more permanent nature, in contrast to the transient ones mentioned above, and involves what economists call real, as against purely monetary, factors. The principal factor in this category was the decline in the terms of trade experienced by most Latin American countries, mainly as a result of the oil price increases of 1973 and 1979.

The third—and very special—group consists of external financing flows, particularly those from international commercial banks. Were it not for financing from these sources, which was growing rapidly and with ever-shorter maturities, an external debt crisis of the proportions experienced could not have developed. But this does not mean that this type of financing was the cause of the crisis. What this financing did was to facilitate the postponement of the measures that, in any event, would have had to be taken to adjust the economies in question to the deterioration in their terms of trade, as well as to the strictly monetary developments that occurred in 1979 and thereafter.

This last point is of particular significance in that it places the economic crisis in a proper perspective and underscores something that has sometimes been overlooked in the debate on recent economic developments, namely, the adjustment that should in any event have taken place beginning in 1974-75. In other words, the current crisis must not be regarded as an unexpected and surprising event that occurred in late 1982. To be sure, it should be set not against some normal or ideal situation but against the difficulties that would have been experienced some time after 1973 or 1979, had it not proved possible to obtain external financing from the international commercial banks in sufficient amounts to postpone corrective measures.

Nature of external financing

The specialization that characterized the external financing of Latin American countries, simply put, was as follows: The countries obtained development credits and long-term loans from multilateral entities and official agencies of the industrial countries (for the financing of capital goods exports). On the other hand, short-term credit, connected mainly with commercial transactions, was provided by suppliers or by international commercial banks. Generally speaking, the first category of loans—development financing—was linked to the feasibility of specific investment projects and was guaranteed by the borrowing country's government. The second category of credit was not government-guaranteed and pertained to commercial transactions between private sectors. This scheme of things began to undergo a rapid and fundamental change from 1975 onward. Although financing by multilateral entities and governments grew rapidly, credits from international commercial banks increased much faster. By the end of 1981, liabilities to international banks accounted for 63 percent of the total external debt of the 20 major borrowing countries. But it was not only the principal lender that had changed; the average maturity of loans had shortened to the point where in early 1982 some 25 percent of these countries' debt was short term (that is, with an initial maturity of less than one year).

Other changes of no less importance were also occurring. An increasing proportion of the loans was no longer linked to the economic feasibility of investment projects. Most of them were being extended to public sectors for the purpose of financing fiscal deficits or investment programs in which the lender was no longer a direct participant in the project risk. This naturally led to a reduction in the application of strictness of project appraisal, while allowing the financing of a higher volume of government expenditure than could be sustained in the longer run. The fundamental role of the risk factor thus underwent a change.

The increase in international bank financing of the public sectors took place on the assumption that the loans involved little, if any, commercial or exchange risk, as a result of which commercial banks did not pay sufficient attention to the global risk represented by the quality of the debtor countries' economic policies as a whole. At the same time, the growing international bank financing of the countries' private sectors was also carried out on the assumption that the operation involved no risk for the public sectors of the debtor countries. This ignored the danger of a possible total and instantaneous suspension of external commercial financing.

It is now clear that all the protagonists were mistaken in their perception of the risk involved. Developments have confirmed at least three postulates: risk is a fundamental factor in market equilibrium; all private external credit involves a certain amount of risk for the public sector of the borrowing country; and private credit to the public sector involves certain risks for the lender. All in all, risk plays a stabilizing role in the maintenance of market equilibrium.

Effect on economic policy

In principle, although foreign credit represents a liability for the borrowing country, it also produces an asset. Unfortunately, this was often not the case in practice in Latin America. Loan proceeds were not always well invested or used to generate foreign exchange or supplement domestic savings. At times, indeed, borrowing financed consumption rather than investment. As a result, the ratio of external debt-service to exports of goods and services rose steeply. It is true that a large part of these increases represented rising interest rates in international markets, but interest rates were also rising for other borrowing countries (i.e., some East Asian countries) that followed different economic strategies and used the external financing to create and expand export industries.

One of the most surprising results of any analysis of Latin America's external debt data is the lack of a direct correlation between the aggregate debt and the deficit on current account and changes in reserves. Theoretically, a country or a region taken as a whole cannot accumulate external debt in excess of the total of its deficits on current account and the changes in its international reserves. It is assumed that external liabilities cannot be greater than the amount of the deficit less the losses in reserves. In the case of Latin America, however, external liabilities exceeded estimated external financing needs. The reason is well known: capital flight.

In its latest *Annual Report*, the Bank for International Settlements estimates that capital flight from Latin America between 1978 and 1983 amounted to possibly $50 billion. These funds, and those previously transferred abroad, are obviously not "lost" and the region's actual aggregate debt position is thus not as serious as it may appear. If the amounts relating to net external debt and net interest payments (received but not repatriated) were known, it could be seen that investment in activities that generate foreign exchange was higher than indicated by the figures for investment in the exporting sectors, but with an important difference: capital flight neither creates jobs nor pays taxes in the country of origin.

The thrust of the foregoing analysis is that the countries in question did not follow the correct policies to take advantage of the increase in external financing made available to them. The surprising fact is that in most of the cases the increased inflow of external funds was accompanied by a drop in domestic savings as a percentage of GDP. Thus, given the imbalance created between the growth of external debt and domestic capital accumulation, a debt crisis was virtually inevitable. In sum, the region lacked not funds but better policies for the use of these funds.

Lessons of the crisis

It is not easy to reach firm conclusions about the experience of the external debt crisis, and perhaps the perspective of a longer period is needed before we can draw the lessons of these events. Nevertheless, a number of broad conclusions are possible.

First, countries do not have an unlimited capacity to absorb external financing and to make proper use of all the funds they may be granted at a given moment. A situation in which a country's absorption, measured in terms of consumption and investment, exceeds its income, must not be confused with the very different situation in which the absorptive capacity for investment limits the total amount of resources that can be economically used. In other words, if there is additional financing, total absorption can exceed income, but the mere availability of financing does not guarantee the economic use of funds. If the availability of the external financing is not contingent on the economic feasibility of specific investment projects, and, consequently, if the risk factor is not sufficiently taken into account, it is highly probable that some irrecoverable loans will be granted. On the other hand, if there is easy availability of finance, it is also highly likely that this will reduce the discipline on countries to adopt better economic policies.

Second, the public sectors of the countries in question had neither the needed taxing capacity nor the domestic savings required to service the external financing offered to them. Fiscal deficits thus rarely contribute to higher total investment. Neither domestic nor external credit can be permanent substitutes for, or alternatives to, fiscal discipline. Sooner or later total expenditure will have to be brought into line with total resources, and financing cannot postpone that adjustment indefinitely.

Third, since external loans must be repaid in foreign exchange, external borrowing decisions must be linked to a general economic policy framework that will guarantee both the profitability of the investment and the generation of sufficient foreign exchange for external debt service. The maintenance of a realistic exchange rate policy is essential to attain this objective.

If these general conclusions lead to a single recommendation, it is that countries must view their external financing policies in the framework of their global macroeconomic policies, and that, within such a framework, adequate financial programming must assure a minimum of consistency between objectives, resources, and instruments.

Latin America's External Debt: The Limits of Regional Cooperation

Esperanza Durán

The problem of Latin America's external debt, which came to the forefront of international attention in 1982 and 1983, continues to be serious. Financial and economic collapse at the domestic and international level has been averted by swift action by the creditor banks and some tough austerity policies in the debtor countries—in many cases under the supervision of the International Monetary fund (IMF). But only temporarily. The "crisis-management" approach adopted to ease the immediate difficulties has worked, but long-term solutions for what remains a potentially explosive situation have not yet been devised.[1]

Within Latin America, a growing awareness has developed that, despite the diversity of their approaches to economic policy-making, the countries in the region are up against the same problems in negotiations over their foreign debt. This realization, plus the deterioration of the external conditions in the world economy (rising interest rates, declining terms of trade, growing protectionism in the industrial countries), has prompted Latin American leaders to make pronouncements and engage in a measure of collective action aimed at easing the conditions imposed on them and increasing their bargaining power. Many have argued that the debt problem is no longer a purely financial question and that it has been transformed into a largely political problem. The leaders of the main Latin American countries have made this clear at a series of meetings held to discuss a common strategy on the debt which resulted in the formation of the 11-strong Cartagena group. The group's aim is to establish a political dialogue among the main actors in the debt drama: banks, governments of creditor and debtor countries, and multilateral institutions. So far, the group has had no success. But there have also been more radical statements from the region. Alan García, on his inauguration as President of Peru in July 1985, declared his intention to make debt repayments not exceed 10 per cent of his country's export earnings. Shortly afterwards, Cuba's Prime Minister, Fidel Castro, in the presence of a host of Latin American personalities in Havana, called for the collective default of the Latin American countries' foreign debt. But these spectacular public statements have not, so far, been followed by radical actions by the Latin American countries. Neither the much-feared formation of a debtors' club nor the collective repudiation of financial obligations by the Latin American countries has occurred, although a few individual—and inevitable—"discreet moratoria" by countries like Bolivia and Ecuador have taken place.

This article describes the efforts by the Latin American countries to present a common front vis-à-vis their creditors, and their successes and failures in achieving more favourable terms in their debt renegotiations; points out the limits to collective action and analyses external obstacles to closer cooperation by Latin American countries on the debt issue;

From the May 1986 issue of *The World Today*, published monthly by the Royal Institute of International Affairs, 10 St James Square, London SW1Y 4LE, UK. Student discounts for subscriptions.

and finally, it examines the prospects for more assertive action by the Latin American debtors in the future.

The Debt Saga: Phase One

When the gravity of the debt problems faced by the Latin American countries was fully realized by the creditor banks and the governments of the industrialised nations, following the summer of 1982, prompt measures were taken to take control of the situation. The governments, as lenders of last resort, tried to convince the banks to keep their credit lines open to the Latin American debtors in order to keep the financial system running smoothly until some longer-term solutions could be found. The common opinion at this early stage was that the problem faced by the debtor countries was one of liquidity, not of insolvency. Therefore, it was believed that short-term assistance combined with a swift return to sound economic management would lead to the creation of the necessary resources to enable debtor countries to meet their debt-servicing obligations.

Adjustment programmes under the guidance of the IMF were demanded by the banks as a precondition for keeping their credit lines to heavily indebted countries open. Thus, they increased an exposure which on purely commercial individual-bank considerations would have been improbable. IMF stabilisation stressed the need for fiscal and monetary caution and tried to put an end to expansionary economic policies in Latin America, which were regarded by many as one of the roots of the debt crisis. The emphasis was on sharp reduction in public expenditure and anti-inflationary measures, the raising of fiscal revenues and the curtailment of capital flight. On the current-account front, measures prescribed included trade (and domestic-markets) liberalisation and the devaluation of the national currency to boost exports and reduce imports. The chief aim was the achievement of a trade surplus which would enable debtor countries to replenish their foreign reserves and meet their debt repayments.

This type of adjustment programme was supposed to restore internal equilibrium to the Latin American countries and put them back on a sound economic basis. The disbursement of stand-by credits by the IMF and the new finance to be provided by commercial banks was to be linked to the performance targets of the countries under treatment. The expectation was that the implementation of this programme would lead to the eventual restoration of the debtors' credit-worthiness which would, in turn, lead to the resumption of voluntary lending.

However, the theory did not match the practice; the IMF-sponsored measures produced a number of negative consequences. The stabilisation policies pursued by the Latin American countries in order to obtain access to further lending created heavy social and political burdens. There was a steady decline in nutritional standards; drastic cuts in public expenditure led to a further reduction of already poor educational, housing and medical services; unemployment increased dramatically. There were food riots and demonstrations in Brazil, violent protests in the Dominican Republic and huge strikes in Bolivia and Peru. Austerity in the eyes of the Latin Americans did not seem a reasonable solution to their problems. Worst of all, these sacrifices did not even look like containing the seeds of a solution in the longer run. The future, just like the present, continued to look dim.

With increasing frequency, over the last year or two, the Latin American leaders kept saying that the region could no longer sacrifice growth in order to repay its $360bn worth of external debt. Latin American officials started voicing their belief that it was not only internal factors that had created the debt crisis. External circumstances and policies in the industrial countries were also to be apportioned part of the blame. Therefore, they argued, it was logical to expect that the burden of responsibility should be more evenly shared. Latin American leaders repeatedly stressed that, despite very high costs in social and political terms, the Latin American countries had made major adjustments in their economies to meet their financial obligations, and called for a parallel reaction by the banks and creditor countries. These declarations seemed to suggest that the way was being paved for a collective Latin American approach to the problem. But it soon became clear that this type of action faced heavy obstacles.

Regional Cooperation: the Latin American Option

What worried commercial bankers and their governments after the Latin American governments started consultations among themselves about debt renegotiation was the possibility of a polarisation in the debtor-creditor relationship and the eventual formation of a debtor club. The danger there lay in the possibility that such a club adopt a radical posture towards common financial obligations, including the imposition of ceilings to debt-servicing linked to each country's export performance; unilateral interest rate-capping; declaration of grace periods when no capital or interest payments would be made; or even, however improbable, a concerted default. These were the developments banks and creditor governments feared and wanted to avoid. At the very least, the formation of a debtors' club would make the present (and preferred) case-by-case approach unworkable. It would also provide the Latin American debtors with a powerful new addition to their bargaining power.

Six months after the 1982 Mexican financial collapse which triggered the crisis, the then president of Ecuador, Osvaldo Hurtado, appealed to two Latin American economic institutions, namely ECLA (United Nations Economic Commission for Latin America) and SELA (Latin American Economic System), to develop a strategy for dealing with the acute economic and financial difficulties the region was undergoing. These institutions drafted a document outlining the "bases for Latin American response to the international economic crisis", and sponsored several meetings of representatives of Latin American governments to discuss possible common action.[2]

A major Latin American economic conference took place in Quito, Ecuador, in January 1984, which was attended by the Presidents of Colombia, Costa Rica, Ecuador, Dominican Republic, the Prime Minister of Jamaica and high level officials from 26 Latin American and Caribbean countries. The conference issued a document called the Quito Declaration and a Plan of Action outlining the steps that the countries in the region should take to ease their economic and financial problems. The Plan of Action stated that the responsibility for the current problems posed by a massive foreign debt was shared between debtor and industrial countries, banks and multilateral financial institutions. It went on to propose a comprehensive programme which covered not only debt-related solutions but considerations on trade, regional food security, cooperation on energy issues and services. Specifically with regard to the debt, the Plan called for a reduction of debt-service repayments, interest rates, commissions and other charges which substantially increased the cost of renegotiation. It proposed the lengthening of repayment and grace periods, the maintenance of an adequate flow of fresh finance for the region, more commercial credits and the elimination of the protectionist barriers imposed by the industrial countries.[3]

At this early stage of regional cooperation on the debt, none of the proposals contained in the Plan of Action translated into effective practice. Nor did they have a direct impact on the bilateral negotiations which were taking place around this time between debtors and creditors to restructure the existing debts. But the Quito meeting had created an atmosphere of regional solidarity and provided a common platform for future negotiations.

The first test of this newly found regional identity came during the annual meeting of the Inter-American Development Bank (IDB) in Punta del Este, Uruguay, in the spring of 1984. The governments of Brazil, Colombia, Mexico and Venezuela took the unprecedented step of putting together a $300m loan for Argentina to help it meet overdue interest payments. This Latin American bail-out was a good sample of the options available to Latin American borrowers if they decided to act collectively. However, the next collective action was triggered yet again by an external factor and not by a regional development.

There had been warnings coming not only from Latin America, but from top policy-makers in the United States, such as the then chairman of the Council of Economic Advisers, Martin Feldstein, and the Chairman of the Federal Reserve Board, Paul Volcker, that rapidly rising interest rates, coupled with the Latin American countries' reluctance to accept economic stagnation as the price for new funds, would make the "crisis-management" approach followed until then unworkable in the medium and long term. Indeed, interest rates had been showing marked increases in a relatively short time. From February to May 1984, the United States prime lending rate increased by one and a half per cent adding up millions to the interest bill of the debtor countries. In May 1984, the prospect of a clash between Latin American debtors and their creditors over interest rates and trade protectionism increased sharply. The Presidents of Argentina, Brazil, Colombia and Mexico issued a joint statement warning western governments that external factors outside the control of their governments, namely high and rising interest rates and the proliferation of protectionism, not only were serious threats to the economic growth of the region, but that they were also jeopardising the progress of democratic trends in Latin America. "Our countries cannot accept these risks indefinitely. We do not accept being pressed into forced bankruptcy and a prolonged economic paralysis. . ." read the statement.[4] The statement was unprecedented not only because of the severity of its tone, but because it was jointly subscribed by three big Latin American debtors.

Reactions to this and other appeals by the Latin American countries to the western governments to adopt a more flexible attitude towards their foreign debt difficulties and to the suggestion that a debt summit should take place came at the tenth annual economic summit of the seven major industrialised countries in London in June 1984. In their communiqué the call for a debtor-creditor summit was ignored, but the third-world debt problems were specifically addressed. The statement regarding the debt problem reiterated the agreed strategy of the industrial countries for dealing with it: to be flexible in its application and to continue the case-by-case approach. It mentioned that the part industrial nations should play was to help debtor countries to implement the necessary economic and financial policy changes with due attention to political and social problems. The industrial nations agreed that the IMF should continue to play a central role in this process in closer cooperation with the World Bank, whose function in fostering medium- and long-term development should be strengthened. Finally, the communiqué stressed the need to extend multi-year reschedulings of commercial debts, as well as those of governments and government agencies, to the countries which made successful efforts to implement the necessary economic reforms.

The "Cartagena Consensus"

The statement on the debt, issued after the 1984 London summit did little to assuage Latin American countries' worries. Shortly afterwards, the majority of the countries in Latin America sent delegations to Cartagena, Colombia, to try to reach a common position on the pressing problems affecting their debt repayments, particularly the rise of interest rates (which increased by another percentage point in June). Of the countries represented at Cartagena, the one most prepared to adopt a radical attitude towards creditors and IMF-imposed austerity programmes was Argentina, with the possible backing of Bolivia, Ecuador and the Dominican Republic.

It was the economic and political situation in these countries that was behind their possible challenge to the whole IMF-centred international financial system and approach to the problem. President Raul Alfonsin, as the first democratically elected Argentine leader after the long period of military dictatorship, was in no position to accept the IMF austerity package as the condition to obtain new finance. He had already issued a refusal to pay interest accrued on Argentina's debt. It was, in fact, the Latin American loan, as mentioned above, that prevented Argentina's debt from becoming non-performing. Bolivia, for its part, had already declared a moratorium on its foreign debt; payments had already been suspended in 1983. Ecuador had also stopped payments on its foreign debt a month before the meeting, while the Dominican Republic had suspended negotiations with the IMF in the wake of riots which followed the introduction of food price increases. Other possible backers of the radical approach were Peru and Chile, both small and perhaps more vulnerable debtors. Chile, for instance, urged the region as a whole to pay no more than 25 per cent of its export earnings on debt-servicing. Bolivia backed this initiative, which became generally accepted by the Cartagena group as a principle, but was never put into operation. Other participants at the meeting were less inclined to take a confrontational attitude, which had a lot to do with their own economic situation and the state of their bilateral negotiations with the banks.

But the real obstacles to achieving a collective clout, were the relatively better conditions then enjoyed by several countries. Mexico was expecting to be the first country to obtain the much-sought multi-year rescheduling of its official debt in exchange for its willingness to abide by the austerity measures directed by the IMF. Brazil was expecting similar treatment, given that it had been making efforts since early 1983 to implement major changes in wage, fiscal and monetary policies and was achieving impressive trade surpluses.

Thus, there was not much common ground among the 11 Latin American countries gathered in Cartagena to take concrete collective actions. There was a strong interest, particularly among the large debtors (with the exception of Argentina), in the maintenance of the autonomy of individual countries in their negotiations with the banks, and in the adoption of only a general declaration of principles. In the end, this position won the day. The moderate line was adopted. All agreed against the creation of a debtors' cartel, and against a general moratorium. The final document, known as the Cartagena Consensus, reiterated the Quito declaration on the need to bring down interest rates and reduce trade protectionism, but also demanded a rate cap on loans to debtor countries, the lowering of the "spreads" (the difference between borrowing and lending rates), the stretching of the maturities of loans and compensatory payments to countries hit by variable interest rates.

A significant concrete result achieved in the process was the institutionalisation of the 11-nation Cartagena group[5] as a permanent regional forum for consultation on debt matters, in particular addressed to securing an efficient exchange of relevant information. The next meeting of the group took place in September 1984 in Mar del Plata, Argentina. There were no new initiatives over the debt as such, but the invitation to the industrialised countries to engage in a direct political dialogue with the debtors was renewed. The Argentinian delegation, in contrast to its attitude at Cartagena, this time adopted a cautious approach, avoiding statements which could harm its own negotiations. The Latin American representatives present at this meeting agreed that the Interim and Development Committees within the IMF and World Bank respectively were inadequate forums to move forward on the debt issue. These committees were essentially of a technical character, whereas the debt problem was firmly placed within the political sphere. Any radical change in strategy would need to involve bodies with a wider competence. The reaction to this proposal was varied. The United States and Britain rejected the idea of a special conference on the debt stressing that it should be kept within the established forums, such as the UN, and the IMF and World Bank committees. However, other governments, including France and Canada, informally supported the idea. Among the proposals the Mar del Plata meeting agreed upon was that for the creation of a compensation fund within the IMF for use by less developed countries whose debt repayments had risen substantially owing to high interest rates. There were also suggestions for increasing the lending capability of the World Bank. Changes were proposed on the guidelines of the IMF for negotiating austerity packages in order to accommodate longer-term solutions as well as considerations of social costs involved. The Latin American representatives also objected to the practice of prior agreement with the IMF before renegotiation of loans that commercial banks have traditionally insisted on.

Between the period of the Mar del Plata meeting and the following gathering of the Cartagena group in Santo Domingo in February 1985, the debt situation of several countries moved in the right direction. Mexico achieved in September 1984 a much publicised restructuring of $48.7bn of its public debt on very favourable terms, and Brazil and Venezuela, and perhaps also Argentina, were in a good position to follow in Mexico's steps. In Santo Domingo, Latin American delegates decided to stop pressing for the idea of a summit with western governments in order to await the results of the IMF's Interim Committee and World Bank's Development Committee due to take place in Washington in April 1985. Some interpreted this moderate position as the result of the fact that Mexico, Argentina and Venezuela had had major successes in their official debt negotiations. But these developments triggered the launching from Santo Domingo of a call for this treatment to be extended to the rest of the debtor countries.

The Maverick Approaches

The summer of 1985 brought some unpleasant surprises for bankers and creditor governments alike. These were: Peru' s decision to limit foreign debt payments to 10 per cent of its export revenues; and Fidel Castro's large and notorious Latin American gathering in Havana, where he made an appeal to the Latin American governments to repudiate their foreign debt. Although no serious immediate consequences ensued from García's and Castro's much publicised statements, they added a new element of urgency to the regional debt negotiations.

Alan García's challenge to Peru's creditors, made in his presidential inaugural address, took everybody by surprise. It was the first case of a major country taking unilateral action to implement one of the proposals suggested by the Latin American countries in their regional meetings—the proposal to put a ceiling on debt payments in relation to the countries' export earnings. Moreover, the ceiling announced by García was far more drastic than the 25 per cent limit proposed by Chile at the Cartagena meeting. Other Latin American debtors reacted quickly to García's statement. High-level delegations were present in Lima for the inauguration, six of them headed by the Presidents of their respective countries. The members of the Cartagena group rejected the Peruvian President's initiative to cap debt repayments. Although the idea of linking debt payments to exports had been endorsed by the Cartagena group as a principle, no country had dared carry it out, let alone announce it, so defiantly. The other tough part of his statement, that Peru would not accept the conditionality of the IMF, did not cause so much consternation. Other countries (for instance Venezuela) had kept their distance from the IMF, while Brazil and Argentina had maintained only intermittent relations with the Fund.

García's statement did not unleash a wave of attacks on the prevailing strategy for managing the debt, but it did serve to reinforce the view that Latin American countries should engage in harder bargaining with the banks and should not accept great sacrifices for their populations and stagnant economies as a matter of course.

Another maverick initiative came from Cuba's leader, Fidel Castro. In Havana at the end of July 1985, Castro hosted a conference for 1,500 delegates, including ex-presidents, ex-prime ministers, political and religious leaders and prominent businessmen, but few of the region's policy-makers. Castro's contention was that the debt was unpayable and that, therefore, Latin America should repudiate all its financial obligations. His appeal fell on deaf ears. The general reaction in Latin America was that it was all very well for Castro to urge a global repudiation of the debt when the bulk of Cuba's debt was to the Soviet Union which was not insisting on regular Cuban repayments. As far as Cuba's $2bn debt to western governments was concerned, it was noted that Cuba had worked hard to achieve a rescheduling agreement with its creditors within the framework of the Paris Club and generally showed that it was most interested in maintaining its creditworthiness.

The Baker Initiative: Too Little, Too Late?

The repeated collective appeals of the Latin American countries for easing the burden of their external debt, and their call for a debt summit with the creditor governments, appeared to go unheeded. Real interest rates remained relatively high. But the debate on the basic nature of the problem began to spill over to the North. There were second thoughts about the strategy advocated until then for handling the debt problems. It is difficult to assess to what extent this change was due to the impact of Cartagena, and its repeated calls for the reactivation of the Latin American economies. However, it was surely no coincidence that the United States appeared to be ready to adopt a new approach to the Latin American debt problem.

The new approach was outlined by the American Secretary of the Treasury, James Baker, at the meetings of the IMF and World Bank in Seoul in October 1985. His proposal was to make available about $29bn net new lending over a three-year period to ease the financial problems of the 15 middle-income most indebted countries. Of this sum, private creditor banks were expected to contribute $20bn, which would be matched by an equal amount in loans from the World Bank and the multilateral development banks (in the case of Latin America, the Inter-American Development Bank), raising lending levels by 50 per cent. This inflow of much needed fresh funds would take place under the continuing supervision of the IMF, although the policies of the debtor countries would be geared at fostering economic growth.

The Latin American response to the Baker initiative was prepared at another meeting of the Cartagena group in December 1985, this time in Montevideo, Uruguay. The group proposed a set of economic "emergency measures" to alleviate the economic stagnation in many countries by fostering the revival of economic activity. The main demands of the group, contained in the so-called "Montevideo Declaration", included a call for larger fresh funds than those envisaged in the Baker initiative. Among their demands, the Cartagena group similarly reiterated the need for reducing American interest rates to "historic levels" by the end of 1986. They also called for a reduction in commercial banks' profit margins, as well as an increase in trade finance and new credits from banks beyond the levels proposed by Baker and the maintenance of their exposure to the region. With regard to the Baker plan, the group described it as "positive and useful" but "insufficient". An ad hoc group composed of Brazil, Mexico, Argentina, Colombia and Venezuela was formed to monitor the progress of the Latin American developments and to propose alternative measures in case of non-fulfillment of the stated objectives.

Similarly, the banks' reaction to the Baker initiative was not enthusiastic. In general, the banks seemed to be reluctant to increase their exposure to deeply indebted third-world countries, and stressed the need for a balance between the contributions of the commercial banks and those from governments and multilateral institutions. A number of banks were not satisfied with the contribution the governments of the industrial countries had made to easing the difficulties created by the Latin American (and third-world) debt. In the banks' view, the governments had not done enough to enlarge the export credits available via export credit guarantee schemes, nor had they matched the banks' offers of multi-year reschedulings of officially guaranteed debts. The banks attached certain conditions to their eventual support of the Baker initiative. Credit would continue to be provided on a case-by-case basis, and this only after the debtor countries had adopted sound economic programmes. A particularly critical and tricky request was that the debtor countries, in the banks' view, should make efforts to halt capital flight as well as to improve the investment climate for prospective foreign investors.

There were some points of coincidence between the two "opposing ends" of the Baker initiative, i.e. the banks and the Latin American debtors. For example, on the necessity for governments of industrial countries to ease the difficult situation by providing more export credit and easing trade flows, and the need for a higher profile to be given to the management of the debt problems. But there were many more points of divergence. This was particularly true of the banks' reluctance to increase their exposure without sufficient guarantees which, in the Latin American view, amounted to the continuation of the much debated and not too successful approach of recent years.

The Impact of Declining Oil Prices

The continuous decline in oil prices, particularly felt at the beginning of 1986, has had a devastating effect on the two major oil producers in Latin America, Mexico and Venezuela. The fact that these two countries are also among the region's big debtors raised international concern over their continued ability to keep servicing their foreign debts.

In an effort to keep its oil market, Mexico was forced to respond to the general level of spot prices and cut its own by an average of $4 per barrel in early February. This price-cut meant that oil revenues (accounting for more than 70 per cent of Mexico's total export revenues) would decrease by $2.2bn on a yearly average. Only a fortnight later, Mexico was again forced to reduce a further $4.68 a barrel, with another possible drop of $3bn in revenue amidst a downward trend expected to continue. Mexico's drastic moves led to speculation that in view of these extremely adverse circumstances Mexico would decide either to declare a moratorium or to ask its creditors to accept a cut in interest payments.

Before reaching a decision, Mexico attempted to involve the Latin American collective forum in dealing with the bitter new phase of the debt problem. A meeting in Cancun, Mexico, between the Presidents of Mexico and Venezuela, Miguel de la Madrid and Jaime Lusinchi respectively, prepared the ground for an emergency meeting of the Cartagena group. A preliminary meeting of the Cartagena group took place in Washington, the first time such a gathering took place outside Latin America, after a call from Mexico and Venezuela. It was agreed then that the members of the monitoring committee should meet again in early March in Punta del Este, Uruguay.

Mexico, Argentina and Brazil seemed to agree on the need to reduce interest rates on past loans, whilst applying market rates to any future borrowing. This was one of the main topics to be discussed at Punta del Este, and Mexico was seen to be on the verge of declaring its intention to cap its interest payments. However, there was no agreement among the monitoring committee as to whether it should spell out a specific rate cap or only to issue vague proposals without specific figures, as had been done in the past.

Nevertheless, when the finance ministers of the steering committee met, after discussions by the foreign ministers on the peace process in Central America, there was a certain lack of rapport among them. Mexico gave the impression of having devoted more time and attention to negotiating bilaterally with its foreign creditors and American Administration officials than to the preparation of a document for discussion at the meeting with its Latin American partners, or to keeping them informed of what strategy it wished to adopt. Perhaps as a result of this, the Punta del Este meeting ended with a short communiqué supporting Mexico in its negotiations with the banks and creditor countries on the emergency financial package.

Declining oil prices, while creating severe problems for oil-exporting countries, help other debtors who have been paying exorbitant oil import bills since 1973. Lower oil prices may have a very positive effect on the world economy, with particular benefits for less developed countries, and even the oil exporters. With low oil prices, world markets will be (and are already being) stimulated. Smaller oil import bills of industrial countries will aid economic recovery, with likely increases in internal demand. This will be a stimulus to international trade, with increased demand for products of less developed countries.

A second possible side-effect of the fall of oil prices may well be an increased readiness in industrial countries to liberalise trade or to grant "preferential" status to debtor countries; indirectly, competitivity may change in their favour. Though Latin American oil exporters may find it very hard to adjust to the drop of oil prices, other Latin American debtors, particularly Brazil, may find this a very welcome development.

Conclusions

The debt crisis, which has engulfed the Latin American countries in severe economic and financial problems since 1982, has led to a marked increase in regional contacts and to the formation of a Latin American forum, the Cartagena group, for the discussion of their financial problems and the adoption of common postures. Latin American countries realised that the formation of a "debtor' s cartel", implying a confrontational attitude vis-à-vis their creditors, was not in their interest. The actions and pronouncements of the Cartagena group have up to now remained within the bounds of moderation.

The Cartagena group's success in having its demands to the international community met has been mixed. On the one hand, the Cartagena group's proposal for a debtor-creditor summit has been rejected; interest rates still remain high; international trade has not so far received the boost necessary to ease the inflow of foreign exchange from exports to the debtor countries; and the increase of fresh loans to the region has not materialised. The amounts offered under the Baker initiative were considered insufficient, and six months after its announcement no country has yet benefited from it. But on the other hand, the Cartagena group's impact has not been negligible. Its repeated appeals for policies that would foster economic recovery and growth in Latin America have been accepted by banks and creditor countries, at least in principle. And, very important, the Cartagena group has helped to keep up the momentum in the search for long-term solutions to the debt problem.

Collective action, however, has met many obstacles. Solidarity and cooperation seem to operate only when no specific commitments are made. Because it is in each debtor's interest to maintain the maximum level of autonomy when negotiating with creditors, cooperation with regional partners takes second place. A commitment to collective action could well limit the scope of the debtor' s bargaining ground. Regional cooperation ends when bilateral negotiations begin.

[1] For general background, see Roland Dallas, "Democracy and debt in Latin America", *The World Today*, April 1984; Andrew Hurrell, "Brazil, the United States and the Debt, *ibid*., March 1985; and Esperanza Durán, "Mexico: economic realism and political efficiency", *ibid*., May 1985.

[2] On the origins of Latin America collective action on the debt issue, see Riordan Roett, "Latin America's response to the debt crisis", *Third World Quarterly*, April 1985, pp. 228-34.

[3] CEPAL, Notas sobre la economia y el desarrollo en America Latina no. 389/390, January 1984, "Declaracion de Quito y Plan de Accion".

[4] Andrew Whitely, " Latin Americans step up demands on debt and trade", *Financial Times*, 21 May, p. 1.

[5] The 11 countries represented at Cartagena were: Argentina, Bolivia, Brazil, Chile, Colombia, the Dominican Republic, Ecuador, Mexico, Peru, Uruguay and Venezuela.

Democracy and Debt in South America: A Continent's Dilemma

Riordan Roett

I

Democracy and debt were a macabre *pas de deux* in South America during 1983. As military regimes withdrew in disgrace (Argentina), further liberalized (Brazil), or tried to cope with vigorous popular pressures to restore democracy (Uruguay and Chile), that welcome news was haunted by the growing social and political implications of the continent's economic difficulties. The growing foreign debt burden has become the most visible manifestation of the current economic crisis, the worst in more than 50 years.

The quality of life has deteriorated dramatically in most of the countries of South America, largely as a result of stabilization programs and austerity measures implemented in 1983. Outbursts of rioting and growing street demonstrations indicate a decreasing tolerance for belt-tightening among the poor and middle sectors of the populations. Many ask if it is possible for fragile democratic institutions to meet the demands of the International Monetary Fund and the international private commercial banks, and simultaneously to respond to the expectations and needs of their citizens.

U.S. policy in the Western Hemisphere in 1983 continued to emphasize what the Reagan Administration has taken to be America's "backyard" in Central America and the Caribbean. Indeed, the early twentieth-century reality of the "big stick" and "gunboat diplomacy" returned for many observers as American troops landed in Grenada, the number of U.S. advisers increased in Central America, U.S. covert aid for guerrillas became overt, and American warships steamed off the coast of Central America. These actions were a warning to unfriendly governments that the Reagan Administration was committed to a reassertion of what it perceived as U.S. vital interests in the region. Headlines trumpeted the meandering of the Contadora Group (a regional peace initiative by Colombia, Mexico, Panama and Venezuela) as well as the deliberations of the Kissinger Commission for Central America.

At the end of the year, the Administration faced multiple problems in this backyard—disengaging and helping to establish viable self-government in Grenada, working toward new elections in El Salvador while seeking to bring right-wing death squads under control, and above all addressing the policy issue of whether it would accept a continued Marxist regime in Nicaragua even under some negotiated structure of restraints on its external behavior. But there could be no doubt that the Administration—and Congress—were fully engaged in these problems.

Reprinted by permission of *Foreign Affairs*, vol. 62, no. 3, 1983. © 1983 by the Council on Foreign Relations Inc.

That was not true for the continent, unfortunately. Preoccupied with at best a stalemate and possibly a rapidly deteriorating situation in Central America, the U.S. government nodded vaguely from time to time in South America's direction, primarily when the financial crisis threatened to boil over. Contadora received only polite lip service. Little else about South America appears to have stirred Washington's emotions in 1983.

Yet, in relation to the potential political dangers to the major nations of South America posed by the economic crisis, a low profile or the absentminded neglect of the continent is surely shortsighted; it is also dangerous. In their mid-term and long-term importance, the countries of South America and Mexico loom far larger than those of Central America and the Caribbean, whether one looks at political, economic and commercial, or financial considerations. The United States has important national interests throughout the hemisphere, not only in the backyard. If we assume that support of democratic regimes is a legitimate goal of U.S. foreign policy in Latin America, there is a grave danger in failing to understand the threat that the current economic crisis, and the foreign debt specifically, pose to the social and political stability of a majority of the states in South America.[1]

There is a risk that these democratic governments will collapse, of course—possibly to be replaced by others prepared to take radical steps such as repudiation of their debts. But an even more basic threat is that the promising trend to greater democracy in the area—an intricate and delicate process of political institutionalization now under way—may be aborted, with the crushing of social expectations that were generated during the 1970s, as South America moved toward middle-class status in the international system. These dangers are, or should be, of the highest importance to U.S. foreign policy in the hemisphere in the 1980s.

II

The high profile of Latin America in the current debt crisis has been carefully reviewed elsewhere.[2] About one-half of the total Third World debt is owed by Latin American states. Two-thirds of the Latin debt has been loaned by private commercial banks. The banks have lent to Latin America at prevailing commercial interest rates, which have fallen from the all-time highs reached in 1980-1981 but remain very onerous; the average term of the loans is also relatively short. Fees and spreads add to the cost of borrowing. To generate the foreign exchange required to service the interest on the private bank debt alone, Latin America has had to mortgage a higher and higher percentage of its export earnings—35 percent in 1983. In 1982, total debt service, both interest and principal, equalled 66 percent of the region's exports. This is at a time when the world recession has cut the demand for the region's exports; merchandise exports in 1983 were estimated at about $87 billion, compared to $97 billion in 1981. The recession has cut into Latin America's traditional export markets in Western Europe as well as newfound openings within Latin America itself and in the Third World. The 1983 payments on the debt—for interest alone—were about $40 billion.[3]

Private commercial banks have reduced the net flow of capital to Latin America at a time when greater flows are needed. New publicly announced syndicated loans (maturities of one year or over) to Latin America fell off sharply from 1981 to 1983. The banks loaned Latin America $30.2 billion in 1981. That figure dropped to $26.7 billion in 1982 and, at the end of 1983, had fallen to half the 1981 number, or $15.3 billion. The trend is similar for other areas of the Third World.

Trade is a crucial link in the chain of repayment. But the trends both for Latin America and for the United States are disturbing. Given the increasing percentage of exports required to finance interest payments on the debt, little is left for buying goods from the industrial countries. The year-end estimate was that U.S. exports to Latin America fell about 40 percent in 1983 from 1981 levels, and it is worth noting that the decline in U.S. exports to Latin America cost nearly 400,000 domestic jobs in 1982 and 1983. While exports to Latin America accounted for only 17 percent of total U.S. exports in 1981, between 1978 and 1981 they had grown more than 50 percent faster than exports to the rest of the world. Thus, the decline since 1981 represents a particularly sharp reversal of past trends.

Meanwhile, the Latin Americans find that the North American market is even more important—with recovery still lagging in Europe and with the Third World barely emerging from deep global recession. According to the Department of Commerce, the United States had an $8-billion trade deficit with Latin America in 1983, compared with negative $3.8 billion in 1982. This trend, especially the resulting loss of employment, has spurred protectionist pressures in the United States against Latin products. Such pressures probably strengthen the hand of those who oppose increased support for the International Monetary Fund, which is seen as "bailing out" the Third World; during 1983 it took many months to persuade the Congress to approve, in November, an IMF quota increase that may still fall short of the need. And any undertaking to support the private commercial banks may be viewed in similar terms. The Fund and the banks are key actors in both the short-term and long-term resolution of the crisis. "Efforts to limit their role or effectiveness will further complicate the debt morass.

Latin America is caught. World markets are inhospitable to the exports which it needs to earn foreign exchange to meet payments on the debt. The U.S. market, absorptive in the present recovery, is under increasing pressure to limit access. Increased lending is vital to maintain a modicum of economic order, but the amounts remain inadequate and are subject to stringent policy conditions of retrenchment that tend to hit particularly hard at the working classes.

III

There is a wide range of opinion about the implications for the private commercial banks and the international financial system of the current debt crisis. Reasonable men disagree. One school of thought argues that a moratorium by one or more nations is possible, indeed likely, if the general economic picture in 1984 remains as gloomy as it was in 1983. Others argue that the debt is manageable, that the problem is liquidity rather than fundamental solvency, and that the capacity to meet debt payments can be adequate—if an overall recovery in the industrial countries becomes a solid reality in 1984 and beyond. The debate about the financial aspects of the debt burden and the timing and magnitude of recovery will continue. It is an important debate, and it is natural that it should be addressed by the IMF, government economic officials and the banks primarily in terms of figures and economic indicators.

But it may be even more important to understand the social costs for Latin America, and especially South America, of the current economic downturn there—and the probable future social price for the people of the continent. If these social costs should lead to political changes that bring in radical governments unwilling to continue the regressive policies required by the IMF and the banks, then and then only might there be not only moratorium but outright debt repudiation—first in one country and then perhaps in others. And even if such repudiation were avoided, so that debt payments continued on an agreed schedule, financial "victory" could be at the price of eventual political defeat.

The economic impact of the debt burden and the belt-tightening measures that accompany IMF lending can be quickly summarized in aggregate terms. The year-end estimate was that, for Latin America as a whole, gross national product (GNP) declined by 3.8 percent in 1983, adjusted for inflation. Per capita income fell for the third straight year in 1983, to a level eight percent below its peak in 1980. On present prospects, even if growth picks up after 1983, per capita income will not return to the 1980 level before the end of the decade.

On their face, these declines may not seem significantly more serious than those experienced in the post-1980 deep global recession by many countries, including the United States itself. Why, then, is the situation in Latin America more threatening and more politically explosive?

The first answer is that continent-wide figures do not reflect significant differences from one country to another. While the Latin American oil-exporting countries, notably Venezuela and Mexico, have had their own steep decline in the standard of living of their citizens, those standards are considerably higher than elsewhere in the hemisphere. More important, even the present price and market for oil are sufficient to give these countries a significant cushion and means of recovery. Mexico in 1983 exceeded expectations in getting on top of its debt problem and now looks a good bet to dig itself out without major internal political disruption.

On the other hand, the much larger number of countries that have no such oil capacity are almost uniformly in bad shape. All of the states of South America have experienced high rates of inflation, escalating unemployment, diminishing fiscal resources for social support programs, and increasing poverty. But this precipitate decline in social and economic wellbeing has been particularly acute in selected cases, of which Peru and Brazil are the most dramatic examples. And it happens that these are the two countries where there were marked outbreaks of social unrest during 1983.

In Peru, the drop in GNP was about 12 percent in 1983. Less than half of the workforce of six million is fully employed. Real wages are only three-fifths of their 1973 levels and inflation doubled to 130 percent in 1983.

Moreover, Peru experienced a series of natural disasters during the year. El Niño reappeared at Christmas 1982—a warm water current that drives away schools of anchovies who thrive on the cold waters of the Humboldt current—and has decimated the world's fourth largest fishing industry. Fish processing, once Peru's major economic activity, fell by two thirds in the first half of 1983, compared with 1982. The climatic changes that accompanied El Niño caused severe floods in the north of Peru and drought in the south.

For Brazil, 1983 was the third year of recession. More than a quarter of the work force of 49 million was out of work, or underemployed; employment levels in São Paulo, the industrial heartland of Brazil and of Latin America, have fallen back to where they were in the early 1970s; over the year food prices rose by 227 percent, with the cost of some staples, such as beans and potatoes, multiplying four-fold.

In short, averages do not by any means tell the whole story. The situation is far graver in several key countries,

Second, the process through which Latin America is passing is particularly hard on working classes and the poor. The need to drastically cut imports has led to a dramatic decrease in production and therefore in job creation. The economic crisis has occurred at the same time that the children born in the 1960s, when birth rates were far higher than now, are entering the job market. The sudden "bulge" in the labor force further aggravates the situation of the working poor. Devaluations have spurred inflation and increased the real cost of living for all, but especially for the poor, who are a majority in each of the countries of the continent. In these circumstances, social assistance programs or public work projects to create employment opportunities are financially infeasible.

In their rush to expand in the 1970s, what were apparently the most successful Latin American countries neglected their safety nets—in Brazil, for example, there is no social security system, nor is there unemployment insurance or a widespread network of social support institutions. In other countries with more comprehensive systems, coverage often extends only to industrial workers. There is little social support for those employed in agriculture, where significant percentages of the economically active population remain: more than 35 percent in Brazil, Colombia, Ecuador, Peru, Bolivia and Paraguay. Only Argentina and Uruguay have less than 20 percent employed in the countryside.

It is possible to overdramatize the social situation in South America. It is also true that poverty and social marginality have been facts of life for decades in the region. But a third factor making the current economic crisis ominous in social and political terms is that it has come so drastically and suddenly, after years of relatively good economic growth in the 1960s and 1970s. During those years many of the key South American countries and Mexico—most notably Brazil—made great economic strides, so that they came to be classified as newly industrialized countries; growth was uneven, and by no means equally distributed throughout the society, but there was a palpable sense of momentum and forward movement. As de Tocqueville pointed out long ago in connection with the French Revolution, and as contemporary history has demonstrated time and again, political danger may be greatest not when an economy remains stagnant, but when it has turned upward and then become disappointing.

These are the factors that lay behind the riots and looting that came abruptly to the world's attention in São Paulo in April, and in Rio de Janeiro during the autumn. Soup kitchens in Lima and Santiago are common occurrences today, as they are in other major cities of the continent. The dramatic victory in the race for the mayoralty of Lima, Peru, in November 1983 indicated the relationship of hunger and deprivation to politics—for the first time, a Marxist candidate won the position. He had promised to provide free milk for children. To the poorer segments of Lima society, his ideology appeared less important than his social message.

The issue is not that one Marxist candidate, of a relatively mild stripe, won an open and competitive election in Lima. It is the generalized stress under which the political systems of South America now labor. And this brings us to the fourth factor, namely that the crisis comes at a time when most Latin American nations have become progressively disillusioned with the performance of authoritarian and military regimes and are in the process of inaugurating or moving toward democratic systems. The very process of democratization runs the risk of being short-circuited if social and economic expectations cannot be met by democratically chosen governments. The slow and tortured consolidation of open and competitive politics, not necessarily a replica of the U.S. system, but representative of the realities and the desires of Latin Americans, may be in jeopardy.

It is this interaction between economic crisis (enormously accentuated by the debt problem) and a political crossroads that is at the core of the situation in South America today. We shall return to a country-by-country examination of the interaction in Sections V and VI—putting Peru and Brazil alongside others in this wider context. For 1983 was a year of paradox—on the one hand, a year of unprecedented economic strains, and on the other hand a time when the possibility of a return to democracy on the continent gained strong momentum.

But first let us take a short look at the historical background against which this important political trend has emerged. This background is also relevant to our discussion because it highlights the dangers for the United States in facilely accepting, in the future, the argument that "weak" democratic regimes are susceptible to subversion and that "strong" military governments will be both efficient and ideologically more amenable to "Western" values.

IV

After a decade or two of populist politics in South America in the 1950s and 1960s, badly managed development (in the face of enormous inherent difficulties, it must be said) led to societal polarization and eventual political breakdown. A wave of military regimes replaced democratic governments—Brazil in 1964, Argentina in 1966 and 1976, Peru in 1968, Ecuador in 1972, Chile and Uruguay in 1973. All of the new regimes, with the exception of Ecuador and Peru, were right-wing authoritarian; those in Ecuador and Peru were military populist experiments. In general, these new regimes rested their right to rule on their efficiency, their capacity to induce economic growth, and their newfound ability to govern without the political stalemate and social class tensions that populist democratic regimes allegedly generated.

From the perspective of many in the United States and the industrial North, those promises appeared to bear fruit. The Brazilian "miracle" of the 1970s led to spectacular rates of growth. The post-1973 Chilean "Chicago School" of economists and bankers modernized the economy and opened it to the winds of world competition. Argentina's classical solutions to traditional problems made economic ministers like José Martinez de Hoz heroes among international bankers and corporate leaders.

The armed forces, in some cases, also justified their overthrow of the democratically elected governments on the grounds that the latter were either willing to tolerate, or unable to control, subversive forces. Radical leftist (and anti-democratic) elements were indeed present in Brazil in 1964, in Chile in 1973, and in Argentina in 1976. In each of those countries, and in others, the military undertook a vigorous campaign to suppress and eliminate such activities. But extra-legal action, such as the cancellation of political rights or exile, soon slid into ominous witchhunts against all who allegedly supported the old government or were in some way thought undesirable by the new one. In Chile, a Santiago soccer stadium and Dawson Island became symbols of how far the armed forces would go to protect that country from the threat of Marxism. The olive-green Ford Falcon sedans that were used to abduct those allegedly guilty of subversion, and the Naval Mechanics School, the location of some of the most savage torture, testified to the efficiency and commitment of the security forces in defending their perverse view of "social peace." By the end of the decade, as human rights violations continued, public protest grew stronger.

After a few years of economic sleight-of-hand, and following the first oil price shock of 1973-74, the economic invincibility of the technocrats in South American societies became questionable. Bloated state bureaucracies borrowed and spent large amounts of money, often without clear guidelines or central government control. Pharoanic projects became the norm in some countries. In many, corruption became endemic. Capital flight and speculation were acceptable business activities. By the late 1970s it was clear that the military regimes had no magic wand with which to modernize their economies. It was also clear that their disdain for political participation and social needs, even in Peru where the military regime claimed to have created a humane revolution, had become intolerable to the average citizen.

The United States also discovered, often to its surprise, that authoritarian regimes had contrary views on international issues. Argentina and Brazil refused to sign the Non-Proliferation Treaty. When President Carter asked them to join the United States in organizing the grain embargo against the Soviets to protest the invasion of Afghanistan, they declined. As regimes diversified their economic and political relations, they turned to other arms suppliers: Soviet weapons suddenly appeared in Peru, for example. Increasingly, military regimes espoused the language of the Third World and entered into the fray of the North-South dialogue—on the side of the South.

Moreover, apart from the tensions created by their human rights violations, the recent authoritarian regimes in Latin America have shown a strong tendency to reopen old scores, initiate or risk armed conflict, and meddle in the internal affairs of other sovereign states in the hemisphere. In earlier periods, the United States had been able to exercise some influence in preventing such activities, and particularly outbreaks of hostilities. But the United States had lost the leverage that went with its earlier role as the sole source of military equipment, first under grant aid and then by sales. Sources of arms are now varied and diverse; indeed, Brazil had become an important Third World arms producer, in part to be independent of the United States and the industrial arms suppliers. Other instruments of policy normally available for purposes of influence and persuasion, such as foreign aid, had diminished or disappeared.

Thus, for the first time in decades, war talk was cheap talk in South America in the 1970s and early 1980s, and the settling of old scores became fashionable, as newly armed military regimes rediscovered old border disputes and territorial claims. Chile and Argentina came perilously close to war over possession of the Beagle Channel islands in 1978. Two military regimes, identifying their prestige with a long-festering claim to sovereignty, spent hundreds of millions of dollars in preparation for a war that neither country could afford and neither people really wanted. In Peru, even after President Fernando Belaunde Terry returned to power in democratic elections in 1980, an autonomous military establishment skirmished with Ecuador in 1981.

And the most devastating example, of course, was the 1982 war in the South Atlantic, initiated by the military regime in Argentina through the forceful seizure from Britain of the Falklands, or Malvinas, Islands.

In none of these conflicts was there parliamentary or political party consultation. Public opinion was shamelessly manipulated. Arms purchases were given highest priority, without regard for the social and economic needs of the domestic population. And the United States appeared powerless to prevent the outbreak of hostilities. Indeed, in the case of the South Atlantic conflict, U.S. mediation was interpreted as duplicitous by many countries in Latin America and momentarily exacerbated diplomatic ties between Washington and the major capitals of the continent.

In short, the record in South America over this period—and indeed in past history—shows that authoritarian regimes have a strong tendency to military aggressiveness and to the forceful assertion of territorial claims. The theme will not go away. The claims are many and diverse.[4] For military regimes war is an obvious and simple response to a simple problem. The difficulty is that people die and causes are lost, as the South Atlantic war clearly demonstrated.

V

It is also true that authoritarian regimes in advanced states of decay can badly misjudge aroused public opinion, especially after a military defeat. The origins of the successful return to democracy in *Argentina*, capped by the election on October 30, 1983 of Raul Alfonsín as constitutional president, lay in a massive public repudiation of the military government following the revelation, first by events and then by progressive disclosures, of its mendacity and fecklessness in conducting the war. The defeat in the Falklands/Malvinas was the straw that broke the Argentine military's back. The conflict had been preceded by widespread economic chaos and increasing public repudiation of "el proceso"—the dirty war that resulted in the disappearance of thousands of Argentine citizens allegedly implicated in subversive action against the state. If the mothers of the Plaza de Mayo, who marched each day in front of the presidential palace demanding information on their missing children, symbolized the personal agony of a nation, the outcome in the Falklands/Malvinas symbolized the incompetence of the armed forces and shattered any remaining claim they had to govern Argentina.

Argentina responded late in 1982 by suddenly joining the countries of the continent moving toward democracy. The promise of free elections, so often confounded in the past, this time became reality. By 1983, the age-old division between the Radical Party and the Peronists, organized in the Justicialista Party, was again the key element in electoral politics. Alfonsín, for many years the leader of a minority faction in the former, captured the nomination by offering an image of competence and energy. After a period of suspense over whether Mrs. Isabel Perón would return from exile in Spain to either lead the Peronists or become their candidate, they selected Italo Luder.

In the country's first campaign season since Perón himself ran and won in 1973, I encountered many who said that while they themselves preferred Alfonsín, Luder would win. However, playing on the need for a change, Alfonsín artfully identified the conservative Peronist labor elite with the military. Images of the violent side of Peronism emerged in the campaign meetings. In a historic shift in direction, the Argentinians gave Alfonsín an extraordinary majority of 52 percent of the popular vote.

Alfonsín's election victory has meaning far beyond Argentina. With close ties to the social democratic parties of Latin America and Western Europe, the Radical Party's victory is viewed as an opportunity to offer a dramatic alternative to the military regimes that remain in power in the Southern Cone. Moreover, it represents a moment in which civil-military relations in Argentina, and by extension in other states, can be redefined to help preclude future coups d'état. Finally, with his popular mandate, there is widespread hope in and out of Argentina that the president will be able to heal the nation and restore the vitality of the state.

The agenda he faces is overwhelming, but not impossible. The military are demoralized and publicly rejected. The Peronists are divided. Alfonsín has widespread support throughout Argentine civil society, even among those who voted for other candidates. What he needs is political space to deal simultaneously with multiple problems. The foreign debt is one of the most immediate.

About $10 billion of the total $40 billion debt comes due in 1984. The Alfonsín government has asked for a six-month grace period and then renegotiation of the debt. The attitude of the private commercial banks, the Central Banks, the IMF, and the U.S. government will be critical in determining whether the space is made available. While the social cost in Argentina has not been as great as in other countries in South America, a 1983 inflation rate of 433.7 percent, the highest in the world, daily price changes, rising unemployment, and widespread uncertainty have created a tense situation. It is simply not realistic to expect Alfonsín and the Radicals in 1984 to successfully restructure the armed forces, to reorganize the unions, and to deal with the punishment of those guilty of the dirty war and the death of at least 6,000 "disappeared" Argentinians—while at the same time imposing further economic hardship on the Argentine nation.

From the point of view of U.S. foreign policy, the first priority should be the consolidation of the democratic process in Argentina. Internal social and institutional questions are of highest priority and must be dealt with successfully to demonstrate that the government is effective. Building legitimacy—over time—can be turned into valuable currency to nurture the democratic system.

Washington must frankly face up to the likelihood that this overriding priority may for the time being mean that a number of issues now dividing Argentina and the United States will have to be put to one side or treated in low key. Argentina's nuclear program, the most advanced in Latin America, appears to be at the point where a nuclear weapon could theoretically be made; this is rightly a cause for growing concern—and not only in Washington—but it cannot be undone, and it is unlikely that Alfonsín will soon change his country's negative posture toward the Non-Proliferation Treaty. The real question is whether Argentina will develop a serious nuclear capability. The Alfonsín government has assigned a low priority to nuclear research and that decision, to hold, requires the continuation of civilian democratic rule.

Likewise, Argentina's strong commercial ties and increasing technological links with the Soviet Union have been an irritant in U.S. foreign policy circles. The new regime may be disposed to dilute these ties but it cannot move rapidly, and again the long-term picture depends on economic recovery and political stability. And the same is true of Argentina's Third World orientation in foreign policy; for the time being this is a "given"—the long-term question is whether it will be pushed in an adversary and abrasive manner.

In short, if an escalation of misunderstanding is to be avoided, the one issue on which there is the possibility of immediate and salutary action is the debt. It behooves policymakers to understand the debt as political and as an opportunity to contribute to the consolidation of democracy in Argentina. Such a determination would strengthen the U.S. position with our social democratic allies in Western Europe, including parties now in opposition.[5]

Above all, it would be seen throughout Latin America as a signal that the United States is able to redefine its foreign policy to meet new and highly relevant circumstances in the hemisphere.[6]

A similar attitude may be needed in the near future in the case of *Brazil*, whose economic situation was outlined earlier. That country's more than $90-billion foreign debt has become increasingly burdensome in both financial and political terms.

Following the remarkably successful national elections of November 1982, 1983 was to be the year of democratic consolidation in Brazil. A new congress, new state governors (the latter directly elected for the first time since 1965) and new municipal officials indicated the vitality of Brazil's political system, now unfettered and looking to indirect presidential elections in 1985 with a real possibility of a civilian candidate at that time.

Simultaneously, 1983 was to be a year of implementing a four-phase program that represented the best thinking of the Brazilian government, the private commercial banks, and the Fund. Apparently successful negotiations surrounding the foreign debt were concluded in December 1982 and agreement reached with the IMF.

Things did not work out so neatly. The December 1982 package contained a number of tough social and economic measures, including the deindexing of wages from inflation, a drastic reduction in inflation, a decrease in government spending in all areas, and the elimination of agricultural subsidies for farmers. Very shortly it became clear that the Brazilian government was having difficulty in meeting the targets established in December. The continuing decline in economic activity and rising unemployment caused an explosion in Sao Paulo in April 1983 with days of rioting and looting. The call for a debt moratorium grew among the opposition parties and eventually spread to members of the government party.

The commercial banks and the Fund announced in May that further payments were suspended until the government complied with the agreements. June and July were months of labor agitation, strikes, and demonstrations against both the austerity package, which focused primarily on wage cuts, and against the private banks and the IMF. Supermarket invasions and looting erupted in Rio de Janeiro in the autumn.

Meanwhile, the government attempted to ramrod a series of decrees through congress to meet the guidelines of the austerity package. Only after a painful period of months, in which the congress voted down a number of wage bills, did the executive branch open negotiations with the legislature. A compromise was reached that pleased no one, but it did comply with a new letter of intent negotiated between Brazil and the IMF in late August, which the private banks accepted.

The tension generated by the crisis surrounding the debt renegotiation intertwined with a deteriorating political situation in 1983. President João Figueiredo developed health problems and had to take a leave of absence in July. Confidence in the country's economic team dropped precipitately as new decisions were abruptly announced and as the austerity measures took their full toll on industry, the middle class, and the poor. The presidential succession became increasingly complicated in late 1983 as the opposition pressed for direct elections in 1985 and the government appeared uncertain of its course of action. Indeed, the music had stopped in Brazil. Gone were hopes of rapid economic modernization and social mobility for millions. The toll on the renewed democratic institutions was not quantifiable, but the fear that extremist political groups would attempt a comeback lurked beneath the surface of conversation in Brazil.

There are few who believe that a threat from the left is imminent. The most likely danger, if one emerges, will be from the right. Unlike the past, a rightist challenge may well be nationalist and populist in tone and in policy, disposed to either nationalize or severely restrict the role of the private banks and direct foreign investment." If 1984 is as traumatic as 1983," one high-ranking government official in Brasília commented to me in late fall, "all bets are off." The severe economic crisis of 1983 made a dramatic turn of events, barely conceivable a year before, at least plausible to some observers. Others are even more pessimistic. They believe that a breakdown in the present political structure will lead to disintegration of the political system and the emergence of a highly unstable stop-go series of temporary governments, none of whom will be able to restore order or establish coherent policies.

Many Brazilians ask: Is it worth the domestic political risks to go on trying to work with the IMF and the banks? It may of course be possible to formally negotiate a new debt package if the existing one doesn't work. New goals are easily established, but they will be increasingly hard to meet when unemployment is rising rapidly; rioting, looting and bank robberies are escalating; industrial output has dropped precipitously; the shrinkage of the industrial park is a cause of real concern to the business community; and tens of thousands of Brazilians are demanding political action to relieve social and economic distress that is affecting millions of citizens. No one wants or predicts a collapse. But the potential is high.

It is in the U.S. interest to do all in its power to prevent a further deterioration of the social situation in Brazil and thereby provide a strong show of support for the fledgling democratic system. There are many who see a scenario in which Brazil will need to open negotiations again early in 1984. Letters of intent between the government and the Fund will be rewritten. New money will be pledged. But the revised guidelines will not be met because of the social cost and rising political opposition. And another breakdown will result.

It is that kind of scenario that calls for a definition of the debt as political and for quick and salutary efforts to reorganize the debt, public and private, on very different terms than those now employed. We shall return in Section VII to how this might be done, recognizing that Brazil is the toughest case and—perhaps even more than Argentina—the bellwether one.

VI

Debt and politics in 1983 were deeply interwoven elsewhere in South America. One of the most vigorous of the continent's democracies, *Venezuela*, had already undergone four years of stress. During the tenure of outgoing president Luís Herrera Campíns, the foreign debt doubled to $34 billion. Overspending and falling oil income led to a precipitate decline in economic activity. Although notoriously unreliable in Latin America, existing data indicated that unemployment was nearing the 20-percent mark.

The December 1983 national elections gave Democratic Action Party candidate Jaime Lusinchi a resounding victory at the polls and a mandate for a new economic policy.[7] The first priority is the renegotiation of the foreign debt. Whatever the outcome, Venezuelans confront years of austerity. Having grown accustomed to a comfortable middle class lifestyle, (the per capita income is $4,700 a year), many will find that the future will little resemble the past. It is at that point that serious strains may appear.

Again, it is in the interest of the United States to do whatever is feasible to provide Lusinchi and his colleagues, who take office in February 1984, as much political space as is possible in the debt renegotiations. Everyone admits that there was bureaucratic inertia and incompetence in the outgoing government, as well as mindless spending and apparent disregard for economic reality. But holding the new government to account for the mistakes of the old will not serve any purpose and might contribute to a weakening of viable political institutions in a key South American nation-state.

In *Peru*, the democratic political system, restored in 1980 with the election of Fernando Belaunde Terry as president, was buffeted by economic and social adversity in 1983—with highlights noted earlier. It is estimated that servicing the foreign debt in 1983 will absorb 47 percent of export earnings. The government has drastically reduced imports, starving industry of essential supplies. Government spending has been cut, taxes will be raised, and the currency devalued. Inflation is running at an annual rate of 130 percent. A key element in Peru's current difficulty is that military expenditures absorb about one-quarter of Peru's annual budget, with the government contending this is essential for the struggle against the Sendero Luminoso (Shining Path) guerrilla movement.

The Belaunde government is trapped by rising social and political discontent, illustrated by the resounding defeat that Lima residents gave to the president's party in November 1983 in electing a Marxist mayor of the capital city. The guerrilla threat, which has moved from the mountains into the cities, has led the government to declare a state of emergency for long periods of time. Black-outs and bombings are frequent, as are labor strikes and protests.

Peru, like others, needs time to initiate a modest economic recovery. The renegotiation of the debt is a prime element in any overall strategy, given current world economic realities. The next presidential elections are scheduled for 1985. There is increasing skepticism in Peru that the elections will take place as scheduled if the government is unable to demonstrate a higher level of political competence and response to popular pressures. The Belaunde government is under siege as much from without as from within. The Peruvian debt is small, only $12 billion, but it looms large in any overall strategy of satisfying both security demands (mostly legitimate, though some of the saber-rattling variety toward Ecuador) and the social needs of the hard-pressed people of Peru.

In both *Chile* and *Uruguay*, the political motif is different. There rigid authoritarian regimes are under mounting pressure to restore democracy. In both countries economic adversity has played an important part in robbing the military of their claim to be efficient modern administrators. But the principal pressure appears to stem from a growing revulsion against repression, torture, and human rights violations, 1983 was an important year for the democratic cause in both countries.

Increasing protest in Uruguay clearly communicated to the armed forces their growing unpopularity. Opposition party leaders were invited to Buenos Aires for the Alfonsín inauguration to emphasize the new Argentine government's interest in change in Uruguay. Public demonstrations continued in Montevideo with thousands of citizens defying the government to march under the slogan of "freedom, work and democracy." The generals have now promised elections in November 1984 and a return to democracy in 1985. The question is whether these elections will be genuinely free—and what parties will contest them.

Chile is more turbulent, with no change yet envisioned. The regime of General Augusto Pinochet confronted in 1983 the most sustained opposition since it came to power a decade ago following the overthrow of Salvador Allende. Buffeted by bank and business failures, rising unemployment, high levels of inflation, and an unmanageable foreign debt, the Chilean middle class appeared ready to support a restoration of democracy. In a series of violent protests that began in May 1983, dozens of people were killed and thousands arrested. The demonstrations were motivated both by economic deprivation and political discontent. In an effort to defuse the tense situation, Pinochet allowed several thousand political exiles to return and lifted a state of emergency, in effect since 1978. A series of cabinet changes gave Pinochet an opportunity to appoint Sergio Onofre Jarpa as Interior Minister. Jarpa set out to construct a package of reforms that would grant greater political freedom in Chile, without opening the issue of whether Pinochet would continue in power until the scheduled end of his term in 1989.

The opposition, organized in a Democratic Alliance composed of the Christian Democrats, an important part of the socialists and the Christian Left, and smaller parties of the center, attempted to negotiate with the government, but talks collapsed in late September and were not renewed. Opposition forces were themselves divided on strategy. There remained great concern among average Chileans about a return to the disorder of the pre-1973 years, in which the Communist and Socialist Parties were key actors. 1984 will be an important year in determining the relative strength of the various opposition groups and the tolerance of the Pinochet regime for continued public protest.

At the Alfonsín inauguration in Buenos Aires in November, Vice President George Bush said: "We would like to see a greater adherence to democratic principles in Chile. If there were, you would see vastly improved relations between the United States and Chile." It was a welcome statement of U.S. policy for supporters of democracy in South America who had seen the Reagan Administration evolve from its early acquiescent and friendly posture toward authoritarian military regimes to the general backing for democracy expressed by President Reagan in his short Latin American trip of late 1982—but who had noted the Administration's failure to apply its position to specific countries, particularly Chile.

The United States in 1984 will have ample opportunity to endorse the process of restoring democracy in both Uruguay and Chile, and of strengthening democratic forces in small countries such as *Paraguay* and *Bolivia*. The former remains the longest standing dictatorship on the continent. While no one expects General Alfredo Stroessner to liberalize his regime in the short term, the movement to democracy in Argentina and elsewhere in the Southern Cone will stimulate opposition to him. Diplomatically, the United States should support those efforts. In Bolivia, where the embattled democratic government of President Hernan Siles Zuazo faces threats from both political opponents and from the armed forces, strong support will be needed to avert a military coup d'état. Economic assistance may also be a key issue for Bolivia's government, as it confronts depressed world markets for its principal mining exports and as it wrestles with the debt incurred under previous military regimes.

In two other countries on the continent, *Colombia* and *Ecuador*, democratic institutions have demonstrated resiliency in dealing with social and economic pressures. Belisario Betancur, the Conservative Party leader elected Colombian president in 1982, has demonstrated a capacity for strong leadership and artful dealings with his opposition. Colombia has withstood the devastating impact of the world crisis better than many of its neighbors; Betancur deserves high marks for continuing the democratic tradition and using it in a responsive and responsible manner.

President Osvaldo Hurtado of Ecuador, elected vice president in 1979, succeeded to the presidency in 1981 with the sudden death of President Jaime Roldós. In conformity with an IMF austerity program, Hurtado took a series of highly unpopular economic measures in 1983 that have produced strong protest. But the democratic institutions of Ecuador withstood the pressures, and prospects are good that the presidential elections scheduled for 1984 will take place and further consolidate that country's commitment to democratic politics. Both countries demonstrate that democratic institutions do function and that they are able to cope with stress, but that reality should not be taken for granted.

VII

In the final analysis, the ability of the United States to come to grips with the big problems in South America is a question of foreign policy management. Our affairs in the hemisphere, at this moment, are dominated by the immediacy of the crisis in Central America. The United States appears unable to manage both the day-to-day activities of defining and protecting our vital interests in Central America and the Caribbean and the elaboration of a strategy, with important variations for individual countries, for the continent of South America.

The United States cannot play either the role of policeman or that of savior in South America. The circumstances call for a much more nuanced management strategy. One major element must be a high diplomatic and political profile that clearly identifies the United States with the return to democracy. No occasion should be lost to reiterate, in specific terms and with reference to specific countries, the posture exemplified by Vice President Bush's statement in Buenos Aires concerning Chile. But the biggest challenge to U.S. policy at the beginning of 1984 is to devise mechanisms to limit the social and economic damage caused by current world economic conditions; in most countries the key problem is external debt. Democratic political institutions in South America are neither strong nor experienced, in most instances, and the continent is undergoing a rapid process of returning to democracy after years of military government. What is needed is time for new governments to consolidate decision-making procedures and programs that will build confidence in democratic politics and reduce the possibility that the armed forces or extreme elements of either the left or the right will bid for power.

It should be clearly understood that support for democracy is not a ruse to allow directly elected governments to walk away from their countries' outstanding financial obligations. Responsible governments in South America need to recognize previously incurred debt as a binding obligation. Just as the private banks should not be "blamed" for the current crisis, the countries of South America should clearly reject the evolving mentality that argues for a unilateral default on the debt or selective responsibility for only part of the debt. And it is precisely to avoid those possibilities that effective political leadership by the United States is required now.

This necessitates a willingness by the Reagan Administration to look beyond the narrow financial aspects of the current economic crisis and take the lead in defining the foreign debt of South America as a foreign policy priority of potential political volatility. Only U.S. government action will bring together the key players to devise short-term and medium-term strategies for defusing the debt issue. Those players include the IMF, the debtor countries, the Federal Reserve System, and the private commercial banks of the United States, Western Europe and Japan.

Increasing concern has been shown by some of these players. It is reported that the Federal Reserve Board supports improved terms for bank lending to countries such as Mexico that have been able to implement austerity programs with success, although at high social cost. The Managing Director of the IMF, in December 1983, stated that credits by the private banks "should be provided on reasonable terms in order not to compound unduly the balance of payments and indebtedness problems of debtor countries." Mr. de Larosière also stated that large and small commercial bank creditors will have to participate in future restructuring efforts; that large countries must not preempt the flow of funds to smaller nations; and that the composition of capital flows must change in order to foster a more viable debt structure. He urged that private bank lending be supplemented by "more basic development oriented financing" such as foreign direct investment and expanded official flows, with new official aid for the poorer countries taking the form of larger concessional assistance.

In the November 1983 legislation approving the new U.S. contribution to the IMF, the U.S. Congress also stated its concern. "Sustaining economic growth" was named a high priority by the Congress, and the President and others were instructed to encourage countries to formulate economic adjustment programs which:

. . .should be designed to safeguard, to the maximum extent feasible, international economic growth, world trade, employment, and the long term solvency of the banks, and to minimize the likelihood of civil disturbances in countries needing economic adjustment programs.

The legislation directed the U.S. executive director of the IMF to recommend and work for changes in Fund policy to "convert short-term bank debt which was made at high interest rates into long-term debt at lower rates of interest" and to "assure that the annual external debt service, which shall include principal, interest, points, fees and other changes required of the country involved, is a manageable and prudent percentage of the projected annual export earnings of such country." In other language, designed to preclude "bailouts" of the banks, the U.S. executive director should "work to insure that the Fund encourage borrowing countries and banking institutions to negotiate, where appropriate, a rescheduling of debt which is consistent with safe and sound banking practices and the country's ability to pay."

Slowly, and reluctantly, the private commercial banks have begun to modify their lending policies. In negotiating a $3.8-billion loan in late 1983, the banks recognized the Mexican government's extraordinary success in imposing an austerity program in the past 18 months. The new loan was for ten years, with repayment scheduled to begin in 1989, compared with more stringent terms earlier in 1983. The banks also stipulated lowered interest rates and fees. Some bankers privately, and editorial opinion publicly, regretted that the loan agreement did not provide even easier terms in recognition of Mexico's performance and as an incentive for other debtor countries attempting to cope with austerity measures. But at least the banks have recognized Mexico's efforts and may be persuaded to negotiate similar or easier agreements with Venezuela and Argentina in 1984 to avoid no-win confrontations with the Alfonsín and Lusinchi governments. Brazil, whose latest $6.5-billion loan ran into bank reluctance until the very last moment, may require even greater private bank understanding if any semblance of an orderly repayment schedule is to be maintained.

All of these actions are welcome, but they are relatively isolated. What is required is a U.S.-led initiative to devise an orderly procedure for evaluating the structure of each country's debt, its ability to repay, and its future borrowing needs. Only leadership by the

U.S. government will succeed in devising and implementing such a mission. The Federal Reserve System is not charged with the formulation of U.S. foreign policy. There are limitations on what the IMF alone can do without raising criticism once again that its actions are little more than an effort to save the private commercial banks and their profits. It is essential that the banks not be made the scapegoat in the debt crisis. Their role in the future is too important to allow ourselves the luxury of seeking victims.

The one player not yet heard from is the U.S. government. Compared to the positive initiatives of 1982—bridging loans, special packages, etc.—1983 saw a return to an attitude of business-as-usual. More ominous were signs that, at the top level of the Reagan Administration, the growing expressions of concern by the IMF, the Federal Reserve, and the U.S. Congress were either misunderstood or, in its preoccupation with the escalating power game in Central America and the Caribbean, ignored.

For example, the Administration announced in December 1983 that the U.S. contribution to the World Bank's International Development Association (IDA), a vehicle for loans to very poor countries, will be $750 million a year over the next three years. The United States had been urged by the Bank and by the members of the Organization for Economic Cooperation and Development to commit a billion dollars a year. And at the end of 1983, the OECD issued a report which indicated that the United States, in 1981 and 1982, allocated proportionately less of its wealth to poor countries than almost any major non-communist state. The report indicated that in a seven-year period beginning in 1976, U.S. assistance as a percentage of GNP declined by a greater factor than in any Western industrial society. While little of this aid is earmarked for South America, the policy does form part of the Administration's attitude toward the developing world.

If the U.S. record on official aid for the poor countries has been stingy, its attitude in 1983 on trade issues appeared to harden and to become more protectionist. The United States, for example, also took the lead in pressing for an agreement among industrialized countries to eliminate subsidies for steel mills built in the Third World. Given world overcapacity, the United States and its industrial allies are moving to bar steel from developing countries to protect domestic producers. In both steel and other products, such as footwear, leather goods and cement, South American countries could find themselves frozen out of U.S. markets at a time when they must export to service their debt and to pay for crucial imports from the United States and the industrial countries.

The Reagan Administration also failed to act on the U.S. budget deficits which are a major cause of the high rates of interest charged by the commercial banks for loans to South America. As South America's need to borrow continues, high interest rates further compound the debt burden and make prompt or manageable repayment more problematical.

In 1983, the United States was thus found wanting in a range of policy areas that would lessen the social cost and possibly avoid political repercussions in South America. What should the U.S. government do?

A strong U.S. position in defense of free trade and against protectionist pressures is critical to South America's recovery. Many believe that an increase in world trade is the only way in which the debt crisis will be stabilized. The United States will need to take the political heat, always difficult in an election year, of carrying the flag for an expansion of world trade. One imaginative proposal calls for the creation of an "Export Development Fund." The new entity, closely allied to the World Bank, "would mobilize support from the export sectors of the industrial countries through joint financing by the national export credit organizations, private commercial banks, and the World Bank."[8]

The Reagan Administration should seriously consider a joint effort by the United States and its West European and Japanese allies to actively encourage exports from South America as the best means of earning the foreign exchange required to meet interest payments on the debt. Such trade, as we have seen, would also generate jobs in the industrial countries, as South America used new foreign exchange earnings to buy their products.

A second U.S. initiative with great merit would emphasize greater lending facilities for the World Bank, the Inter-American Development Bank, and other multilateral agencies, in which the South American states generally have a high degree of confidence. It has been suggested that the leverage of the World Bank be increased, for example. Currently, the Bank borrows and lends an amount roughly equal to its paid-in and callable capital. Various proposals have called for increased facilities for the Bank. U.S. public support for exploring variations on this theme would be welcome and indicate U.S. confidence in an expanded role for the multilateral organizations.

A third area in which the United States should take the lead is in strongly and publicly encouraging the private commercial banks, in the United States and abroad, to reduce the terms of their loans to South America as the governments of the region demonstrate a willingness and ability to take appropriate internal decisions with regard to exchange rate policy, public spending, and other adjustment-related programs. U.S. government action in this regard would support the efforts of the Federal Reserve and others who argue for greater flexibility in lending terms. The Reagan Administration could make a very useful contribution to the present efforts to restructure existing debt obligations by indicating its concern that the smaller banks, in the United States and abroad, remain firmly committed to a renewal of credit for South America and available for new loans, as appropriate, in the future.[9]

Finally, the United States needs to continue providing federal government support through emergency credits and financing as needed. Humanitarian and emergency assistance, in the form of food and medicine primarily, should be given serious consideration for countries like Bolivia, Brazil and Peru.

None of these suggestions is earth-shaking; all have been made before. What is lacking is coordination at the highest political level and a capacity to anticipate new pressures and needs rather than waiting to respond after the fact.

The Reagan Administration has a historic opportunity to seize the debt issue, to define it as political and of immediate concern to U.S. interests in the hemisphere. No one predicts that such an initiative will be either easy or fully successful. But it must be done. Prudent management of the nation's foreign affairs requires prior action, *before* the next and probably inevitable wave of public protest and demonstration, and while responsible governments remain in power. Once a particular political situation starts to go to pieces, the possibilities of action can only become less, and there will be a progressive danger of new and radical regimes, with drastic implications for the ultimate repayment of debt, the spread of democracy, and the security situation in the hemisphere—not to mention sharp and growing anti-U.S. sentiment.

In the last analysis, the consequences of failure to handle the debt issue will be not merely economic, or even confined to the domestic politics of individual Latin American countries and of the continent as a whole: behind both of these lies a crucial security dimension. It would hardly serve U.S. interests to save Central America from a communist threat while allowing major South American countries to become radical, alienated from the United States, and active against it. In a recent study on the debt crisis in Latin America, Ambassador Thomas O. Enders, former Assistant Secretary of State for Inter-American Affairs, put the point well: [10]

. . .When the crisis in some countries drags on with per capita incomes below 1980 levels—as they may be for much of this decade—and without credible promise of relief, it is easy to imagine resentment and frustration exploding in Latin America, turning against governments when they fail to persuade the United States and other industrial countries of the need for more generous terms. Not only would the current broad but weak trend towards democracy falter, but public order and national security could also be at risk.

Whatever the action taken, the Administration must see U.S. relations with the countries of South America in the broadest context. Not to do so is to neglect the potential impact on the international financial system, the U.S. banking system, and the economic and political relations between the United States and the continent, of a possible debt crisis. It is also to overlook the human cost in South America of the current austerity measures. And, ultimately, it fails to understand that U.S. interests in the hemisphere are best served by whatever steps are taken to strengthen democratic institutions and procedures.

Early in 1983, President Osvaldo Hurtado wrote to the executive secretaries of the United Nations Economic Commission for Latin America (ECLA) and of the Latin American Economic System (SELA). Hurtado asked their help in devising a Latin American response to the economic crisis confronting the hemisphere. The deliberations continue, but Hurtado captured the essence of the problem confronting us when he wrote that:

What is at stake, then, as never before, is the social peace of the nations and the stability of the democratic system—in brief, the fate of vast human communities which are seeing their unresolved social problems grow worse day by day, are fearfully becoming aware of the possibility of total disaster.

The president of Ecuador is a wise man. He is also a democratic political leader. On both counts, his message requires a thoughtful hearing by the Reagan Administration.

Notes

[1] The political implications of the debt crisis are as real elsewhere in the Third World as they are in Latin America, of course. The recent coup d'état in Nigeria clearly demonstrated the fragility of democratic systems in Africa in the present economic situation. As *The New York Times* commented, "the oil glut, high interest rate, and recession are squeezing virtually every economy in the third world. That is not an environment in which democracy can flourish, no matter how well laid the plan. If America cares about democracy in the rest of Africa, Asia and Latin America, it will have to lend more than its political structure." (January 4, 1984, p. 20.)

[2] Pedro-Pablo Kuczynski, "Latin American Debt." *Foreign Affairs*, Winter 1982/83, pp. 344-364; and "Latin American Debt: Act Two," *Foreign Affairs*, Fall 1983, pp. 17-38.

[3] In fact, Latin America has become a capital exporter. The amount of money it pays each year for servicing the debt is larger than the amount of new money that flows into the region.

⁴ The Chilean-Argentine dispute over the islands in the Beagle channel is not irrelevant in broader geopolitical terms. The thirty-year freeze on new territorial claims in Antarctica is beginning to wind down and both countries have substantial interest in pursuing competing claims on the Antarctic continent. Possession of the channel islands will determine the outcome of those claims. In early 1984, it was reported that both countries have accepted the 1980 proposals of Pope John Paul II to resolve the dispute which award the islands to Chile.

⁵ The impressive array of west European and Latin American social democratic leaders that attended the Alfonsín inauguration in December 1983 indicated the extraordinary level of interest in the success of the new democratic government in Argentina. As a leading member of the Alfonsín team said to me in late November in Buenos Aires, "Argentina identifies with the west, but we do not necessarily equate the west with the U.S. alone."

Clearly the Reagan Administration needs to understand the great significance for social democracy, worldwide, of the Alfonsín victory. If that implies a further deepening of Argentina's ties within Latin America, and with Western Europe, it should be welcomed by the United States as another source of support for democracy in the southern cone.

⁶ In the case of Argentina, the legacy of past U.S. policy is clearly an impediment. Many Argentinians, including members of the Alfonsín government, believe the Reagan Administration "tilted" toward the military authorities between 1981 and 1983. The United States appeared overly anxious to establish cordial relations with General Leopoldo Galtieri particularly. His government's actions in Central America, in support of the Reagan Administration's policy, were viewed by many as an important factor in Argentina's decision to risk war with England over the Falkland Islands. Galtieri believed that because of this tie the United States would not side with Britain against Argentina. After Galtieri's overthrow, the United States pressed the issue of certifying Argentina for a renewal of military aid and arms sales, even though Alfonsín made clear it was a very low priority for his government. Finally, Alfonsín's strong defense of human rights compares unfavorably with the Reagan Administration's "low profile" on human rights.

⁷ The Democratic Action party is closely allied with the social democratic movement in Latin America and Western Europe. The election in 1983 of governments in Argentina and Venezuela with social democratic affinities may prove to be useful in South American efforts to devise complementary strategies for dealing with global issues.

⁸ William H. Bolin and Jorge Del Canto, "LDC Debt: Beyond Crisis Management," *Foreign Affairs*, Summer 1983, p. 1099.

⁹ There have been a number of more dramatic suggestions made with regard to debt refinancing. Some call for converting existing debt into old-fashioned development bonds with a grace period for both interest and principal and a guaranteed real rate of interest. Others urge the creation of a new international institution which would issue long-term bonds to banks in exchange for accepting Third World debts. A new round of SDRs has been suggested as one way of introducing greater liquidity into the international financial system. None of these ideas has been tested, nor does it appear that the political climate at this moment will support high levels of innovation and creativity in dealing with the debt. More practical suggestions, of late, emphasize subsidization when lending occurs at unduly high interest rates. The private banks oppose this suggestion because of the impact on their earnings. Another proposal would permit debtors to pay half their interest in dollars and the remaining half in local currency. Latin American governments are increasingly interested in schemes to limit interest payments to 20 to 30 percent of export earnings.

¹⁰ Thomas O. Enders and Richard P. Mattione, "Latin America: The Crisis of Debt and Growth", *Brookings Discussion Papers in International Economics*, No. 9, December 1983, Washington: The Brookings Institution. p. 79.

Chapter 10

Crisis in Africa: Famine, Economic Discontinuities and Debt

Introduction

It is now approximately twenty years since the vast majority of African countries achieved political independence. Disenchantment with the economic gains from colonial rule was a major factor in the struggle for independence and the belief was widely held that independence by itself would almost automatically transform a state of poverty to one of economic plenty for all.

By the beginning of the 1980s, the optimism of the early 1960s had been replaced by a profound pessimism. The economic progress of Africa during the 1960s and 1970s was minimal and less than the economic progress made by Asian and Latin American countries in general. More depressing still are some of he forecasts noted by the Organization of African Unity (OAU) heads of state in the preamble to the *Lagos Plan of Action for the Economic Development of Africa: 1980–2000*, adopted in April 1980: "If the world economic forecast for the next decade is to be believed, the overall poor performance of the African economy over the past 20 years may be a golden age compared with future growth rates."[1]

This chapter seeks to shed some light on the problem of why the economic performance of African countries has fallen far below expectations, why they have not done as well as other Third World countries in Asia and in Latin America, and why a select few African countries have performed much better than most of the others.

A first fact to note is that African countries entered the international scene as independent political actors and launched their development efforts at a time when the field was already crowded. Latin American countries achieved independence between 1808 and 1825, while in Asia independence did not come until the immediate post-World War II period. Libya, Morocco, Sudan and Tunisia attained independence between 1951 and 1956, but the vast majority of African countries had to wait until the 1960s to achieve their independence.

All these countries, starting with those in Latin America in the nineteenth century, saw independence not only as an end in itself, but also as an opportunity for the achievement of prosperity and economic development. Given what they perceived as centuries of exploitation and poverty, they made economic development a key goal. Most, if not all, counted on external help to further their development. Already at the Bretton Woods and the San Francisco conferences in 1944-45, the Latin Americans and the few Asian states that were represented insisted that the World Bank be concerned not only with the reconstruction of Europe, but also with the development of the Third World, and that the United States should give more emphasis to problems of development. Within the United Nations itself, even before 1960, Third World countries were urging the creation of a United Nations Capital Development Fund earmarked for capital investments in their respective countries.

Thus when African countries arrived on the scene in the 1960s, they found many other actors already present and competing for scarce resources. In 1961, the underdeveloped countries were estimated to have a population of 1509 million people. Nearly 18% of these people (270 million) were in Africa, excluding South Africa. Even without the entry of over a quarter billion Africans into the race for scarce international development resources, it is doubtful that the international system would have had the resources or political will to satisfy the demands of even those who were on the scene first. The significant increase in the number of those seeking help that resulted from Africa's entry on the scene meant that the available resources had to be spread more thinly. True, the resources made available for development did increase. But the continued push by Third World countries for more international development assistance shows that they did not consider this increase to be enough. Latin America had over a century and Asia around a decade and a half head start in the development competition compared with Africa. Thus, around 1960, the nations of these areas were generally more developed than African countries and so had a competitive edge. Figures provided by the US Agency for International Development (1963) show that in 1961, for example, Latin America had a per capita GNP of $265; the Near East, $205; and Africa excluding South Africa, only $100. The Far East, excluding Japan, had a per capita GNP of $95 and South Asia was at the bottom with a per capita GNP of $80. For adult literacy, however, the same source shows that the rate was 65% in the Far East excluding Japan, 55% in Latin America, 30% for the Near East, 25% in South Asia, and only 15% for Africa, excluding South Africa.

One result of the earlier entry and comparative advantage in level of development of other Third World areas compared with Africa is that they have been more successful in attracting external resources for development. One example of this is the flow of foreign direct investments. In 1967, ten developing countries had 36.5% of the total stock of foreign direct investments in developing countries. They were Brazil, Mexico, India, Malaysia, Argentina, Singapore, Peru, Hong Kong, the Philippines, and Trinidad and Tobago. Venezuela alone had 10.6% of these investments while all OPEC countries had 27.7% out of which Nigeria had 3.3%. The tax havens of the Bahamas, Barbados, Bermuda, Cayman Islands, Antilles, and Panama accounted for another 7.0% of these investments. The remainder of the developing countries had to share the remaining 28.8% among themselves. The clear tendency for transnational corporations to invest in wealthier countries is revealed by the fact that, in 1967, 43.4% of their investments went to countries with per capita incomes of $1000 or more; 23% to countries with per capita incomes of between $500 and $999; 16.4% to countries with per capita incomes of less than $200.[2] And since most African countries fell under the last category in 1967, they got very few of the available direct foreign investments. The situation has changed very little over thirty years. Africa is still at the very bottom of the ladder.[3]

To compound the above situation, the United Nations notes that "the countries that most attract the transnational corporations are also those that have borrowed most on the international capital markets. Just two countries—Brazil and Mexico—together accounted for almost one-third of all the developing countries borrowing in 1976."[3] In 1975, all developing countries had private borrowings amounting to $88,462 million. But African countries had borrowings of only $9088 million, or 10.26% of the total. Brazil, Mexico, the Republic of Korea, Argentina, Peru and the Philippines had 44.22% of this total, while the share of the Middle East was 10.34%. The data in the introduction to Chapter 7 in this volume shows that Africa in 1986 was still as disadvantaged as earlier. Clearly, given its comparatively greater needs, Africa has not been getting a fair share of private loans to developing countries.

Finally, Africa is also comparatively disadvantaged with respect to the distribution of official development assistance. In 1969, the members of the Development Assistance Committee of the Organization for European Cooperation and Development and multilateral aid agencies gave net concessional assistance that amounted to $6452.7 million globally. Out of this amount, Asia received $3047.1 million or 47.2%; Africa, $1582.9 million or 24.5%; and Latin America, 1094.1 million or approximately 17.0%. By the mid-1980s the composition of DAC disbursements had changed considerably, reflecting Africa's dire needs for food and emergency aid. In 1984, of a total ODA of $18722.7 million, Asia received $5981.7 million or 31.9%, Africa $7502.6 million or 40%, and Latin America $2624.7 or 14%.[4]

The population of Africa in 1969 was estimated to be 360 million, while that of Latin America was 260 million and that of Asia, excluding China, 640 million. In 1985 the respective populations stood at 538 million, 263 million and 1.9 billion. Thus the above aid distribution seems to follow roughly the population distribution in these three regions. However, when the comparatively greater degree of absolute poverty in Africa is taken into account, coupled with the fact that Africa receives significantly less private foreign direct investments and foreign private loans, the distribution of official development assistance has been comparatively unfavourable to Africa.

Thus far, the comparatively poor performance of African states in relation to Asian and Latin American countries has been explained on the grounds that African countries arrived later in a crowded field and that the comparative competitive edge of Latin American and Asian countries meant that they received substantially more private foreign direct investments and private loans, while Africa received no compensation in the area of official foreign assistance. But there is more to it than this. The greater success of Asian and Latin American countries in attracting foreign resources is due not only to their relatively higher degree of development, but also to political considerations.

The fact is that on the world diplomatic and strategic scene, Asia and Latin America have been far more important than Africa. The United States is a Pacific power, and one of the most important political partners of the United States, Japan, is an Asian power. In addition another Asian power, China, was until recently one of the United States' arch-enemies. The two major wars the United States has been engaged in since World War II, the Korean and Vietnam wars, have both taken place in Asia. And the second most populous country and the largest democracy in the world is India, also an Asian country. Asia has, therefore, been of major strategic and political importance to the United States, the most powerful member of the western alliance, and the single largest donor of assistance to the Third World.

Latin America has also been of prime importance to the United States. After all, Latin America forms its backyard and the Castro revolution and the Cuban Missile Crisis of 1962 seemed to Americans to represent a strategic threat to the United States. Thus the US military interventions in Latin America and President Kennedy's Alliance for Progress.

As far as Africa is concerned, it remained peripheral to the main focus of US interests and was not regarded as an area offering great opportunities. Beyond a narrow circle of specialists, there was not much interest in Africa even among the elite in the United States. In the early 1960s France was still burdened with the Algerian war, Britain was still engaged in the retreat from empire, and the Federal Republic of Germany had not yet started showing much interest in the Third World. In any event, these countries were no substitute for the United States in terms of the potential resources they could make available for development.

It is plausible to suggest that the comparatively greater flow of resources to Asia and Latin America was the result of the greater importance of these countries to the United States. True, some of these resources came from the private sector. But the US government clearly has the ability to influence the perceptions and behavior of private investors and bank officials. Nor are these individuals insensitive to the importance of Asia and Latin America to the political and therefore corporate interests of the United States, thereby influencing them to do what they can to facilitate the development and thus the stability and continued membership of these countries in the western camp. Both of these factors work together to increase the flow of resources to Asia and Latin America.

In sum then, Asian and Latin American countries had the advantage over African countries of having arrived on the scene earlier and with comparatively higher levels of development. They were also more important strategically and politically to the United States, the leader of the western alliance. As a result, they have been able to attract greater resources to fuel their development.

It now remains for us to explain the differences in the performances among African countries. As noted earlier, the two African countries whose relatively better economic performances we will try to explain are Kenya and the Ivory Coast. Differences in the endowment in natural resources might conceivably play a role, although these two countries are not endowed with much in the form of mineral resources. Differences with respect to the colonial legacy, especially important in the case of Kenya, must also be taken into account, but this is not especially so in the case of the Ivory Coast. The colonial legacies of countries such as Senegal, Uganda, and Ghana are not significantly different from those of Kenya and the Ivory Coast.

External political factors comparable to those which explain variations in performance between Africa and other Third World countries also help to explain the comparatively better performance of these two countries.

In Africa, Kenya and the Ivory Coast enjoyed especially privileged positions as far as the West was concerned. Kenya had gone through a bitter racial and colonial war in the 1950s, but went through a peaceful decolonization process in the early 1960s which sharply limited the feared exodus of the whites. The Kenyatta government pursued moderate policies and was strikingly pro-West and pro free-enterprise. It was important for the West to ensure the success of the Kenyan model. Such success would preserve the already significant western interests in Kenya, prove to countries such as the then Rhodesia, where racial tensions were significantly greater, that multiracialism does work and that whites need not fear majority rule, and persuade other African countries that a pro-Western and a pro-capitalist orientation was more likely to result in greater economic progress than a pro-Soviet one.

The Ivory Coast enjoyed a similar status in French West and Central Africa. After an initial phase of radicalism and communist leaning, President Houphouet-Boigny was by the late 1940s a staunch supporter of maintaining Franco-African ties. He strongly supported the break-up of the Federation of French West Africa which France pushed in the mid-1950s, and he opposed the creation of political federations by independent French West African states. Houphouet-Boigny actively collaborated with France in pressuring Upper Volta and Niger not to join the Mali Federation with Senegal and the then French Sudan. Further, in the 1958 referendum on independence of continued membership in the French Community, Houphouet-Boigny used his considerable influence to ensure that the other colonies stayed in the French Community. In sum, Houphouet-Boigny actively supported and promoted the French policy of dampening African nationalism and African unity.

Like Kenya, the Ivory Coast pursued a pro-capitalist and pro-Western policy, with a striking bias toward France. Houphouet-Boigny was one of the main architects in the creation of the Union Africaine et Malgache which later became the Organization Commune Africaine et Malgache. These organizations served essentially to maintain close ties among French-speaking African states and to keep them within the French orbit. Finally, Houphouet-Boigny led the fight against leaders such as N'Krumah who were pushing for African countries to adopt socialism and radical pan-Africanism. In all these ways, Houphouet-Boigny demonstrated that he was an important and faithful ally of France. This allegiance had to be rewarded in order to promote pro-capitalist and pro-French tendencies in French-speaking Africa.

Because of the political considerations mentioned above, Kenya and the Ivory Coast had to be rewarded with a greater flow of resources. Thus between 1969 and 1971, Kenya received a total of $71.25 million in aid from bilateral and multilateral sources while the aid received by the Ivory Coast was $55.49 million. On the other hand, during these years, Tanzania, with a larger population and a lower per capita income, received only $53.16 million and Ghana, with about twice the population as the Ivory Coast but with more or less the same per capita income, got $61.26 million.

Per capita aid was thus $6.54 million for Kenya, $4.23 million for Tanzania, $11.23 million for the Ivory Coast, and $7.34 million for Ghana.[5]

Kenya and the Ivory Coast benefitted from an additional and related factor. In part, because of their ability to attract external resources, and also because of the external encouragement and support for the retention of regional economic groupings such as the East African Community and the West African Economic Community, these countries came to dominate the exports within the regional groupings to which they belonged and emerged as so-called "sub-imperialist" states.[6] Kenya, for example, accounted for 63.6% of the intraregional exports in 1964, 61.1% in 1967, and 61.8% in 1970.[7] The Ivory Coast also controls a substantial share of regional exports within the West African Economic Community and in 1974, 22% of Ivorian exports went to these countries. In 1970, 1973, and 1975, the Ivory Coast had a healthy balance of trade surplus with these countries.[8] The serious economic difficulties Kenya has been experiencing since the recent break-up of the East African Community, through certainly due to other factors, merely serve to underscore the importance of access to regional markets for countries like Kenya and the Ivory Coast.

In sum, because of political considerations, Kenya and the Ivory Coast enjoyed comparatively more favorable treatment from external factors. They also gained from their ability to play leading roles in the regional groupings to which they belonged. These two factors greatly account for their comparatively better economic performances. The three articles in this chapter illustrate the plight of Africa. Amechi Okolo traces the history of the relationships between Africa and Europe and identifies five successive stages that the African economy has passed through under the impact of this relationship. Okolo concludes that the current stage of dependency was brought about the progressive proletarianization of Africa. Okolo ends with a number of policy proposals to bring an end to this dependence of relationships.

Carl K. Eicher, in his paper, describes Africa's continuing food crisis and its increasing dependency on the United States and the other OECD countries for food aid. He concludes with a plea for a coordinated restructuring of problems of long-term planning, aid, food policy strategies, technology transfer and foreign private enterprises in Africa, by both donor and recipient countries.

In the last article in this chapter, Timothy M. Shaw describes and evaluates three of the current and most salient proposals for solving Africa's debt, food and development problems—the Lagos Plan of Action, the first Brandt report and the World Bank proposals. While expressing a hope that something can yet be done, his conclusions are for the most part pessimistic; they are concisely expressed in the phrase "the dialectics of depression."

Notes

[1] Organization of African Unity [OAU] (1981) Lagos Plan of Action for the Economic Development of Africa: 1980-2000. Geneva: International Institute for Labour Studies.

[2] United Nations, 1978: 254.

[3] See World Bank, *World Development Report*, 1986

[3] United Nations (1978) *Transnational Corporations in World Development Development: A Re-examination*. New York: United Nations.

[4] Organization for Economic Cooperation and Development, *Geographical Distribution of Financial Flows to Developing Countries*. Paris: OECD, 1977 and 1986

[5] Organisation de Cooperation et Developpement Economique *Cooperation Pour le Developpement: Efforts et Politiques Poursuivis ar les Membres du Comite d'Aide au Developpement*. Paris: Organisation de Cooperation et de Developpement Economique, OECD, 1972, p. 284

[6] Shaw, T.M. and M.J. Grieve (1978) "Africa's Future in the Global Environment." *Journal of Modern African Studies*, 16 (March): p. 1-32.

[7] East African Community, *Review of Economic Integration Activities Within the East African Community*, 1973. Arusha, Tanzania: East African Community.

[8] World Bank, 1978 *Ivory Coast: The Challenge of Success*. Washington, DC: 1978, World Bank, pp. 101-102.

Dependency in Africa: Stages of African Political Economy

Amechi Okolo

Historical perspective on domination of Africa

The history of Africa is a history of five centuries of domination by the Western political economy, which created and now dominates and operates the modern world system.[1] The domination has passed through several phases, each unique to a historical epoch, though all were conditioned by the internal logic of capitalism and by the dynamics of the international system.

The process of Western incursion and domination of Africa can be divided into the following five phases:
1. Barbarian domination
2. Imperialist domination
3. Colonial domination
4. Neo-colonial domination
5. Dependency domination.
Each phase was manifested both in the Western nations and in Africa; every capitalist transformation in the West was reflected in the political economy of Africa.

I. Barbarian domination

This was the earliest phase of capitalist domination of Africa. It occurred alongside the epoch in capitalist development called 'primitive accumulation',[2] when the West was breaking free from feudalism but had not yet entered the era of capitalism. Certain technological changes—such as improvement in maritime technology and the invention of the compass—facilitated trade with distant lands by allowing the West to venture into the open seas. According to Hopkins,

In three centuries before the industrial revolution the focus of the trade moved from the Mediterranean to the Atlantic, from Venice and Genoa to Liverpool and Nantes. This momentous shift of economic power was the product of fundamental changes in the economic and technological basis of European society at the close of the Middle Ages.[3]

The boost in trade increased the wealth of merchants and enhanced their power. Barbarian domination of Africa corresponds to this era of mercantilism in Europe – a period which set the stage for the eventual collapse of feudalism.

Originally published in *Alternatives*, vol. IX, no. 2, 1983. Reprinted with permission.

The West used unbridled crudity in penetration, domination and exploitation of the African society. The purpose was not to rule or govern; the purpose was unrestrained loot and plunder without parallel in Africa's history. The most horrendous form of it lasted from the fifteenth century to early eighteenth century.[4] According to Marx, the history of this period is written in the annals of mankind in 'letters of wood and fire'.[5] It was characterized by *the turning of Africa into a warren for the commercial hunting of black skins*.[6]

The effects of this period in Africa can be briefly summarized as follows:

(a) massive depletion of the African population, especially among the most relevant and productive groups;

(b) massive destruction of the entire fabric of African society – disruptions in socio-cultural relationships and, above all, the diversion of interest from productive activities to plunder and loot as a way of life; and

(c) the pillage of the resources of Africa under the guise of international trade.[7] That is how the twin process of the 'development of underdevelopment' in Africa and the corresponding "development of development' in the West was initiated.[8] According to Hopkins, 'The chief effect of the overseas slave trade in the New World was to populate and develop the abundant land resources of the Americas and the West Indies.' He further observes:

It remains true that the slave and sugar trades brought great wealth to the principal entrepots, such as Liverpool and Nantes, and to many other leading cities. It is impossible to account for the economic vitality of these parts in the eighteenth century, their physical and demographic expansion, and the remarkable overflow of money into cultural activities, without stressing the causative, though not exclusive, role of the Atlantic commerce.[10]

The devastating effect of the period was also felt in Latin America but mainly in the form of massive excavations from their mines – the booty then hauled to the West.

II. Imperialist domination

This second phase of Western domination of Africa again corresponds to a definite historical epoch. Marx observes that, driven by its internal dynamics, capitalism must 'nestle everywhere'.

Having fought their national rivals, and having thus established their predominant position in the national economy, capitalists now shifted the theatre of war for profit and power to the international level known as imperialism. Lenin characterized imperialism as the last, monopoly, stage of capitalism, and identified five characteristic features of this phase of capitalism:[11]

(i) the concentration of production and capital developing to such a high stage as to create monopolies with a decisive role in the political economy;

(ii) the merging of bank capital with industrial capital, forming finance capital and a financial oligarchy;

(iii) the export of capital becoming more important than the export of commodities;

(iv) the formation of international capitalist monopolies, which shared the world among themselves; and

(v) the completion of the territorial division of the world between the monopolies.

Lenin, however, saw imperialism as a rather open-ended phenomenon with a discernible beginning but not necessarily an end.

For me, on the other hand, imperialism was the phenomenon of a definite historical epoch. It was time-locked – with the end as discernible as the beginning.

Historically, it corresponded roughly with the abolition of slave trade by Britain, in 1807, till the end of the century, when colonial governments were being established. In the hectic search for cheap materials for its production and captive markets for its products, European capitalist countries began occupying lands and setting up governments. It can thus be seen that while imperialism was the monopoly stage of capitalism in Europe, for Africa it represented the beginning of an epoch when capitalism's first serious attempt was made to create conditions favorable for a more permanent stay. The principal actors were Britain, France and Germany, essentially acting through their chartered companies. In the scramble for a place in the 'colonial sun', large chunks of African hinterland were seized and claimed and counter-claimed by contending European firms. They could well have driven Europe to war for the sake of their ill-begotten possessions. A conference at Berlin was held to avert it. Called at the initiative of the German government under Bismarck, it was attended by all the major, European powers, including the United States which for the first time was participating in a major international conference with European powers. The European *governments* had met to discuss ways and means of controlling the activities of their merchants before the latter plunged all of them into a bloody shooting war.[12]

The Berlin conference resolved the conflicting territorial claims of these firms by making it obligatory for them to respect the territorial ownership if a trade or protectorate treaty had been signed with the African chiefs. More importantly, it worked out a general alliance between the imperialist powers for the balkanization and control of Africa. However, like all such alliances, the Berlin Conference agreement later turned out to be nothing more than a temporary 'truce' which was destined to crack.[13] Relations between these powers continued to deteriorate and, according to Allan Burns, the continued French incursion into the British 'territory' heightened the tension between them to the point where 'even war between France and Britain was not far from the minds of the cabinets'.[14]

Imperialism thus was not, as Lenin had posited, the completion of the division of the world between the monopolies, but the continuation of the territorial struggle for control of raw materials and markets, even though the struggle was being conducted with the open and overt political support of their home governments.

III. Colonial domination

This third phase of capitalist domination in Africa, in the form of colonialism, corresponds to the period between the beginning and middle of the nineteenth century, when colonialism was institutionalized in most seized lands. Colonialism was a unique form of capitalist domination and control which had not existed earlier. The uniqueness consisted in its totality. It was the most complete and the most direct form of Western domination. It was the naked manifestation of foreign dictatorship, arbitrariness and control of other peoples. It was the most comprehensive strategy of capitalist penetration, domination and control because it left no facet of the society untouched.[15] Above all, it involved direct political and military administration of people to effect sustained maximum economic exploitation, through an organized, disciplined and, above all, *administered* capitalism in Africa. Colonialism became the politico-military weapon for effective and institutionalized administration of the territories their companies had earlier 'acquired'.

Colonialism aimed at creating both international and internal order and discipline from an otherwise anarchic imperialist system by means of direct imposition of superior military-political power. The imperialist system had collapsed for of a number of reasons:

(a) an increasing inter-European counter-penetration of the areas;
(b) an increasing African recalcitrance, resistance and hostility to further European penetration and control; and
(c) the rising cost and complexities of administering Africans far beyond what the companies could 'profitably' continue to undertake.

Colonialism attempted to remedy this by:

(a) lending some sort of international credence and/or legitimacy to the ownership of the areas concerned;
(b) gaining better internal control of the Africans through their acquiescence or passivity; and
(c) providing political clout to facilitate the creation of a more efficient system of exploitation to foot the cost of policing the people.

It is therefore colonialism, rather than imperialism, which truly was the monopoly stage of capitalism in Africa. The institutionalization of the metropolitan power over the territories gave it the rationale for keeping other rival powers from its territory and preventing the intrusion of other competing monopoly firms.

In the process, the *laissez-faire* and free trade of the political economy of Adam Smith,[16] which had ruled Europe from the early phases of industrial capitalism, were thrown overboard. The Berlin Conference had reiterated the principle of free trade and put the signatory powers

under obligation to adhere to the principles of free trade by allowing other nationals free access to the area and to protect foreign merchants and all trading nationalities as if they were her own subjects.[17]

The repudiation of the principle signified the death of free trade in the international market and legitimized monopolies at both ends – in Europe as well as in Africa. This distinction between colonialism and the earlier phase of imperialism should not be overlooked. During imperialism, the monopolies' right to territorial exclusivity was recognized neither by their home governments nor by the international community, making it very difficult for companies of one nation to exclude those of others, since they could not count on the official support of their home governments.[18]

The decline of colonialism was fast – indeed, faster than anything the West had imagined; never before had such a complete reversal occurred with such rapidity.[19] Colonialism was a very unstable system, marked by uncertainty and fear and maintained by violence and brute force. It was a situation in which both the settlers and the natives had lived, according to Fanon,

[In keeping with the] rules of pure Aristotelian logic, they both follow the principles of reciprocal exclusivity. The settlers' town is a strongly built town, all made of stone and steel. It is a brightly lit town, the streets are covered with asphalt and the garbage cans swallow all the leavings. The settlers' feet are never visible except perhaps in the sea, but there you are never close by enough to see them. The settlers' town is a well-fed town. . .its belly is always full of good things. The settlers' town is a town of white people, of foreigners.[20]

On the other hand, the town belonging to the natives is

a place of ill fame, peopled by men of ill repute. They are born there, it matters little where or how; they die there, it matters little where or how. It is a world without spaciousness. The native town is a hungry town starved of bread, of meat, of shoes, of light. It is a town of niggers and dirty Arabs.[21]

After World War II, when colonialism came under seige, attacked and surrounded by a global tide of revolution, capitalism evolved a new strategy to stem the tide. And Africa entered the fourth phase of its political economy.

IV. Neo-colonial domination

This fourth phase of capitalist domination was that of neo-colonialism. It appeared on the African scene in the decade following World War II. Its predecessor, colonialism, was destroyed by two convergent pressures – one internal and the other external. Internally, the nationalist sentiments, whipped up in the course of the West's mobilization of African manpower and resources to fight Nazism, turned against the foreign, white, masters. Africans were determined to wrest power from them.[22] Externally, there was, besides world opinion being against colonial domination, the West's fear of communism becoming an attractive alternative to the colonized.

The colonial powers accepted the inevitability of retreat, but cleverly turned it into a *tactical* retreat, giving up the form of domination but retaining its substance. Foreign faces were withdrawn from positions of power, but only after their places had been taken by hand-picked native faces (*interlocuteurs valuables* – negotiators worth talking to[23]). Exploitation continued unabated, the grip remained as tight, the control of the 'new independent nation' was *total* (see Figure), but the system was so sophisticated that it functioned by 'remote control' without the physical presence of the colonialist.

The defining features of neo-colonialism, which lasted for about a decade after the attainment of formal independence, were (i) that the former colonial master still served as the exclusive reference group for the new nation; and (ii) that the former ruler still exercised domination over every aspect of life: political, economic, and cultural. We shall consider them briefly below.

1. Political domination

The new nations emerged out of colonialism usually with constitutions that were drafted at the metropolitan headquarters. The essential government and political institutions – e.g. the executive, the legislature, the judiciary, and political parties, etc. – were modelled on those obtaining in the former ruling nations.

In the international arena, it was the former colonial power which chaperoned the representatives of the new nation through the diplomatic corridors and put them through the paces in diplomatic etiquette – the first principle of which, not unsurprisingly, was that they must endorse the foreign policy of the metropolitan power. The army and other security forces of the new nation were still trained and manned by the former masters who guaranteed the protege's national and international security.

2. Economic domination

The pattern or monopoly domination of the colonial era still operated exactly as in pre-independence days. The foreign exchange reserves of the new nation were still kept in the metropolitan headquarters. A large part of the foreign trade of the new nation was still with the metropolitan country.

3. Cultural domination

To ensure its exclusive domination in the cultural life of the colonized people, the colonial government hammered into them its own values, social norms and social organization. It assiduously inculcated in them the feeling that its own culture and education were superior to those of other Western nations. The indigenous culture the colonialist destroyed was supplanted, not by European culture as such, but by its own particular brand of European culture. Strong bonds of affection and shared values between the 'two' nations were emphasized. The function of media was to disseminate news about the former colonial ruler.

The form and content of education (in fact, the entire educational system) were the same as in the erstwhile ruling nation. Students who got a chance to go overseas for further studies normally went to the metropolitan country: the Senegalese, the Ivorians, etc., to France; the Ghanaians, the Sierra Leonians, the Nigerians, etc., to England; the Angolans, the Mozambicans, etc., to Portugal. Until recently in Nigeria, for instance, if one studied outside Britain, one would be hard put to it to find a job back home.

The neo-colonialism era was supposed to be a period of apprenticeship for the fledgling nation under the tutelage of the former ruler for graduation to full nationhood.

V. Dependency domination

This is the fifth and the latest phase of capitalist domination in Africa. While in the neo-colonialism period the former colonial master still held and exercised the dominating and unchallenged influence in the affairs of the new nation, dependency betokens a shift in the focus of attention till domination becomes truly 'international', the uni-national monopoly control having been broken. It makes possible the expansion of the cultural area of the former colonies.[24]

Most African nations entered the phase of dependency domination in the 1970s – that is, a decade after their political independence. In this phase, the new nations are subjected to a diffused and complex system of control and exploitation in a situation created by the cumulative effects of the various phases of domination. The end product of this process is a retarded African political economy. Retarded in the sense that the political economy (not

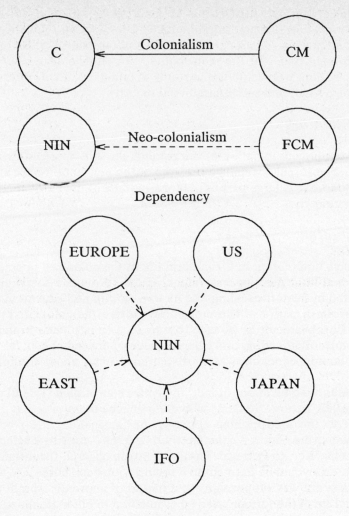

C = Colony
CM = Colonial Master
NIN = New Independent Nations
FCM = Former Colonial Master
IFO = International Finance Organization

the economy) does not and cannot sustain an independent existence. The negative forces have acquired a dynamic of their own and serve to ensure the continued development of underdevelopment in Africa.

Dependency domination is the capitalist strategy of control and exploitation in the modern system where international financial organizations and multinational companies have become vital actors; together they have perfected an intricate and complex control network on which the African nations, as all Third World nations, are hooked. The control mechanisms have been institutionalized, and they have acquired legitimacy within the international system. It is therefore much more difficult to try to break away from the syndrome because it is bound to invite the wrath of the entire capitalist international system.

Figure 1 presents the changing patterns of capitalist domination in Africa from the colonial to the dependency phase. The heavy arrow during the colonial era shows one-to-one relationship between the metropole and the colony. In the neo-colonial phase, the relationship is still essentially one-to-one, but the dotted lines now indicate the 'remote control' in an asymmetrical relationship. The main difference occurs in the dependency era, when the former colony has been subjected to a barrage of competing forces in the dependency stage, the economies of the former colonies have been fully integrated with the international capitalist market economy, making it almost impossible for the new nations to break loose from it even though the odds in the market are all against them. They have been incorporated into the world economic order as mere appendages. Two factors have made this possible: (i) proletarianization of African societies, and (ii) the peonage system imposed on them.

Proletarianization

It is a state in which all that Africans can offer is cheap labour. Having been made dependent on external sources for the satisfaction of even basic needs, the new nations have lost the capacity of feeding themselves, which they were well able to do with their indigenous farming methods. Take for example Nigeria which for ages was a food-surplus country.[25] As of now, Nigeria, like other African nations, has to import grains and other agricultural products. The metropolitan countries supply to African nations not only manufactured goods but also foodstuff.

The peonage system

It is a debt system that ensures continuing servitude of the former slaves after their proclaimed emancipation. In the system, the peons are paid below-subsistence wages; they can meet their very basic needs only by loans given them by their master. Indebtedness keeps them tied to the master; no other employer would hire him without clearance from the former master. So the debts go on mounting and the servitude of the peons is perpetuated.[26] According to Payer,

the worker cannot run away, for other employers and the state recognize the legality of his debt: nor has he any hope of earning his freedom with his low wages, which do not keep pace with what he consumes, let alone the true value of what he produces for his master.[27]

It is the extension of this system of debt slavery to the emergent African states from the period of their political independence to the present day that has continued to ensure, and to worsen, their dependency status.

Table 1
The external debt situation of African countries (million dollars)

Country	Total debt		Total debt % of GNP		Gross int'l reserve		Monthly import	Current a/c bal. before interest payments on external debts		Interest paymt's on external debts	
	1970	1979	1970	1979	1970	1979	1979	1970	1979	1970	1979
Chad	32	172	11.8	30.8	2	17	0.5	2	−72	n.a.	4
Ethiopia	169	620	9.5	15.7	72	321	5.4	−26	−79	6	13
Somalia	77	546	24.4	40.4	21	54	1.4	− 5	−205	n.a.	1
Mali	238	545	88.1	44.2	1	17	0.5	− 2	−64	n.a.	3
Upper Volta	21	256	6.4	25.4	36	67	2.0	9	−68	n.a.	4
Malawi	121	423	38.7	33.1	29	75	1.7	−32	−185	3	16
Benin	41	186	16.0	19.2	16	20	n.a.	− 1	−87	n.a.	3
Tanzania	248	1153	19.4	25.3	65	69	0.9	−29	−457	6	23
Zaire	311	3780	17.1	51.8	189	335	1.4	−55	−463	9	95
Niger	32	234	8.7	14.4	19	137	n.a.	1	−96	1	7
Guinea	314	990	51.7	68.6	13	35	1.0	n.a.	n.a.	4	24
C.A.R.	19	150	11.2	24.0	1	49	2.7	−11	−9	n.a.	n.a.
Madagascar	93	348	10.8	12.6	37	5	0.1	12	−425	2	8
Uganda	128	245	9.8	2.6	57	n.a.	n.a.	24	32	4	5
Mauritania	27	590	16.8	120.9	3	118	3.6	− 5	−70	n.a.	16
Lesotho	8	52	9.2	11.1	n.a.	n.a.	n.a.	n.a.	−22	n.a.	1
Togo	40	851	16.0	85.9	35	71	2.0	− 4	−219	11	16
Sudan	309	2114	11.6	34.5	22	67	0.7	−29	−151	13	86
Kenya	313	1427	20.3	24.3	220	669	3.7	−38	−419	11	60
Ghana	489	977	22.6	9.6	58	404	4.8	−56	282	12	26
Senegal	98	786	11.6	32.3	22	35	n.a.	−14	−394	2	43
Egypt	1644	11409	23.8	60.4	165	1794	2.6	−116	−1316	38	237
Liberia	158	454	49.6	48.4	n.a.	55	n.a.	n.a.	−91	6	22
Zambia	596	1559	34.5	50.5	515	93	1.8	131	264	23	93
Cameroon	131	1634	12.1	32.9	81	141	0.5	−26	−290	4	65
Nigeria	478	3744	6.4	5.0	223	5870	4.5	−348	1429T	20	205
Morocco	711	6227	18.6	40.3	141	916	2.1	−101	−1110	23	411

Table 1 presents the debt situation of African states in the 1970s. It shows that the absolute amount of their debts has been rising astronomically since 1970; that the debts now amount to very high percentages of the states' GNPs; that the very large interest payments which will have to be paid from the very highly deficit current account balances; and, finally, that the international reserves of these countries can hardly sustain their monthly imports.

Table 2

Outstanding external public debts of African countries and types of creditors in US $ million (1975)

Country	Bilateral official	Multi lateral	suppliers	Banks	Others	Total
Benin Republic	83.5	51.5	12.7	13.5	–	161.2
Botswana	113.6	70.9	–	–	–	184.5
Burundi	3.6	22.2	4.2	2.0	2.6	34.7
Cameroon	364.3	239.1	10.1	73.1	1.5	688.1
Central African Emp.	71.5	26.8	8.8	2.4	–	109.5
Chad	104.6	40.0	11.3	7.4	–	163.3
Congo Republic	340.3	53.3	210.8	1.6	10.1	616.0
Ethiopia	288.3	355.7	2.5	26.8	0.4	673.7
Gabon	99.6	46.7	86.9	241.9	40.1	515.1
Gambia, The	13.8	8.3	–	–	–	22.1
Ghana	392.3	221.0	184.1	–	–	797.3
Ivory Coast	313.3	384.5	409.6	373.0	57.1	1537.4
Kenya	460.5	489.1	56.0	26.7	39.0	1071.2
Lesotho	4.2	17.9	–	0.4	0.4	22.8
Liberia	166.1	90.0	10.7	6.9	0.9	274.6
Madagascar	98.7	126.9	3.8	3.9	3.1	236.5
Malawi	196.9	115.3	3.9	5.1	9.0	330.3
Mali	355.6	101.4	13.1	0.8	–	471.0
Mauritania	302.3	46.3	51.9	9.6	–	410.2
Mauritius	66.1	57.7	0.4	–	0.6	124.8
Niger	95.0	31.0	2.3	3.3	–	131.7
Nigeria	513.1	705.8	13.9	12.9	3.1	1248.8
Rwanda	32.5	47.5	1.8	–	0.6	82.5
Senegal	223.8	141.9	14.8	95.6	27.0	503.0
Sierra Leone	67.3	51.3	63.9	–	15.8	198.3
Somalia	353.8	66.4	–	–	3.9	424.2
Sudan	584.1	364.7	172.6	406.4	7.1	1534.8
Swaziland	36.4	28.6	1.5	–	–	66.5
Tanzania	802.2	335.3	29.1	12.3	13.6	1192.5
Togo	53.4	29.6	25.5	44.5	3.7	156.7
Uganda	136.7	73.3	–	2.2	6.2	218.4
Upper Volta	116.7	68.7	0.6	–	–	186.0
Zaire	756.9	286.9	378.5	1273.7	42.5	2738.5
Zambia	513.4	380.8	140.9	407.1	22.5	1464.7

* Source: World Bank: *Public Debt of Developing Countries*, Sept. 1977.

Table 2 shows the sources of credit and the indebtedness of the African countries to each creditor. It dramatizes the complexity of the creditor – debtor relationship which is a cardinal feature of the dependency era.

Dependency and oil

Having lost their agricultural resources, most African states are now fully 'proletarianized', making their manipulation easy. This is equally true of those few African states which have been classified as 'oil exporting states' for no reason other than the accident of oil having been discovered in their territories. It is hoped that these countries have been, or will be, able to transcend dependency and constitute themselves into perhaps regional sub-centres.[28] Nigeria is mentioned as an example. This is misleading. Nigeria's oil income forms 80% of the total government revenue (Table 3); the oil sector is controlled by the foreign oil companies (Table 4); the major buyers of Nigerian oil are the US and other Western countries (Table 5); Nigeria's very existence now depends on the production, transport and marketing of crude oil in the international market, over which Nigeria has no control whatever. This is the reality of modern Nigeria.

Nigeria's fate depends on the vicissitudes of international oil market, the health of the Western capitalist economy and the foreign policies of Western governments as well as the operations of the multinational oil corporations. She is free to frame neither her economic policy nor her foreign policy. Recent convulsions in the Nigerian economy bear eloquent testimony to the vulnerability of the Nigerian state to the international political economy. Nigeria was forced by international oil majors, with the backing of Western governments, to reduce her oil price to an unacceptable level.[29] The objective was internal destabilization of the state and reformulation of its foreign policy.

Table 3
Sources of Nigerian Federal government current revenue 1970-1980
(in million maira)

	Total revenue	Oil related revenue	% oil to total revenue
1970	633.2	166.4	26.0
1971	1169.0	510.2	44.0
1972	1404.8	764.3	54.0
1973	1695.3	1016.0	60.0
1974	4537.0	3726.7	82.0
1975	5514.7	4271.5	77.5
1976	6765.9	5365.2	80.0
1977	8042.4	6080.6	76.0
1978	5111.4	3341.1	76.4
1979	10354.5	8524.9	83.0
1980	11859.8	9922.1	84.0

Source: *Board of Customs and Excise, C.B.N. Economic and Financial Review 1975-1981*

Table 4
Production and export shares of oil companies in Nigeria

Companies	% of Production to total production		% of Exports to total exports	
	1978	1979	1978	1979
Shell	52.74	57.2	19.39	53.8
Gulf	16.86	15.8	17.65	15.9
Mobil	7.09	11.1	8.52	12.8
Agip	13.86	9.6	14.66	12.7
EIF	5.10	3.2	3.82	2.5
Texaco	3.09	2.3	3.10	1.8
Pan Ocean	0.68	0.4	1.62	0.5
Total foreign firms	99.6	99.6	99.4	99.5
NNPC	0.5	0.4	0.6	0.5
Total	100	100	100	100

Source: *NNPC Report* (March 1978)

Table 5
Exports of Nigerian crude oil by destination

Countries		(Percentages) 1978	1979
1.	US	40.21	4.6
2.	France	14.32	9.8
3.	West Germany	8.41	9.5
4.	Netherlands	10.07	8.7
5.	Antilles (Dutch)	5.33	7.6
6.	Curacao	2.50	4.6
7.	Italy	–	2.9
8.	United Kingdom	–	2.9
9.	Bahamas	–	2.0
10.	Gibraltar	–	1.5

Source: *NNPC Report* (Feb. 1979).

Specifically, Britain had attempted to reverse Nigeria's legitimate decision on British Petroleum (BP) by flooding the international oil market with the North Sea oil and thereby creating an artificial glut. It was the timely intervention of OPEC, especially Saudi Arabia, that rescued Nigeria,[30] the 'giant of Africa', from disaster, but not until the president himself had initiated some far-reaching economic measures.[31] Nigeria's indecision about re-establishing diplomatic relations with Israel can be traced to Nigeria's sincere gratitude for Saudi help. However, according to the *National Concord*:

Before much ink and paper is wasted on Israel cum Nigeria cum Black Africa diplomatic relations, it should be noted that according to reports Israel last year had $225 million export dealings with Black Africa with $2 billion contracts (from road building to poultry farming over the next three years) with at least ten African countries. With 'ties' like these, who needs diplomatic relations.[32]

Thus African oil has only helped to tighten the dependency noose round the African neck. This is the essence of the dependency syndrome: the boon that nature grants to a people is turned into a curse for them in the market-place of the existing world economic order. The strands of control are too inextricably woven for the new states of Africa to cope with.

Policy directions to end dependency

The important question for Africans is how Africa, in order to end its dependency, can extricate itself from the modern highly technologized and highly militarized international system, with its sophisticated and complex control network.

There is no simple answer to this. History provides no parallel to the modern dependency-dominance syndrome. True, one colony in the eighteenth century was able to free itself from colonialism and develop into a mature, viable and industrial state to be able to beat the colonizing country in the affluence race: the United States. Even the twentieth century has witnessed the transition from disintegrating political economies to viable, self-reliant political economies; notable examples are Russia (1917) and China (1949).

But the historical conditions in which the two kinds of liberation occurred were different. For one thing, the international system was different – less integrated and less complex. The American colony had to contend with only one power, Britain, which itself was 'developing' at the time. The other members of the 'international system' were either colluding with America or even actively supporting its war of independence; for they were interested in seeing the destruction of the British empire. The other two 'miracles' occurred in the wake of world wars (1914-1918 and 1939-1945).

Today, the international system is much more integrated than ever before, and, moreover, there is a commonality of interest among the major powers in the continued subjugation and exploitation of African societies, whatever the degree of rivalry between them for scarce and dwindling resources.

If, therefore, African political economy desires to disengage itself from the international political economy, it faces a stupendous task. A beginning, however, can be made with the agricultural sector. Without arresting the decay of this sector, no further steps towards liberation can be taken; outlining such steps will be nothing more than an academic exercise. Production of food – indeed, production generally – for *consumption* must be not only re-emphasized but incorporated into concrete policies and vigorously implemented. It is necessary to emphasize *production for consumption* ; for there is a tendency at present to encourage Africans to produce for export. If they are aware of this, they can avoid falling into the trap of 'modern' agricultural technology with its chemical fertilizers, chemical pesticides, and what have you, the combined effect of which is a destabilized ecosystem, eroded soil, damaged human health and a hierarchized, and consequently brutalized, society.

Rejection of modern agricultural technology as a means of liberation from the world market mechanism can provide a key to Africa's autonomy. But it will involve a great deal more. It will involve internal restructuring of African states that will respect indigenous identities and build on them rather than suppress them under the impact of a homogeneous model of modern nationalism, a wholly imported model. It will call for a rejection of elite consumption styles and corrupt politics, brought about by the aggressive salesmanship of Western advertisement media and the politics of aid-givers. This, in turn, will necessitate economic (alongside political) restructuring of African societies, more true to the African tradition than to the cultural trappings of colonialism. It will, above all, call for indigenization of science and technology, learning from the natives and their long rich traditions than from the masters, who, in a very short span, have brainwashed the African mind. The more Africa seeks to become autonomous of colonial vestiges, the more it will need to become itself and discover its true self. Once it realizes this, a whole world can open up before it – a world much larger and deeper than anything that the modern West has offered to Africa.

Notes

This is a revised version of a paper presented at a conference on 'The Future of Africa' organized by the Department of International Relations, University of Ife, Ile-Ife, Nigeria.

[1] See Immanuel Wallerstein, *The Modern World System* (New York: Modern Reader, 1976).

[2] See Karl Marx, *Capital* (New York International Publishers, 1967).

[3] A.G. Hopkins, *Economic History of West Africa* (New York: Colombia University Press, 1973), p. 87.

[4] For details, see Eric Williams, *Capital and Slavery* (New York: Capricorn Books, 1966); A.G. Hopkins (Note 3), pp. 78-117.

[5] Karl Marx (Note 2), *Capital*, vol. 1, p. 714.

[6] ibid., p. 751. (Emphasis added).

[7] See Amechi Okolo, 'The Role of International Trade in the African Political Economy', in Shaw/Ojo (Ed.), *Africa and the International Political System* (Washington, D.C.: University Press of America, 1982), pp. 68-103.

[8] See Walter Rodney, *How Europe Underdeveloped Africa* (Dar-es-Salaam: Tanzania Publishers House, 1973) pp. 103-162.

[9] Hopkins (Note 3), p. 117.

[10] ibid., pp. 117-118.

[11] V.I. Lenin, *Imperialism: The Highest Stage of Capitalism* (New York: International Publishers, 1966).

[12] A.G. Hopkins, 'Economic Imperialism in West Africa 1880-1892', *Economic History Review 21*, December 1968.

[13] R.L. Pfaltzgraff (Ed.), *Politics and the International System* (New York: JBL., 1972), pp. 206-207.

[14] Sir Allan Burns, *The History of Nigeria* (New York: Barnes and Nobles, 1969), pp. 157-171.

[15] I.M. Okonjo, *British Administration in Nigeria 1900-1950* (New York: NOK Publishers, 1974).

[16] Adam Smith, *An Inquiry Into the Nature and Cause of the Wealth of National* (New York, Modern Library Edition, 1937).

[17] John E. Flint, *Sir George Goldie and the Making of Modern Nigeria* (London: Oxford University Press, 1960), pp. 69-73.

[18] A.N. Cook, *British Enterprise in Nigeria* (London: Frank Cass and Co., 1964), pp. 79-110.

[19] G. Barraclough, *An Introduction to Contemporary History* (London: Frank Cass and Co., 1964).

[20] Frantz Fanon, *The Wretched of the Earth* (New York: Grove Press, 1968), p.39.

[21] ibid.

[22] G.O. Olusanya, *The Second World War and the Nigerian Politics 1939-1953* (Lagos: University of Lagos Press, 1973), pp. 70-93.

[23] D.A. Offiong, *Imperialism and Dependency* (Enugu: Fourth Dimension Publishers, 1980), p. 65.

[24] H. M. Hodges, *An Introduction to Sociology* (New York: Harper and Row Publishers, 1971), pp. 99-125.

[25] See Amechi Okolo, 'The Political Economy of the Nigerian Oil Sector and the Civil War', *Quarterly Journal of Administration XV*, 1-2, 1981, p. 108.

[26] Stanley Elkins, *Slavery* (Chicago: University of Chicago Press, 1971); and A. Meier and E.M. Rudwick, *From Plantation to Ghetto* (New York: Hill and Wang, 1969).

[27] Cheryl Payer, *The Debt Trap, the IMF and The Third World* (New York: Monthly Review Press, 1974), p. 49.

[28] Immanuel Wallerstein, *The Capitalist World Economy* (New York: Cambridge University Press, 1979), pp. 66-99 and passim.

[29] President Shagari's speech on the State of the Economy reported in the Nigerian newspapers of April 20 and 21, 1982.

[30] 'Saudi Arabia Warns Oil Companies Not to Cut Oil Buys From Nigeria', *Sunday Sketch*, 28 March, 1982, p. 1; *Sunday Concord*, 4 April, 1982, p. 1.

[31] (Note 29).

[32] *National Concord*, 'Thinking Corner', 3 June, 1982, p. 1.

Facing Up to Africa's Food Crisis

Carl K. Eicher

The most intractable food problem facing the world in the 1980s is the food and hunger crisis in sub-Saharan Africa—the poorest part of the world. Although the crisis follows by less than a decade the prolonged drought of the early 1970s in the Sahelian states of West Africa, the current dilemma is not caused by weather. Nor is the chief problem imminent famine, mass starvation, or the feeding and resettling of refugees. Improved international disaster assistance programs can avert mass starvation and famine and assist with refugee resettlement.

Rather, Africa's current food crisis is long term in nature and it has been building up for two decades; blanketing the entire subcontinent are its two interrelated components—a food production gap and hunger. The food production gap results from an alarming deterioration in food production in the face of a steady increase in the rate of growth of population over the past two decades. The hunger and malnutrition problem is caused by poverty—i.e., even in areas where per capita food production is not declining, the poor do not have the income or resources to cope with hunger and malnutrition.

Twenty-two of the 36 poorest countries in the world are African. After more than two decades of rising commercial food imports and food aid, the region is now experiencing a deep economic malaise, with growing balance-of-payment deficits and external public debts. The world economic recession has imposed a severe constraint on Africa's export-oriented economies. Prospects for meeting Africa's food production deficit through expanded commercial food imports thus appear dismal. African heads of state have held summit meetings to examine their economic, food, and hunger problems, and the Food and Agriculture Organization (FAO), Organization of African Unity (OAU), U.S. Department of Agriculture (USDA), World Bank, World Food Council, and African Ministers of Food and Agriculture agree on the alarming magnitude of the problem.

Donors have responded to these difficult problems by increasing aid flows to the point where African countries now lead the list of the world's aid recipients in per capita terms. Furthermore, the 1981 World Bank report, *Accelerated Development in Sub-Saharan Africa*, advocates a doubling of aid to Africa in real terms by the end of the 1980s. But the crisis cannot be solved through crash food production projects or a doubling of aid. Since the food and hunger crisis has been in the making for 10 to 20 years, viable solutions to the crisis cannot be found without facing up to a number of difficult political, structural and technical problems over the next several decades.

Key questions and policies which must be examined include: Why did the Green Revolution bypass Africa? What lessons have been learned from food production projects in the Sahel and the development strategies of the 1970s—integrated rural development, helping the poorest of the poor, and the basic needs approach? Are technical packages available for small farmers to step up food production in the 1980s? What is the record of agrarian

Reprinted by permission of *Foreign Affairs*, vol. 61, no. 1. © 1982 by the Council on Foreign Relations Inc.

capitalism and socialism? Can the Reagan Administration's foreign aid emphasis on private enterprise, technology transfer, institution building, and manpower development contribute to the alleviation of the food production crisis and economic stagnation in Africa?

II

Despite the fact that Africa is an extremely diverse region, several common features frame the boundaries for addressing its food crisis.[1] First, population densities in Africa are extremely low relative to Asia. The Sudan, for example, is two-thirds the size of India, but it has only 18 million people as compared with 670 million in India. Zaïre is five times the size of France and only has a small percentage of its arable land under cultivation.

Second, most of the economies are small: 24 of the 45 countries have fewer than five million people and only Nigeria has a gross domestic product larger than that of Hong Kong.[2] Small countries have special problems in assembling a critical mass of scientific talent and in financing colleges of agriculture and national agricultural research systems.

Third, the colonial legacy is embedded in the structure of agricultural institutions, the curricula of African universities, and how African policymakers view the role of agriculture in national development. All but two African states—Ethiopia and Liberia-are former colonies.

Fourth, Africa is an agrarian-dominated continent. In most countries, at least three out of five people work in agriculture. For the most part, land ownership is remarkably egalitarian as contrasted with Latin America.[3] Thus, almost all farms are small, with 5 to 15 acres under cultivation by family members. The performance of these small farms (smallholders) is the key to African agricultural development. Moreover, since agricultural output accounts for 30 to 60 percent of the gross domestic product, the poor performance of the agricultural sector over the past two decades has been an overriding constraint on development in the non-petroleum and non-mineral exporting countries.

Fifth, although more than half of the arable land that is idle in the world is in Africa, the land area in some countries is near maximum population density given present agricultural technology and available expertise on soil fertility. Much of the arable land in Africa is not farmed because of natural constraints such as tsetse flies which cause human sleeping sickness and virtually preclude the use of approximately one-third the continent, including some of the best watered and most fertile land.[4]

Looking at Africa's food production trends, population growth, food imports, and poverty, the overriding pattern emerges clearly: since Independence, Africa's historical position of self-sufficiency in staple foods has slowly dissipated. Over the 1960-80 period, aggregate food production in Africa grew very slowly—about 1.8 percent per year—a rate below the aggregate growth rate of Asia or Latin America. However, the critical numbers are not statistics on total food production but per capita figures. The U.S. Department of Agriculture statistics in Figure 1 below show that subSaharan Africa is the only region of the world where per capita food production declined over the past two decades. In addition, the average per capita calorie intake was below minimum nutritional levels in most countries.

The per capita figures reflect the fact that Africa is the only region of the world where the rate of growth of population actually increased in the 1970s. Recent reports show that the annual population growth rate in Africa was 2.1 percent in the mid-1950s, 2.7 percent in the

FIGURE 1
INDEX OF FOOD PRODUCTION PER CAPITA
(percentage of 1961-65 average)

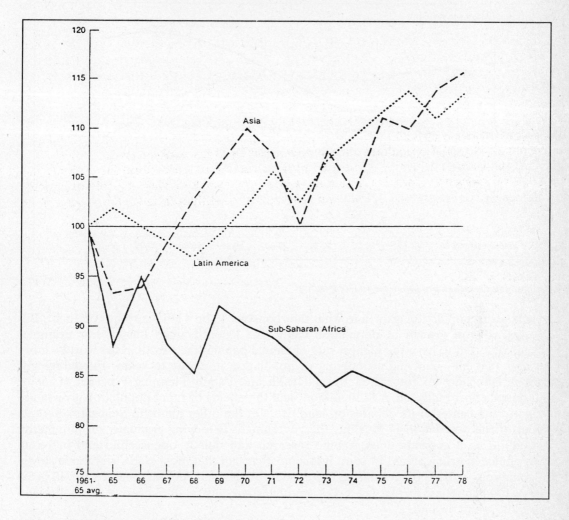

Source: USDA, *Food Problems and Prospects in Sub-Saharan Africa*, 1981.

late 1970s, and as Figure 2 shows, is projected to increase throughout the 1980s until it levels off at about 3 percent by the 1990s. Underlying the upward population trend is a young age structure. The average African woman produces six living children in her reproductive years.

There is little hope for reducing fertility levels in the 1980s because of a complex set of factors, including: the failure of family planning programs to date, the pro-natal policies of some states such as Mauritania, and the indifference of most African heads of state and

FIGURE 2
POPULATION GROWTH RATES, 1950-2000

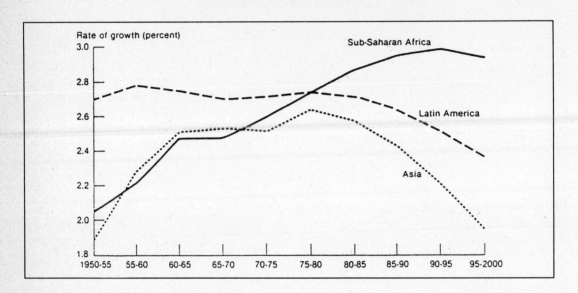

Source: USDA, *Food Problems and Prospects in Sub-Saharan Africa*, 1981.

intellectuals to population growth in what they consider to be a land-surplus continent. But explosive rates of growth of population cannot be ignored much longer. For example, Kenya is reported to have the highest rate of annual population growth in the world—more than four percent—implying a doubling of population in about 16 years. Encouragingly, Kenya is launching an Integrated Rural Health and Family Planning Program, a major multi-donor effort budgeted at $120 million, and the effects of rapid population growth are moving to the center of its debates on land use. On the other hand, in Senegal, where 95 percent of the population is Muslim, the government is moving gradually on population intervention as it expands demographic research and quietly opens child and maternal health clinics in urban areas. In sum, it is almost certain that most states will move slowly on population control policies during this decade. As a result, population growth will press hard on food supplies, forestry reserves, and livestock and wildlife grazing areas throughout the 1980s and beyond.

Food imports are another important dimension of the critical food situation. Many countries which were formerly self-sufficient in food significantly increased their ratio of food imports to total food consumption in the 1960s and 1970s. According to USDA figures, food imports are dominated by grain imports—especially wheat and rice—which have increased from 1.2 million tons a year in 1961-63 to 8 million tons in 1980 at a total cost of $2.1 billion. Significantly, commercial imports of food grain grew more than three times as fast as population over the 1961-79 period. Rising food imports are attributed to many factors: lagging domestic production; increasing urbanization; the accompanying shift of consumer tastes from cassava, yams, millet and sorghum to rice and wheat; availability of food aid; and overvalued foreign exchange rates which often make imported cereals cheaper than domestic supplies. Although data on food aid are imprecise, food aid represents about 20 percent of total food imports. Wheat, wheat flour, and rice dominate overall imports.

Given the intimate linkage of hunger and malnutrition to poverty, economists, nutritionists and food production specialists are coming to agree that food and poverty problems should be tackled together.[5] For if rural and urban incomes are increased, a large increment of the increased income of poor people (50 to 80 percent) will be spent on food. Unless food production is stepped up, an increase in rural and urban incomes will simply lead to increased food imports, possibly inflation, and an increase in hunger and malnutrition. Conversely, while expanded food production should be the centerpiece of food policy in Africa in the 1980s, food policy strategies must go beyond crash food production campaigns to deal with poverty itself because expanded food production by itself will not solve the hunger problem.

III

From this overview, one can see that while most Africans are farmers and Africa has enormous physical potential to feed itself, there are substantial barriers to tapping this potential. Experts from academia, donor organizations, and consulting firms emphasize post-independence corruption, mismanagement, repressive pricing of farm commodities, and the urban bias in development strategies. Year after year, African heads of state point to the unfavorable weather in their appeal for food aid. In fact, the crisis stems from a seamless web of political, technical and structural constraints which are a product of colonial surplus extraction strategies, misguided development plans and priorities of African states since independence, and faulty advice from many expatriate planning advisers. These complex, deep-rooted constraints can only be understood in historical perspective.[6]

Colonial approaches to development facilitated the production and extraction of surpluses—copper, gold, cocoa, coffee, etc.—for external markets while paying little attention to investments in human capital, research on food crops, and strengthening of internal market linkages. For example, colonial governments gave little attention to the training of agricultural scientists and managers. By the time of independence in the early 1960s, there was only one college of agriculture in French-speaking tropical Africa. Between 1952 and 1963, only four university graduates in agriculture were trained in francophone Africa and 150 in English-speaking Africa. By 1964, there was a total of three African scientists working in the research stations in the East African countries of Kenya, Uganda and Tanzania.

Moreover, the effects of colonial policies on contemporary land ownership patterns and agricultural research and training institutions are important contributors to the current food production and poverty problems. Many colonial regimes focused their research and development programs on export crops and the needs of commercial farmers and managers of plantations. The modest investment in research on food crops could be defended during this period because the rate of population growth was low—one to two percent per annum—and surplus land could be "automatically" brought under cultivation by smallholders. But with annual rates of population growth now approaching three to four percent in some countries, research institutions must be restructured to devote more attention to food crops and the needs of smallholders and herders.

The current crisis has also resulted from the low priority that independent African states have assigned to investments in agriculture and to increasing food production over the past 25 years. In that period African states have engaged in five key debates on food and agriculture. The first was over the priority to be given to industry and agriculture in development plans and budget allocations. As African nations became independent in the late 1950s and early 1960s, most of them pursued mixed economies with a heavy emphasis on foreign aid, industrial development, education, and economic diversification. For example, the late president Kenyatta promoted capitalism and encouraged investors "to bring prosperity" to Kenya. A small number of countries such as Mali, Ghana and Guinea shifted abruptly to revolutionary socialism in the early 1960s. But whether political leaders were espousing capitalism or socialism, they generally all gave low priority to agriculture. African leaders tended to view agriculture as a "backward" sector which could provide surpluses—in the form of taxes and labor—to finance industrial and urban development, and thought agricultural development would simply reinforce dependency. Agricultural policies in many countries (both capitalist and socialist) supported plantations, state farms, land settlement schemes, and the replacement of private traders and money lenders with government trading corporations, grain boards, and credit agencies. The effects of these policies on agricultural production were typically inhibiting, and in some cases, highly so.

The second debate was over the relevance of Western models versus the "political economy" (stressing dependency and class structure) and radical models of development. As Western economists assumed important roles in helping to prepare development plans and served as policy advisers in the early 1960s, Western modernization and macroeconomic models were introduced into Africa. The dominant models emphasized the industrial sector as the driving force of development and the need to transfer rural people to the industrial sector. These models had three major shortcomings. First, they assumed that one discipline—economics—could provide answers on how to slay the dragons of poverty, inequality and malnutrition. As Albert Hirschman reminds us, development is a historical, social, political, technical and organizational process which cannot be understood by means of a single discipline.[7] Second, the cities were unable to provide jobs for the rural exodus. Third, the macro models were unable to provide a convincing understanding of the complexity of the agricultural sector—the sector which employs 50 to 95 percent of the labor force in African states. Although these models were technically elegant, they seem remarkably naïve today because they assigned a passive role to the agricultural sector.

The vacuity of the Western models of development and their failure to come to grips with the broad social, political and structural issues, as well as the complexities of the agricultural sector, opened the door for the political economy models of development and underdevelopment to emerge and gain a large following among African intellectuals. Samir Amin, an Egyptian economist who has specialized in African development problems for the past 20 years, has been the preeminent proponent of the dependency and underdevelopment paradigm of development. The political economy models have made a valuable contribution in stressing the need to understand development as a long-term historical process, the need to consider the linkages between national economies and the world economic system, and the importance of structural barriers (e.g., land tenure) to development. But the Achilles' heel of the political economy models is their failure to provide a convincing understanding of the motivations of rural people, and the role of technological change. Furthermore, many political economy scholars have tended to spend more time commenting on the failure of market economics than in generating empirical evidence on farms and in villages in order to verify and refine their models.[8]

The third debate was over the use of pricing and taxation policies to achieve agricultural and food policy objectives. The first issue here is whether Africans are responsive to economic incentives. Empirical research has produced a consensus that African farmers do respond to economic incentives as do farmers in high-income countries, but that Africans rationally give priority to producing enough food for their families for the coming one to two years. The next question is whether African states have pursued positive pricing and taxation policies for agriculture. Numerous empirical studies across the continent have provided conclusive evidence that many countries (both capitalist and socialist) are pursuing negative pricing policies which dampen incentives to produce food and export crops and encourage black market operations.

For example, Tanzania has paid farmers throughout the country a uniformly low price for maize, encouraging the sale of maize in black markets. In Mali, the government pricing policy for small farmers in a large irrigated rice production scheme can be labelled as "extortion." A meticulous two-year study in 1980-81 has shown that it costs farmers 83 Malian francs to produce a kilo of rice but that the government paid farmers only 60 Malian francs per kilo.[9] Does it seem irrational for the rice farmers to smuggle rice across the border into Senegal, Niger and Upper Volta where they can secure 108 to 128 Malian francs per kilo?

Not only food crops are subjected to negative pricing policies—export crops are also heavily taxed. In an analysis of pricing and taxation policies for major crops in 13 countries over the 1971-80 period, the World Bank concluded that, taking the net tax burden and the effect of overvalued currency into account, producers in the 13 countries received less than half of the real value of their export crops.[10] These examples and other studies carried out over the past two decades provide solid evidence that African states are using negative pricing and taxation policies to pump the economic surplus out of agriculture. A simple but powerful conclusion emerges from this experience—African states must overhaul the incentive structure for farmers and adopt increased farm income as an important goal of social policy in the 1980s. Moreover, increasing incentives to farmers is a strategic policy lever for attacking poverty and promoting rural employment.

The fourth debate—agrarian capitalism or socialism—has been one of the most emotional topics over the past 30 years; it will continue to dominate discussions on politics, development strategies, and foreign aid in the 1980s. Even though it is difficult to define African socialism, about one-fourth of the states now espouse socialism as their official ideology. The experiences of Ghana and Tanzania are well documented. Four years after Ghana became independent, President Nkrumah abruptly shifted from capitalism to a socialist strategy which equated modernization with industrialization and large-scale farming. Ghana was unable to assemble the technical and managerial skills and incentive structure to operate its vast system of state farms, parastatals (state corporations) and trading corporations. The failure of agrarian socialism has imposed a heavy toll on the people of Ghana.

Tanzania's shift to socialism in 1967 produced a voluminous literature, international press coverage, massive financial support from international donors—especially Scandinavian countries and the World Bank—and attention from political leaders and intellectuals throughout Africa. The vision of agrarian socialism is set forth in President Nyerere's essay "Socialism and Rural Development." But after 15 years of experimentation, it seems fair to examine the balance sheet on socialism in a country where 80 percent of the population live in rural areas. Knowledgeable observers conclude that Tanzania is in deep financial difficulty in part because of the drought in the mid-1970s, the quantum jump in oil prices, and the conflict in Uganda, but basically because of the stagnant performance of its agricultural sector under socialism. One cannot overlook Tanzania's important gains in literacy and social services, but one may legitimately worry about their sustainability over the longer term without increased rural incomes or exceptionally heavy foreign aid flows. There are many unanswered questions about Tanzania's experiment with agrarian socialism, such as why President Nyerere authorized the use of coercion to round up farmers living in scattered farmsteads and forced them to live in villages. Many pro-Tanzania scholars avoid this topic. But the failure of Tanzania to feed its people explains why Tanzania is no longer taken seriously as a model which other African countries want to emulate.

Agrarian socialism is now under fire throughout Africa: after 20 years of experimentation, there are presently no African models which are performing well. First, and most important, socialist agricultural production requires a vast amount of information and managerial and administrative skills in order to cope with the vagaries of weather, seasonal labor bottlenecks, and the need for on-the-spot decision-making authority. Second, government-operated grain boards have been plagued with overstaffing, corruption, mismanagement and high marketing costs. Because these problems cannot be easily overcome, it is unlikely that Africa will make much progress with socialist agriculture in this century.

As the pendulum swings from socialism to private farming and private traders in the 1980s, it is important to remind the reader that to put all or most of the weight on ideology—capitalism or socialism—is to ignore an important lesson that has been learned over the past 30 years in the Third World—namely, ideology is but one variable influencing the outcome of agricultural development projects. The "correct" choice of ideology cannot in and of itself assure successful development. Examples of failure under both capitalist and socialist models are too numerous to conclude otherwise.

The fifth debate—about the Green Revolution and the African farmer—concerns what can be done to increase the low cereal yields in Africa. There is growing evidence that a dominant cause of rural poverty is the fact that 60 to 80 percent of the agricultural labor force works at very low levels of productivity. As Figure 3 indicates, while yields in Latin America and Asia have increased since 1965, those of Africa have remained stagnant. Over the past 20 years, this debate has focused on whether African states could make use of high-yielding food grain varieties developed in International Agricultural Research Centers in Mexico, the Philippines and other parts of the world, or whether improved cereal varieties could be more efficiently developed through investments in research programs in national and regional research stations in Africa.

Twenty years ago, foreign advisers were optimistic about transferring the Green Revolution technology to Africa, but after two decades of experimentation the results are disappointing. In fact, the Green Revolution has barely touched Africa. For example, hybrid sorghum varieties from India have not been successful in Upper Volta, Niger and Mali because of unforeseen problems such as disease, variability of rainfall, and poor soils. Moreover, the Green Revolution crops—wheat and rice—that produced 40 to 50 percent increases in yields in Asia are not staple foods in Africa. Knowledgeable observers agree that African farming systems are extremely complex and that the development of suitable

FIGURE 3
CEREAL YIELDS

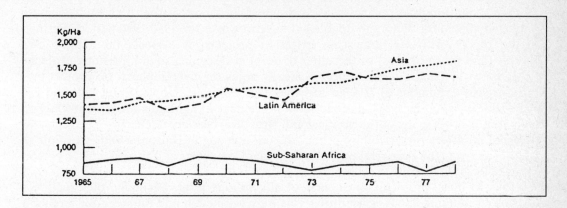

Source: USDA, *Food Problems and Prospects in Sub-Saharan Africa*, 1981.

technical packages requires location-specific research by multidisciplinary research teams, which are supported by strong national research programs on the staple foods of each country.

These five debates illustrate the complex set of problems that have preoccupied African states over the past two decades as they tried to find a meaningful role for the agricultural sector. Throughout much of the post-independence period, most states have viewed agriculture as a backward and low-priority sector, have perpetuated colonial policies of pumping the economic surplus out of agriculture, and have failed to give priority to achieving a reliable food surplus as a prerequisite for basic national, social and economic goals. The failure of most African states to develop an effective set of agricultural policies to deal with the technical, structural, institutional and human resource constraints is at the heart of the present food crisis. Part of the failure must be attributed to the colonial legacy and part to the hundreds of foreign economic advisers who have imported inappropriate models and theories of development from the United States, Europe, Asia and Latin America. In the final analysis, agricultural stagnation in capitalist Zaïre and socialist Tanzania must also be placed before heads of state and planners who have promoted premature industrialization and have exhibited a fundamental misunderstanding of incentives, the motivations of their own rural people, and the necessity to overcome technical constraints and restructure agricultural institutions.

IV

Africa's inability to feed itself amid vast amounts of unused land and record levels of foreign aid is, on the surface, one of the major paradoxes in Third World development. What should be done?

While the several notable recent reports on Africa's food and economic problems agree on the severity of the food and hunger crisis, each of these assessments underemphasizes the mistakes of African states and in a somewhat self-serving fashion overstresses the need for more foreign aid.[11] For example, the World Bank's *Accelerated Development* report correctly singles out domestic policy issues as the heart of the crisis, but it also advances an unsupported appeal for donors to double aid to Africa over the 1980-1990 period. Further, while the report criticizes large-scale irrigation projects, it neglects the Bank's own difficulties (and those of most of the other donors) in designing sound livestock projects. The recent World Food Council report correctly notes the overemphasis on project-type aid, the excessive number of foreign missions (for example, Upper Volta received 340 official donor missions in 1981), and the small percentage of aid funds for food production projects, but it skirts many of the political and structural barriers to change. The report by the African ministers of agriculture at their recent meeting in Nairobi avoids the topic of population growth, the empirical record of agrarian socialism, and the disastrous performance of state grain boards.

Solutions to these problems must, first of all, be long term. Secondly, they require a redirection in thinking about agriculture's role in development and the need for a reliable food surplus as a precondition for national development. In order to buy time to lay a foundation for long-range solutions, it will be necessary to rely on a number of holding actions. Examples include expanded commercial food imports, food aid, and promoting seasonal and international migration until more land is brought under irrigation and higher rainfall areas can be cleared of tsetse flies and river blindness. But these holding actions must not be allowed to substitute for efforts toward long-range solutions.

Two steps should be taken now to start the process of formulating longer term policies. First, African states, donors, and economic advisers should jettison the ambiguous slogans about food self-sufficiency, food first, and basic needs.[12] Although these have a powerful emotional and political appeal they offer little help in answering the key question—what blend of food production, food imports, and export crops should be pursued to achieve both growth and equity objectives?

The second immediate step should be the phasing out or restructuring of some of the crash food production projects—i.e., seed multiplication, irrigated wheat schemes, livestock schemes, and integrated rural development projects—that are floundering. Many of these crash projects were hastily assembled over the past decade without a sound technical package and without being tested in a pilot phase. These unproductive projects consume scarce high-level manpower, perpetuate recurrent cost problems, and create a credibility problem for both African policymakers and international donors. Particularly important is the reassessment of integrated rural development (IRD) projects. The weakness of most IRD projects—their lack of emphasis on food production and income-generating activities—can be corrected by restructuring the projects rather than phasing them out. Other projects which have been implemented in advance of a sound knowledge base, like those in livestock, should either be phased out or scaled down and continued as pilot projects for a five- to ten-year period. A five- to ten-year pilot phase is unheard of in Africa, but in projects like those in livestock it is a necessary period for solving technical problems and developing appropriate local institutions to solve such key issues as overstocking.

The starting point for food policy analysis in each country should be the development of a food policy strategy with two goals in mind: achieving a reliable food surplus (based on domestic production, grain storage, and international trade) and reducing hunger.

Looking toward policy reform, a word of caution is in order. Food policy is every bit as delicate as family planning. The rice riots in Monrovia, which left more than 100 dead in 1979, and the sugar riots in Khartoum and other major cities in the Sudan following the recent doubling of sugar prices, are reminders of the narrow range of options for policymakers on food policy issues. Consequently, as experiences from the Sudan, Zambia and Nigeria illustrate, African countries will move very slowly on policy reforms unless spurred by famine, a reduction in foreign exchange earnings from petroleum, or coordinated donor leverage to link long-term food aid to policy reform.

The Sudan provides a conspicuous example of the difficulty of mobilizing the agricultural sector as an engine of growth and expanded food production. In the mid-1970s, the international press frequently asserted that the Sudan could become the "breadbasket of the Middle East" by drawing on several billion dollars of OPEC loans and gifts to develop its vast reserve of idle land. The issue today, however, is not one of exporting food to the Middle East, but of the Sudan's inability to feed its 18 million people. The Sudan imported $30 million in U.S. P.L. 480 subsidized food last year and it is now facing severe balance-of-payment problems and inflation. Although the Sudan has historically excelled in cotton research, it has devoted only token attention to research on food crops. As long as the Sudan continues to receive food aid and has hopes of striking oil in the southern part of the country, there is little likelihood of policy reforms.

Zambia is importing large quantities of maize, its staple food. In Zambia, about 400 commercial farmers produce an estimated 40 percent of the marketable maize, yet the Ministry of Agriculture does not have proven maize varieties for its half-million small farmers. Should Zambia press on with efforts to achieve self-sufficiency in maize via commercial farmers or small farmers? In any case, the survival of President Kaunda's government will be in doubt if it does not address the most basic policy issue—the achievement of a reliable food surplus.

In the early 1960s, Nigeria was a net exporter of food—mainly oil palm and groundnuts—but by the early 1970s, Nigeria was importing food. Several authoritative reports commissioned by Nigerian policymakers recommended that immediate steps be taken in order to avert Nigeria's impending food crisis. Petroleum exports, however, have enabled Nigeria to buy time. In 1981, Nigeria imported more than one billion dollars of food from the United States. Although Nigeria is far ahead of most francophone African countries in trained agricultural manpower, a 1978 study reported that more than 40 percent of the positions for senior agricultural researchers in the eight major research stations were vacant. The government recently concluded that it will take 15 years to achieve self-sufficiency in food production. Nigeria has now formed a high-level Green Revolution Committee to address its food problem.

Turning to policy reform itself, scaling down the state bureaucracy, the state payroll, and state control over private farmers and private traders are central problems for most African states. After 20 years of experience with parastatals, the record is clear: parastatals are ineffective in stimulating the production of private farmers, are no more efficient than private traders in food grain marketing, and moreover, become a sponge for foreign aid. As the number of parastatal employees increases, the pressure intensifies for donors to commensurately increase their contributions to meet the payroll of the expanded bureaucracy. The parastatal disease is well known, but it is not given much attention in the reports cited above, except in the World Bank's *Accelerated Development* report, which should be applauded for its candor on this topic.

A food policy strategy must tackle the crucial need to raise prices for both food and export crops. Although one cannot generalize for sub-Saharan Africa, donors should withhold project aid unless there is a favorable incentive structure for farmers. In addition, a food policy strategy should not rule out the expansion of export crops because expanded farm income, through food sales, export crops and off-farm income is a prerequisite for solving the poverty and hunger problems.

A major issue in achieving policy reforms is whether donor agencies and countries can or should use food aid leverage to promote the required changes. In existence for almost 30 years, food aid is now a topic of growing interest in Africa. Although there is unanimity on using food aid for humanitarian purposes-for example, feeding refugees—food aid for development is more controversial. The opposition to this sort of food aid—where food is sold at concessional terms and extended as grants for food for work programs—comes from evidence that food aid: (1) can reduce the pressure on recipient countries to carry out policy reforms; (2) depresses farm prices; (3) is unreliable;[13] and (4) promotes an undesirable shift in consumption patterns (i.e., the bulk of U.S. food aid—60 to 70 percent—is in the form of wheat and wheat flour even though wheat is not a staple food in Africa).

Food aid programs are firmly institutionalized with donors. As far as the United States is concerned food aid has accounted for approximately 40 percent of all U.S. economic assistance to Africa over the 1970-80 period. African states find themselves in a strong position to bargain for food aid this year because of large U.S., European Community and Japanese surpluses, and falling international wheat and rice prices.

To date, there has been little solid research on the role of food aid for development purposes in Africa. The food aid experience in Asia and Latin America, however, shows that the availability of food aid can take the pressure off recipient nations to carry out internal policy reforms. Linking food aid with policy reforms in major food deficit countries in Africa would require the development of food policy reform packages for countries such as the Sudan, Mali, Senegal and Tanzania, and agreement by donors to make three- to five-year food aid commitments in exchange for internal policy reforms. Countries such as Mali and the Sudan would be good test cases for linking food aid (which is not used to feed refugees) to tough domestic policy reforms. But unless donors come together and agree to meet minimum forward food aid levels, African states may postpone policy reforms as they continue to rely on a patchwork of bilateral food aid programs.

V

Beyond policy reforms, a long-range solution to food and hunger problems will depend, to a large degree, on achievements in agricultural research. Significant increases are needed over the next 20 years in research expenditures on dry land farming systems with emphasis on food crops (white maize, yams, cassava, millet and sorghum) and on livestock. Authorities on food production and livestock projects in the field now commonly bemoan the lack of proven technical packages for small farmers in dry land farming systems throughout Africa, and the uniformly unfavorable technical coefficients (e.g., low rates of growth, disease) for livestock production.

An expanded research program on food and livestock should be viewed in a 20-year time-frame because problems such as low soil fertility and livestock diseases cannot be resolved through a series of short-term, ad hoc research projects. The U.S. experience, wherein 40 years (1880-1920) were spent developing a productive system of federal and state research programs, should be heeded by U.S. congressmen who are likely to expect major results from the U.S. Agency for International Development financed research projects in Africa in five to ten years.

Research on irrigation is particularly important, and should be accelerated in the coming decades. The knowledge base for irrigation in Africa is meagre. Irrigation has played a minor role in Africa except in large-scale projects in the Sudan and in Madagascar where there is a history of irrigation by small farmers. The cultivated land under irrigation is probably less than five percent in most other countries (as compared with an estimated 30 percent in India). Following the 1968-74 drought in the Sahel, there was considerable optimism about the role of irrigated farming in "drought-proofing" the region. Due to numerous technical and administrative problems, however, the projected expansion of irrigation in the Sahel is behind schedule and it is certain that irrigation will not play a significant role in the Sahelian states until early in the next century.

Although research on the economics of irrigation is fragmentary, the limited results provide support for a smallholder irrigation strategy in the 1980s, with priority given to: ground water development with small pumps; land reclamation through drainage and water control; and an increase in small-scale projects which are developed and maintained by groups of farmers with their own family labor. A small-scale irrigation strategy is advocated because the cost of bringing more rainfed land under cultivation is substantially less than the cost of leveling and preparing land for large-scale irrigation. For example, World Bank data show that recent irrigation projects in Niger, Mauritania and northern Nigeria each had costs of more than $10,000 per hectare at 1980 prices. On the other hand, farmers in Senegal have cleared and prepared their own land for irrigation, expending several hundred hours of family labor per hectare (2.47 acres). Although irrigation will not be a panacea for the recovery of the Sahel, nor for feeding Africa in the 1980s and 1990s, a long-term research program on the human, technical and institutional dimensions of irrigation should be initiated in the immediate future.

An encouraging development on the research front is the recent formation of an informal working group of seven major bilateral donors to plan a long-term program for strengthening national agricultural research systems throughout Africa, with emphasis on food and livestock research. This shift to coordinate bilateral support for research is a welcome innovation, but it remains to be seen whether donors will have the courage to view research as a long-term investment and to provide guaranteed funding for a minimum of ten years. One refreshing change introduced this year by W. Peter McPherson, the Administrator of the U.S. Agency for International Development, is the flexibility to authorize ten-year rather than five-year projects. For example, AID recently authorized funding for a ten-year centrally funded, worldwide water research project and a nine-year tropical soils project.

The question is whether AID's country priorities will remain stable enough to assure African countries of continuity in U.S. funding over a 10- to 20-year period. For example, the proposed allocation to the eight Sahelian states will be slightly reduced in real terms in Fiscal Year 1983 even though Congress had earlier endorsed a 20-year recovery program for the Sahel following the drought. On the other hand, U.S. economic assistance to the Sudan has been dramatically increased this year to over $100 million, exceeding the total U.S. aid for the Sahel. A rule of thumb is that an African country should never embark on a long-term program to upgrade its national agricultural research system with major support from only one bilateral donor.

A third essential component of a long-range strategy is massive investments in human capital formation, including graduate training of several thousand agricultural scientists and managers. This is necessary to replace the foreign advisers, researchers, managers and teachers in African universities and to meet the needs of a science-based agriculture in the next century. Since it takes 10 to 15 years of training and experience beyond high school to develop a research scientist, the investments in human capital will not produce payoffs for Africa until the 1990s.

Building graduate agricultural training programs within Africa necessitates a reexamination of the role of the African university in national development. The time is propitious for African universities to move from undergraduate to graduate training programs in science and agriculture. Before graduate education is expanded, however, some questions must be raised about priorities in undergraduate education. Undergraduate degree programs in agriculture in many universities are still embarrassingly undervalued and underfunded when compared with law, medicine and history. For example, in Senegal, the University of Dakar was formally established in 1957, and in 1960 the Senegalese assumed its administration. Today, there are approximately 12,000 students in the University of Dakar, of whom several thousand specialize in law and economics. Not until 1979 was a National School of Agriculture established at Thies, north of Dakar. Students take their first year science courses at the University of Dakar and the initial group of undergraduates will graduate from the Thies school in 1984-85. That university-level teaching of agriculture was not initiated until 1979, 29 years after independence, reflects an enduring colonial legacy as well as the government's ambivalence about agriculture's role in national development. Although the structural reforms entailed in redesigning African universities to suit their country's needs will require decades to resolve, it is time for donors to stop merely paying lip service to African universities. Whereas donors embraced African universities in the 1960s they generally withdrew their support in the 1970s as they promoted crash food production, IRD projects, and international agricultural research institutes. Money saved ($100 to $200 million) from phasing out the floundering crash projects cited above can be reallocated to selected African universities with emphasis on faculties of agriculture. Donors should press for long-term structural reform of the universities in exchange for long-term aid commitments of 10 to 20 years.

Currently, graduate-level education for African students in the United States costs $1,850 per month, or $35,000-$45,000 for a Master's degree over a 24- to 30-month period. AID should gradually phase out Master's level training programs in agriculture and related fields in the United States. Instead, U.S. faculty members should be sent to Africa to help develop regional centers of excellence in graduate training in eight to ten African universities over the next 10 to 15 years. In order to achieve this goal, AID will have to give greatly increased priority to aiding African universities, including ten-year authorizations to U.S. universities to facilitate this type of training program. In the final analysis, the initiative for this second phase—graduate training in agriculture in African universities—will have to come from within Africa.

The fourth component of a long-range solution to Africa's food crisis will be an ongoing effort to address the hunger/malnutrition/poverty problem. Rural poverty is potentially a much more difficult problem to solve than the food production gap, but self-sufficiency in food production will be a bogus achievement if the poor do not have access to a decent diet. A society cannot expect to move from a low- to middle-income stage of development if two-thirds of its population are producing millet, sorghum, maize and yams at stagnant levels of output. Agricultural research on stagnant food grain production is a prerequisite to solving rural poverty and hunger problems. Moreover, since jobs cannot be created in urban areas for all the unemployed, there must be created in rural areas opportunities in food and cash crop agriculture and rural small-scale industry.

VI

The implications of all this for the foreign assistance community flow quite clearly from the foregoing analysis. Currently, 40 donors are moving funds and technical assistance through a patchwork of several thousand uncoordinated projects in support of agricultural and rural development throughout Africa. Furthermore, donors are continuing to transfer models and slogans-basic needs, appropriate technology, and food first—to Africa. In turn, African states are allocating a high percentage of a scarce resource—trained agricultural professionals—to meet the project reporting requirements of donors. In short, both donors and recipients are prisoners of projects and slogans. Should aid to Africa be doubled in real terms during this decade? The answer depends on how these problems and others are resolved:

1. *Long-term Planning*. Emphasis should be placed on increasing the lifetime of projects, reducing the number of tiny projects (e.g., producing visual aids for the livestock service in a Sahelian country) and increasing the volume of aid in program grants which are tied to policy reforms. Long-term programs like ten-year research projects, five- to ten-year pilot livestock projects, 20-year programs to develop colleges of agriculture, and five-year food aid/policy reform packages—should not be perceived as luxuries, but rather as prerequisites to solving Africa's technical, structural and human capital constraints.

2. *Aid Coordination*. The lack of aid coordination is especially acute in Africa as donors phase out assistance to Latin America and smother Africa with project aid. Most African states have been able to resist the establishment of a formal Consortium of Donors. Such a consortium should be established for large recipient countries such as the Sudan, Senegal, Kenya and Tanzania. Moreover, a strong case could be made for donors to declare a two-year moratorium on certain kinds of projects with poor track records—e.g., livestock projects—in order to sort out the lessons to be learned from the failures over the past two decades.

3. *Developing Food Policy Strategies*. Despite the pleas of journalists who urge donors to increase the number of food production projects, the professional agriculturist knows that a single food policy reform in Mali—raising official farm prices—may be more effective than 20 new food production projects. Donors should concentrate their resources on helping local professionals develop food policy strategies which identify the constraints on achieving a reliable food surplus, with emphasis on food production, storage and international trade.

4. *Technology Transfer.* Analysis of the Green Revolution has shown that donors should shift their emphasis to helping African institutions generate technology within Africa through strengthened national and regional research programs. Although the U.S. and India's food grain varieties are not directly transferable to Africa, some of the processes the two countries used to generate technology appropriate to the needs of their farmers in dry land areas are applicable. The U.S. Dust Bowl crisis in Kansas and Oklahoma in the 1930s gave rise to the U.S. Soil Conservation Service, research on new varieties, irrigation, and other techniques which transformed the Dust Bowl into a highly productive area of American agriculture. In this 30-year process U.S. colleges of agriculture played a strategic role, in cooperation with local and state organizations and with the USDA. The U.S. and Indian experiences in the process of building research programs, colleges of agriculture, and new institutions such as a Soil Conservation Service can contribute to African agricultural development.

5. *Foreign Private Enterprise.* The Reagan Administration has identified the promotion of foreign private investment as one of four areas of concentration in its foreign assistance program. Can foreign private investment contribute to the resolution of Africa's food and poverty problems? Just as the roles of women in African development cannot be analyzed in isolation from those of men, the role of the private sector can only be analyzed in relation to public investments. The poor record of food production projects in the Sahel in the past seven years provides ample proof that many of these projects fail because public sector investments are not made in: agricultural research to develop profitable packages for rainfed farming, prevention and control of animal disease, rural roads, and schools to train agricultural managers. Professional agriculturists know that public sector investments can either facilitate or destroy the conditions for private African capitalists to function in a market-oriented economy. It would be unwise if the Administration pursued a dogmatic private enterprise approach at the expense of public sector investments.

In general, inadequate infrastructure and technical constraints presently limit the scope for foreign private investors. Although some foreign firms prospered in colonial periods when they were given choice land and protected markets, since independence there have been many failures, including the recent efforts of U.S. firms to produce food in Ghana, Liberia and Senegal. As a rule of thumb, if foreign private firms do not receive special subsidies, they cannot compete with African smallholders who have a knowledge of local climate, pests and soils, and are willing to produce food on their own land at rates of return of 75 cents to three dollars per day for family labor. Moreover, the large capital-intensive plantations and ranches emphasized by foreign private firms should be questioned on social grounds because they do not produce the badly needed jobs in an area of the world where seasonal unemployment is widespread. Foreign private enterprise, however, can contribute to Africa's food sector in countries such as Kenya and Zimbabwe which have a good infrastructure and require international managerial skills for investments in food processing plants, and in fertilizer and agricultural input industries. But in the final analysis, the focus of U.S. foreign aid should be on making public investments in roads, universities and research stations to help African capitalists—small farmers and herders—produce food for their families and for urban people.

Aid flows to Africa have grown dramatically in recent years: net official aid in 1980 was $13.70 per capita in Africa compared with an average of $9.60 for all developing countries. In many circles in Africa, there is a feeling that the continent is already too heavily dependent on aid and foreign transactions. The technical specialists in most donor agencies will privately concede that there is currently an excess of donor funds in search of technically sound agricultural production projects. However, if donors take a broad view of the need for massive, long-term public investments in roads, faculties of agriculture in African universities, and land transfer funds (e.g., for Zimbabwe), and if African countries shift their agricultural development strategies and priorities and introduce policy reforms, then it may be desirable for donors to double aid to Africa in real terms over the 1980-90 period.

To sum up, agricultural development is a slow and evolutionary process and it is up to African states and donor agencies to lay the foundation for solving the food production problem over a 10- to 20-year period. Unless steps are taken in the 1980s to solve these basic technical, political, structural and policy constraints, many African states may end up in the 1990s as permanent food aid clients of the United States, the European Economic Community, and Japan.

Notes

[1] Before examining the causes of the food crisis, it is important to remember the complexity of the region and the fallacy of advancing Africa-wide strategies to deal with problems of food and hunger. Sub-Saharan Africa is composed of 45 countries with variable endowments of resources, colonial histories and opportunities for development. Although a few scholars still discuss the "African case," most researchers wisely eschew generalizing about even a subregion such as West Africa—an area as large as the continental United States.

[2] Africa has a shaky data base and there is a need to interpret official statistics with caution. Accurate data on yields and acreage under cultivation are available for only a handful of countries.

[3] The uniform agrarian structure is partially a function of colonial policies which prohibited foreigners from gaining title to land in some parts of the continent, such as West Africa. But in some countries such as Zambia and Zimbabwe, colonial policies promoted a dual structure of large and small farms. In Zambia, 400 large mechanized farms produce an estimated 40 percent of the maize surplus—the staple food—while an estimated 545,000 subsistence farms produce the balance. Zimbabwe is a significant maize exporter following last year's record harvest. But the irony of Zimbabwe's maize surplus is that the bulk of it is being produced by 5,000 large farmers who control approximately one-half of the land at a time when there is political pressure to distribute land to the landless.
[Editor's note: The situation in Zimbabwe, where the government has done a great deal to encourage the small-scale farmer, has changed drastically since this article was written. By 1986 "over 40% of the nation's maize and cotton was produced by small-scale black farmers on communal lands." Jack Shepherd, 'Zimbabwe: Poised on the Brink', *Atlantis*, July 1987).]

[4] Tsetse control is a long-term and costly activity which includes: clearing of vegetation which harbors flies, spraying, release of sterile male flies, and human settlement.

[5] Africa's food and poverty problems should not be allowed to overshadow some impressive achievements of the continent over the past 25 years. Foremost is the increase in average life expectancy—from an estimated 38 years in 1950 to almost 50 years in 1980. This 30 percent increase is often overlooked by those who are mesmerized by rates of growth of gross national product. Moreover, the achievements in education have been impressive in Tanzania and Somalia. Another unheralded achievement is the vast improvement in the capacity of countries such as Nigeria, Kenya and the Ivory Coast to organize, plan and manage their economies.

[6] See Carl K. Eicher and Doyle C. Baker, "Research on Agricultural Development in subSaharan Africa: A Critical Survey," *MSU International Development Papers*, No. 1, East Lansing, Michigan State University, Dept. of Agricultural Economics, 1982.

[7] Albert O. Hirschman, "Rise and Decline of Western Development Economics," in *Essays in Trespassing: Economics to Politics and Beyond*, New York: Cambridge University Press, 1981, Chap. 1.

[8] For a recent assessment of the modernization, dependency and political economy models, see Crawford Young, *Ideology and Development in Africa*, New Haven: Yale University Press (for the Council on Foreign Relations), 1982.

[9] Malumba Kamuanga,"Farm Level study of the Rice Production systems at the Office de Niger in Mali: An Economic Analysis," Ph.D. dissertation, Department of Agricultural Economics, Michigan State University, East Lansing, Michigan, 1982.

[10] *Accelerated Development in Sub-Saharan Africa: An Agenda for Action*, World Bank, Washington, 1981, p. 55.

[11] See Food and Agriculture Organization, *Regional Food Plan for Africa*, Rome, 1978; Organization of African Unity, *Lagos Plan of Action*, Lagos, Nigeria, April 28-29, 1980; U.S. Department of Agriculture, *Food Problems and Prospects in Sub-Saharan Africa. The Decade of the 1980s*, Washington, 1981; *Accelerated Development in Sub-Saharan Africa, op. cit.*; World Food Council of the United Nations. "The African Food Problem and the Role of International Agencies: Report of the Executive Director," Rome, February 22, 1982; and "Nairobi Conclusions and Recommendations of the African Ministers of Food and Agriculture at the World Food Council Regional Consultation for Africa," Nairobi, March 16-17, 1982

[12] Although the World Bank was a staunch advocate of basic needs strategies in the late 1970s it has recently abandoned its support for this dubious concept. Still the International Labor Office continues to confuse African states with recent basic needs missions to Zambia, Nigeria and Tanzania. Is it surprising that African states have so little faith in donors?

[13] For example, U.S. food aid to Mozambique was cut off six months in 1981. See David Anderson, "America in Africa, 1981," *Foreign Affairs, America and the World 1981*, pp. 658-85.

Debates About Africa's Future: the Brandt, World Bank and Lagos Plan blueprints

Timothy M. Shaw

Africa. . . must map out its own strategy for development and must vigorously pursue its implementation; Africa must cultivate the virtue of self-reliance.

Lagos Plan of Action[1]

Prospects for the future are alarming. . . But. . . a defensive reaction will be disastrous, as it was in the years before the Second World War. Since that time the nations of both the South and the North have become far more interdependent. . . The self-interest of nations can now only be effectively pursued through taking account of mutual interests.

North-South: a programme for survival[2]

Academics can, and will, find many flaws in the Brandt Report. However, it is the best Brandt Report we have; and it has got the essentials right. The probable alternative is dwindling North-South flows of trade and capital, leading to chronic slumpflation in the world economy. This will not be cured by chanting the monetarist mantras, whether at poor countries stricken by bad harvests and oil-price explosions, or nearer home. . . If Brandt is unimaginatively shelved, it is more likely that major defaults, starting in the South, will catalyse the Northern-OPEC 'world system' in a different way entirely. And monetarist Tweedledum, protectionist Tweedledee, and 'realist' Scrooge will all be eaten by the Monstrous Crow; and serve them right. But us? And the wretched of the earth?

Michael Lipton[3]

. . . projections by the World Bank's researchers. . . point to. . . an absolute worsening of circumstances for millions of Africans in the years ahead. That outlook simply must be improved!. . . It can be improved through better global economic conditions, through greater development assistance to Africa, through some new policy initiatives by some of the governments here, and by a greater involvement in this region by the World Bank. That greater involvement will demand a new era of more intense partnership between the peoples of Africa and the Bank.

A W Clausen[4]

The major danger is that the [IBRD] Report may well be used to lecture to Africa about its internal policy reforms without providing an increase in financial assistance. It will be very unfortunate if the foreign assistance recommendations of the Report fall through, which looks likely at the moment, and all that remains are generalisations and homilies about Africa's domestic problems.

Mahbub ul-Haq[5]

The current crisis of capitalism—a world system which apparently thrives on crisis and contradiction—appears to be unrelenting: the impacts on and implications for both rich and poor states are fundamental, particularly for the interrelated hard cores of both the OECD (Europe) and the Third World (Africa). The transformations which have occurred in the post-Bretton Woods (dis)order—inflation, recession, unemployment, debt, decay, *etc.*[6]—have already generated a new global hierarchy, in which NICs (Newly Industrialised

Originally published in <u>Third World Quarterly</u>, vol. 5, no. 2, April 1983; reprinted with permission.

or Influential Countries) feature prominently. It has also stimulated a novel global ideology, in which the Brandt Commission and related regional reports feature importantly.

This paper is concerned with the origins and orientations of the ensuing debates as well as with the diplomatic, political and economic forms to which they have given rise. It argues that the simplistic North-South divide overlooks salient divisions among and within countries, especially those in the EurAfrican group, which account for the variety of responses to the Brandt Report and related projections and presumptions.[7] In the post-neocolonial world of the 1980s, old assumptions about international economics and politics need to be discarded if the contemporary conjuncture is to be both understood and transcended.[8] Meanwhile, given the seemingly inescapable nature of the crisis, action is urgent; inaction merely serves to intensify inequalities and difficulties. As Richard Jolly and Susan Joekes argued in 1981:

The prospects for the 1980s in most of the poorer developing countries, but especially in Africa, are extremely dismal. In all these respects the position today, and the prognosis, look even more serious than when the Brandt Report was published a year ago.[9]

However, prospects for a few countries and classes in both Africa and Europe are considerably less bleak; hence the ambiguities of response and the artificialness of negotiation.

Introduction: the coexistence or contradiction of liberalism and protectionism

There now exists, then, a rather sombre consensus that the future developmental prospects for the continent in the post-Bretton Woods world are quite dismal.[10] Not that they were ever particularly bright. As the *Lagos Plan of Action*, the major statement of economic intent to emerge from Africa's landmark April 1980 economic summit, recognised:

. . . in the 20 years from 1960 to 1980 the average annual rate of growth continent wide has been no more than 4.8 per cent, a figure which hides divergent realities ranging from 7 per cent growth rate for the oil exporting countries down to 2.9 per cent for the least developed countries. Yet, if the world economic forecast for the next decade is to be believed, the overall poor performance of the African economy over the past 20 years may even be a golden age compared with future growth rate.[11]

Africa's unpromising future is, from a longer-term perspective, a function of its inheritance of incorporation in the world system: in the shorter term it is a product of the global crisis, which has had a particularly devastating and immediate impact on the continent as a whole. As the World Bank's own report in response to the African condition has indicated:

During the past two decades economic development has been slow in most of the countries of sub-Saharan Africa. When, in the mid-1970s, the world economy experienced inflation and recession, nowhere did the crisis hit with greater impact than in this region.[12]

If the *Lagos Plan of Action* and *Agenda for Action* were responses to the continental crisis, then the Brandt Commission can be conceived as a reaction at the level of policy and ideology to the global conjuncture. All three perspectives embodied projections as well as prescriptions and included implicit explanations of current situations; they also identified and mobilised particular constituencies. Although quite distinctive in terms of direction and association, they shared a sense of disquiet about present and projected development. The Brandt Commission captured the prevalent mood:

Current trends point to a sombre future for the world economy and international relations. . . The 1980s could witness even greater catastrophes than the 1930s.[13]

The character of the current crisis, even if not its origins, are now quite clear—recession with high levels of inflation and unemployment, along with increasing problems with debt and foreign exchange. But the impacts of the successive stages of the crisis have been uneven: in general, the rich, as usual, have been hurt less than the poor, within as well as between countries.

One major result has been that some industries and countries have now become quite marginal: rationalisation of production has confined some states and regions to the rubbish-heap of economic history. Discussions about cartels in chemicals and steel, and the decay of countries like Ghana or Chad are symptomatic. In the relatively optimistic post-war period it was generally assumed that most countries would, eventually, make it; now it is increasingly recognised that most will not, especially the 'late-comers' left stranded in Africa, Confidence in both projections and solutions are consequently very low; only a minority seems to have a future.

The trends towards rationalisation and marginalisation has produced a new set of hierarchies in the world system rather different from established colonial-style North-South distinctions. The essential difference lies between those states and industries in contraction ('the old') and those in expansion ('the new'); 'the old' include Britain and textiles in the North, and Senegal and sisal in the South, while 'the new' include Japan and microchips in the North, and Nigeria and petrochemicals in the South. Such specific changes have been collapsed into a general recognition of NICs, but in reality only a few classes, regions, and peoples are the beneficiaries: there is massive poverty, for instance, in Nigeria, despite its growth, while Britain's decline has remained slow enough to prevent widespread impoverishment.

The rise and fall of 'states'—the conventional shorthand term for dominant classes, industries and regions—is a continuing factor in the political economies of both OECD and ECA communities, as well as in relations between them such as EurAfrica. In the former, considerable attention is paid to rationalisation and restructuring—automobiles, energy, steel, textiles, *etc*.—while, in the latter, considerable effort is made to accelerate development through regional integration, typically centred on one or two NICs with their above-average potential.

In the OECD nexus, reports for the Club of Rome and the RIO Foundation, as well as more official scenarios and suggestions such as *Interfutures* and *Global 2000*, have attempted to respond to environmental and developmental demands as well as to widespread concern over economic recession. In the ECA grouping, such efforts at restructuring and crisis management in the North, combined with minimal or negative growth both of late and for the foreseeable future, have generated the *Lagos Plan of Action* as well as *Agenda for Action*. The Brandt Report in many respects stands as the apex of such activities: a global synthesis about the world's receding future, as Michael Lipton recognises in the opening quotation.

In general, the Brandt Commission can be taken to be reflective of 'internationalist' opinion—the revival of the world economy requires more and equal exchange—and has as its African counterpart the World Bank's *Agenda for Action*:

While the international system has become much more complicated, with more independent nations, more institutions and more centres of influence, it has also become much more interdependent. . . the achievement of economic growth in one country depends increasingly on the performance of others.[14]

By contrast, there is no single global projection which captures the spirit of the 'nationalists', Friedman economics notwithstanding; the essentially contradictory monetarist and protectionist impulses represented by conservative administrations in Washington and London are not based on any single statement. Yet, the *Lagos Plan of Action* does reflect such a spirit as it reveals itself in the African context—the protectionism of the poor:

. . . Africa is unable to point to any significant growth rate, or satisfactory index of general well-being, in the past 20 years. Faced with this situation, and determined to undertake measures for the basic restructuring of our continent, we resolve to adopt a far-reaching regional approach based primarily on collective self-reliance.[15]

There are, of course, significant differences between neo-mercantilism among the rich—protecting industries and jobs from other OECD members, rather than from threats from the Third World—and self-reliance among the poor-disengagement from a tradition of unequal exchange to secure a new basis for trade. Nevertheless, such protectionist impulses in both North and South are reflective of significant domestic pressures and are responsive to the internationalist proclivities of the Brandt Commission and its kind. If the motif of the latter is *interdependence*—'The self-interest of nations can now only be effectively pursued through taking account of mutual interests'[16]—that of the former, in both North and South, is *independence*, from dependence on foreign trade, technology, finance or values.

In general, then, the Brandt Commission's internationalism is closest to the Africa report of the World Bank, *Agenda for Action*, rather than the OAU's *Lagos Plan*. Like the *Agenda*, Brandt does not advocate national or collective self-reliance, or protectionism. Nevertheless, its internationalist impulses are moderated somewhat by its social democratic roots; so it recognises the superior claim of the South compared to that of the North to protectionism:

The South needs and wants to be more self-reliant, to complete the process of political independence. But that does not imply separation from the world economy.[17]

Likewise, there are limits to the nationalist proclivities of the *Lagos Plan of Action* given the continued incorporation of many OAU members and leaders in the world system:

. . . self-reliance. . . is not to say that the continent should totally cut itself off from outside contributions. However, these outside contributions should only supplement our own effort; they should not be the mainstay of our development.[18]

The national or continental self-interest advocated in protectionist schema stands, then, in contrast to the global or mutual interest preferred in interdependence scenarios. However, these alternative nationalist versus internationalist viewpoints do not readily correlate with the North-South divide: different 'national' class and corporate interests cut across such a simple division. There are, clearly, supporters of protectionism in the South as well as the North—the whole *dependencia* school is in some ways the precursor of neomercantilism— as well as advocates of further and fair exchange in the North. As Reginald Green has argued in relation to British responses to the Brandt Commission:

The support and opposition for the Brandt Report—or international structural change more generally—do not fit the simple division between capital and labour (or business and unions). Some businesses see profit in more trade and more aid. Those oriented to Third World markets and those dealing in Third World imports are examples. Inversely, firms affected by imports favour trade restrictions and put pressure on Third World sources in particular because they are seen as politically vulnerable (though calls for restrictions against socialist Europe, Japan and the USA are growing too).[19]

* * *

Nationalist Response: protectionism and self-reliance

For most African states and statesmen, the contemporary crisis is but a further manifestation of the problems of dependence. Africa as a whole never really benefited much from the 'Golden Age' of Bretton Woods. So, it hopes to turn the current conjuncture to advantage: an opportunity (suggested in the first opening quotation) to escape from established 'development' policies and plans. As Adebayo Adedeji, the catalyst behind the *Lagos Plan of Action*, has argued:

. . . the African economy today is the most open and the most exposed in the world, overly dependent on external trade and other external stimuli, foreign technology, and foreign expertise. The very strategies of development the African governments have been pursuing since independence have come from outside, derived as they were from theories of economic development that were developed during the colonial and neo-colonial periods to rationalise the colonial pattern of production in Africa. Not unexpectedly, these foreign theories of development and economic growth reinforce the economic dependence of Africa. . . The cumulative result is that, today, neither high rates of growth or diversification, nor an increasing measure of self-reliance and self-sustainment has been achieved in the African economy.[29]

The collective African response has been, then, to advocate disengagement as a precondition for development, the antithesis of the internationalists' vision.

Given past disappointments and unpromising trends based on present conditions, the *Lagos Plan of Action*, as indicated in the first opening citation, called for the cultivation of 'the virtue of self-reliance':

Africa's huge resources must be applied principally to meet the needs and purposes of its people; Africa's almost total reliance on the export of raw materials must change . . . Africa, therefore, must map out its own strategy for development and must vigorously pursue its implementation.[30]

A somewhat similar set of beliefs motivates protectionists in the North: if the old industrialised countries could only protect themselves against 'unfair' competition, then employment, production and profit would all revive, structural changes in the global economy notwithstanding. Such neo-mercantilism in the North has an ally, recognised or not, in the South: both self-reliance and protectionism seek to regulate and reduce the external exchange which the internationalists see as essential to global welfare. National (or fractional) interests are ranked above the collective; independence is preferred to interdependence.

The general nationalist versus internationalist debate has been joined with a vengeance in Africa over the virtues and intents of the *Lagos Plan of Action*. Before looking at this directly, however, I examine further the interdependence position as projected in the Brandt Commission as well as in the Bank Report.

Internationalist Response: mutual interest and interdependence

The neo-Keynesian response to Africa's crisis is to call for more, not less, aid, trade, technology, and investment. So *Agenda for Action* calls for more, rather than less, attention to agriculture, as well as for increased exports and rapid privatisation. The cause of underdevelopment is seen to be internal rather than external, inefficiency rather than market forces:

. . . agricultural output is the single most important determinant of overall economic growth, and its sluggish record in recent years is the principal factor underlying the poor economic performance of the countries of this region.[31]

To encourage a return to the land, as well as to orthodoxy, the Bank and Brandt both advocate increased aid, although the mobilisation of further public funds from foreign sources is likely to be problematic. Nevertheless, the Brandt Report calls for an immediate antihunger programme with most relevance to Africa and with the greatest likelihood of external 'humanitarian' support:

An action programme must be launched, comprising emergency and longer-term measures, to assist the poverty belts of Africa and Asia and particularly the least developed countries.[32]

Likewise, the Bank asserts that it has already mobilised increased internal and external resources for Africa: more officers, more projects, and more policy attention.[33]

In short, the internationalists would claim that they have readjusted policies, procedures, and priorities in response to the African crisis, despite protectionist and isolationist impulses amongst certain significant OECD donor states. Yet, although some African regimes and fractions would argue that the Bank and the interdependence coalition are not doing enough, many, as indicated in the final opening quotation from Mahbub ul-Haq, would assert that they are still intervening too much. The consensual OAU response, for instance, rejects the 'new' internationalism as the old dependence:

. . . the proposed outward-looking, external-oriented concept of development proposed for our countries in the [IBRD] report is indeed a suggestion that we continue to do what we have been doing all these years. The only difference is that we lose the independence to set our goals, adopt our strategy and determine our policies. Added to this is the glaring arrogant paternalism in the report with no concern shown for the need to increase the capacity of our countries to do in the near future what outsiders are doing for them now.[34]

The continuing African debate about the Bank's *Agenda for Action* and the OAU *Lagos Plan for Action* represents, in part and in microcosm, some of the major differences between internationalist and nationalist responses to the current crisis. In turn, the African response to the Bank is indicative of the continental reaction to Brandt: a new scepticism about the intentions and implications of apparently sympathetic internationalism. Is 'interdependence' a new cover for EurAfricanism—Africa's continued subjugation to EEC and OECD interests?

The African Debate: plan versus agenda

The critical African response (having already designed and sanctified its own continental plan for an African Economic Community by the year 2000) to the Bank's contrary report has implications not only at the levels of theory and policy, but also in terms of *praxis*. For, if one takes the Brandt Commission's position seriously—increased liquidity in the Third World is essential for the revival of production in the first—then any disinclination to reflate in Africa would have implications for prosperity in the OECD. The OAU/ECA rejection of *Agenda for Action* is, of course, on principle—it is the wrong scenario from the wrong source—yet the denial of internationalist ideas erodes their coalition's claims and prospects; it also serves to reduce their amount of support. Conversely, economic nationalism in the South may reinforce such pressures in the North. In short, the outcome of the African debate is of wider interest and impact.

As the continental dispute has already begun to receive such (deservedly) broader notice, I do not intend to rehearse the issues here.[35] Suffice to say that the two sides disagree fundamentally on the causes of and solutions for the current crisis. Ironically, the *Plan* blames external dependence and advocates internal selfreliance whereas the *Agenda* blames internal deficiencies and advocates external exchange. The former also prefers industry over agriculture; the latter encourages private rather than state enterprise. The OAU asserts that 'modernisation' can never produce development; the Bank argues that 'trickle-down' just requires more time, care and input.

The Africans essentially reject the *Agenda's* claims that it is compatible with and builds upon the *Plan*. But they are most angry about its 'new paternalism':

We are. . . concerned about the general tone of the report which tends to suggest that the region's problems are entirely of its own making and that unless outsiders are allowed to come in with aid and new policies, the crisis would get out of hand and the result would be catastrophic.[36]

Even the relatively conservative African governors of the Bank largely rejected the proposals of *Agenda for Action*. They were particularly regretful of its failure to recognise external causes, despite its emphasis on outward-oriented 'solutions'. Africa alone cannot be responsible for its own condition given that it 'imports' many of its difficulties:

. . . certain questions have not been dealt with in the World Bank report: problems such as the soaring of interest rates in the international financial markets, global negotiations with a view to establishing a new international economic order, and stabilisation of commodity prices.[37]

Although most African leaders have been well socialised and incorporated into the world system, they remain ambivalent over what they perceive to be their inadequate share of the benefits. They are also under increasing domestic pressure as recession intensifies, inflation increases, unemployment grows, peasants return to subsistence and foreign exchange becomes unavailable: the spectre of anarchy looms.[38] The *Lagos Plan of Action* may articulate, then, a common fear of decay and disorder which would threaten all fractions of the indigenous bourgeoisie, internationalist and nationalist alike.

Nevertheless, underneath the consensual adoption of the *Plan* certain country and corporate interests remain closely identified with the Bank: the more bourgeois states (the semi-periphery) and classes (the indigenous bourgeoisie, particularly in its *comprador* guise) continue to espouse orthodox *laissez-faire* perspectives. Hence the differences between, for instance, Sierra Leonean and Nigerian, Algerian and Black Francophone, IBRD Governors[39] as well as between more conservative and more progressive ministries. The NICs along with the 'technocrats' and '*compradores*' may move closer to the Bank and the OECD, while the least-developed countries along with more 'political' and 'national' elements will tend to espouse populist OAU values. Whilst the former, internationalist coalition stands to gain if the global recession eases, the latter, nationalist coalition may protect itself against further external depression and future foreign exploitation. Although the OAU *Plan* claims to represent an extension of African nationalist values from the political into the economic realm, in reality the cohesion which underlay the former in the 1950s can never be revived for the latter in the 1980s: differentiation within and between African (political) economies has gone too far, and the world system has evolved from a period of expansion into one of contraction.

Conclusion: the dialectics of depression

Despite the interrelated crises in the African condition and the global economy, resolution through either negotiation or fiat remains unlikely. In the post-Bretton Woods situation, no country, corporation, or coalition has sufficient dominance to enforce a solution. Moreover, no condition is permanent, so both major coalitions face the prospect of both gaining and losing support as the crisis continues to mature in a cyclical fashion. Therefore, a variety of alternative propositions will continue to be presented—reflective particularly of interdependence and dependence dogma—even if none of them ever achieves signal success. Over time, however, the essence of several different proposals may be reflected in sectoral or regional negotiations and resolutions.[40]

The appearance of diverse internationalist and nationalist coalitions, both in opposition to each other and with all their own intricacies and contradictions (e.g., Bank versus Brandt in the former, and protectionism versus self-reliance in the latter), is suggestive of a need to go beyond simple antinomies in both theory and practice. The world is no longer, if ever it was, North-South or rich-poor. Rather, each coalition picks up support from diverse sources within and between countries—the internationalists from both multinational corporations and consumer associations, the nationalists from old industries[41] and new entrepreneurs. Within both there is a continual tension between state and non-state actors[42], as well as within both types (e.g., France versus US[43] and corporations versus trade unions). Yet out of all the debate and discourse comes a clear call for innovative perspectives and policies: as Lipton's opening citation indicates, orthodox approaches are quite inappropriate for the post-Bretton Woods era.[44]

In addition to divergent origins, disparate associations and various tensions, these two coalitions can be situated within two distinct genres of ideas; they may also embody rather different time perspectives. The nationalist viewpoint is rather short-term and reactive, characteristic of traditional 'realist' thought. By contrast, the internationalist position is longer-term and more consistent, characteristic of the 'idealist' strand in international affairs. To be sure, both are considerable updates of more original and general positions which were hardly concerned with developmental issues; yet they do contain points of contact with schools of thought given their economic preoccupations. Such connections may be important in understanding their mutual reactions and antipathies and in explaining the powerful grip which they exert on some of their more committed advocates. As always, the existential crisis has deeper intellectual roots.

Conversely, every prescription is reflective of perceived interests whether these be country, class or corporate.[45] As Selwyn and others recognise, the notion of 'national' interest was inappropriate in the depression of the 1930s; it is even more misleading—a cover for hegemonic fractions, whether these are founded on bureaucratic, military or entrepreneurial formations—in the continuing crisis of capitalism in the 1980s. The need to go beyond declaration and diplomacy to the substructure of international affairs is so for Africa[46] as well as for Europe: 'internationalist' and 'nationalist' coalitions cut across established divides (of actors) and modes (of thought). We need to go beyond current debates and apparent positions to understand the character of the post-Bretton Woods order which, unlike NIEO, is already in the process of formation and foundation. Nineteen Eight-four marks the centenary of the Berlin Conference; it may also mark the beginning of a new age of 'divide and rule' in Africa. Colonialism and neocolonialism are past, but differentiation proceeds relentlessly, notwithstanding the idealistic schemes of nationalists and internationalists alike.

Notes

[1] OAU *Lagos Plan of Action for the Economic Development of Africa, 1980-2000*, Geneva: International Institute for Labour Studies, 1981, p 8.

[2] *North-South: a programme for survival. Report of the Independent Commission on International*

[3] *Development Issues ('Brandt Commission')* London: Pan, 1980, p 269. Michael Lipton 'Brandt: whose common interest?', *International Affairs* 56(2) April 1980, p 327.

[4] Alden W Clausen, 'Looking Towards a Brighter Future', West Africa (3378) 3 May 1982, p 1194. See also, 'Blunt Words from Clausen', *Africa Now* (14), June 1982, pp 94-5.

[5] 'World Bank "stagnant and confused", says former director' *Africa Now* (13) May 1982, p 89.

[6] For an overview of these, see Timothy M Shaw *Towards an International Political Economy for the 1980s: from dependence to (inter)dependence*, Halifax: Centre for Foreign Policy Studies, 1980.

[7] See Hans W Singer 'The British Government and the Brandt Report', *IDS Bulletin* ('Britain on Brandt') 12(2) April 1981, pp 39-41.

[8] see Dudley Seers, 'A Different Kind of Fortress Mentality', *Guardian Third World Review* (London) 16 July 1982, p 16.

[9] Richard Jolly and Susan Joekes, 'Editorial' *IDS Bulletin* 12(2) April 1981, p 1.

[10] See, *inter alia*, Timothy M Shaw (ed) *Alternative Futures for Africa*, Boulder Colorado: Westview, 1982.

[11] *Lagos Plan of Action*, pp 7-8.

[12] IBRD, Accelerated Development in Sub-Saharan Africa: an agenda for action (Washington DC, 1981) p 2.

[13] *Brandt Commission*, p 47.

[14] *ibid*. p 33.

[15] *Lagos Plan of Action*, p 5.

[16] *Brandt Commission*, p 269.

[17] *ibid*, p 42.

[18] *Lagos Plan of Action*, p 8.

[29] Adebayo Adedeji, 'Development and Economic Growth in Africa to the Year 2000: alternative projections and policies', in Timothy M Shaw (ed), *Alternative Futures for Africa op. cit*, p 281.

[30] *Lagos Plan of Action*, p 8.

[31] *Agenda for Action*, p 45.

[32] *Brandt Commission*, p 282.

[33] See 'On the record: Wapenhans on sub-Saharan Africa', *The Bank's World* 1(5) May 1982, pp 11-12, and A W Clausen, "Looking Towards a Brighter Future." *op. cit.*

[34] OAU, 'Report of the Secretary-General on the World Bank Report', (Council of Ministers 38th Ordinary Session, Addis Ababa), 23 February to 1 March 1982, CAU/1177 (xxxxviii), Appendix II, p 3.

[35] See, for instance, Charles Harvey 'Accelerated Development in Sub-Saharan Africa: review article' in Colin Legum (ed), *Africa Contemporary Record: annual survey of events and documents, Volume 14, 1981-82*, New York: Africana, 1982; 'What the World Bank Didn't Say' and 'World Economy: Africans respond to World Bank study', *Africa News* 18(19) 10 May 1982, pp 2, 3 and 11; 'Berg Report Gets Hesitant Welcome', *Africa Now* (14), June 1982, pp 94-5; and Timothy M Shaw 'OAU: the forgotten economic debate', *West Africa* (3375), 12 April 1982, pp 983-4.

[36] 'Report of the Secretary-General on the World Bank report' *op. cit.*, Appendix II, p 1.

[37] 'World Economy: Africans respond to World Bank study', *op. cit.*, p 2.

[38] See Timothy M Shaw, 'Beyond Underdevelopment: the anarchic state in Africa', *African Studies Association*, Washington DC, November 1982.

[39] See Timothy M Shaw, *Which Way Africa: ECA and IBRD responses to the continental crisis*, Uppsala: Scandinavian Institute of African Studies, 1982, and 'Berg Report Gets Hesitant Welcome,' *op. cit.*

[40] For further overviews, see Timothy M Shaw, 'The African Condition: prophecies and possibilities', *Year Book of World Affairs*, London: Stevens, 1982, vol: 36, pp 139-50, and 'From Dependence to Self-reliance: Africa's prospects for the next twenty years', *International Journal* 35(4) Autumn 1980, pp 821-44.

[41] On the case of textiles in the Ivory Coast and Kenya, and their ambiguous relations with European 'parent' corporations, see chapters by Lynn K Mytelka and Steven Langdon in Timothy M Shaw and Olajide Aluko (eds) *Africa Projected: from dependence to self-reliance by the year 2000*, London: Macmillan, 1983.

[42] See Timothy M Shaw, 'Unconventional Conflict in Africa: nuclear, class and guerrilla struggles', *Jerusalem Journal of International Relations* (forthcoming).

[43] For a sensitive overview of Great Power competition see Arthur Gavshon, *Crisis in Africa*, Harmondsworth: Penguin, 1982.

[44] See Wilfred A Ndongko and Sunday O Anyang, 'The political Economy of International Relations and Third World Economic Development', *Jerusalem Journal of International Relations* 5(1) 1980, pp 1-26.

[45] For a thoughtful critical view of North-South which situates the Commission in terms of theory and political economy, see William D Graf 'Anti-Brandt: a critique of Northwestern prescriptions for world order', in *Socialist Register, 1981*, London: Merlin, 1981 pp 20-45.

[46] For earlier pleas for such critical analysis, see Timothy M Shaw 'Review Article: Foreign policy, political economy and the future: reflections on Africa in the world system', *African Affairs* 79(315) April 1980, pp 260-8, and 'Class, Country and Corporation: Africa in the capitalist world system', in Donald I Ray *et al* (eds) *Into the 1980s: proceedings of the 11th annual conference of the Canadian Association of African Studies*, Vancouver: Tantalus, 1981 vol. 2, pp 19-37.

Chapter 11

Asia and the Pacific:
Challenge and Opportunity

Introduction

During the past decade Asia and the Pacific Rim countries have become "glamorous"; in the United States and Canada, they have received a great deal of attention and collectively have come to represent what has been termed the Pacific challenge.

This challenge is led by Japan, which is technologically advanced and appears to be setting the agenda for international technological developments, especially in export-led growth, in the 1980s and into the 1990s. The Asian NICs—South Korea, Singapore, Taiwan and Hong Kong—are not far behind. In fact, in many highly-competitive manufactures, both of mid-level technology (such as textiles, mechanical machinery and automobiles), and high-technology production (such as home entertainment electronic goods and computers, *and* ship-building), they are competing with Japan in the First World markets. In addition, both Japan and the Asian NICs are also opening up markets in other Pacific Rim countries as they introduce competitive merchandising and new production systems to them. In some respects, one could even say that the East Asian Greater Co-Prosperity Sphere envisaged by the imperialist Japanese in the 1930s has today become an economic reality, with the important difference that the Japanese economic domination appears to lead very quickly to raising the Asian partners to worthy competitors.

But there is yet another challenge in Asia—that of China, opened up to the United States by President Nixon in the early 1970s and quickly developed by the Japanese as a consumer market.

The Asian and Pacific Rim countries provide both an opportunity and a challenge. An opportunity, in that new markets in which Western high-technology goods from the United States, Canada and Western Europe can compete as a result of economic development and internal generation of wealth. A challenge, in the sense that the rising, or new in the case of China, competitive manufacturing capability is invading our Western markets, at home as well as abroad. To meet this challenge simply by raising barriers to competitive foreign goods is not only politically short-sighted but economically destructive. For, after all, it was the United States which through two decades, carefully led and nurtured the Japanese miracle. In other words, that which we are seeing in the Pacific is the contemporary flowering of the entrepreneurial spirit of liberal economics.

The articles in this chapter explore the origins and development of the Pacific form of Western entrepreneurship. The examination does not lead to complacency about the success of transplanting Western entrepreneurship.

Cumings, in his article, reviews the three success stories of the Pacific Rim, Japan, Korea, and Taiwan. He demonstrates the shaping and conditioning effects of economic forces on three distinct societies and the effects of industrial product cycles on the regional political economy. All three have come to develop similar economic structures and all three have adopted similar political models and roles for the state. He also argues that industrial development in the three cannot be considered as an individual country phenomenon but that it is a regional one in which a tripartite hierarchy of core, semi-periphery and periphery was created in the first part of the 20th century and then slowly recreated after the Second World War. He notes that developments in the three differ considerably but are nevertheless similar. He also suggests that a hegemonic system is necessary for the functioning of this regional political economy—unilateral colonialism until 1945 and American hegemony since then. Today, however, the Japanese are competing with the Americans for hegemony over "semi-peripheral" Taiwan and South Korea as well as the rest of the area. The question that he ends with is: "Can Americans live at peace with a formidable Japan?"

In the third article here, DeWolfe describes the economic reform that has recently taken place in China both in agriculture and industry, and that is leading to a rapid rate of economic development, especially in the rural areas.

The last article in the chapter, by Stuart L. Smith, provides a brief, hortatory overview of what Canada can do to meet the Pacific economic challenge in redirecting its industry to compete with the Japanese-led Pacific Rim countries.

The Origins and Development of the Northeast Asian Political Economy: Industrial Sectors, Product Cycles and Political Consequences

Bruce Cumings

East Asia today is the center of world economic dynamism. Japan in 1980 became number two in the world in gross national product (GNP). Its achievement is complemented by the "gang of four," South Korea, Taiwan, Singapore, and Hong Kong. These four East Asian developing countries now account for almost twice the export totals of the entire remainder of the Third World, and their growth rates are usually the highest in the entire world. Singapore and Hong Kong are difficult to categorize: are they nations? industrial platforms? city-states? My concern in this article will be with the northeastern portion of the East Asian basin: Japan, Korea, and Taiwan.

These four nations (including the two Koreas) in 1978, before the second oil shock, accounted for a combined GNP of about $ 1.06 trillion, a population of 190 million, an annual growth rate of 10 percent, and perhaps $232 billion of world trade. This compared to a U.S. GNP in 1978 of about $2 trillion, a population of 218 million, a growth rate of 4 percent, and world trade of $326 billion. Apart from the United States, no other region had a higher GNP—the combined GNP of the European Economic Community in 1978 was $ 1.95 trillion, less than double the Northeast Asian figure, and the average growth rate in the EEC was 2.9 percent. The Soviet Union had a larger population but a lower GNP, and a growth rate estimated at 3.1 percent.

Since the onset of export-led growth in the mid 1960s the GNPs of both Taiwan and South Korea have grown by an average of about 10 percent per year, with manufacturing expansion often doubling that figure. North Korea, according to official statistics, had the highest rate of agricultural growth in the entire world in the period 1970-78, and since the Korean War its industrial production has grown at the highest rate in the socialist world.[1] In the space of one generation these countries have transformed their economic structures such that the agrarian sector, including upwards of 60 percent of the population in 1960, now accounts for less than 20 percent of GNP. It is little wonder that American developmentalists speak of miracles in Taiwan and South Korea, or that socialist economists like Joan Robinson speak of a miracle in North Korea. For reasons of space, however, I shall limit this analysis primarily to South Korea and Taiwan.

A glance back before World War II suggests that we may need a longer perspective to capture the true dimensions of this growth. Japan's interwar annual growth rate of 4.5 percent doubled the rates of interwar Europe; colonial manufacturing growth in Korea, 1910-1940, averaged 10 percent per annum, and overall GNP growth was also in the 4 percent

Published with the permission of the author and MIT Press; article originally published in *International Organization*, vol. 38, no. 1, Winter 1984.

range, as was Taiwan's. No nation's heavy-industrial growth rate was steeper than Japan's in the period 1931-1940; in the textile sector, Japan's automation was ahead of Europe's in 1930. Yet new research now suggests that both Korea and Taiwan experienced higher GDP growth rates than Japan between 1911 and 1938 (Japan, 3.36%; Korea, 3.57%; Taiwan, 3.80%).[2]

In the past century Japan, Korea, and Taiwan have also moved fluidly through a classic product-cycle industrialization pattern, Korea and Taiwan following in Japan's wake. Japan's industrialization has gone through three phases, the last of which is just beginning. The first phase began in the 1880s, with textiles the leading sector, and lasted through Japan's rise to world power. In the mid 1930s Japan began the second, heavy phase, based on steel, chemicals, armaments, and ultimately automobiles; it did not begin to end until the mid 1960s. The third phase emphasizes high-technology "knowledge" industries such as electronics, communications, computers, and silicon-chip microprocessors.

Within Japan each phase, in good product-cycle fashion, has been marked by strong state protection for nascent industries, adoption of foreign technologies, and comparative advantages deriving from cheap labor costs, technological innovation, and "lateness" in world time. Each phase involved a bursting forth into the world market that always struck foreign observers as abrupt and unexpected, thus inspiring fear and loathing, awe and admiration.

For Japan the product cycle has not been mere theory; it has melded with conscious practice to make Japan the preeminent example of upward mobility in the world system through successive waves of industrial competition. In the 1930s Kaname Akamatsu elaborated his famous "flying geese" model of industrial development in follower countries, predating Raymond Vernon's work by several decades.[3] Time-series curves for imports, import-substitution for the domestic market, and subsequent exports of given products tend to form a pattern like wild geese flying in ranks. The cycle in given industries—textiles, steel, automobiles, light electronics—of origin, rise, apogee, and decline has not simply been marked, but often mastered, in Japan; in each industrial life cycle there is also an appropriate jumping off place, that is, a point at which it pays to let others make the product or at least provide the labor. Taiwan and Korea have historically been receptacles for declining Japanese industries. Adding agriculture gives a pattern in which in the first quarter of this century Korea and Taiwan substituted for the diminishing Japanese agricultural sector, exporting rice and sugar in great amounts to the mother country (Taiwan was annexed in 1895, Korea in 1910). By the mid 1930s Japan had begun to export iron and steel, chemical, and electric-generation industries, although much more to Korea than to Taiwan. In the 1960s and 1970s, both smaller countries have received declining textile and consumer electronic industries from Japan (as well as from the United States), and in the 1980s some Japanese once again speak of sending steel and autos in the same direction.

Thus if there has been a miracle in East Asia, it has not occurred just since 1960; it would be profoundly ahistorical to think that it did. Furthermore, it is misleading to assess the industrialization pattern in any one of these countries: such an approach misses, through a fallacy of disaggregation, the fundamental unity and integrity of the regional effort in this century. Yet ahistorical disaggregation is the most common approach; it is reinforced by the many differences between the three countries, and by the dominant modernization school in U.S. academic circles, which has produced by far the greatest quantity of literature on East Asian development. The three countries speak different languages, have different histories, different cultures (albeit all traditionally influenced by China), and, in Korea and Japan, two highly homogeneous but quite different ethnic constituencies. Modernization theory and these basic differences have reinforced a tendency, at least since 1945, to view each country apart from the others and to examine single-country trajectories. Furthermore, critical and radical (or nonmodernization) developmentalists have tended to ignore East Asia, focusing instead on Latin America and Africa. Those that do study East Asia usually study the Chinese revolution, which produced many things but not stunning industrial development.

A country-by-country approach is incapable of accounting for the remarkably similar trajectories of Korea and Taiwan. Thus, specialists on Korea argue that its development success "is unique in world history";[4] Taiwan specialists make similar claims. Thus, Taiwan specialists cite the apparent "paradox" of Taiwanese development—that it developed in a fashion that contradicts the assumptions of dependency theorists—while not breathing a word about Korea.[5] Both groups of specialists omit the essential Japanese context of Korean and Taiwanese development. Conventional neoclassical economists attribute growth in Taiwan or Korea to specific attributes of each nation: factor endowments, human capital in the form of a reasonably educated workforce, comparative advantage in labor cost, and so on. Modernization theorists offer a diffuse menu of explanations for Taiwan or Korea, ranging from the discipline or "rationality" of traditional Confucianism, through various cultural arguments, the passion for education, U.S. aid and advice, and the presumed "natural" workings of the product cycle, to the diffusion of advanced education, science, and technology.[6] Political arguments about the alleged big power of small states, while addressing one facet of East Asian political development, beg the question why Korea and Taiwan but not Guatemala or Burma. Product-cycle arguments, unlike the others, do have the virtue of linking Japanese with Korean and Taiwanese development, but their proponents do not explain why the cycle has conformed to theory in Northeast Asia so much better than elsewhere.

This article asserts that an understanding of the Northeast Asian political economy can only emerge from an approach that posits the systemic interaction of each country with the others, and of the region with the world at large. Rapid upward mobility in the world economy has occurred, through the product cycle and other means, within the context of two hegemonic systems: the Japanese imperium to 1945, and intense, if diffuse, American hegemony since the late 1940s. Furthermore, only considerations of context can account for the similarities in the Taiwanese and South Korean political economies. Simultaneously, external hegemonic forces have interacted with different domestic societies in Korea and Taiwan to produce rather different political outcomes: this, too, has been characteristic throughout the century. Korea was more rebellious in 1910; it is more rebellious today. I seek, therefore, to explain both the similarities in economic development and the differences in political consequences in the three countries.

Some theoretical consideration

The concept of the product cycle offers a useful way to understand change and mobility within and among nations. This theory of the middle range has the virtue of being compatible with liberal, neomercantile, and Marxist or world system theories. That is, the neoclassical liberal can make the Ricardian assumption that a system of open exchange (free trade) provides the structure in which nations maximize their comparative advantages and thus create a world-ranging and mutually beneficial division of labor. The mercantilist can make the Listian assumption that free trade is the ideology of the early-arriving hegemonic nation, and that to catch up the follower nation needs not laissez-faire but a strong state, not open systems but protectionist barriers. For a world system analyst the product cycle is one among several means of upward and downward mobility; the core assumption is the existence of a capitalist world economy that, at least in our time, is the only world-ranging system. Thus, the core power pursues an imperialism of free trade, and rising powers use strong states, protectionist barriers, or a period of withdrawal and self-reliant development (the Stalinist or socialist option) as means to compete within the world system.[7]

All three theories assume that the product cycle is a middle-range explanation for the waxing and waning of industrial sectors, and that it is embedded in some larger structure—and international division of labor or a world economy. All likewise assume intense competition—a race—for development; nations swim upstream, against the current, or are carried backward. Both Liberal and Marxist theory postulate a utopia to end the struggle: a world of free trade and the greatest good for the greatest number, or societies submitted to a rational plan under a world socialist government. Mercantilists are content to postulate a survival of the fittest, by whatever means necessary.

The world system perspective posits a tripartite division of the globe: core, semiperiphery, and periphery. A tripartite hierarchy appeals to many analysts: Aristotle was the first to note the social stability provided by a broad middle class, and Charles Kindleberger pointed out many years ago that in a hierarchy of top, middle, and low the middle functions "to discipline the third member in forms of behavior which he should adopt toward the first. The relations of the middle class to the wealthy and to the working classes may partake of this character. . ."[8]

Immanuel Wallerstein, a sociologist by academic origin, casts onto the global system the classic role of the middle class in providing social stability, disciplining and mediating those below to serve the interests of those above, and being an agency of change, through class or individual social mobility.[9] This is the role for the semiperiphery in the world; the means of upward mobility are wars, diplomacy, alliances, product cycles, and so on.[10]

What about the "world upper class," or core? I use the term *hegemony* to refer to core-state behavior. By hegemony I do not mean the Gramscian notion of class ethos, nor a crude Marxist notion of ruling class or imperial domination, nor the diffuse contemporary Chinese usage, referring to big-power domination in all its manifestations. Nor do I use it in Robert Keohane and Joseph Nye's sense "in which one state is able and willing to determine and maintain the essential rules by which relations among states are governed."[11] I mean by hegemony the demarcation of outer limits in economics, politics, and international security relationships, the transgression of which carries grave risks for any nonhegemonic nation.

In the postwar American case, hegemony meant the demarcation of a "grand area."[12] Within that area nations oriented themselves toward Washington rather than Moscow, nations were enmeshed in a hierarchy of economic and political preferences whose ideal goal was free trade, open systems, and liberal democracy but which also encompassed neomercantile states and authoritarian politics; and nations were dealt with by the United States through methods ranging from classic negotiations and trade-offs (in regard to nations sharing Western traditions or approximating American levels of political and economic development) to wars and interventions (in the periphery or Third World), to assure continuing orientation toward Washington. The hegemonic ideology, shared by most Americans but by a few in the rest of the world, was the Tocquevillean or Hartzian ethos of liberalism and internationalism, assuming a born-free country that never knew class conflict. Not a colonial or neocolonial imperialism, it was a new system of empire begun with Wilson and consummated by Roosevelt and Acheson. Its very breadth—its nonterritoriality, its universalism, and its open systems (within the grand area)—made for a style of hegemony that was more open than previous imperialisms to competition from below. Indeed, we may eventually conclude that this was its undoing.

This form of hegemony establishes a hierarchy of nations, therefore, but but not one that is frozen: it may render obsolescent the development of underdevelopment. Instead, far more than the German hegemony of Eastern Europe that Albert Hirschman analyzed of the Japanese unilateral, colonial hegemony, it is open to rising talent from below and particularly to disparities of attention (what Burke, speaking of England and the American colonial revolution, called "wise and salutary neglect") that give leverage and room for maneuver to dependencies. As Hirschman put it more recently, the dependent country "is more likely to pursue its escape from domination more actively and energetically than the dominant country will work on preventing this escape."[13] Finally, this form of hegemony also fused security and economic considerations so inextricably that the United States has never been sure whether economic competition from its allies is good or bad for grand-area security. As a result, inattention often becomes catatonia (witness U.S. policy toward Japan in the past decade). A diffuse hegemony, then, it perhaps merits a diffuse definition: we know it in the doing, and we mark it more in retrospect. American postwar hegemony grew less out of specific human design (although Dean Acheson as architect would come close) than out of the long-term reactions of hegemonic interests to the flow of events.

These various terms and concepts are applicable to the international system. But Kindleberger notes in a seminal paper that foreign-policy actions and reactions are embedded "deep in the structure of society." In one nation (e.g., Germany) class may be important in understanding foreign economic policy; in another (e.g., Britain) it may not.[14] Likewise, in nations the state may be strong or weak, and empirical investigation suggests that this bears little relationship to Wallerstein's strained argument that state power recedes as one climbs down the hierarchy from core to periphery. In Japan, Taiwan, and Korea, much of their success and their variance from one another may be explained by reference to state and society. For the strength of states, we can use Alexander Gerschenkron's sequencing argument and Stephen Krasner's simple scheme: strong states can formulate policy goals independently of particular groups, they can change group or class behavior, and they can change the structure of society.[15] (After all the inflated verbiage, this is fundamentally what Nicos Poulantzas had in mind when he referred to the "relative autonomy" of capitalist states.)[16] Japan, as Krasner notes, rates very strong on this scale; so, in the later periods, do South Korea and Taiwan. Indeed, these three strong states go far toward explaining their product-cycle virtuosity.

Finally, there is society, by which I mean both the conventional notion of a system structured by groups and classes and Karl Polyani's sense of society being the human web that reacts to market penetration, capitalist relations, and industrialization in varying but always critical ways around the globe.[17] Attention to society and its reactions can avoid the reductionism of some Wallersteinians who place inordinate emphases on the structuring effect of the world system on national societies, as if they are putty to be shaped and molded. In fact, in the Northeast Asian case the three different societies deeply affect the development of the national and regional political economies.

The origin of the Northeast Asian political economy, 1900-1945

However much it may pain the majority of Korean nationalists and the minority of Taiwanese nationalists, the place to begin in comprehending the region's economic dynamism is with the advent of Japanese imperialism. Japan's imperial experience differed from the West's in several fundamental respects.[18] It involved the colonization of contiguous territory; it involved the location of industry and an infrastructure of communications and transportation in the colonies, bringing industry to the labor and raw materials rather than vice versa; and it was accomplished by a country that always saw itself as *dis*advantaged and threatened by more advanced countries—Japan was "weak and puny," Professor Etō Shinkichi has written, and this perception affected the entire colonial enterprise. All of these characteristics made themselves felt most strongly in Korea, the closest and always the most important of Japan's possessions.

Japan entered upon colonization late, in a world with hundreds of years of colonial experience and where, as King Leopold of Belgium said three years before the Meiji Restoration, "the world has been pretty well pillaged already." Most of the good colonial territories were already spoken for; indeed, for several decades Japan faced the possibility of becoming a dependency, perhaps even a colony, of one of the Western powers. With imperial attention mostly focused on China and its putative vast market, however, Japan got what E. H. Norman called a "breathing space" in which to mobilize its resources and resist the West. Its success was manifest in victories over China and Russia within the decade 1895 to 1905, but that should blind us neither to Japan's perception of its position as poised between autonomy and dependency in a highly competitive world system nor to the very real threats posed by the West. While the British and the Americans marveled at Japanese industrial and military prowess at the turn of the century, the Kaiser sent his famous "yellow peril" mural to the Tsar and the French worried about Japanese skills being tied to a vast pool of Chinese labor, posing a dire threat to the West. In such circumstances the Japanese were hardly prone to worry about the sensitivities of Taiwanese or Koreans but rather to see them as resources to be deployed in a global struggle; and, of course, Japan never lacked for Westerners (including socialists like Sydney and Beatrice Webb, and hardy Americans like Theodore Roosevelt) who were quick to justify Japanese aggression. [19]

The relative lateness of the endeavor imparted several additional characteristics: first, a posthaste, anticipatory quality in colonial planning; second, an extraordinary interest in and mimicking of previous colonial experience; third, a rather quick anachronism to the whole enterprise; last, little choice but to colonize contiguous neighbors.

Many have spoken of Japan's defensive reform and industrialization after 1868; and so it was with Japan's colonial expansion—offensive to Taiwanese and Koreans, it looked defensive to Japanese planners in a predatory world. And, much like reform at home, the colonial effort had an anticipatory, preconceived, planned aspect. The characteristic figure in this architectonic endeavor was therefore not an adventurous Cecil Rhodes type but an administrator and planner like Goto Shimpei, who played the architect in the Taiwan colony.

Like MITI in the Japanese economy today, the colonizers exercised sharp "administrative guidance" in shaping colonial society. These planners would both mimic the West and seek to avoid its errors. Thus, Ito Hirobumi discovered the secret of the German state, colonial administrators studied French policies of assimilation, architects designed railroad stations in the classic style for Seoul and Taipei. When Europeans witnessed Japanese behavior, they were looking into a mirror of their own behavior.

There was also something anachronistic about Japanese imperialism, perhaps not in the seizure of Taiwan but certainly by 1910 with Korea, and a fortiori 1931 with Manchuria. Japan since the 1880s has always seemed in some vague way to be about twenty years behind European and American developments, and therefore to be persisting in the lathered pursuit of things the West was tiring of; today, for example, an automobile boom runs in Japan some two decades after the boom began ending in the United States. By 1910 strong anti-imperialist movements had developed in England and the United States, and shortly thereafter Woodrow Wilson was not only calling for self-determination in colonies but pursuing an American neoimperialism that envisioned organizing great spaces in the world for free trade and competition, thereby branding the exclusive possession of colonial territory as outmoded or immoral, or both. Another great power, Russia, emerged from World War I with an equally potent idea: self-determination and national revolution for colonial peoples. Wilson and Lenin both changed the rules of the game for latecomers like Japan. The swashbuckling, sword-carrying colonist suddenly looked like a museum exhibit to the modern world that Japan took as its constant reference after 1868. Thus, seeking to anticipate every eventuality, Japan met an unanticipated consequence: progressives proclaimed Japan to be a backward exemplar of 19th century ideas.

In order to acquire colonies in the first place, Japan had to maximize its comparative advantages by seeking territory close to home. The West, always stretched in East Asia, could in judo-like fashion be dispatched in the near reaches of Japan. Thus, unlike most colonial powers Japan colonized neighbouring countries, making feasible a close, tight integration of colony to metropole. Contiguity also facilitated the settling of colonial migrants, especially from among an insular, homogeneous people who abhor distance from the native source, and could raise the potential of extraordinarily rapid exchange-time in market relations. Japan quickly enhanced this potential through laying railroads, opening ports, and making heavy investments in communications.

Lateral expansion also meant that Japan preferred the military, in the form of a land army resident in the colony, as its coercive force—not a navy or a tiny cadre of colonial ministers, à la Britain. As Hannah Arendt once suggested, lateral imperialism is usually more repressive, and this was true of Japanese colonialism.

In Korea and Taiwan the colonial power emphasized not only military and police forms of control but also development under strong-state auspices. This was particularly true after the Depression, when Japan used a "mighty trio" of state organization, central banking, and *zaibatsu* conglomerates to industrialize Korea and parts of Manchuria. Although strong in both colonies, the state in Korea bulked even larger in the economy than in Taiwan, as figures on government capital formation show.[20] Much like its role in the decades after the Meiji Restoration, the state substituted for an absent or at most incipient entrepreneurial class. As David Landes writes of Japan,

It was the State that conceived modernization as a goal and industrialization as a means, that gave birth to the new economy in haste and pushed it unrelentingly as an ambitious mother her child prodigy. And though the child grew and developed its own resources, it never overcame the deformity imposed by this forced nurture.[21]

The deformations were even more marked in Korea and Taiwan, where the colonial state stood above and apart from societies that had not yet reached Japan's level of social, political, and economic development. Thus, a highly articulated, disciplined, penetrating colonial bureaucracy substituted both for the traditional regimes and for indigenous groups and classes that under "normal" conditions would have accomplished development themselves. The colonial state replaced an old weak state, holding society at bay so to speak; this experience goes a long way toward explaining the subsequent (post 1945) pronounced centralization of Taiwan and both Koreas, and has provided a model for state-directed development in all three.

Japan's administrative and coercive colonialism took two quite different societies and political economies, and molded them into look-alikes.[22] The first act was a major cadastral survey and land reform; 1898-1906 in Taiwan, 1910-18 in Korea. North-South trunk railroad lines were laid. Ports were opened. In Taiwan, cane sugar and to a lesser extent rice were promoted; by 1938 Taiwan was second only to Cuba in sugar exports. Korean rice exports expanded by leaps and bounds in the 1920s. Yet agricultural growth was stronger in Taiwan than in Korea; colonial administrators remarked that what could be done with economic incentives in Taiwan required coercion in Korea.

Here we have our first important societal reaction to hegemonic penetration. Whereas Taiwan had for the most part only an aboriginal population until the 18th century, and a small class of Chinese absentee landlords by the end of the 19th century (the ta-tsu-hu), Korea had a powerful landed class of centuries' duration, in which property holding and aristocratic privilege were potently mixed.[23] The Japanese found it expedient to root landlords more firmly to the ground, as a means of disciplining peasants and extracting rice for the export market. The landlord class therefore persisted through to 1945, although by then it was tainted by association with imperial rule. In Taiwan, by contrast, land reform at the turn of the century eliminated absentee lords and fostered a class of entrepreneurial landowners, emerging "from below as they had in Japan. By 1945 most Taiwan landowners held less land than their Korean counterparts and were far more productive. Whereas tenancy increased markedly in Korea, it actually decreased in Taiwan between 1910 and 1941. Samuel Ho has concluded that by 1945 agriculture in Taiwan was quite scientific, and change had occurred "without disrupting the traditional system of peasant cultivation."[24] Korea, on the other hand, had frequent peasant protests and rebellions, guerrilla movements in the border region, and above all a huge population movement off the land that severely disrupted the agrarian political economy.[25] In other words, Korea betrayed most of the features associated with colonial underdevelopment, Taiwan did not. It may be that the very existence of Korea, and subsequently Manchukuo, gave Taiwan its own "breathing space" within the regional imperium. In any case, its experience did not conform to the predictions of dependency theorists. And, of course, Taiwan produced a weak nationalist impulse, Korea an extraordinarily strong one.

In the 1930s Japan largely withdrew from the world system and pursued, with its colonies, a self-reliant, go-it-alone path to development that not only generated remarkably high industrial growth rates but changed the face of Northeast Asia. In this decade what we might call the "natural economy" of the region was created; although it was not natural, its rational division of labor and set of possibilities have skewed East Asian development ever since. Furthermore, during this period, Japan elaborated many of the features of the neomercantile state still seen today. One prescient writer in the mid 1930s speculated that Japan's heavy industrialization spurt was so impressive that "if world trade were not restricted by tariff walls and import quotas. . . Japan might become the largest exporter in the world—and in a very short time." Guenther Stein saw in this spurt "the beginning of a new epoch in the industrialization of the world."[26] He was right on both counts. (This is not the usual dating: the watershed years of 1945-50 are presumed to have remade Japan, but, as we shall see, they did not.)

The definitive work by Kazushi Ohkawa and Henry Rosovsky sees two "long swings" of Japanese industrial growth in this century, one in the 1930s and the other in the post 1955 period; the first was only marginally less successful. The 1930s' development rested on the "two sturdy legs" of cheap labor and "a great inflow of technology," followed by massive state investments or subsidies to zaibatsu investors. Exports were still mostly "light," mainly textiles; but iron and steel, chemicals, hydroelectric power, aluminum, and infrastructure (transport and communications) grew markedly in the imperium.[27] What is so often forgotten is that this spurt located industry in the colonies as well.

Japan is among the very few imperial powers to leave located modern heavy industry in its colonies: steel, chemicals, hydroelectric facilities in Korea and Manchuria, and automobile production for a time in the latter. Even today, China's industry remains skewed toward the Northeast, and North Korea has always had a relatively advanced industrial structure. Samuel Ho remarks that, by the end of the colonial period, Taiwan "had an industrial superstructure to provide a strong foundation for future industrialization"; the main industries were hydroelectric, metallurgy (especially aluminum), chemicals, and an advanced transport system. By 1941, factory employment, including mining, stood at 181,000 in Taiwan. Manufacturing grew at an annual average rate of about 8 percent during the 1930s.[28]

Industrial development was much greater in Korea, perhaps because of the relative failure of agrarian growth compared to Taiwan but certainly because of Korea's closeness both to Japan and to the Chinese hinterland. By 1940, 213,000 Koreans were working in industry, excluding miners, and not counting the hundreds of thousands of Koreans who migrated to factory or mine work in Japan proper and in Manchuria. Net value of mining and manufacturing grew by 266 percent between 1929 and 1941.[29] By 1945 Korea had an industrial infrastructure that, although sharply skewed toward metropolitan interests, was among the best developed in the Third World. Furthermore, both Korea and Taiwan had begun to take on semiperipheral characteristics. Korea's developing periphery was Manchuria, where it sent workers, merchants, soldiers, and bureaucrats who occupied a middle position between Japanese overlords and Chinese peasants; as Korean rice was shipped to Japan, millet was imported from Manchuria to feed Korean peasants in a classic core-semiperiphery-periphery relationship. As for Taiwan, its geographic proximity to Southeast Asia and South China made it "a natural location for processing certain raw materials brought in from, and for producing some manufactured goods for export to, these areas."[30]

The Japanese managed all this by combining a handful of zaibatsu, several big banks, and the colonial state structures. They also foisted upon Koreans and Taiwanese an ideology of incorporation emphasizing a structural family principle and an ethical filiality: the imperium was one (not-so) happy family with Emperor Hirohito as the father. Although the colonized peoples (especially Koreans) remember this period with intense loathing—the forced Emperor worship, the alien Shinto beliefs, the requirement to speak Japanese and take Japanese names—the fact remains that as Taiwan and Korea have industrialized in the postwar period they have fostered *zaibatsu*-like conglomerates, with extensive family inter-penetration, and ideologies of familial hierarchy and filial loyalty (the "New Life" movement in Taiwan, the "New Spirit" movement in 1970s South Korea, a corporate familism in North Korea). [31]

Although Taiwan seemed to emerge from the last phase of colonialism relatively unscathed, with few disruptions, Korea was profoundly transformed. The period from 1935 to 1945 was when Korea's industrial revolution began, with most of the usual characteristics: uprooting of peasants from the land, the emergence of a working class, widespread population mobility, and urbanization. Because the Japanese industrialized from above, however, social change accompanying this revolution was greatest in the lower reaches of society. The social and regional conflicts that racked Korea in the 1945-53 period have their origins in the immense population shifts, agrarian disruptions, and industrial dynamism of the final phase of the Japanese imperium. This was truly a decade-long pressure cooker; the lifting of the lid in 1945 deeply affected Korea.[32] But Japan, too, was deeply changed by the experience. Japan was remade in this period.

The modern Japanese state, well described in its contemporary features elsewhere,[33] was initially the great work of the Meiji oligarchs. But it was in the 1930s that it took on many of the neomercantile features that persist today: its virtuosity in moving through the product cycle, from old to new industries; the extraordinary role for the bureaucracy and key agencies like MITI, exercising "administrative guidance" throughout the economy; the peculiar vehicles for credit, which account for much of the mobility in and out of industries; the role of large conglomerates; the systematic exclusion of labor from most important decision making; and the high rates of exploitation of poorly paid female labor.

The imperatives of late development in a predatory world shaped Japan more in the 1930s than in any other period, amid the general breakdown of the world system. Sharp competition precipitated remarkable unity at home. The militarist aggression and street politics of the young radicals blind us to the formidable coalition that came together within Japan during the decade. Chalmers Johnson argues that this period saw the emergence of three key features. The first was national planning and industrial strategy that extended to most major industries in Japan. Its only American counterparts are isolated experiences like the Manhattan Project or the space program. The second was the structural features of the MITI function in the years 1939-43 (even though MITI had not yet appeared), including key managerial personnel ("old cadres") who persisted long into the postwar period. And the third was the role for the state and credit institutions that is by now the mark of the Japanese model.[34] G. C. Allen has argued that Japan owed industrial success in the 1930s to "structural adaptability" that came from systematic state subsidization and protection of new industries, and credit institutions that treated investment funds in very mobile fashion. Allen suggests that Japan's ability to centralize credit institutions and industry "under a single control" was a great comparative advantage at the time, although such concentration was also a measure of the immaturity of the Japanese economy: with capital weak and many producers still in traditional sectors, the state had to select and foster large industries and banks. Like Johnson, he finds "an identifiable thread of continuity" from this period to the contemporary era.[35] Ohkawa and Rosovsky also trace the practice of administrative guidance to the 1930s, with state planning agencies being central to the surveying of the foreign technology scene, the import of technology, licensing, allocation of foreign exchange to importers, and so on.[36] These early agencies, and their MITI successor, in effect were the directors of Japan's movement through the product cycle.

Behind everything in Japan there seems to have been a bank. In the 1930s the Big Four *zaibatsu* controlled four of the six biggest banks; their integrated financial power made it possible to mobilize and direct capital, achieving great and rapid adaptability. The banks, official and semi-official, along with the *zaibatsu*, "provided the chief means by which the government promoted industries of national importance."[37] Thus, the forerunners of MITI provided the goals, and the banks and corporations the means, for directing and riding the product cycle.

The prewar *zaibatsu* were family-interpenetrated conglomerates that used feudal-holdover ideologies to incorporate workers "as fellow clansmen who devote themselves to the services of their overlord." By the end of the 1930s, Mitsui, Mitsubishi, and Sumitomo controlled half the copper and coal production, half the total ship tonnage, 70 percent of flour milling, 90 percent of paper production, most of the aircraft industry, nearly all sugar refining, and, with some smaller and newer *zaibatsu*, nearly all of the colonial industrialization in Korea, Manchuria, and Taiwan.[38] The *zaibatsu* and the state combined to accomplish a thorough repression and incorporation of labor, leading in the 1940s to a forced military-style discipline in the factories that long left its mark on the working class. Women were particularly exploited: they received much lower wages than men for similar work, and predominated in the older textile sector. Finally, at the bottom were more than a million Korean laborers in Japan, men and women harshly regimented for the most difficult sorts of industrial work and subjected to invidious racial discrimination.

In the postwar period Japan was shorn of a few features of its 1930s political economy. But in Taiwan and, later, South Korea the 1930s model reappeared, in nearly all its aspects, including militarization and harsh repression of labor.

The postwar settlement and the emergence of a new hegemony

In September 1945, as U.S. occupation forces filtered into Japan, an American officer walked into a Mitsui office in Tokyo and introduced himself. A man in the office pointed to a map of the Greater East Asian Coprosperity Sphere and said, "There it is. We tried. See what you can do with it!"[39] It was not until 1948 that the United States would seek to do much with it, however. In the period 1945-47 in Korea, Japan, and Taiwan, society reacted strongly against the effects of imperial militarism and industrial midwifery. American occupation in Japan led by a 19th century liberal also reacted strongly in the early years against the political economy of prewar Japan, seeking to destroy the Japanese Imperial Army, break up the *zaibatsu*, eliminate rural landlords, and bequeath to the world a reformed and chastened Japan that would never again mix aggression with economic prowess. Unions and leftist parties were unleashed and, with Occupation "New Dealers," mustered a challenge to the prewar system strong enough, at minimum, to establish the countervailing power that enables us to call postwar Japan a democracy. Although the main emphasis was on democratization and an end to militarism, narrower interests also asserted themselves. The first head of the Economic and Scientific Section of the Occupation, for example, was Robert C. Kramer, a textile industrialist; he and representatives of American textile, rayon, ceramics, and other industries threatened by Japanese competition opposed reviving Japan's economy, particularly in its potent prewar form.[40] American allies, especially the British, also urged that commitments to reform and reparations be carried through, thereby to weaken Japan's competitiveness in world markets.

From the early 1940s, however, one sector of American official opinion opposed a punitive occupation, for fear that this would play into the hands of the Soviets and make a reintegration of Japan with the world economy impossible. In essence, such people, who included a Japanophile faction in the State Department,[41] wanted a Japan revived to *second-rank* economic status and enrolled in an American-managed free trade regime. Such recommendations remained in the background, however, while Japan's American emperor, Gen. Douglas MacArthur, masterfully imposed a benevolent tutelage upon the Japanese people.

All this began sharply to change in late 1947, leading to what we might call the Kennan Restoration. George Kennan's policy of containment was always limited and parsimonious, based on the idea that four or five industrial structures existed in the world: the Soviets had one and the United States had four, and things should be kept that way. In Asia, only Japan held his interest. The rest were incontinent regimes, and how could one have containment with incontinence? Kennan and his Policy Planning Staff played the key role in pushing through the "reverse course" in Japan.

American policy in the mid 20th century resonated with Jacob Viner's description of British policy in the 18th: it was governed "by joint and harmonized considerations of power and economics."[42] Security and economic considerations were inextricably mixed. A revived Japan was both a bulwark against the Soviets and a critical element in a reformed and revived world economy. What is surprising, in the multitude of formerly classified American documents now available on early postwar Asian policy, is how powerful were the economic voices. In particular, a cluster of bankers and free traders, now dubbed the "Japan Crowd," were instrumental in the ending of the postwar reforms in Japan and the revival of the regional political economy that persists today.[43] Economics bulked so large because, as Charles Maier points out, the defeated Axis powers (Japan and West Germany) were to become world centers of capital accumulation and growth, not of political or military power.[44] Thus Japan's economy was reinforced, while its political and military power (beyond its borders) was shorn. The result is that in the postwar world economy Japan resembles a sector as much as a nation-state. Until the 1970s it was a distinctly secondary sector when compared to the United States, that is, it was returned to semiperipherality as (it was hoped) a permanent second-rank economic power.

The coalition that brought the reverse course to Japan has been well detailed elsewhere. In brief it included, in addition to Kennan, Dean Acheson, Dean Rusk, Max Bishop and others within the government, several journalists, and a powerful lobby of American firms and individuals who had had large investments in prewar Japan: General Electric, Westinghouse, Goodrich, Owens-Libby, American Can, and others.[45] Percy Johnston, head of the pivotal Johnston Committee whose report in April 1948 was instrumental in the reverse course, was chairman of the Chemical Bank; the "Dodge Line" of fiscal austerity was run by a Detroit banker; many Wall Streeters, including the American maker of the Japan Peace Treaty, John Foster Dulles, supported a revival of Japan's economic prowess. As good free traders from the new hegemonic power, they had nothing to fear from Japan. The old hegemonic power, Great Britain, fought unsuccessfully against the changes.

As thinking about a revived Japan evolved in 1948-50, two problems emerged: first, how could Japan's vital but second-rate status be assured; second, how could a prewar political economy that got raw materials and labor from the Northeast Asian periphery survive in the postwar world without a hinterland? George Kennan raised these problems in a 1949 Policy Planning Staff meeting:

You have the terrific problem of how the Japanese are going to get along unless they again reopen some sort of empire toward the south. . .

If we really in the Western world could work out controls. . . foolproof enough and cleverly enough exercised really to have power over what Japan imports in the way of oil and other things. . . we could have veto power over what she does.[46]

Thus, once the decision to revive Japan was made, two questions predominated: the hegemonic problem and the hinterland problem. The CIA in May 1948 suggested NE Asia as the new (old) hinterland:

As in the past, Japan for normal economic functioning on an industrial basis, must have access to the Northeast Asiatic areas—notably North China, Manchuria, and Korea—now under direct, indirect, or potential control of the USSR.[47]

A high official in the Economic Cooperation Administration, a few months later, suggested the same hinterland, and a drastic method of recovering it. Without North China and Manchuria, he argued, Japan would have "no hope of achieving a viable economy"; it (and Korea) would be "doomed to military and industrial impotence except on Russian terms." Therefore, "Our first concern must be the liberation of Manchuria and North China from communist domination."[48] This rollback option, however, was delayed; the victory of Mao's forces throughout China and the possibility in 1949 that Washington might be able to split Moscow and Peking (Acheson's policy) combined to suggest a hinterland for Japan in Southeast Asia.

In July 1949, the CIA asserted that the United States had "an important interest" in "retaining access to Southeast Asia, for its own convenience and because of the great economic importance of that area to Western Europe and Japan." It argued that "the basic problem with respect to Japan is to recreate a viable economy. This in turn requires a stabilization of the situation in Southeast Asia and a *modus vivendi* with Communist China." The latter requirement might be satisfied if China could be drawn away from "vassalage toward the USSR."[49] Southeast Asia was the preferred candidate for Japan's hinterland. It would provide markets for Japan's textile and light industrial exports, in exchange for raw materials Japan badly needed. The problem was that France and Britain sought to hold the countries in the region exclusively, and nationalist movements resisted both the Europeans and a reintroduction of the Japanese. Thus, "Anglo-American consensus over Japan dissolved" as the United States played the hinterland option. Japan was a threat to sterling bloc trade and currency systems, and was "perforce in the dollar bloc"; the United States wanted Japan to earn dollars in the sterling bloc, which would have the dual virtue of supporting Japan's revival while encouraging Britain's retreat from empire.[50]

The Occupation also rearranged Japan's monetary and trade policies to support a revival of trade. The yen was fixed in 1949 at the rate of 360 to $ 1.00, from which it did not depart until 1971; the rate was artificially low to aid Japanese exports. The Dodge Line pursued a strict policy of fiscal restraint. In the same year (1949) the Occupation removed price floors on Japanese exports, raising fears of "dumping" in Southeast Asia.

Particularly important is the *triangular* structure of this arrangement: United States (core), Japan (semiperiphery), and Southeast Asia (periphery). This structure was clearly articulated in the deliberations leading up to the adoption of NSC 48/1 in late December 1949, a document so important that it might be called the NSC 68 for Asia. (With this the United States made the decision to send aid to the Bao Dai regime in Vietnam, not after the Korean War began.) The first draft argued the virtues of a "triangular" trade between the United States, Japan, and Southeast Asia, giving "certain advantages in production costs of various commodities" —that is, comparative advantage in the product cycle. It also called for a positive policy toward Communist-held territory in East Asia: the goal was "to commence the rollback of Soviet control and influence in the area." The final document changed this phrase to read, "to contain and where feasible to reduce the power and influence of the USSR in Asia."[51] The roll-back contingency expressed both the fear of continuing communist encroachment, what with the fall of China in 1949, and the search for a Japanese hinterland.

The Korean War effectively drew the lines of the "grand area" in East Asia. When the war broke out, the Seventh Fleet was interposed between Taiwan and the mainland, suggesting once again an integration of Taiwan with Japan and the world economy. South Korea was almost lost in the summer of 1950. Then, after the Inch'on landing, the course of the fighting opened the realm of feasibility suggested in NSC 48/1; the "contain and reduce" phraseology was used in the State Department to justify the march north and, in passing, to wrench North Korea's industrial base away from the communists. Roll-back met several hundred thousand Chinese "volunteers," however, and that debacle froze the situation. The geopolitical lines, or hegemonic outer limits, were thus fixed and they have survived. Taiwan and South Korea were in, North Korea and Manchuria were out. It remained only to reintroduce Japanese economic influence, which the Kennedy administration did in the early 1960s in both Taiwan and South Korea.

Acheson would remark in 1954 that "Korea came along and saved us," and the *us* included Japan. The Korean War not only boosted the Japanese economy but provided MacArthur with justification for reviving police and military and for excluding labor and the left within Japan. The strategic lines of the new Northeast Asian political economy, however, brought the peculiar nature of American hegemony to the fore. There is a paradox at the heart of it: nonterritorial in contrast to Old World imperialism, organizing great spaces and knocking down barriers to trade, it has outer limits sufficient to keep countries *in* the system but not sufficient to protect the home economy against destructive competition, and not sufficient to maintain effective dependency relationships or a frozen hierarchy. The system permits upward mobility. The United States retrieved South Korea and Taiwan from oblivion in 1950, but invoking the threat of oblivion to keep them in line in later years was unthinkable. The United States keeps Japan on a food, oil, and security dependency, maintaining a light hold on the Japanese jugular; yet to squeeze would be disastrous. Outer limits are not enough to bring recalcitrant allies to heel. Furthermore, within those outer limits a dependent but strong state obtains leverage over the American "weak state," weak in the sense of competing centers of power and economic interest that can be played off against one another.[52] Thus, the postwar settlement simultaneously gave Japan, in particular, dependency and autonomous capability.[53]

Japan is ultradependent on the United States, or on American firms, for oil and security, and significantly dependent on the United States for food. During the Occupation, the Petroleum Board that set policy was made up of members mostly drawn from American oil majors, and even in the mid 1970s Japan was receiving about 70 percent of its oil deliveries from the majors.[54] In the 1960s and 1970s the United States also supplied 60 to 70 percent of Japan's food imports, and in the 1950s used the PL480 program to sell grain in Japan, Taiwan, and South Korea. All three have been protected markets dependent upon American grain. And since 1945 Japan has had no military capability remotely commensurate with its economic power. Even today analysts cannot decide if Japan is a superstate or a puny dependency. When Ezra Vogel began a Harvard seminar on Japan by saying that "I am really very troubled when I think through the consequences of the rise of Japanese power," Samuel Huntington responded that Japan has "these really fundamental weaknesses—energy, food, and military security." It is, he thought, "an extraordinarily weak country."[55] The paradox of the postwar Northeast Asian settlement is that both are right.

Within Japan, after the reverse course took hold, was a formidable political economy for competition in world markets. The *zaibatsu* were less smashed than reformed, prospering again by the mid 1950s if in less concentrated form. More important, they were now under state influence and control, something that prewar bureaucrats had longed for; the role of the big banks was also enhanced.[56] With the *zaibatsu* weakened, the military smashed, and the landlords dispossessed, but with the bureaucracy untouched (the Occupation governed through the existing bureaucracy with few reforms or purges), the Japanese state had more relative autonomy than in the prewar period. Indeed, it was the great victor of the Occupation. Autonomy enabled Japan to pursue neomercantile policies of restricting entry to Japanese markets, resisting the intrusion of foreign capital, and providing various incentives and subsidies to restructure the industrial base in the 1950s, and conquer foreign markets in the 1960s and 1970s.

T. J. Pempel and Jon Halliday both note the low level of internationalization of the Japanese economy. Total foreign assets in Japan in the mid 1970s were only about 2 to 3 percent of total assets, few non-Japanese multinationals operated there, and the major markets for foreign imports remained food and oil. Halliday argues that Japan's "successful isolation" has precipitated greater elite unity than in countries like the United States: Japan does not have major conflicts between firms with national and those with international interests, therefore foreign interests cannot invoke much leverage in domestic Japanese politics. Moving out of declining into advanced sectors is much easier because powerful domestic business interests rarely clash, and a labor force lacking influence at the commanding heights can be eased out of old industries and retrained for new ones. Japan's monetary isolation lessens the influence of foreign lenders, while reliance on bank rather than share capital also promotes mobility and flexibility.[57] Finally, as in the prewar political economy, labor is corralled by docile unions, paternalism, and a large reservoir of workers in traditional sectors. Ohkawa and Rosovsky call Japan a businessman's "heaven on earth" in regard to labor, while Pempel says labor is "a fundamentally excluded sector"; they also note that women continue to bear inferior and exploited positions in the workforce, and that the state still does not spend significant amounts on social welfare.[58]

Postwar Korea and Taiwan

The immediate postwar settlement in Taiwan and Korea fundamentally expressed the differences in the two *societies*. Taiwan "drifted aimlessly" in the late 1940s, having to reorient its trade away from Japan and toward China (until 1949); it sold sugar, cement, aluminum, and food to this now-enlarged periphery.[59] But it remained "an extremely well-ordered society," with "fewer signs of social disintegration" than any place on the Asian mainland.[60] Like Japan, the state emerged stronger after the inflow of the Kuomintang (KMT) and the China mainlanders in 1945-49. The potent colonial bureaucracy was preserved nearly intact; Japanese personnel in many cases stayed on well into 1946, training Taiwanese replacements, and native bureaucrats who had served in the colonial administration continued in office. When the mainlanders took over they added a powerful military component to give the state even more autonomy from society: the Kuomintang had finally found a part of China where its bureaucracy was not hamstrung by provincial warlords and landlords. Thus, for the first time, the Nationalists were able to accomplish a land reform; they could do so because none of them owned any land in Taiwan. The reform, in turn, aided the productivity of agriculture because redistributed land went primarily to entrepreneurial, productive, relatively rich peasants. Furthermore, a disproportionate number of experts, technicians, and well-educated professionals fled the mainland, adding to Taiwan's already significant human capital. The result, once the Seventh Fleet drew the outer limit in 1950, was a state with significant relative autonomy but now far more dependent on the United States than in any previous period of Nationalist rule.

Korea, of course, was divided in 1945. In the North a quick and efficient social and anticolonial revolution occurred under Soviet auspices, the ultimate (but also the predictable) societal response to nearly half a century of Japanese imperialism. The South, however, festered for five years through dissent, disorder, major rebellions in 1946 and 1948, and a significant guerrilla movement in 1948 and 1949. Southern landlords succeeded in recapturing the slate in 1945 and 1946, under American auspices, and used it in traditional fashion to protect social privilege rather than to foster growth. They prevented major land reform until the Korean War began, and showed no interest in developing the economy. Instead, they ruled through draconian police and military organizations. As in Taiwan there was considerable continuity in the bureaucracy from the colonial period, but the Japanese officials had mostly fled when the war ended and those Korean functionaries who remained were largely unable to function, since they were often hated more than the Japanese overlords. The southern state entered a general crisis of legitimacy in the late 1940s: marked by the worst Japanese excesses but unable to carry forward colonial successes, the regime seemed doomed.

When civil war erupted in June 1950 the North had an easy time of it, sweeping the southern regime away until it met massive American intervention. But paradoxically, the three-month northern occupation of the south, which included a revolutionary land reform in several provinces, cleared the way to end landlord dominance in the countryside and to reform landholding on the Taiwan model once the war terminated in 1953. By 1953 South Korea further resembled Taiwan. Its colonial heavy industry had been amputated by Korea's division, most of it now in the north and beyond reach; like Taiwan, southern Korea was the home of light industry and the best rice-producing provinces. During the war many northerners had fled south, also disproportionately including the educated and professional classes. By the war's end the South had a standing army of about 600,000, compared with 75,000 in 1950, so it approximated the distended Nationalist Army. Finally, Syngman Rhee, like Chiang Kai-shek, had won an ironclad commitment of American defense from communism. So, to put it concisely, by 1953 Taiwan and South Korea once more resembled each other, but what was accomplished with ease in Taiwan required a war in Korea.

Import-substituting industrialization

With the underbrush of the early postwar period cleared away, Taiwan and South Korea (ROK) once again began marching in tandem. The Korean War gave Taiwan a head start on postcolonial industrialization on the typical import-substituting pattern, but by 1953 the ROK was doing the same. Both were enmeshed in a system of American hegemony that brought them economic and military aid on an unheard-of scale, but Taiwan's low societal response and the KMT's high relative autonomy gave it more bargaining power with the United States. The Rhee regime, on the other hand, was penetrated from below by superannuated landlords who retained political influence and from above by a huge American political, economic, and military presence. In the years immediately succeeding the devastation of the war, society was quiet and Rhee ruled through a diffuse authoritarian system that was cruel in its domestic political consequences but incapable of mustering the autonomy to direct growth, and unable to withstand the social onslaught that came in 1960. The now-senile Rhee was toppled, the colonial-linked police and military came undone, and the way was clear for a dynamic authoritarian system.

Since 1945 South Korea has received some $13 billion in American military and economic aid, and Taiwan some $5.6 billion ($600 per capita in the ROK, $425 per capita in Taiwan).[61] To gauge the true dimensions of this munificence comparative figures are helpful. The ROK's total of nearly $6 billion in U.S. economic grants and loans, 1946-78, compares with a total for all of Africa of $6.89 billion and for all of Latin America of $14.8 billion; only India, with a population seventeen times that of South Korea, received more ($9.6 billion). U.S. military deliveries to Taiwan and the ROK in 1955-78 (that is, excluding the Korean War) totaled $9.05 billion. All of Latin America and all of Africa received $3.2 billion; only Iran got more, and most of that was pumped in after 1972 (the figure is $10.01 billion). Soviet economic aid to LDCs, 1954-78, was $7.6 billion in drawn aid, that is, little more than American aid to the ROK alone. Total drawn aid for all LDCs from all socialist countries, 1954-78, was $13.4 billion, about 25 percent greater than the total for Taiwan and the ROK since 1945. Soviet military deliveries to all LDCs, 1955-78, totaled $25.3 billion, about 280 percent of the total for Taiwan and the ROK.[62]

During the 1950s U.S. aid accounted for five-sixths of ROK imports. Aid was lavished on Japan as well, and special U.S. military procurements from Japan alone in the period 1952-56 totaled $3.4 billion, one-fourth of American commodity imports at that time.[63] Samuel Ho estimates for Taiwan that foreign savings, much of which was U.S. aid, totaled 40 percent of gross domestic capital formation.[64] This significant figure is low when compared to the ROK; Taiwan's higher rate of domestic savings can be accounted for by less postwar disruption and the Kuomintang's having taken China's gold reserves to the island. Taiwan has also had an additional source of aid and investment unavailable to the ROK, overseas Chinese.

The United States, of course, did not just give military and economic aid to Taiwan and the ROK but deeply influenced economic programs and the societies themselves. Often it was difficult to know if natives or Americans were writing the plans and policies; the aid missions pushed through land reform on Taiwan and forced it through in Korea; here, in short, was by far the best example in the world of what Wallerstein has called "development by invitation." If the principle of upward mobility in this system is "many called, few chosen," Taiwan and the ROK were clearly part of the chosen few.[65] Japan, too, was chosen, if at a higher level in the system: not only were aid totals high, but the United States allowed a "simultaneous technological infusion" in the 1950s that brought backward Japanese industries up to speed and started new ones.[66] American hegemony also had an element of indulgence in the halcyon years of the 1950s—U.S. officials tolerated import substitution in Taiwan and the ROK while chiding both for having the state too involved in the economy (i.e., the typical policy of Republican administrations). Thus, the three Northeast Asian political economies had in the 1950s a rare breathing space, an incubation period allowed to few other peoples in the world. The period set the stage for the breakthroughs of the 1960s, and it may be a capitalist analogue to the radical tonic of withdrawal and reorientation by socialist state machineries and societies.

Taiwan and Korea pushed remarkably similar import-substitution programs, although the Taiwan program was less fitful. The key industries were textiles, cement, flat glass, and so on, protected by and nurtured behind a wall of tariffs, overvalued exchange rates, and other obstacles to foreign entry.[67] In both countries capitalist parvenus, usually mainlanders in Taiwan and northerners in the ROK, interpenetrated the state, official monopolies, and banks, making windfall profits in import-substituting industries through such connections. Both the KMT and the Rhee regime, after all, grew out of agrarian-bureaucratic traditional systems and had pursued so-called "bureaucratic capitalism," with its "total interpenetration of public and private interests."[68] Favored capitalists took over formerly Japanese-held industries in Taiwan and the ROK, laying the basis for many of the conglomerates that would appear in the 1960s and 1970s (especially in Korea). The phase of "easy" import substitution started two or three years earlier in Taiwan and came a cropper in 1958-59; it did the same in the ROK in 1960-62. In both countries a new export-led industrialization began in the early 1960s.

In the 1950s both regimes had absurdly swollen military machines—about 600,000 soldiers in each army, ranking among the highest military/civilian ratios in the world. The United States footed much of the tab in Korea, less so in Taiwan because Americans opposed Taiwan's pretensions to retake the mainland. Thus, Taiwanese defense spending ran at about 12 percent of GNP, Korean at about 4 percent. These large militaries served two important purposes: first, as a perimeter defense for the hegemonic "grand area." Without such military machines and expenditures Japan would have had to spend much more than its less than one percent of GNP on defense. As Paul B. Simpson said of the U.S. aid program to the ROK in the 1950s:

If we were to characterize the program simply, we would say that the Korean consumer has been subsidized by ICA and U.S. military expenditures in return for the maintenance of a large military establishment. The attitude one adopts toward this Korean military program very largely determines one's attitude toward the U.S. aid program in Korea.[69]

Second, the military in both countries gave disciplined training and basic literacy to a mass of young people, while rearing officers and managers who later populated state bureaucracies and big corporations. Of course, both distended militaries have continually devastated democratic impulses.

In the Korean case the military also played a decisive role in the switch from import substitution to export-led growth. The downfall of Syngman Rhee carried the bureaucratic capitalists with it. After the military coup in 1961 those who had profited from import substitution were marched through the streets, carrying sandwich signs with slogans like "I was a parasite on the people." A transition that occurred with difficulty in several Latin American nations transpired quickly, if violently, in South Korea; managed from the top down, it cleared away social and political obstacles to the new program.

The export-led phase and the emergence of BAIRs

Readers who know Latin America and especially the work of Guillermo O'Donnell will have noticed that Taiwan and Korea went through industrialization in phases that resemble the sequence in Brazil, Argentina, and other states, even though the import-substituting phase was much shorter in East Asia. It would have continued longer had it not been for opposition by American aid officials (which demonstrates their superior influence in this region of overwhelming American hegemony). But this phase did not have the political characteristics it had in Brazil and elsewhere. Politics did not stretch to include workers, peasants, or plural competition for power. The political sequence of inclusion followed by exclusion, as the "easy" phase ended and export-led development began, was absent.[70] Labor was excluded in the 1950s and remained excluded in the 1960s; nor did the squeezed middle class of bureaucrats and small businessmen achieve representation in either Taiwan or South Korea. It is possible to argue, however, that the Korean state was more penetrated by society in the 1950s, both because new capitalists gained some influence as the landlord interests receded and because the United States and a small stratum of Korean liberals insisted on a formal democratic structure that was occasionally implemented, if only through students massing in the streets. The democratic facade could occasionally be invoked. Taiwan, of course, has been ruled under martial law since 1947 in a single-party system; the KMT's internal organization principles were on Leninist lines. Its politics could easily translate into the new state requisites for export-led development and deepening import substitution. In Korea, however, such a state had to be reinforced: bureaucratic, secret police, and party power needed to be strengthened.

In both countries the export-led program was decided by the United States. Edward Mason and his associates say that in Korea the United States "basically dictated" the reform programs; Ian Little says that in Taiwan A.I.D. pressure was one of the "clearest cases in economic history of cause and effect."[71] Therefore, early 1960s' policies in Taiwan and the ROK tended to be very similar. Taiwan promulgated a nineteen-point reform package in 1960, containing extensive reforms of monetary, fiscal, taxation, and trade practices. Korea pursued the same package after Park Chung Hee's coup in 1961. It involved downward revaluation of currencies to cheapen exports, drastic lowering of tariff barriers that had protected native industries, tax holidays, exemptions, and reductions across the board for firms willing to export, and state guarantees for foreign investment and foreign loans. Implemented by 1963 or 1964, the package was followed by accelerated depreciation schemes, discounts and subsidies for transportation costs, and monopoly rights for certain firms, usually linked explicitly to export performance.[72] Taiwan established its big Free Export Zone (FEZ) at Kaohsiung in 1965, and Korea followed suit with its Masan FEZ. Both regimes developed long-range planning agencies and multiyear plans; American experts continued riding herd on the planning function (a sort of transnational planning).

Both regimes pursued their comparative advantage in relatively well-educated and skilled, but low-paid, labor. Paul Kuznets notes that Korea's comparative advantage derived from these factors and that labor was "abundant and unorganized"; Wade and Kim estimate Korean labor productivity as higher than American in light industries such as textiles and electronics, at 20 percent the cost. In the FEZs, however, labor-cost savings for foreign firms may be substantially higher: one source puts Korean productivity at 2.5 times American at 10 percent of the cost, for a factor of 25 in cost savings.[73] One Taiwan analyst has argued for the virtues of "splitting up the production process" on a worldwide basis, since capital has much greater mobility than labor.[74] This is, of course, the point. The result of the early 1960s' reforms was that Taiwan and the ROK became suppliers of labor to an increasingly far-flung division of production; in the mid 1960s multinational corporations, the World Bank, and the IMF replaced U.S. aid missions as the conduits to the world economy. This pattern, most marked in East Asia, is well known and need not detain us. More important were the political consequences.

By the mid 1960s both Taiwan and South Korea possessed strong states that bear much comparison to the prewar Japanese model, and to the bureaucratic-authoritarian states in Latin America. Termed NICs (Newly Industrializing Countries) in much of the literature, the Taiwan and Korean variants deserve a more accurate acronym. I shall call them BAIRs, or Bureaucratic-Authoritarian Industrializing Regimes. These states are ubiquitous in economy and society: penetrating, comprehensive, highly articulated, and relatively autonomous of particular groups and classes. Furthermore, especially in Korea, state power accumulated considerably just as the ROK began a deepening industrialization program in steel, chemicals, ships, and automobiles. Taiwan has developed planning agencies and bureaucracies to go with its existing strong state, but with society weak the state has had neither the occasion nor the necessity to deepen or change its features: once strong for retaking the mainland and guaranteeing KMT power, it is today strong for economic development. The best Latin American analogy for Taiwan would be Mexico, where deepening industrialization occurred within the context of an established authoritarian system; Korea is closer to Argentina, where deepening required a much stronger state. In any case, by the mid 1960s Taiwan and South Korea had joined the world: we no longer need area-specific, idiosyncratic explanations for their politics. They now have the politics that their economies—and powerful external forces—demand.

In the creation of the Korean BAIR, there was a poignant moment for American political scientists. Amid Kennedy administration pressure to go civilian and respect human rights, the ROK promulgated a new constitution in 1963. Harvard scholar Rupert Emerson journeyed to Seoul and advised Koreans, in classic American fashion, to disperse power through a strong legislature, a two-party system, and various checks and balances. Five years later Samuel Huntington published a book that cited the ROK for precisely the opposite: he applauded the regime for its accumulation of central power and its stability amid rapid economic and social change. Huntington's concern for order transcended liberal categories: the problem was not to hold elections but to create organizations.[75] Although his preferred vehicle was the party, the logic fitted a strong state power by whatever means necessary. The book was translated into Korean and is widely read there. Huntington's logic was possibly the first piece of political advice from an American that did not fall on deaf ears in Korea.

Shortly after the coup, Park and his allies organized the Democratic Republican Party (DRP) and the Korean Central Intelligence Agency (KCIA). During much of the 1960s the DRP was the designated vehicle for a stable politics; its internal structure mimicked the KMT with its democratic centralism. But when Park's power was shaken in the period 1969-71 (he nearly lost the 1971 election to Kim Dae Jung in spite of manipulation), the KCIA emerged as the preferred organization of order. An arm of the executive, it penetrated nearly every arena of Korean life, with agents in factories, central and local government offices, and university classrooms. Organized with the help of the U.S. CIA, and always working in close liaison with the Seoul CIA station, it was an example of transnational politics to go with the transnational economics. Unfortunately for Park Chung Hee, the KCIA became so strong that every director came to challenge his power (Lee Hu-rak, Kim Jae-gyu, Kim Hyong-uk) until finally its chief shot Park to death over dinner one evening in October 1979.

In the economic sphere the Koreans in the early 1960s set up an Economic Planning Board (EPB), which took on many of the functions of MITI. It took over from a previous ministry the entire budgeting function; it decides which industries and firms to promote, which to phase out; it closely supervises both the development and the implementation of planning; along with an official trade promotion agency (KOTRA) it surveys the world for needed markets, capital, and technology. The main difference from Japan is that the EPB brings in foreigners (Americans and Japanese) as "senior partners" in consultation and planning.[76] Many other state agencies are involved in export promotion, and in both Korea and Taiwan, the achievement of some export target is cause for patriotic hoopla and celebration (this has become the national pastime of these two BAIRs).

Until the mid 1970s, American analysts tended to deny that an authoritarian politics might have much to do with economic growth in Taiwan and the ROK. But more recent writing has discarded the previous assumptions of the modernization literature, that development could proceed amidst or would promote democracy. Kuznets, for example, argues that "because this [Korean] regime has been authoritarian and has no economic interest base, it could hold down wages and consumption, largely ignore rural interests, and concentrate on rapid development through industrialization."[77] He errs only in suggesting that the state has no base. The state's relative autonomy from particularistic economic interests, combined with the exclusion of workers and farmers, gives it the capacity to look after the whole in the interest of, but not necessarily at the behest of, certain of the parts. In this structural sense it resembles the relative autonomy of the Japanese state.

A Harvard project on the Korean economy also breaks with the assumption of inevitable democratic development. The authors find that "Korea, Inc." is "undoubtedly a more apt description of the situation in Korea than is "Japan, Inc." The state is senior, the corporations lesser partners: "It is the government that is Chairman of the Board [of Korea, Inc.], with business holding a few directorships."[78] The Korean *zaibatsu* (the Koreans pronounce it *chaebol*, but the term is the same) have grown up with the new BAIR. Ten of them now appear on *Fortune*'s international 500. Like prewar Japanese *zaibatsu*, there is great family interpenetration: the Harvard project found that of current *chaebol* chief executives, 61.4

percent are firm founders, 7.9 percent are direct descendants of founders, 12 percent are relatives of founders, and only 18.8 percent are unrelated to the founding family.[79] As a Gerschenkronian analysis would suggest, "feudal holdovers" have been an important aspect of late development in East Asia: in the case of prewar Japanese *zaibatsu*, Korean *chaebol*, and the Taiwanese state (the President being the son of Chiang Kai-shek), it is the traditional family structure that provides a basis for organizing industry. The power of this analysis is confirmed in the Northeast Asian socialist case, where the North Korean state is highly interpenetrated by Kim Il Sung's family and where his son has been chosen as successor.

As in Japan, Korean and Taiwanese big firms exercise paternalistic sway over workers with company dormitories, recreation and hospital facilities, uniforms, and company songs. The different labor markets in Korea and Taiwan mean, however, that there is no permanent employment, working hours are much longer (52 hours per week in the big firms, longer in small firms), and wages are much lower in relation to living cost.

Yet there is no question but that the state is the maker and at times the breaker of the conglomerates. They prospered and grew as the economy grew, in close consort with state support. They do not have the credit power of the Japanese *zaibatsu*. At the core of the latter was always a bank, but in Korea and Taiwan it is the state that provides credit. This is one of its greatest weapons. State bureaucracies like the EPB control domestic credit and favor certain export-oriented firms, and they mediate foreign credit through licensing schemes. Thus, they have almost total control over access to investment capital; the *chaebol* are all structured with very low equity and huge debt components.[80] Most are in technical bankruptcy at any given time. Thus, when the Yolsan conglomerate added to Park Chung Hee's difficulties by (reportedly) flirting with the opposition leader Kim Dae Jung in 1979, the president pulled the plug and Yolsan collapsed, taking several small banks with it. Samuel Ho notes the same sort of autonomy for the state in Taiwan: it can move in and out of sectors, promote this or that industry, because it is "relatively neutral to sectoral or regional interest."[81] It is this relative autonomy and promotion of sectoral mobility that makes these BAIRs resemble the Japanese model.

Another similarity with the Japanese model is the exclusion of labor, the exploitation of women, and the low state expenditures on social welfare-all three, of course, are bound to be more extreme in the periphery than in the core. Social spending is minimal in both countries. In 1973, expenditures on social insurance, public health, public assistance, welfare, and veterans' relief represented 0.97 percent of GNP in the ROK, 1.2 percent in Taiwan; this compares with 3 percent in Malaysia and 5.3 percent in Japan.[82] Such figures capture the tradeoff between Japan and Korea and Taiwan: the latter two spend 4 to 10 percent of GNP on defense, and Japan can hold defense expenditures under one percent; but Japan, by virtue of its "New Deal" during the Occupation and its democratic system, must spend 5 percent on social programs (still low by world standards). In any case both the ROK and Japan until recently escaped with spending about 6 percent of GNP on defense and welfare combined. Korean and Taiwanese workers pay the cost in the periphery.

Exploitation of labor, particularly females, is so marked that it is foolish to deny it (even though many American specialists continue to do so). In both the Kaohsiung and the Masan FEZs 80 percent of the workforce is female, and teenage girls are about 60 percent of that total. Most of the work is unskilled assembly, done by girls recruited from peasant families. Their wage rates are at the bottom of the heap in world scales—one-third of

Japan's level, one-fifth to one-tenth of the U.S. level, even one-half of the level in Hong Kong, where similar practices prevail. The state guarantees foreign firms not only various investment subsidies and profit remissions, but prohibition of union organization. In the Kaohsiung FEZ about 85 percent of the 150 or so firms are wholly or partially foreign-owned (including holdings by overseas Chinese).[83] FEZ products include light electronic assemblies (like calculators), textiles, and simple manufactured items like nuts and bolts. Thus these are basically platforms of world production located in countries that can provide cheap and controlled labor. In Korea and Taiwan strikes are usually prohibited (even though they may occur), and unions are company or state-managed in good corporate fashion.

All in all the BAIR provides a potent mix, fusing state and economic power in pursuit of comparative advantage in world markets. To the extent that hegemonic outer limits are not invoked, relative autonomy is at any given time greater in Taiwan and Korea than it is in Japan or the United States. Thus both states sought in the early 1970s to use their autonomous power to upset transnational and free-trade interests by once again import substituting, this time in heavy industry. Both sought not simply to deepen their industrial structures but to deepen their self-reliance and independence vis-à-vis their hegemonic partners. One key enabling factor was the massive reentry of Japanese capital (loans and investments) into the ROK and Taiwan in the mid 1960s. Accomplished relatively easily in Taiwan, in Korea, as we would predict, society reacted strongly and the "normalization" had to be rammed down the throats of protesting students and legislators in 1964-65. But Japan's reentry gave both regimes a strong proxy to play off against American power and capital: a single hegemony began to turn into a dual hegemony.

Park Chung Hee declared in 1972 that "steel = national power," a pithy slogan that symbolizes the deepening industrialization of both countries. The Third Five-Year Plan, 1971-76, inaugurated this phase. During 1969 to 1971 domestic capital formation rose markedly in the ROK, to account for 26 to 30 percent of gross domestic product, compared to 17 to 18 percent in the United States and 36 to 40 percent in Japan during the same years; the manufacturing sector rose from 11 percent to 30 percent between the early 1960s and the mid 1970s. A similar and coterminous deepening occurred in Taiwan. Economist Anthony Michel has also noted that Korean economic nationalists were dominant in constructing the Third Five-Year Plan, bypassing the EPB, which is transnationally penetrated by Western economists with theories opposed to industrial deepening.[84] The ROK got a new integrated steel mill (developed and installed by Japanese technicians), supertanker shipbuilding capacity, heavy chemical factories and refineries, and an auto industry (with GM, Ford, and Japanese technology) that produced 38,000 cars by 1978. American planners and economists resisted these developments, arguing that heavy industry is unsuited to the factor endowments and small domestic markets of both countries; surplus, idle capacity would be the inevitable result.[85] In other words, Korea and Taiwan were violating a rational international division of labor.

The ROK and Taiwan were able to obtain needed financing and technology for these enterprises from the Japanese, in part because the new programs provided the structure necessary to receive declining Japanese heavy industry. This simultaneously increased Taiwanese and Korean autonomy in the world at large while deepening dependency on Japan. The United States was opposed and, indeed, during the same period the Nixon administration dealt the sharpest blows since 1949 to both countries by limiting shoe and textile imports, floating the dollar, recognizing People's China, and pulling a division of U.S. troops out of the ROK. This set the agenda of conflict for the present: would the Northeast Asian political economy continue as a joint hegemony or as an increasingly Japanese preserve?

By the early 1970s, Korea and Taiwan were both in transition between peripheral and semiperipheral status;[86] in a sense they had recovered their structural position of the last years of the Japanese empire. Vietnam was a periphery for both, as each sent construction teams and other industrial personnel, and Korea sent some 300,000 soldiers over a seven-year period (1966-73). The Vietnam War played for the ROK the role that the Korean War played for Japan; labelled "Korea's El Dorado," it accounted for as much as 20 percent of foreign exchange earnings in the late 1960s.[87] Procurements for the war were also important for Taiwan, and, by the 1970s, Taiwan was exporting capital goods, technicians, and foreign aid to several Southeast Asian nations.[88] Both countries sent construction teams to the Middle East to recycle petrodollars after the 1973 oil shock. By the late 1970s both nations were competing for an intermediate position in the world economy, continuing to export labor-intensive goods to advanced countries and capital-intensive goods to LDCs.[89] Firms in both countries sought to go multinational, looking for cheaper labor in Bangladesh, Mexico, and elsewhere, while continuing to supply construction to the Middle East. In these tactics Taiwan and the ROK have been more successful than other industrializing regimes such as Brazil and Argentina. Korea, however, had to bolster its state power and did so in dramatic fashion: the early 1970s were the period of the Yusin Constitution (*yusin* in Korean is *isin* in Japanese, the same characters used to refer to the post 1868 Meiji reforms), KCIA penetration of society, a clump of "emergency decrees," and increasing use of vile tortures against dissidents.

Although Taiwan and Korea sought to escape dependency in the 1970s, what they succeeded in doing was exchanging one form of dependency for another, or enhancing one and reducing the other. The U.S. role has declined; experts no longer dictate to the regimes, as they did in the early 1960s, but "offer suggestions." The direct dependency of the 1950s and early 1960s has changed into an indirect dependency, increasingly like Japan's, within the U.S. hegemony. Both countries remain captive grain markets for the United States, both continue to get much of their oil shipped in and refined by U.S. multinationals, and both remain highly dependent on the United States for security (with Taiwan moving into a less determinate position after the U.S.-China normalization). In both countries direct aid ended in the mid 1960s, but PL480 grain and other supports continue to flow as a trade-off for "voluntary" textile export restraint. In the period 1951-74 Korea alone received $8 billion in U.S. food shipments, most of it under PL480, and surplus American grain has been essential in keeping wages low in Korea and Taiwan.[90]

Japan, by contrast, lacking a military or resource component to foster peripheral dependency, has pursued a trade hegemony that could be a textbook example of Hirschman's schema for Germany in interwar Eastern Europe. Japan's trading practices toward Taiwan and the ROK fit almost perfectly with his outline of techniques a dominant country uses to create an "influence effect" dependency: create groups with vested interest in trade, direct trade toward poorer countries, trade with countries with little mobility of resources, induce discrepancies between production for export and for the home market, and so on.[91] Northeast Asia exemplifies Hirschman's rule that dependency will emerge where country A takes a large percentage of trade from country B, but country B's trade is a small part of country

A's total trade. He illustrates this by reference to Bulgaria's trade with Germany: 52 percent of its imports came from and 59 percent of its exports went to Germany, but that trade only amounted to 1.5 percent of German imports and 1.1 percent of German exports.[92] In the 1970s, Japan accounted for about 25 percent of ROK exports and 38 percent of its imports; Japan and the United States combined accounted for 70 percent of ROK imports and about two-thirds of its exports.[93] Direct Japanese investment in Korea ballooned after the 1965 normalization, which was itself accompanied by a munificent package of loans and credits totaling about $300 million. Within a few years Japanese direct investment outstripped the American total; in the period 1972-76, for example, Japanese investment was more than four times the American total ($396 million to $88 million). Japan's ten largest trading firms handled as much as 50 percent of exports and 60 percent of imports to and from Korea between 1963 and 1972.

Taiwan's trade is similarly skewed; but Taiwan is less dependent on financing from Japan and the United States, whereas the ROK's dependence on Japanese financing since 1965 is, according to Kuznets, "characteristic of Korea's earlier satellite role within the Yen Bloc."[94] Both countries remain almost entirely dependent on American and Japanese multinationals for foreign markets and technology transfer.[95] Although an indirect dual dependency continues to exist, the Japanese are more aggressive than the Americans: as Ezra Vogel argues, the Japanese try "to induce as much technological dependence on Japan. . . as possible."[96] In Taiwan and Korea this takes the form, for example, of letting them assemble color television sets while jealously guarding the technology necessary to make a color picture tube.

Many are called but few are chosen: Korea's export-led trap

Export-led development on the Korean and Taiwan model places four critical obstacles in the way of upward mobility in the world system. First, LDCs need to break into the system of economic exchange at a point other than comparative advantage in labor, that is, in marketing, better technology, or better organization. Yet multinationals provide most of the markets and use "steady-state" or obsolescent technologies—as Lin puts it, technology "is stable in the product-cycle sense."[97] Second, limited factor endowments and the small domestic markets that characterize such offshore production inhibit second-stage industrialization and cause early problems of surplus capacity. Third, rising competition from poorer states means that there is a critical but a short and slim lead over competing LDCs. Multinationals, especially the smaller textile firms, may simply move production facilities to countries offering better labor costs. Finally, core-country protectionism will arise to the extent that declining sectors have representation in the polity. In the late 1970s, Taiwan and Korea met all these problems compounded by inflated oil prices.

In the event, Taiwan was chosen but the ROK was not. Taiwan is beginning to manufacture computers for export (Atari moved a big factory there in 1983), while Korea suffered a loss of 6 percent of GNP in 1980, the first loss since the export-led program began. In 1978, the Korean threat to advanced country industries seemed so palpable that Japanese newspapers were filled with wary editorials about "the Korean challenge," and a middle-level State Department official stated in my earshot that a prime goal of U.S. policy toward Korea was to "manage its articulation with the world economy so that we don't get another Japan there." According to some sources, the Carter administration put off its troop withdrawal plan both to maintain influence in Korea and to stave off ever-increasing Japanese dominance. In June 1979, Jimmy Carter visited Park Chung Hee and toasted him for his stable rule. Six months later Park was assassinated amidst a general political and economic crisis. The timing of the economic crisis may be explained by the second oil wave of early 1979, but the cause of the crisis lay deep in the structure of Korea's economic activity. The late 1970s saw increasing protectionism, declining technology transfer, and a greater need to borrow to meet oil expenses and service previous debt. Furthermore, in dialectical fashion, the remedy that Korea had used to ride out the first oil wave-dispatching construction teams to the Middle East—caused a skilled labor shortage that bid up wages within Korea, thus jeopardizing the ROK's comparative advantage. At the same time, an outward-turning People's China began eating into Korean textile markets. The big steel, shipbuilding, and automobile factories met the very obstacle that free traders had predicted: when ships and cars could not be sold abroad, the small domestic market could not help out. Korean automobile production in late 1979 and 1980 came to a virtual standstill. Thus, as the economist Yung Chul Park stated, all these problems threatened to "bring the export-led industrialization to a rather abrupt end."[98] Korean EPB planners stated publicly that the economy was "uncontrollable" and in a "quandary."

The economic difficulties detonated a political crisis, beginning with vastly enhanced opposition power deployed around Kim Dae Jung. He in turn drew support from textile workers, small businesses and firms with national rather than international interests, and his native southwestern Cholla region, which, historically rebellious and leftist, had been left out of much of the growth of the previous fifteen years. Major urban insurrections occurred in the southeastern cities of Pusan and Masan in the autumn of 1979. Some 700 labor strikes were recorded in 1979-80, and in April 1980 miners took over a small town east of Seoul and held it for several days. In May, hundreds of thousands of students and common people flooded the streets of Seoul, leading to martial law, which in turn touched off a province-wide rebellion in South Cholla and the capture of the provincial capital by rebels who held it for a week. Korea seemed to be on the verge of disintegrating as Iran had done, but unlike Iran the military did not fracture and a new general, Chun Doo Hwan, executed a multistage coup: within the military in December 1979, within the KCIA in April 1980, and throughout the state apparatus in summer 1980. Through withering repression the strong societal reaction was quieted, but at the cost of a deep radicalization of remaining protesters.

In the aftermath of this rebellious period, the Korean state intervened continuously to revive the economy's comparative advantage in the world system. The state sponsored the sectoral reorganization of several large conglomerates, on the principle of one *chaebol* for each industrial sector. For the first time the ROK publicly referred to the "organic" nature of its perimeter defense relationship with Japan, as justification for demanding at least $6 billion in Japanese loans and aid. (In early 1983 Korea and Japan agreed upon a $4 billion package of loans and credits, clearly marking Japan's increasing role as compared to that of the United States.) Finally, the state accomplished a thorough repression of labor in outlawing strikes and unions, closely watching any and all organizing activity, and driving down wages. Thus in 1981 labor productivity increased 16 percent while wages went down 5 percent in real terms. GNP growth of 6.4 percent recovered the loss of 1980.[99] Yet the period 1978-83 has seriously weakened the ROK in its struggle with Taiwan for advantageous position in the world economy.

In 1979, the World Bank reported that "the burden of external debt is being steadily reduced," and agreed with Korean planners that a growth rate for exports of 16 percent and for GNP of 9 to 10 percent per year could be sustained through the 1980s. It noted that "confidence in Korea's ability to meet its external debt service obligations is based on the continuation of rapid export growth."[100] Since the 1980 downturn the economy has grown only in the 5 to 6 percent range, debts have more than doubled since 1979 to a total external debt of $42 billion (third largest in the world), and export growth has tumbled badly. Growing by double-digit rates throughout the 1970s, and by 17 percent in the bad year of 1980 (to $17.2 billion), exports reached $21 billion at the end of 1981 and by mid 1983 were no higher than $22 billion on an annual basis. In other words, export growth has been flat since 1981. Taiwan's exports have not been booming, either, but its external debt is no more than $7 billion and the slowing of export growth has had no apparent effect on internal politics.

Thus, in 1983 as in the rest of this century, Taiwan continues its smooth development, in spite of losing major security guarantees and in spite of structural obstacles to its development. South Korea, on the contrary, plays out its history of economic dynamism mixed with spasmodic social reaction. Today, its development program hangs in the balance.

Conclusions

I have sought to demonstrate the shaping and conditioning effects of economic forces on three distinct societies, peoples, and cultures, and the effects of industrial product cycles on a regional political economy. Japan, Taiwan, and South Korea have come to have similar economic structures (although in different temporal sequences), and all three, with markedly different traditional polities, have adopted quite similar political models and roles for the state. The BAIR model—relative state autonomy, central coordination, bureaucratic short- and long-range planning, high flexibility in moving in and out of industrial sectors, private concentration in big conglomerates, exclusion of labor, exploitation of women, low expenditures on social welfare and, in prewar Japan and contemporary South Korea and Taiwan, militarization and authoritarian repression—is found in all three nations. When one is compared to another the differences will also be salient, but when all three are compared to the rest of the world the similarities are remarkable.

I have also argued that industrial development in Japan, Korea, and Taiwan cannot be considered as an individual country phenomenon; instead, it is a regional phenomenon in which a tripartite hierarchy of core, semiperiphery, and periphery was created in the first part of the 20th century and then slowly recreated after World War II. The smooth development of Taiwan has its counterpart in the spasmodic and troubled development of Korea, and neither can be understood apart from Japan. Not only was Taiwan's society less restive and its state less penetrated by societal constraint, but it also had breathing space occasioned by Japan's greater attention to Korea and Manchuria before 1945, and American "development by invitation" after 1950. In short, the developmental "successes" of Taiwan and Korea are historically and regionally specific, and therefore provide no readily adaptable models for other developing countries interested in emulation.

The evidence also strongly suggests that a hegemonic system is necessary for the functioning of this regional political economy: unilateral colonialism until 1945, U.S. hegemony since 1945. Today there is increasing competition between American and Japanese hegemony over semiperipheral Taiwan and South Korea, but as years pass there may well be sharper competition over a new hinterland, People's China. Will the United States or Japan, or both, organize Chinese labor in the world system? And as Chinese labor-intensive exports increase, whither Taiwan and South Korea? Past history suggests that a triangular structure works best, and so Taiwan and the ROK should move into a middling position between China on the one hand and the United States and Japan on the other. The Chairman of the Korea Exchange Bank, Choon Taik Chung, said in 1981 that "within ten years, Korea will be the bridge. . . between mainland China and the United States." Already, some synthetic textiles made in South Korea are being shipped to China for finishing, taking advantage of cheaper labor cost; the finished product is then sold in American markets. Within Japan, there are voices arguing that Japan should slowly transfer its auto and steel industries to South Korea and Taiwan, placing emphasis instead on high-technology "knowledge industries."[101] The continuing world competitiveness of Japanese auto and steel exports in the early 1980s seems to have slowed this transfer, but it will probably continue. Still, international politics and domestic social forces (especially in Korea) complicate the replication and deepening of this "natural" tripartite hierarchy.

The China connection comes to the heart of the problem. In a recent discussion Raymond Vernon said the Japanese capabilities for exploiting that opportunity are "some orders of magnitude greater than the capacity of the U.S." to deal with it. Jon Halliday argues that Japan is far better positioned than the United States to benefit from the economic opportunities of the 1980s in Northeast Asia.[102] In a situation of stable U.S. hegemony, such as existed from 1951 to 1970 in the region, Japan and the United States could profit equally from such opportunities. Today, in an era of limits, this is not the case. The world system does not provide open access for all. It can tolerate only one or two hegemonies, and only one or two Japans. For the smaller and weaker countries, core-power rivalry spells trouble in the intermediate zone. For Japan, the coming period, like the interwar period, will test its ability both to be successful economically and to live at peace with the world around it: tragically, in the past its striving toward core-power status resembled less flying geese than a moth toward a flame.

Americans, as Vogel suggests, "haven't begun to think about the implications of living in a world where Japan is the most powerful industrial power."[103] They must also decide if they can live at peace with a formidable Japan. And they must contemplate the obvious fact that, in the late 20th century, the race is passing to those who are best organized for competition in a merciless world system. We see this reflected in a poignant observation by Raymond Vernon:

The concept of free access of every country to every market and the gradual reduction of trade barriers and the openness of capital markets, served us well, given our internal political and economic structure, and given our position in the world from 1945 on. All my preferences, all my values argue for retaining this system, for as long as one can. But one observes the way in which Japan has organized itself. . . with a certain unity of purpose, which can easily be exaggerated, but nonetheless at the same time should not be overlooked. One looks at the way in which state enterprises are being used somewhat—*somewhat*. . . by the other advanced industrial countries and now by the developing countries in very considerable degree. Observing these various forms of interference with the operation of market mechanisms, I find myself reluctantly pushed back constantly to the question whether we have to opt for a set of institutional relationships and principles that reflect a second best world from our point of view. We have to somehow organize ourselves.. [104]

Notes

[2] G. C. Allen, *Japan's Economic Policy*, (London: Macmillan, 1980), p. 1; see also Kazushi Ohkawa and Henry Rosovsky, *Japanese Economic Growth: Trend Acceleration in the Twentieth Century* (Stanford, Calif.: Stanford University Press, 1973), pp. 74, 82-83. For the comparisons of growth rates with Korea and Taiwan see Mataji Umemura and Toshiyoki Mizoguchi, eds., *Quantitative Studies on Economic History of Japan Empire* [sic], *1890-1940* (Tokyo: Hitotsubashi University, 1981), p. 64.

[3] Kiyoshi Kojima, *Japan and a New World Economic Order* (Boulder, Colo.: Westview, 1977), pp. 150-51.

[4] L. L. Wade and B. S. Kim, *Economic Development of South Korea: The Political Economy of Success* (New York: Praeger, 1978), p. vi.

[5] See Susan Greenhalgh, "Dependency, Distribution and the Taiwan "Paradox,'" and Denis Simon, "U.S. Assistance, Land Reform, and Taiwan's Political Economy" (both papers presented at the Taiwan Political Economy Workshop, Columbia University, New York, 18-20 December 1980).

[6] For a good example of this line of reasoning see chap. 2 in Edward S. Mason et al., *The Economic and Social Modernization of the Republic of Korea* (Cambridge: Harvard University Press, 1980).

[7] For references, see David P. Calleo and Benjamin M. Rowland, *America and the World Political Economy* (Bloomington: Indiana University Press, 1973), and Jacob Viner, "Power versus Plenty as Objectives of Foreign Policy in the Seventeenth and Eighteenth Centuries," *World Politics* 1 (October 1948), on mercantilism and neomercantilism; Raymond Vernon, *Sovereignty at Bay: The Multinational Spread of U.S. Enterprises* (New York: Basic Books, 1971), on the product cycle and free trade; Immanuel Wallerstein, "The Rise and Future Demise of the World Capitalist System: Concepts for Comparative Analysis," in Wallerstein, ed., *The Capitalist World-Economy* (New York: Cambridge University Press, 1979), for the world system approach.

[8] Charles P. Kindleberger, "Group Behavior and International Trade," *Journal of Political Economy*, February 1951, p. 42.

[9] Wallerstein, "Rise and Future Demise."

[10] Like most interesting concepts, these categories of core, semiperiphery, and periphery have problems of definition and scope, but they are useful for locating nations in the world economy. A similar set of categories is Krasner's tripartite distinction between makers, breakers, and takers among nations. See Stephen D. Krasner, "US Commercial and Monetary Policy: Unravelling the Paradox of External Strength and Internal Weakness," in Peter J. Katzenstein, ed., *Between Power and Plenty: Foreign Economic Policies of Advanced Industrial States* (Madison: University of Wisconsin Press, 1978), pp. 51-52.

[11] See C. Fred Bergsten, Robert O. Keohane, and Joseph S. Nye Jr., "International Politics: a Framework for Analysis," in Bergsten and Lawrence B. Krause, eds., *World Politics and International Economics* (Washington, D.C.: Brookings, 1975), p. 14; also Keohane and Nye, *Power and Interdependence: World Politics in Transition* (Boston: Little, Brown, 1977), pp. 42-46.

[12] The "grand area" was a concept used in Council on Foreign Relations planning in the early 1940s for the postwar period. See Laurence H. Shoup and William Minter, *Imperial Brain Trust: The Council on Foreign Relations and U.S. Foreign Policy* (New York: Monthly Review Press, 1977), pp. 135-40.

[13] Albert O. Hirschman, *National Power and the Structure of Foreign Trade* (1945; rpt. Berkeley: University of California Press, 1980), pp. ix-x; Burke is quoted in Hirschman.

[14] Kindleberger, "Group Behavior," pp. 43-44, 46. The locus classicus for such reasoning is now James R. Kurth, "The Political Consequences of the Product Cycle: Industrial History and Political Outcomes," *International Organization* 33 (Winter 1979), pp. 1-34.

[15] Krasner, "US Commercial and Monetary Policy," p. 60; Alexander Gerschenkron, *Economic Backwardness in Historical Perspective* (Cambridge: Harvard University Press, 1962).

[16] Nicos Poulantzas, *Political Power and the Social Classes* (London: NLB, 1975), part 4.

[17] Karl Polyani, *The Great Transformation* (New York: Farrar & Rinehart, 1944).

[18] See Bruce Cumings, *The Origins of the Korean War: Liberation and the Emergence of Separate Regimes* (Princeton: Princeton University Press, 1981), chap. 1. On Taiwan see Samuel Ho, *The Economic Development of Taiwan 1860-1970* (New Haven: Yale University Press, 1978), pp. 26, 32; he puts a similar emphasis on the role of the colonial state in Taiwan.

[19] Jean-Piene Lehmann, *The Image of Japan: From Feudal Isolation to World Power, 1850-1905* (London: Allen & Unwin, 1978), p. 178; J. M. Winter, "The Webbs and the Non-White World: A Case of Socialist Racialism," *Journal of Contemporary History* 9 (January 1974), pp. 181-92.

[20] Umemura and Mizoguchi, *Quantitative Studies*, pp. 70-77.

[21] David S. Landes, "Japan and Europe: Contrasts in Industrialization," in William W. Lockwood, ed., *The State and Economic Enterprise in Japan* (Princeton: Princeton University Press, 1965), p. 182.

[22] Cumings, *Origins*, chaps. 1 and 2; Ho, *Economic Development*, pp. 28-57; also Chingyuan Lin, *Industrialization in Taiwan, 1946-1972: Trade and Import-Substitute Policies for Developing Countries* (New York: Praeger, 1973), pp. 13-28.

[23] James B. Puluis, *Politics and Policy in Traditional Korea* (Cambridge: Harvard University Press, 1975), pp. 1-19.

[24] Ho, *Economic Development*, pp. 43, 57.

[25] Cumings, *Origins*, chaps. 8-10.

[26] Guenther Stein, *Made in Japan* (London: Methuen, 1935), pp. 181, 191.

[27] Ohkawa and Rosovsky, *Japanese Economic Growth*, pp. 180-83, 197.

[28] Ho, *Economic Development*, pp. 70-90; Lin, *Industrialization in Taiwan*, pp. 19-22.

[29] Mason et al., *Economic and Social Modernization*, pp. 76, 78.

[30] Lin, *Industrialization in Taiwan*, p. 19.

[31] Bruce Cumings, "Corporatism in North Korea," *Journal of Korean Studies* 4 (1983).

[32] Cumings, *Origins*, chaps. 1 and 2.

[33] T. J. Pempel, "Japanese Foreign Economic Policy: The Domestic Bases for International Behavior," in Katzenstein, *Between Power and Plenty*, pp. 139-90.

[34] Chalmers Johnson, "A Japanese Model?" (Paper presented at the Japan Seminar, University of Washington, School of International Studies, Seattle, May 1981); also Johnson, *MITI and the Japanese Miracle* (Stanford, Calif.: Stanford University Press, 1982), pp. 305-24.

[35] Allen, *Japan's Economic Policy*, pp. 42-50, 119-20.

[36] Ohkawa and Rosovsky, *Japanese Economic Growth*, pp. 221-23.

[37] Allen, *Japan's Economic Policy*, pp. 50, 102, 128.

[38] Ibid., pp. 51-54.

[39] John Emmerson, *The Japanese Thread* (New York: Holt, Rinehart & Winston, 1978), p. 256. I am indebted to Michael Schaller for providing me with this quotation.

[40] Jon Halliday, *A Political History of Japanese Capitalism* (New York: Pantheon, 1975), pp. 183-84.

[41] Akira Iriye, "Continuities in U.S.-Japanese Relations, 1941-1949," in Yonosuke Nagai and Iriye. eds., *The Origins of the Cold War in Asia* (Tokyo: University of Tokyo Press, 1977), pp. 378-407.

[42] Viner, "Power versus Plenty," p. 91.

[43] John G. Roberts, "The 'Japan Crowd' and the Zaibatsu Restoration," *Japan Interpreter* 12 (Summer 1979), pp. 384-415.

[44] Charles S. Maier, "The Politics of Productivity: Foundations of American International Economic Policy after World War II," in Katzenstein, *Between Power and Plenty*, p. 45.

[45] Halliday, *Political History*, p. 183.

[46] See Kennan's remarks in "Transcript of Roundtable Discussion," *U.S. Department of State,* 6, 7, and 8 October 1949, pp. 25, 47, in *Carrollton Press Declassified Documents Series,* 1977, 316B.

[47] Central Intelligence Agency, ORE 43-48, 24 May 1948, in HST/PSF file, Memos 1945-49, box 255, Harry S. Truman Library, Independence, Missouri.

[48] Economic Cooperation Administration, unsigned memorandum of 3 November 1948, in Dean Acheson Papers, box 27, Harry S. Truman Library.

[49] *Central Intelligence Agency, ORE 69-49, "Relative US Security Interest in the European-Mediterranean Area and the Far East," 14 July 1949, in HST/PSF file, Memos 1945-49, box 249, Harry S. Truman Library.*

[50] *Calleo and Rowland, America and the World Political Economy, pp. 198-202.*

[51] *Draft paper, NSC 48, 26 October 1949, in NSC materials, box 207, Harry S. Truman Library. For a fuller elaboration see Bruce Cumings, "Introduction: The Course of American Policy toward Korea, 1945-53," in Cumings, ed., Child of Conflict: The Korean-American Relationship, 1945-1953 (Seattle: University of Washington Press, 1983).*

[52] *Krasner, "US Commercial and Monetary Policy," pp. 63-66; Hirschman, National Power, passim.*

[53] *Jon Halliday, "Japan's Changing Position in the Global Political Economy" (Paper presented at the annual meeting of the Association for Asian Studies, 1979, Los Angeles).*

[54] *See ibid.; also Martha Caldwell, "Petroleum Politics in Japan: State and Industry in a Changing Policy Context" (Ph.D. diss., University of Wisconsin, 1980), chap. 2.*

[55] *Ezra F. Vogel, "Growing Japanese Economic Capabilities and the U.S.-Japan Relationship" (Summary of the 1st meeting of the American Discussion Group on U.S. Policy toward Japan, Harvard University, 13 December 1979; hereafter cited as Harvard Seminar 1979).*

[56] *Johnson, "A Japan Model?" Also Allen, Japan's Economic Policy, pp. 108-9.*

[57] *Pempel, "Japanese Foreign Economic Policy," pp. 163-64; Halliday, "Japan's Changing Position"; Halliday, Political History, p. 283.*

[58] *Ohkawa and Rosovsky, Japanese Economic Growth, pp. 118, 235-36; Pempel, "Japanese Foreign Economic Policy," pp. 149-55.*

[59] *Ho, Economic Development, p. 103; Lin, Taiwan's Industrialization, pp. 27-28.*

[60] *Ho, Economic Development, p. 104.*

[61] *CIA, Handbook 1979; also Ho, Economic Development, pp. 108-11; also Mason et al., Economic and Social Modernization, p. 165.*

[62] *CIA, Handbook 1979.*

[63] *Allen, Japan's Economic Policy, p. 130.*

[64] *Ho, Economic Development, p. 237.*

[65] *Immanuel Wallerstein, "Dependence in an Interdependent World," in Wallerstein, Capitalist World-Economy.*

[66] *Ohkawa and Rosovsky, Japanese Economic Development, p. 92.*

[67] *On Korea, see Mason et al., Economic and Social Modernization, pp. 7-8; also Paul W. Kuznets, Economic Growth and Structure in the Republic of Korea (New Haven: Yale University Press, 1977), pp. 48-71; on Taiwan see Lin, Taiwan's Industrialization, pp. 3-4, and Ho, Economic Development, p. 106.*

[68] *Alice H. Amsden, "Taiwan's Economic History: A Case of Etatisme and a Challenge to Dependency Theory," Modern China 5 (July 1979), p. 362.*

[69] *Paul B. Simpson, "Report on the University of Oregon Advisory Mission," mimeo. (Eugene: University of Oregon, 1961), p. 49. I am indebted to Tony Michel for bringing this quotation to my attention.*

[70] *Guillermo A. O'Donnell, Modernization and Bureaucratic-Authoritarianism in South American Politics (Berkeley: University of California Institute for International Studies, 1973); see also the articles by O'Donnell, Fernando Henrique Cardoso, Robert Kaufman, James Kurth, Albert Hirschman, and Jose Serra in David Collier, ed., The New Authoritarianism in Latin America (Princeton: Princeton University Press, 1979). Serra, Hirschman, and, in part, Kaufman challenge the O'Donnell theses.*

[71] *Mason et al., Economic and Social Modernization, p. 47; Ian M. D. Little, "An Economic Renaissance," in Walter Galenson, ed., Economic Growth and Structural Change in Taiwan (Ithaca: Cornell University Press, 1979), p. 474. See also Ho, Economic Development, p. 195.*

[72] *Mason et al., Economic and Social Modernization, pp. 96, 129-32; Kuznets, Economic Growth, pp. 73, 96-97; Lin, Taiwan's Industrialization, pp. 83-93.*

[73] *Kuznets, Economic Growth, p. 103; Wade and Kim, Economic Development, p. 100; Suh Sang Chul, "Development of a New Industry through Exports: The Electronics Industry in Korea," in Wontack Hong and Anne O. Krueger, eds., Trade and Development in Korea (Seoul: Korea Development Institute, 1975).*

[74] Lin, *Taiwan's Industrialization,* p. 134.

[75] Samuel Huntington, *Political Order in Changing Societies* (New Haven: Yale University Press, 1968), pp. 7, 25, 258-61.

[76] Mason et al., *Economic and Social Modernization,* pp. 16-17.

[77] Kuznets, *Economic Growth,* p. 85; see also pp. 105-7.

[78] Mason et al., *Economic and Social Modernization,* pp. 16, 263, 485.

[79] Ibid., p. 277.

[80] Ibid., pp. 19, 486.

[81] Ho, *Economic Development,* p. 251.

[82] Mason et al., *Economic and Social Modernization,* p. 22.

[83] Lin, *Taiwan's Industrialization,* pp. 139-44; Choe Boum Jong, "An Economic Study of the Masan Free Trade Zone," in Hong and Krueger, *Trade and Development.*

[84] Kuznets, *Economic Growth,* p. 67; Mason et al., *Economic and Social Modernization,* p. 99; Greenhalgh, "Dependency, Distribution"; seminar paper by Anthony Michel, University of Washington, Seattle, 5 May 1983.

[85] Kuznets, *Economic Growth,* p. 152; Lin, *Taiwan's Industrialization,* p. 137.

[86] Daniel Chirot, *Social Change in the Twentieth Century* (New York: Harcourt Brace Jovanovich, 1977), pp. 218-20.

[87] David C. Cole and Princeton N. Lyman, *Korean Development: The Interplay of Politics and Economics* (Cambridge: Harvard University Press, 1971), p. 135; also Kuznets, *Economic Growth,* p. 71.

[88] Greenhalgh, "Dependency, Distribution."

[89] Lin, *Taiwan's Industrialization,* pp. 131-32.

[90] Wade and Kim, *Economic Development,* p. 10; Kuznets, *Economic Growth,* p. 103.

[91] Hirschman, *National Power,* pp. 34-35.

[92] Ibid., p. 30.

[93] Mason et al., *Economic and Social Modernization,* pp. 138, 497; Kuznets, *Economic Growth,* p. 73.

[94] Kuznets, *Economic Growth,* p. 85.

[95] Lin, *Taiwan's Industrialization,* p. 173.

[96] Vogel, *Harvard Seminar 1979.*

[97] Lin, *Taiwan's Industrialization,* p. 134.

[98] A good summary of the recent economic problems of the ROK's export-led program can be found in Yung Chul Park, "Recent Economic Developments in Korea" (Paper presented to the Columbia University Seminar on Korea, 24 April 1981).

[99] See "South Korea's New Leader: Off and Running," *Far Eastern Economic Review,* 30 January-5 February 1981; *Christian Science Monitor,* 5 January 1982; *Tonga Ilbo (East Asia Daily),* 26 December 1981.

[100] World Bank, *Korea: A World Bank Country Economic Report,* Parvez Hasan and D. C. Rao, coordinators (Baltimore: Johns Hopkins University Press, 1979), pp. 8-9, 47. This is also a good source on World Bank criticism of Korea's deepening industrialization strategy during the Third Five Year Plan.

[101] Lecture by Norman Thorpe, Seoul correspondent for the Asian Wall Street Journal, Seattle, Wash., 8 January 1982; also John Marcom Jr., "Korea Dents Japanese Dominance in Steel," *Asian Wall Street Journal,* 28 December 1981.

[102] Raymond Vernon, in *Harvard Seminar 1979;* Jon Halliday, "The Struggle for East Asia," *New Left Review* no. 124 (December 1980), pp. 3-24.

[103] Vogel in *Harvard Seminar 1979.*

[104] Vernon in ibid.

Economic Reform in China:
The recent policy changes in perspective

Luc De Wulf

With the Decision on the Reform of the Economic Structure, announced on October 20, 1984, China dramatically consolidated and accelerated a process of reform that had begun more than five years earlier. In the late 1970s, in the years after the "Cultural Revolution" and in the midst of growing official concern with slow improvement in living standards, the Chinese leadership first expressed interest in new approaches to the country's economic development. While overall growth since the 1949 Revolution had been remarkable, it was achieved largely through the application of greater amounts of physical capital and manpower rather than through more efficient use of resources. There was concern that the sacrifices required were becoming disproportionate to the gains achieved. Past economic development, with its emphasis on large-scale investment, growth of heavy industry, mass participation, and egalitarianism, had left workers and peasants with only moderate increases in incomes and inadequate supplies of consumer goods. Citing excessive levels of investment, rigid administrative control over resource allocation, insufficient individual incentives, and undue emphasis on local, regional, and national self-sufficiency, the authorities laid the groundwork for economic reform.

The Four Modernizations Program, launched by the Central Committee of the Communist Party in December 1978, sought to put China on the path of sustained, balanced, and rapid development. It represented a break with past economic policies and announced the process of widespread economic reforms. Although it did not present a blueprint for the new economic system, it did indicate a commitment to trying different methods of resource allocation and distribution. Under this program, experiments were evaluated, modified, and implemented on a national scale when judged beneficial, and changed or eliminated when found inappropriate. From the very beginning, China's economic reforms have been part of a pragmatic and dynamic process, one that combined both bold steps forward and strategic retreats.

The 1984 Decision has distilled the essence of these various earlier reforms and has sketched the direction in which the authorities intend to steer the economy. As such, and for the first time, the reforms have been presented as a comprehensive, continuous undertaking, backed by the full authority of the Central Committee. This is expected to muster the support of those party members who had been opposed to the reform movement on ideological grounds and of those who had been reluctant to implement what they viewed as a passing phenomenon. Although no precise timetable has been presented for the introduction of the reforms, most of them are to be in place within five years. Price, banking, and monetary reforms, however, are expected to require additional time.

Originally published in *Finance and Development*, vol. 21, no. 1, March 1985. Reprinted with permission.

This article surveys the nature and intent of these reforms; its coverage is selective and deals primarily with agricultural and industrial reforms. Reforms in the public finance and banking sectors are mentioned only briefly and, for lack of space, China's efforts to attract foreign direct investment and increase international trade are not examined.

Agriculture

China replaced its agricultural cooperatives with communes in 1958 but the reorganization, followed by two years of disastrous weather, so disrupted agricultural production that it took more than five years for it to regain the 1957-58 level of output. Commune production subsequently realized moderate growth, but often at high costs. More rapid increases in production were hampered by an incentive structure that did not link remuneration to effort, by detailed high-level planning that often neglected to take local circumstances into account, and by political interference in production decisions.

To remedy this, a production responsibility system was introduced on an experimental basis in two provinces as early as 1978. Success there in increasing productivity gradually led to the introduction of the system in most rural areas, including some state farms. Production responsibility systems differ slightly from one another, but all are based on a contractual relationship between the commune and a group of farmers, a household, or an individual. These contracts specify the amount of land to be cultivated, the amount and type of produce the contractor is to deliver to the state, and the required tax payments and contributions to the welfare and investment funds. The contracts, as they refer to access to land, were originally valid for 5 years, and have, since January 1983, been extended to 15 years (50 years for orchards); amounts of produce, and other aspects of the contract, are adjusted more frequently. Contracts can be passed on to children or other beneficiaries, and can be sold with the permission of the commune; compensation for improvements, such as irrigation or application of fertilizer, may be negotiated. The contractor is free to dispose of excess produce in free markets. These free markets, which had all but disappeared during the "Cultural Revolution," have been revived, and their operation has been facilitated by state authorization permitting long distance transportation and marketing for all agricultural produce—even grain, a commodity whose trade had been a state monopoly since 1949. Simultaneously, the commune's production and economic responsibilities have been divorced from its administrative functions, which now reside with the newly revived townships.

The response to these changes has been impressive and is credited with a large share of the 9 percent average annual growth in agricultural production realized in 1981-83. Admittedly, increased procurement prices, which rose 20 to 25 percent in 1979, favorable weather conditions, and the shift back toward greater regional specialization contributed to this performance. Yet both personal observation and reports from experts indicate that the system has infused the rural areas with a new enthusiasm and has been much better able to draw on the resourcefulness of the peasants.

The rural reform, however, has not come without problems. The more efficient utilization of the rural work force has made about one third of the agricultural workers redundant and created the need for alternative forms of employment. In order to avoid the social and economic problems of large-scale rural-urban migration, the authorities continue to control such migration strictly. Therefore, new employment possibilities have had to be created in the rural areas themselves. To meet this need, industrial production in the rural areas and nonagricultural activities, such as livestock breeding, water resource management, commerce, handicrafts, catering, construction, and transportation, have been stimulated and are currently, in fact, the fastest growing sectors in the economy. About 10 percent of the rural work force is now employed in the industrial sector, while between 10 and 15 percent is engaged in various specialized nonagricultural occupations. In more advanced regions, such as Jiangsu, the share of industrial employment is much higher, but further progress will be needed to meet this challenge.

Another problem that followed the success of the production responsibility system has been the emergence of acute shortages of consumer goods, agricultural inputs, and construction materials. The rural population now possesses greater purchasing power, but the supply of goods has not kept pace with demand. Authorities have been making more industrial production available to the countryside, and moderate progress has been made.

Industry

The Four Modernizations Program, which initiated the reforms, gave equal emphasis to urban and rural areas. Yet reforms in the rural areas have proceeded more speedily and are now virtually completed. In the urban areas, where economic relations are much more complex, reforms have been implemented more slowly, with more time devoted to experimenting. On the basis of this experimentation and heartened by the success of the production responsibility system in the rural areas, authorities have indicated in the 1984 Decision a willingness to accelerate urban reforms.

These reforms principally seek to redress inefficiency in the state-owned industrial sector, which the authorities have laid to several interrelated factors. First, mandatory central planning, which was inspired by the Soviet model in the 1950s and may have been proper for the simple economy of that period and in the context of forced growth based on the development of heavy industry, is now seen as insufficiently flexible to deal with the greater complexity of an expanding industrial base. Second, enterprises were constrained in their pursuit of efficiency. Treated as departments of government agencies and managed as such, they were, until recently, required to hand over all their profits to the budget, which in turn covered their losses and provided their investment funds in the form of a grant from the budget. Supply and distribution channels were rigid and unresponsive to shifts in demand; wages were set to give more weight to seniority than job performance or enterprise profitability; bonuses were prohibited; and recruitment and dismissal of workers were outside the purview of the manager. Third, the price structure was greatly distorted. This complicated the assessment of enterprise performance, hampered the introduction of technological innovation and the rationalization of the production mix, distorted consumption patterns, and caused both shortages of goods with low profit margins and excess production of goods with artificially high margins. Because consumer prices for many goods were less than procurement prices, the budget incurred large subsidy expenditures. Fourth, the preeminent role of state-owned and collective enterprises, combined with a disregard for the contributions that could be made by the private sector, deprived the economy of a source of creativity and left whole areas of consumer demand unsatisfied. (The private sector refers to small enterprises run by individuals or groups of individuals.) The purpose of the industrial reforms, therefore, was to modify the economic environment within which enterprises operated so that they would become independent economic entities, responsible for their own profits and losses, and endowed with both the incentives and the authority to improve their efficiency and profitability. The essence of these reforms can best be captured by looking at their impact on planning, enterprise management, prices, and the role of the private sector.

Planning. In the course of the next few years, the scope of mandatory planning in China will be narrowed, while that of guidance planning expanded. Planning will concentrate on outlining the direction the economy should take, while increasing use will be made of macroeconomic policy instruments, such as correct price signals, taxation, credit and interest rates, profits, and wage differentials. The 1984 Directive indicated that in the future mandatory planning will be restricted to major products that have a direct bearing on the national economy and on the standard of living. The central plan will include output targets for energy, rolled steel, cement, basic raw materials for the chemical industry, and synthetic fiber. In agriculture, targets will be used for cereals, cotton, edible oil, tobacco, jute, pigs, and fish products. All in all, mandatory planning will eventually pertain to only 60 industrial and 10 agricultural commodities, down from 120 and 29 at present. Other products will be more broadly regulated through a guidance plan, with state and collective enterprises and the private sector allowed to compete among themselves. Although no statistics are yet available to gauge the importance of the commodities under the mandatory plan, it appears, for the near future at least, that they will continue to constitute the bulk of total production but they will comprise a much smaller share of the number of commodities.

The reform effort has squarely faced the possibility that some enterprises outside the sphere of mandatory planning may not be able to withstand competition. Already a number of enterprises that were unable to meet the required quality or cost standards have been merged with other enterprises, forced to change their line of business, or simply closed down. These consolidations differ, however, from bankruptcy in market economies, since the state attempts to minimize both the loss of productive capacity and the transitional problems for the workers affected.

Enterprise management. The new reforms recognize that in order for enterprises to be run as independent economic entities and assume responsibility for their own results, they must be given greater authority and greater incentives to work efficiently. This has led to the introduction of a whole series of interconnected reforms,

Enterprise management is to be gradually separated from the government agencies that, until now, have taken most managerial decisions. These agencies will now set broad policies, coordinate production, and assist enterprises in the achievement of their own objectives. With this newly acquired independence, enterprises are being made increasingly responsible for their own profits and losses, and a system to determine which share of the profits will be retained by the enterprises is being put into place.

After experimenting with several profitsharing and income tax schemes, an income tax for state-owned enterprises was introduced in mid-1983 and was fully implemented by the end of 1984. The rate of this income tax has been set at 55 percent. But as price distortions affect enterprise profitability often more than does managerial efficiency, an adjustment tax has been applied to the after-tax profits, to bring profits more or less in line with those retained before the introduction of the income tax. The new system also has allowed enterprises that improve their profitability to retain the larger part of increased profits. Although the new tax system is intended to provide a legal basis for the disposal of profits, and therefore streamline the relations between the supervisory agencies and the enterprises, it will not yield its full potential until the price structure has been rationalized.

Directors of enterprises are now to be appointed by supervisory departments, and their authority has been broadened under the new reforms. Workers' Congresses continue to exist, but their role in managerial decision making has been circumscribed. The managers have now been allowed greater discretion in the recruitment and dismissal of workers and do not have to absorb workers assigned by the employment department, as was the practice in the past. They now have the authority to organize job-specific examinations and recruit accordingly. As a corollary, workers have been granted somewhat greater mobility, and school graduates have been encouraged to submit job applications to various employers. Managers have also been given greater discretion to promote better and more qualified workers and to dismiss those that do not perform well.

The wage policy has also undergone rapid change. In 1979 enterprises began to give bonuses to more efficient workers. These bonuses initially could not exceed 2.5 months of basic salary, a restriction abolished in 1984. Now enterprises can grant the bonuses they choose, but a progressive tax has been levied on enterprises that grant bonuses in excess of 2.5 months of basic wages. The regulations specifying that only enterprises that achieve profits and improve their performance can grant bonuses have also been strengthened. A common problem, however, with the bonus system has been that managers often distribute them in a egalitarian fashion, thus undermining their very purpose.

The October 1984 Decision endorsed the policy of bonuses but went one step further and recommended that the wage system itself be reformed, widening the wage differentials between various trades and jobs, and increasing the remuneration for mental work. These deviations from the strict egalitarianism that long had been the hallmark of much of China's development model are deemed necessary as the previous system was felt to have undermined workers' commitment to tasks and bred mediocrity. The authorities, however, do not feel that gearing remuneration of workers to their contribution absolves society from its responsibility of taking care of the less fortunate.

Prices. The present distortions in China's price structure are largely the result of adherence to a system of fixed prices that gradually became divorced from productivity developments and unrelated to international prices. This allowed wages to remain stable for very long periods, but the budget eventually had to absorb the increases in procurement costs for basic necessities. As a result, in 1983, subsidies for basic necessities constituted nearly one fourth of budgetary expenditures.

These shortcomings in the price system were first recognized in 1979 but adjustment was not believed possible within the context of the Sixth Five-Year plan (1981–85). A consensus, however, appeared to develop that price reform would be undertaken in earnest in the Seventh Five-Year Plan (1986–90). Partial measures were taken in the meantime, and some prices were changed. Foremost among these was an increase in agricultural procurement prices in 1979. Since consumer prices were only partially increased, however, budgetary subsidies rose sharply. Selective price increases have also been granted for commodities that were in short supply or whose production costs had increased substantially, while prices for certain other goods were reduced, often to help producers unload overstocks or to keep down increases in the cost of living. In addition to these changes, some producers were authorized to let prices for some of their output fluctuate within a fixed margin around the state-fixed prices or to negotiate the price of a share of their production. These more

Adjustment and reform in the Chongqing Clock and Watch Company, Sichuan Province, China

Here is an example of how one company responded to reforms in the period 1978-82. The Chongqing Clock and Watch Company (CCWC) was one of five state-owned companies chosen by Sichuan province to participate in experimental reforms under the Four Modernizations program. This gave the company some prominence in China's reform of light industry.

CCWC is one of the 12 largest producers of watches in China—a country where over half the urban residents own watches, and whose production and purchase of clocks and watches are unusually high for its per capita income level. The company started producing clocks in 1958, and began full-scale production of watches in 1977. By 1978, it employed 2,600 workers.

In the late 1970s, its output rose rapidly as a result of large investments financed by state grants. But the company suffered from shortages of capital, land, and labor (hiring of new workers being a highly restricted and tedious process); it had little authority to make decisions, and little incentive to expand production or to improve efficiency.

● **The reforms**. These were introduced mainly in 1980, and included:

1. Organizational changes, permitting joint ventures and various forms of association with other enterprises, which gave the company access to more resources, including land for expansion and increased its control over the production of parts and components.

2. CCWC was among the pioneers of a new incentive system replacing the remittance of profits to government with payments of income tax. From 1980 onward CCWC was allowed to retain 60 percent of its total net product, which it used for wages, bonuses, and various benefits to workers, and to invest in expansion.

3. Financing of fixed investment by bank loans and retained profits, rather than by grants from the budget. The terms of the loans were such that the enterprise bore very little of the financial risk of productive investment.

4. The end of guaranteed purchase by commercial units of all the company's output. Permission to market some of its output gave the company a strong reason to base its production decisions on forecasts of market demand. The company could not set its own output prices, however.

5. CCWC was authorized to plan its own production, investment, and investment financing, and could play a significant role in planning sales. It could contract directly with suppliers when its needs exceeded its input allocation quotas. Targets were still set by higher authorities for physical output of the company's main products, product quality, labor productivity, and profit. They were not rigidly enforced, however, and appear to have had little influence on the company's actual production.

6. Since 1978, the company has been allowed to pay bonuses for efficient work, but in other labor matters there was little change. Quotas largely unrelated to the production plan limited the number of workers the firm could hire, and redundant workers could not be dismissed. When several hundred were made redundant by the collapse of the clock market in 1982, the worst that happened was that groups of 300 workers at a time were placed on study leave, with temporary loss of bonuses.

These reforms and policy measures eliminated the most important constraints on CCWC's expansion of production. They also gave the company strong material incentives to increase production and profits. The company has allocated bonuses rather evenly among workers. However, a high proportion of its retained profits could be used to construct subsidized housing for its workers. Housing, which was in extremely short supply, was funded entirely by the company and allocated or the basis of seniority. This gave workers a strong incentive to raise the company's profits.

CCWC responded to the new opportunities with a highly ambitious expansion program supported by heavy borrowing. Gross output nearly tripled between 1979 and 1981. To a large extent, the company geared its decisions to the interests of workers and their dependents. Employment increased by 50 percent, while average annual wages per employee rose from 755 yuan to 950 yuan. The average value of nonproductive fixed assets per worker (mainly housing) more than tripled from 1979 to 1982.

● **Marketing problems emerge.** By the end of 1981 the clock market had become saturated. And there were signs that watch producers, too, had overextended their capacity. National planning authorities intervened, limiting CCWC's targets for watch production to about half those planned by the company, and a reduction in watch prices imposed in April 1982 cut the firm's profit margins. At the end of 1981 CCWC began to have difficulty controlling the quality of its first-grade watches. In 1982, its clock production fell by 50 percent; watch production increased by only 10 percent; gross output rose by only 3.9 percent (compared with 66 percent in both 1980 and 1981); and total profits and retained profits fell by nearly one third.

The government's limitations on watch production and prices forced the company to confront more abruptly a marketing problem that was bound to emerge eventually. Despite this problem—the bane of consumer durables producers worldwide—the company had been left with strong financial incentives. It reacted by changing its development strategy from expansion of existing products to the development of new products and improvements in quality.

● **A change in strategy.** The change was accomplished through: (1) Selective adherence to the rules restricting the company's actions and affecting incentives. It seems likely that in this regard the company received special consideration by virtue of its prominence in the reform program. (2) Vigorously promoting sales. The most extreme example occurred in 1983, when several hundred clock production workers were forced to go out and sell clocks to avoid losing their bonuses and part of their wage. (3) Developing new products and varieties (including a washing machine timer and a gold-plated watch). On the whole, the company has been more successful in diversifying watch production than in finding new products to replace clocks. (4) Price reductions. Where possible, CCWC cut prices directly. Cuts in watch prices were forbidden because, being highly profitable and highly taxed, watch sales helped to maintain government revenue. Here the company disguised price reductions by changing the product mix and improving the quality of each grade of watch.

● **Conclusions.** CCWC's development in the past few years exemplifies how an enterprise can make the transition from extensive growth (by expanding the volume of output) to intensive growth (largely by widening the variety of its products and improving their quality). Promoting this transition is the underlying goal of China's economic reforms. In CCWC's case, the transition was accomplished in response to a mixture of reform in incentives, changes in market conditions, and direct government intervention that hastened the action of underlying market forces.

flexible price practices were largely restricted to overstocked commodities and to production in excess of the state-fixed production quota. But prices of commodities of lesser importance were increasingly freed from state control and were allowed to be determined by market forces. Similarly, the prices agreed upon between buyers and sellers on free markets were totally freed, although in principle the state retained the authority to intervene whenever prices would otherwise increase too fast.

The 1984 Decision has given greater urgency to the implementation of price reform. Although no definite timetable has been announced, it was made clear that prices will change, and change soon, albeit gradually. In essence the Decision announced that the scope of state-controlled prices will be reduced, while that of prices agreed between buyers and sellers will be expanded. The logic of this reform, therefore, is to create a situation in which prices-whether state-controlled or not—will reflect their production cost and take into account the supply and demand forces in the economy. The Decision recognizes that this will lead to increased prices for some commodities and reductions for others, yet it makes clear that the reform will not be allowed to cause a generalized price increase. The message is that the price reform will be introduced gradually, and the various economic agents given time to adjust to the changes by altering their production or input mix, or by absorbing cost increases through productivity gains. To the extent that subsidies will be phased out and prices of previously subsidized goods increased, real incomes of consumers will be protected as wages and other income elements will be increased accordingly. The Decision also predicts that real wages will continue to increase, since the reforms will boost productivity gains. In these circumstances the maintenance of price stability will greatly depend on the implementation of a monetary policy that prevents excessive liquidity growth in the economy.

The implementation of the price reform will be the most difficult element of the whole economic reform movement, since it will have an impact on all segments of economic activity. Financial flows will be affected, as will enterprise profitability, thus putting at risk the lines of production of some enterprises and the survival of others. Similarly, budgetary flows and sectoral credit requirements will be changed. The realization of this pervasive impact of the price reform on the economy explains the authorities' past reluctance to tackle this issue. There is an awareness now, however, that the benefits of the economic reforms will be jeopardized if the price structure is not altered, and this has prompted the authorities to accelerate the price reform.

Diversification of the economic structure. The widely recognized failure of the state and collective production sectors to respond effectively to market demand, to take sufficient advantage of the creativity of the work force, and to absorb growing numbers of people looking for employment led authorities not only to permit private activity to take place but also to stimulate such activities and clarify their scope. In the early years of the reforms, private sector activities were regarded with suspicion by some local authorities, who took arbitrary measures to prevent them from flourishing, but their contributions in providing new employment and new services have been gradually recognized. The number of private establishments has risen sharply in recent years, with these enterprises often absorbing graduates unable to find employment in state or collective enterprises. By the end of 1983 private establishments formed a still small, but rapidly growing, share of the total work force (about 2.3 million workers now, nearly a threefold increase since 1980). They are principally engaged in small-scale commerce, handicraft, catering, transport, and construction. Since early 1983 the private sector has been invited to lease small state-owned enterprises or to run them on a contract basis. As such, the role of the private sector is now firmly established in China, and its contribution is recognized as an irreplaceable element in the continued improvement of China's living standards.

Commerce. As recently as 1978 state and collective sectors accounted for 90 percent of total retail trade, thereby effectively monopolizing distribution channels. Production was largely insulated from distribution, and unsold inventories of some products and shortages of others were frequent. In addition, administrative barriers to trade between regions prevented the free flow of goods, and gave rise to costly local monopolies.

To alleviate these deficiencies, distribution channels were gradually diversified. Since 1979, private sector trade, virtually abolished during the "Cultural Revolution," has been revived and by 1983 it accounted for more than 18 percent of total retail sales and a much larger share of the trade in vegetables, eggs, handicrafts and small industrial commodities. Recent reforms streamlined regulations pertaining to private trade, spelling out registration requirements, tax obligations, and rights.

Efforts have been underway for several years to bring the productive sector more in line with the commercial sectors; these are intended to help producers gear their output more toward market demand. Commercial enterprises are being urged to purchase according to prior orders rather than stock all products that enterprises have to sell. Manufacturers have also been prompted to improve their market research and participate more actively in the work of the commercial sector in selling slow moving commodities. This may require discounts or the repurchase of defective products, both practices that have been extremely rare in the past.

Administrative barriers between jurisdictions and between urban and rural areas, erected when local self-sufficiency was at a premium, are gradually being abolished. These restrictions had given rise to a multi-tiered distribution system that prevented the rationalization of trade transactions, burdened administrative and transport facilities, contributed to the maintenance of excessive inventories, and promoted the existence of small high-cost, regional producers. At present, experiments are under way to merge several levels of wholesale trade and to create an integrated supply network based on central cities, thereby unifying urban and rural markets. Progress has been slow, partly because of entrenched positions and interests but also because many jurisdictions want to protect their inefficient enterprises from the competition of outside producers.

In conclusion. . .

The process of economic reform now under way in China represents a very important development in China's history. It entails not only a realistic assessment of the development model of the past but also a commitment to safeguard the socialist nature of Chinese society while allowing resource allocation to be influenced increasingly by macroeconomic instruments, the forces of supply and demand, and material incentives. In the process, mandatory planning and administrative interference will be reduced.

This shift in gears initiated in 1978 has proceeded rapidly and produced good results in the rural areas; in the urban areas progress has been much slower, and the newest reforms focus attention on this sector. A "blueprint" of the type of economy Chinese authorities want to realize is now available. Its full implementation is still a long way off and a number of obstacles will have to be overcome. Some of these pertain to the manner in which enterprises will adapt to the changed economic environment. Although most of the problems have now been identified, practical solutions are still to be implemented. Other obstacles are more subtle, but may be more intractable. One will be to persuade an established bureaucracy, accustomed to taking nearly all production decisions, that it should relinquish some of its prerogatives, and allow decisions to be taken in a less structured manner and with a less predictable outcome. Another will be to adjust an economic philosophy that, for many years, has emphasized strict adherence to egalitarianism and job security rather than economic efficiency, without alienating the adherents of the previous approach. Furthermore, China recognizes that a successful implementation of the reforms will require further progress in giving greater responsibility to younger and better educated personnel and in accelerating managerial and financial training.

In the years ahead, Chinese leaders will have to steer the country over uncharted territory. While other countries have reformed their economy or are in the process of doing so, no other country has attempted economic reform on this scale affecting one billion people. Under its previous management system, China made considerable progress toward meeting the people's basic needs. Now it wants to do even better.

The Pacific Challenge

Stuart L. Smith

A profound change is underway in the world's economy. The new agenda is being set in Japan, a nation ironically thrust into such a prominent role by the oil shocks of the 1970's. The irony arises out of the fact that Japan was the one nation that was supposed to be least able to sustain those same oil-related adjustments.

Admittedly, while Japan sets the agenda, the United States of America will likely remain dominant in the global economy for the foreseeable future. But the directions set by Japan, and improved upon by the United States, will have enormous implications for Canada. Canada cannot afford to lag too far behind either the United States or Japan in economic performance; too large a lag would mean the loss of our best people south of the border and would reduce our will for national survival. We must therefore examine the new world economic order and find a place within it for a competitive Canada.

The United States is now and always will be Canada's major trading partner. After that, however, Canada's trade with the Pacific is much larger than with the Atlantic and the trend is rapidly accelerating. Never again will Canada's Atlantic trade be even close to that with Pacific nations. The sooner Canada begins to think of itself as a Pacific rather than an Atlantic nation, the better it is likely to do. This should guide the courses taught in universities and in business schools, the sales agencies and trade offices set up, the languages and customs studied. Perhaps it is time to replace the usual Atlantic-centre with a Pacific-centred one in the Canadian consciousness.

The oil shocks caused all countries, but especially Japan, to emphasize products and production methods that saved energy and raw materials, these being commodities for which Japan is dependent upon other nations. Central to these savings have been a number of technologies which, although not altogether new, were brought to a very advanced state in the 1970's: namely, robotics, microelectronics and the development of new materials. The United States, after suffering serious damage to many of its key industries, recognized the importance of innovative technology and has established leadership in additional areas, including information software, life sciences and biotechnology.

As automation advances, it has become easier to move the production of mature, mass-produced items to newly industrializing countries where wages are still low. For the advanced nations, a greater proportion of world trade every year is represented by innovative, high value-added, knowledge-intensive products and related services. In these fields, the United States and Japan are predominant, with Western Europe struggling to keep up.

On the other hand, raw materials are declining as a proportion of world trade. More specifically, Canada has local supply problems in some instances (e.g. forestry and fisheries), and international supply side problems with "unfair" competition from the Third World producers of metals. Beyond, that, however, there are serious long-term demand limitations as a consequence of various factors, including:

Originally published in *International Perspectives*, October 1984. Reprinted with permission.

a) substitution of new materials (e.g. fibreoptics for copper, electronics for newsprint, composites for steel, ceramics for aluminum)

b) increased quality and durability of products; and

c) lightweight, down-sized, energy-efficient items.

To put it succinctly, for Canada, while food and energy production will continue to be a significant source of wealth, many other basic commodities may run into serious problems. As for manufactured goods, products can frequently be more cheaply produced elsewhere. Canada is obliged to automate its industries and to enter into knowledge-intensive industries producing sophisticated, high quality products with a high research content for world markets.

The need for this change must be emphasized as strongly as possible. The world is now poised on the threshold of a golden era in the advance of fundamental and applied knowledge. It is a cascading effect as discoveries in one field permit new doors to open in other seemingly unrelated areas. Fundamental discoveries are being made week by week to the extent that historians will probably look back on the 1980's and 90's as a time of the most accelerated scientific advances in human history.

All this new knowledge will have a major impact on the world's economy. New products, new materials, new machines, new cures, new methods will be discovered, patented and marketed. Canadians cannot simply expect to be purchasers of all these discoveries if we have none to sell. The habit of selling off natural resources will not be sufficient to buy Canada's way into the status of an advanced country in the New World. The way has to be earned by being competitive and successful in at least some of the more advanced industries.

The Canadian record so far is not very encouraging. There have been some real successes in telecommunications, transportation, office equipment, lasers and space. While these prove that Canada can compete successfully we are hardly represented at all, in fine chemicals, pharmaceuticals, advanced software, precision instrumentation, medical devices, fine ceramics and new composites. There is a need to set a serious national priority to have one or more successful companies in each of these fields. It may be necessary for government to share the risk with venture capitalists in setting up some of these companies or in building upon existing small companies. Governments, including those at the provincial level, should assist wherever possible in order to give such new companies a reasonable Canadian market with which to get a start. In some instances, branches of multi-nationals should be singled out and a special effort should be made to acquire genuine world product mandates in one or more of these important fields.

Joint ventures

Two other major thrusts are needed. First, there are enormous opportunities for Canada to enter into joint ventures with Japanese companies; these should be encouraged. The Canadian branch of such a joint venture might well benefit from Japanese production expertise and could logically be assigned the North American market to serve from a Canadian base. The Japanese branch might serve the rest of the world, using Canadian science and technology wherever possible. This kind of arrangement could help Canadians overcome the common problem of having superb science which is rarely turned into successful commercial products. Japan is seriously worried about its lack of basic scientific discoveries, so such partnerships with Canada could be very useful to both sides.

Canadian science is often used, of course, by United States companies but the industrial benefits to Canada are sometimes quite minimal. In some cases, the scientist or his or her invention is simply taken to the United States. perhaps a Canadian branch is set up but it usually does not export. There are exceptions, of course.

Secondly, there is the very delicate matter of how to make use of intellectual property which presently resides in Canadian universities. Universities are rightly wary of permitting their major function to be undermined by the commercialization process. However, Canada has little alternative but to find ways to use its university resources, despite the problems. There is not enough industrial research nor are there the large companies from which new innovative ones can spinoff, ready to go into action as they do in the US. The universities, like it or not, may represent Canada's only important asset in this vital contest.

Business attitudes

Some comment must also be made about Canadian business attitudes. The most important pools of capital, including those controlled by leading business families and institutions, are almost all invested in retailing, finance, real estate and resources. High value-added manufacturing and research-intensive industries are very tiny portions of the portfolios of major capital aggregations. They are invested in conservative investments in industries which would be located here even if Canada were part of the US. For these investors, the market seems to pay an insufficient premium to draw them into the kinds of risky products that are needed to compete in the future. As a result, government plays a larger and larger role in the higher risk, new technology industries. Either by ownership, as in the aircraft industry, or by procurement as in the space industry, or by special financial arrangements such as in the transportation industry, government is drawn more and more into filling the vacuum left by the private sector. This is not a healthy situation and stands in sharp contrast with the Japanese experience.

In Japan, there is constant dialogue among capitalists and the trained business people and government concerning the long term interests of the nation and the ways in which such interest can be maximized. Government does not tell business what to do. In fact, information from the business people that normally forms the basis for whatever national policies are eventually adopted. Once a policy adopted, it guides both government and the private sector. Such teamwork does not prevent fierce competition, lobbying or even complaining. It does focus attention, however, on the strategic interests of the nation. Canada is not Japan but surely it can learn from that process.

In summary, then, Canada's wealth will have to come from new and complex sources, requiring a change in institutional structure and in international orientation. Canada must react to events in the Pacific; be part of the great future of that area and, most of all, learn from its successes. As a Pacific nation, the potential is there to secure the future.

PART IV

DIALOGUES WITH THE SOUTH:
THE POLITICS OF SELF-INTEREST

Chapter 12

The North Views the South

Introduction

The attitudes among the First World countries towards the Third World are varied, mixed and inconsistent. They are an admixture of long-term self-interests, immediate selfish needs, system maintenance approaches which are both ideological and pragmatic, and some idealism, mostly based on the one-world, weakest link adage. They range from the more to the less generous, with the Nordic countries and the Netherlands at the leading edge followed by Canada with the European Community in the middle and Japan and the United States bringing up the rear. This, however, is a gross oversimplification.

Table 1 shows a 35 year retrospective of the complexity of attitudes towards the Third World, as statistically measurable by the volume of Official Development Assistance (ODA), flowing from specific countries and groups of countries to the Third World, their share in World ODA, and ODA as percent of their GNP. This shows that whereas there has been a declining trend of American ODA as a percent of US GNP during the quarter century, the absolute amount of funds distributed to the Third World has remained remarkably constant in terms of of constant prices since 1960. *And*, the United States share of ODA at 22% of World ODA is twice that of its nearest competitors, France and Japan. Of course, the US share of World ODA has declined to half of what it was in 1960; at the same time the Japanese share has increased from 3% to almost 11%. Also, the European Community members share has declined from almost half 35 years ago to just under one-third. Nevertheless, the share of the seventeen members of the Development Assistance Committee (DAC) in World ODA, although declining from nearly 100% in 1950 to 76.8% in 1984 has quadrupled during the same period in constant dollar amounts. The slack has been taken up principally by OPEC since 1970 and by the Council of Mutual Economic Assistance (CMEA) countries of Eastern Europe, whose share in World ODA, however, after an initial increase to 11.3% in 1970 has dropped considerably below 10%. It should also be pointed out that whereas the DAC countries' assistance is broad ranging, the OPEC countries' assistance flows primarily to other Arab countries with small amounts to other known Arab, African and Asian countries. Similarly, the assistance of the CMEA countries is exclusively earmarked for LDC members of CMEA and other communist countries.

The following excerpt from the DAC's 1985 Review, *Twenty-Five Years of Development Cooperation* specifically addresses comparative aid levels, in our opinion describes the mixture of general attitudes toward the Third World among the First World countries:

TABLE 1

LONG-TERM TRENDS IN AID BY MAJOR DONORS

	Volume of ODA ($ million at 1983 prices & exch. rates)					Share in World ODA					ODA as per cent of GNP				
	1950-55	60-61	70-71	75-76	81-84	1950-55	60-61	70-71	75-76	83-84	1950-55	60-61	70-71	75-76	83-84
United States	3 961	8 689	7 045	7 037	8 236	50.2	46.3	30.8	21.7	22.2	0.32	0.56	0.31	0.26	0.24
EEC members combined [a]	3 730	6 476	7 129	8 275	11 834	47.2	34.5	31.2	25.6	31.9	0.52	0.64	0.42	0.45	0.52
EEC members (excl. DOM/TOM)	..	4 084	6 399	7 267	10 512	..	24.9	28.9	23.1	29.4	..	0.40	0.38	0.40	0.49
of which:															
France (incl. DOM/TOM)	2 325	2 827	2 450	2 659	3 939	29.4	15.0	10.7	8.2	10.6	1.24	1.35	0.66	0.62	0.75
France (excl. DOM/TOM)	..	(435)[b]	1 720	1 651	2 617	..	(2.7)[b]	7.8	5.3	7.3	..	(0.21)[b]	0.46	0.38	0.51
Germany	193	1 213	1 684	2 149	3 108	2.4	6.5	7.4	6.6	8.4	0.11	0.38	0.33	0.38	0.47
United Kingdom	888	1 605	1 523	1 583	1 578	11.2	8.6	6.7	4.9	4.3	0.42	0.56	0.42	0.39	0.34
Netherlands	105	220	587	884	1 288	1.3	1.2	2.6	2.7	3.5	0.27	0.38	0.60	0.79	0.96
Italy	183	270	409	326	1 009	2.3	1.4	1.8	1.0	2.7	0.23	0.19	0.17	0.12	0.28
Belgium	36	112	295	400	474	0.5	1.7	1.3	1.2	1.3	0.11	0.82	0.48	0.55	0.58
Denmark	..	29	172	258	438	..	0.2	0.7	0.8	1.2	..	0.11	0.40	0.57	0.79
Japan	67	558	1 568	1 794	4 027	0.8	3.0	6.9	5.5	10.9	0.04	0.22	0.23	0.22	0.34
Canada	91	212	885	1 346	1 544	1.1	1.1	3.9	4.2	4.2	0.10	0.16	0.41	0.50	0.48
Sweden	12	24	277	662	748	0.2	0.1	1.2	2.0	2.0	0.04	0.06	0.41	0.82	0.82
Australia		257	619	665	750	..	1.4	2.7	2.1	2.0	..	0.40	0.59	0.53	0.47
Norway	6	28	114	294	576	0.1	0.1	0.5	0.9	1.6	0.04	0.13	0.33	0.68	1.06
Switzerland	8	37	119	177	315	0.1	0.2	0.5	0.5	0.9	0.02	0.06	0.13	0.19	0.31
Austria	..	6	34	92	177	..	x	0.1	0.3	0.5	..	0.02	0.07	0.17	0.26
Finland	..	3	28	65	166	..	x	0.1	0.2	0.4	..	0.02	0.09	0.17	0.34
New Zealand	..	13	37	89	60	..	0.1	0.2	0.3	0.2	..	0.12	0.23	0.47	0.26
Total DAC	7 875	16 304	17 845	20 480	28 433	99.7	86.9	78.1	63.3	76.8	0.35	0.52	0.34	0.35	0.36
Spain	..	..	15	53	109	..	..	0.1	0.2	0.3	..	..	..	..	0.07
Ireland	..	..	4	11	36	..	..	x	x	0.1	..	..	0.02	0.09	0.22
Luxembourg	..	..	5	5	8	..	..	x	x	x	..	..	..	0.12	0.19
Portugal [c]	22	152	176	..	..	0.3	0.8	0.8	..	..	0.30	1.70	1.05	..	..
Total OECD	7 897	16 456	18 045	20 549	28 586	100.0	87.7	79.0	63.5	77.1	0.34	0.52	0.33	0.34	0.36
OPEC countries															
Saudi Arabia	..	..	486	4 085	3 526	..	..	2.1	12.6	9.5	..	..	5.31	6.86	3.29
Kuwait	..	..	323	1 236	1 023	..	..	1.4	3.8	2.8	..	..	4.79	6.13	3.83
U.A.E.	..	..	63	1 518	411	..	..	0.3	4.7	1.1	..	..	5.36	10.32	0.81
Other	..	..	184	2 141	67	..	..	0.8	6.6	0.2	..	..	..	0.85	(0.07)
Total OPEC	..	..	1 053	8 980	5 027	..	..	4.6	27.8	13.6	..	..	0.78	2.61	0.95
CMEA countries															
USSR	..	(1 605)	2 023	1 776	2 650	..	..	8.9	5.5	7.1	..	..	0.15	0.16	0.26
GDR	..	..	110	98	(169)	..	..	0.5	0.3	0.5	..	..	0.12	0.11	0.16
Eastern Europe, other	..	(250)	457	291	(316)	..	..	2.0	0.9	0.9	..	..	0.15	0.09	0.10
Total CMEA	..	1 855	2 590	2 165	3 135	..	9.9	11.3	6.7	8.5	..	..	0.15	0.14	0.21
LDC donors [d]	..	454	1 149	649	301	..	2.4	5.0	2.0	0.8	..	..	..	..	..
Total World	7 897	18 765	22 837	32 343	37 049	100.0	100.0	100.0	100.0	100.0	(0.30)	(0.41)	0.33	0.40	0.37

a] Excluding Ireland and Luxembourg.
b] In 1960-61 DOM/TOM are defined to include Algeria receiving $1 295 million at 1983 prices and exchange rates.
c] Portugal was a member of DAC up to 1974 and is now on the list of developing countries.
d] China, India, Israel, Yugoslavia.

Source: DAC, *Twenty-five Years of Development Cooperation*, a review, OECD, Paris, 1985, p.93.

While economic strength is a significant factor in explaining comparative aid levels, the size and orientation of national aid programs are determined by many complex factors. These include:

— Support for aid on the part of the political elites and broader public opinion, based on humanitarian concern and understanding of the need to contribute to international economic and social stability;

— Traditional links with the countries of the Third World;

— The importance of developing countries as economic partners (markets, suppliers of raw materials);

— Specific or global foreign policy, security and strategic interests and responsibility;

— Particularities of the political slash constitutional decision-making and budget processes.

The Nordic countries and the Netherlands clearly stand out for an extraordinary degree of public support for strong development assistance programs. This reflects genuine sympathy for underprivileged people, the fact that a large part of the population is conscious of living in an affluent society and an optimism about the feasibility of promoting social justice through public programs. It may be a matter of projecting on the international level the collective sense of responsibility for the less fortunate which seems to be particularly developed at these countries at the national level. The sense of international solidarity may also be favoured by the strong homogeneity of the population in these countries, which are largely free of social, racial, religious or language tensions, and by their relative insulation, as small countries, from international political conflicts that have effective public opinion toward particular developing countries in, for example, the United States. . ... A comparison of official development assistance as a percentage of GNP with privately collected grants by voluntary non-government organizations shows a leading role of Sweden, Norway and the Netherlands in both cases. With respect to private grants, however, these countries are joined at the top by Switzerland and the United States, whose official assistance is much smaller in relation to the GNP. The generous readiness of the American people to help in emergencies is renowned. In Switzerland a traditional suspicion prevails against bureaucratic economic activity by the State. (As witnessed by the negative vote in the National Referendum in 1976 on a possible contribution to IDA). In comparison with a strong humanitarian concern for the problems of the Third World. In Germany too, readiness of the people to participate and direct actions to private organizations exceeds by far, in international comparative terms, the relative position of the FRG with respect to ODA.

In the Nordic countries and the Netherlands active public education has contributed to create a positive public opinion towards development assistance. Although cause or conclusions in this field are difficult it is significant that the public authority spends some 50 US cents per capita for public information on development issues in Sweden and Norway and some 20 cents in Denmark and the Netherlands, whilst the comparable figure in the United States and the United Kingdom is only about 1 cent." [pages 133–4]

Table 2 shows in striking terms the relative stability in the share of ODA in national budgets compared with the wild fluctuations over the same period in ODA/GNP ratios. Even in the case of the Nordic countries the percentage share of the national budget allocated to aid has not significantly increased during the past decade.

The bar graph in Figure 1 illustrates the commitment of the different DAC countries to ODA measured as a percentage of the GNP and compares that to the actual value of the funds donated.

TABLE 2

ODA APPROPRIATION AS PERCENTAGE
OF CENTRAL GOVERNMENT BUDGET EXPENDITURE 1970-83

	Fiscal years (three year averages)			
	1970-72	1975-77	1978-80	1981-83
Australia	2.2	1.6	1.5	1.5
Austria	0.3	0.4	0.4	0.4
Belgium	1.9	1.9	1.7	1.4
Canada	2.8	2.3	2.3	2.1
Denmark	1.5	1.9	1.9	2.0
Finland	0.6	0.6	0.7	1.1
France	3.6	3.3	3.1	3.1[b]
Germany	2.3	2.1	2.4	2.5
Italy	..	..	0.6[a]	1.0
Japan	1.9	1.8	2.0	2.1[b]
Netherlands	2.6	2.7	3.1	3.0
New Zealand	0.7	0.9	0.7	0.6
Norway	1.4	2.5	2.7	2.4
Sweden	2.2	2.7	2.5	2.5
Switzerland	1.9	1.9	2.2	2.6
United Kingdom	1.8	1.5	1.4	1.2
United States	1.2	1.0	1.2	1.0

a) 1980.
b) 1981-1982.

Source: DAC, *Twenty-five Years of Development Cooperation*, a review, OECD, Paris, 1985, p. 132.

The graphs in Figure 2 demonstrate the trends in the ODA/GNP ratios of the DAC members during the past thirty years. As may be seen, apart from the striking decline of French commitment, most countries have remained fairly steady, with the Nordic countries and Canada demonstrating a fairly steady growth during the past twenty years.

It is the objective of the articles in this chapter to examine some of the attitudes of the First World towards the Third World from a policy perspective. Hence, Pinder begins his evaluation by examining the current role of monetary doctrine in American and British, as well as other Western European economic policies during the 1980s. According to him most of these policies are misguided and their impact on the Third World may be disastrous. In so far as trade is concerned, he argues that "the crux, for the health of the Northern economies and the growth of their imports of Southern manufactures will be to ensure that Northern industrial policies focus on the development of industrial activities towards higher added-value, thus moving steadily up the technological ladder and leaving room for the exporting NICs to climb onto." However, he adds, "Third World countries will suffer if

FIGURE 1

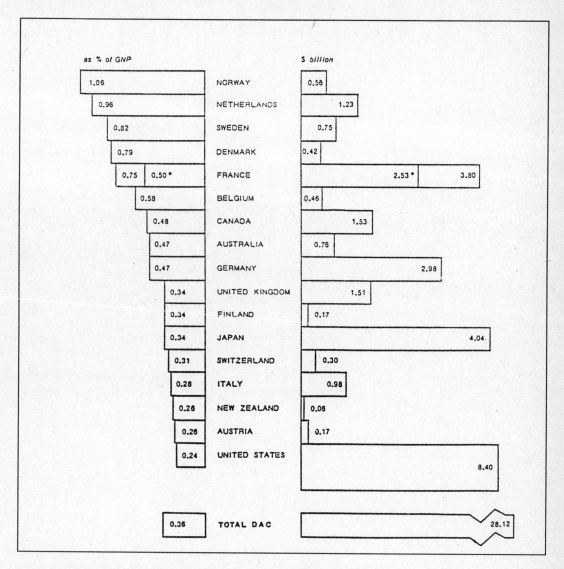

Source: DAC, *Twenty-five Years of Development Cooperation*, a review, OECD, Paris, 1985, p. 96.

they neglect to do what they can to influence European industrial and trade policies by exerting their own bargaining power." [page 127] He concludes that "the EC is. . .both sharply subject to short-term political pressures and well endowed with the capacity to appreciate its long-term enlightened self-interest in well managed interdependence. . . But the long-term interest will certainly have a better chance if some Third World countries respond to the vision of an increasingly interdependent and cooperative system, with insti-

FIGURE 2

TRENDS IN ODA/GNP RATIO OF DAC MEMBERS, 1950/55-1984
(Two-year moving averages)

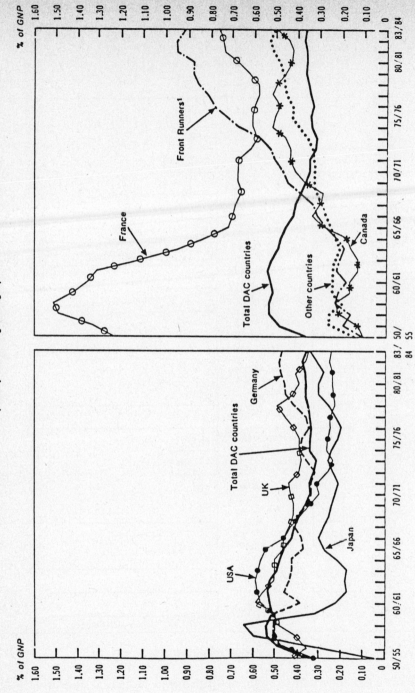

1. Front Runners : Norway, Sweden, Denmark and Netherlands.

Source: DAC, Twenty-five Years of Development Cooperation, a review, OECD, Paris, 1985, p. 97.

tutions that will match the needs of an international mixed economy in the twenty-first century. [page 130]

Blackwell evaluates the Lome III convention and discusses many of its specific provisions of trade, aid as well as Stabex and Sysmin, two measures whereby the EC provides special funding for Third World commodities, the first designed to compensate for decline in export earnings and the second to help maintain production capacity during adverse market conditions. However, it must be remembered that these assistance programs apply only to the sixty-six ACP (Asian Caribbean and Pacific) states which are signatories to the Lome convention. All are former colonies of the major European EC countries, most of the United Kingdom and France, as well as the minor colonists, the Netherlands, Belgium, Portugal and Spain. Hence, it could also be argued that the European Community's programs of assistance to the Third World are mere perpetuations of historic political-economic relationships in modern garb.

The article written by Doug Williams of the North-South Institute takes a somewhat different tack and evaluates the Canadian approach towards the Third World as a recipient of various mixtures of First World assistance and concern. It concludes that although Canada is doing an adequate job in supplying these kinds of assistance, it has by no means reached its potential, nor has it come anywhere near its self-ascribed moral obligations as a leader of First World concern for the Third World.

The observant reader will note that there is no article describing or evaluating American approaches toward the Third World in this chapter. The reason is simple—there are many articles sprinkled through the book which reflect, describe, evaluate and criticize aspects of American policies and demarches on development issues. Moreover, it is difficult to integrate the American experience in a short article such as the preceding Canadian one.

A Question of Political Economy

John Pinder

The external trade of the European Community (EC) comprises about a quarter of world trade. The EC is a giant in the world economy, a greater trading power than the United States, with a powerful influence on most other countries' economies and on the international economy as a whole. As such, we can expect it will be criticised. But we may also hope that the criticism will be useful. Unfortunately, it seldom is.

Most of the criticism is flawed because it is based on the assumption that free trade, and implicitly *laissez-faire*, is a tenable policy for the contemporary economy. It is ironic that many of these critics are Marxist or other central planners who demand that the EC remove its trade barriers but would never dream of shutting a factory or laying off workers in their own countries in order to make room for imports. Yet to dwell on this irony would be to miss the main point, which is that *laissez-faire*, even in the modern dress of Thatcherism or Reaganomics, just does not work in the modern economy. Monetary control without an active industrial or incomes policy can bring down inflation, as in Thatcher's Britain, but only at the cost of decimating investment, industrial production, employment and growth. Reagan's combination of monetarist and supply-side doctrines, with tax cuts causing a budget deficit which, in the context of tight money, pushes interest rates through the roof, may induce a demand-led reflation for a year or two; but with investment constrained by the interest rates and pay push restrained by nothing, the reflation will lead to bottlenecks, over-heating and inflation which will, probably by 1985, run the economy on to the buffers of yet tighter monetary restriction, higher interest rates, and hence renewed recession.

All this may be seen as hard luck on the Americans and the British, or as just retribution for their choice of political leaders. But those who are tempted to indulge in *schadenfreude* should remember that these failures of economic management do not concern their perpetrators alone. In the interdependent international economy, the ripples generated by even small successes or failures of management in a major industrial country can affect the economies of other countries throughout the world; and when the economy is as big as that of the United States and the failure as great as that of Reaganomics is likely to be in a year or two, there can be not just a ripple but a tidal wave that could submerge weak economies and snap the moorings that have held the international economic system together. Reagan's entry on the world stage has given us a preview of this in the current debt crises of so many Third World countries. Real interest rates rose to heights unimagined in the financial markets; demand for imports of both primary products and manufactures fell in the industrial countries as the interest rates piled on the recessionary pressure; and these scissors of high interest rates and low demand cut the developing countries' growth and their means of servicing and repaying their debts. If the US repeats this monetary performance, the Third World's current debt crisis would become the springboard for something much worse.

Originally published in *Third World Quarterly*, vol. 6, no. 1, January 1984. © Third World Quarterly; reprinted with permission.

This introduction is not intended to frighten the reader into turning towards an off-the-peg ideology of economic management from the other superpower. The Soviet Union is in just as much trouble if not more, for the opposite reason: too much centralisation, which suffocates innovation, technological development and progress towards microeconomic efficiency. Nor do the other East Europeans, or the Third World countries of similar orientation, offer an example that should encourage others to adopt the Soviet model. The intention is, rather, to stress that new methods of economic management must be developed in the North if the South is to benefit as it could from North-South economic relations. Thus, in considering the future relationship between the Third World and the European Community, we have first to think about the development of the EC's own economic policies. For if the EC stagnates, its imports cannot give a dynamic impulse to the growth of developing countries. Protection, which is the main target of Third World criticism, is secondary to the stagnation of demand. Britain, in the 1950s and 1960s, allowed free entry for almost all imports from Commonwealth countries; yet their exports to Britain grew much slower than their exports to the continent of Europe and Japan, where protection against the Commonwealth countries was quite high but whose economies, and hence demand for imports, were growing faster. The system of economic policy in the EC, as in other Northern economies, is therefore central to its relations with the Third World. The forces with which modern economic policy has to contend, and which will therefore shape its development, are moreover to be found not only in the EC but also in the wider international economy. So the trend of policy in the EC is likely to show similarities to the trend of policy in the international economy also. These are compelling reasons why analysing the problem of the modern political economy, whether in the EC or elsewhere, is not a digression, but a precondition for understanding the likely course of EC-Third World economic relations.

The Europeans and the Mixed Economy

The economic troubles of the past decade have turned economic policy in Britain and the United States back to a form of market economics that tries to minimize the role of public policy in the economy. The reaction has been less extreme among the EC countries on the continent of Europe. But all of them are relying on old-fashioned deflation to squeeze out the inflation that followed the second oil price shock in 1979; and none has found a way to keep inflation down without depressing employment and growth.

The monetarist doctrine which has taken hold of American and British policy and also increased its influence in other Western countries is based on an assumption of more-or-less perfect markets, in which prices and incomes bring about any necessary economic adjustments by responding to changes in supply and demand. Thus, the money supply is supposed to govern total production and market forces to look after the allocation of resources to production of the various goods and services. But in the industrial economies incomes respond only very imperfectly to changes in the money supply and the pattern of demand, for the division of labour and specialisation of production place so many groups, large or small, in positions of monopoly or quasi-monopoly. All these groups can resist the effect of monetary squeeze on their pay and take more than full advantage of any monetary relaxation. Thus the effect of tight money is not to keep the growth of their pay within the growth of their productivity, but to squeeze investment and reduce the employment of the less strongly placed; while easier money leads to increases of their pay more than of investment and employment. Hence we see the apparent paradox of stagflation, which is not a paradox at all if the importance of these imperfections in the labour market is understood.

With such imperfections built into the structure of the modern economy, the pay push can by controlled only by savage and permanent deflation or by constraints established within the system of pay determination. Such constraints can inhere mainly in pay determination within the firm, as in Japan, with national trends set oligopolistically by a few leading firms; or in collective bargains between trade unions and employers' associations in major industrial sectors, as in West Germany, with the trend set by an oligopolistic price leader (the IG Metall union in the engineering industry); or as in Austria by a comprehensive incomes policy, involving employers, unions and public authorities. In each of these countries, but particularly in Austria and Japan, inflation has been kept low while employment and investment have remained reasonably dynamic. Observers in the Third World may not have regarded the systems of collective bargaining in industrial countries as a matter of prime concern to them; but these systems have come to determine the allocation of resources to investment, growth and the creation of employment, and hence the industrial countries' propensities to import or to protect. Without systems for controlling pay push, which must be based on a consensus between unions and employers' associations and supported by public policy (i.e. incomes policy), the old industrial economies will remain weak importers, strongly protected against the "disruption" of imports from the newly industrialising countries.

A second major imperfection in the modern market economy is the cost of starting new production or winding up the old. In perfect markets, resources would move without cost from one form of production to another. In the modern economy, the winding up of old plant may leave firms with heavy capital charges and redundancy costs, workers with no employment and public authorities with the cost of unemployment assistance and of local infrastructure which is no longer used. The starting of new production may require great expense on research, development, investment, training and marketing. Thus adjustment from old production to new, so far from costless, can be very costly; and the social benefit of economic progress and employment may not be reflected at all in a private benefit for the firms doing the adjusting. With slow-growing economies, as during the past decade, this discrepancy is particularly serious, because the markets for new production are less able to support the costs. But even in Japan, where growth has remained twice as fast as in Europe, the government has found it necessary to help channel resources out of several "structurally depressed industries" and into the sectors of the future. It requires no complicated economic analysis to see the case for an industrial policy that will promote the new lines of production and ease the adjustment away from the old; and the more successful of the industrial countries, such as Japan, France, West Germany, Austria and Sweden, have indeed pursued the more effective industrial policies of this kind. Their most important instruments have lain in macroeconomic policies that give full weight to industry's need for low interest and exchange rates, combined with an array of tax and subsidy incentives for adjustment and development. The Japanese have, in addition, developed the concept of the rationalisation cartel, whereby the firms in a structurally depressed sector receive temporary protection and support on condition that they modernise and adapt their production to the needs of the future.

Such industrial and income policies, together with manpower policies to ensure the workforce is well trained for the new industries and services, are essential elements of the modern mixed economy: mixed in the sense, not of any particular mix of private and public ownership, but of an appropriate involvement of central public policy in a decentralised market economy. Those who wish to know whether the European countries will again become dynamic trading partners should try to judge whether these countries are evolving mixed economies along these lines, as still seems to be the case in continental Western Europe, or whether the doctrine of *laissez-faire* is gaining ground, as has undoubtedly happened in Britain—perhaps for quite specific political reasons.

Trade and Monetary Integration in the European Community

The Europeans' trading stance will depend on their success in restoring employment and growth, which will govern the ease with which they adjust to Third World competition. But their attitude towards protection has also been influenced by their realisation that wider markets were needed to reduce unit costs and enlarge the scope for specialisation and scale, in an epoch when these are becoming increasingly necessary conditions of further economic development. This was a major reason for the establishment of the European Community and of the free trade system surrounding it in Western Europe, and for the maintenance of free trade within Western Europe during a recession that calls to mind the 1930s when each European country retreated into its autarkic shell. Any tendency to repeat that disintegration would hurt the Third World too; autarky would be likely to protect each country against all comers. It can, conversely, be strongly argued that a closer collaboration within the EC, through not only free trade but also a common industrial policy, would improve the economic health of its members and hence benefit its trading partners also.

The question of monetary integration in the EC is particularly significant. The high interest rates, originating in the US, annoy the Europeans as they do the Third World. Dear money in the international capital market means dear money in the European capital markets and thus an obstacle to industrial investment. Protests make little impact on the stubborn forces shaping American budgetary politics. If American policy is to be influenced, if must be done by equally stubborn economic forces that can affect the US economy for better or for worse. In the early 1960s, the US changed its trade policy and initiated the Kennedy Round of far-reaching tariff negotiations because it was confronted by the EC's common tariff which made the Community a trading power on the scale of the US. The only such instruments conceivable in the monetary field would come from strengthening the EC's European Monetary System, by implementing proposals to establish a common reserve fund and move in the direction of a common currency. Such a development would be most significant for the Third World too, as the Europeans would use any such countervailing power to secure a reduction in interest rates that would apply not only in the US and the EC but also in the international economy as a whole.

The EC and the Third World

Prosperity and growth in the North would have more impact on prosperity in the South than all the specific measures of Brandt and the NIEO combined. Indeed, the most pertinent criticism of NIEO proposals may be that they seemed to regard the North as a fat cow that could be milked, or even have juicy steaks hacked out of it, regardless of its health and strength. But although Northern prosperity is a necessary condition of rapid development in the South, it is not a sufficient condition. Just as the structure of the modern economy requires a mixed economy system to manage individual industrial countries or the European Community, so a successful international economy will need to be managed on mixed economy principles.

Capital flows from North to South offer a good example. As it stands today, the international capital market is dominated by a market force which turns out to be a peculiar combination of two theories (monetarist and supply-side) as they affect the American budget and economy. The needs of industry in Europe and of development in the Third World count for little in the face of this political and ideological peculiarity. But in the perspective of an international mixed economy, the needs of industry and development must be the main objective of international policy, and thinking has to focus on the instruments that can further this objective. In monetary policy, the crucial instrument is a reasonable rate of interest; and as we have seen, a strong European Monetary System is the only likely counterweight to American monetary and fiscal policies from which the high interest rates derive—hence the common interest of the EC and the Third World in European monetary integration, creating monetary instruments that can be used to secure interest rates more suitable for their respective development needs.

Beyond the lower interest rates in the international capital market, for which both EC and Third World have a need, the perspective of an international mixed economy points towards special measures to promote investment in the Third World. For just as regional policies are employed in particular countries to break the vicious circle of growth-retarding externalities in the less-favoured regions, so a world regional policy is appropriate to promote Third World investment and growth. Such a policy has of course been embodied in the World Bank and the International Development Association (IDA); but whereas the policy's original impulse came from the US, it is the Europeans who have recently given it the stronger support. The EC has, moreover, become a considerably larger provider of official development aid than the US, partly through the EC's European Development Fund, though mostly still through the member countries' aid programmes.

The old lesson of market economics (that healthy demand is more important for primary products than any measures of official support) applies with particular force in the world commodity markets. But the peculiarities of such markets justify measures at least to cushion producers or consumers against the wilder fluctuations. If policymakers in the industrial countries did not believe this, they would surely abolish their policies of domestic agricultural support; but none of them does so. The most impressive international support measure is the Stabex scheme, through which the EC, under the Lomé Convention, compensates the African, Caribbean and Pacific exporters of a number of commodities if the value of these exports falls below an agreed level. Although the severity of the present recession has overstrained the funds that the EC allocated for this, it remains more far-reaching and imaginative than the IMF's facility for balance-of-payments assistance, which the EC also supports.

The other side of that coin is, however, the EC's own agricultural policy, which supports European farm production at the expense of international trade. This causes the greatest problems for other temperate producers, such as Canada, New Zealand and the US—although the ability of the US to influence Community policy shows again the significance of bargaining power in the international mixed economy. The EC's policy has, however, also caused some difficulties to Third World countries,[1] even if those have been much mitigated for Lomé sugar-exporters by the market guarantees of the Lomé Convention.

Industrial Policies and Trade in Manufactures

For manufactures, trade and industrial policies are the chief manifestations of the contemporary mixed economy. During the years of prosperity, the EC greatly improved its conditions of access for imported manufactures. Its tariff was about halved through successive GATT rounds; tariff-free access was widened under the Lomé Convention to almost all of Africa, as well as to Caribbean and Pacific countries; and it was the EC that pioneered the introduction of the Generalised System of Preferences. In the past ten years of recession, however, the pressures from hard-hit workers, unions, employers and regions have been for more protection; and EC countries have adopted industrial policies that provide protection in new forms as well as, in a more positive vein, promoting industrial development.

At the same time as trade in manufactures has been complicated by national industrial policies, it has also become clear that manufactures will increasingly dominate international trade. First Japan rose to become the supplier of one-tenth of world exports of manufactures; then, during the 1970s, the Newly Industrialising Countries did the same. A process of diffusion of technology throughout the world is evidently in train; and more and more Southern countries will join the NICs of the 1970s until manufactures eventually outweigh primary products in exports from South to North. This makes it the more important to understand the implications of industrial policies for manufacturing trade.

The problems that the international economy poses for industry in developing countries are well known: the competitive weakness of infant industries; the relative strength of foreign investors and multinational companies; and now the crisis of interest rates and debt. Northern worries about international trade are less well understood—and indeed a contemporary Northern fashion writes them off as sinful Keynesian fantasies. But their causes are more objective than that. The market imperfections that we earlier discussed, rooted in the structure of the modern economy, impede adjustment to changes in technology or demand. These impediments are yet harder to overcome when the changes stem from trade with countries that have different economic levels, rates of growth or systems of economic management.

The stereotype of comparative advantage is the cheap textile produced by cheap labour. The danger of such stereotyping in a fast-changing world was shown when the production of cloth became as capital-intensive as that of cars, leaving only clothing, rather than textiles as a whole, as a labour-intensive sector. This point was confirmed when the Economic Commission for Europe found that clothing and footwear were the only major industrial sectors with physical capital intensity far below the average.[2] Useful though the export of textiles and footwear may have been to developing countries, and painful as these imports may have been for many disadvantaged workers and regions in the industrialised countries, the stereotype of labour-intensive sectors does not help much towards understanding the contemporary problem of trade in manufactures.

The advantages of fast-growing countries are far more important. Over an increasing range of production, such countries have newer products, newer equipment and, often, more up-to-date technologies than slower-growing, older industrial economies. When combined with lower-cost labour these advantages can be formidable indeed, as Japan was the first to show in the postwar world economy. The Japanese went on to demonstrate that the virtuous circle of efficiency, investment and rapid development, established while labour was cheap, can be sustained in what has become a high-wage and high-technology economy. But the strength of Japanese competition during the time when they were catching up on the Europeans and Americans has wider significance. For this has already been shown not to be a uniquely Japanese phenomenon, but has been repeated by a dozen Asian, South European and Latin American NICs; and these will surely be joined by a growing number of Third World countries. This must raise the question whether the older industrial economies face a danger of general industrial stagnation when competition from newer ones reaches a critical mass. The British experience of sliding, since the second half of the nineteenth century, from a state of industrial pre-eminence into a vicious circle of weak adjustment and slow growth might have been regarded as unique were there not signs of a similar trend in much of American industry and, more recently, on the continent of Europe.

Before considering the likely response of policy to this question, we should also recognise the effect of differing policy systems on international trade. The arbitrariness of price and investment decisions in the Soviet-type economies has long been seen in the market economies as justifying protection; and, in the last ten years of recession, protection has increasingly been applied. Although superior efficiency is widely recognised as the main source of Japanese competitive strength, the "targeting" of their exports and their cultural and institutional barriers against imports are increasingly held to justify protection against Japanese competition. From the wide range of policy systems among the NICs, a common factor has been observed to enhance the competitiveness of most of them: their relatively free labour markets (in the technical sense of freedom from effective institutional curbs on market forces), combined with official support for capital allocation that promotes industrial investment.[3] American and European trade unions frequently use this as an argument for protection.

So long as recession and stagnation last, European reaction to these structural problems of international trade is likely to be protectionist. Unlike the old issue of labour-intensive sectors, moreover, it is hard, short of the very long term, to discern a limit to the process of catching up by NICs or an end to the differences between their policy systems and those of the Europeans; as the more developed NICs catch up, others will take their place on the lower rungs of the ladder. Thus it is equally hard to envisage a turning of the rising tide of protectionism so long as European industrial stagnation continues. That would point to a fortress EC economy. If, on the other hand, the stagnation is replaced by healthy growth, this will follow, if the earlier argument was sound, from the devising of new methods of economic management which include an industrial policy to overcome the structural barriers to industrial adjustment and development. Such a policy may have to be particularly far-reaching while the economy is being moved out of its long recession; but the experience of Japan, where an active industrial policy has been pursued in the context of an uninterruptedly dynamic economy, confirms our expectation that such a policy will still be needed beyond the present recession, if Europe is to avoid the fate of secular stagnation. Thus a dynamic European economy will still present a new problem for international trade: the accommodation of interests expressed not only in a conventional trade policy but also in a wide variety of industrial policies.

Bargaining about Industrial Policies

A fortress EC would probably gravitate towards controls and even bilateral balancing in its trade with the Third World, with some characteristics of the system practised by the East European COMECON countries. In such circumstances, human ingenuity has devised specialisation agreements, buyback and many other forms of industrial cooperation to alleviate the trading system's inherent viscosity. But its resistance to progress is indicated by the fact that the EC's trade with the six million Swiss is greater than that with the Soviet Union and its associates in Eastern Europe combined, although their population is over fifty times as big. Trade would continue and doubtless even increase, but with such a bias towards separate development, the path of economic progress for the Third World would be longer and rougher. Such a split in the world economy, counter to the secular technological trend towards interdependence, would not only hold back economic development but also exacerbate political conflicts in a world where they are already dangerous enough.

While trade with a fortress Europe would have to be negotiated every step of the way, an EC that recovers enough dynamism to remain an essentially open economy would also be likely to present the Third World with more need to bargain than in the past. The doctrine of non-reciprocity has been common to supporters of both *laissez-faire* and NIEO. Their belief in its practicability was encouraged by the introduction of Part IV of the GATT, the Lomé Convention and the Generalised System of Preferences. But these victories for non-reciprocity were won before Northern industries other than textiles had been seriously hurt by competition from the NICs, before the costs of adjustment to such competition had risen so high and the obstacles to new industrial development in the North became so great, and before the particular interests affected had reacted to these new conditions by asserting their strength against the general principles of the old trading order. The rise of the interest groups must be seen as a social and political concomitant of the market imperfections in the structure of the modern economy. Where change involves economic and social costs or benefits which are not entirely dictated by impersonal market forces, groups will become organised to influence the outcome, whether directly in the market or by securing changes in public policy. Since these groups have become so important, there has been a new wave of literature on their role in the modern economy,[4] which analyses the leverage they exert in pluralist democracies. This shows how industrial and trade policy has become the subject of bargaining within each industrial country, whether any trading partner chooses to bargain about its trading interests or not. Since the livelihoods of people and the prosperity of firms and regions may be at stake, the domestic bargaining can be very tough; and a trading partner that relies on the doctrine of non-reciprocity and refrains from exerting any bargaining power runs a greater risk of losing out. As the French say, *Les absents ont toujours tort* ('Those who are absent are always in the wrong').

There are reasons why the obvious examples of EC protectionism in the past do not reflect the balance of forces that is likely to determine EC policies towards the bulk of imports from the Third World, once the EC has recovered some of its dynamism. The agricultural lobby, despite the dramatic decline of farm population, still represents not much less than a tenth of the EC's voters, concentrated where their gearing in the political system is maximised. The textile lobby also represents a large and fairly concentrated population, in a sector where labour-intensity has favoured, and in clothing still does favour, the Third World competitors. The rapid surge in European imports of a number of products from

Japan has not been reciprocated by an equivalent growth in Japanese imports from Europe. None of these conditions will apply to the bulk of manufactured exports from the Third World to the EC in the future. The EC has a large surplus on its trade with the Third World in manufactures; those who export to the Third World therefore represent a major interest in favour of more such trade, hence of enabling Third World countries to earn money by increasing their own exports to the North. These industrial interests tend to be joined in general industrial associations, with the export interest counter-weighing the import-resisting interest, whereas the agricultural lobby is usually separate. Textile protection, although less tough than the EC's protection of agriculture, shows that there is a limit to this argument. But since clothing and footwear are the only sectors in which labour-intensity is generally pronounced, Third World comparative advantage will in future increasingly be distributed across a range of sectors, at the labour-intensive end of each.[5] The EC exporters will therefore carry their influence within the same sectoral interest groups as the import-resistors; and it follows from the EC's surplus in manufactures trade that the exporters should be better placed to check protectionism than they have been in relation to agriculture, textiles or Japan—especially as they will usually be supported by the still-growing weight of the multinationals.

The crux, for the health of the Northern economies and the growth of their imports of Southern manufactures, will be to ensure that Northern industrial policies focus on the development of industrial activities towards higher added-value, thus moving steadily up the technological ladder and leaving room for the exporting NICs to climb it too. This appears quite feasible in the context of an EC which shows the resilience to evolve a new form of economic management to deal with the new conditions of the modern economy; but threatened interests will remain active, and Third World countries will suffer if they neglect to do what they can to influence European industrial and trade policies by exerting their own bargaining power.

Bargaining power has always been important in the international economy, even if liberal theory has tended to ignore it. The impact of the EC's rise as a trading superpower on US behaviour in tariff negotiations was mentioned earlier, as was the potential of EC monetary integration for influencing American fiscal and monetary policies. The growth of Northern industrial policy, with its special implications for the NICs, adds a new dimension to the Third World's need for bargaining power. In a prosperous international economy, Third World countries conducted some successful negotiations in groups; OPEC and the Lomé countries were examples, although the Group of 77 did not achieve many tangible results. But OPEC's recent experience shows that such groups of sovereign states are less cohesive in bad times. The more solid bargaining power is likely to reside in the large economies such as Brazil, Mexico and India; Nigeria among the Lomé countries; Indonesia in ASEAN; and, among OPEC members, Saudi Arabia. Where the most-favoured nation principle applies, the big countries' negotiating successes will also accrue to the smaller countries; the same will apply where they use their bargaining power as leaders of a group. Where the small countries are poor and weak, moreover, they will draw some benefit from the quantum of generosity that the North increasingly reserves for the least developed. But it must doubtless be accepted as a fact of life that, where there is negotiation, those with the greater bargaining power will gain the more.

The Third World countries seeking access on better terms to Northern markets, whether for their exports of manufactures and primary products or for their imports of capital, can negotiate about the terms of access for Northern exporters or for Northern investors and multinationals to their own markets. As the markets of the major Southern countries grow, these become more significant bargaining counters; and the more these countries use them, rather than relying on non-reciprocal Northern liberalism, the more they will be able to influence Northern policies. Their negotiating will be the more effective, moreover, and their influence the greater, the more they understand and allow for the Northern countries' own industrial development needs. One aspect of this is a readiness to restrain fast-growing exports through orderly marketing agreements when the Northern countries apply industrial policies of a kind likely to secure the adjustments that will facilitate the removal of restraints within a reasonable time. A second aspect would be a recognition of the role that Third World countries could play in expanding the international economy to pull it, North as well as South, out of the recession.[6] A third aspect, long-term and fundamental, would be a consciousness of the mutual need for a constant widening of the market to provide room for the specialisation and scale involved in containing technological development.

Beyond the Immediate Bargains: institutions of interdependence

Enlightened self-interest in international trade usually implies accepting a short-term inconvenience in order to secure a larger, if longer-term, gain. One reason for the growth of Northern protectionism is the lack of a vision of a feasible open trading system for the future.

With the North-South metaphor implanted in the mind, one tends to forget how fast some of the NICs were catching up on the mature industrial countries in the 1970s. Given a revival of health in the international economy, it will again be seen that countries such as Brazil, Mexico and some of the East Asians are not so far behind Greece and Spain, let alone Portugal. Thus their economic levels, and probably consequently their economic systems and rates of growth, will become less different from those of the EC countries. While average living standards in India will long remain much lower, the Indians may also progress rapidly to reduce the industrial and technological gap.

As the divergence of economic levels, rates and systems is reduced, and as the easier adjustment problems of intra-industry trade replace the harder task of adjustment to one-sided pressure on particular sectors, the obstacles to open trading will also be reduced. These are among the conditions that underlie the EC's readiness to negotiate about the accession of Portugal and Spain. Although the membership of these countries may excite some disquiet among the NICs that will be competing with them in the EC market on less favourable terms, the NICs should at the same time carefully observe the process of mutual adjustment of industries in the old and the new EC members. For this may resemble the process that would follow from a later participation of the EC and, say, Brazil, Mexico, and eventually India, in a more open trading system.

With industrial policy as important as trade policy, the consequence of a far-reaching reduction of trade barriers becomes not industrial laissez faire but a coordination of industrial policies, for example, common rules of competition, similar regimes of adjustment assistance and joint participation in rationalisation cartels; and these imply some common institutions and common policy instruments. This would go beyond the degree of cooperation embodied in existing international organisations or the Lomé Convention; and so long as the balance of economic power remains so heavily tilted against all the Third World countries, they rightly resist a stronger dose of policy integration. But as the larger among them, with populations that will then amount to 1-2 hundred million or even many more, come closer to the EC's economic level, the balance of economic power will become more even, and they may become readier to work more closely with a mature industrial economy such as the European Community.

The capacity to cooperate in international institutions is indeed crucial for the effective management of the international mixed economy; and we must also ask how far such a capacity has been shown by the EC. When compared with the behaviour of European nations in the 1930s, the behaviour of the EC member-countries in the postwar period has been remarkably cooperative. Not only have they established the Community itself, which is more far-reaching than any other example of economic cooperation among modern states; but the EC and its member countries have played their full part in all the main international organisations. As was noted earlier, the EC has been more inclined than the US recently to respond to Third World needs, particularly on monetary and commodity issues; and the Lomé Convention was at the time of its inception widely recognised as representing best practice in Northern policies towards the South.

The EC is nevertheless as amenable as other pluralist democratic systems to interest group pressures; the power of each of the ten member-governments to obstruct decisions in the EC's institutions may, indeed, add a dimension to the influence of industrial lobbies. The recent strains in the EC's trading relationships, from agriculture, through the Multi-Fibres Agreements and the argument in GATT over safeguards, to relations with Japan, bear witness to the forces that inhibit cooperation in the present economic climate. Yet given an improving economy, the EC has a number of attributes that will conduce to cooperation with Third World countries. The EC is more apt than the US to understand a mixed economy system. Its member-countries, especially if Portugal and Spain are included, have strong links with almost all parts of the Third World, of a kind that have supported the Lomé Convention. They have their own strong experience of interdependence and its consequences, which will make the idea of a wider interdependence comprehensible to them. As medium powers, they will find the idea of equality with the emerging industrial nations of the Third World easier to accept than the superpowers are likely to do. Strategically and economically exposed as they are, they are acutely conscious of their interest in world peace and economic stability.

The EC is, then, both sharply subject to short-term political pressures and well endowed with the capacity to appreciate its long-term enlightened self-interest in well-managed interdependence. It would be rash to predict whether the short-term or the long-term considerations will prevail. But the long-term interest will certainly have a better chance if some Third World countries respond to the vision of an increasingly interdependent and cooperative system, with institutions that will match the needs of an international mixed economy in the twenty-first century.

Notes

[1] See Mackel, Marsh and Revell, p 131 below.

[2] UN/ECE, *Structure and Change in European Industry*, Part 1, chapter 2 and Part 2, chapter 3, Geneva, 1982, cited in Christopher Saunders, "Changes in the Distribution of World Production and Trade', in John Pinder (ed), *National Industrial Strategies and the World Economy*, Totowa, New Jersey: Allanheld Osmun, 1982, p 21.

[3] See for example Wolfgang Hager, "Little Europe, Wider Europe and Western Economic Cooperation", in *Journal of Common Market Studies Special Issue: The European Community . Past, Present and Future*, September-December 1982, p 186.

[4] For example, Ghita Ionescu, *Centripetal Politics*, London: Hart-Davis, MacGibbon, 1975; Lester C Thurow, *The Zero-Sum Society: distribution and the possibilities of economic change*. New York: Basic Books, 1980: Mancur Olsen, *The Rise and Decline of Nations: economic growth, stagflation and social rigidities*, New Haven: Yale University Press, 1982.

[5] For some of the advantages of intra-industry trade, see Saunders, *op. cit.*, pp 34-6.

[6] See Reginald Herbold Green, "Things Fall Apart": the world economy in the 1980s', *Third World Quarterly* 5(1) 1983, p 93.

Lomé III: The Search for Greater Effectiveness

Michael Blackwell

The Lomé Convention unites the European Community and a group of African, Caribbean, and Pacific (ACP) states in an agreement which includes among its most notable features trade preferences, aid, and special facilities. When it first entered into effect in 1975, it was heralded as the only agreement that brought industrial countries and developing countries together as equal partners in mutual recognition of their interdependence in seeking economic growth and development, and as a step forward in the construction of a New International Economic Order.

Over the years some of the initial optimism has dissipated; indeed, some ACP spokesmen have claimed that the two sides now relate to each other more as aid donors and recipients than as equal partners. Although acknowledging that many ACP states have not derived all of the economic benefits they had hoped for, the European Community has argued that the Convention grants these states greater access to Community markets and the greater share of EC aid flows. In the Community's view, the ideal of partnership has not been abandoned and the failure of many ACP states to derive greater benefits from the Convention is best explained by the inappropriate policy stances adopted by their governments.

The 1983-84 negotiations for the third Lomé Convention were rooted in these contrasting perspectives and often echoed the broader debates that practitioners and scholars alike have lately engaged in on the effectiveness of aid, the respective merits of competitiveness and appropriate domestic policies versus trade preferences in stimulating export growth, and the role of special facilities in helping countries adjust to fluctuating demand for their commodities. This article examines the issues raised and the agreements reached in the course of negotiating the Lomé III Convention and pays particular attention to the changes in its language and emphasis.

Background

Lomé has as its origin the European Community's decision in 1957 to set up a European Development fund (EDF) worth $581 million—quite separate from the general Community budget and from members' bilateral aid budgets—to be used over a five-year period to make development grants to their predominantly African overseas countries and territories. By 1963 many of these had become independent and a more formal agreement, the First Yaoundé Convention, was concluded to specify the nature of trade preferences and development assistance that the Community was prepared to offer its partners. When the United Kingdom formally achieved EC membership in 1973, some of the developing countries of the Commonwealth decided they would join with the Yaoundé Convention participants and some other African countries to form a group of African, Caribbean, and Pacific

Originally published in *Finance and Development*, September 1985. Reprinted with permission.

States that would approach the Community as a common negotiating body and seek a new, wider Convention. The ensuing negotiations resulted in a five-year Convention, which was signed at Lomé, Togo, in 1975 and has subsequently been renewed twice. Lomé III has a financial endowment of ECU 8.5 billion (in June 1985, one ECU or European Currency Unit was worth about $0.73), compared with ECU 5.5 billion under Lomé II and ECU 3.5 billion under Lomé I. The number of signatory ACP countries has risen from 46 in Lomé I to 66 in Lomé III.

Although all three Conventions have contained a wide variety of provisions, ranging from assistance with agricultural development to cultural cooperation, their major features have centered around joint management of trade preferences, aid provisions, and special facilities, namely, STABEX (the system for the stabilization of export earnings) and SYS-MIN (a special facility for mining products). The Lomé III agreement effected changes in each of these areas.

Trade provisions

The drafters of the first Lomé Convention were convinced that the extension of trade preferences to the ACP countries would boost their export capacity and hence encourage economic growth and development. Looked at purely in terms of EC-ACP trading relations, this objective does not seem to have been achieved. Although ACP exports to the Community, excluding crude and refined petroleum products, have increased in value by 51 percent between 1976 and 1983, their share of total EC imports from outside the Community during this period fell from 6.3 percent to 4.5 percent, while their share of imports into the EC from all developing countries remained stable at around 19 percent. During the same period the trade balance in the Community's favor rose from ECU 3.5 billion to ECU 4.4 billion. However, it is not possible to draw definite conclusions from these figures about the effects of the Lomé Convention on trade. For example, they mask the fact that some individual ACP states have considerably increased and diversified their exports to EC markets. The Community view is that these figures—taken in conjunction with the evidence that many ACP states have limited themselves to traditional exports, have failed to match the productivity and quality advances of Asian and Latin American competitors, and have seen a consequent decline in their exports-suggest that the full benefits of trade preferences can only be enjoyed by countries with domestic policies that encourage a dynamic and flexible productive sector.

The ACP states, while not totally rejecting this analysis, argue that some elements of the Convention, in fact, hinder the growth of their exports. They claim, for example, that the Convention's safeguard clause tends to inhibit growth in areas where they could enjoy the greatest dynamic comparative advantage and provides a powerful disincentive to their industrial development. The Community has pointed out that it has never invoked the safeguard clause and has only asked one ACP country—Mauritius—to accept a voluntary export restraint agreement (for textiles). It feels there is room for increased exports of even sensitive products and that the specter of the safeguard clause is used rather unfairly to excuse weakness in the ACP countries' productive capacity.

The ACP countries advance similar arguments with regard to the rules of origin. In their view more lenient rules of origin would encourage greater external investment. The Community's response is that the rules of origin of the Lomé Convention are considerably more generous and flexible than those applied by the Generalized System of Preferences. The Community notes that very few countries have taken advantage of the exceptions that are offered and it is concerned that any further liberalization would probably serve only to open a back door to its markets for its industrial country competitors, while bringing few real economic benefits to the ACP countries themselves.

Several ACP states argue that they could rapidly increase their exports to the Community if the freedom of access granted to manufactured goods applied also to agricultural products covered by the EC Common Agricultural Policy. Special arrangements are provided for beef, rice, sugar, rum, and bananas, which are of great value for a few ACP countries; on the whole, however, access for agricultural products is no more generous than that offered to countries outside the Convention. The Community has made a few minor concessions on agricultural trade in the Lomé III Convention—mainly designed to broaden and speed up consideration of requests for preferential access—but holds out little hope of any major liberalization in this area.

In short, the Community believes that ACP countries are unlikely to increase their exports unless they take action themselves to boost their productive capacity and improve their competitiveness. For this reason, the new Convention offers greater possibilities for the financing of measures to help individual ACP states develop coherent trade strategies; train personnel in export-related jobs; enhance the quality of products, particularly by adapting them to market requirements; and improve infrastructure, notably for transport and storage facilities.

Aid

Under each Lomé Convention the financial endowment of the EDF is divided between the special facilities, regional aid programs, and individual country programs. For the latter category the Commission draws up an indicative program with each ACP country and earmarks specific resources according mainly to the country's population and GDP per capita.

The effectiveness of aid granted under the Lomé Convention has come under close scrutiny in recent years, most notably in the "Pisani memorandum" prepared in 1982 by the Commissioner then in charge of development affairs, Edgard Pisani. In the Lomé III negotiations, both sides recognized that much aid granted under previous Lomé Conventions had been used inefficiently, with only a limited impact on development. The ACP states faulted delays in the selection and financing of development projects and cited an overcentralized decision-making process in Brussels and cumbersome bureaucratic procedures. To the Community the problem was more fundamental. Its evaluation of the effectiveness of Lomé aid led to the conclusion that efficiency was less related to the quality of the goods or services provided than to the degree to which local skills and initiative were stimulated. Pisani went so far as to say that "below" a certain threshold of effectiveness and relevance, aid becomes an evil, for it nourishes illusions and encourages passivity." In this light, it seemed imperative that new Lomé resources should be used less for new capital projects and more for integrated sectoral programs, particularly with a view to agricultural and rural development.

To achieve this shift in emphasis the Community negotiators asked their ACP counterparts to accept a "policy dialogue," which would precede the choice of schemes to be financed from Lomé resources. Initially, many ACP states took grave exception to this term, believing it to be a euphemism for EC control of their development plans and thus an encroachment on their national sovereignty and incompatible with the principle of equal partnership. In the end no direct reference was made to policy dialogue in the new Convention and spokesmen for both sides were at some pains to emphasize that the ACP states retained their contractual right to choose the way in which aid would be used. However, the ACP states agreed to include in the first chapter of the Convention a statement to the effect that "support shall be provided in ACP-EEC cooperation for the ACP state" own efforts to achieve more self-reliant and self-sustained development" and to reach this objective "special efforts shall be made. . . to promote rural development, food security for the people and the revival and strengthening of agricultural production potential in the ACP states." The Community hopes that this language and the new emphasis on programs, sectoral development, and the stimulation of national potential that it implies will lead to a much more detailed consideration of a country's overall objectives and, hence, automatically, to a more thorough dialogue on the policies needed to achieve them. It remains to be seen, however, whether the Community and the individual ACP states will in reality be able to come to a more united appreciation of the optimal way in which the Convention's resources can be used.

STABEX

A major part of the debate on aid efficiency was focused on the utilization of STABEX resources. STABEX is probably the most distinctive feature of the Lomé Convention. It grew out of the Community's recognition in the early 1970s that aid tended to be less effective in countries experiencing instability in their export revenues. STABEX was introduced in the first Lomé Convention as a means of alleviating this problem and now compensates ACP states for loss of export earnings from any of a list of 48 agricultural products and subproducts.

Although there is a certain amount of overlap between STABEX and the IMF's compensatory financing facility, there are many differences, two of the most notable being that (1) STABEX takes no account of earnings from other merchandise exports or of the country's overall balance of payments position in calculating the compensation for a shortfall in earnings from one of the covered commodities (in other words, a country can draw from STABEX even if there is an upward trend in its overall export earnings) and (2) drawings are not limited by any equivalent of the member's quota in the Fund, but by the resources the Community allocates to the scheme for a particular period. Given the limited number of commodities covered, these features of STABEX have led to situations in which a relatively high proportion of the available resources has been directed to a small number of countries.

STABEX worked fairly smoothly during its initial period of operation, 1975-79. The ECU 382 million set aside to finance it met all the eligible claims. Despite an increase in its resources to ECU 557 million, however, the scheme ran into serious difficulties at the beginning of the Lomé II period, as the prices of several commodities dropped rapidly in comparison with the average prices of the reference period. In both 1980 and 1981, claims of up to ECU 1 million were met in full, but transfers to meet larger claims had to be reduced by about one half. The system regained its equilibrium in 1982 and 1983 as the high commodity price years of the late 1970s dropped out of the reference period.

Participants in the Lomé Convention are:

European Community: Belgium, Denmark, France, the Federal Republic of Germany, Greece, Ireland, Italy, Luxembourg, the Netherlands, and the United Kingdom, Portugal and Spain are expected to become participants in 1986.

ACP states: Angola, Antigua and Barbuda, the Bahamas, Barbados, Belize, Benin, Botswana, Burkina Faso, Burundi, Cameroon, Cape Verde, the Central African Republic, Chad, the Comoros, the Congo, Djibouti, Dominica, Equatorial Guinea, Ethiopia, Fiji, Gabon, The Gambia, Ghana, Grenada, Guinea, Guinea Bissau, Guyana, the Ivory Coast, Jamaica, Kenya, Kiribati, Lesotho, Liberia, Madagascar, Malawi, Mali, Mauritania, Mauritius, the People's Republic of Mozambique, Niger, Nigeria, Papua New Guinea, Rwanda St. Christopher and Nevis, St. Lucia, St. Vincent, Sao Tomé and Principe, Senegal, Seychelles, Sierra Leone, Solomon Islands, Somalia, Sudan, Suriname, Swaziland, Tanzania, Togo, Tonga, Trinidad and Tobago, Tuvalu, Uganda, Vanuatu, Western Samoa, Zaïre, Zambia, and Zimbabwe.

Major provisions of the Lomé III Convention

Trade

- Free access to EC market for all manufactured products where materials originate in the ACP states or in the Community.
- Free access for manufactured products containing materials from other sources if, among others, (1) nonoriginating materials account for less than 5 percent of total material costs, and (2) certain types of processing of the nonoriginating materials have been carried out.
- Exception to the rules of origin granted, inter alia, when nonoriginating materials represent at least 60 percent of value of finished product or when these materials originate in UN-designated least developed countries.
- Conditions of access for all agricultural products sometimes more preferential, never less so, than those offered to third countries.
- Community can take safeguard measures if trade provisions result in serious disturbances in economic sector of a member state or jeopardize external financial stability.
- Financial and technical assistance provided to assist development of ACP trade potential.

Aid

STABEX

- Provides compensation for a loss of earnings from exports to the Community and, in some cases, to the rest of the world, if: (1) the product(s) represented at least 6 percent of the claiming country's total exports during claim year (1.5 percent for landlocked, island, and least developed countries); and (2) earnings from product fell at least 6 percent during claim year (1.5 percent for landlocked, island, and least developed countries) compared to earnings during a reference period (generally the preceding four years).
- All claims considered simultaneously in year following claim year.
- Transfers repayable if earnings increase sufficiently during seven-year period following claim year (no such obligation for landlocked, island, and least developed countries).

SYSMIN

- Provides assistance to help overcome adverse consequences of a fall in ability to produce or export copper (and associated cobalt), phosphates, manganese, bauxite (and alumina), tin, iron ore.
- Country eligible if at least 15 percent of total export earnings derived from a covered mineral (10 percent for the landlocked, island, and least developed countries).
- Country can be eligible, by exemption, if 20 percent (12 percent for landlocked, island, and least developed countries) of total export earnings derived from any combination of mining products other than precious minerals, oil, and gas.

Financial endowment for 1985-89	
Grants to individual ACP states	ECU 4,360 million
Emergency aid	210 million
Aid for refugees	80 million
Interest rate subsidies for European Investment Bank loans	210 million
STABEX	925 million
SYSMIN	415 million
Special loans	600 million
Risk capital	600 million
Loans from IEB	1,100 million
Total	**8,500 million**

In preparing for the Lomé III negotiations, the European Community, while acknowledging that many STABEX claims could be attributed to reasons beyond a claiming country's control, such as adverse market or climatic conditions, argued that many others could be explained by falling levels of production and competitiveness. This situation, it believed, was often brought about by the low priority some governments had given to agriculture, notably by policies that set producer prices too low, and by inefficient transportation and other infrastructural problems. The Community felt that several ACP countries had failed to use STABEX resources to tackle these problems, employing these funds instead to meet the most pressing demands on the national budget on the frequently tenuous grounds that this represented a permitted diversification away from the troubled export sector. After long discussions of principle on how free the claiming country's authorities should be to decide the best use to which STABEX payments could be put, it was agreed that financing diversification measures would be permissible; however, the Community obtained the insertion of language that "Every request for a transfer shall, in addition to the necessary statistical data, include substantial information on the loss of earnings and also the programmes and operations to which the ACP state has allocated or undertakes to allocate the funds." This is much stronger than the corresponding Lomé II text, which provided only that the ACP state should give the Community "some indication of the probable use to which the transfer will be put." In addition, the new Convention permits the Community to suspend decisions on subsequent claims if a satisfactory account of the transfer has not been rendered one year after the transfer decision was made. These two new provisions should help the Community to ensure that the use of STABEX funds is directly related to the reasons for the shortfall in export earnings concerned.

SYSMIN

Increasing the efficiency of aid and promoting the productive use of special facility resources were also at the heart of negotiations concerning SYSMIN. SYSMIN was introduced with the Lomé II Convention and came into effect in 1980. It was designed to help ACP countries cope with any serious temporary problems beyond their control which caused, or were projected to cause, a decline in their capacity to export certain specified minerals. Unlike STABEX, SYSMIN was not designed to compensate for a decline in export earnings. Its resources were expected to be used primarily to help maintain production capacity during adverse market conditions and their release was made conditional upon Commission examination and approval. The Community was careful to avoid any element of automaticity, so that multinational mining companies could not organize their activities with the express purpose of becoming eligible for transfers.

In its first four years of operation SYSMIN benefited only four countries—Guyana, Rwanda, Zaïre, and Zambia. During the negotiations for Lomé III, a number of the ACP countries complained about this and noted that under Lomé II only some 12 countries were potential beneficiaries of the system. The Community agreed to go some way toward meeting these concerns. While it was unwilling to change the list of covered minerals, it did agree to open a "second window", to SYSMIN resources. This provided exceptions, on a case-by-case basis, for ACP countries deriving 20 percent of their export earnings (12 percent for the landlocked, island, and least-developed countries) from a combination of mining products other than precious minerals, oil, and gas, but not necessarily those mentioned specifically in the Convention. The opening of this "second window" to SYSMIN resources is expected to benefit a number of ACP states, notably, Botswana, Niger, and Zimbabwe.

The Community also liberalized the detailed criteria for the eligibility of claims by agreeing to consider using SYSMIN funds to remedy problems caused for major development projects, when the financing from the mineral sector on which they depend is seriously cut back or terminated, and also made more explicit that SYSMIN funds can be used to deal with structural as well as cyclical problems. Under the new Convention, the system can be used not only following "accidents" or "grave political events" but also in cases of adverse technological developments (such as the substitution of plastics for copper in traditional copper uses) or adverse economic developments (such as the inflationary impact of an oil price increase on mining operations).

Perhaps the most important change in the provisions for SYSMIN in the Lomé III Convention is in its orientation. Under Lomé II the main purpose of interventions was to maintain production capacity during a difficult period. Under the new convention the aim will be "to reestablish the viability" of the mining sector concerned. This will allow the Community not only to finance improvements to the production infrastructure but also, when it is considered to be in the best interests of the ACP country concerned, to finance orderly reductions in production capacity.

Conclusion

Although some signatories of the Lomé Convention feel that it falls short of what was originally hoped for, all are agreed that its overall effects have been beneficial. There is considerable satisfaction on the ACP side that the real value of the Convention has been maintained at a time when several Community, members have been actively considering cuts in aid budgets and when the real value of some other multilateral funds, such as IDA, has been reduced. There is also satisfaction that the latest Lomé Convention offers some new benefits to the ACP countries and promises a new flexibility and a streamlining of administrative procedures. On the Community side there is hope that the new Convention will be more effective in promoting economic development and that through its institutions it will continue to provide one of the most significant forums for the North-South dialogue.

Critical Issues in Canada—Third World Economic Relations[1]

Doug Williams

1. Introduction

Canada's high profile on North-South issues, a legacy of its tradition of international diplomacy and the interest of former Prime Minister Pierre Trudeau, belies the fact that, by many measures, its economic links to Third World countries are weak. In terms of imports, exports and international lending, for example, Canada has few ties to developing countries, especially in comparison to most other industrial countries. Only in the area of official development assistance (ODA), has Canada made a strong mark, both in absolute terms and in relation to other industrial country donors.

Canada has much more at stake in Third World economic growth and development than statistics would seem to suggest, however. In an increasingly interdependent world, Canada's own economic health and security is closely tied to that of the Third World, as events during the recent recession have clearly indicated. Canadian relations with developing countries have an important bearing on the achievement of Canada's own economic and foreign policy goals, which include job creation, enhanced economic competitiveness and economic and political security, and strengthening the multilateral system of institutions for managing interdependence.

2. Canada's Economic Links to Developing Countries

Although weak, Canada's trading and financial relationships with the Third World had expanded rapidly throughout the 1970s, and developing countries were among Canada's most dynamic economic partners. With the recession of the 1980s, however, this dynamism has been lost, at considerable expense to the Canadian economy. The impact of the recession is now familiar: trade protectionism, increased interest rates, and the reluctance of private lenders to extend further credit to heavily indebted developing countries, particularly following Mexico's suspension of debt repayments in 1982, forced many developing country governments to undertake drastic adjustments. Government expenses were cut, social services reduced, and imports of all kinds drastically cut, in many cases undercutting the very basis of their economic growth. The costs of this economic and development crisis, transmitted through the world's financial and trading system, have hit all countries, however weak or strong their direct ties to developing countries may be.

This paper was written especially for this volume.

Trade Relationships

Table 1
Canada-Third World Trade, 1976-85
($ million)[a]

Year	Exports	Imports	Balance
1976	3,120	5,310	−2,190
1977	3,660	5,290	−1,630
1978	4,580	5,550	− 970
1979	5,640	6,890	−1,250
1980	7,980	9,100	−1,120
1981	8,420	10,900	−2,480
1982	8,230	8,020	+ 210
1983	7,580	8,060	− 480
1984	8,500	9,280	− 780
1985	7,440	9,400	−1,960

Source: General Agreement on Tariffs and Trade, *International Trade*, various years.
[a] Unless otherwise noted, all dollar figures cited in this paper are Canadian dollars.

Canada's trade ties with the Third World, already weak, have been hard hit by recession. The limited extent of Canada's Third World trade relationships can be contrasted to the experience of other industrial countries. The United States, European Community and Japan conduct 35 per cent, 16 per cent and 40 per cent, respectively, of their total trade with developing countries; the Third World's share of Canada's external trade has never exceeded 12 per cent. Reasons often cited for this small share include Canada's distance and lack of historical ties to developing countries, proximity to the United States market, and a narrow and often uncompetitive manufacturing base.

Despite their small share of Canada's trade, Third World countries were among Canada's most dynamic trading partners throughout the 1970s. Their purchases of Canadian products (notably agricultural, resource-based and some manufactured goods) increased more rapidly than those of other Canadian trading partners, and their share of Canadian exports rose rapidly over the decade as a result, from 7 per cent in 1970 to over 12 per cent in 1980. Increases in Canadian exports to Southeast and East Asia were particularly rapid. On the import side, Canadian purchases from developing countries also increased rapidly over the decade, led by imports of textiles and clothing from export-oriented countries of the Pacific rim.

Since 1981, this dynamism has been lost. With recession, the rapid and sustained growth of Canada's Third World trade that characterized the 1970s ceased. Exports, particularly to hard hit countries in Africa and Latin America, fell sharply and the drop in Canadian imports from developing countries was even sharper, as shown in Table 1, exceeding comparable drops recorded by other industrial countries. Recovery has been slow, and both exports and imports in 1985 remained considerably below their 1981 peaks. This lost dynamism and Canada's booming trade with the United States is reflected in the declining share of developing countries in Canada's trade: from a peak of 12.2 per cent in 1980, their share had fallen to 7.7 per cent in 1985.

The shrinkage of developing country markets has been costly for the Canadian economy. Between 1980 and 1983, for example, exports to four major Latin American markets, Argentina, Brazil, Mexico and Venezuela, declined from $2.2 billion to $1.3 billion. The effects of these cutbacks were felt in many regions of the country: exports of machinery and vehicles from central Canada to these four countries declined by more than 50 per cent; forestry products and raw materials from western Canada by half; asbestos and aluminum from Quebec by 70 per cent; and exports of steel rails from Nova Scotia ceased altogether. The job losses associated with this downturn were substantial, at a time when unemployment was already at historically high levels.

Financial Relationships

Table 2
Selected Financial Flows from Canada to Developing Countries
1976-85[a]

Year	Direct Investment $ million	%	Net Private Bank Lending[b] $ million	%	ODA $ million	%	Total Financial Flows
1974-76 average	244	12.2	586	29.2	822	45.5	2,005
1977	415	16.2	524	20.4	1,053	41.0	2,568
1978	637	25.5	343	13.7	1,209	48.3	2,502
1979	−117	−4.4	1,038	38.8	1,237	46.3	2,672
1980	81	2.1	1,485	39.4	1,257	33.3	3,770
1981	369	5.3	2,141	30.7	1,426	20.4	6,979
1982	153	6.6	—	—	1,477	64.2	2,299
1983	705	22.2	248	7.8	1,761	55.5	3,174
1984	613	16.8	256	7.0	2,104	57.8	3,640
1985	116	5.1	58	2.5	2,218	96.6	2,296

[a] Other official flows, including export credits, are not included in this table.
[b] Defined as the change in bilateral claims of resident banks.
Source: Organization for Economic Co-operation and Development, *Development Co-operation, Efforts and Policies of Members of the Development Assistance Committee*, (various years), Paris.

Like trade, financial flows from Canada to developing countries have declined since the onset of recession, marking a sharp reversal of the situation prevailing throughout the 1970s. Private flows, notably direct investment and private bank lending, have virtually ceased. Official development assistance (ODA), stagnant during the late 1970s and early 1980s, has shown some increase in real terms since 1984. As a result of these trends, the flow of financial resources from Canada to developing countries, which has long had a higher component of aid than in the case of other industrial countries, is now even more heavily comprised of ODA.

Prior to 1981, the opposite had been true. The stock of Canadian-based foreign investment in developing countries had increased quickly, more rapidly in fact that Canadian investment anywhere else in the world. With this growth came a shift in the location of Canada's Third World investments (away from Latin America, which accounted for 58 per cent in 1981, and toward Indonesia and other countries of Asia), and the sectors involved (away from utilities and banking, and toward energy and mining and smelting).

Similarly, Canadian private bank lending to developing countries also increased rapidly prior to 1981. As shown in Table 2, the net flow of private bank lending increased from $343 million to $2,121 million between 1978 and 1981, and made up a rising share of the total net flow of financial resources from Canada to developing countries. Third World lending represented a particularly fast growing component of Canadian bank's international activity.

Since the onset of recession, private financial flows to Third World countries have stalled or come to a halt. Private bankers have virtually withdrawn from all but the most attractive Third World markets, preferring to focus their international lending on markets considered less risky, such as the United States. Canadian direct investment in developing countries has been erratic, and suggests considerable hesitancy to undertake new investments in the Third World.

In contrast, Canada's aid effort has increased, both in current dollars and in real terms, and the ODA share of Canada's financial flows to the Third World has risen. Canadian ODA, as reported to the OECD's Development Assistance Committee, stood at $2,296 million in 1985, equal to 0.49 per cent of Gross National Product (GNP). According to this measure of aid effort, Canada placed eighth amongst the seventeen DAC members, and was somewhat above the DAC average of 0.35 per cent. Since 1982, the growth of Canadian ODA has exceeded inflation, and is reflected in increases in the ODA/GNP ratio from a low of 0.41 per cent in 1981. Moreover, it has outpaced the increase in aid flows from other industrial countries, taken as a whole, to developing countries during this decade.

3. Critical Policy Issues in Canada-Third World Economic Relations

Trade Policy Challenges

With the launch of the Uruguay Round of multilateral trade negotiations in September, 1986, under the auspices of the General Agreement on Tariffs and Trade (GATT), it is clear that the multilateral trading system is at a critical turning point, with a future based on either more, and more open, trade, or the kind of immiserizing protectionism which characterized the Great Depression. The negotiations, to be completed within four years, promise to be the most complex and ambitious yet attempted. Their success is vital for the future of North-South trading relationships and economic prosperity of all countries.

The principal issues to be covered over the course of the negotiations include a mix of the old (issues left unresolved at the close of the previous round of negotiations in 1979), and the new.[2] For many developing countries, the issue of quantitative restrictions and other non-tariff barriers that are contrary to basic GATT principles (such as those imposed under the Multi-Fibre Arrangement, of MFA), has been a longstanding concern. Such measures have been used frequently by industrial countries in response to the rapid penetration of their markets by new and competitive suppliers. Typically, the industries involved are labour intensive and vulnerable to import competition, and the suppliers are newly industrializing and, increasingly, other developing countries. Among the other issues left outstanding in 1979 and of particular concern to developing countries are agricultural trade (largely excluded from previous negotiations), and the use of trade distorting domestic and export subsidies.

A unique feature of the Uruguay Round is the inclusion of new trade issues for the first time, among them, trade in services (such as banking, insurance and tourism), trade-related investment issues, and intellectual property rights (patents, copyright and trade in counterfeit goods). A number of developing countries (notably India and Brazil) strongly resisted moves to include such issues in the new round, concerned that their inclusion would jeopardize progress in other areas of particular concern to them, and would represent an unwarranted intrusion into sensitive areas of national economic and cultural sovereignty. Other developing countries, however, were prepared to begin the discussion of new issues if it meant that their outstanding concerns would also be dealt with.

For Canada, the outcome of the negotiations will have important implications for its own economic health. Canada's economic prosperity is critically dependent on open world markets. As one of the most open industrial countries, exports account for thirty per cent of GNP, a share that far exceeds that of most other industrial countries. The negotiations will also have an important bearing on the conduct of Canada's trading relations with developing countries, particularly in such sensitive sectors as textiles, clothing, and footwear.

Like most industrial countries, Canada has made extensive use of quantitative restraints on imports of particular importance for developing countries. Textile and clothing imports from all major Third World and eastern European suppliers are restrained by means of discriminatory 'voluntary export restraint' agreements under the Multi-Fibre Arrangement. In recent years, Canada has also restrained imports of footwear (a product of particular interest to a number of developing countries) with a global quota imposed under GATT Article XIX.

There have been encouraging signs that Canada is taking a more open approach in the case of footwear. Quotas on imports of men's footwear were lifted in late 1985, while quotas on imports of women's and children's shoes are being phased out over a three year period. Although the government had concluded in 1985, at the end of an extensive inquiry, that the industry was able to stand on its own without special measures of import protection, the industry has continued to press for relief. The government has resisted industry calls for a new global quota, but has indicated its intention to seek "voluntary restraints" from a number of major developed country suppliers.

In contrast to its stance on the footwear industry, the Canadian government seems to have acknowledged that the Canadian textile and clothing industry is not, now or in the foreseeable future, able to stand on its own without special measures of protection. Canada's existing battery of restraint agreements controlling 'low cost' textile and clothing imports from over twenty developing country and eastern European suppliers expired in late 1986. The Canadian industry has pressed for a further tightening of the import restraint system, and clearly indicated its preference for a global quota on textile and clothing imports (which would set an absolute limit on the volume of imports), and a guaranteed share of the domestic market. While rejecting this option (which would expose Canada to retaliation from developed country trading partners), the Canadian government did agree to a further tightening of the system of bilateral restraints which now extend for the remainder of the decade.

The government seems to have accepted industry arguments that some form of trade protection is essential for the survival of the Canadian industry. It is now exploring options for protecting the industry in the event that the current MFA is not extended and textiles and clothing trade is brought back under GATT disciplines. To this end, it has launched a three year trial duty remission program for Canadian men's shirt manufacturers. By granting these firms access to duty-free imports of shirts in volumes tied to their Canadian production, it is hoped that Canadian manufacturers will rationalize their product lines and become more efficient and competitive.

A further reflection of the central role of special trade measures in strategy for this industry has been the abandonment of the adjustment assistance program for the industry, the Canadian Industrial Renewal Program, which expired in early 1986.[3] Under this program, funds had been channeled to firms, workers and communities reliant on the textile, clothing, footwear and tanning industries, to promote restructuring and reduce reliance on special import control measures. In the place of this sectoral approach, the government has revamped existing economy-wide programs for workers, firms and communities facing adjustment difficulties and, as noted above, will continue to rely on special trade measures to assist these industries.

Financing Development

Restarting financial flows to Third World countries is no less important for the economic health of both North and South, and equally difficult. Developing countries' access to finance, which had dried up so abruptly during the recession, has yet to be restored. Despite wide acceptance in industrial countries of the "Baker Initiative", there continues to be a general reluctance on the part of commercial banks to undertake new Third World lending activity. Canadian banks are no different in this regard, and have been cutting back on their Third World activity, preferring lower risk markets in Canada and the United States. As a result, many developing countries (and indeed the Third World taken as a whole) are now experiencing net financial *outflows*, due to the withdrawal of private creditors (except as part of official refinancing packages), and the continuation of high real interest rates. Such outflows are difficult, if not impossible, to sustain and have serious implications for developing countries' capacity for economic growth and for the stability of the world's financial system.

Canada has played a prominent role in efforts to increase flows of *official* finance to developing countries. Like many other countries, Canada was disappointed at the U.S. insistence on a three year replenishment of only US $9 billion for the International Development Association (IDA), the World Bank affiliate dealing with the poorest countries, in 1984. This replenishment was much lower than the US $16 billion considered the minimum necessary to maintain the real value of the IDA program. Furthermore, Canada actively supported the creation of a US $1.3 billion special facility for sub-Saharan Africa the following year and pressed for the US $12 billion IDA replenishment successfully negotiated in 1986.

Canada and other industrial countries will be challenged to further increase the capacity of multilateral financial institutions to lend to developing countries, such as by supporting the proposed increase in the capital of the World Bank which will permit it to step up its lending activity. Support will also be needed for changes to the conditions attached to the use of multilateral finance by developing countries, in favour of adjustment programs that contribute to renewed economic growth and protect the poorest and most vulnerable groups in society.

In terms of *private* flows, there are now signs that Canadian banks may be prepared to pursue more innovative approaches in dealing with developing countries. The president of the Bank of Montreal, Canada's third largest bank, has recently put forward a proposal for swapping debt for equity in the case of Brazil (which owes Canadian banks approximately US $5 billion), an approach that would reduce the outstanding debt of Brazil, and private banks' exposure to that country, and result in new infusions of equity investment. Similar approaches have been pursued in a number of other developing countries with some success.

Strengthening the Aid Program

With the drying up of other sources of finance for developing countries, issues concerning official development assistance programs have assumed particular importance. For the Canadian ODA program, two crucial questions are outstanding: the volume of aid, and its quality.

Although Canada's aid program has grown in recent years, both in absolute terms and in relation to GNP, there is still considerable concern about meeting aid targets, and some suggestion that targets may be abandoned. Since 1975, the Canadian government has been committed to meeting the ODA target of 0.7 per cent of GNP first put forward in 1969 by the World Bank sponsored Commission on International Development, chaired by the former Canadian Prime Minister Lester B. Pearson.[4] Since it was announced, however, the date for achieving this target has been postponed several times, from 1985 to 1990, and more recently to 1995. Currently, the Canadian government has indicated its intention to increase ODA in line with the growth of the Canadian economy for the remainder of the decade (and thus maintain the current 0.5 per cent ratio), and to raise the ratio to 0.6 per cent by 1995 and to 0.7 per cent by the end of the century.

As in the past, it is uncertain whether the Canadian government is prepared to increase aid spending by the amounts necessary to meet these targets. In the current atmosphere of government expenditure restraint, ministers have been hard pressed to protect even the current modest aid spending growth. To meet the 1995 target of 0.6 per cent of GNP would entail very rapid increases between 1990 and 1995, increases that current and future governments will find difficult to support in view of the priority placed on deficit reduction. However, the longer progress toward the target is delayed, the more difficult the target is to achieve, and the more likely it is to be further delayed or dropped altogether.

In any case, some aspects of the current structure of the aid program undermine the likelihood that ODA targets can be met as well as undercut the quality of the aid effort. By some measures, Canada's aid has been among the most liberal of the major donors'. A large share of Canadian bilateral (or country-to-country) aid has been extended on very soft financial terms, typically as grants, or loans with low interest rates, long grace periods and extended repayment periods. Since 1986, all bilateral aid has been provided as grants. In 1986, the government also announced the rescheduling of outstanding ODA debts of those African countries implementing adjustment programs.

In other respects, however, the quality of Canadian aid has been found wanting. The program is guided by a number of objectives; although the promotion of development is considered the primary objective, the program is also expected to achieve important political objectives (supporting Canadian allies in the Third World and promoting ties with

Commonwealth and francophone developing countries), and to promote Canada's commercial objectives in the Third World. Inevitably, pressure to simultaneously achieve political and commercial objectives undermines the development effectiveness of the aid program.

Of particular concern is the increased priority currently placed on extracting commercial benefit for Canada from the aid program. Canada has been long recognized as one of the donors placing extremely tight procurement restrictions on the use of its bilateral aid. Since 1970, 80 per cent of Canada's bilateral aid (excluding transportation costs) has had to comprise Canadian goods and services; to qualify as Canadian, a good must have two thirds Canadian content, and a service must be provided by a majority Canadian-owned firm employing primarily Canadian citizens. Furthermore, there have been recent proposals to increase the commercial use of aid by making greater use of aid to subsidize official export credit in "mixed credit" packages. Although 1984 and 1985 proposals for a new mixed credit facility were not implemented, pressures to increase the use of aid in this way continue.

Many consider practices such as procurement tying and mixed credit to have considerable adverse impact on the development effectiveness of Canada's aid. It has been argued they increase project costs (to the extent that Canadian products are not competitive) and skew the types of projects supported (toward those making use of imported inputs and away from those with high local costs). It is further argued that they skew the sectoral distribution of aid, in favour of traditional infrastructure projects in the power and transport sectors for example, and the country distribution, in favour of higher income developing countries of particular export interest to Canada. As well, from the donor perspective, these practices tie the hands of aid planners, limiting their flexibility to respond to the priority needs of developing countries and their capacity to make use of increased financial resources.

4. The Third World in Canada's Foreign Policy Review, 1987

Despite early concerns on the part of many observers that the 1984 election of a new government would mark drastic changes in the traditional foreign policy framework, such has not proved the case. At mid-term, the Conservative government has reaffirmed in its words and actions many key elements of Canadian foreign policy. Of particular importance for developing countries has been Canada's commitment to support for more open world trade and multilateral solutions to pressing economic and political issues. In several key areas for Third World countries, however, Canadian policy has yet to be made clear. The outcome of policy reviews still underway, and the government response to the resulting proposals, will set important policy directions for Canada's Third World relations.

The victory of the Conservative Party in the September 4, 1984 general election launched a period of intensive policy review, consultation and change in Canada. Early indications led some observers to fear a new era of introversion on the part of the federal government, with a narrow preoccupation with domestic economic and political goals. Prominent on the new government's agenda, for example, were increased economic growth and job creation, deficit reduction and improved federal-provincial relations. In the trade sphere, the emphasis placed on striking a bilateral free trade agreement with the United States also alarmed some observers who questioned the new government's commitment to Canada's traditional support for multilateralism.

However, early concerns about policy directions proved somewhat premature, at least in the foreign policy sphere. The new government was quick to acknowledge that the prosperity and security of an open, middle sized country such as Canada are caught up in the changing currents of the wider world. In its first Speech from the Throne, the government reaffirmed Canada's longstanding framework of principles guiding foreign policy: that Canadian interests, whether economic, development or security, are best protected and asserted within the framework of sound multilateral institutions.[5] This approach has been reinforced more recently in the governments response to the report of the Senate-House of Commons Special Joint Committee on Canada's International Relations:

Canada often relies on multilateral institutions...to make its contribution to the national management of world order... 'Going it alone' is never ruled out, but is usually less productive for a country in Canada's circumstances.[6]

The reaffirmation of Canada's commitment to multilateral management of interdependence is one important part of Canadian policy with respect to relations with Third World countries. Like Canada, developing countries have an important stake in an effective set of multilateral institutions to manage international economic and political relationships, and much to lose from the breakdown of the system.

More specifically, the profile of issues related to Canada-Third World relations has risen steadily over the course of the foreign policy review process. In the early stages, little attention was devoted to these questions: the government's initial discussion paper made only cursory reference to them.[7] With each succeeding step in the process, however, the focus on these issues has sharpened. During the deliberations of the Senate-Commons Joint Committee, over 1,000 written briefs were received, and over 600 witnesses appeared, over two thirds of them dealing with just two questions, human rights and Central America. In its report, the Committee called for human rights to be treated as an explicit theme in Canada's external relations and made several recommendations to this end, a number of which have already been acted on by the government.[8]

In two other important areas, review has yet to be completed. The House of Commons Standing Committee on External Affairs and International Trade will submit its report on Canada's development assistance program in late spring, 1987, and is expected to call for increased emphasis on assisting the poorest and supporting human resource development through the aid program. The Senate Foreign Affairs Committee has completed its investigation of Canadian roles in international financial institutions (such as the International Monetary Fund and the World Bank) and its report is awaited. In both cases, the government response to the reports, expected in the fall, will set important policy directions for Canada-Third World relations.

Notes

[1] Much of the material contained in this chapter has appeared previously in the North-South Institute's annual Review/Outlook. The author would like to acknowledge the contributions of Institute staff on which this chapter is based.

[2] For a full description of issues for the new trade round, see "The Uruguay Round: Issues for Multilateral Trade Negotiations", *Briefing 17* (Ottawa: North-South Institute, 1987).

[3] The Components of the Canadian Industrial Renewal Program are outlined in Doug Williams, *Canadian Adjustment Policy: Beyond the Canadian Industrial Renewal Board* (Ottawa: North-South Institute, 1987).

[4] *Partners in Development, Report of the Commission on International Development*, Lester B. Pearson, Chairman (New York: Praeger Publishers, 1969).

[5] Canada, Senate, "Speech from the Throne", *Debates of the Senate*, 1st Session, 33rd Parliament, November 5, 1984, p. 7.

[6] Canada, External Affairs Canada, *Canada's International Relations: Response of the Government of Canada to the Report of the Special Joint Committee of the Senate and the House of Commons* (Ottawa: Supply and Services Canada, December, 1986), p. 5.

[7] Canada, External Affairs Canada, *Competitiveness and Security: Directions for Canada's International Relations* (Ottawa: Supply and Services Canada, 1985).

[8] Canada, Special Joint Committee on Canada's International Relations, *Interdependence Internationalism: Report of the Special Joint Committee on Canada's International Relations* (Ottawa: Queen's Printer for Canada, 1986).

Chapter 13
A Dialogue of Monologues

Introduction

As the Western world entered the last quarter of the 20th century it became evident that the period ahead would be notable for its changeability and flux. The international economic system established following the Second World War, which had served the industrial countries so well for three decades, seemed less and less well-fitted to the new distribution of economic and political power that emerged during the 1960s and 1970s.

Formal recognition of the changed circumstances came most dramatically through the Nixonian shocks of 1971 in the abdication of the US dollar of its regal position. But the shake-up of the international monetary system only reflected the underlying shifts taking place in the global distribution of economic power, the most important of which was the emergence of the European and Japanese economies following their surprisingly brief post-war convalescence. This development was bound to challenge an international system founded upon the comfortable predominance and tutelage of the US economy.

However, the diffusion of economic power was not to be limited only to the traditional group of countries. The successful assertion of OPEC power in 1973 launched a group of developing countries into the big league of economic and political players. The oil-exporters' example fueled the hopes of other Third World commodity exporters that they too might organize and exert similar pressure. For the most part, however, these hopes were extinguished by the very different market realities facing other export commodities. Nevertheless, the magnification of the OPEC role in the world stage did drive home—especially in Europe and Japan—the increasingly critical part played by the developing world in the provision of raw materials and agricultural products to the industrial North. More generally, it became the catalyst initiating what came to be known as the North-South Dialogue.

The 1970s also witnessed the growing vitality of another group of developing countries, located mainly on the Pacific Rim of Asia and in Latin America, whose trading strength was increasingly impressed on the international system and evidenced on the store-shelves and in the factories of the North. As with the OPEC member countries, those labelled "newly industrializing"—NICs—found themselves increasingly dissociated from other Third World countries in development analyses: their economic importance duly, if not always accurately, is used to justify a "graduation" from the general "less developed country" classification.

Underlying many of these changes and the economic dynamism of the period lies an accelerated pace of technological change. The application of science to productive processes and related activities seems today to be reaching a dizzying pace, with no end in sight. Science is making itself felt with a vengeance in economic life, increasing mobility, accelerating obsolescence and, generally, exposing economies to gales of change. With this remarkable impact on productivity comes a strong dose of insecurity and impermanence injected into what were relatively stable patterns of resource distribution and production, both within and among countries.

The final element in the turbulence of our time is the increased interpenetration of national economies, evidenced in the flows of capital, goods, services, technology and labour. The consequences of such a development are mixed. If interpenetration has positive features linked to increased output, free flows of factors of production, specialization and efficiency, it also implies a heightened sensitivity and possible vulnerability of one economy to policies or trends in others, especially the strongest.

The context within which North-South discussions are conducted is thus one permeated by the fact of fluidity and change, only some of which, it must be stressed, is related to the developing countries. The challenge facing governments and their peoples is that of economic, social, political and psychological readjustment at a time when slack economic conditions seem to offer little room for manoeuvre.

The formal North-South dialogue dates from the establishment in 1964 of the first United Nations Conference on Trade and Development (UNCTAD). The dialogue covering development, trade, finance and, more recently, a restructuring of the totality of the world economic system, has taken place in various UN forums. As a direct result of the failure of a decade of negotiations within UNCTAD, the Fourth Conference of Heads of State or Government of Non-aligned Countries meeting in 1973 in Algiers drew up an "economic declaration" which led to the adoption of the Declaration and Programme of Action on the establishment of a New Economic Order in the Sixth Special Session of the United Nations General Assembly held in the Spring of 1974. During the regular session following in December, 1974, the UNGA adopted a complementary text, the Charter of Economic Rights and Duties of States. These documents together form the basis for the principles for what became known as the NIEO (the New International Economic Order) demands. More specifically, these may be conveniently gathered under five heads: 1) the economic development of the Third World cannot be accomplished without structural change in the international economic system; 2) Third World commodity prices must be stabilized at just and remunerative levels; 3) better access for manufactures from the Third World to First World markets must be assured; 4) industry should be developed and diversified in the Third World, mainly through the transfers of technology on favourable terms; and 5) development assistance should be provided in increased volume and on better terms.

Although discussions continued between the First and Third Worlds on the NIEO between 1975 and 1981, the exchange was primarily one of monologues, with the First World disagreeing widely on both the need and the possibility of altering the existing international system. Similarly, the Third World's negotiating agenda has reflected a consensus but lacked priority, basically because the diversity in the Group of 77 (actually 120 Third World countries) is enormous. The poorest African countries have little in common with the NICs of Latin America, for example. In contrast, the First World, although divided on such matters as rates of assistance to the Third World, nevertheless operates on a common industrial, financial, trade, and cultural basis and is therefore relatively united in the need to preserve the existing institutions of the international system which have served it well. Hence, the attempt by the Third World, using its majority in the United Nations General Assembly, to institute so-called "global negotiations" to be carried out in the Eleventh Special Session of UNGA in 1980, failed. The objective was to carry out discussions and eventual negotiations about restructuring the entirety of the international economic system within the United Nations General Assembly, where the Third World has an automatic built-in majority. The First World categorically refused this venue, agreeing only that discussions should continue on different aspects of restructuring within the specific institutions that had responsibility for them: UNCTAD, IMF, FAO, UNIDO (United Nations Industrial Development Organization), and GATT's MTN. There matters have rested since the beginning of the 1980s. In particular, the recession of 1981-2 and the realignments of manufacturing costs have squeezed First World politics, leading to the so-called new protectionism designed to save employment at home. The 1980s may be characterized as a period of First World consolidation of self-interest while the Third World's interests get short-shrift.

This is not to argue that the First World is not conscious of the increasing importance of the Third World's role in its economy. For example, the Third World now receives 35% of U.S. exports, more than the European Common Market and Japan combined; the Third World provides a large quantity of raw materials and energy resources to both the United States and the European Community; and total American direct investment in the Third World exceeds US $50 billion. Hence economic prosperity of the developing countries is clearly in the interest of the United States and Europe. Both, however, argue that access to assistance from the First World is not a right of the Third World, nor is there an agreement that the First World should now correct perceived past inequities. The First World argument is that although many of the poorest countries depend on us to help strengthen their economies and diversify their exports, the major responsibility for development and the well-being of their citizens lies with the developing countries themselves. It is the belief of most of the First World countries that experience has shown that development is achieved when sound, market-oriented domestic economic policies are pursued in a climate that encourages private investment and in a political atmosphere fostering practical solutions to problems. First World countries assert that if the Third World countries pursue such policies, they will benefit from increased international trade and investment.

The three articles in this chapter illustrate the diversity of the First and Third Worlds' approaches to restructuring, or making fairer, the international economic order. Stewart reviews the second Brandt report, published in 1983, after the apparent failure of the NIEO negotiations. The second report is heavily based on the argument that the First and Second and Third Worlds have "common interests" and that addressing the problem of the Third World from this point of view will lead to solutions. Stewart, however, concludes that it is not enough to discover common interests, there must be a matching of imagination and vision with interests. "The Brandt report has tried to provide such a matching, but has failed".

The final article by Langley, followed by a rejoinder by Omo-Fadaka, is an exchange between a representative of the First World's views and a representative of the Third World's views. The exchange demonstrates the wide gulf between the two.

Third World Vulnerabilities and Global Negotiations

Stephen D. Krasner

What do Third World countries want? More wealth. How can they get it? By adopting more economically rational policies. What should the North do? Facilitate these policies. How should the North approach global negotiations? With cautious optimism. What is the long term prognosis for North-South relations? Hopeful, at least if economic development occurs. This is the common wisdom about relations between industrialized and developing areas in the United States and much of the rest of the North. Within this fold there are intense debates among adherents of conventional liberal, reformist liberal, and interdependence viewpoints. But the emphasis on economics at the expense of politics, on material well-being as opposed to power and control, pervades all of these orientations.

This essay elaborates an alternative perspective. It assumes that Third World states, like all states in the international system, are concerned about vulnerability and threat; and it recognizes that political regimes in almost all Third World countries are profoundly weak both internationally and domestically. It offers a very different set of answers to the questions posed in the preceding paragraph. Third World states want power and control as much as wealth. One strategy for achieving this objective is to change the rules of the game in various international issue areas. In general these efforts will be incompatible with long term Northern interests. Relations between industrialized and developing areas are bound to be conflictual over the long term because most Southern countries cannot hope to cope with their international vulnerability except by challenging principles, norms, and rules preferred by industrialized countries.

Conventional views of the South

There has been an intense debate in industrialized countries about the proper attitude that should be taken toward developing areas. This debate has been concerned with a wide range of issues including basic human needs, international institutions, and national policies in the North and the South. Three different orientations—orthodox liberal, reformist liberal, and interdependence—have dominated this exchange. While displaying deep divisions over specific policy issues, all three share a fundamentally economic view of the international system, a view in which wealth is the primary concern and mutual cooperation is the normal condition.

For orthodox liberals the problems of developing countries must be resolved internally. Low per capita incomes are the result of inadequate factor endowments. The rate of capital formation is low; infrastructures are underdeveloped; soil conditions are poor; education is

Originally published by Butterworths, Guildford, U.K., in the *Review of International Studies*, vol. 9, no. 4, October 1983. Reprinted with permission.

inadequate. To some extent these conditions, as well as the poor rate of economic growth of many developing countries, is blamed on inappropriate economic policies. Conditions in underdeveloped countries are of their own making. Orthodox liberals are especially perturbed by the failure to rely on market mechanisms. Trade barriers promote inefficient domestic industries. Investment regulations discourage multinational corporations. Low payments to farmers reduce food production. Inappropriate exchange rates distort production and consumption. Taxes on primary exports encourage smuggling. Enforced collectivization destroys individual incentives. P. T. Bauer and B. S. Yamey, probably the most well known exponents of this orientation conclude that such policies 'have brought about prompt and readily observable reverses or even collapse in large sectors of the economy in many countries, including reversion to subsistence production following the destructions of the trading system'. [1]

The policy implications for the North of orthodox liberal views are readily apparent. The New International Economic Order (NIEO) program should be rejected in its entirety. There is no need to reform the international economic system. Third World policies are responsible for Third World poverty. Indeed, such reform would be counterproductive because it would substitute state activity for the market. The NIEO is seen as a cock-eyed set of proposals inspired by erroneous dependency arguments at best and economic stupidity at worst.

Orthodox liberals have not placed much emphasis on Northern policies which impede the functioning of the market. Such policies are unfortunate, even reprehensible. But the fate of the South will not be determined by anything that the North does; while the present system may be flawed in modest ways, it still offers enormous opportunities to developing countries such as Taiwan, South Korea, Hong Kong, and Singapore, that are prepared to seize them.

Reformist liberal orientations share many of the basic presuppositions of orthodox liberalism, but place more emphasis on the need for more forthcoming Northern policies. Such policies should make markets work more effectively, and therefore increase global efficiency and well-being. Reformist liberals strongly condemn import restrictions imposed by developed countries. Such policies discourage adjustment in the North as well as impeding exports from the South. They are hypocritical given the endorsement of the market by the United States and other industrialized states.

Reformist liberals have also been willing to accept some of the more general criticisms of the existing system that have been made by the South, at least those that point to imperfections in existing markets. For instance, the transfer of technology is carried out largely by multinational corporations. But multinational corporations usually function in oligopolistic markets and can shroud their internal activities in secrecy. Individual developing countries cannot penetrate their innards. Therefore, international agreements concerning technology transfer and business practices are needed. Such agreements, like American antitrust legislation, facilitate the functioning of the market.

Reformist liberals are also more tolerant than their orthodox colleagues of domestic policies in developing countries that do not strictly accord with market principles. They place more emphasis on the infant industry argument. Given market imperfections developing countries' domestic subsidies may be the second best solution. When basic human needs are at stake, the state may have to allocate. But reformist liberals are as unhappy about inefficient domestic policies in developing countries as their orthodox brethren.

This analysis leads reformist liberals to a more sympathetic view of the New International Economic Order. The demands of the Third World are seen as reformist not revolutionary. The Third World is understood to believe that the world economy can provide benefits for all. Rhetoric which condemns the system as a whole is just rhetoric. Compromise is possible at the international level. Moreover, the North needs to reform its own policies. Northern restrictions on imports from the South can seriously impede economic development. Present structures do not necessarily provide the price signals needed to maximize global efficiency. A more efficient system would provide benefits for both industrialized and developing areas.[2]

Observers who emphasize global interdependence adopt an even more forthcoming attitude toward the Third World. Like both orthodox and reformist liberals, poverty is seen as the fundamental problem. However, poverty threatens the North as well as the South. It is not just that economic growth for developing areas would have economic benefits for the North, the position taken by reformist liberals, but also that economic collapse in the South or even a continuation of present inequities would have disastrous consequences for the North.

The Brandt Commission Report, *North-South, A Program for Survival*, offers elegant testimony to this orientation. In his introduction Brandt writes of 'destruction or development?'. He avers that 'War is often thought of in terms of military conflict, or even annihilation. But there is a growing awareness that an equal danger might be chaos—as a result of mass hunger, economic disaster, environmental catastrophes, and terrorism.'[3] 'The world is now a fragile and interlocking system, whether for its people, its ecology or its resources.'[4] The North cannot have stable supplies of a number of raw materials unless developing countries agree to provide them. Failure to develop adequate supplies of food for the South will contribute to inflationary pressures in the North. Increases in population will lead to uncontrolled migration and pressure on the world's limited resource base. Persistent poverty will contribute to political instability which cannot be contained within the countries of the South. The North cannot have peace without the development of the South.

The policy implications emerging from this analysis incorporate the arguments put forth by orthodox and reformist liberals and go beyond them. Domestic policy in developing countries must be improved; equity within countries can only be achieved through national policies. Impediments to developing country exports must be removed, the North must adjust not protect. Large scale resource transfers are needed for the poorest countries to meet basic human needs and promote development. International economic institutions must be restructured to give the South more influence and to provide more resources. International commodity agreements should be concluded to stabilize raw materials prices. MNCs should be more closely controlled so that their technological resources and capital can be better harnessed by both the North and the South. On critical issues of subsistence, market allocation must be subordinate to assuring security of food supplies.

Many of these proposals are already associated with the New International Economic Order, including provisions for commodity agreements, food stocks, export promotion, institutional restructuring, and increased resource transfers. This does not imply that the interdependence position accepts the dependency analysis used by the South to rationalize the NIEO. This analysis implies a higher level of underlying conflict than the interdependence orientation could accept. For the Brandt Commission the present system has not performed adequately. But it is not fundamentally corrupt and exploitive.

United States policy

American policy has partaken of all three conventional orientations, although not in equal measure at the same time. The Reagan administration is more closely aligned with orthodox liberal perspectives than any of its recent predecessors. The President has referred to the 'magic of the market-place' as the key to economic growth. The Agency for International Development has established a Bureau for Private Enterprise. In Congressional testimony in the fall of 1981 the administrator of the Agency for International Development stated that less 'emphasis will be placed on transfer of funds, of taxpayers' dollars. Great emphasis will be placed on the transfer of those things that generate resources—the technology, skills, know-how, and capital of the US private sector.'[5] He argued that AID would encourage sounder economic policies in developing countries including realistic exchange rates, greater private investment, and more technical training. In a recent conference on the World Bank the deputy secretary of the Treasury argued that developing countries must generate their capital internally, that the most important contribution that the United States could make to development would be to achieve its own national economic objectives, and that 'a major focus of development policy must be the generation of non-aid capital flows'.[6]

The Carter administration, in contrast, was more heavily influenced by reformist liberal and interdependence orientations. Greater attention was given to human rights. Developing countries were frequently depicted as junior partners in the world economic system. Heavy emphasis was placed on the concept of graduation—of having more advanced developing countries assume responsibilities like those accepted by the industrialized countries. The growth of resources for international financial institutions were endorsed, although the administration failed to get an aid package through Congress in its last years. The need for 'rules of the game' for multinational corporations was recognized. At least in its first two years there was considerable expression of rhetorical sympathy for the Third World. In his opening statement at the Paris Conference on International Economic Cooperation (CIEC) Secretary of State Vance pledged United States cooperation for 'a new international economic system in which there must be equity, growth, and, above all, justice'.[7] American ambassadors to the United Nations have often been the clearest expression of an administration's underlying attitude toward the Third World. They can say things presidents cannot; Andrew Young and Jeanne Kirkpatrick do not send the same message.

Orthodox and reformist liberal, and interdependence viewpoints have been at the center of American debate about policy toward the Third World. Their disagreements should not obscure the similarity of their interpretations of the underlying dynamics of North-South relations. Economics is the driving element in all three approaches. The assumption, often tacit, is that if the problem of poverty is solved, if developing countries can achieve adequate standards of living for their peoples, then the North-South conflict will fade away. More advanced LDCs will come to resemble the already industrialized countries. Less prosperous ones will at least reconciled to the existing order.

The persistent analogy is to disadvantaged groups within states in the North -especially to the labor movement. Unions were initially scorned by orthodox liberals. But workers are now reconciled to the existing system because the market-place has brought growth and prosperity and organized labor has been able to alter some principles, norms, and laws within the context of capitalism. The labor movement is no longer seen as a fundamental threat in any of the advanced industrial democracies. The analogy of the Third World to the labor movement reinforces the conviction that poorer countries will be satisfied with economic growth alone, a conviction shared by orthodox liberals, reform liberals, and interdependence orientations alike.

Political aspects of Third World behavior

Is this overarching worldview wrong? Will the South be satisfied with the present game if only its winnings increase? It is impossible to give a definitive answer. The present evidence can be read in many ways. But there are a number of considerations that raise questions about relatively optimistic prognoses for North-South relations, at least if economic development is widespread.

The existing system has not worked badly. In fact, economic growth over the last two decades has been better than virtually anyone predicted in 1960. For the period 1960-1979 the average annual growth rate of gross domestic product was 4.6 per cent for low income developing countries, 5.8 per cent for middle income developing countries (excluding capital surplus oil exporters), and 4.2 per cent for industrialized market economy countries. Per capita figures are less favorable for the Third World. Per capita gross national product rose at an average annual rate of 1.6 per cent in low income developing countries, 3.8 per cent in middle income developing countries and 4.0 per cent in industrialized countries. Even though the rate of growth is lower for the developing world it is very high in comparison with their growth rates during earlier periods or with growth rates in the now industrialized areas when they were at comparable levels of development. Furthermore, the rapid increase in population growth, 2.2 per cent in low income developing countries for the period 1960-1979, and 2.4 per cent in middle income developing countries compared with 0.9 per cent in industrialized countries, is an international problem only in the sense that improved knowledge about public health has extended life expectancy. Life expectancy at birth has increased from 42 years in 1960 for low income developing countries to 57 years in 1979, from 53 to 61 years for middle income developing countries, and from 70 to 74 years for market economy industrialized countries.[8] If the Third World countries were only concerned with improving their economic situation, these figures suggest that they would have endorsed the present international economic order, raising their voices at the United Nations and UNCTAD in a muted if not full throated defense of liberalism and the market.

Such tributes have not been voiced. Instead Third World countries have endorsed a set of arguments, associated with the concept of dependency, that reject the basic rules and norms of the existing order. They have contended that their backwardness is a function of the workings of the liberal international economic system not the indigenous characteristics of their own economies and polities. The poverty of the South is seen as a product of the wealth of the North. The terms of trade for raw materials are declining, providing exporters with limited incomes and importers with inexpensive supplies. Multinational corporations enjoy unfair bargaining power; developing countries are compelled to accept arrangements that they would reject if power were distributed more equitably. Major international financial institutions are controlled by the North; developing countries are more or less excluded from significant decision making forums. The level of negative sentiment that accompanies these analytic arguments is very high: the North is depicted as a plunderer and exploiter of the South.

The absence of a concerted Southern reaction to OPEC is also puzzling from a purely economic perspective. The increase in oil prices since 1973 has done more damage to the South than any other single well defined event. In 1973 the oil trade balance for all net oil importing developing countries was – 5.2 billion dollars. The non-oil trade balance was – 4.0 billion dollars. The total current account deficit was 8.9 billion dollars. In 1981 the oil trade balance was –77.5 billion dollars and the non-oil trade balance was – 10.4 billion dollars. The total current account deficit had risen to 81.9 billion dollars. For all non-oil LDCs the debt service ratio (payments as a percentage of the exports of goods and services) increased from 14.0 per cent in 1974 to 26.6 per cent in 1981.[9] The balance of payments consequences of higher oil prices have been more severe for developing countries because surplus oil earnings have been initially placed in the North. Many developing countries have been compelled to borrow on terms less favorable than those enjoyed by actors in more developed areas.

However, the South has not launched any sustained protest against OPEC. It is possible to argue that such protests would fall upon deaf ears, but the same argument could be applied to many aspects of the NIEO program. It is possible to argue that OPEC countries have bought off developing countries, especially in Africa, with higher levels of economic assistance, but with the exception of a few Islamic countries overseas development assistance from oil exporters has been far less than the increased costs of petroleum. A purely economic calculus would have suggested a Southern strategy designed to secure differential treatment in oil pricing, or higher aid, or international taxation of oil earnings. No such program has been presented.

Finally it is difficult to understand the South's ability to present a unified position at international forums from a purely economic perspective. The conventional wisdom is that the Group of 77 engages in horse trading arriving at some kind of compromise position that gives something to each of its members. But this ignores the fact that the benefits of the NIEO, were it fully implemented, would be extremely skewed. Most developing countries would not benefit from commodity agreements because they do not export substantial amounts of raw materials. Most would not benefit from preferential trading arrangements because they export few manufactures. For most developing countries, which do not have long coastlines, a narrow economic zone for the oceans would have promised higher potential returns from the exploitation of minerals and petroleum; instead the Group of 77 accepted the extensive zone proposed by a few of its members. Small countries with limited resources and trade could not develop efficient merchant marines. Only more aid or international taxation would have a substantial impact on all Third World states, but, with the exception of proposals for debt relief, these items have not been at the center of the South's agenda for more than a decade.

The NIEO as an effort to decrease vulnerability

If politics rather than economics, power and vulnerability rather than wealth and well-being, are viewed as the central elements in North-South relations then the positions enunciated by the Third World are more comprehensible.[10] The disparities in the domestic power capabilities of Northern and Southern sides is enormous. If gross national product is taken as a measure of power, then 70 per cent of developing countries have capabilities less than one per cent those of the United States. The number of exceptions is limited. The gross domestic products of China and Brazil are about equal to Canada's; those of India, Mexico and Argentine to Sweden's; those of Indonesia, Saudi Arabia, Nigeria and Venezuela to Norway's. The existing differences in aggregate levels of economic activity are so great that even very rapid growth in the South and relatively slow growth in the North will not close the absolute gap for many countries even though their relative position would improve. The national resources of developing countries rarely provide them with the ability to influence the international environment upon which they must depend.

This international weakness is compounded by the fragility of regimes in many Third World states. The level of legitimacy is low. Political institutions are weak. Coups are frequent. Bureaucratic capacities are limited.

Political leaders often stay in power through more or less direct economic pay-offs. The military is given new equipment. Industrial workers are guaranteed jobs in government-owned plants. The consumption of staples in urban areas is subsidized. Foreign exchange is restricted so that import licences can be granted as political favors. Political leaders in many Third World countries are dependent on government revenue to maintain their position. If revenue falters it poses not just an economic problem but a political one as well.

Taxes on foreign trade are the main source of revenue for most developing countries. With weak bureaucracies, poorly developed internal markets, and limited popular support it is difficult to collect other kinds of tax. Indeed, it is difficult to collect taxes at all. Trade is the most obvious source of revenue because the government can lay its hands on it more easily than on other transactions. Valuation is facilitated by international prices. Goods flow through a limited number of ports of entry. While corruption and smuggling limit the state's ability to extract resources even from the international sector, exports and imports are more accessible than most other economic activities. Hence political leaders in developing countries cannot control international markets, but their political durability (even their physical durability) often depends on revenues that are generated by activities in these same markets. Not a comfortable existence.

Even the OPEC countries should not be taken as being completely exempt from this analysis. As a result of tight market conditions and growing expertise, oil exporting Third World countries were able to seize control of the international energy market in the 1970s. But the domestic political structure in many of these countries remains weak. Struggles over the division of the spoils may even exacerbate internal conflicts. Changes in international demand can severely disrupt domestic development plans and may even threaten political stability. If technological innovation, new discoveries, or a continued decrease in the demand function for petroleum lead to a sharp drop in prices most of the Saudi royal family may be able to settle in Geneva or Beverly Hills, but the ambitious development projects on the Arabian peninsula could be covered with sand.

The programs put forth by the Third World can be seen as an effort to lessen vulnerability and weakness by altering the rules of the game in various international issue areas. These rules were largely established by the United States at the conclusion of the Second World War. They are informed by liberal principles. The governing norm endorses the allocation of goods by markets. Without challenging the wisdom of conventional economic arguments about the benefits of the market, such an allocative mechanism poses the fewest problems for those actors that have substantial mobile resources; for actors that can influence some transaction patterns and adjust to others. Few Third World countries are either large or nimble.

For small and weak states a more attractive way to allocate goods in the international system is through the authoritative decisions of states taken in forums where the principle of sovereign equality provides each with equal voting power. Even if such decisions do not fully satisfy Third World desires they can at least limit the discretion of more powerful Northern actors. Efforts to move from markets to authoritative allocation underlie virtually every position that Third World countries have supported. Proposals for international taxation are the most obvious. In a number of forums, developing countries have called for the generation of aid from some source which Northern states would not control. At the United Nations Conference on Disarmament, for instance, the Group of 77 proposed a tax on arms expenditures which would be used for development assistance. The Law of the Seas Treaty includes provision for the taxation of profits from the exploitation of seabed nodules. The Trust Fund, funded by the International Monetary Fund's sale of gold, has been a source of revenue several steps removed from the discretionary control of industrialized states. Linking the creation of special drawing rights with development assistance would provide a source of capital whose distribution would be governed by an internationally agreed formula rather than the decisions of specific developed states.

Developing countries have supported international codes dealing with business conduct and technology transfer to enhance their leverage over multinational corporations. In dealing with multinationals Third World countries are torn between the desire to attract foreign capital and technology and the fear of losing autonomy and control. The problem is complicated by competition among developing countries for additional direct investment. National regulation is the primary device for limiting the discretion of multinationals. Third World states have promulgated rules governing ownership, profit remittances, imports and exports, technology transfer, and employment of nationals. International agreements can make national policies more effective by legitimating the restrictions imposed by host governments and coordinating policies among Third World countries.

In the area of communication and transportation the developing world has moved to establish rules of the game that would allocate resources according to the preferences of equal sovereign states rather than the dictates of the market. At World Administrative Radio Conferences (WARC) the Third World has argued that radio frequencies should be allocated on the basis of projections of future need rather than present capabilities, a principle that would provide a wider range of frequencies for developing countries while limiting those available to industrialized nations. At numerous UNESCO meetings the Third World has supported rules that would legitimate national restrictions on the western media.[11]

The United Nations Code on Liner Conferences calls for 40–40–20 division of freight among exporting, importing, and third countries. (Liners are freighters that ply regularly scheduled routes. They account for about 20 per cent of world shipping.) The Group of 77 has opposed flags of convenience because they are seen as inhibiting the development of merchant marine fleets in the developing world. Flags of convenience allow shipowners to escape requirements for the national ownership of commercial vessels.[12]

Civil aviation provides an illuminating contrast with shipping. Civil aviation is one issue area where allocative decisions are governed more by state preferences than the market. Routes and fares are subject to explicit government approval. The norm is that national airlines should carry 50 per cent of the passengers embarking or debarking within their territory. This target is, in fact, more or less met by those countries that do have their own international airlines. The rules governing civil aviation have been more heavily influenced by considerations of national security than market efficiency. They have allowed a number of Third World countries to achieve a parity with developed nations that have been denied them in other areas. North-South cleavages have blurred in the IATA where both developing and industrialized country airlines have resisted American efforts to create a more market oriented regime.[13]

In trade the Third World has sought special and differential treatment, a clear violation of the liberal norms of non-discrimination and reciprocity enshrined in the GATT. The General Agreement on Tariffs and Trade has been revised to emphasize the importance of development goals. All of the non-tariff barrier codes negotiated during the Tokyo Round contain special provisions for developing countries. The Generalized Systems of Preference provide for more favorable treatment for a limited number of exports from LDCs. The developing world has persistently called for international commodity agreements which would raise and stabilize prices. Fully enacted, UNCTAD's Integrated Programme for Commodities would have established a common fund with resources to intervene in markets where no explicit agreements had been reached with consumers and to promote greater participation by producing countries in the processing and marketing of raw materials.

The Third World's efforts to enhance its control and reduce its vulnerability is most transparently displayed in efforts to alter international institutions. In some cases the Third World has been able to use its voting power to assume effective control. The United Nations General Assembly is the most notable example. New institutional structures such as UNCTAD have been created when existing ones were thought to be too heavily influenced by the North either ideologically or politically. In international financial institutions developing countries have pressed for greater voting power and more involvement in decision making. Even in these institutions, which are most biased against them because of weighted voting, the South has enjoyed substantial success. Developing countries have at least a blocking veto in all institutions, including the IMF and the World Bank. They have a majority of votes in the Inter-American Development Bank and the African Development Bank, and over 40 per cent of the votes in the Asian Development Bank. They effectively control the United Nations Development Program and the International Fund for Agricultural Development.[14]

In sum, the programs conjoined under the umbrella of the New International Economic Order have not been haphazard. The NIEO is not simply a conglomeration of particular concerns linked together for tactical reasons. It is not designed merely to reform existing institutional structures. Rather, the NIEO is a coherent effort to alter the basic principles guiding resource allocations in the international system. It would replace the market based liberal system established largely by the United States at the conclusion of the Second World War with a system in which equal sovereign states would intervene directly in allocative processes. Equity would replace efficiency as the central norm. Specific rules would be designed to promote growth for the South rather than total global output. Decision making procedures would restrict the discretion of industrialized states. This program is rationalized and legitimated by a more or less fully realized ideology which blames the poverty of the South on the prosperity of the North, and which sees existing arrangements as unfair and exploitative. The NIEO flows from the profound weakness of virtually all Third World states. Lacking both international power and domestic resilience, they are extraordinarily vulnerable to the perturbations of a world market system which they cannot control but upon which they depend. It is fatuous to assume that economic development would end the South's alienation from the existing global order.

Policy prescriptions for the North

If the South, at least at the level of the rules of the game, is after basic restructuring not reform, what policy is most appropriate for the North? Specific arrangements involving clearly defined, short-term economic benefits should be emphasized. Most efforts to secure mutual agreement on general principles and long term arrangements, especially through multi-functional global negotiations, should be downplayed or abandoned. Meetings like the Cancun summit can only serve as platforms for articulating opposing principles.

American economic involvement with the developing world is substantial. In 1980 the United States exported $60 billion worth of goods to non-oil developing countries. This was larger than American exports to the Common Market ($51 billion) and Japan ($20 billion). Exports to non-oil developing countries rose from 24 per cent of total US exports in 1973 to 29 per cent in 1980. If exports to oil exporting countries are included the figures are 28 per cent for 1973 and 38 per cent for 1980. Common Market trade with developing countries, especially the traditional oil exporters, has also grown substantially, increasing from 27 per cent of all exports (excluding intra-EEC trade) in 1973 to 37 per cent in 1980. For Japan exports to developing areas have risen from 39 per cent in 1973 to 43 per cent in 1980.[15]

This growth has occurred despite the political turbulence that characterized North-South relations during the 1970s. It is testimony to the substantial economic benefits accruing to actors in both industrialized and developing areas. It is based on a wide range of specific arrangements, usually between private actors. But this pattern does not imply that the South will reconcile itself to the existing system or that it will agree to new rules of the game that would also be acceptable to the North. There is a fundamental difference between specific short term arrangements based on calculation of immediate economic benefit, and long term commitment to a framework of principles, norms, rules, and decision making procedures. Short term arrangements change when the power or interest of the actors change. Behavior is not constrained by mutual agreement on the rules of the game. There can be high levels of mutually beneficial interaction provided that all parties can extract returns in the short run. But if transactions must be spread over time, or one party must make an irrevocable commitment before the other, then some basic agreement on principles, rules and norms is essential.

The present global pattern of raw materials exploitation offers an example of the consequences of a breakdown of the rules of the game. Multinational corporations have been extremely reluctant to commit themselves to projects in developing countries requiring extensive exploration and large capital outlays. Experience has eroded confidence in long term contracts with developing countries, since such contracts have been constantly renegotiated as the bargaining position of the host country improved. Exploration has increasingly taken place outside the Third World even though developing areas have been much less thoroughly investigated. Multinational oil companies are still active in the Middle East, several substantial investments have been made in Latin American copper mines, but without agreement on the rules of the game the level of interaction between industrialized and developing areas is less than it would have been.[16]

Should the North pursue new rules of the game? Reformist liberals and advocates of interdependence answer in the affirmative. But if the South is aiming at control, not just wealth, and if developing countries want to limit their vulnerability to intended and unintended international pressures, the possibilities for agreement are limited. The North should only attempt to formulate rules of the game in issue areas where there are tangible clearly defined benefits.

Raw materials supplies, including petroleum, offer an example of one area where new rules of the game are politically feasible and economically attractive. The North wants security of supply. Security increases with output and the number of producers. The South needs export earnings. But the South also wants rules of the game that would protect it from the vicissitudes of the market. Terms of trade and price fluctuations are difficult to measure and their impact on economic development is even more problematic. But fluctuations do have political costs for Third World regimes, whose durability depends upon their ability to dispense revenue secured from taxes on international transactions. International commodity agreements designed to limit such fluctuations are attractive to the South for political as well as economic reasons. By providing more stable markets, and thereby encouraging production, they would provide an insurance policy for the North.

Possibilities for mutual agreement also arise in the area of raw materials investments, including energy investments. The Reagan administration's opposition to the creation of a World Bank energy affiliate was ill considered. Most other Northern states supported it. The kindest interpretation of US behavior is that policymakers have misunderstood the impediments to a smoothly functioning market for large nonfungible long term investments in Third World countries. Deputy Secretary of the Treasury R. T McNamar, for instance, explained American opposition to the proposed energy affiliate in the following terms: 'Bluntly put, this was (sic) an area that the private sector can and will adequately serve. The energy affiliate would have simply substituted less expensive public development capital for available private capital.'[17] Given the relatively low level of exploration in the developing world it is difficult to see how this argument can be made.

Private companies are extremely reluctant to commit large sums to Third World countries which have over and over again renegotiated contracts. A World Bank energy affiliate, and similar structures for other raw materials in the World Bank or other international financial institutions, could provide needed capital, including co-financing with private companies. Larger supplies, regardless of their source, would mean greater security for industrialized importing countries. Such facilities could satisfy some of the political concerns of Third World countries. The financial institutions, where developing countries have some influence, could act as a buffer against multinational corporations whose decisions must be guided by global profit concerns rather than the economic development of a particular host country. Projects with heavy involvement from international institutions would also leave political leaders less exposed to accusations that they had sold out to international capitalism. Thus, changing the rules in the area of raw materials investments could be attractive, both politically and economically, for the North and the South.

Working to maintain existing global rules of the game or making new ones is also important in areas where the absence of agreement would lead to chaos. It is useful for the North to have the IMF as an intermediary between borrowing LDCs and private banks; it is easier for debtors to accept conditions imposed by the IMF than those that would be imposed by private institutions. If there were no international institutions to set conditions, private banks would be more reluctant to lend. Some agreement on division of the radio spectrum, accomplished through World Administrative Radio Conferences, is needed to prevent overlapping broadcasts and garbled communications. Agreements to standardize international health forms help to control communicable diseases and in their symmetrical treatment of all states do not pose a threat to developing countries.

However, the North has participated in many global negotiations where failure would not entail any obvious costs. These negotiations have usually been fruitless. Agreements that have been concluded, such as the Common Fund for Commodities, have often been truncated, leaving both sides cynical, embittered, or disappointed. In other cases, such as the UNCTAD Code on Liner Conferences some signatories have had second thoughts.

The United Nations Law of the Seas Conference (UNCLOS) illustrates the pitfalls of multi-purpose global negotiations. In the late 1960s the North accepted the principle that the oceans were part of the common heritage of mankind. Ocean issues could only legitimately be decided by the whole community of nations. Standing to participate in rule making could not be limited to those countries with coastlines or large fleets. UNCLOS formally placed Upper Volta on the same footing with the United States. The negotiations also encompassed a wide range of issues, including scientific activity, passage through straits, coastal zones, and deep seabed mineral nodules, that were not necessarily related.

On the whole, policymakers from the industrialized countries expected that UNCLOS would concern itself with the immediate questions at hand. They believed that the inclusion of a range of issue areas under the same negotiating umbrella would facilitate compromise especially because the economic and strategic concerns of states varied considerably, and the resulting cleavages did not fall along North-South or East-West lines. There are Third World states with extensive coastlines and others with no direct access to the sea. Land based mineral producers whose economic interests could be damaged by the exploitation of deep seabed nodules include Australia, Canada, and South Africa as well as Zaire, Zambia, Chile, and Peru. The leading maritime states including the Soviet Union as well as Great Britain and the United States were particularly worried about the encroachment on freedom of navigation that would result from intensified unilateral assertions of sovereignty over the oceans by littoral states. The Northern expectations that the negotiations would be characterized by cross cutting cleavages, moderation, and compromise were not unreasonable.

In most of the issues included in the UNCLOS negotiations this expectation proved to be well founded. Agreement was reached on questions related to navigation and scientific study. The participants also agreed to the establishment of a 12-mile territorial sea, a 200-mile ocean economic zone, and a continental shelf resources zone of up to 350 miles. This last set of agreements, undoubtedly the most important reached at the conference, reinforce the sovereignty and control of individual states. They benefit not only the Third World countries that initially pressed for greater national control over the oceans, but also advanced states with extensive coastlines including the Soviet Union and the United States.

However, agreement on many central issues did not lead to an atmosphere of moderation and compromise. On the contrary, in time the North-South cleavage became increasingly salient. Differences between land-locked and littoral Third World states were papered over. The South increasingly acted as a coherent block inserting global North-South issues into the UNCLOS setting.

Differences between the Third and First worlds crystallized around the issue of deep seabed mining. As a result of Third World initiatives the final version of the Treaty provided for a regulatory body, the International Seabed Authority, and for the International Seabed Enterprise, which would engage in nodule exploitation along with private corporations. The voting arrangements for the Authority guaranteed a high level of politicization. The United States, especially under the Reagan administration, protested against a number of the final arrangements. American officials objected to provisions that would allow amendments to be passed by a majority vote after fifteen years. They argued that basic American philosophical commitments to free enterprise were violated by requirements that private mining consortia share technology and nodule sites with the Enterprise. Officials, particularly in the Defense Department, feared that the Treaty could restrict American access to strategically important raw materials. (Cobalt and manganese, both essential ingredients for high performance steels, are present in seabed nodules.) In December 1982 the United States refused to sign the Final Act of the Conference, the penultimate step to signing the Treaty itself. In the United States the common acronym for the Law of the Seas Treaty has now become LOST.[18]

One interpretation, the most obvious, is that American rejection of the Treaty reflects the fickleness of partisan politics in the United States. The Carter administration would have acted differently. Private corporations were short-sighted in lobbying against the Treaty, lobbying that would almost certainly have precluded Senate ratification even if the United States had signed.[19] However, this interpretation ignores the fact that a number of other countries also refused to sign the Final Act, including South Korea, Belgium, Italy, Spain, Switzerland and, most importantly, the United Kingdom, West Germany, and Japan.[20] France was the only major market economy country to break ranks. While some of this solidarity can be attributed to American lobbying, the Soviet gas pipeline dispute demonstrates that the United States does not simply call the tune for its allies.

The fundamental problem with the LOST is that it creates a set of rules of the game that are far removed from the underlying power capabilities of the states involved. Such a regime is not likely to function effectively. The ability to exploit deep seabed nodules is possessed by a small number of actors in advanced states that have the requisite technology and capital. At least some of these same states also have the military capability to protect any commercial operation that is mounted. But the Law of the Seas Treaty places power over the rules of the game largely in the hands of Third World countries that have neither economic nor naval capability. It is not likely that such a situation could provide for stability over the long term even if it were endorsed by all states. Should seabed nodules become vitally important to the most powerful states, it is not likely that they would be constrained by an international agreement whose major supporters lacked the national power resources to thwart unilateral action.

There was no inherent reason why the North should have admitted that the oceans were part of the common heritage of mankind. This reflected an interdependence rather than a power oriented or even conventional liberal perspective. There was no reason to lump so many issues into a single forum. There was no necessary reason to include all states in the international community as opposed to those with the capability to upset any agreement they opposed. By accepting a forum in which all states were recognized as having a legitimate voice the industrialized world created an inherently unsatisfactory decision making structure. There will be no stable international regime for the deep seabed. Commercial activity will be chilled by the absence of clearly established property rights. Given the experience of the last decade it is impossible to start de novo. Even if the industrialized states conclude an agreement among themselves, its efficacy would be undermined by the existence of a rival regime.

UNCLOS not to mention CIEC, various United Nations Special Assemblies, UNCTAD general meetings, and the United Nations Committee of the Whole are precisely the kinds of forums where the North can expect little satisfaction. These settings are most conducive to the elaboration of new principles designed to enhance the power and control of the South, often at the expense of actors from the North.

In sum, Northern policy must start from the premise that interests but not principles and norms are shared with the Third World. Basic conflicts over power and control preclude agreement on the rules of the game in many issue areas. Reformist liberals and advocates of interdependence are bound to be disappointed because these conflicts will not be overcome by mutual economic interests. Negotiations about basic principles, norms, and rules are only likely to be successful if they not only provide tangible benefits, but also satisfy Third World concerns about vulnerability.

References and notes

[1] P. T. Bauer and B. S. Yamey, 'Against the New International Economic Order', *Commentary*, 63 (April 1977), p. 29. See also P. T. Bauer, *Equality, The Third World and Economic Delusion* (London, 1981); and Harry Johnson, 'Commodities: Less Developed Countries' Demands and Developed Countries' Responses', in Jagdish N. Bhagwati, *The New International Economic Order: The North-South Debate* (Cambridge, Mass., 1977).

[2] For representative statements of this position see Anne O. Krueger, *Foreign Trade Regimes and Economic Development: Liberalization Attempts and Consequences* (Cambridge, Mass., 1978), which summarizes a larger series on foreign trade regimes sponsored by the National Bureau of Economic Research and edited by Kreuger and Jagdish N. Bhagwati. G. K. Helleiner, 'World Market Imperfections and Developing Countries', in William R. Cline (ed.), *Policy Alternatives for a New International Economic Order* (New York, 1978) is particularly critical of market imperfections. See also Albert Fishlow, 'A New International Economic Order: What Kind?', in Albert Fishlow, *et al.*, *Rich and Poor Nations in the World Economy* (New York, 1978).

[3] Independent Commission on International Development Issues (Brandt Commission), *North-South, A Program for Survival* (Cambridge, Mass., 1981), p. 13. For other examples of interdependence reasoning see Barbara Ward, 'Another Chance for the North', *Foreign Affairs*, 59 (Winter 1980/81); John W. Sewell, 'Can the North Prosper Without Growth and Progress in the South?', in Martin M. McLaughlin, *The United States and World Development, 1979* (New York, 1979); and Thomas Erlich and Catherine Gwin, 'A Third World Strategy', *Foreign Policy*, 44 (Fall 1981).

[4] Brandt Commission, *Report*, p. 33.

[5] US Department of State, Bureau of Public Affairs, *Current Policy*, No. 329, 19 October 1981.

[6] US Department of the Treasury, *Treasury News*, R-560, 7 January 1982.

[7] Quoted in the *Los Angeles Times*, 31 May 1977, 5:1.

[8] All figures derived from World Bank, *World Development Report*, 1981 (Washington, DC, 1981), Tables 1, 2, 17, and 21.

[9] Figures from International Monetary Fund, *World Economic Outlook* (Washington, DC, June 1981), Appendix B, Statistical Tables 13 and 30.

[10] The basic argument developed here and throughout this essay draws heavily on the analysis presented in Robert W. Tucker, *The Inequality of Nations* (New York, 1977).

[11] Rosemary Richter, 'Battle of the Bias', *Foreign Policy*, 34 (Spring 1979); for a general discussion of the information problem see Rita Cruise O'Brien and G. K. Helleiner, 'The Political Economy of Information in a Changing International Economic Order', *International Organization*, 34 (Autumn 1980).

[12] Lawrence Juda, 'World Shipping, UNCTAD, and the New International Economic Order', *International Organization*, 35 (Summer 1981).

[13] Christer Jonsson, 'Sphere of Flying: The Politics of International Aviation', *International Organization*, 35 (Spring 1981).

[14] Stephen D. Krasner, 'Power Structures and Regional Development Banks', *International Organization*, 35 (Spring 1981).

[15] GATT, *International Trade, 1980/81* (Geneva, 1981), Appendix tables.

[16] United Nations, Economic and Social Council, Commission on Transnational Corporations, *Issues Arising from Decisions Taken by the General Assembly and the Economic and Social Council: Progress made Towards the Establishment of the New International Economic Order: The Role of Transnational Corporations*, E/C. 10/74 (16 May 1980), pp. 17-18.

[17] US Department of the Treasury, *Treasury News*, R-560, 7 January 1982.

[18] For two recent discussions, both critical of the American position, see D. C. Watt, 'Ocean Resources: The Need for Agreement', *International Affairs*, 58 (Winter 1981-82); and Leigh S. Ratiner, 'The Law of the Sea: Cross-roads for US Policy', *Foreign Affairs*, 60 (Summer 1982).

[19] Tom Alexander, 'The Reaganites' Misadventures at Sea', *Fortune*, 106 (23 August 1982).

[20] Japan did sign the Convention in early 1983.

Brandt II—The Mirage of Collective Action in a Self-Serving World

Frances Stewart

The second Brandt Report has just been published. Like the first Brandt Report,[1] it is a consensus document signed by distinguished people from North and South.[2] The central thrust of this Report is an Emergency Programme 'directed to averting world economic collapse and the subsequent chaos and human suffering and to creating conditions leading to world economic recovery'. The Emergency Programme consists mainly of financial measures. It includes recommendations to double the quotas of the International Monetary Fund and for a major new allocation of Special Drawing Rights. In addition, it contains familiar proposals on trade (resistance to protectionist pressures, ratification of the Common fund, negotiation of new Commodity Agreements, increased compensation for periodic losses of developing countries' commodity earnings), food (to increase and improve resource flows to agriculture, strengthen the international system of food security, increase food aid) and energy (a new international energy agency to increase energy self-reliance in developing countries.)

A Report of this kind can be assessed from two different points of view. On the one hand, there is the question of the intrinsic value of the proposals and of the analysis on which they are based: on the other, the contribution the Report is likely to make to North-South relations, to negotiations, and to reform. On the first count, the Report scores pretty well, if one takes a progressive/reformist view of the world. This Report, like its predecessor, will be soundly attacked by those who believe that the market by itself produces optimal solutions and that interference, however benign in intent, tends to be malign in results. The Report is decidedly interventionist. But the current state of the world economy, and or national economies that have recently veered towards market solutions—such as the UK, the US, Chile—do not lend support to the view that a 'hands-off' approach is going to rapidly eliminate the world's problems. Equally, the Report contains little of value for those who believe that capitalist relations are at the heart of exploitation, inequality, and poverty both nationally and internationally. Nowhere does the Report consider the international system as one aspect or capitalist relationships. The Report is firmly in the centrist Fabian tradition: viewed within that tradition, while its analysis is often sketchy, its recommendations are difficult to fault. It may be said that they are not especially original, echoing many UNCTAD resolutions, but the point of a Report like this is not to make startling discoveries—it is to nudge the world into reforms. From a Fabian/reformist point of view then, the question at issue is, above all, the impact the Report is likely to have on North-South negotiations. In considering this question, one is inevitably forced to look again at the first Brandt Report and what has happened in the years that have followed its

Originally published in *Third World Quarterly*, vol. 5, no. 3, July 1983. © Third World Quarterly, 1983; reprinted with permission.

publication. An analysis of that experience does more than simply offer a critique of a particular document: it provides insights into the workings of North-South relations. These insights permit a more informed assessment of the value of Brandt II; they also call into question much of the reformist view of North-South relations, a view which has provided the framework within both North and South for most recent discussion, proposals and, especially from the South, demands. The NIEO itself, as well as the pronouncements of the non-aligned countries at their March 1983 meeting in Delhi, are firmly in this tradition. The lessons of Brandt I suggest alternative approaches to North-South relations—alternatives which might prove more effective in securing change.

Brandt I was published after years of futile negotiations between North and South, years in which the Pearson Commission's recommendations had been thrown aside, in which the demands for a New International Economic Order had been launched, discussed and buried.[3] In the context of the failure of North and South to find common ground, the first Brandt Report was a remarkable document—not so much for its contents—which broadly represented the liberal consensus about North-South relations—but for the fact that prominent and potentially (though significantly not actually) powerful people from North and South, people not noted for their radicalism, could agree unanimously on substantive and important proposals for reform in the way the North and South conduct their economic relations.

They agreed, for example, that 'The reform of the international monetary system should be urgently undertaken'; that there should be a massive transfer of resources to the South; that aid should reach and then surpass the 0.7 per cent target; that 'Protectionism by industrialised countries against the exports of developing countries should be rolled back'; that action should be taken, including provision of adequate funds to the Common Fund, for the 'stabilisation of commodity prices at remunerative levels'; they agreed that 'Measures to facilitate the participation of developing countries in processing and marketing should include the removal of tariff and other trade barriers. . .'; they agreed on the need for Codes of Conduct for multinational companies and technology transfer; and they agreed that "There must be an end to mass hunger and malnutrition'.

The agreement of the Commissioners, (who included a former Conservative Prime Minister of Britain and an ex-Chancellor of West Germany) on these proposals, together with the tremendous popularity of the document, seemed to augur well for their acceptance, especially since the Report did not base its recommendations primarily on moral arguments but on self-interest in the form of mutual or common interests between North and South.

Yet on substantive issues there has been little progress, and indeed some regress, on many of the reforms recommended in Brandt I. This is recorded in Brandt II. The second Report notes some positive achievements—an increase in aid to the poorest countries, an expansion of IMF lending and the introduction of the World Bank structural adjustment loans. But IDA funds were cut; no progress was made on commodity agreements and trade barriers worsened. After an initial relaxation, the IMF again hardened its terms; a number of new credits were cancelled in the first half of 1982 during which time there was no increase in the Fund's net disbursements. The World Bank's structural adjustment loans remained limited in quantity, and generally associated with stringent conditionality. On the most important recommendations of Brandt I—international monetary reform, a massive transfer of resources, the 0.7 per cent target, a rolling back of protection, commodity agreements—it is fair to conclude that there has been no progress at all.

The overall position of Third World countries is undoubtedly worse now than when the first Brandt Report was published. This deterioration has three aspects: first, recession in the developed countries has meant stagnant markets and a substantial fall in commodity prices. Non-oil commodity exporters have experienced a 35 per cent drop in the dollar price of commodities since late 1980. Commodity prices are now at their lowest level in real terms for three decades. The newly industrialising countries have found their markets for manufactured exports curtailed by the slow growth of world markets and increasing protectionism. Secondly, the big rise in interest rates has greatly increased the LDCs' debt burden. Thirdly, with the rising ratio of interest payments to export earnings the banks have become reluctant to extend new loans and have increased the proportion of short-term debt in current lending, increasing the LDCs' vulnerability to debt crises.

The deterioration in the world economy cannot, of course, be laid at the door of the first Brandt Report, which had warned that such developments were likely unless international action of the kind recommended w   taken. But it can be concluded that there was something fundamentally wrong with the Report's reasoning since it is argued that its recommendations were in the interest of both North and South. Yet, virtually none of the recommendations were instituted, nor does it look probable that they will be.

The major fallacy underlying the arguments and recommendations of Brandt I concerns its analysis of interests, and the relationship between interests (as defined in Brandt) and international action. To a considerable extent—but not wholly as we shall see—the second Brandt Report makes the same mistakes. Both Reports ultimately stem from outrage, the moral outrage which any person must feel at the world in which we live; an outrage most movingly expressed by Brandt himself in the introduction to the second Report: 'Every two seconds of this year a child will die of hunger or disease. And no statistic can express what it is to see even one child die. . . "to see the uncomprehending panic in eyes which are still the clear and lucid eyes of a child"'.

A sense of outrage pervades the Reports—outrage that people can starve while others suffer from obesity; that massive resources are used for the production of weapons of mass destruction; that defence expenditure in the major economies rises, while aid is cut. . . The Commissioners recognise that such outrage will not produce action. Consequently, they appeal to interests because interests, they believe, do form the basis of action in our immoral world. The mistake they make, however, is in the analysis of interests: it arises because the Commissioners, although they are anxious to come to moral conclusions, justify them by arguments based on interests and are casual and lack rigour in their analysis. As a result, the interests they identify are not the interests which form the basis of political action, so that the appeal to interests is scarcely more effective than if the argument had been left in the realm of morality.

The 'interests' identified by Brandt are the common interests of the North as a whole and the South as a whole. In neither group are policies formed at a collective level, but rather at the level of individual countries. Policies may be in the interests of either or both group(s) as a whole, yet not of particular countries. We have examples of this situation in both the North and the South. Trade protection provides one. Freer trade, it is argued, will be in the interests of the North since additional imports from the South (e.g. textiles) will be offset by additional exports to the South of more advanced goods, such as capital goods. That may well be true at the level of the North as a whole, but individual countries may lose out. For example, liberalised trade would tend to increase imports most into those economies which (i) have a considerable domestic production of goods which are potentially competitive with goods from the South; and, (ii) where low labour productivity and high labour costs lead to production being least competitive with Southern exports. The additional exports of capital goods to Southern economies will come from those economies where the combination of quality and prices is most attractive. It is clear that the economies most likely to import most as a result of liberalisation are not the same economies as those whose exports are likely to rise most. The least competitive Northern economies will tend to be most affected by liberalisation on the import side. Industries in the UK, for example, would tend to be most adversely affected by competition from LDC goods. But the extra exports—of machinery, etc.—going to the South would tend to be concentrated among the most competitive economies in the North, such as Germany and Japan. It may, therefore, be difficult to persuade the weaker Northern economies to liberalise (although it is here that expansion of markets for the South can be expected to be greatest) since these economies may not be potential gainers.

A Southern example of national interest is to be seen in the apparent reluctance of the South to establish its own secretariat. It appears that the strong Southern countries, whose resources of finance and manpower are most needed for such a secretariat, oppose such an institution because it seems they believe that it might more effectively represent the weaker Southern countries in its briefings and recommendations at the expense of the stronger countries.

The fact that decisions are made at a national level, in both North and South, also creates a 'Prisoner's Dilemma'-type paradox concerning action in the common interest. This applies where each country would gain if collective action were taken, but each would lose if they alone take action. An example is arms control. From the point of view of international security, collectively all would gain by reduced arms supplies to countries in conflict. There are dangers to international and regional security from the arms build-up in areas of conflict, such as the Middle East, or the Indian sub-continent. But if just one country holds back on arms sales with no assurance that others will, the restraining country will suffer losses in jobs and revenue without any corresponding gain in international security. The Brandt Reports recognise the common interests in these areas, but fail to note that national interests, the level at which decisions are taken, prevent these common interests effectively determining action.

The nation itself is too high a level to analyse the formation of policies, many of which result from pressure groups within nations. These groups take the form, for example, of trade unions, of food producers, of arms manufacturers, of bankers, of capital goods producers, of multinational companies, and so on. Each is affected by international policies and each lobbies to secure its own interests. Government policies are the outcome of pressures from these particular interests in interaction with the government's ideological bias plus the view it takes of the common interest. Hence the common interest is often offset by the power of particular interests. This is frequently the case, for example, in the field of protection, where consumer interests in low prices is offset by producer interests in protection, in food and manufactures, in the Northern economies.

If the concept of interests is to be effective as a means of securing action, it is essential to appreciate precisely how interests are related to national and international action. The failure of Brandt I can be attributed directly to a lack of understanding of these connections, assuming that the interests of all are equivalent to the interests of each, when in fact these are often in conflict; it is particular, not general, interests which are most closely related to policy formulation. A realistic view of these connections is sufficient to explain why no material progress has been made on any of the major areas identified in Brandt I—on trade, aid, arms, food, etc.

The second Brandt Report shares much of the language and many of the recommendations of the first Report. In many of the fields covered—trade, food, energy and arms—the same defects in reasoning which made Brandt I ineffective also apply to Brandt II. Particular and national interests are likely to defeat the 'common interest' identified in the Report, and no more progress can be expected than after the first Report: indeed, given the high levels of unemployment in the North and the weakening of OPEC, prospects for reduced protection and for commodity agreements seem weaker than before. However, the central part of the second Brandt Report is its Emergency Programme for international recovery. Here the situation is rather different; some action has already been taken and more may be expected.

The Emergency Programme assumes that the North and South share a common interest in the recovery of the international economy. The interests of the South in expanding markets and higher earnings from commodity exports does not need arguing. For the North, the Report contends, large numbers of jobs (one in six industrial jobs in the US) depend on markets in the South. The Report quotes the Morgan Guaranty Trust finding that the OECD growth rate would be 1 per cent higher with a 20 per cent annual growth in bank lending to the South, as compared with zero growth in lending. These arguments are similar to those advanced in the first Report for a massive transfer of resources that would revitalise the North as well as the South. They were not convincing to Northern governments for two reasons—first, because some leading governments deliberately restrained expenditure and growth, preferring to reduce the power of their working classes, control inflation, and to obtain sustained economic growth and full employment. Secondly, governments of industrialised countries have other means at their disposal to generate renewed expansion, without relying on transfer of resources to the South. They may reduce domestic taxes or increase domestic expenditure, each of which is more attractive politically than resource transfers to the South. As a basis for action, the arguments are no more convincing today. But today it seems that action is likely on the financial front, not because of common interests in recovery, but because powerful special interests are threatened by the prospect of Southern collapse.

Some major international banks have a very substantial exposure to the big LDC debtors: 'At the end of 1980 the nine largest UK banks had an exposure to Brazil equal to 43 per cent of shareholders' capital, to Mexico of 38 per cent and to Korea of 19 per cent. . . The figures show that if Brazilian, Mexican and Korean debts had to be written off, all the capital and reserves of the US banks would be wiped out'.[4] These banks are powerful lobbyists. In addition, failure of a major bank could have knock-on effects throughout the world banking community. Politicians are well aware of the connections between financial disaster and political change. Hence the danger posed to the banking system by the present conjuncture, and especially by the problems of a few Latin American countries, have been a powerful lever in persuading the North, and in particular the US, which had been especially unimpressed by appeals to morality and the common interest, of the need for action.

Since August 1982 (when the Mexican debt crisis erupted), there has been considerable progress in altering the international monetary system so as to bail out the big debtor countries and the banks. The Bank of International Settlements has become an important source of bridging finance. In recent months it has extended loans to Hungary, Mexico, Brazil and Argentina. The IMF has been actively encouraging (and at times coercing) the private banks to renew loans and extend new ones. At its January meeting, the Fund's lending capacity was effectively doubled with a 47 per cent increase in quotas and an expansion of the General Agreement to Borrow. The World Bank has also extended its activities in recent months, with a Special Action Programme to enable it to undertake a greater share of project costs to assist in the completion of unfinished projects. The intention is to extend the structural adjustment loans beyond the previously agreed limits. But, whereas the international community has increased the resources available to the IMF, the Bank faces severe resource constraints, and little extra real growth is expected up to 1985. Furthermore the IDA, which provides loans on concessional terms to poorer countries is constrained by the US reluctance to subscribe to it.

The contrast between the changes underway in the financial system, where the West's banking interests are involved, and the failure to provide the World Bank, IDA and the Common fund with much-needed finance is instructive on the way decisions on the international economy are made. In the former case, powerful particular interests are under threat. In the latter, the well-being, and even the survival, of very poor people is at stake, as well as the 'common interest' as identified by Brandt. But as politically effective interest groups are not involved, there is inaction or even retreat.

Viewing the second Brandt Commission Report in this light, it becomes clear that where its recommendations reflect a coincidence of particular interests and the common interest, there is likely to be a response from the international community, as there has already been for some of the financial reforms even before the Report was published. But for the bulk of its recommendations, including a good deal of the Emergency Programme, (e.g. the issue of substantial extra SDRs), which rests on a rather ill-defined "common interest', little can be expected.

This interpretation of developments in North-South relations is suggestive of future negotiating strategies. The experience of the 1970s shows that the South will make negligible gains if it pursues general demands for changes, as with the NIEO, basing its case on the grounds that it is their right and/or that it is in the common interest. Progress will only occur where the South can offer benefit or threaten harm to particular interests which are politically powerful. This conclusion does not render the South powerless; in fact it offers a large arena for action.

In finance it is now abundantly clear that large debtors have powerful leverage over lenders. If sufficiently determined, they can to a large extent dictate their own terms, unilaterally deferring payments. So long as a country does not expect to be a net borrower over the medium term because interest on accumulated debt will exceed new borrowing, the possibility that new lending may dry up as a consequence is not relevant. Meanwhile, the international banks have a considerable interest in coming to an agreement which avoids overt default. Industrialised countries' producers also have a substantial interest in seeing that the high-spending Southern countries have credit to finance purchases from them. Without open confrontation in the shape of a declaration of default,(which could trigger off various counter actions—political as well as economic), countries may quietly use their power as debtors to secure better terms. Individually, a number of countries have done so: Argentina, Brazil and Mexico have deferred payments. Mexico and Brazil are negotiating loans from the Fund on terms which appear generous, as compared with previous Fund programmes negotiated with less powerful countries. While *de facto*, the power of debt is being used on an individual country basis, it has not been used collectively, but it offers considerable potential as a lever to secure international monetary reform.

In trade, Third World countries have power as suppliers of crucial commodities and as buyers of goods from the North. The South (inspired by the example of OPEC) has focused most on the supply aspect. But this power was only successfully used in the case of oil, which is a rather special case, and then, it seems only temporarily. Control of supply is difficult because it requires cooperation among supplying countries, and it is ineffective if substitutes can readily be found. Moreover, the use of supplier-power is less effective during recession when demand is weak. In contrast, the potential power derived from providing markets for Northern goods is greater during recession. Control over markets provides an important source of leverage which can be exercised by individual countries in the South, without cooperation among Southern countries. So long as a particular country buys more from a Northern country than it sells to it, then it may threaten to switch purchases from the Northern country (in a recession there are plenty of alternative sources of supply), unless it gets favourable access for its own goods. Indonesia used this tactic successfully *vis-à-vis* the UK. The trade weapon may also be used for other objectives: Malaysia eschewed British goods in order to secure better treatment for her students in Britain. Mrs Gandhi bargained with major project contracts to persuade the British to replenish IDA. The purchase of military supplies presents opportunities for bargaining, especially since these purchases are generally conducted at governmental level.

The area of potential action is large: here I have only touched on a few possibilities. Detailed information on bilateral and multilateral relationships and interests is needed to establish the full potential.[5] The issues involved are the same as those covered in the Brandt Reports. The objectives are also similar: to secure more resources on better terms. The difference is that the mechanism is to use and make operational particular interests, rather than appeal hopefully to general interests. The area of potential action does not only concern interests already in being, but from a longer term perspective includes the ways in which interests develop. For example, the development of trade and technology links between Western Europe and the Soviet Union has created particular interests in Europe in easing the Cold War, which have proved effective in influencing government policies. Similarly, some large retailers in the North have come to depend on cheap supplies from the South, and have become a significant lobby inside the North for permitting continued market access for Southern products. Policies can then be selected which are likely to produce a favourable constellation of interests.

In many areas, the approach will prove more effective if countries of the South pursue it collectively rather than individually. However, Southern cooperation is beginning to look as elusive as North-South cooperation. Whether or not South-South cooperation develops significantly there are possibilities for action on an individual country basis, and (as for example with the Andean Pact) for regional cooperation on specific issues. The discussion above considered trade and debt: other potentially promising areas are technology transfer and multinational investment, taxation and international reserve policy.

Multilateralists may object that the interest approach sketched here could threaten the multilateral trading system, with the benefits it offers as a spur to static and dynamic efficiency. Moreover, the government interventions required may not only threaten efficiency, but also boost corruption. There is an element of truth in the objections. But against these must be set the poor record of the multilateral approach in recent years, while departures from multilateralism are numerous and growing. Multilateralism offers most of its benefits when there are high levels of employment in the industrialised countries and sustained growth in output and trade. With stagnation in world trade and falling commodity prices the benefits are much less, especially with growing protectionism in the North. It may be true that with a fully liberal multilateral system of trade and payments, the Third World might do better than with bilateral bargaining. But in the present system, in which the North intervenes heavily in trade in agriculture and manufacturing, Southern countries may improve their position by bilateral negotiations.

A more fundamental objection to this view of international relations is that it displaces vision, putting in its place the somewhat cynical process of lobbying and brokerage. Surely, it will be argued, major progress has occurred only when a visionary approach has been adopted and a leap has been taken to pursue grand schemes: this, broadly, is what the Brandt Report is recommending. In the words of Harry Dexter White (quoted in Brandt II): "we must substitute, before it is too late, imagination for tradition; generosity for shrewdness; understanding for bargaining; toughness for caution; and wisdom for prejudice'. And that, it may be argued, is what happened at Bretton Woods and inspired the Marshall Plan, ushering in thirty years of unparalleled prosperity. Contrast the twenty years following World War I, when particular interests were rampant, with the years following World War II, when visionaries triumphed. But while Bretton Woods and the Marshall Plan did require vision, they also reflected the *réalité politique et économique*. It was in the interests of the major power of the day—the US—to provide finance so that others might buy American goods; to secure free trade, where the US would dominate; to obtain the free movement of international capital so that US companies could extend their dominion. Imagination was needed to see that this was so, but interests were also forcefully involved. Hence the dismantling of the system today, as it begins to threaten the interests which previously benefited from it.

If world recovery is to be instituted and the development of the Third World promoted by international action, there must be a matching of imagination, of vision, and of interests. The Brandt Report has tried to provide such a matching, but has failed. Their failure arises on both sides of the equation: their imagination is limited; but of greater importance is the failure to match their vision to the real interests that dominate the world.

Notes

[1] *North-South: a programme for survival*, London: Pan Books, 1980

[2] Perhaps significantly, neither Report contains any signatory from the socialist bloc, while Mr. Peterson of the US 'did not participate in the preparation of this [the second] memorandum'.

[3] The formal burial appears to have taken place at the Delhi meeting.

[4] Overseas Development Institute, *Briefing Paper*, No. 2, March 1983.

[5] A beginning has been made with R. Cassen, R. Jolly, J. Sewell and R. Wood, *Rich Country Interests and Third World Development*, London: Croom Helm, 1982, which summarises the interests of particular rich countries in the Third World. But it does not provide the detailed information needed, from a Third World point of view, to illuminate the potential of the approach suggested above.

The New International Economic Order: An Exchange

In vol. VIII, No. 4, Spring 1983, pp. 543-550, Alternatives *carried an article by Jimoh Omo-Fadaka, entitled 'The Mirage of NIEO: Reflections on a Third World Dystopia'. Omo-Fadaka began the article by noting that the implementation of the 'Declaration on the Establishment of a new International Economic Order' as well as the appended 'Programme of Action' (passed by the special session of the UN General Assembly on 1 May, 1974) was entirely dependent on the willing cooperation of the industrialized West. But soon after the Declaration was passed, the US representative to the UN, Mr. John Scali, obviously speaking for the Western countries in general, had made it absolutely clear that their cooperation in what he characterized as an 'unrealistic' project would not be forthcoming. Hence, it would be futile, Omo-Fadaka argued, for Third World countries to pin their hopes on the NIEO. Further, he contends that even if the industrialized West had agreed, regardless of the considerable sacrifices involved, to extend generous aid, loans on easier terms, better terms of trade, transfer of technology, etc. (which was what the NIEO was all about), the Third World countries would have continued with dependent 'development' without coming anywhere near to dealing with the basic problem of mass poverty and sharp social polarization. Oma-Fadaka therefore pleaded that Third World countries should evolve an alternative strategy of self-reliant, self-sustaining development both singly and collectively, and towards this end bring about on the national planes the kind of structural change they demand on the international plane.*

In the following essay Winston Langley takes issue with Omo-Fadaka on several counts. he argues that since even local social and economic problems are global in scope, they must be addressed globally. In view of this, going it alone is neither feasible nor helpful for Third World societies. He therefore considers the NIEO a step in the right direction. That it has not materialized so far is no reason for abandoning the norms for a just and equitable international order.

Langley's essay is followed by Omo-Fadaka's rejoinder.

—Editors of *Alternatives*

Originally published in *Alternatives*, vol. 10, no. 2, Fall 1984. Reprinted with permission.

An Exception to 'The Mirage of NIEO'

Winston E. Langley

The objective of this note is to take exception to Omo-Fadaka's article, "The Mirage of NIEO: Reflections on a Third World Dystopia."[1] It contends that Omo-Fadaka erred seriously in concluding that the "basic assumptions of the [Brandt] Commission's diagnosis and prescriptions are the same as those of the NIEO" (p. 545), which led in turn to a serious weakness in his proposal for correcting the development problems of Third World states. Further, the note argues that he inadmissibly used his assessed worth of the Brandt Report's proposals to evaluate the merits of the NIEO and that he disregarded a major source of cooperation among states. It will conclude by showing that the significance of the proposed NIEO should not be weighed in proportion to how it satisfies some fixed time for its inauguration, but rather the extent to which it forges a basis for normative changes in the existing international economic order.

Similar to other terms which have gained currency, the meaning of interdependence has been confused and sometimes distorted. In describing their *existing* economic relationship with their industrial counterparts, less developed countries (LDCs) have characterized it as one that is interdependent, which is to say, a relationship in which their economies are linked or cemented with but nevertheless subordinated to and dependent on the economic life of industrial states. The definition also entails a certain negative connotation: that the interlinked economic and political asymmetry (actually interlinked dependency) is one that is ill-suited for the interests of Third World states and their relative contribution to the economic welfare of industrial countries and the world at large. On a normative plane, the primary concern of the LDCs, interdependence is understood as symmetrically reciprocal relationships within which dependency is mutual—that is, equitable sharing of burdens and benefits, responsibilities and rights, vulnerability and power.

To move from that which *is* (the descriptive) to that which *ought* (the normative) or vice versa, is, of course, a logical fallacy. The distinction, however, is often not the clearest; indeed, it is easily obfuscated when the issue is important enough. LDCs conceive of interdependence normatively so that when they contend that there must be a change in the existing *structure* of the international economic order, it must entail fundamental transformations to ensure that the distribution of global socioeconomic opportunities benefits all. Industrial states, on the other hand, use interdependence in the descriptive sense. So even when they speak of reforms, they envision but only modest managerial and other rearrangements *within* the existing asymmetrical economic order—rearrangements which will maintain transnational linkages based on values which are essentially Northern in origin.

The Brandt Report, in employing the term interdependence, uses it, by and large, descriptively. Indeed, far from being "the same as those of the NIEO," as claimed by Omo-Fadaka, the assumptions of its diagnosis and prescriptions are really premises, positions and recommendations which at best consider but promise little by way of the fundamental changes sought by the LDCs. For example, consider the proposals for the "reform of the world monetary system," where the Report called for urgent steps to be undertaken, building on "the large measure of consensus which emerged in the Committee of Twenty, and taking account of current difficulties and dangers."[2] Their recommendations to increase Official Development Assistance, make Special Drawing Rights the principal reserve asset, and improve the participation of LDCs in global monetary affairs appear significant, but it is curious that they anticipate only minor adjustments *within* the current international economic structure.

A more careful study will reveal, however, that the Committee of Twenty, which was set up in 1972 within the International Monetary Fund (IMF) to address monetary reforms, is really derived from the 20-member Executive Board of the IMF. And that Board, in turn, reflects the power structure of the IMF and the international monetary system as controlled by the North. If reforms in the latter system are to be based on a consensus of that Committee, then one can hardly expect fundamental changes. Other instances of such structural constraints would include the Committee's proposals for the establishment of the Oil Facility and the Extended Fund Facility. While these institutions, which came into being in 1974, are ostensibly to help members of the IMF cope with the impact of increased costs of petroleum imports on their balance of payments for periods and amounts in excess of that permitted under the IMF's credit tranches, they are really nothing but "adjustment mechanisms" which do not alter the existing monetary framework.

This is not to say that LDCs are not interested in proposals such as increased Official Development Assistance. They are. But they consider such measures as interim or transitional in nature,[3] as measures that should be implemented pending the creation of a *new* international monetary authority. The new system will be negotiated under the auspices of a UN Conference on International Money and Finance (not through the IMF), and whose principal attributes would include democratic management and control (not a continuation of the present oligarchic system) and an international currency unit (not a system regulated through key currencies of certain industrial states). Of course, together with these attributes would be values that reflect preferences which are not exclusively patterned after the freemarket model of economic development, or the parliamentary model of political democracy.

Because both the Brandt Report and Third World states use the term interdependence, Omo-Fadaka assumes that they mean the same thing. Hence his confusion, as indicated in the following quotation:

None of the spokesmen for the developed countries has spoken of the need for Third World countries to rely on their own efforts. Neither does the Brandt Report. They all speak (including the Brandt Report) of interdependence. Interdependence should be welcome if it is based on justice between and within nations. However, history shows that within the framework of interdependence rich nations have exploited the poor and weak nations. The existing international economic structure is not fortuitously but inherently exploitative and serves the interests of the powerful at both the national and international levels. What is required is an equitable distribution of the world's resources and *not* interdependence as defined by these spokesmen and the Brandt Report (p. 547).

The "framework of interdependence" Omo-Fadaka refers to—supported by the North and through which "poor and weak nations" are exploited—is interdependence of the descriptive kind. And if statements such as "Interdependence *should* be welcome *if* it is based upon justice between and within nations" (emphasis added) are any indication, then Omo-Fadaka is aware of the distinction between the descriptive and normative senses as well. All this said, however, the fact remains that he proceeded to equate the proposals for a NIEO with those of the Brandt Report.

But as mentioned earlier, the interdependence sought by the Brandt Report is of the descriptive type, not one based on any fundamental restructuring of the present world economic system. The NIEO, through which LDCs aspire to cope with their poverty and close the economic gap between them and the industrial states, seeks the opposite. So if Omo-Fadaka had wanted to analyze the position of Third World states, he should have focused on the proposals for a NIEO and on their sought-after interdependence, not the recommendations of the Brandt Report.

The importance of this point, and the magnitude of Omo-Fadaka's error, in overlooking it, cannot be stressed more. For even with all its deficiencies and problems, the NIEO represents a *moral claim* on the rich industrialized countries. And it is this feature which affords the entire NIEO program such dignity and appeal it possesses. After all, there is no other rational basis for the Third World to demand substantial transfers of real resources and a restructuring of the world economy. That the NIEO is currently going nowhere, strictly speaking, is irrelevant here.

The Brandt Report, on the other hand, would have the Third World abdicate this moral claim. Its recommendations, while often substantively similar to those of the NIEO, would have transferred the underlying basis for any action from a right of the Third World to a reliance on the largesse of the North. Put in this light, that the Brandt Report has also been politely buried is an indication not of how radical it is, but rather how grasping and desperate the rich countries are.

Omo-Fadaka's perception of the basis for North-South cooperation in the pursuit of a NIEO is also weak. According to him, if one of two parties is necessary to realize an objective and one of the parties registers strong objections, further pursuit of that objective is useless. For instance, because the US and other Western governments were not "willing" to make the sacrifices the NIEO entailed when it was initially proposed, and their subsequent economic problems hardened their objections to it in Delhi—viz., at the 1980 Conference of the UN Industrial Development Organization held in New Delhi, India—the continued pursuit of the NIEO is seen as naive. Yet, if international relations were conducted on such a basis, there would be few negotiations, let alone agreements and treaties between states. Nation-states do not cooperate because they are by nature altruistic or otherwise favorably disposed to helping others. They cooperate because it is in their interest to do so; and that cooperation is usually brought about via negotiations where initially conflicting premises and anticipations are resolved, become mutually satisfactory, or at least nonantagonistic. The call for global negotiations by the Third World, therefore, should not be abandoned.

Omo-Fadaka concluded his article by suggesting an alternative program for LDCs to correct their ineffective models of economic development. His proposal may be summed up in the following expression: "restructuring at home." According to him, LDCs should reorient their economies from one whose production strategy relies on demand from Western states to one based on domestic demand. It would entail changing from a life-style usually characterized by waste and affluence to one based on eco-development: that is, encouraging self-sufficiency, satisfying the basic needs of the poor before acceding to the claims of the affluent, and a foundation in a symbiosis between people and nature. Third World nations, he states, are right to expose and oppose the injustice at the international level, but they have the corresponding obligation to eliminate the inequalities and injustices in their own societies. There is no reason why structural changes at home should be made to wait on structural changes internationally, and every reason why they should not. For internal social justice is a prerequisite for the creation of a genuine NIEO. Third World countries must put their own house in order if international justice is to benefit their people as a whole (p. 548).

Although one must agree that Third World countries should do at home what they preach abroad,[4] the idea that social justice at home *must precede* a more equitable international economic order is based on faulty logic. Likewise with the view that Third World states can, by relying on their own efforts, and focusing on ecodevelopment, achieve their goal of a NIEO and the elimination of poverty. For if the LDCs are indeed powerless to influence the behavior of industrial states—as Omo-Fadaka contends in citing the weakness of even OPEC-and the economic welfare of the latter countries is linked to the current economic strategies pursued by the former, why then should the North allow the South to reorient their economies so as to be less dependent? Indeed, it is those portions of the NIEO which address issues of nonintervention and a state's right to "exercise full permanent sovereignty, including possession, use and disposal over all its wealth, natural resources and economic activities"[5] which have evoked some of the most forceful objections on the part of industrial states. One has but to look at the reaction on the part of some industrial states to the attempts of Michael Manley to effect limited reorientation of Jamaica's economy to find an apt and chilling illustration.

And what of the view that *intra*national social justice is a prerequisite for *inter*national social justice? An analogous argument would have to hold that international conventions on human rights should come only *after* internal codes are adopted. Operationally, then, each state must pursue the ideals of human rights if we are to have a world where human rights are universally respected. But this realization did not prevent the needed adoption of international conventions. Similarly, each state is obliged to ensure the economic welfare of all its citizens, a matter addressed in Article 7 of the Economic Rights and Duties of States—one of the three documents embodying the proposals of the NIEO—if universal social justice is to be achieved. But an international framework is necessary because the lives and economic welfare of people throughout the world are interlinked, requiring some collectively agreed standard for economic intercourse. Because one of the goals of the proposed NIEO is to promote values reflecting this interjoined economic fate of the world's population, it should not, contra Omo-Fadaka, be so quickly disregarded.

To be sure, Omo-Fadaka is quite correct in urging LDCs to emphasize domestic social justice. Otherwise, "any concessions gained at the international level will tend to be beneficial only to the export sector, thus strengthening the power of the minority which monopolizes economic, social and political power" (p.548). But while cognizant of this dynamic, Omo-Fadaka fails to perceive that it applies just as well to the solution he proposes: that is, just as it is counterproductive for international justice to precede intranational justice, so too with intranational justice preceding international justice. Rather, the more realistic and suitable program will have LDCs working for both international and domestic social justice at the same time.

The bottom line all along in this note is that the NIEO was never intended to work toward merely technical changes, and hence its significance as well as its actual or likely success should not be evaluated on such grounds. The proposals represent and are associated with an attempted departure from an old order which is breaking down, partly because of its inherent inequality. This inequality should be eliminated if for no other reason than that it breeds resentment and even hatred—two emotional states that ill-accord with the promotion of peaceful and friendly relations among states. But it should be eliminated also because the ideal of social justice should guide human conduct. Successful introduction of any new order, however, has historically never come about peacefully, or without postponements, delays and substantial opposition from the old system. There is scant if any reason, therefore, why we should expect that the NIEO would enjoy a different experience.

As such, instead of suggesting that Third World states should seek to "go it alone," or that they should first effect within their borders the social and economic justice for which they agitate internationally, one should first accept the fact that the international as well as domestic social and economic problems are global in scope, and must by necessity be addressed globally. The proposed NIEO is but a step in the right direction. And while its recommendations are weak in some areas, including those of eco-development, they do suggest norms—for example, sharing, cooperation and collective economic security—that can fundamentally change the nature of the present global economic order.

One should also bear in mind that, as recommendations, the principles of the proposed NIEO can, ought to, and will be amended. In fact, necessary as well as desirable foci such as the symbiosis between people and nature, socio-cultural diversity, and opportunities for the unfolding of individual and collective imagination can form the basis for improvements in those proposals. And ultimately, the NIEO cannot be assessed on whether it has succeeded or failed in having its principles implemented so far, but rather on whether the values it stands for might advance normative changes in the existing international economic order.

Notes

[1] Jimoh Omo-Fadaka, "The Mirage of NIEO: Reflections on a Third World Dystopia," *Alternatives VIII* 4, Spring 1983, pp. 543-550.

[2] Willy Brandt et al., *North-South: A Program for Survival* (Cambridge, MA: MIT Press, 1980), p. 219.

[3] See "The Arusha Initiative: A Call for a United Nations Conference on International Money and Finance," *Development Dialogue*, 1980:2, pp. 11-23.

[4] Winston Langley, "The Third World: Towards a Definition," *Third World Law Journal II*, 1, May 1981, pp. 27-28.

[5] *Economic Rights and Duties of States*, UN General Assembly Res. 3281 (XXIX), December 12, 1974, Article 2, Section 1.

A Reply to Winston E. Langley

Jimoh Omo-Fadaka

The difference between Professor Langley and myself is that while he is describing what 'ought' to happen in an 'ideal' world which is still, by any reckoning, even if it can be expected to materialize at all, a long way off, I am dealing with the situation in the 'real' world as it is today. It is, then, understandable that we could not arrive at the same conclusions.

Today Third World countries are critically dependent on industrialized countries. This 'external' dependence manifests itself not only directly in foreign ownership of and control over the key sectors of the economies of these countries (the 'commanding heights' of their economies), but indirectly through aid, capital, technology, consumer goods and arms. The internalization of this 'external' dependence has led to the distortion and disintegration of the socio-economic structures of these countries, thereby leaving them with no other choice but to shape and re-adjust their economies to those of the developed countries. This inevitably thus reinforces the centre-periphery relationship of master and servant.

A continuation of the ideology of 'interdependence' will mean a continuation of this type of asymmetrical relationship, which is bound to worsen the poverty problem of these countries. The prospects for many of these countries now and in future, under the umbrella of 'interdependence' are not very promising. This fact alone should remind us of the urgent need for economic decolonization of these countries. While the worsening economic and social situations in these countries is dominating the attention of many people, including Professor Langley, Third World countries should not lose sight of their long-term development goals: namely, the internalization of the development process in the spirit of collective and local 'self-reliance' and self-sustainment; the democratization of the development process at all levels so that the factors of development—human, capital and natural resources—can effectively and productively interact; and the strengthening of sub-regional and regional cooperation so as to create larger and integrated markets that will permit co-ordinated utilization of the countries' vast potentials.

This was the main thrust of my article. Development policies in Third World countries have, for far too long, been too outward-looking and dependent on bruising external crutches. The need now is for more inward-looking policies, and this within the framework of collective 'self-reliance' and regional integration. After a period of collective de-linking, in order to put their houses in order, they can then re-link on a selective basis to the mutual benefit of both parties. Such a re-orientation of policy is not a choice but a necessity if satisfactory development is to take place. Economic development will have to be increasingly internally-oriented, and growth in internal demand will have to become a major source of growth. This in short is what is termed 'self-reliance'. This is what I advocated in my article, not a policy of 'go it alone' as Professor Langley puts it. Those are his words, not mine.

The question is not whether the North would allow the South to reorientate their economies so as to make them less dependent. The point is that the countries of the South have no other choice but to search for alternative mechanisms and policies. My hope is that it can be achieved peacefully.

Like Professor Langley, I believe that international relations should be guided by morality, brotherhood of man, equity and justice. I have spent half of my life, in conjunction with others, to bring this about and will continue to do so throughout my lifetime. I also believe, like him, that international negotiations, treaties, etc., should be the underpinnings of a just and equitable world that both of us would like to see. But, unfortunately, the world today is not governed by these norms. Treaties and conventions are signed almost every day and broken the next day or by-passed with impunity, and business continues as usual as if the conventions and treaties had never been signed. But, of course, that is no reason for not trying. We must continue to strive for an 'ideal' and humane world. Treaties and conventions should be regarded as guides to action, *not* the action itself. Or else we will be raising false hopes.

Chapter 14

East-South in North-South: The Dominance of Pragmatism over Ideology

Introduction

Thirty-five years ago, the Communist countries of Europe had gone as far as they could to isolate themselves from the world economy and even from one another. Stalin's last year saw the full consequences of their autocratic policies and the severe pressures that he and his local administrators had imposed on the smaller countries of Eastern Europe, as well as on the USSR. The strains proved excessive, the policies impossible to implement consistently, with the result that the new political and economic leadership in the Soviet Union and in several of their satellites took a new course.

For different reasons, pressure also developed to change the Western embargo on sales of "strategic" goods to the East, also at its height in the early 1950s. As trade rapidly expanded within each bloc, East and West gradually turned towards each other, then pushed at the door which the other had already opened. Recently, both East and West have appeared to be trying to maximize the volume of trade between them, constrained only by limits on credit and the residual strategic restrictions. One manifestation of this new climate is the East's hard currency debt to the West, up from a few billion dollars at the beginning of the 1970s to over $50 billion at the end of 1977.

East-South economic relations have not been so dramatically transformed, and it is perhaps more difficult to discern the underlying forces shaping them. Both Western and Eastern analysts have devoted comparatively little attention to East-South trade and payments, and even less to the reciprocal impacts of each of the major relationships upon the others. Indeed, the terminological problem of dividing this triangle of First, Second and Third Worlds from North-South and East-West suggests a fundamental substantive issue: for what purposes, and in what contexts, is the East part of the North?

The East has itself been ambivalent, but it cannot long postpone taking positions as North-South negotiations continue and Eastern involvement in the world economy deepens.

This overall identification of Eastern and Western interests partly arises from, and partly determines, Eastern attitudes towards the major separate issues: debt and the international financial system; trade preferences and restrictions; cartels and stabilisation agreements for primary products; controls over TNCs; etc. It certainly does not preclude East-West conflict on these issues, but it defines the framework in which East-West disagreements can be handled. And if the present argument is accepted, it implies that the long-run bargaining position of the South is weaker than it would otherwise be.

By East or Eastern Europe we mean the socialist, centrally planned economies (CPEs) of the USSR and the smaller countries of Eastern Europe (the Six), excluding Cuba, Yugoslavia, and the Asian CPEs. References to Comecon or CMEA (Council for Mutual Economic Assistance) will normally focus only on its East European members. The West is essentially OECD, the South all non-oil LDCs, and OPEC a separate fourth grouping.

The discussions in this chapter assume certain fundamental geopolitical relations as given, notably that the Warsaw Pact and Sino-Soviet hostility continues with little change for at least a generation and that Soviet ideology remains Marxist, as does that of the Six, which stay in the Soviet sphere of influence, by armed force if necessary.

The Current Role of Eastern Europe in the World Economy

The peculiarities of East European price systems—as well as the non-convertibility of their currencies—invalidate the standard measure of foreign trade dependence (value of trade per capita, share of trade in GNP, etc.). It is generally accepted that the East's trade participation is still relatively low, although in recent years their trade has been growing as fast as that of the rest of the world. The structure of East European trade reflects the distribution of raw materials supplies and manufacturing capacities among the seven countries. Within CMEA, there has been persistent excess demand for most foodstuffs and raw materials (hard goods) and excess supply of low-quality machinery (soft goods) in the past because it has been much easier to sell the former to the West for hard currency. The Soviet Union has supplied raw materials to the Six in exchange for machinery, some semifabricates, industrial consumer goods and food, whereas the Six mainly trade machinery among themselves.

East-West trade, however, is primarily an exchange of raw materials and some simple manufactures from the East for more advanced manufactured goods and materials from the West. And East-South trade is similar to the Western North-South trade: manufactures (including armaments) from the East in exchange for raw materials from the South. Thus in its relations with the West, the East is in a position similar to that of the South, while in its relations with the South, the East plays a role similar to that of the West. From another perspective, trade within the Six is in substitutable goods, as is most trade between the advanced industrial countries of the West; but trade between the USSR and the Six, between East and West, and between East and South is complementary. There are alternative hypotheses to explain these differences: natural resource endowments, or comparative advantage more broadly interpreted; differences in economic systems; and the relative levels of economic development of the regions.

Since the East's own use of raw materials is high, corresponding to its large manufacturing output, even Soviet supplies do not make the region important in world markets for very many commodities. Outside the bloc the USSR is a major supplier of oil, gas, coal, timber, chrome, cotton, industrial diamonds, and gold, and

Poland of coal, copper and sulphur. But otherwise the East holds no strong supplier positions.

Although since the early 1960s the total volume of East European trade has not grown more rapidly than world trade, East-West trade has grown much faster. About a third of East European exports now go to Western industrial countries, and about a third of East European imports have come from the West in the 1980s (up from 23% and 25% respectively in 1965). Of total OECD exports, 5% went to Eastern Europe in 1981, compared with 3% in 1965. Eastern trade with the South has also been rising somewhat faster than intrabloc trade, the share of which has been falling for all seven countries. Even for the Six, which have always had a higher share of their trade within the bloc than the USSR, this share fell to about 55% in 1974, where it has tended to remain.

The most striking figures are provided by the East European hard currency trade deficits, at $1 billion in 1971, $2 billion in 1972, $4 billion in 1973, $6 billion in 1974, $12 billion in 1975, $10 billion in 1976, and about $8 billion in 1977. Eastern Europe (mainly the USSR, but also Romania and Bulgaria) currently runs surpluses with the LDCs, not negligible at $1 to 2 billion annually, but of little help in redressing the very large deficits with the West. Also, much of the surplus with the South either is in inconvertible currencies or is covered by long-term credits (economic aid) which may in the long run be unredeemable.

In other hard currency flows, Eastern Europe has a surplus of about $500 million annually in tourism and roughly the same in invisible transfers, but has a larger and rapidly growing interest payments deficit on its debt to the West. Thus overall there have been large current account deficits for the past several years, reflecting large real capital flows from West to East (with some from East to South) and creating a correspondingly large accumulation of Eastern European debt. Almost two-thirds of this debt has been financed by Western commercial banks without government guarantees.

East, West, and South:
The East and the New International Economic Order

In the past, Western analysts have focused primarily on East-West competition in the LDCs when looking at the relations between the First, Second and Third Worlds. In discussions of proposals for a New International Economic Order, the East has simply avoided taking positions on issues such as debt relief, primary product market 'stabilisation', trade preferences for LDC-manufactured goods exports, etc. In the long run the East is likely to find itself more Northern than Southern in its interests, and hence allied with the West on basic economic issues. This, however, does not entail radically increased East-West economic cooperation in trade, monetary arrangements or investment flaws. Rather, Eastern inability to penetrate Western markets for manufactures will impose tight constraints on such direct economic relations, despite a basic community of interest about the structure and operation of the international economic system.

There are reasons why the East might instead find it appealing to make common cause with the South in its demands on the West. First, there are ideological and geopolitical considerations—the East might naturally feel drawn to stand by the South in the battle against what both might see as exploitation by capitalist imperialism. Second, East and South are currently both primary product exporters to the West, seeking access to Western markets for their basic manufactures. They are also both borrowers in international (Western) capital markets.

These arguments can, however, be taken the other way. The East is in fact more rich than poor (with the low birth rates characteristic of rich and conservative societies). It cannot identify with the South except in opposition to capitalist exploitation, since (a) only a small part of the South is socialist, not capitalist, (b) the pattern of the East's trade relations with the South is also 'exploitive', and (c) China, a truly poor and also socialist country, will certainly align with the South, and it will be impossible to match China's anti-imperialist "bona fides". It would, in fact, be demeaning as well as unconvincing for the East to act as if it were poor. Eastern Europe is and will be seen to be fundamentally conservative, not revolutionary, with a considerable stake in the existing world order and in preserving its own place in the world economy.

Moreover, the East will in fact be a "competitor" with the South in the Western markets for simple manufactures, credit, foodstuffs and technology transfer, and for favorable attentions of the Western transnational corporations. Although the East might want whatever concessions the West may grant to the South, it will probably judge that it is unlikely to get much benefit this way and would be better off (because initially stronger) competitively if the West does not give anyone preferential treatment.

On food, for example, the Soviet agreement to buy at least six million tonnes of grain annually from the United States for several years during the 1980s is the action of a desirable customer whose credit is good and who can make this sort of arrangement to secure supplies, ahead of others (in the South) who cannot afford to make such long-term commitments. The initial Soviet resistance to this arrangement reflected its reluctance to acknowledge formally a long-term inability to be self-sufficient in grain. But the US-USSR grain agreement did not improve the overall stability of the world food market, to which a world food reserve might contribute. And although the Soviets will probably have to continue feed grain imports for some years, in amounts varying widely with harvest vicissitudes, the USSR has so far shown no interest in making a long-term cooperative undertaking with the world's major grain producers. This is an example of the Soviet preference for operating bilaterally, unless there is a clear and strong balance of advantage to it in multilateralism. C. Hosoya, et al., ("Collaboration with Communist Countries in Managing Global Problems," Triangle Paper no. 13, Trilateral Commission [1977]) are therefore correct in judging that the USSR will not participate unless the West proceeds regardless, stressing that unless the Soviets join in, they will find themselves at the end of the line when the current bilateral agreement expires. In exports of simple manufactures, the East currently competes with the South in selling clothing, furniture, shoes and similar items in the West. But only Romania, with its own distinctive strategy, has joined the Group of 77 and The World Bank as an LDC and has qualified for the Generalised System of Preferences. None of the others have any interest in even trying and, in any case, only Bulgaria would be a plausible candidate. Moreover, in the longer run, the East would not wish to specialise in such goods since the opportunities for selling them in Western markets will be limited, given the extent of Southern competition (which will have the advantage of cheaper labour). In any case these are not really highly profitable activities. The Eastern countries will be better off trying to sell to the West the engineering goods in which each specializes for export to the other CMEA countries, since the capital-intensive exports, which they have already developed will also face increasing competition from the more advanced LDCs.

This approach will need the sort of adaptation to Western market requirements which has so far been difficult for the East, but cooperation through sound ventures—for example, with Western firms—could change that. Here also, with no special concessions, the East may have more to offer the transnationals than the South: political stability, relatively high income and growing markets, a well-trained labor force whose unions are oriented towards production rather than wage bargaining—in fact, everything except equity participation, which may progressively become unsustainable in many Southern countries as well.

The borrowing problem is complex. The Eastern countries have so far had better terms in the Euromarket than almost all LDCs except the oil producers. In the Western "gentlemen's agreement" on export credit terms, however, the East Europeans have not been treated as generously as most of the LDCs. The minimum interest rates and down payments and maximum maturities prescribed for the Eastern countries are those applying to the richest LDCs, while most of the South gets preferential terms.

This is another example of the general proposition that the East cannot expect to be dealt with by the West on the same terms as the South. Moreover, the East has a vital interest in keeping the flow of credit going, and it is as afraid as the better-off LDCs that a few defaults by poorer or less responsible countries could endanger access to credit for all.

Thus one can assume a continued East-West strategic opposition and specific economic conflicts but still suppose that the East will seek a predominantly Northern identification in the international economy. The West is likely to see the East in this way as well and to find trade, investment and monetary relations with the East easier as time passes. And as the world moves away from liberal, non-interventionist trade and monetary rules, dealing with CMEA countries will be less a departure from the norm.

It might seem sensible to institutionalize the East's increased role in the world economy, both in trade and capital markets, through the entry of East European countries to GATT, the IMF, and other international organisations. Some framework will be needed for negotiating detailed economic conflicts and problems, which are likely to increase in numbers. But Eastern participation in these organisations could be disruptive, and the USSR will certainly not participate unless the rules treat her as the equal of the USA. The Soviets still seem to think they can do as well bilaterally as multilaterally, without restricting their freedom of action. They may be right for themselves, but clearly not for the smaller Eastern countries, and they do appear to realise this. They are consequently somewhat more complacent now about approaches by their partners to multilateral organisations, perhaps also because they recognize that the centripetal forces in CMEA will be so strong that they need not fear any reduction of Eastern dependence on the USSR.

GATT has become more attractive to the Eastern countries because of its increasing focus on non-tariff barriers to trade. Despite the Soviet Union's historical non-participation, GATT does include Czechoslovakia and Poland (accession in 1967), Romania (1971) and Hungary (1973), so there is no insuperable ideological or practical barrier for the others.

Only Romania, however, belongs to the IMF, and it joined the Fund and World Bank as an LDC, primarily to obtain bank loans (currently amounting to over $600 million). Although there are no great practical obstacles, East European leaders resist the infringement of sovereignty which they see in the weighted voting system of the IMF, dominated by the US and controlled by the combined votes of the US and the EC. In addition there would be no advantage in access to IMF loans if one were unprepared to accept the surveillance which might accompany them, but most East European countries (particularly the USSR) do not wish to give the IMF even the routine information on balance of payments, reserves, etc., which members must supply. They are very sensitive about such data, and Romania in fact reached a compromise with the Fund and Bank whereby the data it submits are kept confidential.

The three articles in this chapter put East Europe and the Marxist Leninist approach to the Third World into the perspective of Western North-South relations. Lothar Brock in his article provides a (West) Eurocentric point of view in which he argues that West Europe is about to come of age and take its rightful place as facilitator of Third World development, especially by cooperating with Eastern Europe, and thereby also contributing to detente. His historical analysis of the developments of the past 40 years in Europe lends credence to the idea; all that is lacking is political will. The second article, by Colin Lawson, describes both the rationale and the failure of the Third World's call **at UNCTAD VI** for great East European involvement in Third World development. Despite initial failure the demands of the Third World have provided a stimulus to Soviet and East European thinking about the South.

The final article in the chapter provides exegesis of the contemporary East European Marxist Leninist view that it is possible to move directly from a pre-capitalist to a socialist society without having to undergo capitalism and the following revolution. The Non-Capitalist Road to socialism (the stage preceding the achievement of communism on earth) has been extensively propagated by the Soviet Union in the

Third World. Professor Graf gives the North-American reader a lucid and interesting account of a theory familiar to all Third World intellectuals—and one that certainly will continue to play a role in the East-West ideological and political conflicts in the South.

The East-West and the North-South Conflicts: The Role of Western Europe

Lothar Brock

Introduction

Compared with the bleak state of conceptual thinking in the fields of peace and development in the mid eighties, the early seventies were days of remarkable vigour and vision. On the one hand, there was détente and the growing confidence that a viable and constructive coexistence between states with different social systems would be possible. On the other hand, new concepts for dealing with the problems of the Third World emerged, culminating in the institutionalization of the North-South dialogue. Thus it appeared that the politics of confrontation and direct or indirect coercion in both, the East-West and the North-South arenas, would come to an end and be replaced by multilateral bargaining.

From the late seventies on, however, the situation and the public mood reflecting it changed dramatically. In the early seventies, it seemed as if the fundamental conflict in international relations has shifted from the Cold War between East and West to one of how to restructure the global economic order.[1] Now there is renewed escalation of East-West tensions and a dramatic acceleration of the arms race. In addition, there has been no progress on all efforts to follow-up the great designs of the early seventies concerning a restructuring of North-South relations with concrete negotiations and workable agreements. While the concept of global negotiations was treated in a dilatory fashion and for all practical purposes has been discarded by now, agreements which were reached on certain issues like the integrated commodities program were not significant. Both tendencies—the renewed tension in East-West relations and the stagnation of North-South deliberations—have come together in intensified East-West quarrels over North-South issues, implying, it seems, not only a reaffirmation of the East-West struggle as the most critical but also its globalization. However, the East-West conflict has been global in nature from the very beginning. What is new today is (merely) that the globality of the East-West struggle has become more visible and more militarized, with the "reassertion" of U.S. foreign policy under the Reagan administration on the one hand, and a more systematic engagement of "real socialism" in the Third World on the other. In addition, the Soviet Union has developed new military capabilities to project its power globally which match those of the United States, thereby increasing the potential of superpower conflict throughout the world.

Of course, not everything that happens in the Third World today can be defined in terms of the East-West conflict. Rather, there is a growing contradiction between the institutionalization of the East-West conflict as a global military conflict, and the increasing complexity of political, military, economic and social developments in the Third World which simply

Originally published in *Alternatives*, vol. 10, no. 4, 1985. Reprinted with permission.

do not fit any dualistic model of world politics. Furthermore, the East-West conflict, for a good part, has turned into sheer power-rivalry between the two superpowers.

Yet, if the East-West conflict has been global in nature from the very beginning, one of the decisive deficiencies of détente is that it was not. Accordingly, what is needed today to stem the tide of further militarization of politics and conflict escalation, seems to be a truly global détente, implying—in the long run-cooperation or at least coexistence between East and West in the Third World, instead of the present costly and dangerous confrontation. Global détente, while cognizant of the globality of the East-West struggle, would approach Third World problems with appropriate awareness of their complexity. This would refute the dualistic conceptualization of world developments that has helped the superpowers especially to legitimize any policy they pursue around the world to be in the interest of national security or world peace, freedom or anti-imperialism.

Presently, Western Europe has neither the ability nor the interest to opt of the East-West conflict, understood as a struggle between OECD-capitalism and COMECON-socialism. But Western Europe does have a special interest in mitigating superpower rivalry and in reviving or reconstituting détente, both under economic and security considerations. At the same time, Western Europe, which is the most important regional group for Third World trade and the biggest source for its development funds, also has a special interest in and capacity for developing new economic opportunities in the Third World to secure its own economic standing in the global competition with the United States and Japan. With a view to these interests, can we expect Western Europe to take up the task of global détente? Would Western Europe be willing, in this respect, to play a more independent role in world politics even at the risk of embarrassing the United States? Is there a West European view of the world which would serve as the basis for a policy of dialogue, instead of confrontation, on the East-West level concerning North-South problems?

This paper does not aspire to answer these questions but attempts to contribute to a debate which eventually may produce some answers or even workable suggestions. In making this attempt, the paper deals with the global role of Western Europe in the East-West context. "Western Europe," in our discussion, refers to the member states of the European Community (EC). It is important to note that neither Western Europe nor the EC countries are being viewed as *one* actor in world politics. Indeed, part of the problem here is that we are dealing with multinational politics. Such multinational politics, on the one hand, offer special chances for innovative thinking. On the other hand, they hamper the decision-making process in the realization of innovative ideas even more so than the complex constellation of domestic political forces does in a big national actor like the United States.

Global Dimensions of the East-West Conflict

The formative stage

From the outset, East-West politics have been global politics: they have always affected "out-of-area" developments in the Third World and have been affected by them. The historic roots of the *global* nature of the East-West conflict are easy to trace. First, the October Revolution that gave birth to the Soviet Union took place at a time when the last colonies had been divided among the colonial powers. From that time on, inner European conflicts had global implications, dramatically demonstrated by that the war breaking out in

Europe in 1914 eventually turned into a *world* war. Second, due to its geographic features, the Soviet Union is multi-regional, stretching from Europe to East Asia and the Pacific. Therefore, any attempt by the new regime to restructure its relations with its neighbors had by necessity wide international repercussions. This was illustrated by the early manifestations of East-West rivalry in China during the 1920s.

Third, though capitalism and socialism are universal concepts, their status continue to depend on a states system where actors tend to pursue individual aims. The universalistic nature of capitalism and socialism has helped their protagonists to define their individual interests in terms of global needs and has led to the creation of what Hans Morgenthau called a "universalistic nationalism" that feels challenged by its adversary anywhere however remote.

The theoretical basis for this perception of world developments was paved by Lenin. By reformulating the Marxian perspective on the world revolutionary process, Lenin brought the Third World into focus as a battleground for the struggle between socialism and capitalism. Lenin advanced the idea that the October Revolution had created an international milieu where national liberation and social transformation can be combined as two mutually reinforcing elements of the struggle against capitalism in its imperialistic stage. If capitalism at this stage depended on the exploitation of the Third World, then a breakdown of capitalist exploitation in the wake of national liberation would unleash a chain reaction that would lead eventually to revolutionary change in the capitalist center as well. Such was the understanding of world political and social developments to which the Comintern was committed.

Lenin was not very familiar with conditions in the different colonial or semicolonial areas. And despite its highly developed sensitivity for contradictions, Leninist theory helped to introduce the perception of zero-sum political and social change in the world—particularly in the Third World—which defined all change in terms of gains and matching losses of influence in the struggle between East and West. In the 1930s, this zero-sum view of the world was quickly modified by the progress of fascism, which called for new alliances. The Communist International adjusted its policy in light of the new global realities, but only temporarily, as became clear at the end of World War II.

Post-World War II institutionalization of global East-West competition

For the United States, its concept of the post-war order was to foster its economic, political and security interests within a cooperative international system as outlined in the Charter of the United Nations. With such a system, the United States, in accordance with the prevailing self-perception of its political tradition, would play the role of a leading power but not of a hegemonic power.[2]

However, the initial agreement between the Allies to continue cooperating in the post-war period did not extend to cooperation in specific matters, and the system broke down before it really got going. In the context of the times, U.S. leaders reacted by assuming the zero-sum perception of world developments that was strongly affirmed by Stalin or Shdanov's Two Worlds thesis; it offered the United States an *explanation* of the turn of events, a *motivation* to do something about it, and a *justification* for doing so (controlling the domestic political and social developments of other countries). Not surprisingly, the resulting U.S. policy was defined in terms of helping those peoples which were threatened by international communism (Truman Doctrine), while the Soviet Union saw itself playing the role of a mere midwife assisting historical necessity come to life as a forceful reality.

The ensuing struggle saw a retreat from collective security and a return to (selective) alliance politics on a global scale. Undoubtedly, the core area of the struggle was Europe. But it was in the Third World that the first regional alliance was formed—in Latin America with the Rio pact of 1947. It was in Latin America, too, where the transformation of an antifascist front into an anticommunist front made the quickest advances.[3] In addition, the areas bordering the Soviet Union and those from which the European colonial powers had to retreat—from Turkey via West and South Asia to China, Korea and Indonesia—immediately became objects of East-West rivalry. After the "loss" of China, the United States went to war to prevent further inroads of communism in these regions. It also installed, partly in cooperation with the old colonial powers, a system of regional alliances in the Third World which were to serve as bases for the containment of the Soviet Union. With this multilateral alliance system in Europe, Latin America and Asia, the East-West conflict was institutionalized as a global conflict from which only parts of Africa remained temporarily unaffected.

Escalation of the East-West conflict in the South

During the Cold War, there were continuous efforts on the part of both East and West to keep up communication and to reach a certain understanding on how to prevent tensions from escalating into a shooting war. In substance, however, despite the rhetoric of "rollback" during the fifties, Western policy toward the East in Europe was already status-quo oriented with the possible exception of German reunification. But even reunification was used much more as an instrument in the East-West struggle than accepted as a task in itself. After the political rearrangement of Europe in the late forties, the real struggle between East and West over the political orientation of states had moved to the Third World where it was not preempted but invigorated by the "Spirit of Bandung" that paved the way for the conception of Non-Alignment.

Of course, there were a number of crises in Europe during the fifties: the GDR crisis in 1953, the Hungarian and Polish crises of 1956, and the Berlin crisis of 1958. But these were crises of adjustment to the socio-political status-quo. In the Third World, the status quo itself was changing rapidly with decolonization and soon wielded a potential for conflict which led to indirect and even direct military confrontations between East and West. Thus, during the Suez crisis when the West was split—United States versus France and Great Britain—the use of military force by France and Great Britain was met with threats by the Soviet Union to defend Egypt and the Nasser regime militarily. If the Soviet Union had not been tied down in Hungary, the Suez situation could well have escalated to the point of a direct East-West military encounter in a most sensitive Third World region.

In the case of the Cuban missile crisis of 1962, the confrontation between the United States and the Soviet Union over the stationing of Soviet missiles in a Third World country led to the brink of a third world war. The situation was, of course, unique and could not have been repeated easily in any other part of the Third World, since no other country outside the Caribbean Basin is as exposed strategically vis-a-vis the United States as Cuba is. But one can also state that no event in Europe since 1945, including the Berlin blockade, had ever taken such dramatic turns as the Cuban missile crisis did. For this very reason, the missile crisis, despite its specific features, gave a most important impetus for the general reorientation of East-West politics from cold war to détente.

The missile crisis did not, however, keep the United States from escalating their military engagement in Vietnam in the following years up to the point where the United States became the main military adversary of the National Liberation Front and the North Vietnamese. As a consequence, U.S. military action in Vietnam became one of the main issues contributing to East-West political tension during the sixties and early seventies. The Soviet government, however, carefully avoided a further internationalization of the conflict beyond its own participation as a weapons supplier.

The era of détente

The initiation of the détente process coincided, remarkably, with the escalation of U.S. military action in Vietnam, giving rise to speculation about whether the increased activity might not actually have taken place under the shield of incipient détente. It might well be that reduced East-West confrontation in Europe was perceived to allow for regional conflicts in the Third World, despite that such conflicts continued to be understood in terms of the universalistic antagonism between the Western world and communism. But U.S. actions in Vietnam were influenced much more by the Sino-Soviet dispute—thence helping bring about the Sino-American rapprochement and allowing the Nixon administration to play the "Chinese card." The Sino-Soviet dispute was an enormous complication for Soviet world policy and modified the whole East-West pattern of conflict.

Still, it is not entirely out of place to have doubts about the meaning of détente for the Third World. The Moscow agreement of 1972 between the Soviet Union and the United States concerning their respective "out-of-area" conduct, could have been interpreted as a barter by which U.S. consent to the sanctity of the status quo in Europe was exchanged against Soviet consent to a continued predominance of Western influence in the Third World. This may have been the understanding of the Nixon administration.[4] As it soon turned out, however, if such was the U.S. understanding of the agreement, it was not that of the Soviet government. From a Marxist ideological perspective, it would not have made sense if the socialist countries had actually consented to freeze the distribution of Western and Eastern influence in the Third World because that would have amounted to a negation of the laws of history. Rather, the Soviet Union regarded détente as an expression of realistic Western politics, that is to say, the West has now given up trying to beat socialism and is adjusting to a world in which the anti-imperialist and socialist forces were gaining ground.[5]

Not surprisingly, the West failed to appreciate Soviet expressions of solidarity with anti-imperialist and socialist forces in Angola, Mozambique, Ethiopia, and Afghanistan as conducive to détente. The complete failure of East and West to reach a working understanding of the Third World and of the nature of underdevelopment, and the shifting balance of East-West military capabilities in favor of the East were very important determinants of the quick demise of détente.

The demise of détente

Détente and the North-South dialogue, at least for a short time, nourished a new confidence that the most pressing world problems could and would be solved cooperatively and that the East-West and the North-South conflict formations would be transformed into a system of viable coexistence on the global level. But this vision quickly faded. The "Vietnam trauma" in the United States had hardly reached its climax when it was superceded by the "Angola shock"—the apparent surprise of Western governments that the Soviet Union, despite the Moscow agreement of 1972, aided socialist liberation groups in the struggle over the liquidation of Portuguese colonialism in Africa.

The "Angola shock" was followed by growing inhibitions about the military presence of "real socialism" in Ethiopia after the fall of Haile Selassie, about the de-Westernization of Indochina, and about the new dimensions of Soviet armament which established the capacity of the Soviet Union for a global military power projection. Finally, the Afghanistan intervention, following the revolutionary changes in Iran, the oil crises, and general disturbances of the world economy, all helped to foster the political and socio-psychological milieu giving rise to a political fundamentalism which, after the election of Reagan, swept away what was left of détente.

Instead of strengthening the feeble but conceptually bold approach to world politics symbolized by détente and the North-South dialogue, the world witnessed a resurgence of superpower rivalry, a return to the worst of zero-sum thinking, a stagnation of global development efforts, an unprecedented acceleration of the East-West armament process and the arms race spreading to the Third World.

Western Europe in Global Politics

The Europeanization of the world and the European retreat

What was the role of Western Europe in these lamentable developments? At the beginning of world politics in the modern sense, there was Europe. It was the industrialization of Europe that led to the establishment of *one* world, in which henceforth the political, economic, social and cultural developments of the different regions would be more or less tightly linked as parts of a global system of social reproduction. In other words, today's international system derives from the projection of the interests of European capital and European nation states onto the world. These interests, again, were determined as much by intra-European rivalries as by the demand for overseas markets and resources.

If World War I was the culminating point of the Europeanization of the world, the Second World War put an end to it. But contrary to Shdanov and Stalin's Two Worlds thesis, the *one* world, established by Europe, persisted even while the European states themselves were reduced to secondary actors. Germany lost its identity as a political entity altogether while the other European states also became objects of global power politics that many had hitherto participated in. Of course, the United Kingdom and, to some degree, France also played an active role in delineating the contours of the post-war order as it was spelled out in the United Nations' Charter. But it was clearly the U.S. perception of the post-war situation that dominated what was henceforth to be understood as the *Western* position. This process was based on the economic and military disparities between the United States and the European countries which prevailed at the end of the war, and enhanced by the accelerating dissolution of former colonial empires.

The retreat from the colonies symbolized more clearly than anything else that Europe, while remaining a major stage for the great political struggles of the day, had lost its place as the center of gravity of world developments. To the extent that the old colonial powers continued to play an important role in world politics, they often did so by causing trouble in the process of their retreat from empire instead of contributing constructively to the solution of problems which they themselves had helped bring about. This was demonstrated in the Suez crisis when France and Great Britain, far from supporting U.N. actions to alleviate the crisis, escalated it by unilaterally landing troops on the very day the General Assembly called for the removal of all foreign troops from the canal area and the Sinai.

Another example of the inability or unwillingness of European colonialists to accept decolonization as a historical necessity, and to adjust to it in a constructive way, is the Algerian war. It was one of the bloodiest wars of the fifties and was finally relinquished by de Gaulle. In the sixties and seventies, again, it was the persistence of European colonialism—this time that of the Portuguese under Salazar—that had most disturbing effects on the international scene. It prepared the way for the counterproductive interaction of East-West and North-South politics which helped to dismantle détente in the second half of the seventies.[6]

The "reassertion" of Western Europe

The wartime destruction, the division of Europe, and the forced and bloody retreat from empire comprised only one side of the post-war development of Europe. The other side was the reassertion of Western Europe by way of integration. This process, in the beginning, was directed inward, spurred by economic advantages and the political drive toward overcoming war in Europe. It resulted not only in speedily stabilizing the political scene but also in the reconstruction of the former colonial powers as an economic bloc that, by its sheer economic weight, wielded considerable power for world economic development.[7]

The drive toward European integration was supported by the United States. But it also increased economic competition between the United States and the Common Market and led to a number of acute conflicts over protectionistic practices and the extent to which economic means, including development aid, should be used as a weapon in the East-West struggle. European economic integration was gradually politicized in this way through its potential or manifest external repercussions.

The politicization process received a big push from the efforts of the European Community (EC) member countries to install the European Political Cooperation (EPC) as a partial compensation for, or a first step toward, European political integration. EPC succeeded in playing an important role in coordinating the policies of EC member countries to negotiate the Helsinki agreement on security and cooperation between the East and the West in Europe. The Helsinki accord, in turn, was accompanied by an impressive upsurge of economic exchanges at an all-European level and a qualitative intensification of East-West economic relations through industrial cooperation.[8]

This success of EPC within the context of East-West politics coincided with a reorganization of its relationship with formerly associated Third World countries and part of the old British colonies through the treaty of Lomé. Both sides, the EC, and the ACP countries, hailed the agreement as a historic step toward a cooperative solution of world problems.[9]

In addition, the EC countries, experiencing what they perceived as a threat to economic security by the oil-exporting countries, began a Euro-Arabian dialogue to minimize further economic pressures within the context of the Middle East conflict.

The EC countries also ventured to formulate a comprehensive concept for an integrated approach to the whole Mediterranean area. They eventually developed contacts and concluded agreements with the Maghreb-states, Latin American sub-regional state groupings like the Cartagena group, as well as with Southeast Asian countries (ASEAN). They also issued declarations on various conflicts around the world such as in the Middle East, Cyprus, Portugal and Southern Africa.

All these activities could and were interpreted as part of the search for a "European identity" in the world,[10] that the European countries were on their way back to playing a global role, and one that is also relatively independent. Of course, adherence to, and the existence of the Atlantic Alliance was never in question.[11] More relevant is the extent to which this search transcended the East-West interpretation of North-South politics that played an increasing role in U.S. policy towards the Third World after 1975.

Transcending the East-West dimension of North-South relations

As mentioned above, it was in the United States where a harsh critique of détente, given Soviet policy in the Third World, emerged barely after the Helsinki agreement. But West European policy-makers, too, were concerned about Soviet policy in the Third World long before "Afghanistan." In particular, the following issues provoked considerable anxiety. First, the political future of Africa in light of Soviet and Cuban involvement in the last stages of the decolonization process and the relevance of this involvement for strategically important areas like Southern Africa and the Horn. Second, the future of the Non-Aligned Movement, especially in the context of the 1979 Havana summit and Cuban attempts to impose a socialist interpretation of Non-Alignment. And third, the security of Europe's supply of raw materials. For example, the "supply security" of oil seemed threatened by a further destabilization of the Middle East region through the revolution in Iran, Soviet intervention in Afghanistan, as well as the Iran-Iraq war.

Nevertheless, West European policy concerning these developments and the whole issue area of interaction between the East-West and the North-South conflicts was different from that of Washington. As a rule, the Europeans attempt to prevent an overdramatization of, and over-reaction to, the Soviet role in Third World developments. Of course, the Europeans could not but agree that Soviet intervention in the Third World was a threat to what was left of détente. Thus, the then president of the European Council, Ruffini, summarized the position of the EC by stating that détente by its very nature is global and consequently indivisible.[12] But concrete reactions, especially the two-phase plan for a political solution of the problems at hand forwarded in June 1981 by the EC, demonstrated a keen interest in preventing further disturbances of East-West relations from Soviet engagement in certain countries or regions of the Third World.[13] To be sure, there was a very controversial debate about how to react to the politics of "real socialism" in the Third World. In general, however, there certainly was more interest among EC countries in the divisibility of tensions than in the indivisibility of détente.[14]

West Europeans, while appreciating U.S. concerns, felt that they had more to lose by horizontal conflict escalation. Consequently, in the EPC declarations and those of the EC Parliament referring to different conflicts in the Third World with East and West involvement, there is a tendency to point to the economic and social causes of such conflicts, to call for substantive conflict resolution which goes to the roots of the respective conflicts, to support intra-regional initiatives for settling disputes, and to modify the influence of the superpowers. For example, in the case of Central America, the EC countries are supporting regional and non-militaristic conflict resolution with the help of the Contadora group. These processes, as far as Western Europe is concerned, should be supported through external economic aid and internal reform, which are supposed to be brought about or intensified through a European-Central American dialogue in the context of a more active Latin American policy of the Community.[15] Of course, the "Kissinger plan" for Central America and the Caribbean, taking up the concept of the Caribbean Basin Initiative, also strongly emphasize the necessity to go to the roots of the turmoil in the region and to embark upon a program of intensive economic aid and social reform.[16] But the motivation behind this notion seems to be legitimizing more military action on the part of the United States.

In contrast, West European declarations and resolutions on the subject stress the inadequacy of military measures and the counter-productivity of such measures as far as preventing intervention (on the part of socialist countries) is concerned. West Europeans do not view Central America so much as a test-case for the credibility of the West vis-a-vis alleged ambitions of "real socialism" to foster world revolution. Rather, they prefer to look at the situation in its historic specificity, and as a test-case for combining social transformation and political democratization, or for the credibility of the Central American left's claim to pursue this end. In this context, West Europeans draw upon their experience with the Portuguese revolution. In the case of Portugal, after the downfall of Salazar, it was not an attempted isolation of, but a critical and rather selective dialogue with the forces of change that helped keep Portugal in the Western camp and paved the way for its final inclusion into the European Community.

Such thinking manifested itself in the refusal of the EC to go along with the U.S. trade and aid embargo against Nicaragua. Nevertheless, there is, of course, a considerable variety of attitudes toward U.S. policy in the region. Some party groups within the EC parliament, especially on the left, and the West European member-parties of the Socialist International in general, are willing to express strong opposition and to risk at least a modest degree of U.S. embarrassment. For example, the European section of Socialist International, under the leadership of Willy Brandt, has set up a committee for the defense of the Nicaraguan revolution and supports the Salvadorean Movimiento Nacional Revolucionario.[17] Among the ruling parties, the Socialists in France under the Mitterrand government are the most outspoken in formulating and implementing an approach to Central American politics which pays little heed to the U.S. definition of the situation. Thus, in 1981, France in a joint declaration with Mexico afforded quasi-diplomatic recognition to the revolutionary forces in El Salvador. Furthermore, France has delivered weapons to the Sandinista government in Nicaragua and even offered it help to remove the U.S. installed minefields off the Nicaraguan coast.

On the other end of the spectrum are Great Britain and West Germany, the latter after the 1982 change of government. The official position of the West German government has always been moderated by its special ties to the United States in security matters. The present government of the Federal Republic, however, went beyond traditional caution to normalize diplomatic relations with El Salvador and stopped bilateral aid to Nicaragua (without preventing multilateral aid on the EC level). It has explicitly rejected the critique that aid was stopped because of the socialist orientation of the Sandinistas, but justified the policy by contending that Nicaragua was intervening in the affairs of its neighbors.[18]

There is, therefore, no uniform European stand on Central America (or any other region of the Third World). But there is the attempt to offer Central America and other regions of the Third World a "European option" that would widen their margin of action and help prevent an all-out projection of the East-West conflict onto the conflicts of the Third World.[19] Along this line, members of the EC Commission and of the EC Parliament have warned that the renewed East-West tensions would detract attention from North-South issues and further worsen the chances for concerted and effective efforts to solve some of the basic problems of underdevelopment. Commission member Pisani in this connection talked of the "marginalization of the North-South Dialogue" through the East-West conflict.[20] Against this danger, after the Cancun conference of 1981, the European Parliament pleaded for a reaffirmation of the necessity and feasibility of transforming the North-South dialogue into the formal global negotiations the developing countries had called for.[21] The arguments in favor of such negotiations were not so much expressed in terms of European economic interests as in terms of a close relationship between persistent underdevelopment and instability as well as the likelihood of violent conflict at the international level. Such language was very much in accord with the analyses offered by the United Nations on the inter-relationship between peace or disarmament and development.[22]

One year after the Cancun conference, however, it became clear to the EC that there is little chance of concrete initiatives leading up to global negotiations.[23] In its memorandum on development policy of October 1982, the EC Commission pointed to the difficulties standing in the way of global negotiations and underlined the necessity of immediate though specific or rather limited action.[24] The urgency of such action, in the view of the Commission, followed from that the East-West conflict in its global dimensions could block the developing countries realizing a meaningful future and this could lead to unintended and uncontrollable consequences for all parties.

Toward this end, the Commission noted again the special role of Western Europe. The East, it argued, had confined its own policy on Third World problems to the critique of Western colonialism and its long term implications. Instead of assisting in the construction of an effective multilateral system for development, they had preferred to work bilaterally to foster their own interest in the way of military aid and ideological influence. As a result, Soviet military aid and ideological influence counteracted Western aid, leading to the North-South dialogue being, in practice, replaced by East-West confrontation.

According to the Commission, the United States under the Reagan administration also were almost exclusively interested in the East-West dimension of world politics. They preferred to exert influence through bilateral interaction instead of supporting collective action in the context of the North-South dialogue. Hence, they failed to put their enormous resources to work and realize overdue tasks.

In contrast to these policies and conceptions, the EC, so the memorandum argued, was very much interested in enhancing the stability of the international system. As a commercial and political power, the EC was not interested in conflict, but in regulating interdependence. In this respect, Europe and the Third World countries are in the same boat. They both profit from peace and suffer under conflict and war, because they are likely to be their victims and/or serve as the battleground on which conflict and war will be fought out.[25]

An Independent Role for Western Europe

Western Europe as a global actor

From the viewpoint of "real socialism," Western Europe as a center of world capitalism will always remain committed to the strategic aim of fighting socialism everywhere. While this may be true, its practical relevance is being modified by many factors, one of them being the dynamics of inter-state politics.

The modern international system which was established in the process of European industrialization remains a nation state system. More precisely, the establishment of the modern international system went hand in hand with the creation of the nation state system and reinforced the latter. This development was not in contradiction to the growing internationalization of production, but rather interacted with it. Also, the projection of the European nation state system onto the world had not been challenged by the advent of "real socialism." To the contrary, "real socialism" is defined by its adaptation to the nation state system; under Stalin, this adaptation was perceived as "socialism in one country." The East-West conflict, therefore, has been an inter-state conflict from the very beginning. Or, to state the case in more general terms, the organization of social formations in what Toynbee called a "system of contending states" has modified and continues to modify all social transformation processes by putting them into the context of a continuous struggle for the accumulation of national power. The one side of this accumulation process is national self-determination, the other hegemony.

Under the specific conditions resulting from the Second World War, it was not only the universal antagonism between capitalism and socialism, but also the dynamics of the power accumulation process as such which led to the dual hegemony of the United States and the Soviet Union. By its very nature, this structure implied a curtailment of the freedom of action of all other states, including the respective allies of the superpowers. Since freedom of action is an essential ingredient of self-determination, and since self-determination is a driving force of politics as long as the nation state system exists, the bipolarization of the world, by itself, unleashed centrifugal countertrends, which did not abolish the antagonism between capitalism and socialism but modified its concrete meaning in international relations.

These centrifugal trends demonstrate a stubborn autonomy of the High Politics of national self-assertion vis-a-vis the seeming imperatives embodied in global interdependence and universalistic value systems. However, since power inequalities between single states are transcended by power inequalities between regions, there is also a tendency to compensate these inequalities through "group politics" at the international level: that is, to coordinate and integrate national policies and to pool national resources in order to strengthen the competitiveness and the bargaining position of their respective societies vis-a-vis other states or regions.

From this viewpoint, the search for a "European identity" in the world is limited but real. Real because it reflects the general dynamics of inter-state politics just mentioned, but also real in the context of present world developments. Given the protracted world economic crisis and the destabilization of the international security system, Western Europe has a genuine interest in preventing horizontal conflict escalation arising from the global projection of military power by the United States and the Soviet Union. It has a genuine interest in strengthening its position in the world economic system and to open up new economic opportunities instead of limiting them through political considerations pertaining to the East-West conflict.

But the search for a European identity in the world is also limited. First, the dynamics of inter-state politics, one of the causes differentiating the interests of Western Europe and the United States, constitute a grave obstacle for the formation of Europe as a single actor on the global stage. After all, the search for a European identity was not only the expression of the necessity to combine forces in the global struggle for scarce resources (including influence and security), but also of the inability of the EC member countries to make substantial progress on the way toward the envisaged European Political Union. The European Political Cooperation was introduced because overall political integration was way behind schedule, if not considered impossible for the time being. This situation was not only the result of a lack of political will to integrate, but also of structural conditions reflecting the concrete differences in growth and development among the Western European countries, the power-disparities between the big and the small EC members, the complicated inter-play between domestic and European politics in every one of the member states, and also different political traditions and value orientations which are, of course, still very much influenced by the historic experiences of bloody intra-European rivalry.

Second, as a correlate to the various problems, potentials and interests among EC member states, their policies towards the United States differ considerably. This has already been mentioned in connection with the case of Central America. But there are also remarkable differences in the degree of cooperation and disagreement with the United States, as demonstrated in the international debates on restructuring the world economic order, the recent transatlantic debates on security matters, the consent to, and critique of Reaganomics, and most recently by openly divergent views on the Strategic Defense Initiative (SDI).

The search for a "European identity" will go on, but the process will be very slow. The same also holds true for the relationship of Western Europe and the United States. We may expect increasing conflicts of interest deriving from different security needs and decreasing margins for compromise on economic matters. Such developments would further a policy of collective self-reliance both economically and in the security field on the part of Western Europe.[26] But they are most unlikely to lead to an economic and military dissociation from the United States in the foreseeable future.

Realignment of economic forces in the West

The Western Alliance was formed in a situation where there was a striking economic and military discrepancy between the United States and the European countries. This situation has changed due to the rapid reconstruction and postwar development of the European countries, and also to a loss of dynamism of the U.S. economy itself. Within the Western Alliance, economic power constellations have shifted to reflect the relative economic decline of the United States vis-a-vis Western Europe.

At the end of the Second World War, the task for U.S. economic policy was to engage its vast productive capacity which had been developed during the war. Due to wartime destruction and trade restrictions, this capacity was matched outside the United States by an equally vast need that, under the Marshall Plan, the U. S. government helped transform into effective demand. Thus, a mutually reinforcing spiral of transatlantic trade and European reconstruction was set in motion, and functioned as an engine of growth for both sides.

Today it is not a vast demand abroad to which the U.S. economy is challenged to respond, but a tremendous capacity that has built up in Europe, Japan and the Newly Industrializing Countries. Due to these capacities, the United States is running a trade deficit of a previously inconceivable magnitude. In addition, the Reagan administration has embarked on a program of astronomical military spending resulting in unprecedented budgetary deficits. These developments could well imply a loss of economic leverage on the part of the U.S. government, making the attainment of its objectives abroad more dependent on political and military leverage. To this extent, new conflicts of interest with Western Europe will arise because continued militarization of U.S. foreign policy will increase the danger of tensions spilling-over from "out-of-area" conflicts to Europe. Such undesired spill-over could come about through U.S. efforts to influence Soviet behavior in one region of the world (somewhere in the "South") by applying pressure in another region (like Europe), or through the development of Western Europe as a logistic entity serving U.S. global strategies without substantial West European influence on strategy formulation and decision-making in concrete cases. In both respects, Western Europe is already being drawn into the global policy of the United States. As the controversy concerning the shipment of pipeline equipment to the Soviet Union demonstrated, West Europeans are quite aware that conflicts of interest arising from application of pressure on the Soviet Union are much higher for them than for the United States.

Such conflicts do not, however, point to a general polarization of interests in the relationship between Western Europe and the United States. The United States remain an economic giant with a remarkable ability to influence European economic development both in a negative and positive way. For instance, the high interest rates in the United States have led to a drain of capital from Europe which Europeans consider to be one of the causes of economic stagnation. On the other hand, the high price of the dollar has opened up export opportunities for the European countries to the United States which in some cases (like Western Germany) were by far the single most important source for their return to economic growth.

The West Europeans are confronted with the same ambiguity in the case of future technology policy and SDI. In the race for a new generation of technology—computers, biotechnology—the United States and Japan clearly lead the way, putting West European governments under high pressure to consider favorably the closer cooperation with the United States it offered in the context of SDI. However, given the ongoing attempts by the U.S. government to restrict the international flow of technological information to deny the Soviets from participating in Western achievements, it is most likely that SDI technological cooperation would help the United States more to tap European capabilities than vice versa. In addition, it is much more costly to depend on civilian spin-off effects from military R & D than to achieve non-military technological advances by working directly on them. Therefore, it made sense when the Mitterrand government offered a European alternative to SDI—the Eureka program. However, the prospects for the closer West European cooperation envisaged in the Eureka program do not seem to be promising enough to convince all the West European governments that they do have an alternative to the militarization of R & D under the leadership of the United States in the context of SDI.

West-West politics and the differentiation of the Third World

Other factors also give substance to the search for a "European identity" in the world, and limit it at the same time. First and foremost, the post-war reorganization of the economic power constellation between the United States and Western Europe has been followed by the formation of an economic triangle, in which Japan has become the strongest corner-stone. There is no single European country that can match the Japanese economic potential today. But Japan has a decisive advantage, even over the combined West European economic potential, accruing from that the Japanese potential unfolds, just like that of the United States, in *one* country. It is, therefore, not hampered by the unnerving complications of multinational politics of the type practised in Western Europe.

Furthermore, Japan is only part of a Pacific challenge to Europe that has been building up for the last five or ten years from the Newly Industrializing Countries of the Far East. These countries have turned the incipient "Asian Drama" into something like a success story in comparison with other parts of the Third World like Africa and Latin America.[27] The impact of this success story has been enhanced by a "Pacific bias" in U.S. domestic politics under the dominance of west coast interests and, to a certain degree, also by the growing importance of the Siberian/Pacific resources for the Soviet economy. The Siberian/Pacific resources were opened up mainly with the help of European technology. But Japanese firms are advancing in this realm and may well help to give the flow of resources from this vast land mass a new direction—toward the East.

These converging developments may lead to the formation of a new center of gravity of the world economy and world politics that would bring with it the danger of a final marginalization of Europe. The Pacific challenge, therefore, is of the utmost importance for the future of Western Europe. Meeting the Pacific challenge will absorb so much public attention and practical skills that, almost by necessity, the East-West conflict in the Third World will lose much of its impact on policy formulation vis-a-vis Third World countries.[28]

The tendency of the East-West conflict to decrease in significance is strengthened by the continuing differentiation of political and economic interests and objectives which Third World governments pursue at the international level today. To be sure, at present there is a more systematic engagement of "real socialism" in the Third World than there was ten years ago. But this engagement is not the expression of striking advances in the attempt to streamline the world in accord with the conceptualization of progress preferred by "real socialism." On the contrary "real socialism," just like the West, has reached the limits of its influence and power vis-a-vis Third World governments and societies.[29] The days of an easy going anti-imperialist optimism, which culminated at the time of the Havana summit of the Non-Aligned Movement in 1979, are gone because it has become quite clear that socialism in Third World countries has had as hard a time to survive *with* Western help as *without* it.

As discussed earlier, reference to the East-West dimension of North-South relations is justified due to the universality and globality of capitalism and socialism. But with a view to the ongoing political and economic differentiation within the Third World, within the OECD group, and also among socialist countries and countries with a socialist orientation, such references usually involve a fair amount of ideology designed to justify intervention or other forms of coercion as action in accord with the right to individual or collective self-defense.[30] The West Europeans could, of course, try to foster their own interests in the

Third World by defining them as part of the struggle between the two world systems. But first, as the experiences of the past ten or fifteen years have shown the socialist orientation of a Third World country does not at all infringe upon its interest to retain or even intensify its economic relations with Western countries. Socialism may even open up special opportunities for those who, like the West Europeans in the face of increased international competition, are very much interested in growth *and* stability of international economic relations.

Second, for Western Europe, trade and economic cooperation with socialist countries has become a matter of routine. Hence it would not be very convincing or practical to politicize economic relations with certain Third World countries because they pursue a policy of socialist transformation. Where there is such a politicization of economic relations, it usually has much more to do with intra-alliance politics than the actual developments in the Third World.

Third, within Western Europe, socialist political groups have played and continue to play an important role (while they play no role at all in the United States). The existence of these political groups has made West Europeans more willing to retreat from a monolithic interpretation of socialism and to accept the fact that there are not only many roads to socialism, but also many forms of socialism, and many forms of social organization that fit neither of the established categories.

In sum, it is very unlikely that Western Europe will eventually find it more profitable to return to a rigid, fundamentalist anti-communism than to try to broaden its relations with Third World countries regardless of their social order.

Global Détente and Western Europe: The Record of the Search for a "European Identity"

The main conclusion to be drawn from the preceding pages is that the reassertion of Europe and the search for a "European identity" in the world are not expressions of a passing mood or of a short term irritation in Euro-American relations. Rather, they express long-term interests. East-West systemic competition is only one of various other settings in which these interests are being defined. Other fora are the dynamics of nation state politics, the reorganization of the economic power constellation within the OECD group, the Pacific challenge to Europe, and a growing differentiation of interests and objectives pursued by Third World political forces on the international level. However, despite all the activities which have developed since the early seventies, the contours of a European identity in the world remain rather blurred and the record of achievements is mixed.

The search for a "European identity" in the world, officially, was considered an attempt to correct the former imbalance between inward and outward directed activities of the EC. In addition, the idea was advanced that such a search could become a new moving force in the progress of European unification.[31] This interpretation of the new outward directed activities did not go unquestioned, especially in connection with the enlargement of the European Community when critical thoughts about the nature of European integration and its functions for the member states and the outside world were being voiced. Such thoughts were developed in the thesis formulated by Johan Galtung that the EC was "a superpower in the making,"[32] on its way to becoming a world power that would fortify the existing structures both in the East-West and the North-South contexts instead of helping to discard them.

The superpower thesis has some appeal, especially within the academic community. But it was soon shown to be overstating or overdramatizing actual developments. Contrary to the expectations of those who hoped that the search for a "European identity" in the world would help to overcome the crisis of integration, the crisis deepened in the following years and even hampered the search itself. In this respect, the failure of the member states to come to grips with the problems of agrarian overproduction that threaten the very existence of the Common Market is of special concern. At the same time, the outward-directed activities, while multiplying, were not very effective. The Euro-Arabian dialogue was of little help in establishing Europe as an effective actor in the Middle East. Indeed, it began to fade in the early eighties when oil lost much of its power as an economic weapon. Also, the global concept of the Mediterranean did not materialize, and the European contribution to crisis management in the Third World at large remained marginal and, for a good part, was reduced to commissioning reports and issuing declarations with modest practical impact.[33]

Nevertheless, in principle, there are a number of arguments pointing to what Karl Mannheim called the "substantial rationality" of a continued search for a more independent role for Western Europe in the world. The first argument is one deriving more or less from the dynamics of power politics: a more independent role for Europe in world politics would, by definition, lead to a further multi-polarization of international relations. It could thereby help to pave the way for the establishment of a new system of checks and balances in world politics which is urgently needed to cushion the global struggle for hegemony among the superpowers.[34]

Second, West Europeans are realizing today that the chances for isolating themselves from conflicts in the Third World are diminishing insofar as superpower rivalry increases and the superpowers have the capacity for simultaneous military action in two or more world regions. Since superpower rivalry in the Third World does not manifest itself as such, but usually only in the context of concrete conflicts arising from conditions in the conflict area, the only dependable way to alleviate oneself from the danger of horizontal conflict escalation is to reduce the sources of conflict in the Third World. Europeans will have much to gain from a new global approach to détente which accepts social change in the Third World as such, and not merely as a tactical move in the East-West struggle. Reduction of global tensions, in the long run, would involve coexistence and preferably indirect or direct cooperation between the East and the West in the Third World. The chances for such a coexistence or cooperation at present are dim. But if there should be any advances in this direction, they are more likely to develop among the European allies of the superpowers than between the superpowers themselves. Global détente thence will enlarge the margin of action for self-determination in the Third World with a view to ideology as well as economic, technological and administrative capacities.

Notes

[1] Klaus Ritter, "Die Dominanz des Ost-West Konflikts," *Europa Archiv*, 1/1985, pp. 1-10.

[2] Daniel Yergin, *Shattered Peace: The Origins of the Cold War and the National Security State* (Boston, 1977); and Ernst Otto Czempiel, *Das amerikanische Sicherheitssystem 1945-1949* (Berlin, 1966).

[3] The Rio Pact of 1947 was the most visible expression of this transformation. Cf. *InterAmerican Conference for the Maintenance of Continental Peace and Security*, Report of the Delegation of the United States of America, (Washington, 1947); and *Ninth International Conference of American States*, Report of the Delegation of the United States of America with Related Documents, (Washington, 1948). Also cf. Lothar Brock, *Entwicklungsnationalismus und Kompradorenpolitik* (Meisenheim, 1974), pp. 150 ff.

[4] Cf. Henry Kissinger, *Memoiren* 1968-1973 (München, 1979), p. 182. For the German translation of the 1972 declaration on American-Soviet relations, see *Europa Archiv*, 27/1972, pp. D 289 ff.

[5] Henry Trofimenko, "The Third World and the US-Soviet Competition: A Soviet View," *Foreign Affairs*, Summer 1981, pp. 1021 ff.

[6] Cf. Alexander Dallin, "Soviet Policy toward the Third World," *Vierteljahresberichte* (Bonn), No. 91, March 1983; and Adrian Quelke, "Southern Africa and the Super-Powers," *International Affairs*, 4/1980. See also J. Seiler, ed., *Southern Africa Since the Portuguese Coup* (Boulder, 1980).

[7] In addition to the direct influence of the EEC on other regions' economic development, the EEC served as the example for effective regional integration.

[8] Alfred Pijpers, "European Political Cooperation and the CSCE Process," *Legal Issues in European Integration*, December 1984, pp. 135-148. Cf. Reinhardt Rummel and Wolfgang Wessels, eds., *Die Europäische Politische Zusammenarbeit* (Bonn, 1979).

[9] Claude Cheysson hailed the Convention as "unique in the world and unique in history." See *Frankfurter Allgemeine Zeitung*, February 4, 1975.

[10] Copenhagen Summit of the EC of 1973; cf. Europäische Gemeinshcaft, *Neunter Gesantbericht 1975*, Brussels 1975, pp. VI ff. (statement by Ortoli).

[11] Rather, it was reaffirmed with special vigor by socialist governments and parties in France, Italy and Spain.

[12] *EG Bulletin*, 1/1980, p. 9.

[13] *Bulletin PE 73862*, July 6, 1981, p. 23.

[14] Hans Adolf Jacobsen, "Bedingungsfaktoren realistischer Entspannungspolitik," Deutsche Gesellschaft für Friedens- und Konfliktforschung, ed., *Zur Entspannungspolitik in Europa*, Jahrbuch 1979/80, (Baden-Baden, 1980), p. 70.

[15] Conference of European and Latin American States, San Jose, Costa Rica, September 28-29, 1984; German text of communique is in *Europa Archiv*, 2/1985, pp. D 41 ff. Cf. also Hans J. Petersen, ed., *Die Beziehungen zwischen der Europüischen Gemeinschaft und Lateinamerika* (Baden-Baden, 1983).

[16] For a critical appraisal, see William M. LeoGrande, "Through the Looking Glass: The Report of the National Bipartisan Commission on Central America," *World Policy Journal*, Winter 1984, pp. 251ff.

[17] Reimund Seidelmann, "Die Sozialistische Internationale und Mittelamerika," Europa Archiv, 5/1985, pp. 145ff. Cf. Arnold M. Silver, *The New Face of the Socialist International* (Washington, 1981), and Paul E. Sigmund, "Latin America: Change or Continuity," *Foreign Affairs*, 3/1981, pp. 629ff.

[18] The German stand on Central America is determined much more by NATO politics than by actual developments in the area. Because of this linkage, there was speculation in 1982 that Americans had offered the Europeans a "horse trade" in that the U.S. would weaken its sanctions on the Euro-Soviet pipeline deal in return for restraint on the part of the Europeans in the Central America policy and especially with a view to aid for Nicaragua. Mark Schenker, "Umstrittene Entwicklungshilfe für Mit-

telamerika," *TagesAnzeiger,* October 18, 1982. The existence of such an offer was denied by a speaker of the EC. Nevertheless, Schenker's article was reprinted in Ministerium für Wirtschaftliche Zusammenarbeit, ed., *Spiegel der Presse* 22/1982, p. 695.

[19] Heidemarie Wieczorek-Zeul, Member of the European Parliament, ibid. Cf. also HansDietrich Genscher, "Europas Rolle in der Weltpolitik," *Europa Archiv,* 4/1982, p. 92.

[20] In a debate of the European Parliament on the North-South dialogue *Amtsblatt der Europäischen Gemeinschafte: Verhandlungen des Europäischen Parlaments,* Sitzungsperiode 1981-1982, Sitzungsberichte vom. 14-18, December 1981, pp. 126, 147, 150 (statements by Poniatowski, Focke, Ferrero).

[21] Katharina Focke stressed the crucial role of Europe in helping the global negotiations off the ground, ibid., p. 147/148.

The Future of East-South Trade
after UNCTAD VI

Colin W. Lawson

UNCTAD VI emphasised the peripheral position of the Soviet Union and Eastern Europe in world trade. The major proposals for changes in the institutions of world trade, aid and finance, foundered on the intransigence of the developed market economies, not on the caution of the Soviet position. Neither is it easy to imagine any Soviet initiative which would have been both realistic and effective in producing a consensus between the North and the South. Only a major programme of concessions by the Soviet bloc would have stood any chance of producing an important shift in the position of the developed market economies, and even then there would have been no certainty of that result. Such speculation is doubly hypothetical, for most countries which are members of the Council for Mutual Economic Assistance (CMEA) have neither the interest nor the ability to make such concessions. Whether or not UNCTAD will survive, whether or not it is replaced by more specialised, perhaps localised, forums, it is clear that CMEA support for the Group of Seventy-Seven (G77) proposals is almost wholly irrelevant to their success.

In the light of the failure of UNCTAD VI, following on from the unsuccessful UNCTAD V, and the disappointing UNCTAD IV, this is an appropriate time to ask what exactly are the benefits for the Third World in trading with CMEA states, to ask why such states are reluctant to make concessions in international trade negotiations, and to ask what is the likely course of future East-South economic relations. We do this by first asking two further questions: what is the role of trade and aid in centrally planned economies, and what are the interests of CMEA members in trading with the South. We then examine the CMEA position at UNCTAD VI, and relate it to the positions taken by the group at earlier meetings. From this we deduce the group's probable position in any future negotiations and discuss the advantages and disadvantages of trade with the East.

Trade and Aid in Centrally Planned Economies

The traditional description of the role of foreign trade in a centrally planned economy (CPE) was extremely simple, and could be encapsulated in the phrase "barter of residuals". Imports, so the story ran, were intended to fill the gaps in what would ideally have been a virtually autarkic system. Exports were simply the goods which were surplus to domestic requirements, and were scraped together to pay for imports. It really mattered very little what was the provenance of imports or the destination of exports, and, as hard currency was scarce, bilateral clearing agreements were extremely common.

Originally published in *Third World Quarterly*, vol. 6, no. 1, 1984. © Third World Quarterly; reprinted with permission.

Whatever truth there might have been in this description, applied to the Soviet Union under Stalin, it is a very misleading categorisation of CPEs today. Not only are the smaller CPEs of Eastern Europe much more trade-oriented than the Soviet Union, but in all CPEs trade has been long accepted as an important growth factor—though from a supply-constrained not a demand-constrained viewpoint. Even before the creation of the CMEA, trade had become an important thread binding Eastern Europe to the Soviet Union. Over time this intra-bloc trade pattern has been reinforced and sustained by, amongst other factors, an inability to produce goods of sufficient quality for sale outside the bloc to satisfy the bloc's demand for hard currency to purchase Western imports, and an intricate system of tariff and non-tariff barriers to trade.

Partly as a response to these difficulties in trade with the West, partly as an attempt to expand markets for their exports, and to diversify their sources of raw materials, CMEA states in the last decade have shown increasing interest in trade with the South. However, the level of such trade has not been as impressive as the parties had hoped. By 1980, trade with developing countries accounted for only 19 per cent of CMEA exports, and 16 per cent of imports. Admittedly starting from a very low level, trade with the South has become important only for Romania and the Soviet Union. For the South, apart from India, and some of the larger Middle Eastern states, trade with the East has remained of minor importance. Not only that, but in the main it has exhibited a very traditional pattern. The South trades raw materials, fuels, food and some semi-fabricates, for industrial products, particularly machinery. Capital flows from the East to the South have been minimal, and have often taken the form of self-liquidating loans, whereby turnkey plants have been paid for by the export of a proportion of their output. Provided, of course, that the price of the plant and its output are acceptable to the developing state, this form of medium-term capital investment has clear advantages over more traditional forms of capital inflow. But, as we shall see below, the East's record on aid is less satisfactory, and generally compares unfavourably with Western efforts.

While initial contacts between the East and the South almost invariably involved bilateral clearing arrangements, in recent years this system has rapidly changed and been replaced by clearance in convertible currencies. This has clearly been of benefit to both parties, just as the initial clearing arrangements also recognised their mutual interest in avoiding the use of scarce foreign exchange. But at a global level the near-universal change to settlement in convertible currencies has probably been of more advantage to the East. Desire for Western goods, coupled to difficulties of selling on Western markets, has often meant a CMEA deficit in trade with the West. That deficit has been financed in the past by borrowings on Western capital markets, and by convertible surpluses in trade with the South. As Western capital markets have been progressively closed to Eastern borrowers, the importance of such surpluses has increased.

When we come to examine the mutual interests of the East and the South in international trade negotiations, the foregoing description should prepare us for the judgement that they are rather limited. Just as increased access to Western markets unites the otherwise potentially disparate interests of the newly industrialising states with those of the remaining members of the G77, so it does the East with the South. The same applies to any other issue where the East might be included in any Western concessions to the South. The reverse applies to any issue where the East would be included with the West as a donor rather than a donee.

UNCTAD VI from the CMEA Viewpoint

We can begin to analyse the Soviet and East European position on UNCTAD VI, and to relate it to earlier policy stances, by disposing of two potential but actually unnecessary complications. First, in what follows any reference to a CMEA position should not be construed as including Romania. Although a member of CMEA, Romania has pursued an independent foreign economic policy for the past two decades. Nowhere has this been clearer than in UNCTAD negotiations, where Romania, after a long and vigorous campaign, finally joined the G77 just before the 1976 UNCTAD IV conference. Long before that meeting Romania was a vociferous supporter of the Group, and membership was an important step in its campaign to be recognised as a developing country.[1]

Second, in terms of UNCTAD meetings, we can speak of *the* Soviet and East European position, for not only have the Group D states issued joint policy statements and maintained a largely united stance, but it is difficult to see why they might have wanted to have differentiated their positions. Thus although the group position is clearly the Soviet position, and we have no information on what, if any, tensions have arisen in the development of the position, this is of no importance for it is clear that Group D policy is of direct advantage to all of its members.

Finance and Aid

On the first of the three issue areas of crucial importance to the South, the East was either impotent to help, or claimed that their current trading practices met, or more than met, the South's requirements. On the requests that the IMF increase its quotas and its SDR allocations, sell a significant part of its gold stock to finance the poorest developing countries, and increase its compensatory financing facility, the CMEA states, as non-members, were powerless to oblige. In response to suggestions for a new framework for dealing with external debt, the South was offered little more than the spectacle of ritual hand-washing. Certainly, no one could seriously claim that CMEA states have any responsibility for the debt problems of the South. Equally, no one could claim that the smaller East European states are in a strong position to incur extra debts at the expense of the South. Even so, some token concessions might have been expected from the Soviet Union, though in the past it is only fair to point out some willingness has been expressed, particularly by Hungary, to engage in bilateral discussions on debt relief.[2]

On the vexed question of aid, a curious *volte-face* occurred. In the past the East has totally rejected any suggestions that a predetermined proportion of GNP should be devoted to foreign aid. At UNCTAD IV the group, in their joint statement, argued that "it [is] unfounded to appeal to [us] to share the responsibility and material costs of eliminating the consequences of colonialism, neo-colonialism and the trade and monetary crisis of the capitalist economy".[3] As the problem was caused by capitalism and imperialism, "There can be no ground whatsoever for presenting to the Soviet Union and other socialist countries the demands which the developing nations present to the developed capitalist states, including the demand for a compulsory transfer of a fixed share of the gross national product to the developing nations by way of economic assistance".[4] A similar angry denial of responsibility followed the re-presentation of the aid demands at UNCTAD V, and during the 1980 Eleventh Special UN Assembly.

During 1982 the response to aid demands changed. In a speech to the Thirty-seventh Session of the UN General Assembly, A A Gromyko stated that "As to our participation in rendering assistance to the newly-free states in overcoming their backwardness, the Soviet Union does not do less but more than any industrial capitalist country".[5] However, even Soviet authors display some caution in dealing with this remarkable claim. For example, Samorodov is quick to hedge the claim by arguing that "The socialist countries do not compete with the industrial capitalist countries on the matters of rendering assistance for development purposes. The qualitative difference between the Western countries "aid" and the socialist countries technical and economic assistance. . . makes their quantitative comparison impossible".[6]

Other statements have been less cautious. Submitting a proposal to UNCTAD on behalf of the Group D countries, the East German government claimed that "the total net volume of the aid furnished by the socialist countries to developing countries is far higher, as a percentage of gross national product, than that furnished by developed market-economy countries".[7] No percentages are quoted in the above document, but in other UN documents the USSR has claimed that it "disbursed 1 per cent of GNP in net aid during 1976-80, with the net aid/GNP ratio at 1.3 per cent in 1980. Separately, the GDR claimed to have disbursed 0.78 per cent of "national income" in net aid in 1981".[8]

As with many questions of measuring aid, there is rather more involved in testing these claims than is immediately apparent. Neither Soviet nor East German sources have stated the precise methodology used to derive these results, but it seems clear that it is not the same methodology as that used to calculate Development Assistance Committee (DAC) members' contributions. The issue is complicated by several factors. First, the recipients of the bulk of CMEA aid are Cuba, Mongolia, Vietnam, Laos, Kampuchea and Afghanistan. The Soviet Union is, of course, quite open about the reasons for this. In an authoritative article written shortly after UNCTAD V, Bogomolov stated that "the socialist countries" cooperation with the developing world. . . is mainly extended to those countries that are most active in the national liberation struggle and have embarked on progressive political development".[9]

In addition to the main aid recipients noted above, Bogomolov singles out Iraq, Angola, Mozambique, Syria and Ethiopia as worthy of support. The concentration of aid flows to a handful of recipients, does not in itself complicate the assessment of the value of the flows. What complicates the assessment is the fact that many of the recipients are embryonic centrally directed economies, which implies that it is difficult to be sure that world market prices are used consistently in trade between themselves and other CMEA members. If world market prices are not used, then implicit subsidies are involved: subsidies which depend upon the deviation of actual from world market prices. And as the former price data is very difficult to acquire, so a reliable estimate of the implicit subsidies is exceptionally difficult to make.

A second problem with assessing comparative levels of aid arises because of the different levels of concessionality and tying of aid. A recent Foreign and Commonwealth Office report concludes that "Western aid commitments in 1981 carried an average grant of 90 per cent, and 97 per cent for the least developed (states). Only 37 per cent of Western aid was tied. . . The grant element of Soviet and East European aid was below 82 per cent and 79 per cent respectively in 1982. Virtually all. . . was tied".[10] The same report, in findings which are consistent with DAC research, concludes that in 1980 the Soviet Union's net aid to GNP ratio was 0.19 per cent, and the GDR's ratio was 0.17 per cent in 1981. Moreover, in 1981, although there was a positive flow of resources from the CMEA to Cuba, Mongolia, Vietnam, Laos, Kampuchea and Afghanistan, because of aid repayments, the flow of net aid to all other developing countries, viewed as a group, was negative.

Commodities

The most optimistic hopes of the G77 on this issue were that UNCTAD VI would hasten the ratification of the Common Fund so that it could become operational by January 1984; that it would encourage the implementation of the Nairobi Integrated Programme for Commodities; that negotiating conferences would be organised which would lead to agreements for cotton, copper, tin and hard fibres, and that preliminary negotiations would begin for other commodity agreements. Because of the lengthy delay in the ratification of the Common Fund, the UNCTAD Secretariat had put forward an interim Immediate Action Programme. This programme was aimed at keeping commodity prices within pre-set target ranges using buffer stocks and supply management. The price ranges were to be taken from the existing commodity agreements or to be derived from the average of the ten years to 1982. The programme was to be funded by multilateral institutions, financial markets and trade levies, rather than by the national governments who were seen as the main contributors to the Common Fund.

Although on this issue nothing of significance emerged from UNCTAD VI, it is worth noting that CMEA states showed no more enthusiasm for the proposals than did the market economies. In this, they have maintained a consistent position since the programmes were first mooted at UNCTAD IV. At that meeting they conceded that developing countries might reasonably ask for improved terms of trade, but they demanded that participants in commodity agreements should be free to choose whether to contribute to the provision of buffer stocks, or to sign bilateral long-term agreements. As most CPE-LDC commodity trade, though by no means all, is governed by such agreements, this would have reduced the cost of the Integrated Programme to CMEA members. Obviously there would still have been a cost, for not only are substantial purchases made through international commodity markets, but clearly developing countries might have been rather reluctant to commit themselves to long-term agreements where prices deviated substantially from the ranges of the main Integrated Programme agreements.[11]

The current Soviet position on the development of commodity agreements has been carefully stated by Polezhayev, in the house journal of the Soviet Ministry of Foreign Trade. He states that "the USSR's participation in international commodity agreements. . . will, as before, be decided in every concrete case with due regard for a just balance of the rights and obligations of the participants in agreements".[12] Moreover, he argues that when it comes to calculations of national contributions to agreements, because of the "planned, long-term and stable basis of intra-CMEA trade", it should be excluded for purposes of calculating interest in an agreement. It is clear from the article, and from other sources, that CMEA states have scarcely a minimal interest in extending the scope of commodity agreements—certainly no more interest than market economies.

Trade

It is perhaps in the general area of trade policy that the most ambitious long-term proposals of the G77 were made. These proposals, elaborated in draft UNCTAD resolutions, called for reduced protectionism on the part of the developed states; demanded improved facilities for structural adjustment; called for more generous GSP concessions and suggested that not only should UNCTAD monitor progress on these issues, but that it should also formulate the principles and rules for a new international trade system.

Taking the issue of protectionism first: when trying to evaluate CMEA statements it is crucially important to bear in mind two related points. First, with the exception of part of Hungarian foreign trade, all CMEA members make centrally managed trade decisions. Not only is the domestic user of an imported good separated from the foreign supplier by the administrative organs of the Ministry of Foreign Trade, but external and internal prices may bear only an erratic relation to each other. The final, and indeed often the initiating decision to import, lies with the ministry or its foreign trade organisations. Thus domestic consumers, both final and intermediate, cannot be certain that their preferences will be reflected in the import bill. Neither can foreign suppliers be assured that their price signals penetrate into the domestic CMEA market.

The second point follows from the first. The existence of detailed external tariff systems in CMEA states, indeed the existence of GSP and other schemes of tariff concessions, in no sense implies that the recipients of such concessions can look forward to increased sales. Whether we view such tariffs as window dressing, sham bargaining counters, or convenient devices to tax the surplus of the domestic economy, is immaterial. Only a signed agreement for increased imports, at an enhanced price, might signal a concession. *Might*, because even then we would want to be sure that any balances could be cleared in convertible currency.

In the light of these points, some CMEA statements read rather oddly. A statement submitted by Czechoslovakia on behalf of Group D argued that "It is possible. . . to maintain the existing posture—that is, to continue the drift towards protectionism, discrimination and managed trade, or to attempt to discontinue and eliminate the protectionist measures and practices which unnecessarily inhibit trade and to evolve responsible, more liberal. . . policies. The socialist countries favour the second option".[13] What is being suggested is that developed market economies should lower tariff and non-tariff barriers to both developing states and CMEA members. This view is supported by the statement of A Manzhulo, a Soviet Deputy Minister of Foreign Trade, who indicates that claims by developing countries for special status, and for reduced discrimination "should be considered in the context of the overall problems of principles, rules and norms of international trade". He would be happier if "UNCTAD's efforts could be concentrated on evaluating how the established principles and rules are being observed. . . [and] on identifying the actual difficulties, processes and causes hindering the normal development of international trade with due regard for the interests of all nations, those of the developing states particularly".[14]

This clear desire to introduce the question of discrimination in East-West trade into UNCTAD discussions is a theme which runs back at least to UNCTAD IV, and links in with the issue of UNCTAD's role amongst international agencies. Manzhulo criticises some Western countries for wanting no more discussion of East-West trade in UNCTAD. Indulging perhaps in wishful thinking, he calls UNCTAD "a universal trade agency", adding that "Any possible reorganisation of the UNCTAD should be aimed at raising its efficiency as a universal trade and economic forum".[15] This statement precisely echoes the concerns of the Soviet Minister of Foreign Trade, N S Patolichev, seven years earlier at UNCTAD IV, when he said that "we. . . do not opt out [of] a possibility of transforming [UNCTAD] into a World Trade Organisation, with its terms of reference covering also GATT problems".[16] At that time Western opposition to the proposal was based in part upon the view that such matters were better dealt with through the GATT, in part upon a reluctance to discuss such issues in a forum where their economic power would not be reflected in a preponderance of votes. LDC opposition reflected a reluctance to allow discussion of issues which would distract attention from their own problems. It is possible that developing countries might now be willing to support the CMEA on this issue—as a way of broadening the constituency of those willing to give UNCTAD executive authority. However, as on all other issues, the opposition or indifference of the developed market economies has doomed the proposal.

Conclusions

In this paper it has been argued that the aftermath of UNCTAD VI provides an appropriate opportunity to assess the state of East-South economic relations. For both partners, the economic exchanges which generally began less than two decades ago, provided a convenient alternative to, in one case, continued dependence upon traditional export markets, in the other, the vicissitudes of trading with political opponents. The development of East-South trade has been less spectacular than the parties hoped, and this to a large extent is the responsibility of the East. Responsibility, only in the sense that its exports of manufactured goods and machinery proved less attractive than it had hoped, and that its own traditions of group self-sufficiency militated against any important integration with the South, through specialisation. Thus, the trade pattern between the two blocs has remained very traditional, and as the South's manufacturing capacity increases, this will not only place a brake on direct exchanges, but will lead to increased competition in third markets. In contrast to earlier sanguine expectations for East-South trade, by the end of the 1970s Bogomolov was regretting that the CMEA share in the South's trade "has not yet, however, become a stable enough trend and tends to fluctuate greatly in response to the world market".[17]

In the period since exchanges began, the Soviet Union's attitude to the South has undergone a radical change: from an almost blanket support for Third World states and independence movements, to a cautious, qualified position which sometimes approaches the agnostic. The UNCTAD negotiations of the past decade have provided a powerful stimulus to Soviet and East European thinking about the South. The consequence of this is an increase in the sophistication of Soviet analyses of the South, and the development of an acute sense of the issues on which the interests of the two groups coincide, but more importantly of those on which they diverge. In part, this recognition flows from a growing awareness of the heterogeneity of developing countries: a recognition which has led to a rejection of the previous orthodoxy that the East and the South were natural allies. It is in the light of this reassessment that Bogomolov has written, "The relations between socialist and developing countries do not rest on the principle of socialist solidarity, since the majority of the developing countries are developing along capitalist lines and only a few have taken a socialist orientation. There are no grounds, therefore, to claim the presence of class solidarity between them and the socialist countries".[18]

If it is true that at UNCTAD VI the G77 presented less ambitious proposals, and presented them in a less antagonistic manner, to win minimal but tangible concessions, then the strategy failed. It is likely that at that time the power disparity between the North and the South was sufficient to exclude the possibility of a successful strategy. Indeed, it is doubtful that such an extensive, complicated global negotiation is the most effective way of pressing the Group's case. If in future such negotiations are conducted on a regional, even bilateral basis, the probability of concessions may be higher, for then individual developed states may be more willing to reveal their preferences, and spell out their own particular reciprocal demands. For negotiations with the East, such smaller scale bargaining is probably essential to win concessions. In specific group to group, or state to state negotiations, CMEA countries cannot adopt the "bit part" roles they have been happy to assume at global negotiations. In addition, such bilateral negotiations can concentrate on the specifics of trade exchanges, in both monetary and physical terms, unhindered by such issues as tariff reductions or a restructuring of the world financial system, which have no direct impact on East-South trade. Should this occur, at least one positive development will have emerged from the Belgrade fiasco.

Notes

[1] The Romanian strategy is analysed in Colin W Lawson, "National Independence and Reciprocal Advantages": the political economy of Romanian-South relations", *Soviet Studies*, 35(3),July 1983.

[2] See C W Lawson, "Socialist Relations with the Third World: a case study of the New International Economic Order", *Economics of Planning* 16(3) 1980, for a general discussion of this issue.

[3] Joint statement by the Socialist Countries at the Fourth Session of the United Nations Conference on Trade and Development, p 14; in supplement to *Foreign Trade* (September 1976).

[4] "On the Restructuring of International Economic Relations"; statement by the Soviet Government to K Waldheim, UN Secretary-General, 4 October 1976, *Foreign Trade* (December 1976). pp 2-5.

[5] Quoted in A Samorodov, "UNCTAD VI: monetary and financial problems", *Foreign Trade* (May 1983), p 41.

[6] *Ibid.*, p 41.

[7] German Democratic Republic: UNCTAD, TD/L.230,18 June 1983,p.11.

[8] Foreign and Commonwealth Office, "Soviet, East European and Western Development Aid 1976,82", Foreign Policy Document No.85, 1983, summary.

[9] O Bogomolov, "CMEA and the Developing World", *International Affairs* (Moscow) July 1979, p 32.

[10] FCO, *op. cit.*, summary.

[11] See Lawson (1980), *op. cit.*

[12] V Polezhayev, "UNCTAD VI: some problems in commodity trade",*Foreign Trade* (April 1983). p 22.

[13] Czechoslovakia: UNCTAD TD(VI)/C.2/CRP.1, p 5.

[14] A Manzhulo, "The 6th UNCTAD Session: objectives and tasks", *Foreign Trade* (April 1983), p 19.

[15] *Ibid.*, p 20.

[16] N S Patolichev, statement by the Head of the USSR Delegation to the Fourth UNCTAD Session, p 9; *Foreign Trade* (July 1976), pp 2-9.

[17] Bogomolov, *op. cit.*, p 27.

[18] *Ibid.*, p 24

The 'Non-Capitalist Road' to Development: Soviet and Eastern European Prescriptions for Overcoming Underdevelopment in the Third World

William Graf

The general concept of *a* non-capitalist road to development (ncr) is an analytical construct, produced by historical reality, to account for the fact that Marxist-based revolutions in this century have not occurred at the peak of a series of stages of socio-historical evolution leading through the full development of the productive forces of advanced capitalism. Lenin's notion of the "weak link" of capitalism, Trotsky's "law of combined development," and Stalin's strategy of "socialism in one country" all represent attempts to come to terms with, and indeed to rationalize and prescribe a revolutionary theory and strategy for undeveloped and underdeveloped areas in the world capitalist system. The theory of *the* Non-Capitalist Road (NCR), building upon but simultaneously transforming the ncr, has been formulated by Stalin's successors as a set of prescriptions evolving over time for socialist-oriented development in the "Third World." With all its variations and nuances— socialist orientation, the national liberation movement, the state of democratic revolution, etc.—it has become something like a leitmotif in the official thinking of the Soviet Union and the People's Democracies in Eastern Europe as a theoretical-ideological underpinning of policies, tasks and prescriptions *for* the South—entirely analogous to the role of modernization theories in the West. And like the ncr, it represents an ideological concession based on a realization that much of the Third World is not (yet?) capable of rapid socialist transformation and that the world capitalist system still functions in some measure as a dominant global force.

In this paper,[1] I first attempt to "reconstruct" the theory of the Non-Capitalist Road from a variety of complementary and occasionally contradictory East European sources. This admittedly tenuous and to some extent subjective endeavour is intended to clarify and elucidate the premises and analytical-ideological core of the theory, which it necessarily simplifies without, one hopes, oversimplifying. An important aspect of this process is to achieve an adequate "periodization" of the evolution of the NCR, since locating it in a temporal and power-political context helps to impose some conceptual order on a number of ostensible inconsistencies and departures. The argument leads into a critical analysis of the functions, interests and effects of the theory, its "fit" with Southern needs and conditions, and its correspondence with the wider complex of state-socialist policies and goals. Throughout, the method of analysis is that of immanent critique, which I take to mean as unbiased an examination as possible of the actual theory, based on its own content, values and prescriptions. While this in no way is to advance a claim to objectivity, it does mean

Published for the first time in this volume.

eschewing any attempt at *a priori* reasoning based on predetermined categories or ideological predispositions.[2] In other words, I will try to present the NCR on its own terms and criticize it within the framework of its proclaimed norms and goals.

The Need for Theory

During the two decades of socialism in one country, the Soviet experience of development was in itself a sufficient model of the non-capitalist road to development, and the Leninist theory of imperialism, revolution and monopoly capitalism an adequate theoretical-ideological explanation for relations between the Soviet Union and the Third World. Before the Second World War, the Soviets' capacities were, apart from their leading role in the Communist International, necessarily directed toward domestic development and the creation of the material preconditions for the transition to socialism. Under the circumstances, Soviet prescriptions for overcoming underdevelopment amounted to vague recommendations for an international anti-imperialist front combined with emulation of the Soviet model: anti-capitalist revolution under the direction of a vanguard party, forced capital accumulation by the state, centralized economic planning and control, mass mobilization guided by democratic centralism, a cultural revolution (as part of the latter) to eliminate illiteracy and traditionalist attitudes, and a system of labour rationalization and intensification.

But after 1945, the changed constellation of world political forces placed the Soviet Union squarely at the intersection of two fundamental historical-political movements—the East West and North-South conflicts. The Soviets rapidly emerged from the period of relative isolation and underdevelopment into the role of hegemonic power in a world communist movement encompassing one-third of the world's population, including the "Third World" countries of China, North Korea and North Viet Nam. At the same time, the postwar period also produced a great variety of independence movements, national liberation fronts and freedom-seeking parties which, despite their diversity, were moving toward an anti-imperialist strategy in that their central goals could be realized only in opposition to the then prevailing system of direct colonialism.

Partly for reasons of ideological ossification, partly because of the material constraints of postwar reconstruction, but mainly inspired by the rapid and successful dissemination of the communist model, the Soviet Union under Stalin persevered in prescribing a Soviet-style non-capitalist road for the decolonizing countries. The assumption underlying this prescription was that "socialism" *had* now been achieved in the USSR, in record time and against imperialist opposition, and was therefore a, if not the sole, model suited to emulation. For Stalin, therefore, the bipolarity of the Cold War directly and unambiguously translated into North-South policy: either a country/party/ movement was in the imperialist camp, in which case it was left more or less to its own devices, or it was in, or inclined towards, the socialist camp and thus deserving of Soviet support, aid and protection from foreign capitalist powers, all of which however, for reasons already suggested, were relatively modest.

Stalin's successors, Khruschev in particular, set out to expand Soviet influence in the South. The "arrival" of the Soviet Union as a superpower, its advances in scientific technology (nuclear weapons, Sputnik), the growth in number and size of communist movements world-wide, and the intensification of the decolonization process throughout the fifties made an increase in the Soviet presence in the South both desirable and feasible. Partly on an *ad hoc* basis, and partly by design, Khruschev transformed the USSR—and in its train the People's Democracies—into a principal actor in North-South relations, from 1953 trade agreements with India and Latin America to 1954 credits to Afghanistan, to the 1955 "B & K" tours up to the substantial aid programmes granted to Indonesia and Egypt in 1956.

The ideological rationale surrounding these foreign policy incursions into the South was at once less consistent and more nuanced than had been the case under Stalin. On one level, Khruschev's policy represented a revision of Stalin's bipolarity thesis. The new global orientation conceded that even those developing countries following a capitalist road were important to Soviet economic, political or strategic interests, since their independence struggles objectively contained certain anti-imperialist tendencies. If such countries could be induced merely to remain neutral—perhaps even brought into a common anticolonial front—this in itself would work to the advantage of the socialist camp, since this "would den[y] capitalist states the monopoly of influence in the Third World, contribute[. . .] to quickening a self-assertive consciousness among the less developed countries, and identif[y] the USSR with the liberationist aspirations of these states."[3] At this level, the means appropriate to the theory included relatively untied aid, assistance for mega-projects in the South (Aswan Dam) as visible evidence of Soviet largesse, and active support for Third World states in their struggles against neocolonial powers (Egypt during the Suez crisis). At the same time, Soviet policies often tended more toward reinforcing friendly bourgeois regimes, even where these were involved in persecuting local communist revolutionaries. Thus even while Khruschev in 1955 was praising Nehru's accomplishments, the CPI was engaged in a serious struggle with the Congress Party. The corresponding theoretical framework for a broad, anti-imperialist alliance between the socialist countries and Third World neutrals was formulated at the XXth Congress of the CPSU with the notion of a global "Zone of Peace"—an extension of the concept of peaceful coexistence enunciated there—comprising these areas.

But on another level, Soviet policy toward the South was also frankly political. In some ways, in fact, Khruschev's policy was more consistently radical-anti-imperialist than Soviet policy has been since, and the application of that policy clearly indicated that the ncr still dominated its prescriptions for overcoming underdevelopment. Aid and support were concentrated on Algeria, Iran, Ghana, Mali and, after 1958, Iraq, as well as Egypt—all states which, it was thought, were potential followers of the ncr and in any event had a strong anti-imperialist orientation. At this point, the two facets of Soviet strategy come together. Selective aid and moral support, coupled with an explicitly anti-imperialist propaganda campaign and a policy of economic competition with capitalism were aimed at nothing less than a fundamental shift in the postwar political status quo and the assertion of the Soviet position as chief articulator and main beneficiary of the revised world order.

In the heyday of Soviet self-confidence and expansion, these policies were relatively functional. But the failure of the USSR to overtake the West in terms of living standards and scientific innovation, combined with its weakening hegemony over international communism—the growing Chinese challenge, uprisings in Poland and Hungary—soon forced the Soviet leadership back toward ideological orthodoxy. For instance, the central revolutionary role of the peasantry which Mao recognized, and the importance of guerrilla warfare as advocated by Che Guevara and Ho Chi Minh, were negated by the Leninist adherence to the proletariat as the sole agent of anticapitalist revolution. Soviet ideology thus began to depart in some measure from actual Third World conditions. Moreover, the *ad hoc* quality of Khruschev's Southern policy left him open to charges of "adventurism" within. For one, he clearly overestimated the speed and efficiency with which socialism could be established, particularly in Africa. Promised revolutionary changes had not taken place, while the costs of supporting the non-capitalist roaders were mounting. Even where Soviet policy appeared to have been borne out, as in Cuba, the $1.5 M daily commitment of support was a substantial drain on Soviet resources.

Thus by the early 1960s, Soviet policy was confronted by the paradox of how to retain hegemony within the nominally revolutionary world communist movement while at the same time maintaining the global status quo of which it was rapidly becoming a central pillar. Attempts to resolve this paradox led directly to the formulation of the theory of the Non-Capitalist Road to Development. The 1960 Moscow Conference of Communist and Workers' Parties transformed the ncr into the NCR, and the theory was further elaborated and refined at the October 1961 XXIInd Congress of the CPSU. By 1963, R.A. Ulyanovsky articulated the systematized doctrine as ". . .that stage of social and economic development. . .in which by noncapitalist means the necessary preconditions for the transition to the construction of socialism are created."[4]

Reconstruction of the Theory—Primacy of the Political

The transition to the NCR as a prescription for development during the 1960s and since has rightly been described as a shift in tactics, from the communist *offensive* to the communist *model*.[5] This concept is useful because it places the NCR into a context of "normalizing" East-West relations, intra-communist differences and Soviet policy reverses in the Third World. With it, the "fit" between ideology and reality is a better one.

At the centre of the NCR stands the concept of the *socialist world system* whose very existence promotes socialism in the South. "Like a shield [the socialist camp] protects the liberated countries from the imperialists' blows, provides them with an example and moral sustenance, is a huge source of enthusiasm and renders economic aid."[6] Thus, the socialist world system functions as an international proletarian avant-garde,[7] as a reliable mentor and protector. It is posited as the strongest, and most determining of the three revolutionary currents in the contemporary world; the others, the international working class in the capitalist countries and the national liberation movements, stand together with international socialism in objective and subjective opposition to imperialism.

This progressive array of anti-imperialist forces suggests two important corollaries. *Explicitly*, the revolutionary struggle is being increasingly internationalized: "Every revolutionary change in an individual country is today simultaneously an international factor. And vice-versa— the totality of international factors is expressed in the development of the socialist struggles of the individual countries."[8] Since this strong, progressive socialist camp has forced decolonization, opposes neocolonialism and exerts a magnet effect on countries striving for independence, it has also caused the advanced capitalist powers to band together in a defensive alliance under US hegemony. Nevertheless, these powers have been compelled to mitigate their classical forms of exploitation of the South and to seek new methods of imperialism, deployed collectively. *Implicitly*, therefore, the NCR also represents a substantial revision of Lenin's thesis that intra-imperialist rivalry is the primary contradiction in the world system.[9] Rather, the conflict between world socialism and world capitalism, particularly as it is enacted in the Third World, has emerged as the primary contradiction, and indeed, capitalist countries are continuously constrained to maintain a united front in the face of socialist solidarity. Hitherto, international contradictions of this magnitude have produced world wars; but technology too, especially arms technology, has progressed so far as to render global conflicts into a zero-sum game. Even the imperialists have come to realize this. Besides, where wars do occur, socialism inevitably gains, as after World Wars I and II. Thus, capitalist-socialist rivalry in the South must be carried out within a context of peaceful competition, the outcome of which naturally favours the socialist camp.

It is this evolving world order that provides the preconditions for developing countries to follow an accelerated capitalist path to development. At this point, the theory becomes rather murky, not least of all due to the differentiated nature of the phenomenon with which it attempts to come to grips. Setting aside several nuances, three often overlapping types of noncapitalist roads can be discerned:

(1) Outright adaptation to, and emulation of the Soviet development model— the ncr— is on the political agenda at any time, and remains the most desirable option for Third World countries. Such regimes *might* develop in countries where imperialism is forced to intervene directly (South Viet Nam) thus intensifying mass opposition under revolutionary leadership, or where for other reasons mass revolutionary enthusiasm is high (the Middle East, certain areas in Latin America).[10] Here, the Leninist concepts of the weak link of the capitalist system, the specificity of individual revolutionary situations, the global nature of the anti-imperialist struggle are obviously still held to be valid. They apply in particular to the less developed "countries" at the periphery of the USSR itself (Mongolia, Uzbekistan, Kazakistan, Transcaucasia, the Soviet North and Far East, etc.) as well as isolated cases such as North Korea, North Viet Nam and (until the late 1960s) the People's Republic of China. A crucial factor is that the revolution should be led by the proletariat who in Soviet theory are the one consistent revolutionary class on account of their social position and objective interests. The ncr model, updated and marginally revised in the seventies as the "State of Socialist Orientation," is the one consistent variant of state-socialist prescriptions for Southern development.[11]

However, the merit of the NCR as ideology, as suggested above, is its recognition that a Marxist-Leninist revolution, for a variety of reasons (differences in resource bases, pace of industrialization, constellation of class conflict and collaboration, etc.), is not imminent in large areas of the South. It therefore allows for two further possibilities, according to the respective scale of capitalist penetration and consequent level of class formation.[12]

(2) Underdeveloped countries characterized by a low degree of class differentiation in which a capitalist class may exist, but does not yet determine the direction and intensity of development. Such countries may *bypass* the stage of capitalism entirely and proceed directly to socialism via the NCR.

(3) Third world countries where capitalist development is underway and a capitalist class exists in a ruling coalition with other pre- or non-capitalist strata. In this case it is necessary to *break off* capitalist development before advancing through the NCR.

Since developing countries today mainly fall into categories (2) and (3), especially the latter, they are of special interest to any analysis of the NCR and its related theories. As these categories suggest, the NCR explains and justifies both the bypassing and acceleration of the classical Marxian developmental scheme— or at least the vulgar Marxist simplification of it—of a historical progression from feudalism via capitalism to socialism. In other words, it can be theoretically demonstrated

. . .not only that one formation necessarily develops through revolution into another formation and one socio-economic structure is transformed into another, but also that they coexist and interact, and that it is possible to bypass in part or in full a historically transcended and hence superfluous stage of development.[13]

Under what conditions can pre-capitalist or incipient capitalist countries at the world periphery embark on a non-capitalist path?

A provisional answer to this question must start from a negation. The NCR is nowhere defined as a distinct socio-economic formation somewhere between Capitalism and feudalism, or between capitalism and socialism. It is, rather, a *transitional process* which, moreover, takes place at a different pace and with different components from country to country. Thus, there is no "formal" point of entry; countries may simply be proclaimed to be, or not yet to be, on the NCR. For all that, however, entry onto the NCR is first and foremost a political step. It can only be taken by a *political* movement - a more or less progressive elite coalition or other anti-imperialist grouping normally described as the National Liberation Movement (NLM)—seizing state power and establishing a State of National Democracy whose mission is to create the political, socio-economic, material-technical and cultural preconditions for a subsequent transition to socialism. In this sense, it is possible to speak of the *primacy of the political*, or the inversion of base and superstructure, since control of state power is the *conditio sine qua non* to economic development and with it the transformation of all other spheres of society. This will become apparent in what follows.

The National Liberation Movement, whose task it is to capture state power, varies considerably from country to country and reflects the economic deformations brought about by colonialism and neocolonialism. The merger of precapitalist forms of exploitation with those of colonialism resulted in the export of any surplus these economies produced and thus blocked the overall development of peripheral societies. As a result, several different modes of production existed, and exist, side by side with few organic linkages. Such heterogeneous, deformed, multi-sectoral economies produced a similarly uncoordinated lumping of social formations, from local-feudal and neocolonial-dependent groups to national and comprador bourgeoisies and progressive socialist movements. Thus, the formation of a modern class structure has also been blocked with no clearly profiled bourgeoisie or proletariat.[14] The challenge to the NLM then, is to mobilize the progressive elements within this social mosaic into a militant, aware, anti-imperialist force as a basis for the State of National Democracy. Though the composition of the NLM varies according to local conditions—and therefore cannot be dealt with in detail here[15]—its universal foundation is seen as "new nationalism" which, in an emergent nation seeking a development path to overcome the socio-economic blockages just alluded to, is *ipso facto* anti-imperialist and hence anticapitalist. There is therefore a "congruence of interests" between the industrialized socialist countries and the NLM, since both are located on the same side of the global struggle against imperialism. Both want continuing peaceful coexistence, need revolutionary changes and support proletarian internationalism.[16]

What distinguishes the National Liberation Revolution from Marxist-Leninist social revolutions is primarily its class basis. Since the distorted economic development of developing countries has not permitted the growth of a numerically significant proletariat, and since the bourgeoisie remains, in Andre Gunder Frank's telling coinage, a "Lumpenbourgeoisie," the peasantry presents itself as a mass base for an anti-imperialist revolution. Numerically representing the overwhelming majority, not yet bourgeoisified (i.e. not owing the land it works), and mainly feudally organized or even living in communal arrangements, the peasantry have a strong *objective* interest in national independence. Their interests are complemented by those of the mass of urban dwellers, particularly artisans, small traders, semi-proletarianized strata and a large "preproletariat" of mainly uneducated first-generation city dwellers, whose elementary goals can only be realized in opposition to imperialism. Leadership of the NLM, however, will have to be assumed by classes who are *subjectively* conscious of the inhibiting effects of the international class struggle, in particular the "civilian and military revolutionary-democratic intelligentsia."[17] Again, the composition of this crucial group necessarily varies, but may take in the urban petit-bourgeoisie, the technocratic intelligentsia, state employees, semi-proletarians in the cities, some sectors among the better-off peasantry, and most workers.

The theory attempts to take account of the limitations of this heterogeneous stratum but preserve it as a leading force by positing at least two radicalizing forces working on it constantly. For one, its continued mass legitimation is provided by peasants and workers; and merely to attempt to represent their interests is to be under permanent constraints toward more radical policies of redistribution and social justice. And second, the alliance, or at least cooperative arrangements with the socialist countries furnishes ready access to the experiences of scientific socialism as well as aid and advice at every stage. This assumed dynamic is an essential aspect of the entire NLM-NCR theory complex, since it does account for the non-existence of a large, militant proletariat, the relatively amorphous quality of class formation (and hence the low level of class struggle) and the necessity for a mass revolutionary basis to emerge *after* the revolution from out of the peculiar conditions of underdevelopment. This will be further dealt with presently.

Once the NLM has gained control of the National Democratic State, the Non-Capitalist Road to Development proceeds quasi-automatically, though subject to setbacks, reverses or plateaux. The centrepiece of the national-democratic stage is the *strong state*, since "the central issue of the Non-Capitalist Road is the issue of power."[18] Political power, concentrated in the hands of the variegated elements of the NLM, is the absolute precondition for the success of the NCR, because:

The special quality of the Non-Capitalist Road is that as it proceeds it solves not only the general democratic tasks but also several tasks of the socialist revolution. Not only does it eliminate the remnants of feudal relations, it also confines and even wipes out the capitalist economy by means of nationalizing foreign capital and contains the activities of private national capital.[19]

The NCR's mission, therefore, is a dual one: the elimination and/or containment of two modes of production. The strong state, created by what amounts to a revolution "from above," must be prepared for resistance from traditional interests and strata, and from both foreign and domestic capital. It thus must be invested with a certain degree of relative autonomy, standing in some measure above the society in which it functions. As a union of "all the healthy forces in the nation,"[20] it must conform to the imperatives of development and concentrate especially on (import-substituting) industry to establish the basis for a growing, balanced industrialization. If the state and cooperative sectors can expand rapidly and efficiently, not only the primary goal, development, will be realized within a comparatively short time perhaps even within a few decades[21]—but further social preconditions for the eventual transition to socialism will be created. A growing proletariat will furnish both the mass basis and driving force of socialism and at the same time prevent the national bourgeoisie from particularizing non-capitalist development. The peasantry, by being involved in the burgeoning state sector and by increases in its material and educational enablements, will be drawn into an alliance with the proletariat. The increasingly revolutionized masses will then act as a spur and inspiration to the other "national" classes, who will polarize into genuinely progressive and reactionary factions. The progressive elements among the "national" leadership, taking their cue from the masses and from their growing nationalist consciousness, will gradually form as a vanguard party and perceive a need for socialist ideology. Therefore:

Like iron to a magnet, left wing revolutionary democrats are drawn to scientific socialist theory and real existing socialism. The historic mission of revolutionary democracy in the "Third World" is to undertake the kind of socioeconomic transformations that will open the door to eventual socialist development. This is very feasible where the unity of all anti-imperialist forces is maintained, and where revolutionary democracy seeks the support of the socialist world system.[22]

Here, the importance of *mass mobilization* to the success of the NCR is evident. There exists in the NLM a sometimes more, sometimes lesser divergence of interests and outlooks between a composite elite that exercises hegemony and a mass on behalf of whom power is held. The resulting incongruence produces a need for constant mutual adaptation or "dialectic." The more rapidly mobilization and social consciousness are effected, therefore, the more likely is the NLM to proceed from the "stage of the revolution for the people" to the "stage of the revolution realized by the people." Conversely, the more the process is delayed or held back—e.g. by imperialist machinations or intra-elite rivalry—the more bleak are prospects for a successful completion of a NCR strategy. "This fact," write Ibrahim and Metze-Mangold, "demonstrates that the class character of the State of National Democracy cannot be determined solely according to *who* leads it, but to an equal degree according to the social *substance* that its concrete measures display."[23]

Of particular analytical relevance here is the fact that a pronounced element of subjectivism—perhaps "voluntarism"— inheres in the theory. There is nothing inevitable about either the class composition of the revolutionary-democratic state nor about the pace and effectiveness of mass mobilization in a progressive direction. Embourgeoisement is possible even as proletarianization proceeds. Reaction may temporarily defeat the movement toward socialism (Ghana, Indonesia). Thus in Nasser's Egypt the dynamics of the NCR were said to have produced an alliance among the leading potentially revolutionary cadres as against the masses, while in the People's Republic of Yemen there ensued a progressive proximation of base (mass following) and superstructure (political elite). However, as the State of National Democracy proceeds toward the fulfillment of its historical tasks—rapid development, creation of a proletariat, forging of links to world socialism, establishment of economic preconditions for socialism, etc.— the contradictions begin to resolve themselves as the progressive forces in the hegemonic alliance coalesce and carry the masses along with them. The now more self-confident, more autochtonous state, having expanded its domestic market on the strength of state-promoted accumulation and raised its level of domestic savings and investment, having as well rationalized agriculture and begun industrialization, would be in a position to "exploit" foreign capital in reverse, as it were. Since the imperialist countries for the time being represent the major source of capital accumulation on a world scale, and since the socialist countries would be faced by an impossible number of requests for aid and investment from the many new non-capitalist roaders—which is another way of accounting for a chronic shortage of deployable capital among the state-socialist countries—it would be possible, under the changed conditions, to utilize capital inflows and technology transfers from the advanced capitalist states for one's own purposes. The resultant more rapid development of the new socialist countries would in a sense make imperialism into a factor strengthening the very forces that will ultimately negate it.[24]

This exploitation of the profit motive by developing countries is of course based on a crucial—and basically non-demonstrable—assumption that the capitalist countries will continue to invest and grant aid to developing countries that nationalize foreign holdings, curtail profits and ally with the advanced communist countries. It also entails a constant political danger alongside its immense potential economic advantages, namely that the developing country adopting such a strategy may be subjected to regressive pressures. Here again, therefore, the major precondition for adopting this strategy is the strengthened state. Careful government regulation of both grants and credits from the West, it is assumed, will lead to further expansion of the state sector and a determining role for it in the national economy. Nevertheless, such capital and technology inflows must be scrupulously weighed beforehand and only accepted under certain well-defined conditions, for instance: (1) absence of any sovereignty-undermining provisions, (2) use of such funds to correct the deformed sectors of the economy, (3) efficiency of operations being financed must be greater than capital costs (interest, services, etc.), (4) markets, both domestic and foreign, must be assured for goods produced with the aid of foreign inputs, (5) bilateral government-to-government credits to be given preference over direct foreign investment in order to monitor the imported capital and ensure its utilization in the interests of national development, (6) joint ventures to be controlled by recipient state, (7) tax breaks, if granted, to be linked to firm time limits, and (8) all investments involve an obligation to train local personnel in the relevant technical and managerial skills.[25] In this way, industrial development and with it class formation of the proletariat and mass mobilization of the population will be accelerated, thus more rapidly eliminating the need for foreign investment/aid/technology, which can then be phased out.

These then represent in simplified form the main components of the NCR theory. To sum up this section, it is worth recalling that, far from a fixed, definable stage of socio-historical development, the NCR is a fluid, dynamic process—"not socialist development proper but a specific period of *creating* the material, social and cultural *conditions* for the transition to socialist development."[26]

Exigencies and Adaptations

Precisely this processual, transitional quality of the NCR model helps to explain its further differentiation and diffusion over time. The admission of foreign capital and technology, just described, is an initial example of the capacity of the theory to adapt to exigency, in this case to the limited availability of capital and know-how—and for that matter, lack of a broad, multi-sectored scientific-technological fund— in the actually existing socialist countries.

From the late sixties onward, external and internal factors have tended to transform and qualify the conditions under which the NCR was originally formulated. From about the fall of Khruschev until the mid-seventies, rigid bipolarity succumbed to peaceful coexistence, and the People's Democracies, faced with economic slowdown and internal structural problems, concentrated more on domestic savings and internal restructuring. At the XXIIIrd Congress of the CPSU, Brezhnev emphasized building communism at home as a precondition for getting on with "international tasks." "Moderation," "gradualism," "pragmatism," and, above all, "economic rationality" became the watchwords of communist development, while relations with the South were characterized more and more in terms of the "international division of labour" and "mutual advantage." The notion of *mnogoukladnost* ("multi-structured" or "multi-layered") was increasingly used to account for the diversity of the Third World and the complexity of state socialism's relations with it.[27] Among other things, these premises rationalized closer links between aid and trade, and the CMEA countries began to register a series of positive trade balances with the South. Indeed, such trade in the 1970s became an instrument to resolve certain problems and dysfunctions of Eastern European economies by means of such techniques as dumping, sale of obsolete technology, purchasing raw materials cheaply at fixed prices then selling them dearly on the world market, etc.[28]

Where Khruschev had held out the prospect of development within a generation, his successors have emphasized its gradual, protracted nature. The new leaders expanded the scope of Soviet foreign policy beyond active support for comparatively few regimes to include the capitalist roaders as well. In the mid-sixties, credits were allocated to Morocco, Nigeria, Iran, Malaysia, Singapore, the Philippines and several conservative Latin American countries. This pragmatic approach actually increased Eastern European prospects for cooperation with the South, since countries hitherto apprehensive about entering into relations with socialist states could now do so with less concern about ideological penetration.[29] Thus, from this perspective, the communist countries acquired a growing interest in the maintenance of the global status quo.

However, it would be rather simplistic to infer from all this that the state-socialist countries' policies toward the Third World somehow began to converge with those of the capitalist West. For one, the means were different. Where capitalism strives toward ownership of whole sectors of the economy and branches of production, state socialism attempts to establish a greater basis of equality between partners and does not seek a systematized extraction of surplus from the less developed countries. And second, although the NCR thus became an apologetic concept to justify, e.g., cooperation with repressive military regimes, an enhanced role in global arms trade, and dealings with reactionary, corrupt and even anticommunist governments in the Third World, massive support was at the same time forthcoming for revolutionary liberation movements. It is important to establish the existence of this two- or three-track model of communist relations with the South, since state-socialist policies cannot be neatly fit into any single category. Indeed, ambiguity and flexibility are the defining characteristics of the model as well as the policies emanating from it.

By the mid-seventies, Soviet economic growth, like economic development throughout the North, was hampered by the global economic crises that characterized this era. At the same time, the newly liberated NCR states in Africa (Angola, Mozambique, Ethiopia) as well as Afghanistan threatened to place impossible financial and military demands on Eastern Europe, even while some relatively advanced NCR states had regressed toward capitalism (Egypt) or fallen stagnant in their evolution toward socialism (Burma). In this context, several revisions to the theory (and hence to praxis as well) were called for:

(1) The two-camps/two-economies theory of the global economy yielded to the more realistic notion of interdependence within a growing international division of labour. Just as the Third World itself was differentiating into OPEC states, NICs, regressively under-developing areas, etc., so the mutual interdependence of all states advanced to the forefront of the theory. The 1974 *Great Soviet Encyclopaedia* confirmed this line of thinking:

In its initial form the world market was based on the capitalist mode of production and was the world capitalist market. At present the world market takes in the full international division of labor as practiced between the world's two socio-economic systems. The world market has expanded in scale as social production has become increasingly internationalized.[30]

(2) State capitalism emerged as a guiding concept. While state capitalism had been coined to apply to certain measures to be taken by the State of National Democracy, and related to state control of the key sectors of the economy, the notion was now coupled with an emphasis on economic incentives, market rationality and comparative advantage (where once state expansion, political rationality and import substitution respectively had made up the essence of the theory). Profitability, in this connection, became a norm and central prescription.

(3) Parallel to these, the role of actually existing socialism as mentor and protector was downplayed in favour of greater "collective self-sufficiency" (e.g. via the Group of 77) and "local self-reliance."[31]

(4) And finally, a "dialectical" dimension entered into several of the organizing concepts of the NCR theory. Nationalism, as a motive force, was no longer presumed to be simply and invariably progressive; it might also and equally operate to reinforce regressive petit-bourgeois class domination. Leadership in the national democratic coalition might therefore be personalistic and arbitrary rather than progressive and consolidating, particularly where neocolonial relations remained effective. Indeed, within each newly independent state, tendencies were at work both to combat imperialism and simultaneously to come to terms with it, and a given country might therefore be anti-imperialist *and* anti-Soviet.[32]

It is this shift in Soviet thinking—if not total revision, then certainly a re-ordering of ideological priorities—in line with changing conditions that leads Richard Lowenthal to speak of a paradigmatic transformation from "anti-imperialism" to "counter-imperialism," where the latter signifies a stable, growing, peaceful and rather complacent anti-imperialist bloc.[33] This counter-imperialist tendency has been reflected in Soviet approaches to the NIEO during the past decade: "The growing integration of the Soviet economy with an acknowledged single world market made Moscow lose zest for a radical restructuring of international economic relations for the benefit of the developing countries."[35] Whereas the communist countries began by supporting the South's demands for a NIEO, that support has been mitigated as the non-ncr South has increasingly styled the industrialized socialist countries as part of the same North against whose interest the NIEO must be realized. The Soviets and East Europeans have countered with several objections to the Brandtian NIEO, *viz.* (1) that it is indifferent to domestic reforms and thus maintains elite rule, (2) that it departs from universalistic principles and works to the exclusive interest of the South, and (3) that it is non-Marxist in as much as it has no anticapitalist goals, leaves the world capitalist economy intact and assists selected underdeveloped countries to develop into "subimperialist" powers.

The state-socialist countries have however consistently supported the non-aligned movement on the grounds that here the anti-imperialist interests of East and South intersect; but they have failed to put forward an alternative radical plan for restructuring global economic relations beyond a continuing advocacy of a leading Soviet role in the Socialist Community of States. In no small part, this failure is seen in the South as rooted in the new concern for gradual change, comparative advantage and world-market stability.

The renewal of the Cold War in the 1980s, coupled with Soviet reverses in agriculture and a shrinking economic base,have merely exacerbated these conservative tendencies and set off a substantial theoretical debate among scholars and politicians. More and more, the "pragmatists" are prevailing with their call for moderation, for a proper mix of state control and private enterprise—reminiscent of Lenin's NEP measures—and their advocacy of "national" capitalism as opposed to "dependent" capitalism.[36]

Analysis and Critique

It is not at all surprising, therefore, that the Eastern European politicians and ideologists find their NCR-based theories increasingly overtaken by world communist movements rooted in Southern conditions—not only by rivals such as Maoists or Guevarists, but by those who see themselves as proceeding along the Non-Capitalist Road as enunciated in the theories of actually existing socialism. For instance, Abdul R.M. Babu, the Tanzanian Marxist-Leninist, advocates an instant revolutionary transformation for Africa based on a presumed militant proletarian class consciousness.[37] The Secretary-General of the Yemeni Socialist Party has also argued for rapid and complete withdrawal of his country from the world capitalist system on the strength of aid and cooperation from the socialist countries.[38] And the Mozambiquean delegate to UNITAR has made a strong and implicitly critical plea for more Soviet assistance in the immediate construction of socialism.[39]

Precisely these kinds of statements, emanating from regimes subjectively following the NCR, tend to undermine the central theoretical proposition and ideological strength of the NCR, namely the anti-imperialism-grounded identity of interests between developed socialism and the Third World. While this premise basically still applies, the socialist division of labour deduced from it and the increasingly divergent views about the timing and intensity of the NCR are nevertheless potential sources of conflict.

Moreover, the Soviet Union also operates as a great power and the Eastern European People's Democracies as components of a power bloc. As such their interests structurally depart in important ways from those of the South. Communist support for despotic, corrupt or anticommunist regimes in the Third World has already been alluded to. Certainly the model, already broadly conceived, is subject to pressures of diplomatic, power-political and economic exigency. Thus if one sets aside the temporal dimension, the NCR appears to contain a whole series of contradictions, as summarized by Clarkson:

. . .there can be no development under capitalism vs. there must be more capitalist development; the proletariat is weak and lacks class consciousness vs. the proletariat must lead an alliance with the peasantry; imperialism resists third world industrialization vs. imperialist aid facilitates important industrial development; independence can only be achieved by breaking ex-colonial ties with imperialism vs. independence is only relative and will grow while maintaining trading relations with the West; the rural bourgeoisie is the enemy of agrarian development vs. the rural bourgeoisie is leading capitalist development in the countryside.[40]

Conversely, this apparent eclecticism finds its counterpart in the tendency in the South to take from the model what is required for local needs. For Nehru it helped to resolve the nationality question and promote industrialization through economic planning; for Nkrumah its attraction was the disciplined one-party system; and for Sekou Touré it provided a strategy of state control of foreign aid.[41]

Another way of examining the NCR paradigm is to recall that it has been formulated in the state-socialist countries, more or less as official ideology, on the basis of their observations of structures and processes prevailing in the South. As such, the NCR is a Northeastern prescription for world order. All its main components—strong state, "modernizing" elite, mass mobilization, socialist orientation—relate isomorphically to the Soviet experience of development and, whichever actual road may be taken due to local conditions, ultimately converge with the interests of the developed communist states whose social, economic and political system it will sooner or later proximate. In fact the theory expressly precludes (1) a "Third Way" or "convergence" of communism and capitalism in Third World societies,[42] (2) development strategies founded on the "basic needs" of the majority of the population, since these are considered to be "utopian,"[43] and (3) any notion of an absolute North-South or "rich-poor" dichotomy in the world system, which masks the real coincidence of interests between East and South and makes actually existing socialism part of the problem rather than the solution.[44]

The theory also precludes a fourth developmental approach: any reliance on traditional values, beliefs, institutions or ways of life as a basis for indigenous or autocentric development. Apart from isolated references to communal ownership, all "precapitalist relations"—which are usually styled as feudal despite the allusions to communal property—are clearly and unambiguously a hinderance to development. Parasitism, corruption, inertia, unproductivity and immobilism are the defining characteristics of this stage, which the NCR means to overcome with a total transformation of "backward" society into an integrated, mobilized, developing society.[45]

The NCR is further hampered by a very imprecise class analysis. The dynamics of the National Liberation Movement are presumed to produce a progressive tendency within its leadership. Yet in practice most Third World liberation regimes have developed into a single party (or military establishment) serving few interests but their own. Far from mobilizing the masses for socialist development, these elite agencies consciously aim at depoliticization, self-aggrandizement and braking any trends toward popular participation in economy and society. Similarly, state capitalism in the South has by and large made the state into a collective capitalist functioning for the benefit of a growing state elite (as in India, Mexico, Nigeria, Argentina, Brazil and the Shah's Iran, to mention a few prominent examples from the literature on the NCR). Rather than acting as an instrument in the transition to socialism, therefore, the state in most cases has become a mere facilitator and legitimator of capitalist development.

Even the NCR's reliance on the "national" elements of the underdeveloped state is highly problematic, since it assumes a link between nationalism and progressiveness. But those groups which are made up of representatives of all the ethnic groups, religions and sectors of society—almost by definition an elite in any case—within the arbitrary, colonially drawn boundaries, may be anything but dynamic and progressive, as the state elites of Nigeria or Indonesia (military or civilian) clearly demonstrate. While such groups often *are* the "modern" harbingers of "national sovereignty" as against neocolonial domination,[46] they are just as often induced to act as compradors, local agents of foreign capital, or counter-revolutionary forces. The NCR's adherence to such categorical concepts too often leads it to ally with repressive, reactionary or particularistic elites at the expense of supporting subnational groups—the Eritreans, Kurds or Pushtus for example—who may represent more progressive revolutionary forces. A more literal interpretation of the logical consequences of this notion would suggest the local military to be the ideal agent of the NCR. Indeed, Bassam Tibi argues that most National Democratic States said to be on the Non-Capitalist Road are in fact military regimes, few of which actually qualify as agents of an NCR-type regime.[47]

Recently, a few authors[48] have begun to abstract the essential features from the NCR—the strong state, an educated and conscious vanguard, state capitalism as motor of accumulation, mobilization from above for a "cultural revolution," rejection of traditional values and forms, a developed Northeast as a model—and to argue that it in fact amounts to an Eastern European variant of "modernization theory." There is actually much in this thesis. Both modernization theory, whether in its stages-of-growth (Rostow), nation-building (Almond, Pye, Verba) or political order (Huntington) formulations, and the NCR in its several varieties, start from the primacy of the political. This suggests elite control of the state apparatus in order to ensure state-directed accumulation. In the one case, the elite is presumed to be educated and capitalist oriented, in the other to contain a revolutionary potential. Either way, the development process is imposed and guided from above and aims at emulation of development processes already accomplished elsewhere. Indigenous starting points, aspirations and potentials are regarded as obstacles to be overcome. Science and technology as well as rationality and efficiency are prescribed as organizing principles of social change. Thus, popular participation, in both models, is reduced even as mass mobilization is advocated, whether the process is described by Huntington as the creation of political order[49] or by Ponomaryov as leadership of a "revolutionary avant-garde."[50] By the same token, both models seek to "create" a sustaining mass basis of legitimacy for the realization of their goals, the one a proletariat, the other a bourgeoisie.

Tibi's relentless critique of the NCR may be further examined in light of Elsenhans' and Lowenthal's observations. For him, the theory of the National Democratic State, the NLN and the NCR are nothing more than "an unhistorical superimposition of the Soviet model of development onto the peripheral countries. . . even though it contains a few modifications." Thus, the National Democratic State is in essence a replica of the Soviet state in so far as "both display a bureaucratic independence of the state apparatus vis-à-vis the classes of society." Moreover, a determining criterion of NCR states is whether or not they share Soviet foreign policy goals; in this way, e.g., the Shah's Iran or the elites of reactionary oil-producing states can be passed off as "anticapitalist" and "national democratic."[51] Following Marcuse and Negt, Tibi also addresses the problematic of the strong state. In his view the NCR confuses state ownership with a Marxian socialization of the means of production, and in this way degrades the liberating function of communal ownership into a means of state-bureaucratic control. The Marxist theory of emancipation is converted into a theory of production, the negative dialectic transformed into a positive one serving merely to legitimate Soviet domination of Third World societies.[52]

A Progressive Core?

A central problem of analytical constructs that posit the NCR as an instrument of domination or as equivalent to modernization theory is that they absolutize and essentialize certain characteristics and goals that may actually be temporally limited, exiguous or transient phenomena, even while they ignore respective starting points and goals. Like the Cold War "theory" of totalitarianism,[53] these approaches—if used for more than simple heuristic purposes—may in fact be deployed more for purposes of demonization of an ideological opponent or vindication of a capitalist-oriented status quo than for insight and understanding.

For instance, the basic premise of modernization theory, namely the prescription of capitalist relations of production for the Third World, stands in stark opposition to the anticapitalist, anti-imperialist premises of the NCR. If the NCR is to be seen as modernization theory, then it is modernization theory with a class content and progressive core. The inflated state of the NCR must be strong in order to withstand the presumed counteroffensive of imperialism without and reaction within. Its elites are assumed to be able to become independent and self-sufficient, while the masses are imputed with a democratic potential. The purpose of the National Democratic State is to create the material preconditions for socialism. All this contrasts with the assumptions and intents of Western modernization theory.

By way of conclusion, this "progressive core" of the NCR may be discerned in terms of at least two fundamental questions: (1) How does the NCR operate *in praxis* to help "liberate" and "guide" countries in the South, and (2) How relevant is the People's Democracy itself to the goals and aspirations of these countries?

In relation to the first question, the anti-imperialist premise of the NCR, just alluded to, has to be further elucidated. The position of the People's Democracies and their elementary interests within the still essentially bipolar world political-economic system compel them to oppose the global manifestations of transnational capital. At the very least, state-socialism is at present the sole alternative socio-economic formation to world capitalism. Without its presence, much different outcomes of the anti-imperialist struggles in, for instance, Viet Nam, Mozambique, Cuba and presently, Nicaragua may be envisioned— even while not losing sight of converse tendencies such as Afghanistan and Czechoslovakia. From this perspective, it is impossible to reject out of hand Castro's "natural alliance" thesis, advanced at the Sixth Summit of Non-Aligned Countries in Havana in 1979, that an objective or structural identity exists between the interests of the developing countries and those of the industrialized communist states.[54]

Following Salua Nour,[55] one might push the progressive core concept to its analytical limits. Even though the Soviet Union must often behave as a great power, he argues, and despite its increasing search for cheap raw materials and outlets for its manufactured goods, it does not produce permanent structural imbalances and systematic dependency in the same way that international capitalism does. This is mainly because the Soviets do need allies in the anticapitalist struggle and their loyalties can only be assured by a consistent anti-imperialist course. The Soviets and their industrialized allies do make errors (friendship treaties with repressive governments, tied development aid, half-hearted support for local revolutionary movements, etc.), but these are insignificant, the argument goes, compared to the means of control utilized by the advanced capitalist countries: corruption, backing coups, reinforcing the repressive apparatus, creation of structural dependency, etc. True, the People's Democracies have increased their global military presence and become a major proliferator of armaments. But again, communist arms aid concentrates on building up the local military with a view to eventual self-sufficiency as opposed to Western attempts to use it as a means of further deepening dependency relations. To be sure, Northeastern and Southern interests do not always converge in this sphere; they often do, as in the case of military harbour construction in Algeria, South Yemen and Somalia or the build-up of the Syrian and Egyptian forces before 1967; but differences arise as well, as when Egypt's interests in offensive weapons to combat Israel clashed with Soviet interests in maintaining the status quo in the Middle East.

However that may be, Soviet interests are served by any and all developments that tend to undermine world capitalist hegemony. Thus, apart from various conservative policies and alliances, the industrialized communist states do continue to concentrate their support behind revolutionary regimes and movements, and other countries and groups of countries attempting to dislodge themselves from the world capitalist order—the same order that Western proposals such as the Brandt Report attempt to vindicate.[56]

The second and final aspect of the NCR relates to the validity of the People's Democracy model for Southern conditions. After all, the end point of both 'Socialist Orientation' and the NCR itself is, it has been shown, state-socialism. Indeed, as Löwenthal has demonstrated, the concept of People's Democracy, as implemented in Eastern Europe in the late forties, very closely corresponds with the model of National Democracy.[57] Although it is quite impossible to discuss actually existing socialism as a development model within the confines of the present topic,[58] it is worth recalling that the elements of communist development outlined above—forced industrialization, vanguard leadership, etc.—do seem to exert an attraction to Third World countries (or at least their elites) in proportion to the degree of their underdevelopment. But as these countries evolve into NICs, OPEC states, export-led developers and the like, the model seems to decline in relevance. This tendency correlates with the increasingly apparent dysfunctions and limitations of the Soviet-type model itself.

On the pathologies of actually existing socialism, a growing body of literature, based on "immanent critique," has already evolved, as linked with names such as Marcuse, Sik, Bahro, Djilas, Medvedev, Deutscher, *et alia*. Setting aside some important differences of emphasis and nuances, these critiques all conclude (1) that state-socialism has nowhere fulfilled the human emancipatory purpose of Marxism, and that (2) real economic growth and development have not proceeded beyond a certain stage. Concerning the former, Rudolf Bahro posits "a new antagonistic order the other side of capitalism" and argues that the elimination of private ownership of the means of production is separated 'by an entire epoch' from universal human emancipation.[59] For him, the "Gordian Knot of bureaucratization and uneven development" ultimately thwarts any chance of realizing socialism in the Marxian sense of human liberation. Thus,

. . .there is no way, Marx implies, that a pre-capitalist country can industrialize without either wage-labour or extra-economic compulsion. One of the two is needed. The abolition of capitalist private property here means a decision in favour of terror—for an unending torment of development, if no stable dictatorship comes into being—and the specific problem then consists in the productive function of this terror.[60]

In this model of industrialization without emancipation, it is precisely this terroristic-bureaucratic structure needed to trigger development in pre-capitalist or underdeveloped society that prevents that development from becoming self-sustaining. For Senghaas, the dysfunctions of actually existing socialism become apparent with the transition of the economy from its extensive to intensive phases, when the excessive controls exerted by the political superstructure produce economic problems such as declining capital productivity, industrial supply bottlenecks and continuing deferral of consumer needs.[61] Or, to cite Bahro once more:

Criticism of the present condition of the Soviet state system can be summed up in the simple fact that it has still not advanced one single step beyond the structures that were created in the very specific conditions of the 1920s for [the dictatorship of the proletariat]. In this rigid continuity, the Soviet Union finds it difficult to complete even the foundations of socialism, precisely because this is not simply a technical task. Soviet society needs a renovated communist party, under whose leadership it can use the productive forces that were developed in the decades of industrializing despotism to break out to new shores, towards genuine socialism.[62]

These concluding considerations by no means negate the NCR, particularly its "progressive core." But they do suggest anew the dynamic quality of "development," its variability over time and space, and the real problems of adapting this, or any, development model formulated under conditions far removed from those where the model is supposed to be applied.

Notes

[1] A few remarks about this paper are in order. I have to thank Professor Toivo Miljan who first prodded me to develop a more or less coherent analysis of the NCR by inviting me, in the fall of 1984, to present a seminar to his international development class at WLU. He then proposed a more careful and comprehensive formulation for inclusion as a chapter in his forthcoming reader tentatively entitled *A Political Economy of North-South Relations* (New York 1986). The present paper is an initial version of that chapter. Ms Sandra Couch, a graduate student at the University of Guelph, produced an outstanding study, "Communism in the Third World: Prescriptions for Development" (Mimeo., April 1985) from which I have learned much. My thinking on the topic has also been influenced by a series of discussions with Brigitte Schulz of the African Studies Centre, Boston University, whose outstanding study of GDR aid to Africa is a comprehensive and concrete examination of the NCR in practice.

In addition to Soviet and other East European sources, I have chosen to rely especially on the East German literature of the NCR, (1) because many key Soviet sources—to which I had no direct access—have only been translated into German, and (2) because GDR development theory is in many areas (mass basis of the anti-imperialist revolution, individual country studies, etc.) more comprehensive—and indeed more 'orthodox'—than that produced elsewhere in Eastern Europe. For analogous reasons, a number of the—surprisingly few, in the West—most informed critiques of the NCR are found in the West German literature.

[2] For instance, reasoning of the kind presented by S.T. Hosmer and T.W. Wolfe (*Soviet Policy and Practice Toward Third World Conflicts*, Lexington 1983) who write (p. 1) that: "The USSR appears to possess an untiring urge to expand its influence and to reduce that of its rivals in the Third World. In addition, the changing and troubled international environment has become increasingly vulnerable to Soviet opportunism at a time when the USSR's capabilities to project power into the Third World have increased." Indeed, the purpose of their study is to justify and rationalize the buildup of American 'countervailing power' to Soviet 'aggression.'

[3] Elizabeth Kridl Valkenier, *The Soviet Union and the Third World* (New York 1984), p. 11

[4] R.A. Ulyanovsky, *Socialism and the Newly Independent Countries* (Moscow 1972), p. 9

[5] Stephen Clarkson, *The Soviet Theory of Development. India and the Third World in Marxist-Leninist Scholarship* (Toronto & Buffalo 1978), p. 4

[6] Authors' Collective, *Klassen und Klassenkampf in den Entwicklungsländern* (E. Berlin 1969), vol. 1, p. 13

[7] *Ibid.*, p. 13; further see the official statement by Erich Honecker which defines the socialist community of states as "the main revolutionary force of our epoch and a reliable bastion against imperialist policies of war and aggression," *Neues Deutschland*, 16 June 1971

[8] Gerhard Hahn, "Das sozialistische Weltsystem und die Entwicklung des anti-imperialistischen Kampfes der Völker Asiens, Afrikas und Lateinamerikas," *Nichtkapitalistischer Entwicklungsweg*, Report of a Conference held in Leipzig 1973 (E. Berlin 1973), 78-79

[9] On this, see Albert Szymanski, *The Logic of Imperialism* (New York 1981), 57-60

[10] *Klassen und Klassenkampf. . .*, 16 et seq.

[11] P. Polshikov, *Capital Accumulation and Economic Growth in Developing Africa* (Moscow 1981), 120-124

[12] See Lothar Rathman & Hartmut Schilling, "Problem des nichtkapitalistischen Entwicklungsweges der Völker Asiens und Afrikas in der gegenwärtigen Etappe der nationalen Befreiungsbewegung," *Nichtkapitalistischer Entwicklungsweg. . .*, 73

[13] I.L. Andreyev, *The Noncapitalist Way. Soviet Experience and the Liberated Countries* (Moscow 1977), 11

[14] See the article by J. Josweg, H. Kroske and H. Schilling in *Grundfragen des antiimperialistischen Kampfes der Völker Asiens, Afrikas und Lateinamerikas in der Gegenwart* (E. Berlin 1974), 279-281

[15] But see N.A. Simonia, *On the Specifics of National Liberation Revolutions* (Moscow 1968); V.L. Tyagunenko, *Problems of Present-Day National Liberation Revolutions* (Moscow 1969); V.L. Tyagunenko, "World Socialism and National Liberation Movements," *Kommunist*, No. 8, 1973; E. Tarabin, "The National Liberation Movement: Problems and Prospects," *International Affairs*, No. 2 (February 1978), 59-68

[16] See Hahn, *op. cit.*, 82

[17] *Klassen und Klassenkampf. . .*, vol. 1, p. 11

[18] *Nichtkapitalistischer Entwicklungsweg. . .*, 21

[19] Klassen und Klassenkampf. . ., vol. 3, p. 295

[20] *Ibid.*, 308

[21] Martin Breetzmann, *Die Industrialisierung der Entwicklungsländer: Stand, Probleme, Perspektiven* (Frankfurt 1970), 8

[22] Clarence J. Munford, "The National Liberation Movement in Theory and Practice—Nine Theses," Paper presented to Socialist Studies Society Conference, Guelph, Ontario, June 1984, Mimeo., p. 67

[23] Salim Ibrahim & Vera Metze-Mangold, *Nichtkapitalistischer Entwicklungsweg: Ideengesischichte und Theoriekonzept* (Cologne 1976), 86 (emphasis in original)

[24] Gert Kück, Zu einigen Zusammenhängen zwischen politischen und ökonomischen Faktoren bei der Gestaltung der Aussenwirtschaftsbeziehungen der Länder auf nichtkapitalistischem Weg," *Nichtkapitalistischer Entwicklungsweg. . .*, 279

[25] This catalogue is inferred from a variety of sources. The conditions are summed up by Heinz Josweg, "Probleme der Finanzierung von Entwicklungsprogrammen durch Inanspruchnahme ausländischer Finanzquellen in Ländern auf nichtkapitalistischem Entwicklungswege," *Nichtkapitalistischer Entwicklungsweg*, 314-315. Further, see Robert S. Jaster, "Foreign Aid and Economic Development: The Shifting Soviet View," *International Affairs*, vol. 45 (1969), esp. 462

[26] R. Ulyanovsky, Foreword to Andreyev, *Op. Cit.*, 26

[27] C.R. Saivetz & S. Woodby, *Soviet-Third World Relations* (Boulder and London 1985), 12

[28] Salua Nour, "Die Beziehung der Sowjetunion zur Dritten Welt: Beitrag zur Emanzipation der Entwicklungslander oder Weg in eine neue Abhangigkeit?" In: Jose Linhard & Klaus Voll (eds.), *Weltmarkt und Entwicklungslander* (Rheinstetten, Neu 1976), 209

[29] *Ibid.*, 206

[30] Valkenier, *Op. Cit.*, 46

[31] "Gap Between the West and Newly-Free Countries," Department of Centralized Materials (Moscow, April 1982), Mimeo., 11-13

[32] Y. Alimov, "The Newly Free Countries in World Politics," *International Affairs*, September 1981, 22-24

[33] Richard Lowenthal, *Model or Ally: The Communist Powers and the Developing Countries* (New York 1977)

[34] Valkenier, *Op. Cit.*, 110

[35] *Ibid.*, 118-120

[36] Thomas J. Zamostny, "Moscow and the Third World: Recent Trends in Soviet Thinking," *Soviet Studies*, XXXVI, No. 2 (April 1984), 227-230

[37] A.R.M. Babu, *African Socialism or Socialist Africa?* (London 1981); for a critique of this work, see my review in *Canadian Journal of African Studies* Vol. 18, No. 2, 1984

[38] Abdel Fattah Ismail, "A New Vanguard Party," *World Marxist Review*, 22 (January 1979), 24

[39] *Working-Class and National Liberation Movements: Joint Struggle Against Imperialism, For Social Progress* (Moscow 1981), 43

[40] Clarkson, *Op. Cit.*, 251-252

[41] Couch, *Op. Cit.*, 5

[42] The authoritative *Klassen und Klassenkampf. . .* invokes Goethe to reject this possibility: "It is said that truth lies between two extreme views. By no means. What lies between them is the problem." (Vol. 3, 331).

[43] Valkenier, *Op. Cit.*, 90

[44] Horst Grienig, "Burgerliche Theorien des Dualismus," *Nichtkapitalistischer Entwicklungsweg. . .*, 349

[45] On this, see Babu, *Op. Cit.*, *passim*; also Rathmann & Schilling, *Op. Cit.*, 46-47

[46] S.I. Tyulpanov, *Essays on Political Economy. The Developing Countries* (Moscow 1969), 88-92

[47] Bassam Tibi, "Zur Kritik der sowjetmarxistischen Entwicklungstheorie," *Handbuch der Dritten Welt 1975* (Stuttgart 1975), 78-79

[48] In particular, Hartmut Elsenhans, *Abhangiger Kapitalismus oder burokratische Entwicklungsgesellschaft? Versuch uber den Staat in der Dritten Welt* (Frankfurt & New York 1981), ch. IV (1); Lowenthal, *Op. Cit.*, *passim*

[49] Samuel Huntington, *Political Order in Changing Society*, New Haven 1976

[50] Boris N. Ponomaryev, "Urgent Theoretical Problems of the World Revolutionary Process," *Kommunist*, No. 15, 1971

[51] Tibi, *Op. Cit.*, 83

[52] See *Ibid.*, 80

[53] For a critique of "totalitarianism" see my "Anticommunism in the Federal Republic of Germany," *Socialist Register 1984* (London 1984), 175-177, and the literature cited there

[54] See Para. 2f of the Economic Declaration of the "Final Declaration of the Conference of Heads of State or Government of the Nonaligned Countries, 3-7 September 1979," Havana, n.d. (Mimeo.)

[55] Nour, *Op. Cit.*, 202-205

[56] On this, see my "Anti-Brandt: A Critique of Northwestern Prescriptions for World Order," *Socialist Register 1981* (London 1981), 22-24

[57] Lowenthal, *Op. Cit.*

[58] But for a synopsis and discussion of the relevant literature, see O.P. Dwivedi, W.D. Graf, J. Nef, "Marxist Contributions to the Theory of the Administrative State," *Indian Journal of Political Science*, XLVI (January-March 1985) No. 1, 1-17

[59] Rudolf Bahro, *The Alternative in Eastern Europe* (London 1977), 20-21

[60] *Ibid.*, 27

[61] Dieter Senghaas, "Sozialismus: Eine entwicklungsgeschichtliche und entwick lungstheoretische Betrachtung," *Leviathan*, No. 1, 1980, 33

[62] Bahro, *Op. Cit.*, 118-119

BIOGRAPHICAL NOTES

Jahangir Amuzegar, a former Executive Director of the I.M.F., is an international economic consultant.

S.J.Anjaria is Assistant Director of the Exchange and Trade Relations Department of the I.M.F.

Alex Asiabor is Director of the Commodities Division of UNCTAD and a former Governor of the Bank of Ghana.

William P. Avery is Associate Professor of Political Science at the University of Nebraska at Lincoln.

Robert L. Ayres served as Principal Staff Member on the Task Force Secretariat and is a member of the World Bank's International Relations Department. He is the author of BANKING ON THE POOR: THE WORLD BANK AND THIRD WORLD POVERTY (M.I.T.,1983).

James A. Baker, III, is the United States Secretary of the Treasury.

Jayantanuja Bandyopadhyaya is Professor of International Relations at Jadaypur University, Calcutta.

Michael Blackwell, from the U.K., is an economist in the Treasury Department at the I.M.F.

Lothar Brock is with the Frankfurt Peace Research Institute.

Shahid Javed Burki is Director of the World Bank's International Relations Department. He served as Secretary on the Task Force on Concessional Flows.

Manuel Castells is Professor of Planning, Department of City and Regional Planning at Berkeley.

Christopher S. Clapham is Senior Lecturer in Politics at the University of Lancaster and author of PRIVATE PATRONAGE AND PUBLIC POWER (Pinter, 1982).

Theodor Cohn is Associate Professor of Political Science at Simon Fraser University, Vancouver, British Columbia and a prolific writer on food and agriculture.

Bruce Cumings is Professor of International Studies at the University of Washington, Seattle, and author of THE ORIGINS OF THE KOREAN WAR (Princeton, 1981).

Luc De Wulf is a senior economist in the Asian Department of the I.M.F.

William Diebold Jr. spent 40 years with the Council on Foreign Relations, of which he was Director until 1983. He is the author of dozens of articles and five books, most recently INDUSTRIAL POLICY AS AN INTERNATIONAL ISSUE.

Esperanza Duran is a research fellow at the Royal Institute of International Affairs. She is the author of the Chatham House paper EUROPEAN INTERESTS IN LATIN AMERICA (1985).

Carl K. Eicher is Professor of Agricultural Economics and Director of the African Rural Economy Program at Michigan State University. He is co-editor of AGRICULTURE IN ECONOMIC DEVELOPMENT and GROWTH AND DEVELOPMENT OF THE NIGERIAN ECONOMY.

David Goldsborough is with the Developing Country Study Division of the I.M.F. Research Division.

William Graf is Associate Professor of Political Studies, University of Guelph, Guelph, Ontario. He writes extensively on Africa.

Hans-Erik Holm, a Senior Lecturer at Darhus University, Denmark, is co-author of THE RECALCITRANT DISH (1982).

Alexander King is President of the Club of Rome. He is the co-editor of BIORESOURCES FOR DEVELOPMENT: THE RENEWABLE WAY OF LIFE, and SCIENCE, TECHNOLOGY AND GLOBAL PROBLEMS: TOWARD A NEW ROLE FOR SCIENCE AND TECHNOLOGY.

Stephen Krasner is a Professor of Political Science at Stanford University and has taught at Howard University and the University of California, Los Angeles. He is the editor of INTERNATIONAL REGIMES.

P.K.Kuruvilla is Professor of Political Science at Wilfrid Laurier University, Waterloo, Ontario. He has written extensively on politics and public administration in the Third World.

Sanjaya Lall is Senior Research officer at the Oxford University Institute of Economics and Statistics. He is the author of THE MULTINATIONAL CORPORATION (1980) and DEVELOPING COUNTRIES AS EXPORTERS OF TECHNOLOGY (1982).

Winston E. Langley is a professor in the Department of Political Science and International Relations at the University of Massachusetts, Boston.

Joslin Landell-Mills is with the External Relations Department of the I.M.F.

Colin W. Lawson is Senior Lecturer and Director of Studies in Economics at the University of Bath. During 1981-2 he was aVisiting Scholar at the Russian Research Center, Harvard University.

Christopher Maule is professor of Economics and International Affairs at Carleton University in Ottawa.

Max Mmuya teaches at Kivukoni College at Dar es Salaam, Tanzania.

Jimoh Omo-Fadaka is Chairman of the Working Group on Conservation and Rural Development of the International Union for Conservation of Nature and Natural Resources, Commission on Ecology, London.

Amechi Okolo is with the Department of International Relations at the University of Ife at Ife, Nigeria.

John Pinder is the Director of the Policy Studies Institute, London and Editor of NATIONAL INDUSTRIAL STRATEGY AND THE WORLD ECONOMY (1982).

David P. Rapkin is with the Department of Political Science at the University of Nebraska at Lincoln.

Anahdarup Ray, an Indian, was educated at Calcutta, Cambridge, and Chicago Universities. He is a senior economist in the World Bank's Latin American and Caribbean Office. His most recent book is COST-BENEFIT ANALYSIS: ISSUES AND METHODOLOGIES (World Bank, 1984).

Riordan Roett is Professor and Director of the Latin American Studies Program, and Director of the Center of Brazilian Studies, at the Johns Hopkins School of Advanced Study in Washington D.C. His works include BRAZIL: POLITICS IN A PATRIMONIAL SOCIETY (1984).

Jim Romahn is the farm editor of the KITCHENER-WATERLOO RECORD, Kitchener, Ontario.

W.W.Rostow is the Rex G. Baker Jr. Professor of Political Economy at the University of Texas (Austin). His best known book is THE STAGES OF ECONOMIC GROWTH (original edition, 1952).

Timothy M. Shaw is Associate Professor of Political Science at Dalhousie University. He has also taught in Nigeria and Zimbabwe. He is co-author of AFRICA AND THE INTERNATIONAL POLITICAL SYSTEM (1982).

Ibrahim F.I. Shihata is the Vice President and General Counsel of the World Bank and former Director General of OPEC Fund for International Development. His publications include THE OTHER FACE OF OPEC (1982).

Stuart L. Smith, a former leader of the Liberal Party of Ontatio, is Chairman of the Science Council of Canada.

Frances Stewart, a Fellow of Somerville College and Senior Research Officer at the Institute of Commonwealth Studies, Oxford, is the author of TECHNOLOGY AND UNDERDEVELOPMENT (1977), and co-author of INTERNATIONAL FINANCIAL COOPERATION ,(1982).

Susan Strange is Professor of International Relations at the London School of Economics and a pioneer in the study of international political economy.

Richard Swedberg is with the Department of Sociology at the University of Stockholm.

Andrew Vanderwal was a graduate student at Carleton University's Norman Paterson School of International Affairs when the article included was written.

Raymond Vernon is Clarence Dillon Professor of International Relations at Harvard University. At various times he has been an official of the United States government and a consultant on trade policy to numerous government and international organizations.

William N.Walker, a lawyer, was deputy U.S. trade representative from 1975-1977.

Charles H. Weitz, a former International Official with the F.A.O., is currently a lecturer and consultant to the United Nations.

Eduardo Wiesner has taught at Universidad Los Andes (Bogota), and was Minister of Finance and Director of National Planning in Columbia. He is currently Director of the I.M.F.'s Western Hemisphere Department.

Doug Williams has been a Research Officer at the North South Institute in Ottawa, Canada, since 1979, with the exception of 1982-3, when he helped set up an extension program for the Government of Botswana. He has published a range of articles for the institute on food security and Canadian industrial adjustment.

Robert E. Wood is Assistant Professor of Anthropology and Sociology at Rutgers State University of New Jersey at Camden.

INDEX